SAFIRE'S POLITICAL DICTIONARY

SAFIRE'S
POLITICAL
DICTIONARY

William Safire

OXFORD
UNIVERSITY PRESS
2008

OXFORD
UNIVERSITY PRESS

Oxford University Press, Inc., publishes works that further
Oxford University's objective of excellence
in research, scholarship, and education.

Oxford   New York
Auckland   Cape Town   Dar es Salaam   Hong Kong   Karachi
Kuala Lumpur   Madrid   Melbourne   Mexico City   Nairobi
New Delhi   Shanghai   Taipei   Toronto

With offices in
Argentina   Austria   Brazil   Chile   Czech Republic   France   Greece
Guatemala   Hungary   Italy   Japan   Poland   Portugal   Singapore
South Korea   Switzerland   Thailand   Turkey   Ukraine   Vietnam

This work was originally published in 1968 as *The New Language of
Politics* by Random House, Inc. Two revised editions were published in 1972 and 1978 as
Safire's Political Dictionary by Random House, Inc. One revised edition was published in 1993 as
Safire's New Political Dictionary by Random House, Inc.

Published by Oxford University Press, Inc.
198 Madison Avenue, New York, NY 10016

www.oup.com

Oxford is a registered trademark of Oxford University Press

Library of Congress Cataloging-in-Publication Data
Safire, William, 1929–
Safire's political dictionary / William Safire.
p. cm.
Rev. ed. of: Safire's new political dictionary / by William Safire.
Includes index.
ISBN 978-0-19-534334-2; 978-0-19-534061-7 (pbk.)
1. United States—Politics and government—Dictionaries.
I. Safire, William, 1929– Safire's new political dictionary. II. Title.
JK9.S2 2008
320.03—dc22   2007033114

1 3 5 7 9 8 6 4 2

Printed in the United States of America
on acid-free paper

The dedication to the first edition of this dictionary, titled in 1968 *The New Language of Politics*, was "To Mark"—our son, then four years old. He is now married and he and his wife have a daughter, so the happily updated dedication of this fifth edition is:

To Mark, Karen, and Lily Safire

CONTENTS

PROLEGOMENON

When the first edition of this political dictionary appeared forty years ago, its opening line was at that time a most appropriate quotation from Benjamin Disraeli: "With words we govern men."

No lexicographer in his right mind would use that today. The reaction on the part of many readers would be "Not women?" Even traditionalists who recoil at political correctness and resist changing *mankind* to *humankind* know that persuasive political language avoids causing any niggling negative reaction in any part of the audience. (Fortunately, the sex-free synonym *humanity* is available.) Entries herein like *the forgotten man* and *century of the common man* must be used with caution, as frozen in the amber of historical usage. *Muckraker* is okay to aim at journalists because few recall that Teddy Roosevelt based it on "the man with the muckrake" in John Bunyan's 1678 *Pilgrim's Progress*, and *man on the wedding cake* was limited to a specific derogation of the stiffness of candidate Thomas E. Dewey, but it would be jarring to call an authoritarian female leader a *man on horseback* or to describe her combative role as a *man in the arena*.

Therefore, in this fifth edition, let's use a more apt quotation from Disraeli. The future Prime Minister, speaking to the House of Commons in 1859, declared: "Finality is not the language of politics."

The always amendable political language (or *polingo*, to try out a neologism), the past and present vocabulary is prelude to coinages and "boostings" of future campaigns. In the course of this updated prolegomenon (a forty-dollar word for "introduction to a lengthy work") of a book that has undergone a stem-to-stern revision and expansion, a poetic allusion will present itself that looks ahead to the political language of tomorrow.

What Is Special about the Language of Politics?

This is a lexicon of conflict and drama, of fulsome praise and fierce ridicule, of emotional pleading and intellectual persuasion. Color and bite permeate a language designed to rally support, to blast opposition, and to mold the minds of multitudes.

Part of it is the private argot politicians use in talking to other insiders, when they *take him to the mountaintop* or *walk back the cat* and wonder if *salami tactics* or the *smell of magnolias* will trigger a *bullet vote*—or if the *goo-goos* of reform will raise a fuss about the traditional distribution to local election-day helpers of *walking-around money*. Such political parlance, using *code words* in the technique of *dog-whistle politics*, has been simultaneously enriched and debased by the *moonbats* and *wingnuts* of the *netroots* as well as the *mainstream media*, many of whom are unfamiliar with the era of the *smoke-filled room* and *whistlestopping* and a *passion for anonymity* .

Another part of today's political language is the patois of the *thumbsuckers* and *spinmeisters* of the *chattering class*. These *talking heads*, often including a *big foot*, sit gingerly on their *talking points* and toss off locutions like *off the record, backgrounder, dope story, leak, plant, not for attribution, sound bite*, even as they feel a *chilling effect* from prosecutors and litigants seeking their *confidential sources*.

Then there is the lingo of the political scientists, the *eggheads* of the *brain trust*—including *neocon* and *theocon*—pulling their scholarly chins over the *blue state/red state* divide, debating whether *multilateralism* is realistic or idealistic, and squaring off over Clintonian *triangulation*.

Speakers of *Pentagonese*—ostensibly eschewing *groupthink* but even when disagreeing saying only that they *nonconcur*—now know that the *shock and awe* leading to *regime change* does not always result in a *slam dunk*. That last borrowing from basketball is CIA-ese, the *spookspeak* that describes a clandestine transmission of secrets as a *brush pass*.

At the center is the memorable public discourse of past and present political figures, participants in what Oliver Wendell Holmes called "the action and passion" of their times. They play the finger-pointing *blame game* at a *vast right-wing conspiracy* or a *loony left*, some urging the nation remember the *Munich analogy* and *stay the course* and not *cut and run*, others ominously recalling the era of the *quagmire*. Their campaign strategists bestow a *big wet kiss* on the boys who *bundle* and promise a feast at the *pork barrel* to those who *deliver*. Speechwriters of every ilk bounce from *gridlock* to *earmark*, and range in rhetoric from an accusatory *rich man's war, poor man's fight* to an evocative *just and lasting peace*.

Effective political language is vivid in its self-mocking exaggeration. *Gutfighters* with an *instinct for the jugular* and *hatchetmen* adept at *nut-cutting* prowl the political jungle amid the howling of *attack dogs* and the shocking behavior of the *skunk at the garden party*. An anonymous voice over a loudspeaker at a convention becomes a *voice from the sewer*, and a bigot is flayed as an *apostle of hate*. A pessimist is derided in rhyme as a *prophet of gloom and doom* or with alliteration as a *nattering nabob of negativism;* a censor is a *bookburner*. Candidates afflicted with the *wimp factor* or a *character issue* often enter the *arena* with *foot-in-mouth disease* and after a *gaffe* leave in a *hail of dead cats*.

Or What's a Metaphor?

The most gripping of the phrases in this dictionary paint word pictures to conjure startling images. Political economists concerned about currency fluctuations can picture the limited wiggling of the *snake in the tunnel* and call an abortive rally a *dead-cat bounce* (not to be confused with the dead-cat hailstorm). Although nobody wants to be inundated by the *wave of the future*, the *panjandrums of the opinion mafia* delight in the metaphors of disaster: *landslides, prairie fires, firestorms, tsunamis*, and *avalanches* are the goals of *whirlwind campaigns*. Long-shot candidates pray that *lightning may strike*.

The language dips into the Bible for St. Paul's *all things to all men* (now edited to all *people*), admonishes intra-party squabblers with an *Eleventh Commandment*, and *stands at Armageddon* to battle for the nominee. It turns to church terms for *party faithful, party elders, bleeding heart*, and *gray eminence;* to poetry for Shakespeare's *strange bedfellows*, Wordsworth's *Happy Warrior*, and T. S. Eliot's *wasteland;* to indigenous Americans for *sachem, mugwump, caucus*, and *muckey-mucks*, as well as *rainmaker* and *off the reservation;* to horse racing for *dark horse, running mate, front runner, bolt*, and *shoo-in*.

The military-linguistic complex is well represented: Left and right *wings* have been on the march since *slogan* was the name for a Scottish war cry. Phrasemakers have turned to the military for *bloody shirt, boom, campaign*, *calculated risk, hundred days, low profile, man on horseback, rally, regular, spoils system, standard-bearer, war horse,* and *old fogy.* War-gaming words like *escalation* and *exit strategy* proliferate even as the fearsome *nuclear option* describes a threatened parliamentary maneuver. *Thinking the unthinkable* is permitted at *think tanks* and the *puzzle palace,* and the old *arsenal of democracy* is updated by stealthy inventions at the *skunk works.*

The political zoo parade offers the most metaphors of all. *Doves* and *hawks* fly in its aviary along with emblematic *bald eagles,* as *lame ducks eat crow* on the *rubber chicken circuit* and all look warily at the *floo-floo bird,* lowest in the *pecking order.* The menagerie features the emblematic *elephant* and *donkey,* with a big cage for *tigers* (both *Tammany* and *paper*) who enjoy *twisting the lion's tail.* The *mossback* ignores the racket of the *watchdog committees* and the *bird dogs* and *kennel dogs* as *attack dogs* quiet their yapping at the *fat cats,* who in turn hunger for a *red herring* and long to hear *shrimps whistle.* The willing *gofer* and the *coon,* whose skin is a prize for presidential walls, shudder at the ominous silence from the *dinosaur wing,* where traitorous *copperheads* slither and twisted *gerrymanders* abound. In the candidates' stable, the *dark horse,* the *wheelhorse,* and the *stalking horse* are hitched in a *troika,* racing past the *old war horse.* All this causes a *feeding frenzy* on the *zoo plane.*

This dictionary is an inventory of inventive invective, a lexicon of the words and phrases that have misled multitudes, blackened reputations, held out false hopes, oversimplified ideas to appeal to the lowest common denominator, shouted down inquiry, and replaced searching debate with stereotypes that trigger applause or hatred. At the same time, this is a lexicon that shows how the choice of a word or metaphor can reveal sensitivity and genius, inspire and uplift a people, and crystallize a mood that gives purpose and direction to a movement. The best political language, as in the Seward-Lincoln *mystic chords of memory* swelling the chorus of the Union (a collaboration I'll address in a moment) or FDR's homespun *garden-hose analogy* justifying lend-lease, captures the essence of an abstraction and makes it understandable and moving to millions.

Not in This Dictionary

As defined here, the language of politics does not include much of the language of government. If a word or short phrase has a good definition available in most dictionaries, this is not the place to look for it. "Amendment" is not here, though *rider* is; "assistant majority leader" is not, but *whip* is; "vice president" is not, though *veep, Throttlebottom,* and *heartbeat away from the Presidency* are; "president" is not, but *awesome burden, loneliest job in the world,* and *POTUS* are; "diplomat" is not, but *cookie pusher* is, as both *shirtsleeve* and *striped-pants diplomacy* accompany the *sherpa* to the *summit.*

In the same way, this discursive, anecdotal, and at times breezily personal exploration of a specialized world of words concerns itself not so much with the historical event but with the language that comes out of it: there is no "Marshall Plan," "Point Four Program," or "Monroe Doctrine" here, though there is an entry on *doctrines;* no "Atlantic Charter," but an entry on *four freedoms;* no "Geneva conference," but entries on *summitry* and *spirit of;* no "Army-McCarthy hearings," but entries on *point of order* and *junketeering gumshoes;* no "government agencies," but entries on *alphabet agencies* and *acronyms.* The *Bay of Pigs* is included because of its association with *fiasco,* the Cuban missile crisis of 1962 is listed under *eyeball to eyeball*, and the vast subject of Social Security reform gets only a definition of *doughnut hole* and the etymology of *third rail of politics.*

Old Phrase, New Context

A linguistic prism on history offers more than a few insights. Promises and appeals to blacks and whites took the shape of economic slogans like "vote yourself a farm," *forty acres and a mule*, "three acres and a cow," *full dinner pail*, and not until a century later *black power* and the lexicon of *civil rights.* For diplomats, there is a lesson in Kennedy's choice of *quarantine* to describe a blockade—a word denoting an act of war—taken from the preconditioning of the medical metaphor by FDR before World War II. In the same way, McKinley used the revered *manifest destiny* to justify his acquisition of Hawaii, destiny expanding westward that was hardly manifest a half-century earlier, when that phrase was coined.

Most of the seemingly "new" language is surprisingly old: Henry IV's *chicken in every pot*, Al Smith's *cooing doves* and Thomas Jefferson's *war hawk* accusation, Henry Clay's struggle against the *can't-win technique*, Alf Landon's borrowing of *New Frontier* from Henry Wallace, Teddy Roosevelt's blast at the *lunatic fringe*—all are old and have been used as new. There is the longevity of the terms *advice and consent*, *vox populi*, Aristotle's *political animal*, and Bacon's *presidential timber*, and the use of *Hottentots* as a symbol of the nations euphemized as underdeveloped. There is a sisters-under-the-skin relationship between Louis XIV's *L'état, c'est moi* and Mayor Frank Hague's *I am the law*, and a resonance in Andrew Jackson's *kitchen cabinet* of FDR's *brain trust* and *privy council.*

Some words are freshly minted and stay: neologisms of the '30s ranged from *boondoggle* to a prescient *weapon of mass destruction*, followed in the '40s by *gobbledygook*, *welfare state*, and war words like *genocide*, *terrorist*, and *freedom fighter*, coinages that stayed with us; in the '50s, *global warming* surfaced, and so did *backlash;* in the '60s, *clout* and *charisma* took on new political meaning; in the '70s, *convention bounce* and *power curve* appeared; the '80s saw *evil empire*, *empowerment*, and *defining moment;* the '90s spread the use of *ankle-biters*, the *bubba vote*, and *is is, the meaning of.* The new millennium offers *faith-based*, *data mining*, *fuzzy math*, *earmark*, *bridge to nowhere*, *Islamofascism*, and the *war on terror* among the entries herein.

The political language is constantly changing: *gutter flyer* replaces *roorback*, and *angry young men* edges aside *Young Turks. Swing voter* takes over for *floater*, *opportunist* for *trimmer*, *plum* for *persimmon*, *barnacle* for *hanger-on*, *henchman* for *fugleman.* (See *obsolete political terms.*) But some words die and are born again: *snollygoster* and *mossback* were resuscitated as Harry Truman favorites, and *philippic* made a reappearance in Eisenhower correspondence.

Phrases are sharpened in use; longer statements by Jefferson and Cleveland became *few die and none resign* and *public office is a public trust.* Bismarck's "iron and blood" wound up as "blood and iron"; Churchill's "blood, toil, tears and sweat" (with a long history of its own) was popularized as "blood, sweat, and tears."

Chorus and Phantom Coinage

Sometimes a word or phrase pops into the political language spontaneously, without an individual coiner. "As Maine goes, so goes the nation" was a well known slogan; when only Maine and Vermont went for Landon in 1936, it was natural for hundreds of politicians to say "As Maine goes, so goes Vermont" in a chorus coinage. More mysterious, however, is the phantom coinage: a word like *backlash*, subtly carrying the slavemaster's whip, was more apt than "backfire," *boomerang*, or "reaction" and was quickly accepted because it filled a linguistic need. The coinage of *Medicare*, also dwelt on at length here, is included because it shows how the right word will triumph over governmental obstacles. Its coiner was neither famous nor had an important national forum: his word grew slowly and inexorably until it could not be stopped. So did the mouth-filling *infrastructure*, despite Churchill's scorn.

"Boosting" and "Heavy Lifting"

The technique of "boosting"—amending a word or phrase slightly to add irony or reverse the meaning—is as old as phrasemaking. Some abolitionists in 1850 called themselves the Know Somethings, providing an antonym for the *Know-Nothings*; the ambivalence of the nineteenth-century "pax Britannica" has been resurrected in a self-critical *pax Americana*. When Adlai Stevenson suggested the Republican slogan should be "throw the rascals in," or Richard Nixon accused Lyndon Johnson of launching a "war on prosperity," they were boosting—playing on familiar phrases. This is a useful device for making a point, and the strength of a phrase can often be determined by how many *turnarounds* have been given it. Allan Nevins's *too little and too late*, for example, went through "enough and on time" to "too much too soon," and is not dead yet (which is more colorfully rendered as "ain't dead yet," attributed to Lincoln's Aunt Sally).

In this way, Lyndon Johnson made *let us continue* an early theme of his Administration, boosting on John Kennedy's "let us begin"; *peacenik* and *Vietnik* (see -NIK SUFFIX) grew out of *beatnik*; "scrambled *eggheads*" appeared as a refinement of the original word; FDR talked of a "sixth column" of gossips and defeatists, going the *fifth column* one better; and *prebuttal* beat *rebuttal* to the debater's punch. Every current phrase offers ammunition for boosting, in which attribution is implicit: *black power* spawned dozens of other powers, including "blackboard power" for militant teachers and "gay power" for outspoken gays and lesbians.

A prime purpose of this book is to make readily available the phrases that built up or tore down politicians and their policies. By showing the sources of these words or on what analogy they were coined, I hope to assuage a certain guilt about borrowing in phrasemaking. When does mere allusion become "heavy lifting" and turn into plagiarism? The political subdivision of the English language has been in business too long for almost any phrase to be totally original; some of the best are twists of, or plays on, others. The many quotations herein, necessary to show usage, are also possible springboards for better usage. Winston Churchill, as he wrote of fighting on the beaches, in the hills, and in the streets of wartime England, was familiar with Clemenceau's defiance in 1918: "I shall fight in front of Paris, within Paris, behind Paris." An apt quotation may make a point, but an apt alteration of a good phrase from the past—with or without scholarly citation—spices a speech and helps in the making of a leader.

Distinctions with Difference

Because the weight of a word can tip political balances, politicians are wise to concern themselves with distinctions. In his final campaign FDR said, "This Administration has made mistakes. That I freely *assert*. And I hope my friends of the press will not change that to *admit.*" Sherman Adams, searching for the right word to characterize his dealings with industrialist Bernard Goldfine, rejected "unwise" and "wrong" to select "imprudent." Harry Truman used *red herring* with impunity, as Al Smith did before him, until he agreed to its use in a Communist context, when suddenly Truman's usage became a costly *blooper.* In the George W. Bush Administration, an astute department-namer apparently rejected the phrase "Domestic Security"—too close to the repressive "internal security"—and chose the warmer Department of *Homeland* Security.

Coinage Disputes

When each of two distinguished sources says the other is "in error," to whom do you grant coinage credit? When the conflicting sources are books, there is recourse to other sources, original letters, or manuscripts. But when flesh-and-blood eyewitnesses disagree, there is no resolving the claims. When queried by the author, Professor Raymond Moley and Judge Samuel Rosenman each stated flatly that he gave *New Deal* to Franklin Roosevelt to coin, citing date and place; in such a case, the historian has to throw up his hands. Both Professor Moley and Judge Rosenman were responsive on several Roosevelt-era entries, and I am grateful to them; the reader can see what each source says and make his or her own decision. Similarly, there were conflicting credits given to the coinage of *New Frontier;* in that case, however, the author was given enough background to make a judgment.

The reader will find no gleeful "Gotcha!" comments from the author regarding inaccurate entries in venerable sources about political sayings. The reason is that new information is constantly turning up showing earlier uses, and it is foolish to play the antedating game because historians and etymologists as well as assiduous bloggers—aided by search engines able to scan everything ever written or recorded as having been said aloud—plow ever deeper into the oratorical snows of yesteryear. Examples: FDR's Harold Ickes is credited with *government by crony*, which he used four days after it had appeared in an Arthur Krock column credited to "a press gallery wit," who Krock much later admitted to the author was himself. That makes Krock the coiner—unless somebody comes up with an earlier citation. There were also varying reports on the context of Dean Rusk's *eyeball to eyeball* remark, two of which are reported under that entry. And when the wife of a speechwriter for Bush the younger proudly let it be known that her husband had created the much-remarked-upon phrase *axis of evil* for the president, White House sources also let it be known that the phrase submitted had been "axis of hatred" and that another writer had offered "evil"—reminiscent of Reagan's *evil empire*—which "Dubya," by choosing to use it, made his own.

Which brings us to—

Presidents and the Phrases of Their Eras

The memories of an administration can be evoked by a look at an inventory of political phrases minted during its years in power. Some are coined by a president, some by his cabinet, while others are coined for use against him by the political opposition or a creative media critic. Here is a balance sheet of phrases by administration, with popularizations included under coinages, over the past century.

Theodore Roosevelt and Woodrow Wilson led the way. "Teddy" gave political coloration to *lunatic fringe* and *hat in the ring*, in active political usage today; he coined *bully pulpit*, took a stand at *Armageddon*, did not always speak softly but wielded a *big stick*, lambasted *malefactors of great wealth*, and coined or gave national currency to *pussyfooting, weasel words, mollycoddle, muckraker, parlor pink, Square Deal*, and *100% American*.

The vigor and combativeness of Theodore Roosevelt's language contrasts with the idealism in most of Woodrow Wilson's phrases. Wilson coined *New Freedom, little group of willful men, too proud to fight, watchful waiting, open covenants, peace without victory, make the world safe for democracy*, and *self-determination* [of nations]; he is often credited with *war to end wars*, a coinage of the historian-novelist H.G. Wells.

The 1920s were not roaring when it came to phrasemaking. Warren Harding, the only media executive to become president, eschewed "normality" to popularize *normalcy*, enshrined alliteration, and was associated with *smoke-filled room*. Calvin Coolidge's "the business of America is business" is generally forgotten today, though he can be credited with popularizing *law and order* and took a forthright stand *against sin*. Herbert Hoover coined *rugged individualism* and *noble experiment*, with *chicken in every pot* and "prosperity is just around the corner" unfairly thrown at him. New York Governor Al Smith, defeated by Hoover for president in 1928, came up with good uses for *baloney, Santa Claus, laundry ticket*, and *lulu*.

Except for the extraordinary spurt of coinage resulting from the Watergate scandal as Nixon's second term began, Franklin Roosevelt's thirteen-year span produced more phrases than any of the other, shorter administrations. The quality and staying power of the coinages and popularizations of FDR stand out over his successors as well. There are at least seven landmark catchphrases of FDR (*New Deal, Good Neighbor Policy, four freedoms, day of infamy, rendezvous with destiny, fireside chat, nothing to fear but fear itself*). Major phrases associated with candidates who lost in this fecund period include Wendell Willkie's *one world, loyal opposition*, and *campaign oratory*, with *barefoot boy from Wall Street* against him, and Dewey's *time for a change*, with *idiot engineer* and *man on the wedding cake* against him.

The most popular target for phrases in the post–World War II period was Senator Joseph McCarthy, who popularized "I have in my hand," *security risk*, and *point of order*, and was hit with *guilt by association, character assassin, McCarthyism, big lie*, and *junketeering gumshoes*.

A giant of political coinage was Abraham Lincoln (*just and lasting peace*, "malice toward none," *don't change horses*, possibly *Presidential bug*, and just about every other line of the *Gettysburg Address*). Thomas Jefferson coined "electioneer" and *entangling alliances* and popularized "the pursuit of happiness." English Conservative Edmund Burke coined such necessary words as "colonial," "diplomacy," and *federalism*. In the twentieth century, Winston Churchill with "pumpernickel principality," *sheep in sheep's clothing, special relationship,* and "parley at the *summit,*" crowned by *iron curtain* (which, alongside Herbert Bayard Swope's *cold war,* was the major post–World War II coinage), carried on the Burke tradition.

FDR's Era

Coinages	Descriptions	Attacks
again and again and again	alphabet agencies	boondoggle
arsenal of democracy	brain trust	clear it with Sidney
day of infamy	dollar-a-year man	court-packing
economic royalists	hundred days	creeping socialism
fellow immigrants	nine old men	indispensable man
fireside chat	pump-priming	spend and spend . . .
forgotten man	voice from the sewer	that man in the White House
four freedoms		traitor to his class
Good Neighbor Policy		
Happy Warrior		
iffy question		
Martin, Barton, and Fish		
my friends		
New Deal		
nothing to fear but fear itself		
one-third of a nation		
quarantine [the aggressor]		
rendezvous with destiny		

The Roosevelt era's phrase record offers a sharp contrast with Harry Truman's:

Coinages	Descriptions	Attacks
do-nothing [80th] Congress	Marshall Plan	five percenter
Fair Deal	Point Four Program	government by crony
give 'em hell, Harry	Truman Doctrine	Had Enough?
red herring		influence peddler
		soft on Communism
		mess in Washington

The Eisenhower years included some from John Foster Dulles:

Coinages	Descriptions	Attacks
agonizing reappraisal	Eisenhower Doctrine	bird dog . . . kennel dog
atoms for peace	new look	brinkmanship
bigger bang for a buck		Eisenhower syntax
curl your hair		security in prison
domino theory		what's good for General Motors . . .
engage in personalities		vicuna coat
[I shall] go to Korea		
massive retaliation		
modern Republicanism		
open-skies proposal		
spirit of		
unleash Chiang		

Of these coinages, *agonizing reappraisal*, *bigger bang for a buck*, *massive retaliation*, and *unleash Chiang* were used for attacks.

A different pattern appears for John F. Kennedy:

Coinages	Descriptions	Attacks
Alliance for Progress	Bailey Memorandum	absentee Senator
ask not	Camelot	fiasco
I am a Berliner	great debates	managed news
life is unfair	Irish Mafia	
missile gap	Kennedy Round	
New Frontier		
profiles in courage		
rising tide lifts all the boats		
torch has been passed		
victory has a hundred fathers		

The balance sheet for Lyndon Johnson:

Coinages	Descriptions	Attacks
chronic campaigner	Johnson treatment	big daddyism
coonskin on the wall	pressing the flesh	credibility gap
creative federalism	smell of magnolias	daisy spot
Great Society		Macbird
let us continue		quagmire
Nervous Nellies		
no wider war		
pressing the flesh		
that dog won't hunt		
war on poverty		

Here are the major coinages or popularizations by the Administration during the pre-Watergate Nixon years:

Coinages	Descriptions	Attacks
black capitalism	heartland	benign neglect
bring us together	machismo	Nixonomics
effete snobs	Middle America	secret plan
game plan	new politics	Southern strategy
hack it	Nixonomics	Tricky Dick
instant analysis	psephology	used car salesman
lift of a driving dream	quality of life	
linkage	reordering priorities	
nattering nabobs of negativism	social issue	
New Federalism	winding down	
Nixon Doctrine	women's lib	
old wine in new bottles		
radic-lib		
silent majority		
strict constructionist		
Vietnamization		
wilderness years		
workfare		

Compare the above to the eruption of coinages produced by the Watergate scandal in only two years, 1972 to 1974. Politicians and historians deal with that period with severity, but to lexicographers, the era of the Watergate vocabulary was a Golden Age of Political Coinage.

Some of the expressions fixed in the public tongue in those days were short-lived—*shredding* has already lost much of its sinister connotation—but a survey of Watergate lingo makes the point that this three-year turmoil had no precedent in its political linguistic fecundity:

at that point in time	damage control
	hardball
big enchilada	inoperative
cover-up	laundered money
CREEP	nobody drowned at Watergate
Deep Throat	not a crook
deep-six	plumbers
dirty tricks	Saturday Night Massacre
enemies list	smoking gun
executive privilege	stonewalling
firestorm	third-rate burglary
-gate construction	twisting slowly, slowly in the wind

This Watergate list ignores the phrases that had already been part of the colloquial tongue ("break-in," "caper," "paper the file," "team player"); locutions unfamiliar to laypeople but that had lives in the law ("obstruction of justice," "abuse of power," "misprision of a felony"); and phrases that seemed unforgettable for the nonce but now have become frozen in time ("sinister force," "expletive deleted," "candy-ass," *limited modified hangout*).

The Watergate investigation leading to the resignation of President Nixon not only popularized expressions that had been little known, but also spawned terms likely to be used for generations: *cover-up*, loosely applied to any obstruction of justice or lesser denial of information, is a political charge that now carries weight; *stonewalling*, an Australian cricket term given new meaning as refusal to comment, is in politics to stay; and *twisting slowly, slowly in the wind* is likely to be used whenever presidents fail to support their nominees or appointees. Any *flap* that turns into a *firestorm* brings out the *damage control*.

The coinage explosion was followed by three years of Gerald Ford presidency, not notable for memorable presidential phrases. "Our long national nightmare is over" was apt and received with relief, and "a time for healing" was recalled in admiration after his death, but Mr. Ford's most newsworthy act, the pardon of his predecessor, contained no phrase that became part of the political language. His "WIN" button—for "Whip Inflation Now"—was derided and soon forgotten. Mr. Ford's language provided a time for lexicographers to digest the tumult of the 1973–74 period. However, during the rapid decline of Nixon following his reelection landslide and the subsequent short term of President Ford, a new producer of coinage had come forward: Henry Kissinger and his circle of articulate aides at Ford's National Security Council and the State Department gave us *quiet diplomacy, shuttle diplomacy, back channel, bargaining chip,* and *step-by-step diplomacy.*

Phrasemaking under Jimmy Carter picked up somewhat:

Coinages	Descriptions	Attacks
born again	Jimmy who?	Billygate
ethnic purity	Magnolia Mafia	killer rabbit
lust in my heart	running against Washington	one-term president
moral equivalent of war (MEOW)		peanut politics
three-martini lunch		steel magnolia
waste, fraud, and abuse		
zero-base budgeting		

Aided by the speaker's professional delivery, phrasemaking rebounded during Ronald Reagan's two-term tenure:

Coinages	Descriptions	Attacks
are you any better off	let Reagan be Reagan	amen corner
cautiously optimistic	supply-side economics	amiable dunce
city on a hill	Teflon-coated presidency	sleaze factor
evil empire		
fatally flawed		
keister		
level playing field		
make my day		
morning in America		
October surprise		
star wars		
stay the course		
there you go again		

For a president whose syntax came frequently under attack, the elder George Bush's presidency left a legacy of several memorable phrases:

Coinages	Descriptions	Attacks
kinder and gentler nation	empowerment	out of the loop
like ugly on an ape	inside the Beltway	Velcro presidency
line in the sand	volunteerism	vision thing
moving the goalposts		voodoo economics
new world order		wimp factor
read my lips		
thousand points of light		

Bill Clinton's campaigns and two terms in office produced a fair share of phrases and neologisms:

Coinages	Descriptions	Attacks
bubba factor	ethnic cleansing	Hillarycare
Comeback Kid	gridlock	Monicagate
didn't inhale	off-message	Whitewater
era of big government is over	war room	
is is, meaning of		
New Covenant		
triangulation		

George W. Bush's presidency, with its roller-coaster popularity, created as well as provided the backdrop for a rich crop of new or freshly repopularized phrases:

Coinages	Descriptions	Attacks
axis of evil	bundling	bridge to nowhere
compassionate conservative	chad	bunker mentality
cut and run	earmarks	chicken hawks
decider	faith-based	culture of corruption
freedom agenda	insurgent	mission accomplished
misunderestimate	jihadist	slam dunk
netroots	long hard slog	waterboarding
soft bigotry of low	regime change	
expectations	shock and awe	
stay the course		
war on terror		

Though political phrases are most often associated with political figures, they are also the province of journalists. Consider William Allen White's *tinhorn politician*, Arthur Krock's *government by crony*, Walter Lippmann's *Atlantic Community*, Stewart Alsop and Charles Bartlett's *hawks and doves*, and Joseph Kraft's *exit strategy*. Professors who wrote for publication often had the knack for phrasemaking, including Raymond Moley's possible coinage of *New Deal*, Allan Nevins's sure coinage of *too little and too late*, John Kenneth Galbraith's *affluent society* and *conventional wisdom*, and Arthur Schlesinger Jr.'s *vital center* and *the politics of*. On the Internet, *blogosphere*, "the universe of blogs," was coined on his weblog in 1999 by Brad L. Graham "as a joke" and was recoined in 2002 by William Quick of the Daily Pundit and quickly adopted.

Hidden Entries

Every lexicographer is faced with the writing of entries about categories that only a determined browser will trip over. We put them in anyway, hoping that reader will follow the cross-references. Some of these are *great, black, wall,* and *new,* and suffixes like *-ism, -nomics, -word, -bashing,* and *-ocracy*. Speech constructions are also hidden entries, and the reader is directed to *I see construction* for a brief history of visionary statements, *contrapuntal phrases* and *turnarounds* for a look at ways to make a phrase more memorable, as well as *Gettysburg Address* for a look at poetic use of a series of images and repetition of words.

Phrases are entered the way they are most often remembered or quoted and not necessarily the way they were spoken. "The only thing we have to fear is fear itself," for example, is entered as *nothing to fear but fear itself*, and FDR's "a date which will live in infamy" is remembered as *day of infamy*.

Euphemisms rate an entry by themselves, but clichés are tagged as such when they appear individually. *Madison Avenue techniques* are always "high-powered," with images "projected," news conferences "hastily called," bloggers derogated as "pajama-clad." Along with *red state/blue state* and "too close to call," the cliché that bounds along most merrily on election-night television is *tantamount to election*.

Words used to describe language have their own problems of fuzzy usage. "Jargon," as used herein, is synonymous with "cliché" and "bromide," as is illustrated in the *Pentagonese* entry; "argot" is used when a word in a specialized vocabulary has not been abused; "lingo," which used to be quite close to "argot," is now used loosely as being synonymous with "language," "tongue," "lexicon," and "vocabulary." *Cant*, however, preserves its meaning as "slang used by insiders with intent to confuse outsiders," as in *strike a blow for freedom.*

Love's Labor Not Lost

This tome is now approaching 550,000 words of text, with 1800 terms defined in some 1400 entries. Since the original edition in 1968, the lexicographer has metamorphosed (yes, that's a verb) from a public relations man in the early '60s (see *flak, selling candidates like soap, Madison Avenue techniques*) to a "special assistant to the president" in the early '70s (see *speechwriter, ghostwriter*) to an Op-Ed columnist for the *New York Times* (see *pundit, thumbsucker*) over the next 30 years, escaping retirement by becoming a philanthropoid at the Dana Foundation and continuing as resident language maven in the weekly *New York Times Magazine.*

In each career incarnation I have kept a hand in the care and feeding of this labor of love, collecting citations for new political words and phrases, digging further into the origins of other entries, filling in gaps by adding words and phrases that should have been covered in the beginning and etymologies recently discovered.

As an Op-Ed columnist, I became more opinionated and polemical in my writing; "vituperative right-wing scandalmonger" is an occasional self-description herein when I grow too modest to cite myself as a source. But partisanship has always stopped at the dictionary's edge: as a lexicographer and language columnist, I have tried—God, how I've tried—to remain nonpartisan, or at least bipartisan. Although the practice of politics pits Democrat against Republican, liberal against conservative, and the tough-minded against the tender-hearted, the study of politics divides the house differently: into the politically active and the politically inert. That is why politically active people of all persuasions, as well as a few ex-colleagues of felony convictions, responded willingly to my queries about who coined what and when. Normal political differences were suspended and tensions dissipated; in tracking the etymology of political language, we are all lexicographers.

Etymology is a kick. On the origins of words, dictionaries and quotation anthologies vie to antedate one another's earliest citations; it used to provide a secret frisson of pleasure to correct *Bartlett's*, which dutifully made the correction in its next edition, and in the past it was lexicographic ecstasy to "trump the *OED*"—the greatest source of the origins and development of the meaning of words spanning the history of the English language—with some arcane "first" use that lasted until the next "first" was unearthed. (Now the *OED* is online and will be tough to beat.) At the biennial gathering of the Judson Welliver Society of former White House speechwriters, where I have been designated a "foundering father," the erstwhile insiders of twelve administrations compare notes on who coined what phrase for whom and under what circumstances, which has led to much original research in this dictionary.

Of course, the computer revolution with its search engines is to etymology what the invention of the shovel was to archeology. We can now zero in on our target phrases in newspapers of centuries ago and survey just about every scholarly treatise ever published. I imagine the day will come when we will be able to sift through every word ever printed, ever recorded on radio and television as well as clandestine wiretaps of tomorrow's most intimate text messages. Terrible for privacy; great for linguistics.

Time was (a locution now replaced by "back in the day"), an individual lexicographer could presume to write a dictionary by himself, though lifting heavily from predecessors. Samuel "Dictionary" Johnson, who did just that, famously defined "lexicographer" as "a harmless drudge"; however, two entries below that, in defining "lexicon," Dr. Johnson cited a passage from the poet Milton to make the point that context—showing the basis of ideas being dressed in words—is key to the definition. "Though a linguist should pride himself to have all the tongues that Babel cleft the world into," wrote Milton, "yet if he have not studied the solid things in them as well as the words and lexicons, he were nothing so much to be esteemed a learned man, as any yeoman competently wise in his mother dialect only." That's why some of the entries in this lexicon run much longer than others: to refer to "the solid things" in the ideas given life and color by the phrases.

Through four decades and five revisions, I had help. Thanks to the "phrasedick brigade" as well as the fearsome "Gotcha! Gang"—readers of my *New York Times* "On Language" column who responded to my public head-scratchings or lexical failings—I was able to track the long-sought origin of such hard-to-find items as the *third rail of American politics*, the Social Security issue, about which politicians are warned "touch it and you're dead." And sometimes the luck of serendipity beats the combined efforts of a legion of experts "drawn up in vast cumbrous array," in Churchill's phrase about *summitry*: when looking for first use of *Oval Office*, I stumbled across an article in the *Times* archive that revealed the first use of *selling candidates like soap*. (Colonel William Procter of the soap family coined it.)

Inspirational help came from Eric Partridge, lone author of the 1961 *Dictionary of Slang and Unconventional English*. When doing some slang research in the British Library in London in the mid-'60s, I asked the librarian in the high-ceilinged Reading Room if I could see a copy; he replied, "That's Mr. Partridge over in the corner. He's here so much we gave him a desk." I introduced myself, told him of my plan for a dictionary of American political slang, and asked about *bashing*, a locution not yet common in the U.S. The gracious gentleman told me all he knew about the combining form, and in our hushed chat and subsequent notes was most encouraging. That gave me a push toward trying to write a dictionary on my own.

Another inspiring force was Fred Cassidy, who came to the U.S. from Jamaica, co-wrote the *Dictionary of Jamaican English* while teaching here, and then organized the most exciting new linguistic project in the twentieth century: *DARE*, the *Dictionary of American Regional English*, carried on after his death by scores of field workers and a staff led by Joan Hall at the University of Wisconsin. Four thick volumes published so far, through *S* (the letter in the alphabet Fred dedicated to me because I've been plugging that cultural phenomenon so relentlessly in my column for years). It has been an invaluable source for this edition of my dictionary, as has J.L. Lighter's *Historical Dictionary of American Slang*, another major multi-volume enterprise nearing completion. Of recent single books, Grant Barrett's *Hatchet Jobs and Hardball* and Paul Dickson's *Slang: The Topical Dictionary of Americanisms* are up-to-date and politically adept.

Now we're into acknowledgments of other help I've received for what I originally thought would be a one-man show, Partridge-style. Previous editions have listed all those who have been sources, researchers, and editors, which I incorporate by this fervent reference, with special thanks to the lexicographer Sol Steinmetz, who vetted and abetted my fourth edition in 1993; to its publisher,

Robert Loomis of Random House, and to Jeffrey McQuain, my longtime *Times* chief researcher who was general editor of that edition, and to executive aman-uenses Ann Elise Wort and Rosemary Shields. My queries were painstakingly answered by Frederick Mish at Merriam-Webster, Joseph Pickett at American Heritage, Michael Agnes at Webster's New World, and Anne Soukhanov at Encarta, as well as by centenarian Jacques Barzun. For this fifth edition, Ste-phen Dodson provided the kind of creative copyediting and a lust for historical accuracy and semantic precision that a political slanguist expects in dealing with the Oxford University Press, world's greatest lexicographic organization; my thanks to Tim Bent and Dayne Poshusta in editorial, Keith Faivre in produc-tion, Pamela Pease in design, and to *OED* editor-at-large Jesse Sheidlower.

This take in 2008 on the ever-changing language of politics has been blessed with the research and editing of Hugh Rawson. I first became acquainted with his good-humored professionalism with the publication of his *Dictionary of Euphemisms and Other Doubletalk* in 1981, which in 1995 was expanded and updated in a second edition. In 2006, Hugh and his wife, Margaret Miner, selected and annotated the second edition of the 900-page *Oxford Dictionary of American Quotations*, which was right down my alley—not only in help-ing me choose the most memorable sayings or gaffes of politicians and others throughout U.S. history, but often putting them in context as few quotation compilations do. Rawson was the perfect collaborator for this work, quick to remember, locate, and verify the accuracy of a citation, and not least because his political tilt is not the same as mine.

On Editing and Eloquence

In researching *musical metaphors,* I came across the derivation of Lincoln's "the mystic chords of memory," which illustrates the way a political leader can take a thought contributed by an aide and shape it to his own style.

The Civil War had not yet begun. In his draft of his first inaugural address, President-elect Lincoln had planned to conclude with a message to his "dis-satisfied friends" in the South that the choice of "peace or the sword" was *in your hands,* and not in his. William Seward, whom Lincoln had beaten for the Republican nomination and after the election had appointed Secre-tary of State, suggested in a letter that this note of defiance be tempered with "a note of fraternal affection," and submitted language for the penultimate paragraphs:

> I close. We are not, we must not be, aliens or enemies, but fellow countrymen and brethren. Although passion has strained our bonds of affection too hardly, they must not, I am sure they will not, be broken. The mystic chords which, proceeding from so many battlefields and so many patriot graves, pass through all the hearts and all hearths in this broad continent of ours, will yet again harmonize in their ancient music when breathed upon by the guardian angel of the nation.

That was fine oratory. Lincoln accepted Seward's idea of seeking to evoke the sentimental ties that could help bind the nation together, and he used Seward's musical metaphor as well. But the president rewrote the suggested passage, lift-ing it from oratory to poetry. He began his editing by turning around Seward's suggested "I close," which was too abrupt for what followed:

I am loath to close. We are not enemies, but friends. We must not be enemies. Though passion may have strained, it must not break our bonds of affection. The mystic chords of memory, stretching from every battlefield and patriot grave, to every living heart and hearthstone, all over this broad land, will yet swell the chorus of the Union, when again touched, as they surely will be, by the better angels of our nature.

Do speakers of political language today make that kind of creative and editing effort to persuade and inspire? Not often. If they did, would it work? Styles change with the times, and Seward's style may seem florid to us now, but Lincoln's improvement—in the rhythm of eight phrases separated by commas, with mystic *chords* swelling the *chorus* leading to the *angels*—produced a soaring simplicity that moved his immediate audience and reverberates in the national memory.

A quick review of how his successors in this century have done: In using the *bully pulpit* of the White House, Theodore Roosevelt tried strenuously and often succeeded; Taft did not try; Wilson succeeded; Harding, except for his burst of alliteration around *normalcy*, failed. Coolidge and Hoover did not try. FDR succeeded in a way not seen since Lincoln. Truman did not do much beyond *do-nothing Congress;* Eisenhower succeeded in his uncharacteristic farewell; Kennedy succeeded in his inaugural and briefly after; Johnson reached but never grasped. Nixon tried hard and on occasion succeeded; Ford went out of his way not to try; Carter contributed an accent but few phrases; Reagan tried and, without seeming effort, succeeded; Bush the elder seemed not to try but registered with a few phrases. Clinton gave it all he had and was better at ad-lib riffs than *stemwinders* or formal speeches; the younger Bush evoked Wilsonian idealism in a Texas twang and his oratorical style, like Truman's, was *misunderestimated.*

Oratorical success does not ensure political success, as this dictionary strives to teach by colorful example. But all those who study and use the political language—and realize what stirring rhetoric and striking metaphor can do not only to rebut and ridicule but to uplift, rally, and lead—know that our history holds out the hope that it helps.

I am loath to close on that four-*h* alliteration. A decade hence, whoever tackles a sixth edition of my lifelong work will be plucking fresh, low-hanging fruit in the garden of controversy. Better for both reader and lexicographer to fulfill the promise of poetic allusion at the start of this introductory survey by turning to lines from the *Four Quartets* of T.S. Eliot:

For last year's words belong to last year's language
And next year's words await another voice.

SAFIRE'S POLITICAL DICTIONARY

A

abolitionist One who advocates the reversal of a policy so entrenched as to have become an institution.

The word, rooted in the Latin for "disappear," was originally applied in politics to those who sought the abolition of slavery. Spelled with an initial capital in 1790, the term was applied most widely during the nineteenth century to fierce opponents of slavery such as the journalist William Lloyd Garrison and the novelist Harriet Beecher Stowe, author of *Uncle Tom's Cabin*, as well as the BARNBURNERS of New York State.

More recent use refers to those who advocate the abolition of capital punishment. In the 1920s, *abolitionist* was revived as the term of choice to label opponents of the death penalty. Opponents of execution at first did not resist and ultimately embraced the label, which recalled the previous victory over slavery. This usage was not limited to the U.S.; a writer to the *Edmonton* (Alberta) *Journal* in 1979 argued that "Abolitionists are convinced that the evidence does not indicate that capital punishment serves as a deterrent or is otherwise useful but is, in fact, simply retribution or revenge."

Countries that have abolished the death penalty, such as Canada, are often called "abolitionist states," a term used in the earlier anti-slavery sense during the Civil War. After limiting capital punishment in 1972, the U.S. Supreme Court re-approved it in 1976, and 38 states of the U.S. still may execute those convicted of capital crimes. Executions yearly peaked in 1999 at 98 in the nation, and by 2007 were about half that total, trending downward.

The word can be applied to any stop-movement in politics. In a 2007 *New York Times* review of a biography of Ronald Reagan, the conservative *National Review* writer Rich Lowry noted that Reagan "hated nuclear weapons; his dream of the Strategic Defense Initiative derived directly from his nuclear abolitionism." See STAR WARS.

Abominable No-Man Sobriquet of Sherman Adams, Eisenhower's chief of staff, who took on the onus of unpleasantness produced by the President's negative decisions.

By becoming the "no-man," the former New Hampshire governor, usually described as "flinty," assumed the role of lightning rod for resentment that would ordinarily have been directed at the Chief Executive. Critics said Adams usurped a portion of the presidential decision-making power by "insulating" Eisenhower. Friends told the lexicographer, a volunteer working with Adams in the 1952 New Hampshire primary campaign, that Adams willingly accepted the role of scapegoat or buffer: "the yes's come from Eisenhower, the no's from Sherman Adams."

This technique of diversion was later applied to other politicians. In 1980, *The Washington Post* wrote of "former Rep. H.R. Gross (R-Iowa), known and feared on Capitol Hill as the 'Abominable No Man' for his resourceful opposition to virtually everything." The term was also applied to John Sununu, President George H.W. Bush's Chief of Staff, when he became the target of press criticism for long limousine rides in 1991. Jack Watson, at one time President Jimmy Carter's Chief of Staff, called the Chief of Staff's job "Javelin Catcher."

The phrase is a play on "Abominable Snowman of the Himalayas," a legendary monster known as the Yeti whose tracks are occasionally "found" and shuddered at by mountain climbers.

See PALACE GUARD; GRAY EMINENCE; BIG FOOT.

above politics A stance taken most often by generals and business executives to dissociate themselves from partisan strife, often in the hope of attracting political support from opposing sides.

Nonpartisan connotes no controversy at all; *above politics* implies that partisanship exists and there is an individual above it.

Applied to issues and not to individuals, however, *nonpartisan* and *above politics* are synonymous.

Politicians occasionally place themselves *above politics* when they feel they no longer need political allies, when they are ready to become elder statesmen, or when they have reached a point described by Francis Bacon in his essay "In Great Place," published in 1612: "All rising to great place is by a winding stair; and if there be factions, it is good to side a man's self whilst he is in the rising, and to balance himself when he is placed."

Among U.S. Presidents, Eisenhower was one of the few able to place himself above politics on many occasions. Another military hero, Admiral George Dewey, was less successful. When asked his party affiliation, the hero of Manila Bay smiled: "I am a sailor. A sailor has no politics." To his chagrin, he soon found himself with no support from either political party.

See BIPARTISAN; NONPARTISAN; PARTISAN; WATER'S EDGE.

absquatulate See CUT AND RUN.

abuse of power See ARROGANCE OF POWER.

academic freedom The assumed right of scholars and students to conduct their studies and express their findings or opinions free of institutional, political, or sectarian control.

The magazine *World's Work* wrote in 1901: "Every right-thinking man will stand firmly for academic freedom of thought." One of its most dramatic evocations came at the 1925 trial of John Scopes, who had taught Charles Darwin's theory of evolution in Rhea County, Tennesee, in defiance of the state's Butler Act, which forbade the teaching of "any theory that denies the story of the Divine Creation of man as taught in the Bible, and to teach instead that man has descended from the lower order of animals."

The new American Civil Liberties Union made this a test case, bringing to the defense the celebrated lawyers Clarence Darrow, Arthur Garfield Hays and Dudley Field Malone, publicized nationally (and one-sidedly) by the pro-evolution journalist H.L. Mencken. Star prosecutor was William Jennings Bryan, three-time candidate for president. The jury decided in favor of the prosecution and the teacher was fined the minimum, $100, enabling Scopes to say: "I will continue ... to oppose this law in any way I can. Any other action would be in violation of my ideal of academic freedom—that is, to teach the truth as guaranteed in our constitution of personal and religious freedom." The ruling was overturned two years later and the fine never collected.

Academic freedom returned as a national issue during the early 1950s. Pressure was exerted by Senator Joseph McCarthy and others not only against leftists, liberals, and dissenters in general, but also against the presence of their books in publicly sponsored libraries. See JUNKETEERING GUMSHOES. In 1953 President Dwight Eisenhower, speaking at Dartmouth, made his widely quoted response: "Don't join the BOOKBURNERS. Don't think you are going to conceal faults by concealing evidence that they ever existed." By the '60s, the passions of the McCarthy period had cooled, but controversy about academic freedom erupted in Vietnam dissent at the University of California's Berkeley campus.

In 1967 concern was raised over the Central Intelligence Agency's subsidization of student groups. After the first round of investigations, Senator Richard Russell, chairman of the Armed Services Committee, said, "all this clamor about impairing academic freedom ... is a lot of hogwash." By the century's end, with legislation passed restricting "hate speech," the academic freedom to infuriate the majority or intimidate a minority became controversial again.

The issue raised in 2004 was a reverse application of the Scopes case: did those who freshly challenged Darwin's theory— who proposed a theory of creation named in 1903 by Ferdinand Canning Scott Schiller "intelligent design"—have the academic freedom to dispute what almost all scientists agreed was settled scientific truth?

The controversy continues with both sides evoking the principle of academic freedom.

access See INFLUENCE PEDDLER.

accommodation Compromise; relaxation of international tensions after a conciliatory, usually unilateral gesture.

President Woodrow Wilson used the word in its present political sense in his "Peace Without Victory" speech early in 1917: "Difficult and delicate as these questions are, they must be faced with the utmost candor and decided with a spirit of real accommodation if peace is to come with healing in its wings, and come to stay." (Wilson made a subtle allusion to a beautiful phrase in the Hebrew Bible's Malachi 4:2: "But for you who fear my name, the sun of righteousness will rise with healing in its wings.")

When labor leader John L. Lewis split with American Federation of Labor chieftain William Green in 1935 to form the Committee (later Congress) of Industrial Organizations, Arthur Krock wrote in *The New York Times*: "After all, as Huck Finn realized when he heard the Child of Calamity and the other braggart on the raft tell what they would do to each other—and didn't—the most-publicized impasses are those which are surest accommodated. Yet this one looks less soluble in an era of realignments." Ultimately, the AFL and CIO reached their "accommodation," though other union realignments followed.

In 1951 Dr. Edward Corwin wrote in *The New Republic* that Congress and President Truman, in the midst of a constitutional dispute over sending troops to Europe to serve in the North Atlantic Treaty Organization, should undertake "a decent consultation and accommodation of views."

As PEACEFUL COEXISTENCE began to be talked of during the post-Stalin era, the terms accommodation, reconciliation, realignment, and DÉTENTE became popular in many liberal journals, and the SOFT ON COMMUNISM attack lost some of its appeal.

Proponents of a policy of accommodation are serious in their stand, but the word was introduced to the political vocabulary by a comic writer, Artemus Ward (Charles Farrar Browne), in 1866: "My pollertics, like my religion, being of an exceedin' accommodatin' character. ..." See DOVES.

accountability See OVERSIGHT; SIGN OFF ON.

acronyms, political Words formed from the initials of agencies, programs or phrases.

Military acronyms have been in the vanguard. *A.W.O.L.* (Absent Without Leave) is a much-used Army term; an unofficial soldiers' term, *snafu* (in bowdlerized form, "Situation Normal: All Fouled Up") was used by U.S. Secretary of State Dean Acheson on a visit to England in 1952 to apologize for an administrative error: "It is only as the result of what in the United States is known as a *snafu* that you were not consulted about it." (Churchill pronounced it "snay-foo.") Among many derivatives were *fubb* (Fouled Up Beyond Belief) and *tuifu* (The Ultimate In Foul-Ups). (British lexicographer Eric Partridge reported that WWII servicemen would write home with the acronym *norwich* on the back of the envelope, which stood for "kNickers Off Ready When I Come Home.") *WAVEs*, *WACs*, and *WRENs* became well-known words, as did *radar* and *sonar*. Troops of the Republic of Korea soon were known as *ROKs*.

VEEP was first applied to Vice President Alben Barkley and then came to mean the vice president of any organization. When President Eisenhower spoke to *ACTION* (American Committee to Improve Our Neighborhoods), he wondered aloud which came first—the initials or the name.

Secretary of Defense Robert A. Lovett told the National Institute of Social Sciences in 1952 that he frankly advocated the use of what he termed "initialese." He noted that time was saved by referring to the Commander in Chief, Far East, as *CINCFE*, and to his counterpart in Europe as *CINCEUR*. However, *CINCUS* (Commander in Chief, U.S. Fleet) was shudderingly dropped when naval officers pronounced the acronym. As for his own position as Secretary of Defense, the initialese was *SECDEF* rather than the more obvious *S.O.D.* "S.O.D. was abandoned," Lovett explained, "because it would require the most careful enunciation in order not to be excessively accurate as a description of the Secretary of Defense."

Political acronyms are designed to cause a smile. "MOM and POP briefings," reported Scripps-Howard in 1967, "are all the rage at Peace Corps Headquarters here. These are acronyms for 'Memo on Marriage' and 'Policy on Pregnancy.'" Some smiles have been caused inadvertently: During the Nixon Administration, top-secret studies were labeled "National Security Study Memoranda," its initialese *NSSM*, pronounced as an acronym, "Nissim." When Zbigniew Brzezinski took over as National Security Adviser in the Carter Administration, he wanted all vestiges of Kissingerese removed; accordingly, the word "Presidential" was substituted for "National Security" in these memos, which became Presidential Study Memoranda. However, after one day of "PISIMs," embarrassed officials changed the name further to "Presidential *Review* Memoranda," and became known throughout the Carter Administration by the more prim initials, *PRM*s.

Acronyms flourished during the Reagan years. To replace *SALT* (Strategic Arms Limitation Talks), *START* became National Security Adviser Richard Allen's acronym for Strategic Arms Reductions Talks. That change had a rationale—object of the talks was to reduce, not merely limit, nuclear weapons—but the last "t"—for *talks*—preserved a redundancy in the commonly used "START talks." (In the same way, *OPEC* stood for Organization of Petroleum Exporting Countries, with "OPEC countries" another redundancy.)

A deliberately jocular acronym making the rounds in the 1980s was *BOGSAT* (sometimes spelled *BOGSATT*), used to describe the process by which a president chooses his team. In 1986, Congressman Les Aspin explained to reporters that the acronym meant "Bunch of guys sitting around the table." This took place in the power corridor called *BOSNYWASH* (Boston, New York, Washington).

Financial terms such as *DINK* ("double income, no kids") and variations of *YUPPIE*

("young, urban preppie") flourished in the late 1980s, and the administration of the elder George Bush helped introduce spook-speak initialese. Acronyms of security clearance include *LIMDIS* ("limited distribution"), *EXDIS* ("exclusive distribution"), and *NOFORN* ("no foreign dissemination"). Operation Desert Storm helped popularize longstanding military acronyms such as *SAM* ("surface-to-air missile") and *MIRV* ("multiple, independently targetable reentry vehicle").

With the advent of the Clinton Administration, an acronym surfaced for Hillary Rodham Clinton: *TMPWA*, pronounced "TUMP-wah," referred to "the most powerful woman in America." This was soon replaced by *FLOTUS*, "First Lady of the United States"; see the entry on POTUS.

The last word on acronyms seemed to belong to a 1977 cartoon in *Punch* showing two angry people marching under a banner titled "COCOA—Council to Outlaw Contrived and Outrageous Acronyms." But ridicule has not stopped the practice of acronymy. Soon after the attacks of 9/11, Congress passed the USA Patriot Act, which few supporters knew stood for "Uniting and Strengthening America by Providing Appropriate Tools Required to Intercept and Obstruct Terrorism."

President George W. Bush, in March of 2003, authorized an Expeditionary Medal for participants in the Global War on Terror, which promptly became known as the *GWOT*, pronounced "gee-what."

(Putting this survey together has been no *PICNIC*, which netties know means Problem In Chair, Not In Computer.)

See CREEP; GULAG; MEGO; RIF.

acting black See RACISM.

activist As a noun, a person willing to work for a cause, to take direct action to accomplish or dramatize its aims; as an adjective, the attitude of that thoroughly involved person.

At the turn of the twentieth century, *activist* was an adjective applied to a philosophy of realism, akin to *pragmatist*, assuming the active existence of everything. By 1920 the adjective's meaning changed to a description of a policy of energetic action; German intellectuals called political engagement *Aktivismus*.

Activist as a noun, with its current meaning, was set forth in 1954 by Arthur Koestler, in *Invisible Writing*: "He was not a politician but a propagandist, not a 'theoretician' but an 'activist.'"

The word replaced *agitator*, now a quaint derogation of a labor organizer, which came into popularity when a high-level committee of English army officers was organized in 1647 to kidnap King Charles I. They called themselves "the Adjutators" (from adjutant, or assistant); the Presbyterians promptly nicknamed them the Agitators, as shakers-up of the status quo. In 1842 "the Agitator" was the sobriquet of Daniel O'Connell, advocate of Irish freedom. In modern times, organized labor has not given up on the word. Lane Kirkland, Secretary-Treasurer of the AFL-CIO, told his convention in 1977: "The founders of the American labor movement left us all with one central theme and doctrine: 'Agitate, Educate, Organize.'" Kirkland, a highly literate former maritime worker who served as speechwriter to the labor leader George Meany, in the same speech defined "militancy" as "an attention-getting device most successfully and easily employed by spearing one's colleagues for the titillation of the press."

Militant is a calibration more active than *activist*. In England in the thirties, the word was often applied to union leaders holding out for high wage demands; by 1960, London's *Economist* was describing "a 'more-militant-than-thou' attitude" on the part of some trade union leaders. In the late sixties the word became popular in the U.S. as a label, usually intended to be pejorative, but not taken that way by those so described, for a demonstrator with "non-negotiable demands." Most of the time, *militant* implied a lack of reasonableness.

In the vocabulary of verbal representation, an *advocate* is a persuasive spokesman, and has a positive connotation, as in the title assumed by Ralph Nader, "consumer advocate"; an *apologist* is a propagandist, a word that once meant "an explicator of God's word" but now denoting "a slavish mouthpiece"; a *spokesman*, *spokeswoman*, or *spokesperson* is a neutral term for a hired hand who presents a point of view in the media for a public figure, or for an executive shunning public exposure.

In the lexicon of activism, an *activist* is one who presses for the idea of direct action or demonstration; a *lobbyist* is a usually pejorative description by an advocate of one side of a paid activist on the other side; a *supporter* is a less active member of the troops, giving rise to the vogue term "supportive"; a *demonstrator* or *protester* is one who participates in street action and may be derogated as a *rioter*; a *dissident* is a heroic description of a demonstrator, noisier than a *dissenter*, not as ideological or likely to harangue as a *demagogue*. A *militant* is a fierce and uncompromising believer in a cause who—when endowed with leadership qualities—can be called a *firebrand* and if armed and dangerous, becomes a *gunman* or an *insurgent*.

During the second Iraq war, Reuters avoided the use of *terrorist* as unduly judgmental, preferring *gunman* (considered by some to be sexist); other media often applied INSURGENT or *violent extremist* to native Iraqis who were bomb-wielding Baathists, suicide bombers killing civilians, or unregenerate followers of Saddam Hussein, reserving *terrorist* for members of Al Qaeda and other non-Iraqi agents provocateur.

See TERRORISM.

adamant for drift See LOYAL OPPOSITION.

administration Members of the Executive Branch; or the government of a specific leader; or regime.

European usage differs from that of the United States on this word. In Europe, "government" is used to describe a particular leader's time in power, as in Britain, where the Brown government replaced the Blair government. When, as in Italy or France, a government is said to "fall," only the leadership of a party or coalition falls; the structure of government, of course, continues.

In the U.S., *administration* is used to designate the time in office of a president, while *government* is used to mean the ongoing constitutional organization. "Administration officials" and "administration policy" are U.S. government men and policies, but the use of the temporary word stresses the temporary tenure of U.S. elected officials.

Regime is the loosest word of the three and can be used for the power-span of an individual ("the Brezhnev regime") or a mode of government (*l'ancien régime*). This is a European word, however; in the U.S. it is mainly applied to foreign governments or eras. Thus, Englishmen in 1978 thought of "the Carter government" in the U.S., and Americans talked of "the Callaghan administration" in Great Britain, each applying his own usage to the other's political system; both, however, referred to a "Gaullist regime," as did the French. In U.S. usage, *regime* is pejorative; Senator George McGovern derogated the Saigon government of South Vietnam in 1972 as "the Thieu regime." See REGIME CHANGE.

A second use of *administration* is in subcabinet-level government agencies, as in *National Recovery Administration* and *Federal Housing Administration*, though there has been a tendency to substitute *agency* for *administration* in these titles. A *commission* differs from an administration or agency in that it is a quasi-judicial board; an *authority* is an organization set up by legislative act, one step removed from political influence or likelihood of change as an administration (in its first, overall sense) changes.

advance man One who arranges for publicity, protocol, transportation, speaking schedules, conferences with local government officials, and minute details of a visit, smoothing the way for a political figure.

Preparations for a campaign or less political trip are known as "advancing." Members of the advance party usually move into a city three or four days ahead of the candidate. At least one professional writer is on hand to draft "local inserts" for the candidate's speeches. He might prepare specific data on how the regional economy was suffering under the opposition administration, or scan local newspapers for issues on which the candidate might comment. Such a writer would also develop a humorous introduction that would have special meaning for local voters or politicians.

Advance men (and women; the phrase of art remains *advance man*, though when the team is mixed it is called *the advance*) work with local party leaders to plan the schedule, determine the motorcade route, decide on platform sites and seating, help get crowds to turn out, arrange for police and handle press, distribute press kits, flags, buttons and banners, and arrange for "spontaneous" hand-lettered signs, etc.

President Dwight D. Eisenhower's advance man at the Republican convention in San Francisco in 1956 was the resourceful Tom Stephens, who, in this note to Sherman Adams, concerned himself with the probable weather:

If the President arrived some time between 8:30 and 9:30 at night I believe it would be most helpful to him. While it is not cold here in the evening, it does get cool, and if you will look at the weather reports for the last couple of years, which I am enclosing, you will find that it has never gone below 50 degrees and seldom over 60 degrees between 8:30 and 9:30 around the 22nd, 23rd or 24th of August.

The predecessor phrase of *advance man* was *advance agent*; in 1897, that circus term was politically applied by Tennessee Congressman H. R. Gibson, who lauded "that great priest and apostle of protection, and that great advance agent of prosperity, William McKinley." See BANDWAGON.

In the lingo of advance men, *newsies* (reporters plus *wires*, *reels*, and *stills*) and *staffers* make up the *caravan* following *the Man* or, if a woman, *Herself*. Sometimes included are *surrogates*, a half-dozen VIPs who can speak for the candidate before, after, or instead of a personal appearance. The advance staff can schedule, or *pencil in*, a hasty *drop-by* or a *visual*, which is a *photo opportunity*, even if this means *lunching him out* (denying the overbooked candidate a midday meal); ears are cocked at the rally for the *wrap-up*, or standard peroration, which is the signal for a dash to buses to beat the crowd out of the hall.

In 1973, during the Watergate investigation, the term "black advance" was used to describe the darker side of advance work. Presidential aide Richard Moore, acting as an investigative counsel, drafted a memo dated March 22, 1973, detailing what he found in interviews with Gordon Strachan and Dwight Chapin about the disruptive activities of Donald Segretti: "They made reference to Dick Tuck [a legendary Democratic prankster] and cited the kind of harassment of the campaign activities of opposition candidates which Tuck has engaged in over the years. At one point, Strachan described the type of activity as 'black advance,' a term used in political campaigning to describe the planning of measures to harass the opposition or to detect and guard against harassment by the opposition." Segretti served a jail term for campaign infractions, and Chapin (who had skillfully advanced the 1972 Nixon trip to China) was sentenced for misleading an official; suddenly, political advance work learned its limits.

A sign frequently displayed in rooms where experienced advance men teach the trade to neophytes eager for FACE TIME with the candidate reads: "If you arrive with the candidate, you're not advancing."

advice and consent The phrase in the U.S. Constitution (Art. II, sec. 2) enabling the Senate to act as a check on the appointive and treaty-making powers of the president.

In its original form, "advice and consent" is one of the oldest political phrases in current use. In 1184, Henry II issued the Forest Assize "by the advice and consent [*per consilium et assensum*] of the archbishops, bishops, barons, earls, and nobles of England," and Henry III ascended the throne "by the common advice and consent of the said king and the magnates."

The English colonies in America preserved the phrase and concept, with the executive acting "by and with the advice and consent" of whatever the legislative body happened to be named.

At the 1787 Constitutional Convention, it was natural for the English-trained lawyers to use the phrase in describing the action of the Senate to review appointments: "He [the President] shall nominate, and by and with the advice and consent of the Senate shall appoint ambassadors, other public ministers, and consuls, etc."

The "advice" function soon atrophied and was merged into "consent." Although the phrase survives intact, in practice its meaning has been halved: the Senate checks, but usually does not share, the presidential power of appointment. See BLUE SLIP.

An omission in the Constitution led to a century-long battle between the executive and legislative arms of the U.S. government: Need the President seek the advice and consent of the Senate in the removal of appointed officials? Though Jefferson grumbled about the offices packed with Federalists when he came to power in 1800 ("few die and none resign"), he displaced only 39 of them. Andrew Jackson, when the Senate refused to amend the civil-service laws to make places for his followers, proceeded to replace more than a thousand political appointees in his first year, and the Senate did not take up the strong president's gauntlet. See SPOILS SYSTEM.

Weaker presidents followed Jackson, however, and "senatorial courtesy" soon encroached on both powers of appointing and removing. See PERSONALLY OBNOXIOUS. The Tenure of Office Act of 1867 seized much power from Andrew Johnson's hands by limiting removal of public officials to reasons of "misconduct or crime." Only slightly modified, the law rankled Presidents Grant, Hayes, and Garfield, but not until 1887 was a president—Grover Cleveland—able to have the act repealed and permanently wrest the power of consent from the Senate. Said Cleveland to the Senate: "my duty to the Chief Magistracy which I must preserve unimpaired in all its dignity and vigor compels me to refuse compliance …"

The most dramatic case of the Senate's withholding advice and consent was its rejection of the League of Nations, despite Woodrow Wilson's pleas; this is inaccurately identified with the LITTLE GROUP OF

WILLFUL MEN. During the Eisenhower Administration, the refusal to confirm the appointment of Admiral Lewis Strauss as Secretary of Commerce was a surprising defeat. In 1969, the Senate rejection of President Nixon's Supreme Court nominees, Clement Haynsworth and then G. Harrold Carswell, was widely interpreted as a reassertion of the "advice" function, as was the 1977 resistance to the Carter nomination of Theodore Sorensen to be Director of Central Intelligence, which caused the famed Kennedy speechwriter to withdraw.

This ancient phrase was popularized in 1959 when it was used as the title of a novel by Allen Drury, later made into a motion picture. The title was *Advise and Consent*, the verb "advise," not the noun "advice," which is in Senate Rule 38: "the final question on every nomination shall be, 'Will the Senate advise and consent to this nomination?'" Although most earlier expressions of the phrase used the noun "advice" rather than the verb "advise," in current use the verb is preferred because it denotes action and automatically changes the companion word, "consent," from a noun to a verb.

During the 1980s, Ronald Reagan's nomination of Judge Robert H. Bork was defeated in the Senate (see the eponymous verb, to BORK). The elder George Bush's nominee, Judge Clarence Thomas, was confirmed but only after nationally televised hearings into charges of sexual harassment made against Thomas by Professor Anita Hill.

advisers (1) Paid political consultants; (2) the unofficial family of longtime friends or "cronies"; (3) informal title of official assistants who wish to upgrade the title of "aide"; (4) military personnel dispatched to a friendly government to train its army, or a euphemism for those armed forces to conceal their combat role.

The agent-noun *adviser* dates back to 1611 for "one who gives counsel or advice." A modifying term, as in *security adviser*, identifies the authority's area of expertise.

Military use began in 1915, when *adviser* first served as a euphemism for "combat soldier," particularly one sent to help a foreign army. The 1915 *Handbook of the Turkish Army* described reserve divisions formed by "Turkish military authorities and their German military advisers," and a 1939 text on Soviet policy stated, "The Russians have kept a number of 'advisers,' military and otherwise, in Sinkiang for several years."

The military assistance of advisers provided to Vietnam in the 1960s and El Salvador in the early 1980s drew sharp criticism. Walt W. Rostow, Lyndon B. Johnson's national security adviser during the Vietnam War, told *The Washington Post* in 1982: "We already have military advisers on the scene in El Salvador—though we have renamed them 'trainers.' Trainers, advisers, whatever—they are our tribute, our tangible contribution meant to make our commitment look good." Rostow added, "Of course, advisers in Vietnam proved inadequate to the task at hand, a task that wasn't carefully measured before the commitment was made."

In the Iraq war beginning in 2002, coalition forces led by the U.S. ultimately sought to become advisers to the regular Iraqi army fighting an insurgency and terrorists, and were "embedded" in Iraqi units as teaching combatants. The term *adviser*, recalling the euphemism used in Vietnam, was avoided.

The term is sometimes spelled *advisor*, on the *-or* analogy of *supervisor*, which is not incorrect, but the predominant spelling is now with an *e*. By the 2008 campaign, the proliferation of advisers reduced the significance of the title; "key advisers" became "strategists."

affirmative action See QUOTA.

affluent society A semi-critical view of the economic condition of the U.S.: rich and booming, with undertones of unrest from those not participating in the affluence.

The publisher's blurb on a reprint of John Kenneth Galbraith's 1958 book reads, "*The Affluent Society* has added a new phrase to our language." It has. Positioned between Walter Lippmann's *The Good Society* and Lyndon Johnson's GREAT SOCIETY, Galbraith's phrase was taken up by critics of America's effort to come to grips with poverty at home. Yet his theme was not pessimistic:

The affluent country which conducts its affairs in accordance with rules of another and poorer age also foregoes opportunities.... The problems of an affluent world, which does not understand itself, may be serious, and they can needlessly threaten the affluence itself. But they are not likely to be as serious as those of a poor world where the simple exigencies of poverty preclude the luxury of misunderstanding but where, also and alas, no solutions are to be had.

Use was made of the phrase by Dr. Martin Luther King, Jr., in a 1963 letter written to ministers from a Birmingham jail: "when you see the vast majority of your twenty million Negro brothers smothering in an air-tight cage of poverty in the midst of an affluent society... then you will understand why we find it difficult to wait."

The phrase has been largely replaced in populist polemics by *the rich*.

African-American See BLACK, POLITICAL USE OF.

again and again and again An oratorical device of FDR's.

During the 1940 campaign, Wendell Willkie's charge that FDR was leading the nation into war annoyed the President and worried his advisers. Bronx boss Ed Flynn wired his demand that Roosevelt reassure the public that he was not going to send Americans into foreign wars.

"But how often do they expect me to say that?" Roosevelt asked Harry Hopkins and speechwriter Robert E. Sherwood. "It's in the Democratic platform and I've repeated it a hundred times."

"Evidently," said Sherwood, "you've got to say it again—and again—and again."

Roosevelt liked the phrase, especially since his own pronunciation of *again* was distinctive in U.S. speech, rhyming with *rain* rather than *when*. He chose to say "Your boys are not going to be sent into any foreign wars," although Judge Samuel Rosenman, another talented speechwriter, wanted to add a cautious "except in case of attack." Roosevelt disagreed: "If we're attacked it's no longer a foreign war." In a famous Boston speech (see MARTIN, BARTON, AND FISH) the President said: "I have said this

before, but I shall say it *again and again and again*: Your boys are not going to be sent into any foreign wars."

Four years later, however, in the campaign against Republican Thomas E. Dewey, FDR found himself on the defensive because he had not used the "except" clause Rosenman had recommended. The President turned a minus to a plus by repeating the phrase originally associated with the statement: "I am sure that any real American would have chosen, as this government did, to fight when our own soil was made the object of a sneak attack. As for myself, under the same circumstances, I would choose to do the same thing *again, and again, and again*." The crowd, remembering, roared its approval.

The phrase continued to reverberate after Roosevelt's death in 1945. The *Chicago Tribune*, its publisher, Col. Robert R. McCormick, the longtime arch-foe of FDR, recalled it in 1948 while lambasting somebody else: "The Great I Am, old Again and Again and Again himself, couldn't possibly have done a better job of bunking the American people. ..."

ageism See SEXISM.

agitprop Obvious propaganda.

In a 1977 theater review in *Time* magazine, T. E. Kalem wrote of a play by Bertolt Brecht: "One word of joyous warning. In *Happy End*, Brecht has dropped agitprop. The show has no redeeming social value save delight."

The word was long a *Time* favorite. In 1935 the newsmagazine reported: "Far more serious, far more earnest is the Depression-born movement of workers' theaters which are currently putting on 'agit-prop' (agitational propaganda) plays in 300 U.S. cities."

Like *apparatchik* ("bureaucrat"), the word has a nicely sinister foreign tone. It comes from the Russian abbreviation of *agitatsiya i propaganda*, "agitation and propaganda," which was the name of a department of the Central Committee of the Communist Party in the former Soviet Union dealing with political persuasion.

Still hyphenated in many dictionaries, it has lost its hyphen in current journalistic use.

Though the word now has an old-fashioned flavor, it has been embraced in the blogosphere, where it has found an eminent new domain in the titles of websites and blogs.

agonizing reappraisal Pained reassessment; phrase used by U.S. Secretary of State John Foster Dulles in December 1953, hinting at a possible change in American policy toward its European allies.

The architect of Eisenhower's foreign policy was well aware that any change in American foreign policy that would weaken the position of American allies in Europe would be very painful both to them and to the U.S.; however, since the U.S. had growing commitments in Asia, Africa, and Latin America, it might have to shift its area of primary concern from the European continent to one of the other major areas of East-West conflict.

He told the National Press Club: "When I was in Paris last week, I said that…the United States would have to undertake an agonizing reappraisal of basic foreign policy in relation to Europe. This statement, I thought, represented a self-evident truth."

The mouth-filling nature of the phrase has kept it in the political language long after its specific Europe-to-Far East meaning died. In 1965, Yale professor Staughton Lynd called presidential security adviser McGeorge Bundy "that unagonized reappraiser."

In 1976, trying to persuade Israel to offer more concessions to Arabs in his SHUTTLE DIPLOMACY, Secretary of State Henry Kissinger called for a "reassessment" of U.S. support, a word that Democratic candidate Jimmy Carter exploited in a televised debate with President Ford.

Agonizing, a headline-grabbing word, was avoided by diplomats afterward. Kissinger's favorite word to express pain was *neuralgic*.

For other Dulles coinages, see BRINKMANSHIP; MASSIVE RETALIATION.

aide-mémoire See POSITION PAPER.

alarmist One who is easily frightened and transmits his panic to others, or one who sounds an alarm for defeatist purposes

The word has an international history of use just before and during wartime. Of French origin (*alarmiste*), the word was coined during the French Revolution. It is attributed to Bertrand Barère de Vieuzac, French lawyer and revolutionist who defended the Terror. It was used in England in 1794 by the Irish dramatist and orator, Richard Brinsley Sheridan, in a speech in Parliament: "Will the train of newly titled alarmists…thank him for remarking to us how profitable his panic has been to themselves, and how expensive to the country?"

In the U.S. the word was employed defensively in 1840 by Representative John White of Kentucky, quoted in the *Congressional Globe*: "Sir, open and bold usurpations never alarm me. I fear no danger of the perpetuity of this Government, from the assaults of the manly tyrant or despot. I can look with some forbearance upon the unjust pretensions to power, asserted and defended upon principle; yet, whilst I protest, I am no alarmist."

"Alarmist cries about the lack of civilian control of the military," said Truman's Secretary of Defense Robert Lovett, "deal with a STRAWMAN issue." Recently, those who present evidence of global warming, as well as doctors who urge drastic public health expenditures to combat the perceived threat of bird flu to humans, have been dismissed as alarmist; their retaliatory words to skeptics are "short-sighted" escalating to "smug" and "complacent" and "blind."

When the Department of Homeland Security issued a warning in 2007 that school buses in the U.S. were threatened, it turned out that its "red cell" teams—assigned to think of exotic scenarios before terrorists do—were the source of the advisory. *Newsweek* came up with a play on the word in its headline: "Warning: Alarmism."

all deliberate speed See WITH ALL DELIBERATE SPEED; ROOT AND BRANCH.

Alliance for Progress John F. Kennedy's Latin American policy, first labeled by him in a campaign speech at Tampa, Florida, in October 1960.

Speechwriter Richard Goodwin recalled that the phrase was born while he was riding in a campaign bus rolling through Texas in September 1960. Trying to think of the words which would express for Kennedy what GOOD NEIGHBOR POLICY had expressed for Franklin D. Roosevelt, Goodwin's eye caught the title of a Spanish-language magazine left on the bus in Arizona: *Alianza.*

Kennedy agreed that *alliance* should be part of the phrase; but alliance for what? Goodwin telephoned Karl Meyer, one of the editors of *The Washington Post*, for suggestions. Meyer, in turn, called Ernesto Betancourt, a Cuban who had broken with Fidel Castro and was working for the Pan American Union in Washington. "Betancourt said to Meyer," Goodwin informs the author, "that it should be Alliance for something, and proposed several alternatives including 'development,' 'freedom,' 'progress,' etc., from which the final version was selected."

Ted Sorensen offers a different version: "I suggested 'Alianza,' assuming that it had broader meaning than 'alliance' because it was the name of an insurance cooperative organized by some of our Mexican-American supporters in Arizona. A Cuban refugee and Latin America expert in Washington, Ernesto Betancourt, suggested through Goodwin the addition of 'para el progreso' (although for some time we mistakenly dropped the 'el'). The candidate liked it—and the Alliance for Progress was born."

The Alliance for Progress was launched officially on March 13, 1961, before the Latin American diplomatic corps assembled for the occasion in the White House. "I have called on all people of the hemisphere," said President Kennedy, "to join in a new Alliance for Progress—*Alianza para Progreso*—a vast cooperative effort, unparalleled in magnitude and nobility of purpose, to satisfy the basic needs of the American people for homes, work and land, health and schools. ... Let us once again transform the American continent into a vast crucible of revolutionary ideas and efforts."

Any grand title lends itself to ridicule. Asked Senator Everett Dirksen in 1967:

"Where is the Alliance? Where is the Progress?"

But the Kennedy phrase continues to resonate: the *Guardian* newspaper in Britain noted in 2007 that Chancellor of the Exchequer Gordon Brown urged that Britain and India "combine in a new 'alliance for progress' to tackle climate change and terrorism."

alliteration Repetition of the same consonant or sound in consecutive words; a device, when used obviously, to coin a slogan or catch phrase; when used subtly, to create a mood rather than a phrase.

"Apt alliteration's artful aid," a 1763 turn of phrase by Charles Churchill always used in discussing alliteration, has been neatly disposed of in Fowler's *Usage:* "not as good an example of alliteration as it looks, since only the first two a's have the same value."

When a Member of Parliament made a snide reference to "fancy franchises," Benjamin Disraeli replied: "Alliteration tickles the ear and is a very popular form of language among savages ... but it is not an argument in legislation."

The careful culling of consonants to pack a punch in politics has long been in U.S. common use, for good and evil. An early Ku Klux Klan slogan: "Kill the Kikes, Koons, and Katholics." In the 1876 campaign: "Hayes, Hard Money and Hard Times." See RUM, ROMANISM AND REBELLION.

In the twenties, politicians tried to emulate the alliterative success of Warren G. Harding, who made history with "not heroics but healing, not nostrums but NORMALCY, not revolution but restoration, not agitation but adjustment, not surgery but serenity, not the dramatic but the dispassionate, not experiment but equipoise, not submergence in internationality but sustainment in triumphant nationality."

In 1952 Adlai Stevenson, stung by the "Korea, Communism and Corruption" slogan of the Republicans (see K_1C_2), attacked all the alliterative phrases: "each of the following words will appear at least once: crime, corruption and cronies; bossism, blundering and bungling; stupidity and socialism ..."

"Words can do more than convey policy," John F. Kennedy wrote in 1961, using alliteration to show what he meant: "They can also convey and create a mood, an attitude, an atmosphere—or an awakening."

President Lyndon Johnson, whose Texas style and accent struck many Eastern intellectuals as corny, addressed a joint session of Congress five days after the Kennedy assassination and used alliteration subtly and effectively: "I profoundly hope that the tragedy and the torment of these terrible days will bind us together ..."

Vice President Spiro Agnew, campaigning in 1970 to elect Republican congressmen, enjoyed smiting Democrats as "pusillanimous pussyfooters" and "vicars of vacillation," reaching a zenith (sometimes derided as a nadir) with NATTERING NABOBS OF NEGATIVISM. In so doing, he made alliteration a campaign issue, but the technique was contagious—Senator George McGovern denounced the Vice President's "foaming fusillades."

Ronald Reagan used EVIL EMPIRE; George H.W. Bush said America had "more will than wallet." In the 1992 debates, Bill Clinton trotted out "heartbreak and hope, more pain and more promise," while Bush—who intended to use "deadbeat dads"—muffed the alliteration by saying "deadbeat fathers."

The technique is still used to gather issues. A half-century after "Korea, Communism and Corruption," Republicans sought to tie moral issues (anti-abortion, pro-prayer in schools) to weaponry for hunting and self-protection (and opposition to control thereof) and the rights of homosexuals (extended as same-sex marriage) into "God, guns, and gays." The repetition of the three "g" sounds was most often used by critics of these conservative positions, as in this use in 2006 by the newly elected Democratic senator from Virginia, James Webb: "Working Americans have been repeatedly seduced at the polls by emotional issues such as the predictable mantra of 'God, guns, gays, abortion and the flag' ..."

all things to all men Deliberate ambivalence; multi-facedness.

The phrase is used against a politician who makes conflicting promises to win an election or gain advantage, but it can also be used to describe public speculation about an unknown quantity. Jonathan Daniels, former press secretary to President Roosevelt, wrote of the reaction to Harry Truman's ascension to the presidency when Roosevelt died: "He seemed all things to all men and all men including New Dealers and anti-New Dealers, Roosevelt friends and Roosevelt enemies, old friends and new ones, Pendergast politicians, Truman committee members, the eager and the ambitious, seemed to expect that he would be all things to them."

The technique is universally condemned but widely practiced; oddly, the phrase is related to concepts like "beauty is in the eye of the beholder" and "a face only a mother could love." In a work of art, an object that generates varying interpretations is often taken to be a mark of greatness; in diplomacy, a studied ambiguity is often admired; but in politics, a man who seeks to be all things to all men runs the risk of being nothing to anybody, and the practitioner can be attacked as "fuzzy" or for being "tall in the STRADDLE."

In 1826 Benjamin Disraeli entitled a chapter of his novel *Vivian Grey* "All Things To All Men," using the phrase in its current sense. The duplicity in the phrase is readily admitted by the Christian saint who coined the term and perfected the art. In the 1611 King James translation of I Corinthians 9:20, Paul the Apostle says: "And unto the Jews I became as a Jew, that I might gain the Jews." On that principle he ordered the circumcision of Timothy, to recommend that follower of Christ's ministry to the Jews, despite Christianity's substitution of baptism for circumcision as a religious rite. St. Paul continues two verses later: "To the weak became I as weak, that I might gain the weak: I am made *all things to all men*, that I might by all means save some." He justifies the means by the end in 10:32–33: "Give none offense, neither to the Jews, nor to the Gentiles, nor to the Church of God: even as I please all men in all things, not seeking mine own profit, but the profit of many, that they may be saved."

The technique of being all things to all men has an effect not only on the voter but often on the candidate. "No man, for any considerable period," Nathaniel Hawthorne wrote, "can wear one face to himself, and another to the multitude, without finally getting bewildered as to which may be the true."

alphabet agencies A mild derogation of the proliferation of government agencies created in the early months of Franklin D. Roosevelt's Administration.

New administrations, authorities, and corps appeared in sudden profusion in 1933: NRA (National Recovery Administration), TVA (Tennessee Valley Authority), CCC (Civilian Conservation Corps), and AAA (Agricultural Adjustment Administration) were among the best known.

The term was originally "alphabetical agencies," used in this manner by Bronx Democratic boss Ed Flynn: "A small informal committee was formed, however, consisting of [James] Farley, [Frank] Walker, [Louis] Howe, and myself. We were primarily interested in taking care of the original group of people who had started out with us in the campaign prior to the convention in Chicago. This group became known as the 'FRBC': 'for Roosevelt before Chicago.' Perhaps this was the first of the New Deal alphabetical agencies."

The alphabet-agency phrase gave color to the charge of excessive bureaucracy. Democrat Al Smith, disenchanted with Roosevelt, described the government as "submerged in a bowl of alphabet soup," and Republican campaigners at their 1936 convention carried an Alfred Landon banner that read "UP WITH ALF—DOWN WITH THE ALPHABET!"

The use of initials in describing government acts and agencies hardly originated in the New Deal. In World War I, Great Britain's Defence of the Realm Act was called DORA, and the American Expeditionary Force was the AEF. In Germany in the 1920s, *Nationalsozialistische* was shortened to Nazi, and in Russia the *Obyedinennoe Gosudarstvennoe Politicheskoe Upravlenie* (United State Political Directorate) was known as the OGPU. In a 1990 review of a book on

the KGB, *Time* magazine described the spy agency's evolution "through an alphabet soup of designations (GPU, OGPU< NKVD< NKGB< MGB<< MVD to the present KGB)." True to tradition, it changes its name every few years.

Today, with the proliferation of government agencies and commissions operative and accepted, the phrase "alphabet agencies" conveys mild amusement but the political sting is gone. See ACRONYMS, POLITICAL.

always falling, never fallen See ADMINISTRATION; SPLINTER GROUP; BUREAUCRACY.

amateurs Professional politician's scornful word for citizens inexperienced in political campaigns who show up near election time only, but without whom most campaigns would be doomed.

The obvious difference between an amateur and a professional in politics is the degree of experience. More important, however, is the willingness to work in what politicians call "the vineyards" on a year-round basis, without the glamour and excitement of a campaign. Amateurs should not be confused with VOLUNTEERS, lower-level campaign workers who are recruited for canvassing, poll-watching, letter-writing, coffee-klatsch-giving, and clerical work. In a professional politician's eyes, amateurs include those top-level businessmen, labor leaders, attorneys, advertising and public relations people who are highly paid and highly successful in their own fields. Many have excellent political judgment and skills beyond most political pros; their enthusiasm and the transient nature of their politicking are their strengths, because they can speak their minds freely. Moreover, they are unaware of obstacles that the professional knows exist; through sheer ignorance of previous failure amateurs sometimes scale heights no sensible pol would ever attempt.

On the other hand, many of these high-level amateurs enter politics with a distaste for the pros, or "hacks" (see HACK) as they call them, and reject out of hand the experience and sensitivity leaders have to the often useful TROOPS.

"An important maxim to remember is 'Don't be an amateur,'" said Senator Henry Cabot Lodge in 1951, when he was the unofficial campaign manager for Eisenhower in battle against the "pros" behind Robert Taft. "The job of being a professional politician, in spite of the odium which some persons have falsely attached to it, is a high and difficult one." In that instance, as in others, amateurs like Tex McCrary acting professionally, in tandem with pros like Len Hall respecting the amateurs, were able to capture the nomination.

See VOLUNTEERS and THOU SHALT NOT STEAL; for antonyms, see OLD PRO; PROFESSIONAL.

amen corner Center of automatic support; political claque that applauds and echoes the party line.

This phrase predates the Civil War. *Harper's Magazine* commented in 1860 that "The Reverend Judson Noth, a local Methodist preacher, ... was one of the best 'scotchers' that occupied the 'Amen Corner.'" The term applied to the part of a church or meetinghouse in which believers sat to respond regularly with "amen" to the preacher's words.

By 1884, the *Congressional Record* cited a transference to politics: "When commiserated upon the fact that he was compelled to go to what is commonly known here as the amen corner, [he] frankly said that any seat in the Senate was better than none." The same publication referred a decade later to "those saintly Republican monopolists who sit in the 'amen corner' of protected privilege."

Although the term was in decline by the late 1970s, it was revived and popularized by Patrick Buchanan before his 1992 presidential campaign. A conservative columnist and former communications aide to Richard Nixon and Ronald Reagan, Buchanan criticized plans for Operation Desert Storm in a 1990 comment: "There are only two groups that are beating the drums for war in the Middle East—the Israeli Defense Ministry and its amen corner in the United States." This position triggered charges that Buchanan was imputing a dual loyalty to Jewish American commentators and was

thus anti-Semitic, a charge reluctantly subscribed to by the conservative columnist William F. Buckley.

The term clung to Buchanan. In 2003, criticism from the anti-interventionist (or isolationist) far right of the decision by President George W. Bush to invade Iraq and oust Saddam Hussein drew this comment from Toronto's *National Post*: "Their resentment of the often-Jewish neos had expressed itself in the form of an ever-more strident hostility to the state of Israel and (in Buchanan's term) Israel's 'amen corner' in the United States." The phrase, now usually lowercased, sparked a smaller controversy when the British television journalist David Frost interviewed Buchanan. Mr. Frost pronounced the interjection as AH-men; Buchanan countered with the *a* in *amen* pronounced as in *say*.

Golfers know the phrase in a wholly different context: that of prayerful contemplation of difficulty. The challenging 11th, 12th, and 13th holes of the Augusta National, annual site of the Masters championship, are known as "the Amen corner."

American boys Oratorical evocation of vulnerability of members of U.S. armed forces, now outdated.

"We want to get the boys out of the trenches," said Henry Ford in 1915, explaining the purpose of his Ford Peace Ship. He did not add, Gilbert Seldes insists, "by Christmas," nor was he referring to "American boys" who were not yet fighting. Nevertheless, the idea of "getting the boys home by Christmas" has become a phrase used in every U.S. war since.

Isolationist Senator Burton K. Wheeler, on January 12, 1941, infuriated FDR by stating, "The lend-lease-give program ... will plow under every fourth American boy." Roosevelt called this remark "the rottenest thing that has been said in public life in my generation."

In the Korean conflict (it was never officially declared a "war"), General Douglas MacArthur, dismissed for insubordination by President Harry Truman, told a Senate investigating committee in May of 1951: "You can't just say 'Let that war go on indefinitely while I prepare for some other war,' unless you pay for it by the thousands and thousands and thousands of American boys."

President Lyndon Johnson probably regretted a "boys" usage made during the 1964 campaign that came back to haunt him. Urging a policy of restraint in Vietnam, on August 12 the President attacked those pressing for escalation: "They call upon us to supply American boys to do the job that Asian boys should do."

The use of *boys* rather than *men* was obviously used to play on the emotions of parents; the word stresses the youth of the troops, thereby seeking to increase the public's desire to protect them from bloody warfare. The word is so obviously loaded, however, that there was a tendency toward the end of the twentieth century to steer away from its use for fear of appearing demagogic. Then, as women entered the armed forces in increasing numbers, serving in dangerous places, the use of *boys* was seen as sexist. "American boys and girls" was a nonstarter—the word *girls* for adult women is taken as offensive—and *servicemembers* lacks the youthful emotional tug. Critics of the conduct of the second Iraq war at first settled on calling for a timetable to bring home "the troops." See BENCHMARKS.

Without the word *American*, the word *boys* acquired a different political meaning. The other boys are "the boys in the backroom"—the political bosses, a usage traceable to 1879: "Stalwartism" [see STALWART], wrote *The Nation*, "includes indifference or hostility to civil-service reform, and a willingness to let 'the boys' have a good time with the offices." That sense of the word is current, though occasional.

American Dream The ideal of freedom and opportunity that motivated the nation's founders; in oratory, an evocation of the great hopes of the nation.

Compared with the AMERICAN WAY OF LIFE or AMERICANISM, the American Dream is much less often satirized or considered corny. The American System is considered the skeleton and the American Dream the soul of the American body politic. The phrase has not crossed the usage line from sacred to sacrosanct.

In 1893 Katherine Lee Bates wrote in "America the Beautiful" of a "patriot dream that sees beyond the years." In 1960 the poet Archibald MacLeish, debating "national purpose," said: "There are those, I know, who will reply that the liberation of humanity, the freedom of man and mind, is nothing but a dream. They are right. It is. It is the American dream."

The American Dream, to some, stresses opportunity. Historian Matthew Josephson wrote of Thomas Alva Edison: "The rise of the former trainboy and tramp telegrapher from rags to riches was an enactment of the American Dream."

The black writer Louis Lomax applied it to equality: "It is the segregationists who are wielding the iron pipes and unleashing the savage dogs ... if the law-abiding rather than the lawbreakers must cease and desist, then the American promise is but a cruel joke on humanity and the American dream dissolves to the most God-awful nightmare."

Both novelist Norman Mailer and playwright Edward Albee have attacked the phrase in titles. Richard Cornuelle, before becoming executive director of the National Association of Manufacturers, wrote a book in 1965 about the "private sector" called *Reclaiming the American Dream*. His central point: "For a long time it seemed that the free society and the good society could be realized together in America. This, I think, was the American dream."

The phrase defies definition as much as it invites discussion. As a force behind government philosophy, it seems to be interpreted by most users as a combination of freedom and opportunity with growing overtones of social justice. In the personal sense, its present meaning can be inferred from the words Richard Nixon wrote in accepting the Republican nomination in 1960: "I can only say tonight to you that I believe in the American dream because I have seen it come true in my own life."

SEE I HAVE A DREAM; LIFT OF A DRIVING DREAM; VISION OF AMERICA; "I SEE" CONSTRUCTION.

Americanism A patriotic political philosophy, sometimes abused by chauvinists; also, a word or phrase peculiarly American.

Theodore Roosevelt popularized "Americanism" in 1909 as "a question of principle, of purpose, of idealism, of character; it is not a matter of birthplace or creed or line of descent." It was Roosevelt who introduced or propagated the phrases "100% American" and "hyphenated American," and he often returned to this theme: "Americanism means the virtues of courage, honor, justice, truth, sincerity, and hardihood—the virtues that made America."

The KNOW-NOTHINGS of the 1840s and 1850s had given the word a different meaning. They were opposed, for example, to waves of immigration and especially to Irish Catholics. Progressives, however, used *Americanism* in the opposite sense—to urge assimilation of immigrants into the U.S. social system. The issue of immigration—one side calling for a protective fence along the Mexican-U.S. border and the other side urging the earning of amnesty for the more than 12 million immigrants estimated to be living illegally in the U.S. now—persists well into the third millennium.

Editor William Allen White wrote of the McKinley-Bryan campaign of 1896: "The election will sustain Americanism or it will plant Socialism." Huey P. Long, U.S. Senator and Governor of Louisiana, frequently accused of secret ambitions to become a dictator, once said that "if fascism comes to America it would be in a program of Americanism." See UN-AMERICAN.

In its other, linguistic sense, the word *Americanism* was first used in 1781 by John Witherspoon, a signer of the Declaration of Independence and president of the College of New Jersey, which became Princeton University:

The first class I call Americanisms, by which I understand an use of phrases or terms, or a construction of sentences, even among people of rank and education, different from the use of the same terms or phrases, or the construction of similar sentences in Great Britain. It does not follow, from a man's using these, that he is ignorant, or his discourse upon the whole inelegant; nay, it does not follow in every case that the terms or the phrases used are worse in themselves, but merely that they are of American and not of English growth. The word *Americanism*, which I have coined for the purpose, is exactly similar in its formation and significance to the word *Scotticism*.

H. L. Mencken, in *The American Language*, a classic of etymology and word study first published in 1919, wrote: "The first American colonists had perforce to invent Americanisms, if only to describe the unfamiliar landscape and weather, flora and fauna confronting them."

See AMNESTY; KNOW-NOTHINGS; LOYALTY OATH.

American system The private enterprise system; occasionally used as a euphemism for capitalism.

"Let the thirteen states," wrote Alexander Hamilton in *The Federalist* Number II, " ... concur in erecting one great American system, superior to the control of all transatlantic force ..." Twenty years later Jefferson wrote: "The history of the last twenty years has been a sufficient lesson for us all to depend for necessaries on ourselves alone; and I hope that twenty years more will place the American hemisphere under a system of its own ..."

In 1824 Senator Henry Clay applied the phrase in a speech defending the protective tariff of that year. To the Kentuckian, the *American system* called up a vision of nationwide economic improvements combined with high tariffs that would reduce America's dependence on imports and expand its domestic market. Hamilton, Jefferson, and Clay used *American system* as a contrast to and defense against the European economy and polity.

In the twentieth century the phrase lost its protective-tariff meaning and has been used in the sense of a political and economic philosophy of life. As Herbert Hoover said in 1945: "The American system of life is unique in the world ... our American system also holds to economic freedom ... we have proved the American system by raising the standards of life higher than any nation on earth." FDR, accused by Hoover of replacing this system with "regimentation," referred in 1936 to "the American system of private enterprise and economic democracy."

In a 1929 interview, underworld overlord Al Capone used the phrase in the current sense: "Don't get the idea that I'm one of these goddam radicals. Don't get the idea that I'm knocking the American system."

For more modern usages, see SYSTEM, THE, and PROCESS, THE.

American way of life Phrase now used mainly in FOURTH OF JULY oratory; earlier, a patriotic characterization of the free enterprise system. Often shortened to "the American Way."

One of the Alf Landon slogans in the campaign of 1936 was "Save the American Way of Life," an appeal to combat the then-radical measures of the New Deal. Telephone operators at the switchboard of the *Chicago Tribune* answered calls with "only__more days to Save the American Way of Life."

American diplomat and motion-picture executive Eric Johnston felt the phrase was a euphemism and in 1958 attacked it head-on: "And the word is *capitalism*. We are too mealy-mouthed. We fear the word capitalism is unpopular. So we talk about the 'free enterprise system' and run to cover in the folds of the flag and talk about the American Way of Life."

In *The Republican Establishment*, Stephen Hess and David Broder described the subjective reaction to the phrase in 1967: "Like [Michigan Governor George] Romney, there is in Nixon a small-town or Western accent on 'the American way' and 'the things that made America great' that seems stodgy to some and pleasantly nostalgic to others."

In the 1980s, the television producer Norman Lear used the phrase in the title of his liberal group, People for the American Way.

amiable dunce Pleasant but incompetent leader; comic or inept politician.

Clark Clifford, the Truman speechwriter, later powerful Washington lawyer, and former Secretary of Defense, originated this clownish configuration when he described President Ronald Reagan in 1981 as "an amiable dunce" with policies that would be "a hopeless failure." Clifford's off-the-record comments, secretly recorded at a Democratic PAC meeting in Averell and Pamela Harriman's Washington home, were reported in *The Wall Street Journal* by James M. Perry.

Levelers of the charge, however, are open to countercharges. Molly Ivins, political analyst for the *Dallas Times Herald*, asked at the end of Reagan's second term: "If, in fact, the President of the United States for the past eight years has been … an 'amiable dunce,' what does it say about the performance of the press that he's leaving office with one of the highest popularity ratings anyone can remember?"

The phrase bit its coiner in 1990. Mr. Clifford, embarrassed by his position as a director of a bank controlled by the corrupt Bank of Commerce and Credit International, asserted that he had been the unwitting dupe of the overseas bankers. A columnist noted that the superlawyer's defense against charges of venality was that he had merely been an "amiable dunce."

amnesty Official declaration of innocence and obliteration of the crime; an attack word on attempts to compromise the "immigration issue."

"Any plan that rewards illegal behavior is amnesty," declared Rep. Brian Bilbray (R-Calif.). "I think the fact that they have to keep saying this is not amnesty, this is not amnesty, shows they really do know it is."

"This word 'amnesty' is often used to create confusion and doubt and anger," responded President George W. Bush, pressing for passage of a bill to deal with the "underground" status of 12 million illegal immigrants living in the U.S. while increasing border security to prevent further unlawful passage into the country. "The definition of amnesty ought to be that you are allowed to become a citizen without paying any price whatsoever. I strongly oppose that."

"Amnesty is where someone comes in illegally and gets in front of others and immediately becomes legal," agreed Gustavo Torres, director of a Maryland group helping illegal immigrants. "This is totally different. You have to pay a fee, learn English, go through the system. It can take up to 13 years to become a resident." Others pointed to the requirement of no criminal record and a return to the native country by the head of the family before applying for permanent residency, in what they labeled "earned citizenship." The strengthening of the border patrol and a construction of a high fence were included as inducements to political fence-straddlers to support the compromise.

One reason that the word *amnesty* became such a trigger for opposition in 2007 was the passage of a 1986 law during the Reagan Administration establishing a one-year amnesty for illegal immigrants who had been in the U.S. for longer than four years; it did nothing to stem the tide of illegal immigration, especially from Mexico; indeed, said many, encouraged it.

Supporters of the compromise between Edward Kennedy (D-Mass.), the liberal leader, and Jon Kyl (R-Ariz.), a strong conservative, charged that another reason for the fierce opposition was anti-immigrant sentiment that represented a throwback to the days of the nativist KNOW-NOTHINGS; in fact, that near-forgotten term was revived to brand all opponents with bigotry.

Senate majority leader Harry Reid (D-Nev.) tried to bring the bill to a vote after nearly two weeks of debate by invoking CLOTURE on June 8, 2007, but got only 45 of the 60 votes needed to pass this motion. In subsequent votes, only a dozen Republican senators stuck with their president, effectively killing Mr. Bush's hope of overhauling immigration policy during his remaining eighteen months in office.

Amnesty abolishes the crime that was committed and declares the person accused or convicted of it to be innocent. A general pardon only relieves the accused or convicted from punishment, and there is dispute over whether acceptance of a pardon is an admission of guilt. President Andrew Johnson's 1868 declaration of amnesty to Confederate war veterans was the most memorable in U.S. history; President Carter's 1977 pardon of Vietnam war draft evaders did not declare their innocence and was not, in this definition, an amnesty.

Like *amnesia*, the word is rooted in the Greek for "not remembering" and is first cited in the *OED* in 1580 as "A law that no man should be called in question nor troubled for things that were past… called *Amnestia*, or law of Oblivion." See AMERICANISM; KNOW-NOTHINGS; and the "damn nasty oath" under LOYALTY OATH.

angry young men A dissatisfied, impatient group of younger people in a party.

When John F. Kennedy achieved his nomination in 1960, he sought to heal the wounds within the party, especially those of older Democrats Harry Truman and Averell Harriman, who would have preferred Stuart Symington or Adlai Stevenson. The nominee explained why he wanted Harriman to second his nomination: "It will be useful for me to have someone who serves as a link to the Roosevelt and Truman administrations; also an older man. I don't want the Convention to think we're just a collection of angry young men."

The *anger* in the phrase had been popularized by British dramatist John Osborne, whose 1956 play *Look Back in Anger* articulated a restlessness and disgust, a rebellion against the "old boy" philosophy prevalent in British politics and business, where young men were trained for careers that they later rejected or that the "Establishment" did not permit them to pursue. After the general use of this phrase began to wane, the political lexicon made "angry young men" its own.

Earlier, in 1951, the religious philosopher Leslie Allen Paul had entitled his autobiography *Angry Young Man*, but it was Jimmy Porter, the hero of Osborne's play, and Lucky Jim, the hero of Kingsley Amis' novel of that name, who became the prototypes of *angry young men*. The phrase crystallized a surly mood. Critic Kenneth Allsop summed it up: "It was as if the pinball that many young people feel themselves to be today, ricocheting in lunatic movement, had hit the right peg. Lights flashed. Bells rang. Overnight 'angry' became the code word."

Allsop went on to define the phrase with some eloquence: "The phrase Angry Young Man carries multiple overtones which might be listed as irreverence, stridency, impatience with tradition, vigour, vulgarity, sulky resentment against the cultivated and a hard-boiled muscling-in on culture, adventurousness ... rude dislike of anything phoney or fey, a broad sense of humour but low on wit, a general intellectual nihilism, honesty, a neurotic discontent and a defeated, reconciled acquiescence that is the last flimsy shelter against complete despondency—a wildly ill-assorted agglomeration of credos which, although without any overall coherence, do belong to this incoherent period of social upheaval."

The exclusion of young women from the phrase limited its use. In America, the phrase for a time eclipsed YOUNG TURKS, with which it is synonymous.

animal See ATTACK DOG; BIRD DOG ... KENNEL DOG; POLITICAL ANIMAL.

animal spirits The entrepreneurial urge; the willingness to embrace risk in generating profit.

The term was first used in English by Bartholomew Traheron, in his 1543 translation of a text on surgery: "There ben thre kindes of spirites, *animal, vital* and *naturall.* The animal spirite hath his seate in the brayne, ... It is called *animal,* bycause it is the first instrument of the soule, whych the Latins call *animam.*"

By the eighteenth century, *animal spirits* found its metaphoric home in economics. William Wood reported in his 1719 *Survey of Trade* on "The Increase of our Foreign Trade ... whence has arisen all those Animal Spirits, those Springs of Riches which has [*sic*] enabled us to spend so many millions for the preservation of our Liberties."

The economist John Maynard Keynes (see NEW ECONOMICS) picked up this noun phrase and used it three times in his 1936 masterwork, *The General Theory of Employment, Interest, and Money.* Lord Keynes supported this risk-taking: "If the animal spirits are dimmed and the spontaneous optimism falters, leaving us to depend on nothing but a mathematical expectation, enterprise will fade and die."

Today's use of the term by political economists varies from "risk-taking investment" to "undue optimism," as in the following statement by economist Larry Kudlow, quoted in the October 15, 1990, issue of *National Review*: "Most of all, the problem with current economic conditions is a decided lack of risk-taking and entrepreneurship. Instead of animal spirits, business and consumers seem possessed by a highly defensive belt-tightening strategy."

The primary sense, however, connotes courage, the nerve that Daniel Defoe celebrated in his 1719 novel, *Robinson Crusoe*: "That the Surprise may not drive the Animal Spirits from the Heart."

ankle-biters Annoying or small-minded bureaucrats; pettifogging aides.

This hyphenated term replaces the 1970s *munchkins* or the 1980s *weenies*. It refers specifically to low-level officials who use minor details and red tape to hamper or annoy superiors.

Usually used in the plural, the noun has been said to come from the name for trousers patterned after the fifteenth-century Hungarian pants of the Hussars, who wore the bottoms tucked inside stockings at the ankle. Since 1850, the term has been used as a slang term for "young children," similar to the mock put-down of *rug rats* and *curtain climbers*. Now *ankle-biters* is used for adults as well. A 1981 *New York Times* report on changes being made at West Point stated that the general in charge "had enough prestige 'to keep the ankle-biters away.'"

From military use, the term was soon transferred to law and then politics. In 1990, Prince Bandar bin Sultan, serving as the Saudi Ambassador to the United States, told *Defense News* of his message to American troops in his country: "Don't let the ankle-biters get to you. ... You are defending your national interest and also you are defending great principles."

Sometimes two words, sometimes one word without a hyphen, the term *ankle-biters* is meant to demean the person so labeled as both small and irritating.

annuit coeptis See UNITED WE STAND.

anti-anti A counter-counterattack prefix, suggesting advocates of the root word may be tacitly "pro."

Dating at least to the COLD WAR era, the double negation has been favored by those on the political right. When Nathan M. Pusey, president of Lawrence College in Wisconsin (and future president of Harvard), criticized Senator Joseph McCarthy in 1952, the red-hunting McCarthy attacked Pusey as "a rabid anti-anti-communist." Almost a half-century later, reverberations of the cold war still echoed. In October 2000, Evan Gahr of the Hudson Institute, a conservative think tank, dubbed Victor Navasky, publisher of a leading liberal magazine, *The Nation*, as "the country's premiere anti-anti-Communist." (Navasky had written an Op-Ed piece about domestic American Communism that Gahr regarded as a "snow job.")

Some charge that *anti-anti-communist* actually is just another way of saying *communist*. Thus, Jill Cohen Walker, in a guest opinion on *News With Views* in 2005, wrote: "A mentor to Bill Clinton, [Senator James] Fulbright was an anti-anti-Communist; and anyone who knows the rules of positive and negative integers understands that an anti-anti-communist is a communist." Taking a less extreme view, columnist Walter E. Williams held in a *WorldNetDaily* posting a year later: "While academic leftists, and I'd include their media allies, are not communists, they are anti-anti communists. In other words, they have contempt for right-wingers, conservatives or libertarians who are anti-communists.... Leftist elites love the ideas of communism so much that they are either blind to, or tolerant of, its many shortcomings."

With the demise of the threat of Soviet communism, the *anti-anti* formulation is mainly used in retrospect as a near-synonym to FELLOW TRAVELER. However, the rebounding prefix has proven to be versatile as well as durable. Variations include *anti-anti-blogofascism, anti-anti-war, anti-anti-global warming*, and *anti-anti-hype. Human Events* asked in 2006: "Does this mean conservatives are anti-anti-Semites while liberals are only anti-Semites?" *Jewish World Review* cast an aspersion in 2006 on libertarian objections to harsh treatment of terrorism suspects: "Today's anti-anti-terrorists assume nefarious intentions of the U.S. government while clamoring to protect the rights of enemy agents." *The New York Times Magazine* headlined a story in January 2007 about the director of the Anti-Defamation League: "Does Abe Foxman Have an Anti-Anti-Semite Problem?"

The term has crept into the political discourse of other nations, where opinions of the United States have been portrayed as divided between those of *anti-Americans* and *anti-anti-Americans*. Reporting from Paris in the summer of 2003, *New Yorker* correspondent Adam Gopnik observed that "Anti-Americanism, though of course it has a life as a muttered feeling, has almost no life as an idea or argument.... Far more lucid and arresting, and just as likely to sell books and get attention, are the views of the anti-anti-Americans—that small but loud bunch of philosophers and journalists who share the American conviction that September 11 was an epoch-making event, and that how open societies react to it will determine how open they get to remain."

In early 2007, Matthew Kaminski, editorial page editor of *The Wall Street Journal Europe*, noted that Nicolas Sarkozy, soon to be elected center-right president of France, wrote that the U.S. "is a country that a part of our elites make a habit of detesting. That is particularly strange since we've never been at war with this nation, which came to help us, defend us, liberate us on two occasions in our recent history, with which we share close democratic values." The *Journal* headlined this as "France's Anti-Anti-Americans."

Anti-anti does not mean *pro-*, stopping just a shade short, but suggests that the enemy of the enemy is the final word's friend.

antithesis See CONTRAPUNTAL PHRASES; TURN-AROUNDS.

anti-Washington See RUNNING AGAINST WASHINGTON.

apartheid See SEGREGATION.

apostle of hate Attack phrase on one who espouses bigotry; a racist.

In the post-Civil War era, those who revived bitter memories of the war to advance their own political fortunes were accused of preaching a "gospel of hate." In 1876 *Harper's Magazine* rejected the use of the phrase: "anybody in this centennial year...who does not confine himself to rejoicing over our happy reunion, but looks to see the facts, is [called] an apostle of hate, delighting to dabble his fingers in the gore of the BLOODY SHIRT."

In *The Education of Henry Adams* the writer in 1907 defined politics as "the systematic organization of hatreds." Sometimes politics organized against haters: At the 1950 convention of the Congress of Industrial Organizations held in Cleveland five years before the union's merger with the American Federation of Labor, the leaders of most of the member unions delivered attacks on the Communists in their ranks. Philip Murray, who was to become the first president of the merged AFL-CIO, called the Communists "apostles of hate" who lied "out of the pits of their dirty bellies." He was primarily attacking the Communists who had seized control of the United Electrical, Radio and Machine Workers Union.

Lyndon B. Johnson, in his speech to a joint session of Congress on November 27, 1963, five days after the assassination of President John F. Kennedy, made a moving plea for unity in dealing with racial bigotry and intolerance: "Let us put an end to the teaching and preaching of hate and evil and violence. Let us turn away from the fanatics of the far left and the far right, from the apostles of bitterness and bigotry, from those defiant of law and those who pour venom into our nation's bloodstream."

See RACISM.

appeasement A policy of acceding to the demands of the aggressive in the hope of satisfying them, but which often leads to more demands and greater concessions.

This inflammatory word, attacking those opposing intervention in the affairs of a country threatening its neighbor, was first used in its pejorative political sense by Philip Henry Kerr, Marquess of Lothian, in a letter to *The Times* of London in 1934. Kerr objected to "a limitation of armaments by political appeasement."

The word had no negative implications for British Prime Minister Neville Chamberlain. When President Franklin D. Roosevelt wanted to call an international conference in Washington on peaceful relations (an idea of Sumner Welles's), Secretary of State Cordell Hull urged him to check it out first with Chamberlain. The British leader, whose tightly rolled umbrella became the symbol of appeasement in the thirties (see UMBRELLA SYMBOL), wrote the President that such a plan would undermine his own efforts at what he termed "a measure of appeasement" of Italy and Germany. At the Munich conference on September 29, 1938, the Sudetenland and all vital Czechoslovakian fortresses were yielded to Germany. Chamberlain proclaimed "PEACE FOR OUR TIME" on his return, as Winston Churchill warned: "Britain and France had to choose between war and dishonour. They chose dishonour. They will have war."

After World War II, in 1950, Churchill, the man most identified as a foe of appeasement (see MUNICH ANALOGY; IRON CURTAIN), surprised the House of Commons with this amelioration of the word: "It requires to be more precisely defined. What we really mean, I think, is no appeasement through weakness or fear. Appeasement in itself may be good or bad according to circumstances. Appeasement from weakness and fear is alike futile and fatal. Appeasement from strength is magnanimous and noble and might be the surest and perhaps the only path to world peace."

The second edition of Fowler's *Modern English Usage* included appeasement in a group of "worsened words" whose meaning gained a new stigma: *collaborator, imperialism, colonialism,* and *academic.* "There is no hint in the *OED* definitions of anything discreditable or humiliating about the word [appeasement]," noted Sir Ernest Gowers. "No one thought any the worse of Aeneas for letting Cerberus [dog guarding the gates of Hades] have his usual sop." In the third edition, editor Robert Burchfield added *egregious*, which slid from "remarkable" to its present state of "outstandingly bad."

The Domesday Dictionary gives an appropriately horrible example of the nature of appeasement in this selection from Leonardo da Vinci: "Of the beaver one reads that when it is pursued, knowing this is to be on account of the virtue of its testicles for medicinal uses, not being able to flee any farther it stops and in order to be at peace with its pursuers bites off its testicles with its sharp teeth and leaves them to its enemies."

arena Place of political combat for the clash of ideologies and personalities.

The original Latin sense of *arena* is "a sandy place," the center of an amphitheater where sand was scattered to absorb the blood of gladiators.

Henry Clay of Kentucky, a three-time loser for the presidency, wrote in 1837 of being "again forced into the presidential arena"; William Jennings Bryan, destined to be a three-time loser, repeated those words sixty years later. Supreme Court Justice Charles Evans Hughes, asked to run against President Woodrow Wilson in 1916, at first declined "to cast off the judicial ermine in order to enter the political arena." Yet, he ran, lost, served as Harding's and Coolidge's Secretary of State, and was appointed Chief Justice by Hoover.

A representative assembly, wrote John Stuart Mill in *Considerations on Representative Government* in 1861, has a responsibility "to be at once the nation's Committee of Grievances, and its Congress of Opinions; an arena in which … every person in the country may count upon finding somebody who speaks his mind, as well or better than he could speak it himself …"

The word's use was broadened to include all political and ideological spheres. President Lyndon Johnson defined Asia as "the crucial arena of man's striving for independence and order." President Eisenhower passed along to friends a copy of a quotation of Theodore Roosevelt's that returned the metaphor to the gladiator's blood-smeared pit:

It is not the Critic who counts, not the one who points out how the strong man stumbled or how the doer of deeds might have done them better.

The credit belongs to the man who is actually in the arena, whose face is marred with sweat and dust and blood; who strives valiantly; who errs and comes short again and again; who knows the great enthusiasms, the great devotions, and spends himself in a worthy cause; who, if he wins, knows the triumph of high achievement; and who, if he fails, at least fails while daring greatly, so that his place shall never be with those cold and timid souls who know neither victory nor defeat.

After his narrow defeat by John F. Kennedy in 1960, Richard Nixon sent reprints of TR's "Man in the Arena" quotation to hundreds of his friends; since that time, supporters of candidates who have lost elections have frequently sent it to their leaders in lieu of a condolence letter. *The Boston Globe* commented in 1992 on the elder George Bush's use of the metaphor: "The man-in-the-arena tactic, pioneered by G.O.P. consultant Roger Ailes for Richard Nixon's 1968 campaign, served Bush well in his comeback victory in New Hampshire in 1988."

"Politics," wrote John F. Kennedy in *Profiles in Courage*, "merely furnishes one arena which imposes special tests of courage. In whatever arena of life one may meet the challenge of courage, whatever may be the sacrifices he faces if he follows his conscience—the loss of his friends, his fortune, his contentment, even the esteem of his fellow men—each man must decide for himself the course he will follow."

See HAT IN THE RING.

are you any better off? Question to measure voter satisfaction (or to trigger dissatisfaction) with political leadership.

The question, first of a series, was burned into the political lexicon by Ronald Reagan at the conclusion of his October 28, 1980, televised debate with President Jimmy Carter in Cleveland. "Next Tuesday all of you will go to the polls," said candidate Reagan. "You'll stand there in the polling place and make a decision. I think when you make that decision, it might be well if you would ask yourself, are you better off than you were four years ago? Is there more or less unemployment in the country than there was four years ago? Is America as respected throughout the world as it was? Do you feel that our security is as safe, that we're as strong as we were four years ago?"

Six years later, George H.W. Bush recalled the phrase as an indicator of comparative comfort in a campaign commercial. Broadcast on the eve of Election Day in 1988, the spot featured the elder Bush saying, "Americans are better off than they were eight years ago, and if you elect me President, you will be better off four years from now than you are today."

The phrase came back to haunt him early in the 1992 campaign against Bill Clinton, as the economy headed into the "double dip" of recession. A poll in *Newsweek* on September 21, 1992, asked, "Are you better off now than you were four years ago?" The response showed 38 percent saying "yes," 58 percent "no." That was close to the ultimate vote for and against President Bush.

Armageddon The ultimate conflict between the forces of good and evil.

The term was popularized in a political sense by former president Theodore Roosevelt in 1912 when he ran as an independent candidate for president (see SPOILER). At the Bull Moose party's Chicago convention on August 5, 1912, amid singing of "Onward, Christian Soldiers" and other stirring hymns, "Teddy" thundered: "We stand at Armageddon, and we battle for the Lord!" His reference was Biblical; in Revelation, chapter XVI, we read that at a place called Armageddon "there were voices, and thunders and lightnings; and there was a great earthquake, such as was not since men were upon the earth ... and every island fled away, and the mountains were not found ... and there fell upon men a great hail out of heaven ..." Babylon was destroyed, Satan was cast into Hell, and "they were judged every man according to their works."

Geographically, the place is probably the mount of Megiddo, where the Canaanites fought and Josiah was slain; the associations of the spot are suitably warlike.

With the development of nuclear power, the possibility of total annihilation loomed larger. The word was thus used more and more often to describe "World War III," which was the title of a novel by Leon Uris about the threat of war generated in Berlin. General Douglas MacArthur, accepting the Japanese surrender on the deck of the battleship *Missouri* in Tokyo Bay, September 2, 1945, used the word in its current sense, that of a battleground that would mean the end of civilization: "Military alliances, balances of power, leagues of nations, all in turn failed, leaving the only path to be by way of the crucible of war. The utter destructiveness of war now blocks out this alternative. We have had our last chance. If we will not devise some greater and more equitable system, Armageddon will be at our door."

armchair strategist A sofa sophist; one who pontificates about world events without participating in them.

The phrase is similar to PARK-BENCH ORATOR, though the armchair strategist might be less inclined to take public positions. The similar *Monday morning quarterback* implies carping criticism with the advantage of hindsight, but an armchair strategist might be enthusiastic as well as critical.

The armchair, a place of comfort from which to make discomfiting remarks, can also be used as a symbol for laziness. Architect Frank Lloyd Wright claimed in 1938 that "armchair education" was the reason Americans did not realize how discredited their culture was in the eyes of the world.

As anti-war fervor began to mount in 1967, Max Frankel wrote in *The New York Times*: "In most wars, the armchairs are full of generals refighting every battle, recasting every strategy, second-guessing every field commander. But Vietnam, being different in virtually every other sense as well, has also produced a new kind of kibitzer—the armchair diplomat. The galleries in this war are crowded mostly with mediators who second-guess, not the warriors but the negotiators, and spin many an intricate design not for winning the war but for ending it."

The attributive noun *armchair* lent itself to an oxymoron in 2007 when bloggers for the liberal TomPaine.com website headlined an appeal for "armchair activism." See *wafflebottom* under CIA-ESE.

arrogance of power The theme of a school of criticism of U.S. foreign policy in the 1960s, questioning the basis of U.S. intervention in some conflicts abroad.

Senator J. William Fulbright of Arkansas, a Democrat, an intellectual, and in 1966 the chairman of the Senate Foreign Relations Committee, was skeptical about more than U.S. involvement in Vietnam and the Dominican Republic. He cast doubt on the validity of the nation's general posture in foreign affairs: "For lack of a clear and precise understanding of exactly what these motives [for going to war] are, I refer to them as the 'arrogance of power'—as a psychological need that nations seem to have … to prove that they are bigger, better, or stronger than other nations."

In the debate over Vietnam, Martin Luther King, Jr., said in 1967: "Honesty impels me to admit that our power has often made us arrogant… We often arrogantly feel that we have some divine, messianic mission to police the whole world. We are arrogant in not allowing young nations to go through the same growing pains, turbulence and revolution that characterizes our history …"

In many of the attacks on Fulbright from both parties, the word "arrogant" was seized upon, as in this comment from Democrat James Farley: "It is arrogant indeed for a Senator to indict the character of the American people in time of war, or in the terms used by their enemy." Fulbright made the controversial phrase the title of a book.

The phrase spawned other book titles— *The Limits of Power* by Eugene McCarthy, *The Abuse of Power* by Theodore Draper, *LBJ: The Exercise of Power* by Rowland Evans and Robert Novak, and *The Accountability of Power* by Walter Mondale—and may have had a hand in Stokely Carmichael's BLACK POWER.

Fulbright might have taken the phrase from John F. Kennedy, who said in 1963: "when power leads a man towards arrogance, poetry reminds him of his limitations …"

The phrase was picked up in a March 2007 article in *The Washington Post* titled "A Russian Plea for Collaboration" by Sergey Rogov, whom the author often interviewed knowing him to be a longtime Soviet spinmeister for Leonid Brezhnev. He later took up propaganda work for President Vladimir Putin at the Russian Academy of Sciences in Moscow. Rogov wrote that "America has failed to resist the temptations of unilateralism and preemption. A new surge of the arrogance of power brought the United States into Iraq."

See POWER CORRUPTS.

arsenal of democracy The role of the U.S. in supplying munitions to the nations opposing the Axis powers in World War II.

The phrase was coined by Jean Monnet, French ambassador to the United States, in a conversation with Supreme Court Justice Felix Frankfurter. Monnet was describing what would be the most effective assistance the U.S. could provide in the struggle against tyranny. Frankfurter, struck by the forcefulness of the phrase, told Monnet it was precisely the sort that should be given world currency by President Franklin Roosevelt. He asked Monnet not to use it again, lest some other statesman pick it up. The Monnet phrase also came to the attention of John J. McCloy, an Assistant Secretary of War, and it was submitted in a draft speech sent to FDR speechwriter Samuel I. Rosenman.

Roosevelt used it on December 29, 1940: "We must be the great arsenal of democracy. For us this is an emergency as serious as war itself. We must apply ourselves to our task with the same resolution, the same sense of urgency, the same spirit of patriotism and sacrifice we would show if we were at war."

art of the possible A frequent definition of politics stressing the need for compromise, asking not "what must be done" but "what can be done."

Political figures, under fire for falling short of attaining lofty goals promised in campaigns, often fall back on the defensive line, "politics is the art of the possible." It emphasizes the practical nature of political rule, with its built-in checks and balances.

The source: the Chancellor of Prussia, Otto von Bismarck (1815–1898), who said, "Politik ist die Kunst des Möglichen," "politics is the art of the possible."

Adlai Stevenson called Lyndon Johnson "a master of the art of the possible in politics," citing Johnson's own stated philosophy on the subject: "Frequently in life I have had to settle for progress short of perfection. I have done so because—despite cynics—I believe that half a loaf is better than none. But my acceptance has always been conditioned upon the premise that the half-loaf is a step toward the full loaf—and that if I go on working, the day of the full loaf will come."

Václav Havel, the Czech dramatist and dissident who became President of Czechoslovakia and later the Czech Republic, gave the phrase profundity in 1990: "Let us teach ourselves and others that politics can be not only the art of the possible, especially if this means the art of speculation, calculation, intrigue, secret deals, and pragmatic maneuvering, but that it can even be the art of the impossible, namely, the art of improving ourselves and the world."

Tony Blair, stepping aside for Gordon Brown as British prime minister, said in his farewell in 2007: "I was, and remain, as a person and a prime minister, an optimist. Politics may be 'the art of the possible,' but at least in life—give the impossible a go."

For a less elevated definition, see WHO GETS WHAT, WHEN, AND HOW.

as is well known See REPORTEDLY.

ask not See CONTRAPUNTAL PHRASES.

as Maine goes See BELLWETHER.

Atlantic Community Defined variously as "the Western world"; the members of the North Atlantic Treaty Organization; or in its most limited sense, the U.S., Great Britain, and Canada.

Walter Lippmann popularized and possibly coined the expression in his 1944 book, *U.S. War Aims.* In May 1945, *Fortune*

magazine commented: "If her rehabilitation results in prosperity, western Europe will merge with what Walter Lippmann, for lack of a better word, baptized the Atlantic Community."

The use of *community* in the sense of a group of nations with mutual interests can be traced to 1888, when English statesman Henry Molyneux Herbert, Earl of Carnarvon, made the prophetic observation: "We are part of the community of Europe, and we must do our duty as such."

attack dog Counterattack phrase accusing a partisan critic of excessive savagery.

Attack dog is strongly derogatory, implying that the source of criticism or revelation is engaged in a vicious SMEAR. Although nineteenth-century cartoons pictured political figures as snarling animals, political use of the phrase has been dated only to 1973. But its use that year by the *Hillsboro* (Ohio) *Press Gazette* suggested that the term was already fairly common: "He cited the *New York Times* as being 'an attack dog' and the Washington press corps for 'bias.'"

Use of the term blossomed in 1991 after the Senate Judiciary Committee hearings on the nomination of Clarence Thomas to the Supreme Court. A former aide to Thomas, Anita Hill, accused the nominee of sexual harassment, drawing an angry response challenging her credibility from Senator Alphonse D'Amato, Republican of New York. Democrat Mario Cuomo, then governor of New York, came to the accuser's defense by calling D'Amato an "attack dog."

Attack dogs may be said to be untethered, unleashed, or sicced on someone or something. Lou Cannon reported in a 1987 column that Patrick J. Buchanan, then communications director at the Reagan White House, had castigated *The Washington Post* as the "untethered attack dog of the American left." In 2004, a *New York Times* editorial unleashed an accusation at the House Republican majority leader Tom (the Hammer) DeLay of Texas, for having "sicced federal agencies on runaway Democratic lawmakers." (*Sic'em* is a mongrelization of "seek them," a command to a real attack dog, and appeared in American dialect as "He doesn't know *sic'em* from *c'mere*.")

As a metaphor, *attack dog* is in a way the modern equivalent of *cat's-paw*, a term than has been dated to the seventeenth century in the sense of "one acting as the tool of another"; it also evokes the nineteenth-century bulldog, typified by T. H. Huxley, who championed the theory of evolution so spiritedly that he was called "Darwin's bulldog."

Vice presidential candidates often fill the *attack-dog* role, though some are not well cast for it. An anonymous adviser to Senator John F. Kerry, the Democratic presidential nominee in 2004, ruefully told *The New York Times* that Kerry's running mate, Senator John Edwards, "was picked for his sunny disposition. He self-consciously eschewed negativity in his own campaign. Consequently, he doesn't make the most effective attack dog." Contrariwise, the *Chicago Tribune* reported that Vice President Dick Cheney "appears to relish the attack role that he and wife Lynne played in town-hall meetings in the final months of the 2004 campaign." The paper quoted David Doak, a veteran Democratic political operative, saying, "What they are trying to do is to keep Bush above the fray, make him more statesmanlike, and let Cheney be the attack dog."

In April 2007, a few days after Senate Majority Leader Harry Reid (D- Nev.) said at a news conference, "this war is lost," Cheney said, "It is cynical to declare that the war is lost because you believe it gives you political advantage." Reid replied within an hour, "I'm not going to get into a name-calling match with the administration's chief attack dog" and in answers to questions repeated the phrase three times.

See BIRD DOG ... KENNEL DOG; CHARACTER ASSASSIN; POLITICAL ANIMAL; RATTLE THE CAGE; STIR UP THE ANIMALS.

at that point in time A circumlocution for "then," carrying a spurious specificity.

In the mid-sixties, "at that point in time" and "in point of fact" were academic-bureaucratic vogue phrases. In a 1968 memo to his political colleagues, the author

urged the Nixon campaign to eschew such vogue words as "at that point in time," "exacerbate," and "eschew."

As the televised WATERGATE hearings began, youthful bureaucrats of the Nixon Administration's campaign committee (see CREEP) popularized the phrase, which is a combination of "at that point" and "at that time" and seemed more precise than the other vogue term "in that time frame." But the linguist Raven McDavid of the University of Chicago wrote to the quarterly *American Speech*: "Since the beginning of the Watergate extravaganza, academicians have amused themselves with the recurrent phrase *at that point in time* ... however, much as it embarrasses me, it seems clear that the burrocrats [the misspelling was intentional] were following the lead of the intellectuals." He provided three citations, one from a 1970 *Daedalus*, an early 1973 use in the *American Anthropologist*, and a 1963 selection from Cleanth Brooks' literary criticism of William Faulkner: "he takes us back to a point in time three years before Isaac's act of renunciation."

But the phrase was closely associated with Watergate language, and was used ironically by minority counsel Fred Thompson, later a senator and a candidate for the Republican presidential nomination, as the title of his book on the hearings. In 1977 a *Washington Star* editorialist complained about the disuse into which the plain words *now* and *then* had fallen. "Even as 'at this (or that) point in time' became an ungainly scrub for *now* or *then*, there was the sudden, curious intrusion of 'presently.' In the old days it meant 'in a short while' but now, we take it, means 'at this point in time' or, if you will pardon the expression, *now*."

Attila the Hun See REACTIONARY.

austerity See AFFLUENT SOCIETY.

autarkic Economically viable; as the noun *autarky*, a nation able to claim self-sufficiency.

This diplomatic word is most often confused with its homonym, *autarchy*, which means "autocratic or totalitarian rule." But *autarky* with a "k" is a nation able to take care of itself, its state of economic affairs brought about by a policy aimed at avoiding dependency on neighboring nations. Samuel Ward in *Balme from Gilead* wrote in 1617 of "the Autarchie and selfe-sufficiencie of God." The spelling changed in the late seventeenth century to separate the word from its autocratic confuser.

Its connotation changed from good (self-sufficient) to bad (isolationist, selfish), especially during the early 1960s when "declarations of interdependence" came into vogue. In the 1970s that word was frequently used in the foreign economic policy addresses of Henry Kissinger while the opposite—independence—was a staple of Nixonian calls for an end to reliance on Middle East imported oil after the 1973 "oil shock."

"What are the prospects for 'energy independence' in the way that Richard Nixon defined it 34 years ago," asked the oil expert Daniel Yergin in a 2007 *Wall Street Journal* commentary, "—that is, 1930s-style 'autarky' and total self-sufficiency? Based on where we are today, very small, at least for a couple of decades."

authoritarian See TOTALITARIAN.

authoritative sources The screen behind which a political figure airs his views without being directly quoted or identified.

Authoritative sources, reliable sources, informed circles, and *a source that cannot be identified but close to* are all signals that a BACKGROUNDER has taken place.

The most authoritative source of all is called the *highest authority.* He is the President of the United States wearing a beard and dark glasses.

See NOT FOR ATTRIBUTION; OFF THE RECORD; LEAK; DOPE STORY; SOURCES.

availability Candidate readiness, but a cut below *electability*; one who has all of the generally accepted qualifications and would offend no significant voting bloc or region. Derogatory when used to describe over-eagerness on the part of an unannounced candidate.

Harold J. Laski, the British political philosopher, wrote: "Out of all this complexity [of preconvention maneuvering] there has emerged the doctrine of 'availability.' The party needs a candidate who, positively, will make the widest appeal and, negatively, will offend the least proportion of the electorate. ... He ought not to possess any nostrum which can be represented as extreme."

Hubert H. Humphrey was one of many possible vice presidential candidates considered by Lyndon B. Johnson in 1964. When newsmen asked him almost daily whether he was in the running, Humphrey would say: "Nobody has to woo me. I'm old reliable, available Hubert," adding: "I'm like the girl next door—always available but you don't necessarily think about marriage."

In courtship, *available* is several cuts below *eligible* in terms of attractiveness; an available person is one not often dated. The pejorative sense appeared as early as 1837, in the *Baltimore Commercial Transcript:* "The New York papers are discussing whether the most talented, or the most available man, shall be reelected as candidate for the next presidency."

Incumbent first-term presidents traditionally seek to disguise their obvious availability to create at least a little suspense. William McKinley stated a position of qualified availability which has been restated in less orotund oratory: "The question of my acquiescence will be based absolutely upon whether the call of duty appears to me clear and well defined."

A play on the word came around the time of its earliest political use. Scorning the selection of William Henry Harrison and John Tyler by the Whigs in 1840 without even the pretense of a party platform, Senator Thomas Hart Benton of Missouri said, "Availability was the only ability sought by the Whigs." The quality of being at hand was satirized in a bumper sticker that set teeth on edge in both major parties: "He's tanned, rested and ready: Nixon in 2000!"

See JOB SEEKS THE MAN.

avalanche Staggering ballot majority; thunderous downpour of votes.

Avalanche, landslide, tidal wave, and *tsunami* are words of natural disaster applied to political disaster. Early use, especially in the "Log Cabin and Hard Cider" campaign of 1840 of Harrison against Van Buren, applied to large crowd turnouts: "It was another of those glorious and enthusiastic Avalanches of the people," said a Harrison handout, "that distinguish this contest from any other in our National History." Later, the word came to mean votes rather than people, and the *New York Tribune* wrote in 1888 of the Vermont Democrats being "buried under an avalanche of Republican ballots." This is the use that is current today; *avalanche* refers specifically to votes, while *landslide* refers to an election as well as to votes. Lyndon Johnson, who won an election in Texas by the skin of his teeth, was given the sarcastic sobriquet "Landslide Lyndon."

An election in which the popular-vote differential is not large, but the electoral-vote difference is considerable, is a landslide without an avalanche.

See DISASTER METAPHORS.

average man See JOHN Q. PUBLIC; COMMON MAN, CENTURY OF THE.

awesome burden See LONELIEST JOB.

axis An alliance of powers, asserted by them or so described by others; specifically, the Axis Powers (Rome, Berlin, later Tokyo just before and during World War II).

The word comes from the imaginary line that can be drawn through a body, and around which that body could revolve. In its political context, the phrase is attributed to Benito Mussolini, who said in 1936 that the German-Italian agreement was "an axis round which all European states, animated by the will to collaboration and peace can also assemble." In 1937, he added: "We have forced the axis to Berlin and Rome. That is the beginning of European consolidation."

The Rome-Berlin axis, around which all Europe presumably was to revolve, became a familiar phrase in 1938; *The New York Times* wrote, "There was a triangle in 1914—Berlin-Vienna-Rome. There is an axis in 1938—Berlin-Rome." *Newsweek* added: "Central Europe regards the Rome-Berlin axis as an artificial structure." In 1939, as war loomed, the Rome-Berlin axis was further undergirded by what Mussolini called "a pact of steel."

Adolf Hitler made reference to the axis in his Sportspalast speech in Berlin while the Munich Pact was being negotiated, as he assured the world he had no more territorial demands: "This relation [between Germany and Italy] has long left a sphere of clear economic and political expediency and over treaties and alliances has turned into a real, strong union of hearts. Here an axis was formed represented by two peoples ..."

With the entry of Japan into the war, the "axis" lost its metaphoric meaning as the alliance became a triangle. But the Axis Powers were the opponents of the Allied Powers; *axis* for a generation meant only "Hitler-Mussolini-Tojo."

When the link between two cities is a function of geography or trade rather than political alliance, the word *corridor* is preferred, unless a new name is devised; the "Boston-New York-Washington corridor" is informally called "Bosnywash."

For the rebirth of the word *axis* with its sinister connotation in the twenty-first century, see the following entry.

axis of evil A group of nations accused of sponsoring terrorism and threatening to develop weapons of mass destruction (WMD).

President George W. Bush focused world attention on an "axis of evil" in his State of the Union Address on January 29, 2002, less than five months after the attacks of 9/11. Referring to Iran, Iraq, and North Korea, he said, "States like these, and their terrorist allies, constitute an axis of evil, arming to threaten the peace of the world. By seeking weapons of mass destruction, these regimes pose a grave and growing danger. They could provide these arms to terrorists, giving them the means to match their hatred.... the price of indifference would be catastrophic...the United States of America will not permit the world's most dangerous regimes to threaten us with the world's most destructive weapons."

The ringing phrase dominated news accounts of the speech. Others soon expanded its cast of regimes: in a speech on May 2, entitled "Beyond the Axis of Evil," Undersecretary of State John R. Bolton added Libya, Syria, and Cuba to the president's trio of what in the Clinton era had been described by Secretary of State Madeleine Albright, with a lesser degree of condemnation, as "rogue nations."

Foreign leaders also adopted the "axis" construction. Israel's defense minister, Shaul Mofaz, referred in January of 2006 to "the axis of terror that operates between Iran and Syria," while that nation's foreign minister, Tzipi Livni, told *The Washington Post* in July of the same year that that the Hezbollah militia in Lebanon formed "part of an axis of hatred and terror" with "Syria, Iran, and Hamas." Others turned the phrase back upon the United States. President Hugo Chávez of Venezuela termed "Washington and its allies" an "axis of evil" (in contrast to the "axis of the good," meaning Cuba, Bolivia, and his own country in Chávez's lexicon). Among the signs at a pro-Hezbollah demonstration in London on July 22, 2006, according to a Reuters report, was one that read, "Axis of evil: Bush, Blair, and Olmert," referring to the American president and his British and Israeli counterparts, prime ministers Tony Blair and Ehud Olmert.

The famous phrase also spawned many variations. *New York Times* columnist Paul Krugman mocked neoconservative journalists in 2002 for their "evils of access." When Germany and France declined to join the "coalition of the willing" in invading Saddam Hussein's Iraq in 2003, they were mocked as the "axis of weasels"; as the war in Iraq lengthened and opposition to it grew, strident critics derided Bush, Vice President Dick Cheney, and Secretary of Defense Donald Rumsfeld as "asses of evil"; environmentalists attacked gas-guzzling sport utility vehicles as "axles of evil"; federal, state, and city taxes were lumped together as

the "axis of taxes"; and on May 11, 2006, *The Economist* magazine heralded "the closing of the Bush-Blair era" with the cover headline, "Axis of feeble."

The power of the original phrase lay in its evocation of our Axis Power enemies in World War II (see above) tied to the unequivocal moral condemnation of "evil." Although the historical analogy was not strictly applicable (Iraq, Iran, and North Korea never cooperated officially as did Germany, Italy, and Japan), additional traction came from the allusion to President Ronald Reagan's denunciation of Soviet-era international Communism as an EVIL EMPIRE. The Bush phrase was a product of a speechwriting team attuned to his style of plain, short, strong words. David Frum, assigned to lay the groundwork for justifying a preventive war against Saddam Hussein's dangerous regime in Iraq, came up with "axis of hatred" after rereading President Franklin D. Roosevelt's DAY OF INFAMY speech. (Frum lost his White House job after his wife emailed friends and family, boasting about his contribution to the presidential address; a PASSION FOR ANONYMITY is no longer required, but some decorum is called for that precludes an aide from staking an instant claim of authorship.)

Head speechwriter Michael Gerson, often credited with drafting religious themes and phrases in Bush speeches, was reported (with no source named) to have changed Frum's phrase "axis of hatred" to "axis of evil." However, this attribution of coinage credit, perhaps based on a reportorial assumption, was angrily disputed by Matthew Scully, another member of the speechwriting staff during Bush's first term, writing in a September 2007 article in *The Atlantic* about what he termed "the sole occasion when credit snatching ever came up for public discussion." "David [Frum] came up with the phrase 'axis of hatred,'" asserted Scully, "and e-mailed it, along with some other lines, to John [McConnell], Mike [Gerson] and me ... Mike thought we should use the phrase, and we added it to the text. I said 'I hate *hatred*'—which brought to mind the ineffectual 'forces of hatred' favored by

Clinton speechwriters—and proposed going with *evil* instead, since we were already confronting *evildoers, wickedness* and the like. It was agreed ... and we moved on."

Even speechwriters not afflicted with a PASSION FOR ANONYMITY considered the episode unseemly, but it had a sort of historical precedent in the conflicting claims of FDR writers Raymond Moley and Samuel Rosenman (see NEW DEAL), as well as Ted Sorensen and Richard Goodwin (see ALLIANCE FOR PROGRESS).

At year's end, in a column headlined "Bush's 'Axis of Evil' Six Years Later," the widely syndicated Charles Krauthammer assessed the policy: "the Bush legacy is clear: one for three ... Bush will have succeeded on Iraq, failed on Iran and fought North Korea to a draw."

B

backbencher A legislator of low seniority; a steadfast supporter of party leaders.

In Great Britain's House of Commons, where this expression originated, a backbencher is one who goes down the line in regular support of the party leadership at the front bench of the House.

As the expression is used with much less frequency in the U.S., the "party regularity" emphasis is dropped, and the "low seniority" aspect is emphasized. In discussing the dark-horse possibilities of freshman Senator Charles Percy, *U.S. News & World Report* wrote in 1967: "Senator John F. Kennedy of Massachusetts was still a 'backbencher' in 1960 when he took the Democratic nomination away from older and more experienced figures in his party." After the victory by congressional Democrats in 2006, the *Kiplinger Letter* reported: "Several new members of Congress will be more than backbenchers right from the get-go."

See SHADOW CABINET.

back channel A seemingly unofficial but direct method of high-level communication, bypassing the usual routes of messages through bureaucracies.

Referring to jockeying between the State Department and the National Security Council, columnist Flora Lewis of *The New York Times* wrote disapprovingly in 1980: "Diplomacy and negotiation are State's function, which it can't perform being constantly short-circuited by a 'back channel' to the White House." But even within FOGGY BOTTOM negotiations may be conducted through different conduits. Thus, Secretary of State George Shultz made a fine distinction when he said in 1984 that "private diplomatic efforts" to explore possible areas of agreement with the Soviet Union weren't "necessarily the same thing as back-channel diplomacy."

Washington Monthly distrusted back-channel diplomacy for other reasons, asserting in 2004 that "The sad but true history of back-channel diplomacy is … one of enemy intelligence agencies showing gullible American presidents only what they want them to see." This disparaging view recalls the earliest example in the *OED* of a channel as a medium for transmitting information: In a 1537 sermon Hugh Latimer, an English Protestant bishop and martyr (burned at the stake for heresy in 1555), found occasion to refer to "A foule filthy chanel of all mischiefes."

The sense of *back channel* as an informal conduit of communication arose in the American military in the 1960s. *Pacific Stars and Stripes* reported in 1970: "Although the military chiefs do not have command authority over military forces, they have exercised such power through their high position and through a system of communications called the 'back channel.' This is a private channel using telephones or cables addressed personally to other military officers that do not go through the official chain of command network." Columnist Jack Anderson also used quotation marks, suggesting previous usage, in a 1971 item about military procurement: "Maj. Gen. Herron Maples … in charge of peanut butter matters for the Army in Europe … registered his compliance in a formal message that he sent to the Pentagon over the 'front channel.' But he put another secret message on the 'back channel' which is reserved for general officers."

During that period, Nixon national security adviser Henry A. Kissinger took a special delight in conducting *back-channel* negotiations with Soviet Ambassador to the U.S. Anatoly Dobrynin on arms control, to the consternation of officials in the Arms Control and Disarmament Agency and the State Department.

When National Security Adviser Henry Kissinger called this Nixon speechwriter into his office to discuss a presidential announcement of the failure of secret Paris negotiations with the North Vietnamese, he introduced the subject with a dramatic: "We have had a back channel in Paris."

E. Howard Hunt (see PLUMBER) told the Watergate grand jury in 1973 of his search for materials to produce a fraudulent cable linking President John F. Kennedy to the assassination ten years before of South Vietnamese President Ngo Dinh Diem: "I had inquiries made of the Pentagon as to whether the so-called back channel had been used."

The noun phrase and compound adjective have been embraced by English-speaking diplomats on the Indian subcontinent. In 2006, former Pakistani prime minister Benazir Bhutto was reported by DailyIndia.com as confirming "having back-channel contacts" with the Musharraf regime the same week that *The Tribune* of Chandigarh, India, reported that "President Pervez Musharraf today said that back-channel talks were on" between his country and India to resolve the Kashmir dispute. (When Bhutto returned to Pakistan in late 2007 to campaign, she was assassinated.)

The diplomatic phrase was taken up by students of linguistics to refer to encouraging grunts and phrases: "uh-huh," "ah, yes," and "I hear you" by listeners to speakers is described as back-channeling.

backer Political supporter, especially a financial contributor.

One who will talk about you admiringly is a *fan;* one who will ring doorbells for you is a *worker,* or one of the TROOPS; one who believes in a cause is an *adherent;* one who will put his money where his vote is, is a *backer*—in substantial sums, a FAT CAT. A general term covering all these activities is a *supporter,* or a (name of candidate) *man.* The collective term is *following.*

According to William Riordon in 1905, George Washington Plunkitt of Tammany Hall explained how to begin to get backers: "I had a cousin, a young man who didn't take any particular interest in politics. I went to him and said: 'Tommy, I'm goin' to be a politician, and I want to get a followin'; can I count on you?' He said, 'Sure, George.' That's how I started in business. I got a marketable commodity—one vote."

backgrounder A news conference, or interview with a single reporter, where the information is on the record but the news source cannot be revealed precisely.

Theodore Sorensen explained the John F. Kennedy rationale for backgrounders:

> During his Christmas holiday in Palm Beach, both in 1961 and 1962, he invited the two dozen or so regular White House correspondents accompanying him to a free-wheeling three-to-four hour "backgrounder"...dividing each session into domestic and foreign affairs discussions. Year-end "think pieces" (which would have been written anyway, he reasoned) were in this way better informed of views attributable to "the highest authority" or "sources close to the administration." Although these phrases deceived no one in the know, it made for a freer and fuller exchange than would have been true of a regular press conference or a larger background group in Washington.

When the technique of the backgrounder is overused, the news media is overloaded with phrases like "a spokesman said," or "a source close to the White House revealed," or "political circles are buzzing with the rumor that," etc. This leaves the impression that the top official concerned does not wish to stand up and be counted, which is true enough, but it is not at all the impression the official wants to leave. During the 1966 dispute between the Kennedy family and the publishers of William Manchester's book *The Death of a President*, there were daily Kennedy family backgrounders throughout the crucial week before serialization, causing columnist Murray Kempton to comment: "One always departs with his gratitude for a Kennedy backgrounder somewhat diluted by the wish that it hadn't left the foreground so foggy."

In December 1971 *The Washington Post* decided this technique was being abused; editor Benjamin Bradlee said, "the public has suffered from this collusion between the government and the press." Particularly offensive was the "deep backgrounder" in which no source at all could be given. Presidential press secretary Ronald Ziegler promptly agreed: "over the years, to some degree, government has misused backgrounders." Newsmen were cautious in their criticism, however, lest the pendulum swing back too far; the abolition of backgrounders would dry up important sources of news, especially in the foreign policy area.

A cartoon in *Frontier* magazine showed a dais of faceless men with a faceless master of ceremonies speaking at a podium labeled "Washington Press Banquet" and saying: "It's an honor this evening to present the nation's Highest Authority, who will be introduced by a Spokesman Close to the President, following remarks by a Highly Placed Official and A Usually Reliable Source ..."

When a reporter files a story from a region or city not recently covered, he or she sometimes reports on the background of events in that area, but that is properly called a *situationer* and not a "backgrounder."

See NOT FOR ATTRIBUTION; THUMBSUCKER; DOPE STORY; SOURCES.

backlash Civil rights recoil: the reaction by whites against the advancement of blacks when its implications—especially in job competition—hit close to home.

Credit for the word's popularization belongs to the Washington columnist team of Rowland Evans and Robert Novak. After the Birmingham, Alabama, riots in the summer of 1963, President Kennedy's depressed-areas bill was defeated in the House. In the June 16, 1963, *New York Herald Tribune*, Evans and Novak wrote that this defeat was due to other causes and was not "the first backlash of civil rights turmoil." The columnists used the word frequently afterward, and—like Walter Lippmann with Herbert Bayard Swope's COLD WAR and the Alsops with EGGHEAD and PECKING ORDER—gave it currency.

Novak tells the author they took the word from a usage earlier that summer of 1963 by economist Eliot Janeway, which he corroborated. He had been discussing the impact of automation on white and black workers, and pointed out that in any economic downturn there was likely to be a breakup in the long-time political alliance between civil rights groups and labor unions, as white workers "lashed back" at competition from African-Americans for the remaining jobs.

The word was used frequently in the 1964 presidential campaign; a SILENT VOTE motivated by the white *backlash* was supposed to materialize, but never did to the extent some backers of Senator Barry Goldwater expected. "For every backlash the Democrats lose," said President Lyndon Johnson, "we pick up three frontlash."

By 2006, the term had joined the general language: after irate feminists on the Harvard faculty made it impossible for Lawrence Summers to continue as President, *The Wall Street Journal* headlined "Harvard Faces a Donor Backlash."

A synonym coming into vogue is *blowback*, perhaps of automotive origin. *New York Times* columnist Tom Friedman wrote in 2006 about international criticism of Israel for its strong military response to the kidnapping of its soldiers and other provocations by Hezbollah terrorists in Lebanon: "It's made these regimes—Saudi Arabia, Jordan, and Egypt—enormously uncomfortable. And now you're seeing the *blowback* from that."

bafflegab Jargon providing more obfuscation than enlightenment, as is often found in ill-written government reports and other official statements.

Bafflegab began appearing in newspapers and conversation in the early 1950s. In a 1952 newspaper interview, Milton Smith, then assistant general counsel of the U.S. Chamber of Commerce, claimed authorship. Smith explained: "I decided we needed a new and catchy word to describe the utter incomprehensibility, ambiguity, verbosity and complexity of government regulations." Before hitting on *bafflegab*, Smith said, he considered "burobabble" and "gabbalia." Smith's contribution surfaces from time to time, as in a 1967 column by Sylvia Porter, the economics writer. She relegated to "this year's batch of bafflegab" such phrases as *healthy slowdown* and *rolling readjustment*. Other euphemisms for recession include *crabwise movement, high-level stagnation, period of basic readjustment,* and *mini-slump.*

Time magazine in 1968 published a "baffle-gab thesaurus" (unnecessarily hyphenating the word) based on a Royal Canadian Air Force collection of fuzzy phraseology. A ringing, three-word phrase, guaranteed to impress, can be assembled from the spare parts in each of these three categories:

A	B	C
Integrated	Management	Options
Total	Organizational	Flexibility
Systematized	Monitored	Capability
Parallel	Reciprocal	Mobility
Functional	Digital	Programming
Responsive	Logistical	Concept
Optional	Transitional	Time-Phase
Synchronized	Incremental	Projection
Compatible	Third-Generation	Hardware
Balanced	Policy	Contingency

In popular usage, *bafflegab* runs behind GOBBLEDYGOOK and OFFICIALESE. Also see PENTAGONESE; ECONOMIC JARGON; CIA-ESE.

bagman Intermediary in a political payoff; one who carries the bribe from the beneficiary of a corrupt deal to the grafter.

The courts have decided that the word is libelous. Harlem Congressman Adam Clayton Powell described Mrs. Esther James as a "bagwoman" in the policy racket, but chose to make the charge outside the libel-proof halls of Congress. The woman sued for libel and was awarded damages. The congressman spent years avoiding payment and ducking service of subpoenas, requiring him to reside outside his district and country, ultimately followed by House exclusion.

In the administration of Mayor William O'Dwyer of New York, a minor officeholder named James Moran was widely reputed to be the bagman, and went tight-lipped to prison. Newsmen Norton Mockridge and Robert Prall wrote in *The Big Fix*: "Nobody believed, either, that Jim Moran kept all the money he collected. For many years he had been known as a bagman, which in political jargon, is literally the man who carries the bag or boodle for somebody higher up. And the bagman never gets to keep the big money."

Another, more recent, use of *bagman* in a different sense is the military officer who follows the President, carrying the secret nuclear retaliation codes in a case called the *football*. See FOOTBALL, POLITICAL.

Bailey Memorandum Document falsely attributed to John Bailey, Connecticut Democratic State Chairman (later National Chairman), demonstrating how useful a Catholic could be on the national ticket.

The Bailey Memorandum was used in an attempt to gain the 1956 vice presidential nomination for John F. Kennedy, who lost to Senator Estes Kefauver. Contrary to the belief at the time, the document was written at least in part by Theodore Sorensen, Kennedy's closest aide.

The sixteen-page memorandum of statistics, quotations, analyses, and arguments sought to answer Democratic fears of "anti-Catholic" votes by raising hopes of recapturing a greater share of the votes of Catholics, especially among conservatives in urban areas who had voted for Eisenhower in 1952. The memo held that a vice presidential nominee of the Catholic faith would do more to swing states with large electoral-vote totals into the Democratic column than any non-Catholic candidate from the south or farm belt.

When the word of the document spread to newsmen and politicians, Kennedy arranged Bailey's assertion of authorship to avoid being accused of personally injecting a religious issue into the political campaign.

The memorandum controversy again mushroomed during the 1960 presidential election when Republicans reprinted it as an example of a blatant appeal to "Catholic voting blocs." Kennedy, fearing a "Protestant bloc," instructed his aides not to talk publicly in terms of Catholic voting strength.

Sorensen wrote in 1965: "The Bailey Memorandum oversimplified, overgeneralized and overextended its premise in order to reach an impressive conclusion." Many Republicans sadly disagreed.

balanced budget See FISCAL INTEGRITY; PAY AS YOU GO.

balanced ticket A slate of candidates nominated so as to appeal to as many voter groups as possible.

Typical considerations in balancing a ticket: the nominees' personal compatibility, geographic origin, race, sex, religion, type of experience, position on specific issues, physical appearance together, and COLORATION.

In American presidential politics, the home state of the candidates for president and vice president was, historically, the weightiest item on the scale. More than local chauvinism was involved; whether the issue was slavery or free silver, tariffs or manifest destiny, sectional interests came into play. As national politics grew more complicated—and sophisticated—so did the question of balance.

Joe Martin, former House Republican Leader, recalled his 1940 sales presentation to Wendell Willkie on behalf of Senator Charles McNary as a vice presidential candidate. "You are known as a utilities man; McNary has sided with the public power boys. You're supposed to represent big business interests; McNary was the sponsor of the McNary-Haugen farm bill. You aren't supposed to know much about the legislative process; McNary is a master of it. I think you'd make a perfect team." Neither Willkie nor McNary liked the other's politics, but in the spirit of balance they ran together.

The phrase has even been applied to foreign politics where no election in the American sense is involved. In 1962, Averell Harriman of New York, then Assistant Secretary of State for Far Eastern Affairs, was attempting to establish a coalition government for Laos that would both bring stability to that country and satisfy the great and interested powers. His controversial solution: a troika consisting of rightists, neutralists, and pro-Communists. President John Kennedy defended Harriman's efforts,

saying: "He's putting together a New York State balanced ticket."

In local politics, balance is struck between religion, ethnicity, and, more recently, race and sex. Most big cities remain not-very-melted pots in which as many lumps as possible must be appealed to. Edward Costikyan, the former leader of Tammany Hall, spoke for the politicians' consensus when he defended the practice of giving the public a *"representative* representation." In *Behind Closed Doors*, Costikyan recalled the apocryphal DREAM TICKET for the Upper West Side of Manhattan when that section was a prosperous ghetto: "one reform Jew, one orthodox Jew, and one agnostic Jew."

The criteria for ticket-balancing may be changing: In the run-up to the 2008 nominations, Democrats were giving serious consideration to a ticket that had no white male on it.

balance of power The theory that peace is best ensured when rival groups are equal in strength.

An object of international diplomacy for centuries, the term was in use as early as 1700. Alexander Pope wrote a poem entitled "The Balance of Europe" in 1715: "Now Europe's balanc'd, neither side prevails; / For nothing's left in either of the scales." The British, in particular, sought to apply it to maintain a relatively durable peace from 1871 to 1914, with a balance between the powers that eventually grouped themselves into the Triple Alliance (Germany, Austria, Italy) and the Triple Entente (Britain, France, Russia).

In the U.S., political writers often use the expression to discuss the CHECKS AND BALANCES among the states of the Union or the three branches of government. "Every project," wrote John Adams in 1789, "has been found to be no better than committing the lamb to the custody of the wolf, except that one which is called a balance of power." Before the Civil War, it referred to a balance between the slave-holding and the free states.

The phrase is also applied to disputes among the branches of the government. Franklin D. Roosevelt said in 1937, while discussing his plan to pack the Supreme Court (see NINE OLD MEN), that over the last half-century "the balance of power between the three great branches of the Federal Government has been tipped out of balance by the courts in direct contradiction of the high purposes of the framers of the Constitution."

Occasionally it has been scorned as a shaky way of keeping peace. Thus, Winston Churchill, in his Fulton, Missouri, IRON CURTAIN speech in 1946, declared that if the English-speaking Commonwealth joined forces with the U.S., "there will be no quivering, precarious balance of power to offer its temptation to ambition or adventure. On the contrary, there will be an overwhelming assurance of security."

In his 1961 inaugural, John F. Kennedy called on both sides in the Cold War to "join in creating a new endeavor—not a new balance of power, but a new world of law, where the strong are just and the weak secure and the peace preserved." Kennedy later came to see the balance of power as the only real way of minimizing the temptation to adventure, as Churchill had put it. During the Cuban missile crisis, Kennedy said: "If we suffer a major defeat, if they suffer a major defeat, it may change the balance of power." Such a change, he said, "also increases possibly the chance of war."

With the advent of nuclear weaponry and later the rise of the terrorist threat, another phrase is often used in place of *balance of power*—*balance of terror*, coined by Canadian Prime Minister Lester Pearson in 1955.

As for *balance of power*, that phrase no longer belongs exclusively to international geopoliticians. It is now also used to describe divisions of authority within governments and corporate empires. *The Wall Street Journal* noted in 2007 that legislation just signed "has given the director of the National Institutes of Health more authority over cutting-edge research, a prospect that worries traditional patient-advocacy groups. The new law ushers in a change in the balance of power at the NIH."

bald eagle The national symbol of the United States; frequent nickname of baldheaded political leaders.

Though references to bald eagles can be traced to 1836, an early patriotic reference is found in the June 19, 1873, *Newton Kansan:* "Let patriots everywhere ... prepare to do the clean thing by Uncle Sam and his baldheaded eagle."

The bald eagle has been on the Great Seal of the United States since 1782, an olive branch with thirteen olives in its right claw, thirteen arrows in the left (after the thirteen original colonies), and a banner in its beak saying "E Pluribus Unum" (From Many, One). It can be found on the back of every dollar bill. Kennedy aide Ted Sorensen used it metaphorically in 1963: "How does a President choose, for example, in a moment of crisis, between the olive branch of peace (clutched in the right talon of the eagle on his Seal) and the arrows of war (which are clutched in the left)?"

The symbol has also been called the *spread eagle* because of its outstretched wings. The *North American Review* after the Civil War defined "spread-eaglism" as "a compound of exaggeration, effrontery, bombast, mixed metaphors, platitudes, defiant threats thrown at the world, and irreverent appeals to the Supreme Being."

Of course, the "bird of Washington" is only white-headed, not bald; but James M. Husted was cited by Charles Ledyard Norton in 1890 as "the Bald Eagle of Westchester County"; Robert A. Lovett, Secretary of Defense under Truman and a State Department veteran, was the "Bald Eagle of Foggy Bottom" (see FOGGY BOTTOM).

The bald eagle on the Presidential Seal has had a curious history. Heraldic custom calls for eagles on coats of arms to be facing to the right, so that the bird will be facing forward, toward the flagstaff, when flown on a flag ahead of marching troops. During the Administration of President Rutherford B. Hayes, when the Presidential Seal originated, a designer became confused copying the Great Seal of the United States, and turned the presidential eagle's head to the left—looking backward, as it were, while the nation marched ahead.

This national emblemic embarrassment could have continued without rectification were it not for President Franklin Roosevelt's concern about the number of stars on the Commander in Chief's flag. As a White House release of October 25, 1945, delicately put it: "It seemed inappropriate to President Roosevelt for the flag of the Commander in Chief to have only four stars when there were five stars in the flags of Fleet Admirals and Generals of the Army, grades which had been created in December 1944."

As this oversight was being corrected, Arthur E. DuBois, chief of the Heraldic Section of the Office of the Quartermaster General of the Army, pounced on the wrong-headed eagle that had been troubling heraldic specialists for years. He designed a new Presidential Coat of Arms, Seal, and Flag, with the bald eagle facing toward the right. In heraldry, that is the "direction of honor," which has no ideological right-left significance but has to do with the way the eagle is facing on the flag of honorably marching troops (and, presumably, is why a hostess seats her guest of honor on her right, and why diplomatic protocol calls for guests at a state dinner to speak first to the dinner partner on the right).

The new flag and seal were completed after President Roosevelt's death. President Truman, who unfurled it for the first time publicly on October 25, 1945, called attention to a more important symbolic change. "Now raise that flag up, there," he said to his military aide, General Harry Vaughan, who was holding the previously used presidential flag. "This flag here—in President Wilson's time there were two flags for the President, an Army flag with a red star and a Navy flag for the President with a blue star. President Wilson ordered a single flag for the President, and this was the result of that [*General Vaughan displays flag*] with the white eagle facing toward the arrows, which is the sinister side of the heraldic form, and no color…This new flag faces the eagle toward the staff which is looking to the front all the time when you are on the march, and also has him looking at the olive branches for peace, instead of the

arrows for war; and taking the 4 stars out of the corner and putting 48 stars around the Presidential seal."

In the abbreviated version of this story often told to visitors on White House tours, President Roosevelt is said to have had the seal changed so that the eagle would be facing the olive branch of peace rather than the arrows of war. That is true as far as it goes, but it was Harry Truman who caught the war-to-peace significance of the turning of the head of the American eagle.

See PARTY EMBLEMS; UNCLE SAM.

Balkanization See VIETNAMIZATION.

ballbuster See NUT-CUTTING.

balloon goes up Signal of an impending campaign; indication of political excitement to begin.

The release of a hot-air balloon signaled to British forces in 1915 that the artillery should begin firing. The phrase floated over into American military slang and became the term to indicate the start of any activity. In advertising, for example, "The balloon goes up next week" would signal the start of a new ad campaign.

Two centuries ago, the phrase *political balloon* referred to empty or inflated discourse in politics. *The Gentleman's Magazine* of London commented on such inflated claims in 1784: "All these are political squibs, or balloons, filled with inflammable air, which have been dispersed gratis in town and country, and having now evaporated, will probably be assigned to oblivion." See TRIAL BALLOON.

The use of *balloon goes up* has not strayed too far from its military origins, however. When the United States prepared to attack Iraq in 1991, Secretary of State James A. Baker III duly informed Bandar bin Sultan, the Saudi Ambassador to the U.S., of the military action: "The balloon is going up. This is your notification."

ballot-box stuffing Vote fraud; originally, the illegal insertion of paper votes into the ballot box, with or without the connivance of local election officials.

The practice flourished in the days of Boss Tweed and the heyday of Tammany Hall in New York City. With the introduction of voting machines the practice was curtailed, however, leaving the phrase to mean "any attempt to falsify the vote count."

Both practice and phrase appear to have started in San Francisco just after the Gold Rush. An advanced form of ballot-box stuffing was described in the House of Representatives in 1882 by Benjamin Butterworth of Ohio: "They had been accustomed to have a box so constructed that the lid would pull out in a groove part of the way, and on election morning pulling the lid part way back, so the bottom of the box could be seen, the judge, or one of them, would say, 'You see there is nothing in the box.' The box would be closed, and the balloting proceed. True, the box would appear to be empty, while under the lid in the top of the box two or three hundred tickets would be fastened. The box being shut with a thud, the tickets would fall down."

Ballot-box stuffing in New York City may have cost James G. Blaine, Republican, the presidency of the United States in 1884. Blaine lost New York State by a margin of 1,143 votes for Grover Cleveland, the Democratic candidate, out of more than 1,100,000 cast. In the Electoral College, Cleveland obtained 219 votes to 182 for Blaine; had Blaine received New York's 36 electoral votes, he would have been elected. According to Henry L. Stoddard, editor and publisher of the *New York Evening Mail*, Tammany politicians arranged for "Battle Ax" Paddy Gleason in Long Island City and John Y. McKane in Coney Island to stuff the ballot boxes to make up Cleveland's 1,143-vote margin of victory.

In the Kennedy-Nixon campaign of 1960, Nixon campaign chairman Leonard Hall was incensed at what he considered flagrant ballot-box stuffing in Texas, some other parts of the South, and particularly Cook County, Illinois. Since a switch of these narrowly won states would have swung the election to Nixon, Hall urged that Nixon declare the election "stolen" and dispute the result, which Nixon declined to do.

In 1966, *New York Post* writer Paul Hoffman recounted the classic story about ballot-box stuffing, updating it to make his central figure "Uncle Dan" O'Connell, a veteran political leader of Albany: " 'Uncle Dan,' President Johnson, and Lady Bird were sailing down the Potomac all alone when their boat sprang a leak. Each grabbed for the lone life preserver. 'Let's settle this the American way, by secret ballot,' suggested the President. Uncle Dan won it the Albany way ... his vote was 17 to 2." See CEMETERY VOTE.

ballyhoo As a verb, to create enthusiasm; to promote colorfully; to "beat the drums"; to tout. As a noun, the material of such efforts.

"Last of the professions on the Midway," wrote Mary Bronson Hartt in *The World's Work* in 1901, "are those of the 'barker,' 'ballyhooer' and 'spieler.' " The circus origin now applies to stunts, "pseudo-events," and exploitation, both commercial and political, using more modern techniques. FDR warned in his second fireside chat: "We cannot ballyhoo our way to prosperity." *The Atlantic Monthly* in March 1948 wrote of candidates that are "ballyhooed, pushed, yelled, screamed and in every way propagandized into the consciousness of the voters."

Wilfred Funk believed the word is traceable to the village of Ballyhooly, in Cork County, Ireland, where, according to the March 1934 *Congressional Record*, "residents engage in a most strenuous debate ... and from the violence of those debates has sprung forth a word known in the English language as ballyhoo."

Slanguist Eric Partridge agreed: "In Erse, *bally* (or *bal*) means 'a dwelling, a village' and it occurs in scores of Celtic place-names. The precise relationship to this glorified village is uncertain: but American colloquial and slangy speech is 'full of' references to Irish joviality and noisy high-spirits."

A synonym is HOOPLA, which politicians regard as a necessary evil to generate artificial fervor that hopefully ignites genuine fervor. An early edition of *Bartlett's Quotations* indicates *hoopla* as having been a driver's hurrying-up to his horse, a meaning that survives in the political sense of a stimulus to excitement. See BANDWAGON.

baloney Nonsense, malarkey; stronger than *blarney*, more politically palatable than unprintable expletives.

"No matter how thin you slice it," said Alfred E. Smith in 1936, "it's still baloney." It was one of the former New York governor's favorite words. Ten years before, when he was asked by a cameraman at a cornerstone-laying ceremony to actually lay a brick for the movies, he had snarled, "That's just baloney. Everybody knows I can't lay bricks." Expressing his opposition to FDR's rumored plan to take the U.S. dollar off the gold standard in 1933, he was widely quoted as saying, "I am for gold dollars as against baloney dollars."

That was not the last *baloney* attack on New Dealers. Clare Boothe Luce, ridiculing Vice President Henry Wallace's foreign policy proposals in 1943 (see HOTTENTOTS, MILK FOR), used the Smith construction with a new twist: "Much of what Mr. Wallace calls his global thinking is, no matter how you slice it, still globaloney."

President Harry Truman picked it up again in 1948, with accurate attribution, to ridicule Thomas E. Dewey's unity campaign: "In the old days, Al Smith would have said: 'That's baloney.' Today, the Happy Warrior would say: 'That's a lot of hooey.' And if that rhymes with anything it's not my fault ..."

As early as 1943, George Allen wrote to General Eisenhower: "How does it feel to be a candidate?" In his memoirs, Eisenhower recalled his answer: "Baloney!"

When a colleague of Winston Churchill stated in 1953 that "economic planning is baloney," the British statesman was called upon to explain his associate's remark in the House of Commons. Majestically, he evaded the question with "I should prefer to have an agreed definition of the meaning of 'baloney' before I attempted to deal with such a topic."

The word, in its political usage, has long been current in the best circles. James Reston, Washington correspondent of *The New York Times*, wrote in 1964: "More harm is done by swallowing political baloney in this country than by swallowing arsenic or smoking reefers."

The word may be spelled *baloney, bolony, balony, bologna*, and in various other ways, but no matter how you spell it ...

For better or wurst, see SALAMI TACTICS.

banana republic Any small country in Central America, with a rudimentary government and presumably once in thrall to the United Fruit Company; by extension, a derogation of any backward or ineffectual regime.

The earliest citation of *banana republic* found so far comes from "The Admiral," an O. Henry short story that became part of his *Cabbages and Kings* (1904): "In the constitution of this small, maritime banana republic was a forgotten section providing for the maintenance of a navy." O. Henry (William Sydney Porter) may have coined the phrase; the novel is derived from his experiences in Central America, where he fled after being indicted in 1896 for embezzlement from a Texas bank. (He returned to stand trial and served more than three years in prison.)

The demeaning phrase quickly entered common parlance in the U.S. and abroad. *The Indianapolis Star* opined in 1911: "When Uncle Sam finally occupies the canal, it is to be hoped that he thrashes out those banana republic disputes and sees that there is only one uprising a month." Arthur Koestler, Hungarian-born but a resident of England from 1940 onward, conveyed the original, insulting sense in *Promise and Fulfillment* (1949) when referring to "The somewhat jerky behavior displayed by the Central American banana republics." The derogation is no longer geographically limited: speaking in 1993 of Croatia, a journalist in Zagreb told *The New York Times*: "I don't blame any outsider who thinks of us as a third-rate banana republic. It's not true, but I understand people who think Croatia is a backward country ruled by an angry old dictator."

Banana republic parallels other derogatory *banana* phrases and perhaps gains some power from them: for example, *banana boat*, a slow one; *banana oil*, flattering nonsense; *to go bananas*, to go crazy, and, less insulting in the context, *top banana*, a leading comedian. Then there is the *banana* that is an economic downturn by another name; see its extreme use as a euphemism in RECESSION.

The derogatory sense of *banana republic* may be verging on obsolescence, but thanks to its adoption as the name of the successful clothing chain, the phrase has gained a fashionable connotation. *Banana Republican* is another matter, however, as exemplified by references to "beige-clad Banana Republicans" and "Banana Republicans wearing cashmere underwear ... living large but easy in the New Age." And from a report in *The Christian Science Monitor* on the crowd scenes in Palm Beach during the recount of presidential votes in 2000: "Professionally printed 'Sore/Loserman' posters, playing off the '[Al] Gore/Lieberman' campaign design, were everywhere. Often they were accompanied by the waving of 'Sore/Loserman' crying towels. The Democratic response was to tack up posters denouncing 'Banana Republicans.'"

bandwagon A movement appealing to the herd instinct of politicians and voters to be on the winning side in any contest.

The word was used in P. T. Barnum's *Life*, published in 1855, to describe a difficult chapter in the life of the circus: "At Vicksburg we sold all our land conveyances excepting four horses and the 'bandwagon.'" The humor magazine *Puck* in 1884 depicted Chester Arthur driving a bandwagon carrying other presidential hopefuls, and in 1896 it published a similar cartoon showing a McKinley bandwagon.

Songs have also helped popularize the notion of bandwagons. A song published in 1851, written by W. Loftin Hargrave, titled "Wait for the Wagon, A New Ethiopian Song and Melody," was still a favorite in 1900. In that year, too, the Prohibitionists helped popularize a temperance song called "The Prohibition Bandwagon," with the words:

And our friends who vote for gin,
Will all scramble to jump in,
When we get our big bandwagon,
*   some sweet day.*

From 1902 onward the word became well established in American political terminology. In Albert Shaw's cartoon history of Theodore Roosevelt's career, a wagon is shown with Roosevelt's friends making musical noises in his favor, but the main character—Senator Thomas C. Platt—is shown running after the wagon frantically trying to jump aboard, with a whip in his hand indicating that he would like to be in the driver's seat.

Most extensive use of a real bandwagon in modern times was the "Eisenhower-Nixon Bandwagon" of 1952, a project conceived by Arthur Gray, Jr., and C. Langhorne Washburn. Three 25-ton trailer trucks, each with a three-man crew, "advanced" Eisenhower appearances throughout the campaign. Each gaily decorated truck contained helium tanks for barrage balloons, twelve "Ike" dresses in sizes ten and twelve with parasols and hats, thousands of buttons and pieces of literature, Navy bosun's whistles, and a jeep with a loudspeaker. In 29 cities over 32 days, the bandwagon rolled ahead of the candidates to organize parades and major receptions, giving a colorful focal point to local activity. Each night, the campaigners set up what they called an "Ethereal Nocturnal Splendor": powerful searchlights played on the barrage balloons with their "Ike" signs, a sight which could be seen from ten miles away. After taking office, President Eisenhower kept one of the bosun's whistles from the bandwagon in the Oval Office as a memento.

The expression is in use in Great Britain as well. Wrote the *Daily Mirror* in 1966, establishing its independent position: "The *Mirror* ... does not jump on bandwagons ... it isn't, never has been, and never will be, a tin can tied to a political party's tail."

See HYMIE'S FERRYBOAT.

banner district The voting unit in which a party or candidate makes a better showing than anywhere else in a single election; also, the section of a larger constituency in which a politician or party has the strongest support.

Crediting an area with banner status was common practice in political reportage and speechmaking during much of the nineteenth century. Political usage seems to have originated in the 1840 presidential election in which the incumbent Democrat, Martin Van Buren, was challenged by William Harrison, a Whig. In the course of the colorful "Log Cabin and Hard Cider" campaign, a Whig group in Louisiana promised a banner to the state giving the most impressive vote to Harrison. The subsequent controversy over which state won outlived Harrison—who died of pneumonia one month after being inaugurated—and helped popularize the phrase.

Historically, a commander's banner or standard served as a rallying point and symbol of success to come. Much of this meaning has been preserved whether *banner* is used as a noun or adjective in a figurative sense. Politically, the term has acquired an antique flavor; STANDARD-BEARER, however, is still current. See MILITARY METAPHORS.

ban the bomb See BETTER RED THAN DEAD.

barefoot boy from Wall Street Description of Republican presidential candidate Wendell L. Willkie reminding voters of Willkie's success in finance.

FDR's Interior Secretary, Harold L. Ickes, derided the "humble" image of the Indianan. Ickes (see CURMUDGEON) laced into Willkie soon after the candidate's 1940 acceptance speech. The Secretary characterized the Republican candidate as "the rich man's Roosevelt; the simple, barefoot Wall Street lawyer," which later was shortened to "the barefoot boy from Wall Street." He poured it on later by charging that the candidate was a "one-spur leather puller who does not even pretend to know anything about the West." Ickes was a master at the art of colorful insult (see MAN ON THE WEDDING CAKE; INVECTIVE, POLITICAL), and occasionally was himself on the receiving end: Governor Huey Long called him "the Chicago chinch bug."

bargain and corruption See KINGMAKER.

bargaining chip A prospective concession; an arms program justified on the theory that it can be used as a device to induce an adversary to give up an equivalent strategic weapon.

This was SALT LINGO, popularized by members of the National Security Council staff during the early '70s, when Henry Kissinger was National Security Adviser, later adopted by congressmen and writers on the Strategic Arms Limitation Talks. Fred R. Shapiro, editor of the *Yale Dictionary of Quotations*, found a 1965 use in a *Boston Globe* column by Chalmers Roberts on L.B.J.: "Mr. Johnson had by then won a massive election victory, but he had just ordered the first bombing of North Viet Nam in an effort to bring Hanoi to a conference table where the bargaining chips on both sides would be more closely matched."

In the April 1973 issue of the Friends Committee on National Legislation's *Washington Newsletter*, the term was used instead of its predecessor, *trade-off*: "Regarding the SALT negotiations, 14 Republican congressmen appealed to President Nixon to go slow on the 'bargaining chip' idea, calling for restraint in development of weapons such as the B-1 bomber and the Trident submarine at this time." In *The New York Times Magazine* a year later, the term was again defined: "Bargaining from strength calls for arms programs that can serve as 'bargaining chips' to trade for concessions that the other side might not otherwise make…The pursuit of hedges and chips brings about an intensification of the arms race just to keep 'bargaining-chip gaps' from developing."

The phrase evokes the metaphor of high-stakes poker and was a favored Kissingerism, along with STEP-BY-STEP DIPLOMACY, QUIET DIPLOMACY, and SHUTTLE DIPLOMACY.

Barnburners Persons demonstrating uncompromising determination, even at risk of total loss; practitioners of the art of the impossible.

The word originally designated the antislavery wing of the Democratic party in New York State in the 1840s led by Martin Van Buren and his son, John. The name was devised by the "Hunkers," a Democratic opposition faction, to ridicule Van Buren's radical approach "in the manner of the Dutch farmer who burned his barn to destroy the rats."

The Barnburners played an important role in the presidential election of 1848. They bolted from the Democratic National Convention and joined the Free-Soilers; their combined vote swung the election to Whig Zachary Taylor. Their antislavery views led them into the Republican party in the mid-1850s.

The term *Barnburners* and its figure of speech reappears from time to time. A letter sent to President Hoover after his term of office included an affirmative appraisal of his policies: "We are grateful during your occupancy of the White House you never got the idea of burning down the temple of our fathers in order to destroy a few cockroaches in the basement." Warning of the danger of MCCARTHYISM in meeting the threat of Communist subversion, Adlai Stevenson said in 1952: "We must take care not to burn down the barn to kill the rats." A *Washington Post* editorial in 1977 revived the word: "Canadian radicals and barn-burners of various denominations have titillated themselves for years with talk of resorting to arms in Quebec."

The expression can be traced to a sermon by Thomas Adams in 1629: "The empiric to cure the fever, destroys the patient; so the wise man, to burn the mice, set fire to his barn."

barnstorm To take an extended electioneering trip with many brief stops.

Barnstorming has been widely used at least since the nineteenth century, deriving from the custom of using a barn for performances by itinerant players; because politicking was something of a rural amusement, the transfer was simple and logical. The term has since been supplemented by WHISTLESTOPPING.

Although politicians rarely speak in barns any longer, the usage persists. In October 1944, the *Chicago Daily News* wrote: "President Roosevelt indignantly denies that his New York and Chicago barnstorming trips violate his pledge not to campaign in the usual sense." Samuel Rosenman later explained that under pressure from Thomas Dewey's strong campaign, "the President

soon began to realize that it was necessary for him to get out and fight hard. He also realized that it was up to him to prove that he could stand the physical and mental rigors of a political campaign."

A "Value Voters Barnstorm" helped Mike Huckabee to a surprise victory in the 2008 Iowa Republican Caucuses.

See NONPOLITICAL TRIP; CHAUTAUQUA CIRCUIT.

base The group of loyal constituencies that are considered to be a party's core of support, and whose members are the prime targets of TURNOUT efforts.

"To be a real boss, and not just a flunky," wrote the political scientist Clinton Rossiter in 1960 about local political leaders, "a politician must have his own base of power and immunity from external discipline, if not from internal revolt."

Early use of the word in politics required the adjective "political" to modify it. In 1879, the *Colorado Springs Gazette* reported that a California politician had just "meditated a change of political base as soon as he fell out of actual support at the hands of the party."

Through the last half of the twentieth century, the idea of the fundament of support was called the POWER BASE; by the turn of the twenty-first, the noun could stand by itself, often attached to the verb *energize*. In the presidential campaigns of 2004, much was made of the Republican ability to energize and turn out its base of social conservatives (evangelicals, opponents of abortion and single-sex marriage, and other "moral values" voters), gun-control opponents, and economic conservatives pressing tax and spending cuts; meanwhile, the Democratic base of labor, greens, civil libertarians, feminists, proponents of gun control and increased entitlements, and—especially as opposition to the second Iraq war heightened—anti-war activists coalesced.

In an October *New York Times* Op-Ed article titled "Ace of Base," Mark Halperin, while suggesting that the Bush base "may have one more victory to give," reported that critics were asserting "that the politics of the base has run its course, and that the Iraq war, the partisan zealousness and the conservative social policies of the administration have made voters yearn for a more centrist, bipartisan government."

"Something seems to have gone off the rails between President Bush and his base," noted National Public Radio commentator and *Christian Science Monitor* columnist Daniel Schorr as early as May of 2006; the 90-year-old journalist defined *base* as "that solid core of political supporters who will stick with you through electoral thick and thin as long as you are perceived as advancing their principles. Most often, the term is applied to religious conservatives." As Schorr predicted, not only did the Republican base shrink in the midterm election of 2006, but the Bush strategist Karl Rove's previously successful strategy of playing to, and turning out, the base was overcome by the surprisingly strong re-emergence of the SWING VOTER (see TRIANGULATION). "The term 'base' is not in William Safire's political dictionary," Schorr informed his listeners and readers, "but he tells me it will be included in the next edition." And so it is.

See PARTY FAITHFUL; REGULAR.

-bashing Excessive criticism; a combining form to derogate rhetorical attacks on a person, group, or principle.

The combining forms of *-bashing* and *-basher* began in Britain. *Bash*, the eighteenth-century verb that led to these forms, may be onomatopoeic (a word that imitates a sound) or a blend of *bang* and *smash*.

British lexicographer Eric Partridge noted the nineteenth-century use of *basher* for a boxer or professional criminal. By 1940, the peeling of potatoes was known as *spud-bashing*. A driving force behind this counterattacking form is *The Economist*, a London weekly. In 1975, this publication coined *Commie-basher* for Jacques Chirac, the French Gaullist leader, and Senator Henry Jackson was labeled "a veteran *Russia-basher*." Recent use in the United States has hit upon numerous objects of vituperation, from *male-bashing* to *Japan-bashing*.

The government, of course, is a favorite target of the bashers. When the Rea-

gan Administration blamed the Federal Reserve Board for rising interest rates, *The Wall Street Journal* reported that "Reagan aides hope their 'Fed-bashing' will pressure the central bank to ease its tight grip on the nation's credit." See BLAME GAME.

Bay of Pigs fiasco The abortive invasion of Cuba in 1961 by U.S.-supported anti-Castro refugees; a reference to catastrophe resulting from poor planning.

Few phrases of recent coinage are so powerfully fused as *Bay of Pigs* and *fiasco*. The invasion is rarely referred to as the Bay of Pigs *disaster*, or the Bay of Pigs *tragedy*, *failure*, *flop*, *botch*, or even *snafu*. Always *fiasco*, of the same root as *flask*, often of wine, which probably caused *fiasco* to gain its connotation of a misbegotten, perhaps drunken attempt to accomplish a pretentious feat that falls flat on its face.

Criticism of President Kennedy following the invasion attempt soon after his inauguration was vicious: "Caroline is a cute kid, but we shouldn't let her plan any more invasions." Even in references later by Kennedy supporters (said Theodore Sorensen: "The Bay of Pigs fiasco had its influence"), the use of *fiasco* was universal. Substituting another word would be as jarring to the ear as "the *attack* of the Light Brigade."

In politics and in other fields, a *Bay of Pigs* now means a monumental flop with an overtone of ultimate redemption (as Kennedy redeemed his reputation in the confrontation with Khrushchev over Cuba a year after the Bay of Pigs, uh, fiasco). Broadway showman David Merrick closed a show in 1966 called *Breakfast at Tiffany's* before opening night, at a loss of $450,000, with the remark: "It's my Bay of Pigs."

In April 1992, when a Clinton aide sought to minimize the President's responsibility for an F.B.I. attack that led to a mass suicide in Waco, Texas, early in his Administration, he said, "This was not a Bay of Pigs." In 2006, Thomas Ricks, *The Washington Post's* senior Pentagon correspondent, titled his book about severe shortcomings of the U.S. campaign in Iraq *Fiasco*.

beanbag What politics ain't.

"His early experience," wrote Finley Peter Dunne of his creation, saloon-keeping philosopher Mr. DOOLEY, "gave him wisdom in discussing public affairs. 'Politics,' he says, 'ain't beanbag. 'Tis a man's game; an' women, childher, an' pro-hybitionists'd do well to keep out iv it.'"

The above quotation in Irish brogue is taken from the preface to *Mr. Dooley in Peace and War*, published in 1898; it had been used earlier by Dunne, on October 5, 1895, in an essay in the *Chicago Evening Post*.

A beanbag is a cloth bag partly filled with beans (or, more recently, with plastic beads), easily catchable, used in a children's game of the same name. In Mr. Dooley's use, the child's play made a dramatic comparison with an adult's game, and has been used for that purpose ever since (though the game has recently been replaced by HARDBALL).

"[President] Carter's flaw as a political leader," wrote Jack Germond and Jules Witcover in 1977, "has always been his massive self-assurance, his total confidence that no one would believe him capable of political knavery or personal weakness. But in the Bert Lance case, what was in question was his sophistication. And, as Mr. Dooley told us long ago, politics ain't beanbag."

The classic Dooley aphorism is current. In a scathing review of a book by John Dean in 2006, Nick Gillespie wrote in *The Washington Post*: "Yeah, yeah, politics ain't beanbag and all that. But our political discourse is rancorous enough without attempting to psychologize our adversaries out of decent debate."

Dooley wasn't playing *beanbag* with what is now called "the MAINSTREAM media": "Th' newspaper does ivrything f'r us," Dunne wrote in 1902. "It runs the polis force an' th' banks, commands th' milishy, controls th' ligislachure, baptizes th' young, marries th' foolish, comforts th' afflicted, afflicts the comfortable, buries th' dead an' roasts thim afterward."

bean counter Accountant; bookkeeper of financial records or statistics; in recent usage, a derogation of one who seeks to hold politicians to perceived promises of racial or sexual quotas.

This phrase comes from the image of a person carefully keeping track of the number of individual beans. A 1975 issue of *Forbes* magazine referred to one numberscruncher as "a smart, tightfisted and austere 'bean-counter' accountant from rural Kentucky." Both the quotation marks and the attributive use before *accountant* were dropped by 1980, as the term was extended from business into military usage. George C. Wilson of *The Washington Post* questioned our military readiness in 1980, pointing out that "the Pentagon's bean counters have rated six of the nation's stateside divisions far from ready to fight."

The term carries a connotation of disapproval or dismissal. Senate Appropriations Committee chairman Mark O. Hatfield criticized the Office of Management and Budget for derogating a 1982 plan: "By no responsible account can this be called a budget buster, as it has been characterized by the bean counters at the OMB."

As President Bill Clinton was naming his Cabinet choices during the 1992–93 interregnum, he was excoriated by women's groups for not appointing enough women. He responded angrily at a news conference in Little Rock on December 21, 1992, calling them "bean counters" more interested in quotas than ability. He was irritated because two of his appointees—to head the Council of Economic Advisers and the Environmental Protection Agency—were not being treated as top-level appointments by advocates of women's advancement because they were not Cabinet posts. "If I had appointed white men to those jobs," he said, "they would have been counting those positions against our Administration, those bean counters who are doing that."

This usage gave a new sense to the relatively recent derogation of accountants: one who puts mere numbers ahead of other substantive evidence.

beatnik See -NIK SUFFIX.

beauty contest See CATTLE SHOW.

bedsheet ballot A lengthy list of candidates and propositions, often confusing to voters.

This phrase is most often used pejoratively, as if an attempt is being made to bamboozle voters with complexity; in modern times, it is often used to complain about the difficulty of choosing among many candidates for delegates to a political convention.

A synonym is *blanket ballot*; both phrases use the analogy of bedcoverings to evoke a picture of an enormous piece of paper, capable of handling a bewildering multiplicity of choices.

before April 9th men See CUFFLINKS GANG; ALPHABET AGENCIES.

bellwether A trend-setter; or, a district with a history of reflecting a nationwide vote; or, a STALKING HORSE.

Literally, a wether is a male sheep; the leading sheep of the flock sometimes wears a bell. In 1878 *Harper's Weekly* observed that the unthinking crowd would "follow the bellwether over any wall and into any pasture, but the independent sheep would not."

The Judas-goat or stalking-horse meaning remains: Cabell Phillips, after describing the machinations within the Democratic party to dump Henry Wallace from the vice presidency in 1944, wrote that James Byrnes felt indignant because the party leadership "had deceived him and used him as a bellwether to undermine Wallace and to create an opening for Truman."

The trend-setting sense has taken over. President Kennedy, struggling to restrain inflation in 1961, described the steel industry as "a bellwether, as well as a major element in industrial costs." A 1988 *New York Times* listing offers "estimates for Treasury's bellwether bonds."

Maine was considered a bellwether state in national elections early in the mid-nineteenth century, largely because its cold weather caused the state to vote two months ahead of other states' November election day. This led to the slogan "As Maine goes, so goes the nation." In the Roosevelt-Landon contest of 1936, however, the only two states to give a majority to Republican Alf Landon were Maine and Vermont. The reaction of "As Maine goes, so goes Vermont" was obvious to many, but FDR's political chief James A. Farley was most often credited as the source.

Beltway bandits A semi-affectionate derogation of consultants in the District of Columbia, especially lawyers, lobbyists, and public relations executives in the defense and telecommunication industries who thrive on federal government contracts.

The term for these consultants, who primarily work for the defense industry, is based on proximity to the Capital Beltway around Washington, D.C. (*Beltway* is a 1951 word for what the British call a *ring-road*.) This 8-lane circumferential highway, which cuts through Maryland and Virginia suburbs, encloses many of these offices as well as Washington area THINK TANKS, a term coined in the late '60s.

Beltway bandits is jocular usage with a sharp edge and a sinister origin; its source was probably the early 1970s usage for thieves who would strike homes near the Beltway and use the high-speed road to make their escape.

The procurement of government contracts is often led by executives who use the "revolving door"—see HONEST GRAFT—from government to more lucrative private service, pausing for whatever term the Congress fixes as ethical before approaching former colleagues. The alliterative *Beltway bandit* was applied to lobbyists in *The Washington Post* on January 25, 1978: "Some 'Beltway bandit' ought to be hired to put one team of computer experts to work designing crime-proof defenses."

For a time in the 1980s, the figurative avenue of access was called *Gucci gulch*, after the expensive Italian shoe design of loafers with a distinctive linked buckle; a 1987 book by Alan Murray and Jeffrey Birnbaum was titled *Showdown at Gucci Gulch*.

A related term to describe the power of lobbyists' moves from the periphery to the heart of the nation's capital is *K Street*: "Lobby-law firms, trade associations, interest groups and labor unions—known collectively as K Street," wrote Jeffrey Birnbaum in *The Washington Post* just before congressional elections in 2006, "have experienced a quantum leap in CLOUT and are now, more than ever, a permanent and pervasive force in Washington, essential to the workings of government and politics." He noted that the number of registered lobbyists had doubled since the turn of the millennium to 30,000. At the same time, *The Hill* newspaper headlined "Dems seek K St. cash."

First to catch the significance of the street as the metaphor for a fourth branch of government permeated by parasitic petitioners was the writer Lynn Rosellini, who reported in *The New York Times* in 1981 that "All along K Street, lobbyists, lawyers, trade associations, special interest groups and national corporation offices are feverishly working to affect parts of [President Reagan's] budget. Their activity illustrates an important point about power in Washington: Saying 'K Street' is almost like saying 'the Hill' or 'the White House'; it seems to be a branch of government."

Since 2000, both *Beltway bandit* and *Gucci gulch* have been eclipsed by *K Street* in the lingo of insiders and those outsiders envious of them.

The use of the name of a street or highway to denote an industry or power center is hardly new. *Madison Avenue* still denotes the advertising industry, though few agencies are still located at that New York City address; same with *Wall Street* for the financial industry and *Fleet Street* in London, once the center of British journalism. In Washington, K Street—lined with new office buildings all built as high as the capital's strict zoning allows—is located between I and L (there is no J Street, and I is often written "Eye," to avoid confusion with the Roman numeral I), only three blocks from the newly fortified White House.

See INFLUENCE PEDDLER; INSIDE THE BELTWAY.

benchmarks Measurement of progress toward a target date.

This word never meant "a mark on a bench"; its early uses included "a hard, flat surface on which a surveyor could hammer in an elevation marker" and "a surveyor's mark cut in some durable material." It came to mean "touchstone, gauge, criterion

used to judge performance," as in an 1884 *Science* quote about "reference points and bench-marks of the universe."

That meaning was taken up by Bush Administration spokesmen to allay concerns about lack of political progress toward unifying and pacifying Iraq in 2004; such measurements as "reduction of the level of violence" and "passage of legislation by the Iraqi parliament to fairly divide the nation's oil resources among Sunnis, Shia, and Kurds" were two of the most frequently cited benchmarks.

A more urgent and specific word was used by those in Congress eager to withdraw U.S. troops soon: *timetable*, which would mandate withdrawal on a fixed schedule, to which White House spokesmen added a denigrating modifier: "artificial timetable." President Bush escalated that to "an artificial deadline." War critics were equally contemptuous of the fuzzy word *goals*, which *benchmarks* had replaced. *Guidelines* and *guideposts* did not enter the debate, as they are associated with economic JAWBONING.

The Deputy Prime Minister of Iraq, Barham Salih, on a visit to Washington, DC, in May 2007, preferred *commitment*, avoided *timetable*, and accepted *benchmark:* the *Washington Times* headline read "Iraqi Backs 'Benchmark' Action."

Synonymy was provided the author by Joe Pickett, editor of the *American Heritage Dictionary*: "*Timetable* is indicative of modernity, hallmark of an industrialized society, originally the train—indicative of the things humans have to follow to achieve success in modern society. *Guideposts* tend toward moral or personal metaphors—life as a journey, pilgrim's progress. *Milestones* is a related term, but one with very positive connotations." *Signposts* are poles for directions but the word has not made the figurative leap, as *road map* has; that locution is used in diplolingo to point "the way forward" in Israeli-Palestinian negotiations. *Schedule* is rarely used, presumably because it is not metaphoric.

The Pentagon's *Dictionary of Military and Associated Terms* has a crisp definition of *target date*, a phrase also used in the withdrawal debate: "The date on which it is desired that an action be accomplished or initiated." However, its specificity is weakened by "desired."

benign neglect A suggestion to allow tensions to ease, interpreted as a plot to abandon the civil rights movement.

Nixon's urban affairs adviser, Daniel Patrick Moynihan, had a predilection for transmitting his advice in long and literate memoranda. On occasion, the President directed that Moynihan memos be circulated to Cabinet members, who then passed copies throughout their departments. On March 2, 1970, this casual method of transmission backfired.

"The time may have come," wrote Moynihan, "when the issue of race could benefit from a period of 'benign neglect.'"

In context, Moynihan's meaning was that blacks would profit if extremists on both sides of the race issue were to lower their voices. But, as *Newsweek* wrote, "to black leaders and their allies, 'neglect'—benign or malign—seemed precisely to describe everything the Administration was and was not doing about race. And they responded with a fury ..."

Moynihan put *benign neglect* within quotes because he thought the phrase came from a report by the Earl of Durham, who wrote Queen Victoria in 1839 saying that Canada had done so well during two generations of non-involvement by the mother country that she ought to be granted self-government. When he asked an aide, William Kristol, to look for the quote, however, it couldn't be found. Moynihan wrote the author about the phrase's origin: "And so I am forced to suppose I may have thought it up myself, as a kind of summation of the Durham report."

The oxymoronic overtone of the phrase made it memorable, but the mischief that its misinterpretation could cause made it a tempting morsel to leak to *The New York Times*. The leak twisted the meaning of Moynihan's advice and hurt him among liberals, of whom he could fairly be considered one of the few close to Nixon. It did not damage him within the Administration; as *The New Republic*'s John Osborne wrote, "The insiders judged the incident

to be an example of how outsiders misjudge insiders and fail to comprehend the intricacies of Presidential counseling and communications."

Columnist Max Lerner could not resist observing, "If anything, he might have used Holmes' 'intelligent neglect.'"

Moynihan, who became a Democratic Senator from New York, could take heart, however, in seeing the phrase used—without reference to him and in the sense it was originally intended—by a *New York Times* editorialist in January 1978: "Early this month, the Carter Administration abandoned its 'benign neglect' of the dollar."

Berlin Wall See WALL, POLITICAL SYMBOL OF.

best and the brightest See WHIZ KIDS.

best man, the Object of a convention choice; claim by all candidates on the basis of qualifications.

Like ARENA and HAT IN THE RING, the phrase is closely associated with boxing, when the referee concludes his instructions to the fighters with "and may the best man win."

The phrase was used as the title of a play by Gore Vidal, later a motion picture, about the selection of a presidential candidate.

In 1964, when President Lyndon Johnson was faced with the choice of a running mate, proponents of Hubert H. Humphrey used a subtle slogan to soft-sell their candidate: "The Next Best Man."

better red than dead Slogan of the British nuclear disarmament movement.

British philosopher Bertrand Russell wrote in 1958 that if "no alternative remains except communist domination or the extinction of the human race, the former alternative is the lesser of the two evils." This was sloganized into "Better Red Than Dead" and became part of the signage at "Ban the Bomb" demonstrations.

John F. Kennedy, speaking at the University of Washington in 1961, took critical note of the phrase: "It is a curious fact that each of these two extreme opposites resembles the other. Each believes that we have only two choices: appeasement or war, suicide or surrender, humiliation or holocaust, to be either Red or dead."

An obvious turnaround was used by British author Stanley Reynolds in 1964, in a book urging an anti-Communist crusade entitled *Better Dead Than Red*. This effectively sabotaged the slogan; after a while, most people did not know which slogan came first or who was for what. Thermonuclear thinker Herman Kahn (see UNTHINKABLE THOUGHTS) wrote: "If somebody says, 'I would rather be Red than dead,' he is a coward, and I think properly an object of contempt and scorn. But if somebody says, 'I would rather have everybody Red than everybody dead,' he is taking a reasonable position with which I agree. While I would rather have everybody Red than everybody dead, we must not allow a situation to develop in which such a choice is the only one we have."

Big Apple New York City.

In his 1938 book, *Hi De Ho*, bandleader Cab Calloway defined "apple" as "the big town, the main stem, Harlem." In a 1976 conversation with the author, Mr. Calloway explained further that The Big Apple—the name of a Harlem night club in the mid-'30s—was a mecca for jazz musicians. A dance that *Life* magazine in 1937 called "a loose-hipped, freehand combination of 'truckin' and the square dance" was named "The Big Apple," an appellation taken from the night club, according to Calloway.

Robert Gold, author of the 1975 *Jazz Talk*, points to a 1966 speculation in *Record Research* as the likely etymology: "My suspicion [is] that *Big Apple* is a transliteration of the older Mexican idiom 'manzana principale' for the main square of the town or the downtown area." However, David W. Maurer's *The Argot of the Racetrack* (Publication of the American Dialect Society #16, 1951) holds that *big apple* comes from "racetrack argot: in big time racing, New York City had a tradition of high purses, excellent tracks, fine horses." Why race-track people would use the phrase *big apple* was unexplained, unless the fruit was a reward for a horse.

Etymologist David Shulman tracked the term to a 1909 book, *The Wayfarer in New York*, by Edward Martin: "It [the Mid-West] inclines to think that the big apple gets a disproportionate share of the national sap." Mr. Calloway may have been on the right track about the term's popularization: the phrase was black-English jazz talk in the mid-'30s.

In the mid-'70s, with New York City in great financial difficulty, the Convention and Visitors Bureau made an attempt to "market" the city by popularizing the phrase as the metropolitan symbol, which seemed more apt than its predecessor, *Fun City*.

big casino The center ring, grand arena, place of major action.

Ronald Reagan introduced this gaming expression to politics, referring in 1974 to the race for the presidency as "the big casino." A casino was originally a public dancing and meeting hall, later a place for gambling; the word is also used for a card game. (The term beginning with a capital C was used in another sense by John Wayne, dying of cancer, who sought to defeat "the big Casino.")

Wendell Rawls Jr. wrote in *The New York Times* in 1978 that a Republican candidate for governor of Pennsylvania, Richard Thornburgh, had "helped remove a complacent Federal prosecutor in Philadelphia and encouraged the replacement, Mr. [David] Marston, to look upon the city as the 'big casino' of political crime." See CARD METAPHORS.

big character posters See GRAFFITI; SNIPE.

Big Daddy See GREAT WHITE FATHER.

big enchilada The top man, or main target; in Watergate terminology, former Attorney General John Mitchell.

Enchilada is a Spanish-American word for a tortilla enclosing chopped meat, topped with a chili-flavored sauce (the root of the en*chil*ada is *chili*).

"I coined the phrase," former White House aide John Ehrlichman informed the author from his incarceration in 1977. "I've cooked my own enchiladas for years. My California upbringing. Could have said 'big fish,' or 'top dog' or 'big cheese,' I guess."

The phrase was heard on the March 27, 1973, Nixon tape in connection with giving the President's pursuers a substantial prize, in the hope they would be satisfied. Of John Mitchell, H. R. Haldeman said, "He is as high up as they've got," and Ehrlichman replied, "He's the Big Enchilada."

The popular food is also used as a synecdoche for the world, similar to "the whole ball of wax." After the election victory of Jimmy Carter in 1976, former California Governor Ronald Reagan said that the Democrats, long in control of Congress, would no longer be able to share responsibility for difficulties with Republicans. "For the first time," Reagan said, "the Democrats can not fuzz up the issue by blaming the White House. They've got the whole enchilada now."

big foot Celebrated journalist; a derogation of a "media biggie" by envious or bemused colleagues.

This jocular term applies to any columnist or editor who temporarily joins the regular staff on a press bus following a presidential candidate. The image suggests an outsider who will trample the territory of "the boys on the bus" (including women) who normally cover that beat.

During the presidential campaign of 1980, T.R. Reid of *The Washington Post* reported that description of Hedrick Smith, then the Washington correspondent (a term then used to designate the Washington bureau chief) of *The New York Times*, who wore a large cast on a broken ankle for several months. Drummond Ayers, his colleague, had good-naturedly dubbed him that.

Media superstars may be pushed beyond this label. Reid wrote of Walter Cronkite's entrance: "The traveling reporters, who have divided political journalists into two categories—junior reporters, known as 'little feet,' and senior political analysts, or 'big feet'—have given Cronkite a designation all his own: 'Ultra Foot.'"

Two years later, President George H.W. Bush was quoted as saying, as if in relief, that he was receiving "very little attention from the 'Big Feet,'" which the *Times* described as "a colloquial reference to national political news commentators."

The expression soon gained a verb form. *New York Magazine* reported in 1986 that Dan Rather of CBS "arrived just before the president went on the air, but Bob Schieffer was in place and [Rather] decided not to bigfoot him."

The noun *Big Foot* (usually written as two words, but on occasion *Bigfoot*, with varying capitalization) is based on the 1960s nickname for Sasquatch, the large, hairy, humanlike creature that supposedly lives in the Pacific Northwest. Purported evidence of the presence of the creature has been fearsome footprints supposedly left by Big Foot. See ABOMINABLE NO-MAN.

bigger bang for a buck More efficient use of defense appropriations, relying largely on nuclear deterrents.

Secretary of State John Foster Dulles laid down the policy of MASSIVE RETALIATION in 1954 and told the Council on Foreign Relations this policy "permits of a selection of military means instead of multiplication of means. As a result, it is now possible to get, and share, more basic security at less cost."

Defense Secretary Charles E. Wilson promptly dubbed the policy the NEW LOOK (after a fashion phrase of the time describing lower hemlines) and said it would provide "a bigger bang for a buck."

Historian and naval expert Samuel Eliot Morison analyzed it this way: "to strengthen American retaliatory power, to 'get a bigger bang for a buck' as the phrase ran, the defense department built up a long-range 'strategic' air force, with a stockpile of atomic bombs, but neglected both navy and ground forces."

Ultimately, the doctrine of massive retaliation was modified to allow for "brushfire wars" or LIMITED WARS and defense budgets allotted more to ground and naval forces, presumably a smaller bang for a buck but useful when smaller bangs avoid nuclear wars. President Kennedy summed up his approach to the budgetary problem during his Administration with a similar counterphrase: "There is no discount price on defense."

big government An attack phrase on centralized federal authority and massive taxation and expenditure.

The phrase probably stemmed from *Big Business*, which also spawned *Big Labor* (both usually capitalized), but the concern about the size and power of the federal authority began with the birth of the nation. Reformer Samuel Tilden, fighting Boss William Marcy Tweed in New York, harked back to the problems of Thomas Jefferson in 1801: "a grasping centralism, absorbing all functions from the local authorities, and assuming to control the industries of individuals by largesses to favored classes from the public treasury … were then, as now, characteristics of the period." Tilden called for a return to Jefferson's way: "He repressed the meddling of government in the concerns of private business."

But the rise of populism (see POPULIST) and the advent of the trust-busters showed that the public felt that "bigness" was a greater threat from business than from government. Lawyer Louis Brandeis inveighed against the CURSE OF BIGNESS in business. He was countered later with William Howard Taft's statement: "Mere size is no sin." As a Supreme Court Justice, Brandeis kept up his campaign against bigness in both business and government. When the Court unanimously decided to strike down the National Industrial Recovery Act in 1935—Black Monday, New Dealers called it—Brandeis warned Roosevelt aide Thomas Corcoran: "Tell the President we're not going to let this government centralize everything."

"Maybe it's unfortunate," wrote an editor of *The New Republic*, "but about the only counterweight the little man has to Big Business is Big Government." Republicans and conservative Democrats sharply disagree. Thomas E. Dewey stated the case against Big Government in 1950: "All-powerful, central government, like dictatorships, can continue only by growing larger and larger. It can never retrench without admitting failure. By absorbing more than half of all the taxing power of the nation, the federal government now deprives the states and local governments of the capacity to support the programs they should conduct … it offers them in exchange the counterfeit currency of federal subsidy."

Dwight Eisenhower deplored what he called "the whole-hog mentality," which "leans toward the creation of a more extensive and stifling monopoly than this country has ever seen … you don't need more supergovernment."

Republican House Minority Leader Gerald Ford, in 1966, blamed it all on the Democrats, labeling them "the party of Big Business, of Big Government, of Big Spending, of Big Deficits, of Big Cost of Living, of Big Labor Trouble, of Big Home Foreclosures, of Big Scandals, of Big Riots in the Streets and of Big Promises."

"The truth about big government," said John F. Kennedy in 1962, "is the truth about any other great activity: it is complex. Certainly it is true that size brings dangers, but it is also true that size also can bring benefits."

A favorite Ronald Reagan line was "Government is not the solution to the problem; government is the problem." President Bill Clinton astonished some followers and delighted some critics with "The era of big government is over."

big lie A falsehood of such magnitude and audacity that it is bound to have an effect on public opinion even if it is not given credence by a majority; a propaganda technique identified with Adolf Hitler.

Hitler wrote in *Mein Kampf*:

The size of the lie is a definite factor in causing it to be believed, for the vast masses of a nation are in the depths of their hearts more easily deceived than they are consciously and intentionally bad. The primitive simplicity of their minds renders them a more easy prey to a big lie than a small one, for they themselves often tell little lies but would be ashamed to tell big ones …

Something therefore always remains and sticks from the most impudent lies, a fact which all bodies and individuals concerned with the art of lying in this world know only too well, and hence they stop at nothing to achieve this end.

In the U.S. during the 1950s, Senator Joseph R. McCarthy's critics accused him of using "the big lie technique" to intimidate his opponents in and out of the Senate. An example is this editorial in the *St. Louis Post-Dispatch* of 1951: "Gloomy Washington prophets are forecasting a period of 'the big lie,' of the furtive informer, of the character assassin, of inquisition, eavesdropping, smear and distrust. They lump the whole under the term MCCARTHYISM."

A Senate committee headed by Millard Tydings of Maryland, following a four-month investigation of McCarthy's charges that there were 81 card-carrying Communists in the State Department, castigated him in terms rarely used about a Senate member: "We are constrained to call the charges, and the methods used to give them ostensible validity, what they truly are: a fraud and a hoax...the totalitarian technique of the 'big lie' on a sustained basis." McCarthy's efforts helped defeat Senator Tydings in the next election.

Some experts in the mass communications field believe that the size of a requested opinion or behavior change is important in the degree of change effected. Herbert Adelson, of Opinion Research Corporation, observed: "The more extreme the opinion change that the communicator asks for, the more actual change he is likely to get...communications that advocate a greater amount of change from an audience's view in fact produce a greater amount of change than communications that advocate a position that is not much different from the position that the audience already holds."

bigot See REDNECK; REVERSE BIGOTRY.

big stick See DETERRENT.

big tent The theory that a political party is a spacious home for debate, and not a cozy bungalow that permits only a narrow political ideology. A TRUE BELIEVER holds that a political party must "stand for principle" and not muddy up its philosophy with ME TOO ideas held by the opposition.

On the contrary, say the advocates of the *big tent*: there is plenty of room for divergence of opinion within any party, which should be a device for getting into power. They point to Jefferson's statement "Not every difference of opinion is a difference of principle."

After his 1976 defeat, Gerald Ford called a meeting of Republican leaders John Connally, Ronald Reagan, and Nelson Rockefeller and said pointedly: "The Republican tent is big enough to encompass the four individuals who were here today."

In the late 1980s, Lee Atwater, the Republican National Chairman known for his slashing style in the 1988 Bush campaign, mellowed and advocated "a big-tent approach" to overcome the split in the Party caused by the abortion issue.

In 1993, the metaphor was extended by Massachusetts State Senator William R. Keating. At a groundbreaking ceremony for a new mosque, the guests included ministers, priests, rabbis, and local officials, all of whom huddled under a white tent when it started to rain; said Keating, "In this world we are all under one tent."

Senator John McCain, beginning a run for president in 2007, put it plainly in appealing to both wings of the Republican party: "I think we have to be a big-tent party."

The phrase is derived from the circus; the big tent has several arenas which can put on separate shows. The current synonym is *the politics of inclusion*.

big wet kiss An ostentatious, figurative sloppy osculation; not always a bracing embrace to the recipient.

Senator Byron Dorgan, Democrat of North Dakota, dismissed President George W. Bush's plan to establish personal investment accounts within Social Security as "a big wet kiss to Wall Street" in March of 2005. Months later, the Democratic minority leader in the Senate, Harry Reid, characterized a proposal by Republican majority leader Bill Frist for limiting filibusters as "a big wet kiss to the far right."

The derisive *big wet kiss* was employed in other arenas before politicians were attracted to it: actor-comedian Eddie Murphy in May of 1985 apologized, left-handedly, for making fun of homosexuals by saying that "anyone who's offended by the kind of thing I've done.... Sorry. A big wet kiss."

A variant appeared in 2007, though moistness remained the central derisive element of the phrase. Kimberly Strassel of *The Wall*

Street Journal reported that the Association of Trial Lawyers—"a billionaire industry that these days would lose a popularity contest with the Mob"—had recently "changed its name to the bland American Association for Justice." The columnist charged that Rep. Barney Frank, Massachusetts Democrat and newly appointed chairman of the House Financial Services Committee, was "bestowing a *big, wet smooch* on the trial bar."

bigwig Party leader; humorous or sardonic reference to the higher-ups.

The derivation is from the British law courts, where persons of importance (judges, barristers) wear large white wigs. Charles Dickens referred to them, defending a man "spoken of by the bigwigs with extreme condescension."

In current political use, the term is most often included in a phrase like "all the party bigwigs were there"; it is used often by reporters but rarely by politicians. In the mid-'70s the word achieved vogue as "biggies," and was extended to "ad biggies" and "media biggies." It is a favorite of the press in India.

See MUCKEY-MUCKS.

bipartisan *Bipartisan* means interparty cooperation on a matter that is essentially political; NONPARTISAN means interparty cooperation on matters nonpolitical.

In bipartisanship, politicians set aside differences to work together on political matters; in nonpartisanship, politicians work together as individuals, as in philanthropic, patriotic, or civil causes.

Bipartisanship in foreign affairs is most closely associated with Senator Arthur Vandenberg, Michigan Republican, an outspoken isolationist of the '30s. A month after the German invasion of Poland, he was saying: "This so-called war is nothing but about 25 people and propaganda." World War II and a trip to blitzed London changed his thinking, and the ranking Republican in the Senate Foreign Relations Committee made a dramatic speech in 1945 that laid the groundwork for foreign-affairs bipartisanship: "I do not believe that any nation hereafter can immunize itself by its

own exclusive action.... I want maximum American cooperation.... I want a new dignity and a new authority for international law. I think American self-interest requires it."

The Vandenberg switch shattered nascent postwar isolationism and the United Nations Charter was approved with only two senatorial votes against it, a far cry from the furor over the League of Nations after World War I. Vandenberg (who preferred the word *unpartisan*) was hailed by most of the U.S. press for his new stand. At the birth of the Truman Doctrine, which aided the Greeks and Turks in combating internal Communism, "Vandenberg," wrote Truman later, "championed this program in a truly bipartisan manner." But the senator was nagged by his own worry about bipartisanship being carried dangerously far. "To me," he wrote a constituent in 1950, "'bipartisan foreign policy' means a mutual effort under our indispensable two-party system to unite our official voice at the water's edge so that America speaks with maximum authority.... It does not involve the remotest surrender of free debate in determining our position. On the contrary, frank cooperation and free debate are indispensable to ultimate unity."

Within a few months, Vandenberg was asking if "bipartisanship meant more Chinas and more Hisses and more messes with Russian bombs hanging over us," a position not all that far from Robert Taft's blast at "the wreckage that is our Far Eastern policy." Thomas E. Dewey, whose own internationalist position ensured bipartisanship in foreign affairs in the 1944 wartime campaign, reasserted the need for such a united front in war but qualified his position with "I am not prepared to assert that, in a normal, peaceful world, foreign policy should always be bipartisan."

The tension underlying any bipartisanship in foreign policy can never really be relieved: on one hand is the need for a single American voice to the world, on the other hand a need for self-examination and criticism that is the obligation of LOYAL OPPOSITION. In fact, what goes under the heading of bipartisanship is usually a coalition of like-minded legislators in both parties.

Though the word has a halo spinning above it, a dose of skepticism occasionally accompanies its use. When President Bush in 2007 announced he would meet with the entire House Democratic delegation at a retreat in Williamsburg, Va., Gerald Seib wrote in *The Wall Street Journal*: "It will be a real 'Kumbaya' moment for the nation's leaders, a sign of a new spirit of bipartisanship in Washington. Well, maybe. To some extent. While it lasts."

And the *bi* prefix has some independents feeling left out. "At the risk of being condemned as unpatriotic and un-American," wrote Earl Gates, a reader of the *Appleton* (Wisc.) *Post-Crescent*, "I suggest that bipartisan anything is potentially undemocratic. The term implies that there are only two meaningful views of the country... in this case, the currently predominant political parties. That's hogwash, and members of the Green and Libertarian parties and voters registered as independents, know it."

Post-partisan was coined in 1976. The *Washington Post* headlined in 2008 "GOP Doubts, Fears 'Post-Partisan' Obama" and later noted that California Governor Arnold Schwarzenegger "preaches a similar postpartisan approach."

See PARTISAN; NONPARTISAN; WATER'S EDGE.

bipolar See POLARIZE.

Bircher A member or supporter of the John Birch Society, which in the 1960s was the best known of the ultraconservative, militantly anticommunist splinter groups.

Secrecy was a Birch tenet and the society did little to publicize itself as an organization. After its founding in 1958, it was discovered gradually by journalists, particularly after the writings of retired candy manufacturer Robert Welch, Jr., founder of the society, became known. Among other things, Welch called Dwight Eisenhower "a willing tool" of the Communist conspiracy.

On the derivation of the title, there is no argument. Captain John Birch was an otherwise obscure USAF officer killed by Chinese Communists in 1945, and is sometimes referred to as "the first casualty of the Cold War." His murder, according to the Society, was hushed up by Communist agents in the U.S.

Arthur M. Schlesinger, Jr., described the Birch Society's mood as "one of longing for a dream world of no communism, no overseas entanglements, no United Nations, no federal government, no Negroes or foreigners—a world in which Chief Justice Warren would be impeached, Cuba invaded, the graduated income tax repealed, fluoridation of drinking water stopped and the import of Polish hams forbidden."

A question often asked of Republican candidates in the '60s was "Do you accept or reject support of the Birchers?" In the 1962 California gubernatorial primary, Richard Nixon specifically rejected them; he won the nomination and lost the election. In 1966, Ronald Reagan refused to take this position, holding that people who supported him bought his views, not he theirs. Reagan—who carefully applied State Chairman Gaylord Parkinson's ELEVENTH COMMANDMENT, which states, "Thou shalt not speak ill of fellow Republicans"—won by close to a million votes.

bird dog ... kennel dog Canine political metaphor contrasting one who works to earn his keep (*bird dog*), rather than one who depends on others (*kennel dog*).

In 1954, pockets of serious unemployment were distressing the Eisenhower Administration; in Flint, Michigan, 22 percent of the labor force was idle. When Secretary of Defense Charles E. Wilson held a press conference in nearby Detroit, he was asked why his department did not allocate more defense contracts to depressed areas. Wilson suggested that unemployed workers would do better to move to those areas where labor shortages existed, and in reaching for a figure of speech came up with a gaffe: "I've always liked bird dogs rather than kennel dogs myself. You know, one who will get out and hunt for food rather than sit on his fanny and yell."

The remark was seized upon as an example of a heartless Administration run by unfeeling businessmen. Union leaders said that workers "wear no leash and will not be muzzled." Wilson promptly apologized: "I admit that I made a mistake... by bringing up those bird dogs at the same time I was talking about people." See FOOT-IN-MOUTH DISEASE.

Wilson's bird-dog remark recalls other canine teeth in political terminology. A "still hunt"—a method of hunting stealthily, with the dogs muted—was adopted by Tilden supporters in 1876, who boasted that their man conducted a secret "still hunt" of Boss Tweed. And the frontiersman-congressman Davy Crockett said: "Are the people like my hounds, that bark when I tell them, and leave off when I stamp my foot at them?" The idea of a dog trailing at his master's heels was probably the derivation of WARD HEELER; the dialect humorist Petroleum V. Nasby used that derogatory simile in 1866: "The bold shivelrous Southner ... and the Dimokrat uv the North foller'n, like a puppy dog, at his heels, takin sich fat things ez he cood snap up."

In British politics, Prime Minister Harold Wilson received a bad press in 1966 when he mocked Conservative leader Edward Heath's Common Market efforts as "rolling on his back like a spaniel at any kind gesture from the French." To many, the best-known French breed of dog is the poodle; four decades later, a British pollster said of Prime Minister Tony Blair, a stalwart backer of the American-led coalition against Saddam Hussein and later al-Qaida and domestic insurgents in Iraq, that "the perception is that he is George Bush's POODLE, and that's a problem for him."

Though not quite as effective as Franklin Roosevelt's FALA SPEECH, a telling use of a dog in oratory was by Winston Churchill, after being invited by the Chamberlain cabinet to meet German Ambassador Joachim von Ribbentrop: "I suppose they asked me to show him that, if they couldn't bark themselves, they kept a dog who could bark and might bite."

Bird-dog, used as a verb, has an entirely different political meaning from the noun: to ferret out facts, or to follow through on a project until it is successfully completed. Usage: "I don't want this bogged down in red tape; bird-dog it and tell me when it's done." *Newsday* reported in July 1992 that "CBS News President Richard Salant said he was 'embarrassed' by Dan Rather's live convention floor bird-dogging of a G.O.P. official."

See HONCHO. For Chinese Communist use of *running dogs*, see FELLOW TRAVELER. For other snarling similes, see ATTACK DOG; POLITICAL ANIMAL.

bird metaphors See FLOO-FLOO BIRD; PECKING ORDER; WAR HAWKS.

bite the bullet Commit to a difficult course of action; make a tough decision.

President Lyndon Johnson popularized—and simultaneously stigmatized—the phrase by using it in connection with the hard decisions of the Vietnam war. Criticizing Congress for inaction on a bill to raise taxes, President Johnson said on May 3, 1968: "But I think the time has come for all the members of Congress to be responsible and, even in an election year, to bite the bullet and stand up and do what ought to be done for their country."

In 1975 President Ford said: "Some have said that instead of asking Congress and the nation to bite the bullet, I have offered only a marshmallow," adding that the Congress "wouldn't even chew that marshmallow." Mr. Ford's metaphoric extension caused columnist David Braaten of *The Washington Star* to analyze "that recent favorite of literary gourmets, the bite-size bullet" in these terms: "Originally, one bit a bullet to distract oneself from the pain of drastic surgery when no anesthetic was available. It supposedly kept the patient from biting his tongue, or screaming so loud the surgeon was unsettled. From that simple beginning, bullet-biting has come to be used in the quite opposite sense of taking one's medicine. It has replaced the bitter pill as something to be swallowed ..."

The author queried *American Heritage* on the etymology; Oliver Jensen (perhaps influenced by Rudyard Kipling's "The Soldiers and Sailors Too") gave this first impression: "I think I have always misunderstood the phrase, thinking it had something to do with an old style of bullet that had to have something bitten off it to free the powder for the spark—indicating, so to speak, that you were making the crucial decision to be ready to shoot. But I begin to lose faith in that theory now." Jensen wrote to Civil War historian Bruce Catton, who sent him this reply:

I can't give you a definite quotation, but it most certainly comes from before the Civil War; I believe it originated with the British army as early as the 18th Century. Here is how it came into being:

It dated from pre-anesthetic days, when a wounded soldier in a field hospital had to have a painful operation, usually the amputation of a limb. (What with the saw and everything, having that done without chloroform, ether or morphine would obviously be pretty agonizing). When they were ready to go, the afflicted soldier (who was either strapped down or held firmly in place by two or three husky comrades) would be given a round, softlead bullet and told to bite on it. This would help him to get through the ordeal without screaming; the fact that the bullet was of soft lead would make it possible for him to clamp down hard without breaking his teeth. So—to "bite the bullet" meant to endure something extremely bad with suitable stoicism and without making unmanly outcries.

This could not be Civil War in origin. First place, in most cases they had anesthetics in that war. They did have to bite the *cartridge*—not the bullet—when loading those muzzle-loading rifles. The bullet was a cylindro-conoidal bit of lead with a tube of paper attached to the base; paper was full of powder, with the lower end crimped. To load his rifle, the soldier bit off the crimped paper, poured the powder down the barrel, rammed the bullet down after it, and was all ready to operate.

The ammunition-munching metaphor, after a flurry of use in the late '60s, settled into a political language that needs alternatives to "make difficult decisions." An unnamed member of President Carter's Cabinet was quoted in 1978 as observing of Mr. Carter: "He's still not ready to admit that some of these things—like 4 percent unemployment and 4 percent inflation and a balanced budget—are irreconcilable. It's terribly painful for him…There's a reluctance on his part to bite the bullet and make the hard choices."

black, political use of Advocates of the civil rights movement reintroduced the term *black* in the '60s. A century before,

BLACK REPUBLICAN had been used to describe the party of abolition and reconstruction, but in the twentieth century the word was used in its racial sense to describe African natives and as a racial slur to imply that American negroes were close to their ancestors in "black Africa."

To avoid giving offense, white writers and politicians had referred to blacks as *Negroes, colored people, nonwhites* (a statistician's word including Hispanics, Chinese, American Indians, etc.), and the euphemism *minority group.*

As black racial pride increased, black civil rights leaders frequently compared "white men and black men" and looked on marketers of skin-whitening and hair-straightening products with disdain. Martin Luther King, Jr., launched a poster campaign around the slogan "Black is beautiful" in 1967. White usage of *black* lagged until the emergence of "black power" as a slogan in 1966.

In 1970, semanticist (later California Senator) S. I. Hayakawa quoted a letter written in 1928 by W. E. B. DuBois to a young man who wanted to stop the use of the word *Negro*:

Historically, of course, your dislike of the word Negro is easily explained: "Negroes" among your grandfathers meant black folk; "colored" people were mulattoes. The mulattoes hated and despised the blacks and were insulted if called "Negroes." But we are not insulted—not you and I. We are quite as proud of our black ancestors as our white. And perhaps a little prouder.

In a 1974 *Psychology Today* article about bigotry in language, Paul Chance listed a few phrases in which *black* is used positively: *Black Beauty, black belt* (karate), *black gold* (oil), *black tie, black soil, black pearls. White*, which is usually used metaphorically for "good," has some reverse connotations: *white trash, whitewash, white flag, white feather, white slave, white elephant.*

Cartoonist Jules Feiffer, alert to language changes (see DISADVANTAGED), pictured a bearded black intellectual in 1967 describing the ring-around-the-rosy of the political use of the word: "As a matter of racial pride we want to be called 'blacks.' Which has replaced the term 'Afro-American'— Which replaced 'Negroes'—Which replaced 'colored people'—Which replaced 'darkies'—Which replaced 'blacks.'"

By the 1990s, the preferred term had become *African-American.*

black advance See ADVANCE.

black capitalism A 1968 campaign phrase pledging government encouragement to African-Americans starting their own businesses.

In the middle of his 1968 primary campaign, Richard Nixon felt the need to address at some length—and in a positive tone—the problem of racial division in America. In two radio addresses, the first on April 25 entitled "Bridges to Human Dignity," he outlined his desire to go beyond programs "that feed the stomach and starve the soul."

In the first six drafts of the April 25 speech, one of the ideas he put forward was "black entrepreneurship." Speechwriter Ray Price felt this phrase was awkward and sought an alternative. In the radio studio where the speech was to be recorded, the author recalled the New York Stock Exchange's recapture of the word *capitalism* from Communist terminology in their "people's capitalism" advertising campaign. Three alternatives—*black entrepreneurship, black enterprise,* and *black capitalism*—were suggested to the candidate, who chose the last.

"A third bridge," he said, "is the development of black capitalism. By providing technical assistance and loan guarantees, by opening new capital sources, we can help Negroes to start new businesses in the ghetto and to expand existing ones."

The phrase and the idea received some attention, which posed a problem for Democratic candidate Hubert Humphrey when he later advocated a similar program. After the campaign, one of the Humphrey writers told this writer "we couldn't use Nixon's phrase, 'black capitalism,' so we had to go with 'black entrepreneurship,' which is a mouthful, and is hell to fit into a headline."

black hats Villains; "heavies."

The extension of the Western-movie metaphor to politics is most pronounced

when a simplistic "us-against-them" mood dominates the political scene. The users of the phrase are conscious of the satire implicit in its usage: in the shades-of-gray real world of political compromise, few hats are all-black, and all-white hats soon become scuff-marked.

A related phrase is *good guys,* easy to spot in a six-gun epic, which writer Jimmy Breslin appropriated for a book title about the Watergate affair: *How the Good Guys Finally Won.*

Elliot Richardson, who as Nixon Attorney General was regarded by many liberals as a white hat in a black-hatted White House, used the phrase in a talk to business leaders in 1977: "Isolated in the corporate fortress, too many businessmen have cast their argument in terms of the traditional interests—profit and capital for investment. But these are the terms of the black hats. They translate, of course, into jobs, prices, consumer satisfaction—even, given responsible political decision-making, into satisfaction of collective wants and ultimately the improved 'quality of life.' But these are all terms which have been expropriated by those now confidently postured in white hats."

See WHITE HATS.

blacklist See GUILT BY ASSOCIATION.

black power A deliberately ambiguous slogan, meaning antiwhite rebellion to some, the use of political and economic "muscle" to others.

The phrase was made famous by Stokely Carmichael, then head of the Student Nonviolent Coordinating Committee (SNCC), on the occasion of a SNCC-organized march through Mississippi. It appeared in *The New York Times* on June 18, 1966, in a report that Carmichael was teaching marchers the use of the slogan. Two weeks before, on May 30, Harlem Congressman Adam Clayton Powell had used the phrase in a speech to students at Howard University: "To demand these God-given rights is to seek black power …"

Dr. Nathan Hare, Carmichael's sociology professor at Howard University, called the slogan not anti-white, but "anti-antiblack." See ANTI-ANTI. He added: " 'Power' is the ability to influence another person—even against his will, if necessary... 'black power' means the exercise by black people of influence on the forces which oppress us.... Assimilation has not worked.... As Malcolm X [the late Black Muslim leader] said, 'we've been praying when we should have been preying, or playing when we should be flaying—you know, skinning alive.' "

Floyd McKissick, head of the Congress of Racial Equality (CORE), told Senator Robert Kennedy in 1967: "I believe that black power will be accepted just like Irish power has been accepted." This was using the phrase in its nonviolent, political-power sense, and liberal columnist Max Lerner argued its fallacy: " ... while the Irish and the Jews... acted as political appeal groups, they never raised the slogans of 'Irish Power' or 'Jewish power,' nor implied hatred for the majority groups. Nor did they ever scorn to share power with non-Irish or non-Jews, even in the big cities where they were heavily represented."

James Farmer, former head of CORE, tried to moderate the expression: "Black power, whatever the coiners of this slogan mean, to me means shared power—otherwise it leads to an illusion." To the Black Muslims, Black Panthers, and other extremist groups, however, the phrase was a rallying cry for guerrilla warfare. When riots erupted in several cities in the summer of 1967, the phrase's more ominous side became apparent.

The slogan was important enough to be quoted in a Supreme Court decision a year after its coinage. The Court upheld (5 to 4) the contempt conviction of Dr. Martin Luther King, Jr., for defying a court injunction against a march he led in Alabama. The dissent was written by Justice William Brennan: "We cannot permit fears of 'riots' and 'civil disobedience' generated by slogans like 'Black Power' to divert our attention from what is here at stake... arming the state courts with the power to punish as a 'contempt' what they otherwise could not punish at all."

Along with ESCALATION, *black power* became one of the major coinages of the '60s. A rhyming variation was *flower power*, a slogan of the hippies who used flowers as a symbol of love. *Power* was used as the phrase-making device for a variety of groups, including *teacher power* or *blackboard power* for militant educators.

black Republican Used as a political imprecation by Southerners and some northern Democrats before and during the Civil War in an attempt to label the new Republican party as fanatically pro-Negro.

Stephen Douglas, who was to be Lincoln's chief antagonist six years later, began denouncing "black Republicans" as early as 1854, when what was to become the Grand Old Party had barely hatched. Other orators used it as well. By 1855–56, when the Republicans and abolitionists generally took BLEEDING KANSAS as a war chant, Democrats and pro-slavery interests answered with "black Republicans."

By 1860 it was so common an angry derogation that candidate Abraham Lincoln devoted part of his address at Cooper Union in New York City to rebuttal. He repeated his party's opposition to slavery but argued that illiterate slaves were largely unaware of the party's stance. Thus, the party could not be responsible for unrest and violence among Negroes. Lincoln said that to dramatize their case, enemies of the new party defined black Republicanism as "insurrection, blood and thunder among the slaves."

Lincoln's defense did no good. He was nominated for the presidency three months after the Cooper Union speech, and in the acrimonious campaign that followed, Lincoln heard himself often attacked as a black Republican. Jefferson Davis used the term in private correspondence.

The phrase might have been adapted from one used in Europe earlier—*red republicans*—to describe radicals in the revolutionary movements of the 1840s. In this country, many then considered the overthrow of slavery just as radical as many Europeans viewed the death of monarchy.

White officer John Pershing led the 10th Negro Cavalry during the Spanish-American

War. Because of his service with Negro troops, he acquired the nickname "Black Jack." Although no longer used seriously in modern American politics—indeed, a major Republican problem has been to retrieve African-American support—*black Republicanism* is still employed occasionally in a bantering way. Joe Martin, the former House Republican leader, recalled requesting of Franklin Roosevelt a new federal road for Massachusetts. Roosevelt promptly instructed an aide to call the appropriate official "and tell him I am sending down a black Republican and I want…to give him a road."

blame America first Attack phrase on a liberal activist who engages in national self-finger-pointing; an interventionist's idea of the ultimate defeatist.

Jeane Kirkpatrick, the columnist and former United Nations Ambassador, introduced this term in 1984. As the Republican National Convention keynote speaker in Dallas, she emphasized the attack tactics of the Democrats at their earlier convention in San Francisco: "When the Soviet Union walked out of arms control negotiations…the San Francisco Democrats did not blame Soviet intransigence. They blamed the United States. But then, they always blame America first."

The attack phrase—later stingingly expressed as "blame-America-first Democrats"—paints those activists as weak or "squishy" liberal doves; those so targeted claim it impugns their patriotism. Although the imperative "blame America first" paralleled the tourism slogan "see America first," it is bottomed on the America-firsters of the late 1930s who failed to see the threat posed by Hitler and espoused isolationism.

Secretary of Defense Donald Rumsfeld, under sustained fire in 2006 from many Democratic candidates and some Republicans for the long and costly delay in pacifying Iraq, fired back with "the struggle is too important to have the luxury of returning to the old mentality of 'blame America first.'"

Michael Gerson, the chief Bush speechwriter who left the Administration in 2006, noted in a *Washington Post* column a year

later that political fundamentalism had gripped both parties. "Talk-radio conservatism assaults a role for government in compassion and a welcoming attitude toward immigrants…Authenticity on the bitter blogs of the left means a revolt against the centrist, Democratic establishment—a ritual patricide…On foreign policy, 'blame America first' has become 'blame America exclusively.'"

When Nancy Pelosi, a Democrat representing the San Francisco area in California, was elected Speaker of the House in 2007, it took much of the pejorative sting out of Kirkpatrick's "San Francisco Democrat." See LEFT FIELD, LEFT COAST.

blame game A method of avoiding responsibility by pointing one's accusing finger at someone else.

Those most adept at the blame game know that it can be won by announcing that one will not stoop to playing it, thereby diffusing responsibility while seizing the high ground of reasonableness and nonpartisanship.

"It's Not a Blame Game," was the headline of a *New York Times* editorial on Sept. 7, 2005, calling for an independent investigation of the government's lack of preparation for a Katrina-size hurricane along the Gulf Coast and its chaotic response when this storm struck New Orleans. The headline was inspired by President George W. Bush's remark the previous day, "One of the things that people want us to do here is to play the blame game." The president stated that he, personally, intended to "find out what went right and what went wrong," but the *Times* doubted that any administration could make a credible investigation of such a large failure on its own watch; hence, the customary call for an independent panel.

Similarly, news stories in 2002 revealing that both the Clinton and Bush administrations had received warnings of possible terrorist attacks prior to 9/11 inspired the *Newsweek* headline "Playing the Blame Game." Simultaneously, *Time* headed a piece by an anonymous F.B.I. man, "An Agent Speaks Out Against the Blame

Game." But some declined to play, reinforcing the belief that blame-gaming is considered to be negative, while working together can be seen as positive. Thus, Senator Dianne Feinstein, Democrat of California, concluded an exchange with White House press secretary Ari Fleischer by saying, "It is my hope that the administration and Congress can work together to solve the critical security problems of our nation, rather than playing the blame game."

Blame game dates in the purely personal, or interpersonal, sense to the '50s, with the earliest example in the *OED* coming from a 1958 review by drama critic Kenneth Tynan: "The family goes round and round in that worst of domestic rituals, the Blame Game. I blame my agony on you; you blame yours on her; she blames hers on me."

The rhyming phrase, an update of *finger-pointing*, was popularized in the political arena by President Ronald Reagan. Fending off accusations that he had not done enough to halt rising unemployment, he said in a televised address on Oct. 14, 1982: "The pounding economic hangover that America is suffering from didn't come about overnight, and there's no single instant cure. In recent weeks, a lot of people have been playing what I call 'the blame game.'" Mr. Reagan also understood that the best way to win the game was to say that he would not play it, adding "The accusing finger has been pointed in every direction of the compass, and a lot of time and hot air have been spent looking for scapegoats."

Parsing this speech in a column entitled "The Blame Game" just three days later, James Reston, of *The New York Times*, laid out the rules of the game: "The President's speech was a clever and brilliant example of 'The Blame Game' he deplored. It was not supposed to be 'political,' but the whole thrust of it was to avoid responsibility for the economic recession and the unemployment, and to blame the Democrats in particular and the tragedy of history in general for the worst unemployment and bankruptcy record since the Depression of the 1930s."

blanket ballot See BEDSHEET BALLOT.

to describe a minor conflict that presages a much larger one involving roughly the same issues. Historian Samuel Eliot Morison juxtaposes bleeding Kansas and the subsequent Civil War with the Spanish Civil War and the subsequent World War II.

Reporter John Gunther wrote in his 1947 *Inside U.S.A.*: "Does 'Bleeding Kansas' still bleed? Will it still rise to fight injustice? I asked this question generally, and one answer I got was, 'Oh, we still have a hemorrhage once in a while.'"

blitz See DEWEY BLITZ.

bloc A group of citizens or organizations gathered to promote some special interest, as in "the farm bloc."

The French popularized the term, applying it to those temporary and shifting combinations of parties in the Chamber of Deputies during the Third Republic. Clemenceau's *Bloc des Gauches*, formed after the Dreyfus Affair, was an example.

In the U.S., the term has been used to convey the idea of selfish interests as well as special ones. Conferring with his advisers soon after his election to the presidency in 1920, Warren G. Harding asked the question that every one of his successors has had to confront since then: "What shall we do about the farm bloc?"

Adlai Stevenson, during his 1952 presidential campaign, deplored another kind of *bloc*: "... the myth of monolithic voting—the idea that all the votes in a bloc go one way or the other in response to the candidate's willingness to go along with the official positions of the bloc." In a similar vein, John F. Kennedy said during his dramatic confrontation with the Greater Houston Ministerial Association in 1960 that he believed in an America "where there is no Catholic vote, no anti-Catholic vote, no bloc voting of any kind." See BAILEY MEMORANDUM. As the Vietnam war grew, its opponents coalesced into what was called the "Peace Bloc."

For Americans, the word long had another association—in the phrase *Sino-Soviet bloc*, similar to an earlier use of *Rome-Berlin* AXIS. With the growing split between Moscow and Beijing in the 1960s,

however, many experts urged abandonment of the phrase as an inaccurate oversimplification. Historian Arthur Schlesinger, Jr., wrote in a memo to the State Department in 1963, when he was serving as a White House aide: "In view of what is going on currently in Moscow, could not the Department bring itself to abolish the usage, 'Sino-Soviet bloc'? The relationship of that phrase to reality grows more tenuous all the time."

blockade See QUARANTINE.

blocks of five See SWING VOTER.

bloody shirt Waved or shaken rhetorically for nearly three decades after the Civil War; an appeal to old wartime emotions to equate Democrats with the Confederacy, and the South with warmongering.

Even before the war, the political antecedents of radical Republicans used the bloody shirt, both literally and in oratory, as a call for retribution. Abolitionist James Baird Weaver recounted how in the 1850s he acquired the stained and shredded linen of a preacher who had been flogged for inflaming slaves. "I waved it before the crowds," said Weaver, "and bellowed: 'under this bloody shirt we propose to march to victory.'"

The term came into wide use in the 1860s and '70s. Both Democrats and moderate Republicans who sought a conciliatory policy used it when attempting to debunk wilder statements of the hard-peace Republicans. Horace Greeley had been a Union man and an abolitionist, but in 1872, when he broke with the Republicans to run for president as an independent, he denounced his former friends for "waving the bloody shirt." Four years later Republican Senator John Logan of Illinois said in a typical speech: "It has come to be a saying... that we are shaking the bloody shirt if we call attention to brutal wholesale murder of colored Republicans. ... When Democrats will stop staining the shirt with blood, we will quit shaking it."

The visible reminder of a need for vengeance and a debt of blood is ancient. In Shakespeare's *Julius Caesar*, Marc Antony whipped up the fury of his fellow Romans by waving his murdered leader's toga. Gibbon mentions that when the Caliph Othman of Damascus was murdered in A.D. 656, his stained clothes were displayed. It appears in literature and in history—in Scotland (a 1603 massacre by the Clan MacGregor), Corsica, France, and eighteenth-century America, where Patrick Henry displayed a victim's clothing in a court case. Abraham Lincoln was said to have employed a similar trick in an Illinois murder trial where he was assisting the district attorney, saying, "… it is better to wave the bloody shirt than to waive justice."

Commenting on American politics in 1880, Britain's *Punch* magazine wrote of candidate James G. Blaine:

> *There was an old stalwart named Blaine,*
> *Who hailed from the region of Maine.*
> *When he felt badly hurt*
> *He would cry "Bloody Shirt"—*
> *And slay over the already slain.*

In 1942, writer Carey McWilliams characterized anti-Orientalism on the West Coast—resulting in the imprisonment of American citizens of Japanese descent during World War II—as "California's Bloody Shirt."

The charge of using the "ensanguined garment" is current. Senator Robert Byrd (D-W.Va.) in 2007 accused the Bush administration of using the technique: "This White House constantly waves the bloody shirt of 9/11, using the shadow of that terrible day to scare the American people into quiet submission."

blooper An exploitable spoken mistake; a slip of the tongue, or unthinking comment, that can be seized upon by the opposition.

In the synonymy of slips, a *blooper* is more exploitable than a *goof*, not as damaging as a *boo-boo*, *flub*, or *slip of the tongue*, the last explained away with the locution "the president *misspoke*."

Nelson Rockefeller was asked, as he campaigned for reelection as New York governor in 1966, about his campaign promise of 1962 not to raise taxes—which he had broken. Campaign strategists worried about how to meet this most serious opposition charge; their decision was to admit the tax increases had been a mistake, but present the response in a colorfully frank manner. Said Rockefeller of his tax reversal: "That was the biggest blooper I ever made."

A retrospective blooper was George H.W. Bush's promise to the 1988 Republican convention, "Read my lips—no new taxes"; it was a powerful applause-getter at the time, written by Peggy Noonan, but Bush went on to raise taxes as president, and his old crowd-pleaser haunted him in the campaign of 1992 against Bill Clinton.

Blooper is adapted from early radio announcers' slang for a spoonerism or slip of the tongue, derived from *bloop*, a high-pitched howling sound caused by sudden radio interference. ("Ladies and gentlemen," said NBC's Harry von Zell, "the President of the United States, Hoobert Heever.") But the act of blooping has been in politics since the game, science, business, or art began. "Hancock the Superb"—General Winfield Scott Hancock—had a good chance to beat James Garfield in 1880. When asked about tariffs, the most spirited international controversy of the day, he replied, "The tariff is a local issue," and was pleased that he did not get embroiled. "The Republicans, however," wrote editor Henry Stoddard, "made much ado about a soldier's ignorance of economics. Hancock's long dream of the Presidency dissolved in these five inopportune but truthful words." Stoddard suggested that it was only a *blooper*.

Winners' bloopers are seldom remembered; losers' bloopers gain in importance with the years. In the Truman-Dewey campaign of 1948, Truman's whistlestop appearances were seldom on time and Democratic scheduling was less than airtight. See WHISTLESTOPPING. But the Dewey "Victory Special" campaign train rolled on with awesome efficiency, schedules met, speech texts promptly available. At one of the local stops, the Dewey train suddenly jerked away from the station, such a change from the usual smooth start that the candidate exclaimed: "What's the matter with that idiot engineer?" Cabell Phillips of *The New York Times* wrote, "This turned out to be a magnificent blooper. In the skilled hands of the Democratic propagandists, it became overnight a jeering anti-Dewey slogan in railroad roundhouses and Union halls all across the country."

A British example: in the general election of 1964, Conservative Prime Minister Sir Alec Douglas-Home faced a tough interrogation on BBC television. In answering a question about a proposed supplement for older pensioners, Sir Alec used the word *donation*. Labor supporters of Harold Wilson seized the usage, cartoonists illustrated it, and it was used throughout the campaign to exploit the apparently patrician attitude of the Conservatives.

American examples: In the summer of 1971 Senator Ed Muskie told a group of black leaders that he did not believe the American electorate was ready yet for a black on the national ticket. Milton Viorst, a liberal columnist, observed: "Judged by the conventional political code of conduct, Muskie committed a blooper, perhaps a serious one." One less serious—a mere slip of the lip—took place in 2004, when Senator John Kerry, campaigning for president, referred to a fundamentalist Islamic sect, the *Wahhabi*, as *wasabi*, a spicy Japanese condiment. This did not cause a furor because it was a "fluff," an understandable mistake for an English-speaker using a word in a foreign language.

George W. Bush's verbal bloopers quickly became known as *Bushisms*, a reprise of a word used by *Slate* magazine editor Jacob Weisberg about the elder Bush's linguistic lapses. In suggesting his critics were mistaken to underestimate him, "Dubya" came up with the non-word *misunderestimate*, at worst a redundancy, at best an accidental coinage that he defiantly repeated in his next sentence. A more evident blooper, also repeated, was "We cannot let terrorists and rogue nations hold this nation hostile or hold our allies hostile." In a 2001 appearance at his alma mater, Yale University, President Bush kidded himself about such malapropisms: "My critics don't realize I don't make verbal gaffes; I'm speaking in the perfect forms and rhythms of ancient haiku."

In 2006, George Allen (R-Va.), favored in polls to win reelection, called an Indian-American videographer on his opponent's staff "macaca." This is a variant spelling of the rhesus *macaque* (*Macaca mulata*), a monkey widely used in medical research because of its physiological similarity to humans. The word, though unfamiliar to most, is taken to be an anti-Indian slur. It required repeated apologies, terminally weakened his campaign, and with Allen's unexpected defeat cost the GOP its Senate majority, profoundly affecting the balance of power in Washington. See TRACKER.

The campaign for the 2008 Democratic presidential nomination began with Senator Joseph Biden complimenting Senator Barack Obama as being "clean" and "articulate," adjectives intended to be complimentary but that were taken by many blacks to be insufferably patronizing, and widely characterized as a *blooper*.

A *blooper* is equivalent to a *gaffe* (from the Old French, meaning "hook") but far less serious than a *strategic blunder*. A *faux pas*, French for "false step," is a forgivable social *misstep* and a *lapse* connotes momentary forgetfulness, but a *howler* is a ludicrous error that causes much derisive laughter. (Another longtime synonym, *boner*, is avoided because of possible confusion with a modern sexual slang sense of the term.) Repeated commission of any or all of these embarrassments results in the perpetrator being described as having FOOT-IN-MOUTH DISEASE.

Of the above words for inadvertent self-embarrassment, the French *gaffe* is gaining popularity, having crossed from diplomatic to political usage. "A gaffe, it has been said," wrote Michael Kinsley in 2007, quoting himself, "is when a politician tells the truth—or more precisely, when he or she accidentally reveals something truthful about what is going on in his or her head … Journalists enjoy gaffes as a slight taste of human reality at the banquet of artifice where they sup."

On the international scene, diplomatic errors may be serious or amusing, as when U.S. Ambassador to the UN, Warren Austin, hoped during the 1948 war in Palestine that the Jews and the Arabs would settle their differences "like good Christians."

bloviate To speak with unabashed pomposity; to add bombast to oratory and bluster to grandiloquence.

Warren G. Harding gave this word currency; his biographer, Francis Russell, claimed it was an old Ohio term meaning "to loaf," and, as Harding said, "The world has no use for a loafer." Perhaps Harding used *bloviation* in that sense; however, the word soon became applied to his own oratory, and today is best remembered as a description of Harding's forensic fatuousness. (For Harding's awesome abuse of ALLITERATION, see that entry; for his popularization of a useful phrase, see FOUNDING FATHERS.)

The word has had that empty-oratory meaning for more than a century, cited by Albert Barrère and Charles G. Leland in their 1889 *Dictionary of Slang, Jargon and Cant*: "Bloviate (American): a made up or 'factitious' word, which has been used since 1850, and is perhaps older. It is irregularly used to signify verbosity, wandering from the subject, and idle or inflated oratory or blowing, by which word it was probably suggested, being partially influenced by 'deviate.'"

The pioneer slanguists were right: earlier uses have been found. In 1845, the *Huron Reflector* (Norwalk, Ohio) wrote of a lawyer who "will with open throat reiterate the slang of the resolution...and bloviate about the farmers being taxed upon the full value of their farms."

In its October 23, 1909, edition, *Literary Digest* derided a proposal to create a separate state of Southern California by quoting a *Louisville Courier-Journal* suggestion to make Los Angeles a state, an arrangement "which would rid California of a maximum of bluster and bloviation and a minimum of territory."

In current usage, that definition stands. A recent example of *bloviation* appeared in September 1992 in the "Hers" column of *The New York Times Magazine*: "men in Washington talk too much. Everywhere

you look, there are men talking. It's like a giant Bloviation Bee." Another noun form was used by Alexandra Pelosi in *Time* after her mother Nancy's triumph in the 2006 midterm elections, "watching the bloviators pontificate."

blowback See CIA-ESE.

blue book See WHITE PAPER.

Blue Dog Democrats Members of the House of Representatives of moderate to conservative views who see themselves as a coalition of bridge-builders.

The "Blue-Dog Coalition" was formed in 1995, led by Rep. Charles Stenholm of Texas, soon after Republicans became a majority for the first time since 1952, rallied by Rep. Newt Gingrich's CONTRACT WITH AMERICA. "The 'Blue-Dog' moniker was taken," said Rep. Mike Ross of Arizona, the Whip of the Blue Dog Caucus, "because their moderate-to-conservative views had been 'choked blue' by their party in the years leading up to the 1994 election." The "choked blue" statement had been made by former Rep. Pete Geren (D-Tex.), but the maverick group's name was taken in recollection of YELLOW DOG DEMOCRAT, a 1928 assertion by party loyalists of extreme regularity: "I'd vote for a yellow dog if he ran on the Democratic ticket." Rep. Stenholm, formerly self-identified as a BOLL WEEVIL, said that a Blue Dog "has a better sense of smell than a yellow dog, and sometimes will bite you, which a yellow dog won't do."

The political pendulum swung back in 2006. In the election of the 110th Congress, the centrist group increased its original number to 47 members, a majority of whom won their seats from Republican incumbents and made possible the achievement of the blue-state majority. (See RED STATE/BLUE STATE.) It headlined its post-election announcement "Blue Dogs Howl in Victory," and asserted "as moderates and fiscal hawks...the Blue Dog Coalition...appeal to the mainstream values of the American public...promoting positions which bridge the gap between ideological extremes."

Conservative columnist Charles Krauthammer of *The Washington Post* saw them as a silver lining in the dark gray cloud enveloping the GOP after its electoral debacle brought on by lack of progress in the Iraq war and voter disgust at a spate of Republican corruption scandals. "Democratic gains included the addition of many conservative Democrats, brilliantly recruited by Rep. Rahm Emanuel with classic Clinton TRIANGULATION ... The result is that *both* parties have moved to the right. The Republicans have shed the last vestiges of their centrist past, the Rockefeller Republicans. And the Democrats have widened their tent to bring in a new crop of blue-dog conservatives."

The name was derived from the work of a Louisiana artist, George Rodrique, who earned a reputation doing paintings of a blue dog with yellow eyes; a large signboard with one of those dogs advertising his home and studio became familiar to motorists along Interstate 10 near Lafayette. Reached by the lexicographer in 1995, the artist said "The dog I paint was my dog for ten years. He died, and I started to paint him as a ghost dog, on his journey to try and find me. I've been painting him now for seven years. His name was Tiffany."

See BRASS-COLLAR DEMOCRAT.

blue law Legislation considered puritanical, such as the prohibition of the sale of liquor or other business activities on Sunday.

Once common in the United States, particularly in New England, *blue laws* were first reported in 1781 by Rev. Samuel Peters in his *General History of Connecticut:* "Even the religious fanatics of Boston and the mad zealots of Hertford ... christened them the 'Blue Laws.'" Intended to keep people from following their everyday pursuits on the Sabbath, they were reinforced by the Prohibition movement in the nineteenth and early twentieth centuries. Some people objected, of course, as indicated by a report in the *New York Evening Post* in 1904, "Mr. York claimed that conditions were not the same as when the 'blue laws' were passed, and characterized Sunday ball playing as a harmless recreation, encour-

aged in Chicago and Cincinnati with beneficial results."

Today, with local exceptions (particularly where religious fundamentalism is strong), *blue laws* are fading away, either repealed, softened with exceptions, honored in the breach, or obviated by electronic ways of doing business. While regretting the failure of the New York and American stock exchanges to extend their trading hours, a columnist in *The Wall Street Journal* noted the trend in 1999: "Blue laws, which once prohibited or restricted Sunday business in most states, have given way to 24-hour supermarkets, drugstores, theaters, and restaurants. Any time of day, toll-free numbers and Web sites allow consumers to book tickets and buy goods from thousands of merchants at the flick of a finger."

The Supreme Court of the United States has upheld blue laws in principle, however. In *McGowan v. Maryland* (1961), the court ruled that the state had a legitimate interest in promoting public "health, safety, recreation, and general well-being" through a common day of rest. The fact that this day coincided with the Christian Sabbath did not violate the Constitution, in the court's view, since the law did not prevent members of other religions from observing their own holy days.

The original *blue laws* described by Rev. Peters were distributed in 1656 to households in the colony of New Haven (which merged with Connecticut in 1665). They regulated almost all aspects of daily life, forbidding—among many other things— running on the Sabbath day, bringing cards or dice into the colony, and giving food or lodging to Quakers. Mothers were forbidden from kissing their children on the Sabbath or another fasting day. Similar codes were adopted in other places, but Connecticut's primacy was recognized by its onetime nickname, *The Blue Law State.*

blue-ribbon panel A jury or committee chosen on the basis of expertise or reputation for probity to investigate particularly complex or important matters.

The compound adjective denotes exclusivity and comes from the blue ribbons worn by members of the Order of the Garter in Great Britain and the *cordon bleu* of the ancient Order of the Holy Spirit (*l'Ordre du Saint-Esprit*) in France; ribbons of that color are awarded to prizewinners, animal and human alike. Though properly applied to juries, *blue-ribbon panel* has become something of a cliché for any government-appointed committee, from the Hoover Commission that recommended sweeping reforms in the U.S. executive branch after World War II to Lyndon Johnson's commission on the draft and the 1983 Greenspan commission to recommend changes in Social Security—all of which have been described in the press as blue-ribbon panels.

Columnist Art Buchwald spoofed the phrase in 1967: "While Art Buchwald is taking a few days off, a blue ribbon panel has selected some of his articles from the past …"

The term is tiring. In 1992, Hillary Clinton called her panel to come up with health care legislation a "task force," broken down into "work groups." In 2006, a bipartisan panel commissioned by Congress was named the Iraq Study Group.

blue slip An individual senator's approval of a presidential nomination, the lack of which, in some cases, results in withdrawal of a nomination.

The *blue slip* is the currency of SENATORIAL COURTESY. If a senator objects to a nomination the president has made, he can cast a blackball by simply not returning the approval forms sent out by the Majority Leader. If the appointee is from the senator's state, and if the senator and the appointee, or the senator and the president, are in the same party, the likelihood of further Senate consideration is small. The *Los Angeles Times* reported in 1950 that "'Blue slips' are forms supplied by the Judiciary Committee to permit Senators to note their endorsement or objection to nominees."

Here is the text of a blue slip, 1978 vintage, from the Committee on the Judiciary, Senator James Eastland (D-Miss.) chairman: "Dear Senator: Will you kindly give me, for the use of the Committee, your opinion and information concerning the nomination of [blank]. Under a rule of the Committee, unless a reply is received from you within a week from this date, it will be assumed that you have no objection to this nomination. Respectfully …" The second sentence is understood by sender and recipient to be the opposite of the truth. If the blue slip is not returned, a committee secretary calls the senator who has not returned it, to make sure the slip did not get lost in the mail; if the senator's office says, simply, that the senator has not yet acted upon it, the blackball has been cast and the nominee has been "blue-slipped."

In recent decades, both Democratic and Republican chairmen of the Senate Judiciary Committee have eased the *blue-slip policy* or *tradition* when doing so was to their party's advantage. Under the more relaxed rule, a candidate for a federal judgeship might get a hearing if only one senator from his or her home state failed to return the *blue slip*. "I'll give great weight to negative blue slips, but you can't have one senator holding up, for instance, circuit nominees," judiciary chairman Orrin Hatch (R-Utah) told *The Washington Post* in 2003. If both senators *blue-slip* a nomination, though, it is almost certainly dead no matter which party is in the majority.

The term gained a more general use as a device to delay or kill legislation. *The Hill*, a Capitol Hill newspaper, reported in 2007 that "Charles Rangel (D-N.Y.), chairman of the House Ways and Means Committee, has been less sanguine about the tax cuts. He has threatened to file a procedural objection, known as a 'blue slip,' against them, forcing Senate leaders to postpone further action."

By 2007, the technique of blocking nominations had gained several refinements. "Nowhere in the ponderous rules of the United States Senate," wrote Carl Hulse in *The New York Times*, "is there any reference to the Mae West hold, the chokehold or the rotating hold."

The *rotating hold* is used by a group of senators who make themselves hard to identify by switching the objecting among themselves. The *choke hold*, imported from wrestling, is an extreme parliamentary maneuver designed to kill a bill or nomination. And the *Mae West hold*?

Mae West, the buxom siren who satirized sex as an actress and writer ("Is that a gun in your pocket or are you just glad to see me?") was immortalized in survival nomenclature by the "Mae West jacket," an inflatable cushion to be worn around the neck and chest as a lifesaving device to save the wearer from drowning, so called in reference to her physical endowment. "The Mae West version of the Senate hold," defined Hulse, "occurs when the senator behind the objection is open to negotiation, inviting the author to 'come up and see me sometime,'" a version of a famous movie line directed at a youthful Cary Grant by Miss West.

See PATRONAGE; PERSONALLY OBNOXIOUS.

blunder See BLOOPER.

Board of Education A House of Representatives leadership group that gathered on occasion to persuade less senior members of the leadership's wisdom.

In a profile of the new Speaker of the House in 1962, the *New York Times* headline read: "Rayburn's 'Board of Education' Keeps Role Under McCormack." Citing evidence that John McCormack of Massachusetts was a conservative on preserving traditions, the article pointed out: "The latest is his decision to continue the 'Board of Education.' Under Speaker Rayburn, the group—partly social, partly political and entirely private—met about sundown in an out-of-the-way room on the ground floor of the Capitol…Under Speaker McCormack, the same room is used, and the same customs, including the pouring of bourbon and scotch, are maintained." Members included Representative Carl Albert (who succeeded McCormack as Speaker) and Lewis Deschler, parliamentarian of the House. "The only new member…is Rep. Thomas P. O'Neill of Massachusetts. He is a longtime close friend and political associate of Speaker McCormack." "Tip" O'Neill later became Speaker and was associated with, but did not coin, the adage that Social Security was the THIRD RAIL of politics.

See STRIKE A BLOW FOR FREEDOM.

body man See HANDLERS.

body politic Any group governed by any means; a governmental system, with the word *body* used in the unitary sense of "body of laws" or "body of facts."

The metaphor linking the human anatomy to the system of government can be found in Plato's *Republic*. An early use occurred in Thomas Hobbes's *Leviathan*, published in 1651: "Of systems subordinate, some are political and some private. Political (otherwise called *bodies politic* and persons in law) are those which are made by authority from the sovereign power of the Commonwealth."

In Jean-Jacques Rousseau's *Discourse on Political Economy*, the metaphoric use was extended: "The body politic, taken individually, may be considered as an organised, living body, resembling that of a man. The sovereign power represents the head; the laws and customs are the brain…commerce, industry, and agriculture are the mouth and stomach…the public income is the blood…the citizens are the body and the members, which make the machine live, move, and work. …" Rousseau held that "the body politic, therefore, is also a moral being possessed of a will." In *Social Contract* he wondered, "Has the body politic an organ to declare its will?" and warned, "The body politic, like the human body, begins to die from its birth, and bears in itself the causes of its own destruction." (In other translations, the famous phrase reads "seeds of its own destruction.")

The comparison to the human body offered many American politicians an opportunity to be eloquent. James Garfield, a future president speaking just after the Civil War, pressed for the black man's right to vote: "the inequality of rights before the law, which is now a part of our system, is more dangerous to us than to the black man whom it disenfranchises. It is like a foreign substance in the body, a thorn in the flesh; it will wound and disease the body politic."

Dwight Eisenhower helped his audience by defining it in passing: "As we see difficulties and defects in the body politic, in the social order, we must never attempt before our own consciences to dodge our own responsibilities." Columbia University, conferring its Doctorate of Laws on Adlai Stevenson in 1954, took an extreme metaphoric route: "Physician extraordinary to the body politic, skilled in diagnosis, bold in prognosis, forthright in prescription, buoyant of bedside manner ..."

Franklin Roosevelt discarded the phrase but also used an extended version of the metaphor. "A nation, like a person, has a body," he said in his Third Inaugural Address in 1941, which must be fed and housed and clothed in accordance with American standards, and "a nation, like a person, has a mind" which must be kept informed and be understanding. Finally, "a nation, like a person, has something deeper, something more permanent, something larger than the sum of its parts. It is that something that matters most to its future.... It is a thing for which we find it difficult—even impossible—to hit upon a single simple word. And yet, we all understand what it is: the spirit...the faith of America ..." Like Rousseau, FDR found in the body politic "a moral being possessed of a will."

boll weevil A Southern conservative Democrat.

Boll in this noun phrase refers to the seed pod of a plant, such as cotton. *Boll weevil*, first used in 1895, is a small beetle with a prolonged snout; the bug, which can be controlled but not eliminated, infests and destroys cotton plants.

The name of this Southern pest became a self-applied label by conservative Democrats in the 1950s. During Eisenhower's Administration, Rep. Howard Smith of Virginia and, later, Rep. Omar Burleson of Texas advanced the boll weevil as the symbol of their unstoppable group.

In the 1980s, Rep. Charles Stenholm, a Democrat from Texas, reapplied the term, linking himself with other tenacious conservative Democrats: "People have been trying to eradicate boll weevils for a long, long time."

The use of insects for nicknames has also been tried by moderate Northern Republicans, who in the early '80s began to call themselves *Gypsy Moths*. First used during the Reagan Administration by Rep. Lawrence DeNardis of Connecticut, the term contains a promise of change; as Representative DeNardis told columnist David Broder, "The gypsy moth goes through a unique metamorphosis from worm to fly."

For a more recent self-description by conservative Democrats, see BLUE DOG DEMOCRAT.

bolt To desert one's party or faction; as a noun, the act of such desertion.

This is a venerable word in the political lexicon, not surprising because the term goes to the heart of party politics: the never-ending cycle of sundering and solidifying loyalties. In 1884 the *Boston Journal* posed this definition: "a bolter's one...who can't command and won't obey." That spoke for PARTY LOYALTY. Contrariwise, many have upheld the primacy of personal principle. Raymond Moley, who bolted the Democratic party after the 1936 election of Franklin Roosevelt, gave the classic reply: "I was frequently asked why I left the Democratic party. My answer was that the Democratic party had left me."

The equestrian word-picture has kept its original meaning, as well as its currency, perhaps because there is no real difference between its political or figurative sense and its literal or physical meaning ("the horse *bolted* out of control"). Harry Truman, discussing the defection in 1948 of the Progressives on his left and the Dixiecrats on his right, said, "I was confronted not with one major defection in the Democratic party but with two bolts ..."

A synonymous phrase was dropped into the political vocabulary in 1936 by Alfred E. Smith when he publicly broke with Roosevelt, saying he would TAKE A WALK. "Red" Barber, then the broadcaster for the Brooklyn Dodgers, was able to tie baseball, domestic politics, and the Cold War together during the United Nations' early years when the Russian delegation, led by Andrei Gromyko, occasionally bolted, or took a walk. Barber would say of a recipient of a base on balls: "He's taking a Gromyko."

In British political usage, to *bolt* a bill is to pass it without close consideration, which in American usage is *railroad it through.* For other horse-racing metaphors in politics, see DARK HORSE; SHOO-IN; FRONT RUNNER. For a milder form of bolting, see OFF THE RESERVATION; for organized bolting, see SPLINTER GROUP and DIXIECRAT.

bombing pause A temporary cessation of bombing to determine whether the opponent wishes to negotiate; a concession to create an atmosphere for compromise.

The phrase was probably introduced into debate about the war in Vietnam by Canadian Prime Minister Lester Pearson, in a speech in Philadelphia on April 2, 1965. Pearson, who as Canada's Minister of External Affairs had won a Nobel Peace Prize, suggested that President Johnson ought to order a "pause" in bombing North Vietnam, which might bring about peace talks. The phrase gave focus, and the sponsor gave weight, to much previous pressure from what was called the "Peace Bloc" to halt the bombing. Six weeks after Pearson's speech, the first "bombing pause" began, lasted for six days, and was followed by longer and shorter pauses in subsequent years. DOVES complained that the pauses were too short; "hawks" (see WAR HAWKS) criticized the pauses as a show of weakness, allowing the North Vietnamese to regroup and resupply.

Pause is a word with a curious history in politics. President James Buchanan remarked on the eve of the Civil War, "Let us pause at this momentous point and afford the people an opportunity for reflection"— by which he meant a general election that would relieve him of responsibility. German propagandists in 1941 described the lull in fighting after the Nazi conquest of Crete as a "creative pause," and *Time* magazine in 1942 referred to any cessation of hostilities as the "creative pauses of Adolf Hitler." The phrase was an ominous one, implying a build-up of power for a fresh attack (and offering an excuse for inactivity).

Pause hurt the Conservatives in the 1964 general elections in Great Britain. Chancellor of the Exchequer Selwyn Lloyd, in an effort to meet Britain's balance-of-trade crisis, said of wages and salaries: "There must be a pause until productivity has caught up." The "pay pause" was used by Labour to attack the government; after Labour had won, the "pause" went into effect and became known as a "freeze."

In a book by Richard V. Allen on peaceful coexistence published by the American Bar Association, the Russian word *peredyshka* is defined: "Breathing Space (Peredyshka)—Period of rest in which forces are regrouped in preparation for another offensive against the West, which usually occurs after a Communist advance has been halted and the 'enemy' has become alert to further Communist aggression; a period designed to relax the enemy's defenses so as to facilitate the next offensive. 'Peredyshka' means 'pause.'" During the Gorbachev era in the Soviet Union, this *peredyshka* was contrasted with the more famous PERESTROIKA, "restructuring."

bomfog A high-sounding, glittering generality.

The ACRONYM comes from reporters' shorthand covering Governor Nelson Rockefeller's speeches in his 1964 campaign against Barry Goldwater in the New Hampshire primary, which resulted in an upset victory in New Hampshire for Henry Cabot Lodge.

Nancy Shea, then of Rockefeller's staff, informed the author:

> Bomfog was originated by Hy Sheffer who was at one time the Governor's stenotypist. Hy told me he started using it in the late 1959–60 national effort. Since the Governor used the phrase "the brotherhood of man under the fatherhood of God," so often, Hy began to simplify it on the stenotype machine. *Bomfog* took only two strokes on the machine compared to several more strokes for the whole phrase. The reporters traveling with the Governor's party picked it up and made it famous.

"Brotherhood of man, fatherhood of God" is part of the Rockefeller family credo, a speech by John D. Rockefeller, Jr., etched in marble near the statue of Prometheus in New York's Rockefeller Center: "These are the principles upon which alone a new world recognizing the brotherhood of man and the fatherhood of God can be established."

Bomfog had an appeal as a political word because it seemed to combine *bombast* with *fog*, or amorphous oratory. Its use is current, no longer limited to critics of Nelson Rockefeller.

boneless wonder See INVECTIVE, POLITICAL.

boodle Graft; illicit profit derived from holding public office, usually in the form of bribes; more loosely, loot of any type.

This durable word of several meanings came into wide political use in New York during the early 1880s, when the construction of the Brooklyn Bridge was hotly debated. A number of publications used the term around the same time and with the same meaning. Typical was the spoof in *Puck* in 1883, quoting an unnamed alderman in local dialect: "They say there's a power of boodle in the building av it; so yous needn't bother about what they'll do wid it." The following year the *New York World* derided the lobbyists' activities with: "It has been a double-barrelled shotgun of boodle."

Boodle went national in the presidential election of 1884 and was used most tellingly against James G. Blaine, the unsuccessful Republican candidate. When he attended a Delmonico's dinner in his honor—given by some of the country's richest men—the newspapers dubbed the event the "boodle banquet." A Thomas Nast cartoon depicted Blaine defending "Fort Boodle." Benjamin Harrison, the Republican nominee four years later, absorbed similar attacks, but won anyway. Said *The New York Times* when Harrison took Indiana: "There seems to be no good reason to doubt that boodle and bulldozing have carried the state for Harrison."

At the 1948 Republican convention, Illinois Governor Dwight Green lambasted the Democrats as an alliance of "bosses, boodle, buncombe and blarney."

Although the word stems from the Dutch *boedel*, "property," its American use seems always to have had a larcenous or facetious connotation. At least three decades before it became synonymous with political swag,

it was used to denote counterfeit money. Although GRAFT, *fix*, *payoff*, and *bribe* are more frequently used words, *boodle* is still current. "Each time there was a payment," wrote *Life* magazine in a 1968 story on organized crime in New York, "there was this ritual cutting up of the boodle." In 1996, Charles Levendosky charged in the *Casper* (Wyo.) *Star-Tribune* that tobacco lobbyists made contributions to members of Congress to continue a subsidy: "Sound grim to you—our representatives taking money for their votes? You and I might call that bribery. Payola. Boodle. Members of Congress call it lobbying."

In an era of electronic eavesdropping, another synonym is a "wordless word": in lieu of the question "Can he be bribed?" the potential briber says nothing but rubs his thumb against his index and middle finger and raises his eyebrows.

See REACHED; LITTLE TIN BOX; BELTWAY BANDITS.

bookburners Extreme censors; self-appointed guardians of what may and may not be read; anti-intellectuals.

The burning of books offensive to the group in power had often occurred in the Middle Ages, but *bookburning* became a political word on the evening of May 10, 1933, less than five months after Hitler came to power. William L. Shirer described the scene in Berlin:

> At about midnight a torchlight parade of thousands of students ended at a square on Unter den Linden opposite the University of Berlin. Torches were put to a huge pile of books that had been gathered there, and as the flames enveloped them more books were thrown on the fire until some twenty thousand had been consumed. Similar scenes took place in several other cities. The book burning had begun.

Propaganda Minister Joseph Goebbels addressed the students in the light of the pyre: "The soul of the German people can express itself. These flames not only illuminate the final end of an old era; they also light up the new." See NIGHT OF THE LONG KNIVES.

FDR, in a message to the American Booksellers Association in 1942, wrote: "We all know that books burn—yet we have the greater knowledge that books cannot be killed by fire. ... in this war, we know, books are weapons."

Senator Joseph McCarthy, investigating the State Department's predecessor to the U.S. Information Agency, sent two of his assistants, Roy M. Cohn and G. David Schine, abroad to investigate alleged inefficiency and cases of doubtful loyalty. Their tour (see JUNKETEERING GUMSHOES) aroused controversy; subsequently the State Department excluded "the works of all Communist authors" from U.S. libraries abroad. One news report chose the slanted word "burned" rather than "removed," evoking memories of the Nazi experience.

President Eisenhower, who refused to ENGAGE IN PERSONALITIES, made this observation on the campus of Dartmouth College: "Don't join the bookburners! Don't think you are going to conceal faults by concealing evidence that they ever existed. Don't be afraid to go in your library and read every book as long as that document does not offend your own ideas of decency. That should be the only censorship."

History's first recorded bookburning was ordered by the first emperor of the Qin dynasty in China around 220 B.C. The emperor, who was responsible for the construction of much of the Great Wall, not merely burned books but also buried alive scholars in pits mainly to suppress Confucianism. In China "bookburning and scholar pitting" became a familiar phrase. In 2007, the civil libertarian columnist Nat Hentoff called on Ray Bradbury, author of *Fahrenheit 451*, to protest the jailing of librarians by Cuba's Fidel Castro. Bradbury responded promptly: "I plead with Castro and his government to release all those librarians in prison and send them back into Cuban culture to inform the people." A group was formed that launched a "Read a Burned Book" campaign.

The most prescient early comment on the practice was from the German poet Heinrich Heine in 1823: "Wherever they burn books they will also, in the end, burn human beings." What will happen in the distant future, when paper books will be replaced by portable electronic screens able to access everything that has been published throughout history? Surely tomorrow's bookburners will try to expunge dangerous ideas from all databases, but dissident geeks of the future will also be able to copy the complete works of everything on chips that can be squirreled away.

boom (boomlet) A well-publicized movement to promote a political candidate.

Booms may be artificially induced, but those that have voter appeal often turn into the real thing. The word gained political currency in the late 1870s when it was used to describe the noise and hullabaloo associated with the growing sentiment for General Ulysses S. Grant for another Republican presidential nomination. An 1879 story in the *San Diego Daily Union:* "Mr. McCullagh, editor of the *St. Louis Globe-Democrat*, who first applied the word 'boom' to the Grant movement, says he used the term in the sense that it is applied to a sudden and irresistible rise in a river. He wanted a term to imply that the Grant movement was sweeping everything before it, and he chose the word 'boom.'"

The magazine *Puck* speculated in 1879 about the origin of the phrase:

> Lately has been added to our American political vocabulary the word "boom," which sprang up nobody knows where, and means nobody knows exactly what. The term may have arisen from the system of booming great rafts of logs on our rivers; or the term may refer to the boom which is spread out from the mast to extend the canvas to the favoring breeze. Our opinion is that it is the "boom" of cannon which has given rise to the phrase.

A year later *Puck* posed the question that puzzles practical politicians to this day: "Can a boom once boomed be reboomed, or does it boom itself out at the first boom?"

A *boomlet* is a boom that makes only a plaintive, popping sound. Boomlets are started for candidates with little real hope of achieving a nomination. Generally they die out and the person for whom the boomlet was launched throws support to someone else, possibly in return for a place on the ticket—which might have been the reason for the boomlet all along.

An *economic boom* is similar in meaning to a political boom: both are off and running, though there is less connotation of manipulation in an economic boom.

boom and bust Severe cyclical movement of an economy; apparent prosperity followed by extreme depression; a manic-depressive economy.

The phrase always means a prospect to be avoided. In his 1948 State of the Union message, President Harry Truman used the familiar phrase calling for a comprehensive anti-inflation program "to protect our economy against the evils of boom and bust." Eisenhower economic adviser Arthur Burns said in 1960: "The American people have of late been more conscious of the business cycle, more sensitive to every wrinkle of economic curves, more alert to the need for contracyclical action on the part of government, than ever before in our history." Unfortunately for the Republicans, economic expansion programs were not pressed at that time and the 1960 election was held in the midst of an economic slump. Burns, as Federal Reserve Chairman in 1972, did not make that mistake again.

The NEW ECONOMICS of John Maynard Keynes did much to encourage the public to believe that government action could indeed eliminate the wide swings of boom and bust. Walter Heller, economic adviser to Presidents Kennedy and Johnson, held that economists had to go beyond contracyclical planning. "Policy thinking," he wrote in criticism of the Eisenhower years, "had been centered more on minimizing the fluctuations of the business cycle than on realizing the economy's great and growing potential."

Steady, non-inflationary economic growth, relieved of sharp movements in either direction, became the goal of the new economists. Kennedy aide Theodore Sorensen characterized a long-faced conclave of the Council of Economic Advisors in 1961 with "There they are, contemplating the dangers of an upturn!"

boomerang A political statement or policy that unexpectedly damages its perpetrator; a disastrous reaction.

In the 1936 presidential campaign, many companies printed flyers for insertion into pay envelopes opposing Roosevelt's Social Security program. "The whole campaign of propaganda turned out to be a boomerang," wrote Samuel Rosenman. "There may have been a time … as in the Bryan campaigns, when the workers of the nation, either willingly or unwillingly, took political advice from their employers; by 1936 they were voting on their own."

The derivation of *boomerang* is familiar: the crescent-shaped hunting weapon used by Australian natives. When hurled, it comes back to the thrower. The metaphor was probably introduced by poet Oliver Wendell Holmes in 1845: "Like the strange missile which the Australian throws / Your verbal boomerang slaps you on the nose." Cartoonist Thomas Nast used it politically in 1877 against Carl Schurz, who made a politically unwise protest against the sale of arms to France. Nast showed Schurz firing a gun which explodes in his face, with the caption: "Carl's Boomerang. Little Children Should Not Investigate (French) Firearms."

In political usage, the word differs from BLOOPER, *blunder, goof, fluff,* and *gaffe,* which are more slips of the tongue than errors in judgment; a boomerang connotes a conscious policy willingly undertaken that turns out to be mistaken because of the unexpected adverse reaction.

Defense Secretary Charles E. Wilson, victim of several bloopers (see BIRD DOG … KENNEL DOG; WHAT'S GOOD FOR GENERAL MOTORS …), learned late in his career to be more careful of his statements. Treading carefully in a 1957 press conference, he ducked a question by observing, "I somehow feel there's a boomerang loose in the room."

In 1967 Alan Otten wrote an article titled "The Grating Society" and observed: "Slogans are an established ingredient of political public relations. Probably they are initially helpful in selling a program. But they have a way of wearing out their welcome, even boomeranging. They begin to sound contrived or corny; they provide a rallying cry for a program's foes as well as friends."

For a boomerang with racial overtones, see BACKLASH.

boondoggle Any project on which government funds are wasted through inefficiency or political favoritism; originally a make-work project, using government funds to stimulate the economy.

When New York City's Board of Aldermen (now City Council) was investigating relief payments in 1935, they discovered money was being spent for the teaching of tap dancing, manipulation of shadow puppets, and the geographical distribution of safety pins. One Robert Marshall told the aldermen he was paid for teaching "boon doggles."

The word livened up the hearings, and Marshall explained to *The New York Times:* "Boon doggles is simply a term applied back in the pioneer days to what we call gadgets today … no, it is not named for Daniel Boone … it is spelled differently."

H. L. Mencken tracked the phrase back into scouting, as the name given to the braided leather lanyard worn by Boy Scouts. The *Chicago Tribune* wrote that "to the cowboy it meant the making of saddle trappings out of odds and ends of leather, and they boon doggled when there was nothing else to do on the ranch."

Brewer's *Dictionary of Phrase and Fable* gives as the derivation the identical word in Scottish—*boondoggle*—which is a marble given as a gift without the recipient's having worked for it.

The word has lost its Depression-born connotation of keeping the idle busy with government funds, though it always implied waste of money. Now the word is used in attacks on government bureaucracy on all levels, and has acquired a new connotation of favoritism. The Defense Department's TFX bomber program was denounced as a "huge boondoggle," and in 1966, a full-page advertisement appeared in *The New York Times* attacking a proposal for the construction of government-owned merchant ships as "a $2 billion government-aerospace boondoggle."

The word *boon* means gift, or favor, and might have played a role in the word's formation; *doggle,* however, appears to be the operative verb and can be used to make the term more specific. For example, when the American Legion in 1966 pressed for an expansion of national cemeteries to include all Vietnam veterans and their families, the *New Republic* headlined its comment "The Gravedoggle."

boring from within Infiltration of a group or society by agents dedicated to its overthrow; a FIFTH COLUMN.

Communists have long been accused of using a technique of takeover borrowed from nature: a tree-destroying beetle embeds its eggs as deeply as it can in a notch in the tree's bark, and the hatching insect instinctively bores its way through the wood.

In *Suite 3505*, published in 1967, Goldwater organizer F. Clifton White wrote about "how Communist agents and their dupes incessantly bore from within in their untiring efforts to destroy our democratic society …" Nelson Rockefeller, in 1963, accused the Goldwater men of doing exactly the same within the Republican party, in his first MAINSTREAM statement: "the vociferous and well-drilled extremist elements boring within the party utterly reject these fundamental principles of our heritage."

Borer is an obsolete term for political lobbyist; the *Cincinnati National Republican* wrote in 1923 that Pennsylvanians "have applied to each other the elegant appellations of logrollers and borers …"

The accusation has not been limited to Communists and extremists. *Chicago Tribune* publisher Robert McCormick, America's leading Britain-hater in the '40s, explained his estimate of the reason behind Rhodes scholarships: "The infamous Cecil Rhodes conceived the plan to give free education to Americans in Oxford and make them into English cells, boring from within."

bork To viciously attack a presidential nominee, blackening his name in an all-out effort to defeat his confirmation by the Senate.

A contemporary example of eponymy (using proper names to create words) like *lynch* and *boycott*, this verb is based on the name of Judge Robert H. Bork, whose nomination to the United States Supreme Court in 1987 by Ronald Reagan was rejected by the Senate after an extensive media campaign by his opponents. Senator Ted Kennedy (D-Mass.) led the charge at the confirmation hearing with "Robert Bork's America is a land in which women would be forced into back-alley abortions, blacks would sit at segregated lunch counters, rogue police could break down citizens' doors in midnight raids …" (The brilliant and prickly Bork—insufficiently deferential to the Senators examining him—was a constitutional "originalist" who then believed, as he later wrote, that the Court's decision in *Roe v. Wade* was "a radical deformation of the Constitution.")

The verb first appeared in print in 1988, enclosed in quotation marks, as in the *Chicago Tribune* of November 20, 1988: "Honest disagreement is one thing: 'borking' is something else." In February 1989, Republican Senator Malcolm Wallop of Wyoming commented on *CBS This Morning*: "I feel strongly that he [Senator John Tower] is being borked.… The charges that have been leveled at him have all proved groundless, baseless." On the same program on July 9, 1990, it was reported that in considering another conservative nominee to the Supreme Court, "An opponent of Judge Clarence Thomas said yesterday, 'We're going to bork him.'"

The verb later proved useful to conservatives seeking to retaliate for Judge Bork's defeat. A *New Republic* essay by Ruth Shalit discussing potential Democratic nominees to the Supreme Court was headlined "Borking Back," with the subhead "The right gets even." In contexts other than Senate confirmation, users of the verb sometimes allude or refer to the word's eponymous source, as in the article in the *Los Angeles Times* of August 23, 1992: "Perhaps … Hillary Clinton is being 'borked'—attacked in the same orchestrated manner which ultimately undermined the U.S. Supreme Court nomination of Judge Robert H. Bork."

As public opinion turned against the Bush Administration's conduct of Iraq War II, the former Undersecretary of Defense for Policy, Douglas Feith, was rebuked by Democratic senators for having conducted an administration briefing that challenged CIA consensus, which the agency's Inspector General reported was not illegal or unauthorized but "inappropriate." Former White House national security aides Robert Blackwill and Ed Rogers defended Feith in a *Washington Times* Op-Ed headlined "Borking Doug Feith: Is it wrong to question the intelligence community?"

The word is similar to an earlier eponymous verb, to *burke*, originally meaning "to murder someone by suffocation, especially in order to sell the body for dissection," and later used figuratively to mean "to smother or suppress (a book, a debate, an issue, etc.)." The verb was taken from the name of William Burke, executed in Edinburgh in 1829 for smothering his victims so as to leave no mark on their bodies that would make them unacceptable for anatomical dissection. At his hanging, spectators shouted, "Burke him, Burke him! Give him no rope!"

To *burke* is to murder, leaving no trace; to *bork* is to murder a nominee's chances. See also SWIFT BOAT SPOT.

born again In its non-religious, political sense, freshly convinced; or, newly returned to the fold.

Born again is a phrase central to evangelical Christianity, referring to "a spiritual experience resulting in a commitment to Christ." Convicted White House counsel Charles Colson used the phrase in that sense as the title of his 1976 bestseller about the formation of his ministry, the Prison Fellowship. When Jimmy Carter became a serious contender for the Democratic presidential nomination, questions were raised about his religiosity: he freely asserted that he was a "born-again Christian" and his sister, Ruth Stapleton, was an eminent evangelist. This strong assertion of religious belief was regarded by some politicians as a negative, since it was met with suspicion by some voters and with guilt by others. But the threat of "too much religion" in the candidate turned out to be a political old wives' tale, similar to the shibboleth that no Catholic could run successfully for president, which persisted until John Kennedy won. However, Mitt Romney's Mormonism troubled a portion of the "evangelical vote" in the 2008 presidential primaries.

Born again was taken into the political terminology as a compound adjective: Democrats returning to the party were hailed as "born-again Democrats," and liberals reluctant to make decisions that required new taxation were dubbed "born-again conservatives."

The phrase is now often used in politics with an ironic Carteresque connotation, to mean "newborn" or suddenly converted. Anthony Lake, who was a member of the National Security Council staff in the late '60s and who broke with Henry Kissinger in 1970 to become an outspoken DOVE, became a top policy planner in the Carter State Department. In 1978 the Department dissociated itself from some dovish positions taken by UN Ambassador Andrew Young; although continuing to espouse noninvolvement, Lake "put some daylight" between himself and Young. This led to his being identified by columnists Evans and Novak in June 1978 as a "born-again hawk." In 2007, *Human Events* ran a Robert Novak column that suggested Senator John McCain had been changing his position on tax policy to reflect more closely the position of his tax-resistant economic adviser, Arthur Laffer, under the headline: "Born-again Supply Sider?"

In its theological sense of "being born of God" or becoming a child of God, the phrase first appeared in English in John Wyclif's 1382 translation of the Bible: "But a man schal be born agen."

Bosnywash See AXIS.

boss, bossism A *boss* is a party leader who may not hold public office himself but who, through his control of the party organization, exerts great power over those of his party who do; *bossism* is a political system so organized. Both terms are almost always used in a pejorative sense.

Rooted in the Dutch *baas*, "master," *bosses* and *bossism* had their first major impact on the lexicon in the mid-nineteenth century, as big-city political organizations came into vogue. William Marcy Tweed of New York's Democratic party became nationally notorious as "Boss Tweed." A statement generally attributed to him sums up the boss's credo: "You may elect whichever candidates you please to office, if you allow me to select the candidates." He was said to have stolen uncounted millions in public funds, although recent research disputes this. Upon entering prison he gave his occupation as "statesman."

Few bosses before or since have equaled Tweed in either avarice or self-esteem. But they have played a crucial part in American politics, both in their function of building strong party organizations on the county, city, and state level and as a recurrent election issue and target for reformers.

Just as the nation is a federal union, each major American party is really a collection of state and local party organizations. The men who tend the machinery get as their principal wage—unless they personally hold public office—power. This power is tangible in the form of PATRONAGE, influence on nominations for great and small posts, and such matters as where a new road is to be built. But one thing that leaders of this kind rarely obtain is a good public face. Regardless of their honesty, they are often thought of as the gross, evil, Tweed type or as the insatiable tiger clawing over his victims' bodies, as Thomas Nast drew the TAMMANY TIGER in Tweed's day.

The relatively unknown Woodrow Wilson was nominated for governor of New Jersey in 1910 largely through the efforts of boss James Smith of Newark and the state's lesser Democratic captains. Even before he took office, Wilson cooled toward Smith and, as James MacGregor Burns tells it, pictured Smith "not as he really was—a run-of-the-mill party boss—but as evil personified, a party despot, a symbol of corruption and predatory control.... Frantically Smith charged Wilson with dishonesty...but few would take the word of a boss over the word of a high-minded professor."

A similar instance: Mayor Robert Wagner of New York won nomination for a third term (and then reelection) on a beat-the-boss platform. The irony was that the principal Democratic boss, Tammany Hall's Carmine De Sapio, had himself come to power as something of a reformer, had liberalized Tammany's internal practices, and had been a much-valued ally of Wagner's for years. The moral was clear: De Sapio was stripped of power by the very reform processes he introduced.

Harry Truman said sarcastically in 1959: "When a leader is in the Democratic Party, he's a boss; when he's in the Republican Party, he's a leader."

bounce See CONVENTION BOUNCE.

Boy Scout A naive politician; one with a head-in-the-clouds approach to government. "Boy Scout" is a derisive comment, made by cynical reporters or politicians, about those who do not bear the scars of compromise.

The best definition is Disraeli's remark about Gladstone: "honest in the most odious sense of the word." An early political use was by Frank Kent of *The Baltimore Sun*, describing the parade of planners and Ph.D.s into the new Roosevelt Administration in 1933: "Boy Scouts in the White House ... a government by Pink Pollyannas, first-name slingers, mothers' little helpers." At a ball given by New York newspaper reporters soon after the election of John Lindsay as mayor, the new mayor was played onstage by a reporter (Edward O'Neill of the *Daily News*) in a Boy Scout uniform. After Michigan Governor George Romney visited New York's City Hall, Lindsay confided to associates: "You know, they call me a Boy Scout. If I am, Romney's an Eagle Scout." In *The Arrogance of Power* (1967), Senate Foreign Relations Committee chairman J. William Fulbright used *Boy Scouts* in a story illustrating America's misplaced missionary zeal: "I am reminded of the three Boy Scouts who reported to their scoutmaster that as their good deed for the day they had helped an old lady to cross the street. 'That's fine,' said the scoutmaster, 'but why did it take three of you?' 'Well,' they explained, 'she didn't want to go.'"

Politicians who make an important point about integrity in government during their campaigns, or who frequently use the word *reform*, are often tagged with the title of the current comic-strip or television hero (Lindsay, for example, was often called "Batman"). Another similar appellation is "Mr. Clean," the name of a household detergent. *Newsweek* wrote of Ronald Reagan in November 1967: "At times as governor he comes on like Mr. Clean and Captain Nice rolled into one." A month later, when a kickback scandal embarrassed the Lindsay administration, columnist William F. Buckley Jr. wrote: "It is always piquant when it turns out that Mr. Clean never bathes." See MR. NICE GUY.

The political derogation of *Boy Scout* had its effect; in 1977 the Boy Scouts of America changed its venerable name to "Scouting/USA."

boys in the backroom See AMERICAN BOYS.

bracketing Organized opposition to a candidate before and after each campaign stop; surrounding of a campaign visit by a TRUTH SQUAD. See also TRACKER.

The gerund comes from the 1580 noun used in architecture to denote a projecting piece that gives support. Writers use *brackets* to add information or to let error stand with [*sic*].

The political sense of *bracketing* first appeared during the presidential race of 1988, when surrogates for George Bush tracked the Dukakis campaign. A Republican TRUTH SQUAD, staking out cities in which Governor Dukakis was scheduled to appear, would offer questions in advance about the candidate's record and remain after his departure to challenge his remarks.

An unidentified Bush aide told *The Washington Post* that, by using the technique of *bracketing*, the Bush campaign intended to "be in front" of Dukakis at rallies until the last day of the campaign.

Brahmin Aloof elite; a social, intellectual, or political aristocracy that manipulates power from non-elective positions.

The Brahmans of India were members of the highest Hindu caste, at the other end of the scale from the "untouchables"; *Brahmanism* is the word for the often-attacked but never really removed caste system in that country.

When the word arrived in Boston in the late nineteenth century, the spelling was changed. Oliver Wendell Holmes was the importer of the word in *Elsie Venner*: "He comes of the Brahmin caste of New England. This is the harmless, inoffensive, untitled aristocracy referred to, and which many readers will at once acknowledge."

Irish politicians in Boston took the "harmless" and "inoffensive" out of the word's meaning and used it as an epithet. Boston Mayor James M. Curley's biographer headed one chapter "The Boston Brahmin-baiter" and quoted a Curley-watcher as saying: "Jim can make the term 'blue blood' sound like the vilest epithet known to man. He shows the people why it would be a catastrophe to permit the 'Brahmins,' as he terms the wealthy and socially prominent, to obtain a foothold in politics."

"The Brahmins today," wrote John Gunther in 1947, "make a wonderfully close-knit archaic group, which nothing in the United States quite rivals. Harvard and trusteeships; the world placidly revolving around Back Bay; the Apley-Pulham spirit; aridity and charm and a Bloomsbury cultivation; above all, profound family interweavings."

The term is no longer limited to Boston; Brahmins are everywhere, raising money and pulling strings, being occasionally denounced as part of the EASTERN ESTABLISHMENT by those who are not "in." But a Brahmin is a power, and it is no longer considered an insult to be called one.

brain trust A group of advisers to a candidate or incumbent, prized more for their expertise in particular fields and intimacy with their patron than for their official position or rank.

"Since everything else is tending to trusts," wrote the *Marion* (Ohio) *Daily Star* in 1899, early in the era of trust-busting, "why not a brain trust? Our various and sundry supplies of gray matter may as well be controlled by a central syndicate." This could have been a play on *beef trust*, which in the early 1900s meant a monopoly on meat but later was a jocular reference to hefty chorines. In 1928 *Time* headlined an article on a meeting of the American Council on Learned Societies "Brain Trust."

The phrase was first applied politically to the group of university professors whose brains Franklin Roosevelt picked and trusted during the 1932 presidential campaign. Raymond Moley, one of the original "brain trusters," says that James Kieran, a *New York Times* reporter, coined the phrase. But Samuel Rosenman, the lawyer turned speechwriter who advised Roosevelt to recruit academic help, contends that Louis Howe, Roosevelt's earliest close adviser, used the term derisively in a conversation with the chief; Roosevelt himself then used it at a press conference. This was not the only time that the recollections of Moley and Rosenman differed (see NEW DEAL). In any event, *brain trust* caught on and stuck through the New Deal and beyond with little change in meaning. Roosevelt himself had preferred calling the original group his "privy council." Many of the president's critics, to give it a leftist tinge, called it "the Professoriat."

See KITCHEN CABINET, IRISH MAFIA and PALACE GUARD for other views of advisers, and EGGHEAD for a derogation of intellectuals.

brainwash To change drastically someone's outlook and opinion pattern; to convince thoroughly, usually through nefarious means.

Totally committed supporters of an opponent's point of view are derided as *brainwashed*; that is, it is a waste of time to try to convince them of another cause. The scare word is used in political argument, a frequent warning against being converted.

When the American Medical Association chose Dr. Edward Roland Ennis to "answer" President Kennedy on the subject of MEDI-CARE, the doctor claimed that "the American public is in danger of being blitzed, brainwashed and bandwagoned into swallowing the idea that the King-Anderson Bill is the only proposal ..."

The word first began to appear in 1950 to describe the technique of mental and physical torture and concentrated indoctrination of prisoners of war held in Communist countries. "In the newly authoritarian countries," wrote the *American Journal of Psychiatry* in February 1951, "the term 'brainwashing' is born to indicate this systematic breaking down of old loyalties and paternal ties."

The word—a translation from a Chinese term for "thought reform"—gained currency during prisoner-of-war exchanges at the conclusion of the Korean conflict. Americans were shocked when 21 U.S. soldiers expressed a wish not to be repatriated. Subsequently, a new code of conduct for U.S. armed services personnel was issued to clarify a prisoner's responsibilities under the inducements and threats of "brainwashing." (For a 1941 use by a Chinese leader, see Theodore H. White's memoir under CONSCIOUSNESS-RAISING.)

Michigan Governor George Romney's use of the term, in September 1967, illustrated its power. "When I came back from Vietnam [in 1965]," he told a TV interviewer, "I had just had the greatest brainwashing that anybody can get when you go over to Vietnam ... not only by the generals but also by the diplomatic corps over there, and they do a very thorough job ..." He had intended to imply that the reason for his change of position about the war in 1967 was that he had been misled two years before. But Romney's use of *brainwash* was, in his campaign manager Len Hall's words, "not a plus"; ally Jacob Javits called it "inartistic"; Eugene McCarthy said "a light rinse would have been sufficient"; and the *Chicago Daily News* used several current synonyms as they asked whether the U.S. "can afford as its leader a man who, whatever his positive virtues, is subject to being cozened, flim-flammed and taken into camp." See BLOOPER.

His son Mitt Romney, a successful entrepreneur and Republican governor of Democratic Massachusetts, surely expected to be teased with that word through much of the presidential campaign of 2008. "Lack of foreign policy experience will hurt," wrote Wayne Woodlief, a *Boston Herald* columnist soon after Romney announced. "He came back from a quickie trip to Iraq singing the White House's STAY-THE-COURSE tune. Given his dad's misfortune in 1968, Romney would never breathe the B word. But I'd say they brainwashed him."

brass-collar Democrat One who slavishly follows the party line; used mainly in the southern U.S., especially Texas.

Reader's Digest editor Earl Mazo, in a 1972 letter to the author disclaiming coinage of BACKLASH, referred to *brass-collar Democrat* as his favorite bit of political slang. A possible allusion is to those newly freed blacks in Reconstruction days who did not vote Republican. An early slang dictionary (Barrère and Leland's *A Dictionary of Slang, Jargon & Cant*, 1889) defines "Big dog with a brass collar" as a leader, now shortened to "top dog." See BLUE DOG DEMOCRAT; YELLOW DOG DEMOCRAT.

Bravo Zulu Job well done; a commendable performance.

This military term was popularized by National Security Adviser Robert C. McFarlane's use of the phrase in documents widely quoted during the Iran-contra hearings. "Bravo Zulu on Jenco's release," Colonel McFarlane wrote to Vice Admiral John M. Poindexter after the freeing of an American held hostage in Lebanon in late July of 1986. McFarlane again used the phrase in ending a memo to praise the performance of Lt. Col. Oliver L. North.

Taken from Navy signal code, the word *Bravo* stands for the letter B and *Zulu* for Z. These signals started with semaphore, using flags to indicate the letters. It remains unclear why this particular combination of B and Z is used to represent "job well done."

Originally, *Bravo Zulu* was expressed as *Baker Zebra*. The North Atlantic Treaty Organization changed the code words in 1952, choosing to represent Z with *Zulu*, for a member of the Bantu-speaking people of South Africa. More appropriate to the message is *Bravo*, an interjection based on the Italian for "brave, excellent," and used in English since the eighteenth century to applaud or praise.

bread-and-butter issue One that affects voters' personal budgets; a POCKETBOOK ISSUE.

Bread and butter, the staff of life slightly greased, had a stronger political meaning in 1840 when an Ohio politician named John Brough switched his vote on a bill with the explanation: "I have my bread and butter to look after." Earlier, Washington Irving had referred to these "little, beardless bread-and-butter politicians." The phrase is related to "knowing which side your bread is buttered on."

"The Bread and Butter Brigade" was the derisive term applied to the appointees of President Andrew Johnson. Senator Zachary Chandler of Michigan lashed into Johnson in 1867: "[These offices] were filled by Mr. Lincoln with good, responsible, reliable Union Republicans. [They] were removed by Andrew Johnson to make place for unreliable, irresponsible Copperheads in most cases, or bread-and-butter men, who are worse." Theodore Roosevelt, in his Bull Moose campaign, wrote: "They represent the bread-and-butter politicians and the office holders. And we stand for the future."

Bread-and-butter politician fell into disuse in recent years, and when the phrase reappeared as *bread-and-butter issue*, the pejorative meaning had disappeared. It is still in current political use, though its meaning is more usually expressed as *pocketbook issue*, or one that hits the voter where it hurts. Neither is as strong as the PARAMOUNT ISSUE phrase of the late nineteenth century, or the GUT ISSUE of today. See ISSUES, THE.

break all the china Carry out an order regardless of obstacles.

"Break all the china in this building," White House counsel Charles Colson wrote that President Richard Nixon told him, "but have an order for me to sign on my desk Monday morning."

This favorite Nixon locution was probably based on *a bull in a china shop* and was taken by some aides to mean "cut through the red tape and usual objections," but by more literal aides as the equivalent of "march over a cliff."

The phrase is occasionally used without reference to the Nixon period to describe a bureaucratic shaker-upper, with a connotation of insensitivity: "Criticism of [Director of Central Intelligence Stansfield] Turner as a breaker of china in his own agency," wrote columnists Evans and Novak in December 1977, "is hurting him in the administration."

When George W. Bush's nominee as ambassador to the U.N. was blocked in the Senate in 2005, the president gave him an interim appointment that circumvented the senators. Asked about this on MSNBC's *Hardball* show by Chris Matthews, David Gregory of NBC explained "Every time somebody accuses John Bolton about being abrasive or abusive to subordinates or difficult to work with—as somebody who is just going to *break all the china in the place*—the president says 'ah yes, this is why I like this guy. This is exactly what I want at the United Nations.'"

Brezhnev Doctrine See DOCTRINES.

bridge building Measures to reduce the tensions and dangers of the cold war, both between the United States and the Soviet Union and, more generally, between any peoples of differing ideologies.

The bridge as a symbol of peaceful intercourse has a long history; *bridging the bloody chasm* was a phrase used by post-Civil War leaders. Its applications to American foreign policy came into wide use after Lyndon Johnson became president in 1963. In his first State of the Union message, Johnson said: "We must develop with our allies new means of bridging the gap between east and west." He and other officials repeated the phrase often enough—although with variations—to give it wide currency. Senator William Fulbright phrased it this way: "Bridges can be built across the chasm of ideology."

The expression reflected the specific and limited agreements sought, and sometimes achieved, during the Eisenhower, Kennedy, and Johnson Administrations. The partial nuclear test-ban treaty of 1963, the consular treaty ratified in 1967, increased trade relations with Eastern Europe, and other measures were significant, but they hardly constituted a general settlement. Newspaper use of the phrase without explanation indicated its general acceptance; *The New York Times* noted in 1967: "The Senate Foreign Relations Committee advanced the Administration's East-West bridge-building program today by approving the United States-Soviet consular treaty."

Like so many political terms, *bridge building* can be overused, as Soviet Premier Nikita Khrushchev pointed out: "Politicians are the same all over. They promise to build a bridge even where there is no river."

Foreign relations applications of the metaphor declined after the Johnson Administration left office. But Richard Nixon, in the campaign of 1968, titled two of his key speeches "Bridges to Human Dignity" and used the phrase from time to time in his Administration to describe welfare reform and BLACK CAPITALISM.

After the 1969 episode at the Chappaquiddick bridge involving Senator Edward Kennedy, the bridge metaphor gained a tragic connotation and was temporarily dropped from political discourse, replaced by *dialogue*. However, metaphoric bridges returned as a favorite in the Clinton Administration, as the president declared his intent to "build a bridge to the 21st century."

bridge to nowhere A symbol to derogate extravagant government spending on a project that would benefit relatively few people.

As *The Washington Post* put it (April 30, 2006): "Last fall, after House Transportation Committee Chairman Don Young (R-Alaska) and Senate Appropriations Chairman Ted Stevens (R-Alaska) earmarked $223 million to link the remote town of Ketchikan (population 8900) to the more remote island of Gravina (population 50), the Bridge to Nowhere became a national symbol of congressional porkmania."

The $223 million was an installment payment on a proposed 200-foot-high, mile-long bridge (only twenty feet shorter than the Golden Gate). Another $230 million was earmarked for a second bridge, this one two miles long, across an inlet to link Anchorage to a port with almost no present business or homes. Total cost of this bridge, to be named Don Young Way, was expected to run from $1.5 to $2 billion. Rep. Young was not fazed by the cost. The *Post* quoted him as boasting that he had stuffed the highway bill "like a turkey."

The *Post* picked up *bridge to nowhere* from Keith Ashdown, a lobbyist for a public-interest lobby, Taxpayers for Common Sense. Searching for a way to get people worked up about EARMARKS, he had cited the proposed Ketchikan-Gravina bridge three years earlier as a prime example of how Congress directs federal tax dollars to be spent on obscure local projects. The idea that *bridge to nowhere* could become a rallying cry came to him in "a moment of sheer focus" while sipping beer at a local pub, the Hawk 'n' Dove, Ashdown told the Capitol Hill newspaper, *Roll Call*.

The phrase has been used before. *Bridge to Nowhere* is the title of a 1986 New Zealand–made horror-thriller as well as the nickname of an actual bridge in that country, so called because by the time it was completed in 1936, there was no longer any need for it; farmers had deserted the settlement it was supposed to serve. *Bridge to Nowhere* also has been applied unofficially to several U.S. structures, including the span between Middle and Lower Hooper Islands in Maryland's Chesapeake Bay, the Fort Duquesne Bridge in Pittsburgh (which nonetheless gets heavy traffic on Sundays when the Steelers play at nearby Heinz Field), and a bridge over the east fork of California's San Gabriel River that was left in majestic isolation (it is a popular hiking destination) when roads to and from it were washed out by floods in 1938.

Faced with the devastation of New Orleans and its environs, many members of Congress had second thoughts about this allocation to Alaska and considered redirecting the funds to Louisiana. Alaskans objected vehemently: "I don't kid people," said Ted Stevens, a member of Congress for 37 years and president pro tem of the Senate, "If the Senate decides to discriminate against our state...I will resign from this body."

In the end, the Alaskans lost—except that their loss was more apparent than real. Congress removed the earmarks, but allocated $452 million to Alaska anyway. Proponents of the appropriation held that this showed that local projects are best decided upon by local elected officials answerable to their constituents rather than by "bureaucrats in Washington," and that these bridges would stimulate economic development and provide jobs. But the phrase stung the G.O.P. "Our BASE didn't desert us because of the war in Iraq," said John McCain in late 2007. "Our BASE deserted us because of the Bridge to Nowhere.... That bridge is more famous than the Brooklyn Bridge."

See also PORK BARREL.

briefing book Notes in a black binder to prepare a candidate or official on wide-ranging subjects, often including a political GAME PLAN.

Before President Jimmy Carter's inaugural in 1977, *The Washington Post* commented on the nation's capital and "the real U.S. government here, something that isn't in any of the *briefing books* and transition papers that have been developed for him."

The term became embroiled in controversy after Carter's failed second presidential campaign. A briefing book prepared for President Carter in 1980 to help him in debating challenger Ronald Reagan came into the hands of the Reagan campaign. In 1983, the "Debategate" story surfaced, and at first Reagan commented, "Is it stolen if someone gives it to you?"

Still in use, *briefing book*—shorter and punchier than a collection of POSITION PAPERS, but more detailed than *talking points*—is particularly prominent during election years. In September 1992, *Newsday* reported that "Budget Director Richard Darman already has debate briefing books in the works" for the Bush campaign, and that Clinton's staff "has begun collecting facts and figures and drafting witty rejoinders for the briefing books."

This term, though, can also suggest a crutch, indicating a candidate's need for coaching in areas of weakness (see HANDLERS). Lawrence J. Haas, writing for *National Journal* in 1987, implied this negative connotation in complimenting David Stockman of the Reagan Office of Management and Budget: "On Capitol Hill, longtime budget experts say that, yes, Stockman could be sly, but his knowledge was phenomenal. In testimony, he rarely consulted briefing books."

Sometimes the briefing book can work in reverse, informing the staff about what the leader is thinking. On occasion, the lexicographer prepared the briefing book for a Richard Nixon news conference. All likely questions were drawn up; answers solicited from departments and agencies and rewritten in 90-second bites for the president's review. He would then accept some and rewrite others, often revealing his thinking and making timely decisions before the Q and A session. One question I posed in early 1971 was "Will you ask Vice President Agnew to be your running mate again?" Nixon prepared his answer in the affirmative but the reporters did not ask that question for three months until Dan Rather of CBS popped it—during which time Agnew, not knowing, sweated it out.

bring us together A unifying theme used by President-elect Nixon on the day after his 1968 election, which critics later interpreted as a promise and frequently derided.

"I saw many signs in this campaign," said Richard Nixon on the morning after he had been elected president. "Some of them were not friendly and some were very friendly. But the one that touched me the most was one that I saw in Deshler, Ohio, at the end of a long day of whistle-stopping, a little town, I suppose five times the population was there in the dusk, almost impossible to see—but a teenager held up a sign, 'Bring Us Together.' And that will be the great objective of this Administration at the outset, to bring the American people together. This will be an open Administration, open to new ideas, open to men and women of both parties, open to the critics as well as those who support us. We want to bridge the generation gap. We want to bridge the gap between the races. We want to bring America together."

It was Richard Moore, a California communications lawyer and longtime Nixon friend, culling "local color" items for the candidate on the campaign trail, who got off the train in Deshler to mingle with the crowd listening to Nixon speak from the rear platform. He said he spotted a girl with the sign, hand-lettered and obviously not produced by the local Republican organization, and recounted his sighting to this speechwriter's attention.

Nixon used the short phrase at the conclusion of a Madison Square Garden speech in New York City on October 31, 1968, recollecting it as "Bring us together again." This phrase, briefly used and relatively unnoticed, was not used again in the campaign's final weekend. National unity was not the dominant theme of either candidate, as the country was so torn at the time of Vietnam demonstrations that such a theme would have been received with scorn. (The initial Democratic posters, "United with Humphrey," had been quickly scrapped.)

On Election Day, flying from California to New York aboard the *Tricia*, while the nation's citizens voted below, and frustrated at having no writing assignment after months of heavy production, the author drafted a victory statement. To have sent it to the candidate would have been an invitation to bad luck, so I passed it to Communications Director Herb Klein, who was sure to be around Nixon before he went before the cameras the next day. (No concession statement was drafted by anybody.)

Just before taking the Waldorf-Astoria elevator down to the press room, Nixon glanced at the draft. The "Bring Us Together" suggestion registered.

The New York Times headed the transcript "Statement by Nixon Pledging to 'Bring America Together,'" and the Inaugural Committee promptly made it the theme of their festivities. Several Nixon staff aides, this writer included, objected to this, pointing out that while "Bring Us Together" was appropriate for a victory statement, the need for unity should not suddenly be placed ahead of the need for progress; also, the quoted phrase was a call *to* a candidate rather than a call *from* a President. The solution was "Forward Together," which served as the inaugural slogan (but which did not catch on).

The *Times* had sent a reporter and photographer to Deshler to find the little girl; they came up with Vicki Lane and a picture of the sign. The reporter quoted her saying that she saw it lying on the ground and held it up when Nixon was speaking. Since there was no reason to doubt her claim, she was brought to Washington with her family for the inaugural. When I asked Dick Moore years later if he had really spotted that girl or whether he had imagined the sign that day, his eyes took on a faraway look.

As might have been expected, whenever President Nixon took an action that aroused sharp differences of opinion, a common critical refrain was "He promised to bring us together." The phrase was used in this sarcastic sense as the title of a book by Leon Panetta and Peter Gall, once again proving that a phrase with an emotional charge can charge both ways.

brinkmanship A national security policy dictating that the nation be willing to risk large-scale—or even total—war in order to force an adversary to back down during a confrontation; when used derisively by the policy makers' critics, a reckless gamble or hollow bluff.

During the 1956 presidential campaign, Democrats led by Adlai Stevenson accused the Eisenhower Administration, and particularly Secretary of State John Foster Dulles, of *brinkmanship*.

Dulles coined only part of the term in an interview with correspondent James Shepley published by *Life* in January 1956. Said Dulles: "The ability to get to the verge without getting into the war is the necessary art. If you cannot master it, you inevitably get into war. If you try to run away from it, if you are scared to go to the brink, you are lost." Citing the 1953 Korean peace-talk crisis and the 1954 threats of major war over Formosa and Indochina, Dulles added: "We walked to the brink and we looked it in the face."

Republicans won the election, but the debate over brinkmanship went on, keeping alive the new term. Even Sherman Adams, Eisenhower's White House aide, questioned Dulles' argument. "I doubt," Adams wrote after leaving office, "that Eisenhower was as close to the brink of war in any of these three crises as Dulles made him out to be."

The metaphor depicting nations falling into war as if plunging over the edge, or *brink*, of a cliff is old and much used. In 1850 Henry Clay, appealing in the U.S. Senate for amity between North and South over the slavery issue, said, "Solemnly I ask you to pause at the edge of the precipice."

Adding the -*manship* to construct a "facetious formation" is contemporary. *The New Fowler's Modern English Usage* (3rd edition) compares *brinkmanship*—which editor Robert Burchfield attributed to Adlai Stevenson in 1956—with earlier Stephen Potterisms such as *one-upmanship* and *gamesmanship*. However, *Fowler's* takes *brinkmanship* seriously as a useful addition to the vocabulary. Webster's *New International Dictionary* (3rd edition) also accepts it as standard English rather than slang.

John Kennedy referred to "the brink" after his 1961 meeting in Vienna with Nikita Khrushchev and went to the brink the following year during the Cuban missile confrontation. See EYEBALL TO EYEBALL. At the 1964 Republican convention in San Francisco, some hawkish Goldwater placard carriers waved the slogan "Better brinkmanship than chickenship."

brokered convention A party convention at which many key delegations are committed to FAVORITE SONS, thus cutting down the first-ballot strength of the serious contenders for the nomination, and resulting in bloc bargaining.

In recent generations, as states have held caucuses or primary elections to select delegates to national party conventions, a brokered convention—or more exciting still, an OPEN CONVENTION in which individual delegates are free to vote their personal choice and the outcome is in doubt—has been a vain dream of the media.

In the past, brokered conventions were dominated by factional party leaders and favorite sons, who dealt directly or through "neutral leaders" (see POWER BROKERS). Under the "unit rule" in which some state delegations begin by casting all their votes for the candidate that commands the majority of the delegation, states could throw their total delegate strength to one or another candidate in return for promised positions on the ticket or in the cabinet, or simply to be with the winner.

As the state primary or caucus system has taken over, the outcome has become rarely in doubt. In 2008, with a rush by state legislatures to get in on the early-primary publicity and the sense of being decisive in the contest, the national candidate known to "have the tickets"—a majority of delegates pledged—could well be chosen five or six months before the convention. The convention then becomes more of a coronation, much like what usually happens when an incumbent president is a candidate for renomination. (The previously rarely used verb *coronate*, meaning "crown," has been gaining in usage as conventions "anoint" the selection of the primary voters; the royalism is jocular.)

Most modern conventions are brokered to some degree, if only to gain position on the platform or in the selection of the vice presidential nominee; only when two or more candidates show real strength and when no STAMPEDE can be started does a genuine brokered or open convention take place. But since 1972, with the proliferation of primaries, caucuses "front-loaded" to January, as well as erosion of the "unit rule," brokerage has become more difficult, though not impossible.

brother Jonathan Early symbol for the U.S.

George Washington referred to his adviser Jonathan Trumbull, governor of Connecticut, as "brother Jonathan," recalling the second book of Samuel in the Hebrew Bible. He may have taken this from the 1787 play *The Contrast*, by Royall Tyler, in which a character named "brother Jonathan" is portrayed as a Yankee trader.

Because a nation needs a symbol for its collective citizenry or for its average person—as the British have *John Bull* and the French *Marianne—brother Jonathan* became the first appellation of the typical American.

James Russell Lowell contrasted Englishmen and Americans in 1848 in this way: "To move John you must make your fulcrum of solid beef and pudding; an abstract idea will do for Jonathan." Rarely used now, the phrase has been replaced by UNCLE SAM.

brouhaha See UNFLAPPABLE.

brown derby symbol See TAKE A WALK.

brush pass See GAP, IN THE under CIA-ESE.

bubba factor The potential influence of Southern conservatives on an issue or election.

Bubba is a noun of direct address (a name or nickname for the person being spoken to). It comes from *bub*, a century-old term of endearment formed from a shortening of *brother*. The *u* of this *bubba* is short, pronounced as in *cub* and *rub*.

The *Dictionary of American Regional English* reports primary use of this *bubba* among African-Americans, particularly in Southern usage. Professional football players, such as Bubba Smith of the Baltimore Colts, helped popularize the name. Although the term is widely used by blacks, the political *bubba factor* primarily takes into account the influence of Southern conservative whites. When applied to poor rural whites in the South, *bubba* may be used as a synonym for REDNECK, *cracker*, and *good ol' boy*.

A step beyond the *bubba factor* is the *bubba vote*, denoting the political power of Southern white conservatives, primarily rural males. When the elder George Bush's campaign for reelection was challenged from the far right by television commentator Pat Buchanan, *Newsweek* commented in December 1991 that "The media…wondered whether the president could still speak to the all-important 'Bubba vote.'" In early 1992 *The Wall Street Journal* reported that Buchanan was "making inroads into the 'Bubba' vote—conservative whites, many of them Democrats." A follow-up bulletin from the *Journal* added: "Now the word appears to apply to Southern good ol' boys in general. It is akin in meaning to 'redneck,' and it may connote bigotry, but not necessarily."

Bubba Magazine offered a quotation from Bill Clinton on the Clinton-Gore ticket in 1992: "There's a little Bubba in both of us—in the sense that we both come from small towns, where people have old-fashioned values and want their country to be the best country in the world—and I don't think that's all bad."

bubble The security zone around the president that at once insulates and isolates the chief executive from the outside world; formerly called the *cocoon*.

"The *bubble* is what surrounds the traveling road show of any Presidential campaign," wrote *Washington Post* reporter David Maraniss, as the 1992 race between George H. W. Bush and Bill Clinton wound down. "It includes the candidate, the staff, the press, the plane, the bus and all the electronic gear of the 20th-century hustle …" Bill Clinton, asked at a press conference after winning the '92 election if he was frustrated by the press and security "bubble" that enveloped him, said: "I would hope…to maintain some greater level of ongoing personal contact with folks than is typically the case." Clinton managed to do this from time to time, as demonstrated by a *Washington Post* headline on a report about his visit to India in 2000: "Letter from Bombay; Bill Clinton Bursts His Security Bubble."

The metaphoric, metaphysical bubble almost certainly derives from the transparent shield for protecting presidents when riding in open cars. The limousine bubble was an innovation of the Eisenhower Administration, perhaps inspired by the transparent canopy, also called a bubble, over the cockpit of an airplane. The lack of a bubble on the limousine in which John F. Kennedy rode when he was assassinated in Dallas in 1963 was widely noted. The plastic bubble used for presidential motorcades at the time would not have saved him, however; it was neither bullet-proof nor bullet-resistant.

The bubble as metaphor appeared in the early 1970s. The bubble—a plastic encasement—became a metaphor for protection in the case of David Vetter, a boy born in 1971 with "severe combined immunodeficiency," in effect the lack of an immune system. The poignant story of "the boy in the bubble" became familiar to a wide public through news reports and a movie. When he left his bubble in 1984 for medical treatment following a bone marrow transplant, he died.

After John Hinckley shot and wounded President Ronald Reagan in 1981, *The New York Times* editorialized: "Many are beginning to say America must do more to protect its Presidents.... the idea is...get down, get back in the bubble." It did not displace *cocoon* right away, however, which was employed along with *bubble* in the 1992 presidential campaign. Reporting on a western swing by the president, Lloyd Grove wrote in *The Washington Post*: "George [H.W.] Bush, try as he might to get close to the ground, views the country and its problems from a perch of cozy isolation—the perennial perspective of American presidents who perforce live their lives in a beautiful cocoon." The transition from one metaphor to the other was encapsulated that year by *Los Angeles Times* film critic Kenneth Turan, who felt Bush's apparent isolation was due "in considerable part to the bubble-like, enviably efficient security cocoon the President must travel in to ensure his physical safety."

His son, George W. Bush, was characterized by *Newsweek* as perhaps "the most isolated president in modern history" in a 2006 cover story, titled "Bush in the Bubble."

The extreme of the cocoon or bubble as symbolic of isolation is the *bunker*, an evocation of the final hiding place of Adolf Hitler and Eva Braun just south of the Brandenburg Gate in Berlin, where the dictator and his mistress took their lives in 1945. Modern usage is *bunker mentality*: a writer in the *Jerusalem Post* in 2007 noted "the Nixonesque *bunker mentality* that appears to characterize [Prime Minister Ehud] Olmert's continuing grip on power as his poll ratings dip." At the same time, as the Bush administration resisted subpoenas to presidential aides, California Democratic senator Diane Feinstein charged that "the White House is in a *bunker mentality*—won't listen, won't change." At year's end, as the first 2008 caucus loomed in Iowa, Mike Huckabee, a former Arkansas governor seeking the Republican nomination, wrote in *Foreign Affairs* that "The Bush administration's arrogant *bunker mentality* has been counterproductive at home and abroad"; his chief opponent, Mitt Romney, berated him on television for insulting the Republican president.

buck stops here, the Motto of President Harry S. Truman, who briefly kept a sign with these words on his desk.

The motto meant that the presidency was, in Calvin Coolidge's words, "the place of last resort." It was especially appropriate for Truman, who had to make some momentous decisions: to drop the first atomic bomb; to order U.S. forces to South Korea; to fire General Douglas MacArthur.

Arthur Schlesinger, Jr., writing about John F. Kennedy, observed that "the Constitution made it clear where the buck stopped," and quoted Kennedy as saying: "The President bears the burden of the responsibility.... The advisers may move on to new advice." In a BBC interview soon after taking office, Kennedy said, "President Truman used to have a sign on this desk which said: 'The buck stops here'—these matters which involve national security and our national strength finally come to rest here."

The motto comes from the phrase *passing the buck*, which is a poker-playing expression. See CARD METAPHORS. The *buck* was a marker to show who next had the deal; it could be passed by someone who did not want the responsibility of dealing to the man on his left. (The marker was occasionally a silver dollar, which may be how the dollar became known as a *buck*.)

The motto was adopted by President Jimmy Carter, who placed a small sign with those words on a table near his desk in the Oval Office. In 1992, the phrase was used by Clinton Administration Attorney General Janet Reno, in assuming responsibility for the failure of the F.B.I. to avoid casualties in ending the siege of a religious cult in Waco, Texas. When President George W. Bush said in 2006 "I am the decider," he sent the same message but did not strike the same note.

See DECISION-MAKING PROCESS.

buffer state See GLACIS.

bug As a verb, to eavesdrop by means of a concealed transmitter; as a noun, the tiny device used for that purpose.

"Does it have the bug?" That was a question asked by campaign managers of their advertising and printing aides, to make sure that the *union bug*—the oval emblem of the printers' union—was on all campaign literature. This innocent meaning has been replaced by the more sinister slang meaning of "electronic eavesdropping."

An 1883 citation in the *Historical Dictionary of American Slang* shows that a *bug* was a card stuck by a gambler to the underside of the gambling table, to be substituted when profitable for a card in hand; the concealed-item meaning was switched over to the little microphone-transmitters, which bore some resemblance to an insect of the same name.

Another slang meaning, the verb to *bug*, means "to annoy"; when Attorney General John Mitchell spoke at a press dinner in 1970, he said facetiously, "If you quit bugging me, I'll quit bugging you." The quip, containing both senses of the term, turned out to be the opposite of prophetic.

In 1993, a White House tape was released that had been made four days after the Watergate burglary. On the tape, Richard Nixon used *bug* as a verb to make the most shortsighted prediction of his life: "I don't think you're going to see a great, great uproar in this country about the Republican committee trying to bug the Democratic headquarters."

See TAPS AND BUGS.

bullet vote One in which the voter enters the booth determined to pull the lever for one candidate and no other on the same or any competing ticket.

Such a vote is based on personal magnetism and voter service within the district rather than ideology. According to *New York Herald Tribune* reporter Tom O'Hara, with whom the author worked in the early 1950s, left-wing New York Congressman Vito Marcantonio claimed a large portion of his support came from *bullet votes*. Voters with no interest in the candidates for other offices (and who probably would not have voted at all) lined up to cast their ballots for their favorite congressman. As a result, Marcantonio's total in the '40s bulged beyond the others on his ticket. After voting for Marcantonio, many voters then left the American Labor Party line to choose Republican or Democratic candidates for other offices, or else cast no other votes for other offices at all. When they cast other votes on other lines, they became SPLIT TICKET voters; when they cast no other votes they were considered *bullet voters*.

A *Boston Globe* article in 1991 repeated the expression. During a local election, the *Globe* wrote, "operatives were watching closely to see how many 'bullet' votes—votes for only one candidate on the ballot—were cast." A year earlier, Long Island's *Newsday* had turned the term into a verb, reporting that a local candidate "is asking residents to 'bullet vote' by casting ballots only for him, rather than for two candidates."

Political leaders may plan bullet voting campaigns in runoffs or in at-large elections. When a voter has a selection of six out of twelve candidates to vote for, or when there are weights assigned to his first, second, and third choices, he may be directed to choose only one, giving no assistance to any other candidate running. When this technique is applied within a single party, it is called a *jungle primary*.

bully pulpit Active use of the presidency's prestige and high visibility to inspire or moralize.

Theodore Roosevelt, a president of expansive character, took an unrestricted view of his job. "Yes, Haven, most of us enjoy preaching," he told the publisher George Haven Putnam, who had accused him of a tendency to preach, "and I've got such a bully pulpit." In the many controversies during his two administrations, he never hesitated to take his case directly to the people from a presidency he liked to call a *bully pulpit.*

The image of the White House as a pulpit with the whole nation as congregation—linked with the zesty adjective *bully,* meaning first-rate, or admirable—has been frequently used ever since. It has special pertinence in the seemingly endless analysis of active presidents, or those who take the largest possible view of their office and powers, versus the more restrained chief executives. James MacGregor Burns, discussing the influences that helped form Franklin Roosevelt's political views, says: "T.R. and Wilson were both moral leaders ... who used the presidency as a pulpit." FDR used the theme in 1932, calling the presidency "preeminently a place of moral leadership."

A pulpit is a platform from which to preach to worshipers. Sally Quinn, in a 2007 *Washington Post* Op-Ed, criticized as improper a resolution passed by the House hailing Christianity. Her headline: "Congress's Bullying Pulpit."

bundling The collection of political donations from many individuals for delivery to a candidate in a single batch.

Bundling came into vogue after post-Watergate campaign finance laws put limits on individual contributions (in 2007, $2,300 per person in elections and primary campaigns for federal offices). Critics of the practice argue that bundling honors the letter of the law while evading its spirit. Legally, checks in the bundle are counted as coming from the people who wrote them. In practice, however, the organiza-

tion or person who does the bundling gets credit with the candidate for the entire amount. As noted by Charles Babcock in a 1992 *Washington Post* report on political fundraising: "Though political action committees (PACS) have long been the symbol of special-interest influence in congressional races, it's been well-known—but rarely documented—that interest groups can add to their clout by 'bundling' together donations for favored candidates."

The bundles may be hefty even for local elections: Rudolph Giuliani received more than $1 million from a group of 205 "intermediaries" in his 1993 campaign for mayor of New York City, according to a report ("Bundles of Trouble?") by the city's campaign finance board, which pointed out: "Like direct contributions, bundled contributions can be a means for buying access, influence, and political power."

Individual checks in the bundles are marked with tracking numbers, so that the bundlers—"Rangers," as they were called in George W. Bush's presidential campaigns, and "Hill-raisers" in Hillary Clinton's run for the 2008 Democratic presidential nomination—can get major credit for the total, typically on the order of $100,000 per bundle.

Just when the political sense of *bundling* was coined, and by whom, is not known. Rick Bielke, of Public Campaign, spotted the term in a 1972 letter to *The Washington Post.* No direct connection has been made between this kind of bundling and the quaint custom of *bundling,* in which a courting Dutch couple in the North American city of New Amsterdam was permitted to lie beside each other in bed, fully clothed and sometimes separated by a long wooden *bundling board.* More prosaically, the campaign finance bundle derives from the nineteenth-century slang sense of *bundle,* meaning "a bankroll" and, by extension today, "a large sum of money."

The assessment by Will Rogers in a mid-1920s newspaper column has never been truer: "Politics has got so expensive that it takes lots of money even to get beat with."

bunk Pretentious nonsense; claptrap; a long-winded oration meant for hometown consumption.

"Religion is all bunk," declared Thomas Alva Edison.

"History is bunk," stated his friend Henry Ford.

Bunk is an Americanism with a history almost as rich and colorful as *OK*. It is a shortening of *bunkum*, which is an altered shortening of *Buncombe*, a county in North Carolina that made up part of the district represented by Felix Walker, who sat in the House of Representatives in 1820. Walker interrupted a debate on the Missouri Compromise with a long, dull, irrelevant speech, apologizing to his impatient colleagues with the statement "I'm talking for Buncombe."

By 1828, according to *Niles' Weekly Register, talking to* (or *for*) *Buncombe* was well known. The *Wilmington* (N.C.) *Commercial* referred in 1849 to "the Buncombe politicians—those who go for re-election merely," and British author Thomas Carlyle showed that the expression traveled the Atlantic with its meaning intact: "A parliament speaking through reporters to Buncombe and the twenty seven millions, mostly fools."

The word was clipped to *bunk* toward the end of the nineteenth century, and in George Ade's *More Fables in Slang*, published in 1900, it appeared as "he surmised that the Bunk was about to be handed to him." In 1923 William E. Woodward wrote a book titled *Bunk*, and introduced the verb to *de*bunk. A school of historians were named *debunkers* for the way they tore down the myths other historians had built up. *Hokum*, according to the *OED*, is a blend of *hocus-pocus* and *bunkum*.

Another verb occasionally used is to *bunko* or *bunco*; to be *buncoed* means to be cheated or swindled. The well-meaning politician from Buncombe is not the villain here; more likely, the pejorative meaning comes from the Spanish *banco*, a game of cards. Senator Frank Brandegee of Connecticut, one of the anti-Wilson LITTLE GROUP OF WILLFUL MEN, said in the League of Nations debate: "I am not to be buncoed by any oleaginous lingo about 'humanity' or 'men everywhere.'"

bunker busters See SURGICAL STRIKE.

bunker mentality See BUBBLE.

bureaucracy Administrative agencies of government (or large private institutions) manned for the most part by career personnel and characterized by rigid adherence to rules and established procedure; almost always used in a derogatory sense.

Bureaucratic is a nineteenth-century adjective that describes a phenomenon that goes back to ancient Rome. The first echelon below the top has typically been a kind of aristocracy, whether by appointment, heredity, or election. Below that comes the civil service, or *bureaucracy*.

In impact on both vocabulary and life, the bureaucracy looms ever larger as the functions of government multiply. The bureaucracy is supposed to administer laws and policies framed by its superiors, but often the manner of administration looms more important than the policy handed down. "The executive bureaucrat," wrote sociologist C. Wright Mills, "becomes not only the center of decision but also the arena within which major conflicts of power are resolved or denied resolution."

The term comes from *bureau*, the French word for office, and was commonly applied to government agencies. After Napoleon's reign, a relatively permanent and quasi-autonomous civil service took firm hold in France and is generally credited with maintaining government functions through the upheavals at the top that make up so much of French history ("always falling, never fallen"). But the French system also produced the evils generally ascribed to bureaucracy. "Wherever possible," wrote sociologist Max Weber, "political democracy strives to shorten the term of office by election and recall.... Thereby democracy inevitably comes into conflict with the bureaucratic tendencies which, by its fight against notable (i.e., patrician) rule, democracy has produced."

Self-starters see bureaucrats as self-stoppers. But the criticism of public servants, as they call themselves, is often politically inspired: Alben Barkley, in the 1948 Democratic convention keynote address, said "a bureaucrat is a Democrat who holds a job a Republican wants."

Bureaucrats speak *bureaucratese*, which is often called GOBBLEDYGOOK, BAFFLEGAB, PENTAGONESE, or BUZZWORDS. Adjectives most frequently associated with bureaucracy's noun are *entrenched, swollen*, and the alliterative *bloated*. A favored form of communication is *touching base*. When they cannot be reached, bureaucrats are *in the field* or *on travel status*. For their most frequent method of protecting their posteriors for posterity, see CYA.

burning question See TOPIC A; PARAMOUNT ISSUE.

Bushisms See BLOOPER.

business as usual Complacency; unconcern for imminent danger: or, determination to carry on despite danger.

Winston Churchill, speaking at the Guildhall in London in the opening days of World War I, said, "The maxim of the British people is 'Business as usual.'" This carried the same kind of bravery-in-adversity message that he restated more eloquently in the early days of World War II.

In the generation between the wars, however, the meaning of the phrase changed. During the Depression "no business as usual" was a wry slogan. As war approached again, a *business-as-usual policy* was denounced as unworthy of a people aware of the unusual requirements of a wartime economy. Traces of the previous defiant meaning lingered on, however; during the Battle of Britain, with London under almost constant bombardment, a small sign in the Piccadilly window of Albert A. Julius, jeweler, read: "Business as Usual."

The phrase has since been synonymous with complacency. The 1962 Port Huron Statement of Students for a Democratic Society derogated the "familiar campus" as "a place of commitment to business-as-usual, getting ahead, playing it cool." Richard Neustadt in *Presidential Power* (1960) characterized the Truman-Eisenhower years as "emergencies in policy with politics as usual."

busing to achieve racial balance The phrase that became the battleground between forces believing in the primacy of the "neighborhood school" versus those who held that physical transportation of students was necessary to break down segregation.

The most controversy-laden CODE WORD of the late '60s and early '70s was *busing*. (The spelling with one *s*, which looks as if it could rhyme with *confusing*, triumphed over *bussing*, which is synonymous with *kissing*.) To many supporters of desegregation in theory, busing meant carrying the battle for civil rights into their own neighborhoods, and affected their own children; some activists felt cognitive dissonance at that point, and many parents who had been lukewarm about desegregation felt the abandonment of the tradition of keeping children in schools close to their residences was a serious mistake.

The crucial part of the phrase was *racial balance*. In the legislative history of Title IV of the 1964 Civil Rights Act, the phrase first appeared (as "racial imbalance") in a 1963 message from President John F. Kennedy recommending federal technical and financial assistance to schools which were "engaged in the process of meeting the educational problems flowing from desegregation or racial imbalance ..." In the House hearings on this bill, Congressman William Cramer (R-Fla.) tried to get witnesses to define "racial imbalance" with no success; accordingly, the House on January 31, 1964, adopted an amendment he submitted to provide that any definition of *desegregation* in the Civil Rights Act "shall not mean the assignment of students to public schools in order to overcome racial imbalance."

In the Senate, Hubert Humphrey (D-Minn.)—after an 83-day debate had made clear that "busing to achieving racial balance" would have to be sacrificed if any civil rights bill was to be passed—said on June 4 that the amendments dealing with busing "preclude an inference that the title confers new authority to deal with 'racial imbalance' in schools, and should serve to soothe fears that Title IV might be read to empower the Federal Government to order the busing of children around a city in order to achieve a certain racial balance or mix in schools."

The Supreme Court, in *Swann v. Charlotte-Mecklenburg Board of Education,* held in 1971 that this language limiting the Civil Rights Act foreclosed the granting of new powers to the courts to redress *de facto* segregation (caused by residential patterns), but did not withdraw from the courts "their historic equitable remedial powers" to strike down *de jure* segregation (caused by discriminatory action by state authorities).

In most of the political debate on the issue of busing, only the most dedicated civil rights activists defended the idea of transporting students to overcome the segregation brought about by living patterns. Changing *de facto* segregation was described as *integration*, while most public opinion preferred *desegregation*, which stopped short of "busing to achieve racial balance."

A litmus test of the political leanings of the speaker could be found in the adjective used to describe busing. Liberals used *involuntary* busing; conservatives or anti-busing liberals preferred *forced* busing.

The word first came into the language with the double-*s* spelling, and was usually associated with military transport: "They were instructed in march-discipline," wrote Rudyard Kipling in 1923, "as well as bussing and de-bussing against time into motor-buses."

See SEGREGATION; SEPARATE BUT EQUAL.

buttonhole To stop a moving delegate, engage his attention, and press for the support of a candidate or cause; in more general terms, to electioneer.

The verb is colorful because it describes the act of holding on to the persuadee's button, lapel, or any grabbable part of his clothing. The *OED* reports a pre-political usage: "Charles Lamb, being buttonheld one day by Coleridge … cut off the button." The word was adopted by politicians in the mid-nineteenth century. Mark Twain, in *The Gilded Age,* recorded a friend who "bussed and 'buttonholed' Congressmen in the interest of the Columbia River scheme."

The term is being limited in application to delegates on a convention floor. In the raucous 1940 Republican convention that nominated Wendell Willkie, the Willkie supporters who overflowed onto the convention floor (see PACKING THE GALLERIES) caused the head of the New Hampshire delegation to shout into the microphone: "Mr. Chairman! I call the attention of the chair to the fact that many people are in the aisles and buttonholing delegates, who have no right to be on the floor of the convention." The chairman's gavel cut off the buttonholers.

A related phrase is *nickel-and-diming,* the pursuit of support down to the small change of personal persuasion of individual delegates by the candidate. Gerald Ford's press secretary, Ron Nessen, wrote in his 1978 memoir *It Sure Looks Different from the Inside* of the 1976 Republican delegate hunt: "Ford … appealed to individual uncommitted delegates by phone. He invited many delegates to the White House. … it was called 'nickel-and-diming,' trying to win the necessary delegates one by one … A joke went around illustrating how some uncommitted delegates played hard-to-get. It seems one delegate from New Jersey received a phone call from the President inviting him to a reception and state banquet for Queen Elizabeth at the White House. There was a long pause of indecision and then, according to the gag, the delegate asked Ford, 'What's for dinner?'"

buttons, campaign A device for a shy voter to communicate his preference; one of the few "absolute musts" in a campaign budget that managers agree is largely a waste of money; a stimulus to enthusiasm of workers.

When the wearing of campaign buttons was spoken of as inelegant in 1900,

Congressman E. L. Hamilton of Michigan angrily rose to his feet in the House of Representatives. "The wearing of a campaign button is a harmless sort of decoration," he began, "but a social condition that dictates to a man what kind of a button he shall wear approaches a condition of tyranny, and makes a man want to stick campaign buttons all over him, and protect his privilege with a Gatling gun!"

With the freedom to wear buttons given this First Amendment umbrella, their use proliferated. Button manufacturers like Emanuel Ress ("The Button King") recalled an upsurge in 1940 ("Eleanor Start Packing—The Willkies are Coming," "No Third Term," "Two Good Terms Deserve Another").

Rhyme has always been important to button-makers. "I Like Ike" appeared on buttons manufactured in 1947 (as Eisenhower began to be spoken of as a possible Democratic nominee); "Who Else But Nelse" (Rockefeller), "Madly for Adlai" (Stevenson), "All the Way with LBJ" (Johnson), "Who but Hubert" (Humphrey), and "The Grin Will Win" (Carter) followed.

The style of button showing the candidate's picture and name with some patriotic symbol was replaced by the picture-plus-slogan button in the '40s, and gradually the use of pictures on buttons has declined. In 1964, anti-Goldwater forces sported "Extremism in the Pursuit of Vice is No Virtue." When General Eisenhower told that convention to beware of "sensation-seeking columnists," button men within three hours turned out "Sensation Seeking Press" buttons for reporters, along with "Stamp Out Huntley-Brinkley."

In the 1965 John Lindsay campaign for mayor of New York, Adam Mark Lawrence came in with "a great idea for a Lindsay button," which was a button with the copy "Lindsay button." This was followed by buttons that simply said "Button" ("for the sort of people who like to call their dog 'dog'").

Gold lapel pins and cufflinks, elitist forms of buttonry, are often used as fund-raising devices. "The most successful 'button,'" wrote Ted Sorensen, "was a tie clasp in the form of Kennedy's old PT boat. It became a popular badge for Kennedy supporters and a fast-selling item in the 'Dollars for Democrats' drive." See CUFFLINKS GANG.

There was a tendency in the mid-'60s to use campaign buttons when there was no political campaign. Many carried a social rather than political message: "Make Love Not War," "I Am A Human Being: Do Not Fold, Spindle or Mutilate," "Turn On, Tune In, Drop Out." A wide variety of gag buttons were sold: "Support Mental Health Or I'll Kill You," "Kill a Commie for Christ," "Leisure Suits Make You Sterile." The author sported his favorite in 1972: "Agnew and Eagleton—Nobody's Perfect."

Many hardened political operatives who would never be caught wearing any button cannot resist one sold at the end of campaigns: "Good Job, Kid ... Now Get Lost."

buzzword A snippet of jargon; or, a vague vogue word intended to trigger a stereotyped response.

A buzzword can be a CODE WORD that subtly appeals to the emotions of those who "get it." When President Carter, angered at the congressional mangling of his energy proposals in October 1977, lashed the oil-industry lobbyists in tones reminiscent of Harry Truman, American Gas Association president George Lawrence replied, "While buzzwords like 'war profiteers' and 'rob' and 'ripoff' might prove successful in inflaming public opinion, they cannot substitute for the production incentives so flagrantly lacking in the Administration's energy plan."

The more common meaning of *buzzword* comes from the derivation of *buzz* as a verbalized hum or hiss: a sense-dulling bit of jargon that puts the outsider to sleep. (*The buzz* represents the latest word or rumor.) In a 1974 book, *Buzzwords*, Robert Kirk Mueller defined the word on the cover as "words, phrases or zingo-lingo used by an ingroup, a cult, or the cognoscenti for rapid communication within the group ... it refers also to the verbal, intellectual one-upmanship of the cant, slang, jargon, argot and pseudo-tribal language, used by relatively small groups for their own benefit and to help isolate the group from the hoi polloi ... a sort of pro's prose." He credits the word's coinage to Professor Ralph Hower of Harvard, who "used the label *buzzwords* for those phrases that have a pleasant buzzing sound in your ears while you roll them on your tongue and that may overwhelm you into believing you know what you're talking about when you don't."

Buzz phrases include "conceptual framework" (a grand-design favorite of Henry Kissinger's); "going toes up" or "going down the tubes" (to fail, except when used by surfers); "junior angel" (euphemism for the euphemism "senior citizen"); and in 2007, "the way forward" (formerly "the road ahead"). For others, see PENTAGONESE; BAFFLEGAB; GOBBLEDYGOOK; CIA-ESE.

by-election An election in a locality between general elections.

This is British usage; Americans prefer *special election* to describe a race that takes place when an incumbent dies or resigns. *By-electioneering* is campaigning by or for candidates during these times, and it is interpreted as a test for the popularity of the party in power.

Byzantine Convoluted; Machiavellian; characterized by scheming, double-crossing, backbiting, and similarly nefarious behavior often attributed to the denizens of the center of power; or, labyrinthine, arcane, mysteriously complex.

The word was probably introduced to politics by Theodore Roosevelt about 1916, criticizing President Woodrow Wilson as a "Byzantine logothete." Since a logothete in Byzantium was an accountant or collector of revenues (from the Greek "to put to account"), former President Roosevelt was derogating President Wilson as one who fiddled with a pencil while World War I called for American intervention.

But *Byzantine* in that phrase only located the main word, which was *logothete*; the Machiavellian nature of the word *Byzantine* did not appear until later. Arthur Koestler was fond of using this word to describe intricate political workings: "In the old days people often smiled at the Byzantine structure of the Spanish Army," he wrote in 1937, adding in another work eight years later, "The antidote to Eastern Byzantinism is Western revolutionary humanism." A different, if related, meaning prevails in the U.S. "Was French party politics," Peter Braestrup wrote in 1966, "with its Byzantine maneuvers and its feuding factions, really en route to a transformation?" To most U.S. political writers, the synonym for *Byzantine* is "deviously complicated."

To some in the clergy, *Byzantinism* has an altogether different meaning: the denial of religious freedom, or the belief that the civil power controls the spiritual power.

The adjective comes from the city of *Byzantium*, later Constantinople, now Istanbul, which became the capital of the Roman Empire around A.D. 330, and for seven hundred years was the main repository of Roman and Greek civilization. However, the court of the emperor—usually named Constantine—was marked by rivalries, duplicity, and violence, giving the word a bad name today.

C

cabal Group hatching a dark political plot; always carries a sinister connotation.

Derived from the Hebrew word *qabbalah*, "received doctrine," the mystical interpretation of Scripture said to be handed down to the rabbis by Moses, the word was popularized in the Middle Ages by *Cabbalists*, a splinter movement in Judaism protesting against religious formalism. The system degenerated into occult formulas and medieval magic.

An inner group of advisers to Charles II of England was known as the *Cabal*, because the initials of the five key ministers—Chudleigh, Ashley, Buckingham, Arlington, and Lauderdale—formed the word. An anonymous pamphleteer applied the label to the five in the 1673 *England's Appeal from the private Cabal at Whitehall to the Great Council of the nation*, but they were not a conspiracy in the sinister sense of the term.

John Quincy Adams wrote in his diary of 1821: "I would take no one step to advance or promote pretensions to the Presidency. If that office was to be the prize of cabal and intrigue, of purchasing newspapers, bribing by appointments, or bargaining for foreign missions, I had no ticket in that lottery."

George Brinton McClellan Harvey, editor of *Harper's Weekly*, used the term to describe the group of "irreconcilables" (including Senators Lodge, Brandegee, and McCormack) who opposed Woodrow Wilson's League of Nations just after World War I. William Allen White of the *Emporia Gazette* believed a cabal was responsible for Warren Gamaliel Harding's nomination during the 1920 Republican National Convention. He wrote: "Oil controlled the convention of 1920. It worked through the 'Senate cabal' whose members were so busy hating Wilson that they became easy victims of the greed for oil."

Former President Dwight D. Eisenhower refused to join what he termed a *cabal* organized prior to the 1964 Republican convention. Refuting newspaper statements claiming he was supporting Governor William Scranton of Pennsylvania for the presidential nomination, the General informed Governor Scranton that he would be no part of a "stop Goldwater" movement forming within party ranks: the movement promptly collapsed.

Conspiracy theorists abound on the Internet, where rumors of nasty plots and nefarious schemes can easily be spread and ricochet around the world. One group on Usenet, however, with a sense of humor, disseminated an acronym that became famous among bloggers: TINC, standing for "There Is No Cabal." By insisting on denying a cabal's existence, it fanned the suspicion that cabals were everywhere, satisfying many who enjoy believing that cabals are manipulating everything.

Caesarism See ELEPHANT, REPUBLICAN.

calculated risk Action taken when inaction or an alternate course offer greater possibilities of danger; a step soberly taken after the likely consequences have been assessed.

This is believed to be a World War II phrase of Army Air Force origin; risks of possible bomber losses were calculated before missions were decided upon, and the risk weighed against the potential reward if the mission was successful and the target destroyed. A play by Joseph Hayes, *Calculated Risk*, appeared on Broadway in 1961. Mrs. Omar Bradley told the author in 1978 that the phrase was coined by her husband, second in command to General Eisenhower, in a wartime briefing.

Whenever a political figure takes a chancy step, he often labels it a *calculated risk*, indicating he fully understands what he is likely to suffer. In a sense, it is a pre-alibi statement. Humorist James Thurber, writing in *Punch*, put it this way: "I have made some study of the smoke-screen phrases of the political terminologists, and they have to be described rather than defined. *Calculated Risk*, then, goes like this: 'We have every hope and assurance that the plan will be successful, but if it doesn't work we knew all the time it wouldn't and said so.'"

"With what he [President Kennedy] privately acknowledged to be a 'calculated risk,'" wrote Ted Sorensen, the president's alter ego, "he named a panel of conservative private enterprise skeptics to review his 1963 A.I.D. request. That panel, under General Lucius Clay, recommended cuts while strongly defending the program. [Appropriations Subcommittee Chairman Otto] Passman and Company ignored the defense, accepted the cuts and made still more cuts—and Kennedy's gamble backfired."

Camelot An idealization of the administration of President John F. Kennedy; now usually used in irony.

Camelot, in the legend of King Arthur, was the city that was home to the Knights of the Round Table. A Lerner-Loewe musical drama of that title starring Richard Burton and Julie Andrews was popular on Broadway at the beginning of the Kennedy Administration, and its evocation of excellence, hope, taste, and high courage was seized upon as symptomatic of the idealism of the "new generation" to whom the torch had been passed in Washington, D.C.

Satirist Vic Gold defined the word in 1969 as "mythical U.S. Liberal era" when all men were equal, all women were beautiful, witty, and well-groomed, and Republicans knew their place. By the 1980s, in light of revelations of peccadilloes and Mafia relationships, *Newsweek* was referring to "Camelittle." See GOVERNMENT-IN-EXILE.

CHARISMA was much spoken of at the time, but the years brought a sober reassessment. "Lyndon Johnson suffered to the end," wrote *New York Times* columnist Russell Baker in 1974, after the Nixon resignation, "from the suspicion that he lacked both 'charisma' and 'style,' and often seemed deluded by the notion that but for their lack he could have raised a higher 'Camelot.'" Deriding the public relations style of the

Nixon men and alluding to the development of this kind of "p.r." in the Kennedy days, Baker observed: "Politicians will not revive 'Camelot' for a while now. Every disaster has its bright side."

When President Bill Clinton spoke glowingly of his chance as a teenager to meet JFK in Washington, Curtis Wilkie wrote in *The Boston Globe*: "That was the last summer of Camelot, when Washington seemed to young Democrats to be suffused with earnest enthusiasm and perpetually decorated with cherry blossoms."

campaign As a noun, the term is applied to virtually all phases of an effort to win any kind of election, but most particularly the phase involving open, active electioneering; as a verb, to strive for a political nomination or office.

This term has been part of American politics at least since the turn of the nineteenth century. In Massachusetts, John Quincy Adams observed that the 1816 "parliamentary campaign hitherto has been consumed in one laborious effort to suppress the reformers." To provincial journals inland, the term was familiar.

Campaign comes from the French word for open, level country and evolved from there into the military vocabulary, where it was first used to denote the amount of time an army was kept in the field; later it denoted a particular military operation. In seventeenth-century England, the term was extended to politics and usually meant "a session of a legislative body." The meaning further evolved in transatlantic passage as the business of getting elected to public office grew more complex. But the idea that politics is a form of combat remains. When he accepted the Democratic nomination for president in 1932, Franklin Roosevelt told the convention: "This is more than a political campaign. It is a call to arms." See ARENA.

For other political terms with military origins, see ON THE POINT and MILITARY METAPHORS.

campaign oratory Exaggerated charges, promises, or claims made during the heat of a campaign, expected by the speaker to be taken with a grain of salt, to be deprecated and softened after the campaign is over.

Thomas Macaulay observed: "The object of oratory alone is not truth, but persuasion." Theodore Roosevelt told Henry L. Stimson, in regard to William Howard Taft's campaigning: "Darn it, Harry, a campaign speech is a poster, not an etching!" Stimson got the point, and FDR's Secretary of War later wrote: "A man's campaign speeches are no proper subject for the study of a friendly biographer."

Ted Sorensen agreed: "John Kennedy would not want to be measured solely by the speeches we ground out day and night across the country—and neither would I…some, particularly near the close, were overly caustic and captious in their criticism of Nixon." Arthur Schlesinger, Jr., made the same point: "[Kennedy] began by appearing to adopt the thesis that the State Department should have listened to its pro-Batista ambassadors and recognized the revolution as a communist conspiracy from the outset. This differed markedly from his interpretation in *The Strategy of Peace*. Doubtless it was campaign oratory."

The phrase, in exactly that meaning, was firmly fixed in the political lexicon by Wendell Willkie during the campaign of 1940. His hoarse voice had rasped: "if the present Administration is restored to power for a third term our democratic system will not outlast another four years." And "on the basis of his past performance with pledges to the people, you may expect war by April, 1941 if he [FDR] is elected." After his defeat, Willkie traveled to England at FDR's behest, held long talks with Winston Churchill, and returned to the U.S. to urge that the U.S. send Britain all available bombers. In Lend-Lease hearings, Senator Gerald P. Nye (R-N.D.) asked how he could square that position with his earlier charges against FDR. Willkie took a long pause in his testimony, grinned and shrugged: "It was just a bit of campaign oratory." Representative Joseph P. Martin, then Republican National Chairman, recalls: "Republicans in Congress were particularly incensed…it undermined all the criticism that had been

made of the President's foreign policy in the campaign."

Just as there is an unwritten law that takes for granted campaign exaggerations, there is also an unwritten law that a candidate may not afterward disown his campaign statements and leave his supporters in exposed positions.

In its pejorative sense, *oratory* has been overtaken by RHETORIC.

campaign promises Pledges made by a candidate to gain certain things for his constituents after election.

This has been central to politicking since elections began. Said a sign on a first-century Roman wall: "Genialis urges the election of Bruttius Balbus as duovir [commission member]. He will protect the treasury." A candidate's promises, like a party platform, are rarely taken as literal commitments. Often they seem part of a game in which candidates out-promise each other, accuse each other of making rash promises and cite the opposition's unfulfilled promises left over from previous elections.

Occasionally a particular promise takes on major—even historic—importance. One such was Dwight Eisenhower's pledge to "go to Korea" if elected in 1952, taken by most voters to mean he would end the war. But for the most part, Bernard Baruch's admonition seems valid. "Vote for the man who promises least," said Baruch. "He'll be the least disappointing."

The classic campaign-promise story is recounted by Senator Russell Long (D-La.) about his uncle, Governor Earl Long. He had promised voters the right to elect their local sheriffs, but once in office, went in the opposite direction. When a delegation came to "Uncle Earl's" office to protest, Senator Long told the author, "Uncle Earl told his right-hand man, 'I don't want to see 'em—you see 'em.' His aide said, 'What'll I tell 'em?' And Uncle Earl said, right out, 'Tell 'em I lied!' "

campaign songs Ditties using the candidates' names, usually putting words to melodies already popular and whipped up for use at rallies, conventions, and similar events; occasionally, a tune and set of lyrics adopted whole as a candidate's theme.

Although few major campaigns run their course today without producing a song or two, original political music had its zenith in the nineteenth century, when not only was one's candidate boosted, but the opposition roundly and rhythmically knocked. William Henry Harrison became famous in the Indian battle of Tippecanoe, Indiana Territory, in 1811. Thus the song when he ran for President against the more citified Martin Van Buren in 1840: "Old Tip he wears a homespun coat. / He has no ruffled shirt-wirt; / But Mat he has a golden plate, / And he's a little squirt-wirt-wirt." Said a contemporary journalist: "It was a ceaseless torrent of [Whig] music. ... If a Democrat tried to speak, argue or answer...he was only saluted with a fresh deluge." When Harrison's grandson Benjamin ran in 1888, the Republicans sang: "Yes, Grandfather's hat fits Ben—fits Ben; / He wears it with dignified grace, oh yes!"

The "Battle Hymn of the Republic" provided music for songs both pro and con. The opposition in 1872 sang: "We'll hang Horace Greeley to a sour apple tree ..." Four years later, the Republican supporters of Rutherford Hayes and William Wheeler offered this chorus: "Glory, glory Hayes and Wheeler. / As we go voting on." Candidates generally grin and bear the songs invented for them. Growled U. S. Grant: "I know but two tunes; one of them is Yankee Doodle and the other isn't." (A century later, the melody of the "Battle Hymn" provided the somber background for a Kennedy funeral cortege.)

Ring Lardner wrote a number called "Teddy, You're a Bear" in honor of Bull Mooser Theodore Roosevelt. Some of the most famous campaign songs of the twentieth century were Al Smith's theme, "Sidewalks of New York," FDR's "Happy Days Are Here Again," and Eisenhower's "I Like Ike," written for him by Irving Berlin. The rousing melody of "Hello, Dolly" became "Hello, Lyndon" for political purposes in 1964; when Goldwater enthusiasts tried to use "Hello, Barry," producer David Merrick, a Democrat, threatened to sue.

In the 1961 New York mayoralty campaign, a songwriter came up with "Lefkowitz, Gilhooley and Fino," an original ditty which—when translated and sung in Spanish from sound trucks for the city's Puerto Rican residents—was astonishing in its lack of impact.

Rather than create new songs, hard for amateurs to learn, managers now prefer to adapt and identify with popular music. Robert Kennedy started this trend with "This Land Is Our Land"; Bill Clinton continued it with Fleetwood Mac's "Don't Stop (Thinking About Tomorrow)," sung at the 1992 convention that nominated him.

campaign trail See STUMP; HUSTINGS.

campaign train A caravan on rails, containing candidate, political advisers, press, local candidates, and financial supporters, with an aura of "going to the people."

There are no free train rides for candidates, including presidents who are campaigning. The Interstate Commerce Commission in the Taft Administration laid down the rule to stop "deadheading" by politicians. This rule was bent slightly in the case of presidents requiring Secret Service accompaniment, after Calvin Coolidge decided to save some money by traveling to the Black Hills of South Dakota as a drawing-room passenger.

FDR, not especially remembered for his railroad campaigning, covered more than 350,000 miles in 399 railroad trips during his presidency, many on campaign jaunts. "On his trips," wrote White House correspondent Charles Hurd, "Roosevelt normally had to buy from six to eight tickets—for himself, Mrs. Roosevelt or other family members, and for two or three actual staff members. Newspapers were billed for the transportation of their representatives. The Treasury Department paid for the Secret Service agents. ... Thus in pinch-penny luxury the President toured the country in what was euphemistically described as 'The Presidential Special Train.'"

Thomas E. Dewey called his campaign train "The Victory Special," and it was the scene of a grievous error (see his "idiot engineer" gaffe in BLOOPER); Harry Truman popularized a new political word (see WHISTLESTOPPING) in his 21,000-mile, 300-speech GIVE 'EM HELL campaign of 1948; Barry Goldwater named his train the "Baa Hozhnilne" (Navaho for "to win over"); and Lyndon Johnson, campaigning for Vice President in 1960, cut a swath through the South in his "Corn Pone Special." (Naming the mode of transportation is traditional; in 2000, John McCain called his bus "the Straight Talk Express.")

The pressures of life on a campaign train were described by PERENNIAL CANDIDATE Harold Stassen, explaining why General Eisenhower in 1952 allowed himself to be persuaded to remove a statement about General George Marshall from a speech in an area friendly to Senator Joseph McCarthy. "It's easy to judge harshly," Stassen said, "sitting back here in New York and not knowing the pressures that go on inside that insane campaign train. You are trapped there. There are just a few people near you whom you trust. You don't have a chance to get out in the clean air and think things through.... And when all of them around you gang up, to insist you do this or that, it is just about impossible to fight back."

A campaign train, in an era of television and jet airplanes, symbolizes the old virtues of face-to-face personal campaigning, of "life on the campaign trail," of "being out on the hustings." A candidate seeking votes in this manner shows how much he or she wants the job. Because television crews accompany the train, the *whistle-stop* audiences "fill the screen." The campaign train has become a useful, expensive "prop" or backdrop for speeches aimed at a national television audience. See BRING US TOGETHER.

Camp David See SPIRIT OF.

candidate An office seeker, often the object of scorn, but *the* candidate is the party's chosen standard-bearer, cherished and adulated by supporters, a worrisome threat to opponents.

Candidates for high office come in all sizes, from James Madison (five feet four inches, 100 pounds) to Abraham Lincoln (six feet four inches) to William Howard Taft (332 pounds).

The word comes from the Latin *candidatus*, wearer of a white toga, which the Roman office seekers always wore as a symbol of purity. The same root gave the language *candor* and *incandescence*, qualities that candidates occasionally have.

Candidates have a variety of styles and methods of campaigning (see WHISTLESTOPPING; FRONT-PORCH CAMPAIGN; WHIRLWIND CAMPAIGN; WHISPERING CAMPAIGN) and surround themselves in different ways (see BRAIN TRUST; PALACE GUARD; HANDLER).

Few candidates will confess that they hate the idea of meeting people (see PRESSING THE FLESH) or attending dinners (see RUBBER-CHICKEN CIRCUIT). All claim to find campaigning exhilarating and a "great opportunity to meet the people"; some actually find it so. Many have to grit their teeth to crack a smile and some would rather shake a fist than shake a hand.

In Shakespeare's *Coriolanus*, the proud Roman general becomes a candidate for consul and must submit to the indignity of soliciting votes from common citizens. He puts on the white toga and asks a citizen: "Well then, I pray, your price of the consulship?" The imperious general is startled by the citizen's mild, perceptive reply: "The price is to ask it kindly."

Candidates may be *undeclared* (example: Edmund Muskie in 1971) or DARK HORSE (James Polk in 1844, Wendell Willkie in 1940) or *perennial* (see PERENNIAL CANDIDATE); they may be *reluctant*, as Adlai Stevenson was described in 1952, or *captive* (see CAPTIVE CANDIDATE), as Stevenson called Eisenhower in 1952; they may style themselves as *unbossed* candidates or *no-deal* candidates, or be styled by their opponents as "the candidate of the LUNATIC FRINGE." In current use an *undeclared* candidate needs only a formal announcement, usually after a half-dozen broad hints that he intends to announce, at which point he becomes an *avowed* candidate.

At a Republican governors conference in 1967, Nelson Rockefeller declined to hold a press conference because, as he said, "I am not a candidate." When reporters complained that another noncandidate, Ronald Reagan, had held a press conference earlier that week, Rockefeller smiled and said, "Well, he's a different kind of not-a-candidate."

canine metaphors See ATTACK DOG; BIRD DOG ... KENNEL DOG; CHECKERS SPEECH; FALA SPEECH; WATCHDOG COMMITTEE.

cannibalism See IDEOLOGY.

cant Favorite words of public figures.

Eighteenth-century English theologian William Paley declared: "There is such a thing as a peculiar word or phrase cleaving, as it were, to the memory of a writer or speaker, and presenting itself to his utterance at every turn. When we observe this, we call it a *cant* word or *cant* phrase." This is not the shortening of *cannot;* rather, the word calls up the secret slang of thieves, the jargon of bureaucrats, or the favored vogue words of politicians.

A word that keeps popping up in Thomas Jefferson's writings is *boisterous:* "Timid men ... prefer the calm of despotism to the *boisterous* sea of liberty." "The whole commerce between master and slave is a perpetual exercise of the most *boisterous* passions." And Theodore Roosevelt, exponent of "the *strenuous* life," used the word *strenuous* repeatedly.

Adlai Stevenson had an addiction to *felicitous;* his friend, Arthur Schlesinger, Jr., turned often to *odious*. John F. Kennedy used *vigor* so often and with such a distinctive Boston accent ("vigah") that it became the butt of jokes; Dwight Eisenhower harped on *deeds;* Lyndon Johnson probably used *must* more often than any other President (thirty-one times in his 1964 message to Congress alone); and Richard Nixon liked to say *perfectly clear* until it became too much of a trademark. Jimmy Carter laid great stress on his aversion to *disharmoniousness* and *incompatibility*, and substituted *reticent* for *reluctant*. Ronald Reagan began most sentences with "Well, ..."; the elder George Bush liked *prudent;* Bill Clinton liked *hope* and tried hard to sell

covenant; and Bush the younger changed *decision-maker* to *decider* and resuscitated *heck.*

can't-win technique A method of pouring cold water on a hot candidacy; an appeal to delegates to set aside affection and loyalty and even their judgment of ability, to concentrate on the man with "electability."

"Perhaps the most important single influence in the decision of the delegates," observed Thomas E. Dewey in 1950, "is whether they believe a candidate can win if he is nominated."

Henry Clay was among the first to find that out. As a national figure in 1840 and as leader of one of the Whig factions opposing Martin Van Buren and the Jacksonian Democrats, the senator from Kentucky had considerable delegate strength. Thurlow Weed of New York, a powerful editor and behind-the-scenes political figure, decided on the anti-Clay strategy: "Clay can't win." To undermine Clay's support, Weed organized a "triangular correspondence": men professing to be Clay supporters wrote to other state leaders hoping they were having better luck drumming up Clay support than the writer. The men who received the letters were also in on the plot: they in turn showed the letters to genuine Clay supporters with a sorrowful "we like him, but *Clay can't win.*" It worked and Martin Van Buren got the Whig nomination.

In more recent times, Ohio Senator Robert A. Taft—"Mr. Republican"—lost the nomination to Willkie in 1940, let Ohio's John Bricker make the race in 1944 (on the Dewey ticket), lost to Dewey in 1948, and lost his last chance to Eisenhower in 1952.

Taft had been given a taste of the *Taft can't win* treatment in 1948, and tried to bury it forever in a landslide senatorial victory in 1950. He carried Ohio by 430,000 votes that year, in the teeth of vigorous labor opposition; despite the impressive demonstration, he was met in the 1952 convention with the same headshaking from Eisenhower supporters—"*Taft can't win.*"

To be accused of being "one of life's losers" is difficult to shake off, especially in a field where the graceful acceptance of defeat is not widely admired. ("Show me a good loser, and I'll show you a loser" is listed under LOSER.) Only election victory can dispose of a loser image; curiously, a triumph over a "can't win" charge in gaining a nomination is itself a long step toward establishing "electability." After his defeat for president and then for governor, Richard Nixon showed that in his comeback of 1968; he was later accused of being a "sore winner."

Senator Mike Monroney (D-Okla.), as a congressman in the '60s, captured the essence of the effect of the *can't-win* charge: "They can say you are a liar, a cheat, a crackpot, and a licentious old man, and most politicians don't care. But if they say you can't win, you're through."

Canucks French Canadians; sometimes, but less frequently, taken to be a slur.

In the primary campaign of 1972, Democratic Senator Edmund Muskie of Maine, campaigning in the snows of New Hampshire, was hit by a charge scrawled in a letter to the *Manchester Union Leader* that the candidate, while in Florida, had laughed at a description of French-Canadians as *Canucks*.

The "Canuck letter" is now judged to have been spurious, and the Florida incident denied; a White House aide was charged with the DIRTY TRICK, and denied it. But the *Canuck* charge, along with printed derogation of his wife, brought a reaction from Muskie that was seen as excessively tearful and cost him much support.

The author, in an Op-Ed column, used *Canuck* in passing and received an objection from a fellow writer who said it was a racial or national slur. The *Oxford English Dictionary* labels it "in U.S. usage, gen[erally] derogatory." A query to the *Régie de la langue française* in Quebec brought this response from Jacques Robichaud, Secretary: "French-Canadians do not use the word 'Canuck.' English-speaking Canadians use it sparingly in familiar speech, for example: 'The Vancouver Canuck Hockey Team.' I am personally unaware that the use of this word by Canadians of either language offends Canadians of French descent...In the final analysis, the context in which a word is used

is the only, the real guide as to whether or not it is derogatory."

The then Prime Minister of Canada, Pierre Trudeau, also queried, also responded in welcome detail in 1977:

As with all slang, and especially that of nationality, the implications of the word vary a great deal according to the context and the intent of the speaker or writer. Opinion also varies as to who exactly is designated by the word Canuck. Many Canadians feel it refers to all Canadians, some believe it is Eastern Canadians, others that it is French Canadians, while the majority have rarely heard it used in any context.

Although much less widely used than the word "Yankee," its connotations have more or less the same range. We have a hockey team called the Vancouver Canucks, as you have a baseball team called the New York Yankees. "Johnny Canuck" was the personification of an English Canadian war hero in a comic strip. The Yankee of "I'm a Yankee doodle dandy" ... is not the same as "Yankee, go home." Thus, you can see that the question you have posed is not easily answered. Whether or not you committed an ethnic slur would depend entirely on the way the word was used.

You asked more precisely about French Canadians' attitude to this word. Personally, I have never heard it used pejoratively in connection with French Canadians, nor have I ever heard or read the term being used by French Canadians.

These comments are not intended as an official definition but rather as my own feelings in this regard. I think that in closing I might mention that, to me, a slang term applied to a nationality by a person of a different nationality could, under certain conditions, be construed as a slur.

Mitford Mathews, editor of the *Dictionary of Americanisms*, wrote in *American Speech* magazine in 1974 that he suspected the word came from the South Sea Island *kanakas*, as reported by Richard Henry Dana in his 1840 *Two Years Before the Mast*. He cited M. Schele de Vere's 1872 entry in *Americanisms: The English of the New World*: "*Canacks, Canucks*, and even *K'nucks*, are slang terms by which the Canadians are known in the United States and among themselves."

canvass As a verb, to determine the degree of support for a candidate, and sometimes in so doing, to solicit support for the candidate; as a noun, an election or a survey.

The meaning of this word has been changing. The root may be the Old French *canabasser*, "to scrutinize," or literally "to sift through canvas." For many years, the political meaning of the noun *canvass* was the final scrutiny of an election count, resulting in certification or if necessary recount. Lord Bryce used this meaning in 1888. "If all the returns have not been received, the canvass must be postponed." The noun also used to mean "election," as in Theodore Roosevelt's boast to Henry Cabot Lodge that he had made "a rattling canvass, with heavy inroads into the Democratic vote."

In recent years, a second meaning for both noun and verb has been developing: "finding out voter sentiment before the votes are cast." Pollsters *canvass* voters to find out their attitudes. The third—and newest—meaning carries over some of the polling connotation: *canvassers* are "supporters of a candidate who survey other voters with the intent of persuading the doubtful and making sure those committed get a reminder telephone call to turn out on Election Day."

Frances Costikyan, a Manhattan district leader and wife of the former leader of Tammany Hall, described some of the techniques:

Canvassing in person is infinitely more effective than a telephone campaign. As any salesman can tell you, it is much harder for people to say "no" face to face. A personal visit gives the voter a chance to size up the worker, to ask questions that bother him in a quiet conversational tone.… Most captains have discovered that those who live in the lower floors of the walk-ups (which are the slightly more expensive apartments) and the lower floors of the high-rise buildings (which are the slightly less expensive apartments) are much easier people to talk to. The very poor on the top floors of the walk-ups and the very rich on the top floors of the elevator buildings are too reluctant to commit themselves to anything as public or "controversial" as politics, or too uninterested, to be bothered with us.

A British canvasser is a *knocker-up*.

capitalism See AMERICAN WAY OF LIFE; FREE ENTERPRISE.

captive candidate One under the domination of others; an attack phrase used when the opponent is too well liked for direct assault.

The phrase came into prominence during the 1952 presidential campaign. Republicans first attacked Adlai Stevenson as being "the captive of the big-city bosses," particularly Jake Arvey of Chicago. Stevenson took up the phrase and turned it around: "They describe me as a 'captive' candidate. They say I am the 'captive' of the big city bosses, and then of the CIO, and then of the Dixiecrats, and then of Wall Street, and then of an organization called A.D.A.… I had no idea I was so popular, and I hope I can bear this multiple courtship and captivity with becoming modesty… meanwhile, it's not too uncomfortable to be captured by most everybody—except the Republican Old Guard!"

After General Eisenhower had won the 1952 Republican nomination in Chicago and had a unity meeting with his opponent, Senator Robert A. Taft (see SURRENDER ON MORNINGSIDE HEIGHTS), Democrats pressed hard on the "captive" idea, since it was difficult to attack Eisenhower directly. "I am beginning to wonder who won at Chicago," said Stevenson. "Perhaps there is a six-star general somewhere in the Republican party." In 1984, Walter Mondale tried hard to counter Republican attacks that he was a captive of organized labor, known as "the union bosses."

The phrase harks back to images of Harding manipulated by the predatory "Ohio gang" around him; it has been used on all levels of politics when a popular candidate offers a difficult target to attack.

card-carrying Committed; firmly a member of; dedicated.

The phrase gained currency in the '30s, used to differentiate "hardcore" Communist party members from FELLOW TRAVELERS, "left-wingers," and others without actual membership who sympathized with Communist party aims.

Senator Joseph McCarthy revived the phrase in the early '50s with his charge that there were "card-carrying Communists" in the State Department.

The phrase was adopted, in a jocular way, to describe dedicated, ROCK-RIBBED Republicans; "one Chicago newspaperman last week characterized him [Robert A. Taft]," wrote a *New York Times* reporter in 1952, "as a 'card-carrying Republican.'" Syndicated columnist William S. White wrote in 1967 of Richard Nixon that "he is still Mr. Republican to the regular and, so to speak, card-carrying Republicans." That tongue-in-cheek use would be considered a smear if applied to liberals, but is permissible to be applied to conservatives because of the sharpness of the contrast with Communists.

In the 1988 presidential campaign, Vice President George H.W. Bush used the phrase against Governor Michael Dukakis, pointing to his membership in the American Civil Liberties Union; *The Washington Post* noted "there is hardly a state in which Bush has not called Dukakis 'a card-carrying member of the ACLU,'" which the editorialist charged was "evocative of McCarthyism." Bush did not let up.

A candidate who has suffered through defeats or has labored for the party through thick and thin is said to have "paid his dues."

card metaphors

"The bizarre world of cards," wrote Ely Culbertson, bridge expert active in public affairs, is "a world of pure power politics where rewards and punishments were meted out immediately. A deck of cards was built like the purest of hierarchies, with every card a master to those below it, a lackey to those above it. And there were 'masses'—long suits—which always asserted themselves in the end, triumphing over the kings and aces."

Because of the play of power in card games, the metaphor has been applied to politics for centuries. A German poet in 1521 talked of rearranging the affairs of men by "shuffling the cards in a better way," and Thomas Hobbes, in his *Leviathan* (1651), wrote: "there is no honour military but by war, nor any such hope to mend an ill game, as by causing a new shuffle."

In U.S. politics, John Quincy Adams referred to Henry Clay, a renowned poker player, as "a gamester in politics as well as cards." A poker player a century later, Warren G. Harding, explained his own selection as a candidate in the SMOKE-FILLED ROOM in these terms: "We drew to a pair of deuces and filled."

FDR pointed to Mark Twain's *Connecticut Yankee* as the source of the best-known card metaphor, *new deal*: "in a country where only six people out of a thousand have any voice in the government," says Twain's Yankee, "what the 994 dupes need is a new deal." But the phrase was used in a political context throughout the nineteenth century. See NEW DEAL; SQUARE DEAL.

Terms like *ace in the hole, a fast shuffle, dealing from the bottom of the deck, up his sleeve, call a bluff,* etc., are all card expressions used as commonly in politics as in everyday speech. *Wheeler-dealer*, however, seems limited to big business and national politics, and Lyndon Johnson was attacked by Michigan Governor George Romney in 1967 as he compared the New Deal and Fair Deal with the "Fast Deal."

When President Carter's National Security Adviser, Zbigniew Brzezinski, picked up a term several Washington columnists were using in 1978 to describe the leverage on the Soviets of a move toward Beijing, Soviet leader Leonid I. Brezhnev charged that "attempts are being made lately in the U.S.A., at a higher level and in a rather cynical form, to play the 'Chinese card' against the U.S.S.R."

John Ehrlichman, director of the Domestic Council in the Nixon White House and jailed after the Watergate scandal, wrote an embittered roman à clef in 1986 titled *The China Card*.

In 2007, Gerald Horne, an editor of politicalaffairs.net, "Marxist thought online," in giving his hard-left take on *China card*, included this research: "Let me begin by quoting the fortunately retired NY Times right-wing hack columnist William Safire: 'Before Nixon died,' he said, 'I asked him—on the record—if perhaps we had gone a bit overboard on selling the American public on the political benefits of increased trade with China. That old realist who had played the *China card* to exploit the split in the Communist world, replied with some sadness that he was not as hopeful as he had once been: "We may have created a Frankenstein [monster]," said Nixon.'"

See STAND PAT; BUCK STOPS HERE, THE; GO IT ALONE; SLEEPER; FINESSE; BIG CASINO.

caretaker One placed in power only to save or protect the position for another; a seat-warmer.

Despondent Democratic leaders in 1948, certain that Truman could not defeat Dewey, insisted that Senator Alben W. Barkley go on the Truman ticket as vice presidential nominee, so that—in Arthur Krock's words—"he would be in a position to act as 'caretaker' of the Democratic organization during four and perhaps eight years out of power."

When John F. Kennedy was elected president, Governor Foster Furcolo of Massachusetts appointed Benjamin Smith II to replace him as senator; columnists pointed out that it was common knowledge that Smith was acting as *caretaker* of the seat to be sought later by Ted Kennedy.

Meanwhile, the same word was used to needle President Johnson, as the president who would simply warm the seat of power until another Kennedy (Robert) could run for the office. By quickly adopting his own style and asserting the "LBJ brand" of leadership, he dispensed with the notion that he would ever be a *caretaker president*. The word was used to disparage Gerald Ford in 1976.

A *caretaker government*, however, is not a derogatory label; it is one set in place during parliamentary interregnums to maintain order, pay bills, and await the incoming administration.

carpetbagger An outlander moving into a new area to seek political power at the expense of local politicians.

"We see that the Republican caucus has resolved to let loose upon us twenty more men armed with carpet bags," noted an editorialist of the December 14, 1867 issue of the Galveston (Texas) *Flake's Bulletin*. The irate opinion piece, unearthed through a computer search of "America's Historical Newspapers" by Newsbank and

the American Antiquarian Society, was headed "The Carpet Baggers" and gave the definition:

"A carpet bagger in the political nomenclature of the day is an itinerant lecturer and political speaker. They come from the North and journey Southward. Their ostensible mission is to open the political eyes of the blind black men and to comfort the hearts of heart-broken loyalists." Calling the carpetbagger "an ignoramus of the first water," Flake added fervently, "We wish from the very bottom of our hearts that every one of these wandering lecturers would sprain his ankle joint, get the gout, the sour apple complaint or any other mild form of physical ill for the balance of his born days, or at least until after reconstruction is completed."

The carpetbag was a symbol of the man who traveled light, and hence of the man on the make. Before the Civil War, a carpetbagger was an itinerant banker with meager assets who operated in sparsely settled areas. The term *carpetbagger* gained wide currency in the South during the Reconstruction period as Northerners of the period were able to control many public offices with the help of federal troops and discriminatory laws. Congressman S. S. Cox of New York said in 1875, "The carpetbagger had little to go on and much to get. He made out of Negro credulity a living and he made the Negro his prey."

Even during Reconstruction, the term began to be applied outside the South to any non-native politician. Representative James Brooks found it necessary to defend himself in 1868 with this statement: "I was born in the State of Maine and went to New York with a trunk 30 years ago. I did not go there three months ago with a carpet bag." In 1964, another New Englander went to New York and found himself accused of being a carpetbagger. Robert Kennedy was so freshly arrived in the state when he ran for senator that he was repeatedly spoofed: one gag had him appearing before an audience of New Yorkers saying, "Fellow New Yorkites ..." and another clever canard had him asking, "Where *are* the Bronx?" He won a Senate seat anyway, as did Hillary

Clinton, who came to New York from Illinois via Arkansas and the White House.

Alan Otten, chief of the *Wall Street Journal's* Washington bureau, wrote on April 29, 1970, about the decline of the carpetbagger issue. One case was the youthful Jay Rockefeller, who campaigned in 1968 for secretary of state of West Virginia, hardly Rockefeller family territory. To blunt the carpetbagger charge, the candidate told audiences of a phone call he made to advise his uncle Nelson of his intention to introduce Senator Robert Kennedy at a Charleston rally. "There was a long pause at my uncle's end of the line, so I asked him whether he had anything against the senator. There was another long pause at my uncle's end of the line, till finally he said, 'Well, you know he *is* a carpetbagger.' And then there was a long pause at my end of the line." Otten concluded: "Jay Rockefeller won handily, and perhaps this disarming anecdote helped. Or perhaps people are not quite so concerned any more about voting for men who weren't born and bred right in the locality.... In short, 'carpetbagger' just doesn't seem as dirty a word as it once was."

See SCALAWAG.

cartoonists' symbols Reporters found Franklin Delano Roosevelt's cigarette holder an infallible press-conference barometer. Wrote Associated Press White House correspondent Jack Bell, "If the cigarette in his holder was pointed toward the ceiling and his head was thrown back, the news would be good. If he was hunched over his desk and the cigarette pointed downward, look out, somebody was going to get hell." Jonathan Daniels, a Roosevelt press aide, described Roosevelt's exultation after triumph at the polls in 1936: "His cigarette holder seemed not merely a scepter but a wand." (In 1993, the Clintons banned smoking in the White House.)

Other cartoonists' symbols include Churchill's cigar, Senator Joseph McCarthy's "five o'clock shadow," John F. Kennedy's rocking chair, John L. Lewis' eyebrows, Senator Everett Dirksen's "basset" jowls, Lincoln's stovepipe hat, Theodore Roosevelt's teeth, Coolidge's high collar, Grant's cigar stub, Robert F. Kennedy's shock of hair, Hitler's and Stalin's mustaches, Al Smith's brown derby, Nixon's ski-jump nose, Gerald Ford's Band-Aid (from bumping his head), Jimmy Carter's teeth, Margaret Thatcher's pocketbook, Reagan's forelock, Clinton's cheeks, and the younger Bush's close-set eyes.

catchword A word that crystallizes an issue, sparks a response; a technique condemned by those not imaginative enough to master it.

"Normalcy" was a *catchword*; "not nostrums but normalcy" a *catchphrase*; "back to normalcy" a *slogan*.

Catchwords and catchphrases can be dead serious, as FDR's use of DAY OF INFAMY and STAB IN THE BACK illustrates; they may take a popular expression and give it political application: "YOU NEVER HAD IT SO GOOD," "HAD ENOUGH?" Or they may build upon previous phrases, as Lyndon Johnson's "LET US CONTINUE" was built upon John F. Kennedy's "Let Us Begin."

At their best, catchphrases used as slogans summarize and dramatize a genuine appeal, the way "Vote As You Shot" did for Civil War veterans. At their worst, they are plain silly—"We Polked You in 1844, We Shall Pierce You in 1852" tried too hard.

A slogan need not contain a catchword to be effective, as "He Can Do More for Massachusetts" proved for two Kennedys, and a catchword need not be sloganized with a verb (see LEBENSRAUM).

Catchphrases rely heavily on alliteration ("Burn, Baby, Burn!"; "Tippecanoe and Tyler, Too"; "Rum, Romanism and Rebellion"), and both catchphrases and slogans often make use of rhyme ("All the Way with LBJ"; "I Like Ike"; "Jim Crow Must Go "; and Jimmy Carter's "The Grin Will Win"). For a more thorough analysis of these techniques, see SLOGAN and ALLITERATION.

At the turn of the century, Epiphanius Wilson wrote:

> To make the effect of an oration lasting in the memory of the hearers it is good to use some telling phrase or catchword in which the point of the contention is summarized or suggested. Unlettered people carry all their knowledge or wisdom in short rhymes and proverbs, which

are delightful even to the most cultivated as being portable, racy, and seasoned with a kind of wit. As models of this sort of watchword we may point to the "Peace with honor" of Beaconsfield, the "toujours l'audace" [always to dare] of Danton, "the Cross of Gold" of W. J. Bryan, the "Plumed Knight" of Ingersoll, and the "iridescent dream" of Ingalls.

The word *catchword* comes from printing. To make reading easier, John de Spira in 1469 printed at the foot of each page the first word of the next page, a boon to those who read aloud to their families. This was called the *catchword*; the main entry words in a dictionary were also printed in bold type or capital letters to catch the eye, as *catchword* is at the start of this entry and atop each page. In the theater, it has occasionally been used as a substitute for *cue*.

The greatness of a catchword or catchphrase is often its ambivalence, leaving it open to controversial interpretations for years. "A good catchword," said Wendell L. Willkie in a 1938 Town Hall debate, "can obscure analysis for fifty years." (For one obscure analysis, see ONE WORLD; also MAN IN THE STREET.)

Catholic candidate See BAILEY MEMORANDUM.

cattle show Public gathering of presidential candidates during a primary.

This derisive term has been a favorite of the political media—but not of politicians—since the late 1970s. In February 1980 *The Atlantic* poked light fun at "Another of those Saturday Republican 'cattle shows' where all the G.O.P. contenders...make brief speeches to the assembled throngs." In 1983, the TV show "Good Morning America" reported, "Democrats gathered...for the first cattle show of the 1984 campaign."

On March 3, 1983, *The New York Times* described such an event in satirical terms: "In a cattle show, national candidates are herded into a ballroom, which then becomes a kind of stockyard-showcase. Local politicians poke them to see if their flesh is pressable; national pundits prod them to find variances in their views; the local party profits on ticket sales."

When Republican Senator Robert Dole considered running for the presidency in 1984, he decided to consult with former President Richard Nixon about the strategy he should use as a candidate. *Time* magazine described in August 1985 Dole's visit to Nixon: "Dole went up to New Jersey...and found the old campaigner with candidate lists and vote projections. He advised Dole to keep his job in the Senate and stay away from the candidate 'cattle show.' Dole loved it all."

The predecessor term was *beauty contest*. An even more derisive term cropped up in the '90s about second-tier candidates, based on characters in an old tale made famous by the Grimm Brothers: the *Seven Dwarfs*.

In Ames, Iowa, in the summer before the winter caucus (more a poll of party activists than a primary election), a "straw poll" is taken at an event attended by more than 10,000 Iowans to which all announced candidates are invited. The turnout is seen as a test of the organization ability of each of the candidates.

"The lower-tier candidates," wrote the columnist Roger Simon in 2007, "—the Republican Seven Dwarfs—imagine they will go to Ames, make a terrific speech, win over the crowd, finish well, and get media attention and campaign contributions...Don't do well, and your money and support can dry up. And after this year's straw poll, the Seven Dwarfs could quickly be reduced to the Three Stooges."

caucus A closed meeting of party policy makers, originally to nominate candidates and now, more typically, to agree on a legislative program; as a verb, so to meet.

The term is genuinely American, deriving from an Indian word meaning "elder" or "counselor." John Adams in 1763 noted the existence of a discussion group in Boston called the Caucus Club. See SACHEM.

In the early days of the Republic, party machinery was rudimentary and even presidential nominations were decided in small meetings, usually of a party's congressional delegation. What is a partisan's chief duty? an Ohio paper asked rhetorically: "To obey the decrees of King Caucus." (It was common to ascribe monarchical attributes to powerful institutions: King Cotton controlled the South's agricultural economy, and the first King Cong was not an ape but the Continental Congress.)

Andrew Jackson helped start the convention system that took the caucus down several notches in importance, although small groups can sometimes still control a convention. The word once carried the connotation of "secret meeting," no outsiders from the public present, where nefarious deals were made. Henry Adams, author of the political novel *Democracy*, confided his disillusionment in a letter to Senator Henry Cabot Lodge in 1876: "When the day comes when it will be considered as disgraceful to be seen in a caucus as to be seen in a gambling house or brothel, then my interest will wake up again and legitimate politics will get a new birth."

The caucus system today, as exemplified in Iowa, which holds its position as "the earliest caucus" in presidential races, is an amalgam of votes taken at open meetings of party activists in a single state—not as representative as the primary system of enlisting all voters registered in an election of delegates to support a given candidate at a national convention, but hardly as disgraceful as what Adams imagined it had become.

cautiously optimistic The hopeful politician's straddle; having a well-guarded sense of well-being.

This phrase restricts the adjective *optimistic* by modifying it with the wary adverb *cautiously*. President Reagan, asked how he felt about the possibility of approval for his sale of AWACS aircraft to Saudi Arabia, often answered, "Cautiously optimistic." Overused by politicians who picked up Reagan's use, the phrase has become a cliché to reflect an upbeat attitude that is not imprudent. In contrast, "cautiously pessimistic" is used as rarely as "incautiously optimistic."

cell A secret unit of political activity, taking direction from a central authority but not directly connected to other units.

The word was long identified with the Communist party; exposés of membership in "Communist cells" were frequent in the '30s and '40s, culminating in the Chambers-Hiss confrontation of 1948.

Stephen Shadegg, an early Barry Goldwater supporter, discussed the value of a cellular political structure in *How to Win an Election*. He pointed to Mao Zedong's statement "Give me just two or three men in a village and I will take the village" and adapted "The Cell Group" to Goldwater's 1952 and 1958 Senate campaigns: "The individuals we enlisted became a secret weapon possessing strength, mobility, and real impact. They were able to infiltrate centers of opposition support, keep us informed of opposition tactics, disseminate information, enlist other supporters, and to do all these things completely unnoticed by the opposition.... Mao Tse-tung might have been able to take a village with just two or three men. I have learned that to guarantee success in the political effort it is desirable to have three to five per cent of the voting population enlisted in the Cell Group."

The cell imparts a sense of conspiracy to its members, a greater receptivity to ideological discipline, a direct organizational control from the top to workers at the grassroots; equally important, the seizure of one isolated cell need not lead to capture of others. In the 1990s, it became the favored organizational device of worldwide terrorist groups such as Al Qaeda and Hezbollah (the "party of God"). See BORING FROM WITHIN.

cemetery vote A fraudulent vote cast in the name of a voter who has died, but who continues to be listed on the registration rolls; generally, an extreme form of BALLOT-BOX STUFFING.

Vote fraud was long treated lightly by many politicians; "Vote early and often" is a familiar, jocular phrase on Election Day, as was "He's out jotting down the names from the tombstones," a lighthearted reference to the corrupt practices of the past.

Franklin D. Roosevelt was elected governor of New York in 1928 by a margin of 25,000 votes out of a total of 4,235,000, even as Democrat Al Smith was being trounced by Herbert Hoover in the presidential campaign. On election night he told Samuel Rosenman, "I have an idea that some of the boys upstate are up to their old tricks of delaying the vote and stealing as many as they can from us." Worried about the "cemetery vote" and illegal Republican tampering with voting machines, he put in a call to several sheriffs in upstate counties. "This is Franklin Roosevelt," he said, "the returns from your county are coming in mighty slowly, and I don't like it.... If you need assistance to keep order or to see that the vote is counted right, call me here at the Biltmore Hotel and I shall ask Governor Smith to authorize the State Troopers to assist you."

In his memoirs, Rosenman pointed out that FDR was bluffing: "There was really little that Roosevelt could do if those instructions were not followed, especially if he were not elected. But it worked—the returns began to come in more quickly. And they were better."

Few modern get-out-the-vote campaigns can compare with the results of the drive in New York in 1844. There were 41,000 people qualified to vote that year. Allowing for those who were ill that day, the turnout was heartwarming: 55,000. Reviewing that history, Bruce Felknor of the Fair Campaign Practices Committee explained wryly: "The dead filled in for the sick."

In the 1964 presidential campaign, Lyndon Johnson was under severe attack regarding previous vote-stealing episodes that worked both for him and against him. The old cemetery-vote joke, traceable back to Rutherford B. Hayes, was used again. Little boy is asked why he is crying. "For my poor dead father," he replies. "But your father's been dead for ten years." Sobbing, the boy answers, "Last night he came back to vote for Lyndon Johnson and he never came to see me."

Warren Moscow, in *Politics in the Empire State*, tells of Hudson Valley political boss Lou Payne, who admitted that he sometimes voted tombstones, but added, "We never vote a man unless he would have voted our way if he were still alive. We respect a man's convictions." More recently,

Jack Valenti, LBJ's longtime aide, who died in 2007, told friends gathered at his annual Christmas dinner the year before, "When I die, bury me in Texas, because I want to remain politically active."

censure See VOTE OF CONFIDENCE; QUOTED OUT OF CONTEXT.

center of power See POWER BROKERS; OVAL OFFICE.

centralized government See BIG GOVERNMENT; CREEPING SOCIALISM.

centrist An ideological position between extremes within a party; a member of a center party; or one closely attuned to the thinking of the majority.

Colloquial definition is MIDDLE-OF-THE-ROADER comfortable with the CONSENSUS, in the MAINSTREAM. Sometimes mistakenly used to mean a believer in centralized government. During the Truman Administration, political scientist Julius Turner wrote: "Only a Democrat who rejects a part of the Fair Deal can carry Kansas, and only a Republican who moderates the Republican platform can carry Massachusetts."

Centrist is gaining in use as a more sophisticated self-definition than *middle-of-the-roader*. A more vigorous phrase is *the vital center*, coined in 1949 by Arthur Schlesinger, Jr., as the place for pragmatic liberals to be.

The word is now used to define the area where the swing voter likes to swing and where the big decisions are made; a politician who is a centrist can attract both mildly liberal and mildly conservative votes, and can develop a pattern of positions that encompass points on both sides of an ideological fence. But historian Clinton Rossiter held that a concern for this kind of centrism need not stultify debate between parties: "The unwritten laws of American politics command that the differences between the parties be relatively few and modest, but it does not follow that those differences also be obscure. Let the parties compete for the millions of Americans in the vital center by offering alternatives that do not wrench our minds too violently in one direction or the other, but let them also offer us alternatives that can be clearly grasped."

See MIDDLE OF THE ROAD; ME, TOO; OPPORTUNIST.

century of the common man See COMMON MAN, CENTURY OF THE.

chad The tiny splinter of waste cardboard created by punching a hole in a card that became an issue in counting votes in the 2000 presidential election in Florida.

As officials in Florida scrambled to count and recount punch-card ballots in the "squeaker" race for president in 2000 between George W. Bush and Albert Gore, Jr., *The New York Times* led its report with "The leadership of the FREE WORLD may be decided by chads."

The principle of the punch-card voting machine is simple: The voter uses a metal stylus to make a hole in a rectangular box adjacent to the name of the candidate of his or her choice. This creates litter—the *chads*—left as trash in the voting machine after ballots are removed for reading and counting by an optical scanner. Unpunched boxes are regarded as nonvotes. However, the practical difficulty is that not all chads become fully detached. They are known as *hanging chads*, and they may be hinged on different sides and dangle at different angles. Moreover, the stylus sometimes does not punch through the box at all but merely leaves an indentation—making what is referred to as a *dimpled chad*. Because light does not pass through the intended perforations in the proper way, the scanner does not count such votes. They also are regarded as nonvotes, just as if the voter had made a conscious decision not to vote at all.

In Florida in 2000, the stakes were immense, and the margin of victory was minute. On November 8, the day after the election, the Republican candidate, George W. Bush, appeared to have won the state by some 1,700 votes out of six million cast. At the same time, a great many punch-card ballots—perhaps 10,000 in Palm Beach County alone—did not

show votes for president. And many of these "nonvotes" were the result of hanging chads.

Recounting the votes, whether by machine, as required by Florida law in such a close election, or manually, as demanded by the losing Democrats, raised more difficulties. Rerunning ballots through machines causes some hanging chads to open, close, or detach completely, and the more often the ballots are rerun, the more likely it is that chads will be lost. Meanwhile, human eyes may be better than optical scanners at assessing ballots to determine voters' intentions, but even when ballots are handled carefully, chads may be opened or closed. Also, people of different political persuasions may come to different conclusions when examining individual ballots.

The recount proceeded, with Bush's lead in the state dropping at one point to 327 votes. Both parties went to court, with Republicans arguing for recounts in particular counties by machines, which they felt would be unbiased, while Democrats urged that ballots throughout the state that did not show a choice for president be recounted manually, a process that they contended would produce a more accurate result. Not until December 12 did the Supreme Court of the United States rule 5–4 that variations in counting methods from county to county violated the equal-protection clause of the U.S. constitution. The justices proceeded to halt the recounting process on the grounds that the nation could not afford to wait for as long as it would take to remedy the constitutional inequity. Thus, the election was decided in Bush's favor.

Congress attempted to fix the problem in 2002 with the Help America Vote Act, but few states and localities replaced older voting systems. Newer techniques, including optical scanning of paper ballots and ATM-like touch-screen and push-button systems, are difficult for some voters to use. It seems unlikely, therefore, that voters have heard the last of *chads*.

The origin of *chad* remains unknown. The oldest example of the word found so far comes from a 1930 patent application for a "coupon printer" that featured "a receptacle or chad box ... to receive the chips cut from the edge of the tape."

At the 2001 white-tie Gridiron Club dinner in Washington, DC, the first diplomatic dignitary called on to take a bow was the ambassador from the African nation of Chad.

chameleon on plaid See UNHOLY ALLIANCE.

changing horses See DON'T CHANGE HORSES.

channels See RED TAPE.

character assassin One who wages political warfare by seeking to destroy his adversary's reputation, usually by scurrilous means.

The phrase may have originated in the *Burlington* (Iowa) *Weekly Hawkeye* in 1874: "If Tilton is a libeler and character assassin, we would like to see suit commenced against him." It came into vogue during the early 1950s, when Senator Joseph McCarthy's red-hunting forays brought down game of many hues. Besides calling the Communists-in-government issue a RED HERRING, Harry Truman, in a 1950 speech to the American Legion, denounced "scandal mongers and character assassins." Although McCarthy was a fellow Republican, Dwight Eisenhower later criticized those who "assassinate you or your character from behind." See PHILIPPIC.

Toward the end of McCarthy's period of influence, his feud with the Army itself became the subject of a congressional investigation. Joseph N. Welch, an attorney retained by the congressional committee, appeared to be shocked when the senator related how a young lawyer in Welch's firm had belonged to a tainted organization. At a poignant moment of the televised hearings, Welch—well prepared in advance for the revelation—counterattacked with "Let us not assassinate this lad further, Senator. Have you no sense of decency, sir? At long last, have you left no sense of decency?"

The congressional committee has often been a forum for character assassination. Courtroom rules of evidence do not apply. Defamation laws offer no protection because nothing said during official proceedings is actionable. Thus as early as 1876 one member of Congress complained of critics who "say that our committees of investigation are intended to strike down some loyal men, or assassinate character." The Democratic senators who began probing the Teapot Dome situation soon after the death of Warren G. Harding were described by the *New York Tribune* as "the Montana scandalmongers," by the *Post* as "mud-gunners," and by the *Times* as "assassins of character." Over the years, their stock rose as Harding's fell.

George H. W. Bush, whose supporters raised the CHARACTER ISSUE against challenger Bill Clinton, had the destructive term aimed at him during the 1992 campaign. The liberal Thomas Oliphant wrote in *The Boston Globe* of the elder Bush's body language during the televised debates: "In St. Louis, the character assassin had trouble looking straight at the camera; in Richmond, the off-his-game, disengaged President kept looking at his watch."

The use of "assassin" in the phrase gave rise to a phrase popularized in novels and movies about the Mafia: *hit job*. Gangland assassins were given assignments to "hit" or "whack" victims—that is, to kill them. In politics, *hit job* became a less sanguine trope for an attack or SMEAR. In a September 2006 interview of former president Clinton on the Fox network by Chris Wallace, the reporter dared to bring up the sensitive subject of current accusations that the Clinton administration had failed to aggressively pursue Osama bin Laden—a newsworthy question, hardly a smear; Clinton exploded with "So you did Fox's bidding on this show. You did your nice little conservative *hit job* on me." See ATTACK DOG.

character issue The question of the moral uprightness of a candidate; or, a euphemism for an attack on a candidate for philandering.

Almost always used in a verbal attack, *character issue* insinuates a negative evaluation of a candidate's personal background. The raising of this issue is meant to stimulate suspicions about a politician's ability to lead, based on information or innuendo about his or her private life. The attacker usually claims the issue is not whether the candidate committed some ethical slip or moral sin, but whether he or she lied about it—when, of course, forthright admission of a peccadillo would sink the candidacy. See ZIPPER PROBLEM.

The modern phrase has ancient roots, demonstrated by Shakespeare's study of a leader's aloofness to the opinions of voters in *Coriolanus*. The word *character*, used attributively in this noun phrase, comes from ancient Greek for "engraving tool," its meaning extended to the mark that a person makes, or the distinguishing qualities of an individual.

Character issue appeared in a September 1979 letter to *The New York Times*: "I have been impressed by the way you have handled the character issue in the cases of Bert Lance, Hamilton Jordan, Dr. Peter Bourne and others." A month later, *Newsweek* magazine quoted an unidentified Democrat warning that Senator Edward M. Kennedy's challenge to President Jimmy Carter's renomination would harm the party: "If Kennedy is the nominee, the 'character' issue will be 'fair game for the Republicans in the fall.'"

Other political phrases employing *issue* abound. These terms include *burning issue* (William Jennings Bryan's forceful replacement in the campaign of 1900 for *leading issue* and PARAMOUNT ISSUE); the 1964 *gut issue* (a visceral appeal to emotions); BREAD-AND-BUTTER ISSUE (a basic or economic issue, described in 1840 by the attributive noun phrase *bread-and-butter*); SWITCHER *issue* (a controversial topic such as gun control, same-sex marriage, abortion rights, or war policy that causes a *single-issue* voter to switch to the opposition); *social issue* (the 1970 coinage of sociologists Ben J. Wattenberg and Richard M. Scammon for the replacement of economic concerns by changing morality and social concerns); HOT-BUTTON *issue* (a 1980s term for issues that incense voters, such as perks for politicians); DIVORCE ISSUE, fading since the days of Nelson Rockefeller; and WEDGE ISSUE (used to divide coalitions). Also see ISSUES, THE.

charisma Political sex appeal; that "certain something" that campaign managers look for: a combination of attractiveness, empathy, sincerity, and smarts that turns a candidate into The Candidate.

Charisma, pronounced with a *k*, is an ancient Greek word for "gift." In theology, it is defined as a grace, such as the power to heal or to prophesy. Earlier in history, charismatic ascetics and "holy men," relying on begging for support, troubled the early Christians; St. Paul's warning "If a man does not work, neither shall he eat" was directed against the alarming spread of charismatic missionaries.

Charisma determined the fate of Chinese monarchs. If war, flood, or famine afflicted the land, it was a sign that the monarch did not possess the charismatic virtue, that he was not indeed a "son of Heaven." Max Weber, in a chapter on charismatic authority in *The Theory of Social and Economic Organization*, wrote: "The term 'charisma' will be applied to a certain quality of an individual personality by virtue of which he is set apart from ordinary men and treated as endowed with supernatural, superhuman, or at least specifically exceptional powers or qualities."

A politician with charisma can build a personal following outside his party, while developing special attachments within his party. Both Roosevelts had it; Eisenhower had it; Kennedy had it; Reagan had it. It is less spiritual than "vision" and more elemental than "style." Thomas P. F. Hoving, when director of the Metropolitan Museum of Art, said: "The man with the most charisma I ever saw, is Muñoz Marín of Puerto Rico. The minute he walks into the room, you feel it, whether you know who he is or not. The same is true of Picasso, of Haile Selassie, and de Gaulle and Chiang. Pope John had it and Pope Paul doesn't. Khrushchev had it and Stalin didn't."

Columnist Stewart Alsop, covering Ted Kennedy's Massachusetts campaign for the Senate in 1962, spoke of the candidate's *charisma* to a woman reporter, and reported her reply: "Charisma, hell. It's just plain old sex appeal." A psychological study in *The Washington Post* in 1992 tied *charisma* to sexual energy: "Indeed, a candidate's ability to generate the kind of political charisma some people crave may be psychologically inseparable from an aggressive sex drive."

In recent years, the phrase *like a rock star* has often been substituted for *charisma*. Whatever the gift is called, many Democrats preparing early for the 2008 campaign hoped that Senator Barack Obama had it.

Charles River Gang Jocular derogation of the academic-political-scientific elite in Boston, Mass.

Both Harvard University and the Massachusetts Institute of Technology have, in recent generations, been sources of valued counsel to administrations in Washington, D.C.—most often Democratic. In the mid-'70s the power of this intellectual-technological establishment was recognized by hard-liners on the staff of the Senate Armed Services Committee, led by its ranking Democrat, Senator Henry "Scoop" Jackson. Richard Perle, an acolyte of Jackson's and later a leader of neoconservative hawks, may have been the first to dub it the *Charles River Gang*; the term was picked up in the press in the late '70s and remains a mild conservative needle to liberal thinkers.

The Charles River, about 47 miles long, has an estuary which separates Boston from Cambridge. For other "gangs," see CUL-TURAL REVOLUTION and the more recent GANG OF FOURTEEN.

Charlie Name used to designate the letter *C*; also, black nickname for whites.

Three uses of *Charlie* beyond a male first name:

Checkpoint Charlie, in Berlin, was the key point of interchange between the American and Soviet sectors. It was named as part of the normal Army use of words to designate letters clearly, as Able, Baker, Charlie, Dog, etc. The significance of this particular checkpoint, plus the alliteration, made the name famous.

Victor Charlie: Members of the armed forces in Vietnam referred to the Viet Cong as "VC" or "C," which naturally became *Victor Charlie*, or simply *Charlie*. Correspon-

dent Kuno Knoebl wrote a book in 1967 titled *Victor Charlie: The Face of War in Vietnam*.

Mr. Charlie was a derisive nickname for the white man in the lexicon of the civil rights movement; author James Baldwin used the phrase in one of his most important works, *Blues for Mr. Charlie*. There appears to be no connection with the letter *C* in this use, although there might have been a derivation from *white Charley*, a name for right-wing Whig party members. The *Congressional Globe* of 1842 reported: "There seems to me as much prospect of the ultra Whigs—the 'White Charlies'—coalescing with the Democrats, as there is of Tyler and his friends."

Charlie Regan A straw man used to absorb resentment in political campaigns.

Every headquarters must turn down a certain number of well-meaning volunteers without offending them. Clunky campaign songs, meaningless or double-meaninged slogans, and painful pamphlets are submitted; these must be rejected in a way that will not diminish enthusiasm. At other times, strategic delays are necessary. That is why this phrase is so often heard: "I'll give you a firm go-ahead just as soon as Regan gets back."

Charlie Regan never does get back. He is the little man who isn't there, a fictional character, a secret known only to the three or four people at the helm of the campaign. He has a place on the Table of Organization, in a little box near the top, but off to the side with a title like "General Campaign Coordination and Liaison," his own desk, a telephone, a listing in the directory at headquarters. He has a raincoat, which is sometimes draped over his chair, sometimes neatly hung up.

But there is no Charlie Regan. Whenever anybody calls, he is "down at the printer's." Somehow, being down at a political printer's shop implies exploration of the Mindanao Deep: nobody questions its importance or total inaccessibility. More recently, he is said to be "working on the website."

At the end of the campaign, like all the other top headquarters personnel, Charlie

Regan receives a spiritually uplifting letter from the candidate, win or lose. ("Have I ever met Regan? I just can't visualize him." "Oh, you've been in a dozen meetings with him, the little balding guy who never looks up." "Sure, I remember now.") Countless public officials throughout America think they owe a favor to a man named Charlie Regan, and countless frustrated candidates blame their losses entirely on him.

James Hagerty, White House press secretary in the Eisenhower Administration, told the lexicographer, "Our Charlie Regan went by the name of Frank Pierce."

The device might have been derived from "George Spelvin," the name that a hungry actor adopts as a pseudonym when he accepts a role so minor that playing it under his own name would hurt his reputation, or the name an impecunious theatrical producer uses in a program when the same actor is playing two parts.

chattering classes A collective term for journalists, critics, pundits, "talking heads," and other members of the liberal intelligentsia, regarded dismissively as talkers rather than doers.

"When, just a week ago, Barack Obama [Democratic Senator from Illinois] showed a bit of ankle and declared the mere possibility of his running for the presidency, the chattering classes swooned," conservative columnist Charles Krauthammer wrote in *The Washington Post* in October of 2006.

The singular *class* may also be employed. Earlier in 2006, when President George W. Bush changed chiefs of staff, the *Post* reported that while the president "has by no means changed his view of what he derisively calls the 'chattering class,' the shift showed that he was paying attention to it."

The precise composition of the *chattering classes* varies according to the observer. Lawrence O'Donnell, executive producer of the TV series *The West Wing* and onetime Democratic Senate staff aide, told Anne Kornblut of *The New York Times* in 2006 that many people in government "secretly belong to the chattering classes.... When there's a change in personnel in the White House, no one talks about it more than the people working in the White House."

The reporter also sought the views of a pair labeled widely as a political "odd couple," Democratic strategist James Carville and his wife, Mary Matalin, a GOP adviser. When Carville began defining the *chattering classes* in a telephone interview as "A loose confederation of journalists, ex-government officials, attorneys," his wife shouted in the background: "And people who have never done it!" Matalin added CCCW for the *Chattering Classes' Conventional Wisdom*. "Where the chattering classes get dangerous is when something becomes an article of faith among the CCCW. Then it becomes static and immutable and absolutely detached from reality," she said. See CONVENTIONAL WISDOM.

The *chattering classes* are also known as the *Gang of 500*, a term coined by Mark Halperin, political director of ABC News and founder of its website's daily political tip sheet, "The Note." Explaining his editorial approach, Halperin told *The New Yorker* in 2004: "We try to channel what the chattering class is chattering about, and to capture the sensibility, ethos, and rituals of the Gang of 500, which still largely sets the political agenda for the country."

Chattering classes—a play upon *working classes*—is inherently derogatory because of its associations with *idle chatter, chitter chatter,* and *chatterbox*. The implication is that the *chatter* of the *classes* makes as much sense as that of birds or children. *Chatter* also acquires some additional spin as an attack term from its parallel in sound and sense with *natter;* see NATTERING NABOBS OF NEGATIVISM.

The term is a British import. Aubrey Watkins of *The Observer,* who popularized *chattering classes* in the 1980s, attributed the phrase in a 1989 article in *The Guardian* to Frank Johnson, another journalist, who coined it during a conversation with Watkins when the two lived in neighboring apartments. The earliest example in the *OED* is from a piece by Johnson in the March 21, 1980, issue of *Now!*: "The peculiar need for something to be frightened about only seems to affect those of us who are part of the chattering classes." Reporting in 1986 from Blackpool, England, Joseph Lelyveld, of *The New York Times*, noted that "Political commentators and supposed insiders [are] sometimes referred to in Britain as 'the chattering classes.'"

Chautauqua circuit Speaking to culturally active groups in small towns; old-fashioned BARNSTORMING.

On the shores of Lake Chautauqua, New York, Methodist clergyman John Vincent and Lewis Miller called an assembly in the summer of 1874 to promote Bible study in Sunday School. In a few years a permanent summer camp was formed that led to home-study courses in a variety of subjects. The institution was widely imitated, and after 1900, a "traveling Chautauqua" was begun—a series of lectures and concerts held in tents around the country—which lasted until the Depression.

The word came to connote grassroots intellectualism and mobile speechifying. In *The Economist* in 1931, the capitalization was dropped as the word became generic: "The Chequers [the British Prime Minister's residence] conversations proved to be the first of a series of statesmen's chautauquas in the capitals of Europe." While in Britain the word has a Sunday-school flavor, in the U.S. the meaning is more political. "It seems only fitting," wrote *The Atlantic* about Senator Hubert Humphrey in 1968, "that the boy from behind the drug counter in Huron, South Dakota, should wow a Chamber of Commerce convention, that the Chautauqua tent and Grange hall populist can make a Deep Southern audience jump to its feet."

The word is evocative of a bygone era, campaigning to attentive audiences with neither the tedium of the RUBBER-CHICKEN CIRCUIT nor the phoniness of the MEDIA EVENT.

chauvinism See WOMEN'S LIB; SUPERPATRIOTS.

Checkers speech The address Richard Nixon gave on nationwide television to defend himself against charges that he was the beneficiary of a "secret" political fund; now, any such emotionally charged speech.

During the 1952 campaign the Republicans were having a field day with Truman Administration scandals when word got out of the existence of a "secret Nixon fund," as the pro-Democratic *New York Post* called it. The reaction was explosive, including demands not just from the *Post* but from the Republican *New York Herald Tribune* that Nixon resign his candidacy. Dwight Eisenhower at first appeared to give Nixon little support; Thomas Dewey proposed that Nixon bare all in a television speech, leaving the decision to the public, thereby taking Eisenhower out of criticism for supporting or dumping his running mate. Ike called and, according to Nixon's memoirs, said, "go on a nationwide television program and tell them everything there is to tell ..." The Republican National Committee bought a half hour on NBC for $75,000. Just before airtime, Dewey called to say that the Eisenhower advisers urged Nixon to end the speech with his resignation, but would not say it came directly from Ike. Nixon said to tell them to watch the telecast.

The speech began with what speechwriters call a "grabber." Nixon said "My fellow Americans, I come before you tonight as a candidate for the vice presidency and as a man whose honesty and integrity have been questioned." He then explained that the collection was neither secret nor sinister, but a well-audited fund from supporters to pay legitimate political expenses such as travel costs. He spoke from notes rather than a text, covering four points: the facts of the fund and his personal finances; a counter-attack at Adlai Stevenson; praise of Eisenhower; and a dramatic call to the audience to write and wire the RNC to say whether or not he should stay on the ticket. Although he ran overtime and didn't get a chance to give the RNC's address, the reaction was strongly favorable. Eisenhower sent word he would like to see him in Wheeling, W.Va., on the campaign trail, which worried Nixon, but when he arrived there the president-to-be said, "You're my boy!"

In the course of the speech, however, Nixon tugged at a few heartstrings. He pointed out that he was too poor for his wife to have anything but a cloth coat. He also admitted his family had accepted a present—a cocker spaniel puppy named Checkers. "And you know," he went on, "the kids, like all kids, loved the dog, and I just want to say this, right now, that regardless of what they say about it, we are going to keep it."

In his 1962 book *Six Crises* (required reading for Nixon speechwriters years later), Nixon wrote: "It was labeled as the 'Checkers speech,' as though the mention of my dog was the only thing that saved my career. Many of the critics glided over the fact that the fund was thoroughly explained, my personal finances laid bare, and an admittedly emotional but honest appeal made for public support."

But many in the press felt that Nixon's approach was overly emotional, corny, even smarmy. "I regarded what had been done to me as character assassination," he wrote later, "and the experience permanently and powerfully affected my attitude toward the press in particular and the news media in general." In his 1968 campaign that led him to the White House, he would frequently remind his senior aides and writers "the press is the enemy," the hatred of which played a part in his downfall.

Nixon took the idea of injecting Checkers into his speech from Franklin Roosevelt's FALA SPEECH of 1944. The Republicans had accused FDR of sending a U.S. Navy destroyer to fetch his Scots terrier. Roosevelt did more than deny the charge; he turned it around to make it seem a libel on an innocent and appealing pet. Fala, he concluded, "has not been the same dog since."

Great men do well to have small dogs. Thomas E. Dewey's majestic Great Dane did not help project his master as a warm human being, but Winston Churchill's brown poodle, Rufus, was the kind of endearing small animal that appeals to the public. George H.W. Bush did well with a spaniel, Millie (Barbara Bush ghostwrote its book); Bill Clinton was the first to reach out to cat lovers, with Socks. George W. Bush returned to the FDR tradition with a Scottie, and when his pursuit of victory in the Iraq war led to a loss of popularity, said

he would stick with it if his only supporters were his wife Laura and dog Barney. See Ruark quote under COMMON MAN.

checks and balances The power of each of the three branches of government to limit the power of the other two, aimed at making certain that neither the president nor the congress nor the judges "rule."

The federal Constitution's authors feared concentrations of power of all kinds, from monarchism to mob rule. During the nationwide debate over creating a federal union in the 1780s, *checks and balances* emerged as the Federalists' prescription for protecting all sectors of the pluralistic American society.

The term was probably coined by seventeenth-century British political philosopher James Harrington. Among the early users was James Madison, one of the primary Federalist advocates. During the ratification debate, he explained how the landed gentry's rights would be protected: "our government ought to secure the permanent interests of the country against innovation. Landholders ought to have a share in the government, to support these invaluable interests, and to balance and check the other [numerically larger groups]."

This reflected the new government's embrace of the division of power. The House of Representatives was popularly elected, but the Senate was not. The President could veto congressional action, but only Congress could appropriate funds for him to spend. Federal judges depended on the President for appointment and on Congress for money, but the judges serve for life.

Because it describes simply a fundamental and enduring principle of the American system, *checks and balances* has survived as a term, too. Abraham Lincoln, in his first inaugural address on March 4, 1861, said, "A majority held in restraint by constitutional checks and balances and always changing easily with deliberate changes of popular opinions and sentiments is the only sovereign of a free people."

More recently, James MacGregor Burns described the "system of checks and balances that would use man's essential human nature—his interests, his passions, his ambitions—to control itself."

chicken in every pot An easily attackable Republican slogan created by and exploited by Democrats.

King Henry IV of France (1553–1610) was the champion phrasemaker of his era. He was responsible for the *white plume* or *plumed knight* expression used by supporters of James Blaine in the late nineteenth century; he coined *le Grand Dessein*, the "great design" for world peace that Franklin Roosevelt appropriated (see GRAND DESIGN); and as a result of his statement "Je veux qu'il n'y ait si pauvre paysan en mon royaume qu'il n'ait tous les diamanches sa poule au pot" ("I wish that there would not be a peasant so poor in all my realm who would not have a chicken in his pot every Sunday"), he was given the sobriquet of *le Roi de la poule au pot* ("King of the chicken in the pot").

Herbert Hoover never said or quoted it. What he did say, on October 22, 1928, was "The slogan of progress is changing from the 'FULL DINNER PAIL' to the full garage." The former president's secretary wrote to quotation-etymologist George Seldes in 1958: "No one has ever been able to find, in Mr. Hoover's speeches or writings, of which a very careful file has been kept over the years, the expression 'a chicken in every pot.' Mr. Hoover also never promised or even expressed his hope of two cars in every garage."

The repopularization of the phrase, and Hoover's supposed connection with it, can be traced to a Republican campaign flyer of 1928 titled "A Chicken In Every Pot." Democratic candidate Al Smith, in a Boston campaign speech, held up the flyer and quoted from it: " 'Republican prosperity has reduced hours and increased earning capacity.' And then it goes on to say Republican prosperity has put a chicken in every pot and a car in every backyard to boot. ... Here's another good one for you. 'Republican efficiency has filled the working-man's dinner pail and his gasoline tank besides, and placed the whole nation in the SILK STOCKING class.' ... Now just draw on your imagination for a moment,

and see if you can in your mind's eye picture a man working at $17.50 a week going out to a chicken dinner in his own automobile with silk socks on."

Let's look at the record: By 1932, reminders of promises of prosperity were particularly embarrassing to Republicans; Hoover's reference to a "full garage" was combined with Smith's characterization of the Hoover campaign flyer to manufacture a Hoover promise: "A chicken in every pot and two cars in every garage."

FDR loved the misquotation and never let it go. In a letter dated March 21, 1940, and marked in his handwriting "Very private—don't use!" President Roosevelt wrote to a Miss Gertrude Ely of Bryn Mawr, Pennsylvania: "Dear Gertrude: Thank you for your grand pamphlet proving for businessmen that we are in for another 'three or four chickens in the pot era.' "

Democratic campaigners do not let it die. In 1960 John F. Kennedy misquoted the phony quotation in Bristol, Tennessee: "It is my understanding that the last candidate for the presidency to visit this community in a presidential year was Herbert Hoover in 1928. President Hoover initiated on the occasion of his visit the slogan 'Two chickens for every pot,' and it is no accident that no presidential candidate has ever dared come back to this community since."

Comedian Dick Gregory played on a more recent meaning of *pot* with this TURN-AROUND in 1972: "A chicken in every pot will probably not be revived as a campaign slogan. With the eighteen-year-old vote now in effect, some folks feel the new battle cry is more likely to be 'some pot in every chicken.' "

Chicken Kiev See SELF-DETERMINATION.

chilling effect An action or situation that inhibits free speech, or threatens to intimidate, quieten, or dispirit the press; indirect censorship.

Justice William Brennan, author of the Supreme Court's 1965 opinion in *Dombrowski v. Pfister* (380 U.S. 479), popularized the phrase in its current meaning. A civil rights group in Louisiana had protested that the state's Subversive Activities and Communist Control Law subjected its members to harassment by local authorities. Instead of deciding on the basis of bad-faith harassment, the Court found intimidation inherent in "the existence of a penal statute susceptible of sweeping and improper application...the chilling effect upon the exercise of First Amendment rights may derive from the fact of the prosecution, unaffected by the prospects of its success or failure."

Chilling effect made its next appearance in 1967, in *Walker v. City of Birmingham*, this time in a dissent by Justice Brennan to a majority opinion written by Justice Potter Stewart. Since the lexicographer heard that the phrase might have stemmed from Justice Stewart's decision, my letter to that jurist elicited this letter from Justice Brennan to Justice Stewart dated March 7, 1974, describing the derivation:

There is a note in 69 Columbia Law Review 808–842 (1969) entitled "The Chilling Effect in Constitutional Law." That Note traces the concept of "chilling effect" to a concurring opinion by Felix Frankfurter in *Wieman v. Updegraff*, 344 U.S. 183, 195 (1952) where Felix, joined by Bill Douglas, said of a teacher's loyalty oath: "Such unwarranted inhibition upon the free spirit of teachers affects not only those who, like the appellants, are immediately before the Court. It has an unmistakable tendency to *chill* that free play of the spirit which all teachers ought especially to cultivate and practice; it makes for caution and timidity in their associations by potential teachers"

Brennan continued, in his note to Stewart:

Frankly, I have no recollection of bottoming the phrase on Felix's "Wieman" opinion nor upon the opinions of lower courts dating back to 1939 and cited in footnote 2 of the Law Review Note. I would suppose that the Note would help meet Mr. Safire's desire for its history.

And so it does, showing how the term *chilling* had been used since 1939 in cases regarding judicially regulated sales. The metaphor can be traced to the sixteenth century to mean "to affect as with cold": the *OED* cites Hooker's *Of the Lawes of Ecclesiastical Politie* with "chilleth...all warmth

of zeal." According to the *Columbia Law Review*, the author of that article, written in 1969, was New York attorney Herbert T. Weinstein, and his conclusions in that piece show how the Court has used Brennan's phrase to extend the First Amendment:

At first blush, the doctrine seems merely to indicate a rational relationship between constitutionally protected conduct and the law sought to be held unconstitutional. But if this is the function of the chilling doctrine, the words "deters" and "inhibits" would serve as well as the word "chills." It appears, however, that the Court uses the chilling doctrine for more far-reaching purposes. First it uses the doctrine to justify activism in restricting and eliminating laws which proscribe protected conduct. Here the chilling effect reverses the usual presumption of federalism that federal courts should defer to state courts and open their doors only when state judicial and administrative procedures have been exhausted.

The second function of the chilling effect doctrine is to indicate the abridgement of a constitutional right. Here the chilling effect appears to emphasize a presumption in favor of the protected conduct and against the state regulation which deters it.

In current political, rather than legal, use, the phrase is used by reporters who complain that other journalists might be intimidated by "leak-plugging" efforts of government officials. In 1992, *Roll Call* discussed stricter codes on sexual harassment: "If and when this policy is adopted, it will have a chilling effect on free speech around the Capitol Dome." (See PLUMBER.)

The ability of journalists to protect their sources was eroded as a result of the investigation into the leaking in 2003 of the name of an undercover CIA employee, Valerie Plame, supposedly in an effort to undercut the charge by her husband, retired ambassador Joseph C. Wilson IV, that the Bush administration had misrepresented intelligence findings in order to justify attacking Iraq in 2003.

Patrick J. Fitzgerald, the special prosecutor appointed to handle the case, subpoenaed a number of journalists as well as their notes in order to determine whether a government official had committed a crime by identifying Plame. He increased the pressure by getting officials with whom the reporters had been in contact to release them from any pledges of confidentiality.

Many journalists believed that the releases had been coerced, but Fitzgerald threatened to send two of them, Matthew Cooper, of *Time* magazine, and Judith Miller, of *The New York Times*, to jail for contempt of court if they did not testify about their sources. Cooper avoided jail time after his source, presidential adviser Karl Rove, gave him permission to testify, and after his *Time* employer had handed over his subpoenaed notes. Miller, who had written nothing about the case, spent 85 days in jail before agreeing to testify on the basis of what were called "Miller rules": first, a personal telephone call from her source, I. Lewis "Scooter" Libby, Jr., chief of staff to Vice President Dick Cheney, releasing her from her pledge; second, an agreement from the prosecutor to allow Miller's attorneys to redact her subpoenaed notes so that no other source on other articles would be compromised; and finally, assurance that her testimony would be limited to this subject and no "fishing expedition" would lead into any other. She was then released from federal prison and testified to the grand jury.

Libby's defense counsel argued he had suffered an understandable lapse of memory in denying being part of a White House campaign to discredit a critic. After it was revealed that the "leaker," Deputy Secretary of State Richard Armitage—characterized by columnist Robert Novak, who broke the story, as "no gunslinger" (meaning no political partisan)—had admitted to the Justice Department before the investigation by a special counsel began that he was the inadvertent source of the original source of the leak, pro-administration columnists charged that Vice President Cheney's top aide had been the object of a politically motivated prosecution by a special counsel not bound by Justice Department guidelines. They noted that no charge was ever brought that the law protecting the identity of covert operatives (and requiring proof of criminal intent to injure the United States) had been broken.

Libby was found guilty by a jury not for leaking Plame's name but for committing what his defenders had called "process crimes"—perjury and lying to FBI agents—triggered by the prosecutor as a result of the unnecessary investigation into a leak that had already been admitted and based on no underlying crime. The trial judge sentenced Libby in 2007 to 30 months in prison and a quarter-million dollars in penalties; President Bush subsequently commuted the jail sentence, an act that drew widespread criticism about a lack of accountability from political opponents.

Many journalists feared in the wake of this case and others not only that "whistleblowers" and others with inside information about the workings of government and business would become reluctant to speak to them confidentially, but that prosecutors, as well as civil litigators, would start regarding subpoenas of journalists as a conventional fact-finding tool. Bipartisan bills to create a federal shield law—labeled "The Free Flow of Information Act"—were introduced in both the House and the Senate to require federal courts to meet strict standards before compelling journalists to reveal confidential sources in testimony. As of 2008, such statutes are in effect in 32 states and the District of Columbia; in 17 other states, a reporter's privilege—similar to that granted doctors, lawyers, clergy, mental health workers, and spouses—has been recognized through judicial decisions. State prosecutors noted to congressional committees that this protection of the identity of confidential sources has helped rather than hindered law enforcement, especially of government corruption, as low-level officials often tend to trust reporters more than their superiors.

State shield laws tend to be porous, however. Whenever judges are forced to choose between the First Amendment, which includes freedom of the press, and the Sixth Amendment, which guarantees the right to a speedy trial, including obtaining evidence from witnesses, they almost invariably decide that the First must give way to the

Sixth. Another knotty problem is the question of just who is a journalist. Do shield laws apply to people who are not employed by the established media—to authors of books, say, or to Internet bloggers, successors to "the lonely pamphleteers" (in Justice Byron White's phrase) of centuries ago? The answers are not clear, but the questions probably must be addressed in some detail, if not resolved completely, before a federal shield law is enacted.

See CONFIDENTIAL SOURCE and FISHING EXPEDITION.

China card See CARD METAPHORS.

China lobby Attack phrase used against those urging support of Chiang Kai-shek against Mao Zedong, and later pressing for aid to Chiang on Taiwan.

In February 1946 a mission to China headed by General George Marshall had arranged for a cease-fire and a coalition government, which began to break up within three months. General Patrick Hurley, in an angry resignation from his ambassadorial post, warned that "subversives" in the State Department were secretly plotting a Communist victory. "Around the country," wrote Cabell Phillips in *The Truman Presidency*, "a 'China lobby' was forming, controlled largely by zealots of the right beating the gongs of public opinion to 'save' China."

General Marshall returned from his mission in January 1947, and American aid to the Chiang government soon began to dry up. Friends of Chiang in the U.S. bitterly criticized this decision, and President Truman in July 1947 sent General Albert Wedemeyer to China for another look. Wedemeyer filed an ambivalent report, which the Truman Administration suppressed, further whipping up the attacks of Chiang's American supporters.

After Chiang retreated from the mainland to Formosa (now Taiwan), the efforts of the "China lobby" were directed to his support on Formosa and the rejection of any attempt to replace the Chiang government in the UN by the Communist Chinese.

During the Eisenhower Administration, Senate Minority Leader William Knowland of California was often attacked as a captive of the "China lobby" and was labeled "the Senator from Formosa." When mainland China replaced Taiwan in the UN in 1971, and Richard Nixon paid his presidential visit to Beijing in 1972, the influence of the China lobby was seen to have been overrated. When President Nixon arranged for "liaison offices" in Beijing and Washington, the name of the "China lobby" began to change to "supporters of Taiwan"; the vogue phrase became "normalization of relations" with the PRC. President Carter pledged to carry it forward in his campaign, based on the Nixon-Mao "Shanghai Communiqué" that cleverly recognized that Chinese on both sides of the Formosa Straits agreed there was but "one China."

By the mid-'70s, another "lobby"—again carrying the pejorative connotation of manipulation—was spoken of in the U.S. This was the "Israel lobby," which gained much attention when the Chairman of the Joint Chiefs of Staff, General George Brown, said in 1976 that Jewish groups made their influence felt on U.S. policy makers, who considered the defense of Israel "a burden." In the 1980s, as Egyptian and Saudi Arabian embassies in Washington became more sophisticated in dealing with U.S. public opinion, hiring lobbyists for that purpose, a counterphrase appeared: the "Arab lobby."

Supporters of Israel were able to calibrate the degree of animus in those who opposed their views: mildest was identification as "the pro-Israel lobby," followed by "the Israel lobby," and most virulent "the Jewish lobby." In 2007, *The Wall Street Journal* headlined an Op-Ed piece "Anti-Semitism and the Anti-Israel lobby."

China watchers Outside observers of political customs inside Communist China; sifters of official statements for hidden meanings.

This phrase is probably derived from *bird watching* with its connotation of intense concentration, intricate analysis, and observation from a distance. It replaced OLD CHINA HANDS—reporters and businessmen who made their careers in Asia before the rise of Communism there.

A synonym is *Pekingologist*—or, new style, *Beijingologist*—coined on the analogy of KREMLINOLOGIST, referring to those who made their living trying to decipher the puzzles of the former Soviet government, a word that has carried on beyond the collapse of the U.S.S.R., as the center of power in Russia remains the Kremlin. The creed of the China watcher, Kremlinologist, and Pekingologist was summed up by Winston Churchill's description of the Soviet Union: "It is a riddle wrapped in a mystery inside an enigma."

China watching is a construction that has been borrowed for use to describe any group of analysts who laboriously pick over the movements of their subject for hidden meanings—thus, *Bobby watchers* (Kennedy), *Hillary watchers* (Clinton), etc.

choice, not an echo Attack on "me-tooism" (see ME, TOO); a call for a division of parties along ideological lines.

"We think the American people want a clear-cut choice," said Peter O'Donnell, chairman of the Draft Goldwater Committee in April 1963, "between the New Frontier of the Kennedys and Republican principles." On January 3, 1964, candidate Goldwater announced: "I will offer a choice, not an echo. This will not be an engagement of personalities. It will be an engagement of principles."

Phyllis Schlafly chose the phrase for her book title, published soon afterward; Democrats called this one of the "three dirty books" of the campaign. (The others were *None Dare Call It Treason* by John Stormer and *A Texan Looks at Lyndon* by J. Evetts Haley.) At the 1964 Republican convention, Pennsylvania Governor William Scranton, taking the liberal baton after Nelson Rockefeller's defeat in the California primary, played on the phrase: "I have come here to offer our party a choice. I reject the echo we have thus far been handed ... the echo of fear, or reaction ... the echo from the Never Never Land that puts our nation backward to a lesser place in the world of free men."

The Goldwater strategy relied on the presence of a strong SILENT VOTE that had supposedly stayed home up to then because Republicans had not drawn a sharp ideological line in the campaigns of Willkie, Dewey, or Nixon.

The desire for such a restructuring of the two-party system has not been limited to conservatives. Felix Frankfurter, explaining his vote for third-party candidate Robert La Follette in 1924, quoted English observer James Bryce's comparison of the two American parties: "Both have certainly war cries, organizations, interests enlisted in their support. But those interests are in the main getting or keeping the patronage of the government. Distinctive tenets and policies, points of political practice have all but vanished."

See TWO-PARTY SYSTEM; BIG TENT; IDEOLOGY; TRUE BELIEVER; DIME'S WORTH OF DIFFERENCE, NOT A.

chop Approval, whether in the form of an actual mark or seal or a nod of the head.

Secretary of State Colin Powell told the Senate Governmental Affairs committee in 2004 that the CIA had vetted his presentation the previous year to the United Nations of American reasons for attacking Iraq, saying, "The CIA chopped off, or concurred, in everything that I said." The expression has been employed in military and diplomatic circles for at least several decades. In 1989, one of Powell's predecessors at State, James Baker, promised to give Israel "a chop on the representation" of Palestinians at a meeting to arrange for elections in the West Bank and Gaza. Discussing Baker's use of the word, Major David Super, a Pentagon spokesman, told this columnist: "Chop has been in use here for some time. When we circulate a paper for coordination, the cover sheet will have a series of boxes for comments or signatures. We'll say, 'Please put your chop on this,' or just 'Chop this.'"

Chop derives from the Hindi *chhap*, a stamp or brand. The term was carried by European traders to China, where it was used to refer to an official seal, a permit or license bearing such a seal, or a mark on goods to indicate their quality (*first chop, second chop*). The word entered English in the early seventeenth century. *Purchas*

His Pilgrimage, a 1614 collection of writings about foreign lands, includes *chop* in the sense of a seal or stamp: "The King [of Achen] sent us his Chop." Marco Polo would have understood the modern bureaucratese. See SIGN OFF ON.

Christmas tree bill Proposed legislation likely to pass that is then festooned with amendments not germane to its purpose.

The New York Times in 1967 deplored the attempts by protectionists "to tack a series of riders sought by domestic industry onto the Administration's proposals for higher old-age benefits. Their hope is that Congress will give its approval to the entire 'Christmas tree' package.... The only sure way to stop the Christmas-tree bill is to chop it down before it is planted." That was a misunderstanding of "package"; a PACKAGE DEAL is the result of compromise; this is more of an abuse of RIDER amendments.

Elliot Richardson, then Secretary of Health, Education, and Welfare, said in 1970: "Until I became Secretary, I had never heard 'Christmas tree' used as a transitive verb." Explained Alan Otten in *The Wall Street Journal*: "On Capitol Hill, the practice of tagging a host of special-interest amendments to a popular bill is known as 'Christmas-treeing' the bill."

By 2006, *Times* editorialists got the metaphor straight and came up with an imaginative trope. A must-pass half-billion-dollar defense budget was being held up by a small group of House Republicans with an addition to empower evangelical chaplains to speak in the name of Jesus at nonreligious gatherings of the military. The *Times* called this "part of the annual attempt to make a 'Christmas tree' of the measure by weighting it with nonessential favors for political patrons." The editorial's headline: "Keep Christ out of the Christmas Tree." See RIDER.

chronic campaigner Characterization of Richard Nixon by President Lyndon Johnson, in angry dismissal of a Nixon analysis of Vietnam policy.

In the 1966 congressional campaign, former Vice President Richard Nixon was the foremost campaigner for Republican candidates nationally. As a private citizen eager to make a political comeback in 1968, he carried the attack to President Johnson, who pursued the same strategy he had used so successfully two years earlier on Barry Goldwater: to remain "ABOVE POLITICS." Two weeks before the midterm election day, with polls showing a drop in his popularity that was endangering Democratic congressional candidates, Johnson chose to make a dramatic trip to visit to U.S. troops in Vietnam. Nixon held his fire while the President was overseas, but on his return put out a closely reasoned, critical analysis of the Manila Communiqué that had been issued by Johnson and Southeast Asia leaders.

Harrison Salisbury, who later became the first Op-Ed editor of *The New York Times*, was importuned by the Nixon aide (the author) who had written much of the document at white heat to run the full text of the Nixon critique. (Added to the *Times* editor's sound editorial judgment was a journalistic debt to the aide; see KITCHEN DEBATE). Salisbury's decision to print the Nixon text—beyond normal coverage— gave it national importance. Next morning, at the President's news conference, Johnson startled his audience and dismayed his aides by losing his temper. He denounced Nixon as "a chronic campaigner" who was "playing politics with peace."

The alliteration and petulance of LBJ's "chronic campaigner" phrase (see PERENNIAL CANDIDATE) focused national attention on Nixon's role in the campaign and guaranteed him a superb opportunity to counter on television with studied calm, thereby out-above-politicking the president.

A similar attack, though less emotional, was made by John Quincy Adams on Henry Clay: "His opposition to Monroe and myself arises out of a disappointed ambition, a determination to run down the administration and become president by hook or crook in 1824." See CAN'T WIN.

church and state See WALL, POLITICAL SYMBOL OF.

CIA See INVISIBLE GOVERNMENT; DIRTY TRICKS, DEPARTMENT OF.

CIA-ese Spookspeak; the language of the intelligence community (formerly the intelligence establishment), partly based on a glossary compiled in 1976 by the Senate Select Committee to Study Governmental Operations with Respect to Intelligence Activities, with many subsequent additions:

account: Assignment or area of responsibility, typically a nation, as in "the Israeli account" or "the Russian account." Richard Helms, a former director of Central Intelligence, told the author that this sense of *account* might have been introduced into intelligence lingo by a former adman, which, as it happens, Helms also once was.

agent: A foreign recruit of the CIA, considered to be an agency *asset;* see below.

annuitant: A retired CIA employee, still on the payroll and readily available for work.

asset: Any resource—a person, group, relationship, instrument, installation, or supply—at the disposition of an intelligence agency for use in an operational or support role. The term is normally applied to a person who is contributing to a CIA clandestine mission but is not a fully controlled agent of the CIA.

backstopping: Providing verification and support of cover arrangements for an agent or asset in anticipation of inquiries or other actions which might test the credibility of his or its cover.

bigot lists: Uses *bigot* in the sense of "narrow"; a roster of people allowed to know a particular secret—for instance, the existence of a "black" program, a military or intelligence project whose existence is not acknowledged. This is helpful in detecting leaks. Origin: officers being sent to Gibraltar in preparation for the invasion of North Africa in World War II had orders stamped TO GIB; later, according to Henry Becket's 1986 *Dictionary of Espionage,* "when planning commenced for the Normandy invasion, the letters were reversed to read BIGOT and used to list persons with a need-to-know sensitive details of the invasion."

black bag job: Warrantless surreptitious entry, especially an entry conducted for purposes other than microphone installation, such as physical search and seizure or photographing of documents; also called (a later variant) a *U.P.S.,* meaning *uncontested physical search.*

blowback: False information intended for foreign consumption that makes its way into domestic news reports, coined on the analogy of the automotive *blow by* and the electronic *feedback,* or from the wind-shift danger in the use of poison gas. In what was called "psychological warfare" in the '50s, the Soviets pioneered in "disinformation"—falsehoods, widely disseminated, distinguished from "misinformation" by the intent to misinform—and U.S. "black propaganda" has done the same, notably in the implantation of bogus material in Khrushchev's "secret speech" in 1956 denouncing Joseph Stalin. Synonyms of *blowback* are *fallout* and *domestic replay.*

brush pass: See *gap, in the.*

bug: A concealed listening device or microphone for eavesdropping; as a verb, to install audio surveillance of a subject or target.

case officer: A CIA operative, also called an *intelligence* or *operations officer,* recruited domestically, as distinguished from a foreign *agent;* see above.

clandestine operation: undercover activity with emphasis on concealing the operation itself rather than, as in the case of *covert action* below, on concealing responsibility for the action.

code word: A word which has been assigned a classification above "top secret" and a classified meaning to safeguard intentions and information regarding a planned operation. In 1987, *The Washington Post* reported florid terms for attacks on Libya: "In the White House and N.S.C., the top-secret plan to oust Gadhafi was given the code word 'Flower'; a C.I.A. component to undermine Gadhafi covertly was called 'Tulip,' and the plan for a U.S.-Egyptian military action was 'Rose.'" For political uses of this term, see CODE WORDS.

Company, the: Informal, in-house name for the CIA; also called *the Agency* or *Langley,* after the Virginia town where it is headquartered. *Company* follows the precedent of the older British Secret Intelligence

Service, referred to by its employees as *The Firm*, or *The Old Firm*. That *cia* means "company" in Spanish is coincidental.

cover: A protective guise to prevent identification with clandestine activities and to conceal the true affiliation of personnel and the true sponsorship of their activities.

covert action: Any clandestine activity designed to influence foreign governments, events, organizations, or persons in support of United States foreign policy. May include political, economic, propaganda, and paramilitary activities. Requires a formal presidential finding and notification of congressional intelligence committee leaders, but is supposed to be carried out in such a way that the United States can deny responsibility.

cut-out: Go-between used to conceal contact between members of a clandestine activity or organization.

dangle (n): A defector or *walk-in* (see below) who is not truly defecting but pretending to be, on behalf of a foreign intelligence service. The *dangle* may provide tempting tidbits of truthful data, along with much disinformation, and become a penetration agent, or *mole.*

double agent: A person engaging in clandestine activity for two or more intelligence or security services who provides information to one service about the other, or about each service to the other, and who is wittingly or unwittingly manipulated by one service against the other.

executive action: A euphemism for assassination, used by the CIA to describe a program aimed at overthrowing certain foreign leaders, by assassinating them if necessary. Known jocularly as the Health Alteration Committee.

family jewels: An informal phrase for the CIA's darkest secrets. When James Schlesinger was appointed Director of Central Intelligence in 1973, he asked employees to come forward with information about activities "which might be construed to be outside the legislative charter of this agency." Wrote Schlesinger's successor, William Colby, in his 1978 book *Honorable Men*: "Presented to the Director so that he would know about them, they were promptly dubbed by a wag the 'family jewels'; I referred to them as 'our skeletons in the closet.' Among them were the Chaos Operation against the antiwar movement, the surveillance and bugging of American journalists in hope of locating the sources of leaks of sensitive materials, and all the connections with the Watergate conspirators and White House 'plumbers.'" (The phrase *family jewels* has a long-time taboo slang use meaning "testicles," a source of pride as well as a source of progeny.)

finding: See separate entry.

fluttering: Giving a lie-detector test to one's own agents to find out if they are telling the truth. "Investigators for the Church committee," reported Rudy Maxa in *The Washington Post*, "learned—but never revealed—that many of the journalists who had cooperated with the CIA were given lie-detector tests. In the spy business that's called 'fluttering,' and some reporters were fluttered more often than regular agency employees to test their loyalty."

FORMICA: Acronym for Foreign Military Intelligence Collection Activity.

FUSS: Acronym for Fleet Undersea Surveillance System.

gap, in the: Out of sight, momentarily free of surveillance, whether from satellites or from observation by humans on the ground. The ability to operate *in the gap* is essential to the *brush pass* (or contact) for handing something—a package or envelope, say—to another person while under surveillance. The idea is to make one or more quick right-hand turns around the corners of buildings, thus getting out of view of any followers for a second or so, and effecting the brush pass while in the gap. The technique was developed by Haviland Smith, a former CIA station chief in Prague, according to Benjamin Weiser's *A Secret Life*, the story of a Polish colonel, Ryszard Kuklinski, who passed many Soviet-bloc secrets to the CIA from 1973 to 1981.

green door, behind the: Out of public view, in secret, as in Central Intelligence Director George Tenet's testimony to the 9/11 commission: "Well, we sit behind the green door. And for the bang for the buck, the American taxpayer gets a lot for what we give them."

The metaphor comes from the military practice of painting the doors of intelligence units green in order to alert people that they should not enter those offices without proper security clearances. The phrase was introduced into the world of espionage during World War II by code breakers at Britain's Bletchley Park, where the Green Door Problem referred to information that might help units in the field but could not be passed along to them because this would have signaled to the Germans that their Enigma code had been cracked. One of the earlier sources is a story by O. Henry in his 1906 collection, *The Four Million*, about a young man who finds Romance and Adventure by daring to open—as the story is entitled—The Green Door.

HIPSEE: A rough acronym for the "House Permanent Select Committee on Intelligence."

HUMINT: Melding of the collocation *human intelligence*, as distinguished from inanimate *SIGINT*, *signal intelligence*, meaning intercepted communications as well as clues obtained from foreign radar signals or telemetry, and *MASINT*, *measurement and signature intelligence*, referring to information gained from acoustic, nuclear, and seismic sensors. An unofficial category is *RUMINT*, *rumor intelligence*, also called *gossip*, which is sometimes surprisingly reliable. A Defense Intelligence Agency bureaucratization was renaming its *Humint Augmentation* teams, a hush-hush group that gathers intelligence on battlefields, as *Strategic Support* teams.

informant: A person who wittingly or not provides information to an agent, a clandestine service, or police. In reporting such information, this informant will often be cited as the source.

informer: One who intentionally discloses information about other persons or activities to police or a security service (such as the FBI), usually for a financial reward.

keyhole: Code word for data derived from satellite imagery.

mole: An operative planted in another country's intelligence community; a specific form of *agent in place*. This is a coinage by novelist David Cornwall, pen name John Le Carré, which has burrowed its way into intelligence jargon. Former CIA chief Richard Helms told the author he never heard *mole* used in his tenure; the terms used for that most feared prospect, he said, were *penetration* and *penetration agent*.

NIC: Abbreviation for National Intelligence Council. People who work for the NIC are *NIOs*, or National Intelligence Officers. They coordinate their efforts with *SIB*, the Strategic Intelligence Board, and all share *SNIEs*, Special National Intelligence Estimates.

notionals: Fictitious private commercial entities which exist on paper only. They serve as the ostensible employer of intelligence personnel, or as the ostensible sponsor of certain activities in support of clandestine operations. (Not to be confused with *nationals*, citizens of a given country.)

plausible denial: A cover story that enables high government officials to disclaim knowledge of an intelligence activity. Curiously, this term was listed but not defined in the glossary compiled by the Senate Select Committee in 1976. Asked about the oversight committee's oversight, a staff member said merely, "We closed out the report in such a rush we just forgot that definition," itself a plausible denial.

plumbing: The development of assets or services supporting the clandestine operations of CIA field stations—such as safe houses, unaccountable funds, investigative persons, surveillance teams.

proprietaries: Ostensibly private commercial entities capable of doing business that are established and controlled by intelligence services to conceal governmental affiliation of intelligence personnel and/or governmental sponsorship of actions in support of clandestine operations. Also sometimes known as *notionals*.

rendition: See separate entry.

safe house: Innocent-appearing premises established by an intelligence organization for conducting clandestine or covert activity or hiding informants.

sanitize: To delete or revise a document to prevent identification of the intelligence sources and methods that contributed to or are dealt with in the report. Not to be confused with *redaction,* a blackening-out of material that calls attention to its excision.

sheep dipping: Utilization of a military instrument (such as an airplane) or officer in clandestine operations, usually in a civilian capacity or under civilian cover, although the instrument or officer will covertly retain its or his military ownership or standing. The term is also applied to the placement of individuals in organizations or groups in which they can become active in order to establish credentials so that they can be used to collect information of intelligence interest on similar groups.

source: A person, thing, or activity which provides intelligence information. In clandestine activities, the term applies to an *agent* or *asset,* usually a foreign national, being used in an intelligence activity for intelligence purposes. In interrogations, it refers to a person who furnishes intelligence information with or without knowledge that the information is being used for intelligence purposes.

sterilize: To remove from material to be used in covert and clandestine actions any marks or devices which can identify it as originating with the sponsoring organization or nation.

suit: A *P.C.,* that is, a military intelligence officer in *plain clothes* or, in British English, in *mufti* (perhaps from *mufti,* meaning a Muslim legal expert having authority to issue rulings, called *fatwas,* on religious matters).

synecdoche: Pronounced "sin-EK-do-key," the word means a rhetorical device that uses a part to stand for the whole, or a small thing to symbolize a big thing: the BIG APPLE, a nickname for New York City, uses an apple as a synecdoche for the world. CIA Inspector General Lyman Kirkpatrick said in an internal report in 1967 dealing with assassination that intelligence professionals also used the term: "The point is that of frequent resort to synecdoche—the mention of a part when the whole is to be understood, or vice versa. Thus, we encounter repeated references to phrases such as 'disposing of Castro,' which may be read in the narrow literal sense of assassinating him, when it is intended that it be read in the

broader figurative sense of dislodging the Castro regime. Reversing the coin," the CIA man continued, "we find people speaking vaguely of 'doing something about Castro' when it is clear that what they have specifically in mind is killing him."

target of opportunity: Description of an entity (e.g., governmental entity, installation, political organization, or individual) that becomes available to an intelligence agency or service by chance, and provides the opportunity for the collection of needed information.

technical means: Originally reference to a *bug*; now spy satellites and electronic eavesdropping and surveillance stations costing billions of dollars.

terminate with extreme prejudice: To murder; for example, from *The New York Times Encyclopedia Almanac* (1970): "Other reports said that the Green Berets had been advised by a CIA official in Saigon to 'terminate with extreme prejudice'—an official euphemism for murder—the suspect, and had done so with an injection of morphine, two .22 caliber pistol shots in the head, and the disposal of the weighted corpse in the sea." The extreme form of termination most likely derives from the more routine job-related distinction made by the agency in the 1960s between agents who were terminated without prejudice, meaning they were not needed at the moment but could be rehired because they were known to be loyal and reliable, and those who were terminated with prejudice, meaning they should not be rehired for any of a variety of reasons, such as alcoholism, lack of discretion, or suspicion of being double agents. CIA officials and retired operatives insist the "extreme prejudice" phrase is "espionage mythology," a fictional slur on the agency.

treff: A contact, from the German *treffen,* "to meet."

triangulation: Originally a method of locating secret radio transmitters by the intersection of three roving receivers. Later, a technique of finding the source of leaks. Each suspect is given data in slightly changed form; feedback from sources in the opposing force targets people who had been entrusted with the data. A second test with variant forms of secret data is undertaken, enabling the feedback to *triangulate* on the leaker. For the political meaning of this word, see TRIANGULATION.

United States country team: The senior in-country U.S. coordinating and supervising body, headed by the chief of the U.S. diplomatic mission (usually an ambassador) and composed of the senior member of each represented United States department or agency.

wafflebottom: An intelligence officer involved in technical work, including one specially cleared for dealing with codes and ciphers. In the CIA's predecessor agency during World War II, the OSS (Office of Strategic Services), also known as Oh So Secret and Oh So Social (on account of the many upper-crust Ivy Leaguers in its ranks), *wafflebottom* was slang for a communications engineer. The allusion is to the imprint of a chair on the buttocks of a person who sits in one for long hours.

walk-in: A defector, who may or may not be what he (or she) seems. *Spy Book: The Encyclopedia of Espionage*, by Norman Polmar and Thomas B. Allen, defined *walk-in* as "An unheralded defector or dangle … a potential agent or mole who literally walks into an embassy or intelligence agency without prior contact or recruitment."

washfax: An encrypted telephone fax line that is supposedly secure, but that no one in the intelligence business really trusts.

watch list: A list of words—such as names, entities, or phrases—which can be employed by a computer to select out required information from a mass of data.

wet operation (or *work* or *affair*): Russian euphemisms for intelligence operations in which blood is shed, especially political murders, carried out by the *wet squad*, on orders of the former Komitet Gosurdarstvennoi Bezopasnosti (Committee for State Security), more commonly known by its initials, KGB. The Russian expressions parallel the American military *get wet* (from the Vietnam era), meaning to kill someone with a bayonet or knife.

See DESTABILIZE; DIRTY TRICKS; INVISIBLE GOVERNMENT; WATERBOARDING.

circumlocution See RED TAPE.

citizen of the world An internationalist as opposed to an isolationist; more loosely, one concerned with universal issues, whether they apply at home or abroad.

Historian Richard Hofstadter credits Woodrow Wilson with being the first major American figure to urge Americans to be "citizens of the world." During World War I and the ensuing fight over U.S. membership in the League of Nations, Wilson tried to combat the isolationist argument that European affairs were no concern of this country. Wilson contended that American principles were not "the principles of a province or of a single continent … [but] the principles of a liberated mankind."

Neither the sentiment nor the phrase was original with Wilson. In 1762 Oliver Goldsmith wrote a satire entitled *Citizen of the World*, and a similar expression was used in the fourth century B.C. by Socrates. Plutarch says Socrates called himself "*ouk Athenaios, oude Hellen, alla kosmios*"—"neither Athenian nor Greek, but *kosmios*"; *kosmios*, (the adjective from *kosmos*, "order; ornament; world") usually means "well-ordered," but is here used as a synonym of *kosmopolites* "world-citizen" (which turns up in English as *cosmopolite*). American abolitionist William Lloyd Garrison wrote: "My country is the world; my countrymen are mankind."

President Franklin D. Roosevelt, who had problems with "America First" isolationists, especially before the Japanese attack on Pearl Harbor in 1941 brought the U.S. into World War II, said in his fourth and final Inaugural address on January 20, 1945: "We have learned that we cannot live alone, at peace; that our own well-being is dependent on the well-being of other nations, far away. We have learned that we must live as men, and not as ostriches, nor as dogs in the manger. We have learned to be citizens of the world, members of the world community."

See ONE WORLD; MULTILATERALISM.

John Kennedy expanded the phrase still further in a parallel to his famous "ask not" passage when at his Inaugural he said, "My fellow citizens of the world, ask not what America will do for you, but what together we can do for the freedom of man."

City Hall See GO FIGHT CITY HALL.

city on a hill The ideal or shining example of government; a paragon of civic success or virtue.

This metaphor was introduced in one of history's greatest speeches. In Matthew 5:14, Jesus tells his followers during the Sermon on the Mount, "Ye are the light of the world. A city that is set on an hill cannot be hid."

John Winthrop, aboard the *Arabella* bound for the New World, included the expression in a 1630 sermon. The founder of the settlement that became Boston warned his fellow settlers of the Massachusetts Bay Colony that "We shall be as a city upon a hill, the eyes of all people are upon us."

John F. Kennedy, who must have seen that quotation on the pedestal of the statue of Winthrop on Boston Common, used the expression often; eleven days before taking the presidential oath, he told a Massachusetts gathering: "I have been guided by the standard John Winthrop set ... 'that we shall be as a city upon a hill ... ' "

Ronald Reagan used the phrase as well, adding an adjective that made it more luminous but also controversial: in both his inaugural addresses, he spoke of "a *shining* city on a hill." New York Governor Mario Cuomo, in addressing the 1984 Democratic convention, sought to take off some of the shine: "the hard truth is that not everyone is sharing in this city's splendor and glory."

Reagan's amendment to the phrase in Jesus' sermon and Winthrop's unattributed citation seems to be permanent. In the 2004 Kerry-Bush contest, liberal Jonathan Alter wrote in *Newsweek*: " The real issue is how Bush wears. We know his city is heavily fortified and sits well to the right on the hill. But does it shine?" Columnist Gregory Rodriguez of *The Los Angeles Times* noted that Reagan had been "borrowing—and embroi-

dering—a famous line ... Winthrop didn't use the word 'shining' in his original 1630 sermon; his message was not triumphalist."

However, in early 2007, when Deval Patrick gave his inaugural address after being elected Governor of Massachusetts, he said, "To this kid from the South Side of Chicago, this Commonwealth is my shining city on a hill ... for every one of God's children who calls Massachusetts home—let's rebuild our 'city on a hill' and make it shine again."

See CAMELOT.

civil disobedience A doctrine requiring the individual to act against the law, accepting the law's punishment, if that principled person believes the law to be morally wrong or politically unjust.

English utilitarian philosopher Jeremy Bentham expressed the position clearly: that it was "allowable to, if not incumbent on, every man ... to enter into measures of resistance ... when ... the probable mischiefs of resistance (speaking with respect to the community in general) appear less to him than the probable mischiefs of obedience."

In the Declaration of Independence, Thomas Jefferson carried the thought to its political extreme: "that whenever any Form of Government becomes destructive of these Ends it is the Right of the People to alter or abolish it, and to institute new Government ..."

Political philosophers have long held that a "natural law" or HIGHER LAW exists that has precedence over man-made laws, and when these come in conflict the individual has the duty to disobey and resist the man-made laws. But this means that the law may be legally disobeyed, a contradiction in terms that has led to bloody dispute. William Seward of New York said in 1850: "There is a higher law than the Constitution," and his words became an abolitionist rallying cry.

The phrase *civil disobedience* was popularized in the U.S. by Henry David Thoreau's 1848 essay of that title, and in India by Mohandas K. Gandhi in his long, nonviolent campaign against British rule. As one of the cornerstones of the civil rights movement, it was expressed by the Rev. Martin Luther

King, Jr., in his "Letter from a Birmingham Jail":

> I submit that an individual who breaks a law that conscience tells him is unjust, and willingly accepts the penalty by staying in jail to arouse the conscience of the community over its injustice, is in reality expressing the very highest respect for law...Of course there is nothing new about this kind of civil disobedience.... It was practiced superbly by the early Christians...We can never forget that everything Hitler did in Germany was "legal" and everything the Hungarian freedom fighters did in Hungary was "illegal."

The noble connotation of the phrase was undermined somewhat in 1967 by the violence of the LONG HOT SUMMER. *Civil disobedience* was abruptly equated with "race riot" by some, but current usage continues to carry a nonviolent overtone. Stewart Alsop wrote in his *Newsweek* column in 1971: "'Civil disobedience'—a euphemism for breaking those laws in which the law breaker does not believe—has become both respectable and relatively safe. The civil-rights movement of the early '60s began to make it respectable, and the increasing unpopularity of the Vietnam war has helped to make it safe as well as respectable."

civilian review Oversight by a semijudicial board made up of citizens who are not police officers, to investigate complaints made against the police.

Police brutality was one of the earliest and most impassioned phrases of the civil rights movement. Photographs of police dogs being loosed on black demonstrators caused a national revulsion that lent impetus to the movement; it also lent credibility to unfair charges of brutality against police officers enforcing the law.

To lessen racial tensions, several cities adopted civilian review boards to assure minorities of independent control of police activities. In New York City, the issue of civilian review was put to the voters in 1966, with the concept enthusiastically endorsed by Senators Javits and Kennedy and Mayor John Lindsay. The proposal was overwhelmingly defeated. The police had argued that their own civil liberties were being violated by such a board. However, since 1993 New York's Civilian Complaint Review Board has been active and made up entirely of civilians.

An amateur videotape of Rodney King, a speeding motorist, being beaten by a quartet of Los Angeles policemen brought the issue of police brutality to the fore in 1992; after a state trial of the officers resulted in acquittal, the worst riot of the century in the U.S. ensued, leaving 50 dead. The accused were tried again under a federal civil rights statute; two were convicted.

civil rights Those rights guaranteed to an individual as a member of society; most often applied to the movement for black equality.

Civil rights (a phrase usually construed as plural) refer to positive legal prerogatives—the right to equal treatment before the law, the right to vote, the right to share equally with other citizens in such benefits as jobs, housing, education, and public accommodations. In their 1914 *Cyclopedia of American Government*, A. C. McLaughlin and A. B. Hart defined civil rights as "those which belong to the individual as a result of his membership in organized society, that is, as a subject of civil government."

The term is sometimes substituted for *civil liberties*, which refer to more negative rights: those actions an individual is legally free to take without government interference. Spelled out in the Constitution and the Bill of Rights, the more notable civil liberties include freedom of speech, press, assembly, and religion and protection against unreasonable searches and seizures.

Virtually interchangeable with *civil rights*, though broader, is the seldom-used *civic rights*. At the 1924 Democratic convention, liberals who wanted to condemn the Ku Klux Klan for its discrimination against Jews and Catholics as well as Negroes introduced a plank opposing any attempts "to limit the civic rights of any citizen or body of citizens because of religion, birthplace, or racial origin." The plank was narrowly defeated by Southern Democratic votes, and the issue was bitterly divisive in the Democratic party for two subsequent generations.

Civil rights is a term more closely associated with the struggle of African-Americans for equal treatment since the Civil War (though for a time it was used often by labor union organizers). In 1875, Congress passed a Civil Rights Act outlawing discrimination in public accommodations. By 1883, a reaction had set in, and the Supreme Court found key sections of the act unconstitutional. Not until 1957 was another Civil Rights Act passed. See SEPARATE BUT EQUAL; WE SHALL OVERCOME; FREEDOM RIDERS; HUMAN RIGHTS.

class warfare A charge of seeking power by dividing economic groups into predatory rich and oppressed poor.

Senator John Edwards, Democrat of North Carolina, made "two Americas" his central theme in campaigning as John Kerry's running mate in 2004. President Bush noted that "Angry talk, and class warfare rhetoric, and economic isolationism won't get anybody hired." When Edwards in 2007 began his campaign for the top spot in 2008, he was quickly attacked by conservative commentators as pitting the rich (of which there are few) against the poor (of which there are many, though a lower percentage vote). David Limbaugh in *The Washington Times* wrote that liberals "loudly profess their allegiance to capitalism, but resent the inequitable monetary results it produces. Isn't that what John Edwards' 'two Americas' theme is all about?" Columnist Robert Novak quoted an unnamed "party insider" saying that Edwards "came to Washington as a 'New Democrat,' but he's not that kind of Democrat anymore. He's into class warfare."

The liberal E. J. Dionne of *The Washington Post* Writers Group countered with "If, as is likely, Bush's path to a 'balanced budget' combines tax cuts with freezes or reductions in programs for the needy, Democrats should risk being accused of 'class warfare' by pointing out that the president's path will produce not fiscal health but further social decline."

Class warfare was introduced in 1848 as *class struggle*. In their *Communist Manifesto*, Karl Marx and Friedrich Engels wrote, "The history of all hitherto existing society is the history of *class struggle*"; in German, *Klassenkampf.* The German *Kampf* is translated as "struggle," short of *Krieg*, "war." However, four years later, the word was escalated by *The Times* of London: "Lord Henry Lennox thinks that the pressure of taxation is unequal, and he hopes for an amicable settlement of our fatal *class warfare.*" In 1927, Aldous Huxley denounced "those who would interpret all social phenomena in terms of *class warfare.*"

Struggle lost the struggle; in blazing away at populists and others who sought to redistribute income in ways that favored what used to be called "the lower classes," the users of *class warfare* won the phrasemakers' war.

clean sweep A smashing, across-the-board victory; a wide-ranging change of officeholders.

In the synonymy of success in politics, *landslide* refers more often to a great individual victory, *avalanche* to a great number of votes, and *clean sweep* to the success of many candidates belonging to a single party. See DISASTER METAPHORS.

The phrase stems from the expression "a new broom sweeps clean," an English proverb traceable to 1546. In Andrew Jackson's presidential campaigns, "Old Hickory" promised that his hickory broom would sweep out the "Augean stables" of corruption—specifically the "corrupt bargain" of John Quincy Adams and Henry Clay. In 1840 Clay was quoted as saying, "General Jackson was a bold and fearless reaper carrying a wide row, but he did not gather the whole harvest; he left some gleanings to his faithful successor, and he seems resolved to sweep clean the field of power."

Soon after Jackson's inauguration, the phrase's meaning changed. The SPOILS SYSTEM entered American politics and a *clean sweep* came to mean a total change of appointive officeholders. In the twentieth century, however, the meaning reverted to its original sense of broad party victory.

clear it with Sidney A remark of FDR's used by his critics to illustrate how strongly the President was dominated by organized labor.

Arthur Krock reported in *The New York Times* on July 25, 1944, that Roosevelt had said, in connection with the choice of a Vice President in 1944, "Clear everything with Sidney." (The choice turned out to be Harry Truman to replace the more radical Henry Wallace. Others being considered at the time were James F. Byrnes, William O. Douglas, Sam Rayburn, Paul McNutt, Scott Lucas, Alben Barkley, and John G. Winant.)

"Sidney" was Sidney Hillman, head of the Political Action Committee of the CIO, a Roosevelt adviser. The remark was officially denied, but in a book published fourteen years later James F. Byrnes, probably Krock's source, said the remark was made between July 15 and 17, 1944.

Hillman strongly urged that Wallace be kept on the ticket, but it never "cleared" FDR. Truman was Hillman's second choice. The attack on Hillman, according to counsel and speechwriter Samuel Rosenman, "was obviously an unvarnished, unabashed appeal to anti-Jewish prejudices.... The President did not try to defend Sidney Hillman, or say that there was no truth to the charge that things had to be 'cleared with Sidney.' Instead, he carried the attack right to his opponent." Roosevelt's attack came early in the campaign, slamming into religious intolerance in a Boston speech: "big as this country is, there is no room in it for racial or religious intolerance ... and there is no room for snobbery."

Writing about Hillman a decade later, C. Wright Mills gave the phrase sociological significance: "his awareness of himself as a member of the national elite, and the real and imagined recognition he achieved as a member ('Clear it with Sidney') signaled the larger entrance, after the great expansion of the unions and after the New Deal, of labor leaders into the POWER ELITE."

In the Eisenhower Administration, a frequent remark was "Clear it with Sherm" (Sherman Adams, see ABOMINABLE NO-MAN). In 1967, a *New York Times* story began:

"The 'clear it with Hubert' [Humphrey] order was issued by the President at a cabinet meeting last Wednesday."

In current usage, *run it past* is overtaking *clear it with*. See SIGN OFF ON.

climate change See GLOBAL WARMING.

cloakroom Congressional meeting places just off the Senate and House floors, where congressmen confer, trade, and gossip.

English journalist George Rose wrote to his countrymen in 1868 about "a rush to the cloakroom amid the shouts and laughter of the House." The *cloakrooms* of the Capitol came to mean not a place to hang a hat but a place to bargain. "In the quiet councils of committee rooms and cloakrooms," wrote former White House correspondent Charles Hurd in 1965, "they negotiate, compromise and trade their votes."

The sense of trading in the cloakrooms appears to be switching more to a sense of gossiping. "The cloakrooms of Congress resounded with a lurid account," reported the *Chicago Daily News* in 1947, "of what General Eisenhower there proposed as a solution." In 2006, the *Los Angeles Times* reported the reaction of Susan Duran, a House page: "Susan said that while working in the Democratic cloakroom—a members-only inner sanctum for lawmakers just off the House floor—she got a candid view of the daily routines of politicians...'I was behind closed doors, and I got to see it all.'"

Congressional cloakrooms are tending to become synonymous with *rumor mill* and *rumor factory.* See LOBBY.

closed shop A place of work where only union members may be employed.

The *closed shop*—so called because it excludes unorganized workers from the workshop—goes back to labor troubles in Philadelphia's shoe industry in the early nineteenth century, but did not gain wide circulation until a century later. Unionists prefer *union shop*, because it sounds less restrictive. *American Federationist* wrote in 1904: "The object of the union shop is not to create a monopoly of opportunity. It is not a *closed shop*." But the phrase has stuck. In 1948, the *Chicago Daily News* wrote, "A 'closed shop' violates the fundamental rights of the individual."

Recent usage extended the term to professional sports. In 1989, *Newsday* reported on negotiations by teams seeking to sign Dallas Cowboys running back Herschel Walker: "Until they heard Walker had vetoed a deal with the Vikings on Wednesday, said a source close to the negotiations, 'a lot of them thought it was a closed shop.'"

See RIGHT TO WORK.

closed society See OPEN SOCIETY.

closing ranks The act of healing wounds after a battle for nomination in time to achieve PARTY UNITY in the general election.

After a particularly bitter primary, there are always those who will speak up for the importance of the two-party system and the need to *close ranks*. Customarily, the victor in a nomination fight extends the invitation to his previous opposition; many political analysts were astounded at Barry Goldwater's 1964 acceptance speech at the Republican convention, when no such invitation was offered. (The author was present at the Cow Palace in San Francisco that year, and noted how the spectator Richard Nixon sat on his hands during the explosion of applause at Goldwater's "extremism is no vice" line.)

Like many other political expressions (see ON THE POINT), this is a MILITARY METAPHOR, referring to the scattering of troops during a skirmish and the subsequent need to come together to form a cohesive fighting unit once again.

The act of forcing a smile and supporting the man who defeated you or your candidate is a humbling, often teeth-gnashing experience. Two Republicans who opposed William McKinley's nomination in 1896—Henry Cabot Lodge and Theodore Roosevelt—traveled to Canton, Ohio, where the candidate was conducting his FRONT-PORCH CAMPAIGN, and made the necessary obeisances. Statesman John Hay used a colorful, if extreme, metaphor: "Cabot

and Teddy have been to Canton to offer their heads to the axe and their tummies to the harikari knife."

cloth coat See CHECKERS SPEECH.

clothespin vote A loyalist's vote cast without enthusiasm or with outright displeasure.

A *clothespin*—as was formerly well known—is a wooden peg or clip used to fasten wet clothes to a line for drying. This type of pin, its name an Americanism first found in print in 1846 and for a century an indispensable household item before the onset of electric driers, was long used to signal disgust. Cartoons from the turn of the twentieth century show a person's nose clamped tight with a clothespin to keep from inhaling unpleasant odors.

Clothespin's use as an attributive noun in the phrase *clothespin vote* is of mid-twentieth-century origin. This type of ballot is often cast by those who find the party's candidates obnoxious, but decide to stick with their party out of habit or loyalty (see YELLOW DOG DEMOCRAT) or because the alternative seems to them even worse. See HOBSON'S CHOICE. As the 1996 presidential primaries approached, the *Albany Times Union* asked: "Are they now to look askance at a field of their second choices cynical about Clinton, dissatisfied with Dole, gagging on Gingrich, bored with all the rest, in the end forced to cast a 'clothespin vote'?"

cloture The cutting-off of debate; the majority's forced ending of discussion to produce a vote.

Based on a French noun with a circumflex over the *o*, this term denoted the closing of debate in the French Assembly by majority vote. *Edinburgh Review* wrote in 1871 of the prolonged debate "before the establishment of the cloture in the French Chamber." An etymological relative of *cloister* and *claustrophobia* (the fear of enclosed spaces), *cloture* comes from Latin *claustura*, based on the verb *claudere*, "to close."

Before its 1882 introduction into the British House of Commons, cloture caused political observers to fear the effects of cutting short the debate. *The Spectator* commented in 1881, "Might not an unscrupulous party chief…use the cloture to arrest necessary discussion." Following its introduction, this method of shutting off debate became known in England as *closure*, spelled with an *s*.

Cloture entered American politics during the First World War. On March 8, 1917, the Senate adopted the *cloture rule*, which allowed the will of a majority to end debate; however, any Senator was allowed to speak for an hour after invoking the rule.

Still invoked in the 1990s, the cloture rule can lead to a *cloture vote*. Senator Warren Rudman, Republican of New Hampshire, told television interviewer Larry King in June 1992 about the result of debate on balancing the budget: "Well, this is actually a procedural vote, Larry. It's a so-called cloture vote, and if 60 votes are achieved, then we will have a final vote tomorrow on the balanced budget amendment." Two months later, Democratic Senator Harris Wofford of Pennsylvania expressed the hope on Cable News Network for "the cloture votes, beyond the 57 [Democratic votes], to get something on the floor of the Senate."

For more recent cloture developments, see GANG OF FOURTEEN.

Cloud-Cuckoo-Land Dream world; an area of unrealistic expectations and foolish behavior.

The eponym of this unreal world is the *cuckoo*, a thirteenth-century noun that imitates the bird's call. The cuckoo's common European species is a grayish-brown bird that builds no nest and instead expects other birds to hatch and raise its young.

The hyphenated noun phrase comes from the Greek *Nephelokokkygia*, the name for a dream world in Aristophanes' ancient comedy *The Birds*. The Greek term was translated into English in 1824 as *Cuckoo-cloudland*; however, the British journalist Richard Whiteing reworked the name in his 1899 novel, *No. 5 John Street:* "All his thinking processes fade off into the logic of Cloud Cuckoo Land."

Variations include a 1903 comment in *The Daily Chronicle* about "our new school of economists (sort of cloud-cuckoo-town),"

but nowadays the term most often used is Cloud-Cuckoo-Land, capitalized and hyphenated.

In 1988, when the elder George Bush proposed an expensive child-care plan during his first presidential campaign, Michael Dukakis countered that the Republican plan belonged in "financial Cloud-Cuckoo-Land."

cloud no bigger than a man's hand See STRAW POLL.

clout Power, or in a less potent sense, influence.

When applied to a candidate for high office or celebrated political personage, *clout* means political power; when used to describe a political leader not in the public eye, a large contributor, or member of a palace guard, it means influence. Because the word can be used to define both power and influence, the word has a clear meaning only in context.

Clout, in its power sense, applies to the ability of an individual or group to put across a program, decide a nomination, sway votes. In its influence sense, *clout* means the ability to reach and persuade those at the top; it is one step removed from the power source.

Although the etymologist Grant Barrett unearthed an 1868 use in New York City—about fellows in Brooklyn "that always think they are going to be deprived of office and '*clout*'"—the political use of the word has long been associated with Chicago politics. A precinct captain in that city was quoted in Harold Gaswell's *Machine Politics* in 1937 saying, "No one…gets anywhere in politics or business on his merits. He has to have the '*clout*' from behind."

Earlier senses are "cloth," specifically "handkerchief," and the unrelated "a blow on the head," and from that is derived its use in baseball, for a hard-hit drive. Atcheson Hench in *American Speech* magazine (October 1959) pointed out that a *clouter* was originally a handkerchief thief, the noun *clout* later covering any petty thievery. In recent underworld lingo, to *clout heaps* means "to steal automobiles."

Columnist Irv Kupcinet, in the *Chicago Sun-Times*, December 14, 1958, said: "Defendants in Chicago, as in Los Angeles, are found innocent on the age-old legal premise of 'reasonable doubt'—not, as the judge insinuated, 'reasonable clout.'"

Theodore Bernstein, in his word-watching column, provided a nice distinction between *clout* and *muscle:* "The two words mean virtually the same thing: power or effectiveness, particularly in the areas of government or business. But...there is a shade of difference between the two. The accumulation of *muscle* leads to the possession of *clout.*"

Current use stresses the loss rather than possession of clout. Xinhua, the Chinese news agency, reported in 2007 that Les Gelb, president emeritus of the Council on Foreign Relations, said, "There's no doubt that [Vice President Richard] Cheney has lost clout." At the same time, Egypt's *Middle East Times* observed that Russian President "Putin's words came as part of a deliberate effort to reclaim lost Russian clout."

In that context of loss of power, the word has recently been applied to entire states rather than individuals. As large states moved their primary elections earlier in the year to better influence the selection of candidates for national office, the *San Francisco Chronicle* headlined in 2007: "Early primary—too much, too soon? State's bid to gain political clout may be diluted as others join the bandwagon." Which they did. See JUICE.

club See INNER CLUB.

coalition A grouping of often disparate political elements into a major party, or of several nations into an ad hoc alliance.

"A political aspirant in the United States," Alexis de Tocqueville wrote, "begins by discovering his own interest, and discovering those other interests which may be collected around and amalgamated with it." According to political scientist James MacGregor Burns, "Tocqueville was describing one of the oldest and simplest acts of politics—the effort of the Greek magistrate or the Roman senator, of the Russian revolutionary or the British squire, to piece together a following big enough to win power in a legislative assembly or a political party or a popular election."

One example is the formation of the Republican party. It drew its strength, Clinton Rossiter wrote, "from almost every party and group on the American scene—from the Whigs, yes, but also from the Democrats, Free-Soilers, Abolitionists, Know-Nothings, local third parties and, lest we forget, the temperance movement."

In multiparty nations abroad, a coalition involves the fusion of a number of individual parties into a working majority. West Germany's "Grand Coalition" of the Socialist and Christian Democratic parties was an example. In the U.S., by contrast, the major parties are themselves coalitions, combining liberals, moderates, and conservatives, thereby helping Democrats and Republicans to avoid extremes. For this reason, most politicians instinctively reject suggestions that U.S. politics be realigned into liberal and conservative parties.

The word was incorporated into a political movement in the '80s as part of Jesse Jackson's "Rainbow Coalition," a reference to people of different colors. During the second war in Iraq, President George W. Bush, unable to assemble the support of all NATO nations in obtaining REGIME CHANGE, called the group of nations he did assemble "the coalition of the willing."

Words of praise for coalitions are BIG TENT, *united front*, and *umbrella*; attack phrases are STRANGE BEDFELLOWS and UNHOLY ALLIANCE.

coattails Political carrying power; the ability to attract and hold support, not only for oneself but for other members of a ticket; for a weak candidate on a ticket, somebody to grimly hang onto.

Congressman Abraham Lincoln popularized the phrase in a speech in the House on July 27, 1848, after the metaphor had been introduced by Alfred Iverson of Georgia:

> But the gentleman from Georgia further says, we have deserted all our principles, and taken shelter under General Taylor's military coat tail. ...

Has he no acquaintance with the ample military coat tail of General Jackson? Does he not know that his own party have run the last five Presidential races under that coat tail, and that they are now running the sixth, under the same cover?... Mr. Speaker, old horses and military coat tails, or tails of any sort, are not figures of speech, such as I would be the first to introduce into discussions here; but ...

The military connotation soon fell by the wayside and *coattails* came to mean an inducement to straight-ticket voting. In the 1960 presidential campaign, Kennedy supporter Adlai Stevenson said of the Republican nominee, "Nixon is finding out there are no tails on an Eisenhower jacket." (The General had introduced a tail-free military jacket during World War II.) In the 1966 congressional campaign, when Nixon began a political comeback stumping the country for congressional candidates, he also found use for the metaphor, attacking Lyndon B. Johnson's sagging popularity: "There is a new fashion sweeping the country: skirts are shorter, pants are tighter and the LBJ coattails are going out of style." See HYMIE'S FERRYBOAT.

cocoon See BUBBLE.

code words A charge that particular phrases, innocuous in themselves, are intended to transmit hidden meanings.

Charles P. Taft, chairman of the Fair Campaign Practices Committee, said in 1968: "We cannot prevent voters from casting ballots based on racist sentiment, but we can spotlight those campaigners who appeal to that sentiment. We can, that is, if we point to an objective study of the understood meanings of the campaign code words—the current shorthand of racial bigotry." Among conservative phrases considered part of the "code" at that time were LAW AND ORDER, CRIME IN THE STREETS, and BUSING.

In many cases the use of these words was intended to, and did, cloak appeal to racial prejudice. However, they were also often used in good faith to discuss controversial topics, and the *code word* charge could be, and was, used as a smear. The code is sometimes only in the eye of the beholder: in some areas, whenever the phrase *Roman*

Catholic is used rather than *Catholic*, anti-Catholic prejudice is suspected—since *Roman* (as in the 1884 "Rum, Romanism, and Rebellion," which ruined its user) is occasionally perceived as a word intended to show domination from the Vatican (see UNPACK).

"Every campaign becomes, at some point, a battle of coded words and ideas," wrote *New York Post* columnist Max Lerner in 1972, "in which the issues are somehow scooped out and only the verbal husk remains. [Senator George McGovern's] code words are 'precious young lives' and 'dying far from home for a corrupt dictatorship.'" In 1977, the neoconservative Irving Kristol objected in the *Wall Street Journal* to the use of biased code words in news broadcasts: "the neatest ploy of all is the selective use of the word 'controversial'; legislation to regulate the price of natural gas is not controversial. Anita Bryant is controversial; leaders of Gay Rights groups are not. This is the subtlest code word of them all. Watch for it."

The language of diplomacy is catnip for codebreakers. In the Middle East, the phrase "defensible borders" is taken by Israelis and Arabs to mean not returning some of the land taken by Israel in its 1967 defensive war. The phrase "legitimate rights of the Palestinian people" was long seen as a commitment to the "right" to a sovereign state of Palestine, and its use by President Carter in 1977 angered many supporters of Israel, until its use by Israeli Prime Minister Menachem Begin at a breakfast in Blair House in Washington, DC. (The author, who was present, asked if that was a slip, and Begin replied "Has my right hand lost its cunning?"—quoting Psalms 137:5.) In the same way, "West Bank" was considered pro-Arab code; Israelis then preferred "disputed territories." In 2005, Israelis built an anti-suicide bomber "fence"; Palestinians called it a "wall," evoking memories of the Berlin wall.

In 1970 the author, preparing a speech for President Nixon, slipped up on a diplomatic code word. The U.S. and the Soviet Union had been negotiating in a desultory fashion about the removal of each other's troops from central Europe. The Americans called this Mutual and Balanced Force Reduction (MBFR); the Soviets called it Mutual Force Reduction (MFR). In the Nixon speech, the writer left out "and balanced"; Secretary of State William Rogers called to ask that the two words be inserted in the written version of the speech as finally released for publication. The reason is that the U.S. argued that the removal of one American all the way across the Atlantic Ocean should be "balanced" by the removal of more than one Russian from nearby Europe; as Secretary Rogers put it, "those two code words could mean a couple hundred thousand troops." (European diplomats careful not to offend either superpower referred to the talks in 1978 as "M (B) FR" talks, while Americans said wryly the initials stood for "More Better For Russia.")

In 1977, writing in *The New Yorker* about the victory of Ed Koch in New York City's mayoral race, Andy Logan quoted the mayor-elect as saying, "The code word of my Administration will be 'reality.'" The writer noted parenthetically, "code word is now itself a kind of code word." Koch probably intended an up-to-date version of *byword*. FAMILY VALUES became code words in 1992 for opposition to approving homosexuality and abortion; after the attack on the phrase, Republicans behind George H.W. Bush and Dan Quayle preferred to use *traditional values*. For an Australian synonym for code words, see DOG-WHISTLE POLITICS.

coffee-klatsch campaign A method of campaigning in urban areas where the candidate meets small groups of voters at a "coffee hour," often in a supporter's home.

Cocktail parties lend themselves to fundraising, but less to campaigning with the candidate present; they tend to degenerate into bona fide cocktail parties, noisy and inattentive. The coffee-klatsch (*Klatsch* is German for "noise," akin to the English *clatter*) offers a candidate an opportunity to meet about twenty-five people personally, make a brief talk, and move on. The coffee-klatsch costs the host little and is an especially effective technique for apartment-house dwellers.

cold war Nonmilitary conflict; ideological hostilities; now used to indicate outmoded or unwanted policies.

Capitalized, *the* Cold War refers to international tension and jockeying for power between the Soviet Union (and its satellites) and the Western nations; lower case, a *cold war* is any adversary activity short of open conflict; behind-the-scenes struggle; tension and deadlock beneath the political surface, as "the cold war between the Johnsons and the Kennedys."

Coiner of the phrase in its modern sense, though not its all-time originator, was Herbert Bayard Swope, publicist, three-time winner of the Pulitzer Prize, and occasional speechwriter for elder statesman (and Port Washington, N.Y., neighbor) Bernard Baruch. In 1946, about the time Churchill was speaking of an IRON CURTAIN, Swope used *cold war* in a draft speech for Baruch to describe U.S.-Soviet relations (as contrasted to the recent "hot" or "shooting" war). Baruch felt it was too strong, but used it one year later in a speech at Columbia, South Carolina: "Let us not be deceived—today we are in the midst of a cold war." He repeated the phrase, by that time picked up and popularized by columnist Walter Lippmann, to the Senate War Investigating Committee on October 24, 1948.

Because *cold war*, along with IRON CURTAIN, is one of the great coinages of the post-World War II period, its birth as description of the ideological and economic struggle between communism and capitalism, between the U.S.S.R. and its satellites and the U.S. and its allies, deserves close examination. The late Mr. Swope's secretary, Kathleen Gilmour, provided the author with a file of correspondence on the early use.

From Bernard Baruch (see ELDER STATESMAN) to Swope, August 17, 1949:

The first time I ever heard the expression "cold war" was when you first said it some time about June 1946. We decided not to use it at that time. I first used the phrase in April 1947 on the occasion of the presentation of my portrait to South Carolina. This was the first time it was given currency or was publicly uttered so far as I know. Immediately afterward, it was very much commented upon, especially in an editorial in the *New York Daily News*. I then called Mr. [Reuben] Maury and told him I had gotten it from you. Later on, he wrote an editorial giving you credit. In other words, you coined the expression and I gave it currency.

Baruch freely credited Swope with the coinage in several interviews; the probable reason Swope elicited the credit in writing was that the columnist Walter Lippmann was being given credit as coiner rather than as disseminator. Lippmann, after a while, mentioned to Swope that he recalled a French expression in the 1930s, *la guerre froide*, and on May 10, 1950, Swope wrote Lippmann to set him straight:

The first time the idea of the cold war came to me was probably in '39 or '40 when America was talking about a "shooting" war. I had never heard that sort of qualification. To me "shooting" war was like saying a death murder—rather tautologous, verbose and redundant. I thought the proper opposite of the so-called hot war was cold war, and I used that adjective in the early '40's in some letters I wrote, before our war.

Swope drove home his claim of credit to the man he felt was usurping his place in rhetorical history:

I may have been subconsciously affected by the term cold pogrom which was used to describe the attitude of the Nazis toward the Jews in the middle '30s. I never heard the French expressions to which you refer. The description became timely again when the Russians were putting pressure on us for the second front, but I used it first in a little talk I made in '45, just before the war ended. Then in '46 at the time BMB made his speech to the United Nations on the American attitude toward the atomic bomb, I used the phrase in the first draft of his speech that I prepared in March or April. Baruch, Eberstadt and Hancock thought it was too severe to describe our relations with the Russians, even though they had been attenuated for a long time, so it was taken out of the speech.

But the words were put in an important speech which Baruch delivered at the end of '46 or the beginning of '47 at the State Capitol in South Carolina when his portrait was unveiled. ...

I hope this answers your question. I've always believed that I happened to be the first to use the phrase.

As part of the American political language, the phrase gained international currency when Deputy Premier Nikolai Bulganin used it in his opening speech at the Big Four Conference in Geneva on July 18, 1955. Calling for a lessening of international tensions in accord with the "spirit of Geneva" (see SPIRIT OF), Bulganin spoke of the Soviet "desire for a settlement of the outstanding international problems and for the termination of the 'Cold War.'"

Sir Ernest Gowers, who attributed the phrase to Walter Lippmann in his 1965 revision of Henry Fowler's *Modern English Usage*, made this point on its usage: "the metaphor places politicians in a dilemma when they try to follow it up. Are they to advocate a rise or a fall in the temperature of the cold war? The latter would seem to intensify an already alarming crisis; the former to bring the hot war a stage nearer. This problem has to be dodged by doing violence to the metaphor." The metaphoric problem he raised was solved by the use of "a thaw in the Cold War," a melting of the frozen positions without the increased danger of a hot, or shooting, war.

Cold warrior became a term of derogation used by supporters of DÉTENTE and proponents of "convergence" between the two systems. "We won the Cold War," said George H.W. Bush in 1992, campaigning vainly for re-election, following the breakup of the Soviet Union. This led to "post-Cold War" and the emergence of the nomenclature of "the WAR ON TERROR."

Regression from the disorganized democracy in the brief Boris Yeltsin era to the tightly controlled autocracy of Vladimir Putin, with its murders of dissident journalists, led many in the West to concerns about a return to cold-war tensions. "I don't throw around terms like 'new Cold War,'" said Secretary of State Condoleezza Rice in 2007. "It is a big, complicated relationship, but it is not one that is anything like the implacable hostility" of the past. "Russia is not the Soviet Union ..."

Who actually "coined" the phrase? In the 2006 *Yale Book of Quotations*, editor Fred Shapiro used some of the above information and added more, including "In 1938 'the Nation' magazine had a headline 'Hitler's Coldwar' (28 March 1938). According to

Luis Garcia Arias … (1956), a thirteenth-century Spanish writer, Don Juan Manuel, used *guerra fria* to refer to the coexistence of Islam and Christendom in medieval Spain." That takes it back eight centuries, and search engines are still in their infancy.

College of Cardinals See POWERHOUSE.

coloration Ideological identification based on political associations, record, and statements.

This has remained an inside political word. When a political team is being set up around a candidate, or a ticket is being BALANCED, consideration is given to *coloration*: RIGHT WING, LEFT WING, private or public power, EASTERN ESTABLISHMENT, Southern Conservative or other region, known for any beliefs, slogans, or evidence of flakiness.

Coloration is purely appearance, not necessarily substance; many times, honest, outspoken men acquire—through region, association, family name—a coloration totally different from their point of view.

"The most striking discovery one makes in examining the Johnson history," wrote Selig Harrison in *The New Republic* in 1960, "is how little he has changed. Unlike Kennedy—whose political coloration is not at all what it was ten years ago—Johnson seems to have been from the beginning more or less what he is today."

color metaphors Those who supported black causes in the mid-nineteenth century were derided as BLACK REPUBLICANS. See BLACK, POLITICAL USE OF. The *Black and Tans* were opposed by the *Lily-Whites*, and BLACK POWER emerged in the 1960s. *White*, as in the '60s' "white power structure," is also used racially; a *white hope* stems from the futile attempts by a line of white fighters to defeat black champion Jack Johnson. And the word CANDIDATE comes from the Latin "wearing a white toga," the color symbolizing purity of motive.

However, issues are not all black and white; *gray* areas are known to exist, often providing the best atmosphere for a GRAY EMINENCE like a monk who controls a cardinal who controls a king. The gray uniforms of the Confederate soldiers led to the phrase *the grays and the blues*.

Blue has a sexual overtone. *Blue jokes* offend *bluenoses*, who pass BLUE LAWS closing stores on Sundays.

Green is the color of the environmentalist; also the amateur, the newcomer. The *greenhorn* was carefully cultivated by big-city machines, which also provided cash, or *long green*, or *greenbacks*. The *Green Berets* of the U.S. Special Forces gave the color professionalism.

Purple symbolizes royalty, *yellow* cowardice, *orange* describes atomic explosions, and radical *red* has a separate entry herein. Red stood for communism; after the Soviet disintegration, the color returned to its original symbol of radicalism in general as well as China's government.

For "color-blind," see QUOTA. For differentiation of states by party, see RED STATE/BLUE STATE.

colossus of the north See GOOD NEIGHBOR POLICY.

come now, and let us reason together A Biblical invitation identified with Lyndon B. Johnson's CONSENSUS.

Adlai Stevenson, introducing a book of Johnson speeches, wrote: " 'Come now, and let us reason together' is Lyndon Johnson's favorite quotation and his best characterization … for the thirty years I have known him—as a Congressional secretary, Congressman, Senate Majority leader, Vice President, and now President—reasoning together, face to face, has been his method and his strength."

Arthur Schlesinger, Jr., later wrote of a meeting between Johnson and Philip Graham, then publisher of *The Washington Post* in the hectic days before the 1960 Democratic convention: "Graham had meanwhile arranged to lunch that day with Johnson in the double hope of persuading him to release Stevenson from his neutrality pledge in order to nominate Kennedy and also of persuading Johnson to accept the Vice Presidency. But he found the Senate leader far from Isaiah and in no mood for reasoning together." The paragraph is footnoted "Isaiah 1:18, L.B.J., *passim*." When Republicans were attacking Johnson's assumption of the centrist position and difficult-to-assail consensus, they occasionally pointed to more of the same Isaiah quotation, a prophet's threat: "If ye be willing and obedient, ye shall eat the good of the land; but if ye refuse and rebel ye shall be devoured with the sword."

Although the prophet's words were used derisively against memories of the Johnson Administration in the early '70s, they were recalled with affection by Senator Hubert Humphrey in October 1977, as LBJ's former Vice President, dying of cancer, addressed the Senate: "What a wonderful place this is, where we can argue, fight, have different points of view, and still have a great respect for one another and, many times, deep affection...now my plea to us is, in the words of Isaiah, as a former President used to say,—and I mean it very sincerely— 'Come, let us reason together.'"

common man, century of the Utopian ideal popularized by Henry A. Wallace in a 1942 speech.

"The century on which we are entering can be and must be the century of the common man," said Wallace, who was FDR's Vice President at the time he made the speech. "Everywhere the common people are on the march."

In the middle third of the century, the "common man" was the subject of fulsome flattery. Even Adolf Hitler sought to embrace him. "National Socialism," said the Nazi dictator, "is the revolution of the common man." But political thinkers soon began recalling that commonness had not always been a cherished value—far from it. "The superior man," Confucius said, "thinks always of virtue; the common man thinks of comfort."

In 1956, former President Herbert Hoover warned that "we are in danger of developing a cult of the Common Man, which means a cult of mediocrity." Essayist Joseph Wood Krutch wrote:

From defending the common man we pass on to exalting him and we find ourselves beginning to imply not merely that he is as good as anybody

else but that he is actually better. Instead of demanding only that the common man be given an opportunity to become as uncommon as possible, we make his commonness a virtue and, even in the case of candidates for high office, we sometimes praise them for being nearly indistinguishable from the average man in the street.

To Lyndon Johnson, speaking at the Tufts University commencement in 1963, "it seems no longer adequate to describe this as the Century of the Common Man." For, he explained, a "revolution of education" was underway that was "changing the capabilities of the common man," so much so that the period "should henceforth be known as the Century of the Educated Man."

Still, the idea of the *common man* (the phrase has not been amended to "the common person") did not lose its appeal, particularly for politicians. After Richard Nixon's 1952 CHECKERS SPEECH, Scripps-Howard columnist Robert Ruark wrote: "Tuesday night the nation saw a little man, squirming his way out of a dilemma, and laying bare his most private hopes, fears and liabilities. This time the common man was a Republican, for a change."

Communism with a human face See EUROCOMMUNISM.

Communist terminology There are separate entries in this dictionary for PROLETARIAT, PARTY LINE, PEACEFUL COEXISTENCE, and WAR OF NATIONAL LIBERATION. Some of the following smattering of Communist terms are adapted from a glossary prepared by Richard V. Allen in *Peace or Peaceful Co-Existence?*, published by the American Bar Association in 1966.

adventurism: "Excess revolutionary zeal" that leads to taking unnecessary risks and increases the possibility of error.

as is well known: Assumption as fact requiring no further explanation; see REPORTEDLY.

bourgeoisie: Originally the middle class, as distinguished from the very wealthy; Lenin later enlarged this group to include all property owners. In later use it meant all non-Communists.

class enemy: A class that holds political power or which stood between the proletariat and its achievement of power; also, anti-Communists within Communist countries.

class struggle: From Marx and Engels in their *Communist Manifesto*— "The history of all hitherto existing society is the history of class struggles." See CLASS WARFARE.

counterrevolution: Opposing an accomplished Communist revolution or seeking to crush a developing Communist revolution.

oppressed peoples: Citizens of colonial or nonself-governing areas, as well as those emerging nations which maintain too close ties with their former developers.

For a group of communist terms about deviation from the party line, see REVISIONISM. For post-communist terms, see GLASNOST and PERESTROIKA.

community A kindly lumping together of related organizations, instilling by euphemism a sense of shared purpose not always reflecting reality.

The *defense establishment* was a term used by defenders of expanded budgets for the armed services, who were derided by critics of the MILITARY-INDUSTRIAL COMPLEX. However, when *establishment* became pejorative—as in EASTERN ESTABLISHMENT—military people and their supporters began talking (in the early '60s) of the *defense community*, influenced by Walter Lippmann's mid-'40s ATLANTIC COMMUNITY.

Community had a less elitist connotation, and had been a favored term of home builders, who had changed *tract developers* to *community developers*. Similarly, the term *business leaders* was followed by the *business community* as arbiters of whether an Administration possessed "business confidence." The communal euphemism also came to the rescue of beleaguered members of the espionage world in the '70s. The *cloak-and-dagger crowd*, also known as the *intelligence establishment*, became the *intelligence community*. As in real communities, resentments soon developed among people living on different sides of the tracks.

A related word, *set* is always used pejoratively in politics, from the isolationist *Cliveden set* in Great Britain before World War II to the *Georgetown cocktail party set* (more dens of inequity than iniquity) in Washington. *Wine and cheese set* and *brie and chablis set* marked John Anderson's 1980 campaign; a generation later, the set was derogated as "the chardonnay-sipping, bicoastal hipster crowd."

compact of Fifth Avenue An agreement between Governor Nelson Rockefeller and Vice President Richard Nixon before the Republican convention in 1960.

The platform committee, headed by Charles Percy, had drafted a platform acceptable to Republican conservatives and middle-of-the-roaders, but the Rockefeller forces let it be known that—unless the document was changed—they would launch a floor fight. Without informing his Chicago convention staff, Nixon went to Rockefeller's New York apartment; over dinner, he offered the governor the vice-presidential nomination, which was declined; then the two men went over a draft memo submitted by Rockefeller's staff.

The 14-point "compact" that emerged advocated increased defense expenditures, took a cautiously liberal view on education as well as health care for the aged, and adopted a forthright civil rights position. When the manifesto was passed on to the delegates in Chicago, many were furious at Rockefeller's "high-handedness"; others charged Nixon with a SELLOUT. To many conservatives, this appeared to be the opposite side of the coin minted eight years before between Eisenhower and Taft at the SURRENDER ON MORNINGSIDE HEIGHTS. In fact, those positions advocated in the compact were on the whole those taken by Nixon before and much later. He took personal charge of selling the platform committee on the changes needed, and the furor died, though Senator Goldwater had branded the compact "the Munich of the Republican party." (See MUNICH ANALOGY.) President Eisenhower felt that the defense suggestions were an affront to his administration, although Nixon had removed Rockefeller's proposal that $3 billion in additional defense expenditure was immediately necessary.

As with all platforms, compromises were made; the term *sit-in*, part of the Rockefeller statement, was left out of the final plank, but the plank was strongly enough worded to satisfy liberals; the "compact of Fifth Avenue" reshaped the 1960 platform.

compassionate conservatism Centrist slogan popularized by George W. Bush in his campaign to win the Republican Party's presidential nomination for the 2000 election. This was "W's" version of his father's previous KINDER AND GENTLER NATION. The alliterative phrase was suggested to the younger Bush by Marvin Olasky, a journalism professor at the University of Texas at Austin.

Mr. Bush was not the first conservative to recognize the political virtues of boldly expressed compassion. Sen. Orrin Hatch (R-Utah) had objected to a proposed cut in the budget of the Jobs Corps by the Reagan Administration, telling *New York Times* reporter Judith Miller in 1981: "I'm a conservative and proud of it, but I'm a compassionate conservative. I'm not some kind of rightwing maniac, despite some portrayals in the press."

Under the headline "Compassion Becomes a Republican Theme," Roger Ailes (later Fox News chief, see FAIR AND BALANCED), media consultant to Richard Nixon in 1968 and later to Vice President George H. W. Bush, was quoted in 1987: "George Bush is a conservative and a compassionate man. There's nothing mutually exclusive about it."

The alliterative phrase dates back nearly a half-century. The *Times* used the seeming oxymoron in 1962, describing House Speaker Sam Rayburn, a Texas Democrat, "in action a compassionate Conservative." A few years later, the *Appleton* (Wisc.) *Post-Crescent* gave much of the credit for passage of the 1964 civil rights bill to Rep. William M. McCullough of Ohio, the ranking Republican on the House Judiciary Committee: "On fiscal matters, McCullough is a strict conservative. But he is compassionate to the point of boldness on human values involving individual liberties." The editorial's headline: "A Compassionate Conservative."

Before that, another editorialist, this one for the Chicago *Daily Herald*, asserted in 1960 that "the Republican party…must reverse its big business image and bring conservatism to the man in the street. It must champion a 'compassionate conservatism,' a phrase coined by a young Republican friend of ours." The editorial continued, in the words of the anonymous friend, "In the end, you can be a compassionate conservative and still be frugal economically; you can be generous to mankind, but by sound administrative practice, be conservative of the taxpayers' dollar." The elder Bush's Secretary of Housing and Urban Development, Jack Kemp, called himself "a BLEEDING HEART conservative."

See DYNAMIC CONSERVATISM.

Comsymp Compressed form of Communist sympathizer; FELLOW TRAVELER.

California's Robert Welch, founder of the ultraconservative John Birch Society, argued in the late 1950s that the leadership of American corporations, universities, foundations, communications media, and government was riddled with Communists as well as those who "sympathized" with Communist aims. The amalgam of first syllables was useful to Birchers because it avoided having to say if any particular person under attack was a CARD-CARRYING Communist party member or not. The technique of compression was used by Vice President Spiro Agnew in 1970, attacking "radical liberals" as "radic-libs." See PINKO; BIRCHER.

concession speech Remarks of a candidate in the process of being defeated, recognizing the inevitable loss and permitting the winner to make his victory speech.

The two men with the greatest opportunity to refine Presidential concession speeches reacted quite differently. Henry Clay said, "I would rather be right than be President" (see I'D RATHER BE RIGHT), which had the flavor of sour grapes. William Jennings Bryan, after his third defeat, said, "I am reminded of the drunk who, when he had been thrown down the stairs of a club for the third time, gathered himself up, and said, 'I am on to those people. They don't want me in there.'"

To show that defeat need not mean failure, politicians who lose often turn to the comments of sportsmen. Sportswriter Grantland Rice produced this classic: "For when the One Great Scorer comes to mark against your name, he writes—not that you won or lost—but how you played the game." (Green Bay Packers coach Vince Lombardi, in a succeeding generation, took a harder line: "Winning is not the most important thing about football—it's the only thing.")

Napoleon, after Waterloo, said, "My downfall raises me to infinite heights." Winston Churchill began an aphorism with "In defeat, defiance"; Ernest Hemingway, injured in an air crash in 1954, remarked, "I am a little beat up, but I assure you it is only temporary," a modern version of John Paul Jones's "I have just begun to fight."

Although the speech conceding defeat is as old as politics, the modern concession speech began to come into its own with network radio election coverage and blossomed fully in the atmosphere of television. Rapid reporting and analysis of election returns on election night, with computerized "decisions" by commentators (with propagation of phrases like "probable winner" and "too close to call"), resulted in the opportunity to have both concession and victory statement on the same night.

The televised concession speech can be poignant (Hubert Humphrey after his West Virginia primary defeat by John F. Kennedy in 1960, with a folk singer strumming a melancholy song) or even nonexistent (Nixon in 1960, with the tide appearing to turn in his favor after midnight, as West Coast results made the race one of the closest in U.S. presidential history, but prompting Kennedy's caustic comment: "No class").

One of the most eloquent of the televised concession speeches was Adlai Stevenson's in 1952; after reading his congratulatory telegram to General Eisenhower, he concluded: "Someone asked me, as I came in, down on the street, how I felt, and I was reminded of a story that a fellow-townsman of ours used to tell—Abraham Lincoln. They asked him how he felt once after an unsuccessful election. He said he felt like a little boy who had stubbed his toe in the dark. He said that he was too old to cry, but it hurt too much to laugh."

condition, not a theory See PRACTICAL POLITICS.

confederate As a verb, to form an alliance that acts more as a coalition of interests than as a single sovereignty; as a verb, one allied in a struggle or conspiracy.

Federate, based on the Latin *foedus*, "compact, league," means "to form a union that acts as one," but *confederate* (the older verb in English) means "to create an alliance that acts as a group, not as individual entities."

The Founders moved from the Articles of Confederation, in effect from 1781 to 1789, to a more unified Constitution that would federate, or more thoroughly combine, the states. Southerners in rebellion during the Civil War preferred the word *confederacy* to emphasize the looser alliance of Southern states.

The nouns corresponding to these verbs are also not exact synonyms. *Federation* refers to a single sovereignty; a *confederation*, in which each participating power may hold onto its sovereignty, is weaker than a federation.

Of the political ties that bind, the most tightly bound words are *union* and *united*; then comes *federation*, followed by the looser *confederation*, the association of independent states called a *commonwealth*, and the loosest, *league*. The *United States* and *United Kingdom* are unions; the *United Nations* is a league.

confidential source An anonymous informant, hailed as a principled WHISTLEBLOWER or derided as a disgruntled or disloyal employee.

A *confidential source* is sometimes modified by journalists as *reliable* (meaning "this person has supplied accurate information before") or *usually reliable* (a delicate admission that the information supplied has not always been trustworthy). Other variations, typically reserved for government officials, include *highly-placed source* and *responsible* (or *well-informed*) *source* (as opposed, apparently, to sources that are irresponsible or ill-informed).

The FBI and other law enforcement agencies also make use of *confidential sources* (or *informants*), as in this 2007 *Washington Post* report on the use of body-building drugs by athletes: "The search warrant alleged that a confidential source received five orders of anabolic steroids from [former New York Mets employee Kirk J.] Radmoski." The FBI also has employed *highly confidential* (or *sensitive*) *sources*, which are hidden microphones and wiretaps. During the decades that J. Edgar Hoover served as FBI director (1924–72), electronic bugs often were placed without benefit of court order. In order to avoid mentioning the illegal devices, agents had to cast their reports in round-about terms, such as "a highly placed sensitive source of known reliability was contacted and furnished items of personality."

The news business could not function without *confidential sources*. In a great many cases, people will not speak on the record to reporters. Their reasons are diverse and frequently self-serving. Some are WHISTLEBLOWERS, who have information that merits public disclosure, but fear losing their jobs, or being prosecuted, if their identities are known. Others, involved in law enforcement, may be limited legally in what they can say publicly. Still others may occupy high offices in government, or be aides to those who hold such positions, and wish to launch TRIAL BALLOONS without associating themselves with ideas that may go "pop" or to LEAK information for many different reasons. And sometimes the sources just want to help reporters produce better-informed stories.

Different formulations may be used to help readers evaluate the credibility of *confidential sources*. An October 2005 report in *The New York Times* specified that "Three Democratic aides [spoke] on condition of anonymity to avoid reprisals from their bosses." Journalists, as their part of the bargain—whether explicit or implicit—typically go to considerable lengths to shield the identities of their sources in return for retaining access to them. Exceptions

occur. Michael Kinsley wrote in *The Wall Street Journal* in 1987: "Newsweek magazine is in big trouble with a lot of journalists for breaking the cardinal rule of the great Washington leakathon and revealing the name of a confidential source. Provoked beyond endurance by Lt. Col. Oliver North's testimony that leaks by Congress about the capture of the *Achille Lauro* terrorists had 'very seriously compromised our intelligence activities,' Newsweek revealed in its July 27 issue that Col. North himself was a Newsweek source about the operation."

Typically, however, the names of *confidential sources* are revealed only under pressure of subpoenas and threat of jail time for journalists and fines for their corporate employers, as happened in the Libby-Plame case; see CHILLING EFFECT; NOT FOR ATTRIBUTION; SOURCES.

conflict of interest The dilemma of a person trying to serve two masters, sometimes leading to cognitive dissonance and occasionally to jail.

"As a phrase, 'conflict of interest' is a relative newcomer to the American lexicon of wrongdoing," noted *Newsweek* in January 1969, "but as a political problem, it is as ancient as public servants with private incomes, secret holdings or conveniently placed kin." Senator Daniel Webster's 1832 letter to Nicholas Biddle, president of the Bank of the United States, was cited: "I believe my retainer has not been renewed or refreshed as usual." At the time of Webster's dunning, the Senate and the bank were in a battle over the bank's charter.

The phrase gained currency during World War II. In a letter to the Secretary of War on March 31, 1942, Acting Attorney General Charles Fahy gave an opinion about the suggestion that an Army officer be permitted to maintain liaison with a corporation in which he held stock. "Conflict between the interests of the U.S.," wrote Fahy, "the interests of the corporation and the interests of the Army officer as an officer and stockholder of the corporation are more than likely to arise." The Justice official quoted Section 41 of the Criminal Code and a statute forbidding government employees from accepting salary from outside sources for government work, adding: "Both are intended to prevent a conflict between self-interest and the interests of the government."

The phrase has been adopted in the criminal code: Chapter 11 of Title 18 of the U.S. Code is entitled "Bribery, Graft and Conflicts of Interest."

congenital liar Intemperate accusation by a columnist aroused by what he considered to be sustained prevarication by a political figure.

"Americans of all political persuasions are coming to the sad realization," wrote a *New York Times* columnist in 1996, "that our First Lady—a woman of undoubted talents who was a role model for many in her generation—is a congenital liar."

Basis for the charge was her challengeable explanation of highly profitable commodity trades through a disreputable broker, her evasion of responsibility for the firing of White House travel aides, and her reported order to disallow the Justice Department to search the office of a friend for Rose Law Firm records following his suicide.

The response of Hillary Clinton's press aide was to suggest that the word *congenital* was a slur on Mrs. Clinton's mother. (Though *congenital liar* was the example used in *Merriam-Webster's Collegiate Dictionary* to define the sense of "by nature," the columnist—this dictionary's author—would have been more precise had I used the synonymous adjective *habitual*.)

President Clinton's press secretary, Michael McCurry, denounced the "outrageous personal attack that has no basis in fact" and added, "The President, if he were not president, would have delivered a more forceful response to that on the bridge of Mr. Safire's nose." Asked by reporters later that day to confirm this, Mr. Clinton himself did so obliquely with "If I were an ordinary citizen, I might give that article the response it deserves."

This defense of a presidential family member reminded reporters of the note written by President Harry Truman to a music critic who had panned the performance of his daughter Margaret: "Someday, I hope to meet you. When that happens you'll need a new nose, a lot of beefsteak for black eyes and perhaps a supporter below!"

Amusement at the Clintons-vs.-Safire brouhaha peaked when Tim Russert, host of *Meet the Press*, presented the writer with a pair of red boxing gloves on the television program with which to defend himself when he met Mr. Clinton after his presidency.

Ten years later, Mrs. Clinton and the columnist found themselves as "roasters" of Rep. Rahm Emanuel at a charity dinner in Washington, DC. I was able to repeat the humorist Mark Russell's amelioration of the long-ago ruckus: that I had filed not the phrase "congenital liar" but the similar "congenial lawyer" and the fault had been in the computer transmission. Mrs. Clinton, then a senator from New York, topped that with the equally fanciful explanation that Bill Clinton had never referred to my nose, but to my "pitiful prose," and thus the hatchet was buried.

connect the dots See DATA MINING.

consciousness-raising Inciting to enthusiastic involvement; awakening the need for political activity; a recognition of suppressed resentments that call for redress.

"Consciousness," wrote John Locke in his 1690 *Essay on Human Understanding*, "is the perception of what passes in a Man's own mind." That quality of cognition—involving perception, memory, and judgment—combined with self-awareness is usually involved in the many uses of the word.

Although moral philosophers, and later psychologists, popularized the term, in mid-twentieth century politicians made it their own.

It has early Communist associations. Former Moscow correspondents, including Daniel Schorr, have reported to this lexicographer its frequent use in ideological discussions in the '50s, and Theodore H. White, in his 1978 book *In Search of History*, writes of an interview held in 1941, in the Chinese

Communist redoubt in Yenan, with Peng Dehuai, a close ally of Mao Zedong:

> The men who came in from the field, he said ... had to have their minds washed out, had to be remolded in ideology. [See BRAINWASH.] At first he thought this could be done in only three months; he had now learned that a full year was necessary to "remold the brain" before they could go on to study military matters, or economics, or heal, or administration. His interpreter and I searched for a word better than "brain remolding" and finally the interpreter came up with the phrase "raising the level of consciousness." This was the first time I heard that phrase, which, over the years, moved out of China and on to the streets and fashions of America in the 1960s.

Whether it stemmed from Chinese or Russian use, or has another origin, the idea of *raising* the level of consciousness (as distinct from "expanding" consciousness through the use of psychedelic drugs) came into use strongly in the '60s in the U.S., in the civil rights movement and most especially in the women's liberation movement. It may have been influenced by its use in psychology: "encounter groups" and "sensitivity training" also used *consciousness-raising* in their terminology.

By the mid-'70s, the word had been taken over by the women's movement—see WOMEN'S LIB and SEXISM—and the use by Locke in this entry would be frowned on.

consensus Broad agreement which, while not necessarily all-embracing, does embrace enough elements to enable a group to come to a decision.

Though Lyndon B. Johnson put his special brand on the term *consensus*, politicians and thinkers have been pondering its uses and abuses for millennia. The Roman orator Cicero declared, "The consensus of opinion among all nations, on whatever matter, may be taken for the law of nature." (That is a dated translation from the Latin *consensio*; in modern English, "consensus of opinion" is redundant.) Sir Francis Bacon, in his essay "Of Faction," wrote: "When factions are carried too high and too violently, it is a sign of weakness in princes, and much to the prejudice both of their authority and business."

Not everybody considers the quest for consensus the best *modus operandi*. Activist liberal advisers urged on John F. Kennedy the "superiority of the politics of combat as against the politics of consensus." Nonetheless, consensus has its clear uses in a nation as diverse as the U.S. President Eisenhower found himself in 1958 forced to back down from a proposed reform of the Pentagon because "my personal convictions, no matter how strong, cannot be the final answer. There must be a consensus reached with the Congress, with the people that have the job of operating the services."

Consensus is not total agreement. "When President [Lyndon] Johnson speaks about seeking a consensus he is not saying that he expects every one to vote for him and to agree with him," wrote Walter Lippmann. "But he is saying that the great internal problems cannot be solved successfully and satisfactorily until and unless they have the support of a very big majority. In the American political tradition, a very big majority is taken to lie between 60 and 75%. An American consensus is more than a bare 51%." What Johnson was seeking to do, wrote the AP's Jack Bell, was to effect cooperation among "the liberals, who believed in big government, the conservatives, who wanted federal power diffused, the representatives of big business, big labor, the minorities most vocally represented by the Negroes and the poverty-stricken." (This would be termed a COALITION today.)

After the Republican party's big gains in the 1966 elections, New York's Governor Nelson Rockefeller urged the twenty-five GOP governors to work toward a consensus on their objectives before worrying about picking a candidate for the 1968 presidential race. Michigan's Governor George Romney, flying to Puerto Rico for a meeting with Rockefeller, took umbrage at his host's remark. Consensus? "That is Rockefeller's word," snapped Romney. "I associate it with someone else"—namely Lyndon Johnson—"who hasn't fared too well with leadership." Later Romney and Rockefeller made up, and Romney apologetically explained his outburst by saying,

"I was just a little allergic to the previous association of the word."

Even with its connotation of papering over differences, the word is still able to bring about confrontations. The school of political historians who disputed the long-held "conflict" school—which held that the study of U.S. history was in the conflict between institutions and ideas—called itself the "consensus" school. See COME NOW, AND LET US REASON TOGETHER.

conservation See ENVIRONMENTALIST.

conservative A defender of a beneficial status quo who, when change becomes necessary in tested institutions or practices, prefers that it come slowly, in moderation, and preferably not resulting in centralization of government power.

In modern U.S. politics, as in the past, *conservative* is a term of opprobrium to some and of veneration to others. Edmund Burke, the early articulator of the conservative philosophy, argued that the only way to preserve political stability was by carefully controlling change and seeking a slow, careful integration of new forces into venerable institutions. In his *Reflections on the Revolution in France* he wrote: "It is with infinite caution that any man ought to venture upon pulling down an edifice which has answered in any tolerable degree for ages the common purposes of society, or on building it up again without having models and patterns of approved utility before his eyes." Abraham Lincoln called it "adherence to the old and tried, against the new and untried."

The philosophy has had some famous detractors as well. Disraeli, who was later to become a Tory Prime Minister, wrote in his sprightly 1844 novel *Coningsby*: "Conservatism discards Prescription, shrinks from Principle, disavows Progress; having rejected all respect for antiquity, it offers no redress for the present, and makes no preparation for the future." Lord Bryce was of two minds about it in *The American Commonwealth*: "This conservative spirit, jealously watchful even in small matters, sometimes prevents reforms, but it assures the people an easy mind, and a trust in

their future which they feel to be not only a present satisfaction but a reservoir of strength."

The political origin of the word can be traced to the *Conservateur* in the 1799 French Constitution, and was used in its present English sense by British statesman and later Prime Minister George Canning in 1820. J. Wilson Croker, in the *Quarterly Review* of January 1830, made the concrete proposal: "We have always been conscientiously attached to what is called the Tory, and which might with more propriety be called the Conservative party."

In America, it was soon applied to the Whigs, amid some derision: "The *Pennsylvania Reporter*," wrote the *Ohio Statesman* in 1837, "speaking of a probable change in the name of the opposition from Whig to 'Conservative,' says the best cognomen they could adopt would be the 'Fast and Loose' party."

Today many who call themselves *conservative* resist most governmental regulation of the economy. They favor free trade and local and state action over federal action and emphasize fiscal responsibility, most notably in the form of budgets balanced by spending restraint, and frown mightily on Republican political figures who raise taxes or seem profligate in non-defense expenditures. William Allen White, the Kansas editor, described this type of conservative when he wrote of Charles Evans Hughes as "a businessman's candidate, hovering around the status quo like a sick kitten around a hot brick."

There exists a less doctrinaire conservative who admits the need for government action in some fields—anti-monopoly measures to protect small business, for example—and for a steadiness and predictability of change in many areas. Instead of fighting a rear-guard action, they seek to achieve such change within the framework of existing institutions, occasionally changing those institutions when there seems to be a need for change.

Economic conservatives frequently disagree strongly with social conservatives, often giving "the movement" a split personality. Social conservatives favor government support of "faith-based" institutions, often frown on gun control, and oppose abortion and same-sex marriage, positions alliteratively summarized as "God, guns, and gays," but these stands were not taken by such Republican political figures as California Governor Arnold Schwarzenegger and former New York Mayor Rudy Giuliani. See NEOCONSERVATISM; HIDEBOUND; ROCK-RIBBED; LEFT WING, RIGHT WING.

conspiracy theorist See UNHOLY ALLIANCE.

constituent Voter or elector; formal term for resident of a represented district.

A *constituent* is a component of a whole; in grammar, it is a unit of the construction of a sentence, like a verb, a phrase or a clause; in politics, it is a person who is a voting unit in an electoral district. Since 1622, this word has been used for anybody who appoints another as a proxy or representative. A century later, the term took the specific meaning of "one who elects another to public office," particularly a representative to a legislature.

From the Latin *constituere*, "to constitute," the political noun (with a more mouth-filling ring than *voter*) is related to *constituency*, an elected official's district or—spoken of even more reverently—the assembled units of that district that have the power to make or break an elected official.

A spokesman for the 1992 Connecticut delegation to the Republican National Convention used the noun in a way that suggested that constituents are to be communicated with, but their views were not necessarily to be followed: "We encourage candidates to talk to their constituents, elected officials to talk to their constituents—and vote their conscience." In this, he was paraphrasing Edmund Burke's 1774 speech to the electors of Bristol, in which the English statesman said that a representative should have "the strictest union, the closest correspondence, and the most unreserved communication with his constituents," adding "Your representative owes you, not his industry only, but his judgment; and he betrays, instead of serving you, if he sacrifices it to your opinion." His constituency defeated him in the next election. (See FENCE MENDING.)

containment Policy of limiting the aggressive expansion of Soviet Communism by military means, in the hope that its failure to expand would weaken the Communist system.

In February 1946 George F. Kennan, a little-known scholar of Russian history who was counselor of the U.S. embassy in Moscow, wrote an 8,000-word "long telegram" to his State Department superiors that was to change the course of U.S. foreign policy. Later printed in shortened form in the July 1947 issue of *Foreign Affairs* under the title "The Sources of Soviet Conduct" and signed by "Mr. X," Kennan's memo argued:

> Soviet pressure against the free institutions of the western world is something that can be contained by the adroit and vigilant application of counterforce at a series of constantly shifting geographical and political points, corresponding to the shifts and maneuvers of Soviet policy, but which cannot be talked or charmed out of existence. …
>
> … no mystical, Messianic movement—and particularly not that of the Kremlin—can face frustration indefinitely without eventually adjusting itself in one way or another to the logic of that state of affairs.

The policy of containment—to establish "situations of strength" around the world so as to stop Soviet expansion caused by "the traditional Russian sense of insecurity" —came to encompass the establishment of U.S. military bases in friendly countries, the Marshall Plan, Point Four aid to underdeveloped countries, and a rebuilding of U.S. military power.

But containment was essentially a defensive policy with little political appeal. Ultimate victory was decades away. There seemed to be no clean-cut, decisive end to the problem of aggressive Communism.

With the loss of China to the Communists in the late '40s, American restlessness with containment increased. In the 1952 presidential campaign, General Eisenhower's foreign policy adviser, John Foster Dulles, expounded a policy that went beyond containment to the LIBERATION OF CAPTIVE PEOPLES. After Eisenhower's victory, Secretary of State Dulles explained it to the Senate Committee on Foreign Relations: "a policy which only aims at containing Russia... is bound to fail because a purely defensive policy never wins against an aggressive policy.... It is only by keeping alive the hope of liberation... that we will end this terrible peril ..."

When no liberations took place, a general disillusionment set in. Senator George Aiken of Vermont said in 1967 regarding Communist China: "I don't know how you go about containing an idea. I also don't know how you go about containing 700 million people."

Curiously, the appeal of *containment* as a geopolitical philosophy, more than a policy, was undermined in the Administration that many expected to espouse it. Earl Ravenal wrote in *Foreign Policy* in 1977 that President Nixon's policies in the early '70s had helped transform the international system from "bipolar confrontation" to a more diffused balance of power: "If Nixon and Kissinger did not quite end 'containment,' at least they devalued it, making it an item of strategy rather than ideology, blurring its once-sharp focus of hostility, and generalizing it into the more neutral concept of international 'stability.'" In the late '80s, the White House chose "Beyond Containment" as the label for George H.W. Bush's foreign policy.

contract An agreement to deliver a political favor; an accepted political assignment.

Though *contract* in political lingo has been defined "a political or business favor; a bribe; the fix," the usage cited in G.Y. Wells's 1958 *Station House Slang* captures the essential insiders' meaning: "Contract—any favor one policeman says he'll do for another."

In the underworld, a *contract* is an assignment to a *torpedo* to make a *hit*; that is, an agreement to commit a murder. That probably explains the sinister connotation in the nonpolitician's mind when hearing the more innocent use of *contract* by a politician.

Joseph Pearson, long the principal doorkeeper of the House of Commons, defined *contract* in his 1792 *Political Dictionary* as "A thing that will make a man vote either way. I never found it fail yet." That was in the

sense of corrupt payoff. In current political use, the "fix" connotation is disappearing; *contract* now is used to mean "a promise to perform," with no bribe necessarily implied. A contract is not a *deal*, which clearly implies a two-way transaction, while a *contract* is merely an assignment accepted with no specific return favor demanded, at least not immediately as a quid pro quo.

Sample: "You'll sit me on the dais next to the Governor?" "I'll try." "No—make it a contract." "Okay, it's a contract, you'll sit there and be able to bend his ear all night."

For an 1893 usage, see DELIVER.

Contract with America Republican campaign document that set the agenda for the 104th Congress after sweeping GOP gains in the 1994 mid-term elections gave that party control of both the Senate and House of Representatives for the first time since 1952.

The *Contract with America* was the work of Republican representatives, led by New Gingrich (Ga.), Dick Armey (Tex.), and Tom DeLay (Tex.), who went on to become Speaker of the House, Majority Leader, and Majority Whip, respectively, after the GOP election victory. Released on September 27, 1994, the contract was signed by 367 Republican candidates for the House. Following a preamble of eight structural reforms "aimed at restoring the faith and trust of the American people in their government," it listed ten specific measures that the signatories promised to bring to the House floor within the first 100 days of the new Congress.

The "contract" embodied a wish list of ideas that had been fermenting since 1964, when conservatives gained control of the Republican Party and nominated Arizona Senator Barry Goldwater for president. The thrust of the document, which drew on President Ronald Reagan's 1985 State of the Union message, was to reduce the role of government in American life, lower taxes, encourage private enterprise, and promote individual responsibility. Rep. Gingrich, a history professor before he became a congressman, claimed "there is no comparable congressional document in our two-hundred-year history."

The structural reforms in the document's preamble included requirements that all laws that apply to the rest of the country apply equally to Congress, that the number of House committees be reduced and committee staff cut by a third, that terms of committee chairs be limited, and that a super-majority of three-fifths be required to enact any tax increase. Among the ten specific measures: a "fiscal responsibility act" to require a balanced budget, limit taxes, and provide for a line-item veto; a "taking back our streets act" that included a package of anti-crime measures; a "personal responsibility act" to discourage illegitimacy and teen pregnancy by prohibiting welfare payments to minor mothers and cutting other welfare spending; a "national security restoration act" to strengthen national defense and prohibit placement of American troops under U.N. command, and a "citizen legislature act" to establish "term limits to replace career politicians with citizen legislators."

The ambitious program outlined in the Contract with America was not fully realized. House Republicans made good on contract promises by approving nine of the ten specific measures by the beginning of April 1995 (the term-limits bill failed to obtain the two-thirds majority required by the Constitution), but much of the steam went out of the legislative effort after the GOP was largely blamed for a shutdown of the government at the end of the year. Most of the House-approved bills eventually died either in the Senate or in conference committee. Others were vetoed by President Bill Clinton or enacted only in altered form after the President insisted on changes.

The *contract* idea lives on. In 2007, Gingrich's newt.org website—he retired from Congress at the beginning of 1999—featured a 10-point "21st Century Contract with America" that was written as though he might have an eye on the presidency. House Democrats, while carefully avoiding the word *contract*, produced a similar document when preparing for the 2006 mid-term elections. Billed as "A New Direction for America," it outlined a half-dozen legislative priorities that Rep. Nancy Pelosi (Calif.), promised to address "In the first hundred hours of a new Congress if elected." The "Six for '06," a phrase of Rep. Rahm Emanuel of Illinois, head of the Democratic congressional campaign committee, included such topics as: "Real Security at Home and Overseas," "Energy Independence—Lower Gas Prices," and "Affordable Health Care—Life-Saving Science" (the last referring to stem-cell research).

The "New Direction" echoed FDR's NEW DEAL and JFK's NEW FRONTIER (see NEW, POLITICAL USE OF), while Pelosi's "100 hours" improved upon the *Contract with America's* "100 days," at the same time evoking memories of JFK's call for action in his 1961 inaugural address: "All this will not be finished in the first hundred days. Nor will it be finished in the first thousand days, nor in the lifetime of this administration, nor even perhaps in our lifetime on this planet. But let us begin." See HUNDRED DAYS.

House Democrats, following their sweeping victory in 2006 (the Senate also returned to Democratic control), also made good on their "non-contractual" promises, passing their six bills within two weeks, though most were stymied or watered down in the Senate. On the face of it, two weeks appears to be much longer than 100 hours, but since the Democrats counted only hours that the House was in session, it turned out that they finished the job with thirteen hours to spare.

contrapuntal phrases A phrase-making technique that uses a repeated rhythm with an inversion or substitution of words for emphasis; rhetorical antithesis.

Good speechwriters often make phrases memorable by placing contrasting nouns, verbs, or adjectives in counterpoint. Gilbert Highet pointed out in an analysis of the Gettysburg Address that Lincoln was especially fond of such counterpoint: "The world will little note nor long *remember* what we *say* here; but it can never *forget* what they *did* here."

This contrapuntal description of Harry Truman has been attributed to Speaker Sam Rayburn: "*Right* on all the *big* things, *wrong* on most of the *little* ones." FDR in his Four Freedoms speech said, "As men do not *live* by *bread* alone, they do not *fight* by *armaments* alone." In the contrapuntal use of a single word, the possibility for oratorical error is a danger: when, in 1933, FDR shaped a sentence that read "Hard-*head*edness will not so easily excuse hard-*heart*edness," he drew a tiny picture of a head over the first word on the reading copy of the speech, and a heart with an arrow through it over the balancing word.

John F. Kennedy used the device, especially its TURNAROUND variant, more than any other U.S. president. "Let us never negotiate out of fear, but let us never fear to negotiate." "A willingness to resist force, unaccompanied by a willingness to talk, could provoke belligerence—while a willingness to talk, unaccompanied by a willingness to resist force, could invite disaster." "While we shall negotiate freely, we shall not negotiate freedom." And, of course, "Ask not what your country can do for you—ask what you can do for your country." (That last line may have been modeled on a phrase in an 1884 Memorial Day address delivered by Oliver Wendell Holmes in Keene, New Hampshire: "it is now the moment…to recall what our country has done for each of us, and to ask ourselves what we can do for our country in return.")

The "Sorensen style" used by Kennedy did not go unnoticed. Columnist William F. Buckley Jr., writing in 1967 about the Communist world revolution, obliquely referred to a single form of contrapuntal inversion: "And unless we learn how to cope with it, it will—as Theodore Sorensen would put it—cope with us."

"In Ted Sorensen," observed *Washington Star* editorialist Edwin M. Yoder Jr. in February 1978, "Mr. Kennedy had a speechwriter of excellent style with a fondness for antithesis, so that it became a sort of rhetorical tic. Like all the rhetorical devices that we inherit from Latin by way of the 18th Century, antithesis needs a strict sense of occasion. It can be absurdly trivialized: 'Always close the door before you leave, but never leave after you have opened the window.'"

contrarian One who deliberately takes issue with popular trends, takes pleasure

in devil's advocacy, or gleefully goes up against CONVENTIONAL WISDOM.

Humphrey Neill, the financial adviser who wrote the 1954 *Art of Contrary Thinking*, began using *contrarian* in the 1960s to promote financial investment against the current of general investor thinking. Elizabeth M. Fowler wrote in *The New York Times* in 1966 that "Mr. Neill, who calls himself a contrarian, which means he tends to act just the opposite of the crowd or general public, now advises caution."

A builder used this new sense in explaining his company's increased activity after the 1987 stock-market crash: "We took a contrarian view. We decided to go full steam ahead. We figured that if other developers were holding back, there would be less competition."

Based, like *contrary*, on the Latin *contra*, "opposite," the term has moved from financial jargon to political term as both noun and adjective. It is applied to pollsters who defy CONVENTIONAL WISDOM and to candidates who run against the ideological grain of their party. *Contrarian*, however, differs from merely being habitually in the minority or betting on long shots; the word also suggests opposing popular opinion in order to make a profit or to profit politically from being a MAVERICK.

controversial See CODE WORDS.

convention See SPONTANEOUS DEMONSTRATION; PACKING THE GALLERIES; VOICE FROM THE SEWER; BROKERED CONVENTION.

convention bounce A temporary rise in opinion polls following widespread coverage of a party's national convention.

Following the Democratic National Convention in the summer of 1992, Bill Clinton took a realistic and expectation-dampening view of his rising ratings in the polls: "It's partly a convention bounce." After the Republican National Convention in August, President George H.W. Bush's ratings also improved, and *The Christian Science Monitor* commented, "It represents a routine convention bounce." This led *Newsweek* to ask in its Conventional Wisdom Watch,

"Why does the CW worry about the 'convention bounce' if the CW also says the bounce dissipates within two weeks?'"

The term was used as early as 1980 by Jody Powell, Jimmy Carter's presidential spokesman. Powell described the psychological lift from Carter's increase in ratings as "the post-convention bounce we hoped for." (The prefix *post-* is no longer used with the phrase.)

A derivative term is the *New Hampshire bounce*, describing the short-term increase in popularity following that state's earliest presidential primary. *The Washington Post* commented in February 1988 on Bob Dole's showing in Iowa: "Dole's victory may set up a New Hampshire bounce over Bush." In both phrases, the noun *bounce* became more popular than its variant, *bump*.

conventional wisdom Generally accepted but often shortsighted conceptions; stodgy consensus subject to sharp changes of vogue opinion.

The economist John Kenneth Galbraith coined the term in a chapter title of *The Affluent Society*, a bestseller in 1958: "The Concept of the Conventional Wisdom." Galbraith wrote that "the hallmark of the conventional wisdom is acceptability. It has the approval of those to whom it is addressed." To indicate the pejorative sense of the term, Galbraith added, "Ideas need to be tested by their ability, in combination with events, to overcome inertia and resistance. This inertia and resistance the conventional wisdom provides."

This noun phrase, which flourished for a while with the neutral sense of "general view," was probably bottomed on a phrase in ecclesiastical use, *received wisdom*, from a 1382 phrase *received custom*, meaning "the teaching of tradition"; today, both *received* and *conventional* modifiers of *wisdom* carry the negative connotation that Galbraith intended.

Usually derogated in the phrase "contrary to the conventional wisdom," the term has been popularized by *Newsweek* magazine in its weekly feature, "ConventionalWisdomWatch" (its headline three words compressed into one, a voguish convention in typography). *Newsweek* indicates with arrows whether political figures are up or down according to current estimates, but includes this disclaimer at the bottom of the page in the tiniest of type: "The CW is not *Newsweek*'s opinion, but an informal distillation of the ever-changing thinking of Beltway pundits and the chattering classes." See PUNDIT; CHATTERING CLASSES; CONTRARIAN.

cookie pusher A foreign-service Pharisee; an effete, or "striped-pants," diplomat, one concerned with form rather than substance; opposite of SHIRTSLEEVE DIPLOMAT.

Under the headline "No 'Cookie Pushers' for Diplomatic Corps," *The Washington Post* of January 18, 1924 ran an article by George Rothwell Brown with the lede that sets diplomatic teeth on edge to this day: "Hugh Gibson, our Minister to Finland, advocates chasing the tea hounds and cookie pushers out of the diplomatic services." Nine days later, *The New York Times* coverage was headed "Gibson for new diplomacy without white spats and tea" that verified the coiner but missed the memorable phrase.

The phrase graphically describes one who attends social teas; in 1934, Weseen's slang dictionary defined it as "a male student who seeks female companions"—hardly a criticism in later times—but added Gibson's usage of "a tea hound." In 1943, the *Saturday Review of Literature* gave it the definition that demeans and infuriates dedicated foreign service personnel to this day: "'Cookie pushers' is a newspaper men's term for thwarted 'career' men in the State Department ... who wear striped trousers and know the proper gambits for unattractive wives of foreign secretaries." After World War II, the derisive term was popularized by New York Democratic Congressman John J. Rooney, chairman of the House subcommittee on appropriations that oversees State Department spending. "While I have used the expression 'cookie pusher' many times during my years in the U.S. House of Representatives," Congressman Rooney wrote the author in 1967, "I cannot at all claim authorship."

Adlai Stevenson's biographer, Kenneth S. Davis, wrote that the lifted-pinkie phrase was used against Stevenson and his associates in the Committee to Defend America by Aiding the Allies in 1940: "Nor could [Stevenson] fail to resent being dubbed, with his colleagues, a 'cookie pusher,' a 'professional bleeding heart,' a 'warmonger,' day after day in [Chicago] Tribune news and editorial columns ..."

The phrase is closely associated with the compound adjective *striped-pants*, a symbol or stereotype of false formality (although gray striped pants go well with a black morning coat in winter). "You put the Peace Corps into the Foreign Service," warned D. W. Drazner in a political science journal in 2000, "and they'll put striped pants on your people."

cooling-off period In labor disputes, a time allowed management and labor to negotiate with neither strikes nor lockouts permitted.

The phrase has earlier usage in diplomacy. William Jennings Bryan, Woodrow Wilson's Secretary of State in 1913, took the initiative in providing for a method of arbitration on all international disputes, referring these to a permanent investigating commission. He negotiated agreements with thirty-one nations which became known as "Bryan's 'cooling off' treaties."

President Woodrow Wilson, campaigning for the League of Nations in 1919, used an eloquent metaphor in the last major speech before his stroke:

With a cooling space of nine months for human passion, not much of it will keep hot. I had a couple of friends who were in the habit of losing their tempers, and when they lost their tempers they were in the habit of using very unparliamentary language. Some of their friends induced them to make a promise that they never would swear inside the town limits. When the impulse next came upon them, they took a street car to go out of town to swear, and by the time they got out of town they did not want to swear. ... Now, illustrating the great by the small, that is true of the passions of nations. It is true of the passions of men however you combine them. Give them space to cool off.

The *cooling-off period* became locked into the political language with the pas-

sage of the Taft-Hartley Act of 1947. The law specified that sixty days' notice must be given before a labor contract can be changed or terminated; if no agreement is reached within thirty days, the Federal Mediation and Conciliation Service steps in. When a dispute threatens what the president considers to be the national welfare, he is authorized to seek a court injunction to maintain the status quo for eighty days. At the end of this eighty-day pause for reflection, a strike or lockout is permitted.

cooling the rhetoric See RHETORIC.

coonskin on the wall Symbol of victory; similar to *scalp*.

At Cam Ranh Bay in South Vietnam, just before the November 1966 elections in the U.S., President Johnson visited U.S. troops in the field and told them, "I salute you. Come home with that coonskin on the wall."

The expression jarred many members of the President's party, as limited objectives and limited war were the basis of diplomatic feelers, and the President's colorful remark appeared close to the MacArthur NO SUBSTITUTE FOR VICTORY statement.

Columnist Walter Lippmann wrote three months later: "Lyndon Johnson is a complicated human being. There are at least two spirits wrestling within him. One is that of the peacemaker and reformer and herald of a better world. The other is that of the primitive frontiersman who wants to nail the coonskin to the wall. ... It is this second spirit which is now tempting him, and on the outcome of the ordeal depends more than it is pleasant to contemplate."

The hide of the raccoon or opossum has had a long background in American speech, and was the symbol of frontiersman Daniel Boone. Estes Kefauver, senator from Tennessee and Democratic vice-presidential candidate in 1956, wore the coonskin cap for photographers and used it as a symbol on many of his handshaking tours. "The irony of Kefauver," wrote Russell Baker of *The New York Times*, "was that the coonskin cap, by which the country at large knew him, was a fraud. It implied a log cabin rustic bred to the cracker barrel circle, but it concealed one of the authentic EGGHEADS of American politics."

co-opt To convert by absorption; or, to subvert or take over by suffocating agreement.

In general speech, *co-opt* as a verb, or *co-optation* as a noun, used to mean "to elect an outsider to a group by a vote of the membership."

In politics, its meaning is more dramatic. To *co-opt* is "to lure an opponent into becoming a supporter" and in its extreme usage, "to ensnare the victor." Subtly, the Establishment reaches out for the election winner; the bureaucracy enfolds its supervisory appointee, and in the guise of wanting to help or offering to educate, takes the election victor over by changing that person's cultural or political outlook. Such an absorption of outlook seems to occur by osmosis, as the "outsider" thinks he is convincing or changing the "insiders." *Co-opt* was used frequently in discussions about the incoming Carter Administration—held to be "anti-Washington"—by congressional Democrats in 1977.

Cathy Young of *Reason* magazine gave an example of extreme co-optation in *The Boston Globe* in 2007 discussing the Kremlin's backing of an anti-American youth group named Nashi, meaning "ours" in Russian. "With Nashi and several smaller pro-Kremlin youth groups," she wrote, "the Putin regime is hoping not only to co-opt political activism among the younger generation but to use it as a club against its enemies."

Both sides of the hyphenated word came from voguish forebears. *Co* has been used frequently in recent years, with *co-host* a popular television term and *co-equal* taken to mean more equal than the usual *equal*. *Opt* is the vogue form for "choose," without its impulsive differential.

"If you can't lick 'em, join 'em" is an old political axiom; in the case of *co-opt*, the axiom becomes "If you can't lick 'em, flatter 'em, meet 'em half way, and they'll join you." For an earlier form of stealing the opposition's clothes, see DISH THE WHIGS.

copperhead Near-traitor; DEFEATIST; less angrily, dissident; spokesman for an unpopular cause.

The copperheads were those Northerners who opposed the Union cause during the Civil War. The copperhead snake is considered by many to be the lowest of a low breed: it strikes without warning, contrasted with the fair-minded, noisy rattlesnake.

The word was used in America preceding the Civil War as a synonym for *sneaky*, but in the off-year elections of 1862 it became the epithet for Southern sympathizers in the North. The *Lawrence* (Kan.) *Republican* surveyed the epithet list: "That faction of the Democracy who sympathize with the rebels are known in Ohio as 'Vallandinghamers,' in Illinois as 'guerrillas,' in Missouri as 'butternuts,' in Kansas as 'jayhawkers,' in Kentucky as 'bushwhackers,' and in Indiana as 'copperheads.'"

The word atrophied after the Civil War resentments died down, though the progressive politicians at the turn of the century were derided as "copper-streaked" by their foes. Franklin Roosevelt renewed its use in 1938, at the suggestion of Thomas Corcoran, to apply it to those Democrats who wished to drag their feet on New Deal legislation: "Never in our lifetime has such a concerted campaign of defeatism been thrown at the heads of the President and Senators and Congressmen as in the case of this Seventy-Fifth Congress. Never before have we had so many Copperheads—and you will remember that it was the Copperheads who, in the days of the War between the States, tried their best to make Lincoln and his Congress give up the fight ..."

Roosevelt liked the historical epithet and used it again just before World War II as a label for Colonel Charles A. Lindbergh and the America Firsters. When a form of isolationism was articulated in 1990 by Patrick Buchanan, opposed to U.S. intervention in the Persian Gulf, some of his official targets (see AMEN CORNER) retaliated with a charge of "Copperhead."

cordon sanitaire See IRON CURTAIN.

corn pone Symbol of folksiness and Southern voter appeal.

Mark Twain wrote in his essay "Corn Pone Opinions": "You tell me whar a man gits his corn pone, en I'll tell you what his 'pinions are."

Corn pone can be a bread made of corn meal, milk, and eggs; or a cereal whose alternative name is *hominy grits*; or a cakelike bakery product made of pounded corn, pounded sunflower seeds, and boiled beans. *Pone* can be a wide variety of products made from corn, and can stir as many heated debates about what it is and how it is made as does *egg cream* (seltzer with a squirt of milk and chocolate) in the Bronx, New York.

Governor Huey Long brought it into politics as part of his lighthearted but effective campaign to identify himself with rural voters in Louisiana. He started a debate over the proper method of eating corn pone with pot liquor, a juice that remains in the pot after turnip greens are boiled with a piece of salt pork. "Kingfish" Long solemnly held that the pone should be "dunked" in the pot liquor, and not "crumbled" in and then elegantly eaten with a spoon. Governor Franklin Roosevelt of New York wired the *Atlanta Constitution* that he sided with the "crumblers," and Oklahoma's "Alfalfa Bill" Murray called for a wider investigation to include "poke" salad and hog jowl. The matter reached the Solomon's Temple of Emily Post, who decreed: "When in Rome, do as the Romans do."

Corn pone has come to mean "sweet talk" and gentle persuasion. See SMELL OF MAGNO-LIAS. Non-Southerners tend to consider it synonymous with "corny" or "cornball," cloyingly folksy, but in the South there is a more gallant political connotation. In 1960 Lyndon Johnson named his CAMPAIGN TRAIN, which did so much to hold the South for the Kennedy-Johnson ticket, "The Corn Pone Special."

corporate state See FASCIST; TRAINS RAN ON TIME.

corridors of power See POWER BROKERS.

corruption See GRAFT.

cost-benefit analysis Study of cost efficiency; assessment of a project's price in relation to its value.

Cost-benefit was a 1928 term from industrial management; by 1963, economists had added *analysis* in studying social projects; a *Times* of London article explained, "Cost-benefit analysis … constitutes an endeavour to bring into relationship with 'the measuring rod of money' all the social consequences either of introducing a new project or removing an old one."

Such studying of efficiency was sometimes criticized. Stephen Kurkjian of *The Boston Globe* discussed the views of George H.W. Bush's critics in 1988 on his environmental background, adding, "They stressed that during the early months of the Reagan Administration, Bush played a key role in bringing 'cost-benefit analysis' to the field of federal regulation. No longer would the environmental impact be the sole measure of whether a regulation should take effect."

In 1992, British Prime Minister Margaret Thatcher was profiled in *The Washington Post* by Glenn Frankel, who wrote that although "Thatcher showed great reverence for the throne as the repository of Victorian values, many of her followers tend to apply a rigid cost-benefit analysis, in which the royals come out looking like a luxury that Britain can no longer afford."

Not every cost undergoing analysis can be measured in monetary units. The *San Francisco Chronicle* in July 1992 assessed Bill Clinton's choice of Al Gore as his running mate; the study was introduced by "Here is a quick cost-benefit analysis on the major issues."

During the Kennedy Administration, Defense Secretary Robert McNamara introduced to the Pentagon the related term *cost-effective*. Henry Brandon of London's *Sunday Times* wrote in his 1988 book *Special Relationship* about the passing of this term from American to British English. When members of the British defense staff visited Washington during the Kennedy years, John Thompson, a defense aide to the British Ambassador, sought to explain this new usage.

"At a dinner he gave for them," Brandon wrote, Thompson "therefore served three different red wines and asked them to tell him how, according to their taste, they rated each. After they had done that, he told them how much each cost and then he asked them which, taking the cost into consideration, they would buy."

Brandon added, "The wine samples did what wine does not always do, it cleared their minds, and thus *cost-effectiveness* entered the English vocabulary."

cost of living See HIGH COST OF LIVING.

cost-push See INFLATION.

countdown Period of crisis before a decision or event; the last few days before an election.

The word was popularized as the nation watched televised rocket blast-offs from Cape Canaveral, Fla., and announcers in ominous tones said: "Countdown four minutes, thirty seconds and counting," or "two minutes, twenty seconds and holding," with the last ten seconds counted backward to "Ignition. Blast-off."

In 1959 Majority Leader Lyndon Johnson was quoted as saying, "The countdown has begun" in regard to pending legislation; in 1960 General John Medaris wrote a book titled *Countdown for Decision* about the confusion in the missile program; the *New York Times Book Review* headlined a review in 1967 "Countdown for the Minds of Men."

For a time the word was used in lieu of *roll call* by television commentators (many of whom covered the astronaut blast-offs) as the states were called at national conventions. An AP dispatch in July 1960 said that "they professed to believe that Kennedy would lose support in Indiana, Maryland and Ohio in a second countdown." The word, still used in NASA coverage, is also used to describe the final, tense moments of a close campaign.

court-packing See NINE OLD MEN.

cover-up Any plan to avoid detection of wrongdoing; or, an act to conceal a mistake; historically, the conspiracy to obstruct justice in the Watergate case.

Mystery writer Raymond Chandler, in *Black Mask* magazine in 1935, gave a character this line: "I don't have to tell you how a police department looks at that kind of a cover-up on a murder." The law enforcement slang term soon crossed into the political language, to mean a general—not necessarily illegal—concealment of the truth. In a telephone conversation with financier Louis Wolfson in 1968, Supreme Court Justice Abe Fortas told his former law client (who was recording the call) that a conflict-of-interest charge could be made if their relationship was misconstrued: "That your giving me and my accepting the foundation post was nothing but a cover-up and that what was really happening was that I was taking a gratuity from you ... and that is very bad."

In the Watergate case, the charge of *cover-up* (hyphenated as a noun but two words as a verb) gained currency early in the spring of 1973. On April 30, according to a transcript of a taped conversation with former Attorney General John Mitchell in the Oval Office, President Nixon said: "I want you all to stonewall it, let them plead the Fifth Amendment, cover up or anything else, if it'll save it—save the plan."

That transcript was released in the summer of 1974, and the words were used on the July 22, 1974, cover of *Newsweek*. In an interview with David Frost in 1977, the former President allowed as how a reasonable person could construe his actions "as a cover-up," but denied that the concealment had involved criminal action on his part.

Because of its Watergate connotation, the word is now frequently used to attach sinister implications to any attempt to withhold information. To HANG TOUGH is permissible; to STONEWALL implies grounds for suspicion; to *cover up* (verb) or to engage in a *cover-up* (noun) imputes improper concealment or, if combined with criminal intent, unlawful obstruction.

cover your ass See CYA.

cowboy A political rebel; usually one flamboyantly opposed to party discipline.

Cowboy never enjoyed the political currency of such synonyms as MAVERICK and

MUGWUMP and is only occasionally heard today. Its most famous use came just after the death of President William McKinley. Senator Mark Hanna, the leading Republican strategist while McKinley lived, said of Vice President Theodore Roosevelt: "Now look, that damned cowboy is President of the United States!"

It is uncertain precisely how Hanna applied the term because Roosevelt had actually lived and worked in cattle country for a time, and was also considered most unfaithful by orthodox GOP chiefs. In fact, it was their attitude that made him President. He was serving as governor of New York in 1900, assiduously earning the enmity of the Republican organization with his reforms. The vice presidency was vacant and the New York Republican leadership promoted Roosevelt's candidacy, some say to get him out of the state. He won the nomination when men favored by McKinley pulled out. "We did our best," Hanna told McKinley, "but they nominated that madman. Now it's up to you to live." He did not.

Cowboy took on unpleasant connotations during the American Revolution. Tory irregulars in the New York area were called *cowboys*, while rebel marauders were known as *skinners*. The idea of a cowboy being someone unreliable stuck. Senator James G. Blaine in 1879 explained his dislike for "those fellows who are between the parties" by saying that "they are the cowboys of modern days."

After the election of Ronald Reagan in 1980, the European press wrote that the U.S. had elected a "cowboy"; the image was reinforced by Mr. Reagan's role as host of the TV series *Death Valley Days*. The cowboy charge slowly wore off.

The word was reapplied to the George W. Bush style because of his Texas background as well as his willingness to take unilateral action. In an interview in 2007 with Jeffrey Goldberg of *The New Yorker*, former Director of Central Intelligence George Tenet was asked about reporter Bob Woodward's charge that he was derelict in his duty in not going to President Bush directly in mid-2001 with the CIA's fears of an imminent terrorist attack. Tenet

replied: "There's a disciplined process of governance. I got enough cowboy to last me a lifetime that spring and summer." See LONER.

cow-waddle See FILIBUSTER.

crackdown The use of harsh disciplinary action; repression through suddenly severe enforcement of laws.

This noun, along with its verb phrase *to crack down*, appeared during the Depression. The phrase appeared in a 1933 article in *Newsweek* about the National Recovery Administration: "The 'cracking down' phase of the Blue Eagle's career opened last week." In 1935, *The Washington Post* used the noun in writing about the "threat of a 'crack-down' by the middle-class group against those who put forward the legislation for abolishing public utility holding companies."

Now written without a hyphen, *crackdown* is less powerful than *purge* (the Russian *chistka*) but more forceful than *strong measures* (Russian *zhostkiye mery*). Evoking Stalin, the Russian term *zheleznaya ruka*, or "iron hand," is usually parallel to the English word.

cradle-to-the-grave Lifetime security: a phrase used to attack welfare statism.

Cradles and graves are mentioned in the same breath as far back as the early seventeenth century. Joseph Hall, Bishop of Norwich, wrote: "Death borders upon our birth and our cradle stands in the grave."

Poet John Dyer wrote in 1726:

A little rule, a little sway,
A sunbeam in a winter's day,
Is all the proud and mighty have
Between the cradle and the grave.

This was parodied by Samuel Hoffenstein in the 1930s:

Babies haven't any hair;
old men's heads are just as bare;—
Between the cradle and the grave
lies a haircut and a shave.

A 1931 political use was by District Attorney Crain of New York, inveighing against racketeers who "have their hands in everything from the cradle to the grave—from babies' milk to funeral coaches."

Throughout the 1930s, the compound adjective *cradle-to-the-grave* was used to attack the New Deal's Social Security measures. Democratic candidate Adlai Stevenson referred to these attacks in the campaign of 1952: "Republican leadership has opposed us almost every step of the way and now, while adopting everything and proposing to repeal nothing, at least publicly, their orators still sneer at everything we now have and shout about socialism. They call our lives of pride and dignity 'cradle-to-the-grave rides through the welfare state.'"

Other spoofs have included "womb to tomb," the most extreme being "erection to resurrection."

See WELFARE STATE.

creative federalism Federal stimulation and encouragement of state and local action rather than direct federal action to meet human needs.

Governor Nelson Rockefeller of New York put forth the idea of a modified form of federalism in a series of lectures and a 1964 campaign document (distributed as a paperback book) called *The Future of Federalism.* The word *federalism,* with its Founding Fathers connotation overshadowing its too-much-centralization connotation, was thus given new currency and next appeared as the *creative federalism* concept of President Johnson. *Fortune* magazine editor Max Ways wrote a piece on the subject in 1966.

Both the phrase and the concept appeared to be a defense against the charge of BIG GOVERNMENT domination of American life; the "creative" approach proposed to enhance the role of those state and local governments willing to undertake responsibilities assumed in recent years by the federal government.

Proponents considered it an advance into new areas with the localities serving as the cutting edge; critics like Raymond Moley said, "The expression 'creative federalism'... serves as an impressive screen to cover the retreat of those who, since the presidency of the first Roosevelt, have urged the projection of federal authority into the areas traditionally reserved to the state and local governments."

As for the phrase, President Johnson took something old (the federalism of Jefferson, Hamilton, Jay, and Madison, resuscitated by Rockefeller) and something new ("creative"). In California in 1966, Ronald Reagan took *creative*, added it to the mature *society* from Johnson's Great Society, and came up with "the creative society." Rockefeller then countered with an inaugural speech on "the just society." And so it went.

Federalism itself was coined by British conservative Edmund Burke, who also minted *diplomacy, expenditure, municipality,* and *electioneer.* See NEW FEDERALISM; TAX SHARING.

credibility gap The chasm that sometimes exists between public office and the public's trust.

President Johnson suffered from a lack of public trust when he came to his office; a long career as Senate majority leader, during which he was known as a master manipulator and crafty compromiser, was responsible. Only a few weeks after becoming President, he opened the gap wider when he hinted to newsmen that his first budget would probably exceed $102 billion, then produced a budget of under $98 billion. A number of other actions opened it into a yawning abyss (most abysses yawn): the excessive secretiveness and frequent over-optimism surrounding the Vietnam war; his charade in 1964 over his choice of a running mate, which he insisted was not decided until only minutes before he selected Hubert Humphrey; his scheduling a campaign swing in 1966 on the eve of the election, then canceling it and insisting that he had never really planned the trip at all.

Coinage of the phrase in print probably belongs to an anonymous *New York Herald Tribune* headline writer. On May 23, 1965, reporter David Wise wrote a piece that had the word *credibility* in the same lead with the word *gap,* though not tied together. The headline read "Dilemma in 'Credibility Gap.' " The phrase was given currency by *Washington Post* reporter Murray Marder on December 5, 1965, in a story about "growing doubt and cynicism concerning Administration pronouncements. ... The problem could be called a credibility gap."

In a whimsical mood on the eve of his departure as White House press secretary, Bill Moyers remarked that "the credibility gap ... is getting so bad we can't even believe our own leaks." In a more somber mood, Moyers defined the gap as "the difference between what the President says and what the people would like him to say or what they think he should say."

Walter Lippmann, a less sympathetic observer, wrote in 1967 that "the credibility gap today is not the result of honest misunderstanding between the President and the press in this complicated world. It is the result of a deliberate policy of artificial manipulation of official news." *The Baltimore Sun*'s Henry Trewhitt defined it as "the degree of refusal by the public to accept at face value what the government says and does." *The New York Times*'s columnist James Reston wrote: "The most serious problem in America today is that there is widespread doubt in the public mind about its major leaders and institutions. There is more troubled questioning of the veracity of statements out of the White House today than at any time in recent memory."

Johnson's credibility gap developed into a major political theme and was accordingly seized upon by leading Republican contenders for the 1968 presidential nomination. "For years now," said Michigan's Governor George Romney, "we haven't been told the whole facts, and when you begin to find yourself in the position where you can't have confidence in what those who have a public trust are saying about fateful and vital situations, well, you are really in a tough spot."

Credibility also assumed a significant meaning in the geopolitics of the postwar world. The *credible deterrent* refers to the degree to which a country convinces a potential enemy of its strength. See GAP.

CREEP The belatedly discredited Nixon campaign committee of 1972.

The story of how CREEP came into being was recounted in the author's 1975 book, *Before the Fall: An Inside View of the Pre-Watergate White House*:

My only real contribution to the committee had been a recommendation to stress Nixon's incumbency in its title. When Jeb Magruder came into my office in late 1971, the President had not yet publicly chosen Agnew as his running mate again. ... Magruder said, "We can't call it 'Citizens for Nixon-Agnew' because that announces Agnew, and we can't call it 'Citizens for Nixon,' because that will be seen as throwing Agnew overboard, so what do we call the committee?" I remembered the 1966 Rockefeller campaign in New York, when the slogan was "Governor Rockefeller for Governor" ... and I suggested, simply, the Committee to Re-elect the President. "That's the best you can do?" Magruder inquired. I started to remind him that I was charging clients $90,000 a year for advice when he was selling pancake makeup for a local cosmetics house, but then I thought for a moment: any acronym problem? You always have to watch that. C, R, P. Democrats would have to try to stick an "A" in there to make fun of it, which would be in bad taste and they wouldn't try that; if you made it C, R, E, P, using the "election" as a non-hyphenated capital, you would have a french pancake, and that's even too effete for snobs. It would be safe, solid, and stress the incumbency. And so "CREEP" was created.

The CRP was dubbed "CREEP" not by a Democrat, but by Republican National Committee Chairman Robert Dole, who felt the RNC was being shunted aside by the brash young men of the Nixon White House. An early printed reference was in the September 15, 1972, issue of *Life* magazine: "The CRP—or 'CREEP,' as some members of the Republican National Committee call it—occupies five floors of one building and spills across the street onto three floors [of another]." On May 21, 1973, *Time* wrote: "But during the campaign he [Dole] fought many a gallant losing battle with the Committee for the Re-Election of the President; in fact it was he who dubbed it CREEP."

Senator Dole's crack had been aimed at the play on the word *creep*, which is taken from a person who gives one "the creeps" or who causes the flesh to crawl—a derogation that can be found in a 1930 James T. Farrell story. But after it was discovered that the Nixon committee had financed the break-in to Democratic headquarters at the Watergate office complex, CREEP gained a different and far more sinister connotation—as one who enters by stealth—and what had begun as an intraparty gibe became a weapon in the hands of everyone eager to attack anything associated with the overwhelming 1972 Nixon reelection.

creeping socialism Measures increasing the sphere of government activity that are accused of having the cumulative effect of undermining private enterprise.

Republicans during Franklin Roosevelt's NEW DEAL and Harry Truman's FAIR DEAL frequently used *creeping socialism* to describe Democratic programs, especially in the economic and social welfare areas. Historian Samuel Eliot Morison observed later: "Republican orators played this theme in elections and in Congress. ... [but] postwar developments, especially under Eisenhower, justify the quip that instead of creeping socialism, galloping capitalism emerged from the New Deal and the war."

Indeed, *creeping socialism* survives as a term not so much because of Republican or conservative affection for it, but because liberals find it an easy target. See Adlai Stevenson's gibe under DINOSAUR WING. Walter Lippmann, for instance, wrote in 1962: "The so-called socialism which is supposed to be creeping up on us is in fact nothing more than the work of making life safe and decent for a mass society collected in great cities."

When Dwight Eisenhower used the phrase in 1953 ("in the last 20 years creeping socialism has been striking in the United States"), one of his aides wrote him a memo saying the phrase had been "the hallmark of the Old Guard Republicans" and that modern Republicans should have "their own idiom." Eisenhower agreed and dropped the phrase.

The word *socialism* may have been first used politically in 1835 in England by followers of Robert Owen. *Creeping* is now a

jocular equivalent of *incipient*, not limited to ideology, and can be applied to any "ism" for a piquant effect. "After all the amateurish, impromptu diplomacy," wrote columnists Evans and Novak in 1978 satirically about President Carter's use of carefully prepared remarks upon returning from his first trip abroad, "it could be a sign of creeping professionalism."

crime in the streets Initially, urban crime; later a phrase used to derogate the emphasis of LAW AND ORDER as an issue.

Although the words *law and order* were described for a time in the late '60s as "code words for racism," the severe increase in crime—of special concern to black victims in slums—soon erased the pejorative connotation. However, *crime in the streets* was used not so much to describe the situation itself as the political issue arising from it, and this has come to mean "making a political issue out of law enforcement."

Law and order ceased to be regarded as CODE WORDS by 1971, while *crime in the streets* retained the political, though not especially racist, connotation. The term was often used during the Clinton Administration. A rhyming derogation of white-collar crime was expressed in a 1993 White House briefing as "crime in the suites as well as crime in the streets."

Language expert Mario Pei offered this sidelight in *Modern Age: A Quarterly Review*, in 1969: "'Crime in the streets' is a very ancient phenomenon, widespread even in such a world-renowned city as imperial Rome. It gave rise, curiously, to French *crier*, which in turn has become English 'cry.' The root word is '*Quirites!*,' 'Citizens!' a cry of distress corresponding to our 'Help!' used by Romans attacked in the streets."

cronyism See GOVERNMENT BY CRONY.

crossover vote A theory that a primary in one party can be affected substantially by the votes of members of an opposition party.

During the 1976 Republican primaries, supporters of President Ford explained several losses in state primaries in this way: In those states that did not limit voting in primaries to voters registered in that party, many Democratic voters—who would ultimately vote for the Democratic candidate in November—were "crossing over" to vote for Ronald Reagan in the Republican primaries. "Among those who described themselves as Republicans," wrote R. W. Apple Jr. in *The New York Times*, describing a post-primary poll, "Mr. Reagan and President Ford fought on almost equal terms, but the California conservative swept the Democratic crossover voters and beat the President by about 3 to 2 among the independents."

The *crossover theory* holds that the crossover voter is fickle, or mischievous, or interested only in voting in the more hotly contested primary, but who intends to come "home" to the party in which he is registered later in the general election. See NOVEMBER REPUBLICANS. The theory was challenged by Michael Barone, writing in *The Washington Post* under the headline "That 'Crossover' Nonsense!" "All but an insignificant number of the people who will vote for Gerald Ford or Ronald Reagan or Jimmy Carter or Morris Udall in Michigan," he argued, "will be people who are quite ready to vote for them in the general election. In that sense, and it is the only one that matters, they will be legitimate Republican and Democratic voters, not mischievous 'crossovers.' The 'crossover' theory is nonsense."

As the influence of ever-earlier state primaries grows in the selection of presidential candidates, the idea of the crossover vote will be offered as an explanation or an excuse by primary losers, who will insist they were defeated by a vote that did not really reflect the wishes of regular party members. Indeed, in states permitting crossovers, some Democratic voters will vote in the Republican primary, and vice versa, to choose the most "beatable" candidate in the general election in November.

crunch A short period of high tension that becomes a political or economic moment of truth, when participants display courage or cowardice.

The verb *to crunch*, probably of imitative origin (as "the ship *crunched* through the ice"), was introduced to politics by Winston Churchill in 1939, as he warned of "The outcome of the European crunch." Businessmen, editorialized *The New York Times* in 1967, "will lose their fears of a credit crunch when it becomes clear that we are not headed for another 1966 [credit crisis]." That alliterative phrase *credit crunch* has reinforced the politico-economic use of the term. *The Boston Globe* wrote of Bush's Treasury Secretary Nicholas F. Brady in 1991: "he labeled the credit crunch the Administration's 'number one economic priority.'" In 2007, speculation in subprime mortgages led to what was widely described as a *credit crunch* in which the banking system faced the danger of *seizing up*.

In the synonymy of political crisis, *squeeze* is almost exclusively an economic word for tightening; FLAP is transitory; *pinch*, as in Shakespeare's use of "necessity's sharp pinch," is a time of mild hardship; NUT-CUTTING implies action in a crisis toward an individual; *moment of truth*, with its bullfighting origin, has acquired a literary connotation; the *clutch*, with a baseball derivation, is the decisive moment in a close contest; the *crunch* is the pressure of a political or economic nutcracker.

The word was given new meaning when it was changed from its familiar verb form to a noun. Another example of this semantic shift is *hurting;* to *hurt* (or to *be hurt*) means "to inflict (or receive) physical pain," while *hurting* (Dean Rusk in 1967: "the North Vietnamese are hurting") means to be in political or military difficulties. When the *crunch* comes, many straddlers find themselves *hurting*.

crusade A political movement characterized by moral fervor; a word used to endow a campaign with a religious-moral tone.

Americans long identified the word with Dwight D. Eisenhower, but it has had other political resonance. "A crusade against ignorance" was urged by Thomas Jefferson in 1786. "Spend and be spent in an endless crusade," Theodore Roosevelt exhorted his supporters. Franklin D. Roosevelt agreed;

in his acceptance speech to the 1932 Democratic convention, he not only called for a NEW DEAL, but issued "a call to arms ... a crusade to restore America to its own." Three years later, in a cabinet meeting, FDR talked about prospects for re-election: "We will win easily next year, but we are going to make it a crusade." FDR's 1940 opponent, Wendell Willkie, took a page from "that man's" book; in his speech accepting the Republican nomination, Willkie pledged: "We go into this campaign as into a crusade ... on the basis of American liberty, not on the basis of hate, jealousy or personalities."

Eisenhower first used the word in its traditional moral-military context in his June 6, 1944, "Order of the Day" to the Allied troops poised to invade Europe: "Soldiers, sailors and airmen of the Allied Expeditionary Force: You are about to embark upon a great crusade, toward which we have striven these many months. ... The hopes and prayers of liberty-loving people everywhere march with you."

The General entitled his best-selling memoirs *Crusade in Europe*, and it was natural for his political advisers to seize on the word so closely identified with their candidate. Throughout the campaign of 1952 he reiterated the word, perhaps most dramatically in his "I shall go to Korea" speech on October 24: "I do not believe it a presumption for me to call the effort of all those who have enlisted with me—a crusade. I use that word only to signify two facts. First: We are united and devoted to a just cause of the purest meaning to all humankind. Second: We know that—for all the might of our effort—victory can come only with the gift of God's help. In this spirit—humble servants of a proud ideal—we do soberly say: This is a crusade."

That Detroit speech was prepared by Emmet Hughes, and its use of *crusade* was limited to the quest for peace, a narrowing down of its earlier use by Eisenhower to apply to anything on the domestic scene as well. Hughes wrote later: "I struck from the current vocabulary any use of 'Crusade' on the national scene, and 'liberation' on the world scene. Their presumption seemed to me offensive, and they nowhere appeared

in any passage of any speech that I prepared for the rest of the campaign." This attitude might have been in response to Adlai Stevenson's gibes about Eisenhower's oft-repeated dedication to a crusade: "The General has dedicated himself so many times, he must feel like the cornerstone of a public building."

President John F. Kennedy used the word in a negative context in 1961: "Let our patriotism be reflected in the creation of confidence in one another, rather than in crusades of suspicion."

The BBC's Alistair Cooke, writing in *The Listener* in 1963, made an astute observation about crusades and Presidents: "All Presidents start out pretending to run a crusade, but after a couple of years they find they are running something much less heroic, much more intractable: namely, the Presidency."

The word's moral fervor is built in; its literal meaning is "taking the cross," coined in the eleventh century to describe the first military expedition by European Christians to recover the Holy Land from the Muslims. That historical resonance got President George W. Bush in rhetorical trouble one week after 9/11. After identifying Osama bin Laden as the leading suspect in the terrorist attacks, he said "this crusade, this war on terrorism, is going to take a while." The AP reported "with that comment, he stoked suspicion in some Arab and Muslim quarters where 'crusade' is a loaded term that recalls the Christians' medieval wars against Muslims in the Holy Land." The White House press secretary, Ari Fleischer, expressed Bush's concern about such a reaction: "To the degree that that word has many connotations that would upset many of our partners or anybody else in the world, the president would regret if anything like that was conveyed." From then on, the word *crusade* was dropped from the presidential vocabulary.

C THREE C 3 See K_1C_2.

cufflinks gang A group of early supporters of FDR in his unsuccessful run for the vice presidency in 1920, tied together later by the postcampaign gift of gold cufflinks from the candidate.

FDR White House aide Marvin McIntyre wore his cufflinks throughout the 1930s, symbol of his membership in the "original" group; later Bronx Democratic boss Ed Flynn echoed the sentiment by forming an FRBC Club (For Roosevelt Before Chicago) of those who supported FDR before the 1932 Chicago convention. Twenty years before, Theodore Roosevelt's manager, Senator Joseph Dixon of Montana, used "Before April 9th Men" to hail Roosevelt supporters who spoke up for him before the April 9, 1912, Illinois primary brightened his chances.

Mementos like the cufflinks are cherished by the recipients as a badge of being an early insider, with presumably some slight prerogative over the Johnny-come-latelies. John F. Kennedy gave his aides a PT-109 tie clasp, which became the highest status symbol of the New Frontier.

Cufflinks and tie clasps, chosen for these gifts because of their high visibility and portability, are customarily presented by winners (Nelson Rockefeller's post-1966 gubernatorial campaign gift was a pair of cufflinks with a tiny "rock of Gibraltar" embedded in each). After the 1952 campaign Vice President Richard Nixon presented "Order of the Hound's Tooth" scrolls to his intimates, suitable for framing, and KITCHEN CABINET scrolls to those who accompanied him to the KITCHEN DEBATE in Moscow in 1959. After his 1960 defeat, Nixon sent a desk memento to one hundred key men: a clay replica of the life cast taken of Abraham Lincoln's right hand. Ironically, most of these were not wrapped securely and arrived broken in the mail; the Nixon aide responsible (author of this dictionary) spent six months apologizing, having new hands cast and reshipped to impatient, fuming recipients. After his successful campaigning for congressional candidates in 1966, Nixon aides, who had learned a lesson, sent out unbreakable "Churchill crowns" to helpers across the nation with a quotation from Churchill about the dangers of appeasement.

cult of personality Promotion of personal adulation, as contrasted with collective leadership.

At a secret session of the Communist Party Congress on February 25, 1956, Party Secretary Nikita Khrushchev rose to denounce Joseph Stalin, startling the world and leading to a drastic revision of Soviet history books. A transcript of the speech was obtained by Israel's espionage agency, the Mossad, and passed on to James Jesus Angleton of the CIA, who distributed it around the world. It was in the anti-Communist interest to be able to quote Khrushchev saying that a "cult of personality" had been promoted by Stalin after Lenin's death, and that Stalin had abused his personal prestige by using it to undermine collective leadership of the Presidium. *Pravda* followed up a month later with de facto confirmation of the accuracy of the transcript: "Stalin's disregard of the principle of collective leadership, and the frequent decisions taken by him personally, led to the distortion of party principles and party democracy, to the violation of revolutionary law, and to repression."

In later years there was criticism in Communist circles (the word *circles* was a favorite of Moscow translators) of a *cult of personality* growing up around Khrushchev, which ultimately contributed to his own downfall. In the Western world, the phrase is occasionally used in an ironic or joking way.

The idea of extending power through a personality cult, of course, was not original with either Stalin or Khrushchev. Alexander Hamilton, in an 1802 letter, outlined a plan for a "Christian Constitutional Society," appealing to people "through a development of a 'cult' of Washington and benevolent activities." The cult that Hamilton had proposed was formed in 1808—the Washington Benevolent Society—too late to help the sagging Federalists.

Columnist Murray Kempton, writing in 1967 about the first U.S. press conference of Stalin's daughter, Svetlana Alliluyeva, commented: "Of all Russians, the daughter of Joseph Stalin is the one to remind his replacements that the Cult of Personality can no more decently be employed to lay all the guilt on one man than it can be to give him all the credit."

Cultural Revolution Political and social upheaval in the People's Republic of China, fostered by Mao Zedong to forestall bureaucratization and to preserve the purity of the revolution as he knew it.

What troubled Party Chairman Mao when he launched the "Great Proletarian Cultural Revolution" in May of 1966 was the growing gap in China between city and village, intellectual and peasant. Instead of devotion to the Communist cause, there were signs of REVISIONISM, "backsliding," and "bureaucratism," along with yearnings for such bourgeois things as comfort, status, and education. *Toronto Star* correspondent Mark Gayn wrote in the January 1967 *Foreign Affairs* that Mao sought "nothing less than the rejuvenation of a great revolution, the rebirth in middle age of the drive, the passion, the selflessness and the discipline it had in its youth a third of a century ago."

The Cultural Revolution had its origin in November 1965 when a Shanghai newspaper attacked the deputy mayor of Beijing, Wu Han, for having written a play in 1959, *Hai Rui Dismissed from Office*, which was taken to be a veiled attack on Mao. The following year Mao and his then heir-apparent, Marshal Lin Biao, created the Red Guards as instruments to restore ideological purity. Patterned after the peasant youth movement of Hunan in the late 1920s, the Red Guard movement created a reign of terror, with public humiliations of those who opposed Mao, including kangaroo trials, public beatings, and executions.

The faction that Westerners described as "antiradical" ultimately made a comeback under Deng Xiaoping. After Mao's death a short, fierce struggle took place between the "Shanghai radicals" led by Mao's widow and the successor to Mao, Hua Guofeng, who had the army's backing. As a result, the group that had gained power during the Cultural Revolution was arrested and denounced as the *Gang of Four*, while Deng agreed to serve under Hua, whom he soon pushed aside to became what was called "paramount leader."

curmudgeon A likeably irascible old man. In politics, a cantankerous, outspoken older politician with a talent for invective.

FDR's Interior Secretary, Harold Ickes, earned the title "The Old Curmudgeon." New York Parks Commissioner Robert Moses was often identified as a *curmudgeon*, but the word still evokes memories of "Harold the Ick." Among his memorable blasts, he tagged Wendell Willkie as "the simple, BAREFOOT BOY FROM WALL STREET," and is sometimes credited (inaccurately) with labeling Thomas E. Dewey as "the little man on the wedding cake"; Alfred Landon was "a strong but silenced man." When Huey Long called Ickes "the Chicago Chinch-Bug," Ickes replied, "The trouble with Senator Long is that he is suffering from halitosis of the intellect. That's presuming Senator Long has an intellect." He denounced opponents of academic freedom as "intellectual Dillingers," proponents of the Liberty League as "vestal virgins," and Governor Talmadge of Georgia as "His Chain Gang Excellency." He intended to deliver a speech about Rep. Martin Dies, head of the House Un-American Activities Committee, entitled "A Case of Loaded Dies," but Roosevelt restrained him.

A curmudgeon may expect to be attacked in kind. Ickes was described as "the New Deal blackjack squad," "blunderbuss Ickes," and (by House Speaker Joe Martin) "Comrade Harold L. Ickes, Overlord of the Interior and Commissar of the P.W.A."

The definition of *curmudgeon* in most dictionaries is "cantankerous, bad-tempered"; in Samuel Johnson's dictionary it is "churlish, avaricious" (Johnson, in a famous etymological mistake, thought it came from the French for "unknown correspondent," somehow rooted in *coeur méchant*, "wicked heart"). That sense of "grasping" does not apply in politics; "irascible" and "cantankerous" are the right adjectives. The curmudgeon is liked and his irascibility admired because he is a throwback to the days when politicians had fewer advisers telling them to soften their words.

In 1969, *Life* magazine columnist Hugh Sidey referred to publisher John Knight, then seventy-five, as "an old curmudgeon."

Knight looked up the definition in the third edition of Merriam-Webster's *New International Dictionary* and was distressed to see "a miser; niggard; churl" among other disparagements. Sidey quickly wrote one of Knight's perturbed associates: "Word meanings are fluid, like history. Dictionaries are often inaccurate guides to the moment. William Safire's book, The New Language of Politics, … says 'Curmudgeon—a likeably irascible old man.' That is precisely how I feel about Mr. Knight. I believe he is a splendid journalist, a delightful skeptic, a wonderful human being. Nothing you wrote changes my opinion of this old curmudgeon." Knight replied to Sidey, "I guess that calls for a drink," and wrote this author: "I have had a lot of fun with being called a 'curmudgeon' but I much prefer your definition to the one in Webster's."

curse of bigness An attack phrase on monopoly, unlawful combinations, and the power of predatory corporate chieftains.

Labor unrest and violence shocked the nation in 1911, culminating in the dynamiting of the then antilabor *Los Angeles Times* by three union officials. Boston attorney Louis D. Brandeis (later a Supreme Court Justice) wrote the editor of the magazine *Survey* on December 30, 1911: "Is there not a causal connection between the development of these huge, indomitable trusts and the horrible crimes now under investigation? Is it not irony to speak of equality of opportunity in a country cursed with bigness?"

Brandeis' phrase caused a stir; he used it again as the title of an essay published in *Harper's Weekly:* "The Curse of Bigness." The classic answer to Brandeis' phrase is one of the few memorable phrases of President William Howard Taft: "Mere size is no sin against the law." (A double meaning was noticed in that statement: Taft weighed over 300 pounds.) Both phrases are used in discussions of antitrust cases; David Lilienthal switched the Brandeis phrase around in the 1950s in discussing the "curse of smallness."

cut and run To retreat hastily and shamefully; to "bug out."

This counterattacking phrase is strongly pejorative, compared to the euphemistic *strategic withdrawal, redeployment, retrograde movement,* or (as Union Gen. George McClellan put it when backing away from General Robert E. Lee's Confederate army at Richmond in 1862) *change of base.*

Cut and run became a highly charged catchphrase as the war in Iraq—which had begun with the SHOCK AND AWE of a quick military victory in 2003—began looking to many critics of the war like a QUAGMIRE. "We're not going to cut and run from the people who long for freedom," responded President George W. Bush in April of 2004. Once the case was framed in this manner, those who had opposed going to war in the first place, or the way it was being conducted, had little choice but to adopt the same terminology: It was not politically possible for them to grasp what amounted to a red-hot poker and say, "Yes—let's *cut and run*." A day after the president spoke, Republican Senator John McCain asked rhetorically, "Is it time to panic, to cut and run?" Not surprisingly, his answer was "Absolutely not." A week later, Senator John Kerry, then closing in on the Democratic nomination for president, used the term as a compound adjective: "I don't believe in a cut-and-run philosophy."

When opponents of the war began to talk of *timetables* for a withdrawal of American forces, the Bush policy's defenders, though willing to accept the more general *benchmarks* to measure success, applied the label that rejected a rout. The liberal Jonathan Alter objected in a 2006 column in *Newsweek:* "Anyone who dares criticize President Bush's Iraq policy is a 'cut-and-run' Democrat."

Cut and run has been used in connection with American involvements abroad since at least World War II. When engagement in Somalia led to casualties in 1993, then-General Colin Powell said, "I don't think we should cut and run because things have gotten a little tough." Vice President Spiro T. Agnew declared during the Vietnam conflict in 1970 that "if we were to cut and run before the South Vietnamese can adjust to defend themselves, South Vietnam would fall." Just over a decade earlier, in 1959, columnist Holmes Alexander wrote that the Eisenhower Administration "should no more cut and run from Berlin than we ran last summer from Quemoy," referring to a group of Taiwanese islands whose bombardment of mainland China by cannon led to the deployment of the U.S. Seventh Fleet in the area. In 1945, columnist Samuel Grafton complained when an isolationist senator, Kenneth Wherry of Nebraska, threatened to vote against the U.S. joining the United Nations: "We have become the only nation in the world in which ratification of key instruments is a doubtful issue. The world knows now that many of us have an intense belief that we are ultimately uninvolved, that we can always cut and run."

Cut and run is of nautical origin. The earliest example comes from the *Boston News-Letter* of June 12, 1704: "Cap. Vaughn rode by said Ship, but cut & run." A reference work for sailors, *Elements and Practice of Rigging and Seamanship*, defined the phrase in 1794: "to cut the cable and make sail instantly, without waiting to weigh anchor." The meaning was extended by the mid-nineteenth century to include other kinds of quick departures, not necessarily in panic. "Jack Chase cut and run," reports a midshipman in Herman Melville's 1850 novel *White Jacket*, referring to a friend who has jumped ship (to join the Peruvian navy, as it turned out). Alfred Lord Tennyson wrote to his wife, Emily, in 1864: "I dined at Gladstone's yesterday—Duke and Duchess there…but I can't abide the dinners.… I shall soon have to cut and run."

As fighting in Iraq continued through 2006, David Sanger, of *The New York Times*, suggested a variation on the *cut-and-run* theme: "The most talked-about alternatives now include renewed efforts to prepare the Iraqi forces while preparing to pull American combat brigades back to their bases, or back home.… those are options still redolent of timetables—at best cut and walk." Leon Panetta, a member of the bipartisan Iraq Study Group commissioned by Congress to suggest alternatives, said "If this war is consumed by partisan attacks, if the choice is presented as simply one between 'stay the course' and 'cut and run,' we will never be able to do what is right."

A deliciously archaic Americanism was introduced on the Senate floor in July 2007 as a synonym for *cut and run* by Senator Orrin Hatch, Republican of Utah. After warning that "our enemies will be emboldened" because "the majority is waving the flag of withdrawal," Hatch concluded his speech with "Absquatulation is not a policy." In his 1951 *A Dictionary of Americanisms*, Mitford Matthews cited the first known use of the obsolete *absquatulate* in a June 15, 1830 issue of the *Painesville* (Ohio) *Telegraph*, which defined the term as "to mosey, to abscond." Matthews analyzed it as "Of fanciful classical formation as if based on *ab* + *squat*, meaning the reverse of to squat, i.e. to decamp, make off…to depart, go away, esp. in a clandestine, surreptitious or hurried manner."

See also EXIT STRATEGY; STAY THE COURSE; SURGE; VIETNAM SYNDROME.

cutting edge See ON THE POINT.

C.Y.A. The initialized euphemism for "cover your ass."

This initialism was frequently euphemized by the lexicographer, aware of *The New York Times*'s antipathy to the use of the vulgarism *ass*, as "posterior protection," the bureaucratic technique of averting future accusations of policy error or wrongdoing by deflecting responsibility in advance.

Rear Admiral John M. Poindexter testified at the Iran-contra hearings that he destroyed a secret Presidential finding, which "had been prepared essentially by the C.I.A. as a—what we call a C.Y.A. effort."

C.I.A. (or *CIA*, without periods) is the Central Intelligence Agency; *C.Y.A.* is a military-bureaucratic abbreviation defined by Democratic Senator Sam Nunn of Georgia during the same hearings: "Isn't this cable in effect a C.Y.A. cable?… They were covering their rear end back in Washington, weren't they?"

This use of capitalized initialese stands for an imperative clause and points to the fuzzing of responsibility. A bureaucrat adept at *C.Y.A.* (a) likes to employ passive constructions (see MISTAKES WERE MADE), (b) follows up a meeting or phone call with a self-serving *memcon*—"memorandum of conversation," (c) routes memos to and through as many other bureaucrats as possible, thereby spreading the risk of future criticism, and (d) "papers the file" with memoranda supporting and sometimes contradicting his or her position.

The political usage has been adopted in journalism. At the *Detroit Free Press*, Joe Grimm notified his colleagues in 2007: "You've just learned that a story you're writing for the newspaper is likely to bring complaints from a particular group...So, while the story is being edited, you tell the editor that you think people might complain...Your boss is then informed and involved in helping you make the story as bulletproof as possible...the editor has not been blind-sided. Had you not covered your ass by telling the editor what was up, some of the readers' wrath would have rained down on your head...editors, by investing in the process, put their butts on the line with yours. (I can't explain why this part of the human anatomy has so much to do with this particular exercise unless it has something to do with avoiding a good butt-kicking. Or chewing.)"

D

daisy spot Political advertising; anti-war commercial.

This term, in which *spot* is used in the advertising sense of "brief commercial announcement," comes from an ad used by Lyndon B. Johnson in his 1964 presidential campaign. To torpedo his Republican opponent Barry Goldwater, Johnson used an advertisement aimed at underscoring the challenger as a warmongering extremist.

The ad showed a young girl counting as she picked petals from a daisy. A military voice began a different type of countdown, leading to a nuclear explosion that mushroomed across the screen, and LBJ's voice was heard discussing "the stakes" of the election. Shown only once, on September 7, 1964, the commercial drew immediate outcries from Republicans about its unfairness. Republican National Committee chairman Dean Burch complained, "This horrible commercial is designed to arouse basic emotions," and it was immediately withdrawn, but its impact lingered.

The ad's creator, political consultant Tony Schwartz, was quoted in *Newsday* in 1992 as saying that the daisy spot "was the first national Rorschach test," with its implications that Goldwater, who wasn't even mentioned, would start a third world war.

Said Schwartz:

> When this commercial was shown, it was against a backdrop of what was out in the environment about Goldwater, that he had spoken for the use of nuclear weapons to defoliate the jungles of East Asia, and for letting field commanders use them at their discretion. ... People say political commercials manipulate viewers, but viewers have to participate in the manipulation—projecting their own frames of reference onto commercials, filling in the message's blanks.

In current usage, negative advertising is often measured against the impact of, and fierce reaction to, the *daisy spot*. See SWIFT BOAT SPOT.

damage control Minimization of public reaction to mistakes, accidents, or other adverse events without the appearance of panic or despair.

"Call it a campaign code red," wrote Thomas Beaumont in *The Politico* in the spring of 2007, after Rudy Giuliani was a no-show at an Iowa farm event, John Edwards had a $400 haircut, and Barack Obama misstated a Kansas tornado death toll. "A clumsy campaign move, an embarrassing development or an awkward moment makes it way into the press and on the Internet. The blogs crackle. And before top aides can say 'damage control,' the candidate has a big, puffy black eye."

Damage control was associated with accidents aboard ships at sea before being applied to the ship of state. *Chambers's Encyclopedia* defined the term in 1959: "Damage control, the principles by which a certain degree of control may be exercised over the stability and buoyancy of a ship which has received serious underwater damage." Putting the definition into practice, the *Oakland Tribune* reported colorfully the following year on five women members of the Marine Cooks and Stewards Union: "Their fingernails were broken, their coiffures were soaked and their makeup was smeared but with their male companions they fought the sea for more than an hour. ... the first of more than 200 female members of the union to attend a three-day course in damage control and fire-fighting."

The noun phrase came to Washington, D.C., when adopted by the CIA to describe its minimization of fallout after an aborted mission. Political *damage control* was popularized during the Watergate period. An AP writer, Lawrence Knutson, made the connection to maritime affairs explicit when questioning Sen. Lowell Weicker (R-Conn.) in 1974: "Sen. Barry Goldwater [R-Ariz.] has been acting almost in the role of a damage control officer on a submarine in assessing

Watergate's political fallout on Republicans. Do you agree with his predictions of a Republican catastrophe in the fall elections?" Weicker said, "No." He predicted a catastrophe of "untold proportions" for all candidates—Democrats as well as Republicans—who were "incapable or unwilling to undergo a public microscope." Characterizing White House efforts to survive the Watergate scandal, Nicholas Horrock, of *The New York Times*, wrote in 1977: "In the White House jargon of the Nixon Years, they called it 'damage control'—the art of containing, minimizing or if all else fails, riding out political criticism. Damage control in the extreme, of course, became COVER-UP and cover-up destroyed the Nixon presidency."

Subsequent administrations have resorted to *damage control* techniques with varying degrees of success. Speaking of "Billygate" (see -GATE CONSTRUCTION), the Doylestown, Pa., *Daily Intelligencer* editorialized in 1980: "When faced with potential scandal, the wise politician gets it all out into the open as quickly as possible and thus puts the embarrassment behind him. But it appears too late for President Carter to follow that strategy of damage control in the Billy Carter-Libyan affair." Referring to Carter's successor, UPI reported in January of 1982: "President Reagan's stumbling into a thicket of errors at his news conference is keeping his spokesmen at their damage control stations."

A generation later, as Justice Department officials in the George W. Bush Administration scrambled to explain the dismissals in 2007 of eight federal prosecutors, David Gergen, longtime adviser to presidents of both parties, echoed the Doylestown *Intelligencer:* "The first rule of damage control is to get to the bottom of it, figure out what the worst is, conduct an internal investigation, collect all the information and then dump it out in one fell swoop."

dark horse A long-shot candidate for nomination, usually the second or third choice of many delegates, whose best chance for selection lies in a deadlock of the leading candidates.

The first *dark horse* appeared at one of the earliest Democratic conventions. Indeed, the choice of James Polk of Tennessee proved the usefulness of political party conventions. An impasse had been reached between former President Martin Van Buren of New York and Lewis Cass of Michigan in the convention held in Baltimore in 1844. On the eighth ballot, with neither leader willing to give way to the other, a compromise of Polk was suggested. He received 44 votes, Cass 114, Van Buren 104, Calhoun and Buchanan 2 each, with 134 needed to nominate. On the ninth ballot, the convention stampeded to the "dark horse." Polk received all 266 votes.

Like most compromise candidates who followed him, Polk was not well known nationally. "Who's Polk?" became a slogan of the 1844 campaign, in which Polk narrowly defeated the Whigs' Henry Clay. The next dark horse to win was Franklin Pierce, who was not considered as a candidate until the 35th ballot, winning on the 49th. The Democrats' slogan then became "We Polked You in 1844, We'll Pierce You in 1852." He, too, defeated the Whig candidate, General Winfield Scott. In 1876, Rutherford B. Hayes was another successful dark horse.

The phrase *dark horse* probably first entered the political language after Polk and before Pierce. The first direct reference I can find is from a biography of Hamilton Fish by Alan Nevins, quoting New York's Fish, campaigning in support of Lincoln in 1860: "We want a log-splitter, not a hair-splitter; a flat-boatman, not a flat-statesman; log-cabin, coonskin, hard cider, old Abe and dark horse—hurrah!"

In the twentieth century, Warren Gamaliel Harding of Ohio was the most successful dark horse. Army hero Leonard Wood and Governor Frank Lowden of Illinois deadlocked the Republican convention of 1920 for nine ballots. In a suite on the top floor of Chicago's Blackstone Hotel, party leaders selected Harding, a man with apparently no enemies. See SMOKE-FILLED ROOM.

Wendell Willkie in 1940 began his campaign for the nomination as a dark horse against the favorites, Thomas E. Dewey and Robert A. Taft. William Allen White extended the metaphor in a profile in *The New Republic*: "What sort of man personally is this unknown dark horse who is being groomed in the Augean stables of our plutocracy?" See CLEAN SWEEP.

The phrase was used non-politically in a novel by the young Benjamin Disraeli, *The Young Duke*, published in 1831: "A dark horse which had never been thought of, and which the careless St. James had never even observed in the list, rushed past the grandstand in sweeping triumph." Reviewing the first edition of this dictionary in *Encounter* magazine in 1968, historian Sir Denis Brogan added: "in a moment of patriotic pride, I should like to suggest that the most brilliant use of the term 'dark horse' was made by John Morley (known to good Radicals as 'honest John Morley,' no doubt to distinguish him from his colleagues); he called Lord Rosebery (who was as proud of having won the Derby as of having been Prime Minister) 'a dark horse in a loose box.' (The term 'loose box' was also used to describe the special accommodation provided for the mistresses of Edward VII at his coronation in Westminster Abbey in 1902.)"

A darker equine metaphor was put forward by the terrorist leader Osama bin Laden from his hiding place after al-Qaeda's attacks of 9/11, casting aspersions on what was seen as a weak American response to earlier attacks: "When people see a strong horse and a weak horse, by nature, they will like the strong horse."

Other horse-racing metaphors common to politics are BOLT, SHOO-IN, RUNNING MATE, NON-STARTER and FRONT RUNNER. Winners *take the reins* of government; losers are known as *also-rans*.

data mining Extraction of information from large databases by sorting through them to discover previously unknown relationships; "connecting the dots" through potential abuse of privacy.

Financial institutions and direct-mail catalog companies pioneered the field in the 1990s. Where earlier computer programs required that searchers pose specific questions, such as "Find every male under 30 with income over $60,000 in suburban Maryland who has purchased a new car within the last six months," more sophisticated *data miners* are now capable of analyzing patterns of behavior by assessing thousands of variables. In an article with the subhead "Advances in data mining allow companies to find more specific information about target consumers," Scripps-Howard reported in 1997: "With data mining, companies can merely tell the software to sift through a data warehouse in search of interesting but previously unknown relationships such as a tendency for motorcycle owners to buy lobsters."

Application of the same techniques by the government, eager to "connect the dots" in tracing potential terrorists, raised privacy concerns. A children's game of over a century ago was to draw a line between numbered dots until a figure or scene appeared; thus, *connecting the dots* came to mean "making a pattern out of seemingly unconnected information." After 9/11, when it became apparent that data from intelligence sources had not been shared with law enforcement—because of a "firewall" between the CIA and National Security Agency on one side and the FBI and state and local police on the other—demands were made to *connect the dots*, despite previous safeguards that prevented the "tainting" of evidence of crimes by methods not admissible in court.

Under pressure not to let terrorists operate as freely as before, the Pentagon began developing what it called a "Total Information Awareness" program in 2002. The project was headed by retired admiral John Poindexter, former national security adviser under President Reagan.

A vituperative right-wing columnist for *The New York Times* characterized it harshly:

Every purchase you make with a credit card, every magazine subscription you buy and medical prescription you fill, every website you visit and e-mail you send or receive, every academic grade you receive, every bank deposit you make, every trip you book and every event you attend— all these transactions and communications will go into what the Defense Department describes as "a virtual, centralized grand database." To this computerized dossier on your private life from commercial sources, add every piece of information that government has about you—passport application, driver's license and bridge toll records, judicial and divorce records, complaints from nosy neighbors to the F.B.I., your lifetime paper trail plus the latest hidden camera surveillance—and you have a supersnoop's dream: a "Total Information Awareness" about every U.S. citizen.

This is not some far-out Orwellian scenario. It is what will happen to your personal freedom in the next few weeks if John Poindexter gets the unprecedented power he seeks.

This diatribe stirred the ire of writers who put security concerns first. "Blather, nonsense, piffle, and flapdoodle," argued Stuart Taylor in *National Journal* about such "hyperventilating." William Kristol's *Weekly Standard* sneered at "the ravings of privacy fanatics like the *New York Times* columnist William Safire, who triggered the anti-T.I.A. stampede."

The scope of the program worried civil libertarians all along the political spectrum. Questions also were raised about whether Poindexter was the right man for the job, since he had been convicted on five felony counts for his role in the Iran-Contra scandal of 1984–86, even though the convictions—for lying to Congress, destroying official documents, and obstructing the congressional inquiry—were overturned on appeal. In January of 2003, Senators Russ Feingold (D-Wisc.), Jon Corzine (D-N.J.), and Ron Wyden (D-Ore.) introduced a bill to place a moratorium on "data-mining" until Congress could review the TIA program. "This unchecked system is a dangerous step that threatens one of the values we are fighting for—freedom," said Feingold.

Funds for TIA were cut off later in 2003, but data mining continues unabated under different officials and entities. *The Washington Post* reported in February of 2007 that the Department of Homeland Security was testing "a data-mining program that would attempt to spot terrorists by combing vast amounts of information about average Americans, such as flight and hotel reservations," along with audio and visual records.

Called ADVISE (an acronym for Analysis, Dissemination, Visualization, Insight, and Scientific Enhancement), this program was said to be "on the cutting edge of analytical technology that applies mathematical algorithms to uncover hidden relationships in data." ADVISE appeared at the time to be further along in development than the TIA program when it was killed—and already, the *Post* reported, according to a congressional source, researchers probably had violated privacy laws by using real information in their tests rather than fake data.

day of infamy Franklin Roosevelt's condemnation of the attack on Pearl Harbor on December 7, 1941, in requesting Congress to declare war on Japan.

The speech was drafted by Roosevelt himself, without the aid of either Robert E. Sherwood or Samuel Rosenman, his major speechwriters at that time. The first draft's first sentence read: "Yesterday, December 7, 1941, a date which will live in world history, the United States was simultaneously and deliberately attacked by naval and air forces of the Empire of Japan." In his second draft, FDR crossed out "world history" and substituted "infamy"; he crossed out "simultaneously" and used "suddenly."

The third draft includes insertions in FDR's handwriting: "Last night Japanese forces attacked Hong Kong. Last night Japanese forces attacked Wake Island. This morning the Japanese attacked Midway Island." While the President was preparing to go to Congress, he added the latest news as it came in. Harry Hopkins suggested a sentence, which Roosevelt approved, expressing confidence that we would "gain the inevitable triumph—so help us God."

"The remarkable thing," wrote Judge Rosenman later, "is that on one of the busiest and most turbulent days of his life he was able to spend so much time and give so much thought to this speech." Secretary of State Cordell Hull had argued for a long speech, detailing the history of Japanese-American relations. Roosevelt said that he would go into detail in a fireside chat the next day, and decided on his own six-minute dramatic message to Congress.

Roosevelt's revision from "world history" to "infamy" is intriguing; the word was seldom used (Voltaire had written to a friend in 1760: "I wish that you would crush this infamy"), but the change of the word made the phrase memorable.

dead cat bounce An aborted economic recovery.

This macabre metaphor suggests a slight rise after the first economic decline, followed in fast order by a second decline. This bounce of the body of a cat is a graphic depiction of what economists call a DOUBLE DIP.

Usually hyphenated, *dead-cat bounce* first appeared in the *Financial Times* of December 7, 1985, without a hyphen; in this article, investment experts in the Far East described a slight rise in economic indicators as "partly technical and cautioned against concluding that the recent falls in the market were at an end. 'This is what we call a dead cat bounce,' one broker said flatly."

The Associated Press reported the term's use in New York a year later, when a broker, Raymond DeVoe Jr., warned, "Beware the dead-cat bounce." He offered a definition for the term: "This applies to stocks or commodities that have gone into free-fall descent and then rallied briefly. If you threw a dead cat off a 50-story building, it might bounce when it hit the sidewalk. But don't confuse that bounce with renewed life. It is still a dead cat."

The feline figure of speech is alive and well. "A dead cat bounce is a term adopted for a rally in a bear market," wrote Britain's *The Independent* in 2001. "In the U.S. they call it a 'sucker's rally.'" See RECESSION.

dead end, political The mayoralty of any large city; supposedly a thankless job that makes major enemies and aborts a political career.

When New York Congressman John V. Lindsay was being urged to run for mayor in 1965 his friends pointed to the careers of Fiorello La Guardia and Robert Wagner as evidence that the job was "a political dead end." *Newsweek* wrote in 1967: "Democrat Richardson Dilworth won national acclaim during the 1950s as Mayor of Philadelphia only to learn the hard way that City Hall is more often a dead end than a STEPPINGSTONE for promising political careers."

Hubert Humphrey's rise from mayor of Minneapolis, Minnesota, to Vice President of the U.S. was dismissed as an exception that proved the rule. President Eisenhower in 1956 asked Vice President Richard Nixon whether he felt that a cabinet post would be more helpful in furthering his own career. "The President explained to Nixon," reported Sherman Adams, "that history had shown the vice presidency to be somewhat of a political dead end; no vice president in this century had gone on to the presidency except through accidental succession." That changed with the election of Vice President George H.W. Bush in 1988. But with the accidental succession to power of Harry Truman, Lyndon Johnson, and Gerald Ford, the phrase is rarely used today in relation to the office a HEARTBEAT AWAY FROM THE PRESIDENCY.

In 2007, when former New York Mayor Rudy Giuliani became a strong contender for the GOP nomination for president, and as some independents were urging the race on the current Mayor, Michael Bloomberg—a billionaire who could afford a delayed entry in 2008—suddenly the mayoralty of a big city no longer looked like a *political dead end*.

The phrase is derived from the 1935 Sidney Kingsley play *Dead End*; its movie version starred a group of tough-talking young actors who became known as "the Dead End Kids." The title was taken from a traffic sign that indicated no exit at the far end of the street, and was used to symbolize the lack of opportunity available to young men from poor neighborhoods. The sign's message, stunningly accurate, apparently offended fainthearted traffic officials; it has been changed to "No Outlet." See DISADVANTAGED; GRAVEYARD.

deal A political trade of favors or support. When either discovered or imagined, an effective attack word that turns what some consider an honorable arrangement into what others suspect is a bribe.

In 1824, the "era of good feeling" began to sour when John Quincy Adams made a deal with Henry Clay. Andrew Jackson had won a plurality of the popular and electoral votes, but not a majority, and the election had to be decided in the House of Representatives. Speaker of the House Clay threw his support behind Adams, who then won, and promptly named Clay his Secretary of State. In the 1828 election, Jackson's slogan was "Bargain and Corruption" and he won handily.

After that, *deals*—pronounced with a sneer—became something to be denounced by all candidates, especially regarding cabinet posts and other appointments, a point that rarely discouraged campaign managers from dealing in realities. Lincoln piously wired his convention floor manager in 1860, David Davis: "Make no deals in my name." Davis is reported to have remarked, "Hell, we're here and he's not," and dealt freely with the Blair and Cameron forces, promising Cabinet posts in return for delegate support. As President, Lincoln fulfilled the promises made by Davis, who was rewarded with a seat on the Supreme Court.

At the Republican convention of 1880, former President U.S. Grant went a little too far in denying a deal. "It was my intention, if nominated and elected, to appoint John Sherman Secretary of the Treasury. Now you may be certain I shall not. Not to be President of the United States would I consent that a bargain should be made." No bargain, no support; James Garfield was nominated.

Probably the most monumental deal in U.S. political history occurred in the disputed election between Rutherford B. Hayes, Republican of Ohio, and Samuel J. Tilden, Democrat of New York, in 1876. Tilden had won a majority of the popular vote and led Hayes in the electoral vote 184 to 165, with 185 the necessary majority. Twenty votes, from "carpetbag" governments in Florida, Louisiana, and South Carolina, as well as one from Oregon, were in dispute. The Republican-controlled Senate and the Democratic-controlled House could not agree on how the disputed votes were to be counted. An electoral commission was appointed, with seven men from each party plus one "independent"—Supreme Court Justice David Davis, the same man who made the convention deals for Lincoln. He resigned in favor of an eighth Republican, who threw the election, predictably, to Hayes.

Why did the Democrats hold still for this decision to substitute a Republican for the independent swing man? Because the Republicans agreed to a simple deal: the election of Hayes, in return for the withdrawal of federal troops from the "carpetbag" states, ending Reconstruction governments and giving the Democrats control of the South. In the long run, the Democrats got the better of the deal.

William Randolph Hearst received the Democratic nomination for governor of New York in 1906 from the hands of Tammany Leader Charles Murphy, whom Hearst papers had attacked a few months before as "The Colossus of Graft" and "The Black Hand." Suspecting a deal, writer Edmund Wetmore put into poetry what Hearst might have said: "So I lashed him and I thrashed him in my hot reforming zeal, / Then I clasped him to my bosom in a most artistic deal."

At the 1948 Republican convention, Robert Taft (beaten by Thomas E. Dewey for the nomination) agreed to the vice-presidential nomination of his fellow Ohioan, John Bricker, in return for the pledge of Bricker forces for active support of Taft in 1952 (which was forthcoming, though Taft lost to Eisenhower).

As a noun, *deal* takes its coloration from its adjective: a *square deal* is good and a *fast deal* is bad. Its definition depends on the point of view: what is a "cynical bargain" to your adversary is an "honorable compromise" to you. Oklahoma Democratic Senator Robert Kerr, a noted wheeler-dealer, liked to say: "I'm against any deal I'm not in on."

decision-making process The way a political executive makes up his mind; or a cliché used by press secretaries to block access to information about the conflicting pressures involved in the formulation of policy; or a high-sounding phrase to describe whatever inside information reporters can unearth about who gave what advice to whom.

Victor Navasky described in his 1971 book, *Kennedy Justice*, "a series of forays into what is forbiddingly known as the Decision-making Process, a look at how an institution makes up its mind ..." In that sense, the process is institutional, showing how the top executives cannot be totally blamed or credited for their conclusions.

The phrase can be used positively, as in "we must involve more of the people in the decision-making process." It can also carry a negative connotation as a difficult-to-penetrate wall, as in this usage by Attorney General William P. Rogers to a Senate judiciary subcommittee on March 6, 1958, about EXECUTIVE PRIVILEGE: "I appreciate the opportunity... to present my views as to the extent of the inquiry which can be made by the legislative branch of the Government concerning the decision-making process and documents of the Executive Branch."

The process itself can be amorphous and mysterious, as in President Truman's decision to launch a war-ending nuclear strike, or formally laid out with options, projected consequences, and recommendations, as in many of the decisions that are made through the present National Security Council system. Or it can represent the workings of one person's mind, little influenced by staff.

There is commercial value to its understanding. "The regulatory process in Washington is influenced by political factors," former Deputy Attorney General and later Judge Laurence Silberman told reporter Steven Roberts in 1978. "It's awfully important to understand the nature of the decision-making process, to know what is decided at what level and by whom."

Despite the American system of CHECKS AND BALANCES, some major government decisions are vested in the judgment of the elected president, especially in his constitutional role as commander-in-chief. In April 2006, George W. Bush, under fire from Iraq war critics as the pawn of Defense Secretary Donald Rumsfeld, fired back at a news conference with "I hear the voices, and I read the front page and I know the specu-

lation. I'm the decider, and I decide what is best." When phrased as "the BUCK STOPS HERE" by President Harry Truman, that was taken as the proper assumption of responsibility for great decisions; indeed, if Mr. Bush had said, "I'm the decision-maker," it would have raised fewer hackles, but when phrased as "I'm the decider" by Mr. Bush, using an unfamiliar and blunt word, it did not sit well with many senators, including Republican Arlen Specter of Pennsylvania: "I would suggest respectfully to the president that he is not the sole decider. The decider is a shared and joint responsibility."

See BITE THE BULLET; PROCESS, THE; TICK-TOCK.

decouple Separate, split up, unlink.

This verb became popular in the late 1970s as a strategic synonym for *disjoin*. In 1979, Fred Kaplan wrote in *The New York Times Magazine* about the suspicion that "America was 'decoupling' its own defense from that of NATO."

As Vice President, George H.W. Bush used the term to warn against division in alliance: "The Soviet Union, having already deployed sufficient missiles to intimidate Western Europe, is now trying to decouple our security from each other." Secretary of Defense Caspar W. Weinberger commented a year later, "There's not the slightest possibility that America would be decoupled from Europe by the pursuit of this vital initiative."

First used in 1602, the verb *decouple* (from the French verb *découpler*) became a railroad term for unhooking a train's cars. Scientists and economists picked up the word in the 1970s before its rise in popularity as military-diplomatic lingo.

deeds not words A platitudinous attack on platitudes; a clichéd demand for specific action instead of verbal or written assurances.

The phrase was a favorite of Dwight Eisenhower, who used it often in speeches. Returning from his promised trip to Korea after his 1952 election, he told reporters: "We face an enemy whom we cannot hope to impress by words, however eloquent, but only by deeds—executed under circumstances of our own choosing." Before the American Society of Newspaper Editors in 1953, he said: "We welcome every honest act of peace. We care nothing for mere rhetoric. We are only for sincerity of peaceful purpose attested by deeds." He returned to the theme again and again, as in a UN speech in 1953 after a Bermuda Conference: "These are not idle words or shallow visions.... These are deeds of peace."

The word *word*, especially when capitalized to indicate the word of God, gets a good press; the word *words*, however, takes a lot of abuse. The phrase can be found in Samuel Butler's *Hudibras*, a poem satirizing the Puritans, with these lines written before the execution of King Charles I in 1649: "we must give the world a proof / Of deeds, not words." Shakespeare's Richard III said, "Talkers are no good doers"; Hamlet, asked what he was reading, replied dismissively, "Words, words, words." British Prime Minister Neville Chamberlain used the word *words* in the same derisive sense in a rebuff to Franklin Roosevelt in 1938: "It is always best and safest to count on nothing from the Americans but words." In 1966, the British Conservative party slogan was "Action not words."

A long form of *deeds not words* was used by President Grover Cleveland: "It is not the mere slothful acceptance of righteous political ideas, but the call to action for their enforcement and application, that tests the endurance and moral courage of men." A common variation on the phrase is *in deed as well as word*, as used by a translator of Mao Zedong: "Whoever sides with the revolutionary people in deed as well as in word is a revolutionary in the full sense."

Word and deed have gone hand in hand throughout history. The Roman Catholic confession, traceable to 1075 in something like its present form, talks of sinning "in thought, word and deed." And Plautus, in *Pseudolus*, written about 190 B.C., said, "Let deeds match words." "Deeds are males, words females are," written by John Davies in 1610, was adopted in Italian by the first Baron Baltimore *(fatti maschii; parole femine)* and is the motto of the State of Maryland. With the rise of feminism in language, The State of Maryland motto was retranslated in 1993:

"Strong deeds, gentle words." That translation, however, renders a different Latin saying (in reverse order), which was Dwight Eisenhower's motto: *Suaviter in modo, fortiter in re.*

deep background See NOT FOR ATTRIBUTION.

deep freeze See INFLUENCE PEDDLER.

deep-six To dispose of, with emphasis; to destroy or deliberately lose.

In Watergate testimony on June 25, 1973, former White House counsel John Dean attributed the use of the phrase to John Ehrlichman: "He told me to shred the documents and 'deep-six' the briefcase. I asked him what he meant by 'deep-six.' He leaned back in his chair and said: 'You drive across the river on your way home at night, don't you? Well, when you cross over the bridge on your way home, just toss the briefcase into the river.'"

Before entering prison in 1976, John Ehrlichman disputed Dean's testimony in this interview with reporter Nick Thimmesch: "The specific acts by me were supposed to be the conversations with Dean where he said I told him to get Howard Hunt out of the country, and later to 'deep-six' the contents of Hunt's safe. A conversation with Herbert Kalmbach was the basis of another charge. Those conversations never took place."

Deep-six is naval slang. "As an ex-Navy type," Joseph Ross of the Congressional Research Service wrote in answer to the author's query, "I know that this is Navy talk, meaning 'to jettison.' It comes from the leadsman's (fellow who took the soundings) call for six fathoms (36 feet) of depth: 'by the deep six.'"

Lexicographer Peter Tamony supplied a 1927 citation in *A Glossary of Sea Terms*, by Gershom Bradford: "Deep six—overboard." Thus, to *deep-six* anything is to throw it overboard, literally or figuratively, with an eye toward making its recovery unlikely. When used as a noun, the phrase is not hyphenated; as a verb, it takes a hyphen, contrary to COVER-UP, which is hyphenated only as a noun.

defeatist Attack word against those urging sensible caution, or debatably unnecessary retreat, or craven surrender.

Defeatism may be a state of mind about a social program, or a specific position (so labeled by the opposition) on a particular policy. In his 1936 campaign, Franklin Roosevelt recalled "the many cruel years" of the "era of tooth and claw" when poverty was accepted by "the defeatist attitude."

Charles A. Lindbergh and the "America First" group, with their worries about the invincibility of Nazism in Europe in the late 1930s, were attacked as *defeatist*. Then, as in the '60s, the word was often used in conjunction with APPEASEMENT. In 2004, the term derogating those calling for a "new direction"—that is, out of Iraq—was used frequently by Vice President Dick Cheney. His characterization stung and was often met with a vilifying response. In April 2007, Senate Majority Leader Harry Reid, eager to withdraw U.S. troops from Iraq, spoke the four words that encapsulated defeatist judgment: "this war is lost."

See COPPERHEAD; NATTERING NABOBS OF NEGATIVISM; NERVOUS NELLIES; PROPHETS OF GLOOM AND DOOM; CUT AND RUN.

defining moment Significant action or event that illustrates character.

The phrase was coined by Howell Raines, then a reporter for *The New York Times*, in a 1983 article on John Glenn: "Confronted by Glenn and his 'constituency of the whole' candidacy, Walter Mondale has rallied the Democratic establishment. It is a defining moment."

Raines, later the hard-driving Executive Editor of the *Times* who led the paper's coverage of the 9/11 attacks to a record number of Pulitzer prizes (and was subsequently deposed after a newsroom revolt), provided the lexicographer with this definition of the term: " 'Defining moment' is that point at which the essential character of a candidate or campaign stands revealed to the individual or political organization and to the external world."

The phrase was used frequently during the 1988 campaign, usually applied to the character of an individual. By the time Secretary of State James A. Baker III appeared before the House Foreign Affairs Committee in 1990, however, the phrase was being used as a plural and applied to larger contexts. "The Iraqi invasion of Kuwait," Secretary Baker testified, "is one of the defining moments of a new era. ... If we are to build a stable and more comprehensive peace, we must respond to the defining moments of this new era."

During the 1990s, the widespread use of the phrase elevated the status of the participle *defining* to a widely used modifier, spawning such collocations as *defining event* (as in "the *defining event* of mid-twentieth-century America") and *defining achievement*. On January 29, 1991, President George H.W. Bush began his State of the Union message with these ringing words: "I come to this house of the people to speak to you and all Americans, certain that we stand at a defining hour."

defoliate To expose jungle supply lines with the use of chemical, incendiary, or even atomic weapons; one of the words used by Senator Goldwater in the 1964 presidential campaign that damaged him most.

Several times in the course of the presidential primaries of 1964, Barry Goldwater raised the possibility of "defoliating the jungle with low-yield atomic weapons" to interdict supplies to the Viet Cong from North Vietnam. When he repeated the point in a television interview, he tried to take some of the alarming edge off it by adding that he did not think it was a course the United States should follow. Democrats who were pressing the TRIGGER-HAPPY charge overlooked the senator's reservation in quoting his statement of the possibility of defoliation; Goldwater adherents cried foul play and QUOTING OUT OF CONTEXT. However, the senator's previous references to the possibility without the reservation gave the critics' charge credence.

At the Republican convention in San Francisco in 1964, civil rights demonstrators marched in front of the Cow Palace carrying signs that included "Defoliate Goldwater."

As the Vietnam war developed, napalm was used to defoliate areas suspected of covering trails or Viet Cong emplacements.

In early 1967 the *Saturday Evening Post* reported the "slogan of the Air Force's flying defoliators: 'Only you can prevent forests.'"

deliberate speed See WITH ALL DELIBERATE SPEED.

deliver To make good on a political promise, especially the promise to turn out a vote for a candidate.

"Heaven help the legislator who does not deliver," said Illinois Democratic Senator Paul Douglas, shortly after his defeat by Charles Percy in 1966. He was talking about the PORK BARREL and the need for a legislator to promise and get federal projects built in his state.

Early use of the word in a political sense was in an 1893 issue of *The Nation:* "No man is so fierce in his Americanism as … a boss who has 'delivered' the vote of his district as per contract." In that sense, *deliver the vote* was similar to *deliver the goods,* a phrase traceable to 1879. But a pejorative connotation was added when "the vote" did not mean all the votes in an area, but an individual vote or another man's influence. "The basis of the break," wrote the *Brooklyn Standard Union* in 1904, "is said to have been a charge that Shevlin 'delivered' Boss McLaughlin in some deal without the latter's knowledge."

Politicians treat the word with great respect because it touches on the essence of power. "There are no alibis in politics," said Kansas City boss Thomas Pendergast. "The delivery of votes is what counts.… All the ballyhoo and showmanship such as they have at the national conventions is all right. It's a great show. It gives folks a run for their money. It makes everybody feel good. But the man who makes the organization possible is the man who delivers the votes, and he doesn't deliver them by oratory. Politics is a business, just like anything else."

In its broader sense—to keep a political pledge—the word was used in the 1948 presidential campaign. Republican Thomas E. Dewey said, "The 80th Congress delivered as no other Congress ever did for the future of our country." President Harry Truman quoted that line to his "whistle-stop" (see WHISTLESTOPPING) audiences, and punched: "I'll say it delivered. It delivered for the private power lobby. It delivered for the big oil company lobby. It delivered for the railroad lobby. It delivered for the real estate lobby. That's what the Republican candidate calls 'delivering for the future.' Is that the kind of future you want?"

Senate Majority Leader Lyndon Johnson in 1958 used the word (in its deliver-the-vote sense) in international relations. After Johnson's statement on outer space to the U.N. Political Committee, India's acerbic V. K. Krishna Menon commented, "I wish that your country would give as much time to disarming as you give to preparations for arming." Johnson shot back, "Well now, Mr. Ambassador, we're ready. We'll disarm tomorrow. Can you deliver the disarmament of the Communist bloc?"

Deliver is the put-up-or-shut-up word of politics. It calls the bluffs of political leaders and calls to account big-promising candidates. Reporter John Gunther, covering the unpredictable state of Ohio in his 1947 *Inside USA*, wrote: "… nobody is ever sure of Ohio. Once the manager of a presidential candidate, arriving in Columbus, asked the local boss if he could 'deliver' Ohio. The legend is that the local boss took a deep protesting breath, curled up his toes, and on the spot died of heart failure." See EARMARK.

demagogue One who appeals to the brain's amygdala, thought to be the seat of emotions like fear, hatred, and greed; a spellbinding orator, careless with facts and a danger to rational decision.

This is one of the enduring, slashing attack words of politics, in use since the American republic began. John Adams in 1808: "It is to no purpose to declaim against 'demagogues.' … Milo was as much an agitator for the patricians as Clodius for the plebeians; and Hamilton was as much a demagogue as Burr."

Being denounced as a *demagogue* is a sure sign to a speaker that he is making powerful points with some part of the public. In different historical periods, those most often denounced were General Ben Butler, perennial candidate William Jennings Bryan, Governor Huey Long, and Senator Joseph McCarthy. Reverend Thomas Dixon's attack on Bryan was typical: "a slobbering, mouthing demagogue, whose patriotism is in his jawbone."

Theodore Roosevelt and William Howard Taft, after their falling-out, exchanged charges of "fathead" and "demagogue." Roosevelt observed in a letter to Henry Cabot Lodge: "When there is a great unrest, partly reasoning and partly utterly unreasoning and unreasonable, it becomes extremely difficult to beat a loudmouthed demagogue, especially if he is a demagogue of great wealth."

The appeal to emotion is not the only hallmark of the demagogue; an appeal to class is often included. When Democrat Al Smith broke with FDR, he made this point in words reminiscent of the earlier Roosevelt-Taft break: "I will take off my coat and fight to the end against any candidate who persists in any demagogic appeal to the masses of the working people of this country to destroy themselves by setting class against class and rich against poor!" See CLASS WARFARE.

The word has had its defenders. It is from the Greek *demagogos* (leader of the people), which referred to the popular leaders who appeared in Athens during its period of decay. English journalist George Steevens, writing about the U.S. in 1897, held that "in a free country every politician must be something of a demagogue. Disraeli and Gladstone were both finished demagogues, and until we have two more great demagogues in England, politics will continue to be as dishwater." Muckraker Lincoln Steffens wrote in his autobiography: "I had begun to suspect that, whenever a man in public life was called a demagogue, there was something good in him, something dangerous to the system."

The popular conception of the word, however, was given most eloquently by a President not known for his eloquence, Calvin Coolidge: "… the final approval of the people is given not to demagogues, slavishly pandering to their selfishness,

merchandising with the clamor of the hour, but to statesmen, ministering to their welfare, representing their deep, silent, abiding convictions."

Demagogue retains its original sting. Relations between Presidents Truman and Eisenhower permanently cooled when Truman referred to Eisenhower's "I shall go to Korea" statement as "a piece of demagoguery."

The final *g* in the adjective *demagogic* is soft; the more difficult to pronounce and spell *demagoguery*, with its final *g* hard, is more commonly used in the U.S. than *demagogy*, final *g* soft, which is British usage.

demand-pull See INFLATION.

démarche See DÉTENTE.

Democrat A member of a political party favoring greater government action than its conservative opposition does, to direct and promote the welfare of the people in the republic it often governs.

When comparing *Democrat*, a noun, with *Republican*, a word that functions both as a noun (a member of a party) and an adjective (construed as the description of that party or as a form of government), this problem arises: The word *Democrat* is like *apple* (the fruit, a noun) and the word *Republican* is like *orange* (both the fruit, a noun, and the color, an adjective). That is at the heart of the *ic* controversy, about which more in a moment.

Under President Andrew Jackson, the Democratic party, founded in 1828, began using its present name, but the noun *democrat* was current long before that. "Washington," wrote President John Adams in criticism of his predecessor toward the end of the eighteenth century, "appointed a multitude of democrats and jacobins of the deepest dye. I have been more cautious in this respect." Others shared Adams's low esteem. A popular poem in the early days of the Republic was Fessenden's "Democracy Unveiled":

And I'll unmask the democrat,
Your sometimes this thing, sometimes that,
Whose life is one dishonest shuffle,
Lest he perchance the mob should ruffle.

The Federalists sneered at Thomas Jefferson's Republicans as *democrats*, at the time a noun with a meaning to many of "panderers to the mob"; those so called in turn scorned the Federalists as *aristocrats*. Still, by 1856 the Middletown, N.Y., *Banner of Liberty* could capitalize the noun and write that "the name Democrat has become so honorable that all sorts of isms and new-fangled parties claim the name."

Probably the best-known modern quote involving the word was that of the humorist Will Rogers: "I belong to no organized party. I am a Democrat."

In 1955 Leonard Hall, a former Republican National Chairman, began referring to the "Democrat" rather than the "Democratic" party, a habit begun by Thomas E. Dewey. Hall dropped the "ic," he said, because "I think their claims that they represent the great mass of the people, and we don't, is just a lot of bunk." Atcheson Hench wrote of this usage in *American Speech* magazine: "Whether they have meant to imply that the party was no longer democratic, or whether they banked on the harsher sound pattern of the new name; whether they wanted to strengthen the impression that they were speaking for a new Republican party by using a new name for the opposition, or whether they had other reasons, the fact remains that…highly influential speakers…used the shorter adjective."

The "harsher sound pattern," I think, refers to the *crat* ending, which usually has a pejorative connotation, as in *bureaucrat, autocrat, aristocrat*. The *ic* ending takes the sting out of it. More likely, Hall gave the simpler and (according to Occam's razor) the better explanation: why let the opposition get away with taking a beloved adjective, *democratic*, and use it as a noun, endowing their party with the name of the foundation of our political philosophy?

Some Democrats suggested retaliating by shortening REPUBLICAN to Publican, but the National Committee overruled them, explaining that *Republican* "is the name by which our opponents' product is known and mistrusted." However, the habit of some Republicans in removing the *ic* persisted, most notably in the 1996 campaign for president by Senator Bob Dole, a former Republican National Chairman. (Another reason it persisted was that it annoyed Democrats, and GOP partisans delighted in their opponents' public irritation.)

When a reader of *The Washington Post* wrote in 2006 in grammatical defense of President George W. Bush's habit of dropping the *ic*, another reader, Scott Rogers of Alexandria, Virginia, riposted, turning the reasoning above on its head: "The word 'democrat' is a noun; the word 'democratic' is an adjective…Using a noun in place of an adjective is wrong." But Bush persisted; in his 2007 State of the Union address, which was supposed to reach out to Democrats for a bipartisan approach to his final two years in office, he referred to members of "the Democrat party." A few weeks later, speaking to an audience of Democrats, he explained, "Look, my diction isn't all that good. I have been accused of occasionally mangling the English language, so appreciate you inviting the head of the Republic Party."

Republican Theodore Roosevelt, campaigning in the Deep South, supposedly told the classic why-I'm-a-Democrat story. When asked why he was a Democrat, a Southerner replied, "Because my father was a Democrat and my grandfather was a Democrat." A Northerner countered, "What if your father was a horse thief and your grandfather was a horse thief, what would you have been then?" The Southerner's reply: "In that case, I guess I'd have been a Republican."

demonstration See MARCH ON WASHINGTON.

deniability See SIGN OFF ON.

Depression party Recurrent Democratic attack against the Republican party since the 1932 campaign; considered demagogic now, often compared to the Republican charge that Democrats are the WAR PARTY.

After Herbert Hoover had been defeated largely by the *Depression party* charge, some Republicans in 1933 sought to attach the Depression label on the Democrats. The feeble effort was devastated by FDR:

... although I rubbed my eyes when I read it, we have been told that it was not a Republican depression but a Democratic depression.... Now, there is an old and somewhat lugubrious adage that says: "Never speak of rope in the house of a man who has been hanged." In the same way, if I were a Republican leader speaking to a mixed audience, the last word in the whole dictionary that I think I would use is that word "depression."

Harry Truman took up the *Depression party* charge in his GIVE 'EM HELL campaign of 1948, especially relating it to the DO-NOTHING CONGRESS: "The Republican party has shown in the Congress of the last two years that the leopard does not change its spots. It is still the party of the Harding-Coolidge boom and Hoover depression."

Republican Dwight Eisenhower deplored what he felt was an outmoded and unfair attack on his party. In his memoirs he wrote: "For more than twenty years economic depression had been the skeleton in the Republican closet, locked in by demagogues. In many minds [in 1954] the suspicion lurked that this problem might once again prove to be the party's undoing."

See RUNNING AGAINST WASHINGTON.

depth polling Motivation research; pollsters' questions that go beyond voting intention.

Voters' current attitudes and opinions, studied alongside their previous voting behavior and social and ethnic background, help behavioral scientists predict the way they are likely to vote and—more important—what political appeals may get them to vote another way. *Depth polling* has been adopted as the operative phrase by some political communications experts because *motivation research* has acquired such a bad image. The latter phrase, used by Dr. Ernest Dichter and others, excoriated by author Vance Packard in *The Hidden Persuaders*, led to criticism like this by Professor (later Senator) S. I. Hayakawa, a leading linguist: "Motivation researchers are those harlot social scientists who, in impressive psycho-analytic and/or sociological jargon, tell their clients what their clients want to hear, namely, that appeals to human irrationality are likely to be far more profitable than appeals to rationality."

Polling pioneer Dr. Elmo Roper answered the author's query: "The phrase which is usually used is 'polling in depth' and what that means is nothing more than a check to learn the difference in attitude by various sub-groups in the population and even more particularly, *why* they hold whatever attitude they do hold. As a matter of fact, the first term applied generally to this type of probe was 'depth interview.' Apparently the newspapers insist on the word 'poll,' and 'depth interview' became 'polling in depth.'"

Dr. George Gallup responded as well, also resisting *depth polling*, the phrase used by laymen: "Usually the expression is 'interviewing in depth'—or this may be shortened to 'depth interviewing.' This term goes back to 1935. Dr. Paul Lazarsfeld introduced this concept into American research. It typically refers to the long cross-examination of a person with many questions to get at his thinking on a given issue. Today many persons use the term 'depth interviewing' when they have asked more than a few questions on the same subject."

Three levels of polling are currently used, occasionally by the same pollsters: STRAW POLLS or nose counts; *issues polls*, indicating voter feelings about specific topics being debated; and *depth polls*. When a poll's forecast is accurate, it is not news; when it is mistaken or otherwise fails to take into account last-minute changes in voters' minds, the words of Jesus to the Pharisees (Matthew 16:3) are recalled: "O ye hypocrites, ye can discern the face of the sky; but can ye not discern the signs of the times?" See POLLSTER.

deserving Democrats Party workers who believe themselves to be worthy of patronage reward.

Three-time candidate William Jennings Bryan, when he became Woodrow Wilson's Secretary of State, tried to take care of a few old friends. He wrote to the receiver-general of the Dominican Republic, Walter W. Vick, on August 20, 1913, asking if he could find some places in the customs administration of that country. Bryan's letter contained the phrase in the following question: "Can you let me know what positions you have at your disposal with which to reward deserving Democrats?"

The letter was indiscreet; Republicans denounced it as an attempted extension of the SPOILS SYSTEM into the administration of a foreign country under U.S. domination.

Democrat Felix Frankfurter explained in 1924 why he was bolting to vote for a third party: "The Republican party is frankly standpat—things are all right. To the Democrats, also, things are all right, only those who administer them are not. What the country needs is 'honest' Democrats and, doubtless, William J. Bryan would add, 'deserving Democrats.'" George Bernard Shaw, in his play *Pygmalion*, remembered in the U.S. in its musical form, *My Fair Lady*, came up with a character who pointed out that a group being overlooked by government was "the undeserving poor."

Deserving Democrats long ago lost its sting and is now used affectionately; Republicans appeal to *discerning Democrats* for crossover support.

destabilize Euphemism for "overthrow."

Director of Central Intelligence William Colby disclosed to a congressional committee in April 1974 that the CIA had spent $8 million in Chile between 1970 and 1973 in an effort to make it difficult for Marxist Salvatore Allende Gossens to govern.

"The goal of the clandestine CIA activities," wrote Seymour Hersh in *The New York Times* in September 1974, "…was to 'destabilize' the Marxist government …"

Because the word was a freshly coined euphemism, and appeared to conflict with the testimony of Secretary of State Kissinger that "the CIA had nothing to do with the coup," the term was used with force and glee by critics of covert U.S. activities. Curiously, when the word was used early in the Carter Administration, it was in its positive sense, without the *de:* U.S. Ambassador to the UN Andrew Young (see POINT MAN) discussed Cuban intervention in Africa as possibly proving to be a "stabilizing force." As Cuban troop strength grew in Africa in

1978, critics of the Carter foreign policy used *stabilizing force* against the Carter officials, much as critics of Mr. Kissinger had used *destabilization* against him.

See CIA-ESE.

details. See DEVIL IS IN THE DETAILS.

détente A relaxation of tense relations between nations, warmer than *accommodation*, cooler than *rapprochement*.

Woven through the history of the post–World War II period was the French word *détente* or such rough equivalents as *thaw*, ACCOMMODATION, *normalization of relations*, or *opening to the East*. When President Eisenhower met the Soviet Union's dual leaders, Nikolai Bulganin and Nikita Khrushchev, at Geneva in July 1955, he told them, "We have come to find a basis for accommodation which will make life safer and happier not only for the nations we represent but for the people elsewhere."

The seeming thaw in the Cold War begun at Geneva later froze over; during the Cuban missile crisis of 1962, President Kennedy wrote Khrushchev: "If your letter signifies that you are prepared to discuss a détente affecting NATO and the Warsaw Pact, we are quite prepared to consider with our allies any useful proposals." In his book *Kennedy*, Ted Sorensen described the subsequent search for areas of agreement as "the emerging détente," adding: "The breathing spell had become a pause, the pause was becoming a détente and no one could foresee what further changes lay ahead."

Ahead lay the escalation of the war in Vietnam; not until 1971, with the progress of arms-limitation talks and the announcement of a visit to mainland China, did détente become an active possibility. The heyday of *détente*, in policy and in the word's usage, was in 1972 and 1973, as U.S. and Soviet leaders held summit conferences and launched arms-control agreements. After the Nixon resignation, President Ford found both policy and word becoming a burden, as hard-liners previously kept at bay by Nixon attacked détente as a SELLOUT, a GIVEAWAY (a charge to return during the Reagan administration in the debate over return of the Panama Canal), and a *one-way street*. Henry Kissinger's policy was described as "like going to a wife-swapping party and coming home alone."

The Soviet leaders resented the attack on the word, rightly interpreting it as an attack on the Brezhnev policies. As 1976 began, *Pravda* denounced those in the U.S. who were critical of "one-way advantages" won by the Soviets. "Some people with weak nerves," said the Soviet official organ, "losing self-control, are even speaking in extremes. The pseudo-oracle William Safire, who spread himself across the pages of *The New York Times* on New Year's Eve, croaked: 'Détente is dead. The second cold war has begun.'"

President Carter in 1977 tried to take some of the onus off the now-controversial word by defining it in a Notre Dame speech as "progress toward peace." In a *Foreign Affairs* piece (December 1977) gutsily titled "Russia, America and Détente," the former Ford State Department counselor Helmut Sonnenfeldt wrote: "Some of our debates about Soviet policy have tended to turn more on the definition of the labels that have been attached to it than on substance. 'CONTAINMENT,' 'COLD WAR,' 'an era of negotiation,' 'détente'... all caught elements of the complex realities... but over time they came to obscure rather than illuminate them." In the late 1980s, *détente* was lightly referred to around Washington as *the D-word* (see -WORD).

The word had its tongue-in-cheek defenders. David Braaten of *The Washington Star* wrote in 1973: "In the world of clichés, it is always comforting to have a reliable, steady favorite like détente." Pointing to its use in Bizet's eighteenth-century translation of Herodotus about a period preceding the Spartan sack of Athens, and to its resuscitation by the *New York Sun* editorialist Mortimer Lovelace rhapsodizing in the 1920s about the Locarno Pact, Braaten added: "It meets all the requirements: it is French, and therefore impossible for Americans to pronounce with any degree of certainty; it is short enough to fit in a one-column

headline, should that unfortunate necessity arise, yet full-bodied enough to add solidity and a sense of importance to a four-column head-cum-kicker; its meaning is only hazily grasped by its users, and, perhaps most important of all, it means nothing whatever to the reader."

Strangely, a cousin of *détente* is rarely used, except among diplomats: *démarche* means "step forward," or improvement of relations, and cliché-markers hope that its day will come.

deterrent A military force or weapons system whose strength, real or feigned, is capable of forestalling an enemy attack by the threat of devastating retaliation.

"The major deterrent is in a man's mind," wrote Admiral Arleigh Burke in 1960. "The major deterrent in the future is going to be not only what we have, but what we do, what we are willing to do, what they think we will do. Stamina, guts, standing up for the things that we say—those are deterrents."

The concept of preparedness as a deterrent is an old one. In his first annual address to both houses of Congress, George Washington said in 1790: "To be prepared for war is one of the most effectual means of preserving peace." James Monroe, a follower of Thomas Jefferson, argued otherwise. "Preparation for war," he said in 1818, "is a constant stimulus to suspicion and illwill." But many later agreed with Washington. "Speak softly and carry a big stick," Theodore Roosevelt said in 1901. "You will go far." (TR identified this as a West African proverb.)

In 1940, FDR defended the draft by stressing its deterrent effect: "Your boys are not going to be sent into any foreign wars. They are going into training to form a force so strong that, by its very existence, it will keep the threat of war far away from our shores." See AGAIN AND AGAIN AND AGAIN.

Nuclear weapons were believed by many to be the most powerful deterrent of all against a major war. Though they did not prevent minor wars, they kept them from "escalating" into major conflicts. "What has really happened," Walter Lippmann wrote of the Korean truce in 1953, "is that both sides and all concerned have been held within a condition of mutual deterrent."

Israeli Foreign Minister Abba Eban gave a new wrinkle to the definition in 1966 after his country attacked a Jordanian town in an effort to halt Arab terrorism. He called it "demonstrative deterrence"; a year later the Israelis preferred "pre-emptive strike." This was, however, short of PREVENTIVE WAR—an idea put forward as a means of preventing China from growing too menacing. See MASSIVE RETALIATION; DOOMSDAY MACHINE.

deviationism See REVISIONISM.

Devil is in the details The nitpickers' creed, holding that the smallest particulars may prove the most troubling, requiring close attendance to the most minute details.

A key comment about all arms negotiations, this phrase also appeared as early as 1978 in economic reporting, when Hobart Rowen of *The Washington Post* was told in Bremen, "There is an old German saying that the Devil is in the details."

By 1987, the saying was being used by Max M. Kampelman, the United States arms negotiator; he acknowledged to Reuters that agreement with the Soviets was being reached on intrusive verification, but he added, "You know the Devil is in the details." The expression was picked up that year by *Newsweek* as "the old arms-negotiation maxim, 'The Devil is in the details.'"

Written often with a small *d*, the *Devil* in this case should be capitalized to signify the figure of Satan, not some minor vexation. The Devil, however, may not have been part of this quotation's source: A variant form of this saying is *God is in the details*. That version was used by the German Bauhaus architect Ludwig Mies van der Rohe, by art historian Aby Wauburg in 1925, and is sometimes attributed to the nineteenth-century French novelist Gustave Flaubert, but no specific citation for Flaubert's use has been found.

devolution Transfer of power from a central government to a region or locality; sometimes used as a euphemism for secession or separation.

Devolution is associated with "power sharing," a movement that grew popular in the '60s and '70s as charges of "distant bureaucracy" were often leveled at centralized authority and TAX SHARING came into vogue.

Frequent use of the word began in connection with HOME RULE in Ireland, and extended to the calls for "more local say" to outright independence, from Scotland to Quebec. Most early citations in the '70s are from the *Times Literary Supplement*.

In Canada, separatists in Quebec—who wanted to withdraw from English-speaking Canada and to set up their own French-speaking state—used *devolution* as a less revolutionary-sounding word than *secession*.

In 1975 *The Wall Street Journal* described British Prime Minister Harold Wilson's moves to meet Scottish demands: "The government policy is called 'devolution'—the decentralizing of many government powers and functions." In 1976 columnist C. L. Sulzberger of *The New York Times* wrote: "Arguments over 'devolution' versus local 'nationalism' rage in non-English sections of the United Kingdom including Scotland, Wales and Northern Ireland. It is not merely a matter of reviving relatively little-used languages like Gaelic and Welsh but of actually shifting major authority including title to mineral wealth into regional hands." A generation later, in 2007, Peter Hain of the pro-British party in Northern Ireland adopted the mantra "it's devolution or dissolution"; the words were headlined in the *Belfast Telegraph*.

Because the word seems closer to "evolution" than "revolution," it is useful to those who want to maintain a moderate-sounding position before threatening or declaring "independence."

Dewey blitz The second-ballot pressure by the Dewey forces that enabled them to wrest the nomination from Senator Robert Taft in the 1948 Republican convention.

Three Republican candidates led the field in 1948: Dewey, Taft, and Harold Stassen. 548 convention votes meant nomination. On the first ballot, Dewey received

434, Taft 224, and Stassen 157. The favorite-son delegations of Senator Arthur Vandenberg (Michigan) and Governor Earl Warren (California) were considered least likely to change on the second ballot; the favorite-son delegations of Illinois and Tennessee were likely to switch to Taft. That meant Dewey had to pick up other favorite-son delegations, plus strength from Stassen, to hold his momentum.

Led by New York attorney Herbert Brownell, the Dewey organization "leaned on" (see FEET TO THE FIRE) the Stassen voters; important defections were achieved from the Iowa, Maryland, Nebraska, and South Dakota delegations. Though Stassen picked up scattered votes elsewhere, his second-ballot total dropped to 149; Dewey's increased to 515, and Taft's to 274. Thus, the Dewey second-ballot increase was 81 to Taft's 50—and the STAMPEDE was on.

If liberal columnist Max Lerner did not coin the phrase *Dewey blitz*, he was at least an early user. Lerner wrote that Dewey won the nomination "not because he had principles or even appeal, but because he had a machine. The machine was ruthless and well oiled, run by a group of slick and modern operators. It combined the age-old methods of power politics with the newest strategies of blitz warfare and the precision tools of American industry and administration."

The word *Blitz* (German for "lightning") was still relatively new in its military context and referred to fast-moving mechanized warfare carried out by Nazi armored divisions in early World War II. In 1941 the Birmingham (U.K.) *Sunday Mercury* asked: "If the last war's *strafe* is this war's *blitz*, what will it become in the war after next?" See QUAGMIRE.

In its English form—*lightning*—the word enjoyed a brief political vogue in the 1880s. Alabama Democrats adopted a "lightning creed" in 1880, to turn out the Reconstruction Republicans and blacks. "No man can be appointed (in Alabama)," Illinois Representative J. H. Rowell told the House in 1890, "to hold a precinct election unless he is known to be a 'lightning man,' a ballot-box stuffer, a false counter."

The *Dewey blitz* brought the word into U.S. politics; the phrase is still used by elderly politicians to refer to excellent convention organization, and *blitz* has been adopted to describe saturation television campaigns. A *TV blitz* in politics is a concentration of advertising in the last week of the campaign, aimed at the "undecided" and at turning out the vote of the committed. Since 1952, when admen Al Hollender and Rosser Reeves created the Eisenhower "spot" campaign, half-hour speeches have given way to spots of one-minute, twenty-second, or ten-second duration, selling hard to huge audiences. But like all MADISON AVENUE TECHNIQUES, they are troubling. "These new techniques," wrote James Perry in the *National Observer*, "are so overwhelming, so terribly effective. Some day, maybe they will elect a truly dangerous and sinister man to high office." See SELLING CANDIDATES LIKE SOAP.

As political use of the Internet increases in fundraising, persuasion-by-website turn-out campaigns, *e-mail blitzes* have emerged, and the alliterative *blog blitz* cannot be far behind.

dialogue Genuine two-way communication, or the pretense thereof; often a civil, unheated argument.

The phrase *national dialogue* was popularized by Adlai Stevenson in his 1952 campaign as part of his theme, "let's talk sense to the American people." The word appealed to John F. Kennedy, who used it often, as in a 1962 Yale speech: "the dialogue between the parties—between business and government—is clogged by illusion and platitude ..."

In current political usage, the word has an intellectual, slightly wistful connotation. A dialogue is more pointed than a *discussion* or *conversation*, less pointed than an *exchange*; less heated than an *argument*, less formal than a *debate*. It is used to describe the establishment of wary communication between divergent groups; when modified by *meaningful*, the word becomes meaningless. It is hard for a careful speaker to have a dialogue with someone who uses the word as a verb. See ISSUES, THE.

diaper in the ring See HAT IN THE RING.

diehards Dwindling handful committed to a losing cause, fighting long after hope of victory is gone.

In 1911 British Prime Minister Herbert Henry Asquith was determined to reduce the veto power of the House of Lords over the House of Commons. He extracted a trump card from the previous King, Edward VII, and held George V to it as well: if the House of Lords would not go along with a reduction of power, the King would appoint as many new peers to that House as necessary to get the deciding vote. A substantial group in the House of Lords, led by Lord Halsbury, refused to go along; they said they would "die in the last ditch," and became known as the *Diehards*. But other peers were not prepared to die hard; they accepted a two-year veto compromise and deserted the Diehards. The King recorded in his diary: "The Halsburyites were, Thank God, beaten. It is indeed a great relief to me—I am spared any further humiliation by a creation of peers."

The British political use of *diehard* was taken from the nickname of the Middlesex Regiment, the 57th Foot; at the Battle of Albuera in 1811, Colonel William Inglis was badly wounded and refused to be taken to the rear, crying, "Die hard, men, die hard!" The phrase was reinforced in America because George Washington's last words were reported to be "It is well. I die hard, but am not afraid to go."

After the fall of Baghdad in the second Iraq war, Defense Secretary Donald Rumsfeld characterized the remaining resistance by insurgents and terrorists as "dead-enders" and "diehards"; as the war wore on and he remained resolute, war opponents applied *diehard* to him and other high administration officials.

dime's worth of difference A minor-party sneer at the similarity between the two major parties.

The phrase was central to the 1968 independent presidential campaign of Alabama Governor George Corley Wallace, who stressed the need to SEND THEM A MESSAGE: "them," in Governor Wallace's eyes, were the "pointed-headed professors" in Washington who dominated the planning of both the Democratic and the Republican parties. He ran third to Richard Nixon and Hubert Humphrey, but the Southern politician who said after an early local defeat by a segregationist "I'll never be out-segged again" won 13% of the national popular vote.

Governor Wallace informed the author in 1976:

I do not recall the exact date that we first used the phrases "dime's worth of difference" and "pointed-headed." Both of these, I am sure, were used initially in 1967 as we were preparing for the third party campaign and gaining ballot positions. To the best of my knowledge, both of these expressions were original with me and something that I just thought of and put into an extemporaneous speech. The expressions were received well by the crowds and I continued to use them.

Campaigning for the Democratic nomination for president in early 1972, Wallace was shot in the spine by a would-be assassin and was too crippled to continue. By late July, however, he was thinking of running as an independent again, which would have attracted voters who preferred President Nixon over the Democratic nominee, Senator George McGovern. Nixon remembered how the 1968 Wallace vote—sending the *not a dime's worth of difference* message about the two major parties—almost cost him the close 1968 victory over Hubert Humphrey. Nixon sent John Connally of Texas to see Wallace and followed up with a personal telephone call on July 26, 1972; Wallace asked Nixon for an assurance that his "message on issues would be heard." Nixon told him that Connally, his closest political adviser, would be available to listen at all times, and that White House Chief of Staff Alexander Haig would give him regular foreign-policy briefings. Wallace agreed not to run, which contributed to the size of the 1972 Nixon landslide.

See ME, TOO; TWEEDLEDUM AND TWEEDLEDEE.

dinosaur wing An attack phrase aimed at "paleoconservatives"—those considered by liberals to be on the extreme right wing.

A parenthetical remark by Adlai Stevenson in a speech at the Mormon Tabernacle, Salt Lake City, Utah, on October 14, 1952, either coined or popularized the phrase: "Yet the same Republicans (the dinosaurwing of that party) who object to service from our Government—who call everything 'CREEPING SOCIALISM,'who talk darkly of 'dictatorship'—these same men begin to hint that we are 'subversive,' or at best the tools of our country's enemies, when we boast of the great strides toward social justice and security we have already made …"

Stevenson may have seen the phrase used in *The New York Times* the day before, quoting a Democrat complaining about the GOP attacks on corruption and cronyism in the Truman Administration: "Anybody who gets indignant is a hypocritical old dinosaur."

A similar metaphor was used in the mid-nineteenth century to describe former Whigs, "the fossil remains of an extinct party."

The predecessor phrase was *Neanderthal wing*. And columnists Evans and Novak liked *Stone Age Republican*. The Truman Library has an unsigned memorandum dated June 29, 1948, probably written by Judge Samuel Rosenman, FDR's speechwriting counselor, urging Truman to call back Congress after the Democratic convention because "it would keep a steady glare of publicity on the Neanderthal men of the Republican party" (the advice was followed: see "Turnip Day" under DO-NOTHING CONGRESS).

In a 1964 story on Chicago Mayor Richard J. Daley, the *Saturday Evening Post* in 1964 gave the word a bipartisan connotation: "The last dinosaur wins again."

The dinosaur made another foray out of extinction in American business lingo when George Romney, then president of American Motors, launched a compact-car campaign attacking the "gas-guzzling dinosaurs" of the road. When Romney entered politics, it was just a question of time before he adapted his best-known phrase, and the time came in the spring of 1967 when he told a political audience "the Great Society has become a tax-guzzling dinosaur."

The word *dinosaur* was coined by Sir Richard Owen in 1841 from the Greek *dei-nos* (fearsome) and *sauros* (lizard) before it was discovered that the beast, no carnivore, would have registered as a vegetarian.

See RADICAL RIGHT; BIRCHER; LITTLE OLD LADIES IN TENNIS SHOES; KOOKS, NUTS AND; TROGLODYTIC. In the other direction, see PINKO; FELLOW TRAVELER; FLAMING LIBERAL.

diplomacy When used as the second element in a phrase, originally a disparagement of the handling of negotiations between nations; now a combining form to characterize the type or level of relations.

This noun, first cited in 1796, comes from the Greek *diploma*, meaning "folded paper," a letter or passport folded so that its contents remain secret. Within the last century, however, the term has become the basis of noun phrases, usually derogatory, that reflect various approaches to international relations.

DOLLAR DIPLOMACY first appeared in *Harper's Weekly* in 1910; during the Taft Administration, Secretary of State Philander C. Knox was criticized for throwing money at politicians in Honduras. By 1912, though, William Howard Taft spoke in favor of "substituting dollars for bullets" in a talk that became known as his "Dollar Diplomacy" speech.

GUNBOAT DIPLOMACY was first used in 1927. This phrase referred to the use of military force for Western domination of China in the early twentieth century, when American and British interests were protected by the threatened force of gunboats.

Media diplomacy, which can denote the use of satellite telecasts for diplomatic meetings of opposing nations, is more often used to cast aspersion on the attempts of diplomats to use television interviews to conduct foreign relations.

Ping-Pong diplomacy named the first efforts of the Nixon administration to open relations between China and the U.S. In 1971, at the World Table Tennis Championships in Japan, the People's Republic of China's team invited the U.S. team to visit China. On April 12, 1971, the Americans became the first officially approved American group to enter mainland China since 1949, after Mao Zedong's forces overthrew the Nationalist government. Thus *Ping-Pong*, a trademark for table tennis, was used to pave the way for Sino-American diplomatic moves. On a visit to China in 2006, Senator Norm Coleman (R-Minn.) arranged to play with Zhang Xielin, a former world champion who the Senator pointed out was "a member of the 1971 ping pong diplomacy team."

Public diplomacy appeared by early 1976 in the Republican Party's platform. Richard Allen, the foreign-policy analyst, used the term in the platform's section on national security: "A strong and effective program of global public diplomacy is a vital component of U.S. foreign policy." During the Reagan Administration, Ambassador Gilbert A. Robinson, deputy director of the United States Information Agency, said, "A television special on a given policy can often have more impact on a foreign government's actions than a host of traditional diplomatic exchanges."

Quiet diplomacy was Henry Kissinger's preference. (See STEP-BY-STEP DIPLOMACY.) This phrase, with its suggestion of furious diplomatic activity behind the scenes, was also used on occasion by President Reagan.

Shuttle diplomacy appeared in 1973. *Time* magazine reported a year later that Henry A. Kissinger traveled to the Middle East "for another round of 'shuttle diplomacy.'" Airlines were using the word *shuttle* to describe regular short flights back and forth between cities, and in the news at the time was the National Aeronautics and Space Administration's "space shuttle."

See *diplolingo* in PENTAGONESE.

dirty politics Unethical practices in campaigning: ballot-box stuffing, MUDSLINGING, CHARACTER ASSASSINATION, and other chicanery.

Franklin D. Roosevelt Jr.'s characterization of Hubert Humphrey as a *draft-dodger* in the 1960 West Virginia primary (while FDR's son was campaigning for John F. Kennedy) was described by the *Washington Star* as "a new low in dirty politics." Bruce Felknor, executive director of the Fair Campaign Practices Committee, in 1966 compiled a volume of low tricks, smears, and unethical attacks entitled *Dirty Politics*.

American slang includes *dirty pool, dirty wash, dirty linen, dirty work,* and *dirty word*. With a small addition of water, dirt becomes *mud*, leading to MUDSLINGING.

Oddly, there is no antonym for *dirty politics*: *clean politics* is not a phrase in use. PRACTICAL POLITICS carries a connotation of cynicism, *power politics* and *smart politics* slightly more, and *dirty politics* the most. Each phrase is purely subjective.

Often a campaign manager will wire a protest about his opposition's radio or TV spots to the station manager just before an election, with a copy to the Federal Communications Commission and various fair campaign practices committees. Unless the spots contain the candidate's own voice, the station will ordinarily take them off the air for at least several hours until a decision is made or the spots modified. The spots might have been accurate or innocuous, but the protest knocks them off for a while. To the party pulling the trick, it is smart politics; to the party on the receiving end, it is *dirty politics*. "Late hits" on the Internet, whether newsworthy revelations or low smears, are so far uncontrolled.

dirty tricks As "Department of Dirty Tricks," the nickname of the covert operations of the Central Intelligence Agency; since the Watergate scandals, a disapproving term for campaign smears and disruptive activities of a "black advance."

In the 1960s, applied to the CIA, the phrase had a ring of derring-do, since it was felt that democracies had to fight cold-war fire with fire of their own: a *Time* magazine cover story on Richard Helms (February 24, 1967) described a post he had once held as "deputy chief of the plans division, the so-called 'dirty tricks' department." Soon after criticism mounted of our support of South Vietnam, columnist Walter Lippmann began to wonder about those activities: "The question before us today is whether the activities of the CIA which are outside genuine intelligence, that is to say its black propaganda, its interventionist operations, its 'dirty tricks,' are truly in the national interest."

The phrase *dirty trick* can be traced back to 1674, but was rarely used politically, and if so, as a lighthearted description of serious, sometimes nefarious, acts. In 1972 it was used in a general sense by Margaret Truman in a biography of her father: "Along with the smears and lies Dad was continually rebutting, the Republicans threw in a few dirty tricks aimed specifically at our campaign train. A 'TRUTH SQUAD' followed us around the country, issuing statements that supposedly countered Dad's speeches. In Buffalo they hired a horde of school children who tried to drown out Dad with screams and catcalls, anticipating by twenty years the Students for a Democratic Society."

In 1973, however, the phrase in the CIA sense was applied to politics in the Watergate scandals. "Money from the safe, it is alleged," observed the *National Observer* on March 10, "was used to finance Republican 'dirty tricks' during the campaign." *The New York Times* on April 29: "Last week, it was disclosed that a third private treasury of about $600,000 [was] used to finance a variety of dirty tricks." In the July 23 *New Yorker*, Common Cause president John Gardner told reporter Elizabeth Drew that the activity could not be minimized by using the ironic phrase: "Some of the highest officials of this nation carried on a sustained and systematic attempt to destroy our form of government. It wasn't 'dirty tricks' within the system—it was an attempt to subvert the system …"

Although Nixon speechwriter Patrick Buchanan sought to draw distinctions between time-honored pranks and illegal campaign practices, the phrase *dirty tricks* lost its smirk and became a serious term for criminal, or at least obviously unethical, politicking.

A euphemism arose: *opposition research*, soon shortened to *oppo research*. This was initially defined as the legitimate examination of an opponent's record, searching for vulnerabilities in votes and weaknesses in previous positions. However, it had its dark side in the retention of private investigators to dig up embarrassing information about arrests, divorce settlements, peccadilloes, and financial difficulties. A 2005 CNN story about politics as a career had a category listed as "Opposition Researcher" with the lead sentence "If you like digging up dirt, opposition research may be a field for you." A year later, Rep. Thomas Reynolds (R-N.Y.), chairman of the National Republican Campaign Committee, candidly gave the field sanction: "Opposition research is power," he told *The Washington Post*, "Opposition research is the key to defining untested opponents." See HARDBALL.

With the rise of political blogs at the turn of the millennium, such probing of political pasts and earlier records became a more universal pastime. Research challenging Senator John Kerry's medal for heroism during the Vietnam war by "the Swift Boat veterans" on weblogs, although denounced by Democrats as a "dirty trick," all but derailed his campaign for the presidency in 2004. See SWIFT BOAT SPOT.

After the midterm campaigns of 2006, *The Washington Post* noted "the introduction of sleazy new practices such as ROBO-CALLS designed to annoy and deceive voters and a greater use of *push polls* aimed at spreading inaccurate information about candidates."

A *push poll* is a nefarious telemarketing technique designed to spread negative information about an opposition candidate. During the South Carolina primary of 2000, a caller from the George W. Bush campaign asked 300 potential voters: "John McCain calls the campaign finance system corrupt, but as chairman of the Senate Commerce Committee, he raises money and travels on the private jets of corporations with legislative proposals before his committee. In view of this, are you much more likely to vote for him … or much more likely to vote against him?" A push poll is not a legitimate public opinion survey because its purpose is not to obtain an opinion but to influence it, which qualifies the device as a *dirty trick*.

In 2006, the C.I.A.'s Directorate of Operations, unhappy at being called "the department of dirty tricks," renamed itself the National Clandestine Service. (*Clandestine* means "surreptitious; underhanded.")

See DAISY SPOT; GUTTER FLYER; ROORBACK; ROBOCALL; SMEAR.

disadvantaged A euphemism for "poor," replacing *underprivileged* in social workers' jargon, in turn replaced by *underclass* and *low-income.*

As a result of the civil rights movement of the '50s and '60s, it was felt that no citizen was *privileged*, though many were *advantaged*, thus the substitution. Since *underadvantaged* is cumbersome, *disadvantaged*—without the advantages of education and opportunity—was selected. (In the same way, what used to be called a *slum* became "a culturally deprived environment.")

Just as he had done with BLACK, the political cartoonist Jules Feiffer in 1965 showed language change with a man saying to himself: "I used to think I was poor. Then they told me I wasn't poor, I was needy. They told me it was self-defeating to think of myself as needy, I was deprived. Then they told me underprivileged was overused. I was disadvantaged. I still don't have a dime. But I have a great vocabulary."

disaster metaphors Natural catastrophe is commonplace in political language. Beginning with a mild GROUNDSWELL (a heavy rolling sea due to a distant storm), a candidate's fortunes may move forward like a *prairie fire*, his headquarters *flooded* with telegrams of support, leading him to a WHIRLWIND CAMPAIGN, but a *tidal wave* or *tsunami* (Japanese) or FIRESTORM of criticism after a scandal has *erupted* may lead to an AVALANCHE of votes against him and an electoral LANDSLIDE for his opponent, leaving him *snowed under* and wondering how he could have been *blitzed* (*Blitz* is German for "lightning," which candidates hope will strike—see DEWEY BLITZ) by a threat that seemed, at the beginning, *like a cloud no bigger than a man's hand* (I Kings 18:44).

Typical of a political disaster comment was William Allen White's assessment of the defeat of Alfred Landon in the presidential election of 1936: "It was not an election the country has just undergone, but a political Johnstown flood."

disgrace to the human race See THREE-MARTINI LUNCH.

dish the Whigs To steal the opposition's clothes; to win by reversing long-held stands.

In nineteenth-century English slang, to *dish* was to defeat decisively, especially by trickery; the term probably came from the notion of cooking something and serving it well-done.

When England's Conservative party surprised itself and the world by passing the radical Reform Bill of 1867—thereby enfranchising two million workingmen, a goal of its Whig opposition for many years—the Prime Minister, Lord Derby, said delightedly, "Don't you see we have dished the Whigs?" With the aid of Benjamin Disraeli, who was to succeed him as head of the Tories, Derby had indeed won support that had been taken for granted by the opposition.

The British phrase was a favorite of *Newsweek* columnist Stewart Alsop's, and is still used by history buffs to describe cooptation: "Seldom in Western politics since Disraeli's Reform Bill of 1867," declared a *New York Times* editorial about Nixon summiteering on February 10, 1972, "—when Lord Derby boasted, 'We've dished the Whigs'—has a national leader so completely turned his back on a lifetime of beliefs to adopt those of his political opponents."

The Derby reference was especially piquant, since his only other famous remark was: "When I first came into Parliament, Mr. Tierney, a great Whig authority, used always to say that the duty of an Opposition was very simple—it was, to oppose everything, and propose nothing." That statement has been shortened to "the duty of an Opposition is to oppose" and, with poetic injustice, is attributed to the politician who won by adopting the tenets of his opposition.

disinformation See PROPAGANDA.

disintermediation See ECONOMIC JARGON.

dissent See PRESIDENT OF ALL THE PEOPLE; ACTIVIST.

divorce issue The question raised by the married or single voter about the "morality" of a candidate who has been divorced.

The *youth issue* and *religious issue* were largely resolved by Kennedy's victory; the *age issue* declined with the wins by Reagan; the *character issue* remains strong. But what about the *divorce issue?*

In the nineteenth century, the marriage of Andrew Jackson to divorcee Rachel Donelson Robards caused a considerable stir, particularly since her divorce was in question. In the twentieth, Wallis Simpson's divorced status made it necessary for King Edward VIII to abdicate in order to marry her.

The first divorced man to run for president in the U.S. was Democrat James Cox in 1920 (the youthful FDR was his running mate). According to some accounts, a deal between the parties was suspected: the GOP would not mention Cox's divorce, and the Democrats would not whisper about Harding's mistresses.

In modern times, divorce itself is not the issue; Adlai Stevenson had been divorced when he ran for President in 1952, and that fact was not a major factor in his loss to the popular Eisenhower. It is remarriage after a divorce that used to rankle a portion of the public, and still troubles some; "home-wrecking" is considered the worst sin of all.

Nelson Rockefeller, divorced in 1961, was reelected governor of New York a year later by a comfortable half-million votes. Before the election, social critic Cleveland Amory observed that "he's certain to get the divorce vote and remember that's one in four these days." But in May 1963 Rockefeller married Margaretta Fitler ("Happy") Murphy, herself recently divorced, and without assured custody of her five children; there was a measurable reaction.

"People will forgive a politician they love almost any sin," wrote Theodore White, "—as witness James Michael Curley, Huey Long, Adam Clayton Powell, Jimmy Walker, and a score of others; in matters of romance, particularly, they will forgive him almost any peccadillo … so long as the peccadillo is not flaunted. But the frank and open acceptance of a new marriage was a breach with the general indulgence of the hypocrisy of politics."

In the crucial California Republican primary against Barry Goldwater in 1964, the divorce issue hurt Rockefeller—but until the final weekend, the polls showed him ahead. That weekend, "Happy" Rockefeller bore the candidate a son; the newspapers were filled with the story of Rockefeller's flying visit to the hospital, a fresh reminder of the divorce and remarriage. An insidious slogan, "Elect a leader, not a lover," was pressed home by word of mouth, and Rockefeller lost by a narrow margin. Jack Wells, the Rockefeller campaign chairman, later looking at a picture of robust Nelson, Jr. playing with his toys, told the author with a sigh, "If only that little boy were three days younger, he'd be the son of the President of the United States."

Since that time, with more marriages ending in divorce than not, the impact of a politician's divorce on his campaign chances has lessened considerably. A *Newsweek* poll in 2007 reported that "only 5% of evangelicals say they would not vote for a candidate who had divorced," adding about Ronald Reagan, "Though he divorced his first wife and had difficult relationships with his children, he was a hero to evangelicals." With thrice-married, once-annulled, and once angrily divorced Rudy Giuliani surging in polls of Republicans, a cartoon showed Mitt Romney, a Mormon married to the same woman for 37 years, saying to Giuliani standing in front of three women standing behind him, "Tell me about polygamy."

New York Mayor Michael Bloomberg, asked frequently about his availability as an independent candidate for president in 2008, had an answer that encompassed issues of height, marital status, economic position, religion, political affiliation, and geography in a single sentence: "How can a 5-foot-7, divorced billionaire Jew running as an independent from New York have a chance?"

Dixiecrat Southern Democrat who bolted the national party in 1948 in opposition to President Truman's CIVIL RIGHTS platform.

In a fiery speech to the 1948 Democratic convention, an ebullient Hubert Humphrey posed the central issue to face his party in the decades ahead: "It is time for the Democratic party to step out of the shadow of state's rights—and to walk forthrightly into the bright sunshine of HUMAN RIGHTS." Most Democrats followed his lead (although, twenty years later, many liberals—angered by the Vietnam policy of Lyndon Johnson, whom Humphrey served as Vice President—were reluctant to support him).

The States Rights Democrats from Alabama, Mississippi, Louisiana, and other Southern states held a convention of their own in 1948, nominating Senator J. Strom Thurmond as their candidate for President to oppose President Truman and Republican nominee Dewey. The votes that were lost to the Democrats in the South were probably offset by votes Democrats gained in the North, no longer embarrassed by their party's civil rights divisions.

Coinage of *Dixiecrat* was attributed to William Weismer, telegraph editor of the *Charlotte* (N.C.) *News*, who had difficulty squeezing *States Rights Democrats* into a headline. Alabama Governor Frank Dixon did not like the new nickname: "Dixiecrats leaves the wrong impression," he complained. "Our contention is that we are returning to the original concepts of the founding fathers of our nation and the Democratic party." Harry Truman was having none of that. He wrote: "The States Rights Democrats claim that this was not a BOLT from the Democratic party. They said they represented the true Democrats of the Southland. It was a bolt."

See TAKE A WALK; OFF THE RESERVATION.

Dr. Fell syndrome Inexplicable voters' distaste for the personality of a candidate whose positions would ordinarily command their support.

Stewart Alsop, writing in *Newsweek* in 1970, identified the "Dr. Fell Syndrome" as the cause of President Nixon's greatest political weakness—many of the people who liked what he stood for didn't like the way he stood.

The phrase is from the poem by Thomas (Tom) Brown written while he was a student at Christ Church, Oxford, during the 1600s. It is a loose translation of a Martial epigram from the first century A.D.:

I do not love thee, Dr. Fell.
The reason why I cannot tell;
But this alone I know full well,
I do not love thee, Dr. Fell.

The real Dr. Fell, a seventeenth-century English divine, was able to maintain Church of England services despite the rise of Oliver Cromwell and was made dean of Christ Church after the Restoration. Though he was generally acknowledged to be a man of courage, rectitude, and vision, some people just couldn't warm up to him.

doctrines Foreign policies that have hardened with acceptance.

When the word is applied in retrospect, it usually sticks; when it is announced with a policy, it usually fades. President Monroe's decision to deny European influence in the Americas was not laid down as the *Monroe Doctrine;* it became known as that many years later. On the other hand, most Americans do not remember what was contained in the *Truman Doctrine* (aid to Greece and Turkey to fight Communism) or the *Eisenhower Doctrine* (the same kind of CONTAINMENT policy in the Middle East).

Two of the most hotly debated doctrines in American history have all but disappeared from today's political language: the *Freeport Doctrine* of Stephen Douglas, which held that the people of a territory could exclude slavery prior to the formation of a state constitution, and Senator John Calhoun's *Doctrine of Non-Interference,* declaring that federal intervention on the slavery issue in a state was illegal.

In the Communist world, the *One Glass of Water Doctrine* was long remembered, but more in the breach than the observance. This held that good Communists should regard sexual desire as being "no more important than a glass of water." Lenin revoked this doctrine after the Bolsheviks took power, but it remained for many years as gospel to Chinese Communists under the name *bei-shui-zhuyi.* It was the cause of some disaffection among the Viet Cong in South Vietnam.

The *Brezhnev Doctrine*, expounded by General Secretary Leonid Brezhnev on November 12, 1968, after Soviet arms had crushed a turning toward freedom in Czechoslovakia earlier that year, held that "the Socialist community as a whole"—that is, the Soviet Union—had the right to intervene in otherwise sovereign states when it detected a tendency toward capitalism subverting an already Communist state. This asserted Soviet military control of its satellites: "to protect Communist regimes even if it means the use of force."

"The Carter approach to foreign policy," said the State Department's Leslie Gelb in 1977, "rests in a belief that not only is the world far too complex to be reduced to a doctrine, but there is something inherently wrong in having a doctrine at all."

Asked on June 20, 1999, by CNN's Wolf Blitzer "Is there, in your mind, a *Clinton Doctrine*?" the President gave a multilateral reply: "While there may well be a great deal of ethnic and religious conflict in the world ... whether within or beyond the borders of a country, if the world community has the power to stop it, we ought to stop genocide and ethnic cleansing."

George W. Bush preferred to call his doctrine of extending democracy abroad "the freedom agenda," an evocation of Woodrow Wilson's idealism; after "regime change" in Iraq turned into what Secretary of Defense Donald Rumsfeld called "the long war," the interventionist policy was attacked by those calling themselves "realists." See REALISM.

For Henry Kissinger's classic response to the author's question about the April 1970 incursion into, or brief invasion of, Cambodia—"We wrote the goddam Doctrine, we can change it!"—see NIXON DOCTRINE.

dog metaphors See ANKLE-BITERS; ATTACK DOG; BIRD DOG, KENNEL DOG.

do-gooder Derisive name by professional politicians and cynical journalists for annoying reformers and civic-action nonpartisans.

The phrase *do-goods* was traced by the *OED* to 1654, and the use of the compound word in a political context can be found in a 1923 issue of *The Nation:* "There is nothing wrong with the United States except ... the parlor socialists, uplifters, and do-goods." Tracing the use of *good* back in political history, the pattern seems to be "Good Government Clubs," "goo-goos," "goody-goody"—with a separate branch for "holier than thou."

The City Club of New York came up with a district-level network of local action groups called "Good Government Clubs" in the 1890s. Promptly dubbed the *goo-goos* by the *New York Sun*, the reformers raised the ire of Theodore Roosevelt: "The Republican machine men have been loudly demanding a straight ticket; and those prize idiots, the Goo-Goos, have just played into their hands by capering off and nominating an independent ticket of their own."

That hyphenated variant of *do-gooder* has lasted well over a century; in commenting on what it considered the belated S.E.C. exoneration of Senator Bill Frist on spurious charges of insider trading, *The Wall Street Journal* wrote in 2007: "These are the kind of people that the goo-goo Naderites end up driving from public office ... as former U.S. Secretary of Labor Ray Donovan asked after his legal ordeal, 'Which office do I go to, to get my reputation back?'"

Like so many reform groups, the Good Government Clubs atrophied and died in a few years; Democratic and Republican machines skillfully redistricted the city so that the reformers no longer knew which club they belonged to. However, the term *do-gooder* retained its pristine connotation and is current throughout the political English-speaking world: a film role played by the actress Hilary Swank was described in 2007 by the U.K.'s *Barking and Dagenham Post* as "such a golly gosh liberal do-gooder in a prim suit and string of pearls ..."

Just before the rise of the *goo-goos*, "holier-than-thou" was the name given the independent Republicans in 1884. This was derived from Isaiah 65:5, in which the prophet derisively quotes hypocrites as saying: "Stand by thyself, come not near to me; for I am holier than thou."

dog-whistle politics The use of messages embedded in speeches that seem innocent to a general audience but resonate with a specific public attuned to receive them.

Sheepherders have long known that dogs are able to hear high-frequency sounds inaudible to sheep as well as to normal adult humans.

President George W. Bush's criticism, during his 2004 campaign for re-election, of the U.S. Supreme Court's 1857 *Dred Scott* decision upholding slavery seemed innocuous on one level. After all, who today would argue in favor of slavery? But sharp-eared observers interpreted his remark as a signal that he might nominate to the Supreme Court a justice who would vote to overturn *Roe v. Wade*, the 1973 decision that legalized abortion under many circumstances. The unspoken point—*the dog whistle*—was that Supreme Court decisions can be reversed: If the *Dred Scott* decision could be overturned (as it was by Amendment XIII to the Constitution), then *Roe v. Wade* might be reversed by a court that included more Bush appointees.

Commenting on the President's historical reference, David D. Kirkpatrick wrote in *The New York Times:* "The potential double meaning rekindled speculation among Mr. Bush's critics that he communicates with his conservative Christian base with a dog whistle of CODE WORDS and symbols, deliberately incomprehensible to secular liberals." The message would be pitched high enough to rally the whistler's core constituency without unduly arousing the opposition.

Dog-whistle politics have been practiced in other English-speaking countries. "Beware the nasty nudge and wink," warned the Manchester *Guardian* in April of 2005: "Every election introduces a new phrase into the political lexicon and the 'dog-whistle issue' is 2005's early contribution." Credit for introducing the term to the U.K. generally is given to Lynton Crosby, a Conservative Party adviser, who had previously managed election campaigns in Australia for Prime Minister John Howard. As *The Dominion* reported in New Zealand toward the end of 1997: "Labor's spokesman on aboriginal affairs has already accused Mr. Howard of

'dog-whistle politics'—in rejecting a race election, he actually sent a high-pitched signal to those attuned to hear it."

The political *dog whistle* may have derived from the term's use by pollsters. Richard Morin, director of polling for *The Washington Post,* observed in a 1988 article that "Subtle changes in question-wording sometimes produce remarkably different results. ... researchers call this the 'Dog Whistle Effect': Respondents hear something in the question that researchers do not."

The effect has been noticed in other fields. In 1989, Russell Smith noted in the *Dallas Morning News* that an MTV spot "which has no obvious reason to exist, is like a secret signal, a dog whistle blown on a thirtysomething frequency. Come back, MTV beckons, in a language it hasn't spoken in years." Two years earlier, in *New York* magazine, Geraldine Stutz, three-decade president of Henri Bendel in New York City, described her taste in "Dog-whistle fashion," meaning that she specialized in stocking in her store "clothes with a pitch so high and special that only the thinnest and most sophisticated women would hear their call."

dollar diplomacy Use of U.S. military and political power to further the interest of U.S. entrepreneurs in Latin America; or, enticement of foreign nations to follow U.S. political leadership with promises of economic aid.

Early in the twentieth century, under the Roosevelt Corollary to the Monroe Doctrine, U.S. Marines helped U.S. businessmen open new markets in Latin America and protected those interests; protectorates were established over Cuba, Haiti, Nicaragua, and Santo Domingo. *Harper's Weekly* in 1910 referred to the phrase as it was then being applied to Secretary of State Philander C. Knox: "An attempt is made, necessarily sketchy, to outline simply and clearly what is meant by the term 'Dollar Diplomacy' as it has come to be commonly applied to certain of the activities of Secretary Knox as manifested in Honduras, in Liberia, and in negotiations now in progress looking to the participation of American capital in railway construction in the Far East."

President William Howard Taft, in his annual message on December 3, 1912, defended the philosophy in what came to be known as his "Dollar Diplomacy" speech: "The diplomacy of the present administration has sought to respond to modern ideas of commercial intercourse. This policy has been characterized as substituting dollars for bullets. It is one that appeals alike to idealistic humanitarian sentiments, to the dictates of sound policy and strategy, and to legitimate commercial aims."

Dollar diplomacy became a term of criticism used by Latin American diplomats who resented economic arm-twisting. In its more general sense, the phrase has come to mean the dangling of economic plums in front of a hungry neutral or unfriendly nation. In 1965 President Lyndon Johnson offered a billion-dollar investment program in Southeast Asia if only the Communists would replace aggression with "peaceful cooperation." The columnist Arthur Krock observed: "Only from members of the small Republican minority … was any question raised … of the political psychology of a proposal reminiscent by its attendant circumstances of the crude era of American 'dollar diplomacy.'"

In late 1971, the phrase was used in derogation of hard-bargaining Treasury Secretary John Connally, but temporarily lost its pejorative connotation after a realignment of currency rates favorable to the U.S.

domino theory The argument that if one strategically placed nation in an area went Communist, others would quickly follow.

In 1954 Dwight Eisenhower used the metaphor, a favorite of the columnist Joseph Alsop, in explaining his decision to offer economic aid to the South Vietnamese government of Ngo Dinh Diem. "You have a row of dominoes set up," said the President at a press conference, "you knock over the first one, and what will happen to the last one is that it will go over very quickly. So you have the beginning of a disintegration that would have the most profound influences." The theory derives from what historian Arthur Schlesinger, Jr., describes as "a popular construction, or misconstruction, of the Munich analogy." (See MUNICH ANALOGY.) In any event, the idea was accepted widely. As Eisenhower told Churchill: "We failed to halt Hirohito, Mussolini and Hitler by not acting in unity and in time."

John F. Kennedy had reservations about the theory. *New York Times* columnist Arthur Krock wrote after an interview: "I asked him what he thought of the 'falling domino' theory—that is, if Laos and Vietnam go Communist, the rest of Southeast Asia will fall to them in orderly succession. The President expressed doubts that this theory had much point any more because, he remarked, the Chinese Communists were bound to get nuclear weapons in time, and from that moment on the nations of Southeast Asia would seek to be on good terms with Peking."

Some of Kennedy's closest advisers, nevertheless, accepted the theory. His former Chairman of the Joint Chiefs of Staff, General Maxwell Taylor, told a House subcommittee shortly after Kennedy's death that if the U.S. withdrew from Vietnam, the country would quickly go Communist, and "the remainder of Southeast Asia would very shortly thereafter go neutralist, possibly even Communist. Burma would be affected, India also. Indonesia would soon line up with the Communists. We would be pushed out of the Western Pacific back to Honolulu."

One of the most persistent critics of the theory, Senate Foreign Relations Committee Chairman J. William Fulbright, wrote in *The Arrogance of Power:* "The inference we have drawn from this is that we must fight in one country in order to avoid having to fight in another, although we could with equal logic have inferred that it is useless to fight in one country when the same conditions of conflict are present in another." A graphic metaphoric attack was made by novelist Norman Mailer during a 1965 anti-Vietnam demonstration at the University of California, Berkeley: "They are not dominoes but sand castles. Sand castles. And a tide of nationalism is on the way in." *U.S. News & World Report* in 1968 termed the phrase "a cornerstone of U.S. reasoning about Vietnam since the Eisenhower years."

The phrase has retrospective currency. A 1993 letter to the editor in *The Washington Post* commented on an Op-Ed piece whose authors called for American intervention in Bosnia's civil war: "Their arguments remind one of the domino theory for intervention in Vietnam in 1965: That failure to act will lead to a wider European war, perhaps war between Europe and the Muslim world."

As congressional elections approached in 2006, President Bush stepped up his warnings that defeat in Iraq would threaten Americans "in the streets of our own cities" and that "a generation from now, our children will face a region dominated by terrorist states and radical dictators armed with nuclear weapons." This followed a statement by General John Abizaid, head of U.S. forces in Iraq, that "If we leave, they will follow us." Reporter David Sanger of *The New York Times* noted that "it is reminiscent of—updated for a different war, and a different time—President Lyndon B. Johnson's adoption of the 'domino theory'" and concluded that "he is trying to focus voters not on the high price of winning but on the harder-to-define cost of letting the dominoes fall."

The phrase was parodied in 1968 by columnist Art Buchwald. He held that BRINK-MANSHIP was named after a man named Brinkman, and the domino theory after one Sam Domino, who explained how he coined it: "Well, one evening we were having a buffet and there were about twenty people lined up with plates waiting for some chicken cacciatore when my uncle, who was first in line, slipped and fell backward. He knocked over my aunt standing in back of him and she, in turn, knocked over my cousin, who knocked over my son and so on until all twenty people were on the floor. It suddenly occurred to me that if this could happen to people, it could happen to countries."

donkey, Democratic Symbol of the Democratic party.

"A live jackass kicking a dead lion" was the caption of a Thomas Nast cartoon in an 1870 *Harper's Weekly*. The donkey was labeled "Copperhead papers" and the lion was the Republican Edward M. Stanton, who had been Lincoln's Secretary of War. Nast kept using the donkey as his symbol of Democrats, most famously in 1874 showing legislators blowing up a balloon labeled "inflation" from a dish of "soft soap" with the scene captioned "Fine-ass committee." The donkey gained its acceptance as the Democratic symbol—though not welcomed by Democrats, who preferred the Tammany tiger—as a result of Thomas Nast's cartoons (see ELEPHANT, REPUBLICAN), despite Ignatius Donnelly's remark in the Minnesota Legislature: "The Democratic party is like a mule—without pride of ancestry or hope of posterity."

The donkey has provided cartoonists and speechwriters with an invaluable metaphor. For example, when the Democrats at their 1928 Houston convention nominated Al Smith (who favored repeal of Prohibition) and Senator Joseph T. Robinson of Arkansas (who favored Prohibition), the wisecrack was "the Democratic donkey with a wet head and wagging a dry tail left Houston."

In retrospect, many political observers feel that Nast exercised good judgment in his selection of symbols. Historian Clinton Rossiter wrote that the difference between the two parties "is caught vividly in the choice of beastly emblems that was made for all of us long ago: the slightly ridiculous but tough and long-lived Donkey—the perfect symbol of the rowdy Democrats; the majestic but ponderous Elephant—the perfect symbol of respectable Republicans. Can anyone imagine the Donkey as a Republican and the Elephant as a Democrat?"

do-nothing Congress Harry Truman's epithet for the 1947–1948 Republican-controlled session that rejected much of his program.

"Do-nothing" is associated with Truman's criticism of the 80th Congress, since it was so instrumental in giving him an upset victory over Thomas E. Dewey in 1948. But the term was in use as early as the sixteenth century, and Franklin Roosevelt used it in referring to the "do-nothing policy of Hoover."

In his memoirs, Truman quoted Will Rogers' addition to an old slogan: "'Keep Cool with Coolidge'—and Do Nothing."

Truman picked up the compound adjective when, crossing the U.S. in June 1948, he found audiences responding to his attacks on "the good-for-nothing, do nothing, Taft-Hartley 80th Congress" and the "worst Congress" ever. When he accepted the Democratic nomination, he declared: "On the 26th day of July, which out in Missouri we call 'Turnip Day,' I am going to call that Congress back in session, and I am going to ask them to pass some of these laws they say they are for in their platform. Now, my friends, if there is any reality behind that Republican platform, we ought to get some action out of the short session of the 80th Congress. They could do this job in 15 days if they wanted to. ... What that worst 80th Congress does in its special session will be the test. The American people will decide on the record."

Dominated by Ohio Senator Robert A. Taft and his followers disappointed by the GOP nomination of Dewey, the special session accomplished nothing; President Truman was able to continue campaigning on what he considered its obstructionism and on the fact that he had to use the veto 62 times against it. It was a bold move for, as Truman speechwriter Clark Clifford recalled: "We were on our own 20-yard line. We had to be bold. If we kept plugging away in moderate terms, the best we could have done would have been to reach midfield when the gun went off. So we had to throw long passes."

Instead of the traditional defense of the record of the Administration in power, the Truman strategy was to turn his own frustrations and defeats into an asset by furiously attacking those who had effectively hamstrung the Administration. The strategy of unexpected offense helped produce the most stunning upset in modern American political history.

don't change horses A metaphor urging voters to continue an Administration during a period of crisis.

The figure of speech was Lincoln's, spoken at the Republican convention of 1864 to a delegation from the Union League Club which had hailed the action of the convention in nominating Lincoln. Reported his secretaries, Nicolai and Hay: "The President answered them more informally, saying that he did not allow himself to suppose that either the Convention or the League had concluded that he was either the greatest or the best man in America, but rather that they had decided it was not best to 'swap horses while crossing the river.'"

Etymologists Sperber and Trittschuh traced the origin to an 1846 newspaper: "There is a story of an Irishman who was crossing a stream with mare and colt when finding it deeper than he expected, and falling off the old mare, he seized the colt's tail to aid him in reaching the shore. Some persons on the bank called to him, advising him to take hold of the mare's tail, as she was the ablest to bring him out. His reply was, that it was a very unseasonable time for swapping horses."

The expression was edited by usage into "Don't change horses in midstream," or "Don't swap horses while crossing the stream." Heavy use of the phrase was made in the Hoover-Roosevelt campaign of 1932. *The New Republic* characterized the Republican campaign theme as "Don't change barrels while going over Niagara." Roosevelt supporters countered with "Swap horses or drown!"

Its best-known use was in the Roosevelt campaigns of 1940 and 1944. Republican Chairman Joe Martin remained convinced that the unwillingness to shift leadership in a crisis was the root cause of the Willkie defeat in 1940: "The fall of France and the imminent danger to Britain filled the American people with a fear of switching administrations. 'Don't change horses in the middle of the stream' was never a more potent argument in American history than it was then. Not even the third-term issue could prevail against it."

Irving Stone wrote of the 1944 Roosevelt-Dewey campaign: "The Democrats could not seem to fight their way out of the hard crust of inertia in Washington, and the only effort they cared to make was the negative cry of 'Don't change horses in midstream.'" Dewey's stirring slogan was "TIME FOR A

CHANGE," and public opinion polls showed him closing the gap on the President. Dewey's 1944 campaign (in contrast to his second effort in 1948) was slashing and vigorous; Roosevelt supporters, viewing the erosion of their margin of safety, urged FDR to drop his above-the-battle stance and hit hard. The FALA SPEECH soon followed, infuriating Republicans and reminding independents that the Old Master had not lost his political touch.

don't let them take it away An unofficial Democratic campaign slogan of 1948 and 1952.

The phrase appeared in the *New York Journal-American* of December 28, 1946, as a kind of belated answer to the Republican "HAD ENOUGH?" that had been so successful in the 1946 off-year elections. It was used in the 1948 Truman campaign, though not nearly as much as "DO-NOTHING CONGRESS."

In 1952, Adlai Stevenson treated it lightly: "There have been times when I have wondered whether you, my friends here in Illinois, couldn't have found some easier way of getting rid of me. In fact, before the Convention I wrote a song about it, only the Democratic party took the song and changed the words. My song was called 'Don't Let Them Take Me Away.'"

This is a defensive slogan, similar to the British Conservative party's 1964 slogan: "It's your standard of living—keep it with the Conservatives." That did not catch on, either. For one that did, see YOU NEVER HAD IT SO GOOD.

don't waste your vote Slogan of a major party attempting to win back support lost to splinter parties; usually accompanied by the statement "A vote for [splinter party candidate name] is a vote for [major opposition party name]."

President Harry Truman, fighting his uphill battle in 1948, knew that Henry Wallace's Progressive party was drawing votes from people who would ordinarily vote Democratic. As Truman ripped into the DO-NOTHING CONGRESS and its MOSSBACK committee chairmen, he said in Los Ange-

les: "a vote for the third party plays into the hands of the Republican forces of reaction whose aims are directly opposed to the aim of American liberalism."

A classic example of a double *don't-waste-your-vote* effort was the four-way New York gubernatorial race in 1966. Republican Rockefeller was urging members of the splinter Conservative party not to waste their votes on Paul Adams, while Democrat Frank O'Connor was urging Liberal party members not to waste their votes on Liberal candidate Franklin D. Roosevelt, Jr. At the last minute, word was passed to Liberal district leaders that their party members should switch to the Democrat, though too few did so to influence the result.

Reformer William Evarts, who helped break up New York's Tweed ring, was running for U.S. Senator in 1884 and came up with a phrase to dissuade New Yorkers from paying attention to the man running on the Prohibition ticket. He called it "voting in the air."

In the 1992 Presidential election, both major parties revived the expression *don't waste your vote*. Republicans staunchly for George H.W. Bush and Democrats wanting Bill Clinton to garner the votes of the dissatisfied argued that votes for Ross Perot would be wasted, although Perot's forces denied it.

The answer to the *don't-waste-your-vote* plea is, of course, a stand on principle. Said Hearst's *San Francisco Examiner* in support of a hopeless cause in 1908: "The vote for principle is never thrown away. It is the only vote that isn't thrown away." Felix Frankfurter, explaining his vote for Robert La Follette in 1924, agreed: "If clarification of American politics through the formation of a new party is required to make our politics more honest and more real, then all the talk of 'throwing one's vote away' is the cowardly philosophy of the BANDWAGON."

A question in the minds of many American voters is: "Is my vote really needed?" Third parties play on this nagging doubt by urging voters to "make your vote count" by registering a protest. Major parties appeal on these grounds as well. Recalling the importance of "a single vote in each election district" in the 1960 election as well as the cliffhanger in 2000, they point out that each vote is important and the front runner could lose if that particular voter did not turn out.

Worry about the wasted vote is particularly strong in Japan. "For some reason," wrote Nobutake Ike in 1958, "Japanese voters do not like to 'waste' their votes. They are therefore reluctant to vote for a candidate who clearly has no chance to win. By the same token, if they believe that a particular candidate will win by a wide margin, they might shift their vote to someone else. They feel that 'he is going to win anyway, so why shouldn't I make my vote count by giving it to another candidate.'"

For the opposite appeal, see SEND THEM A MESSAGE.

Dooley, Mr. A fictional creation of author Finley Peter Dunne, who made sage political observations in a thick Irish brogue.

Mr. Dooley first appeared in a Chicago newspaper in the 1890s and dispensed his wisdom up to World War I.

Dunne lifted his character out of his hometown Chicago sixth-ward commentary in the Spanish-American War, and gained national recognition in 1896 by commenting on the William Jennings Bryan campaign. Skepticism kept his epigrams astringent: "I see gr-reat changes takin' place ivry day, but no change at all ivry fifty years." His best-known line, now used after being rendered into proper English, was: "No matther whether th' Constitution follows th' flag or not, th' Supreme Coort follows th' iliction returns." See SUPREME COURT FOLLOWS THE ELECTION RETURNS.

Nowadays the phonetic representation of dialect is often considered demeaning to an ethnic, racial, or geographic group. However, the Dooley brogue was used by Dunne to add flavor to political wisdom, and as such is freely quoted today.

A typical Dooley comment is this view of the vice presidency: "Ye can't be sint to jail f'r it, but it's a kind iv a disgrace. ... It is princip'lly because iv th' vice-prisidint that most iv our prisidints have enjoyed such rugged health. Th' vice-prisidint guards th'

prisidint, an' th' prisidint, afther sizin' up th' vice-prisidint, con-cludes that it wud be betther f'r th' counthry if he shud live yet awhile."

The tradition of political humor in dialect is that of Petroleum V. Nasby and Artemus Ward. Mark Twain placed political observations in the mouths of Huck Finn, Tom Sawyer, and Pudd'nhead Wilson. Will Rogers carried the torch for a while, and in the '70s and '80s, without dialect, the field was dominated by Art Buchwald, Dave Barry, and Russell Baker. Since then, political speechwriters have learned to tune in to late-night TV hosts like Jay Leno, Jon Stewart and David Letterman to see who would be the butt of jokes. In today's politics, as in Mr. Dooley's day, humor is serious business.

See BEANBAG.

Doomsday Machine A computer programmed to set off a nuclear war based on another nation's actions; carrying DETERRENT to the extreme.

The *Doomsday Machine*, properly constructed, should be capable of wiping out life on earth. It sits in the nation that built it, but its behavior is controlled by an enemy nation.

This means that the enemy nation knows that certain actions will trigger the machine, and that no fears or false hopes in the nation that built the machine can stop its use. The enemy is thus provided with a list of restraints which have been programmed into the computer and knows where the line is drawn. One such restraint could be "You may not build a Doomsday Machine."

"Although it is most unlikely that any nation would build such a device in the next ten to twenty years," wrote Herman Kahn, author of *On Thermonuclear War*, "there clearly are some circumstances in which a nation might wish it had built one."

A related expression, the *Doomsday Clock*, has led to the use of the urgent phrase "two minutes to midnight." Since 1945, the Doomsday Clock appears monthly on the cover of the *Bulletin of the Atomic Scientists*. Powered by mankind's activities regarding atomic energy, the clock ticks toward the world's midnight when, presumably, all bets are off. The clock was originally set at seven minutes to twelve; by September 1953, when both the Soviet Union and the U.S. had thermonuclear capability, the hands were moved ahead to two minutes to midnight. After the 1963 nuclear test-ban treaty, it was moved back to twelve minutes; in 2007 it was set at five minutes, but now it also includes the threat of climate change.

The *Domesday Dictionary* was published in England in 1964, defining the more frightening nuclear words in a deadpan manner; *domesday* is pronounced *doomsday*, and refers to the survey of England for taxing purposes made by William the Conqueror in 1085, which was recorded in the *Domesday Book.*

doorbell-ringing House-to-house canvassing for votes; personal persuasion by party workers of individual voters, hallmark of a well-organized campaign.

A *doorbell-ringing campaign* is one in which the party's workers are mobilized to make a personal appeal to individuals in their residence. Some of the rules: (1) an index-card file must be prepared of all registered voters, with party preference checked and need for babysitter or transportation on election day indicated; (2) no calls before 8 A.M. or after 9 P.M.; (3) teams of men and women to do the actual doorbell-ringing, to reassure the voter of his safety and to provide for the safety of canvassers.

A follow-up to, but not a substitute for, a doorbell-ringing campaign is a *telephone blitz*—calls made from a "boiler room" to remind favorably inclined voters to turn out on election day. Theodore White, in *The Making of the President 1964*, held that it was the influence of strangers ringing the doorbells of lonely newcomers in California that tipped the scales from Rockefeller to Goldwater in the closing days of the 1964 primary campaign that decided the Republican nomination.

See CANVASS.

dope story A speculative article based on information from a supposedly "inside"

source, sometimes leaked to a reporter and published as his own analysis; a useful method of launching TRIAL BALLOONS to test the waters or condition public opinion.

A President's special message to Congress used to be closely held within an administration until delivery. But President Harry Truman handled the special "turnip day" session of what he termed the "DO-NOTHING CONGRESS" in the campaign of 1948 with an original bit of media manipulation (see MANAGED NEWS). Presidential press secretary Charles Ross leaked the message's contents the week preceding its delivery. "Thus the Truman program got double exposure in the nation's press," wrote biographer Cabell Phillips, "first in the provocative form of 'dope stories,' and again when the message was made officially public. As a publicity gimmick, it was a small triumph."

Dope has a dual root in American slang. As a synonym for narcotics, it is extended to one who appears drugged or stupid, as *dopey*. As slang for information, it spawned *inside dope, dope out, dope sheet*, and *dope story. Dope*'s sense as "data" is not new; the *Dictionary of Americanisms* has a 1901 citation, from a book by George Hobart: "I've known Tommy for a long time, so he feels free to read his dope to me."

Former N.Y. Governor Al Smith, soon after his defeat by Herbert Hoover for the presidency, introduced *dope story* to politics on January 2, 1929, in brushing off queries about "these reports that I'm going to take all sorts of jobs ... there's nothing to all these dope stories." Richard Nixon was the first president to use the phrase publicly; on January 28, 1969, he told a large group of State Department employees: "I have been reading some dope stories lately about the rivalries that may develop between the various departments in Government ..."

The slightly pejorative phrase is current in criticism of leaks or sketchily informed articles purporting to reveal thoughts or plans of insiders. A *Washington Post* editorial in late 1992 cautioned President-elect Clinton against appointing Cabinet members based solely on "help from the press, dope stories fed by various sources and the lobbying groups themselves." See BACK-

GROUNDER; NOT FOR ATTRIBUTION; LEAK; PLANT; THUMBSUCKER.

double digit Inflation of 10 percent or higher.

A *digit*, from the Latin *digitus*, is a finger. Children start counting on their fingers, which is how the word for "finger" became the word for "number." A *double digit* is made up of two figures—10 or more.

The phrase began as *double-figure inflation* in England in the sixties, taken from *double figures* in cricket scores. In the U.S., the coiner of *double digit* was Leonard Silk, member of the editorial board of *The New York Times*, who wrote this lead editorial on March 22, 1974: "For American consumers, it is slaughter at the checkout counters and the gasoline pumps. Food and fuel prices soared again in February, giving another big thrust to skyrocketing consumer prices. With last month's increase of 1.3 percent, the cost of living has climbed 10 percent in the past twelve months—the first double-digit rate of inflation in consumer prices since the Korean War." Mr. Silk, a colleague of the author, recalled: "I remember coming up with the phrase and noticing how fast it was picked up afterward. Of course, we all know that coincidences happen, but I'd be surprised if there was prior publication, since my piece was right on the news, when the digits went double."

Though the phrase is usually confined to inflation, it can be used to describe any high, or inflationary, price. In an essay in *The Washington Post* about the too-casual names given expensive places, Frank Mankiewicz wrote in 1977: "Joe's Place, which used to guarantee...a friendly roadhouse with live music on Saturday nights, now could signal anything from an elegant boutique to a restaurant with double-digit entree prices."

See HIGH COST OF LIVING; INFLATION.

double dip Two economic downturns or drops in the stock market in quick succession, possibly followed by a recovery, a steeper decline, or a DEAD CAT BOUNCE.

Dip began as a verb in Old English, akin to Germanic words for "deep." By 1599, *dip* was used as a noun, usually for a brief plunge or dive into water. That downward movement led to an economic sense of "financial downturn."

In February 1975, *Business Week* attributed the first use of *double dip* to an unidentified economist in the Ford Administration: "What is now likely is a 'double-dip recession,' as one Administration economist puts it." Three months later, the same publication offered a financial view that "portrays a double-dip recession in which the economy recovers in the second half of 1975 but lapses into decline again in 1976," but this double dip did not occur.

Double dip, the noun, began as a sign not of decline but of lavish or excessive offering. An ice-cream store clerk, to provide a *double dip*, would place two scoops on a single cone. Such excess probably led to the popularization of *double dipping*, the participle; for its definition, see below.

double dipping The taking of income from two government sources simultaneously

A more complete definition was given to the author by CPA P. K. Seidman: "The practice of collecting a government salary or other money benefit on top of a pension from the same government, or using the same salary as the base of securing two pensions from related governments such as state and county."

Civilian employees who retire and then return to government service in a different capacity forfeit their pension during their working years. But this does not apply to members of the armed forces. A *New York Times* editorial in 1977 argued: "Double dippers are members of the military who retire young, then take civilian jobs with the Federal government and collect both a military pension and a civilian salary. There are already 150,000 of them...Double dipping is indefensible."

The defense put forward is that retired servicemembers ought not to be penalized by losing their military pension income for the act of later entering the civilian labor force of the government. On September 19, 1977, Harry W. Quillian wrote this letter to *The Washington Post:* "As one who has no prospect of becoming a 'double dipper' I suggest that term be banished from reporting on and discussion of the dual compensation controversy. The implication it seems to carry—that it is reprehensible to earn a salary while receiving a pension—is absurd and doubtless painful to some honorably retired people supplementing their pensions by working at a second job."

When Admiral Stansfield Turner was appointed Director of Central Intelligence by his Annapolis classmate, President Jimmy Carter, he returned to the government payroll while continuing to draw his naval pension: dual compensation from the government, or "double dipping." A Naval Academy graduate often wears a large ring with the naval insignia; when two of them meet in civilian life, they often knock these rings together in lieu of a handshake. The author, then a columnist, merrily referred to the new CIA chief as a "ring-knocking double dipper"; unable thereafter to obtain an interview, the columnist arranged with Milton Pitts, the White House barber, to tip him off when the Director came into his private shop for a haircut. Pitts did so; I sat in the next chair and popped a question out of the side of my mouth about some intelligence matter. The Admiral froze, said "Ring-knocking double dipper, huh?" and made no further response.

At a Mexican-themed cocktail party, two passes at a guacamole bowl with a single potato chip is also called *double dipping*, and is frowned upon as a social error. As noted in DOUBLE DIP, the previous entry, the phrase comes from the ice cream parlor: a cone with two scoops of ice cream is a *double dip*. Additional pension benefits have not yet been termed *sprinkles*.

doughnut hole The gap in coverage for prescription drug expenses under Medicare Part D.

The *doughnut hole* in 2007 amounted to $3,051. After a deductible of $265, Medicare covered 75 percent of the first $2,400 of an individual's yearly drug expenses. Then coverage ceased until total expenses hit $5,451, at which point Medicare began paying 95 percent of additional drug costs.

The metaphor was popularized in 2002. The Alliance for Retired Americans, a union group, zeroed in on *doughnut hole* while looking for a catchy phrase that members could use when disrupting a hearing on the drug bill by the House Ways and Means Committee. Robin Toner, of *The New York Times*, reported that union protesters at the June hearing shouted "Time to stop the doughnut!" in "allusion to the coverage gap—known to health policy aficionados as a hole in the doughnut—in the Republican bill."

The phrase appears to have been coined the preceding year by Rep. Billy Tauzin (R-La.), then chairman of the House Committee on Energy and Commerce. *Congressional Daily* reported that Tauzin told reporters at a briefing on March 22, 2001, that he realized President George W. Bush had not set aside enough money in his budget to cover the proposed prescription drug benefit. Tauzin wanted to build upon a bill that the House had passed the previous year. Referring to the gap in insurance coverage, he said: "Everybody agrees there's a problem with the hole in that doughnut."

The literal *doughnut hole* is much older, of course. The earliest known example of the term in print comes from *The Boston Globe* of March 18, 1886, which ran a letter to the editor in which an anonymous correspondent posed the rhetorical question "Can a man get fat on a diet of doughnut holes?" and promptly supplied the answer: "Doughnut holes can only be introduced into the stomach by swallowing the doughnut whole."

Credit for inventing the *doughnut hole* itself usually goes to a Maine seafarer, Capt. Hanson Gregory (1831–1923). Doughnuts started out as round or nut-shaped balls of dough that did not always cook evenly. One story, probably apocryphal, has it that while sailing through a storm, steering with one hand and holding an old-style doughnut in the other, Gregory suddenly had to grab the wheel with both hands. Not wanting to toss aside the doughnut, he impaled it on one of the spokes of the wheel, and told the ship's cook to keep making doughnuts with holes for convenience's sake.

The captain himself said in an interview in *The Washington Post* in 1916 that he invented the doughnut hole while at sea about 1847, when he was 16. While chewing away at a doughnut ball with an uncooked center, he said to himself: "Why wouldn't a space inside solve the difficulty?" He experimented with strips of dough, then had an inspiration: "I took the cover off the ship's tin pepper box, and—I cut into the middle of that doughnut the first hole ever seen by mortal eyes!" Capt. Gregory's memory is still honored in his hometown of Camden, Maine, but contrary to some websites, a 23½-foot-tall marble statue of him was never erected. The statue part, at least, is a myth.

See also GAP and MEDICARE.

doves Believers in ACCOMMODATION as the route to peace, who reject the "appeasement leads to war" argument of the *hawks* (see WAR HAWKS).

Perched on the arm of Aphrodite, Greek goddess of love and beauty, the dove has been a symbol of peace and gentleness since ancient times. When the painter Pablo Picasso lent his prestige and his palette to the Communist movement, the dove was seized upon as the symbol of peace used in Communist posters and at international conferences.

In the Soviet-American confrontation over the placement of missiles on Cuban soil in 1962, the "dove versus hawk" metaphor came to the fore. In the deliberations of the Kennedy cabinet, UN Ambassador Adlai Stevenson was represented as a *dove* by reporters Stewart Alsop and Charles Bartlett; Robert Kennedy, Dean Rusk, and McGeorge Bundy were identified as the leading *hawks*. Since a firm U.S. line resulted in a Russian backdown, subsequent identification as a *dove* in this crisis was in essence an attack at unwise softness, and friends of Stevenson objected strenuously to such leaks.

Concurrently, debate on the U.S. position in Vietnam was beginning. Those who wished to extricate the U.S. from what they felt was a hopeless QUAGMIRE were labeled *doves*, and those who felt it necessary to contain Communism and resist the new "wars of national liberation" at the South Vietnamese border were called *hawks*. With many exceptions, most liberals favored what came to be known as a "dovelike position," and most conservatives, with a history of attacking liberals as SOFT ON COMMUNISM, willingly identified themselves as hawks. (Senator George Aiken of Vermont preferred to describe himself as an owl.)

In the 1966 elections, many conservative candidates found it possible to adopt far more liberal domestic positions without losing their conservative support as long as they held to a "hard line" in Vietnam, and vice versa.

Edmund Burke's address to Parliament on "conciliation with America" in 1775 made a basic point that applied to the position of the doves of the 1960s: "Terror is not always the effect of force: and an armament is not a victory. If you do not succeed, you are without recourse; for, conciliation failing, force remains; but, force failing, no further hope of reconciliation is left."

McGeorge Bundy, after he resigned as Johnson's chief adviser on national security matters to head the Ford Foundation, made a dovelike (or *dove-ish*, usually spelled *dovish*) differentiation for one so intimately identified with the hawks: "The real choice is not between 'doves' and 'hawks.' It is between those who would keep close and careful civilian control over a difficult and demanding contest, and those who would use whatever force is thought necessary by any military leader in any service." In this manner, he sought to label the center position as "dovelike," pushing *hawk* over to the extreme military-solution position. This would put the "moderate hawks" into dove's feathers, but Bundy's formulation never caught on.

Such POLARIZED positions are traditional in U.S. politics: the *hards* versus *softs*, *lily-whites* versus *black and tans*, and *doves* versus *hawks* are summed up in this analysis of the *tough-minded* and *tender-minded* by philosopher William James: "The tough think of the tender as sentimentalists and softheads. The tender feel the tough to be unrefined, callous, or brutal. Their mutual reaction is very much like that that takes place when Bostonian tourists mingle with a population like that of Cripple Creek. Each type believes the other to be inferior to itself; but disdain in the one is mingled with amusement, in the other it has a dash of fear."

Before its recent usage, *dove* was best known for the use New York Democratic Governor Al Smith made of a remark by his opponent in 1926 in which the luckless Republican said: "If I am elected Governor, I will get along with the Legislature like a cooing dove." Retorted Smith: "Had I gotten along with the Legislature like a cooing dove, there would have been no automobile regulation...the people of New York want clear-headed, strong-minded fighting men at the head of the government and not doves. Let the doves roost in the eaves of the Capitol—not in the Executive Chamber. So much for the doves ..."

Appropriately, the goddess Aphrodite is associated with two symbols: the dove and the "apple of discord."

For the British equivalents of doves, see WETS.

draft, presidential A demand by a party that a man not seeking the nomination accept it; upon rare occasion, and not recently, applies to one who did not encourage his own candidacy.

The most recent authentic draft was at the Democratic convention of 1952. At that time a reluctant Adlai Stevenson, who was President Harry Truman's early choice, was drafted by the delegates who felt uncomfortable with Tennessee Senator Estes Kefauver (who led on the first two ballots). Historian Richard Morris contended that "Stevenson, who did not seek the nomination, was the first Presidential nominee to be drafted since Garfield (1880)."

The Garfield draft (see PRESIDENTIAL FEVER) was a classic example of a man putting himself forward without appearing to do so. Supporters of former President U.S. Grant, led by party leader Roscoe Conkling, had the most convention strength; James Blaine of Maine and John Cooper of Ohio trailed close behind. Before the ballot-

ing began, a floor fight broke out over the seating of delegates who refused to take a party-loyalty pledge. Congressman James Garfield of Ohio, in a graceful speech, suggested a face-saving compromise. As he agreed to the compromise, Conkling sent Garfield a note on his potential nomination for the presidency.

The three-man deadlock lasted for 34 ballots when Wisconsin, whose votes had been scattered between Grant, Blaine, and Cooper, suddenly cast 16 votes for Garfield. Garfield jumped up to exclaim, "No man has a right, without the consent of the person voted for, to announce that person's name, and vote for him in this Convention." However, Garfield had not objected when two Pennsylvania delegates voted for him on 30 previous ballots; his sudden protestation of unavailability triggered more support. On the 36th ballot, Garfield was drafted.

FDR felt he had to seem to be drafted in 1940 by the Democratic convention, to prove he had no dictatorial ambitions and to blunt the no-third-term issue. For his technique in arranging the draft, see VOICE FROM THE SEWER. Though FDR used the word *muster* rather than *draft* when referring to military conscription, he embraced *draft* in his acceptance speech in 1940: "Only the people themselves can draft a president. If such a draft should be made upon me, I say to you, in the utmost simplicity, I will, with God's help, continue to serve ..."

As a political word, *draft* remains best known for military conscription, and the *Draft Riots* in New York during the Civil War locked the word in the lexicon. In 1966, amid Vietnam protests, students chalked walls and wore buttons that played on another meaning of the word: "Draft beer not men."

draw a line in the sand Set a limit; a dramatic figure of speech to conjure the phrase "this far, no farther."

After Saddam Hussein's Iraqi troops invaded Kuwait in 1990, President George H.W. Bush announced in a televised speech that "A line has been drawn in the sand," which, despite the passive construction, presented a vivid figurative marker of limits in the Arabian desert. *The New York Times* followed the President's usage with a headline that read "Worried Nation Backs U.S. Line in the Sand."

The infinitive phrase *to draw the line* is "to mark a limit or boundary," as in a children's game that dares opponents to cross a line. This expression may have come from the lines of farm boundaries that were plowed in medieval England or from the lines of tennis courts that were established in fourteenth-century France. The phrase first appeared in print in 1793, in the trial of Fyshe Palmer: "It is difficult...to draw the line."

The figurative *line in the sand* may have come from a literal use of the phrase. In 168 B.C. the Seleucid king Antiochus Epiphanes invaded Egypt, then ruled by the Ptolemies, but was stopped by Popillius Laenas, a Roman senator who ordered the king to turn back. When Antiochus hesitated, the Roman drew a circle in the ground around him and told the king that he would never step out of the circle until he agreed to withdraw his army. It might have been a bluff, but the king turned and took his army home to Syria.

Among the Texas legends of the Alamo, the fortified mission besieged by the Mexican army in 1836, is that of William Barret Travis, who used his sword to *draw a line in the ground* (or *sand*) and reportedly said, "Those prepared to die for freedom's cause, come across to me," and 189 of the 190 Texas fighters did; the 190th lived to tell the story.

dream ticket Politician's vision of a combination of candidates with an unbeatable appeal, simultaneously unifying the party's divergent wings; rarely comes true.

"GOP Dream Ticket," *Newsweek* headlined in 1967, "Reagan and Brooke." Dreamily, the magazine continued: "Some professional Democrats now say privately that the strongest team the GOP can field in '68 is one headed by Ronald Reagan and Edward Brooke. The Negro Senator from Massachusetts might cost the ticket some Southern votes, they admit. But these would be more than offset by the votes he

could capture for Reagan in the populous industrial states of the U.S. where elections are usually won or lost."

A dream ticket not only balances geography, ideology, age, and religion but also puts together two personalities that are famous—neither of which is ever likely to accept the other at the top of the ticket. Republicans in 1960 talked of a dream ticket of Nixon and Rockefeller, and Nixon did urge the New York governor to be his running mate; Rockefeller, as most realists predicted, turned it down. See COMPACT OF FIFTH AVENUE. (It worked for Kennedy and Johnson.)

In 1988, former President Nixon wrote a think piece for the *Christian Science Monitor* about the Democrats' choice of Massachusetts' Michael Dukakis and Texas's Lloyd Bentsen titled "The Odd Couple—Dream Ticket or Nightmare?" (He thought choosing the conservative Bentsen was smart politics.) In 2000, *The Washington Post* headlined "McCain's Resistance Doesn't Stop Talk of Kerry Dream Ticket."

The dream ticket means one that is especially strong; *a* dream ticket is one that is striking in its juxtaposition of personalities, but is PIE IN THE SKY.

drop-by. See ADVANCE MAN; FACE TIME; PULL-ASIDE.

drop-off voter See OFF-YEAR.

duck See PROVERBS AND AXIOMS, POLITICAL.

dump See JOE SMITH; KINGMAKER.

dustbin of history Relegation to oblivion; lack of historical significance or fame.

Leon Trotsky popularized the term when he shouted after the Mensheviks departing from the 1917 Second Congress of Soviets in protest at the Bolshevik seizure of power, "Go to the place where you belong from now on—the dustbin of history!" This expression, with the Russian for "dustbin" given as *musornyi yashchik*, appeared in the English translation of Trotsky's autobiography; an eyewitness, Nikolai Sukhanov, quoted Trotsky's phrase as *v sornuyu korzinu istorii*, but the meaning is the same.

Synonyms for *dustbin* are used in various translations. In 1982, for example, Ronald Reagan used the term in a London speech: "The march of freedom and democracy...will leave Marxist Leninism on the *ash heap* of history." A year later, the Soviet leader Yuri Andropov used the expression with a different synonym in the Tass translation: "Those who encroached on the integrity of our state...found themselves on the *garbage* heap of history."

Dust heap was the original term used in English by the British essayist Augustine Birrell, who coined the expression in *Obiter Dicta*, his 1887 collection of essays: "that great dust heap called 'history.'" As the Soviet Union disintegrated more than a century later, *The International Herald Tribune* provided a synonym familiar to both British and American readers in a 1991 headline: "*Scrap Heap* of History." Translations not yet tried include *trash can, dumpster, wastebasket, rubbish bin, refuse container ...*

dyed-in-the-wool An all-out partisan, proud of his party label; most often applied to ardent members of the Democratic FAITHFUL.

The expression comes from the coloring of textiles while the material is in a raw, unfinished state; wool so dyed is likely to be more colorfast than that with color added later in the process.

The use can be traced to 1830, and likely originated earlier; in current use, alliteration has consigned *dyed-in-the-wool* to Democrats, and ROCK-RIBBED to Republicans. *Whole hog*, with its Jacksonian origin, is applied mainly to Democrats, *staunch* to Republicans; HIDEBOUND belongs to extreme conservatives.

Senator Huey Long of Louisiana had some fun with the phrase. "I am a dyed-in-the-wool party man," he told the Senate in 1935. "I do not know just what party I am in right now, but I am for the party."

dynamic conservatism Eisenhower's attempt to define his approach to the economic and social needs of the nation.

The President and conservative Republican congressmen became more disillusioned with one another as his Administration drew on. He found that Democratic votes were often needed to save measures he thought necessary; the Republicans found a New Dealish tinge to many of those same measures. The result was a President who thought many of his party members were too Republican to be progressive, and a number of conservatives who found him too progressive to be a very good Republican.

Searching for a phrase in 1955 that would have the right sound and sum up his basic philosophy, Eisenhower tried out "conservative dynamism." In his speech before the finance committee of the Republican National Committee on February 17, 1955, President Eisenhower turned it around before using it: "I have said we were 'progressive moderates.' Right at the moment I rather favor the term 'dynamic conservatism.' I believe we should conserve on everything that is basic to our system. We should be dynamic in applying it to the problems of the day so that all our 165,000,000 Americans will profit from it." (A half-century later, that number had risen to 300 million.)

This term, too, failed to satisfy his centrist, or oxymoronic, desires and went the way of *progressive moderation* and *moderate progressivism*. To his once and future opponent Adlai Stevenson, this fuzzy sloganeering was the subject of a 1955 Chicago press conference: "I have never been sure what 'progressive moderation' means, or was it 'conservative progressivism'? I have forgotten and I am not sure what 'dynamic moderation' or 'moderate dynamism' means. I am not even sure what it means when one says that he is a conservative in fiscal affairs and a liberal in human affairs. I assume what it means is that you will strongly recommend the building of a great many schools to accommodate the needs of our children, but not provide the money."

dynasty The recurrence of political power in generations of a single family; previously, the passing of power among a small group of the political elite.

In the U.S., the first *dynasty* to be denounced was the Virginia Dynasty—the succession of power from Jefferson to Madison to Monroe. The Jacksonian Democrats tagged a *dynasty* label on what was then an Establishment, and on their second try for national power, broke it up.

The *dynasty* charge, sometimes called the *nepotism issue*, was an important part of the election of Benjamin Harrison, grandson of President William Henry Harrison. In 1888 the Democratic song was "Grandpa's pants won't fit Benny," and the Republican refrain went "Yes, Grandfather's hat fits Ben—fits Ben."

For his study of *American Political Dynasties*, Stephen Hess chose the following families: Adams, Lee, Livingston, Washburn, Muhlenberg, Roosevelt, Harrison, Breckenridge, Bayard, Taft, Frelinghuysen, Tucker, Stockton, Long, Lodge, and Kennedy.

Sociologist C. Wright Mills pointed out: "There are of course political dynasties in elite American politics—the Adams family being only the outstanding and best known. Yet, it can be safely said that throughout U.S. history well over half of the American political elite have come from families not previously connected with political affairs. They come more frequently from families highly placed in terms of money and position than political influence."

A startling cover of *Esquire* magazine in March 1967 capsuled the hopes and worries of many Americans about the Kennedy "dynasty." It showed four men in rocking chairs—John F. Kennedy, 35th President; Robert Kennedy, 37th President; Ted Kennedy, 38th President; and John-John Kennedy (John F.'s son), 39th President. This kind of frightening satire was long associated with the Kennedy clan. John F. Kennedy was quoted as saying: "Joe [Junior] was supposed to be the politician. When he died, I took his place. If anything happened to me, Bobby would take my place. If something happened to Bobby, Teddy would take his place."

Despite two assassinations, because of their willingness and ability to have a great many children, the Kennedys had an especially strong chance at creating a dynasty. When Mrs. Robert F. (Ethel) Kennedy had her tenth child in 1967, her mother-in-law, Rose Kennedy, commented, "If I knew there was going to be a contest, I never would have stopped at nine."

With Senator Hillary Rodham Clinton an early frontrunner for the Democratic 2008 nomination, columnist Nicholas Kristof noted that "if Mrs. Clinton were elected and served two terms, then for seven consecutive presidential terms the White House would have been in the hands of just two families." That was a thought-provoker: the elder Bush one term, the male Clinton two terms, the younger Bush two terms, and the female Clinton two terms—28 years, from 1988 to 2016—two families alternating in power. Although he thought Mrs. Clinton would make "a terrific president," the columnist argued, "That's just not the equal-opportunity democracy we aspire to."

E

eagle symbol See BALD EAGLE.

earmark As a verb, to set aside funds for a special project or purpose; as a noun, the money so designated.

In a sense, almost all government appropriations are *earmarked*. Appropriations for the Defense Department, for instance, typically specify how much money will be spent on a particular missile, plane, or weapons system. As commonly used in Congress, however, *earmark* has a narrower meaning: funds that individual senators or representatives specify be directed to projects and activities that will benefit particular people, institutions, or locations in their home constituencies. By earmarking appropriations, legislators force departments and agencies to fund projects that the president did not include in the Administration's budget request to Congress.

The practice of earmarking has mushroomed in recent years. The Congressional Research Service estimated that from Fiscal Year 1994 (the year of the Gingrich "revolution," when the GOP gained control of Congress) to Fiscal Year 2005 the number of earmarks for agriculture appropriations, for example, more than doubled.

The $388 billion Consolidated Appropriations Act for 2005 had more than 12,000 earmarks distributed throughout its nearly 1,700 pages. They ranged from such small items as $25,000 for studying the development of mariachi music in Las Vegas schools and $100,000 for a weather discovery center in Punxsutawney, Pa., home of that well-publicized groundhog, Punxsutawney Phil, to, most famously, the proposal to spend $433 million in Alaska on two BRIDGES TO NOWHERE. Many local projects are surely worthy, and a strong case can be made for local decision-making about local needs. However, most editorialists made the counter-case that the inclusion of thousands of earmarks in a huge bill, without public review, invites corruption of the sort demonstrated in 2006 by the guilty pleas of "K Street" lobbyist Jack Abramoff and two congressmen to the giving and receiving of kickbacks in return for legislative favors. See BELTWAY BANDITS.

The financial sense of *earmark* stems directly from the word's original, straightforward meaning (from 1523, *OED*) of a mark or brand in the ear of a sheep or another domestic animal to indicate ownership. The application of the term to money or other property set aside or limited to a particular purpose arose in England in the nineteenth century but seems not have become common in the U.S. until the opening decades of the twentieth. An early American example, from a 1931 statement by prohibitionist ("dry") leaders about money going to pro-liquor ("wet") leaders: "Dry Democrats should earmark their gifts to the party with the stipulation that their money shall not pay Mr. Shouse's salary [he was executive director of the Democratic National Committee] either as a wet speech-maker, or a wet statement-issuer, or pay for any other wet propaganda activities."

Earmark became popular in a congressional context as senators and representatives scrambled in the 1930s to reserve portions of Depression-era relief bills for their states and districts. "Republican plans for a fight to re turn of relief administration to the states was added today to a strong bi-partisan drive to earmark nearly half of the proposed $1,500,000,000 work relief appropriation," reported the United Press in 1936, and four years later made the connection to PORK BARREL politics: "President Roosevelt today called for quick congressional approval of the $1,111,000,000 relief appropriations and asserted that proposals to earmark the funds for specific projects approached 'pork barrel' methods of appropriation."

Abuse of *earmarks* has given the term a bad name. But much depends on who decides who gets what. When Senator Joseph Lieberman, of Connecticut, was challenged in a 2006 Democratic primary-campaign debate by anti-war Ned Lamont: "You support the earmarks, you work with the lobbyists, and that's what needs to be changed," Lieberman (who narrowly lost the primary but easily won re-election as an independent) replied with equanimity, "The earmarks are great for Connecticut." Defenders of the practice argue that control of federal spending in localities is more responsibly lodged with locally elected legislators than with "Washington bureaucrats" in the executive branch.

With Democrats taking control of Congress in 2007 pledged to "earmark reform," hopes rose for major change in the system. However, when a Michigan Republican proposed striking a $23 million earmark for a "drug intelligence" facility in the home district of Rep. Jack Murtha, a Democratic "cardinal" on the House Appropriations committee, Murtha told the upstart reformer, "I hope you don't have any earmarks in the defense appropriations bills, because they are gone and you will not get any earmarks now and forever." By year's end, 9000 earmarks studded the budget. "The gusher of earmarks was a triumph of bipartisanship," wrote George Will, "which often is a synonym for kleptocracy."

Curiously, given the controversy about *earmarks*, the glossary of words relating to Congress on the official website of the United States Senate did not acknowledge the existence of the term in 2006, skipping from *discretionary spending* to *enacted* with nary a stop in between.

Eastern Establishment A cluster of legal, financial, and communications talent centered in New York, formerly liberal Republican in politics; not an organized group but influential all the same.

Senator Robert A. Taft spoke of the Eastern Establishment when, after again losing the 1952 GOP nomination, he complained: "Every Republican candidate for president since 1936 has been nominated by the Chase National Bank." Barry Goldwater was another critic, as evidenced by his frequent, only half-jesting remark during the 1964 campaign that he would like to "saw off the Eastern seaboard" and set it adrift in the Atlantic.

Historian Arthur Schlesinger, Jr., offered an apt description of the Eastern Establishment in his Kennedy memoir, *A Thousand Days*:

> Its household deities were Henry L. Stimson and Elihu Root; its present leaders, Robert A. Lovett and John J. McCloy; its front organizations, the Rockefeller, Ford and Carnegie Foundations and the Council on Foreign Relations; its organs, *The New York Times* and *Foreign Affairs*. Its politics were predominantly Republican; but it possessed what its admirers saw as a commitment to public service and its critics as an appetite for power which impelled its members to serve Presidents of whatever political faith.

In *The Making of the President 1964*, Theodore White wrote:

> From beyond the Alleghenies, the Eastern Establishment seems to inhabit a belt that runs from Boston through Connecticut to Philadelphia and Washington. Its capital is New York, a city shrouded in symbolic words like "Wall Street," "international finance," "Madison Avenue," "Harvard," "*The New York Times*," "The Bankers Club," "Ivy League prep schools," all of which seem more sinister and suspect the farther one withdraws West or South.

Eastern Establishment is a specific political term; *establishment* alone is a general sociological term, originally coined in Great Britain by Henry Fairlie. See ANGRY YOUNG MEN. The *National Observer* objected to the overuse of the general term at the end of 1967: "If someone wishes to complain about something but hasn't a very clear idea of what, all he needs do is blame the problem on the 'establishment' and people will sagely wag their heads. ... It is one of the great blessings of America that it has no 'establishment.'" In 1987, *Newsweek* commented that "Bush's native political tribe—the Eastern-establishment wing of the G.O.P.—is nearly extinct today."

With American as its modifier, however, the noun continues in international political jargon. In January 1993, an Official Kremlin International News broadcast commented, "The American establishment is linking the success of Russia's reform and the prospects of democracy in Russia to the political fate of Boris Yeltsin." A month later, *The Times* of London wrote of "the American establishment already alarmed by Mrs. Clinton's forthright display of her political power."

Its geographic corridor of power, connected by hourly airline shuttles, goes by the acronym BOSNYWASH. See COMMUNITY.

eat crow To admit freely a mistaken prediction or erroneous choice and to offer to accept the consequences.

The San Francisco *Picayune* in 1851 printed a story that had been making the rounds about a man who boasted he could eat anything: "The bet was made, the crow was caught and nicely roasted…he took a good bite, and began to chew away.… 'Yes, I can eat a crow!… but I'll be darned if I hanker after it.'" This joke's punch line became a part of American folklore.

The political use of the phrase took hold in 1872, when a splinter group calling themselves Liberal Republicans bolted to the Democrats and persuaded them to nominate renegade Republican Horace Greeley to run against Republican President Ulysses Grant. "Mr. Greeley appears to be 'boiled crow' to more of his fellow-citizens," wrote *The Nation*, "than any other candidate for office in this or any other age…boiled crow he is to his former Republican associates; and now the Democrats are saying in a curious way that to them also he is boiled crow." By 1885, the *Magazine of American History* was saying: "'To eat crow' means to recant, or to humiliate oneself. To 'eat dirt' is nearly equivalent."

While the expression has been adopted throughout the language, it appears to have a special place in politics. The New York *World* in 1881 reprinted the original story and gave it a political base: "the delectable old story of the political sneak who, having been caught and convicted of slander and fed upon his own words, looked up piteously from the unsavory meal and murmured: 'I hev eat crow, and I kin eat crow, but I don't hanker arter crow.'" Its use in a cartoon without the complete punch line indicates its widespread use in 1900; Carl Schurz and his friends were shown eating a "silver" crow with the caption "We can eat it, but—"

In recent use, *boiled* has been dropped and the phrase used mostly about "experts" who have been wrong in political prognostications. The most poll-shaking example of this came in 1948, when Harry Truman amazed the pundits by defeating Thomas E. Dewey. As Truman and Vice President-elect Alben Barkley rode up Pennsylvania Avenue in their "home-coming" celebration, they saw a sign hung from the *Washington Post* building that read: "Mr. President, we are ready to eat crow whenever you are ready to serve it." Truman wrote in his memoirs: "I sent that great newspaper word that I did not want anyone to eat crow, that I was not elated or in a mood myself to crow over anyone."

That was a nice turn of phrase; *crow over* is another use of the image of the tough, intelligent, raucous black crow. For another use, see JIM CROW.

ecology See ENVIRONMENTALIST.

economic jargon

Stagflation "applause and acclaim awaits the creator of the newest star of economic slang: 'stagflation,'" wrote *Washington Post* reporter Robert J. Samuelson in 1971. "The word is everywhere these days—in the London *Economist*, in speeches, in newspaper columns." But no claimant to the coinage came forward; Peter Jay, financial editor of *The Times* of London and later ambassador to the U.S., used the term in a 1969 article, but thought it came from the U.S.; economists here are inclined to attribute the word to a British use. The word describes a situation of unrelenting inflation combined with low (stagnant) economic growth and high unemployment—often called "the worst of both worlds," just the opposite of the *Goldilocks economy* (with the porridge "just right.")

Nixonomics: A pejorative term used to label the economic policy of the Nixon

Administration, coined by Walter Heller in the summer of 1969 and popularized by Larry O'Brien, chairman of the Democratic National Committee. O'Brien's definition: "Nixonomics means that all the things that should go up—the stock market, corporate profits, real spendable income, productivity—go down, and all the things that should go down—unemployment, prices, interest rates—go up." (The neologism had been independently suggested to Nixon by this writer in early 1969 as a catchphrase to replace the dreary *gradualism*, but was turned down as too contrived.) See -NOMICS.

Liquidity crisis: Along with *credit crunch*, this describes a lack of ready cash in banks for lending to companies. In the summer of 1970, with the Federal Reserve restraining the growth of the money supply to combat inflation, there were fears this would lead to a drying up of the funds needed for the conduct of business; at a White House dinner at that time, Federal Reserve Chairman Arthur Burns told a group of businessmen in plain terms, "There will be no liquidity crisis," and there was not. In the summer of 2007, when a downturn in housing revealed excessive risk in subprime mortgage lending, the Fed under Chairman Ben Bernanke moved swiftly to make money available to banks, in order to avert a liquidity crisis. The phrase used to describe the situation was that the credit market had "seized up," using the metaphor of muscular contraction or more serious physical convulsion.

Disintermediation: This word was popularized in 1969, and again in 1971, by Federal Reserve Governor Andrew Brimmer and Assistant Budget Director Maurice Mann. When interest rates are rising and the rates that may be paid by banks and savings and loan associations are restricted by legal ceilings, investors shift their funds from banks and S&Ls to bonds and other financial instruments that pay higher rates. *Intermediation* is the process by which lenders use an intermediary in passing funds to a borrower; an individual puts his money in a bank, and the bank lends it to a homebuyer. *Disinterme-*

diation cuts out the middleman, or bank, as the lender lends his money directly to the borrower by purchasing a bond.

See BAFFLEGAB; DEAD CAT BOUNCE; HOLD THE LINE; INFLATION; GAME PLAN; JAWBONING; NEW ECONOMICS; GUIDELINES (GUIDEPOSTS); WE ARE ALL … ; SNAKE IN THE TUNNEL; HIGH COST OF LIVING; DOUBLE DIGIT.

economic   royalists   FDR's derogation of those with great wealth who, he warned, hoped to control the activities of government.

In his acceptance of renomination at the 1936 Democratic convention in Philadelphia, Mr. Roosevelt said: "The economic royalists complain that we seek to overthrow the institution of America. What they really complain of is that we seek to take away their power."

The speech was written by Samuel I. Rosenman and Stanley High, although Judge Rosenman gives credit for the phrase—much repeated thereafter—to Mr. High. However, FDR fund-raiser Sidney Weinberg of Goldman Sachs recalled that *economic royalist* was originally suggested by Robert Jackson, who later became a Supreme Court Justice.

The phrase awakened memories of MALEFACTORS OF GREAT WEALTH, *robber barons*, and VESTED INTERESTS.

In 1977 President Carter lambasted oil-industry lobbyists for "the greatest rip-off in history" in opposing his energy proposals. His selection of an amorphous, faceless villain—rather than an opponent like Louisiana Senator Russell Long—recalled the FDR tactic to many. "A President enters a slanging match," editorialized the *Washington Star*, "with the 'economic royalists' of the moment at his own risk, although most Democratic chief executives find the temptation to do so irresistible."

See CLASS WARFARE.

edifice complex A monumental desire by a politician to leave behind great, expensive buildings.

When the Albany Mall was under construction in the sixties, New York Governor Nelson Rockefeller came under fire for spending too much taxpayer revenue on Ozymandian buildings. The governor, who in his youth helped manage Rockefeller Center in New York City, was accused of having an *edifice complex*.

In a 1990 interview about his record, New York Governor Mario Cuomo said, "If I had wanted to be the guy with the edifice complex... I could have talked only about the state university building I've rebuilt and the roads and bridges I've rebuilt."

The pun is, of course, a play on *Oedipus complex*, the yearning a child feels toward a parent of the opposite sex.

effect When used as the second element in a phrase, a change made in something because of its being studied.

Scientific parlance has contributed several phrases employing *effect* to the study of politics.

The *Heisenberg effect*, formally known as the *Heisenberg uncertainty principle*, came from the German physicist Werner Karl Heisenberg, who died in 1976. Applications of his effect in financial marketing and media studies led to its political usage. The columnist Richard Reeves applied it to President Jimmy Carter's activities in 1977: "No one does or can do the same things onstage that he does unobserved. It's the popularized Heisenberg effect: the act of observing inevitably changes the process under observation."

Opinion polls taken immediately after the first Reagan-Mondale debate in 1984 showed Mondale the winner by a small margin; the discussion of the debate by political commentators vastly increased that margin in later polls. To explain the increase, George Church wrote in *Time* magazine, "This seemed to be a political application of what in physics is known as the Heisenberg uncertainty principle: the very act of measuring a phenomenon changes the phenomenon being measured in such a way as to make future readings unpredictable."

The *Hawthorne effect* offers a similar conclusion. This effect came from experiments during the 1920s at the Western Electric Company's Hawthorne Works of Cicero, Illinois. The performance of work-

ers, according to this effect, will be affected by the study of that performance. When lights were turned up, worker productivity increased; when lights were lowered, productivity again increased, primarily from the effect on workers of being included in the experiment.

effete snobs An Agnevian attack on the arrogance of pseudo-intellectuals that backfired.

"A spirit of national masochism prevails," Vice President Agnew told a dinner at New Orleans on October 19, 1969, "encouraged by an effete corps of impudent snobs who characterize themselves as intellectuals."

Headline writers dropped "corps of impudent" to compress the epithet to *effete snobs*, which is how it is remembered today. One reason the phrase caused such a fierce reaction was that many readers interpreted *effete* to mean "effeminate," which is not its meaning—"enervated," "wrung out," "intellectually barren" define the term properly and fit the context of his remarks.

The New Orleans speech was a lengthy, fairly dull exposition of the Nixon Administration's foreign and economic policies; however, the opening—including the controversial phrase—was prepared by the Vice President and gripped the audience. In it, he tried to blunt the expected countercharge of anti-intellectualism: "Persuasion through speeches and books is too often discarded for disruptive demonstrations aimed at bludgeoning the unconvinced into action.... Subtlety is lost, and fine distinctions based on acute reasoning are carelessly ignored in a headlong jump to a predetermined conclusion. Life is visceral rather than intellectual, and the most visceral practitioners of life are those who characterize themselves as intellectuals."

However, the term was used by Agnew critics as an example of POLARIZATION, "escalating the rhetoric," and—as expected—anti-intellectualism.

The former CBS newsman John Hart in 2000 sent along this bit of dialogue in Margery Allingham's *Death of a Ghost*, a novel written in 1934: "Fustian, did you write this disgusting piece of effete snobbery?"

Hart asked: "Was somebody reading old English mysteries?" Answer: no, "great minds think alike." (That quotation, repeated by plagiarists for four centuries, is cited in the *Oxford Dictionary of Proverbs* as the 1618 "good wits jump," with *jump*'s obsolete meaning of "agree," or "think alike.")

egghead An intellectual; a highbrow. When used derogatively, an effete, bookish person with intellectual pretensions; when used affirmatively, a person with brains.

The term, which dates back to the early 1900s, appears in a circa-1918 letter by the poet Carl Sandburg. The letter in the Toledo, Ohio, public library is from the poet to his former newspaper boss, Negley Dakin Cochran: "'Egg heads' is the slang here for editorial writers here.—I have handed in five editorials on Russia and two on the packers, voicing what 95 percent of the readers of The News are saying on the [trolley] cars and in the groceries and saloons but they have been ditched for hot anti-bolshevik stuff.... At that it isn't so much the policies of the papers as the bigotry and superstition and flunkeyism of the Egg Heads."

Stewart Alsop, in his syndicated column, reported in September 1952:

> After [Adlai] Stevenson's serious and rather difficult atomic energy speech in Hartford, Conn., this reporter remarked to a rising young Connecticut Republican that a good many intelligent people, who would be considered normally Republican, obviously admired Stevenson. "Sure," was the reply, "all the eggheads love Stevenson. But how many eggheads do you think there are?"

Alsop went on to define the word as "what the Europeans would call 'intellectuals' ... [someone] interested in ideas and in the words used to express those ideas." Years later he revealed that the "rising young Connecticut Republican" was his brother, John (not the columnist Joseph): "John says the word sprang unbidden into his mind, with the mental image of a thin outer shell with mushy white stuff underneath." *Newsweek* quoted the source, John Alsop, as recalling "Egghead ... dredged up out of my unconscious ... is a visual picture

of speech, tending to depict a large, oval head, smooth, faceless, unemotional but a little haughty and condescending."

The Baltimore *Sun* observed: "Writers on the lower levels of the trade have sought in vain for a new way of saying 'highbrow.' 'Loftydome' was about the best they could do, until 'egghead' came along."

Stevenson tried to laugh it off. A month before the 1952 election brought Dwight Eisenhower to the White House, he paraphrased the famous conclusion to the Communist Manifesto with "Eggheads of the world, unite; you have nothing to lose but your yolks." But, as the MAN ON THE WEDDING CAKE hurt Dewey, and the BAREFOOT BOY FROM WALL STREET hurt Willkie, *egghead* hurt Stevenson.

The familiar image had long gone unnamed, but was nonetheless etched in many minds. From the huge, bald head of the scientist in the comic strip *Buck Rogers* to the description of an intellectual by Mao Zedong ("swollen in head, weak in legs, sharp in tongue but empty in belly"), a stereotype existed of a balding, top-heavy head bulging with brains and shaped like an egg. For a while, subdivisions were made of label that included "scrambled eggheads" for the confused variety to "hard-boiled eggheads" for the more tough-minded type. President Eisenhower, when asked about a Latin motto on his desk—*Suaviter in modo fortiter in re* (Gentle in manner, strong indeed)—smiled, "That proves I'm an egghead."

In the late '60s Alabama Governor George C. Wallace sharpened the top of the egg to label his target "pointed-headed professors." See DIME'S WORTH OF DIFFERENCE; SEND THEM A MESSAGE.

eight millionaires and a plumber Description of the original Eisenhower cabinet.

In selecting his cabinet, President Dwight Eisenhower turned for administrative talent to the business community. Democrats naturally sniped at the business-weighted cabinet. When it came to choosing a Labor Secretary, Eisenhower later wrote: "I hoped to find a satisfactory man from the ranks of labor itself. Long before, the old Department of Commerce and Labor had been divided, and Commerce was now traditionally headed by a businessman; I thought as a counterbalance the Labor Department should be headed by one actually experienced in the labor movement."

Adviser Herbert Brownell suggested Martin Durkin, a Chicago Democrat, head of the Journeyman Plumbers and Steamfitters Union. The contrast of Durkin with the other cabinet members only served to accentuate the business orientation; Richard Strout, under the pseudonym "TRB" in *The New Republic*, wrote in the December 15, 1952, issue: "The next four years may see the biggest lobby drive since Grant's day to loot the public domain, reverse history and crown big business. Ike has picked a cabinet of eight millionaires and a plumber."

The phrase caught the media fancy; writing a follow-up on February 2, 1953, Strout observed: "We often ask ourselves how much influence a weekly column like ours has, and we still don't know the answer, though it is curious to note the following. In the December 15 issue of this magazine we commented casually, 'Ike has picked a cabinet of eight millionaires and one plumber.' The result was rather astonishing. We find the comment still traveling outward after being included by such excellent columnists as Alsop, Childs, Stokes, Fleeson and goodness knows how many others; it bounded the Atlantic into the London *Economist* and bounced back to America again in the *St. Louis Post-Dispatch*. Well, good luck, little quip—keep flying! Everybody in Washington, of course, likes to see his ephemeral comment take into the air and buzz away; no question of paternity is ever asked."

Asked by the lexicographer about its paternity in 1977, Mr. Strout recalled: "It came to me in the bar of the National Press Club and I carefully husbanded it, knowing that if I loosed it there it would be around before I had reached 14th Street."

Oddly, the phrase is now usually misquoted as "nine" millionaires and a plumber, perhaps because of the growth of the cabinet.

Eisenhower doctrine See DOCTRINES.

Eisenhower syntax Convoluted extemporaneous remarks; ad libs that appear confused.

Spoken English differs from written English. Good secretaries rephrase their bosses' dictation before presenting it for signature. John Steinbeck was one of the rare authors who occasionally dictate rather than write or type their prose. Journalists have often "covered" for extemporaneous speakers by adding punctuation for clarification and even rearranging sentences. (The preceding paragraph of four consecutive declarative sentences is in "spoken" English; written prose should be more fluid.)

Dwight Eisenhower had good days and bad days with unprepared remarks. His off-the-cuff addition to a speech before the American Society of Newspaper Editors in 1956 was a model of clarity; in many press conferences, however, the written transcript was both fuzzy and contorted. (Earlier Presidents refused to permit direct quotation, and reporters often edited their sentences.)

Oliver Jensen, later an editor of *American Heritage*, rewrote the GETTYSBURG ADDRESS as Eisenhower might have ad-libbed it, satirizing both Eisenhower syntax and vocabulary:

I haven't checked these figures, but 87 years ago, I think it was, a number of individuals organized a governmental setup here in this country. ... Well, now of course we are dealing with this big difference of opinion, civil disturbance you might say, although I don't like to appear to take sides or name any individuals. ... But if you look at the overall picture of this, we can't pay any tribute—we can't sanctify this area—we can't hallow, according to whatever individual creeds or faiths or sort of religious outlooks are involved, like I said about this particular area. It was those individuals themselves, including the enlisted men—very brave individuals—who have given this religious character to the area. ... We have to make up our minds right here and now, as I see it, they didn't put out all that blood, perspiration and—well, that they didn't just make a dry run here, that all of us, under God, that is, the God of our choice, shall beef up this idea about freedom and liberty and those kind of arrangements, and that government of all individuals, by all individuals and for the individuals shall not pass out of the world picture.

Columnist Arthur Krock observed that this kind of criticism dimmed the Eisenhower glory. "One reason is that glory withers in the controversial fires of politics. Others were supplied by the General himself: his frequent revelations at news conferences that he had not done his homework, his often blind and always labyrinthian syntax when extemporizing. These were gleefully seized on by the articulate 'liberals' who were his principal critics to lampoon him as an OLD FOGY ..."

It may be surprising to some that Eisenhower was a sharp and accurate editor of written copy; speech texts corrected by him show sensible tightening and clarifying. His first official words, following a brief prayer, spoken after taking his oath of office on January 20, 1953, were: "The world and we have passed the midway point of a century of continuing challenge." He had written on the margin of a draft: "I hate this sentence. Who challenges whom? About what?" He resisted the rhetoric, then agreed to use it.

The author kept a copy of an Eisenhower statement in 1952 after the General had edited it in pencil. Here is a sentence I drafted during the presidential campaign: "The Federal Government can make a tremendous contribution through the example it sets in how it conducts its business." Here is how candidate Eisenhower tightened it: "The Federal Government can make tremendous contributions including the example it sets in the conduct of its business." Nothing drastic, but sound editing.

Reporter Tom Wicker, reviewing William Manchester's *Death of a President*, about the Kennedy assassination, showed that rambling ad libs were not confined to the Eisenhower era: "Kennedy gets only the best of verbs, adjectives and similes. Thus, a certain day was 'as clear and crisp as a Kennedy order'; this may be an allowable descriptive, but not to those who tried to decipher a large part of the Kennedy syntax as recorded at many news conferences."

elder statesman An older politician or aging adviser to presidents, who is treated with public respect and sometimes veneration.

"You can always get the truth," said abolitionist Wendell Phillips in 1860, "from an American statesman after he has turned seventy, or given up all hope of the Presidency."

As a dead or retired reporter becomes a *journalist*, many politicians who leave the arena become known as *statesmen*; and those who grow old in this often active limbo are sometimes dubbed *elder statesmen*.

Like PUNDIT, the phrase was popularized in the U.S. by *Time* magazine. An early use in that publication was September 16, 1929: "Last spring Elihu Root, gray Elder Statesman of U.S. diplomacy, good friend of Herbert Hoover, went to Geneva ..." Best known of the breed was financier Bernard Baruch, who in his Wall Street days gave new respectability to the word *speculator*. A typical accolade was Arthur Krock's in 1943:

> Though others have titles, he has none. Yet he is the President's counselor, philosopher and guide.... He is an honored visitor at the Pentagon, the Navy Department, the Department of State.... His rooms at the Carleton and the Shoreham, and the bench in Lafayette Square where he likes to warm his old bones in the sunshine, are the gathering places for all those with problems growing out of the State's business.... He is the nation's elder statesman. He is Bernard Mannes Baruch.

Baruch himself defined what stylists call the bogus title this way: "An elder statesman is somebody old enough to know his own mind and keep quiet about it." But President Harry Truman had a more acerbic view of B.M.B. "He had always seen to it that his suggestions and recommendations, not always requested by the President, would be given publicity.... Baruch is the only man to my knowledge who has built a reputation on a self-assumed unofficial status as 'adviser.'"

Elder statesmen are occasionally PARTY ELDERS as well; Harry Truman and Herbert Hoover, in their later years, qualified for both. But normally, an elder statesman is ABOVE POLITICS; he is turned to for advice and photographs by Presidents who wish to show the breadth and depth of their brain-picking, and he lends his prestige to projects like international arms control, efficiency in government, and GLOBAL WARMING.

Eleanor Roosevelt, writing about her husband's soul-searching before deciding to run for a third term, showed how the elder-statesman role has a powerful appeal: "it became clearly evident to me, from little things he said at different times, that he would really like to be in Hyde Park, and that the role of elder statesman appealed to him. He thought he would enjoy being in a position to sit back and offer suggestions and criticisms." Unlike Theodore Roosevelt, who left the presidency and then changed his mind about being an elder statesman, Franklin Roosevelt decided that the edge of power was no substitute for the center of power.

electability See SEND THEM A MESSAGE; CAN'T WIN.

elect a leader, not a lover See DIVORCE ISSUE.

electioneer To campaign crassly; to appear to intrigue or try too hard to get votes.

"All the world here is occupied in electioneering," wrote Thomas Jefferson in 1789, immediately defining the word he had just coined: "in choosing or being chosen." Nearly a decade later, his fellow Founder and political opponent agreed: "The whole judicial authority," wrote John Adams in 1798, "as well as the executive, will be employed, perverted and prostituted to the purpose of electioneering."

From those revolutionary times to these, the verb continues to bear the connotation of "too narrowly a partisan approach to the polls." Its tone of disapproval—with the last syllable ending *eer*, as in *profiteer* or *domineer*—is reinforced today by signs posted some fifty yards from voting places by Boards of Elections that read: "No Electioneering between this point and the Polls."

Criticizing President Lyndon Johnson's diplomacy, reporters Edward Weintal and Charles Bartlett set forth their account of a meeting between the President and the British Prime Minister, Harold Wilson: "The President blasted the Prime Minister in no uncertain terms. 'I won't have you electioneering on my doorstep,' he stormed. 'Every time you get in trouble in Parliament you run over here with your shirttail hanging out ...'"

electronic eavesdropping See TAPS; BUG.

elephant, Republican Symbol of the Grand Old Party.

An 1860 issue of *Railsplitter* and an 1872 cartoon in *Harper's Weekly* connected elephants with Republicans, but it was the cartoonist Thomas Nast—creator of the DONKEY, DEMOCRATIC in 1870—who provided the GOP with its permanent symbol in *Harper's Weekly* on November 7, 1874.

Two unconnected events led to the birth of the Republican elephant. James Gordon Bennett's *New York Herald* raised the cry of "Caesarism" in connection with the possibility of a third-term try for President Ulysses S. Grant. The issue was taken up by Democratic politicians in 1874, halfway through Grant's second term and just before the midterm elections, and helped disaffect Republican voters. While the illustrated journals were depicting Grant wearing a crown, the *Herald* involved itself in another circulation-builder in an entirely different, nonpolitical area. This was the Central Park Menagerie Scare of 1874, a delightful hoax perpetrated by the *Herald*. They ran a story, totally untrue, that the animals in the zoo had broken loose and were roaming the wilds of New York's Central Park in search of prey.

Cartoonist Thomas Nast took these two examples of *Herald* enterprise and put them together in a cartoon titled "The Third-Term Panic" for *Harper's Weekly*. He showed an ass (symbolizing the *Herald*, as well as the Democrats) wearing a lion's skin (the scary prospect of Caesarism) frightening away the other animals in the forest (Central Park). His caption quoted a familiar fable: "'An Ass, having put on a Lion's skin, roamed about in the Forest, and amused himself by frightening all the foolish Animals he met with in his wanderings'—Shakespeare or Bacon."

One of the foolish animals in the 1874 cartoon was an elephant, representing the Republican vote—not the party, the vote—which was being frightened away from its normal ties by the phony scare of Caesarism. In a subsequent cartoon a year later, Nast showed the Republican elephant with its trunk raised in triumph, trampling the "reform" signs of New York's Tammany Hall. Other cartoonists picked up the symbol, and the elephant soon ceased to be the vote and became the party itself; the jackass, now referred to more respectably as a donkey, made a natural transition from representing the *Herald* to representing the Democratic party.

Why the choice of an elephant? New York State Senator N. A. Elsberg in Francis Curtis' 1904 book, *The Republican Party*, explained: "Among the elephant's known characteristics are cleverness and unwieldiness. He is an animal easy to control until he is aroused; but when frightened or stirred up, he becomes absolutely unmanageable. Here we have all the characteristics of the Republican vote ..."

A less sympathetic explanation came from Adlai Stevenson: "The elephant has a thick skin, a head full of ivory, and as everyone who has seen a circus parade knows, proceeds best by grasping the tail of its predecessor."

Eleventh Commandment "Thou Shalt Not Speak Ill of Fellow Republicans."

When Dr. Gaylord E. Parkinson, a San Diego obstetrician, became California State Republican Chairman, he inherited a party that had been torn apart with internecine warfare every two years. Just before the contest between actor Ronald Reagan and San Francisco Mayor George Christopher for the Republican gubernatorial nomination in 1966, Parkinson laid down the rule that he named the *Eleventh Commandment*. Reagan, who had most to lose in a bitter battle and whose strategy was to "unify the party behind a candidate who can win," accepted the rule with alacrity; Christopher followed along and never really raised the "inexperience" issue against the actor.

The term may also be used to modify a noun. In the 1988 primaries, Vice President George H.W. Bush announced his intention not to badmouth Bob Dole. Said Bush: "I'm going back to being the old George Bush. I'm going to be the nice, benign guy that I was, an 11th-commandment guy; never say anything bad about another Republican and all that stuff."

Party chairmen traditionally try to heal breaches in primaries before they become so irreparable as to make a nomination valueless. Boss Frank Hague of Jersey City, plumping for Al Smith against FDR for the Democratic nomination in 1932, declared that Franklin Roosevelt would not carry a single state east of the Mississippi. FDR's manager, Jim Farley, made a mild reply, calculated to win the respect of the professionals: "Governor Roosevelt's friends have not come to Chicago to criticize, cry down or defame any Democrat from any part of the country."

Calling a truism a *commandment*, or endowing a fiat with commandment status, gives a jocular lift to any political advice. In July 1977 Vernon Jordan, head of the National Urban League, criticized President Carter for failing to remember his strong black support at the polls, for "not living up to the first commandment of politics—help those who help you."

elitism Leadership by an aristocracy—whether of the intellectual, the wealthy, the tastemaking, the meritorious, or the merely powerful.

In the Nixon Administration attempt to identify and rally a cross-party SILENT MAJORITY, a useful bête noire in 1970 was *elitism*. (That use of the French term for "black beast" instead of the choice of the plain word *villain* is an example of literary elitism.) In 1968 Alabama Governor George Wallace had successfully exploited the resentment of lower-middle-class voters against unseen forces in faraway Washington that manipulated their lives (see SEND THEM A MESSAGE); in the midterm congressional campaign President Nixon directed Vice President Spiro Agnew to "crack those elitists" who ran the power centers most critical of his

Administration: the Establishment media, the Ivy League academy, the liberal foundations. This was an attempt at a turnabout: leftist political philosophy, which espoused the redistribution of income for the benefit of the greatest number of people, could be attacked as being guided by a small and well-to-do clique (whose children were usually sent to private schools). The target was the liberal leadership, not the millions of recipients of entitlements that flowed from liberalism's liberality.

The word, which had been popularized in sociology by C. Wright Mills (see POWER ELITE), gained its *-ist* and *-ism* forms in the early fifties in the writings of sociologist David Riesman. Sigmund Freud, he wrote in 1950, "shared with…Nietzsche and Carlyle elements of an elitist position." Although some in the rising conservative elite preferred the term *illuminati*, the word *elitist* soon became a kind of imprecation. Defenders of the idea of intellectual leadership (see EGGHEAD) shied away from the now-pejorative *elite* and substituted *meritocracy*, not always a synonym.

In 1972 the editors of the pre-neoconservative quarterly *The Public Interest* surveyed the emergence of the new sociopoliticological favorite:

> *Elitist*, of course, is closest to the surface. Perhaps it has already lost its esoteric quality. Who knows, any longer, that it derives from Mosca, Michels, and Pareto, and achieved a bastardized American birth through the midwifery of Harold Lasswell, James Burnham, and C. Wright Mills. But in a populist society, *elitist* is a handy stick for all sides and for all seasons. In the *New York Times* Op-Ed page, that elitist sounding board for the vox populi, Jeffrey St. John denounces "public broadcasting" as appealing only to elitists, and concludes that therefore the U.S. Government should not provide a subsidy. In the *Village Voice*, where the radical chic meet to read and devour each other, Jimmy Breslin calls his fellow McGovern delegates who had voted for Sissy Farenthold instead of Tom Eagleton "elitist bastards."

In the 1992 presidential campaign, William Kristol, chief of staff to Vice President Dan Quayle, introduced in his boss's name the term *cultural elite*; in what some conservatives considered a reach for readers in the illuminati, *Newsweek* promptly published its choices for that list.

empowerment The gaining of influence and authority to the point of control; the comforting collection of clout.

This forceful noun gained political and economic meaning after its adoption by the Students for a Democratic Society in the '60s. Especially resonant among blacks, the word was used in 1976 by Vernon E. Jordan Jr., when he headed the National Urban League: "That goes to economic security, income maintenance, economic empowerment—the real basic issues of equal opportunity."

In politics, the term has been applied in voter registration as *electoral empowerment*. Pat Caddell, the political pollster who advised Gary Hart during the Democratic primaries of 1984, offered the word in a rueful commentary after Republican Ronald Reagan's re-election: "The issue was the empowerment of a generation. …"

The elder George Bush employed the noun in 1990, during an awards ceremony in the Rose Garden. "Each of these seven Americans," said Bush, "provides a definition of the word that I have learned to respect so much, learned from Jack Kemp—empowerment." Kemp, Bush's Secretary of Housing and Urban Development, was foremost among the word's supporters in Washington, urging enterprise zones, school vouchers, and tax credits for the poor; he called himself a "bleeding heart conservative." Kemp's own definition of *empowerment*: "Giving people the opportunity to gain greater control over their own destiny through access to assets of private property, jobs and education."

empty chair The little candidate who isn't there: a phrase dramatizing an opponent's refusal to debate.

In 1924, while running for vice president on Robert La Follette's Progressive ticket, Burton K. Wheeler attacked President Calvin Coolidge in a way Wheeler described in his *Yankee From the West*:

> In Des Moines, I hit on an original showmanship gimmick. The hall was jammed to the rafters…

I said, "You people have a right to know how a candidate for President stands on issues, and so far President Coolidge has not told you where he stands on anything...so I am going to call him before you tonight and ask him to take this chair and tell me where he stands." People in the auditorium began to crane their necks to see if Coolidge really was somewhere on the premises. I pulled a vacant chair and addressed it as though it had an occupant. "President Coolidge," I began, "tell us where you stand on Prohibition." I went on with rhetorical questions in this vein, pausing after each for a short period. Then I wound up: "There, my friends, is the usual silence that emanates from the White House." The crowd roared in appreciation.

In 1949 the international lawyer John Foster Dulles ran against the former New York Governor Herbert Lehman for the Senate, but he was unable to draw Lehman into debate. To make his point, Dulles traveled with a "prop"—an empty chair he debated in lieu of Lehman, who won the seat.

In the four-man gubernatorial race in New York in 1966 (Rockefeller, O'Connor, Roosevelt, Jr., and Adams), negotiations for a debate appeared interminable to Frank O'Connor's representative, Peter Straus. Straus threatened John Trubin, Rockefeller's representative and a law partner of Senator Jacob Javits, that O'Connor would go on alone and debate an empty chair. Trubin shook his head. "That's against FCC regulations," he said with a straight face. "This is a four-man race. You'd have to debate *three* empty chairs."

The symbol is not limited to the United States. Gaby Rado of Independent Television News reported in June 1991 on Soviet newspapers and their criticism of Boris Yeltsin: "Yeltsin's also been criticized for refusing to take part in last night's pre-election TV debate. An empty chair was pointedly left for him on the studio floor." See EQUAL TIME.

empty suit See STRAW MAN.

end game See EXIT STRATEGY.

enemies list Originally, Nixon White House counsel John Dean's roster of Administration opponents to be harassed or uninvited; now used as a counter-attack by any person considering himself targeted for criticism by those in power.

"This memorandum," Dean wrote on August 16, 1971, "addresses the matter of how we can maximize the fact of our incumbency in dealing with persons known to be active in their opposition to our Administration. Stated a bit more bluntly—how we can use the available federal machinery to screw our political enemies."

George Bell, an aide to presidential counsel Charles Colson, compiled a list in response to Dean's memo, which Colson forwarded to Dean under the heading "Opponents List." However, when Dean revealed his own memo and its answer in testimony before the Senate Watergate Committee, he renamed it an "enemies list"; the word *enemies*, which he had used in his original memo, carried a far more savage connotation than *opponents*. Curiously, the revulsion at this device exempted its author, Dean, and concentrated on Nixon, Colson, and the rest of "the President's men" (a play on "all the king's men" in the Humpty Dumpty tale). Among those opponents on the *enemies list* were a fund-raiser (Arnold Picker of United Artists Corp.), a large contributor (Howard Stein of the Dreyfus Corporation), a labor leader (Leonard Woodcock of the United Auto Workers), a black congressman (John Conyers, D-Mich.), and "a real media enemy"(Daniel Schorr, CBS).

Enemies list became one of the phrases associated with the abuses of power charged during the Watergate investigation. Colson argued that it had been compiled "for the use of the social office" to exclude opponents from White House dinners, but it was widely assumed that the underlying nefarious intent was to use the power of government to punish political adversaries. William Sullivan, a former deputy to J. Edgar Hoover at the FBI, insisted that the freeze-out idea "originated in the Bureau. In the Bureau it was called the 'No Contact List'... On the No Contact List went all individuals who had criticized the Bureau or Hoover personally."

The phrase has become generic, applying to any targets (under HIT LIST, see FDR's "sinners' roll") of political or economic retribution. In September 1977, when supporters in the Senate of President Jimmy

Carter's natural-gas program were filibustering against deregulation—and were unexpectedly abandoned by the White House—Senator James Abourezk (D-S.D.) cracked: "This Administration doesn't have an enemies list—it has a friends list."

As Watergate memories recede, the phrase has been used in gentle spoofs. On April 10, 1978, *The New York Times* editorialized: "We have been compiling an enemies list: uppity words." The ten on the list were *absent* ("when disguised as a synonym for 'without'"), FEEDBACK, *governance* ("except when accompanied by ELDER STATESMEN"), *hold harmless, in place, massive* ("except in case of nuclear attack"), OPTION, *posture, thrust*, and *viable*.

engage in personalities Phrase used to evade personal political clashes; always disappointing to journalists and bloggers.

Most closely associated with Dwight Eisenhower, this rather formal locution is consistent with his frequent ABOVE POLITICS stance. At one of the early press conferences of his 1952 campaign, he was reminded of his comment that the loss of China must not be repeated, and asked on whom he would pin responsibility for that loss. "I am not … going to engage in personalities in anything I have to say. I believe in certain principles, certain procedures and methods that I will discuss with anybody at any time. I am not going to talk personalities."

In office, Eisenhower held to his rule. Looking over a draft of a presidential message to Congress that implied criticism of some congressional leader's motives, he is reported to have said, "Look here, you and I can argue issues all day and it won't affect our friendship, but the minute I question your motives you will never forgive me." A good many Democrats questioned Eisenhower's motives in refusing to tangle with Senator Joseph McCarthy in the tumult of MCCARTHYISM. In his memoirs, Eisenhower answered this criticism: "McCarthyism was a much larger issue than McCarthy. This was the truth that I constantly held before me as I listened to the many exhortations that I should 'demolish' the Senator him-

self. … Lashing back at one man, which is easy enough for a President, was not as important to me as the long-term value of restraint, the due process of law, and the basic rights of free men." See PHILIPPIC.

In his informal memoir, *At Ease*, he wrote: "I make it a practice to avoid hating anyone. If someone's been guilty of despicable actions toward me, I used to write his name on a piece of scrap paper, drop it in the lowest drawer of my desk, and say to myself: 'That finishes the incident … and that fellow.' The drawer became over the years a sort of private wastebasket for crumbled-up spite and discarded personalities."

The phrase, as it stands, is confusing; it is a compression of "engage in a criticism of personalities," and really means "You won't get me in the gutter with that guy."

enlightened self-interest The theory that actions taken seemingly at variance with personal gain can ultimately benefit society, including the individual making the sacrifice.

Self-interest dates to the mid-1600s, primarily in religious contexts condemning sinful self-absorption. Edmund Burke, the Irish-born political writer and British statesman, used the longer phrase in his 1790 *Reflections on the Revolution in France*. In refusing to support the French Revolution, Burke—who dared to sympathize with Marie Antoinette—wrote of "an enlightened self-interest, which, when well understood, they tell us, will identify with an interest more enlarged and publick."

Within a decade the longer term was being used to rationalize personal benefit or profit. *Farmer's Magazine* in 1801 wrote of "an enlightened sense of self-interest." In this context, with *enlightened* as a modifier, the phrase can suggest bowing to persuasion or pressure. George Beall, a Baltimore attorney and former prosecutor, told *The Washington Post* in 1977 about business deals being cut with cooperating witnesses. According to Beall, those witnesses cooperated out of "enlightened self-interest. It's not a very nice business—it's a dirty business."

On Cable News Network in 1992, the enlightening phrase was used by Michael

Young, spokesman of the United States delegation to an environmental summit: "It's enlightened self-interest that will produce precisely the kinds of technical breakthroughs that we need to save the environment. Business is part of the problem, but business is also a very good part of the potential solution."

Enlightened is also a political modifier of nouns that might otherwise draw criticism. In 1989, former Senator Gary Hart proposed "enlightened engagement" justifying selective intervention to those who, a generation ago, opposed Vietnam involvement. The elder Bush's Secretary of State, James Baker III, unaware of the Democratic source, picked up the term in speeches.

entangling alliances A phrase of Jefferson's that is threaded through American history, most often used to justify a policy of ISOLATIONISM.

President George Washington, who many people think first used *entangling alliances*, only came close to using the phrase in his Farewell Address in 1796: "It is our true policy to steer clear of permanent alliance with any portion of the foreign world." In the same speech he also said: "Why, by interweaving our destiny with that of any part of Europe, *entangle* our peace and prosperity in the toils of European ambition, rivalship, interest, humor, or caprice?"

Two years later, Thomas Jefferson wrote to Thomas Lomax: "Commerce with all nations, *alliance with none*, should be our motto." He had lost the presidential election of 1796 to John Adams, but by running second became the Vice President. Jefferson ran again and won in 1800, and in his inaugural address in 1801, reworked that idea derogating alliances, this time using Washington's pejorative word *entangling*, calling for "Peace, commerce, and honest friendship, with all nations; *entangling alliances* with none."

Jefferson's crystallization of Washington's point became a rock of American foreign policy for over a century. When Woodrow Wilson tried to persuade Americans to accept the League of Nations, Wilson addressed himself to the one phrase that

most stood in his way, and tried to identify himself with it: "I am proposing that all nations henceforth avoid entangling alliances which would draw them into competitions of power.... There is no entangling alliance in a concert of power."

The Jeffersonian phrase was handled just as gingerly by Franklin Roosevelt and his Secretary of State, Cordell Hull, in the mid-thirties. While denouncing *entanglements* (which everybody is automatically against) they had to lay the groundwork for *alliances* (which most people more or less favor). FDR said in 1935: "Our national determination to keep free of foreign wars and entanglements cannot prevent us from feeling deep concern when ideals and principles that we have cherished are challenged." Hull added in 1936: "While carefully avoiding any political entanglements, my Government strives at all times to cooperate with other nations to every practical extent in support of peace objectives ..."

Entanglement has lost none of its effectiveness as an attack word. Walter Lippmann (see ATLANTIC COMMUNITY) wrote in 1965 that if Lyndon Johnson's conception of the Great Society were to fail, "it would not be because the conception is false. It would be because of some external cause—possibly because we had become diverted by some entanglement in another continent."

A serious threat of entanglement without end is now called a QUAGMIRE or "long war."

entitlement A right to benefits mandated to be provided by government or—to opponents of the growth of federal spending—a euphemism for *welfare*.

The term appeared in a law passed by Congress in 1944: "it should be clearly provided that entitlement to pay and allowances is not to be terminated on the actual date of death. ..." After a few decades of limited use, the word was revived by congressional aides in the late 1960s, at the end of the GREAT SOCIETY, to defend against attacks on "welfare cheats."

The word was used synonymously for *welfare*, which was once a euphemism for *relief*; a generation after its introduction, though, *welfare* became a pejorative term because of its abuses. (In New York City, *Welfare Island* was renamed *Roosevelt Island*.)

Not everybody accepts the equating of *entitlement* and *welfare*. Ceil Frank at the Office of Family Assistance in Washington said in 1982, "Entitlement includes both earned benefits and unearned benefits. Social Security and veterans' benefits are earned benefits and unearned benefits are what *welfare* refers to."

Liberals prefer to differentiate between *welfare* as being "public assistance" and *entitlements* as being earned or deserved. Conservatives prefer to lump the two together and call for SPENDING CAPS; Ross Baker, a political science professor at Rutgers, called *entitlements* "tenure for the underclass."

In a June 1993 speech in Milwaukee, as his policies were being criticized as too liberal, Bill Clinton attacked what he characterized as the Reagan era's "politics of abandonment" and juxtaposed that extremist position with *entitlement* as the opposite extreme: "We have to move beyond entitlement and abandonment. I ran for President basically on the same things that I found had worked for me when I was governor—not entitlement, not abandonment, but EMPOWERMENT. ..."

Entitlement is now a noun that cuts both ways: reassuring the middle-aged "baby boomers" facing retirement but worrying the following generation who will be paying most of the rising costs. "A generational backlash is inevitable," wrote *The Washington Post*'s Robert Samuelson in 2007 in a piece about "the coming 'entitlements' crisis." The economics columnist argued that "the idea that younger workers will meekly bear the huge tax increases needed to pay all boomers promised benefits is delusional."

The verb *entitle*—"to provide a right or claim"—now includes an entitlement to work beyond 65 and to defer some taxes to provide an incentive to save and invest. This also involves painful "Social Security reform" (see THIRD RAIL; WELFARE STATE).

environmentalist An anti-pollutionary; a "green" who puts the values of the preservation of the earth and its atmosphere ahead of economic development.

At the turn of the twentieth century, an environmentalist was a scientist who believed that a human being's behavior was determined more by his surroundings than by his genetic inheritance.

Until the '60s, the battle of heredity versus environment colored the use of the word. However, as that verbal face-off was being replaced by the alliterative *nature versus nurture*, another battle was beginning that gave *environmentalist* new surroundings. Keith Mellanby, in *Pesticides and Pollution* in 1967, wrote of pesticides "which have recently been shown to constitute such an important contribution to environmental pollution." In 1970 a group of marine biologists wrote *The Times* of London that "we are actively involved in various facets of environmental science—a less emotive and more encompassing term than pollution studies."

By the '70s, *environmental impact* became a rallying phrase for a loose alliance of scientists and political activists who were worried about the encroachments of immediate comfort upon the long-term life of man; the word *ecology*, which had meant a balance in nature of organisms and their environment, became a vogue term. *Ecologist*, a term coined in 1873 by biologist Ernst Haeckel to describe the relationship of organisms to their environments, may replace *environmentalist* in time. However, *ecologist* has a more scientific connotation, and *environmentalist* still encompasses people who have been winning victories in legislatures or courts over chemicals in their drinking water or cigarette smoke indoors. The construction of phrases concluding with the word *free* preceded by a hyphen has proliferated; "quiet cars" on railroad trains are said to be *conversation-free* from auditory pollution by cell phone.

Conservationist, the predecessor term, survives; perhaps it has been avoided by liberals interested in the restraint of technology because of its resemblance to *con-*

servatism. George Reiger, conservation editor of *Field & Stream*, wrote *The New York Times* in 1978:

> you should permit the record to be set straight on conservation, a word popularized in America by Gifford Pinchot (a hunter) after it had been used in Great Britain for half a century to describe "the wise use of renewable resources." ... People who believe that no creatures should be killed, that no forests should be cut, that, in fact, the goldfinch that comes to their feeder this winter is the very same bird that visited them a decade ago should be called ultra-preservationists, radical environmentalists, unrealistic extremists, or residents of the twilight zone, but please, please, don't call them conservationists. They are not.

Political environmentalism inherited schizoid tendencies: a stance that is outspokenly anti-development, pro-wilderness, and suspicious of technology's "advances" (which is seen as anti-business) often comes into conflict with such developments as shopping centers that generate new jobs, and is thus attacked by organized labor as ELITIST. "If there's ever a flat choice between smoke and jobs," President Nixon told this speechwriter in 1970, "tilt toward jobs."

Demanding "a more vigorous approach to supply expansion," the NAACP issued a statement at the end of 1977 saying: "We cannot accept the notion that our people are best served by a policy based on the inevitability of energy shortage and the need for the government to allocate an ever-diminishing supply among competing interests."(See ZERO-SUM GAME). Republican Ronald Reagan seized on this statement as indicative of the "elitism" of environmentalists, whose best-known publication was *The Limits to Growth.* "The limits-to-growth people," said Reagan, "who are so influential in the Carter Administration are telling us, in effect, that the American economic pie is shrinking, that we all have to settle for a smaller slice ... the best way ... is for government to get out of the way while the rest of us make a bigger pie so that everybody can have a bigger slice."

Environmentalists, sometimes derided as *tree huggers,* found a more politically appealing approach in pointing to scientific concerns about GLOBAL WARMING. During the Clinton Administration, Vice President Al Gore took the lead in promoting green issues. (Environmental activists the world over are known as *greens;* it became the name of a potent German party.) In 2007, Gore led the production of a film, *An Inconvenient Truth,* which won an Academy Award for best documentary and—along with his Nobel Peace Prize—stirred talk of his potential political recovery.

Greens rarely use the word *world;* their locution of choice is *planet.*

eponymy See QUISLING; MAVERICK; GERRYMANDER; SOLON; PHILIPPIC.

equal time A doctrine requiring radio- and television-station licensees to exercise fair play in making air time available to opposing candidates for public office or views differing from the station's editorial policies.

Curiously, the phrase *equal time* does not appear in the statutes or decisions of the Federal Communications Commission, the agency charged with regulating stations. In a 1968 letter to the author, FCC Secretary Ben F. Waple explained:

> As you point out, in Section 315 of the Communications Act of 1934, as amended (47 U.S.C. 315), the phrase "equal opportunities" is used in reference to broadcasts by candidates for public office. The same phrase is used in the Commission's Rules regarding that subject (47 CFR 73.-120). The term *equal time* is used popularly in the broadcasting industry as an equivalent to "equal opportunities." *Equal time* has no official status and does not appear in the Commission statute, rules, or interpretive rulings; however, it may appear in press releases for the Commission's Office of Reports and Information.

(For an example of reluctant official adoption of a popular phrase, see MEDICARE.)

In essence, *equal time* requires broadcasting stations to make provision for all candidates if they make their airwaves available to any, *unless* the coverage is part of a regularly scheduled news broadcast, interview, documentary, or on-the-spot coverage of a news event. To be on the safe side, most stations lean backward to provide equal time on interviews and regularly scheduled news broadcasts (over a period of time) as well.

Under its "historical notes," the FCC does use *equal time* to describe the special provision made in the 1960 presidential campaign to permit the Kennedy-Nixon debates without offering time to the splinter-party candidates.

The phrase, as used today, applies only to free, public-service time offered by broadcast stations and networks to candidates; on purchased time, candidates can and do obtain unequal time, depending on the financial capability and media choices of the political parties. However, if one party "reserves the time" in a period shortly before Election Day, and the opposition decides to spend some money that night, stations must bend every effort to make equal "commercial" time available for sale, even though it might already be sold to others. The FCC rules have not been applied to cable channels, although most cable companies go along with the equal-time rules partly to appear FAIR AND BALANCED but mainly to avoid a court case that might set an unwelcome precedent.

What about television stars who run for office? In California, when Ronald Reagan ran for governor, stations dropped re-runs of his movie, *Bedtime for Bonzo*, in which the actor played opposite a charming chimpanzee. "During the 2003 gubernatorial race in California," noted *The Washington Post*, "television stations dropped all Arnold Schwarzenegger movies out of fear that showing them would require them to give countless hours of free airtime to all 134 other candidates for Governor." In 2007, as Republicans looked for a candidate who could succeed President Bush, some supported Fred Thompson, an actor and former Senator who played a District Attorney in the popular television series *Law and Order*; it was feared his candidacy might knock the show off the broadcast network (and possibly cable, if those stations did not want to test their freedom), as other candidates would have demanded *equal time*.

Era of Good Feeling The years 1817 to 1825, when James Monroe was President of the United States and there was, in effect, no organized political opposition.

The term was probably first used by Benjamin Russell in the *Columbian Centinel* in 1817 while Monroe was making a northern tour. Russell, speaking for the defeated Federalists, expressed a wish that the Federalist faction, now practically defunct, should be treated as though past differences had never existed.

The *Good Feeling* was more apparent than real. Monroe's victory was largely the product of political organization, the Federalists' complete loss of credit because of their opposition to the War of 1812, and an attempt in New England to secede during that war. The result had been the sweeping Monroe victory in 1820 in which only one elector voted against him.

During the Era, factions were forming which eventually gave rise to political parties as we know them today. At that time there was the "Adamite" faction, Eastern-oriented, looking toward Europe and the sea. They were merchants and the new manufacturers, followers of John Quincy Adams, who would soon become the Whigs. Opposing them were the Jacksonites, farmers and frontiersmen, who were soon to become the leaders of the Democratic party.

The term has been continually revived. Victorious Northern Republicans used it after the Civil War, meaning by an *Era of Good Feeling* the hope that the Democrats and the South would accept defeat gracefully.

Franklin D. Roosevelt used it in 1928 when, upon being elected New York governor, he described "a period in our history known in all our school books as the 'era of good feeling.' It is my hope that we stand on the threshold of another such era in this State." As President, Roosevelt called in his second inaugural address for "a genuine period of good feeling." And Lyndon Johnson, after his overwhelming victory over Senator Barry Goldwater in 1964, expressed the hope that a new Era of Good Feeling would result.

It did not; and in the cut-and-thrust of debate in a political democracy, feelings soon fray after a HONEYMOON PERIOD. Even in the days of Monroe there was continual conflict between individual supporters of John Quincy Adams and Andrew Jackson. President Lyndon Johnson's hopes were based on the continued success of his policy of CONSENSUS and this, too, was frustrated. Long wars beget ill feeling, as President George W. Bush discovered.

See PRESIDENT OF ALL THE PEOPLE; DEAL.

erring brethren See EUPHEMISMS, POLITICAL.

escalate the rhetoric See RHETORIC.

escalation An increase in military activity, either in preparation for or during an armed conflict; by extension, acceleration of effort in any kind of campaign.

Escalation is one of the linguistic products of the COLD WAR and the nuclear age. Scientists and strategists began writing what they called SCENARIOS of how nuclear war might occur and how it might be avoided. Herman Kahn, one of the most articulate of the thermonuclear thinkers, put it this way: "War by miscalculation might also result from the process ... called 'escalation.' A limited move may appear safe, but set into motion a disastrous sequence of decisions and actions." Kahn even postulated a sixteen-step "escalation ladder" leading from "subcrisis disagreement" to the aftermath of "all-out war." See UNTHINKABLE THOUGHTS. Through the writings of Kahn and others in the 1950s, the term came into wide use as one of the relatively unusual cases in which both experts and laymen could share the same snippet of jargon. "But wars, large or small, are fought for victory," opined *The Nation* early in 1961. "That means you pound the enemy with every available lethal assistance, with the inevitable result—to use the fancy new term—of escalation to all-out war."

Centuries ago, there had been another military term for an elevating device or act. *Escalade*, from the French, was used as a verb meaning "to scale a wall or fortification." Sir Ernest Gowers' edition of Fowler's *Modern English Usage* explains the preference for *escalation* over the older term by pointing out that *escalation* "has the advantage of novelty and a more native look, and

a moving staircase provides a more up-to-date metaphor than a scaling ladder."

Escalation gained its widest currency not because of nuclear conflict but because of the war in Vietnam. Each time one side or the other introduced reinforcements or a type of weapon previously unused in the war, the act was branded as *escalation*. In the U.S., the word took on political overtones and a pejorative shading, first because Washington was pledged to seeking peace rather than "widening" the war, and second because it gave opponents of the war a universally understood term with which to attack the Administration. Official spokesmen, editorialized *The New York Times*, "have generally shied away from describing each new expansion of the air war as 'escalation' because of political sensitivity ... [they] prefer to say that the air war is being widened, that pressure is being increased or that the war is being increased."

Time magazine lost all patience with the term in April 1967, calling it in a lead article "one of those windy words that are foisted on the public by military bureaucrats, interminably parroted by the press and kept in the vernacular long after losing any real meaning." Nonetheless, *escalation* seemed too deeply entrenched for exorcism. Dr. Martin Luther King, Jr., an opponent of the war, called on his followers for "an escalation of our opposition to the war in Vietnam."

Although real escalators run both up and down, the political term heads only upward. The antonym is the awkward *de-escalate*. After the Vietnam era, *escalate* became part of a new cliche, "don't escalate the rhetoric," an admonition honored largely in the breach.

After four years of the second Iraq war, when the Bush military planners recommended an increase of over 30,000 troops for a concerted push in Baghdad and a few other areas of intense sectarian warfare, the White House staff chose a Pentagonism to avoid the dreaded *escalation*. See SURGE. However, Rep. Rahm Emanuel, a rising Democrat in the House, was having none of that avoidance and passed word to all Democrats and opponents of any increase in troop commitments to use *escalation*. See also WINDING DOWN; VIETNAMIZATION.

establishment See EASTERN ESTABLISHMENT.

ethnic cleansing The removal, sometimes by mass murder, of an ethnic group—whether troublesome or hated because of being "different"—by another ethnic group, usually in the majority.

This is a euphemism for GENOCIDE, the systematic murder of an entire people. In 1988, Armenians and Azerbaijanis were fighting for control of the autonomous enclave of Nagorno-Karabakh; Yugoslav sources said that Soviet officials used this term—in Russian, *etnicheskie chistki*, "ethnic purges"—to describe the attempts by one group to drive out the other.

Slobodan Milošević, then head of the Communist party in Serbia and later Serbia's president, said in an April 1987 speech in the town of Kosovo Polje that ethnic Albanians were trying to drive Serbs and Montenegrins from the province of Kosovo, where Albanians predominate: "Albanian separatists and nationalists are counting on the time factor, and that conditions are working for them." He added ominously, "There is the political view that the request for an ethnically clean Kosovo is justified and possible." *The Washington Post* reported in February 1993 on Vojislav Šešelj, the Serb leader in the former Yugoslavia, who increased "his demands for ethnic purity. He says he wants at least 360,000 ethnic Albanians to clear out of Kosovo. According to Helsinki Watch, the human rights group, Šešelj has said that children of mixed Serb-Croat marriages are 'illegitimate' and have to be 'eliminated.'" Questioned at a news conference about killings in Bosnia in April 1993, President Clinton responded, "The principle of ethnic cleansing is something we ought to stand up against."

Milošević was tried for genocide and crimes against humanity at the International Court of Justice in The Hague, insisted on defending himself with much bravado, and died in prison in 2007 before the four-year trial ended, depriving his victims of a verdict.

In Iraqi Kurdistan in March of 1988, Saddam Hussein's forces attacked the town of Halabja with poison gas, killing upward of 5,000 civilians. Kurdish sources at the time provided the author with a short film, taken by an Iranian cameraman, of the helicopter gas attack; I passed this on to Dan Rather of CBS News, who telecast a portion of the clip some months later; this first documented use of poison gas since World War I went largely ignored at the time. The Halabja massacre was part of a campaign to suppress opposition to Saddam by Kurds, which included the removal of Kurdish Iraqis from their ancient provincial capital of Kirkuk, site of major oil deposits. Arab families were moved into the homes of Kurds, who were driven out to the mountains.

After Saddam was deposed by U.S. forces and hanged by the elected Iraqi government, partial reversal of that ethnic cleansing began. Many Arab families implanted in Kurdish homes and farms by Saddam's Baathists were compensated and moved back to their previous villages; insurgents claimed this itself was ethnic cleansing. Dr. Barham Salih, deputy Prime Minister and a Kurd, told the author that such a complaint by the intruders was a perversion of the phrase, and "Kirkuk is our Jerusalem."

Ethnics Americans who take pride in their national origin; now broadening to any group conscious of a cultural heritage that is not White Anglo-Saxon Protestant or black.

Ethnic began as an adjective, meaning "pagan" or "heathen." At the start the meaning was limited to people neither Jewish nor Christian; later, in social science, the meaning was "racial" or "ethnological." In 1941, sociologists W. Lloyd Warner and Paul Lunt, in *The Social Life of a Modern Community*, used the adjective for the first time as a noun, calling attention to their coinage by using quotation marks: "These groups ... we have called 'ethnics.'"

By 1970, as a white BACKLASH took political form, a word was needed for lower-middle-class whites who felt threatened by the advancement of minorities. In a 1973 promotional piece for the *American*

Heritage Dictionary, associate editor Alma Trinor wrote: "There is among many groups in the population a new sense of group identity and pride that has given rise to changes in nomenclature. Now we read not about HYPHENATED AMERICANS, second-generation Americans, or religious minorities, but about *ethnics*."

David Guralnik, when he was editor of *Webster's New World Dictionary*, recalled: "Originally the term was created to refer specifically to Jews, Italians, and Irish in the large cities, but in Cleveland it is now pretty well restricted to people of central European extraction, but specifically excluding Jews."

As *ethnic groups* changed to a breezier *the ethnics*, the term at first took on an anti–civil rights connotation and then lost it. In 1972 *Newsweek* columnist Stewart Alsop, an unabashed WASP, wrote of the rules of television situation comedies: "The rules are: 'ethnics' are okay, Jews are okay, blacks are very okay, white Anglo-Saxon Protestants are a bunch of bigoted boobies."

By the presidential campaign of 1976, every campaign had ways of reaching the *ethnics*. In a televised debate on foreign policy, President Ford blundered by insisting that the East European nations were not under Soviet domination, and a "captive nations" spokesmen denounced this as inaccurate. At the inauguration of President Carter, an inaugural official used two vogue words in his complaint: "There's no outreach to the ethnics."

Ethnics, the plural noun, is a slightly clinical, neutral, and inoffensive way of identifying national groups, though it carries a note of condescension to some ears. In a 1974 *Atlantic Monthly* article, Henry Fairlie, coiner of *Establishment*, drew a useful distinction between the polemically loaded *ethnic* and the more clinical *ethnic group*. "One *belongs* to an ethnic group, one *is* an ethnic, and there is a world of difference. To say that someone is a member of an ethnic group is implicitly to say that one is describing only one of his characteristics. To say that he is an ethnic is to imply that this is the most important characteristic about him, the determining characteristic ..."

In recent years, "ethnic politics" has centered on the "immigration issue."

eunuch rule Provision in state constitutions forbidding governors from succeeding themselves, except after the lapse of another term.

In most states, particularly in the South, governors are rendered politically impotent—LAME DUCKS from the moment they enter the Statehouse—by the *eunuch rule*. This was designed to prevent four-year governors from building long-lasting machines. (In two-year-term states, like Texas and Arkansas, succession is permitted.)

Wherever the eunuch rule applies, the governor starts thinking about (1) running for senator, (2) laying the groundwork for a career in private business, or (3) "modernizing" the state constitution to permit reelection.

Alabama Governor George Wallace, unable to achieve the necessary modernization that would have enabled him to succeed himself, beat the eunuch system by running his wife, Lurleen, in his place in 1966. She was elected, and the state received "two Governors for the price of one." Wallace himself was later re-elected.

euphemisms, political Avoidance of hard words; or, obvious avoidance to use a cliché with irony or humor.

Classic political euphemisms come out of the Civil War, which was delicately referred to as "the late unpleasantness" by humorist Petroleum V. Nasby. The Confederate states were sarcastically called "our erring brethren" by Northerners, or "our wayward sisters" (a phrase of General Winfield Scott's, repeated by Horace Greeley to seceding states with "wayward sisters, depart in peace"). After the war, the BLOODY SHIRT was called "the ensanguined undergarment." (A fine euphemistic difference is still drawn about this war. Northerners say *Civil War*, but many Southerners say *War Between the States* or a tongue-in-cheek *War of Northern Aggression*.)

During the cold war, Pentagon officials estimated that a World War III would cause 120 million deaths in the U.S., and more than 120 "megadeaths" (million deaths) in the Soviet Union; the euphemism for this cataclysm is an "All-Out Strategic Exchange," similar to a "future unpleasantness." Similarly, Hitler's genocidal campaign against the Jews was called the FINAL SOLUTION.

On the domestic scene, politicians dealing with the problem of the aged shy away from *old people, the aged,* or even *the elderly.* An *Esquire* cartoon showed one of these people shouting at a television set: "Call me Gramps, call me an Old Fogy—call me anything except a Senior Citizen!" Environmental issues have inspired deceptive euphemisms. The Clean Air Working Group lobbied against amendments to strengthen the Clean Air Act; the Washington Forest Protection Association sought to ease environmental restrictions on logging. Tax increases are paraded as "revenue enhancement"; President Clinton called them "contributions."

A much-derided euphemism of the Vietnam era was "protective reaction," a military term for bombing raids against anti-aircraft installations, along with "reconnaissance in force" in lieu of *search and destroy,* "specified strike zone" for *free-fire zone,* and "soft ordnance" for *napalm.* In South Africa, apartheid was given the name of "plural relations"; in Bosnia and Herzegovina, Serbian nationalists murdered and expelled Muslims and Croats under the guise of ETHNIC CLEANSING; the ironhanded generals who run Myanmar (their name for Burma) call themselves the "State Peace and Development Council."

The influx of "illegal aliens" into the U.S. has long been recognized as a problem. Since most of these were Mexicans, formerly derogated as "wetbacks" (from having to swim the Rio Grande River), many Americans felt they should be given legal status and changed their appellation to "noncitizens"; that still did not remove the stigma, and was further euphemized with "undocumented persons." (Spanish-speaking Americans usually eschew the euphemisms and call them *ilegales.*) Another lobbying group, the Federation for American Immigration Reform, favored restrictions on immigration that

seemed somewhat at odds with its acronym, FAIR.

A U.S. Department of Labor dictionary of job definitions, published at the end of 1977, enshrined euphemism in a government document. To eliminate sex and age references, occupational analysts changed *busboy* to "dining-room attendant"; *batboy* to "bat handler"; *governess* to "children's tutor"; *repairman* to "repairer." Faced with deciding what to call people who wait on tables, the Labor Department eschewed "waitron" and surrendered to "waiter-waitress." In the continuing effort to upgrade job titles, nightclub bouncers have been elevated into "security," sales clerks into "associates," shipping clerks into "traffic expediters," and soda jerks into "fountain attendants."

Hugh Rawson, author of *A Dictionary of Euphemisms and Other Doubletalk,* notes the way the military continues to produce its own spate of euphemisms: "collateral damage" (civilian casualties resulting from bombing military targets), "assets" (weapons), "discriminate deterrence" (pinpoint bombing), "blue on blue" (friendly fire, itself a euphemism of the Vietnam War; the phrase alludes to the Civil War), and "persons in transit" (refugees). Those who disagree say "I non-concur." The WAR ON TERROR engendered "enhanced interrogation techniques" and "alternative interrogation practices," which critics called abuse and torture. Interrogators at Guantanamo were advised by Behavioral Science Consultation Teams, or B.S.C.T.s, informally known as Biscuits. Prisoners who attempted to commit suicide were described as being involved in "self-injurious behavior incidents"; those who tried to starve themselves to death were subjected to "internal nutrition," or force-feeding.

See DISADVANTAGED; POLICE ACTION; POLITICALLY CORRECT; PENTAGONESE; RENDITION.

Eurocommunism The form of un-international Communism espoused in the 1970s by leaders in West European nations who purported to be independent of the line set forth by the Communist party in the Soviet Union.

"The striking fact about Eurocommunism," said anti-Titoist Yugoslav Milovan Djilas in 1977, "is that for the first time opposition to Moscow flows from the democratic process." Eurocommunism received its biggest boost in Italy, where political pluralism was embraced by Italian Communist leader Enrico Berlinguer, who recommended a HISTORIC COMPROMISE whereby Communists could share power in the national government of Italy. In France, Communist party chief Georges Marchais set back the cause of Eurocommunism in September 1977 by dramatically breaking with the Socialists, driving a wedge in the Union of the Left with a demand for specifics in the nationalization of industry; as a result, the right was able to turn back the challenge from the left in 1978.

The phrase was a major post–Cold War coinage. Arrigo Levi, editor of *La Stampa*, informed foreign correspondent Flora Lewis that the originator of the phrase was Frane Barbieri, a high-ranking Yugoslav Communist who settled in Italy in the early '70s. It was lost in all the other *euro-* coinages, from *euromarketing* to the currency denomination as the *euro*.

everyman See JOHN Q. PUBLIC.

every man a king Populist slogan of Louisiana Governor Huey P. Long.

This was the trigger phrase of Governor Long's Share-the-Wealth program, which he espoused from 1928 until his assassination in 1935. It was taken from William Jennings Bryan's "Cross of Gold" speech to the 1896 Democratic National Convention.

Long held that 10 percent of the people in the U.S. owned 70 percent of the wealth, taking most of his populist ideas from Senator S. J. Harper. The full slogan used "Every Man" as one word: "Everyman a King, but No Man Wears a Crown."

evil empire A moral attack on the worldwide corruption of Communism, criticized as simplistic when made but now seen by many to be a defensible historical judgment.

Ronald Reagan introduced this alliterative-looking phrase on March 8, 1983. Speaking at a National Association of Evangelists convention in Orlando, Florida, Reagan delivered what amounted to a political sermon on the sources of evil in the modern world. In the speech's peroration he stressed his anti-Soviet theme: "in your discussions of the nuclear freeze proposals, I urge you to beware the temptation of pride—the temptation blithely to declare yourselves above it all and label both sides equally at fault, to ignore the facts of history and the aggressive impulses of an evil empire."

Western accommodationists found the phrase extreme, and the liberal historian Henry Steele Commager labeled this speech "the worst ever given by a President." Reagan and his aides, however, had managed to couch the U.S.-Soviet superpower geostrategic competition in stark moral terms: "the struggle between right and wrong, good and evil."

Anthony R. Dolan, Reagan's chief speechwriter, provided him with the colorful collocation to denounce Soviet totalitarianism. Writing for *The American Enterprise* a decade after the speech, Dolan observed: "The President's critics and many foreign-policy analysts were vastly uncomfortable with conservatives like Reagan who used such words as 'evil' about a regime toward which their own priorities were ordered not so much by a concern for moral distinctions as by the pursuit of a modus vivendi—an accommodation with Soviet power." (The phrase's importance is underscored in the title of a book by Dolan, *Undoing the Evil Empire: How Reagan Won the Cold War*.)

Other political voices continue to echo the Reagan usage. Richard Nixon stated in *Time* magazine in 1992, "The nations of the former evil empire lost faith in communism both because of its inhumanity and because it did not work." See AXIS OF EVIL.

exchange rates See SNAKE IN THE TUNNEL.

executive privilege The right claimed by a President to withhold information from Congress or the judiciary.

"The doctrine of Executive privilege is well established," President Nixon said publicly on March 12, 1973, as the Watergate case was about to break. Citing its use since George Washington, he said that both members and former members of his White House staff "shall follow the well-established precedent and decline a request for a formal appearance before a committee of the Congress."

Historian and former Kennedy aide Arthur Schlesinger, Jr., took sharp issue with this in the March 30, 1973, *Wall Street Journal*:

> the very term "Executive privilege" seems itself to be of fairly recent American usage ... You will look in vain for it as an entry in such standard reference works as the Smith-Zurcher "Dictionary of American Politics," or the "Oxford Companion to American History" or Scribner's "Concise Dictionary of American History." It is not even to be found, I was dismayed to discover, in "The New Language of Politics," compiled by William Safire of Mr. Nixon's very own White House staff.

To correct that omission from the earlier editions, here is the history of the phrase taken from Schlesinger's observations, a tracking of the term in *American Speech* (Fall-Winter 1973), and a contribution by an early user.

"In May 1954," Schlesinger recounted, "in the midst of the Army-McCarthy hearings, President Eisenhower instructed employees of the Department of Defense that, if asked by the McCarthy Committee about internal exchanges within the Department, they were 'not to testify to any such conversations or communications or to produce any such documents or reproductions.' This was an unprecedentedly sweeping denial to Congress. But it had a certain moral justification in the atrocious character of the McCarthy inquisition, and it was given legal color by an accompanying memorandum from Herbert Brownell, the Attorney General ..."

That was a point that was to trouble many scholars: if Mr. Eisenhower's evocation of executive privilege (the idea, not the phrase) was constitutionally right in the case of withholding data from the "atrocious" Senator McCarthy, how could Mr. Nixon's repetition of that maneuver be constitutionally wrong in withholding informa-

tion from a Congress operating with more public support? Judge John Sirica supplied the answer. As *Time* magazine reported in 1973, Sirica "noted that the Supreme Court in 1953 had recognized an Executive privilege for military secrets ... But he made it clear that Executive privilege does not cover conversations relevant to a criminal investigation and not involving performance of official duties."

The practice of withholding information from Congress, without the modern phrase, did begin with George Washington. In the 1792 House inquiry into the St. Clair expedition, President Washington gave the House the documents it requested, and sent his cabinet members to testify, but—according to Thomas Jefferson's diary—agreed with his cabinet officers that "the Executive ought to communicate such papers as the public good would permit, and ought to refuse those, the disclosure of which would injure the public; consequently were to exercise a discretion."

The phrase grew out of the use of the word *privilege* in law to mean "the royal prerogative," or privilege of clergy, or the privilege of Parliament. The 1953 citation by Judge Sirica was in the Supreme Court decision of *U.S. v. Reynolds*, when the Court referred to the government's "privilege against revealing military secrets." On May 17, 1954, Attorney General Herbert Brownell wrote: "Presidents have established, by precedent, that they and members of their Cabinets, and other heads of executive departments have an undoubted privilege and discretion to keep confidential, in the public interest, papers and information which require secrecy." Raoul Berger, in his 1974 *Executive Privilege: A Constitutional Myth*, traced the phrase to a 1958 article by Conrad D. Philos in the *Federal Bar Journal* (14:113) titled "Executive Privilege and the Release of Military Records," and a *Federal Supplement* (157:943/2), "The position taken rests on the claim of executive privilege."

The earliest judicial use of the term was tracked by Fred R. Shapiro, the editor of the *Oxford Dictionary of Legal Quotations* (1993), to August of 1940, in an opinion handed down by the U.S. Court of

Appeals in *Glass v. Ickes*. The court held that Harold Ickes, F.D.R.'s Secretary of the Interior, was immune from the charge of defamation because "a communication, released generally to the press, [was] within this executive privilege."

The earliest use of the phrase by a high official of the executive branch that this lexicographer can find is in testimony by William P. Rogers (who, as Deputy Attorney General under Herbert Brownell, helped draft the 1954 memorandum) before the Senate Judiciary Subcommittee on Constitutional Rights on March 6, 1958, objecting to new disclosure requirements on administrative procedure legislation.

The phrase was used three times in Rogers' summary: "(1) the executive privilege applies to the executive functions of the independent agencies; (2) the executive privilege obviously does not apply to judicial functions; similarly (3) legislative inquiry into the legislative functions of the independent agencies is not limited by any executive privilege, but there are other restraining considerations ..."

Coincidentally, Rogers was Richard Nixon's Secretary of State when the dispute arose in 1973 over the Nixon use of the separation-of-powers doctrine to keep Congress from digging into the Watergate scandal. When Nixon turned to Rogers, his friend and longtime colleague, for legal support of his claim of executive privilege, Rogers advised that in having already directed aides to testify on related matters, the President had waived his claim to privilege.

Because its use was discredited in Watergate, recent presidents have tended to employ the phrase (with the *e* not capitalized, as it should be if referring to the Office of the President) with care, using it either as a last resort for withholding information from Congress and the courts or as a negotiating chip to obtain concessions in demands made upon them.

President George H. W. Bush's national security adviser, Brent Scowcroft, cited *executive privilege* when declining to testify before the Senate banking committee in 1992 about exports of American technology to Iraq prior to the first Gulf War. Independent Counsel Kenneth Starr included President Bill Clinton's frequent assertions of *executive privilege* as a reason for impeaching him (this particular charge was dropped), but Clinton and his lawyers shied away from using this privilege when they thought they could, instead claiming *lawyer-client privilege* or, in a failed effort to prevent Secret Service agents from testifying about him, *protective privilege*.

President George W. Bush also invoked *executive privilege* a number of times. For example, he cited *executive privilege* in 2001 when blocking the release of internal Justice Department documents relating to the misuse of mob informants by the FBI's Boston office and in 2007 when refusing to allow his former counsel, Harriet Miers, and his political adviser, Karl Rove, to testify under oath to a Senate panel investigating the firing of eight federal district attorneys. (He would have permitted them to testify in private sessions, without taking oaths and without making transcripts of what they had to say, but the senators did not accept these conditions.) However, he chose not to assert *executive privilege* in 2001 when blocking release of the records of Vice President Dick Cheney's energy task force, relying instead on the separation-of-powers doctrine—and was upheld by the U.S. Supreme Court.

Tarnished though it was in the Watergate years, the phrase did not escape commercialization. Bloomingdale's department store brought out a gift for Christmas, 1973, which it called "Executive Privilege": an electric paper shredder with a smoky Plexiglas shell to catch the shreds. Lynne Cheney, the Vice President's wife, whose talents include novel writing, also anticipated her husband's desire to keep the deliberations of his energy task force from public view in a 1979 political thriller that argued for executive secrecy. Her book's title: *Executive Privilege*.

exit strategy A plan for extricating military forces from a foreign country, more slowly and with greater deliberation, than if they were forced to CUT AND RUN; often, a euphemism for a hasty retreat.

"On Tuesday, the voters told President Bush that they wanted him to come up with an exit strategy in Iraq," editorialized *The New York Times* in November 2006, following Democratic gains in the midterm elections. Later that month, a Republican senator, Charles Hagel of Nebraska, criticized his party's president in *The Washington Post:* "If the president fails to build a bipartisan foundation for an exit strategy, America will pay a high price for this blunder—one that we will have difficulty recovering from in the years ahead."

Ten months later, in testimony before several congressional committees, General David Petraeus did lay out the Bush Administration's military strategy to begin a staged withdrawal of U.S. forces in Iraq. The expectation was that the "exit" would not be complete until well into the next president's term.

The issue of having or, more frequently, not having an *exit strategy* has been raised in connection with most American commitments abroad in recent years. In the case of Bosnia-Herzegovina, columnist Thomas L. Friedman asserted in April 1996: "Ever since the Clinton Administration dispatched 20,000 troops to Bosnia to implement the security provisions of the Dayton peace accord, it has never been clear what the U.S. exit strategy was." In the case of Haiti in 1994, *The New York Times* reported: "Administration officials hope that by defining limited goals and an exit strategy for Haiti, they can deflect mounting criticism of the prospect of putting American troops in harm's way." In the case of Somalia in 1993, columnist Richard Cohen wrote in *The Washington Post* in October: "The new buzz phrase here is 'exit strategy.' It applies, of course, to Somalia where something has gone tragically awry."

An *exit strategy* may be part of an *end game* (or *endgame*, as it is often spelled), which in chess is the stage after most of the minor pieces have been removed from the board. A headline for a *Washington Post* editorial in July of 2006 posed the question: "Endgame in Lebanon: Everyone agrees on how the war should end, but does anyone know how to get there?" Strobe Talbott employed the term in the title of his 1979 book about arms control negotiations between the U.S. and Russia: *Endgame: The Inside Story of SALT II.*

Both *exit strategy* and *end game* arose—and continue to be used—in nonpolitical contexts. *Exit strategy* began as a business term, with the earliest example in the *OED* coming from 1973: "Stephen A. Wakefield of the Interior Department said Phase IV controls on oil and gas are 'intended as an exit strategy from the whole wretched, frustrating business over the free exchange of goods and services.'"

The columnist Joseph Kraft introduced the phrase to the political lexicon on February 2, 1984, regarding U.S. involvement in Lebanon: "It is time to think about an exit strategy which can be applied unilaterally to limit the gains that will accrue to radical nationalists and the Soviet Union."

The humorist Art Buchwald, told he had but a short time to live, checked into a hospice in early 2006 and notified his friends that they should come for a final visit. Many did; however, he did not die on schedule. "Dying isn't hard," he wrote, "getting paid by Medicaid is." Though in life he had suffered from severe depression, in his long death Art cheered others with newfound optimism, titling one of his last columns "A New Exit Strategy."

The difference between *end game*, coined in 1881, and *exit strategy*, which entered politics a century later, is this: *End game* does not suggest withdrawal or extrication, as does *exit strategy*. Analyzing a game in the 1987 world championship match between Garry Kasparov and Anatoly Karpov, *The Washington Post* reported in 1987 that "Kasparov was merely trying to prove that his position is so strong that he can afford to enter an end game a pawn down." Samuel Beckett collapsed the two words into a single one as the title of a one-act play, *Endgame*, first produced in 1957; the main character is, in effect, a king in a chess game who knows he is making senseless moves in a game that is lost from the start.

Drawing a direct connection between endgames in chess and politics, Richard Cohen began an analysis of the implications for President Bill Clinton of the Lewinsky scandal in a 1998 *Washington Post* Op-Ed piece this way: "Bill Clinton's game is golf. It's a game of some skill and some luck. Not so chess. It is a game of pure skill in which the slightest misstep early on can determine the outcome. If President Clinton were a chess player, he would know he had made such a mistake. The endgame of his presidency has begun."

extremism A position at the either end of the ideological spectrum; home of the politically far-out.

Senator Barry Goldwater, accepting the Republican nomination for president at the national convention at the Cow Palace in San Francisco in 1964, drew a roar from his adherents and a gasp from his opponents in the party with this line in his acceptance speech: "I would remind you that extremism in the defense of liberty is no vice. And let me remind you also that moderation in the pursuit of justice is no virtue!"

In his text, Goldwater underlined the two sentences. (Authorship of these CON-TRAPUNTAL PHRASES has been attributed to speechwriter Karl Hess.) In their campaign for Lyndon Johnson, Democratic speakers underlined it as well, stunned at their luck in garnering from their chief opponent's own mouth a phrase unequaled in its service to the opponent since 1884. (That was when a Protestant clergyman supporting nominee James Blaine infuriated Irish Catholics in tightly contested New York by blasting Democrats as the party of "Rum, Romanism and Rebellion," thereby electing Grover Cleveland.)

Supporters of Goldwater, and the Senator himself, had been annoyed at the "extreme" label applied to them by the Republican MODERATES in the primary campaign. Some saw Goldwater's use of *extremism* as a way of rubbing it in to the defeated liberals; others felt it was an affirmation of his personal identity and point of view, as opposed to the usual unity approach after a difficult division. "My God," cried a reporter, "he's going to run as Goldwater!"

Republican Nelson Rockefeller, leader of the liberal wing, issued this statement the following day: "To extol extremism whether 'in defense of liberty' or 'in pursuit of justice' is dangerous, irresponsible and frightening. Any sanction of lawlessness, of the vigilante and of the unruly mob can only be deplored.... I shall continue to fight extremism within the Republican party. It has no place in the party. It has no place in America."

Richard Nixon, who sat on his hands during the enthusiastic demonstration after Goldwater's line, sought some unifying clarification from Goldwater three weeks later. Nixon and others pointed out to the candidate that his statement was being construed as a blanket endorsement of extremism. In a letter to Nixon, Goldwater backtracked to this extent: "If I were to paraphrase the two sentences in question in the context in which I uttered them I would do it by saying that wholehearted devotion to liberty is unassailable and that half-hearted devotion to justice is indefensible."

But that was not what he had said to the convention, and the original statement could not be glossed over. Lyndon B. Johnson hammered it home at the conclusion of the campaign: "Extremism in the pursuit of the Presidency is an unpardonable vice. Moderation in the affairs of the nation is the highest virtue."

Extremism today remains as frowned upon by most people as in this 1639 English proverb: "Extremity of right is wrong." However, Martin Luther King Jr., in his "Letter from a Birmingham Jail," wrote that "though I was initially disappointed at being categorized as an extremist, as I continued to think about the matter I gradually gained a measure of satisfaction from the label ... the question is not whether we will be extremists, but what kind of extremists we will be. Will we be extremists for hate or for love? Will we be extremists for the preservation of injustice or for the extension of justice? ... Perhaps the South, the nation and the world are in dire need of creative extremists."

That letter was dated April 16, 1963, more than a year before the GOP convention in San Francisco. What would the reaction have been if Goldwater had cited it?

See RADICAL RIGHT; CODE WORDS; MOONBAT; WINGNUT. Even so, MODERATION can lead to accusations of ME, TOO and raise the WIMP FACTOR.

eyeball to eyeball At the brink of a direct international confrontation; a diplomatic crisis with war a distinct possibility.

Senator Kenneth B. Keating (R-N.Y.) charged in 1962 that Russian missiles were being established in Cuba. Within weeks, the "Cuban missile crisis" had come to test the will of the Kennedy Administration, which was still smarting from its earlier Cuban errors. See BAY OF PIGS FIASCO.

Reconstructing the events that led to the strong stand by the U.S., writers Charles Bartlett and Stewart Alsop, in the *Saturday Evening Post*, quoted Secretary of State Dean Rusk as saying: "We're eyeball to eyeball and the other fellow just blinked." Roger Hilsman of the State Department reported that the statement was made by Rusk to ABC newsman John Scali, who had helped in the negotiations, and the words used were: "Remember when you report this—that, eyeball to eyeball, they blinked first."

The metaphor, closer than *face-to-face* with its vivid picture of two men, foreheads pressed together, glaring into each other's eyes, soon became synonymous with *confrontation* and was as well known as BRINKMANSHIP in the Eisenhower years.

In current usage, an *eyeball-to-eyeball* situation is something that far-sighted diplomatic policy seeks to avoid. However, both the idea of confrontation and the phrase that so vividly describes it are not likely to disappear. In September of 1977, when U.S. Secretary of State Cyrus Vance became embroiled with eyepatch-wearing Israeli Foreign Minister Moshe Dayan in dispute over the makeup of a Geneva conference, columnist Joseph Kraft wrote: "They're eyeball to eye patch, and you can't tell who blinked." Charles Bierbauer of Cable News Network reported in early 1993 that "Iraq and the United States have gone eyeball to eyeball again, and Baghdad may have blinked."

The expression has a military origin, and is a contribution of Black English. General Harold Johnson, U.S. Army Chief of Staff in the mid-sixties, tells the author he first heard the term used—and widely quoted—in November 1950, during the Korean conflict. Before President Truman desegregated the armed forces, the 24th Infantry Regiment was all-black; after a counterattack had caused a retreat of U.S. forces, MacArthur's headquarters sent an inquiry to the 24th Regiment, which was expected to bear the brunt of the fighting: "Do you have contact with the enemy?" The reported reply: "We is eyeball to eyeball."

F

face time Impressing a superior or employer by being in his or her presence; or, being noticed by a significant audience.

U.S. News & World Report wrote in 1978 that Jimmy Carter "drops by the White House press room…guaranteeing himself a few precious seconds of 'face time' on the evening TV news."

In 1981, Lois Romano of *The Washington Post* wrote that Presidential adviser Ed Meese attended a book party "for what is commonly referred to in Washington as 'face-time,'" which she defined as "a handshake, a walk around the room and one drink." (In political jargon, that brief appearance is known as a *drop-by*.)

That sense of appearing in person rather than on television was mentioned by Jeffrey Schmalz in a *New York Times* article about the 1983 hockey season at Cornell University: "'Going to the games is positive face time,' said Alan Baren, a senior. (Translation: Having your face seen at the right place, at the right time, with the right people.)"

The lexicographer included the phrase in a 1985 survey of college slang: "Happily, a recent term for necking—*sucking face*—is on the decline, replaced by the more romantic *doing face time*." Kara B. Kerker, then a senior at Cornell, disputed that definition, defining *face time* as "the art of seeing and being seen." She wrote that undergraduates collected F.T.U.'s (face time units) in various ways, including "occupying the window seat in a popular town bar and throwing dead fish at the Harvard players during their hockey team's annual visit to Ithaca."

In Pentagonese, the term took on a sense of "apple-polishing." Maj. Gen. Perry M. Smith provided a glossary of insider lingo at "Fort Fumble" in the 1989 book *Assignment: Pentagon*. He defined *face time* as "time spent near big bosses in attempts to impress them with your diligence and loyalty," adding that *night face* (after-hours

contact) counts double and *weekend face* counts triple.

Campaign staffs use the term to derogate aides who think they can do best by being physically near the candidate: their fear is "out of sight, out of mind." During Persian Gulf war preparations in 1990, Maureen Dowd of *The New York Times* reported that a White House aide being thrust into the limelight was "getting a lot of face time on national television." The politically active phrase was the title of a 1998 novel by Erik Tarloff about a White House speechwriter whose girlfriend, also on the presidential staff, is having an affair with the president.

In 2006, Jim Hoagland of *The Washington Post* applauded the ascension of Josh Bolten to the post of White House Chief of Staff because his predecessor had been "deferential to Cabinet members eager for face time with a president famous for not being interested in details." *Time* magazine reported in 2007 that President Bush "personally rejiggered the seating chart at a White House luncheon" because, in his effort to denuclearize the Korean Peninsula, "he wanted some extra face time" with China's Hu Jintao.

fact-finding trip A serious effort to obtain firsthand information; or, a ploy designed to impress the folks back home with a spurious interest in foreign affairs.

An overseas tour by a congressman or candidate is described by him as a *fact-finding trip*, but as a *junket* by his opponents, who usually add "at taxpayers' expense." A good test of whether a trip abroad is politically motivated is whether it covers the THREE-EYE LEAGUE: Ireland, Italy, and Israel, points of origin or antecedence for many ethnic voters.

The appeal of a "see for myself" attitude was demonstrated by Eisenhower's "I SHALL GO TO KOREA" pledge, which was heightened by the fact that he was a general going to study a war. But it works for civilians as well, and the year before a national convention, world leaders find their calendars filled with visits by aspiring U.S. politicians: a trip to Baghdad was a "must" on the schedule of most candidates for the 2008 presidential nomination.

Another important use of a fact-finding trip is to keep a national political figure out of trouble for weeks at a time; when he returns for a ship- or plane-side interview, he is "fresh" news copy. In labor negotiations, parties who do not wish to be bound by arbitration occasionally agree to a *fact-finding panel*, or one may be imposed by government. On rare occasions the phrase is used in its past tense, as in this 1967 comment on my *New York Times* column by the great usagist, Professor Jacques Barzun, then provost of Columbia University (and in 2007, at age 100, still a perceptive member of OLBOM, the *On Language* Board of Mentors), on the subject of the spread of social research studies: "Judging from what is being studied, researched, and fact-found all over the world, it is clear that as a civilization we no longer know how to do anything... we repeatedly analyze the familiar and suspend action." See NONPOLITICAL TRIP; JUNKETEERING GUMSHOES.

fail-safe A retaliatory strike that can be recalled if the original signal was a mistake; a system whereby bombers may be launched on an ambiguous warning.

Bombers operating on a *fail-safe* system can take off if an enemy attack appears to be under way, fly to a point of no return, and there get instructions from a central control whether or not to continue on to target. "In this way," wrote Herman Kahn, thinker of UNTHINKABLE THOUGHTS, "the central authorities have additional time to confirm or deny the validity of the original warning."

When UPI in the '60s disclosed the existence of fail-safe in a story of the Strategic Air Command's operations in the Arctic, the revelation was soon followed by a book and motion picture on the sensational subject. "It should have been possible," wrote Douglass Cater, later a White House aide, "to describe our military precautions without resorting to the phoney dramatics about bombers headed toward Moscow which alarmed our allies and provided propaganda material for the Soviets."

Fail-safe refers to a system with two signals: one to take off, the other to verify. If bombers headed for enemy territory *fail* to receive a confirmation signal, they return home, placing the communications failure on the *safe* side.

fair and balanced Slogan of Fox cable-news network, extolling even-handedness.

Owned by media magnate Rupert Murdoch and started up in October of 1996 by longtime Republican campaign strategist Roger Ailes, Fox News, with its flag-rippling graphics and conservative point of view, soon dominated its field, attracting many more viewers than its principal rival, CNN. Some media observers interpreted the slogan as an intentional put-down of Fox's rivals, implying that they do not provide fair and balanced news. But this was not what Ailes said he had in mind as he introduced the slogan at the press conference on January 30, 1996, when the plan for Fox News was announced. Asked about the genesis of the phrase, he said that the fairness idea had been percolating in his mind since at least the early 1990s when his consulting firm, Ailes Communications, had devised "Fast, Fresh, and Fair" to describe news gathering at WDIV, a TV station in Detroit. Having watched many media outlets as they bent all their efforts to be first with the news, he decided that fairness was more important as a standard—as well as being a good marketing tool. "Democracy guarantees freedom of the press, and freedom demands fairness," he said.

Fair and balanced has been used in broadcasting as well as in other contexts over the years. A 1948 decision of the FCC involving the renewal of the license of radio station WHLS in Port Huron, Mich., cited the importance of "insuring a fair and balanced discussion of the relative merits of candidates for political office." President Ronald Reagan described a budget proposal for 1985 as a "fair and balanced package," and President Gerald Ford used the phrase in hailing the 1975 Sinai agreement between Israel and Egypt. The *Burlington*

(N.C.) *Daily Times* reported in 1931 that a paper presented at a meeting of the local Mentor Book Club was distinguished by a "very fair and balanced criticism" of the novels of James Fenimore Cooper.

Of course, fairness, like beauty, is in the eye of the beholder. Fox News sought an injunction in 2003 to prevent distribution of comedian Al Franken's book, *Lies and the Lying Liars Who Tell Them: A Fair and Balanced Look at the Right.* Fox contended that Franken (later a Democratic Senate hopeful) could not use *fair and balanced* because it had trademarked the phrase in 1998. While the trademark prevented other news organizations from adopting the motto, partisans on the left and media competitors attacked the suit as an attempt by Fox to use commercial law to make an end run around the First Amendment. The case was dismissed.

Ailes's *fair and balanced* slogan appealed to many on the political right convinced that the organs of what used to be called "the EASTERN ESTABLISHMENT media"—including broadcast networks and a newspaper headquartered in New York City—were afflicted with liberal bias. That accounted, at least partially, for the ratings popularity of Fox network news and opinion panels; its commentators made conservatives and many centrists feel that their views were better represented in the programming. Its existence did offer a counterweight to many other media, so that in its entirety it contributed to "balance."

The reader will note that this entry is carefully balanced; whether it is "fair" is for the reader to judge.

fair deal The theme of President Truman's State of the Union message in 1949, updating the NEW DEAL inherited from Roosevelt.

During his first eighteen months in office, President Truman worked under the shadow and confining legacy of Franklin Roosevelt's New Deal policies. Truman needed a phrase and an image of his own. These he established in his first message to the 81st Congress: "Every segment of our population and every individual has a right to expect from his government a fair deal."

The press picked up the phrase—a natural progression from the New Deal of FDR—and used it to label the domestic policies of the Truman Administration. (Two generations before, Woodrow Wilson had used *Fair Deal* as a counterpart to Theodore Roosevelt's *Square Deal.*)

In 1967, Michigan's Republican Governor George Romney made a punning reference to the progression of "the Deals": "There was the New Deal of Franklin Roosevelt, the Fair Deal of Harry Truman and the ordeal of Lyndon Johnson."

See CARD METAPHORS.

faith-based Rooted in religion.

The choice of the more general *faith* rather than *religion* received official sanction at the start of President George W. Bush's first administration in January 2001 with the creation of an Office of Faith-Based and Community Initiatives. Announcing formation of the new White House office, Mr. Bush said: "Government will never be replaced by charities and community groups. Yet when we see social needs in America, my administration will look first to faith-based programs and community groups.... We will not fund the religious activities of any group, but when people of faith provide social services, we will not discriminate against them." The President's point about discrimination was amplified the following August when the new office issued a report, "Unlevel Playing Field," which held that restrictive agency rules undermined the civil rights of faith-based groups. See LEVEL PLAYING FIELD.

Leaders of both major parties had begun employing the faith-based modifier in the 1990s. Republicans in the House of Representatives supported a plan in 1996 to provide new tax deductions to those who contributed to charities run by religious organizations in poor communities. "If you don't start with a faith-based approach, you aren't starting," said Newt Gingrich, then Speaker of the House. Mr. Bush, then Governor of Texas, weighed in that year, saying, "Government should welcome the help of faith-based institutions." A welfare law enacted in 1996 included a provision to allow, as *The New York Times* reported, "so-called faith-based groups to receive government money without having to hide or compromise their religious character." The following year, the Senate adopted by unanimous consent a resolution, proposed by Paul Wellstone (D-Minn.), urging "the President, Congress, the states, and faith-based and other organizations" to work together to assist elderly and disabled legal immigrants.

Both candidates in the 2000 presidential campaign favored faith-based programs. Mr. Bush's Democratic opponent, Vice President Al Gore, told a Salvation Army meeting in Atlanta in 1999 that "For too long, faith-based organizations have wrought miracles on a shoestring. With the steps I am proposing today, they will no longer need to depend on faith alone."

Previously, *faith-based* had been used primarily by people who believe in God as an overarching modifier for the broad spectrum of religious organizations. Leaders of Protestant, Roman Catholic, and Jewish organizations pointed out at a meeting in Washington, D.C., in 1989, according to an AP dispatch, that "churches and faith-based organizations provide $20.3 billion annually for community education, health and social benefit programs."

The earliest use of the hyphenated modifier, however, came in a criticism of the intrusion of religion into public life. Clarence Martin, a lobbyist for the Association for the Advancement of Psychology, wrote in 1981 that social scientists, as intellectual heirs to Darwin, Marx, and Freud, "are the empirical left who may challenge the views, or more importantly reject the faith-based values, of the creationists, the Moral Majority, the laissez-faire industrialists, the economic determinists, the sexists, the militarists, the coalition who put Reagan into office."

Etymology helps explain the attraction for politicians of *faith-based* vs. *religion-based*. *Faith* derives from Latin *fides*, "trust," and is often used in non-religious contexts, while *religion* has no such non-faith-based meaning. The modifier thus evades traditional objections to "religion in politics" by emphasizing a belief in val-

ues and not necessarily an organized set of beliefs. The Reverend Bill Callahan, co-founder of the Quixote Center in Maryland, said, "The language of faith-based signals to people our motivation while separating us from institutions."

When employed outside political and religious contexts, the modifier usually has a disparaging connotation. *The New York Times* headlined a 2004 editorial about the Bush Administration's missile defense system "The Faith-Based Missile Shield." And a reported sighting of an ivory-billed woodpecker, a bird long thought to be extinct, was dismissed in 2006 by Jerome A. Jackson, an ivory-bill specialist at Florida Gulf Coast University, as "faith-based ornithology." The implication in each instance is that faith alone is not enough.

See FAMILY VALUES; WALL, POLITICAL SYMBOL OF.

faithful See PARTY FAITHFUL.

Fala speech A Franklin D. Roosevelt campaign speech in 1944 that marked a return to partisan politicking from a previous "ABOVE POLITICS" posture.

In the summer of 1944 many Republican newspapers were printing a rumor that President Roosevelt's Scottie, Fala, had been left in Alaska after a presidential visit and that an American destroyer had to be turned around and sent back for him. More factual policy charges were being made, but FDR seized on this one to ridicule and cast doubt on all the others.

In a campaign speech to the Teamsters Union in Washington, President Roosevelt answered the Republican attacks:

> Republican leaders have not been content with attacks on me, or my wife, or on my sons. No, not content with that, they now include my little dog, Fala. Well, of course, I don't resent attacks, and my family doesn't resent attacks, but Fala does resent them. You know, Fala is Scotch, and being a Scottie, as soon as he learned that the Republican fiction writers in Congress and out had concocted a story that I had left him behind on the Aleutian Islands and had sent a destroyer back to find him—at a cost to the taxpayers of two or three or eight or twenty million dollars—his Scotch soul was furious. He has not been the same dog since.

I am accustomed to hearing malicious false-hoods about myself. ... But I think I have a right to resent, to object to libelous statements about my dog.

The rest of the *Fala speech* was a serious enumeration of the problems facing the U.S., and those points had considerable effect on the campaign of '44. However, the Fala reference made the speech come alive; speechwriter Samuel Rosenman, in retrospect, felt it was FDR's most effective single political speech.

The Democratic National Committee issued a cheerful statement after the speech: "The race is between Roosevelt's dog and Dewey's goat."

See CHECKERS SPEECH; BIRD DOG ... KENNEL DOG; DEWEY BLITZ.

fallback position A planned line of retreat.

Late in 1966, as liberal Republican leaders sought to avoid the divisions of 1964 that led to the nomination of conservative Barry Goldwater and the ensuing debacle, *fallback position* came into political use. New York Governor Nelson Rockefeller announced his support of Michigan's Governor George Romney, urging all Republican MODERATES to do the same. Romney pegged his campaign on his "winability," a dangerous route presupposing no slump in his popularity rating. When the slump came in early 1967, talk of a secret "fallback position" began as *New York Times* reporter Warren Weaver referred to Illinois freshman Senator Charles Percy as "the backup candidate." This implied no active support for him unless Romney faltered, at which point the combined moderate forces would move—in impossibly disciplined fashion—to a second candidate.

A year before the 1968 convention, Senator Jacob K. Javits used the phrase in an interview with *Time* magazine, reiterating his and Rockefeller's support of Romney. Obviously recognizing the weakening effect of the admission of any secret second choice, he insisted: "We have no fallback position. There are no alternatives." *Time*'s editors added: "None, that is, unless Romney happens to stumble." When he did (see BRAINWASH), it became apparent that not Percy but Rockefeller occupied the *fall-back position*. See PENTAGONESE.

Jimmy Carter was the first President to use the phrase in diplomatic negotiation. In July 1978 he warned Israel that if direct negotiations between Egypt and Israel did not produce results, the matter could be placed in the anti-Israel U.N.: "The Geneva conference is ... the basic framework for peace and that is always a fallback position if we fail as an intermediary or mediator."

fallout Unfortunate side effects of a political policy or event; a negative chain reaction.

Senator William Fulbright wrote in 1966: "the Vietnamese war thus far has had three major 'fallout' effects on East-West relations: first, it has generated a degree of mistrust and antagonism toward the United States ... second, it has weakened the drive of the Eastern European countries toward greater independence of the Soviet Union; third, it has put a severe strain on the Soviet-American detente ..."

The political use is an extension of the scientific term coined in 1950, well after the explosion of the first atomic bombs in 1945. *Fallout* is defined in the April 1953 issue of the *Bulletin of the Atomic Scientists* as "the descent of the [radioactive] particles back to earth—[that] may occur in the immediate vicinity of the detonation or as far as several thousand miles away ... although it is heaviest near the site."

Political usage should not be confused with *falling-out*, a disagreement sometimes leading to a split.

family jewels See CIA-ESE.

family values The unifying power of traditional home life in American culture; or, CODE WORDS to counter supporters of abortion and gay rights.

The Rev. Andrew M. Greeley and Peter H. Rossi wrote in their 1966 book, *The Education of Catholic Americans*, that "Marriage and family values do show some relationship with Catholic education; however, the relationship is in most instances not a strong one."

Political usage of the phrase began a decade later. The 1976 Republican Party platform stated: "Divorce rates, threatened neighborhoods and schools and public scandal all create a hostile atmosphere that erodes family structures and family values."

Mario Cuomo used the words *family* and *values* in a warm, positive sense during his speech to the 1984 Democratic National Convention. But fused in a collocation, the phrase became the G.O.P. attack term of the 1992 campaign. Pat Robertson, the religious broadcaster who had campaigned in 1988 for the Presidency, railed against the Democratic use of the term: "When Bill and Hillary Clinton talk about family values, they are not talking about either families or values. They are talking about a radical plan to destroy the traditional family and transfer its functions to the Federal Government."

The traditional family is that of father and mother (of opposite sexes), legally married, with children under 18 at home. In 1992, according to the Census Bureau, only 26 percent of American households met this definition, labeled the *nuclear family* by anthropologist George P. Murdock in 1949. In 2006, this group seemed to have leveled off at just under 25%, populated mainly by the college-educated and affluent.

Implicit in the phrase's celebration is that the opposite side takes a permissive attitude regarding abortion and homosexual rights, undermining the institution of the family. *Family values* echoes the use of *social issue* (see PSEPHOLOGY; ISSUE, THE) for concern about the drug culture and changing moral standards.

This powerful campaign theme, however, can backfire. At the 1988 Republican convention, the elder George Bush and his running mate, Dan Quayle, gathered their families onstage to assert traditionalism (while, unknown to them, the background music playing was "The Best of Times" from *La Cage Aux Folles*, a Broadway musical about accepting homosexuality). After Patrick Buchanan's hard-right convention speech declaring "cultural war" seemed harsh to many centrist Republicans, the Bush-Quayle campaign team backed away

from the phrase *family values*, which was drawing fire from Democrats as a code phrase for intolerance, and adopted instead "traditional values." See FAITH-BASED.

fascist Originally, a believer in the corporate state; now a smear word to impute a lust for totalitarianism on the right.

Fascio is the Italian word for "bundle, group." Radical workers' organizations called *fasci dei lavoratori* were common in Sicily in the 1880s, joining together in the early 1890s as a political group called *Fasci siciliani* before being suppressed by the government. In 1914 Benito Mussolini created the militaristic *Fasci d'azione rivoluzionaria*, called the "Milan *fascio*," whose members were called *fascisti*, and in 1919 he reconstituted it as the *Fasci italiani di combattimento*, transformed in 1921 into a political party, the *Partito Nazionale Fascista*. The movement grew in the early twenties as an especially brutal alternative to Communism, and under Mussolini controlled Italy from 1922 to 1943.

In current use, the word is an epithet directed often from the angriest far left toward anyone on the right; in Communist terminology, it was the worst insult short of *revisionist*. During the demonstrations of the '60s in the U.S., the phrase "fascist pig" (with *pig* the preferred term for "police officer") was used so often that the phrase and its adjective lost some of its sting.

See ISLAMOFASCISM; TRAINS RAN ON TIME.

fatally flawed Containing too much error for correction; damaged beyond repair.

This treaty-knocking cliché began to be overused when Ronald Reagan charged that the Carter Administration's SALT II treaty was "fatally flawed," unable to reduce the numbers of large Soviet land-based missiles. Reagan repeated the alliterative term in 1987 when President Oscar Arias Sánchez of Costa Rica proposed a plan in Guatemala; an accommodationist editorial countered, "The Guatemala plan, whatever its weaknesses, is not fatally flawed."

Dun's Review was an early medium for the phrase in 1975 when a job-hunter wrote, "He said my resume was fatally flawed because it failed to tell a prospective employer what I could do for him." By the early 1980s, the hyperbolic term had become trite. In 1983, for example, the United States Ambassador to UNESCO, Jean Gerard, recommended leaving the organization that had become "so skewed, so far off course, so fatally flawed."

The participial phrase's adverb (*fatally*) modifies a past participle (*flawed*). Also frequently used is "*seriously* flawed," but that adverb is seriously weaker than *fatally* and implies the possibility of overhaul and correction.

Sir Arthur Quiller-Couch, in his 1916 *On the Art of Writing*, criticizes a work for "the one fatal flaw that it imports emotion into a theme which does not properly admit of emotion." It may be that *fatal flaw* is patterned after *tragic flaw*, known as *hamartia* in Greek tragedy: in Aristotle's view, it is that inescapable weakness that leads to a tragic hero's downfall.

fat cat A person of wealth, especially an important contributor to political campaigns. Though derogatory, the phrase is respectful at the same time, since few politicians can go far without such supporters.

The phrase was popularized by Frank R. Kent of the *Baltimore Sun* in his 1928 book *Political Behavior:* "these capitalists have what the organization needs—money to finance the campaign. Such men are known in political circles as 'fat cats.'"

In politics, *fat* means "money." The word was used in that sense in the nineteenth century: high-pressure fund-raising was called "fat-frying" in the presidential campaign of 1888. Publisher Henry L. Stoddard wrote historian Mark Sullivan: "[Mark] Hanna was *a* fat-fryer. *The* fat-fryer was John P. Forster, President of the League of Young Republican Clubs. It was in 1888 that he wrote a letter suggesting 'to fry the fat out of the manufacturers.'" Hanna was the Ohio political boss, later appointed Senator, who collected enough money from his wealthy friends to help elect William McKinley in 1896 by outspending his rival, William Jennings Bryan, by ten to one. This pioneering of "BUNDLING" con-

tributions made Hanna the patron saint of today's fundraisers, who remember his words spoken in 1895: "There are two things that are important in politics. The first is money and I can't remember what the second one is."

The word is not always used in the campaign-contributor sense. FDR in 1937 wrote to Ambassador Bowers in Spain: "All the fat-cat newspapers—85% of the whole—have been utterly opposed to everything the Administration is seeking ..."

By the forties, politicians had developed a taste for biting the hand that greased them. Republican Party Finance Chairman Ernest T. Weir tried to oust National Chairman Joe Martin after the Willkie defeat in 1940 by putting on a financial "freeze." At a private luncheon in the Capitol, in 1941, Wendell Willkie said, "The thing I like about Joe Martin is that he has the guts to tell those fat cats to go to hell."

Fundraisers for John F. Kennedy organized the President's Club, with a membership gained by a donation of $1,000. This was denounced by Republicans as evidence of "fat cats with axes to grind" getting contracts as special recognition for their contributions to Kennedy's campaign. Despite the negative publicity, Governor's Clubs, County Chairman's Clubs, etc., were formed by both parties to give the *fat cats* a warm hearth and a feeling that their purrings were heard by the man at the top. By 2007, despite reforms that limited individual contributions and the publication of the names of major donors, the BUNDLING successors to Hanna were called by George W. Bush "Rangers" ($100,000 and up bundled) and by Hillary Clinton "Hill-raisers" ($200,000 and up). See GREASE.

fat-frying See SLUSH FUND; FAT CAT.

favorite son A candidate who holds a state's votes together at a convention for brokerage purposes; not a serious candidate for the presidency, but one who seeks a trading position with a chance as a compromise candidate or vice president.

The phrase was first applied to George Washington as "Freedom's Favorite Son" in the late 1780s. Its early use in a more partisan sense applied to Martin Van Buren, "New York's favorite son" in the 1830s, and Henry Clay, "Kentucky's favorite son" a decade later.

In current use, a state's political leader often announces his intention of going to a convention as a *favorite son*. In that way he appears not to be seeking the nomination seriously; he can be promoting the interests of his own state (Hiram Fong's demonstration at the 1964 Republican convention extolled the delights of Hawaii on national television), avoiding a divisive primary fight in his home state, or simply holding his delegates in line to act more influentially as a bloc in a BROKERED CONVENTION or the even more unlikely OPEN CONVENTION.

The favorite-son candidacy gives an alibi to the potentially serious candidate for refusing to withdraw his name from preferential primaries in other states—such a disavowal would be "inconsistent" with being a favorite son. Contrariwise, it gives a leading national candidate an excuse not to enter a certain state's primary so as not to "offend the favorite son." Because of its usefulness, the scornful implication of the phrase, prevalent in the later part of the nineteenth century, has disappeared.

Though *favorite son* is understood throughout the political U.S., *native son* is also used to mean the same, particularly in the Midwest. Harry Truman wrote in his memoirs: "I recalled the 1928 Democratic convention in Houston. There were two or three native-son nominations that year, including Jim Reed of Missouri ..."

The locution will either be dropped or edited as women have become national candidates. "Favorite daughter" is the logical replacement, but some believe that any reference to sex (or gender, as it is called in politics) is discriminatory.

fear itself See NOTHING TO FEAR.

-feasance Accountability in public office; the taking of public responsibility.

Without a prefix, the noun *feasance* (*OED*: "The doing or execution of a condition, obligation, feudal service, etc.") is labeled "obsolete." Nouns formed from this vestigial *feasance* are formed by adding negative prefixes: *mis*feasance, *mal*feasance, and *non*feasance.

Misfeasance is perceptible but minor wrongdoing; the prefix *mis-* means "badly" or "wrongly." Reckless decisions by those in power may raise questions of misfeasance but not of outright corruption. For example, a public company that dumps waste materials damaging to the environment out of ignorance may be guilty of *misfeasance*.

Malfeasance contains the French prefix for "evil" and refers to deliberate acts of serious wrongdoing, as in illegal dumping of waste materials to save costs despite knowledge of the law. Somebody who commits *misfeasance* may be unsuitable for public office, but a deliberate abuse of public office, bordering on criminal activity, is *malfeasance*.

Nonfeasance means "a failure to carry out one's responsibility," that is, failure to act when one has a duty to act. Not filing a tax return on taxable income is an example; in a different order of magnitude, a president who fails to fulfill the duties of office may also be held responsible for *nonfeasance*.

When some journalists telephone politicians and are asked by their secretaries "What is this in reference to?" they sometimes avoid tipping their hand by responding "Nonfeasance"; it usually gets a fast call back. When the author tried this attention-getting technique on an Assistant Attorney General, he returned my call a few days later saying, "I call back quickly only on '*mis*feasance.'"

federalese See PENTAGONESE; CIA-ESE; GOBBLE-DYGOOK.

federalism See CREATIVE FEDERALISM; NEW FEDERALISM.

feedback Response; voter reaction; information resulting from a TRIAL BALLOON.

In radio engineers' vocabulary, *feedback* describes the loud squeak that jars the nerves of an audience when loudspeakers are misplaced in such a way that they feed sound waves back into the microphone.

In automation, the word is the essence of automatic control: the return to input of part of the output of a machine, system, or process.

In politics, feedback is the information candidates get when they have probed in a given direction. Approving or critical, it registers the first test reaction before a major commitment. Example: "Put out a rumor that I'm supporting so-and-so and see what kind of feedback we get." A recent offshoot of the term is *blowback*.

A second political meaning is negative reaction, similar to but not synonymous with FALLOUT; see also FLAK. Most often, *feedback* encompasses both bouquets and brickbats.

feeding frenzy Intense media interest; excessive attacks by the media.

This derogation of oppressive press and broadcast reporters began in the 1970s. An Associated Press article of March 9, 1977, reported a speech by Gerald L. Warren, who was editor of *The San Diego Union* and a former Nixon press secretary. In the speech, he called for the end of "jugular journalism" that leads some reporters to behave like "sharks in a feeding frenzy."

The literal sense dates back to *Shark Attack*, a 1958 book by V.M. Coppleson, who discusses "slow feeding" as "distinct from 'collective behavior' or 'frenzied feeding,' seen under somewhat rare conditions. In this case, sharks compete with others for possession of the prey and attack everything within range."

Thomas P. Murphy, commenting on the business use of the term, wrote in *Forbes* magazine in 1983: "A feeding frenzy, in case you are not a fisherman, occurs when bait is thrown to a school of hungry fish. They go wild, slashing at the bait, each other and anything else with the temerity to move."

Political use of the noun phrase resurfaced in 1988, after Senator Dan Quayle was introduced as George Bush's vice presidential candidate. His expression when told of his selection for nominee was widely described as "like a deer caught in the headlights." Don Kowet wrote in *The Washington Times* about what he saw as the media's savaging of Quayle: "In a piranha-like feeding frenzy, yesterday television news tossed away any pretense of fairness."

feet to the fire Pressure to fulfill a commitment.

The phrase is customarily used in regard to persuading delegates to conventions to honor their promises, and often implies economic coercion. "Who knows his banker? Who's his boss? Who does he do most of his business with? Put his feet to the fire."

Governor Ronald Reagan of California said in 1967 he would approve a withholding system of taxation only if "they held a hot iron to my feet." Senator Stephen Young told of a colleague who had switched his vote, and was congratulated by a friend for having "seen the light." The reply: "I didn't see the light, but I felt the heat."

The New York Times in 1968 used the phrase in this way: "Senator Robert F. Kennedy has been squirming rather uncomfortably at the edge of the national arena of late, and the man who has been putting his feet to the political fire has been his supposed comrade-in-arms, Senator Eugene F. McCarthy of Minnesota."

Gradations of political pressure begin with a mild *talk to him*, rise to *twist his arm*, then *lean on him*, and finally *put his feet to the fire*. See LEVERAGE.

fellow countrymen See MY FRIENDS.

fellow immigrants A pointed, though apocryphal, reminder to "bluebloods" that the status of their ancestors was no different from those who recently emigrated to America.

This salutation, to some in the audience more grating than ingratiating, is used to hail one's compatriots while alluding to the variety of ethnic backgrounds.

President Franklin Delano Roosevelt's April 21, 1938, speech to the Daughters of the American Revolution is remembered as the "My fellow immigrants" speech, although F.D.R.—often derided as "a traitor to his class"—did not use the salutation.

F.D.R. first reminded the audience that he was one of them: "it so happens, through no fault of my own, that I am descended from a number of people who came over in the *Mayflower.*" Then he made the point that modern aristocrats must not forget their non-aristocratic heritage; the closest he came to "my fellow immigrants" was this passage: "Remember always that all of us, and you and I especially, are descended from immigrants and revolutionists."

The purpose of the ad-libbed remark, made the day after the upper-class audience had adopted resolutions denouncing his leftist proposals, was to assure his "class" that his New Deal was not traitorous to its immigrant heritage, and to suggest gently that the members of the D.A.R. not forget their roots.

Variants of the phrase have also been tried. Vice President Dan Quayle, addressing the American-Israeli Public Affairs Committee in 1992, used the phrase "fellow Zionists."

The compression of FDR's message into "my fellow immigrants" was done by "the editing of history" as a play on the standard salutation "my fellow Americans," or more specifically in Roosevelt's case, his fireside-chat radio salutation "MY FRIENDS."

fellow traveler One who accepted most Communist doctrine, but was not a member of the Communist party; in current use, one who agrees with a philosophy or group but does not publicly work for it.

Leon Trotsky was troubled by some Russian authors of the 1920s who showed an interest in the Bolshevik Revolution, but were not dedicated to it. The disciple of Lenin, later murdered on Stalin's orders, made the distinction in 1924: "They are not the artists of the proletarian revolution, but only its artistic *fellow travelers.*" That quote continues "in the sense in which this word was used by the old Socialists," indicating Trotsky was not the originator of the phrase.

The columnist Max Lerner, in an article in *The Nation* in 1936 titled "Mr. Roosevelt and his *Fellow Travelers,*" explained: "The term has a Russian background and means someone who does not accept all your aims but has enough in common with you to

accompany you in a comradely fashion part of the way." After World War II, the term was most often applied to those accused of having been in general agreement with the Communist party.

The word in Russian is *poputchik.* Another word for "fellow traveler" is *sputnik,* used as the name for a Russian space satellite, as something (the satellite) accompanying a traveler (the earth).

Fellow traveler was an attack phrase on leftists; the Chinese Communist attack phrase on rightist "lackeys of capitalism" has been *running dogs.* V. I. Lenin has been frequently quoted as referring to "the USE-FUL IDIOTS OF THE WEST," but a lengthy search at the author's request by the Library of Congress of all his writings has not turned up a source. The political synonym of *fellow traveler* is "sympathizer"; when Muslim extremists replaced Communists as geopolitical villains, one phrase used was "Islamofascist *sympathizers.*"

See "when it walks like a duck" under PROVERBS AND AXIOMS, POLITICAL.

feminazi See WOMEN'S LIB.

fence To place restrictions on; to limit by using conditions or requirements.

In political use, *fence* as a verb took on a sense of "to limit by legislation." During the Reagan Administration, Senator John Tower of Texas announced that "funding for production of the MX missile would be retained in the bill but would be fenced." A spokeswoman explained, "In Senator Tower's statement, the word *fence* was used to mean 'restrict.' The money for the MX was to be approved, but before it could be used, certain requirements had to be met—that was the restriction, or the fence." Tower's usage was probably dialectal, similar to that of the western-flavored song "Don't Fence Me In."

This verb began in the fifteenth century with the literal sense of "to enclose with a fence." One of the verb's various figurative senses has been "to sell stolen property to a fence," the slang noun meaning "a receiver of stolen goods."

Almost synonymous with *fence* is the verb *cap,* which politicians borrowed from the oil industry's use of "to place a cap on," as in *capping* a gusher. *Cap* means "to restrict in height" and is usually used with amounts of money in spending; *fence* restricts in width by applying conditions or requirements that must be met.

fence, on the Undecided; unwilling to take a position; straddling.

In its original use, *on the fence* meant refusing to take a firm stand for or against a candidate or issue and was an attack phrase. That sense continues, but a new use has arisen: to be "on the fence" is not all bad, because it shows that a political figure is considering all the alternatives.

The term blossomed in 1828 and was probably in use before then. The *Ohio Journal* in that year summed up the Senate split between supporters of President John Quincy Adams and Andrew Jackson:

> Administration 22
> Jackson   13
> On the fence   1

The *Georgia Journal* in 1840 suggested a position that was later termed ALL THINGS TO ALL MEN to politicians of the time: "Our advice to all politicians who have a hankering after the praise of all … is to take a position near the fence, on the fence, or above the fence."

Carl Schurz, insisting on political independence, described his position (according to James Blaine) "as that of a man sitting on a fence, with clean boots, watching carefully which way he may leap to keep out of the mud."

This defense of fence-sitting as the best place to be before all the facts are in remains a secondary meaning of the phrase. Daniel P. Moynihan told the Americans for Democratic Action in 1967:

> President Johnson is said to be fond of relating the experience of an out-of-work school teacher who applied for a position in a small town on the Texas plains at the very depths of the depression. After a series of questions one puckered rancher on the school board looked at him and asked, did he teach that the world was round or that the world was flat. Finding no clues in the faces of the other members of the board, the teacher swallowed hard and allowed he could teach it either way.

Johnson's Texas background led to his being criticized as "tall in the STRADDLE," a play on *saddle*, when he took a position on the fence. *Straddle*, its political use traced to 1843, carries a more negative connotation than being *on the fence*. See ALL THINGS TO ALL MEN.

fence mending Looking after interests in one's POWER BASE; taking good care of the folks back home.

When Senator John Sherman of Ohio made a trip home in 1879, ostensibly to look after his farm but actually to see to his political interests, he insisted to reporters that he was home "only to repair my fences."

The following interchange took place in the House of Representatives on August 16, 1888:

> Mr. Dougherty:—I presume [the absent members] are at home seeking renomination or looking after their fences…. Mr. Weaver:—I have "fences" as well as other gentlemen; but my friends will look after my "fences" while I am here…Mr. Springer:—I am very anxious that the public business would be dispatched as early as possible, and that we may return to our constituents; and then, if there are any "fences" to be mended, … we shall have our own time in which to attend to such matters.

A deeper sense of *fence mending* was given in Robert Frost's poem "Mending Wall." In it the poet explains the comradeship and sense of mutual respect between two men who recognize each other's limitations:

> *Before I built a wall I'd ask to know*
> *What I was walling in or walling out …*
> *Something there is that doesn't love a wall,*
> *That wants it down …*
> *He says again, "Good fences make good*
>   *neighbors."*

Fences have an important place in politics. *Fence mending*—talking to local politicians, contributors, workers, and newsmen—is considered good and necessary, but *sitting on the fence* is often considered cowardly, and *fence straddling* is opportunistic. See FENCE, ON THE.

The underworld use of *fence*—as an intermediary for stolen goods—is not used in politics; however, a baseball metaphor, *hitting it over the fence*, is occasionally used in politics to describe a successful speech, and politicians parry questions while *fencing* with reporters.

The British equivalent to *fence-mending* is "nursing a constituency."

fetcher bill A legislative proposal designed to attract a bribe to bury it.

Like RIPPER BILL, this is statehouse lingo. Frank Trippet, in *The States: United They Fell* (1967), defined a *fetcher bill* as "a measure that, by threatening to curtail some commercial interest, provides incentive for a payoff to obtain the death of the bill."

Its origin is in old English slang. The *OED* has a meaning for *fetch*, beyond the usual verb "go get," as a noun to mean "contrivance, stratagem or trick." A 1745 citation reads: "This might be another of their politick Fetches." A *fetcher bill* is one that *fetches*—or solicits, or goes and brings back—a bribe.

few die and none resign See ADVICE AND CONSENT.

fiasco See BAY OF PIGS FIASCO.

field expedient An alteration in plans made on the stump without consulting campaign headquarters.

A *field expedient* is an army term for a makeshift substitute: an ingenious device, made from materials at hand, to take the place of a manufactured item. A rifle barrel can be cleaned with a government-issue item consisting of a small lead weight, a chain, and a square of chamois cloth. When this is lost, soldiers come up with a "field expedient" of a small pebble, a string, and a piece of shirt-tail.

When General Eisenhower was campaigning through upstate New York in 1952, he was scheduled to broadcast to a New York City fund-raising dinner from Governor Thomas E. Dewey's mansion in Albany. A microphone and loudspeaker were set up in Dewey's office for the two-way broadcast of a conversation between dinner chairman Paul Hoffman in New York City and Eisenhower and Dewey in Albany.

A moment before the broadcast was to begin, the line went dead. The author, then on furlough from the Army, was the director of this event and looked at the radio engineer; thinking quickly, the engineer made a telephone call to the Grand Ballroom of the Waldorf-Astoria, got Hoffman on that end of the line, and jammed earphones on the heads of Dewey and Eisenhower. The earphones were too small for Dewey and hurt his head; angrily, he muttered, "Save us from AMATEURS."

Eisenhower, who had been tense at the sudden change in technical setup and worried looks of the engineer and director, immediately relaxed when the director explained, "Field expedient, General." "Nothing to worry about," the nominee reassured Dewey. "This is a field expedient." Since the General seemed to expect him to understand the term, Dewey stopped glaring and coolly proceeded to introduce the broadcast.

fifth column Any secret group of traitors, or sympathizers with an enemy, prepared to rise up and strike on his behalf from behind the lines at the most propitious moment.

The term was coined by Emilio Mola, a rebel general in the Spanish Civil War. The term was used during an interview granted by General Mola while his troops were advancing on the then Loyalist-held capital of Madrid in October 1936. Mola described how four rebel columns were converging on the city; when asked by a reporter which column he believed would actually capture the city, he replied, "the fifth."

The phrase was used again and elaborated on in a radio broadcast on October 16, 1936. The exact words have been lost, but General Mola made it clear that by a "fifth column" he meant sympathizers of the Franco cause who would rise within the city at the appropriate time. General Mola died in an airplane crash on June 3, 1937, before the fifth column of which he boasted achieved the results he had predicted.

The world, wrote *Time* magazine in 1947, "pounced on the phrase with the eagerness of a man who has been groping for an important word." Ernest Hemingway titled his only play *The Fifth Column*; it was presented in a 1937 performance at Madrid's Florida Hotel, a center for foreigners sympathetic with the Loyalist cause.

The phrase was later used to describe the secret Hitler sympathizers in Western Europe, then to identify almost any hidden group of enemies. *Chicago Daily News* correspondent Leland Stowe, covering the fall of Norway to the Nazis in World War II, broadcast a description of that country's collapse in which he charged Norway had fallen "to its fifth column of QUISLINGS and others."

President Roosevelt used "sixth column" to describe the "gossips and defeatists" during World War II. In his 1946 IRON CURTAIN speech, Winston Churchill described Communist parties in Western countries as "Communist fifth columns [which] are established and work in complete unity and absolute obedience to the directive they receive from the Communist center."

The metaphor's use is current. In late 2002, the defeated Democratic presidential candidate, Al Gore, told the *New York Observer* that "conservatives in the media like the Fox News Network, the *Washington Times*, and Rush Limbaugh are financed by wealthy ultra-conservative billionaires who make political deals with Republican administrations and most of the media has been slow to recognize the pervasive impact of this fifth column in their ranks."

Fifty-Four Forty or Fight See WAR HORSE.

fighting the problem Refusal to come to grips with a situation that requires action; pettifogging delay.

This military expression gained some currency in political life. An army recruit who explains to the mess sergeant that unpeeled potatoes have more vitamins and better flavor than peeled potatoes is "fighting the problem": sooner or later, he will have to peel the potatoes.

"As Secretary of State," wrote Harry Truman in his memoirs, "[General George C.] Marshall had to listen to more staff talk than when he was Chief of Staff. He would listen for a long time without comment, but when the debates between members of his staff seemed destined to go on interminably and he could stand it no longer, he would say, 'Gentlemen, don't fight the problem; decide it.'"

Defense Secretary Robert Lovett used another line in the same kind of situation: "Gentlemen, as one rat said to the other, 'To hell with the cheese, let's get out of the trap.'"

fight the good fight To stand up for one's convictions; a lifelong battle for principle.

The Bible is known as "the good book," and "the good fight" is an ethical fight. The outcome is less important to the definition than the idea of taking a stand on a question of principle. The phrase comes from the second epistle of Paul to Timothy (4:7): "I have fought a good fight, I have finished my course, I have kept the faith."

Senator George Norris of Nebraska, a leader in battles to overthrow the arbitrary rule of House Speaker "Uncle Joe" Cannon, to introduce federal power in the Tennessee Valley, and to abolish the LAME DUCK Congress with the Twentieth Amendment, put it this way toward the end of his life: "I have fought the good fight with all that was in me. Now there is no strength left. Other hands must take up the burden. Remember, the battle against injustice is never won."

Adlai Stevenson, with his defeat all but certain, titled his final television appeal of the 1952 campaign "The Good Fight." In political use, it has come to connote a worthwhile but losing battle, and was the title of a 1993 book by former Senator Gary Hart. The point to remember is that it is not the fight that is good but it is the good that is worth fighting for.

filibuster A technique by which a minority of senators attempts to defeat or alter a measure favored by the majority through the device of continuous talking, or when a senator dramatically calls public attention to a bill he considers is being "railroaded through."

The entire process rests upon the Senate's pride in itself as the world's foremost chamber of enlightened debate. Until 1917 speeches could go on and on, preventing measures from being brought to a vote. Then, in reaction to the LITTLE GROUP OF WILLFUL MEN who had filibustered to death Woodrow Wilson's proposal to deter U-boat attacks by arming merchant vessels, the Senate adopted Rule 22, which provided for cloture (more often used than *closure*), a two-thirds vote to end debate (amended to three-fifths in 1975). Filibusters are not possible in the House of Representatives, where the rules limit the duration of any individual's right to speak, or in Great Britain's House of Commons, where Rule 20 permits the Speaker to direct a member "who persists in irrelevance" to "discontinue his speech."

The usual strategy is for the group of senators involved in a filibuster to follow one another in planned succession. As the vocal cords or imagination of one begins to tire, he yields to a successor. Subject matter need not be relevant—a common phrase is "reading the telephone book"; a synonym is "talkathon," or marathon talk.

The word was first used to describe the sixteenth-century English and French privateers who began by raiding Spanish treasure ships in the waters of the Caribbean, then known as the Spanish Main, and who ended up, more often than not, as pirates.

The word is derived from the Dutch *vrijbuiter* (*vrij*, "free," and *buiter*, "booter") or "freebooter," a word commonly used to describe pirates. *Freebooter* was borrowed into French as *flibustier* and into Spanish as *filibustero*, and then back to English as *filibuster*.

Whatever the origin, the term was already common in American politics in its present sense by the time of the Civil War. It was first used during a debate on the floor of the House on Jan. 3, 1853. A group of Southerners had been organizing expeditions to seize Cuba from Spain and annex it to the U.S.; the Democrats were in favor of this, the Whigs were opposed. Abraham W. Venable (D-N.C.) broke with his party to support the Whig policy of nonintervention, saying that if the U.S. were to acquire Cuba, it should not be through filibustering (that is, piracy): "Originally freebooter in Old English, ... [it] is now in our tongue filibuster, but still a freebooter; and it will not be surprising if it should become one day the watchword of a party... If the policy of any Administration is to make the United States the brigands of the world ... I utterly denounce the policy." Albert G. Brown (D-Miss.) responded: "When I saw my friend standing on the other side of the House, filibustering, as I thought, against the United States, surrounded, as he was, by admiring Whigs, I did not know what to think." The vivid word quickly became attached to the practice of making speeches to block legislation.

Until 1957, Southern senators were able to defeat proposed civil rights legislation by filibustering, and often merely by threatening to filibuster. The countermeasures employed by the majority were round-the-clock sessions, intended to wear the minority down, and cloture, which required a super-majority; in this manner the 1957 Civil Rights Bill was finally passed.

The all-time champion filibusterer was Republican—formerly Democratic—Senator Strom Thurmond of South Carolina, who talked for more than twenty-four hours in his losing battle against the 1957 bill. The man considered to be his closest challenger was Democratic—formerly Republican—Senator Wayne Morse of Oregon. However, Senator Morse rejected the role, claiming his most strenuous long-talking efforts made in opposition to the Kennedy Administration's space satellite communication bill was not filibustering but merely "education."

In 1967 Senator Albert Gore (D-Tenn.), attempting to stop the tax checkoff measure for financing political campaigns, protested a delaying action taken by Louisiana Senator Russell Long. Long (whose father Huey set the then-record of sixteen hours in 1935) replied with an expression reminiscent of Alice in Wonderland's "curiouser and curiouser": "When the Senator talks about delaying tactics," he said, "he is speaking as one filibusterer to another filibusterer."

A similar technique in the Japanese Diet is the "cow-waddle," used to delay a vote and express minority displeasure. As the vote is called, opposition members individually waddle—with infinite slowness, stopping to chat along the way—to the ballot box on the rostrum.

For a recent threat to stop the filibuster in the Senate, see NUCLEAR OPTION and the GANG OF FOURTEEN who averted the confrontation. Also see GAG RULE, GRIDLOCK, and UP-OR-DOWN VOTE.

Final Solution Hitler's planned extermination of the Jews; now used to mean any plan whose carrying out would lead to a neat, if morally corrupt, conclusion.

This euphemism for mass murder was used by Reinhard ("The Hangman") Heydrich, then head of the Reich Security Police, in a letter of November 6, 1941, to the Nazi Quartermaster General. He had previously used the term (in German, *Endlösung*) in a secret report about Polish Jews to the German military officials in Poland in September of 1939.

"At the Nuremberg trials," Charles Whittier of the Library of Congress informed the author, "a memorandum from Hermann Goering to Heydrich, dated July 31, 1941, was cited: Goering claimed that *Endlösung* in that memo meant 'total' solution and not 'final' (*Gesamtlösung*, rather than *Endlösung*)."

Another user of the term was Franz Stuckart, who drafted the Nuremberg decrees in 1938, but in his use it probably did not mean what has come to be called "GENOCIDE": Stuckart recommended the deportation of all Jews from Germany so as to make the Reich "*Judenrein*," or free of Jewish taint.

The earliest use the author can find is in the March 10, 1920, *Völkischer Beobachter* ("Racial Observer"), using the term *Endziel*, or "final goal," and proposing concentration camps for Jews.

The phrase is now used ironically in the U.S., as an example of the furthest reach of euphemism. In the late 1980s, another term was popularized for genocide: ETHNIC CLEANSING. The Armenians and Azerbaijanis were fighting for control of the autonomous enclave of Azerbaijan called Nagorno-Karabakh in 1988; according to Serbo-Croatian sources, Soviet officials used this term—in Russian, *etnicheskaya chistka*—to describe the attempts of one group to drive out the other.

See HOLOCAUST.

finding The decision within the executive branch that allows a president secretly to suspend a law involving national security.

Finding is a gerund (a verb form functioning as a noun) that was first used in the fourteenth century for "the act of locating." Shoemakers picked up the term and applied it to parts and materials, such as laces and buckles, used in the making of shoes. By 1859, the noun had received a legal sense: "the result of an official inquiry or investigation; a judicial decision."

From that judicial sense comes the political use of *finding*, often capitalized in security use. The National Security Act of 1947 allows a president to make the decision about when to obey or to suspend a law, but requires the chief executive to report the finding to the Congress in timely fashion. Subsequent legislation required the president to inform the Intelligence committees of House and Senate of findings in a timely fashion. Presidents and congressional leaders traditionally differed on the meaning of "timely."

Ronald Reagan's Finding (capitalized when referring to a specific document) on arms sales to Iran was released almost a year after its signing. This Finding, a secret document when signed by the President on January 17, 1986, stated in part: "I hereby find that the following operation ... is important ... and direct the Director of Central Intelligence to refrain from reporting this Finding to the Congress." In 1991, the law was changed to require the President to inform the committees of a finding "before the initiation of the covert action authorized by the finding."

finesse As a verb, to use a stratagem of applying only as much power as is absolutely necessary to accomplish a political goal, yet not so much power as to induce a counterattack; as a noun, style (as viewed by an ally), trickiness, guile (as seen by an enemy).

In establishing the right of judicial review, Chief Justice John Marshall "finessed" President Thomas Jefferson. At the start of Jefferson's Administration, the Supreme Court was filled with Federalists appointed by John Adams. Jeffersonian Republicans let it be known that if the Court tried to invalidate important Republican measures, the President would defy the judges, thereby denying the Court the power to declare laws unconstitutional.

Marshall selected the case of *Marbury v. Madison* to finesse the President. He invalidated a minor part of a bill that, ironically, would have given certain technical powers to the Supreme Court. Had he chosen an important Republican measure to declare unconstitutional, Jefferson would have joined the issue and disputed judicial review. But this was a minor, technical matter at hand, without even a specific court order for Jefferson to refuse to obey. The President was finessed, and the vital precedent was set.

On the point of applying "just enough" power, a common expression is: "You don't use an elephant gun to shoot a rabbit."

Finesse entered political language through cardplaying (as did NEW DEAL). In bridge, a *finesse* is the withholding of a higher card in the hope that a lower card will take the trick. Also, in croquet, an opponent is *finessed* by placing the ball in a difficult position for him to make a shot, which is what Marshall did to Jefferson. See CARD METAPHORS.

finger on the button Ready to launch an atomic war; a scare phrase used in attacking candidates who complain of a NO-WIN POLICY.

President Lyndon Johnson, campaigning on television in 1964, let the nation know that he considered Barry Goldwater TRIGGER-HAPPY: "You must have strength, and you must always keep your guard up, but you must always have your hand out and be willing to go anywhere, talk to anybody, listen to anything they have to say, do anything that is honorable, in order to avoid pulling that trigger, mashing that button that will blow up the world."

Former President Dwight Eisenhower, in a televised conversation with candidate Goldwater, did what he could to refute the implication: "This is actual tommyrot…you're not going to be doing those things that are going to be—what do they call it?—push button, you're not going to push a button here and start a war." In a 1954 press conference, Eisenhower gave a more eloquent explanation of the restraints a president must keep on himself: "In many ways the easy course for a president, for the administration, is to adopt a truculent, publicly bold, almost insulting attitude. A president experiences exactly the same resentments, the same anger, the same kind of sense of frustration almost, when things like this occur to other Americans, and his impulse is to lash out."

Kennedy aide Ted Sorensen called the president "custodian of the nuclear trigger." *Trigger* and *button* are interchangeable in this sense, in both the U.S. and Britain. In the 1951 British election, the Labour party accused the Conservatives of being warmongers, an attack led by the *Daily Mirror*'s article, "Whose Finger on the Trigger?"

This use of *trigger* is related to the Western "hair-trigger" (see TRIGGER-HAPPY); *button*, as in *push-button war*, is becoming preferred, and is probably derived from the *panic button* of World War II. Writing in *American Speech* magazine, Lt. Col. James L. Jackson, USAF, suggests:

The actual source seems probably to have been the bell system used in bombers (B-17, B-24) for emergency procedures such as bailout and ditching. In case of fighter or flak damage so extensive that the bomber had to be abandoned, the pilot rang a "prepare-to-abandon" ring and then a ring meaning "jump." The bell system was used since the intercom was apt to be out if there was extensive damage. The implications of the phrase seem to have come from those few times when pilots hit the panic button too soon and rang for emergency procedures over minor damage, causing their crews to bail out unnecessarily.

Eddie Mahe, an adviser to the Reagan campaign, said in 1992 about his candidate's success: "The only thing he had to prove to people was that they did not have to be scared if he had his finger on the button.... When he proved that, it was over."

Soon after taking office in 1969, Richard Nixon removed an electric push-button window-opener from his White House bedroom, which had been installed by President Johnson. "I took that out," President Nixon told the author and others, "because I was afraid if I pushed the button, I'd blow up the world."

fire in the belly A thirst for power; the burning drive to achieve a goal.

In political lingo, the expression is usually used to indicate a presidential candidate's burning (in the sense of "fierce") desire to win, particularly the willingness to endure the long contest. It first appeared in print in 1882, in an essay by Robert Louis Stevenson, in which he compared historians Thomas Carlyle and Thomas Babington Macaulay. "Carlyle," wrote Stevenson, "had a fire in his belly so much more hotly burning than the patent reading-lamp by which Macaulay studied, that it seems at first sight hardly fair to bracket them together."

When Senator Howard Baker, a laid-back and unflappable politician, coolly campaigned for the Republican presidential nomination in 1984, he countered suspicions about his willingness to go the distance by insisting: "I have the fire in the belly."

To assure voters he was not too cooly cerebral, Senator Barak Obama closed his 2008 presidential campaign speeches with a rousing "Fired up! Ready to go!"

How to turn the cliché upside down was demonstrated in 1989 by Dianne Feinstein, then mayor of San Francisco. At the start of her campaign for the governorship of California, her longtime political consultant resigned from the campaign, claiming that the candidate lacked "fire in the belly." When shortly afterward she underwent a hysterectomy, the future Senator Feinstein quipped, "I had a fire in the belly and had it removed."

fireside chat A warm talk by a leader to a few million of his intimate friends.

In 1938, President Roosevelt allowed as how he wasn't sure how the term *fireside chat* began to be applied to his radio talks. "The name 'fireside chat,'" he said, "seems to be used by the press even when the radio talk is delivered on a very hot mid-summer evening."

FDR's first fireside chat as president was made on March 12, 1933, dealing with the opening of banks the next day. However, he had used radio talks in the same way during his first term as governor of New York State, principally to woo upstate Republicans who received most of their information from Republican newspapers.

The title of the first speech made no mention of firesides; it was "An Intimate Talk with the People of the United States on Banking." In a letter dated October 30, 1933, FDR recalled the audience he had in mind: "I tried to picture a mason at work on a new building, a girl behind a counter, and a farmer in his field." Joseph Abrell pointed out in an unpublished study of Roosevelt's radio usage, "the term 'Fireside Chat' was not applied to his first such address but in promoting the second. Harry C. Butcher, who in 1933 was head of the CBS office in Washington, D.C., suggested the name, and from then on they were identified as such by everybody from the 'girl behind the counter' to Roosevelt himself."

Will Rogers thought the talk had so simply explained banking that "even bankers understood it." *The New York Times* editorialized: "His use of this new instrument of political discussion is a plain hint to Congress of a recourse which the President may employ if it proves necessary to rally support for legislation which he asks for and which the lawmakers might be reluctant to give him." Backhanded testimony came from defeated Republican candidate Alf Landon in 1938: "The Presidency is primarily an executive office, not a broadcasting station." (See BULLY PULPIT.)

Roosevelt was so effective as a radio speaker that succeeding presidents were urged by their advisers to give more radio and TV reports to the nation. President Kennedy's journalist friends urged him so strongly to use the airwaves more often that he commented, "People seem to think Roosevelt gave a fireside chat once a week." Kennedy's staff found that Roosevelt gave only thirty fireside chats during his twelve years as President; before World War II, he averaged only two a year. See OVEREXPOSURE.

The collocation (words placed together that become familiar as a phrase, as in *fireside* and *chat*) was used as the basis for a gag in 1976 poking fun at Senator Henry Jackson's lackluster speech delivery, used later about Senators Sam Nunn and Bill Bradley, and again in the '90s about an FDR successor as New York Governor, George Pataki: "If he gave a fireside chat, the fire would go out."

When President Carter made a televised "fireside chat"—complete with crackling fire—in 1977, he included a wrinkle of his own: a cardigan sweater.

firestorm Sudden, fierce controversy; a surge of public fury.

"Richard Nixon clung tenuously to office last week," wrote *Newsweek* in November 1973, "in the face of the most devastating assault that any American President has endured in a century—a nationwide rebuke of such magnitude that one of Mr. Nixon's principal aides described it as 'a fire storm.'"

The anonymous source was probably White House chief of staff Alexander Haig, a lifelong Army officer accustomed to the vocabulary of military catastrophe. The following April, *Newsweek* reprised the word to describe the scene: "It was a full five months since the Saturday-night massacre—the firing of Special Prosecutor Archibald Cox, the resignation of Attorney General Elliot Richardson and the ouster of his deputy, William Ruckelshaus—touched off the fire storm of public outrage that made the impeachment of a U.S. President a real possibility."

General Haig was familiar with the term from its use in the language of atomic warfare. After a heavy incendiary attack, or the dropping of an atomic bomb, rising hot air creates a vacuum that causes a "storm" of air to rush in, causing further devastation. In 1959 *The New York Times* estimated casualties in an atomic attack in this way: "Nearly half of these could be expected to die instantly, killed by blast or incinerated in the fire-storms caused by the explosions."(The *OED* tracks the word back to 1581 in a similar upward-sucking metaphor: "Helias…was taken vp into Heauen in a fire storme.")

Although the word was occasionally used in its political sense before Watergate (columnist James J. Kilpatrick wrote in 1970 that "the next revolutionary who strikes a match in Seattle may ignite a political firestorm"), its association with the most crucial moment in the Nixon decline annealed it to political crisis terminology. When President Gerald Ford issued his surprise pardon of Mr. Nixon, CBS correspondent Bruce Morton quoted a congressman as saying he predicted "a firestorm of criticism," a calibration more dire than criticism's usual *storm*. The *Wall Street Journal* used the same word for the same event the next month: "It may well be, as some of Mr. Ford's oldest and closest advisers say privately, that the President will soon recover from the fire storm that followed the Nixon pardon."

As in most catastrophic figures of speech—see DISASTER METAPHORS—the new word was soon trivialized. When Secretary of Agriculture Earl Butz made a racial slur in a joke told privately during the 1976 campaign, John Fialka wrote in *The Washington Star*: "What began as a casual conversation among three airline passengers—John Dean, Pat Boone and Earl Butz—has ended in a political firestorm that has cost Butz his job …" In this way, *firestorm* (now usually one word, sometimes hyphenated) has almost become synonymous with FLAP, which is unfortunate, since a word for a sudden public-opinion rage is useful.

first in war "To the memory of the man," read the resolution presented to the House of Representatives by Henry (Light Horse Harry) Lee on the death of George Washington in 1799, "first in war, first in peace, first in the hearts of his countrymen."

The line is as famous as any in American history primarily because of the circumstances in which it was spoken; at the death of a great president, the nation is attuned to a memorable phrase (attributed to Stanton on Lincoln: "Now he belongs to the ages"). The line also scans in three-syllable beats like the hoofbeats of a galloping horse: first-in-war / first-in-peace / first-in-the / hearts-of-his / countrymen. This rhythm has led to parroting, which overlooks the truth in the phrase: Washington was indeed the man who was most responsible for winning the Revolutionary War, for setting up a republic, and refusing a monarchy, and was the most popular American.

When Tammany Hall scandals began to embarrass New York Governor Franklin Roosevelt in 1931, *Time* magazine wrote of Tammany: "First in war, first in peace, first in pockets of its countrymen." And in 1967, cartoonist Conrad in the *Los Angeles Times* pictured a colonial-looking Lyndon Johnson as "First in War, second in Peace, and 46% in the Polls of his countrymen." The former Washington Senators baseball team was derided as "First in war, first in peace, and last in the American League."

first lady The wife of the President of the U.S.

British war correspondent William Howard Russell (who coined the phrase *thin red line* in the 1877 edition of his book about the Crimean War, *The War: From the Landing at Gallipoli*) used *first lady* in *My Diary North and South*, in 1863. "The gentleman who furnished fashionable paragraphs for the Washington paper has some charming little pieces of gossip about 'the first Lady in the Land.'" (For the history of *thin red line*, see http://www.oed.com/learning/word-stories/red-line.html.) His use of the phrase in quotations indicates an earlier usage than this reference to Mary Todd Lincoln. Carl Sferrazza Anthony points out a possible coinage in his book *First Ladies* when President Zachary Taylor eulogized Dolley Madison in 1849: "She will never be forgotten, because she was truly our First Lady for a half-century." The British novelist Edward Bulwer-Lytton used the expression in his

1853 book *My Novel*: "she looked like the first lady in the land."

American poet and novelist Mary Clemmer Ames used the phrase in describing the inauguration of President Rutherford B. Hayes on March 5, 1877. It was popularized when playwright Charles Nirdlinger wrote a comedy about Dolley Madison in 1911, entitled *The First Lady in the Land*, which enjoyed a good run at New York's Gaiety Theatre. She was the first presidential wife also to be a public figure. In recent administrations, Nancy Reagan was noted (and occasionally criticized) for her influence on White House business, and Hillary Clinton's active role in health care reform for a time earned her the title of TMPWA (see ACRONYMS, POLITICAL), for "the most powerful woman in America."

When the president dies, the first lady ceases to be "first," but may remain a celebrity. Eleanor Roosevelt was consistently on the "most admired American" lists after 1945, and was often introduced as "First Lady of the World." Jacqueline Kennedy remained the center of some attention after Lady Bird Johnson became first lady in 1963.

In the '80s, the wife of the vice president began to be called "the second lady," despite its ambiguous meaning, with the acronym SLOTUS. This was dropped in the late '90s, in light of the Monica Lewinsky scandal; Hillary Rodham Clinton was often referred to as FLOTUS, "First Lady of the United States," on the analogy of POTUS, applied to her husband. In early primaries of 2008, as the possibility loomed of Bill Clinton returning to the White House as husband of the president, the title suggested was "First Laddie."

fiscal integrity The "motherhood" of budgetary policy—everybody is for the goal, but differs on ways to get there.

Fiscal policy has to do with budgeting the government's taxes against its expenditures; *monetary* policy concerns itself with the interest rates that reflect and guide the flow of funds in a nation. *Balanced budget* and *deficit financing* are phrases in the fiscal area; *easy* money and *hard* money belong in the monetary area.

Fiscal integrity, then, has been used most often to describe a balanced budget. It is stressed more often by conservatives, who usually charge liberals with budgetary recklessness and "fiscal irresponsibility." With the advent of Lord Keynes (see NEW ECONOMICS), the rules appeared to change on fiscal integrity: in recessions, perhaps fiscal integrity required deficit financing. (See PUMP-PRIMING.)

"I think the virtues of a 'balanced budget' can at times be exaggerated," wrote Harry Truman. "Andrew Jackson paid off the national debt entirely, and the budget was balanced when the unprecedented Panic of 1837 struck. Even the depression following the crash of 1929 overtook a government which was operating in the black."

Such a comment would have been considered heresy for a politician only a generation before. Its acceptance as a position without blinking—although with some gulping—indicated that "fiscal integrity" was shifting away from balancing the budget and toward some amorphous "doing the right thing for the economy to ensure prosperity, full employment, and no inflation." See PAY AS YOU GO. Both Presidents Bill Clinton and George W. Bush promised to "cut the deficit in half"—in the "out" years, recalling the words of St. Augustine: "O Lord, help me to be pure—but not yet."

fishing expedition Investigation without a legislative goal; a probe undertaken usually by a committee dominated by one party into the affairs of another party, for the purposes of unearthing whatever "bait" might be useful in a campaign.

The phrase can be used as a defensive smear of a legitimate investigation. Thomas L. Stokes wrote in 1940 about the Harding–Teapot Dome investigation of 1924: "many voters, undoubtedly, were willing to accept the Republican explanation that it was just a 'political fishing expedition.'"

In a 1955 Eisenhower cabinet meeting, Philip Ray, general counsel to the Department of Commerce, explained why he refused to turn over department records

to the House Judiciary Anti-Trust subcommittee, headed by Democrat Emmanuel Celler. Ray said that Celler seemed bent on a "fishing expedition," and Eisenhower agreed that the department should draw a line between what could and could not be released to a committee of Congress. According to reporter Robert Donovan's reading of the minutes of that meeting, Eisenhower said "he was never going to yield to the point where he would become known as a President who had practically crippled the Presidency." Supporters of Presidents Bush and Clinton used the phrase when asserting EXECUTIVE PRIVILEGE and seeking to impugn the constitutional basis for investigations by committees of the opposite party.

Judith Miller of *The New York Times* in 2006 resisted a subpoena from a special counsel prosecuting I. Lewis "Scooter" Libby, Vice President Cheney's top aide, for perjury, holding that she could not reveal a confidential source; to coerce her to testify, she was jailed for contempt of court for 85 days. Only when the prosecutor agreed to allow her attorney to redact any other sources from her notes, and not to question her about sources other than Libby—who toward the end of her incarceration personally released her from a pledge of confidentiality—did she agree to testify, having averted what she and her lawyers called "a FISHING EXPEDITION." See CHILLING EFFECT.

Other fishing metaphors in politics include the familiar *fish or cut bait,* the graphic *floundering around,* and an angler's expression adopted by politicians, *going fishing,* which means sitting out a campaign—not quite BOLTing but refusing to help. The July 2, 1876, *Cincinnati Commercial* wrote: "There has been a great deal of inquiry as to whom Carl Schurz was going for in the presidential campaign. Perhaps he is not going for anybody, but is going a-fishing." Writing on California Republican politics in *The New Republic* ninety years later, Andrew Kopkind observed: "[Senator Thomas] Kuchel supported [Mayor George] Christopher against [candidate for Governor Ronald] Reagan, and 'went fishing' in the general election."

To *fish for votes* is a common construction, leading to this frequent admonition to candidates too willing to spend time on citizens too young to vote or too deeply committed to either side: "Fish where the fish are."

five percenter One who claims to know officials in high places and can be "helpful" for a fee of five percent of a government contract.

Republicans, notably Senator Joseph McCarthy of Wisconsin, popularized the phrase in the friends-in-high-places scandals during the Truman Administration.

A New England furniture manufacturer, Paul Grindle, triggered a congressional investigation in 1949 by charging that James V. Hunt, a management counselor in Washington, assured him that he could introduce him to influential people for $1,000 down, $500 a month and five percent of any contract. Grindle closed the deal and then put reporters for the *New York Herald Tribune* on to the story.

Subsequent investigations uncovered other emoluments: the wife of an examiner of loans for the Reconstruction Finance Corporation received a $10,000 mink coat after the RFC had approved a loan for a Florida motel; Major General Harry Vaughan, President Truman's military aide, and other Washington notables received deep freezers as gifts. Truman refused to get drawn into a detailed discussion of the five-percenter investigations, and Vaughan said he was "bewildered and baffled" by the uproar about doing a few favors for friends. As a result of the Senate investigations, the RFC was reorganized, and there were some purges in both the Department of Justice and the Internal Revenue Service. For related attacks on the Truman Administration, see INFLUENCE PEDDLER; MESS IN WASHINGTON.. For more recent derogations of corrupt expediters of federal largesse, see BELTWAY BANDITS.

flak Opposition, especially noisy opposition to a new idea or program. To *run into flak* means to encounter some unexpected but not devastating criticism.

The word was coined in World War II to describe anti-aircraft gunfire, an acronym for the German *Flieger* (aircraft) *Abwehr* (defense) *Kanone* (gunfire). In politics, flak serves to bring down TRIAL BALLOONS.

The puffs of smoke of the exploding anti-aircraft shells may have also given rise to a similar word, *flack:* "press agent," or "public information officer," and more recently, "media adviser." The puffs refer derogatorily to "puffed-up" or inflated, exaggerated information; *puff pieces* are articles that flatter and swell the head of the subject. Fred Shapiro, editor of the *Yale Book of Quotations*, traced *flack* to a note in the June 1939 issue of *Better English* magazine: "That alert weekly, 'Variety,' birthplace of numerous Americanisms, is trying to coin the word 'flack' as a synonym for publicity agent. The word is said to be derived from Gene Flack, a movie publicity agent. Something Variety may have overlooked, however, is that a Yiddish word similar in sound means 'one who goes around talking about the other fellow's business.'"

The two meanings came together in a footnote to history. While working on a speech in the White House one day in 1969, the author received a call from David Young, an assistant to Henry Kissinger (who later went on to phrasemaking fame as the coiner of PLUMBER). The young aide wanted to know what *flack* meant. Because the first rule of bureaucratic survival is not to pass out any information without knowing its intended use, I deliberately misinterpreted the question and gave an answer that explained the German derivation of the acronym *flak*.

Moments later the aide called back to say, "Dr. Kissinger doesn't need you to teach him German, but he says a columnist named Joe Kraft just called him 'an Administration flack' and he wants to know whether he should take offense." With the background understood, the current meaning of *flack* with a *c*—"apologist, or paid proponent"—was passed along, with its pejorative but sometimes madcap connotation. To cheer up Dr. Kissinger, the thought was added that the role, if not the word, could be an honorable one, since a skilled advocate was needed to explicate foreign policy. However, when Dr. Kissinger next saw the author, he gloomed: "I decided to take offense." Perhaps he was wrong to worry about the relatively innocuous *flack*; in a few years he was to learn what it was to be the object of *flak* without a *c*, from this writer and others.

Flak, without the *c*, continues to be useful in political commentary. *National Journal* reported in February 1993, discussing the line-item veto, that "Clinton took some flak for his views"; a week earlier, the *Los Angeles Times* had commented on Hillary Clinton that "If she's going to catch flak...she might as well catch flak over something that matters, and health care does."

In 2007, after Senator John McCain (R-Ariz.) charged that Senators Barack Obama (D-Ill.) and Hillary Clinton (D-N.Y.) had "embraced the policy of surrender by voting against funds to support our brave men and women fighting in Iran and Afghanistan," Obama issued a written statement reminding voters that "Senator McCain required a flack jacket, 10 armored Humvees, 2 Apache attack helicopters and 100 soldiers with rifles by his side to stroll through a market in Baghdad just a few weeks ago." The Vietnam war hero McCain's rejoinder was, "By the way, Senator Obama, it's a 'flak' jacket, not a 'flack' jacket."

flaming liberal Attack phrase on a member of the political left; more colorful than *radical*.

Fire is often used to characterize radicalism. A *fiery* orator, or *firebrand, fires up* his audience; with *fire in his eyes*, he *inflames* their passions to *heated* argument about his *infernal* opinions about *burning* issues. (Smoke, on the other hand, implies deviousness: see SMOKE-FILLED ROOM and SMOKE SCREEN.) In politics, where there is smoke, there is often no fire.

The phrase arose parallel to the "flaming youth" of the 1920s. Labels like LIBERAL require adjectives to make a description more exact. During Prohibition, those who went along with repeal were called "Wets," and they opposed the "Drys"; but those who felt strongly about repeal were labeled "dripping Wets." (In Britain, ultra-accomodationists are called "wringing wets.") Similarly, liberals are tagged KNEE-JERK LIBERALS (who react without thinking), *professional* liberals (a favorite Harry Truman criticism of those who only talked liberalism), or *bleeding-heart* liberal (passionately caring), its religious root explicated under BLEEDING HEART.

A flyer put out by an extreme right-wing group in 1964 attacked "Hubert Humphrey: The FLAMING LIBERAL" as a member of "a semisecret, New York-based, Communist-appeasing group called the Council on Foreign Relations." The flyer did not add that other members of this group included Dwight Eisenhower, Lucius Clay, Edward Teller, and several of Barry Goldwater's foreign policy advisers.

flap See UNFLAPPABLE.

flat-out Maximum effort applied from the beginning, with no consideration given to rest, overexposure, or saving a last burst of energy and money for the end.

The phrase is probably derived from auto racing, where it means "maximum speed, accelerator flat on the floor."

The *flat-out* campaigner runs the risk of being spent, physically and financially, on the crucial weekend before election; the campaigner concerned with *peaking* runs the risk of having energy and money left over when it is too late to use them.

The phrase, now current, is often misused for the shorter word *flat*. When Robert Kennedy and FBI Director J. Edgar Hoover began trading charges in 1966 on who was responsible for electronic eavesdropping, one former Justice Department aide accused Hoover of "a flat-out lie." Prescriptive slanguists hold that lies and denials can be *flat* or *out-and-out*; campaigns and races are *flat-out*, hyphenated.

Opposite of *flat-out* is PEAKING, planning a campaign so that all activity, expenditure, and voter interest reach a crescendo just before election day. FDR began the 1936 campaign by going on a leisurely two-week cruise, allowing the Republicans to take center stage; his time would come nearer the decision date. "The Republican high command," he wrote his running mate, John Nance Garner, "is doing altogether too much talking at this stage of the game." See OVEREXPOSURE. In the campaign of 1960, Kennedy began as the underdog and ran a flat-out campaign, as an underdog must do; Nixon, who dropped back after the first debate on television, came on with a rush at the end, peaking just a few days too late to win. Wrote Arthur Schlesinger, Jr.: "Some close to Kennedy believed that, if the campaign had gone on three days more, he would have been beaten. The candidate himself knew the tide was shifting."

San Francisco Mayor George Christopher, Nelson Rockefeller's Northern California chairman in the 1964 Republican primary ultimately won by Barry Goldwater, gave this description of what it is like to be involved in an intense, flat-out campaign: "This morning I was sitting on the edge of the bed just holding a sock in my hand. My wife asked me what I was doing. I told her I was trying to figure out whether I was getting up or going to bed."

flat tax A single tax rate for all.

Proposals for a *flat tax* surface periodically in American politics, though usually with modifications that preserve some elements of the progressive, or graduated, income tax system by limiting the *flat tax* to wages or exempting people with incomes below a threshold amount. Five states—Illinois, Colorado, Massachusetts, Michigan, and Pennsylvania—had *flat taxes* in 2008.

Steve Forbes is the media-political figure associated most closely with this tax idea; he made it the centerpiece of his campaigns for the Republican presidential nomination in 1996 and 2000. Forbes initially proposed a flat rate of 17% of consumption, which he defined as income minus savings, with exemptions to be determined by size and type of household; the threshold for a family of four was $42,000. Senators Sam Brownback (R-Kans.) and Trent Lott (R-Miss.) have supported *flat tax* plans, as has Jerry Brown, former Democratic governor of California. When Brown advanced such a plan while running for his party's presiden-

tial nomination in 1992, one of his rivals, Sen. Tom Harkin of Iowa, said the idea must have originated with the Flat Earth Society. Former New York City Mayor Rudolph Giuliani, who dismissed Forbes' plan in 1996 as "a disaster," endorsed the idea of a flat tax when campaigning for the Republican presidential nomination in 2007—and in return received Forbes' endorsement of his candidacy.

The appeal of a *flat tax* resides largely in its simplicity for the taxpayer and low cost of collection by the Internal Revenue Service: taxes could be paid by filling out one or two forms the size of postcards. To raise as much money for the government as the progressive tax, however, the flat tax would have to be set high enough so that middle-class taxpayers would pay more than under the existing progressive system. Because *flat tax* proposals would leave wealthier people with more money to save or invest, thereby stimulating economic growth, they generally are favored by conservative SUPPLY-SIDE economists.

Flat taxes have been adopted abroad, notably by Russia (to overcome massive tax evasion) and other nations in eastern Europe. When the possibility of establishing such a system was raised by the Conservative Party in the U.K., Gordon Brown, then the Labor Chancellor of the Exchequer (he became Prime Minister in 2007), dismissed the *flat tax* as "An idea that they say is sweeping the world; well, sweeping Estonia; well, a wing of the neo-conservatives in Estonia."

flatteries of hope See GLOOM AND DOOM, PROPHETS OF.

flip-flop A dramatic reversal of position; a charge that a political figure, with a finger to the winds of change, has completely changed his mind.

Both noun and verb have become common in political attacks. In supporting a tax increase, President Reagan was asked whether he had "flip-flopped on the tax issue"; he replied, "There is not any flip-flop on this at all."

The reduplication *flip-flop* has been used in English for more than four centuries. Its original senses—describing large ears or imitating the sound on slippers as they slap the floor—have been replaced by the image of a somersault. George Lorimer applied that somersault image in 1902: "When a fellow's turning flip-flops up among the clouds, he's naturally going to have the farmers gaping at him." By the 1940s, a metaphorical use described romantic fickleness as "heart flip-flops."

At a Camp David meeting in August of 1971 (attended by the author) to curb inflation and to stem the sudden outflow of gold, Richard Nixon was warned by Treasury Secretary John Connally and others that a decision to impose wage and price controls—long an anathema to conservatives—would trigger a charge of *flip-flopping*. He dismissed this with a curt "Circumstances change." The reduplication's use in political vituperation has continued: In the 1988 presidential primary campaign, Gov. Michael Dukakis pointed to Rep. Richard Gephardt and said, "There's a flip-flopper over here," adding, "I'm not a flip-flopper."

In the 2004 presidential campaign, Democratic candidate John Kerry—a Senator accustomed to the arcane workings of Senate votes—sought to mitigate his support of an appropriation for the war in Iraq by saying defensively, "I actually voted against the $87 billion before I voted for it." This was shortened in attacks on him to "I was against the war before I was for it." A *Washington Post* editorial, headed "Flip-Flop, Hedge and Straddle," noted that "flip-flops aren't always bad; there's nothing to admire in politicians who never change their minds and never learn from experience," adding that "his supporters can find a Bush *flip* for every Kerry *flop*." But there was no doubt that the charge of *flip-flop* was a factor in his defeat.

On Christmas Eve 2006, with public impatience with the conduct of the Iraq war on the rise and a bipartisan commission urging a change of course, Senator Kerry wrote in a *Washington Post* Op-Ed: "There's something much worse than being accused of 'flip-flopping': refusing to flip when it's obvious that your course of action is a flop."

Although the term is always pejorative and is often difficult to refute, a refusal to flip-flop in the light of changing circumstances can be a sign of rigidity; a willingness to flip-flop is expressed by supporters as evidence of flexibility and an ability to "evolve." That was the position taken by supporters of former Massachusetts Governor Mitt Romney in 2007, explaining his change of mind from "pro-choice" to "pro-life," which pleased social conservatives who are a force in the Republican party.

In the synonymy of about-turns, WAFFLE, *waver*, and *vacillate* mean "to swing back and forth between opinions," while *hedge* means "to take both sides simultaneously." A neutral term for a change of mind as circumstances change is *a reversal of views*; to *dither* and *falter* signal "irresolution," while the ringing *tergiversate* (pronounced with a soft *g*, from the Latin verb *tergiversari*, "to turn one's back") means "to switch sides like an apostate."

floater See SWING VOTER.

floo-floo bird A symbolic creature that flies backward, more interested in where it has been than where it is going; liberal's description of a conservative.

The architect Frank Lloyd Wright referred to this curious bird in a 1938 speech to architects in Washington, D.C.:

> The cultural influences in our country are like the "floo floo" bird. I am referring to the peculiar and especial bird who always flew backward. To keep the wind out of its eyes? No. Just because it didn't give a darn where it was going, but just had to see where it had been. Now, in the "floo floo" bird you have the true symbol of our Government architecture ... and in consequence, how discredited American culture stands in the present time. All the world knows it to be funny except America.

Just after Dwight Eisenhower's re-election in 1956, Senate Majority Leader Lyndon Johnson said the country supported the President because it felt that Eisenhower "was more interested in where he is going than where he has been." The lack of wisdom present in backward-looking was expressed by Negro League baseball pitcher Satchel Paige, who was reported by Richard Donovan of *Collier's* magazine to have counseled: "Never look back. Someone may be gaining on you."

Other birds in the mythical heavens include the "worry bird," a small desk ornament that does the worrying for executives; the "gooney bird," or weekend Air Force reservist flying around for practice; and the extinct dodo, subject of the alliteration "dead as a dodo." The Johnson family's names (wife "Lady Bird" and daughter Lynda Bird) gave rise to some satire, as in Barbara Garson's antiwar play *MacBird!*, produced in New York in 1966, parodying Shakespeare's *Macbeth.*

For the political menagerie's aviary, see this dictionary's Introduction. Architect Wright did not hyphenate *floo-floo bird* in his written remarks. Better usage calls for the hyphen, which looks both ways.

floor fight An argument, usually about platform demands or delegate credentials, that cannot be settled in committee and is taken to the floor of the convention for decision.

Floor fights are despised by most political professionals: they mean that compromise has failed, and sections of the party will consider themselves losers at the convention and may go home and sit on their hands.

Historian Stefan Lorant wrote of the day in 1896 when a man burst into Republican boss Mark Hanna's St. Louis hotel room and announced: "Mr. Hanna, I insist on a positive declaration for a gold-standard plank in the platform." Hanna looked up and said, "Who the hell are you?" The man replied, "Senator Henry Cabot Lodge of Massachusetts." "Well, Senator Henry Cabot Lodge of Massachusetts, you can go plumb to hell. You have nothing to say about it." "All right, sir," bristled Lodge. "I will make my fight on the convention floor." Replied Hanna: "I don't care a damn where you make your fight." But cooler heads prevailed, and a floor fight was averted. When it became known that the Democrats would declare for free silver, the platform committee placed the Republicans dead against it. ("Avert a floor fight,"

as used above, is a cliché. For an example of how to stop a floor fight before it starts, see COMPACT OF FIFTH AVENUE.)

A floor fight in the 1952 Republican convention over contested credentials swung the nomination away from Taft to Eisenhower (see THOU SHALT NOT STEAL); a floor fight on ideological grounds in the 1948 Democratic convention resulted in the BOLT of the DIXIECRATS.

The meaning of *floor* as "forum," or "right to speak," predates American political history and comes from English parliamentary tradition. See HUSTINGS.

flugie A rule that only benefits the maker of the rule, and can be changed to avoid having it benefit his opponent.

When Senator Russell Long (D-La.) wanted to get special legislation passed for a constituent and a fellow senator objected, Senator Long explained patiently that his proposal is "just like a flugie." When the objector wonders what that is, Senator Long eagerly told the story, as recounted by former senator Bob Packwood:

Two men are playing poker; one gets a full house and starts to gather in the winnings, when another player—with not even two of a kind in his hand—stops him. "This is my pot," says the full-house man, "you don't have a thing." "Ah," says his opponent, "but nothing is a 'flugie.' Read the sign on the wall behind me." Sure enough, the sign says: "A Flugie Beats Everything." The man with nothing in his hand takes in the pot. On the next hand, the man who just held the full house comes up with nothing, and starts to rake in his pot. "Wait," says the flugie expert, who this time has a pair. "Read the sign behind you." On the wall, the sign reads: "Just One Flugie Per Evening."

Washington Star reporter James Dickenson, referring to this in 1977, added: "The widespread notion of the U.S. Senate is that when it comes to tax legislation, what Long really wants, which very often benefits oil and gas producers, he consistently gets the only flugie of the evening."

flyer A small handbill or circular with a brief political message.

Political literature includes *handbills*, *handcards*, *doorknob-hangers*, *flyers*, *brochures*, *reprints*, *blogs*, and *mailers* (and, increasingly, *e-mails*). See also SNIPE.

In current use, *flyer* and *handbill* are used interchangeably to mean a cheap circular about an issue or one calling attention to an upcoming event or visit; a *handcard* is a picture of a candidate on heavier stock paper with a brief description of his background and occasionally a summary of his platform; a *brochure* is an expanded version of the handcard, often using pictures of the candidate in action and with improved graphic design, usually more elaborate than a flyer; a *doorknob-hanger* is a flyer saying that a volunteer called and giving some brief information about a candidate, with the top of the flyer slit or shaped so that it can be hung on a doorknob; a *reprint* is a photo-offset reproduction of a favorable article about the candidate or a transcript of a broadcast or cable praise in flyer form to be handed out; a *mailer* is a brochure designed, with space left for address and stamp, to be mailed without an envelope. *Circular* is no longer in current use in politics. HAND-OUT is rarely used in this sense; its current meanings are "a welfare payment" or a "press release."

Flyer (when not used to mean "aviator" or "speculative, small venture in the stock market") is the most frequently used word for political literature. It can be traced to an 1888 speech in the House by Congressman T. E. Tarsney of Michigan: "[My opponent] placed upon every doorstep of every house in the city [of Saginaw] a flyer. 'Do not vote for Tim Tarsney: he is a freetrader.'"

For examples of how flyers can get far more vicious than the kind Tarsney complained about, see GUTTER FLYER; ROORBACK.

Foggy Bottom Nickname for the offices of the State Department in Washington, D.C.

The new headquarters of the State Department was built at the end of World War II on once-miasmic land that had originally been called "Foggy Bottom," and the name was reapplied because it recalled a fogginess of official language.

Columnist James "Scotty" Reston told his *New York Times* colleague, the lexicographer, that the reporter who first applied the phrase to the State Department was Edward Folliard of *The Washington Post*: "Eddie grew up down by the gasworks, between what is now the New State Department building and the K Street bridge," Reston recalled. "The coinage took place soon after State moved out of the building across the street from the White House, that's now the Old Executive Office Building." Reston reported in the *Times* in 1947: "The State Department has moved its principal offices ... from Pennsylvania Avenue to Foggy Bottom, which, for the benefit of any cynics, is not an intellectual condition but a geographical area down by the Potomac."

The Library of Congress provides a description of the derivation, from George R. Brown's 1930 book, *Washington:*

> Over in the old First Ward of an earlier day ... where originally had been the little town of Hamburgh, which existed before Washington was even conceived, was—and still is—Foggy Bottom, lying west of Twenty-third Street and extending to Rock Creek and stretching from the river nearly to Pennsylvania Avenue. In its southern reaches it was formerly a section of swamps and flats, from which arose at night miasmatic vapors which gave to it its colorful cognomen.

Arthur Schlesinger, Jr., in his Kennedy memoir, *A Thousand Days*: "The State Department sent over a document. ... In addition to the usual defects of Foggy Bottom prose, the paper was filled with bad spelling and grammar." Robert A. Lovett, who served as Secretary of Defense in the Truman Administration, had been dubbed "the Bald Eagle of Foggy Bottom"(see BALD EAGLE) from his earlier State Department days.

The nickname for the old neighborhood is now journalese for the center of American diplomacy: when Condoleezza Rice relocated from her office in the West Wing as National Security Adviser in the George W. Bush administration to become Secretary of State, the *Chicago Tribune*'s shorthand described her move "from the White House to Foggy Bottom."

Puzzle Palace is the nickname of the National Security Agency near Laurel, Maryland; its initials are jocularly said to refer to "No Such Agency." The Pentagon is *Fort Fumble.*

following See BACKER.

follow the money A rule for finding guilty parties by pursuing their financial trails.

The phrase became a rallying cry for reporters investigating corruption in high places years after the WATERGATE scandal. It was popularized in the 1976 film, *All the President's Men,* based on the 1974 book by Bob Woodward and Carl Bernstein, the *Washington Post* reporters (so closely joined at the keyboard that they sometimes were referred to as *Woodstein*) who broke key elements of the Watergate story. In the film, the words are uttered by "Deep Throat," the long-anonymous source now known to have been FBI associate director W. Mark Felt, in a meeting with Woodward (played by Robert Redford) in an underground parking garage in Washington, D.C.

The money trail in this case began with some $5,500 in consecutively numbered $100 bills possessed by the men who been arrested on June 17, 1972, while breaking into the offices of the Democratic National Committee in the capital's Watergate complex. The money was traced from the burglars to contributors to the Nixon campaign, with detours through banks in Florida and Mexico, and, most damagingly, to the Committee to Re-Elect the President (see CREEP), whose chairman, former Attorney General John Mitchell, had approved the break-in.

Most movie-goers assumed that the memorable line appeared in the Woodstein book; not so. It comes from the screenplay written by William Goldman, and was not a phrase spoken by the real Deep Throat. Asked about the provenance of the quote by NPR commentator Daniel Schorr, Goldman said: "I can't believe I made it up. I was in constant contact with Woodward while writing the screenplay. I guess he must have made it up." Following the linguistic trail, Schorr proceeded to query Woodward, who

then went back through all his notes of all his interviews. Unable to fund the phrase in his records, Woodward passed the buck back to Goldman, telling Schorr that he was inclined to think the screenwriter had made it up.

There the matter lay until 1997 when Stephen Lesher, who had covered the Justice Department for *Newsweek* in 1973, suggested in a letter to this lexicographer that *follow the money* probably should be credited to the late Henry Peterson, Assistant Attorney General for the Criminal Division, who headed the Watergate investigation prior to the appointment of Archibald Cox as special prosecutor. A principal source for many reporters, Peterson told Lesher that "from day one" he had instructed his chief lieutenants, Earl Silbert and Seymour Glanzer, "to follow the money. If they followed the money, they'd get to the bottom of the case." Lesher continued: "If Peterson used the 'follow the money' expression with me, who was new to the story, he certainly must have used it with other reporters who, like Woodward, had been there from the start."

Money trails also are of international importance. Criticizing major newspapers for revealing a hitherto secret anti-terrorist program for tracing international bank transfers in 2006, Stuart Levey, Under Secretary of the Treasury for Terrorism and Financial Intelligence, said "It's one thing to say you are following the money. It's quite another to tell people exactly what they're looking at."

In non-political usage, in commenting on news personality Katie Couric's decision in 2006 to leave NBC's *Today* show for a much larger salary as anchor on the "CBS Evening News," one network insider was reported saying: "In the television business you've got to follow the money."

football, political A controversial associate, or an innocent civic or philanthropic project, used by the political opposition to concoct a political issue.

Pity the low-flying, nonpolitical bird that finds itself the shuttlecock in a game of political badminton. This, to mix a SPORTS METAPHOR, is the *political football*, and it means "unfair use of a pure project for crass partisan gain." The attack phrase, however, often draws sympathy to the nonpartisan ball that is getting kicked.

In 1800 Abraham Bishop wrote in *Connecticut Republicanism:* "Multitudes of rational men are for destroying that kind of religion which is made a football [soccer ball today] or stalking horse, and which operates only to dishonor God and ruin man."

Fiorello La Guardia, former New York mayor who headed the United Nations Relief and Rehabilitation Administration, got into a debate with Adlai Stevenson in 1946 over methods of providing emergency relief. Taking the offensive, the "Little Flower" accused Stevenson of "making a political football out of food." In the same way, Harry Truman said of Dwight Eisenhower's actions in the campaign of 1952: "Hard as it was for us to understand this side of Eisenhower now revealed to us, it was even more of a jolt to see our foreign policy used as a political football."

Mobster Charles "Lucky" Luciano, recording an interview with the author, in 1953 a U.S. Army correspondent in Europe, sat in the bar of the Hotel Vesuvio in Naples and claimed to be an innocent and bored retiree. What did he do all day? "I get up inna morning, I go to the barber, I go to the track, and the day is shot." Was he released from jail in New York by Governor Thomas Dewey because he had ordered the mob-influenced longshoremen's union to make certain that no Nazi saboteur in World War II inflicted damage in the port of New York? "Lucky" glowered and gloomily reviewed the cause of what he maintained was his persecution: "I was sent to jail, I was sprung, and I was deported, all because I was a political football."

A new, more ominous use of *football* refers to the small, thirty-pound metal suitcase containing codes that can launch a nuclear attack. It is carried by a military aide to the President and follows the Chief Executive wherever he goes. See BAGMAN. For the use of football terminology in politics, see GAME PLAN; SPORTS METAPHORS.

foot-in-mouth disease Tendency to blunder when ad-libbing; error-proneness.

The day after Eisenhower's Defense Secretary Charles E. Wilson made his famous BIRD DOG … KENNEL DOG comparison, he admitted his error and told reporters that some of his cabinet colleagues "seem to think I have foot-in-mouth disease."

This is a combined colloquialism of interesting parentage, now almost exclusively applied to political figures.

To put one's foot in it, to step into a foul substance or tread heavily on thin ice, has long been slang for "misstep; mistake; blunder." On matters verbal, the expression was narrowed *to put your foot in your mouth.* This was language akin to the cattleman's problem, *foot-and-mouth disease* or *hoof-and-mouth disease*, a serious contagion affecting livestock, especially of cloven-hoofed animals. *Foot and mouth* and *foot in mouth* sound identical when spoken quickly, thus spreading the political "disease."

The metaphor can be mixed. Newbold Morris, wealthy reform associate of Fiorello La Guardia and at one time president of New York's City Council, was derided as a man "born with a silver foot in his mouth." The keynote speaker at the Democratic convention of 1988, Texan Ann Richards, got a big laugh when she derided the misspeakings of President George H.W. Bush with "poor George … he cain't he'p it . . he was born with a silver foot in his mouth." See BLOOPER.

footnote to history A seemingly insignificant detail, contributed long afterward to illuminate a great event or a historic person's life.

Judge Samuel Rosenman felt that his accounts of FDR's use of language were important, "not only as a footnote to history, but as an aid to the better understanding of the leadership exercised by Franklin D. Roosevelt." By designating his information as a footnote to history, the contributor strikes a modest pose; in addition, he calls attention to the detail—most people, like it or not, find their eyes dragged down to the bottom of a page by a footnote.

Criteria for a footnote to history are that it be (1) hitherto unpublished, (2) from firsthand knowledge, (3) illustrative of character or mood, and (4) unpretentious. See the Kissinger story in FLAK as an example.

The phrase is from an 1892 non-fiction book of that title by the English novelist (and Samoan devotee) Robert Louis Stevenson.

foreign wars See AGAIN AND AGAIN AND AGAIN.

forgotten man Single image for the millions left in economic desperation by the Depression.

Governor Franklin D. Roosevelt of New York, campaigning in 1932 for the Democratic presidential nomination, used this phrase in a short speech containing several ideas which would become basic during the first years of his presidency. The theme of this address was the need to come up with plans that "rest upon the forgotten, the unorganized but the indispensable units of economic power... that build from the bottom up and not from the top down, that put their faith once more in the forgotten man at the bottom of the economic pyramid."

The party's 1928 presidential candidate, former New York Governor Alfred E. Smith, saw this phrase as a radical attack on business: "At a time like this, when millions of men, women and children are starving throughout the land, there is always a temptation to some men to stir up class prejudice ..." See CLASS WARFARE. To the man out of work in a time of prosperity, however, already suffering and fearful of what lay ahead, the "forgotten man" was himself; the phrase played a part in Roosevelt's victory over Smith at the Democratic convention and then, after the stock market crash and onset of the Depression, over President Herbert Hoover.

The future president was not the man who coined the phrase, nor was Professor Raymond Moley, though he picked it up and inserted it into FDR's speech. A sociologist at Yale University, William Graham Sumner, first used the phrase in an article written in 1883. Far from intending it to describe the destitute, Sumner had in mind the sturdy middle-class citizen who bears society's greatest loads: "Such is the Forgotten Man... he is not in any way a hero (like a popular orator); nor a problem (like tramps and outcasts); nor an object of sentiment (like the poor and weak); nor a burden (like paupers and loafers)... therefore, he is forgotten. All the burdens fall on him ..."

Just how important FDR's use of the phrase was at the time is shown by a bitter verse printed in the *New York Sun*, a paper whose unyielding Republicanism was never in doubt, after Roosevelt's victory and just before his inauguration. The President had gone on a fishing cruise on Vincent Astor's yacht, the *Normahal*. The party included other well-to-do friends, which inspired the newspaper's poet to write:

> *They were just good friends with no selfish ends*
> *To serve as they paced the decks;*
> *They were George and Fred and the son of Ted*
> *And Vincent (he signed the checks);*
> *On the splendid yacht in a climate hot*
> *To tropical seas they ran;*
> *Among those behind they dismissed from mind*
> *Was the well-known Forgotten Man!*

In 1972, on the 90th anniversary of Roosevelt's birth, *The New York Times* editorialized: "...to anyone under the age of 40, his name is likely to evoke nothing more than the shadow outline of a wartime statesman... Roosevelt is in danger of himself becoming America's greatest 'forgotten man.'"

For Roosevelt Before Chicago See CUFFLINKS GANG; ALPHABET AGENCIES.

Fort Fumble See PENTAGONESE.

forty acres and a mule Illusory political promise to secure black votes.

This Civil War term began as "ten acres and a mule" in 1862. Northern propagandists offered a promise, later broken, that Southern plantations would be confiscated and divided among the slaves after the Civil War. The acreage increased after Union General William Tecumseh Sherman issued a special field order on January 16, 1865: "Every family shall have a plot of not more than forty acres of tillable ground."

Forty acres, one-sixteenth of a section, appeared frequently as a measure of land.

The *Congressional Globe* stated in 1871, "The slaves only appreciated the advantages of fighting for freedom when this privilege was accompanied with a present bounty or future prospect of 'forty acres and a mule.'"

This expression was featured in *Gone With the Wind*. The 1939 film based on the Margaret Mitchell novel showed a CARPET-BAGGER on a soapbox addressing a group of freed blacks in Atlanta; identified in the screenplay as the Orator, he pledges, "We're goin' to give every last one of you forty acres and a mule. ... Because we're your friends and you're going to become voters—and you're going to vote like your friends do."

Modern uses of the phrase point back to the Reconstruction promises. In 1978, *The Washington Post* commented on the difficulty facing black entrepreneurs in securing loans: "Success would redeem government's post-Civil War pledge of '40 acres and a mule' for blacks." The phrase became a symbol of broken promises and dashed expectations: the production company for the African-American filmmaker Spike Lee's *Malcolm X* in 1992 was "40 Acres and a Mule Filmworks."

Not only blacks, however, have been disappointed by broken pledges. John Powers of *The Boston Globe* commented in a 1992 essay on a series of American political promises to entice or bamboozle voters: "We elect politicians who vow to make EVERY MAN A KING, who promise us 40 acres and a mule, a CHICKEN IN EVERY POT and a car in every garage."

In British political usage, it was taken up by land reformers in 1885 as "three acres and a cow." The power of the phrase lies in its single-syllable evocation of a barnyard animal.

Founding Fathers A group of revolutionaries who took their chances on treason to pursue the course of independency, who are today viewed reverently as sage signers of the documents of U.S. freedom.

Although the phrase has the feel of an early Americanism, it is of twentieth-century origin.

At the instigation of Richard Hanser, television writer and phrase hunter, the Library of Congress researched the subject and came up with the unlikely popularizer: Warren Gamaliel Harding. On George Washington's birthday in 1918, then Senator Harding told the Sons and Daughters of the American Revolution: "It is good to meet and drink at the fountains of wisdom inherited from the founding fathers of the republic." He repeated it in his campaign for the presidency in 1920 and used the phrase again in his inaugural address: "I must utter my belief in the divine inspiration of the founding fathers."

Earliest use of the phrase in the *Oxford English Dictionary* is in the title of a 1914 book by K.B. Umbriet: *Founding Fathers: Men Who Shaped Our Tradition*. It was later used, in a dynastic sense, by Richard Whelan in his 1964 biography of Joseph P. Kennedy.

Without capitalization, the phrase now means the originator of any movement or organization; capitalized, the reference is primarily to the men who gathered at the Constitutional Convention in Philadelphia in 1787. After feminists in the 1980s objected to the paternalism of the phrase and pointed to the participation in the parentage of the nation by Abigail Adams and others, it became more acceptable to drop the "fathers" and refer to the *Founders* or the *framers*.

President Harding was fond of matching up words with the same beginning letter (see his "not nostrum but normalcy" line-up under ALLITERATION), and "Founding Fathers" functioned as the fulfillment of his forensic fancy.

four freedoms Objectives of U.S. policy as summarized by President Franklin D. Roosevelt in his message to Congress, January 6, 1941: freedom of speech, of religion, from want, and from fear.

In his State of the Union message, eleven months before the U.S. entered World War II, President Roosevelt suggested the Lend-Lease program to supply Great Britain with war equipment to fight the Axis Powers. He also outlined the "four freedoms":

In the future days, which we seek to make secure, we look forward to a world founded upon four essential human freedoms.

The first is freedom of speech and expression—everywhere in the world. The second is freedom of every person to worship God in his own way—everywhere in the world.

The third is freedom from want—which, translated into world terms, means economic understandings which will secure to every nation a healthy peaceful life for its inhabitants—everywhere in the world.

The fourth is freedom from fear—which, translated into world terms, means a worldwide reduction of armaments to such a point and in such a thorough fashion that no nation will be in a position to commit an act of physical aggression against any neighbor—anywhere in the world.

President Roosevelt, his speech writers, and his personal secretary, Dorothy Brady, were working over the fourth draft of his 1941 State of the Union message when FDR turned to his secretary and asked her to take down an addition. The addition was the passage he must have had in mind since the previous July, when he briefly mentioned the four freedoms in a news conference.

One of the speechwriters who was present at the meeting, Samuel Rosenman, later wrote that only a few words were changed from the way FDR dictated the four-freedoms passage to the final draft as it was delivered. In his dictation, Mr. Roosevelt added "everywhere in the world" only to the first two freedoms.

Harry Hopkins suggested that "everywhere in the world" covered a lot of territory. He doubted that the American people were interested in "the people in Java." The president, according to Rosenman, answered, "They'll have to be some day. The world is getting so small that even the people in Java are getting to be our neighbors now." In the final draft Mr. Roosevelt added "everywhere in the world" and "anywhere in the world" to the last two freedoms. The four freedoms were later incorporated into the Atlantic Charter.

fourth estate The press; a dated phrase now often used in sarcasm.

Books of quotations usually credit Edmund Burke with coinage, thanks to a citation by historian Thomas Carlyle in *Heroes and Hero-Worship*, written in 1839: "Burke said that there were three estates in Parliament; but, in the Reporters' Gallery yonder, there sat a Fourth Estate more important far than them all." When diligent research failed to turn up the phrase in anything Burke said or wrote, some quotation detectives assumed Carlyle was referring to Lord Macaulay, who said in 1828: "The gallery in which the reporters sit has become a fourth estate of the realm."

"Fourth estate" had been used much earlier in both England and France, usually in reference to "the mob" (the other estates being the king, the clergy, and the commons, all powers whose agreement was necessary for legislation). The *OED* reports that Lord Brougham was said to have applied it to the press in a speech in the House of Commons in 1823 or 1824, and "it was at that time treated as original."

The vote of this lexicographer for the coiner of the phrase as a definition of the press goes to English essayist William Hazlitt, who wrote on the character of William Cobbett in an 1821 "Table Talk" essay. Cobbett was a pamphleteer and editor, vituperative and often in trouble for libel both in England and America. Hazlitt wrote of this early media giant: "One has no notion of him as making use of a fine pen, but a great mutton-fist; his style stuns his readers...He is too much for any single newspaper antagonist; 'lays waste' a city orator or Member of Parliament, and bears hard upon the government itself. He is a kind of *fourth estate* in the politics of the country."

The phrase was used to put the press on an equal footing with the greatest powers in a nation; in the twentieth century it was taken up by many editors in descriptions of the importance of journalism. The phrase lost its vividness as the other "estates" faded from memory, and now has a musty connotation. In current use "the press" usually carries with it the aura of "freedom of the press" enshrined in the U.S. Constitution, while critics of the press usually label it, with a sneer, "the MEDIA," originally popularized as an advertising term. For a related etymology, see THIRD WORLD.

Fourth of July speech An emotional appeal to the spirit of patriotism; a flag-waver.

A speech made on the Fourth of July is expected to be patriotic; when the term *Fourth of July speech* is used to describe a speech made on any other day, it is patronizing, even derogatory.

The expression dates far back in American history. Ohio Senator Stanley Matthews, on Feb. 13, 1879, asked his fellow senators: "Has the oratory that is peculiar to the Fourth of July come to be a hissing and a byword, a scorn and a reproach…is it enough to smother opposition and put down argument, to say that that is merely the sentimentality of a Fourth of July oratory?"

One example of how Fourth of July oratory came to have a bad name can be seen in this excerpt from a speech on July 4, 1827, by Edward Everett, Massachusetts governor, U.S. Secretary of State, and Harvard president (best known for his forgotten speech before Lincoln spoke at Gettysburg): "Let us then, as we assemble on the birthday of the nation, as we gather upon the green turf, once wet with precious blood, let us devote ourselves to the sacred cause of Constitutional Liberty! Let us abjure the interests and passions which divide the great family of American freemen! Let us resolve …" He went on at length in this vein.

James Russell Lowell, a poet who served as ambassador to England, abjured that approach in his Independence Day speech in London in 1883: "Now the Fourth of July has several times been alluded to, and I believe it is generally thought on that anniversary the spirit of a certain bird known to heraldic ornithologists—and I believe to them alone—as the spread eagle, enters into every American's breast, and compels him, whether he will or no, to pour forth a flood of national self-laudation." Lest his English listeners think him unpatriotic, Lowell added: "I ask you, is there any other people who have confined their national self-laudation to one day in the year?"

Although Americans are traditionally self-conscious about excessive displays of patriotism (see SUPERPATRIOTS), and will deride such excess as "Fourth of July," there are limits to how far derision is allowed to go. When Rufus Choate denounced the "glittering and sounding generalities that make up the Declaration of Independence" in 1856, Ralph Waldo Emerson snapped back with "Glittering generalities! They are blazing ubiquities."

freebie A gift or pass; something of value that is cost-free to the recipient.

This slang noun is first found in print in Rudolph Fischer's 1928 novel *The Walls of Jericho*, where it is spelled *freeby*. This spelling and the variant *freebee* are recorded in Berrey and Van den Bark's 1942 *American Thesaurus of Slang*. Louis Armstrong defined it in his 1954 autobiography: "That meal was a freebie and didn't cost me anything."

The noun uses a popular *ie* ending, with the *b* inserted between the vowels to ease the pronunciation (such an insert is called a *paragogic infix*). By 1990, the term had entered the political lexicon. Matthew Lesko wrote a book that year publicized as "how to tap into the thousands of freebies and cheapies among 30,000 government goodies." When the elder President Bush was asked whether preparations for the first Persian Gulf war would change his projections on cutting the budget deficit, he replied, "It may cause for a rearrangement in how money is spent, because this is not a freebie."

freedom agenda See DOCTRINES.

freedom fighter See CIVIL DISOBEDIENCE; ACTIVIST; TERRORISM.

Freedom Now Slogan of the civil rights movement, criticizing delay in achieving equality in fact after achieving it in law.

"To the Negro demand for 'now,'" wrote Murray Friedman in the *Atlantic Monthly* in 1963, "to which the deep South has replied 'never,' many liberal whites are increasingly responding, 'later.' But the Negro will accept nothing short of first-class citizenship, now."

"Now" became one of the "in" words of the mid-'60s, stemming from its use in "Freedom Now," a militant civil rights slogan that preceded Stokely Carmichael's BLACK POWER. Its structural sloganeering predecessor was Clarence Streit's pre–World War II call for an international federation, "Union Now." In 1966, there were *now* dresses (miniskirts), *now* dances, and the *Now* Generation (from the "Lost Generation" via the "Beat Generation").

Freedom, like democracy, justice, and peace, is a Humpty Dumpty word, meaning whatever the user or abuser chooses it to mean. In phrases, it was used in *freedom fighters* in Hungary in the early '50s, FREEDOM RIDERS in the U.S. a decade later.

Theodore White wrote in 1965: "Perhaps the most necessary intellectual operation in American life is some redefinition of the word 'freedom.' I have attended as many civil rights rallies as Goldwater rallies. The dominant word of these two groups, which loathe each other, is 'freedom.' Both demand either Freedom Now or Freedom for All. ... It is quite possible that these two groups may kill each other in cold blood, both waving banners bearing the same word." The French existentialist philosopher and writer Jean-Paul Sartre came up with a startling oxymoron to describe the dread felt by humans on whom responsibility was thrust in a hostile universe: *inescapable freedom*.

freedom of the press See RIGHT TO KNOW.

freedom riders Groups of blacks and whites that rode buses through the South in the summer of 1961 testing the segregation of public facilities in interstate bus terminals.

In February 1960, four Negro (so called before *African-American* was preferred on first reference) students attempted to sit and eat at a lunch counter in Greensboro, North Carolina. They were evicted. For the next year, the director of the Congress of Racial Equality (CORE), James Farmer, raised money to hire buses and recruited black and white volunteers to ride them through the South to demand the right to sit and eat in a public place or to use facilities that the general public was permitted to use. CORE dubbed the buses "freedom buses," and those who rode them "freedom riders." See FREEDOM NOW.

"The most nightmarish day of our freedom ride," wrote CORE's James Peck, who took 53 stitches after a beating, "was Sunday, May 14, 1961, Mother's Day. I identify the date with Mother's Day because when Police Chief Connor was asked why there was not a single policeman at the Birmingham Trailways terminal to avert mob violence, he explained that since it was Mother's Day, most of the police were off-duty visiting their mothers."

In September 1961, the Interstate Commerce Commission desegregated all facilities in terminals used in interstate bus travel and the Justice Department ordered the desegregation of public transportation. See SEGREGATION.

The phrase became secure enough to be parodied. When a New York State law threatened to invalidate "quickie" Mexican divorces, a stampede of unhappy spouses poured into Juárez, Mexico, before the law took effect. "Most of the New Yorkers flocking here are women," reported *The Wall Street Journal* in 1967, "and many arrive on American Airlines flight 295 (which they call 'the Freedom Riders Special') ..."

free enterprise The practice of capitalism under representative government.

A British economist, Alfred Marshall, wrote in 1890 of tracing "the growth of free enterprise in England." President Woodrow Wilson used it in 1913 first as "freedom of enterprise" and then, at the time the Federal Reserve System was being set up, he said it was to help "resourceful businessmen ... deal with the new circumstances of free enterprise ..." The Republican platform in 1936 charged President Roosevelt with having displaced "free enterprise with regulated monopoly." FDR fired back: "Private enterprise, indeed, became too private. It became privileged enterprise, not free enterprise."

The term has been most popular with conservatives distressed when the capitalistic system is challenged by government regulation. *Newsweek* wrote in 1938: "Management leaders representing the world's democratic countries agreed that free enterprise, not government control, is the key to better times." Roosevelt, under fire from the right, felt the need to reaffirm his faith in 1944: "I believe in free enterprise—and always have. I believe in the profit system—and always have."

When the term *laissez-faire* (derived from French *laisser faire*, "to allow to do," or "to let alone") lost political acceptability, and *capitalism* was a target of communism, *free enterprise* became the banner that centrists as well as those who identified with FDR's position as "a little left of center" could embrace. See AMERICAN SYSTEM; AMERICAN WAY OF LIFE; BLACK CAPITALISM.

free lunch As to which there is no such thing.

Nobel economics laureate Milton Friedman, who died in 2006 at the age of 94, published articles, a book, and lectures using the title "There Is No Such Thing as a Free Lunch." His meaning was that everything, even what is seemingly "free," had a cost; it must be paid for by somebody in some way and there is no sense in hiding that economic reality. The bars that offered "free lunch" to patrons made their profit on the drinks that accompanied the food.

Reached by the author in 1993, Dr. Friedman replied that had no idea where his much-quoted phrase comes from: "I wish I did, but if wishes were horses ..." (An allusion to the saying "If wishes were horses, beggars would ride," to which novelist Vladimir Nabokov once replied, "I'd wish for Pegasus.") The illusion-shattering phrase was also popularized by science fiction writer Robert A. Heinlein in his 1966 novel *The Moon Is a Harsh Mistress*. Heinlein coined TANSTAAFL, its lengthy acronym changing Friedman's *is* to *ain't*.

Referring to the once-common practice of offering patrons "free" food, slanguist Stuart Berg Flexner offered the author this help: "*Free lunch* dates from the 1840s and was supposed to have moved from the West to the East, getting fancier as it approached eastern bars and hotels, so sometime after the late 1840s I can just see some bartender slapping the hands of a customer and asking him to buy that 5-cent beer before shoveling in the victuals ..."

Thanks to the Friedman popularization, as well as to the trend begun in the 1970s toward a fresh acceptance of conservative economic ideas, the phrase's use mushroomed. When a bill favoring the maritime industry was defeated in a surprise vote in Congress in 1977, Common Cause president David Cohen explained: "The maritime industry has had a free lunch on Capital Hill before this, because there'd been no publicity." In November 1977, reporter Fox Butterfield wrote in *The New York Times Magazine* about an improbable welfare state in Micronesia, especially on the island of Yap: "Yap is a living refutation that there is no such thing as a free lunch," a U.S. official was quoted as saying. "Here it's a smorgasbord."

The phrase returned to its literal meaning in the aftermath of the 2006 congressional elections, which turned in part on voter revulsion of evidence of G.O.P. lobbyists like Jack Abramoff entertaining politicians and corruptly influencing legislation. When the House passed rules banning the wining and dining of elected officials by lobbyists, a "toothpick rule" was put into effect, limiting free food to hors d'oeuvres that had to be eaten standing up. The *Wall Street Journal* headline: "No Free Lunch: New Ethics Rules Vex Capitol Hill." For a 1964 Goldwater use, see SANTA CLAUS, NOBODY SHOOTS AT.

free ride A campaign undertaken by an officeholder who runs for a higher office without giving up his own; if the candidate loses, he or she continues to serve in the first office.

Senators, serving six-year terms, have the best opportunity for "free rides" running for governor of their states, or on a national ticket. In the election of 1960, for example, Senator John F. Kennedy, whose term did not expire until 1964, had a free ride; in 1964 Senator Barry Goldwater, whose term expired that year, did not. Lyndon Johnson solved the problem in 1960 by running simultaneously for both senator and vice president. Senators Hillary Clinton, John McCain, Joe Biden, Barack Obama, and Chris Dodd did not have to give up their Senate seats in campaigning for president in 2008.

In a more general sense, the phrase means "any effort that requires no sacrifice." Robert F. Kennedy, announcing his 1968 challenge to Lyndon Johnson's renomination, said, "I can't believe that anybody thinks that this is a pleasant struggle from now on, or that I'm asking for a free ride ... I'm going into primaries ... I'm not asking for a free ride ..." Another sense is "an open field": In July 1992, the *Washington Post* commented, "This is an odd time in the campaign, providing something of a free ride for the Democratic ticket before the Republican National Convention is held next month."

free soil, free men, Frémont See REPUBLICAN.

free world In the eyes of democracies, an amorphous agglomeration of nations not under dictatorship.

The free world gained currency in the early 1940s as the AXIS threat loomed and in the early '50s as realization of the Communist expansion dawned.

In October 1941, two months before the attack on Pearl Harbor, an obscure economic adviser in FDR's Department of Agriculture named Mordecai J.B. Ezekiel started a monthly publication named *Free World*, headquarters at 55 W. 42nd St. in New York City. Its directors included Clark Eichelberger and *The Nation* editor Freda Kirchwey, and contributors were well-known liberal internationalists, from Robert Nathan to Henry Wallace to the columnist Dorothy Thompson. It was a project of the Free World Association, its slogan "For Victory and for World Organization," and hailed "the immense superiority of the United Nations" in a March 1942 issue; in 1946, *Free World* merged with *United Nations World*.

In January 1951, Volume 24, issue #2 of the *Proceedings of the Academy of Political Science* was titled "The Defense of the Free World," with articles by Gladwyn Jebb,

Raymond Dennett, and Herman Beukema, which popularized the collocation in academia. A 1955 Edwin Marcus cartoon was typical: an upstanding-looking gentleman labeled "free world," with his arm in a sling labeled "violation of Yalta agreements," is spurning the blandishments of a bear labeled "Russian honor," with the caption "Once bitten, twice shy."

Dwight Eisenhower used the phrase frequently: "I believe that the situation and actions best calculated to sustain the interests of ourselves and the free world ..." (memo to John Foster Dulles, 1955).

Its constant use by Western orators made it uniquely an anti-Communist phrase that could not be turned around, as the Communists did with the phrase "people's democracy." This was revealed in Chairman Nikita Khrushchev's preface of the phrase with a SNEER WORD in an address to the 21st Congress of the Communist party, January 27, 1959: "The so-called free world constitutes the kingdom of the dollar ..."

The breakup of the Soviet Union changed the perception of the phrase. In 1992, *Newsday* discussed the success of Bill Clinton's campaign: "He portrayed Bush as a man who sees the world locked in a struggle between communism and the free world, and implied that Bush was unable to make the transition to the post-Cold War world."

Senator Barack Obama (D-Ill.), speaking in 2007 to the Chicago Council on Global Affairs, heartened Robert Kagan—one of Senator John McCain's advisers, who were under fire from the REALISTS deriding interventionists—when Obama referred to the U.S. as "leader of the free world." Kagan wrote in *The Washington Post*: "No one speaks of the 'free world' these days, and Obama's insistence that we not 'cede our claim of leadership in world affairs' will sound like an anachronistic conceit to many Europeans ... but Obama believes the world yearns to follow us, if only we restore our worthiness to lead. Personally, I like it ... of course, it's just a speech."

freeze Stop or halt; the discontinuance or suspension of political or economic action.

This verb, which goes back to Old English, took the sense of "to become solid or congealed by cold." Police jargon picked up the imperative use of "Freeze!" to stop suspects from fleeing.

The noun *freeze*, first used in the fifteenth century, gained modern prominence in the phrase *nuclear freeze*, used in 1980 by DOVES displeased with lack of progress in the Strategic Arms Limitation Talks (SALT) who called for a "mutual freeze" on nuclear weapons and the means of delivering them. In March of 1982 Judith Miller of *The New York Times* reported, "A congressional resolution urging the United States and the Soviet Union to negotiate a freeze in their nuclear arsenals has touched off an intense debate among Democrats"; Republicans behind President Reagan sided with the hawkish Democrats who believed "that the freeze proposal would endanger national security by giving the Soviet Union a permanent advantage in, for example, land-based, long-range missiles."

In Reagan's second term, with his "trust but verify" philosophy, and Mikhail Gorbachev replacing the more rigid Kremlin leadership, the superpowers negotiated the Strategic Arms Reduction Treaty (START) and the *freeze* figure of speech turned to other issues. Economic uses of the noun date back to the October 1942 use of *price freeze*, based on a 1930s concept of *price control*. From that use of the term came the *COLA freeze*, an attempt to end the cost-of-living adjustment of Social Security benefits. The *wage-price freeze* of the Nixon administration served only to demonstrate that government control of the economy is not a good idea. See GAME PLAN.

After a freeze has been in effect for a while, critics of the policy usually want to unfreeze, or to lift the freeze, or, in extended imagery of ice, to *thaw*.

frontlash See BACKLASH.

front-porch campaign Originally, a dignified campaign technique, eminently successful; now, a pompous approach to voters by a lazy candidate.

"McKinley stayed at home," wrote Harry Truman, "and spoke only to such delegations as came to his house from time to time. This was the first of the 'front porch' campaigns. I do not approve of 'front porch' campaigns. I never liked to see any man elected to office who did not go out and meet the people in person and work for their votes."

Although Harry Truman, in his 1948 campaign (see WHISTLESTOPPING), laid to rest for modern campaigners any thoughts of relaxed campaigning at home, his historical analysis is open to debate. There were three front-porch campaigns—Harrison in 1888, McKinley in 1896, and Harding in 1920—and the last two resulted in landslides for the frontporcher. McKinley, especially, had good reason to stay at home and entertain delegations to Canton, Ohio—he was not the stemwinding orator that his opponent, William Jennings Bryan was. It made more political sense to play to his strength, which was a homely, conservative, heartland-of-America stability.

Benjamin Harrison made speeches from his front porch in 1888, narrowly defeating Grover Cleveland, and repeated the technique in 1892, losing to Cleveland. But it was McKinley's campaign that perfected the technique and coined the phrase. The delegations to Canton organized by Mark Hanna's Republican organization included railroad excursion fares, which made such a trip, in the *Cleveland Plain Dealer*'s disgusted opinion, "cheaper than staying at home." Though the candidate said he was "averse to anything like an effort being made to bring the crowds here," the delegations were met at the depot by a gaily uniformed escort of horsemen, conducted to the McKinley home in a noisy parade, and treated to a fine display of rustic Americana; they returned home with excellent word-of-mouth to pass on about the charming gentleman who shook each visitor's hand.

In his next campaign, in 1900, McKinley felt more confident about Bryan's opposition, and agreed to travel more. In 1920, the Harding managers thought it would be safer to keep their man mainly at home and out of the kind of trouble possible in a STUMP campaign.

What makes a front-porch campaign impossible today is that a candidate must never seem remote and inaccessible. But William McKinley's accessibility—to those who would travel to see him—added to his appeal. English journalist George Steevens wrote: "If you want to see a Presidential candidate you ring the bell and walk in and see him. That is what he is there for. I rang and walked in; Mr. McKinley was sitting on a rocking-chair not ten feet from the door... he is gifted with a kindly courtesy that is plainly genuine and completely winning."

front runner The leading contender for a nomination.

Another racing term describes the front runner: "shows early foot." This means that the horse (or candidate) is capable of getting out of the starting gate well and sets the pace for the others in the field. Occasionally his lead becomes insurmountable, as Barry Goldwater's nomination race showed in 1964, and Jimmy Carter's capture of many convention states and early primaries showed in 1976, but the phrase as used today in politics carries ominous overtones of a possibility of fading in the homestretch.

FDR, the front runner in 1932, received this letter from Robert W. Wooley about his leadership so early in the campaign: "Herein lies the danger... automatically you become the target of the other candidates, real and potential. There isn't a single FAVORITE SON whose delegation won't be held out of the Roosevelt column so long as there is a reasonable chance of getting something for that favorite son, even at your expense."

Ted Sorensen echoed this point about John F. Kennedy a generation later: "There were disadvantages in being the 'front runner.' The Senator's critics became more open and vocal and his every word was politically interpreted."

The front runner must come thundering into the convention increasing his speed and with enough "kick" left for a final spurt. "When the balloting starts," wrote Thomas E. Dewey, "every candidate wants to show enough strength to be one of the leaders on the first ballot. He also wants to have enough strength in reserve so he can gain on the psychologically important second ballot. For example, in 1940, I led on the first three ballots out of six—the wrong three. I lost ground on the second ballot. That was the beginning of the end and everybody knew it." See DEWEY BLITZ.

Front runners like to stress the "inevitability factor," part of the BANDWAGON effect: if you go up against the one whose selection is seemingly inevitable, you will be marked for political life as a "loser." George W. Bush in 2000 seemed to have the nomination locked up before the primaries began, which gave him in polling and fundraising what Bush's father had called "the Big Mo"—momentum—but was set back by John McCain's surprise win in the first primary in New Hampshire. Peter Hart, the Democratic pollster who advised Walter Mondale in 1984—who also found his inevitability shattered for a time by Gary Hart's upset victory in New Hampshire—said in 2007, "Inevitability is not a message... there needs to be something to grab on to. Inevitability is not a tune that people can march to." Adam Nagourney of *The New York Times* observed that "nothing invites a teardown more than being perceived as the front-runner. Being on top makes you a big target for your opponents and the news media, and sets you up for buyer's remorse, a common phenomenon in the nomination process, even before the sale is done."

Despite all the protestations of danger in being the front runner, candidates prefer that position to DARK HORSE, or, worse, *long shot*. However, the racing analogy is not complete. In 1953, a sports page pictured a victorious jockey completely splattered with mud. The caption explained that "it is evident McCreary's mount had to come from way back to win—front runners stay clean." Not so in politics.

frying the fat See FAT CAT.

fudge factory See WAFFLE.

full-court press An all-out effort.

"Something dramatic was in order," wrote *Time* in October 1977, describing Carter Administration plans for a counterattack on opponents of its energy legislation. "[Vice President Walter] Mondale spoke up and, using a basketball image, urged a 'full-court press' on energy. Carter liked the idea."

The basketball phrase became White House lingo in the late '60s; one of its most frequent users was Nixon counsel Charles Colson. In politics, the term has come to mean a strenuous effort to get legislation passed, probably because of its resemblance to *all-out pressure.*

In basketball, however, the phrase is used only to describe a defense. When a professional team takes the ball into play from behind its own basket, it has ten seconds to cross mid-court; the defense sometimes employs a *full-court press* to harass and otherwise delay the offense from bringing the ball across. Other "presses" are *half-court* and (in college ball) *zone*; in each case, the intent is to concentrate delaying pressure on the offense (in hockey, this is known as a *forecheck*).

However, in political usage the defensive image has dribbled away, and only the aggressiveness remains. The Associated Press reported in March 1993 that "President Clinton promised a 'full-court press' against Bosnian Serbs to secure their agreement to the peace plan." On the political court, *The Washington Post* reported in 2007 that "Democratic Senatorial Committee Chairman Chuck Schumer (NY) is putting the full court press on former Gov. Jeanne Shaheen to take on Sen. John Sununu for the second time ..." See SPORTS METAPHORS, and specifically basketball, SLAM DUNK.

full dinner pail Symbol of prosperity, turn-of-the-century equivalent of a cornucopia, or horn of plenty; slogan of the 1900 William McKinley campaign.

"Hurrah for a full ballot-box, a full dinner-pail, and continued prosperity!" The *Review of Reviews* in 1900 showed a picture of a large dinner pail featured in a Youngstown,

Ohio, parade, with a caption: "Four more Years of the Full Dinner Pail."

William Jennings Bryan, in his second campaign against McKinley, stressed imperialism as the PARAMOUNT ISSUE: "Immediate Freedom for the Philippines" was the Democratic slogan. The Republicans emphasized prosperity, with vice presidential candidate Theodore Roosevelt doing much of the campaigning, assuring the workingman that Republicanism and high tariffs would continue to keep the dinner pails full.

The dinner pail had long been a symbol in the growing labor movement. Thomas Nast used it in an 1880 *Harper's Weekly* cartoon, and Theodore Roosevelt wrote a friend in 1894: "I hear all around that the working men intend to vote for 'the policy of the full dinner pail' ..." In 1928 Herbert Hoover tried to update the phrase, holding the symbol for the "party of prosperity": "The slogan of progress is changing from the full dinner pail to the full garage." Writing about his defeat a year later, Democrat Al Smith described Republican strategy that had "brought down from the garret the old full dinner pail, polished it up and pressed it into service."

Since the Depression, most Republicans have stayed away from symbols of prosperity in campaigning, though they have used the word *prosperity* itself; Democrats have hammered away at the "CHICKEN IN EVERY POT" (which Hoover never said), denying Republicans the *full dinner pail* as a symbol. Since dinner pails are blue-collar rather than white-collar, and the packaging of food has changed, the symbol may be expected to reappear as a nutritious, portable snack.

full disclosure Complete candidness; an apparently total release of information.

This revealing phrase has appeared in all areas of governmental information, the release of which has been governed by both the Freedom of Information Act of 1966 and the Privacy Act of 1974. Its use of the modifier *full* suggests the built-in skepticism about disclosing information.

The Securities and Exchange Commission provides the origin of the term. Its first official appearance was in the preamble to the Securities Act of 1933: "An act to provide full and fair disclosure of the character of securities sold in interstate and foreign commerce and through the mails, and to prevent frauds and the sale thereof, and for other purposes."

William Futrell, a spokesman for the environmentalist Sierra Club, told *National Journal* in 1977 that "the full disclosure of the impact statement is our most valuable tool for environmental coalitions." Almost a decade later, Ronald Reagan urged Congress to give limited immunity to John Poindexter and Oliver North for their Iran-contra testimony. Reagan's statement read in part, "There is an urgent need for full disclosure of all facts surrounding the Iranian controversy."

Most often, in recent years, the collocation is used in parentheses to show an avoidance of conflict of interest, as in (*full disclosure*); the lexicographer used the phrase to title his 1977 novel about the 25th Amendment, concerning a blinded president's inability to carry out his duties.

full generation of peace The central theme and highest ideal of the Nixon presidency.

Richard Nixon attributed the phrase to Jawaharlal Nehru. As Vice President in 1953, on his first trip to India, Nixon told his aides he had asked the Indian Prime Minister what was his nation's greatest single need. According to Nixon, Nehru replied, "The greatest need for India, and for any newly independent country is for twenty-five years of peace—a generation of peace."

Six months earlier (on May 11, 1953), soon after the death of Stalin, Winston Churchill had told the House of Commons that a "conference on the highest level" should be convened: "At the worst, the participants in the meeting could have established more intimate contacts, and at best we might have a generation of peace."

At a speech to the Air Force Academy in June 1969, Nixon began contrasting the record of the past generation with his hopes for the next: "In the past generation,

since 1941, this Nation has paid for fourteen years of peace with fourteen years of war. In terms of human suffering, this has been the costliest generation in the two centuries of our history. Perhaps this is why my generation is so determined to pass on a different legacy. We want to redeem that sacrifice. We want to be remembered, not as the generation that suffered in war, but as the generation that was tempered in its fire for a great purpose: to make the kind of peace that the next generation will be able to keep."

On his arrival in India on July 31, 1969, Nixon referred to the Nehru observation, and made it his own theme: "It is essential, absolutely essential, that we have a generation of peace for Asia and the world."

By using the phrase again in his speech to the 25th anniversary of the United Nations, and repeating it in the 1971 State of the Union message, the President made it plain that he had found his central theme. There was one oddity about it: the limited nature of the goal retained the possibility of war in a later generation—considerably short of "permanent peace," or in Lincoln's phrase, a JUST AND LASTING PEACE. Nixon dealt with that single-generation goal at the dedication of the Woodrow Wilson Center in Washington, D.C., on February 18, 1971:

Every war-time President since Woodrow Wilson has been tempted to describe the current war as "the WAR TO END WARS." But they have not done so because of the derision that the phrase evoked, a reminder of lost dreams, of lights that failed, of hopes that were raised and dashed.

What I am striving for … is something America has never experienced in this century, a full generation of peace.… That is why I have set our sights on a span of time that men in positions of power today can cope with, just one generation, but one long step on the path away from perennial war.

fur ball Fierce dogfight; a difficult problem.

As military aviation slang for close aerial combat, this phrase gained popularity during the first Persian Gulf war. In January 1991, The Associated Press reported the use of *fur ball* by military pilots to mean "the hectic tangle of air-to-air dogfights."

The term was used seven years before by an air traffic expert who told *Aviation Week and Space Technology* of "a fur ball of airplanes, so many that Patrick radar approach control can't handle them." Within three years, the term was also used for the engagement of enemy aircraft. Mike Spick wrote in *Defense & Foreign Affairs* in June 1987 about the improved training of aerial fighters: "Should they get trapped in the fur ball, and there are no absolutes in air combat, then they are better equipped both to win and to survive than their predecessors."

An extension of the metaphoric *dogfight*, the term *fur ball* (sometimes written solid as *furball*) suggests any tangle, military or political, too tight for the participants to be differentiated. A related expression for fighting, *to make the fur fly*, began in American slang in the early nineteenth century; *Niles' Register* of 1814 warned, "Smugglers look out, or you will soon see 'the fur fly.'"

Fur ball has also been used for any difficulty, from cats to spies. Junette A. Pinkney wrote in *The Washington Post* in 1984: "The only fur ball in the whole business was that Brenno had to get an allergy shot." In May 2006, General Michael Hayden, appearing before the Senate Intelligence Committee considering his confirmation as Director of Central Intelligence, said that reports of wireless surveillance conducted by the CIA were a "furball." A year later, as warrantless tapping of overseas calls was revealed, the fur flew.

fusion Coalition before election; a combination of minority parties to defeat the majority party.

Coalition is used to describe the alliance of different political groups who combine to form a government after an election, and therefore is mainly a word to describe non-American politics. *Fusion*, on the other hand, is a welding of interests before an election in the U.S. and particularly in big cities.

As a young novelist, Benjamin Disraeli described the usage in the 1840s in England: "Political conciliation became the slang of the day, and the fusion of the parties the babble of the clubs."

Bronx boss Ed Flynn expressed the feeling of the Democratic politician in New York for the two groups that caused him the most trouble: "the 'other party,' which in New York is the Republican party; and the motley mob of political hacks that cluster periodically about benign old jurists and smart young boy gangbusters who raise the flag of 'Fusion.'" Edward Costikyan, a new-era Tammany leader, offered this definition: "*Reformer* was a term of opprobrium within the machine, and reformers looked ... to the occasional creation of an *ad hoc* political force which would sporadically 'throw the rascals out' and enjoy four years or so of steadily deteriorating governmental power, until the machine returned to power. In New York, this tradition became known as *fusion*."

New York City fusion succeeded five times: in 1901, when Seth Low became a one-term mayor; in 1913, when John Purroy Mitchel became a one-term mayor; in 1933, Fiorello La Guardia for three terms; John Lindsay in 1965; and a form of Democratic-Republican fusion electing Ed Koch in 1981. Michael Bloomberg fused himself: elected as a Republican, he became an independent in 2007. Lindsay was fond of quoting La Guardia's appeal to nonpartisanship when speaking to voters registered Democratic: "There is no Republican way or Democratic way to clean the streets."

future and it works See WAVE OF THE FUTURE.

fuzziness See ALL THINGS TO ALL MEN.

fuzzy math Arithmetic that doesn't add up correctly; attack phrase for disputing governmental tax and spending programs.

Fuzzy math made its national political debut on October 3, 2000, during the first debate between Vice President Al Gore, the Democratic candidate for president, and Texas Governor George W. Bush, the Republican nominee. Gore came to the debate in Boston brimming over with so many facts, figures, and statistics that the moderator often had to cut him off. Gore charged, among other things, that Bush's proposed tax cuts would give more money to the wealthiest one percent of the population than he planned to spend on health care, prescription drugs, education, and national defense combined. Rather than attempt to refute Gore's criticisms in any detail, Bush dismissed them as "fuzzy math." The retort became a refrain, with Bush saying at different points in the debate, "The man is practicing fuzzy math again," "The man has been disparaging my planning with all this fuzzy math," and "I can't let the man continue with fuzzy math."

Most pundits judged the debate to be a draw, but the *fuzzy math* sound bite struck a chord. The next day, when Bush observed sarcastically during a campaign stop at a college outside Philadelphia that Gore "loves to talk numbers," the young people began chanting "No fuzzy math. No fuzzy math."

Attempts were made to turn *fuzzy math* back on Bush. Paul Krugman dissected Bush's tax proposals in a 2001 book entitled *Fuzzy Math*. CBS News reported in February of 2004: "In a presidential debate nearly four years ago, George W. Bush accused Al Gore of employing 'fuzzy math.' But increasingly, it's the White House that's being accused of fuzziness on Medicare, the deficit and jobs." Senator John Kerry, the Democratic candidate for president in 2004, posed the rhetorical question to reporters later that April, "Do you trust the Bush administration's math?" and answered it immediately: "I think it's fuzzy math as usual, and they're not telling the truth."

Fuzzy math most likely resonates with the public as well as it does because of the controversy surrounding attempts to introduce it into the nation's classrooms. Also known as "whole math" and "new-new math," *fuzzy math* was promoted by the National Council of Teachers of Mathematics starting in 1989. The object of this approach, particularly popular in California, was to teach students basic concepts through discussion of word problems rather than require them to master chores, such as memorizing multiplication tables, which are handled easily by calculators. Many parents and teachers rebelled, however, when they found that their children were having difficulty performing such routine operations as addition and subtraction. The NCTM subsequently backed off from this approach.

The expression has crossed the U.S. border. A spokesman for Mexico's Felipe Calderón, in his narrowly successful campaign for president of Mexico in 2006, attacked his leftist opponent, Andrés Manuel López Obrador, as being unfriendly to business: "He calls bankers 'parasites,' tells businessmen they will see their 'unfair advantages' end, then he expects their help.... at the end of the day, it's simply a case of fuzzy math." See NUMBERS GAME.

G

gaffe See BLOOPER.

gag rule Attack phrase on a parliamentary device or resolution to limit debate.

Both in England and America, sedition acts at the end of the eighteenth century were labeled "gags" by critics. The most famous American example of "gag rule" was a resolution passed by the House of Representatives in 1836 to cut off debate on the subject of abolishing or curtailing the institution of slavery. In 1833, after the American Anti-Slavery Society was founded, the House of Representatives was deluged by thousands of antislavery petitions and proposed measures, particularly bills demanding the abolition of slavery in the District of Columbia. The answer of the slaveholding interests, operating within the Democratic party, was the "gag rule." The measure was actually proposed by a Northerner, C. G. Atherton of New Hampshire, and Northerners within the Democratic ranks supported it. It tabled (in the American sense of "set aside," not the opposite British sense) any measures dealing with the subject.

Former President John Quincy Adams, who had entered the House as a representative after his term as Chief Executive, opposed it at the beginning of every session of Congress, writing later: "then came Atherton of New Hampshire, the man of the mongrel gag." In 1844 the "gag" was finally defeated, but not before it had become a national issue publicizing the antislavery forces. Adams was anathematized by some; however, John F. Kennedy, in his book *Profiles in Courage,* refers to the Adams fight against the measure as "the brightest chapter of his history."

During FDR's first term, newly empowered Democratic leaders in the House employed the iron discipline reminiscent of turn-of-the-century Speaker "Uncle Joe" Cannon. "They can determine how much debate, if any, they shall permit," wrote Ray Tucker of *The New York Times* in 1935.

"If they feel so inclined—and they often do these days—they can bar any amendments except those offered by their side. This is what is known as the 'gag rule.'" In 1995, this was recalled with a vengeance by Republicans taking control of the House for the first time in 40 years; in 2007, when Democrats who took back control, it was turnabout time again: Speaker Nancy Pelosi pledged to ram though a series of Democratic proposals and new rules in "the first 100 hours," employing tactics the GOP members denounced as "gag rule." See HUNDRED DAYS

Rule is a word that harkens to the historical American distaste of monarchy, and—with the exception of *majority rule*—is used pejoratively in politics. In addition to *gag rule,* there is *mob rule,* which usually means anarchy following a breakdown of law and order but occasionally is used in regard to organized racketeering; *boss rule,* the object of reformers' scorn; *rule-or-ruin,* from English poet John Dryden's "resolved to ruin or to rule the state," used in the U.S. in 1836 against the Whigs and now a condemnation of sore losers and bolters in primaries or conventions; *one-man rule,* first used against "King Andrew" Jackson; and *one-party rule,* the object of ridicule by advocates of a TWO-PARTY SYSTEM. In Great Britain the sovereign *reigns but does not rule;* a positive use of the word is in the aforesaid *majority rule,* but even that came under attack with de Tocqueville's "tyranny of the majority." About the only rules held sacred are the biblical Golden Rule, the RULE OF LAW, and HOME RULE.

game plan Strategy; a blueprint for action with all tactics designed to achieve the ultimate goal.

Paul McCracken, chairman of the Council of Economic Advisers, told the American Statistical Association on August 21, 1969: "There is one thing that perhaps the Council Chairman can do. That is to outline for you the Washington *game plan* for economic policy." McCracken had used a phrase that was current in Administration circles because President Nixon used it often in private conversation with his aides, usually as a verb: "We have to game-plan this." This was natural enough, as he was both an avid football fan and a believer in the GRAND DESIGN.

The expression soon became hackneyed. Every suggestion had to be "game-planned," and when the author suggested the term be banned he was told sympathetically to submit a game plan on how *game plan* was to be abolished. Alan Otten wrote in *The Wall Street Journal* on December 23, 1970: "Government also tends to become infatuated with a phrase, and then abuse or misuse it. Thus officials in both foreign and economic policy areas have too eagerly embraced the 'game plan' image of the sports world. They now constantly project their 'economic game plan' or 'Vietnam game plan,' even though the phrase carries overtones of fun and frivolity that don't quite suit the serious business of ending the war in Southeast Asia or restoring economic vigor at home."

In professional football, a detailed game plan is drawn up for both the offensive and defensive units to exploit the weaknesses of the opposition. The quarterback is told what to do under a variety of circumstances before the game begins: first down deep in his own territory, third and short yardage at midfield, etc. "Part of the game plan deals with reactions to varying defenses," Edward Bennett Williams, one of the owners of the Washington Redskins in the '70s, informed the author. "A game plan is quite detailed, even computerized. Of course, when you get behind, you sometimes have to scrub the game plan."

Thus, in football, the phrase has a more detailed, tactical connotation than in politics, where the meaning is more strategic. But in politics, too, when you get behind, you often scrub the game plan: At a meeting in Camp David on Friday, August 13, 1971, the game plan was interred and a new economic policy—suspending the convertibility of the dollar into gold and, unfortunately, imposing wage and price controls—was born. The lexicographer who drafted the speech that sent economic shock waves around the world substituted "new economic plan" for "game plan," but somebody remembered that Vladimir Lenin had proposed a New Economic Plan for the Soviet Union. With a gulp, I struck it out without naming the plan.

The cliché lingers on but has been downgraded. *American Banker* wrote in 1985 about a trend "away from political game plans and toward business strategies."

Gang of Four See CHINA WATCHERS; CULTURAL REVOLUTION.

Gang of Fourteen Group of centrist U.S. Senators, seven Democrats and seven Republicans, who made a pact in 2005 to allow votes on six of President George W. Bush's nominees for federal judgeships while defusing the threat by the Republican majority of employing the mock NUCLEAR OPTION to prevent filibusters.

Democratic members of the bipartisan group agreed not to filibuster either the nominations at hand or future ones except under vague "extraordinary circumstances." In return, the Republicans promised not to support a proposed rule change that would have deprived the Democrats of a traditional parliamentary tactic by lowering the number of votes required to halt filibusters on all judicial nominations from sixty to a simple majority of fifty-one.

The emergence of the so-called *gang* made headlines at the time and set something of a precedent for bipartisan coalitions. When two Republican senators, John W. Warner of Virginia and Susan Collins of Maine, met with a Democrat, Ben Nelson of Nebraska, in January 2007, to discuss a possible Senate resolution on President Bush's Iraq policy, *The New York Times* reported: "Senators Warner, Collins, and Nelson, in a move reminiscent of the 'Gang of 14' meetings that helped avert a showdown over judicial filibusters in 2005, began meeting this week after they saw the language of the initial bipartisan resolution." As the 2006 midterm election approached, partisanship returned.

In political terms, *Gang of Fourteen* plays upon the *Gang of Four* that attempted to gain power in China following Mao Zedong's death in 1976. See CULTURAL REVOLUTION and OPPORTUNIST.

Though *gang* may be employed jocularly by U.S. senators when referring to one another, the term is essentially pejorative, having been applied to bands of pirates and other criminals since the seventeenth century. Curiously, its derivative, *gangster*, an Americanism, appears first in a political context, with the earliest examples coming from Ohio newspapers in the 1880s. The *Newark Daily Advocate* referred disparagingly to "a very tall Republican gangster" in 1887. Two years later, the *Advocate* characterized another Republican in terms that would be considered excessive today: "[George B.] Cox is the worst political boss and gangster the city of Cincinnati or the State has ever known. He is representative of all that is vicious and vile in politics."

gap A phrasemaking word to illustrate shortage, lack, insufficiency, a falling short, or a gulf between.

The original rhetorical gap was the MISSILE GAP, a Democratic charge in 1959 and 1960; educators used *reading gap*, businessmen *experience gap*, and political critics used CREDIBILITY GAP against Lyndon Johnson, who talked of "bridging the gap between East and West" in his 1964 State of the Union message. For a gap in Medicare coverage, see DOUGHNUT HOLE.

Russell Baker, the "Observer" columnist of *The New York Times*, needled the gapsters in 1967, calling attention to

> the so-called gap gap, one of the most pressing problems confronting the Government today. Several of Washington's most important Cabinet officials illustrate the enormous range of gaps that have already been dealt with in intensive, two-year studies conducted by the nation's leading universities, and make a convincing argument that if the present rate of two-year studies is maintained the country will be out of gaps to keep its blue-ribbon committees employed by the end of 1969. The inescapable sociologist, Sean Moynihan, controversial as always, proposes solving the problem by lengthening all two-year gap studies to four years.

Generation gap can be a frustrating lack of communication between young and old, or a useful stretch of time that separates cultures within a society, allowing them to develop their own character. *Generation gap* was not sired by *missile gap* out of *credibility gap*, though gapsmanship in general reinforced all three. The originator was Winston Churchill, who wrote in *My Early Life* (1930): "Come on now, all you young men, all over the world. You are needed more than ever now to fill the gap of a generation shorn by the war ..." The future British leader went on to write: "Don't take no for an answer, never submit to failure. Do not be fobbed off by mere personal success or acceptance. You will make all kinds of mistakes; but as long as you are generous and true, and also fierce, you cannot hurt the world or even seriously distress her. She was made to be wooed and won by youth."

garden-hose analogy FDR's homely parable to explain Lend-Lease to the American people.

Late in 1940, Prime Minister Churchill wrote a 4,000-word letter to President Roosevelt reviewing Britain's military and financial position, and hoping—without using the words *loan* or *lend*—that the U.S. would not "confine the help which they have so generously promised only to such munitions of war and accommodations as could be immediately paid for." At a press conference in Washington on December 17, 1940, Roosevelt pointed out that the more supplies Britain took—paid or not—the more quickly our own productive capacity would grow, and the war materials were more useful "if they were used in Great Britain, than if they were kept in storage here."

FDR went on extemporaneously telling a kind of parable:

> Suppose my neighbor's home catches fire, and I have a length of garden hose four or five hundred feet away. If he can take my garden hose and connect it up with his hydrant, I may help him to put out his fire. Now, what do I do? I don't say to him before the operation, "Neighbor, my garden hose cost me $15; you have to pay me $15 for it." What is the transaction that goes on?

I don't want $15—I want my garden hose back after the fire is over.

After the fire is put out, he puts the garden hose back, and if it is damaged beyond repair in putting out the fire, he (my neighbor) says, "All right, I will replace it." Now, if I get a nice garden hose back, I am in pretty good shape.

The plain words about lending a garden hose to a neighbor to put out a fire—which, incidentally, might well spread to your own home—and later getting the garden hose back, or a duplicate, was Lend-Lease in its simplest terms. As complex a scheme as Lend-Lease turned out to be, it could not have been more effectively placed before the American people.

Of course, the hose was never returned, nor did FDR ever expect it would be.

garrison state See WELFARE STATE.

-gate construction A device to provide a sinister label to a possible scandal.

After WATERGATE, a scandal in France dealing with the adulteration of Bordeaux wines was promptly dubbed "Winegate." This led to the adoption of the -*gate* suffix as a scandalizer in other fields.

When it became known in 1976 that an investigation had been launched into corruption of members of the U.S. Congress by the South Korean CIA, this writer started referring automatically to "Koreagate." When mayoral candidate Mario Cuomo attacked New York Mayor Abe Beame for seeking to suppress an SEC report on the finances of the BIG APPLE—New York City— he called it "Applegate." More aptly, charges leveled at Congressman Daniel Flood in 1978 were called "Floodgate," and charges that some contractors were double-billing the government reminded those acquainted with British English of the possibilities of *double-billingsgate*. The formulation with the -*gate* suffix is too useful to fade quickly.

genocide See HOLOCAUST; FINAL SOLUTION.

geopolitics See HEARTLAND; LEBENSRAUM.

gerrymander Drawing of political lines by the party in power so as to perpetuate its power; designing a district to fit a voting pattern.

This is one of the most triumphant political expressions, traceable to the early days of the Republic and still in current use.

Charles Ledyard Norton selected a picture of a gerrymander for the cover of his 1890 book, *Political Americanisms*—initial inspiration to the writer of this dictionary—and gave this etymology:

The term is derived from the name of Governor [Elbridge] Gerry, of Massachusetts, who, in 1811, signed a bill readjusting the representative districts so as to favor the Democrats and weaken the Federalists, although the last named party polled nearly two-thirds of the votes cast. A fancied resemblance of a map of the districts thus treated led [Gilbert] Stuart, the painter, to add a few lines with his pencil, and say to Mr. [Benjamin] Russell, editor of the Boston *Centinel*, "That will do for a salamander." Russell glanced at it: "Salamander?" said he, "Call it a Gerrymander!" The epithet took at once and became a Federalist warcry, the map caricature being published as a campaign document.

Gerry's name was pronounced with a hard *g;* but because of the similarity of the word with *jerry-built* (meaning rickety, no connection with *gerrymander*) the letter *g* is pronounced as *j*.

Governor Gerry, a signer of the Declaration of Independence and later one of James Madison's Vice Presidents, has become— thanks to linguistics—a kind of villain in American history, although he never sponsored the redistricting bill and is said to have signed it reluctantly. But his name has been perpetuated in denunciations like this: "See where the hateful serpent of the gerrymander has wound his sinuous course," said an Indiana congressman in 1893. "See where in his glittering folds he has strangled the life out of the spirit of liberty." In 1993, the *Los Angeles Times* printed this comment on a school board redistricting plan: "A gerrymander by any other name is still a gerrymander. This is one of the problems of the board. Too much self-interest instead of interest where it ought to be—the education of our children."

Gerrymandering created some odd-looking districts, such as the "Monkey-Wrench" district of Iowa, the "Dumb-bell" district of Pennsylvania, the "Horseshoe" district of New York, and the "Shoestring" district of Mississippi. For a modern use of the ancient technique, see ONE MAN, ONE VOTE. For other examples of eponymy, see MAVERICK; SOLON; PHILIPPIC; BORK; and QUISLING.

Gettysburg Address The Sermon on the Mount of politics, often quoted, not always understood.

To most Americans, Lincoln's Gettysburg Address is a string of revered catchphrases, beginning with "four-score and seven years ago" (a solemn way of saying eighty-seven) and ending with the familiar "of the people, by the people, for the people." (See IDEAS.) Some who memorized it in grammar school will also recall "the last full measure of devotion" and "that these dead shall not have died in vain."

The Gettysburg Address is a poem based on the theme of national resurrection. Its opening sentence contains a triad of images of birth—of a nation "*conceived* in liberty" and "*brought forth*" (born), with all "*created* equal." The speech then uses the forum of a national cemetery and the images of death ("final resting place," "brave men, living and dead") to symbolize purification and resurrection—that out of this scene of death, "this nation, under God, shall have a *new birth* of freedom."

Rather than addressing himself at length to the dead men in that cemetery, Lincoln used the occasion to recount the conception, birth, death, and rebirth of the nation. But the metaphor, central to Christianity, is never labored.

In his 266 words, Lincoln used the word *dedicate* six times. The first and second times refer to the nation's dedication to an ideal—"that all men are created equal." The third and fourth refer to the specific purpose of the occasion, honoring the dead men buried at Gettysburg—"to dedicate a portion of that field as a final resting place," and noting that their sacrifice had already consecrated it. The fifth and sixth times refer to the ideals—"to the unfinished work" and "to the great tasks remaining before us."

The structure of this speech can be based on these uses of *dedicate*—a strong dedication to ideals first, then a dedication of ground for the dead, and finally a ringing rededication to the ideals.

The structure of the speech is so deceptively simple and its choice of words so plain that it spawned the "jotted-on-the-back-of-an-envelope" legend. Most speechwriters believe that its theme was far too carefully constructed and its sentences too rhythmically biblical to have been written so casually.

Everything can be parodied; for one, see EISENHOWER SYNTAX. For earlier uses of the structure of its famous conclusion, see IDEAS.

ghostwriter One who writes another's speeches, articles, and planned "ad libs."

Eight categories of ghost (or "spook") haunt the political scene:

1. SPEECHWRITER, who operates out in the open. The public has come to recognize that a president and a few other high officials are too busy—or are not talented enough writers—to prepare all their own messages, and consider it an act of honesty for these speechmakers to let it become known who writes their speeches.
2. *Ghostwriter*, or *ghost*, is one who surreptitiously prepares written and oral messages for public figures below the highest levels.
3. *Phrasemaker*, one who improves upon speeches already drafted, who "punches up" or adds impact to remarks that contain no quotable passages.
4. *Sloganeer*, which can be a pejorative word for *phrasemaker*, or may refer to an advertising copywriter whose assignment is to create slogans and define issues in a short headline.
5. *Wordsmith*, a hack ghostwriter able to transcribe thoughts into speakable English but with few ideas of his own.
6. *Research assistant*, who can be one ferreting out the facts on which to base a speech or with which a general speech can be made more specific, or a *ghost* or *wordsmith* on the public payroll whose

euphemistic title conceals his public-relations or writing activities.

7. *Press Secretary*, capitalized if in the White House, or *press aide* (downmouthed as *press agent* or *flack* by some reporters who could not handle that job), also writes material for his employer, though the higher the public office becomes, the less likely the press aide is to handle the speechwriting function.

8. *As-told-to*, a writer with a well-known byline who is identified on the cover of a book written with the active cooperation of the subject, who vouches for its authenticity.

giveaway Attack word against those who propose private development of natural resources, made by those who feel that public development would be more in the public interest.

If there is any counter to the conservative's charge of CREEPING SOCIALISM, it is the liberal's charge of *giveaway*. The word became popular in the controversy in 1953–55 over who should provide power to the city of Memphis, Tenn.: the public Tennessee Valley Authority (proud product of the New Deal), or a combine of private companies called "Dixon-Yates" after the names of the two company presidents. Democrats charged that the Dixon-Yates proposal would "give away" some $5 million in profits annually to private enterprise, which could be "saved" if the TVA did the job.

Giveaway, SELLOUT, and *steal* were the excoriations most often used in the attack. Eisenhower in 1954 attempted to explain his position: "The issue is not…public power versus unregulated private power. The issue posed to us is federal monopoly of power, as against public or regulated power, freely chosen in each instance by the citizens of each area, with the federal government coming in as a cooperating partner where this seems necessary or desirable."

However, after a contract had been signed with Dixon-Yates, it was revealed that a consultant to the Bureau of the Bud-get was also an official of the banking firm that was to finance the deal, and the City of Memphis decided to build its own power plant.

Democrats felt they had a good campaign issue against the Eisenhower policy on power and conservation, but it became confused when the "natural gas lobby" overstepped the bounds of propriety in fighting for their bill in 1956. While agreeing with the purpose of the natural gas bill, Eisenhower vetoed it because of the nature of the lobbying, which left Majority Leader Lyndon Johnson, who supported the bill, holding the bag. After that, *giveaway* lost its bite, and Dixon-Yates gave way to new issues.

Many conservatives, though not Ronald Reagan, finally found use for the word in 1977: they charged that the Panama Canal treaty was a *giveaway* of U.S. sovereignty.

give 'em hell, Harry A Truman campaign battle cry in 1948, now used to typify a hard-hitting campaign.

Enthusiasm for Harry Truman's candidacy was notably lacking among Democrats early in the 1948 campaign; signs at the convention read: "I'm just mild about Harry." On September 17, as he began barnstorming the country (see WHISTLESTOPPING), Truman recalled that he told his running mate, Alben Barkley: "I'm going to fight hard. I'm going to give them hell." As he ripped into the "gluttons of privilege" (see VESTED INTERESTS and the DO-NOTHING CONGRESS), the crowds responded to the scrappiness of the underdog with welcome interruptions of "Give 'em hell, Harry!"

"I never give them hell," Truman smiled as he reviewed his technique in 1956. "I just tell the truth, and they think it is hell."

The phrase became closely identified with the former president in an affectionate way. When Oxford University presented him with an honorary degree in 1956 ("to Harricum Truman, Doctoris in Iure Civili") the student cheer was "Harricum! Harricum! Give 'em hell, Harricum!"

The current generic use of the phrase is illustrated by this passage from Sherman Adams' memoirs: "[Len] Hall and I realized that it was futile to expect Eisenhower as the head of the party to make a 'give 'em hell' tour of the countryside ..." An informal slogan of Senator Hillary Clinton's 2008 presidential campaign was "Give 'em Hill."

glacis Buffer state; a defensive land barrier between potential enemies.

Unfamiliar words travel fast in Washington. Sahabzada Yaqub Khan, foreign minister of Pakistan, presciently used the term in an interview with the author in 1982 to discuss the country that lay between the Soviet Union and its Persian Gulf strategic interests: "Afghanistan might one day be intended by the Soviets to be a glacis." Soon afterward, William J. Casey, the Director of Central Intelligence and my longtime friend, dropped by the house one Sunday and gruffed, "You got a map of Afghanistan? It's a glacis, you know." (I got out a world atlas for him and a dictionary for me.)

Pronounced "GLASS-ee" or "GLAY-sis," this term is derived from a French word originally meaning "slippery place" and related to the Old French verb *glacier*, "to slip or slide." The English noun was first used in 1672 for "a gentle slope or inclined embankment"; that sense soon led to the more specific military use for "a fortification that slopes to ground level," recalling Pickett's charge up toward Cemetery Ridge in the battle of Gettysburg.

Its figurative sense, however, developed in the mid-'50s. *The Times* of London reported in 1955 that East Germany was seen "as part of Russia's defensive glacis"; in 1960, *The Observer* commented that Eastern European countries "form the glacis between the Soviet Union and the West."

The phrase *glacis state* indicates a barrier of defense, but it suggests more than *buffer state* or *zone*, which merely lies between two powerful countries. A *glacis* forms part of the defense system of one or both of those powers. The word is in a state of desuetude but is in this dictionary in case it surfaces again one day.

glasnost Openness; eagerness to display the public release of information.

Translated from the Russian as "openness" or "publicity," *glasnost* was the declared policy of the former Soviet Union in allowing freedom of speech and the press. Closely identified with Mikhail Gorbachev, the noun emphasized his attempts to reform the Soviet-era suppression of free speech, a reform reversed under Vladimir Putin.

This term, derived from the archaic Russian word *glas*, meaning "voice," was in use long before Gorbachev popularized it. It was a favorite of reformist bureaucrats in the mid-nineteenth century, and Prince Petr Dolgorukov said in 1857, "Without the broad development of *glasnost*, the government will never have the opportunity to recognize all the abuses and thus will never have the opportunity to eradicate them." In *Deception: The Invisible War Between the KGB and the CIA*, Edward Jay Epstein noted that Lenin used the term more than 40 times in his writings. To achieve occasional purges, Lenin would use *glasnost* to force local officials into confessing their own ideological errors as well as informing on the mistakes of others; his urging of *glasnost* strengthened the dictatorship and at the same time offered the appearance of a movement toward free speech. Lenin's eloquent expression of this policy stated that "*Glasnost* is a sword which itself heals the wound it inflicts."

The word is used in the West today in nostalgia: "Once again the chilly winds are blowing across the steppes and over the rest of the world," noted the U.K.'s *Times Online* in 2007; "perestroika and glasnost are little more than memories ..." See PERESTROIKA.

glitch A mechanical or electronic failure that afflicts campaigns and can rattle campaigners.

A monkey wrench that finds its way into a "well-oiled political machine"; the piercing sound of feedback when a speaker reaches a climactic moment in a speech; the loss of baggage on a campaign tour—all these come under the heading of *glitches*, a term with electronic-error connotations.

Glitch, the mischief of a computerized gremlin, fills a linguistic need for an annoying and usually inexplicable failure of normal operations which results in a candidate's toe-stubbing or diplomatic BLUNDER. On Jimmy Carter's first trip abroad as President in December of 1977, he was unexpectedly troubled by a State Department mistranslation of his "desire" to be in Poland as a "lust" for Poles, and of his "leaving" the U.S. garbled by the interpreter as "abandoning" the U.S. This was followed in India by the worldwide coverage of President Carter's whispered, private suggestion to Secretary of State Cyrus Vance that he send a "cold, very blunt" letter to the Indian Prime Minister upon their return to the U.S.; unknown to the President, a microphone was open nearby during a "photo opportunity," and the broadcast whisper required fast backtracking by Press Secretary Jody Powell.

"That private talk with Vance," wrote Vernon A. Guidry Jr. of *The Washington Star* on January 2, 1978, "is now likely to become a source of embarrassment to Carter. It became public through another one of the glitches that have plagued the President's foreign tour." (A copy editor, unfamiliar with "glitches," changed the word in the second edition to "snafus.")

The word probably originated in the German and Yiddish *glitschen*, meaning "slip." According to the *Polyglot's Lexicon*, it entered the language in 1966, as a false signal, mishap, or malfunction in spacecraft, and by 2006 was standard jargon in telecasts of delayed NASA rocket launches.

It still carries weight in political campaigns. The *Los Angeles Times* wrote in 1992: "What if an advance man stumbles? What if the sound system fails, a setting sun makes the candidate squint, the motorcade breaks down or passing air traffic drowns out a speech? ... One such glitch can stain or spoil a campaign appearance, leaving a poor impression that can be hard to shake."

For a locomotive glitch, see the "idiot engineer" who helped undo candidate Thomas E. Dewey, under BLOOPER. An example of overcoming a glitch is in FIELD EXPEDIENT.

glittering generality See FOURTH OF JULY SPEECH.

globaloney See BALONEY.

global warming Planetary climate change, which most scientists and all ecologists are convinced is under way.

Global warming rings alarm bells—pushes the "hot" button—while *climate change* is a cooler warning. The first phrase is alarming, the second neutral, but the two are used interchangeably. According to the National Academy of Sciences, "the phrase 'climate change' is growing in preferred use to 'global warming' because it helps convey that there are changes [in precipitation, for instance] in addition to rising temperatures."

President George W. Bush, who long resisted the idea that people contribute to global warming, preferred to speak in terms of *climate change*. At the start of a press conference on June 11, 2001, he announced: "Climate change, with its potential to impact every corner of the world, is an issue that must be addressed by the world." While citing a report by the National Academy that attributed global warming in large part to human activity, he focused on the uncertainties: "Yet the Academy's report tells us that we do not know how much effect natural fluctuations in climate may have had on warming. We do not know how much our climate could, or will, change in the future. We do not know how fast change will occur, or even how some of our actions could impact it." In July of 2005, he acknowledged a connection between human activities and global warming, remarking at a press conference in Denmark: "Listen, I recognize that the surface of the earth is warmer and that an increase in greenhouse gases caused by humans is contributing to the problem."

Global warming is older than *global climate change*. The *Hammond* (Indiana) *Times* reported on November 6, 1957: "Now our scientists, particularly those of Southern California, are studying the possibility that this continued pouring forth of waste gases may upset the rather delicate carbon dioxide balance in the earth's general atmosphere and that a large scale global warming, with radical climate changes may result." The idea of *global climate change* does not appear to have surfaced in the public consciousness until the 1980s, at least not by that name. In April of 1988 a group of forty-two U.S. senators, led by Lincoln Chafee (R-R.I.), used both phrases in a letter to President Ronald Reagan. Noting that "scientists predict that, as a result of past pollution, we are already committed to significant global warming," the senators asked the President to use an upcoming summit meeting with Soviet leader Mikhail Gorbachev "as a forum to call for the negotiation of a convention on global climate change."

The National Academy's opinion about nomenclature to the contrary, *global warming* remains a keen competitor in usage. A Google search in January 2008 showed almost three times as many hits for *global warming* as for *climate change*. See ENVIRONMENTALIST.

gloom and doom, prophets of The airy dismissal by the optimistic "Ins" of the viewing-with-alarm of the "Outs."

"My theory has always been," wrote Thomas Jefferson, "that if we are to dream, the flatteries of hope are as cheap, and pleasanter than the gloom of despair." Not so to a group of political pundits, or to almost any candidate running for another man's seat. The man seeking to oust the incumbent must convince voters that all is not rosy, that we are indeed in grave danger of a variety of catastrophes that could only be averted by a change of administration or representation.

Alliteration and rhyme help the sloganeering. Incumbent Democrats described Republicans in the campaign of 1936 as "disciples of despair" floundering in a "fountain of fear"; during the Eisenhower years, Republican Clare Boothe Luce denounced Democrats as "troubadours of trouble and crooners of catastrophe." Most common, however, is prophets of, or peddlers of, "gloom and doom."

One of the leading prophets, consistent through changes in Administrations, was the *New York Herald Tribune* columnist Joseph Alsop. After World War II ended, Alsop predicted to Harvard's Signet Club that the cause of Western man was lost; he urged free men today to emulate the brave action of the Spartans at Thermopylae, to "comb their golden hair in the sunlight and prepare to die bravely." *The Miami News* in 1967 wrote about its rival, *The Miami Herald:* "A gloom-and-doom piece in a Sunday newspaper here is rather typical of the nitpicking ..."

The phrase was coined in 1954, at the start of the first midterm congressional election campaign during the Eisenhower Administration. At the Springfield, Illinois State Fair, Democrat Adlai Stevenson—whom "Ike" had defeated in 1952 and would defeat again in 1956—derided incendiary political accusations of Senator Joseph McCarthy about Communists in high places, and said he hoped the president, in his appearance at the fair, would tell Republicans that their campaign "should not be just smile and smear—his smiles and their smears." Next night, on August 21, 1954, Eisenhower appeared before a larger crowd and chided the Democrats as "prophets of gloom and doom."

This was the exchange the author had in mind when, in the midterm campaign of 1970, he submitted a similar anti-pessimism phrase to Vice President Spiro Agnew. See NATTERING NABOBS OF NEGATIVISM.

gluttons of privilege See VESTED INTERESTS.

gnomes of Zurich International bankers.

Popularized by British Foreign Secretary George Brown in 1964, this gnarly trope paints a picture of busy elves in the Swiss financial capital, and was aimed at derogating the speculators who—by questioning Great Britain's credit standing—forced unpopular austerity measures on the government. Brown felt the "gnomes of Zurich" were out to make a killing at the expense of the pound sterling. "The term is a misnomer," wrote reporter Paul Hoffman, "since George Brown was actually referring to the Bank for International Settlements, which is in Basel."

The word *gnome* was coined (possibly from Greek *ge-nomos*, "earth dweller") by Philippus Aureolus Paracelsus, a sixteenth-century Swiss alchemist and physician, while investigating the mechanics of mining and the diseases of miners, and originally meant a misshapen being who guarded the mines and quarries of the inner earth, able to move through earth as a fish moves through water.

The mining derivation of *gnome* made Brown's phrase especially apt: in Zurich, the gnomes deal in gold, a metal that was the quest of the alchemists. (Besides, Basel is often pronounced "Bahl," following the French Bâle, which would have made the phrase with the correct city confusing to the reader.)

Unlike MALEFACTORS OF GREAT WEALTH and ECONOMIC ROYALISTS, *gnomes of Zurich* has a manipulative rather than a predatory connotation. By 1968, the phrase had gained the top rank of bogeymen, as in this use in *The Wall Street Journal*: "Frankly, we had enough to worry about with the MILITARY-INDUSTRIAL COMPLEX, the ESTABLISHMENT, the gnomes of Zurich, the *illuminati* and the POWER ELITE. Now the arbiters of instant demonology have added the *jet set*."

George J. W. Goodman, using the pseudonym Adam Smith in his 1968 book *The Money Game*, called one character the Gnome of Zurich. His pessimistic credo: since men cannot long manage their affairs rationally, politicians make costly promises, trade surpluses evaporate, gold reserves trickle away, and a "dollar crisis" periodically results.

James Pinkerton, an adviser to the elder Bush, commented in 1993 on President Clinton's earliest days in office: "The gnomes of Zurich and Tokyo are all tuned in, and they react in ways that clearly are catching Clinton by surprise."

The expression was used jocularly in 2007 to express one of the three historic achievements of the three-languaged Alpine nation: "Switzerland is what was left over when the Europeans founded their nation-states," wrote the Norwegian journalist Kjetil Wiedswang in a commentary for the BBC. "Italian , French and German

ultra-conservatives escaped to the mountains, joined forces and created 500 years of peace, the cuckoo clock and the gnomes of Zurich." This was an updating of a line in Orson Welles' movie *The Third Man:* "In Switzerland they had brotherly love, 500 years of democracy and peace, and what did that produce? The cuckoo clock."

go along See HOLD STILL … GO ALONG.

goals See QUOTA.

gobbledygook Stilted circumlocution in official directives, sometimes intended to be hard to comprehend but usually the result of a lazy lapse into legalese.

The coiner of this classic Americanism was Texas Congressman Maury Maverick, whose grandfather Samuel lent his name to the word for "rambunctious loner." See MAVERICK.

"People ask me where I got *gobbledygook*," Rep. Maverick wrote in 1944. "Perhaps I was thinking of the old bearded turkey gobbler back in Texas, who was always gobbledy gobbling and strutting with ludicrous pomposity. At the end of this gobble there was a sort of gook."

The congressman defined the term as "talk or writing which is long, pompous, vague, involved, usually with Latinized words. It is also talk or writing which is merely long, even though the words are fairly simple, with repetition over and over again, all of which could have been said in a few words." The congressman found a text from the Bible: "except ye utter by the tongue words easy to be understood, how shall it be known what is spoken? for ye shall speak into the air."

Maverick must have been using the word in early 1943; it appeared in *American Notes and Queries* in April of that year as "Maury Maverick's name for the long high-sounding words of Washington's red-tape language," and in *Time* a year later: "Maury Maverick … railed against what he called Washington's 'gobbledygook' language."

The slang lexicographer Eric Partridge, in his 1952 *Chamber of Horrors: A Glossary of Official Jargon Both English and*

American, satirized speculative etymology by imagining what might have been going through the Maverick mind: "When a term is so devastatingly apposite as *gobbledygook*, it walks unquestioned into the vocabulary, as *quisling* had done four years earlier in Britain. The allusion is to the gobbling noise made by a turkey cock; probably the word was an unconscious yet none the less inspired adaptation of *gobble* of the turkey cock, the *de* in imitation of stage foreigners' pronunciation, and *cock* becoming *gock* by assimilation to the *g* of *gobble* and *gock* becoming *gook* perhaps under the influence of *goon*."

In 1975 *The Washington Star* began a series called "Gobbledygook" regularly exposing to ridicule some blatant examples of federal prose. With the word thus regularly featured, President Jimmy Carter (like King Edward VIII making official the word *radio* rather than *wireless* in his Churchill-written abdication) enshrined it in the Official Papers of the Presidents in 1978 as part of his first State of the Union address: "We have made a good start on turning the gobbledygook of federal regulations into plain English that people can understand, but we still have a long way to go."

Synonyms are OFFICIALESE; *federalese*; PENTAGONESE; BAFFLEGAB.

God, guns and gays See ALLITERATION.

God is in the details See DEVIL IS IN THE DETAILS.

godless Communism See OPIUM OF THE PEOPLE.

gofer One who will "go for" coffee and run errands in a political headquarters.

Eager to be seen at headquarters by a candidate, many district leaders, minor officeholders and even fundraisers willingly assume menial tasks. The need for the sustenance fetched by gofers was recognized in 1712 by Alexander Pope in *The Rape of the Lock*, when the British poet wrote of "coffee, which makes the politicians wise."

As John Lindsay took office as New York Mayor in 1966, a controversy arose when it was charged that city police officers were being used as gofers, which was vigorously denied by the new mayoral staff. In 1974, doggerel was used by Fred Bruhn in *The Wall Street Journal* to deride a proposal for a permanent special prosecutor for accused top officials:

> *It's not the big black cars with chauffeurs,*
> *It's not the maids, the aides, the gofers,*
> *… What stamps a man of power and wealth:*
> *A prosecutor for himself.*

In Texas the word used for *gofer* (a homonym of *gopher*) is *Billy-do-boy*. A similar-sounding word, coined on the same analogy as *gofer*, is *two-fer*, which originally meant two tickets for the price of one; in politics, it is used to indicate that a candidate or appointee is both a member of a minority group and a woman, thereby pleasing two constituencies.

go fight City Hall An expression of helplessness in the face of bureaucracy; a shrugging acceptance of the insuperable difficulties of organized society.

The expression, which probably originated in New York City, is not to be taken literally and assumed to be a call to action. On the contrary, it means that one *cannot* fight City Hall. The speaker is really saying, "Don't bother me with your problem; take it up with the powers that be in government—and you won't get anywhere with them, either." The expression implies the same futility as *tilting at windmills*, a reference to the foolish gallantry of Don Quixote.

In 1967, when the elder Al Gore, then senator from Tennessee, was able to attach a rider calling for repeal of a campaign fund measure favored by Majority Whip Russell Long (D-La.), a Gore aide was quoted as saying happily, "You don't beat City Hall too often."

When the phrase is used to mean the real City Hall, it is a joke, as in this *Newsweek* usage about a New York City crackdown on diplomatic parking abuses: "For the smouldering diplomats, the encounter was a new lesson in international relations. Around the U.N., the word was being passed that you can say what you like about the United States, but you can't fight City Hall."

go fishing See FISHING EXPEDITION.

go it alone To stand by oneself as a person or a nation; to practice unilateralism.

American politicians have been either proud of themselves or critical of others for "going it alone" since about 1850, when card players began using the phrase to describe one who wanted to play the game of euchre single-handed. In the card game of four-handed euchre (not three-handed, or "cutthroat," euchre), a player's point total is doubled if he takes in his tricks by rejecting the help of a partner and "goes it alone."

In 1874 Senator G. F. Edmunds of Vermont said, "Our forefathers [did not act] upon the idea that a member of Congress was to take his carpet-bag and go it alone [in Washington]."

Early in 1953, Ohio Republican Senator Robert A. Taft suggested that "the U.S. might as well forget the United Nations as far as the Korean war is concerned. I believe we might as well abandon any idea of working with the United Nations in the East and reserve to ourselves a completely free hand." President Eisenhower didn't like Taft's idea and said so at a news conference: "If you are going to go it alone in one place, you have to go it alone everywhere." Taft later denied that he was advocating a policy of "go-it-alone."

A half-century later, the phrase was going strong. In 2007, as Nicolas Sarkozy took over the presidency of France from Jacques Chirac, following the replacement of Gerhard Schröder as German Chancellor by Angela Merkel in 2005, a warmer relationship with the Bush Administration was predicted. *The Washington Post*'s Molly Moore observed that many Europeans believe that in recent years, "the divided capitals of Europe and the go-it-alone foreign policy of the Bush Administration aggravated rather than quelled some of the globe's most dangerous conflicts and disputes."

See CARD METAPHORS; ISOLATIONISM; UNILATER-ALISM.

gold window See WINDOW OF OPPORTUNITY.

good fight See FIGHT THE GOOD FIGHT.

good guys See DO-GOODER; MR. NICE GUY; WHITE HATS.

Good Neighbor Policy Franklin Roosevelt's program for relations with Latin American nations.

FDR set forth the phrase *good neighbor* in a portion of his inaugural address drafted by brain truster Raymond Moley in March 1933: "In the field of world policy I would dedicate this nation to the policy of the good neighbor—the neighbor who resolutely respects himself and, because he does so, respects the rights of others." A month later he told the Pan-American Union: "Never before has the significance of the words 'good neighbor' been so manifest in international relations. Never have the need and benefit of neighborly cooperation in every form of human activity been so evident ..."

The time was ripe for a fresh approach to Latin American relations. Phrases like "colossus of the north," "Yankee imperialists," and DOLLAR DIPLOMACY were in common use in Central and South America to show resentment toward the "big brother" in the north. At a conference in Montevideo, Uruguay, on December 26, 1933, Secretary of State Cordell Hull supported a pact declaring, "No state has the right to intervene in the internal or external affairs of another." FDR added two days later: "The definite policy of the U.S. from now on is one opposed to armed intervention."

This did not met with universal approval at home. The Republican candidate in 1936, Kansas governor Alfred Landon, commented, "We can be a good neighbor without giving away the latch-key to our door." But the Latin American policy turned out to be the least controversial of all Roosevelt's foreign policies, supported by both isolationists and internationalists. The internationalists felt that a united hemisphere was useful in maintaining world peace; isolationists held that cross-hemispheric relations fell within a kind of "regional isolationism."

The policy was bolstered by the Act of Chapultepec in 1945, the Rio Treaty of 1947 (both pacts of mutual military assistance), and the creation of the Organization of American States. The policy was strained in U.S. dealings with dictators like Argentina's Juan Perón and, later, Cuba's Fidel Castro.

President Eisenhower felt it necessary to amend the phrase. "Our Good Partner Policy," he said in 1960, "is a permanent guide encompassing nonintervention, mutual respect and juridical equality of States." The *partner* phrase never took hold.

John F. Kennedy, reported Theodore Sorensen, "requested suggestions for a policy label as meaningful for the sixties as Roosevelt's 'Good Neighbor Policy' had been for the thirties. I suggested 'alianza.' …" (For speechwriter Richard Goodwin's recollection of that coinage, see ALLIANCE FOR PROGRESS.)

The neighborhood is being extended. A Pentagon official in 1993 described joint military training with the Royal Thai Armed Forces "conducted under Thailand's good neighbor policy with observers from other countries in the region." However, the phrase is still most closely associated with Latin America.

good ole boy See REDNECK.

good soldier A politician willing to place the good of the party first; one who swallows personal pride and falls in line.

The phrase is often preceded by a gulp. In 1956, Ohio favorite son Michael Di Salle announced that he was throwing his support to Senator John Kennedy for vice-presidential nominee (he lost to Senator Estes Kefauver). William Coleman, Ohio state chairman, did not like Di Salle's decision but decided to go along. A *Columbus Dispatch* reporter asked him, "Mr. Coleman, is Senator Kennedy really your choice?" The grim-faced state chairman replied, "I am a good soldier."

He was echoing a phrase made famous by Missouri Senator James Reed at the 1932 Democratic convention. Reed, who had bitterly opposed Franklin Roosevelt, sat on the platform with what was described as "an expressionless face" while the final ballot showed 945 votes for Roosevelt, 190 1/2 for Al Smith. The convention chairman asked him to address the convention in a display of unity, and he refused. FDR aide Arthur Mullen went to him and said, "We're all Democrats, Jim." Reed went to the microphone and calmed the disappointed Smith supporters: "At a time like this, every man who claims to be a Democrat should banish from his heart all feeling of disappointment, all sense of chagrin, and like a good soldier, fall in line, salute the colors and face the enemy."

Speaker of the House Sam Rayburn also used the phrase at a convention. In 1960, when John Kennedy urged him to convince his fellow Texan, Lyndon Johnson, to take second spot on the ticket, "Mr. Sam" replied, "Well, there is always the thought in a fellow's mind that he might get to be President. Lyndon is a good soldier, and he will hear the call of duty."

Good soldier is a high accolade among professional politicians, a decoration for regularity. The ringing phrase must not be confused with *old soldier,* "a funky cigar butt," or *dead soldier,* "an empty whiskey bottle." See OLD SOLDIERS NEVER DIE; MILITARY METAPHORS.

goo-goo See DO-GOODER; REFORM.

GOP Republican; initials for Grand Old Party.

In the 1870s, "grand old party" and "gallant old party" were in use, mostly referring to Republicans. Meanwhile, in England, Prime Minister William Gladstone was being dubbed "the Grand Old Man," first used in 1882. Soon after, Gladstone was "the G.O.M." Soon after that, GOP made its bow. On October 15, 1884, the *New York Tribune* reported "'The G.O.P. Doomed,' shouted the Boston Post"; nobody has yet found the earlier *Boston Post* usage.

In early motorcar days, the letters also stood for "get out and push"; in the sixties, the Republican National Committee launched a modernization program for the old acronym, referring to themselves as "the GO-Party," which went nowhere, and in 1972 pointed to "Generation of Peace," a favorite Nixon theme. Democrat Harry Truman said the Republican initials meant "Grand Old Platitudes."

gopher See GOFER.

gospel of hate See APOSTLE OF HATE.

go to the well Expect public revenues to finance; look to the public treasury for support.

The political use of the verb phrase became popular during Ronald Reagan's Administration. In May 1988, *National Journal* reported that "privatization supporters say that as government officials go to the well to pay for new constituent services, they are discovering that the well is dry and are beginning to see the wisdom of private-sector initiatives." As that usage indicates, the phrase usually suggests that the well's resources are diminishing.

However, the phrase's meaning changes when the word *with* is added. Lyndon Johnson was reported to have asked of potential aides, "Is he someone you can go to the well with?" This is a Southwestern phrase, rooted in pioneer days when the danger from Indians required two men to get water from wells far from the house. One person would draw the water, and the other would stand guard; the phrase came to mean "someone who can be trusted."

governance See PUNDIT.

government See ADMINISTRATION.

government by crony An Administration in which advisers qualify not by experience or talent but by their longtime friendship with the Chief Executive.

Washington columnist Arthur Krock, in a February 9, 1946, piece in *The New York Times* titled "Government by Crony," wrote: "During the Truman administration, New Dealers and Conservatives found themselves together in opposition to what a press gallery wit has called a 'government by crony.'" Krock suggested that many New Dealers held over from the Roosevelt Administration "opposed many of Truman's intimate White House circle because, they say, they are of courthouse caliber." The columnist added: "Government by crony is not new in Washington. President Roosevelt appointed many persons of doubtful competence or eligibility because of personal relationships."

Soon after Krock's use of the phrase, Secretary of the Interior Harold Ickes (see CURMUDGEON) resigned with a blast at Truman: "I am against government by crony."

In 1973, I suspected that the anonymous "press gallery wit" quoted by Krock might be similar to "Western observer"—the reporter himself. Mr. Krock, whose office in retirement was down the hall from mine at the *Times*'s Washington bureau, admitted it in response to my query: "As I recall, I was referring modestly to myself in that reference to 'a press gallery wit,' though I couldn't document that I am the originator. But I, too, have seen no previous use of the expression in the public prints." (A predecessor phrase to the current *the media*—almost as old as *the press*—is *the public prints*.)

Other "government by" phrases used in the pejorative sense: "Government by organized money" (FDR in referring to the Republican Administration before 1932); "Government by epilepsy" (Brazilian President Jânio Quadros describing Fidel Castro's Cuba in 1961); "Government by injunction" (John L. Lewis after the U.S. government found him guilty of abrogating the United Mine Workers contract with the government in 1946); "Government by golly" (anti-Eisenhower); "Government by IRISH MAFIA" (anti-Kennedy); "Government by Texans" (anti-Johnson).

Most of the "government by" phrases of the last century were probably coined to compare unfavorably with the phrase Lincoln popularized, "government of the people, by the people, for the people." For the derivation of that phrase, see IDEAS.

government-in-exile In U.S. politics, a description of the Kennedy family and their close associates during the Administration of President Lyndon Johnson.

"On Capitol Hill," wrote the historian William Manchester in 1967, "the two brothers [Robert and Ted Kennedy] inevitably came to be regarded as the nucleus of a government-in-exile."

Although President Johnson asked most of the Kennedy men (see IRISH MAFIA) to stay on after the assassination of John F. Kennedy ("I need you more than he ever did"), most left the White House to write books and form a coterie around other Kennedys. Ted Sorensen, Arthur Schlesinger, Jr., Richard Goodwin, Kenneth O'Donnell, Stephen Smith, and others of the "Clan" formed a circle around Robert, Ted, and Jacqueline Kennedy; Postmaster General Lawrence O'Brien, Poverty War head Sargent Shriver, and Defense Secretary Robert McNamara refrained from going into "exile."

The use of the phrase indicated an estrangement that grew within the Democratic party, which author Manchester reported—and was accused of exaggerating—in his book *The Death of a President.*

In its traditional use, a *government-in-exile* has either been forced out by revolution or usurpation or invaded and taken over by another nation, with the "legitimate" government taking refuge elsewhere. The use of the phrase in the Johnson-Kennedy context served to further polarize Democratic factions. Tension between the two groups, which led to a nomination contest in 1968, was described by White House adviser John Roche (see INTELLECTUAL-IN-RESIDENCE) the year before: "[LBJ] plainly enjoyed the recent row about the 'government in exile' at Harvard and candidly confesses that he has never had anything in common with 'that crowd of cold Kennedy cats operating exclusively on the star system.'"

After its use in the Johnson Administration, the phrase was applied to the usually liberal Brookings Institution during the Nixon-Ford years, then to the conservative American Enterprise Institute in the Carter years, then to the Bush family in the later Clinton years. It was revived in 2005 with the group of Clintonites gravitating to the support of New York Senator Hillary Clinton and the prospect of a White House run that led to talk of a Clinton "restoration" in 2009.

government of laws, not of men A maxim holding that favoritism or human weakness has no place in the administration of justice; that all persons stand equal before the bar.

The idea can be found in Baron Montesquieu's *Spirit of Laws,* a work written in 1748 that influenced many of the founders of the U.S. Constitution: "The rulers of republics establish institutions, and afterwards the institutions mould the rulers."

John Adams, in his draft of the Massachusetts Constitution in 1778, used the phrase as his ultimate political goal: "In the government of the Commonwealth of Massachusetts the legislative, executive, and judicial power shall be placed in separate departments, to the end that it might be a government of laws, not of men." Chief Justice John Marshall picked up the Adams phrase in his decision in the landmark *Marbury v. Madison:* "The government of the United States has been emphatically termed a government of laws, and not of men." In Britain, the phrase for the same idea is alliterative: MEASURES, NOT MEN. In the U.S., it is often replaced by the august RULE OF LAW.

During the year preceding Richard Nixon's resignation in 1974, the phrase was used both as an admonishment to the Nixon men (charged with putting themselves above the law) and as a spur to the forces favoring impeachment (holding the law above the elected officials). Its most dramatic use came on the night of October 20, 1973, when Special Prosecutor Archibald Cox—just fired by the President in what came to be known as the SATURDAY NIGHT MASSACRE—issued a challenging statement from his home: "Whether ours shall continue to be a government of laws and not of men is now for Congress and ultimately for the American people."

At his swearing-in on August 9, 1974, Gerald Ford, who saw his mission to be a "healer," answered that challenge in his first speech to Americans as their new president: "our long national nightmare is over. Our Constitution works. Our great Republic is a government of laws and not of men."

gradualism See SALAMI TACTICS.

graffiti Slogans and messages scrawled on walls.

"Cuba Sí—Yanqui No" and "Ami Go Home," in paint or chalk on walls in the U.S. and abroad, first brought this ancient art to the attention of U.S. politicians. The word originally applied to all scrawled messages, from "Kilroy Was Here" to the names of a boy and a girl with an arrow and heart, to outright smut, but its meaning includes messages with some social or political content.

A 1967 advertisement for Books USA, a government-endorsed project to mail books abroad, showed a picture of a U.S. soldier standing next to graffiti that read "Go Home Yankee Dog," with this copy: "Read any good walls lately? Probably not. Few flattering things have ever been written on walls about anyone. And the unflattering truth is that there are walls like this in many countries, covered with words written in anger, mistrust and ignorance …"

The word is the plural of *graffito*, which refers to a method of ornamenting architectural plaster surfaces by scratching the top coat to reveal colored layers underneath, used in ancient cultures and refined in fifteenth-century Italian decorative art.

The spreading of slogans by graffiti recalls the dissemination of news via wall posters in China. "Posters written in big characters," said Mao Zedong, "are an extremely useful new type of weapon." See SNIPE. During the upheavals of the CULTURAL REVOLUTION, *dazibao*, "big-character posters," served as one of the few ways of getting news to the people.

graft Money or property gained through political corruption.

A *grafter* is the one who receives the money, or seeks the payment. Standard English construction would ordinarily make him the *graftee*, and the one who makes the payment the *grafter*; this is not current usage, because the corrupter is considered less sinful than the official who "betrays a public trust."

The word is traceable as thieves' argot back to a *Police Gazette* of 1865: "'Twas handy that we were so related, as, when about a 'graft,' or 'doing stur,' both sisters could keep each other company." Josiah Flynt in his *Tramping with Tramps* (1899) and *World of Graft* (1901) defined the word as "a generic slang term for all kinds of theft and illegal practices generally."

St. Louis circuit attorney Joseph W. Folk gave the word its political flavor soon after the turn of the century, and his war on what he called "grafters" took him to the governorship of Missouri in 1905. As politics took over the word, thieves' argot shifted to *grift*.

Richard Leche, Louisiana governor who succeeded Huey Long, turned out to have an income in 1938 of $282,000 on a salary of $7,500. Shortly before he went to jail, Leche earned his place in political history with the comment: "When I took the oath as Governor, I didn't take any vows of poverty."

Graft is specific, *corruption* general; graft is the currency of corruption. In 1914 Walter Lippmann overlooked the differentiation in explaining the emerging meaning of both words:

> We can see, I think, what people meant by the word graft. They did not mean robbery. It is rather confused rhetoric to call a grafter a thief. His crime is not that he filches money from the safe but that he betrays a trust. The grafter is a man whose loyalty is divided and whose motives are mixed. A lawyer who takes a fee from both sides in some case; a public official who serves a private interest; a railroad director who is also a director in the supply company; a policeman in league with outlawed vice; these are the relationships which the American people denounce as "corrupt." The attempt to serve at the same time two antagonistic interests is what constitutes "corruption."

The author, fulminating in 2004 about the billions intended for the Iraqi people gone down the drain in the corrupted U.N. oil-for-food program, asked readers "What's French for *kickback?*" A Parisian responded: *pots de vin*, "jugs of wine," apparently a metaphor for a percentage of the payment corruptly returned, done *dessous de table*, "under the table." A Persian word borrowed into Turkish and Arabic, *baksheesh*, which can mean "tip, gratuity," is also understood in France to describe a more sinister payment. A Russian slang term is *otkat*—literally, "recoil (of a gun)"— originally criminal slang and now used by new dissidents in Moscow to mean "graft" and "kickback." See BOODLE; GREASE; HONEST GRAFT; REACHED; WHIPSAW.

grand design Diplomatic master plan; a broad strategy to shape historical forces.

This phrase comes from the French, *Les Grands Desseins*, and *grand* can be translated as "great" or "grand." The phrase, from the time of the French King Henry IV, was reintroduced by Franklin D. Roosevelt at the Tehran Conference in Iran, December 1943, where Stalin, Churchill, and Roosevelt planned an invasion of France and received a commitment from Stalin that Russia would enter the war against Japan. Roosevelt used "Great Design" and Churchill, in his war memoirs, "Grand Alliance" (after the English-Dutch-Hapsburg "Grand Alliance" of 1701).

At the 1944 Republican convention, former President Herbert Hoover traced the derivation: "During the past month Forrest Davis has published a circumstantial account of the Teheran Conference ... It relates to President Roosevelt's new peace method, called by him, the Great Design. A peace method under this same name, the Great Design, was proposed by Henry the Fourth, a French monarch, some 350 years ago. It has some similarities to Mr. Roosevelt's idea. ... The American people deserve a much fuller exposition of this Great Design." This point was indicative of a Republican charge of "secret agreements" made after later Big Three conferences, especially Yalta.

FDR may have taken the phrase from its use by Theodore Roosevelt, who received a letter from some prominent Frenchman congratulating him on his efforts in international conciliation. TR later wrote: "They believe that the action of President Roosevelt, which has realized the most generous hopes to be found in history, should be classed as a continuance of similar illustrious attempts of former times, notably the project for international concord known under the name of 'The Great Design of

Henry IV' in the memoirs of his Prime Minister, the Duke de Sully." (Sully's memoirs refer to vague *Grands Desseins* based on the King's wish to avoid another European war.)

For another contribution to American political terminology by Henry IV, see CHICKEN IN EVERY POT.

grandpa's pants won't fit Benny See DYNASTY.

grants-in-aid See TAX SHARING.

grapevine Rumor factory; word-of-mouth communication of political secrets or background; source of useful tips as well as salacious innuendo.

The old mouth-to-ear grapevine is falling into disuse because bloggers rush onto the Internet with all the latest rumors and the mainstream media competes with constantly updated Web sites. The adage "rumor races round the world before truth can get its boots on" has never been more apt; reporters learn and print most gossip and tips before politicians have a chance to pass them along. "I hear by the grapevine" was replaced a century ago by Mr. DOOLEY's "I see by the papers," which has in turn been superseded by "I caught it on Drudge that ..."

The phrase persists mainly in the hints of jobs available and personnel shifts. Etymologist Hans Sperber thought *grapevine* may have had its origin in an episode told by Charles Howard Shinn, in a mining book about the Great Comstock lode in Nevada:

That curious and vivid Western phrase, "grapevine telegraph," originated in 1859. Colonel Bee constructed a telegraph line between Placerville and Virginia City, attaching the wire to the trees; their swaying stretched it until it lay in loops on the ground, resembling the trailing California wild grapevines. Frequent breaks occurred from falling trees and avalanches, till the line became almost useless, being sometimes beaten into Sacramento by the Pony Express. California and Nevada papers took it up, and whenever a journalist wished to cast doubts on the freshness of his opponent's news he forthwith accused him of running a grapevine telegraph.

The metaphor was used before 1859, however, in connection with the Underground Railroad, the abolitionists' method of aiding escaped slaves. The grapevine was their communications system, often used interchangeably with "the clothesline telegraph." Grapevines, it may be assumed, were used as a substitute for rope and the two phrases came into being together. Union Captain John Truesdale, in an 1867 collection of Civil War anecdotes called *The Blue Coats*, showed how the clothesline could be used as an intelligence device: clotheslines were used as visual transmitters of espionage, with shirts of different colors hung out to dry used as a code to reveal the order of battle of the Confederate troops.

grassroots The ultimate source of power, usually patronized, occasionally feared; the rank and file of a party, or voters not normally politically active.

The term (often hyphenated) began with a rural flavor, implying simple virtues of the land as against city-slicker qualities. Recently the anti-big-city connotation has been disappearing, leaving only an anti-boss, up-from-the-people meaning. Accordingly, politicians seek support "from the grassroots and the sidewalks of the nation" to cover everybody.

The word has its own roots in mining terminology, used in 1876 to mean the soil just beneath the surface. An early metaphoric use was by Rudyard Kipling, in *Kim*, published in 1901: "Not till I came to Shamlegh could I meditate upon the Course of Things, or trace the running grassroots of Evil." (Why "running"? Philip Howard of the *Times* of London wrote in 1977 that Kipling was probably referring to "*Agropyron repens*, the common couch or switch grass, whose long creeping root-stalks or rhizomes run below the surface and make it a pestilential and ineradicable garden weed.")

An early political use was in 1912, when Senator Albert J. Beveridge told the Bull Moose convention in Chicago: "This party comes from the grass roots. It has grown from the soil of the people's hard necessities." The Farmer-Labor party used it as a slogan in 1920.

The phrase came into prominence with a Republican effort to organize a massive thrust to unseat FDR. In Springfield, Ill., on June 10, 1935, the Grass Roots Conference was held. "Issues are hard to find," reported *Common Sense*, "and the 'Grass Roots' Conference in Springfield, Illinois, found itself stumped." Three decades later, Republican Chairman Ray Bliss called a similar conference to mobilize grassroots (by then one word) support in the big cities, and claimed better results.

Most candidates now claim to run *grassroots campaigns*, where they get out to meet the people, just the opposite of a sedentary FRONT-PORCH CAMPAIGN. However, the best way to reach the grassroots is from a radio or television studio, posing a semantic problem. Senator George McGovern used the word as the title of his memoirs.

Reporting on Attorney General Robert Kennedy's trip to the Far East in 1962, *Newsweek* came up with a good play on the phrase: "He sought to make U.S. policies understandable at the rice-roots level." See STREET SMARTS.

The grass and the rice were replaced by the Internet in the new millennium, and NETROOTS became the vogue word in political organizing. However, the grass portion of the original metaphor is still green: During the debate on immigration legislation in 2007, Colin Hanna, of a conservative group named Let Freedom Ring, claimed that "Technologically enhanced grass-roots activism is what turned this around," defining his supporters as "people empowered by the Internet and talk radio."

grass will grow in the streets A threat of financial ruin if the opposition is elected, and specifically if a protective tariff is removed.

The grass-in-the-streets prophecy was a part of the most famous of all convention speeches: William Jennings Bryan's 1896 "Cross of Gold" address, which had a strong agrarian flavor. "Burn down your cities and leave our farms, and your cities will spring up again as if by magic," he orated, "but destroy our farms and the grass will grow in the streets of every city in the country."

Bryan rephrased a metaphor used frequently before, especially in regard to tariffs. An 1892 issue of *The Nation* warned that an argument for a protective tariff "is the old 'howling wilderness' and 'grass-in-the-streets' argument for protection."

An earlier use was in a speech by Jefferson Davis, shortly after his inauguration as President of the Confederate States of America. He predicted a short, victorious war, because soon "Grass will grow in the Northern cities."

The phrase was reprised in the twentieth century by Herbert Hoover in the campaign of 1932 as he was defending the Smoot-Hawley tariff against a suggested Democratic tariff proposal: "The grass will grow in the streets of a hundred cities, a thousand towns; the weeds will overrun the fields of millions of farms if that protection is taken away." This was fairly colorful language for Hoover, but it came with the election only a week away and did little good. Roosevelt used it in 1936, however, reminding responsive audiences: "I look for the grass which was to grow on city streets."

The phrase is now obsolescent, partially because so many park-hungry urbanites would welcome grass wherever it grew within a city's limits. Interestingly, Petrograd was in such straits after the First World War, the Revolution, the removal of the government to Moscow, and the Civil War, losing almost two-thirds of its population, that grass actually did start growing in its streets, inspiring this bitterly celebratory paragraph from Osip Mandelstam, beginning his 1921 article "The Word and Culture": "The grass in the streets of Petersburg is the first sprouting of the virgin forest that will cover the site of contemporary cities. This vivid, tender greenery, with its surprising freshness, belongs to a new, spiritualized nature. Truly Petersburg is the most advanced city in the world. It's not by subways or skyscrapers that modernity's run, speed, is measured, but by the cheerful grass that pushes out from under city stones."

See GLOOM AND DOOM, PROPHETS OF.

gratitude, political Favors done now in anticipation of return favors to come.

Unlike normal gratitude, political gratitude looks forward and not backward. The phrase is used usually when a politician turns down a request from someone who helped him in the past. The rejected former helper, understandably cynical, murmurs, "That's political gratitude for you," meaning that the politician will be "grateful"—receptive—only to those who can help him in the future. English essayist William Hazlitt ascribed to Horace Walpole the following maxim, similar to one of La Rochefoucauld's: "The gratitude of place expectants is a lively sense of future favors."

President Kennedy is reported to have said that "politicians do not have friends, they have allies." This was an adaptation of "the British Empire has no friends, only interests." FDR aide and later *Newsweek* columnist Raymond Moley wrote: "Sam Rayburn once told me that whenever he secured a job for a political applicant, he 'made nine enemies and one ingrate.'" Rayburn was passing along a comment of Louis XIV, in Voltaire's *Siècle de Louis Quatorze*: "Every time I fill a vacant office I make ten malcontents and one ingrate." Thomas Jefferson in 1807 increased the enemies tenfold as he quoted obliquely: "Every office becoming vacant, every appointment made, *me donne un ingrat, et cent ennemis.*"

graveyard Profoundly secret; an unbreakable confidence; or, a DEAD END.

Political secrets are often transmitted with the prefatory admonition: "This is graveyard." It appears to have gained currency in the 1950s and is occasional political usage today, although it rarely is seen in print. Presumably the metaphor connotes a place of darkness, whispers, and trepidation, the proper atmosphere for a political confidence.

A second meaning of the word is "final political resting place," or "dead end." A reporter in 1967 asked New York Mayor John Lindsay, "Isn't the mayor's office a political graveyard?" Lindsay replied with a reference to two New York mayors who departed office under clouds of suspicion,

James Walker and William O'Dwyer: "Some mayors have gone on to international fame. One went to Europe, one went to Mexico …" Rudy Giuliani has a loftier goal, as perhaps does Michael Bloomberg.

gray eminence A shadowy figure who exercises power through another; a manipulative adviser.

Armand Jean du Plessis, duc de Richelieu, French statesman and cardinal, wore a red habit (unique at the time) that made him known as *l'Eminence rouge*, "the Red Cardinal." As Prime Minister, he controlled Louis XIII, directing both foreign and domestic policy, successfully shifting the balance of power from the Hapsburgs to the Bourbons. Cardinal Richelieu's private secretary, Père Joseph de Trembley, a Capuchin monk attired in a gray habit, became known as *l'Eminence grise*—"the Gray Cardinal," who, while not a cardinal at all, often exercised the power of a prince of the Church because of his influence on Richelieu.

The title's ghostly connotation made it eminently suitable for political use; a gray eminence is now used to describe any POWER BEHIND THE THRONE or KINGMAKER who has the ear of a political leader but does not often appear publicly.

The description was often applied to Louis Howe, a brilliant, gnomelike, lifelong adviser and confidant of Franklin Roosevelt. "Roosevelt's election," wrote Jonathan Daniels, "was, of course, Howe's final, unique triumph. He was to be remembered as the long-time friend, the Warwick, the alter ego, *l'éminence grise*."

Other figures have also received this description. The late newsman Eric Sevareid was called "an in-house wise man and gray eminence of CBS News" in *The Washington Post* in 1992, and *National Journal* referred to Brent Scowcroft in 1989 as "Washington's preeminent 'gray eminence' on national security."

Japanese Liberal party leader Tsuji Karouki, a behind-the-scene power, was described as a *kuromaku*, or "black curtain," a term that goes back to the nineteenth century and is derived from kabuki

theater, where costumes and scenery are changed behind such a curtain. In the younger Bush's White House, Vice President Dick Cheney was sometimes described by reporters as a *gray eminence*, but because a VP is too prominent, and Cheney is balding, the informal title, along with *guru*, fell to the main political strategist behind the scenes, Karl Rove. See RUSTLING BEHIND THE JALOUSIES.

grease As a verb, to smooth the way by bribery; as a noun, the money used in such corruption.

"Cash…is a necessary article in their business," wrote the *Columbian Centinel* in 1797, "and without daily application of this specific grease their wheels must roll heavily on."

Grease's meaning can limited to "money"—"We must have grease to run a campaign," Democratic leader John Thompson told the Ohio Central Committee in 1881—but the overtone that the money is corruptly obtained is more often present.

After a period in which the word was considered an archaism, it appears to be making a modest comeback: "U.S. Attorney Thomas P. Sullivan said yesterday," went a UPI report from Chicago in 1977, "a federal investigation is under way on charges that Mayor Michael A. Bilandic 'greased' an 11.7 percent city taxi fare increase last summer."

For the derivation of the monetary meaning of "fat," see FAT CAT: another, earlier use of *grease* is "to grease the fat pig," or to give to those who need it least, a proverb found in John Heywood's 1566 collection of sayings.

great, political use of In the sense of GREAT SOCIETY, magnanimous; in the sense of GREAT UNWASHED, a large body; in the sense of GREAT DEBATES, important; as an adjective modifying *statesman* or *leader*, eminent.

Historians who compare the greatness of presidents use a variety of criteria, especially the ability to meet crises, make progress, and verbally exalt and inspire the nation. In this connection, they have created the comparative word "near-great."

In its political use, the word cannot be used as a synonym for *big*: Big Government is not at all Great Government, and Great Business and Great Labor are never used, indicating that the political meaning of *great* does not usually include the idea of size.

As an adjective in introductions, the word is intended to mean "noble" or "outstanding," but the meaning has been prostituted by its frequent application to nonentities and hacks.

Bitterness at its overuse in convention oratory was illustrated in this passage by novelist John Dos Passos about jobless men sleeping on the streets in 1932. "Try to tell one of them that the gre-eat Franklin D. Roosevelt, Governor of the gre-eat state of New York, has been nominated by the gre-eat Democratic party. ... Hoover or Roosevelt, it'll be the same cops."

In diplomacy, *greater*, capitalized in front of the name of a country, is a way of warning of plans for expansion beyond territorial lines. Secretary of State James Baker's critical reference in 1989 to a "Greater Israel" troubled many supporters of the Jewish state; in 1993, *The Washington Post* warned of threats to Bosnia posed not only by "aggressive Serbs seeking a Greater Serbia but also by treacherous Croats seeking a Greater Croatia."

Great Communicator See SOBRIQUETS.

great debates In recent times, the series of televised debates first between Kennedy and Nixon and later among all presidential aspirants; earlier, the debates among Calhoun, Clay, and Webster.

Because *great* rhymes with *debate*, there is a tendency to label important national discussions as "great debates." The first known widely by this title was the Senate debate of Henry Clay's package of compromises regarding slavery, including admission of California as a free state and no restrictions on slavery in the territory acquired from Mexico. In the debate that lasted through February and March 1850, Clay occupied the middle position, Daniel Webster spoke for the Union without slavery, and John C. Calhoun (enfeebled by illness, his final speech read by another) advocated the halting of agitation on the slavery issue and opposed the compromise. During this debate Webster said, "I wish to speak today not as a Massachusetts man, not as a Northern man, but as an American. ... I speak today for the preservation of the Union. 'Hear me for my cause.'"

Oddly, the debates between Lincoln and Douglas were not known as "great debates," but simply as the Lincoln-Douglas debates. In recent times, a "great debate" was held at the United Nations in 1946 over the adoption of the Baruch plan for atomic control.

Senator Blair Moody, a Michigan newsman serving out the unexpired term of Senator Arthur Vandenberg in 1952, had the idea of a national confrontation of major presidential candidates. This failed to interest either Eisenhower or Stevenson in 1952; Stevenson was said to feel that a challenge to Eisenhower would be regarded as a gimmick. And Section 315 of the Federal Communications Act requiring EQUAL TIME for all candidates stood in the way. In August 1960, however, Congress temporarily suspended Section 315, and on the night of Richard Nixon's nomination, NBC board chairman Robert Sarnoff offered Democrats and Republicans eight hours of prime time for what he called "The Great Debate." Kennedy, lesser known, promptly accepted; four days later, Nixon did the same.

Nixon's gaunt appearance surprised many viewers on the first debate of four; "Was Nixon Sabotaged by TV Make-Up Artist?" asked *The Chicago Daily News*. When asked "Who won?" after the first debate, viewers tended to go along with the candidate they had previously supported, and radio listeners gave Nixon the edge. But the first debate gave the Kennedy campaign a powerful boost, and in retrospect, many viewers later said they thought Kennedy won the first debate.

"As they approached this brave new frontier of television," wrote Douglass Cater years later, "the two candidates were far more concerned about their images than their arguments. Both proved remarkably adaptable to the new art form. They were marvels at extemporization, wasting none of their precious time by reflective pauses ... the flowering of television in politics had coincided with the flowering of politicians particularly adapted to its special demands." Pollster Samuel Lubell found "the overwhelming majority responded in terms of how the candidates looked and handled themselves rather than in terms of the issues that were argued about."

Theodore White wrote that what the debates did best "was to give the voters of a great democracy a living portrait of two men under stress and let the voters decide, by instinct and emotion, which style and pattern of behavior under stress they preferred in their leader." White added: "The salient fact of the great TV debates is not what the two candidates said, nor how they behaved, but how many of the candidates' fellow Americans gave up their evening hours to ponder the choice between the two."

In 1976, the series we know today began with President Ford and Jimmy Carter and a lengthy delay caused by a GLITCH that was labeled "the Great Silence." Ford's answer to the question posed by Max Frankel of *The New York Times*—"There is no Soviet domination of Eastern Europe"—cost him reelection. The most memorable lines in the Reagan-Carter debates of 1980 were the challenger's "ARE YOU ANY BETTER OFF than you were four years ago?" and, with a shake of the head, "THERE YOU GO AGAIN," both spoken by Reagan. Former Vice President Walter Mondale did well against Reagan in 1984 with his adoption of the advertising slogan "Where's the beef?" but his cause was hopeless.

The shuddering moment in the Bush-Dukakis debate of 1988 was the cool, bloodless answer by Dukakis of a panelist's question about a hypothetical rape and murder of his wife; in the vice presidential debate that year, the Democratic candidate, Lloyd Bentsen, almost destroyed his opponent, Vice President Dan Quayle, with his riposte after Quayle compared his Senate experience with John F. Kennedy's (see YOU'RE NO JACK KENNEDY).

In 1992, the third-party candidate H. Ross Perot's colorful personality all but stole the show from the major-party nominees and helped him win 19% of the vote; he was disinvited next time out and finished poorly. The most damaging moment to President George H.W. Bush in his debate with Bill Clinton was Bush's looking at his watch as if hoping the ordeal would all soon end.

In 1996, challenger Bob Dole came across as negative against a confident President Clinton. In 2000, it was the underestimation of the younger Bush that boosted his surprisingly likeable performance, while the rolling of Vice President Gore's eyes and heavy sighing hurt his presentation. Four years later, in the three debates between Bush and Senator John Kerry, the most damaging to the Democratic challenger was his well-meaning reference to Vice President Cheney's daughter as a lesbian, which GOP staffers in "spin alley" (the press room of the telecast site) exploited mercilessly after the debate.

In these joint meetings called "great debates," sometimes the high points or amusing lines are remembered; in most, the blunders are what affect election outcomes.

Great Leap Forward A Chinese Communist plan for dramatic economic advance, notable for its failure; now, any audacious diplomatic move, especially in the Far East.

Mao Zedong's "Great Leap Forward" began to be mentioned in the Chinese media in 1957, not as part of any five-year plan but as a special effort to dramatically advance the Chinese economy. It was officially adopted at the second session of the eighth Party Congress between May and July of 1958, and is generally considered to have ended in mid-1960.

Westerners regarded the "leap" as a colossal flop, causing the expression to be used in derision throughout the '60s. However, when President Nixon announced his acceptance of the invitation of the People's Republic of China to visit Beijing, U.S. media turned to the phrase and set aside its previously pejorative connotation. In *The New York Times*, Max Frankel wrote: "President Nixon's success in arranging a trip to China evoked the widespread judgment here today that American policy, in Mao Zedong's phrase, was taking a great leap forward." Columnist Mary McGrory: "Some are saying the trip to China is merely a step in the right direction. For Richard Nixon it could be the 'great leap forward' that could not only bring a long-deferred encounter with reality, but also carry him back to the White House."

Relatedly, President Nixon began substituting "mainland China" for "Red China" or "Communist China" in private meetings in 1970. In a toast to Romanian President Ceausescu in the White House State Dining Room on October 26, 1970, Nixon used "People's Republic of China" for the first time publicly. In his report to Congress on foreign policy of February 25, 1971, the President used the official name again, which was taken as a gesture of respect by those who had been previously known in the U.S. as "the Red Chinese."

A long generation later, the phrase continued in use bereft of its Chinese association and ironic twist, giving rise to an uncapitalized reversal: In early 2007, Senator Barbara Boxer (D-Cal.) told Secretary of State Condoleezza Rice at a contentious hearing about a planned U.S. troop "surge" in Iraq: "You're not going to pay a particular price, as I understand it, with an immediate family." Rice said later, "I thought you could still make good decisions on behalf of the country if you were single and didn't have children." Bush press secretary Tony Snow fanned the criticism of Boxer's remark with "It's a *great leap backward* for feminism."

great seal of U.S. See UNITED WE STAND; BALD EAGLE.

Great Society Slogan of the administration of President Lyndon B. Johnson.

President Johnson's first approach to the theme was made three months after he took office. When asked on a television program if he had a slogan as yet, he replied, "I haven't thought of any slogan, but I suppose all of us want a better deal, don't we?"

He tried "Better Deal" a few times in subsequent speeches, but it didn't catch on.

The SQUARE DEAL–NEW DEAL–FAIR DEAL lemon had been squeezed dry.

Meanwhile Richard Goodwin, a Kennedy speechwriting holdover, had suggested "Great Society." He prepared a draft of a speech presenting the first Eleanor Roosevelt Memorial Award to Judge Anna M. Cross on March 4, 1964. Jack Valenti, then the President's chief speechwriter, preferred another draft without the phrase, but held the thought for later trial.

When the "better deal" fizzled, the "Great Society" began popping up in Johnson speeches; the President was obviously anxious to drop the label "Kennedy-Johnson programs." At a White House ceremony on March 17, 1964, he tried: "We want to have the glorious kind of society." He asked a group of editors on April 21 to "accept with me the responsibility of developing a greater society." He told a Democratic fund-raising dinner on April 23: "We have been called upon—are you listening?—to build a great society of the highest order, a society not just for today or tomorrow, but for three or four generations to come." That "are you listening?" was a heavy-handed way of signaling that a slogan was being loosed upon the public.

Johnson liked the feel of the phrase and he used it at least sixteen times publicly thereafter. Goodwin, who was writing the May 22 speech at graduation exercises of the University of Michigan, then developed it in detail. The advance tests of the speech capitalized the phrase—"Great Society"—a clear signal to the press that the President had found his slogan.

We have the opportunity to move not only toward the rich society and the powerful society, but upward to the Great Society.

The Great Society rests on abundance and liberty for all. It demands an end to poverty and racial injustice ... a place where every child can find knowledge to enrich his mind and to enlarge his talents. It is a place where leisure is a welcome chance to build and reflect, not a feared cause of boredom and restlessness. It is a place where the city of man serves not only the needs of the body and the demands of commerce but the desire for beauty and the hunger for community ...

But most of all, the Great Society is not a safe harbor, a resting place, a final objective, a finished world. It is a challenge constantly renewed, beckoning us toward a destiny where the meaning of our lives matches the marvelous products of our labor.

Republican researchers pounced on a previous use of the phrase by English Fabian socialist Graham Wallas, in a book titled *The Great Society*, published in 1914. Wallas told one of his Harvard students, Walter Lippmann, that the book was "an analysis of the general social organization of a large modern state ..." Lippmann later amended the title for a more influential book of his own, *The Good Society*. Goodwin said he had never heard of Wallas' work.

Wallas, in turn, probably never read another use of the phrase in Blackstone's *Commentaries* of the 1760s: "Man was formed for society; and, as is demonstrated by the writers on the subject, is neither capable of living alone, nor indeed has the courage to do it. However, as it is impossible for the whole race of mankind to be united in one great society, they must necessarily divide into many, and form separate states, commonwealths, and nations, entirely independent of each other, and yet liable to a mutual intercourse."

In 1931 English socialist Harold Laski, in his *Introduction to Politics*, titled a chapter "The Place of the State in the Great Society." Sir William Blackstone and Harold Laski used "great" as meaning "whole," or "total"; Wallas and later Johnson meant it as "noble" or "grand."

Adaptation is the sincerest form of recognition; Ronald Reagan used the phrase "creative society" in his campaign for California governor in 1966, Nelson Rockefeller used "a just society" after his reelection as governor of New York that year, and Senator J. William Fulbright said in 1967 that our preoccupation with Southeast Asia was making the U.S. a "sick society." Over the next generation, the noun's modifier dwindled down to the title of a comic strip, *The Small Society*.

great unwashed Condescending view of the lower classes; now used ironically and not publicly by politicians.

Current use is typified in this passage from black novelist James Baldwin's *The Fire Next Time* (1963): "as long as we in the West place on color the value that we do, we make it impossible for the great unwashed to consolidate themselves according to any other principle."

The phrase had been used in 1864 to describe the English lower classes of an earlier time by English novelist James Payn: "There were no such things as 'skilled workmen' or 'respectable artisans,' in those days. The 'people' were 'the Great Unwashed.'"

The phrase may have been used before that by Edmund Burke. In the U.S., political observer George Julian wrote in 1884 about the Polk-Clay race that the Whigs "insisted that ... the larger element of ignorance and 'unwashed' humanity, including our foreign-born population, gave victory to Mr. Polk."

Throughout the nineteenth century the phrase was used to mean Democratic voters, and was often a self-description of some pride. A *Cleveland Leader* headline in 1884 read "Thomas A. Hendricks Addresses the Great Unwashed at Cincinnati." The editor William Allen White used the word in its Democratic sense as late as 1946: "When election time came around, this black abolition Republican, who was my mother, and this Stephen Douglas Copperhead Democrat, who was my father, still unwashed, still voting for Jackson, had their purple moments."

The phrase's party affiliation is no longer exclusive. "The liberal left controlled the culture for decades," wrote Wesley Pruden, editor in chief of *The Washington Times*, in 2007, "with the great unwashed—the rednecks, the evangelicals, Joe Sixpack and his friends—kept on the sidelines ... That changed with talk radio, the ascent of 'conservative media,' ... then cable television ... and the great unwashed finally had an effective voice."

In his perceptive, thousand-page 2007 biography of Richard Nixon, Conrad Black quoted the originator of "beat generation" in applying the phrase: "Nixon was the people. He was the representative inhabitant of what Jack Kerouac called the 'great unwashed body of America' ... climbing, falling, climbing again, and never ceasing to struggle."

See VAST WASTELAND; SILENT MAJORITY; MIDDLE AMERICA.

Great White Father A term ridiculing the paternalism of the President of the United States.

Just after the 1936 Democratic convention, publicist Herbert Bayard Swope wrote to his friend Felix Frankfurter: "Probably you and I are the only ones left who have no hope of reward, or fear of punishment, from the Great White Father." (Frankfurter was rewarded with a Supreme Court Justiceship three years later; Swope—coiner of COLD WAR—never found a government role.)

The phrase is used either in a spirit of mild affection, which was Swope's usage, or in a blast at all-powerful, centralized government. "It is devouring the substance of self-supporting people," wrote *Reader's Digest* in 1949, "to render them self-supporting no longer and to establish a condition of universal reliance upon the biased paternalism of a Great White Father."

In the early days of the Republic, the Great White Father was the name given the president by the American Indians subjugated by the new nation, and the treatment was paternal indeed. President Thomas Jefferson, in 1808, nearing his retirement told a group of Indian chiefs gathered to bid him farewell:

> Sensible that I am become too old to watch over the extensive concerns of the seventeen states and their territories, I requested my fellow citizens to permit me to live with my family, and to choose another President for themselves, and father for you. ... Be assured, my children, that he will have the same friendly dispositions towards you which I have had, and that you will find in him a true and affectionate father. ... Tell your people ... that during my administration I have held their hand in mine; and that I will put it into the hand of their new father, who will hold it as I have done.

The phrase is sometimes associated with Big Daddy (the name of a character in Tennessee Williams's *Cat on a Hot Tin Roof*), which was used by critics of Lyndon Johnson. "Big Daddyism" meant stiflingly paternalistic government.

The tag was a natural for President Johnson because he frequently used the word himself, as when he claimed FDR had been "like a daddy to me." In California, the term has most often been applied to the Democratic Speaker of the Assembly, Jesse M. Unruh. In 1968, after Unruh had reduced his weight from 285 to 200 pounds, Governor Ronald Reagan remarked, "It seems like it takes more than a tailor to change the image of Big Daddy," a comment that Unruh felt was "sort of poor taste on his part."

Political analyst Morton Kondracke used the phrase on television's *The McLaughlin Group*. Discussing the civil rights movement, he said, "They look to the great white father, the President, to somehow bail out the black community." The novelist James Baldwin was quoted in *The New Republic* in 1992 as saying of his earlier activism, "I was, in some way, in those years, without entirely realizing it, the Great Black Hope of the Great White Father."

gridlock Legislative logjam.

This highway engineering term for a massive automobile traffic jam gained notoriety as "grid lock" during a transit strike in New York City in April of 1980. It entered the language of politics compressed to one word later that year. In the wake of the 1980 presidential election, the *Chicago Sun-Times* used the word prophetically: "The instant analysis of election night raised the possibility of political gridlock, a government unable to function because of the division between the Republican President-Senate and the Democratic House of Representatives."

Throughout the Reagan and Bush Administrations, legislative gridlock, brought on by the tug-of-war between the Republican executive branch and the liberal Democratic Congress, blocked the passage of many crucial bills.

In 1992, Ross Perot capitalized on this issue with his third-party campaign using the word gridlock to make his point, pledging to put an end to the impasse that had characterized the government for 12 years. After Bill Clinton's election, even before his "honeymoon" period had been consummated, he was confronted by the very bugbear he had joined Perot in pledging to eliminate: gridlock. In April 1993, Republican Senators staged a filibuster to stop passage of Clinton's economic-stimulus bill which they described as a PORK BARREL bill. "The Administration has earnestly shouted 'gridlock,'" reported *The New York Times* on April 19, "... saying Republicans were thwarting efforts to create jobs." Republicans, led by Bob Dole, had the last word. "If you're against something," he told some editors in Concord, New Hampshire, "you'd better hope there is a little gridlock." See GO FIGHT CITY HALL.

groundswell Popular support; enthusiasm for a policy or candidate from the lower levels of a party or from the general public.

To a sailor, a *groundswell* is a heavy undulation of the ocean, caused by a far-off gale or earthquake. The sense of depth and inexorability is kept in the political metaphor; when a genuine groundswell develops for one candidate, all the others are in choppy water.

"A ground swell, however," wrote President-to-be James Buchanan in 1856, "among a noble people who had sustained me for more than thirty years forced me reluctantly into the field." In March 1968, a weathered observer noted: "By the politico-meteorological standards of New Hampshire, the sudden Rockefeller candidacy not only failed to qualify as a ground swell, but fell considerably short of a frost heave."

In current use, the two words are usually wedded, as with the similar GRASSROOTS and its offshoot NETROOTS; the word continues to refer to a freely formed, un-manipulated public opinion. For examples of other natural phenomena used in politics, see DISASTER METAPHORS.

guaranteed annual wage See LIVING WAGE.

Gucci gulch See BELTWAY BANDITS.

guidelines (guideposts) A general standard of measuring wage and price increases to determine whether they are in what the federal government considers to be the national economic interest.

National wage-price guidelines (suggesting a limit of 3.2 percent rise per year) were set forth by President Kennedy in 1962; he resisted the charge that wages and prices were none of his business by pointing out "when things go badly ... if we have another recession, the President of the United States is to blame. So I think it is our business."

The economist Walter Heller called the guidelines (which he usually termed *guideposts*) "the jawbone method" of holding wages and prices down, since they were founded on no statute and included no specific sanctions for violators. Kennedy never picked up the usage, probably suspecting that some critic would point out that Samson used "the jawbone of an ass."

Heller informed the author that he felt the word *guidelines* sounded "too interventionist—*guideposts* seemed to me less constricting." However, the press and public preferred the more activist *guidelines*. See JAWBONING.

The rationale for guidelines was that high wage demands, passed on as price increases, would inflate the economy and dissipate any real wage increase. Opponents argued that government intervention was in effect wage-price control and a long step toward a "managed economy." As guidelines began to erode in 1966, Heller took a more modest view of their intent: "First, the guideposts have been a useful moderating influence in 1961–1965. Second, since they are designed to function as a supplement rather than an alternative to overall fiscal monetary policy, they should not be expected to carry the burden of stabilization—nor should they be judged by the performance of wages and prices—in a period of excessive total demand."

Guidelines was not a new word in the use of presidential power; Eisenhower told a cabinet meeting in 1954 that he wanted guidelines laid out for departmental handling of congressional requests for information.

Franklin Roosevelt used another word for a more limited economic purpose: before he became president, he called for public competition with private power utilities, "at least as a yardstick." As President, he demanded that the Tennessee and Columbia rivers be the sites of federal power projects for use as *yardsticks* in measuring private utility services and costs.

The *guideline* phrase traveled. In the British general election of 1964, the Conservatives were saddled with a "pay pause" phrase that one of their leaders had mistakenly used; Labour Minister John Hare announced that any pay pause would soon give way to a more flexible "guiding light." See BENCHMARKS.

guilt by association Insinuation of wrongdoing by a person because of the wrongdoing—or extremist connections—of those with whom he associates.

The phrase was used by civil libertarians against what they considered the WITCH HUNTS of the early fifties, when blacklists such as *Red Channels* cast doubts on the loyalty of many who belonged to Communist or Communist-front organizations, or were associated with or related to those who did.

The Supreme Court, however, in *Adler v. Board of Education*, 342 US 485 (1952), noted that people are indeed often judged by the company they keep, and a person's associations may be considered in determining loyalty. See SECURITY RISK.

The charge of using *guilt by association* was most often made against Senator Joseph McCarthy, when he headed the Senate Subcommittee on Permanent Investigations. J. B. Matthews, staff director, wrote an article for the *American Mercury* magazine in 1953 charging that "the largest single group supporting the Communist apparatus in the United States today is composed of Protestant clergymen." There was protest from areas that had earlier kept silent about McCarthy; Eisenhower denounced the attack in a telegram to clergymen, and Matthews resigned. "There was irony in this, too," wrote Robert Donovan, "because McCarthy, so far as anyone knows, had

nothing whatsoever to do with Matthews' article. He was simply trapped in a case of guilt by association, which had been his own favorite snare for catching others."

Those who rely too heavily on character references are sometimes accused of seeking "innocence by association." See LOVED FOR THE ENEMIES HE MADE. The phrase is secure enough to resist punning: during hearings to confirm Nelson Rockefeller as Vice President in 1974, it was revealed that he forgave large loans to his former government aides. This was dubbed "gilt by association."

Gulag Acronym for the Soviet slave labor camps; now a symbol of harsh banishment or imprisonment.

When Russian novelist Alexander Solzhenitsyn published *The Gulag Archipelago 1918–1956* in Paris in 1973, the word *gulag* entered the English language. It is an acronym for the main administration of correctional labor camps—in Russian, *Glavnoye Upravleniye Ispravitelno-trudovykh Lagerei*. (It is not strictly an acronym; although the G and U are word initials, the remainder represents the first three letters of *Lagerei*, which is why on rare occasions it is written *GULag*.) When the U.S. State Department referred to this system, the abbreviation was spelled as a long acronym ought to be—all in caps—but in most other use, the word was merely capitalized as *Gulag*, as if it were a place. This led to a widespread impression that the Gulag was a large prison, a Siberian Lubyanka. But the metaphor Solzhenitsyn had in mind was a series of islands—or camps—in the sea of the USSR.

The term was soon linked to almost any discussion of forced labor or the absence of human rights in the Soviet Union. See SAMIZDAT.

This expression is not often used in humor. In April 1993, however, Bruce W. Nelan wrote in *Time* magazine that a Russian referendum of Boris Yeltsin has been "a listless campaign in which both candidate and voters have acted as if a week in the Gulag would be preferable to enduring one more speech."

But the acronym still stings. In 2006, with many critics of the conduct of the war in Iraq calling for his resignation, Secretary of Defense Donald Rumsfeld told an American Legion convention, "When Amnesty International refers to the military facility at Guantanamo Bay—which holds terrorists who have vowed to kill Americans and which is arguably the best-run and most scrutinized detention facility in the history of warfare—'the gulag of our times,' it's inexcusable."

gumshoe campaign See JUNKETEERING GUMSHOES.

gunboat diplomacy The iron fist of threatened force inside the velvet glove of diplomatic relations.

The expression is always derogatory, and has always been used in the sense of those days being long gone. "It has been said that the days of 'gunboat diplomacy' in China are over," goes an *OED* citation from the U.S. Naval Institute's *Proceedings* dated February 1927. In the United Nations in 1961, an Iraqi delegate termed a British action in Kuwait "gunboat diplomacy at its worst."

The phrase began in a description of Western domination of China in the early twentieth century, with U.S. and British interests maintained by gunboats on the main rivers and patrolling harbors. In 1937 the *"Panay* incident" took place when a Japanese bomber sank a U.S. gunboat 27 miles north of Nanking on the Yangtse River, but that was an example of a gunboat being on the receiving end of force.

The gunboat has a long tradition in American naval history. The "gunboat system"—small armed craft manned by local seamen—was preferred by Thomas Jefferson to a more expensive regular navy for the defense of U.S. harbors, and in the war of 1812 it defended New Orleans from the British until Andrew Jackson arrived. But the term gained an oppressive or imperialistic connotation from the Chinese experience.

Now the phrase is used exclusively to express dismay at what is considered JINGO-

ISM. In 1976, when Republican Ronald Reagan charged that the Ford Administration's advocacy of black majority rule in Rhodesia "risks increased violence and bloodshed," Senator Joe Biden (D-Del.) commented: "There is a good deal of gunboat rhetoric that is misleading the American people."

A *Washington Post* editorial in 1992 criticized George H.W. Bush's attempts at this form of diplomatic relations: "he has fared poorly in developing intermediate policies that persuade or coerce other nations to avoid looming confrontation. He is not a skillful practitioner of gunboat diplomacy, in an era when that talent would be of great utility."

For a rundown of the way the phrase has been used to make other phrases, see DIPLOMACY and SHUTTLE DIPLOMACY.

gun control See MERCHANTS OF DEATH.

gung ho Enthusiasm undampened by experience, often shown by a political volunteer.

When a political operative is *gung ho*, he is willing to undertake the impossible cheerfully, often overcoming obstacles that "old pros" consider too difficult to attack.

Gung ho was used by Allied armed forces in World War II to express a spirit of cooperation and enthusiasm, popularized by Colonel Evans F. Carlson's Marine raiders. The term was drawn from Chinese, where it was an abbreviation (now rendered *gonghe* in pinyin) of the name of the industrial cooperatives set up by missionaries in China in the mid-thirties, the equivalent of English *Indusco*; it was taken as meaning "work together" (based on the meanings of the characters taken separately) and used by the Marines as such.

Nym Wales, an authority on Chinese affairs, wrote in 1938:

the Gung Ho industrial cooperatives were to be neutral politically—to start co-ops for both Kuomintang and communists to help win the war—and to bring about the industrial revolution in the village, not in the treaty-port cities, as before. Would Henry Luce sponsor the Gung Ho industrial cooperatives? This was a vital question. *Time* did give publicity to the infant Gung Ho cooperatives and Henry Luce agreed to be on the advisory board of the America Committee in Aid of Chinese Industrial Cooperatives along with Mrs. Franklin Roosevelt.

The phrase may be used to deride boosterism, as a modernization of Talleyrand's advice to diplomats: "Above all, not too much zeal."

guns before butter The strain placed on consumer products and social-welfare projects by a nation that must place a higher priority on war supplies.

The phrase is generally attributed to Hermann Göring, who said in a radio broadcast in 1936: "Guns will make us powerful; butter will only make us fat." Earlier that year, Nazi Propaganda Minister Joseph Goebbels had said: "We can do without butter, but, despite all our love of peace, not without arms. One cannot shoot with butter but with guns."

The "guns before butter" slogan came to mean the domestic economic sacrifices any nation must face in preparing for war. In the U.S., however, the phrase has changed to "guns *and* butter," which is a charge that the president is refusing to face up to the sacrifices required. Senator Lyndon Johnson made this charge against President Harry Truman in the early stages of the Korean conflict; he was on the receiving end during his own presidency.

In his 1966 State of the Union message, Johnson told the joint session of Congress: "Time may require further sacrifices. If so, we will make them. But we will not heed those who will wring it from the hopes of the unfortunate in a land of plenty. I believe we can continue the Great Society while we fight in Viet Nam." No signal was needed; editorial writers and Johnson critics across the country called this "a guns and butter policy." A year later, following a House Appropriations committee's gentle handling of a public-works project (see PORK BARREL) bill, *The New York Times* asked: "If the nation can't afford guns and butter, can it afford guns and pork?"

In 1993, Ariel Cohen of the Heritage Foundation told Reuters' Steve Holland of the need for American aid to the former Soviet Union: "We can pay a little bit now, or we can pay hundreds of billions of dollars later for a new arms race. It's better to send butter to Russia now, than to build guns against Russia later."

The phrase is still applied to the choice of balancing a budget or spending into deficit on arms procurement. "As long as the grown-ups are away," noted the liberal *Guardian* of the UK in 2007, "you can have all the guns and butter you want. Well, paygo means the grownups are back in the room." See PAY AS YOU GO.

guns, God and gays See HOT BUTTON.

Guru See RABBI.

gutfighter A tough-minded, no-holds-barred, sometimes mean-spirited political operative prepared to go for the soft underbelly of his opponent.

"The people voted for the homely, rumpled, irrational gutfighter, Harry Truman," wrote *New York Times* reporter Cabell Phillips.

Gutfighter is generally used admiringly, unlike MUDSLINGER or CHARACTER ASSASSIN, and is not to be confused with *gutter fighter*, which means one who drags a campaign down to the lowest level of the street.

Politicians consider a gutfighter to be one who is totally committed, intensely loyal, and willing to do almost anything for his cause or candidate. Gutfighters are at their best dealing with *gut issues*.

See INSTINCT FOR THE JUGULAR; HATCHETMAN; HARDBALL.

gutter flyer The lowest variety of political literature, vicious and untraceable.

The "coffin handbill" of 1828 was the first important example of this genre. The one-page flyer, recounting "some of the Bloody Deeds of General Jackson," was decorated with coffins, illustrating the murders of soldiers and others while he was commanding troops. Philadelphia publisher John Binns was credited later with the authorship of the handbill, which contained the text of the execution order for six men signed by Lieutenant Colonel (later Senator) Thomas Hart Benton and approved by Jackson.

Most of the "victims" represented by coffins had been court-martialed for mutiny or desertion. One man Jackson had slain himself; the general had been tried, pleaded self-defense, and was acquitted. The handbill was effective, but Jackson won.

A later gutter flyer was the "Nixon deed" used in the 1960 campaign. This was a blowup of the deed of the house in which Richard Nixon lived in Washington; like all other houses in that area, it contained a restrictive covenant. The flyer, clearly implying a racial bias by the candidate, was distributed widely in African-American neighborhoods in New York, Philadelphia, Detroit, and other urban areas. Democratic headquarters claimed no knowledge of the effort, but it appeared to Nixon supporters to be too well organized and financed to be the work of a single vicious entrepreneur. To force a halt, a Republican volunteer thought of getting a similar deed on Kennedy-family homes in the Washington, D.C., area, most of which contained a similar restrictive covenant at that time. But wherever he looked in the town records, the sheet had been destroyed; the organizer of the "Nixon deed" plot had thought ahead.

In November 1963, John F. Kennedy was welcomed to Dallas with a gutter flyer in the form of a Bertillon police poster, with front and side views of Kennedy and the headline "Wanted for Treason."

In most cases, gutter flyers are unsigned; federal law prohibits the use of unsigned literature in a campaign for federal office. However, angry "flaming" blogs can be hard to trace and can perform the same function in the less regulated blogosphere.

For an early example of the printed flyer, see ROORBACK; for recent episodes, see DIRTY TRICKS.

H

hack A harmless political drudge; attack word on a long-time hanger-on.

The word is derived from the *hackney* horse in England, an animal that was let out for hire, usually mistreated, and became dull, broken-down, and exhausted. See HOBSON'S CHOICE. The word was especially apt for politics because political hacks were disciplined by a party WHIP.

After the death of William Pitt in 1806, England was governed by a star-studded "Ministry of All the Talents," as the administration headed by Lord Grenville was dubbed. However, this was followed in 1807 by a less eminent—if more practical—group, soon derided as "All the Hacks."

The English usage made the transition to American politics in the early years of the new nation; in 1828 the *New York Enquirer* observed that other publications were calling those "friendly to Gen. Jackson 'political hacks.'"

A *hack* is one who works mechanically; he differs from a HENCHMAN, who works under clear direction, and a HATCHETMAN, who works ruthlessly, and is closest to a *hanger-on*, who does not work at all.

Although disdained in intellectual circles, a *hack writer* is sometimes sought after in politics despite his hackneyed prose. "Find me a good hack writer," one local candidate told the author, "who will put down what I think, and you can keep all your Sorensens and Emmet Hugheses with their fancy ideas." For the PECKING ORDER of political writers, see SPEECHWRITER; GHOSTWRITER.

In 2005, Senator Harry Reid (D-Nev.) denounced Alan Greenspan, then the widely respected chairman of the Federal Reserve Board (see IRRATIONAL EXUBERANCE), as "one of the biggest political hacks we have here in Washington," to which the *Washington Post* columnist David Broder responded after the Nevadan became Senate Majority Leader, "Reid is assuredly not a man who misses many opportunities to put his foot in his mouth." See FOOT-IN-MOUTH DISEASE.

As a verb, *to hack it* means "to succeed; to come through," synonymous with *to cut it*, probably from *cut the mustard*.

"Had Enough?" Republican campaign slogan in the midterm-year elections of 1946.

The phrase *had enough*, with a modern variant *had it*, is an old expression of mild disgust. When Theodore Roosevelt decided not to run for a third term in 1908, he said, "I don't want it. I've had enough ..."

In 1946 Harry Truman's young presidency was in trouble. The cost-of-living index was climbing rapidly; more unions were striking than usual; postwar shortages of meat, autos, and housing were continuing. The White House was the scapegoat. The creation of an advertising slogan that reflected the public mood—"Had Enough?"—is credited to the Harry M. Frost agency of Boston. "A nation which had quite enough of inflation and the Russians," wrote the historian Eric Goldman, "of strikes, shortages, and the atom bomb, of everlasting maybe's about peace and prosperity, rose up in a hiss of exasperation and elected the first Republican Congress since the far-distant days of Herbert Hoover." For the opposite campaign slogan, see DON'T LET THEM TAKE IT AWAY.

hail of dead cats Criticism accompanying the exit of an unpopular figure from public life.

The National Recovery Administration, a New Deal project, ran into severe criticism soon after Roosevelt's HUNDRED DAYS had ended, and was frequently labeled "the National Run-Around." A series of strikes, especially in the textile industry, required National Guard action that resulted in a list of dead and wounded on the labor front. In the fall of 1934 General Hugh Johnson, controversial head of the NRA, resigned in what he called "a hail of dead cats."

Precipitation has an affinity for resignations. A "*rain* (or *flood* or *deluge*) of complaints" leads to a resignation "under a *cloud*"; a "*storm* of criticism" is followed by the most colorful expression of all, "a *hail* of dead cats." These felines are not related to the *dead cats* of the circus (nonperforming lions and tigers) but may be akin to *catcall*, a raucous noise expressing disapproval.

"A general hail of dead cats has greeted the Congressional Democrats' lawsuit charging House Majority Whip Tom DeLay over campaign redistricting," wrote a legal newsletter in 2000. DeLay shook them off, but six years later, stimulated by scandalous influence-peddling by lobbyists, the cats of criticism won. For another use of a fatal-feline image, see DEAD CAT BOUNCE.

half-breeds See STALWART.

handlers Managers of political candidates; also, lesser aides who "handle" the needs of candidates.

In the 1300s, handlers were money-changers, those who handled silver. A century later, the noun was used figuratively in criticizing a preacher as "an unreverent handler of God's word." By the nineteenth century, the term was used in animal fighting; a handler held a fighting dog or gamecock. During the twentieth century, the word was applied to the person who shows off the best points of dogs to the judges of dog shows.

The word entered boxing by mid-century, labeling the seconds who offer backrubs and advice between rounds. Former heavyweight champion Jack Dempsey wrote in 1950, "His handlers threw in the towel," meaning that a boxer's seconds asked the referee to stop the fight.

As a political term, *handlers* first became prominent during the 1988 Presidential campaign. This sense, however, suggested negative control and manipulation of the candidate. A.M. Rosenthal wrote in *The New York Times*: "I do not believe in the genius of the handlers. They are all brilliant during the campaigns. How come 50 percent of them turn out to be so wrong on election night, when their man loses?"

Dan Quayle, in his campaign for the vice presidency that year, sought to avoid the appearance of being robotically "programmed," and he announced: "Now it's my turn. I'm my own handler." A year later, President George Bush rankled at the suggestion that White House handlers were in charge of political nominees. Bush the elder said in 1991 he considered it demeaning "to suggest that handlers are telling everybody what to say or not to say," and showed his knowledge of the term's etymology by adding, "Somehow I don't like the word *handlers*. Like the prizefighter—'O.K., go in there and slug him again.'"

Those in the business of coaching political figures never call themselves *handlers*; they prefer *consultants, strategists, gurus, advisers,* or *key aides.* In recent campaigns, the handler handling the more menial chores has been designated the *body man:* "Every candidate has a body man," noted *The Boston Globe* in 1988, "someone who fulfills a kind of mothering role on the trail. The body man makes sure the candidate's tie is straight for the TV debate, keeps his mood up, and makes sure he gets his favorite cereal for breakfast."

Female candidates do not have "body women"; their GOFERS are still called *handlers*, and male friends sometimes called *walkers*.

Handout is an attack word on welfare payments. A conservative political cliché is "People want a hand up, not a handout." The word has connotations of begging; the usage began in the late nineteenth century as hobo lingo, referring to the bundle of clothes or plate of food given at the back door. See HOTTENTOTS, MILK FOR.

A press or media handout is a story written by a political figure's press aide to be given to reporters at a news (formerly press) conference to save them the trouble of taking notes or asking questions. Many reporters disdain handouts as self-serving, which they unabashedly are; however, an informative handout can be helpful and timesaving. A *handout* is often directly given—handed—by press aides to reporters; a *release* may be handed out, e-mailed, or posted on a website.

Handout is still an infrequently used word for political handbill; see FLYER. Its use for "welfare payment" is in the league with *relief* and has long been outdated, except in the cliché "a hand up, not a handout."

hand-picked A candidate chosen or an appointment made by a powerful person; an allusion to boss rule.

Among sneer words—*so-called, purported, self-anointed, supposed, once-powerful—hand-picked* is a favorite. In the 1958 Democratic convention in New York State, the choice of the respected, veteran Manhattan District Attorney Frank Hogan for senatorial candidate was dictated by Tammany chief Carmine De Sapio. Hogan was promptly depicted by Republicans as "Boss De Sapio's hand-picked candidate" and was roundly defeated by Kenneth Keating.

In agriculture, *hand-picked* (vs. *machine-picked*) means carefully chosen, resulting in an unbruised fruit or berry, or, more commonly, selected by hand from a larger group of the same product for quality. In politics, the opposite has come to be the meaning. *Hand-picked successor* implies autocratic domination, subverting democratic processes, and is a charge hurled by whatever group refuses to hold still or go along. The vice presidential candidate is usually hand-picked by the presidential candidate, though Adlai Stevenson in 1956 made a point of permitting an "open convention" to allow the choice of Senator Estes Kefauver over Senator John F. Kennedy.

"In 1908," wrote Harry Truman, "William Howard Taft had been hand-picked by [Theodore] Roosevelt as his successor." He did not add that he himself had been hand-picked by another Roosevelt in 1944.

See HEIR APPARENT.

hanger-on See HACK.

hang tough Strike a determined pose; or, remain grimly resolute.

Eugene Landy's 1971 *Underground Dictionary* traced the phrase to the world of narcotics rehabilitation: "It is used to encourage individuals during a stressful situation, such as a period of withdrawal from a drug. *Hang tough* was commonly used at Synanon Foundation during the foundation's initial stages when addicts were allowed to withdraw after entering Synanon. Synanon's house in Santa Monica, California has a ship's white life preserver upon which is written 'S.S. Hang Tough' hanging on the wall."

The phrase, which has variant readings of *hang in there* and *tough it out*, was used by Hugh Sidey in *Life* magazine in 1970 about the revelation that President Nixon's favorite movie in the White House was *Patton*, starring George C. Scott, about the pistol-packing, profane fighting general of World War II: "In sum, they agree that the emergence of 'Patton' as a major figure in the Nixon Pantheon is a good sign, meaning that he will continue to hang tough in the crunches."

During the sixteen months of Watergate siege, President Nixon was urged by some, including his wife Pat, to "hang tough," and the phrase has been used in reference to presidential resolution or irresolution ever since. Ross Baker, a Rutgers University political analyst, commented in February 1993 to *USA Today* on President Clinton's performance early in his Administration: "Whether he has the capacity to hang tough is still an open question. He seems to fold at the slightest sign of disaffection by some interest groups."

Hang loose is an older locution, from *hang it easy*, a teenage phrase from the early fifties. Some slang authorities speculate that both *hang loose* and *hang tough* are sexual in origin, referring to the relaxed or tense condition of the genitals. Steven Weisman defined *hang loose* in *The New York Times* in 1976 as "the period when a legislator has not made up his mind." Columnist Tom Wicker speculated in a 1973 note to the author: "I believe *hang in there* will be found to be a prize-fight term meaning that someone—momentarily rocked by the other guy—should 'hang in there,' maybe even literally hanging on to the ropes or hanging on to the other guy in a clinch."

Tough it out has a longer lineage in slang. R. L. Thornton has six citations in his *American Glossary*, beginning with an 1824 memoir: "We little fellows had to tuff it out as well as we could."

happy camper Satisfied person; team player pleased with the status quo.

Print citations for the term date back at least to 1981, when David Bird wrote in *The New York Times* about homeless people: "It is not a group of happy campers that gets off the bus after its 70-mile journey." A year later, the columnist Mary McGrory applied the term to politics; observing a Reagan-era Republican television ad about prosperity in a region of high unemployment, she wrote, "The happy campers of the commercial have few counterparts in the Peoria area today."

The phrase in its literal sense probably sprung from its use at summer camps. Its reverse, *unhappy camper*, has long described the homesick city child.

By the mid-'80s, the two types of camper were part of political jargon. Representative Thomas J. Tauke of Iowa commented in 1985 about a toxic-cleanup proposal: "I want the authors of the bill to know that I am not a happy camper." Representative Billy Tauzin of Louisiana responded, "This is the most unhappy campsite in America." In 1988, when the *Discovery* space shuttle successfully followed the *Challenger* disaster, flight commander Frederick Hauck signaled the crew's jubilation to Mission Control: "You got a bunch of happy campers up here."

When the State Department in 2004 had to admit that its statistic about the number of terrorist attacks around the world was inaccurate, Secretary of State Colin Powell insisted that it was not the result of political manipulation; however, coming on the heels of his admission that information from intelligence sources that he had presented to the U.N. Security Council about weaponry in Iraq "was inaccurate and wrong and in some cases, deliberately misleading," the Secretary was embarrassed. "I am not a happy camper over this," he said.

Happy Days Are Here Again Campaign song of FDR in 1932.

Hit songs during the Depression ranged from the downbeat "Brother, Can You Spare a Dime?" to the determinedly upbeat "Happy Days Are Here Again."

Bronx Democratic boss Edward J. Flynn felt that the music to be played when FDR was nominated should be lighthearted and optimistic. Flynn and FDR confidant Louis Howe were lying on the floor of Howe's hotel suite in Chicago listening to the nomination on the radio. Roosevelt, a former Secretary of the Navy, had suggested that at the moment of nomination the convention band should play "Anchors Aweigh." When the musicians began to play the Navy song slowly, Flynn groaned to Howe: "That sounds like a funeral march. Why don't we get them to play something peppy, like 'Happy Days are Here Again'?" The gnome-like Howe agreed and had the self-confidence to countermand FDR's wish. Flynn telephoned the convention floor manager to suggest that the band switch to a lively rendition of "Happy Days." Flynn wrote later: "In a moment it began to come over the air. To me, it certainly sounded more cheerful and appropriate to the occasion."

The song soon came to mean for Roosevelt campaigns what "Sidewalks of New York" meant to Al Smith's. Nobody bothered to point out that the song was written just before the crash of 1929 by Jack Yellen and Milton Agar for use in an MGM movie titled *Chasing Rainbows*.

At the 1976 Democratic convention, the song was played to recall past Democratic glories for candidate Jimmy Carter. At the 1992 convention nominating Bill Clinton, the theme song was "Don't Stop (Thinking About Tomorrow)."

Happy Warrior Franklin Roosevelt's reluctant characterization of Al Smith, which became his sobriquet.

Franklin Delano Roosevelt, who had been nominee for vice president on the losing Democratic ticket in 1920 and was crippled by poliomyelitis in 1921, made his political comeback in a nomination speech for Alfred E. Smith in 1924. Leaning on crutches, he struggled to the podium and said of Smith toward the end of his speech: "He is the Happy Warrior of the political battlefield." The entire address, columnist Walter Lippmann wrote Roosevelt later, "was a moving and distinguished thing. I am utterly hard-boiled about speeches, but yours seems to me perfect in temper and manner and most eloquent in its effect."

Roosevelt's reference was to English poet William Wordsworth's "Character of the Happy Warrior":

Who is the happy Warrior? Who is he
That every man in arms should wish to be? ...
But who if he be called upon to face
Some awful moment to which Heaven has
*   joined*
Great issues, good or bad for human kind,
Is happy as a lover ...

Writer of the speech was Judge Joseph Proskauer, who died in 1971 at the age of ninety-four. As an aide to Governor Al Smith, Proskauer drafted the nominating speech for the man nominating him to give (a practice widely followed today). Roosevelt objected, "You can't give poetry to a political convention," and drafted a speech of his own.

Recalled Proskauer:

So I took Herbert Bayard Swope, the editor, with me to Roosevelt's place up the Hudson so that we could work it out. Swope made the mistake of the century. He picked up Roosevelt's speech, turned to me and said, "Joe, this is awful. It's dull. It won't do." And he flung it down on the floor. Then he picked up my "happy warrior" speech. "This is great, Frank," he said to Roosevelt. "You've done it just the way it ought to be." Well, Roosevelt damn near went through the roof. We fought and fought. Finally I told him, "Frank, I have this message from the Governor: Either you give this speech or you don't nominate him."

Roosevelt gave the speech Proskauer had prepared rather than the draft he had written himself. "It's a good question whether it did Smith or Roosevelt the most good," grumbled the judge years later, "but I wrote the speech."

At that 1924 convention, Smith deadlocked with McAdoo, and John W. Davis received the nomination, only to lose to the Republican, Calvin Coolidge. Four years later, FDR was glad to repeat the well-received "Happy Warrior" theme to the Democratic convention in Houston, this time to fifteen million Americans listening on radio. This time Smith's bid for the Democratic presidential nomination was successful, thanks largely to Republican-turned-Democrat John Raskob, who ran the Smith campaign. He lost to Republican Herbert Hoover.

In 1932 Smith and Roosevelt competed for the Democratic nomination and bitterness developed between the two. Smith "took a walk" (see TAKE A WALK; OFF THE RESERVATION) during the first term of the New Deal. When the embittered "Brown Derby" attacked Roosevelt in his 1936 reelection campaign, FDR selected Senator Joseph Robinson, Smith's running mate in 1928, to answer the Democrat who had bolted. Robinson hit where it hurt most with the famous phrase: for deserting his party, Al Smith was labeled "The Unhappy Warrior." In 1992, after George H.W. Bush was defeated for reelection, *Newsweek* noted that "Bush had never been a very happy warrior, and his appetite had been further dulled by the pasting he had taken for the nastiness of his 1988 campaign [against Michael Dukakis]." The headline on the article: "Unhappy Warrior."

The original Wordsworth sobriquet was often cheerfully applied to Senator Hubert Humphrey, who liked to espouse "the politics of joy."

hardball Aggressive, rough-and-tumble political tactics; stronger than *practical politics* or *pranks*, but not as over-the-line as DIRTY TRICKS.

The author first heard the word used on December 20, 1972, by attorney (later Secretary of HEW) Joseph Califano, complaining of Republican tactics during the campaign that trounced Senator George McGovern: "Nobody ever played hardball like you guys." (He was unaware at the time that previous presidents had used the FBI and CIA for campaign intelligence purposes.)

"The hardest hardball that's ever been played in this town" was a line in the 1973 book by Bob Woodward and Carl Bernstein, *All the President's Men*. The word is fixed in U.S. archives as used in a recording of an

Oval Office discussion on March 21, 1973. President Nixon, chief of staff H.R. Haldeman, and counsel John Dean were troubled by how damaging the knowledge held by Howard Hunt might become if his demands were not met. After Nixon worried, "I think Hunt knows a hell of a lot more," Dean replied, "He is playing hardball. He wouldn't be playing hardball unless he were pretty confident that he could cause an awful lot of grief."

In hearings on September 26, 1973, before the Senate Watergate Committee, Nixon speechwriter Patrick J. Buchanan gave a declension of rough tactics in politics: "My own view is that there are four gradations." He began with what he argued was an example of the worst, practiced by leftist anti-war demonstrators in the 1968 Democratic primaries: "There are things that are certainly utterly outrageous and I would put that in with the kind of demonstrations against Vice President Humphrey in 1968 which denied him an opportunity to speak for almost a month." He then listed lesser categories of attack: "Then, there is 'dirty tricks.' Then, there is political hardball. Then, there is pranks."

Soon after that, in straining to show that hardball, as the term was understood in the campaign marred by the Watergate scandal, was not necessarily immoral or illegal, the author wrote in his Op-Ed column "not every hardball is a beanball." (In baseball, a beanball is a pitch deliberately thrown at the batter's head.) The sports columnist Walter "Red" Smith promptly corrected the misusage: "In sports terminology there is no such thing as 'a hardball.' When the word is used, which is seldom, 'hardball' means the game of baseball as distinct from softball. It does not mean a high, fast pitch. Probably Mr. Safire should be excused, for this was a column applauding Richard Nixon's forthright behavior in the Watergate case. It had an understandably agitated tone."

The word gained a sense of "aggressive questioning" as the title of a political interview program on MSNBC, *Hardball with Chris Matthews*, its host a former aide to Democratic Speaker of the House "Tip" O'Neill and author of a perceptive book about the relationship between senators Nixon and Kennedy.

A frequent euphemism for hardball is *opposition research*, to describe the ferreting out of information embarrassing to opposing candidates. In 1992, *The New York Times* reported on some of the crews getting material for rumormongering: "Officially, their job is drearily called 'opposition research'—or 'oppo' for short." See DIRTY TRICKS.

In political journalese, a *softball* or *fat pitch* is a question designed to give an interviewee a rest, deferential but considerably short of a BIG WET KISS. For other uses of games in figures of political speech, see BEANBAG; FULL-COURT PRESS; GAME PLAN; and also SPORTS METAPHORS.

hard line A firm, unwavering stand; when used pejoratively, intransigence.

During the Cold War, *hardliners* expressed strong support of the CONTAINMENT of Communism, a policy criticized as "rigid" by those who foresaw "convergence" of the Communist and capitalist systems and favored ACCOMMODATION.

The *line* in *hard line* appears to have come from PARTY LINE. Historian Samuel Eliot Morison wrote: "Thus the cold war began as soon as the hot war was over. Earl Browder, head of the Communist party in the United States, was the first victim of the 'hard line.' For his continuing to preach friendly collaboration between the United States and Russia, which he had been ordered to do in 1941, he was contemptuously deposed in May 1945, by orders from Moscow."

Western powers, led by the U.S., took note of the new Russian line and of Winston Churchill's IRON CURTAIN warning in 1946; NATO was formed, and the policy of containment originally formulated by the diplomat George Kennan followed. (See MR. X.) The *hard line* was pursued in the Korean War, and was subsequently identified with Secretary of State John Foster Dulles throughout the Eisenhower years.

At the onset of the war in Vietnam, however, the wisdom of the hard line came under increasing attack in the U.S. and abroad. In 1967, *The Wall Street Journal* noted:

Such hard-liners as Sens. Bourke Hickenlooper (R-Iowa) and Frank Lausche (D-Ohio) can't shake the fear that the various national Communist parties around the world still want to seize political and social control everywhere, that they still have the common goal of toppling capitals. Former Ambassador Kennan, a hard-liner himself during Stalin's day, contended that this economic goal is becoming increasingly theoretical.

The *Hards* vs. the *Softs* date back at least a century and a half in U.S. history. New York State sent two competing political factions to the 1848 Democratic convention in Baltimore: the Hunkers, known as the *Hard Shells* or *Hards*, and the BARNBURN-ERS, known as the *Soft Shells* or *Softs*. The Hards supported the Polk Administration's policy opposing the Wilmot Proviso prohibiting slavery in California and the rest of the Mexican Cession; the Softs were against the Democratic Administration's opposition, and fought to limit the extension of slavery. Efforts at a compromise failed, and neither faction took part in the convention.

The early political etymologist Charles Ledyard Norton in 1890 traced the hard and soft "shells" to sects of the Baptist denomination, so called by their critics because of their supposed similarity to crabs in different stages of development.

Hard-liners are often described as *hard-nosed*, but for some reason, soft-liners are never described as *soft-nosed*. According to lexicographer Kenneth Hudson, *hard-nosed* was originally applied to bulls: "A hard-nosed bull is one who does not respond when the ring through the cartilage of his nose is twitched by the person leading him on a pole or rope."

American conservatives found the noun *hardliner* useful after the collapse of Communism and the breakup of the Soviet Union. Russian Communists resisting democratic reform were being labeled "conservatives"; this angered U.S. political

journalists on the right, who thought of the Russian opponents of change as unreconstructed old radicals. When the reformist but unstable Boris Yeltsin was succeeded by the longtime KGB operative Vladimir Putin and dissidence fell out of favor, the wielders of power in the Kremlin were described by U.S. conservatives as *hardliners*.

hard money Historically, metallic versus paper currency; recently, applied symbolically to anti-inflationists.

One of the great debates of early U.S. history pitted the "hard-money" against the "soft-money" men. In an 1816 debate, Senator Daniel Webster formulated the classical defense of gold and silver currencies: "The framers of the Constitution, and those who enacted the early statutes on this subject, were hard-money men; they had felt and therefore duly appreciated the evils of a paper medium."

Andrew Jackson tied the Democratic party to a hard-money policy during his battle with the banks, and they became known as "Perish Credit, Perish Commerce" men. But in 1840 the party split into hard- and soft-money factions. Greenbacks were introduced during the Civil War with some trepidation; President Lincoln was said to fear he would have to sign every U.S. banknote. In retrospect, "paper money" turned out to be a useful way for the Treasury to borrow large sums from a trusting citizenry.

Nowadays, paper currency is universally accepted, but the *hard* and *soft* terms are still applied symbolically. The *hard-money* men favor a slow, measured expansion of the money supply, generally no more than 2 or 3 percent a year. The *soft-money* men— often Democrats, Keynesians, or both— traditionally approve pumping greater quantities of currency into circulation as a stimulus to employment and consumption.

The terms are also applied to campaign fundraising. Leslie Phillips wrote in *USA Today* in March 1993 that "The heart of President Clinton's campaign finance reform is based on a trade-off: converting unlimited 'soft' money, donations used by political parties to help elect candidates, into regulated—and limited—'hard' money." For a new-millennium innovation to get around campaign finance reform laws that put a cap on individual contributions of hard money, see BUNDLING.

As the chairmanship of the Federal Reserve System passed from Alan Greenspan (see IRRATIONAL EXUBERANCE) to Ben Bernanke in 2006, the tightening of money by raising interest rates was named "policy firming."

hatched Removed from political activity by virtue of the Hatch Act.

The Act of Congress bearing the name of Senator Carl Hatch, a Democrat from New Mexico whose bill was passed in 1939, says: "It shall be unlawful for any person employed in any administrative position by the United States, or by any department, independent agency, or other agency of the United States ... to use his official authority for the purpose of interfering with, or affecting the election or the nomination of any candidate ..." Its purpose was to prevent political appointees from unduly influencing government workers.

The phrase "subject to the restrictions of the Hatch Act" was soon shortened to the verb *hatched*, which present usage no longer capitalizes.

In 1970 George Shultz, who had been promoted from Secretary of Labor in the Nixon cabinet to Director of the Office of Management and Budget, was routinely asked to make a speech supporting a candidate in his home state. This White House speechwriter, who carried the message to him from the President, volunteered to help him with the speech. Shultz looked up from his desk as if he had just pecked his way out of an eggshell and replied, "I can't. I've been hatched."

Presidential advisers use this rule of thumb: if you are on the White House payroll, or you are in a job that has called for Senate confirmation—you've not *hatched*. In the late 1970s, there was agitation to repeal the Hatch Act because it limited some people's rights to political expression; in this way, reformers were calling for reform of reform.

hatchetman An insider close to an office-holder who revels in the unpleasant assignment of forcing supporters into line; also a public figure who engages in strong partisan attacks.

In FDR's political campaigns, Louis Howe was his private hatchetman, Harold Ickes his public hatchetman. Sherman Adams was occasionally Eisenhower's private hatchetman; Richard Nixon was often accused of being Eisenhower's public hatchetman because of the Vice President's willingness to lead the partisan charge in contrast to Eisenhower's nonpolitical stance.

Robert Kennedy was often accused of being John Kennedy's hatchetman, though Kenneth O'Donnell often had to perform that function. Lyndon Johnson occasionally used Hubert Humphrey as a public hatchetman; privately, White House aide Marvin Watson did much of the necessary hatcheting, although President Johnson—with his Senate Majority experience—did not flinch from the job himself. In 1971 *The Wall Street Journal* sunk the fearsome sobriquet in the head of Nixon counsel Charles Colson. In recent years, the title has been infrequently awarded.

The derivation indicates both the public and private senses of the expression. In the public sense—one who engages in partisan attacks to clear a path for the above-politics leader—the root is in colonial military vocabulary. A hatchetman, or ax-man, was used to chop foliage in advance of a military group operating in woods or jungle. General George Washington wrote to a subordinate: "I think it will be advisable to detain both mulattoes and negroes in your company, and employ them as Pioneers or Hatchetmen."

In the sense of the short-handled ax being swung to intimidate or decapitate an opponent, the derivation is from the Chinese tong wars of the 1880s, where "hatchet-armed killers" were the "enforcers" of their era, murdering enemies of the tongs for pay.

In current political usage, a politician differentiates between the *hatchetman* who operates in public and the *insider* who does the unseen dirty work for a public figure.

A HENCHMAN is one cut above a *hanger-on* but one cut below a hatchetman, though he may be used for hatcheting chores from time to time. The work performed is called a *hatchet job* as well as *hatcheting*. Harry Truman's 1948 blast at GOP attackers: "Gluttons of privilege...all set to do a hatchet job on the New Deal."

As noted above, the quintessential hatchetman (and privately so identified by Nixon Chief of Staff H.R. Haldeman) was Charles Colson. When the AFL-CIO insulted President Nixon with a second-row seat on the dais during its annual convention at Bal Harbour, Florida, it was Counsel Chuck Colson who set out to punish labor's lobbyists in following years with his bitterly amusing slogan "Remember Bal Harbour." As Watergate unfolded, he was made a target of prosecutors, copped a guilty plea and was jailed.

In 2006, however, the following invitation to a testimonial dinner was received by the lexicographer:

Almost 30 years ago, Charles W. Colson was known as the White House "hatchet man," a man feared by even the most powerful politicos...When news of Colson's conversion to Christianity leaked to the press in 1973, the *Boston Globe* reported "If Mr. Colson can repent of his sins, there just has to be hope for everybody." After leaving prison, Colson founded Prison Fellowship Ministries in 1976, which has since become the world's largest outreach to prisoners, ex-prisoners, and their families. In recognition of his work, Colson received the prestigious Templeton Prize for progress in religion in 1993, donating the $1 million prize to Prison Fellowship.

By his example, Colson proved to pols that there is redemption possible for even the most feared and despised hatchetman, recalling the symbol of frontiersmen and Indians: When peace is made, the hatchet is buried. See GUTFIGHTER; ATTACK DOG.

hat in the ring Announcement of active candidacy.

Former President Theodore Roosevelt was actively working to get the Republican presidential nomination in 1912, but had not yet announced that he really wanted to run against his protégé, William Howard Taft.

When Republican governors signed a petition asking Roosevelt to take hold of the progressive forces in the GOP and make a run for the nomination, Roosevelt couldn't help answering a reporter's question about his possible candidacy one cold night in Cleveland. "My hat's in the ring. The fight is on, and I'm stripped to the buff."

Roosevelt, a sportsman, popularized a boxing phrase used on the American frontier. When a Westerner decided he was willing to fight all comers, he threw his hat in the prize ring, similar to "throwing down the gauntlet" in the days of chivalry. After newspapers had picked up Roosevelt's "hat in the ring" quote, *Harper's Weekly* said of the bitter feud between Roosevelt and Taft: "Hate, not hat, is in the ring."

The construction is flexible and current. Harold Ickes derided young Thomas E. Dewey for "throwing his diaper in the ring," and it was said in 1967 that congressional candidate Shirley Temple Black "threw her curls in the ring." The *Los Angeles Times* reported in January 1993 a debate among approximately 40 candidates for mayor of L.A.; Faye Fiore wrote of that vast field, "But if former Gov. Edmund G. (Jerry) Brown Jr. had thrown his hat in the ring, you can bet they would have found an extra chair." In late 2006, as a boomlet was launched for freshman Illinois Senator Barack Obama, a Tom Toles cartoon had him with a halo over his head and a hat in front of him labeled "'08," with the beatific candidate saying, "I am considering throwing my ring into the hat."

have and have-not nations. Phrase used to dramatize the gulf between the nations rich in resources and industry and those yet undeveloped and dependent.

Miguel de Cervantes gave currency to the proverbial Spanish phrase. In the second book of *Don Quixote*, Sancho Panza observes that his grandmother always used to say, "There are only two families in the world, the Haves and the Have-Nots." The Spanish *el tener y el no tener* is sometimes translated "have-much and have-little." A parallel aphorism is Rabelais's "one half of the world knows not how the other half lives."

The phrase has always filled a need. Lord Bryce used it in *The American Commonwealth*: "In the hostility of rich and poor, or of capital and labour, in the fears of the Haves and the desire of the Have-nots ..." Theodore Roosevelt wrote in 1918: "... to oscillate between the sheer brutal greed of the haves and sheer brutal greed of the have-nots means to plumb the depths of degradation."

The phrase is used in its general sense defining the chasm between economic classes, and in a more specific sense pointing to the difference between rich and poor nations. H. L. Mencken used the general sense in his blast at Democratic candidate John Davis in the 1924 campaign: "Dr. Coolidge is for the Haves and Dr. La Follette is for the Have Nots. But whom is Dr. Davis for? ... himself."

Talking about foreign affairs in 1948, Harry Truman used the more specific: "The world was undergoing a major readjustment, with revolution stalking most of the 'have-not' nations. Communism was making the most of this opportunity, thriving on misery as it always does."

America's responsibility toward the *have-not nations* has been a running controversy (see HOTTENTOTS, MILK FOR) in domestic politics. Frequently, when the *have-nots* bite the hand of the *haves* that are trying to feed them, there is a reluctance to continue the largesse (or fulfill the social responsibility, depending on the point of view).

In the 1980s, as the East-West superpower competition came to an end, the *haves* were referred to as the North, the *have-nots* as the South. See CLASS WARFARE; THIRD WORLD.

have the tickets See TICKET.

hawks See WAR HAWKS.

heartbeat away from the presidency A macabre reminder to voters to examine the shortcomings of a vice presidential candidate.

"The Republican Vice Presidential candidate," Adlai Stevenson said in the Cleveland Arena in 1952, "—who asks you to place him a heartbeat from the Presidency—has attacked me for saying in a court deposition that the character of Alger Hiss was good." Stevenson then launched into a blast at Richard Nixon.

Nixon supporters in the 1960 campaign took a leaf from Stevenson's text. They compiled a list of every one of vice presidential candidate Lyndon Johnson's votes against civil rights legislation as a representative and senator and circulated a flyer in black neighborhoods entitled "Only a Heartbeat from the Presidency."

McKinley manager Mark Hanna of Ohio, seeking to block "that cowboy" Theodore Roosevelt from the vice presidential nomination, used the thought but not the phrase in 1900. "It must always be remembered," one report quoted him—"that there is only one life between the Vice President and the Chief Magistracy of the nation." Another report of the same statement by Hanna: "Don't any of you realize that there's only one life between this madman and the White House?"

U.S. history to date has shown that there are about two chances in ten that the president's heartbeat will stop during his term in office. Tyler took over for Harrison; Fillmore for Taylor; Johnson for Lincoln; Arthur for Garfield; Roosevelt for McKinley; Coolidge for Harding; Truman for Roosevelt; Johnson for Kennedy. The scary phrase was used by reporter Jules Witcover as the title of a book about the forced resignation of Spiro Agnew: *A Heartbeat Away*.

heartland The strategic central area of a nation or a land mass; in American political usage, those noncoastal sections where spiritual and moral values are said to be most revered.

The geopolitical theory expounded by Halford Mackinder in 1904 held that Eastern Europe's "heartland" could dominate the continent of Eurasia. From the Elbe to the Amur, the idea went, a self-sufficient area existed that could not be challenged by British mastery of the seas, and held the key to world domination. Naturally, this theory was vigorously disputed by exponents of British seapower.

The modern political use of the word stemmed from Dwight Eisenhower's 1945 Guildhall speech in London, where he referred to his boyhood in Abilene, Kan.: "I come from the very heart of America." Political analyst Kevin Phillips applied the old geopolitical word to modern U.S. politics in his 1969 book, *The Emerging Republican Majority*: "Twenty-one of the twenty-five Heartland states supported Richard Nixon in 1968. ... Over the remainder of the century, the Heartland should dominate American politics in tandem with suburbia, the South, and Sun Belt-swayed California."

Although the word continues to have this geopolitical meaning, it is more commonly used in a less specific context. "I am always pleased to be here in this great heartland of America," President Nixon told a group of Indiana's elderly citizens in 1971. *New York Times* correspondent Seymour Topping wrote on July 16, 1971: "The willingness of the President to travel to Peking, to the heartland of the Asian Communist world, cannot fail to impress the Chinese ..."

The word is used not just to identify a place, but a state of mind and repository of "old-fashioned" values. In his first year in office, George W. Bush told a group of Future Farmers of America, "You should never be afraid of embracing the values you find in the heartland of America, of worship and faith, the importance of family, the values of hard work, the values of taking a risk, the values of understanding that if you own a farm or a ranch, every day is Earth Day." See HOMELAND; MIDDLE AMERICA; PLAY IN PEORIA.

hearts and minds See SLOGAN.

heckle To harass a speaker with comments or questions with intent to rattle, embarrass, or silence him.

Nikita Khrushchev was heckled at a dinner of the Economics Club of New York in 1959, and won the respect of his audience by skillfully handling the heckler: "I am an old sparrow, so to say, and you cannot muddle me by your cries."

The Middle English verb *hekelen* meant "to comb flax, to tease or ruffle hemp." (A *hekele* was what you heckled flax or hemp with.) As early as 1808, Jamieson's Scottish dictionary began carrying a second definition for *heckle*—"to tease with questions."

Few hecklers today stop at teasing. Most try to make the heckled angry. If the heckled loses his temper, the heckler has won his point. In 1906 *The New York Times* considered the word fit enough to use in that way and ran a headline: "Hearst is Heckled Into Talking Taxes."

Campaigning politicians are continually heckled. Their retorts, often carefully written ad libs, if clever enough, can quiet the hecklers quickly. During the 1960 campaign John F. Kennedy was often met by determined and loud young Republican hecklers. Whenever he was faced with a "We want Nixon!" chant, he replied with a good-humored "I don't think you're going to get him." This was not brilliant repartee, but it pleased crowds and eased the tension and embarrassment of a crowd toward the hecklers within it.

In the same campaign Richard Nixon found that all heckling need not be audible, nor even in English. In Chinatown, Los Angeles, courtesy of Democratic "prankster" Dick Tuck, there was a huge billboard with a smiling picture of Nixon with the words "Welcome Nixon." However, in Chinese characters the sign asked, "What about the Hughes loan?," a Democratic allegation that Nixon had abused the trust of his office to obtain financial aid for his family. See DIRTY TRICKS.

Sometimes a hard answer is needed to turn away a wrathful heckler. 1964 Republican presidential candidate Barry Goldwater was giving a relatively quiet speech at Rutgers University when a young man leapt to his feet and shouted, "You goddam Fascist bastard!" Goldwater won cheers from a generally hostile audience when he replied, "If you call me a bastard again, I'll meet you outside." Some observers noted at which word he took offense.

Most American politicians, accustomed to what they consider the art of heckling, are amazed at the virulence of the harassment in England. On the stump, British candidates often have great difficulty in making themselves heard over the shouts and catcalls of groups of men who come equipped with loudspeakers. However, heckling with charm is also a British trait. Sir Alec Douglas-Home, when he was a British Foreign Secretary, said he received the following telegram from an irate citizen: "To hell with you. Offensive letter follows."

For an example of how a speaker's overreaction to heckling or tracking can have a stunning political effect—loss of a Senate majority in 2006—see the *macaca* remark under BLOOPER. See also TRACKER.

heft, political Gravitas; weight or substance as a candidate, based on experience or intellectual capacity, or the seriousness with which the public treats his candidacy.

This is a word used frequently in discussions of a candidate's potential, with written citations dating back to 1969 when *Business Week* wrote of "twenty-four House Democrats with political heft." "He's got heft," the opposite of "He's a LIGHTWEIGHT," is usually accompanied by a rising and falling motion of the hand, as if the pleasurable weight of a roll of dimes was being hefted.

The term can be used to cast doubts on a political staff as well as the politician himself. *Time* magazine wrote of the new Clinton Administration in January 1993: "Several party veterans predict privately that the President-elect will need to be far more decisive.... Last week many of the same officials questioned whether Clinton had chosen a staff of sufficient depth and heft to meet the challenge."

An ancient meaning of the word is "raised aloft" ("Inflamed with wrath his raging blade he heft"—Spenser), a past tense of *heave*; a colloquial meaning has long been "influence," which is figurative weight.

hegemony Domination by one state over others.

Hegemony (preferred accent on the "gem") is the dirty word for leadership. In Greek, a *hegemon* is a leader; among the warring Greek city-states, Athens sought hegemony. Among individuals, this sort of leadership is often seen as laudable, but among states it has always been perceived as predatory. In 1860 the *Times* of London wrote: "No doubt it is a glorious ambition which drives Prussia to assert her claim to the leadership, or as that land of professors phrases it, the 'hegemony' of the German Confederation." In the U.S., *Forum* wrote in 1904: "The hegemon of the Western Hemisphere is the United States."

The word was popularized more recently by Mao Zedong. "Dig tunnels deep," he counseled, "store grain, and never seek hegemony." As the Sino-Soviet split developed in the Communist world, the crucial epithet became *hegemony*—secondarily the domination of imperialism, but primarily Mao's denunciation of the attempt by the Soviet Union to dominate China. When Communist parties in Western Europe sought to show their independence from Moscow so as to improve their appeal locally, *hegemony* was their attack word as well. One Italian Communist suggested that the Marxist "dictatorship of the proletariat" be changed to "the hegemony of the working class." See EUROCOMMUNISM.

The term resurfaced in early 1993 in charges that the U.S. and Britain were manipulating the world's currency markets. Pierre Bérégovoy, the Socialist prime minister of France, wrote in *Le Monde* "that America was engaged in a drive for global economic hegemony, leaving it bound to oppose a single European currency." In 2007, the *Daily Observer* in Banjul, Gambia, took the long view from Africa: "The Cold War is now history, but politics, like nature, hates a vacuum: there now emerges the 'hegemony war' between the U.S. and China. It is a battle not for ideas, but for oil, raw materials and markets, and for military bases."

heir apparent The chosen successor, who does not always succeed in a democratic society.

If the man at the top feels secure enough, he will designate an *heir apparent* to carry on his policies after his term or life is over. From the boss's viewpoint, the advantage is a cessation of bickering below; the disadvantage is boredom below, or an unexpected bid for power by the second in command. See HAND-PICKED.

Martin Van Buren was Andrew Jackson's heir apparent, but "Little Van" could not carry the Jacksonian tradition past a single term. William Howard Taft had been publicly tapped by Theodore Roosevelt to be his successor as president, but later Roosevelt turned on Taft and ran as a "Bull Moose" independent against him, splitting the Republican vote enough to elect Woodrow Wilson.

Splitting heirs, the *heir expectant* is one who is simply in line for some inheritance; the *heir presumptive* is one who will succeed if the top man dies or quits immediately, but who can be replaced by the birth of a closer relative; and the *heir apparent* is the one to stop when the top dog lets his power slip.

Heisenberg effect See EFFECT.

Hell before breakfast See RIGHT TO KNOW.

hell-bent for election Determined to the point of recklessness; lickety-split; evoking an image of a spirited, horn-blowing, flag-flying campaign.

The phrase had its political origin in Maine in 1840, year of the "Tippecanoe and Tyler Too" election. Edward Kent won the gubernatorial election handily, and a ditty ran: "Maine went Hell-bent for Governor Kent." It was reprised by Mark Twain in a 1860 letter: "To use an expression which is commonly ignored in polite society, they were 'hell-bent' on stealing some of the ... oranges"; by Stephen Crane in an 1899 short story; and in a 1904 *Boston Herald:* "The populist Democrats are going 'hell-bent,' as the old song says, for [Theodore] Roosevelt."

When Chuck Jones, cartoon animator of *Bugs Bunny* and *Road Runner*, died in 2002, his obituary in London's *Daily Telegraph* noted that during World War II, "Jones directed the pro-Roosevelt campaign cartoon Hell Bent for Election, using two trains to symbolise the forthcoming 1944 election."

Hell-bent was defined early as "fiendishly," and is also heard as *hell-bent for leather,* suggesting a whip on a racehorse. The derivation is a mystery, but the political meaning is clear and colorful. See FLAT-OUT.

henchman In fact, a member of the staff of a candidate or party; in an attack, a stooge, hatchetman, hanger-on.

This word has deep roots, starting with the Anglo-Saxon *hengest,* or horse; a hengestman was a groom, squire, or page. In the Scottish Highlands, the henchman became a *gillie,* or right-hand man, to the clan leader, where the word picked up its political meaning of a loyal supporter and active worker.

The word is now only used pejoratively; when all assistants preen at being a *key aide,* nobody ever claims to be anybody else's *henchman.* Typical use was by Alfred Landon in 1936: "Idealists may have been at the front door preaching social justice, but party henchmen have been at the back door handing out jobs."

A rare but colorful synonym is *janissary,* taken from the sultan's guard in Turkey. For differentiation in current usage, see HACK; HATCHETMAN.

hidebound Narrow-minded, stubborn; an attack word on conservatives, with the adjective all but married to the noun *reactionary.*

In a cliché fight, a *hidebound conservative* could square off with a *bleeding-heart liberal. Cooper's Thesaurus* of 1559 notes a "sickenesse of cattall...that their skynnes dooe cleve fast to their bodies, hyde bounde."

The term is current. *Business Week* wrote in April 1993 about teachers' unions, including "the larger and more hidebound National Education Association." More often, it is applied to the right: "Like the Democrats during the 1970s," wrote the *Washington Monthly* in 2007, "today's GOP is hidebound and out of touch." See DYED-IN-THE-WOOL; ROCK-RIBBED; MOSSBACK.

highbinder See SPELLBINDER.

high cost of living Perennial political complaint about inflation; standard charge by the party out of power.

The *OED* credits American author William Dean Howells with the earliest use of *cost of living* in 1896: "The pay is not only increased in proportion to the cost of living, but it is really greater."

The earliest political use that this lexicographer independently spotted is in the 1912 *Republican Campaign Textbook*, where the subject is addressed as "The Advance in the Cost of Living." The Taft Administration was under attack by Democrats on the tariff issue, and the Republican National Committee defended itself in this tough-all-over way:

> The increasing cost in recent years of the common necessaries and comforts of life has presented a serious problem to the masses of the people ... The most striking feature of the situation, however, is that the advance is not confined to this country or to the countries having protective tariffs, but is world wide, and that in every country the same kind of an agitation is going on, with more or less effort to lay the blame upon "the party in power" ...

Republicans, split by Teddy Roosevelt's "Bull Moose" party, lost in 1912 to the Democrat Woodrow Wilson.

By 1920, after eight Democratic years, the Republican textbook added an adjective and made the issue its own, using "The High Cost of Living" as its chapter heading: "To the plain citizen of the United States the term 'High Cost of Living' has a clear and definite meaning. It sums up the hardship and suffering that the American people have borne during the past five years, because of the great rise in the prices of the goods and of the services upon which their income is ordinarily spent." The Republicans had the reason: "The prime cause of the 'High Cost of Living' has been, first and foremost, a fifty percent depreciation of the purchasing power of the dollar, due to a gross expansion of our currency and credit." The party also blamed "reduced production, burdensome taxation, wage advances and the increased demand for goods."

Three generations later the charge and phrase are in current use. The word INFLATION is used when the consumer price index is approaching DOUBLE DIGIT proportions, and the plainer *high cost of living* (no longer capitalized)—with its vague suggestion that the cost can be brought down—is used to express general dissatisfaction when inflation is not so high.

higher law An appeal to moral or spiritual authority to excuse a principled refusal to obey the laws of man.

This is an ABOLITIONIST phrase, probably used first by William Ellery Channing in 1842: "On this point the Constitution, and a still higher law, that of nature and God, speak the same language; and we must insist that these high authorities shall be revered." Senator Daniel Webster agreed. The phrase was taken up by William Seward, of New York, in an antislavery speech in the Senate in 1850: "I know that there are laws of various kinds, which regulate the conduct of men ... But there is a higher law than the Constitution, which regulates our authority over the domain."

Democrats and Whigs (including Abraham Lincoln) thought Seward had gone too far; later this phrase, along with Seward's 1858 characterization of the slavery issue as "an irrepressible conflict," led to Seward's defeat and Lincoln's victory at the Republican convention of 1860.

The idea of a *higher law* has usually conflicted with the RULE OF LAW and a GOVERNMENT OF LAWS, NOT OF MEN. It has been used by dissenters from established laws as justification for CIVIL DISOBEDIENCE. In 1968 *The National Observer* wrote: "America must renounce the popular and poisonous philosophies that glorify anarchy as a heroic response to a 'higher law.'"

The phrase, however, has an idealistic or moralistic ring, and is not usually considered anarchic, or—as used against Seward—anticonstitutional.

highest authority See AUTHORITATIVE SOURCES; BACKGROUNDER.

highest note in the scale theory See OVEREXPOSURE.

high muckey-mucks See MUCKEY-MUCKS.

high road ... low road Rational argument versus emotional appeal; appealing to the intellect versus going for the jugular; Marquess of Queensberry rules versus no-holds-barred.

The phrase became popular in the presidential campaign of 1948, when Republican Thomas E. Dewey selected "the high road" and let voters draw their own conclusions as to what road President Harry Truman was trudging. When Truman compared Dewey's mustache to Adolf Hitler's, Dewey wired Republican state chairmen to see if they thought he should take off the gloves and reply in kind (in earlier campaigns, Dewey had gained a reputation as a slashing speaker). "They all agreed," said GOP speechwriter John Franklin Carter, "that the proper thing for Dewey to do was to ignore Truman's personal attack and continue along the high road to the White House."

Politicians do not consider a "low road" charge the worst kind of insult. In 1958's off-year elections, Eisenhower aide Sherman Adams rehashed charges of Democratic catastrophes such as losing our atomic secrets, losing China to the Communists, and described the Korean War as the one "they couldn't end." In Adams' memoirs, he admits: "I was loudly (and not quite inaccurately) accused of 'taking the low road' while the President was keeping his campaign oratory on a high and dignified level."

The low road, however, is not always smart politics. In the Democratic primary contest for Massachusetts senator in 1962 between Attorney General Edward McCormack and Ted Kennedy, McCormack, trailing, decided to go on the attack against Kennedy in a televised debate. The political editor of *The Boston Herald* wrote: "[McCormack's] attack on Kennedy, and the latter's refusal to be drawn into an Army base brawl, apparently created unfavorable reaction to the Attorney General among many viewers, especially women.... Kennedy took the high road, and, although he was battered and mauled by McCormack,

probably won a strategic victory with the huge TV audience."

Ted Kennedy was following John F. Kennedy's strategy at the 1960 Democratic convention, when Lyndon Johnson baited him in a debate before a joint caucus of the Texas and Massachusetts delegations. *Washington Post* publisher Philip Graham urged Johnson to present himself as a man of wide experience in defense and foreign affairs and avoid the kind of comments about Kennedy's health and his father's alleged pro-Nazi record that Johnson supporters were spreading. Pro-Kennedy historian Arthur Schlesinger, Jr., wrote later: "During the debate Johnson opened with Graham's 'high road' but went on to attempt the personal thrusts which Kennedy parried with such ease and mastery."

Derivation: a *high road*, or *high way*, is the easy way in English usage. In London today the *high streets* are the main traffic arteries. However, the takers of low roads can sometimes make better time, as the balladeer in "Loch Lomond" indicates: "O ye'll take the high road and I'll take the low road and I'll be in Scotland afore ye ..."

Hill, the Capitol Hill, location of the House and Senate; familiar term for the legislative branch of U.S. government, as *White House* is for the executive branch.

"On the Hill" is frequently used in roundups of news from Washington, D.C.; White House aides for legislative liaison take messages "up to the Hill." (The judiciary has a similar metaphor, with indictments being handed "up"—to the bench—and decisions handed "down"—from the bench. And Israelis say, "I'm going up to Jerusalem," which sits on high land.)

The Hill is both real and figurative. The base of the Capitol sits 88 feet above sea level, as compared with the White House's 55 feet, with lower areas in between. Before November 21, 1800, when Congress moved from Philadelphia and held its first session in the new Capitol, the eminence was known as Jenkins Hill, presumably from Thomas Jenkins, who rented the land from one Daniel Carroll, who owned it. Both George Washington and Pierre L'Enfant, who laid out the city of Washington, referred to Jenkins Hill in letters. It is by no means the tallest hill in Washington—the hill on which the National Cathedral stands is over 300 feet—but it is the one that dominates the scene.

When Martin Tolchin, veteran Washington correspondent of *The New York Times*, was approached by the publisher Jerry Finkelstein about starting a biweekly newspaper directed at an audience centered on news of the House and Senate and their staffs—to compete with the successful *Roll Call*—he met at Loeb's delicatessen in D.C. with the author and posed the question of what to name the new enterprise. When asked where the basic readership would be, Tolchin replied "the Hill"; thus was the newspaper named.

Although *the Hill* implies the seat of power, an unrelated metaphor, *over the hill*, implies the diminution of power, as even legislators become as *old as the hills*.

historic compromise A promise of resolving a longstanding and sometimes bloody disagreement.

In the early '70s, as the Italian Communist party grew in voting strength in local elections, the idea was broached that a coalition might be possible with the long-ruling rightist party, the Christian Democrats. Arrigo Levi, editor of Italy's *La Stampa*, replied to the author's query with this derivation of the phrase:

As to "historic compromise": this was coined by [Enrico] Berlinguer himself, in the famous articles which appeared in the pci PCI's [Italian Communist Party] weekly *Rinascita* in 1973...after the end of [Chilean President Salvatore] Allende, as a comment on the reasons that had led to his fall. Fundamentally, Berlinguer criticized Allende's policy of trying to split Chilean Christian Democracy, stated that the PCI's policy in Italy was to try and achieve a "historical compromise" with the whole of Democrazia Cristiana, in order to prevent the kind of reaction which happened in Chile.

See EUROCOMMUNISM.

Uses of the phrase in other contexts are frequent. At a Capitol Hill hearing on the Middle East: "Perhaps most encouraging for the PEACE PROCESS is the evidence that many Israelis and many Arabs are tired of the conflict and are finally ready for a *historic compromise*." That was in 1993, and the phrase has been used about this often bloody dispute ever since. Another compromise billed as *historic* has been a proposal for an autonomous Kurdistan within a unitary Iraq. Yet another may turn out to be historic: U.S. congressman Richard Neal, long interested in resolving the Northern Ireland "troubles," said in 2007 "I would like to congratulate Rev. Ian Paisley and Gerry Adams...the historic compromise they reached took courage and vision."

hit job See CHARACTER ASSASSIN.

hit list Persons or projects targeted for removal.

In underworld lingo, a *hit* is a murder and a *hit man* a hired assassin. On the analogy of an older phrase, *shit list*, it followed that a *hit list* was a group of individuals to be exterminated.

In politics, the phrase is usually used at a time of transition between administrations, when the new "Ins" are avidly examining a publication called "the Plum Book" and other rosters to see what appointments (political PLUMS) are available for replacement with the FAITHFUL. If those who are selected for removal can claim any civil service protection, they charge that they have been placed on an Administration *hit list*, giving a sinister connotation to old-fashioned PATRONAGE.

Postmaster General James A. Farley was FDR's major dispenser of federal largesse. According to Jean Edward Smith's 2007 biography of Roosevelt, "Farley had a 'white list' of Democrats who had consistently supported the president and a 'sinners' roll' of party members who had deserted on crucial roll calls. The constituents of those on the 'sinners' roll could expect slim pickings."

The opposite of a *hit list* for projects is a *must list*, a term for top-priority legislation. *New York Times* reporter Steven Weisman, then assigned to Albany, wrote in 1976: "In the Capitol, where one man's 'must' is another man's 'maybe,' all the leaders circulate their 'must lists' among themselves to make sure that the bills that 'must' be passed are, in fact, passed. Lists are so popular in Albany that some aides keep lists of their lists." (See ENEMIES LIST.)

The nonmurderous, but besmearing, use of *hit* is growing. Carter Administration Attorney General Griffin Bell denounced a 1977 newspaper story about him as "nothing less than a 'hit job,'" thus being the first to marry *hit* to *hatchet job*, and the writer so accused reportedly "resented [the story] being characterized, even without naming her, as a 'hit job.'"

The *list* end of the collocation is alive and hitting. In 2007, a new near-daily publication about Capitol Hill titled *The Politico* front-paged an article by Carrie Budoff about "parties growing increasingly bold in their hunt for prey." It featured plans of the new majority party to put money and a strong candidate up against the Senate Minority Leader Mitch McConnell (R-Ky.), whose current 6-year term ended in 2008. The headline: "Democratic Activists Put McConnell on Hit List."

In politics, a list is usually something to avoid being on. A *blacklist* evokes the McCarthy era; an ENEMIES LIST created a furor during the Watergate investigation; and a *hit list* makes an officeholder a target for unseating. (On the other hand, a *short list* is a roster of those being most actively considered for a top appointment, and *Emily's List* is a women's political fundraising organization.)

hizzoner A sobriquet bestowed on all mayors by writers with an instinct for the jocular.

"Hizzoner the Mayor," New York dialect for *His Honor the Mayor*, was a frequent heralding sound in that city during the incumbency of Fiorello H. La Guardia. Since "the Little Flower" was not stuffy, the playful derogation of the honorific title seemed in place, and has become a part of big-city mayoralties, much as "Veep" loosely attached itself to the vice presidency.

A refinement was introduced when Mayor Richard Daley of Chicago became known as "Hizzoner duh Mare." *Washingtonian* magazine resurrected the Daley usage in 1993: "'Vote early, vote often.' The most famous axiom of machine politics has already been encoded in your Motor Voter bill, which will extend a uniquely Chicago privilege to all corners of America. Hizzoner would be proud."

Time magazine reported that the West Virginia town of Coalton was having trouble finding a citizen to serve as mayor because the salary was only $100 a year. The headline: "It's No Honor to Be Hizzoner."

Hobson's choice A take-it-or-leave it proposition; in politics a situation in which you vote for one candidate or do not vote at all.

English poet Thomas Ward wrote in 1630: "Where to elect there is but one / 'Tis Hobson's choice,—take that or none."

Sir Richard Steele, in *The Spectator* No. 509, explained the derivation:

> Mr. Tobias Hobson [Thomas Hobson, 1544–1631] from whom we have the expression … was a carrier … the first in the Island who let out hackney-horses. He lived in Cambridge, and observing that the scholars rid hard, his manner was to keep a large stable of horses, with boots, bridles, and whips. … When a man came for a horse, he was led into the stable, where there was great choice, but he obliged him to take the horse which stood next to the stable-door; so that every customer was alike well served according to his chance, and every horse ridden with the same justice. From whence it became a proverb, when what ought to be your election was forced upon you, to say Hobson's Choice.

In *The Careful Writer*, Theodore Bernstein pointed out that it is incorrect to use the phrase as if it meant the kind of choice involved in a dilemma, as in this sentence: "But how long, in Berlin, must we rely on this cruel Hobson's choice between honoring pledges and eviscerating the world?" The correct use was in this 1910 New Jersey campaign address by Woodrow Wilson, which marked an early use of NEW DEAL as well: "If it is reorganization, a new deal and a change you are seeking, it is Hobson's choice. I am sorry for you, but it is really vote for me or not vote at all."

A political synonym is CLOTHESPIN VOTE, in which the voter puts a metaphorical clothespin on his nose and votes for a candidate he does not like as the lesser of two evils.

hold still ... go along The grudging willingness of a politician to accept publicly, or not to fight privately, a proposed project.

Hold still indicates a greater degree of personal objection and an unwillingness to offer public support; *go along* in current usage means the political leader will remain passive and indicate his support when asked. For example, "We can't get him to go along, but he'll hold still—he'll have to BITE THE BULLET, but he won't BOLT."

When Alice Roosevelt Longworth expressed doubts to George Harvey about the selection of Warren Harding as a candidate for president, Harvey explained that Harding was best because he would "go along." See SMOKE-FILLED ROOM.

In *Profiles in Courage* John F. Kennedy (and Ted Sorensen) wrote: "The question is how we will compromise and with whom. For it is easy to seize upon unnecessary concessions, not as means of legitimately resolving conflicts but as methods of 'going along.'"

An old saying in the U.S. Congress is: "The way to get along is to go along." In 1958 Arthur Krock wrote a bit of doggerel called "Wisdom of a House Freshman" that sums up the point:

I love Speaker Rayburn,
His heart is so warm,
And if I obey him
He'll do me no harm.
So I shan't sass the Speaker
One least little bitty
And then I'll wind up
On a major committee.

Degrees of *going along* range from "willingly" to "grudgingly" to "kicking and screaming." (The last cannot be used with *hold still*.)

hold the line Government efforts to restrain the economy; anti-inflation moves.

Four months after he became president, Harry Truman issued an Executive Order gradually relaxing controls over prices, wages, and production as the wartime economy made its transition to peace. This became known as the "hold-the-line order."

"Holding the line against inflation" remains a cliché, taken from a football metaphor ("Hold that line!"), which in turn comes from a military expression (a line of soldiers trying to prevent an enemy breakthrough). Other inflation bromides include *inflationary spiral* and *runaway inflation* that *erodes the purchasing power of your dollars* and hurts most *those on fixed incomes*. See INFLATION; DOUBLE DIGIT.

Columnist Art Buchwald quoted a mythical professor of the "Grim Economic Institute" as predicting for 1968: "An inflationary spiral followed by a wage and price merry-go-round which will eventually lead to a roller coaster ride ending on a Ferris wheel cycle of high interest rates."

holier than thou See DO-GOODER; RELIGIOUS METAPHORS.

Holocaust, the The systematic murder of six million Jews during the Nazi regime in Germany.

Toward the end of World War II, the slaughter of the Jews spawned a new word, *genocide*, the 1944 coinage of U.S. scholar Raphael Lemkin. The United Nations in 1948 passed a Convention on the Prevention and Punishment of the Crime of Genocide.

Somehow, *genocide* struck many as too clinical a description of what had happened; the similar *homicide* is a bureaucratic word for "murder." *Holocaust* first appeared in English around 1250, in a biblical song recounting the story of Abraham's willingness to sacrifice his son, Isaac, as a burnt offering to God.

In his 1856 account of the mass executions of Protestants in the Netherlands by the Duke of Alva in 1567, John Lothrop Motley, in Volume II of *The Rise of the Dutch*

Republic, wrote that while the Duke's secretary "declined to dip his own fingers in the innocent blood which was about to flow in torrents, he did not object to officiate at the initiatory preliminaries of the great Netherland holocaust."

In modern times, *holocaust* appeared on page 157 of Chapter XIII, titled "The League of Nations," in *The Aftermath*, a sequel to *The World Crisis*, by Winston S. Churchill, published in March 1929: "As for Turkish atrocities: marching till they dropped dead the greater part of the garrison at Kut; massacring uncounted thousands of helpless Armenians, men, women, and children together, whole districts blotted out in one administrative *holocaust*—these were beyond human redress." To this day, the Turkish government takes great umbrage at anyone using *holocaust* to describe the century-old suppression of Armenians, and cracks down on Turkish citizens who write about it.

The *OED* has three citations of the use of the word in connection with the Nazi war crimes in 1942, 1943, and 1945, but none before an influential audience at a major news center. However, on January 9, 1946—eight months after V-E Day, five months before World War II's end—in Washington, D.C., the attorney (and former FDR adviser, see HAPPY WARRIOR) Joseph Proskauer spoke to the Anglo-American Committee of Inquiry on Palestine on behalf of the American Jewish Committee. "No one can forget," he said, "that there remain in Germany and Austria today the scattered remnants of a people who were once upstanding, loyal citizens of their countries and who were stricken down not in the thousands but in the millions. There has been no such *holocaust* since our forefathers wept by the waters of Babylon ..." The text was provided to the author by Proskauer's family.

In 1965 Alexander Donat published a book titled *The Holocaust Kingdom* about the Warsaw ghetto, and two years later Norman Cohn, in *Warrant for Genocide*, wrote that "by the end of 1944 the holocaust was nearing its conclusion." In 1968 the Manchester *Guardian* reported: "There is now within modern history a compartment of 'holocaust studies'—dealing with the wholesale destruction by the Nazis of European Jewry."

Holocaust is rooted in the Greek *holokaustos*, "burnt whole"; a holocaust is a burnt offering, extended to an all-consuming conflagration. In 1977, when Egyptian President Anwar el-Sadat became the first Arab chief of state to visit Israel, Prime Minister Menachem Begin conducted him to the mausoleum of Yad Vashem, the shrine to the six million Jews who died in what—since only the mid-sixties—has come to be known widely as the *Holocaust*. When capitalized, the word refers specifically to mass murder by the Nazis, often including Gypsies and homosexuals.

The word has been extended to encompass more than the mass murder of Jews. From casualties in our Civil War (reportedly described then as "a holocaust of lives") to the genocide inflicted by the Khmer Rouge in Cambodia, the term has not been limited to any single group. Jews seeking a term for their twentieth-century tragedy have used *shoah*, the Hebrew word for "catastrophe." Clause Lanzmann entitled his 1985 documentary *Shoah*, a nine-hour history of the killing. In the mid-sixties a group of militant U.S. Jews formed the Jewish Defense League to demonstrate against those they considered anti-Semites. Though most established Jewish organizations disavowed its sometimes violent activity, they could not dispute its slogan, based on the Holocaust: "Never Again."

When the Holocaust Memorial opened in Washington, D.C., in 1993, Bosnians were being subjected to ETHNIC CLEANSING by Serbs; speakers recalled the "Never Again" pledge, and some sought to embarrass President Clinton for allowing genocide to happen again.

Neo-Nazi "skinheads" and assorted anti-Semitic groups and gangs have claimed since the end of World War II that the incontrovertible evidence of Hitlerite war criminality was manufactured or exaggerated. In 1984, the phrase *Holocaust denial* was first used.

See FINAL SOLUTION.

homeland Word used by a group seeking an independent state to assert a moral or historic claim to the territory.

This incendiary, evocative term was first used in a political context by Theodor Herzl, at the First Zionist Congress in Basel, Switzerland, in 1897. The Basel Declaration called for a Jewish homeland: the German word used was *Heimstatte*, which translates more as "homestead" than the more common *Heimatland*, or "homeland." In 1917, in an effort to marshal Jewish support for the Allies in World War I, British Prime Minister Arthur Balfour embraced the idea in a communication to the second Baron Rothschild.

The Balfour Declaration came close to using the word: "His Majesty's Government view with favor the establishment in Palestine of a national home for the Jewish people...nothing shall be done which may prejudice the civil and religious rights of existing non-Jewish communities in Palestine ..." Formally approved at Versailles in 1919, Balfour's pledge of a "national home" became the basis of the League of Nations Mandate for Palestine. After World War II, a combination of guilt felt by the Allied powers at their inability to stop the murder of six million Jews in Europe (see HOLOCAUST), gratitude for Jewish efforts in North Africa in the face of some Arab support of the Axis powers, and a fierce determination by Jews for *eretz Israel* led to the U.N. resolution creating a state out of the Jewish "homeland."

When Arabs on Israel's borders failed, after four wars, to conquer the new nation, they made demands for the "civil and religious rights" mentioned in the Balfour Declaration. Although the Palestine Liberation Organization interpreted those rights as a return of Israel to Arab rule, other Arabs—and their U.N. supporters—saw "the legitimate rights of the Palestinian people" as meaning a separate state in the West Bank of the Jordan River and in the Gaza Strip. This "moderate" demand took the form, in the mid-'70s, of a call by third parties for a "homeland" for the Palestinian refugees. Israelis pointed out that the Jewish state had absorbed all Jewish refugees from Arab states, while Arab states had refused to absorb the Palestinians, using the festering camps as a weapon against Israel. Jewish leaders took umbrage at the use of "homeland"—their word—against them.

Israel's supporters were dismayed when, on March 21, 1977, President Carter told a Clinton, Mass., audience: "There has to be a homeland provided for the Palestinian refugees who have suffered for many, many years." Later he denied that "homeland" meant a separate state, as most people construed it; the President said he preferred an "entity," of ambiguous nature, tied to Jordan.

Not until 2001 did a U.S. president—George W. Bush, a strong and valued supporter of Israel—declare U.S. policy to call for the creation of an independent state for Palestinians, a step beyond the amorphous *homeland*.

Another example of the power of the word (which stirs feelings akin to, though not as aggressive as, LEBENSRAUM) was in its appropriation in the early '70s by the white leadership of the Union of South Africa. Under the policy of apartheid—racial separation—some tribal Bantustans, occupied by blacks, were made politically independent, though they remained economically dependent upon South Africa. Columnist William Raspberry wrote in 1978: "They will play at 'reform'—removing racial barriers at only the country's most expensive hotels, for instance—because they value world opinion. For the same reason, they will put new names on old policies—'homelands' instead of 'Bantustans' or 'native reserves.'"

When the Office (later Department) of Homeland Security was created in the months following the 9/11/2001 attacks—first on the U.S. continental homeland—the names considered were *domestic security* and *internal security*. Evidently *homeland* was considered less bureaucratic—closer to home.

See HEARTLAND.

home rule The demand that a state government grant more autonomy and local self-government to cities and counties.

"In campaign season," wrote the *New York Sun* in 1905, "politicians of all stripes and kinds howl for 'Home Rule!' Then they flood to Albany and ask the Legislature to tinker up what they consider imperfect in the city government."

Injection of the phrase into big-city politics was probably begun by Tom Loftin Johnson in his campaigns for mayor of Cleveland, Ohio, in the early 1900s. The full slogan of the Democratic ticket was: "Home Rule; Three Cent Fare; and Just Taxation."

In Jersey City, N.J., opponents of Frank "I AM THE LAW" Hague in 1939 elected five anti-Hague commissioners in Bayonne, N.J., on the slogan "Home Rule—Not Hague Rule."

The argument for home rule has always been, "the best government is that government closest to the people." The argument against it is that many local political figures are hesitant to take locally unpopular but necessary steps in taxation, school construction, etc. The argument reaches its highest pitch when a major city in a state is controlled by one party and the state government by another.

Origin of the phrase is English, about 1860, in connection with agitation for self-government in Ireland. Benjamin Disraeli, speaking in Manchester in 1872, suggested that with international troubles brewing, England might be wise to have a loyal Ireland to call upon: "Our connection with Ireland will then be brought painfully to our consciousness, and I should not be at all surprised if the visor of Home Rule should fall off some day, and you beheld a very different countenance." The Home Rule movement, led by Sinn Féin, ultimately founded the Irish Free State; Northern Ireland remained a part of Great Britain, operating under a Home Rule Act. Modern descendants of the Home Rule movement made a breakthrough toward a peaceful settlement of power sharing and devolution disputes in 2007. See DEVOLUTION.

honcho As a noun, the one in charge; as a verb, to follow through.

This Japanese word for "squad leader" was popularized in the White House in the late '60s by Nixon staffers from Califor-nia and soon became part of political and business mediaspeak. It began as a noun—"who's the honcho on this project?"—and soon acquired a verb usage: "Honcho this and don't let it get lost in the bureaucracy."

When Marcus Brauchli was appointed Editor of *The Wall Street Journal* in 2007, the *New York Press* headlined "Familiar Face Is New Head Honcho at WSJ."

honest graft Money made as a result of political power, without doing anything illegal—no longer considered honest.

New York newspaperman William Riordon took down and reshaped the thoughts of Tammany leader George Washington Plunkitt as he held court on his favorite rostrum, the New York County Court House bootblack stand, in 1905:

> Everybody is talkin' these days about Tammany men growin' rich on graft, but nobody thinks of drawin' the distinction between honest graft and dishonest graft. There's all the difference in the world between the two.
>
> I might sum up the whole thing by sayin': "I seen my opportunities and took 'em." …
>
> I'll tell you of one case. They were goin' to fix up a big park, no matter where. I got on to it, and went lookin' about for land in that neighborhood.
>
> I could get nothin' at a bargain but a big piece of swamp, but I took it fast enough and held on to it. What turned out was just what I counted on. They couldn't make the park complete without Plunkitt's swamp, and they had to pay a good price for it. Anything dishonest in that?

Times have changed, and profitable action taken based on inside information is no longer considered "honest." Such gains by a politician or any member of his family are now considered ill-gotten; bribery is said to be permissible only to the extent of "something that can be eaten or smoked in a single day." That is stretching a point.

Today's "honest graft" is more payoff postponed: many government officials, when they retire, take lucrative jobs with private industry. Admirals who have steered government cargo to certain steamship lines, planning commissioners who have pressed certain zoning matters, find themselves recompensed in a way that arouses little or no criticism. In the late '70s this practice was derided in the media as the "revolving door," and laws were passed requiring a decent interval between regulating an industry and taking a lucrative job in it, curbing one modern version of Plunkitt's technique.

The term, however, continues to be used. *National Journal* commented in 1990 on Congress and campaign contributions: "The question is whether the system of 'honest graft' ... is gridlocking legislation and squeezing the competition out of Congressional elections." In 2006, ethicists zeroed in on lavish entertaining by lobbyists of mainly Republican congressional figures and staff, leading to jail terms when a quid pro quo was proven. See BOODLE; GRAFT.

honeymoon period The short time after first taking office during which a public official is not set upon by the press.

"Kingdoms have their honeymoon," wrote Thomas Fuller in 1655, "when new Princes are married unto them." The political use is among the first *OED* citations of the word.

"The honeymoon is over." This darkly declarative sentence is heard as election elation turns to fresh targeting and returning disenchantment. During the honeymoon, news generated by an administration on any level of government is primarily that of appointments, announcements of plans, often a quick vacation that the public considers well deserved. The opposition cannot yet carp without appearing to be sore losers; the media have little to criticize, and many reporters are even willing to give the new man the benefit of the doubt. In historian Charles Beard's phrase, a "golden glow" emanates from the press; the cartoonist Herblock, who had always drawn Richard Nixon with a sinister "five o'clock shadow," announced that he had given the new president a shave.

"Every newly elected Governor," wrote Adlai Stevenson's biographer, Kenneth S. Davis, "has his 'honeymoon' period with the press of the State. Stevenson's [in Illinois] was unusually ecstatic and unusually prolonged." On the other hand, California Governor Ronald Reagan took some controversial steps regarding the University of California soon after assuming office in 1967 and was promptly blasted by many newspapers. After four months in office, he said: "If this has been a honeymoon, then I've been sleeping alone."

The shortest honeymoon on record for any President was recounted by columnist Murray Kempton in the *New York Post* in December 1977. Colonel Robert McCormick, late publisher of the *Chicago Tribune*, was watching the news tickers in his office in March of 1929 as President Herbert Hoover's inaugural address was being dispatched. After the fourth paragraph he fired his response to his Washington bureau: "This man won't do. McCormick."

The word refers, of course, to the vacation after a marriage and before settling down, and is derived from the all-too-practical thought that the *honeymoon*, or full moon, begins to wane from the moment it is full.

hoopla Devices and techniques to stimulate enthusiasm at rallies when crowds are turned off by long speeches (see MEGO).

Hoo is the sound of excitement and gaiety. *Hooray* and *Hoohah!*, along with *Whoopee* and *Whoop-de-do*, all probably derive from the excited squeals of children.

In politics, hoopla is a necessary ingredient to campaigns to give them bounce, youthfulness, and a sense of fun. At the opening of Rockefeller headquarters at the New York Hilton in the 1966 campaign for governor, the publicist Gilbert Robinson was in charge of attracting and whipping up a crowd; discussing budget with the Rockefeller manager, he pointed out that an opening rally required balloons, buttons, a sound truck with bunting, and hats and sashes for the "Rockyettes." Multicolored confetti, he explained, cost 10 cents a package, but it was cheaper if you bought it by the pound, at 50 cents per pound.

"I can't give you a budget," Robinson explained, "until I know how big a rally you want."

"Figure a thousand people," the office manager said.

"You want a lot of hoopla?"

The man in charge of the budget took out a requisition slip and calculated rapidly. "Give me fifty pounds of hoopla."

See BALLYHOO; BANDWAGON.

horse-and-buggy Not merely out-of-date, but hopelessly old-fashioned.

The phrase became political parlance when Franklin Roosevelt denounced the Supreme Court decision in 1935 striking down the National Recovery Act (see NINE OLD MEN). FDR called the decision "horse-and-buggy law."

A generation later, Rev. Martin Luther King, Jr., used the metaphor in his letter from a Birmingham, Alabama, jail: "The nations of Asia and Africa are moving with jetlike speed toward the goal of political independence, and we still creep at horse-and-buggy pace toward the gaining of a cup of coffee at a lunch counter."

horse-trading Hard political bargaining to a conclusion of a deal.

Horse-trading, with its no-nonsense connotation, implies a more naked display of power than *bargaining* or *negotiating*, with a greater intent to close the deal. A good example of the technique was outlined by William V. Reichel, Republican national committeeman from California, to the California delegation committed to Earl Warren in 1944: "We have fifty convention delegates and we're going to get something. At the convention, our votes will get us a Western cabinet member, a Western Supreme Court Justice, and a Western man on every high policy-making body in the government. That's what Warren will be bargaining for. We'll get them or they won't get our votes." As it happened, Warren wound up the vice presidential nominee on the Dewey ticket, but its loss to Democrats Truman and Barkley meant that the horse-trading was all for naught.

In a 2007 article on the 1787 Constitutional Convention, Christine Gibson wrote on AmericanHeritage.com that "The delegates' debates, after-hours vote-scrounging and political horse-trading found compromises between immiscible interests."

(*Immiscible* is a chemical term meaning "unable to be mixed," like oil and water.)

hot button Word or issue that ignites anger, fear, enthusiasm, or other passionate response.

The noun phrase is often hyphenated and used adjectivally in *hot-button issue*. Such an issue, involving values or morals, lifts an audience out of its seats in protest or approval.

Perhaps related to *panic button*, which led to *finger on the button, hot button* began as a marketing term. Walter Kiechel III wrote in a September 1978 issue of *Fortune*: "The marketers are searching for what they call 'consumer hot buttons'—needs to be satisfied, desires to be slaked—and the means to push those buttons."

Real-estate brokers picked up the term for fine detailing in home sales; saunas or gold-plated fixtures are examples of *hot buttons* to help close a deal. Computer users have *hot buttons* that can split a screen into two windows with a single keystroke, allowing various sets of data to be seen simultaneously.

Since 1981, the collocation has been a staple of political jargon. John L. Stevens, then director of the Republican Governors Association, told *The Washington Post* in 1981, "There are a whole lot of hot buttons waiting to be pushed; we're still trying to find out what those buttons are."

For the following generation, politics became the primary area concerned with incendiary triggers. *Newsweek* wrote during the 1988 campaign: "What's a hot button? It's something a candidate says to instantly show that his values are the voters' values." The magazine listed resistance to abortion rights and gun control as Republican hot buttons, and reforming (or tampering with) Social Security among those of the Democrats.

In the 1992 campaign for the Democratic Presidential nomination, Edmund G. "Jerry" Brown Jr. was asked if his call to cut foreign aid included a reduction in aid to Israel. The former California Governor replied evasively: "You know, that Israel thing is a hot-button issue."

"After years in the political wilderness," ABC News reported in April of 2007, "Democrats are wary of engaging in hot-button social issues such as the three G's—guns, God and gays."

For earlier versions of *hot-button issue*, see SWITCHER ISSUE and STIR UP THE ANIMALS; for a later version, see WEDGE ISSUE.

hot line Direct teletype link between world leaders, designed to prevent "accidental war."

The idea for a direct communications link between the heads of government in Washington and Moscow was proposed by the journalist Jess Gorkin, editor of the Sunday supplement *Parade*, in 1960. He told the author he got the idea from the Strategic Air Command's "red telephone" system; in his October 30, 1960, issue, Gorkin referred to a "hot line" that provided the SAC controller with "instant contact with 70 bases in ten countries on four continents."

President John F. Kennedy gave Gorkin credit for the idea: "It is heartening to me that the Soviet Government has agreed in principle to the United States suggestion for a 'hot line' between our two countries. I remember when you first brought this new and imaginative idea to my attention back in 1960 ... your advocacy of faster communications between the United States and the Soviet Union was sharply underlined during the Cuban crisis ..."

Jack Raymond, in *Power at the Pentagon*, wrote: "The proposal was made by the United States in the light of the Cuba experience, during which, at times, the President and his aides were uncertain whether the Soviet leaders fully understood the import of steps that could lead to nuclear war." After negotiations in Geneva, the "hot line" was set up in September 1963.

The first non-test use of the first hot line (other lines between different capitals followed the White House-to-Kremlin line) was in the Arab-Israeli war in 1967. Responding to a question from Alexei Kosygin, President Johnson told the Soviet Premier Kosygin on the new direct teletype link that an American ship had been attacked in the Mediterranean and planes from the U.S. Sixth Fleet were flying to its aid; this made sure that the Soviets did not misinterpret the scrambling of American planes as a threat to them.

Since then, hotlines have proliferated, usually phone numbers like 911 to call police or fire departments in emergencies (the number spoken as "nine-one-one" rather than "nine-eleven" to avoid confusion with the 9/11 terrorist attacks). Although the cell telephone has made communication between foreign capitals instantaneous, China—attached to strategic doctrine that calls for surprise—has resisted any official communications link with the U.S. similar to the Washington-Moscow "hot line."

Hottentots, milk for Attack on U.S. foreign aid to underdeveloped (HAVE-NOT) nations.

Harry Truman's Vice President, Henry Wallace, made his "century of the common man" speech in 1942 (see COMMON MAN, CENTURY OF THE), disputing the point of view of the Luce publications—*Time, Life* and *Fortune*—that the coming hundred years would be "the American Century." Wallace had been raising the hackles of conservatives with his demand for full employment ("60 million jobs") and pressing forward on New Deal legislation that had been eclipsed by the war effort. During his speech, Wallace said that he had told the wife of the Soviet ambassador, half in fun and half seriously: "The object of this war is to make sure that everybody in the world has the privilege of drinking a quart of milk a day."

The statement was used as a weapon against the liberal Wallace, often accused of being a FELLOW TRAVELER of the Communists. The Hottentots, a nomadic southwest African tribe with a catchy name (now considered offensive and usually replaced by Khoikhoi), had been used as a symbol of an undeveloped people even before Lord Salisbury's "Hottentot Speech" in Parliament in 1886 opposing Irish HOME RULE. Dutch explorers named the African tribe *Hottentot*, according to a 1670 Dutch lexicographer, because of the "clucking speech" of the aborigines. Edgar Allan Poe, in 1840, had used the tribal name as typical of preposterous-sounding words: "The Hottentots and Kickapoos are very well in their way. The Yankees alone are preposterous." Wallace's statement was stretched by conservatives into a policy of "milk for the Hottentots."

"Many of Wallace's progressive and well-meaning speeches," wrote Samuel Rosenman, counsel to FDR, "about improving the standards of living in backward areas of the world had been so unfortunately phrased that they were distorted by the isolationist press into a statement of readiness to embark on crackbrained and unrealistic projects of worldwide charity handouts."

The phrase remains a symbol of selfless aid, with a mocking connotation of hopelessly impractical idealism. Herman Kahn, listing typical U.S. foreign policy aims in 1962, chose four for discussion: "RULE OF LAW, JUST AND LASTING PEACE, FOUR FREEDOMS, and Milk for the Hottentots."

See THIRD WORLD.

house An ideological, business, or political entity or movement.

Like *covenant, house* is a Biblical word borrowed for political use. "All the house of Israel," "dwell in the House of the Lord," and reference to a church as a *House of Prayer* or *House of God* laid the groundwork for the metaphor.

Lincoln in 1858 took a quotation from Mark 3:25, "If a house be divided against itself, that house cannot stand," shortened it to "A house divided against itself cannot stand," and added, "I believe this government cannot endure permanently half slave and half free."

Houses of Parliament and *houses of Congress* refer more to the political bodies than to the buildings containing them. European business empires such as Rothschild and Krupp referred to themselves as *houses*, and a young American banker or broker still seeks a position in a "fine old Wall Street house."

In May 1937, a strike at the Republic Steel plant in Chicago erupted into violence in which thirty strikers were shot, ten of whom died. This "Memorial Day Massacre," low point of labor relations in the "sit-down strike" era of the thirties, brought a surprising remark from FDR: "A plague on both your houses." Later the President tried to explain his quotation from Shakespeare as applying only to extremists of both sides, but CIO president John L. Lewis, beginning with a Biblical allusion, turned Roosevelt's use of "house" into the familiar "House of Labor." Lewis, with bushy black eyebrows and a mellifluous voice, intoned over nationwide radio: "Labor, like Israel, has many sorrows. It ill behooves one who has supped at labor's table and who has been sheltered in labor's house to curse—with equal fervor and fine impartiality—both labor and its adversaries when they become locked in deadly embrace."

(The lexicographer wrote the foregoing paragraph in a large room of a historic building in Washington, D.C., that for many years was the office of John L. Lewis. It is now the library of the Dana Foundation and my current place of work. A famous photograph of the leader of the United Mine Workers emerging, covered with coal dust, from a visit to a mine disaster dominates the room; I can hear his Stentorian tones in my head right now.)

Woodrow Wilson used a variation on the housing theme when he referred to Warren G. Harding as a man with "a bungalow mind." When Barry Goldwater in 1960 urged his conservative followers to work within the Republican party, despite their dissatisfaction with the Rockefeller-Nixon COMPACT OF FIFTH AVENUE that ensured a more liberal platform, he told the G.O.P. convention: "This great Republican party is our historic house. This is our home." President Lyndon Johnson told a group of reporters during a 1964 stroll: "The Democratic party has been the House of Protest since it was born."

The shelter metaphor (price *ceilings, tariff walls, floor* fights, *walls* of separation, *parlor* pink, *fireside* chats) is used as often as the anatomical metaphor. See BODY POLITIC.

household word A satiric reference to a political figure's high or low "recognition factor."

Like RED HERRING, this was a phrase that gained fame when used by a reporter in a question and accepted and repeated by the man being interviewed.

Richard Nixon's choice of the reputedly centrist Maryland Governor Spiro T. Agnew to be his running mate came as a shock to newsmen covering the Republican convention in 1968. On August 8, just after Nixon's decision had been announced, the VP-to-be held a news conference at the Hilton Hotel in Miami Beach. Mike Wallace of CBS observed, "The name of Spiro Agnew is hardly a household political word across the nation." Agnew replied, "I would certainly agree with that, yes." Wallace went on to ask, "what political strength do you actually bring to the ticket?" The candidate answered, "I can't analyze any strength I bring, and I agree with you that the name of Spiro Agnew is not a household name. I certainly hope that it will become one within the next couple of months."

It did. Two years later, columnist James J. Kilpatrick used the now-famous phrase as a sobriquet for the Vice President: "The Household Word said some things about higher education, and especially about the folly of 'black quotas' that needed badly to be said."

In use, *household name* became transmuted to the more familiar *household word*. With Agnew's forced resignation in 1973 during an investigation into Maryland payoffs, use of the phrase diminished and is recalled now with irony or shame; on his leaving office to avoid prosecution, he popularized the Latin phrase *nolo contendere*, a plea of guilty without an admission of guilt.

human element Personal quirks or characteristics that must be taken into consideration in a political plan; one element over which detailed strategies have no control.

Airline accident reports occasionally give as a reason for a disaster "human error," often a euphemism for "the pilot dozed off." In political planning, on a tight schedule, time must be allotted for the human element: a trip to the restroom, or a short belt of gin, or a yen for Japanese food, or a quick phone call to an old friend in the city visited. Allowances must be made for the distressing fact that not all politicians act logically; a known grafter can upset his enemies' plans with an inexplicable burst of altruism or social responsibility. "Stuff happens," as Thomas Bowdler would put it; the celebrity supporter counted on for a crowd-pleasing introduction can get laryngitis.

When Arthur Schlesinger, Jr., at the 1960 Democratic convention, urged Robert Kennedy to move quickly to conciliate the disappointed Stevenson supporters, Kennedy replied, "Arthur, human nature requires that you allow us forty-eight hours. Adlai has given us a rough time over the last three days. In forty-eight hours, I will do anything you want, but right now I don't want to hear anything about the Stevensonians. You must allow for human nature."

At the same convention, a classic example of the human element was Robert Kennedy's comment regarding the confusion around the selection of Lyndon Johnson as the vice presidential nominee: "My God, this wouldn't have happened except that we were all too tired last night."

The human element enters into far less consequential political matters. Ambassador Richard C. Patterson, New York City's official greeter during the Robert Wagner administration, called his speechwriter late one night with a problem. He was to introduce South Korean President Syngman Rhee at a Waldorf-Astoria luncheon the next day; part of the introduction was to be a telegram from General Douglas MacArthur praising Rhee's "courage and his indomitable will."

"So you'll read the telegram," the speechwriter said, "and everybody will clap. What's the problem?"

"You're forgetting the human element," said Patterson. "Nine people out of ten will flub on the word 'indomitable'—including me. I can just hear myself saying 'indominitabubble' and everybody laughing and embarrassing the guest of honor. Go ahead—you try it."

"Easy," said the speechwriter, "Indominit-abubble."

"You see? Let's substitute another word. We can release the General's accurate text in written form."

The speechwriter thought a moment. "I have the word. You got a pencil? 'Indefatigable.'" Long silence as Patterson considered hiring a new speechwriter. Then we settled on "steadfast," and the human element in politics triumphed again.

human rights The idea that each person is born with the moral claim on some degree of political freedom which, by right, ought not to be denied by any government.

"Ignorance, neglect or contempt of human rights," read a declaration of the first National Assembly of France, "are the sole causes of public misfortunes and corruptions of government." The phrase in French was *droits de l'homme* ("the rights of man"), taken from the concept of "natural rights" espoused by English political philosopher John Locke in the seventeenth century.

Locke held that man, in a theoretical state of nature, was born free; after he mixed his labor with the common property of nature's abundance, he had property of his own. Man then traded part of his absolute freedom to government in return for protection of his person and his property "rights."

Locke's "natural rights" were also called "inherent" and "imprescriptible"; when Thomas Jefferson referred to them in the Declaration of Independence, they were "unalienable." When people were denied these rights by kings, Locke argued with some discretion, they could "appeal to Heaven"—a euphemism for revolution, since the cautiously couched theory struck at the root of the divine right of kings.

For nearly two centuries after the American and French revolutions, human rights were called "the rights of man." That was the title of Thomas Paine's powerful and best-selling book on the subject; in Herman Melville's *Billy Budd*, the name of the ship on which his moral tale took place was *The Rights of Man*.

In his 1967 book *Political Theory and the Rights of Man*, Professor D. D. Raphael, of the University of Glasgow, explained why the name was changed:

The concept of Human Rights, as they are called in the English text of the [U.N.] Universal Declaration of 1948, is of course a revival of the eighteenth-century concept of the Rights of Man. According to Eleanor Roosevelt, who was Chairman of the United Nations Commission on Human Rights, the old phrase was changed because of an interpretation given to it, at an early stage of international discussion, by a delegate from some benighted country. "I assume," he blandly remarked, "that when we speak of the rights of man, we mean what we say. My government, of course, could not agree to extend these rights to women." The French text of the Universal Declaration retains the traditional *droits de l'homme*, perhaps because the French ... are familiar with the dictum that, in the language of the law, "the male is presumed to embrace the female."

Mrs. Roosevelt was not the first to reject the apparent, and often real, discrimination in the phrase. Mary Wollstonecraft, one of the earliest feminists, had taken the side of the French radicals in the French Revolution and in 1791 was the first to publish a refutation of Edmund Burke's book sympathetic to the monarchy. She called her pamphlet *A Vindication of the Rights of Men*; however, when she learned to her dismay that her friend Thomas Paine was unconcerned about equal rights for the other half of the human race, in 1792 she wrote a subsequent book that made her both famous and bitterly resented among radicals in France and conservatives in England: *A Vindication of the Rights of Woman*. (She chose the word *woman*, not *women*, to draw a contrast with Paine's *Rights of Man*.)

In the U.S. throughout the 1950s and '60s, however, the movement for "rights" was directed at the *civil* rights of American blacks; having achieved their fundamental "human" right to freedom, blacks demanded the equality in voting, education and housing that belonged to them in civil law. The phrase "*human* rights" was, in those decades—as it was when Woodrow Wilson used it—treated as a ho-hum expression of idealism.

Although President Harry Truman had told the U.N. conference at San Francisco in 1945 that "the Charter is dedicated to the achievement and observance of human rights and freedoms," the Charter's Article 2, section 7, limits that dedication in this way: "Nothing contained in the present Charter shall authorize the United Nations to intervene in matters which are essentially within the domestic jurisdiction of any state ..."

Hubert Humphrey, in a DEFINING MOMENT of his career, used the term in his defense of civil rights, when he spoke to the Democratic National Convention of 1948: "There are those who say to you—we are rushing this issue of civil rights. I say we are 172 years late. There are those who say—this issue of civil rights is an infringement on states' rights. The time has arrived for the Democratic Party to get out of the shadow of states' rights and walk forthrightly into the bright sunshine of human rights." See DIXIECRAT.

Daniel Patrick Moynihan, one of the most outspoken of the American U.N. ambassadors, became most closely identified with the articulation of human rights in a world grown more statist. He challenged many other diplomats who had hitherto criticized the U.S. with impunity, while their own countries routinely denied citizens basic human rights.

At that time, the policies of Secretary of State Henry Kissinger, promoting DETENTE with its QUIET DIPLOMACY and pragmatic acceptance of the differences between societies, were coming under widening attack. By the beginning of the election primaries of 1976, "the human rights issue" began to flower, offering hardline conservatives and moralistic liberals common ground: the assertion of American values in a world made up of so many totalitarian states.

Among conservatives, Ronald Reagan picked up the issue in his nearly successful attempt to wrest the Republican nomination from President Gerald Ford. During that 1976 primary season, Democratic candidate Jimmy Carter also embraced the subject and the phrase in his desire to incorporate a different approach into his foreign policy statements.

In his inaugural address, President Carter put forward the idea in ringing terms: "Our commitment to human rights must be absolute." When the new president corresponded with Soviet dissenter Andrei Sakharov, this displeased the Soviet Union, which responded angrily in its propaganda, identifying the American human rights campaign as a part of the hawkish "anti-DÉTENTE faction of Senator Henry Jackson." At the urging of many foreign policy professionals, and to the dismay of some of his early supporters, President Carter moderated the tone of his speaking out about human rights by the end of his first year in office.

The term is now often used in diplomacy; intervention is debated by those who believe the U.S. has a responsibility to lead the world in enforcing human rights (Bosnia, Iraq) versus those who limit involvement to national interests or through multilateral organizations (Rwanda, Darfur).

In current political usage, *human rights* means more liberty for dissenters in totalitarian lands; *civil rights* is associated with equality for minority groups and women; and *civil liberties* connotes lip-biting approval for the free speech of people espousing unpopular causes. In the '90s, human rights became one basis for advocacy of intervention across national borders by those who had overcome the VIETNAM SYNDROME, and subsequently became one of the bases for the rationale for George W. Bush's decision to bring about REGIME CHANGE in Baghdad. But that suffered as the war in Iraq dragged on. See REALISM.

By 2007, hopes for human rights in Russia were set back by the authoritarian governance of Vladimir Putin, successor to the democratic but erratic Boris Yeltsin as that nation's elected president. Thanks to an economic boom led by the rising price of oil, Putin's popularity remained high even as he squelched other political parties, maintained iron control over mass media, and made little effort to find the killers of dissidents. At a meeting with Western journalists, he rejected human rights criticisms, criticized Britain for giving refuge to "scoundrels," and added sarcastically, "I am an absolutely pure democrat. The real tragedy is that I am the only one. Since Mahatma Gandhi died, there's just nobody left to talk to."

humor, self-deprecating A politician's attempt to take the sting out of a charge by kidding about it; acknowledging a disadvantage in such a charming way as to turn it to an advantage.

Abraham Lincoln joked about his height and plain looks. "Here am I and here is Mrs. Lincoln. That's the long and short of it." And "The Lord prefers common-looking people. That's the reason he makes so many of them."

Humor has been used often in politics, especially in ridiculing an opponent (Churchill re MacDonald: "sheep in sheep's clothing," see INVECTIVE, POLITICAL) but not until the 1950s did the Lincolnesque technique of poking fun at oneself come into such universal political vogue. Adlai Stevenson led the way in defeat, quoting Lincoln's story about the little boy who stubbed his toe and was too big to cry and hurt too much to laugh.

John F. Kennedy carried self-deprecating humor forward. Criticized for appointing his younger brother Attorney General, he innocently observed, "I see nothing wrong with giving Robert some legal experience before he goes out to practice law." (According to Arthur Schlesinger, Jr., Robert protested that this joke was not funny, and his brother told him to get used to kidding himself, because people liked it. "Yes, but you weren't kidding yourself," Robert responded, "you were kidding *me*.") Robert Kennedy took up the technique, introducing candidate Adlai Stevenson III in Illinois with the remark, "If there's one thing I can't stand, it's a fellow running on his family name."

Senator Ted Kennedy, who bore the brunt of a "nepotism" and "dynasty" charge in Massachusetts, said that he wanted to be judged on his own so much that he thought of changing his name—from Teddy Kennedy to Teddy Roosevelt. Defusing the "born with a silver spoon" bomb, Ted Kennedy quoted a factory worker who said to him, "Senator, I hear you never worked a day in your life, and this is what a lot of people have against you. I want to tell you, you haven't missed a thing."

Bill Clinton, in 1993 at his first Gridiron Club dinner—where media biggies in white tie and other absurd costumes make fun of top officials in attendance—took some of the sting out of criticism of the role of the First Lady by saying, "The views I express here are those of my wife."

Alan Otten, *Wall Street Journal* political analyst, wrote: "This type of humor has obvious advantages. It's usually a quick throwaway line, less likely to bore an audience than the old-fashioned long anecdote. It disarms critics by making their target appear unafraid of the criticism. It makes the listener feel this can't be such a bad fellow after all."

In the 1992 campaign debates, Ross Perot—who had been caricatured with jug-ears—began an answer with "I'm all ears." Mitt Romney, in 2007 the first Mormon to be a serious presidential candidate, told a Gridiron audience that it was untrue that Mormons were squares and stiffs. He told of an outing with Senate Majority Leader Harry Reid, Democrat of Nevada, and Orrin Hatch, Republican of Utah, both Mormons, at which "we really let 'er rip." But nobody would ever read about their secret escapade or see a picture of it on any screen because, he confided, "What happens in Disneyland stays in Disneyland."

Today's one-liners at "roasts" and such mutual-kidding affairs are prepared by professional gagwriters. Politicians know it makes good sense to laugh at themselves, but a well-delivered joke does not necessarily indicate a sense of humor.

Humpty Dumpty Sure loser; a sacrificial lamb.

This nursery rhyme character who "sat on a wall" and "had a great fall" was popularized by Lewis Carroll as an early example of anything-goes linguistics: a word, to Humpty Dumpty, meant anything he chose it to mean.

In politics, a Humpty Dumpty is selected to take a great fall in a hopeless race against an unbeatable opponent. The appellation, always contemptuous, may be connected to *fall guy*, a "sucker, scapegoat, or member of a conspiracy selected to take the punishment for all."

The *dump* in the phrase was given a twist in 1967 by Florida Governor Claude Kirk, who predicted that President Lyndon Johnson would replace Hubert Humphrey with a more exciting running mate in 1968, calling the gambit "Humphrey Dumphrey." In this way, the ancient Mother Goose phrase may have come full circle: it is believed that the rhyming compound's first word was originally a pet form of "Humphrey."

The name was subtly revived after Nixon's fall by reporters Bob Woodward and Carl Bernstein in their book title *All the President's Men*; the allusion was to "all the king's men" in the Humpty Dumpty tale, and the inability of Nixon's aides to put together the Nixon presidency after the cracks of Watergate appeared.

A related term, opposite in meaning, is *Mickey Mouse*, used when any candidate chosen to run could beat the unpopular opponent (see LAUNDRY TICKET). This phrase is also used to mean "inadequate" in more general terms; Roy Innes, director of the Congress of Racial Equality, told a CBS interviewer, "I am disgusted with the Mickey Mouse welfare programs …"

For the political use of related folklore characters, see TWEEDLEDUM AND TWEEDLEDEE.

hundred days Most often applied to the productive special session of Congress summoned by Franklin D. Roosevelt in 1933 to cope with the Depression.

The historical parallel to FDR's Hundred Days was Napoleon's escape from Elba and his triumphant march across Europe that finally culminated in disaster at Waterloo. The time span between Napoleon's Elba escape and ultimate abdication, however, was 116 days; the *hundred days* was applied to Louis XVIII's absence from Paris beginning March 20, 1815, as Napoleon arrived, to June 28, when the King returned in state after Napoleon's defeat. The Count de Chambord, prefect of Paris, coined the phrase: "A hundred days, sire, have elapsed since the fatal moment when your Majesty was forced to quit your capital in the midst of tears." When used in reference to that period, the phrase has now come to mean the time of Napoleon's return rather than the King's exile.

Roosevelt's Hundred Days were equally eventful. During the period from March 9 to June 16—exactly one hundred days— the 73rd Congress enacted such milestone legislation as vast public works and relief measures, guarantees of bank deposits and tighter federal regulation of the banks, agricultural subsidies, and the Tennessee Valley Authority. "The legislative record it set," wrote Raymond Moley, a member of FDR's BRAIN TRUST, "the impression it created on the public, its impact upon the economy of the nation, and the incredible speed with which important legislation was planned, considered, proposed and enacted has no parallel in the earlier history of the Republic. Nor has there been any parallel since, except under the exigencies of the war that began eight years later." Not even Lyndon Johnson's 89th Congress was comparable, argued Moley, because much of its program "had been inherited from the Kennedy years" or was traceable to the Roosevelt era.

While John F. Kennedy was working on his inaugural address, Theodore Sorensen wrote in his memoir *Kennedy*, the president at one point said impatiently, "I'm sick of reading how we're planning another 'Hundred Days' of miracles. Let's put in that this won't all be finished in a hundred days or a thousand." His finished speech thus read: "All this will not be finished in the first hundred days. Nor will it be finished in the first thousand days, nor in the life of this Administration, nor even perhaps in our lifetime on this planet. But let us begin." Historian Arthur Schlesinger, Jr., chose *A Thousand Days*—the approximate length of the Kennedy Administration—as the title of his history of the period. See "LET US CONTINUE."

Britain's Harold Wilson was less reluctant to exploit what had become a cliché. "What we are going to need," he said during his successful 1964 campaign to lead Labour to power and himself to the prime ministership, "is something like what President Kennedy had after years of stagnation—a program of a hundred days of dynamic action." At a news conference in April 1993, *Washington Post* columnist Mary McGrory asked President Clinton: "Would you care to assess your first hundred days before we do?"

Speaker Nancy Pelosi, on assuming the gavel in 2007 as Democrats became the majority party, announced her intention to pass rule changes and promised legislation "in the first 100 hours," some of which Democrats proceeded to do, provoking Republican charges of GAG RULE. Nobody has yet used the pledge of "one hundred minutes," but that will come.

hundred flowers A governing promise that seems to permit open disagreement within an administration.

Chinese communist leader Mao Zedong made a speech in 1957 that appeared to embrace sweet reason: "Ideological struggle is not like other forms of struggle. Crude, coercive methods should not be used in this struggle, but only the method of painstaking reasoning." He went on to use a charming metaphor: "Let a hundred flowers bloom and a hundred schools of thought contend."

When the flowers were foolish enough to bloom, they were ruthlessly cut down. Historian Sidney Hook wrote: "The Communist Party loosed another fierce campaign of PURGE and suppression, branding these flowers of doctrine as poisonous weeds which must be chopped down." Beijing's *People's Daily*, four months after Mao's speech, completed the metaphor: "Only by letting poisonous weeds show themselves above ground can they be uprooted." Two decades later, after Mao's death and the fall of the radical Gang of Four, a limited amount of debate was permitted, especially in the form of wall posters. This recalled the "hundred flowers" phrase, but Chinese leaders disagreed with great circumspection: they had learned their lesson.

In American political usage, the phrase is employed—usually sardonically—in descriptions of public disagreements by Administration leaders. This is often referred to in the press as a "let-a-hundred-flowers-bloom technique," and is more frequently condemned for its seeming confusion than praised for its acceptance of open debate.

The Washington Post quoted an unidentified military officer in November 1982 about Ronald Reagan's leadership: "Reagan, in essence, let a hundred flowers bloom early in his Administration and that has caused many of the problems with the anti-nuclear movement in Europe and the United States."

hunker See BARNBURNERS; HARD LINE.

hurting See CRUNCH.

hustings Specifically, any place from which a campaign speech is made; generally, the campaign trail.

The original meaning was "an assembly, any deliberative body"; before written ballots became the law in England in 1872, the *husting* was the place from which candidates for Parliament addressed the electorate. The best-known husting was the upper end or platform of the Guildhall, where the Mayor held court.

In Scandinavian countries the word *thing* is the name of legislative assemblies and courts of law; *husting* is taken from the Old Norse *hús-thing*, literally "house meeting." In a classic English translation of Demosthenes' "Oration on the Crown," the Greek orator says: "In what spirit was I to mount the hustings? In the spirit of one having unworthy counsel to offer?—I should have deserved to perish!"

In current use, *on the hustings*, *on the stump*, and *on the campaign trail* are synonymous, though the archaic *hustings* is more often used semihumorously. Stephen Chapman used the term in a 1993 commentary on the new Administration: "During the Presidential campaign, Bill Clinton had all the answers. He's since learned that a variety of problems—gays in the military, Haitian refugees, middle-class taxes—are a lot easier to solve from the hustings than from the Oval Office."

In Scotland, Wales, and India, the word is used currently with considerable respect as a description of personal, rather than media, campaigning.

Hymie's ferryboat An earthy analogy about the COATTAIL effect of a strong candidate.

"Hymie" Schorenstein, a Brooklyn Democratic district leader in the 1920s, received a complaint from one of his candidates for a local elective office: "Why is it, Hymie, that your whole budget for posters and literature is for Governor Roosevelt, and nothing for the candidates on the local level? I need to become better known, Roosevelt doesn't. How about a few signs for me?"

Schorenstein did not answer directly. "You ever watch the ferries come in from Staten Island?" The candidate allowed as how he had, and waited for Hymie's point.

"When that big ferry from Staten Island sails into the ferry slip, it never comes in strictly alone. It drags in all the crap from the harbor behind it." Hymie let the message sink in before adding, "FDR is our Staten Island Ferry."

That is the way the story is most frequently recounted as it worked its way into political legend. When political reporter Richard Reeves used the anecdote (citing an early edition of this dictionary as a source), he received a letter in 1976 from John Rae of New York City, an eyewitness to its telling: "I was at a party with Jimmy Walker and Hymie Schorenstein. The ferry story concerned Hymie's nonentity nephew running for the Assembly at the time Walker was running for Mayor. Walker assuaged Hymie by saying he would pull Hymie's nephew in—he coined the ferryslip story which Hymie loved to repeat as did Beau James."

Schorenstein, who despite an inability to read operated most effectively as a county clerk, was preceded in the use of this metaphor by the president of Columbia University, Nicholas Murray Butler, who heard it from Boies Penrose, a leader of the Pennsylvania delegation in the Republican convention of 1912. In the midst of a fistfight between supporters of former President Theodore Roosevelt and President William Howard Taft, Butler wondered how men of that type ever were selected for the responsibility of choosing a presidential nominee. Penrose replied, "Oh, those are the corks, bottles and banana peels washed up by the Roosevelt tide." See BANDWAGON.

hymn book See ON MESSAGE; TALKING POINTS.

hype See MEDIA EVENT.

hyphenated American Identification of an American's racial or ethnic heritage, a phrase now dated.

African-American (in place of *black* on first reference, which replaced *Negro*) and *Asian-American* have become the foremost use of this hyphenation, although ethnic examples of the formulation range from *Irish-American* to *Italian-American*. It allows the designation of a person's racial or ethnic background by using a capitalized modifier linked to American with a hyphen. Curiously, Americans of Mexican or other Spanish-speaking extraction are known informally as *Hispanics* or *Latinos* (*Latinas* for women), with no hyphen needed.

The phrase was first defined in Farmer & Henley's slang dictionary in 1893 as "a naturalized citizen." In the early 1900s, *hyphenated American* was used contemptuously to question the allegiance of immigrants to their adopted country. This was less of a slur than *wetback* (from swimming the Rio Grande) and was later changed to *undocumented worker*, and more recently to *guest worker*.

Relatedly, the racial appellation *American Indian* was objected to by many aboriginal Americans, some of whom preferred *Native American* (not hyphenated), although that was a source of confusion with all citizens born in the United States and native thereto, and *Indian-American* denotes U.S. citizens born in India. This confusion has not been resolved; however, hyphenation with an *American* ending is primarily a self-description and is considered a source of pride in the user's heritage. See ETHNICS.

Jewish American is not hyphenated because Jewish is an adjective modifying the noun, rather than a combination of nationalities like *Asian-American*. (In the same way, *Arab-American* takes the hyphen, *Muslim American* does not.) When asked if he prefers to be identified as a Jewish American or as an American Jew, the author replies, "In temple, I am an American Jew; in the voting booth, I am a Jewish American." No hyphen either way.

Half-breed is considered a slur on a combination of Native American (aboriginal or American Indian) and white; the term *half-Native American, half-Anglo* is occasionally used but seems awkward. Although *colored* is considered by some African-Americans as a mild slur, *of color* is proudly embraced; it may be that *colored* will make a comeback as acceptable.

Senator Barack Obama (D-Ill.), as the son of a white American mother and a father from Kenya, has identified himself as *of mixed heritage*, which—if his political ambitions are realized—might replace much past hyphenation.

I

I am the law Arrogant assertion of political imperiousness.

Mayor Frank Hague of Jersey City, big-city boss and full-time autocrat, received a bum rap from history on this quotation. The episode involved two youths who wanted to change from day school to night school so that they could go to work, but who had been denied working papers by the Board of Education's Special Services Director because the law required them to stay in day school. Mayor Hague cut through the red tape and ordered the official to give the boys working papers. As he proudly recounted the matter before the Men's Club of Emory Church in Jersey City on November 10, 1937: when the school official told him, "That's the law," Hague replied, "Listen, here is the law. I am the law! Those boys go to work!"

Today such an action would be lauded as the action of a public official pushing aside an unresponsive bureaucracy to "meet human needs"; but Hague had a well-deserved reputation for high-handedness, and the phrase soon lost its context and was used against him.

During World War II Charles de Gaulle irritated Churchill and Roosevelt with his insistent remark, *"Je suis la France"* ("I am France"). This phrase reminded them of Louis XIV's supposed remark to the 1665 Parliament of Paris, *"L'état, c'est moi"* ("I am the state"). In his 1825 Bunker Hill Monument oration, Daniel Webster gave this interpretation, which could also apply to Hague's remark: "When Louis XIV said 'I am the state,' he expressed the essence of the doctrine of unlimited power. These ideas, founded in the love of power, and long supported by the excess and abuse of it, are yielding in our age to other opinions …"

The phrase is current. On April 1, 1978, after L. Patrick Gray and other former FBI officials were indicted for violating the civil rights of members of a terrorist group, cartoonist Herblock pictured two agents in raincoats carrying a black bag labeled "illegal operations" and asking: "We broke the law? We *are* the law!"

Political figures use *I am* at their peril. George W. Bush told a questioner in 2006, "I am the decider." That, for the nation's Chief Executive, is indisputable regarding the executive branch—see the BUCK STOPS HERE—but had a touch of swagger to it and was gleefully used against him.

ideas A catchword for political movements that enjoyed some fame in the U.S.

"One-idea parties" was a nineteenth-century label placed first on anti-Masons and then all minority or splinter parties by members of larger parties. However, some of the ideas were worth looking into:

The idea of freedom: Associated with the abolitionist cause, the phrase was introduced by Theodore Parker at a New England antislavery convention held in Boston on May 29, 1850. Parker's idea was of "a democracy, that is, a government of all the people, by all the people, for all the people; of course, a government after the principles of eternal justice, the unchanging law of God; for shortness' sake, I will call it the idea of freedom." (Part of this statement was later adopted by Lincoln at Gettysburg. Earlier, on January 26, 1830, in his widely read "reply to Hayne," Senator Daniel Webster described the Union as "made for the people, made by the people, answerable to the people.")

The Ohio idea: The Democratic platform of 1868 stressed the redemption of national debts in specie—not paper money but gold and silver coin. Senator George H. Pendleton summed up this "Ohio Idea" in 1881: "the absolute equality of all men before the law; absolute and equal justice to all men by the law; and … the administration of the few powers committed to our State legislature by the Constitution in such wise that every man may pursue his own avocations and his own scheme of domestic life according to his tastes...as is consistent with the order of society and the peace of the community."

The Plattsburg idea: With World War I under way, those who advocated preparedness for the U.S. introduced the Plattsburg idea in April, 1915—two years before America's entry into the war. Named for the northern New York State site of a training camp, it called for military training for civilians at similar spots.

The Wisconsin idea: Graduates of the enlightened University of Wisconsin, which encouraged its students to seek wealth, power, and influence for the betterment of society, fostered the idea. They envisioned a progressive, agrarian-democratic commonwealth—and from 1900 to 1914 they went a long way toward making the idea a reality. With Robert La Follette, Sr., as governor, advocates of the Wisconsin idea enacted a direct primary, tax reform, laws controlling the railroads, initiative and referendum provisions, a corrupt-practices act, child- and female-labor laws, workmen's compensation, regulatory agencies for utilities and transportation, and laws covering campaign expenditures, civil service, lobbying, safety, public health, conservation, and the schools. Tommy G. Thompson, a Republican who became Governor of Wisconsin in 1987, defined a *New Wisconsin Idea* "aimed at moving away from intrusive government, and putting responsibility and initiative back in the hands of people." (He briefly announced for president in 2007.)

Current campaign oratory tends to discard the word *idea* on the grounds that it appears too sudden a notion, substituting the less exciting *plan* or *program;* George W. Bush expressed his idea as the freedom *agenda.*

ideologue See IDEOLOGY.

ideology Originally, a system of ideas for political or social action; in current political attacks, a mental straitjacket, or rigid rules for the philosophically narrow-minded.

French philosopher Destutt de Tracy coined the word in 1796, to mean a modern, rationalist "science of ideas" opposed to ancient metaphysics, and made it the title of his 1801 book, *Idéologie.* Napoleon Bonaparte was the first to give the word a bad name: "It is to the doctrine of the ideologues...one must attribute all the misfortunes which have befallen our beautiful France." British historian Thomas Carlyle tried to rescue the word from its pejoration in 1839: "Does the British reader...call this unpleasant doctrine of ours 'ideology'?" However, after Karl Marx and Friedrich Engels in 1845 joined Napoleon's semantic side in condemning the word in their attack on German radicals, titling their book *The German Ideology*, the term could never shake its connotation of rigidity. When the Marx book was finally printed in English in 1927, the word gained currency in the U.S.

"I think 'ideology' is a scare word to most Americans," observed former California Governor Ronald Reagan to columnists Evans and Novak in 1978. "But a basic political philosophy is the reason for a party existing."

Reagan's observation, taking *ideology* to its root as a synonym for *philosophy*, was etymologically accurate but semantically outdated. To most current political writers, *ideology* carries the connotation of rigid theory, and *ideologue* is used to mean "demagogue hawking an extreme point of view."

In 2006, Douglas Feith, who had served in the Pentagon as Undersecretary of Defense for Policy, and had been vilified by critics of the war as an "ideologue" for his active advocacy of REGIME CHANGE in Iraq, asked the author: "What's happened to the word 'ideologue'? It's come to be an epithet, meaning 'one to whom the facts don't matter.' That's not reflected in the dictionaries. Is it wrong to espouse an ideology? Isn't every philosophical system an ideology?" The 11th edition of Merriam-Webster's Collegiate defines *ideology* as "visionary theorizing" and "a systematic body of concepts esp. about human life or culture," but, as Feith suggested, also defines *ideologue* as "an impractical idealist" and "an often blindly partisan advocate or adherent of a particular ideology."

idiot engineer See BLOOPER.

I'd rather be right Henry Clay's statement that began as an example of his idealism but now has a flavor of sour grapes.

"I would rather be right than be President." Kentucky Senator Clay made this statement several times to his friends, in a letter in 1839, and in a Senate speech in 1850. "The Great Compromiser" and "The Great Pacificator" achieved major-party presidential nominations twice and was defeated both times. See CAN'T-WIN TECHNIQUE. Like Ohio Republican Senator Robert A. Taft a century later, Clay was too strictly a congressional leader to build nationwide coalitions beyond Congress. After losing the presidency, he tired of hearing his immortal words about rather being right quoted and said dryly that this particular sentiment "had been applauded beyond its merit."

Clay's use of the statement in a Senate speech was in reply to those that said his Missouri Compromise would hurt his chances for the presidency. For years, congressmen quoted the remark until it became a political bromide; House Speaker Thomas B. Reed answered a Clay-quoter with "the gentleman need not be disturbed; he will never be either."

George M. Cohan wrote a Broadway musical entitled *I'd Rather Be Right* in the 1930s, kidding the Administration of Franklin Roosevelt. In it, the President in the show would turn to his secretary and say, "Mac, take a law." FDR enjoyed this and often turned to his secretary, Grace Tully, and said, "Grace, take a law."

Variations on Clay's remark can be found before and after he first sounded it. William McKinley, before his 1896 election, told a friend, "If I cannot be President without promising to make Tom Platt Secretary of the Treasury, I will never be President." Marcus Tullius Cicero (106–43 B.C.) said of the Pythagoreans, "I would rather be wrong with Plato than right with such men as these."

On the eve of the 1952 election, Democratic candidate Adlai Stevenson kept rewriting his speech in the television studio before the telecast. His finished product was five minutes too long and the network cut him off. His aide, George Ball, noted sadly in his memoir: "We used to tell him he'd rather write than be president."

if by whiskey… Taking both sides of an issue; equivocating; a political STRADDLE.

These three words, followed by an ellipsis, refer to the classic speech of equivocation on the issue of prohibition. Now used as a compound modifier—"He gave an if-by-whiskey speech"—the expression may be applied to any political position that fails to take a position.

The originator of this speech is Judge Noah S. Sweat Jr. of Corinth, Mississippi. Judge Sweat, nicknamed "Soggy" for "Sorghum Top" (his hair resembling the tassels atop sugar cane), copyrighted his speech in 1952. The satiric straddling purports to answer the question of a politician's stance on the controversial matter of drinking whiskey.

"If when you say whiskey," the politician begins, "you mean the Devil's brew, the poison scourge, the bloody monster that defiles innocence…then certainly I am against it.

"But, if when you say whiskey," the speechmaker continues, "you mean the oil of conversation, the philosophic wine,… that drink the sale of which pours into our treasuries untold millions of dollars, which are used to provide tender care for our little crippled children, our blind, our deaf, our dumb, our pitiful aged and infirm; to build highways and hospitals and schools, then certainly I am for it."

iffy question A hypothetical question; phrase used by Franklin Roosevelt to avoid giving iffy answers.

"If you run next year, who will your vice president be?" This type of question directed at a sitting president is designed to elicit not one answer, but two (Who will be the vice president? Will you run next year?). Many press conference traps of this kind were neatly avoided by FDR, who merely smiled and said, "That's an iffy question."

New York Governor Averell Harriman, campaigning against Nelson Rockefeller in 1958, was asked if he planned to retain Tammany leader Carmine De Sapio as

Secretary of State, and replied, "I think that's an iffy question that doesn't—that I needn't deal with today." Because "boss-ism" was an important thrust of Rock-efeller's campaign, and since the "if" in the question was hardly hypothetical but pertinent to post-election plans, the Harriman use of *iffy question* was an ill-advised evasion.

The phrase appears to work only when the question is indeed hypothetical, or "iffy." Robert Kennedy was asked by reporters in 1964 if he would accept a vice presidential nomination. He answered such obvious speculation with: "The question reminds me of my brother. When he was posed with such a question, he used to say that is like asking a girl if she would marry that man *if* he proposed."

Other types of questions include: *loaded, slanted, planted, tricky, penetrating, stupid* and *innocent*.

if it ain't broke, don't fix it Leave well enough alone; avoid creating unnecessary trouble or controversy.

Bert Lance, former director of the Office of Management and Budget, introduced this down-home Southernism to political usage in Washington early in the Carter Admin-istration. *National Journal* indicated its widespread use by 1978 in referring to Dem-ocrats who "follow the advice of…Bert Lance: 'If it ain't broke, don't fix it.'"

A proverbial equivalent of the hoary punch line "don't make waves," this expres-sion uses the nonstandard *ain't* but still fits a traditional grammatical pattern. The con-ditional *if*-clause (the protasis) leads into a main clause (the apodosis) *don't fix it,* which is expressed in the imperative (with its subject *you* understood).

In 1977, *The Washington Post* reported a comment by a Virginia Democrat, state del-egate Ira M. Lechner, suggesting an earlier origin: "I support reorganization, but not these helter-skelter efforts. As my father used to say, 'if it ain't broke, don't fix it.'"

Democrats have not been alone, however, in using this nonpartisan rephrasing of the already updated "let sleeping dogmas lie." Cathy Mickels, a Republican delegate from

Washington, on *The MacNeil/Lehrer News Hour* in 1992, pushed for a continuation of the Party's previously winning ways: "The old adage that states, 'If it ain't broke, don't fix it' applies here. I think it would be foolish to change our platform in any way to devi-ate from the 1988 winning platform that we have." It was broken and needed fixing.

if you can't lick 'em … join 'em. A fre-quent bit of advice, origin obscure, given in areas dominated by one party.

Akin to the Scottish proverb "Better bend than break," the sentence carries no conno-tation of surrender; it advises that the way to take over the opposition's strength is to adopt their positions and platform. See ME, TOO; CO-OPT.

President Harry Truman in his 1948 cam-paign warned farmers about a variation of this technique supposedly practiced by Republicans: "It's an old political trick: 'If you can't convince 'em, confuse 'em.' But this time it won't work."

if you can't stand the heat … get out of the kitchen A motto often attributed to President Harry S. Truman.

President Truman stressed two facets of the presidency with colorful phrases: "The BUCK STOPS HERE" on the need for decisive-ness, and "If you can't stand the heat, get out of the kitchen" on the cheerful expec-tancy of pressure. As a senator, Lyndon Baines Johnson phrased the same philoso-phy in this way: "My daddy told me that if I didn't want to get shot at, I should stay off the firing lines. This is politics." (In Winston Churchill's first book, *The Story of the Mal-akand Field Force* [1898], he wrote, "Noth-ing in life is so exhilarating as to be shot at without result.")

This standing-the-heat advice is as closely associated with Truman as GIVE 'EM HELL, DO-NOTHING CONGRESS, and RED HERRING, all needing no specific attribution to him for identification. Daniel P. Moynihan, then of the Joint Center for Urban Studies, wrote complaining of an attack on him in *Trans-action* in 1967: "A better political scientist than I said the final word on government executives either standing the heat or getting out of the kitchen, but there are levels of personal abuse that make one wonder whether it is worth it." (It was; Moynihan went on to be an influence for progressive domestic policy in the Nixon White House and to become senator from New York.)

In 1984, the Reverend Jesse Jackson used the saying to emphasize the need for toughness in a presidential candidate; commenting on his opponents' performance in a three-way debate, he said, "If you can't stand the heat, get out of the kitchen."

When Sir Walter Raleigh, nibbling his nails, wrote, "Fain would I climb, yet fear to fall," the more direct Queen Elizabeth I is said to have written in reply: "If thy heart fails thee, climb not at all."

I have a dream A memorable speech construction by Rev. Martin Luther King, Jr., at the Lincoln Memorial during the March on Washington, August 28, 1963.

> I say to you today, my friends, that in spite of the difficulties and frustrations of the moment I still have a dream. It is a dream deeply rooted in the American dream...I have a dream that one day on the red hills of Georgia the sons of former slaves and the sons of former slaveowners will be able to sit down together at the table of brotherhood...I have a dream that my four little children will one day live in a nation where they will not be judged by the color of their skin but by the content of their character...I have a dream today ...

For other examples of vision and inspiration in speeches, see "I SEE" CONSTRUCTION; AMERICAN DREAM; VISION OF AMERICA.

illegitimi non carborundum A pseudo-Latin phrase meaning "Don't let the bastards grind you down."

Small signs and plaques carrying this message have appeared in U.S. business offices and army posts for two generations, since General "Vinegar Joe" Stilwell used it as his motto in World War II. The slanguist Eric Partridge speculated it originated among officers in Britain's World War II Intelligence Corps: "I wonder which Oxford 'Classic,' exacerbated almost to desperation, coined this trenchant piece of exquisite Latinity?"

Carborundum is a trademark for silicon carbide, a leading commercial grinding substance, probably a blend of the words *carbon* or *carbide* and *corundum* (the hardest mineral except for the diamond), also used as an abrasive.

In politics, the motto was popularized by 1964 Republican nominee Senator Barry Goldwater, who hung the sign in his office in one of its many variations: *Noli Permittere Illegitimi Carborundum*. It expressed a suitable be-yourself, don't-compromise attitude that fit "Mr. Conservative." It may be a great motto, but users of it should remember it is not Latin.

The New Republic in 1967 used an egregiously bowdlerized translation in reporting on its use by a group of senators who had been characterized as DOVES: "The Administration brought General Westmoreland all the way from Vietnam to overawe its critics, but the Senate's Democratic and Republican dissenters appropriated Barry Goldwater's old dog-Latin motto, 'Illegitimi non Carborundum,' which roughly means, 'Don't let the so-and-so's shut you up.'"

illuminati See POWER ELITE.

image The impression of self that a public figure attempts to convey; the merchandising of reputation.

Political images and image-makers are post–World War II offspring of television and big-league advertising and public relations. All politicians in all times, of course, seek public affection and respect. But turning this search into a constant and major effort is a recent innovation. John Brooks observed that the preoccupation with "image" sprang from an "unholy...liaison between promotion and psychology" that "invaded American politics about the time Eisenhower came to the White House." Almost as one, political writers picked up the term and have yet to put it down. Sir Ernest Gowers in his second edition of Fowler's *Modern English Usage* called it an overused "vogue word" but still a valid one in an era when "politicians and advertisers and other advocates of themselves or other causes can ... project their images into our very homes" via TV.

The personal use of the word, to mean more than a reflection in a glass, was begun by psychologists; *father image* has long been a familiar psychiatric term. The word was picked up by advertising men as *brand image*, meaning the conception on the part of the consumer of a manufacturer's trade name or product; this led to *corporate image*, a conception that a public (stockholders, employees, suppliers, financiers, local community, the competition, etc.) has of a corporation. "A brand image is what you say you are," public relations practitioners like to say, "but a corporate image is what you really are." That's debatable.

As *image* became a sales tool for opinion shapers, it became a handy and modern-sounding word to describe the total public posture and impression of a public figure. Many politicians misuse the word to mean something that belongs to them, much like Peter Pan's shadow, and feel lost without it; the fact is that an image belongs to the public.

The activating verb used with *image* goes back to the use of the word as a reflection, or picture. Images are *projected*, as one would project a film on a screen.

The seventeenth-century English aphorist Thomas Fuller lamented that "Fame sometimes has created something of nothing." It has also created political myths. Charles Evans Hughes, the Republican candidate for president in 1916, was the victim of the "ice myth" that portrayed him as so withdrawn from the common man that he "communed in the Alps with Kant, solid geometry and Lycurgus." Hughes replied, "I'll plead guilty to knowing Kant, but not guilty as to the solid geometry charge. As to Lycurgus ... do you think it is anything intoxicating?" Hughes lost the election.

News media play a major part in image-making, of course. Calvin Coolidge gave reporters so little good copy that embroidery became necessary to keep editors and readers awake. Henry Suydam, recalling his days as a Washington correspondent, wrote: "Mr. Coolidge would observe, with respect to a certain bill, 'I'm not in favor of this legislation.' The next morning

Washington dispatches began as follows: 'President Coolidge, in a fighting mood, today served notice on Congress that he intended to combat, with all the resources at his command ...' "

A politician's attitude toward his image was famously expressed by Oliver Cromwell to the man painting his portrait: "I desire you will use all your skill to paint my picture truly like me, and not to flatter me at all; but remark all those roughnesses, pimples, warts, and everything as you see me: otherwise I will never pay one farthing for it." Through the centuries, that statement has helped that regicide's image. See MADISON AVENUE TECHNIQUES; SELLING CANDIDATES LIKE SOAP.

immigration issue See AMNESTY; KNOW-NOTHINGS.

imperial presidency A charge that the executive branch has gained more power than the Constitution warrants.

At the end of 1973 Arthur Schlesinger, Jr.—historian of the Jackson era and the New Deal who served as a White House aide during the presidency of John Kennedy—published *The Imperial Presidency*, which was taken to be an attack on the growth of presidential power. Because the book came out in the midst of the fall of Richard Nixon, it provided an intellectual underpinning to those liberals who otherwise were having problems of consistency with their previous enthusiasm for the growth of executive power under FDR and their fierce disapproval of its growth under Nixon.

Schlesinger, who was then unaware of many of the abuses of civil liberty that a Senate committee in 1975 showed to have taken place in the '60s, was careful in his introduction to disclaim any desire to cripple the powers of the President: "The answer to the runaway Presidency is not the messenger-boy Presidency. The American democracy must discover a middle ground between making the President a czar and making him a puppet." His timely book confronted the dilemma of all those who had long urged an "activist" presidency and who had been dismayed when too much activism had led to Vietnam and Watergate.

As in the POLITICS OF, a Schlesinger book title became the basis for many variations in phrase-making. Laurence Silberman, at the American Enterprise Institute and later an appellate judge, published a critique of expanding judicial power, which he called "the imperial judiciary." After the War Powers Act and the forced resignation of Nixon, Congress gained much power and was frequently criticized as "the imperial Congress"; in May 1978 Robert Manning wrote in *The Atlantic* (which had printed some of Schlesinger's original material in its pages): "Americans wanted no part of an Imperial Presidency. Neither will they tolerate an Imperial Press." In a 1993 opinion piece in *The Chicago Tribune*, David Evans wrote of the need to "restore some overdue constraints on the imperial Presidency's war-making powers." The pendulum was to swing back again in 2006 as Congress gained the opposition strength to challenge, for at least a year, an unpopular president's refusal to accept defeat in Iraq.

impudent snobs See EFFETE SNOBS.

incomes policy Government influence upon or regulation of wages, prices, and profits, ranging from mild JAWBONING to direct wage-price controls.

In the late '50s, U.S. economists, who had been using *wage-price policy* to describe pressure to restrain inflation, switched to the British usage, *incomes policy*. This was because labor economists felt that wages and prices did not cover the subject of dividends and profits.

The new phrase came to public attention in the late '60s, when inflation persisted longer than most economists had expected. Because of its vagueness, it was especially popular as a solution to inflation by those who wanted to go beyond the customary methods of fiscal and monetary policy, without advocating wage and price controls.

Incomes policy was given a more specific definition, and the policy a strong boost, by Arthur Burns, who in 1970 became Chairman of the Board of Governors of the Federal Reserve System. He called for an incomes policy, centering his proposal on a wage-price stabilization board—relying on voluntary compliance, short of mandatory controls. Dr. Burns's espousal of a stabilization board, at a time when the Administration was using a milder form of incomes policy, moved the definition of the phrase in popular usage toward a more activist meaning. When the author pointed out to the Federal Reserve Chairman that the policy he was proposing was directly in conflict with all he had written in the past, Burns replied, "I am not afflicted with the notion that what I write is chiseled in granite."

"Incomes *strategy*" has a different meaning, having to do with providing money, rather than services or food, to those dependent on public support. Proponents of an incomes strategy hold that the least demeaning way to help the needy is to give them the cash to buy their own essentials; opponents point to ignorance about nutrition standards and the danger of misuse of the welfare money by the recipients.

incumbent In office; an elected official running against a challenger.

In its original sense, *incumbent* means "lying down on," with the same Latin root as *recumbent* and *succumb*. The idea of resting is illustrated in the phrase *It is incumbent upon us*, which means "It rests with us" and is as stilted as *It behooves us*. When an incumbent official is seen to be lying down on the job, voters end the incumbency.

Based on past performance, the odds are two to one that an incumbent president will be re-elected. Sixteen have succeeded (FDR three times) out of twenty-two attempts. Those who failed were John Adams in 1800, John Quincy Adams in 1828, Martin Van Buren in 1840, Grover Cleveland in 1888, Benjamin Harrison in 1892, William Howard Taft in 1912, Herbert Hoover in 1932, Gerald Ford in 1976, Jimmy Carter in 1980, and George H.W. Bush in 1992. See SITTING PRESIDENT. Those who failed of later nomination by their own party were John Tyler in 1844, Millard Fillmore in 1852, Franklin Pierce in 1856, Andrew Johnson in 1868, and Chester Arthur in 1884; of these, only Pierce had already been elected president "in his own right." Theodore Roosevelt tried to return to the presidency in 1912, failed to win renomination, ran as an independent, and lost to Woodrow Wilson.

In almost every political race, the incumbent has an edge. Incumbent congressmen have a franking privilege that enables them to regularly report to or survey their constituents, showing themselves busily at work without incurring direct-mail advertising costs. Officeholders can also use their title as part of their name in campaign posters. The extreme example of this was the advertising approach of Jack Tinker & Partners in the 1966 New York campaign for governor: "Governor Rockefeller for Governor." (Campaign aide Harry O'Donnell, explaining the choice of the slogan to reporters, said, "It was either that or 'Nelson Rockefeller for Nelson.'")

With the same thought of extending incumbency in mind, Republicans in 1971 called their citizens' committee Committee for the Re-election of the President. Republican National Chairman Bob Dole dubbed its near-acronym CREEP, which gained a sinister connotation after the revelations of Watergate.

independents See SWING VOTER; SWITCHER.

indispensable man A spurious claim, made to be denied, that the U.S. government cannot get along without a particular person, including the sitting President.

FDR repeated this statement of Woodrow Wilson's, who was running against both a sitting President, William Howard Taft, and former President Theodore Roosevelt seeking a comeback as a third-party candidate: "There is no indispensable man. The government will not collapse and go to pieces if any one of the gentlemen seeking to be entrusted with its guidance should be left at home."

Just before President Eisenhower's heart attack in 1955, as Republicans were urging him to announce his intentions of running again in 1956, he told a gathering of Republican state chairmen at the Brown Palace Hotel in Denver, "We don't believe for a minute that the Republican party is so lacking

in inspiration, high-quality personnel and leadership that we are dependent on one man ... humans are frail and they are mortal. Finally you never pin your flag so tightly to one mast that if a ship sinks, you cannot rip it off and nail it to another. It is sometimes good to remember." Within two weeks, the President suffered a heart attack, and his words sounded suddenly prophetic. (On the other hand, when Eisenhower wrote about General Alfred M. Gruenther, who succeeded him as Allied Commander in Europe, Ike referred to him as "practically an indispensable individual.")

Origin of the phrase is in the French proverb: *"Il n'y a point d'homme nécessaire."*

inflation Loss of the purchasing power of money; in politics, an issue of greatest concern to those on fixed incomes or dependent on savings.

Basically, there are two forms of inflation: *demand-pull*, when there are too many dollars chasing too few goods, and *cost-push*, when wage increases sharply exceed productivity increases, pushing prices ever higher.

The first great quarrel in the U.S. over inflation started the long-running debate between hard- and soft-money men. The hards warned in 1837 that "a bubble will be inflated more disastrous in its explosion than the present one." See HARD MONEY.

In 1933, after the burst of a particularly great bubble led to the Great Depression, the government began talking of "reflationary" measures, such as massive deficit spending. Raymond Moley wrote: "One zealot said to me at the time that the $3.3 billion"—the amount appropriated for the National Industrial Recovery Act's "reflationary" public works program—"would be better used if it were scattered by aircraft over the country in $1 bills. I suggested that $2 bills would be more appropriate because in the resulting inflation a dollar would mean so little."

During his 1952 campaign, Dwight Eisenhower hit hard at Democratic inflation and promised to correct it. He later wrote: "To illustrate inflation I had used a length of board (sawed to the breaking point in two places) to represent the buying power of a 1949 dollar. To demonstrate the decline in the dollar between 1945 and 1952, I would break off the first third of the board. To illustrate the decline that was probable with eight more years of Fair Deal policies, I would break off another chunk of the board, ending up with a wooden equivalent of a 33-cent dollar in terms of 1945 values. We expended a large pile of lumber in this lesson, but the point got across."

With John F. Kennedy's Administration the Keynes-oriented "new economists" (see NEW ECONOMICS) made deficit spending and a moderate dose of controlled, continuing inflation official policy. After inflation gained momentum in the late '60s under pressure of heavy defense spending, the federal government moved to a "full-employment budget" concept, the limit on spending set at the amount that the tax system would produce at "full"—that is, about 96%—employment.

The word most closely associated with inflation is *spiral*; *inflationary spiral*, like *Vandyke beard*, is a phrase that is most often defined by a gesture of the fingers (pulling for Vandyke, twirling for inflation). The pace of inflation ranges from *creeping* to *galloping*, and orators denounce the way it "eats away" at the purchasing power of the dollar. Campaigns using the theme often print tiny replicas of dollar bills and call them "(whoever the opponent is) dollars."

In the '70s, *stagflation* came into use, which *Fortune* magazine defined as "continuing inflation under conditions of stagnant output and rising unemployment." This situation was also described, in a reversal of Voltaire's Dr. Pangloss, as "the worst of both worlds."

See HOLD THE LINE; HIGH COST OF LIVING; DOUBLE DIGIT.

influence peddler One who has, or claims to have, the contacts and "pull" supposedly necessary to get government contracts and favors from public officials, for a fee.

Testifying before a special Senate subcommittee in 1949, one of many of the FIVE PERCENTERS being investigated said, "I have nothing to sell but influence."

The phrase became common during the concluding years of the Truman Administration as Republicans sought to discredit the Democrats. See MESS IN WASHINGTON; GOVERNMENT BY CRONY. President Truman was never accused of profiting personally by corruption. Testimony showed, however, that his military aide and close friend, Major General Harry Vaughan, had been active on behalf of people interested in getting to France to bring in perfume base at a time when transportation for such activities was not available. General Vaughan had also interceded successfully for others wanting structural steel, then in short supply, in order to put up a race track in California and, in fact, had helped others get military contracts.

Vaughan denied having kept anything for himself, and President Truman staunchly sustained him, as he did special assistant and fellow Missourian Donald Dawson, who was charged by another committee (headed by Senator J. William Fulbright) with being the man to see if a loan was wanted from the Reconstruction Finance Corporation.

Synonymous with *influence peddler* was *five percenter*, a man who claimed to be able to get government contracts for which he wanted, in return, 5 percent of the value. During that period, sixty-six employees of the Bureau of Internal Revenue were purged and nine went to prison.

Nothing, however, had quite the impact as gifts of deep-freeze units made by a former Army officer, Colonel James V. Hunt, at the suggestion of General Vaughan. They were sent to Mr. Truman's Independence, Missouri, home, to Chief Justice Fred Vinson, and to Secretary of the Treasury John Snyder. Their value was much less than other examples of giving or getting things to which one was not entitled, but the "deep freeze" gifts gripped the public mind, as did the "vicuña coat" from Bernard Goldfine to Sherman Adams during the Eisenhower administration and through to lavish trips to St. Andrews golf course in Scotland and other "freebies" leading to corruption prosecutions in subsequent decades.

The predecessor of *influence* was *pull*, which Charles Ledyard Norton described in 1890 as "what influence, honorable or dishonorable, can he bring to bear to secure his election, or further party interests." That word, a shortening of *wirepulling*, can be found in "The Boss," a poem by the nineteenth-century conservative James Russell Lowell:

Skilled to pull wires, he baffles Nature's hope
Who sure intended him to stretch a rope.

See BELTWAY BANDITS.

infrastructure A political entity's skeleton: the roads, communications systems, schools, power plants, and other facilities on which a modern community depends.

This word, coined in 1927, proves that nobody—not even a great world leader and master of language—can kill a really tenacious bit of jargon.

Winston Churchill tried. Emanuel Shinwell, Labour Minister of Defence, reviewed for the House of Commons in 1950 the results of a meeting of the Consultative Council of the Brussels Treaty Western Union, a predecessor of the Common Market. Shinwell explained that the installation of signal communications, preparation of the headquarters, and division of the airfields were activities now known collectively as working on the "infrastructure."

Churchill rose and gave the use of the word fair warning: "As to this new word with which he has dignified our language, but which perhaps was imposed upon him internationally, I can only say that we must have full opportunity to consider it and to consult the dictionary."

Two months later, in a debate on the Schuman plan to pool European coal and steel, the word appeared again and Sir Winston was ready for it: "In this debate we have had the usual jargon about 'the infrastructure of a supranational authority.' The original authorship is obscure; but it may well be that these words 'infra' and 'supra' have been introduced into our current political parlance by the band of intellectual highbrows who are naturally anxious to impress British labour with the fact that they learned Latin at Winchester."

Considering the prestigious source of the ridicule, *infrastructure* lay seemingly dormant, but crouched in the weeds. In the American diplomatic community in Vietnam in the '60s, the word reared its head cautiously. In discussing the need for winning the "hearts and minds" of the people, diplomats and generals briefed correspondents on the need for a "viable indigenous governmental apparat"—that is, a local Vietnamese government that would be accepted by the citizenry, able to continue after U.S. forces left. This became known as the "viable infrastructure." Defense Secretary Robert McNamara said "That 'viable' phrase drives me mad. I keep trying to comb it out, but it keeps coming back." But with Churchill gone, linguistic defense collapsed and *infrastructure* triumphed.

Typical home-front use was in this 1967 *New Republic* article by Andrew Kopkind: "If [Governor Ronald] Reagan had appeased the people, he had also alienated the major economic interests. California's corporatism, perhaps more than any other state's, relies heavily on the production of technicians and intellectuals to support its 'infrastructure.' Huge technological parks go up around every new campus, the better to feed off the state-subsidized resources."

This indicates that the word has also absorbed the pejorative bureaucratic sense of *superstructure:* "excess organization." John Kenneth Galbraith, in *The New Industrial State*, labeled the "organized intelligence" directing modern industrial production as the *technostructure*. But in his 1992 campaign, Bill Clinton emphasized "investment in our infrastructure," by which he meant stimulating public-works spending.

For another coinage that met early resistance but could not be stopped, see MEDICARE.

initialese See ACRONYMS, POLITICAL; ALPHABET AGENCIES.

initials, presidential A contribution made by newspaper-headline writers to American history.

Before 1932, the President was referred to in headlines as the President, or by his last name, occasionally by his nickname

("Teddy," "Cal"), once by his initials (T.R. for Theodore Roosevelt). Presidents, in signing brief memos, would often use the initial of their first name (A. Lincoln).

Franklin D. Roosevelt initialed memos "FDR" and his staff referred to him that way. This proved a boon to headline writers, saving six spaces on both "Roosevelt" and "President." Use of initials was terse but not disrespectful, as "Frank" might have been. English newspapers had long followed the practice: Gladstone was headlined as "GOM" (Grand Old Man). Following FDR, HST was immediately adopted as short for Harry S. Truman. Though Eisenhower initialed short notes "DE," his nickname was short and famous enough to take the place of initials, though "Ike" was considered too familiar for *The New York Times*.

Irreverent headline writers who referred to John F. Kennedy as "Jack" before his election quickly switched to "JFK" afterward. Ted Sorensen wrote: "JFK—as he persuaded the headline writers to call him, not to imitate FDR but to avoid the youthful 'Jack.'"

Even before his association with FDR, LBJ was preoccupied with initials: Lady Bird Johnson, Lynda Bird, and Luci Baines all carried the same initials, as did his ranch. "All the Way With LBJ" was used as a preconvention slogan in 1960, but achieved little national recognition. Johnson became LBJ outside his own circle only after he became President. In 1964 he used his initials in campaign advertising: "USA for LBJ."

Jimmy Carter avoided using his initials because "J.C." is usually associated with Jesus Christ. Richard Nixon's last name was short, which meant headline writers did not need "RN"; miffed, the former President used the initials as the title of his 1978 memoirs. Jerry Ford's name was even shorter, doing away with the need for a gruff "GRF." Neither Reagan nor the elder Bush used their initials widely, but initialese cropped up in the Clinton term as FOB—not "freight on board," but "Friends of Bill." Headline writers seized on the middle initial of the younger Bush's name, both because it differentiated him from his father and because the irreverent, drawling "Dubya" came with him from Texas.

Inner Club A small, informal group once holding leadership power in both the House of Representatives and the Senate, especially the Senate.

The phrase is attributed to columnist William S. White, who wrote in 1956 of the "Inner Club where emphasis is still put on seniority and skill in negotiation." It is a relative of the much older description of the U.S. Senate as "the most exclusive gentlemen's club in the world."

Its members, whatever their political affiliation, have in common some degree of seniority and a secure seat; a working belief in compromise; the quality and force of their personality; and a willingness to do solid, difficult work in the committees where legislation is forged. The members of the Inner Club are by no means always the best known or eventually the best rewarded. During their senatorial years, neither Richard Nixon nor his next-office neighbor, John Kennedy, was considered a member of the Senate's Inner Club.

An example of the group's cohesive power occurred in Hubert Humphrey's first term in the Senate. He came to the upper house as an outspoken liberal, proceeded to launch an attack on Virginia's conservative but highly respected Senator Harry Byrd, and was firmly squelched for his presumption. Senator Humphrey's attitude to the Club organization underwent so strong a change that a few years later he was Assistant Majority Leader under the most ardent exponent of Clubmanship of all, Senate Democratic Majority Leader Lyndon B. Johnson.

The phrase applied beyond the Senate. Kennedy-appointed State Department official Roger Hilsman wrote of the time he and two other aides waited until a large group left the President's office. "The three of us trooped into his oval office through the curved side door from the room his private secretary, Mrs. Lincoln, occupied and found the President rocking away in his chair before the fireplace, reading and signing the last of a pile of letters. He looked up and grinned. 'And now,' he said, 'we have the 'inner club.'" (That is usually described as "the inner circle.")

The senatorial Club's "folkways" included apprenticeship, reciprocity, issue specialization, deference to a core group of southern Democrats, reverence for seniority and tradition, and personal courtesy. However, the desire of many non-Club senators for media exposure with an eye toward the presidency, accelerated by the rise of partisanship, led to the lessening of dealmaking across the aisle engineered by a core of "heavyweights." There has not been a pairing of powerful, dealmaking clubbers since Lyndon Johnson and Everett Dirksen, which has led to the decline of inner-clubbiness.

For the closest gathering of a bipartisan group acting in concert, see the formation in 2007 of the centrist GANG OF FOURTEEN to avert the NUCLEAR OPTION of weakening the filibuster.

inoperative A correction without an apology, leaving the corrector in a deep hole.

On April 17, 1973, press secretary Ronald Ziegler came before the White House press corps just after President Nixon had announced "new developments" were forthcoming in the Watergate case. When asked about his own previous statements on the case, as well as the President's earlier speeches denying that anyone on the White House staff was involved, the press secretary said—six separate times—that the "operative" statement was the most recent one issued by the President.

Then, in a situation similar to the one that ensnared Harry Truman on RED HERRING, a reporter used the word that later became famous and asked the spokesman if he would adopt it. R. W. "Johnny" Apple of *The New York Times* asked, "Ron, could I follow up on your comment on the 'operative' statement? Would it be fair for us to infer, since what the President said today is now considered the operative statement, to quote you, that the other statement is no longer operative, that it is now inoperative?"

Ziegler, as columnist Nick Thimmesch later put it, "dropped his guard and took the sucker punch." After a minute's fencing, the press secretary replied using the word the reporter knew would provide a devastating lead: "The President refers to the fact that there is new material," Ziegler explained. "Therefore, this is the operative statement. The others are inoperative."

The bit of jargon, with its mechanistic metaphor, stirred great derision. The *New York Daily News* White House correspondent, Paul Healy, said, "I think he should resign. His credibility has been ruined." The National Press Club professional relations committee denounced the way Ziegler "has misled the public and affronted the professional standards of the Washington Press Corps." Seven weeks later, the battered press secretary turned over the briefing function to his deputy, Gerald Warren. Although never accused of telling a lie by the Special Prosecution force, Ziegler was saddled in history by the word he allowed a reporter to lead him into saying.

Inoperative, with its Watergate cover-up connotation, continues to carry a burden of coldly brushing off the past; in 1975, in a *New York* magazine competition, *inoperative statement* was defined as "a lie that no longer works." It has become part of the general vocabulary of the commentariat: "A looming leadership change and urgent domestic problems in France," wrote the columnist Jim Hoagland in 2006, "render inoperative the French-German duopoly that often runs European affairs."

The first known use of the word is by the poet John Donne, who wrote before his death in 1631 about "a dead faith, as all faith is that is inoperative." It can be found four times in amendments to the U.S. Constitution, and until the Ziegler usage was best remembered from Abraham Lincoln's statement on September 13, 1862, explaining why he had not issued an Emancipation Proclamation: "What good would a proclamation of emancipation from me do, especially as we are now situated? I do not want to issue a document that the whole world will see must necessarily be inoperative, like the Pope's bull against the comet." The Proclamation was announced nine days later; Lincoln had deliberately misled his abolitionist callers. He misled himself about the papal bull (meaning "edict"): though Pope Calixtus III decreed "several days of prayer for averting the wrath of God" when Halley's Comet appeared in 1456, the story that the Pope excommunicated the comet by papal bull has been disproved and is theologically inoperative.

in place An informer situated in a position of trust in the enemy camp.

The word is taken from espionage, where to have an *agent in place* is the most productive form of covert operation. Spy novels and movies gave the phrase currency, and the occasional political use of the idea has kept it current. See the sub-entry on *mole* under CIA-ESE.

In many large campaigns, a covert operation put a secretary, office boy, or messenger into the opposition headquarters. This *agent in place* often did nothing more than bring copies of press releases to opposition headquarters as they were delivered to the press, giving the opposing camp time to prepare a counter-release. Post-Watergate, this practice was usually seen to be more trouble than it was worth, since it ran the risk of a DIRTY TRICKS charge.

The phrase had an antecedent political use before it shifted in meaning to become part of the undercover intelligence lexicon. Abolitionist Wendell Phillips, welcoming the crisis caused by Lincoln's election in 1860, told his followers: "Not an abolitionist, hardly an anti-slavery man, Mr. Lincoln consents to represent an anti-slavery idea.... He seems to govern; he only reigns.... Lincoln is in place, Garrison in power."

input See DECISION-MAKING PROCESS.

Ins and Outs The party in power and the party out of power; used to show basic similarity in political ideology.

Democrats in 1892 sang this song for the return of Grover Cleveland: "Grover, Grover, four more years of Grover—In we'll go, Out they'll go, Then we'll be in clover!"

When asked "What is the difference between Republicans and Democrats?" a host of political figures have been credited with the remark: "The only difference is— they're In and we're Out." Herbert Hoover, campaigning against Franklin Roosevelt, in 1932, tried to draw a wider distinction: "This election is not a mere shift from the ins to the outs. It means deciding the directions our nation will take over a century to come." Adlai Stevenson in 1952 derided Republicans for "being out of patience, out of sorts, and ... out of office."

Attorney General Griffin Bell, criticized for replacing Republican U.S. Attorneys with Democrats despite campaign pledges by Jimmy Carter as candidate to keep politics out of such appointments, surprised reporters with his frankness in January 1978: "We have two parties in this country. The 'in' party right now happens to be the Democrats." No such disarming candor came from Bush Attorney General Alberto Gonzales in 2007 when faced with a similar, though more serious, accusation.

There are other meanings to the phrase. An experienced politician is one who knows the *ins and outs* of politics. An *in-and-outer*, however, is a "trimmer," one who trims his sails to catch the prevailing winds and who cannot be trusted to stand fast in times of trouble. But in the sense of "in power," and usually capitalized, the Ins of today are the Outs of tomorrow.

One common denominator of the Outs has always been an envy of the Ins. The British political lexicographer Joseph Pearson wrote in 1793: "If I was stone blind, and sitting my chair, I could tell whether any of the *Ins* were coming, from the Minister himself down to the King's letter-carrier. Damn me, they're all as proud as the Devil."

inside baseball Specialized or private knowledge; the minute details savored by those in the know, found boring by most others.

This prepositional phrase began as a synonym for scientific baseball, the tactical approach to playing that emphasizes nuances like the steal or the hit-and-run. The Baltimore Orioles of the 1890s were known for this playing style. Red Barber, the radio broadcaster known as the voice of the Brooklyn Dodgers, said of the term, "I've heard 'inside baseball' ever since I've been in baseball. The idea of an inner circle, or sanctum sanctorum, goes back all the way to the days of tribal government."

The sports term was transferred to politics as early as 1978. Myra MacPherson wrote in *The Washington Post* that year about Senator Edward M. Kennedy: "He chairs endlessly boring hearings, ... then cuts through testimony with inside baseball jokes that no visitors understand but laugh at anyway."

Describing an intimate interest in fine details and minutiae, *inside baseball* may be used admiringly. Michael Kramer wrote in *U.S. News & World Report* in 1988, "It is one of those underappreciated, 'inside baseball' moments that ratify politics as the Ultimate Game."

The same phrase, however, can suggest an excess of concern with trivia. Richard Weiner, chairman of Michigan's Democratic Party, commented: "The people in my state are interested in jobs, the economy, and education. The rest is inside baseball."

inside the beltway Geographically, within the Capital Beltway surrounding Washington, D.C.; metaphorically, minutiae of government gossip of interest mainly to pundits and lobbyists, but a yawner to those in the Real World Out There.

The delicious details of insiderdom, cherished by insiders, are derided as "inside-the-beltway stuff" by those professing to be in touch with the more important feelings of the GREAT UNWASHED, SILENT MAJORITY, and folks in the HEARTLAND.

The phrase first appeared as a hyphenated modifier in a 1977 *Washington Post* headline on a fishing story: "Inside-the-Beltway Trout Fishing Nears." It was based on the 1951 coinage *beltway* for the surrounding road the British call a *ring road* or *orbital road*; the center of Moscow is similarly circled by the *Sadovoye koltso*, meaning "garden ring." Malcolm Dill, Baltimore County's first planning director, coined the noun to replace *circumferential route*, the term then being used for what is now the Baltimore Beltway. (For a different use of

that word, applicable to "K Street" lobbyists, see BELTWAY BANDITS.)

Its political sense overwhelmed its geographical meaning in the 1980s. A *Newsweek* article in 1984 quoted a Democratic campaign manager who refused to dismiss a possible comeback by George McGovern in 1984, and needed to identify the location of the word in brackets: "If he's perceived as a man on a fool's errand, that's still inside the [Washington] Beltway, not the world as a whole." Later that year, Vice President George H.W. Bush helped popularize the term on *Meet the Press*, discounting a dispute between Treasury Secretary Donald Regan and economist Martin Feldstein, redundantly calling it "an inside-the-Beltway thing that nobody really cares about." Bush urged his interviewers to listen to President Reagan, not to "the who's-up, who's-down, inside-the-Beltway stuff."

Although the term may be used to derogate narrowed interests, some give it a positive spin as "the inside skinny" (also redundant, as *skinny* means "inside dope"). A gossip column in *The Washington Times* used "Inside the Beltway" as its title, and during the 1992 Presidential campaign the neutral phrase was picked up by the pundit Mark Shields in discussing the candidacy of Bill Clinton before official primaries began: "He won the inside-the-Beltway primary."

The negative connotation of insular or elite thinking still colors the expression. During the 1991 confirmation hearings of Clarence Thomas for the Supreme Court, Senator Charles Grassley of Iowa spoke of "ordinary American people, who look at things differently than are looked at here inside the Beltway." Senator John Sununu (R-N.H.) doubted the wisdom of GOP strategy emphasizing national security in the 2006 congressional elections, which drew counter-fire from offended Democrats: "I don't think the inside-the-beltway discussion about political tit-for-tat makes any difference in the majority of races."

The phrase should be hyphenated when used as a modifier before a noun (*inside-the-Beltway wisdom*), and *Beltway* has been losing its capitalization as a specific reference to the Capital Beltway. However, in the attack on lobbyists as BELTWAY BANDITS, the capitalization should remain, as the consultants on K Street, three blocks from the White House and symbolizing the nerve center of influence, operate inside the specific highway ringing the District. For a similar term on interest limited to political junkies, see INSIDE BASEBALL.

instant analysis The reaction of television commentators following a presidential speech.

The phrase was coined by Vice President Spiro Agnew in his first speech castigating much of the media, in Des Moines, Iowa, on November 13, 1969: "a week ago, President Nixon delivered the most important address of his Administration, one of the most important in our decade. His subject was Vietnam. His hope was to rally the American people to see the conflict through to a lasting and just peace in the Pacific. ... When the President completed his address—an address that he spent weeks in preparing—his words and policies were subjected to instant analysis and querulous criticism. The audience of seventy million Americans—gathered to hear the President of the United States—was inherited by a small band of network commentators and self-appointed analysts ..."

This speech, which was written by Nixon aide Patrick Buchanan, was telecast in its entirety on prime time and did much to make the Vice President both a rallying point and a lightning rod. The phrase grew out of *instant history*, a pejorative term for articles and books about current events on recent Administrations, which in turn percolated from *instant coffee*. The use of *instant*—similar to the description of a graduate of Officers Candidate School as a "90-day wonder"—plays on the suspicion of any quick assumption of expertise.

Although Agnew's remarks were roundly denounced by many television journalists as an abridgement of freedom of the press, the subsequent character of analyses following presidential addresses changed markedly from rebuttal to wrap-up, and the frequent showing of a rebuttal by the political opposition.

instinct for the jugular Ability to ferret out and attack the hidden weakness of the opponent; willingness to launch an attack that will do lasting damage; a quality of an ATTACK DOG.

To the tough-minded, the phrase is a compliment; to the tender-hearted, it is a reference to the cruelty of wolves who slash at the vulnerable jugular vein of their quarry to guarantee a kill. Most politicians admire an *instinct for the jugular* in other politicians, but do not like it to show publicly in their candidates.

The vivid phrase, still current but with the bloodiness faded, is one of the oldest in U.S. politics. It was coined by Massachusetts Senator Rufus Choate (coiner of *glittering generalities*), directed at another Massachusetts man, John Quincy Adams, sixth President of the U.S: "He has peculiar powers as an assailant, and almost always, even when attacked, gets himself into that attitude by making war upon his accuser; and he has, withal, an instinct for the jugular and the carotid artery, as unerring as that of any carnivorous animal."

The metaphor used as the opposite of this was reported by Eliot Marshall in *The New Republic* in 1977: "One former [Henry] Kissinger aide told Les Gelb of *The New York Times*, 'Neither Henry nor I in the first years thought [James] Schlesinger was a man to be taken seriously. Given Jim's turn of mind, his interest in the technical rather than policy issues, we thought he had an instinct for the capillaries.'"

No phrase is so horrifying that it cannot be punned upon: humorist Russell Baker was referred to by a colleague as a man with "an instinct for the jocular." See GUTFIGHTER; HATCHETMAN.

insurgent In a positive sense, a political reformer trying to win control of a party; less positively, a rebel or revolutionary seeking to seize control of a government; pejoratively, a euphemism for a terrorist.

Following the defeat and disbandment of Saddam Hussein's army in 2003, *insurgent* was adopted as the broadest label for characterizing a variety of enemy factions that were united only in opposing the occupation of Iraq by the U.S. and its allies. The *Los Angeles Times* headlined a report in November 2003 on a briefing by Gen. John Abizaid: "Head of the Central Command calls the insurgents a mix of ex-regime loyalists, extremists, terrorists and foreign fighters." Edward Wong of *The New York Times* listed *insurgent* as one of a number of possible labels the following month: "The foreign news media has had to grope for an easy way to describe them: do you call them guerrillas, insurgents, resistance fighters, terrorists, mujahideen, rebels, jihadists or loyalists of Saddam Hussein?" To that could be added *Baathists*, members of the political party of mainly Sunni Arabs dominated by Saddam. Secretary of Defense Donald Rumsfeld called them *diehards*, resisting the use of *insurgent* probably because it could imply a legitimate political movement.

Earlier, in Afghanistan, *insurgents* were regarded as allies because they fought on the side of the NATO forces against the Taliban regime. A 30-year veteran of the CIA, Milt Bearden, recalled, "My own experience has largely been on the side of the insurgents." See also ISLAMOFASCISM and JIHADIST.

Stemming from the Latin *insurgere*, to rise up, *insurgent* arose in the mid-eighteenth century as a way of distinguishing an irregular combatant in an undeclared war from a *belligerent* in an officially declared one. Reporting in 1859 on the rapidly dis-Uniting States, the Middletown (N.Y.) *Banner of Liberty* used the term in an approving sense, headlining a follow-up account of John Brown's raid in 1859 on a federal arsenal in what was then Virginia (now West Virginia): "The Harper's Ferry Insurgents." Four decades later, at the beginning of a sequel to the quickly won Spanish-American War, *insurgents* were viewed as the enemy. The Lowell (Mass.) *Sun* carried a report from Manila in September 1898: "The correspondent of the Associated Press had an interview with Aguinaldo, who said there were 67,000 insurgents armed with rifles. He added he could raise 100,000 men. Indeed, the insurgent leader pointed out that the whole population of the Philippine Islands was willing to fight for their independence."

The military *insurgent* was applied to dissidents in domestic politics before the end of the nineteenth century, again with positive or negative connotations depending on the observer's point of view. With Republicans in Pennsylvania fighting each other in 1899, *The Indiana* (Pa.) *Weekly Messenger* left no doubt about which side it was on: "Finding that they are woefully in the minority among Republicans of the Keystone state, these insurgents, as they have since shown themselves to be, have been carrying on a guerrilla warfare against stalwart Republicans in every section of the state. They have a newspaper bureau, which circulates their weekly budget of misrepresentation among the insurgent newspapers."

In Kansas ten years later, the contest in Republican primaries was between *insurgents* and *stand-patters* (see STAND PAT), with the *insurgents* sweeping to victory. *The Fort Wayne Sentinel* reported election results in August of 1910: "Six out of eight insurgent congressmen have been nominated in spite of everything the congressional organization in Washington and the regulars in Kansas could do to save their men."

Another highly successful political *insurgent* was Franklin D. Roosevelt, whose rebellion against the Democratic Party machine was viewed positively. In a profile of FDR just after he won his party's nomination for president in 1932, the *Syracuse Herald* noted: "Within two seeks after reaching Albany, [state] Senator Roosevelt was at the head of an insurgent movement which blocked the election to the United States Senate of William F. (Blue-Eyed Billie) Sheehan, a powerful standpat traction and public utility lawyer who had the backing of Tammany Hall."

Insurgents conduct *insurgencies*. As *insurgent* Ned Lamont contested Sen. Joe Lieberman for the Democratic senatorial nomination in Connecticut in 2006 (Lieberman lost the primary but won the election), former Speaker of the House Newt Gingrich told Fox News: "You have what

I think is a legitimate insurgency in Connecticut, which needs to be met head on and debated head on."

It is hard to visualize American politics without such periodic bouts of intramural warfare. An absence of *insurgencies* upsetting party hierarchies would be a sign of hardening of political arteries.

integration See WITH ALL DELIBERATE SPEED; SEGREGATION; BUSING.

intellectual-in-residence A presidential adviser hired in the Johnson Administration to bridge the gap between the White House and the "intellectual community."

First to hold the job was Princeton professor Eric Goldman, who resigned after a year with a blast at the President's unwillingness to accept new ideas. He was succeeded by John P. Roche, former chairman of Americans for Democratic Action. "I am not a governess to the intelligentsia," Roche said in describing his duties. "I am not the President's ambassador to the 'Partisan Review' or the Metropolitan Opera." His assignment was primarily as a bridge-builder to such outspoken intellectual critics of the Administration as University of Chicago professor Hans Morgenthau, who promptly said: "He conceives his official task to be the HATCHETMAN who will try to ruin the reputation of those intellectuals who dare openly to disagree with his master."

The phrase originated with *poet-in-residence* and *writer-in-residence*, a method used by some colleges to provide the upkeep for a well-known poet or author while enhancing the school's reputation. The whatever-in-residence is rarely expected to teach, but is expected to inspire students with his creative presence.

A misunderstood word contributed to intellectual estrangement soon after Roche took office. To an interviewer, he referred to "the West Side [of New York] Jacobins"; most intellectuals would have taken this allusion to the radicals of the French Revolution in stride, but the word was reported in the *Partisan Review* (quoting a "nationally syndicated column") as "jackal bins," which started a

mild furor in the intellectual community reminiscent of Charles E. Wilson's BIRD DOG … KENNEL DOG.

intellectuals See BRAIN TRUST; EGGHEAD.

interests See VESTED INTERESTS.

intransigent Unwilling to compromise; obstructionist, especially regarding peace negotiations.

During the Mideast SHUTTLE DIPLOMACY of 1974, a "senior official aboard the Secretary's plane" (the phrase denoting Secretary of State Henry Kissinger speaking on background) complained that the Israelis were being *intransigent* in his attempt to negotiate an agreement with Arab states. Since this was the first overt criticism of Israel by a high U.S. official, and was soon accompanied by a threat of a "reassessment" of U.S. support, the word received much attention.

Although hard to pronounce, *intransigence* is a word deeply rooted in diplomacy. *Transigere* is Latin for "carry through; come to terms" and its past participle is *transactus*, the basis for *transact*: thus, *intransigent* is etymologically "unwilling to do business." In diplomacy, this has been interpreted as "uncompromising," and it has long been used as a criticism of one party in peace negotiations.

invective, political Personal abuse, vituperation, and ridicule of another; usually wistfully referred to as "a dying art," but never quite dead.

John Randolph of Virginia, who coined *doughface* to describe the supporters of the Missouri Compromise, served as a power in the House and Senate from 1799 to 1829. Recognized as the master of American political invective, Randolph said of Edward Livingstone, then a House member and later Secretary of State: "He is a man of splendid abilities, but utterly corrupt. Like rotten mackerel by moonlight, he shines and stinks."

Throughout his life it was rumored that Randolph was impotent. Congressman Tristram Burges of Rhode Island said in the

House about Randolph, "I rejoice that the Father of Lies can never become the Father of Liars," to which he replied, "You pride yourself upon an animal faculty, in respect to which the slave is your equal and the jackass infinitely your superior."

Public blows as low as this were commonplace in England and America in the eighteenth and nineteenth centuries. John Montagu, fourth Earl of Sandwich, predicted that his former friend John Wilkes "would either die on the gallows or of a loathsome disease." Wilkes, in a reply sometimes credited to Disraeli, lashed back: "That depends, my lord, on whether I embrace your principles or your mistress."

Modern American invective has often been reduced to simple name-calling, as with John L. Lewis' description of John Nance Garner: "a poker-playing, whisky-drinking, evil old man." In the 1930s, name-calling and invective flourished, with General Hugh Johnson, Westbrook Pegler, and Harold Ickes (for Ickes' contributions, see CURMUDGEON). Johnson, a New Dealer turned against Roosevelt, called New Dealers "economic pansies" and "a cock-eyed crew of wand-waving wizards," and selected Senator Sherman Minton to be "the messenger-boy in chief for the White House janissariat." For farewells, see HAIL OF DEAD CATS.

Hugh Johnson should not be confused with Hiram Johnson, first two-term (of four years) governor of California, who held this opinion of *Los Angeles Times* publisher Harrison Grey Otis: "He sits there in senile dementia with a gangrene heart and rotting brain, grimacing at every reform, chattering impotently at all things that are decent, frothing, fuming, violently gibbering, going down to his grave in snarling infamy ... disgraceful, depraved ... and putrescent."

Westbrook Pegler, whose most frequent target was Eleanor Roosevelt, did much to popularize the phrase *bleeding-heart liberal* (see BLEEDING HEARTS), hit gossip columnists as "gents-room journalists," hit intellectuals as "double domes," and infuriated the FBI by widely disseminating left-wing Congressman Vito Marcantonio's description of Director J. Edgar Hoover as

"a Stork Club detective," a reference to a New York City restaurant frequented by Hoover, columnist Walter Winchell, and assorted celebrities.

Winston Churchill is commonly thought to have directed his famous dig "sheep in sheep's clothing" at Clement Attlee. In a review of the first edition of this dictionary, British historian D. W. Brogan set the record straight: "Sir Winston Churchill never said of Clement Attlee that he was a 'sheep in sheep's clothing.' I have this on the excellent authority of Sir Winston himself. The phrase was totally inapplicable to Mr. Attlee. It was applicable, and applied, to J. Ramsay MacDonald, a very different kind of Labour leader." MacDonald was a favorite target of Churchill's, as illustrated in the following classic of invective without rancor, on a low key: "I remember, when I was a child, being taken to the celebrated Barnum's Circus, which contained an exhibition of freaks and monstrosities, but the exhibit on the programme which I most desired to see was the one described as 'The Boneless Wonder.' My parents judged that that spectacle would be too revolting and demoralising for my youthful eyes, and I have waited fifty years to see the Boneless Wonder sitting on the Treasury Bench."

In current use, political invective has become more decorous; personal attacks are whispered rather than spoken publicly, for fear they will boomerang. (During the 1992 campaign, however, *Newsday* wrote of "the biting sarcasm, that breathtaking invective" from Republican Pat Buchanan, who said, "Bill Clinton's foreign policy experience is pretty much confined to having had breakfast once at the International House of Pancakes.") Perhaps Francis Bacon's words are being considered: "Anger makes dull men witty, but it keeps them poor." ,

investigative reporter See MUCKRAKER.

invisible government Any group accused of creating public policy immune from public criticism or electoral recall.

"The Invisible Government," wrote David Wise and Thomas B. Ross in their 1964 book of that title, "is not a formal body. It is a loose, amorphous grouping of individuals and agencies drawn from many parts of the visible government. It is not limited to the Central Intelligence Agency, although the CIA is at its heart.... This shadow government is shaping the lives of 190,000,000 Americans. Major decisions involving peace or war are taking place out of public view."

In 1967 the editors of *Ramparts* magazine disclosed that foundations acting as conduits for CIA funds had secretly subsidized trips abroad of U.S. student groups. The public reacted severely to this disclosure of a covert operation, and President Johnson ordered it ended. A political cartoon showed a scruffy-looking, bearded beatnik trudging along on a campus, observed by a pair of young women students, one of whom says, "Oh, is he CIA? I thought he was FBI."

After reporter Seymour Hersh broke the story of the CIA's illegal activities in 1975, the "agency"—or as it was also known, "the company"—lost some of its mystery. With repeated disclosures (see *family jewels* under CIA-ESE), the intelligence organization ceased to be known as an *invisible government* and adopted the benign term *intelligence community*.

The term has visibly spread to describe other bureaucracies. A 1991 editorial in *The Seattle Times* wrote of a term-limits initiative that the measure would "not limit power, only transfer it to a permanent, invisible government of legislative staffs and special-interest lobbyists, elected by no one."

Invisible is a word with deep and mistrusted roots in American history. Albert Beveridge, senator, orator, and Lincoln biographer, used the phrase at the 1912 Progressive Party convention that nominated Theodore Roosevelt: "These special interests, which suck the people's substance, are bipartisan. They use both parties. They are the invisible government behind the visible government...it is this invisible government which is the real danger to American institutions." The phrase was used heavily in the three-man Taft-Roosevelt-Wilson campaign; Wilson joined in denouncing the "special interests"and added: "an invisible empire had been set up above the forms of democracy."

In 1923 the *Review of Reviews* reported that "Governor Parker of Louisiana appeared in Washington to consult with President Harding and the Department of Justice regarding an 'invisible government' that was alleged to be interfering with the administration of justice in his own state and in other parts of the South." The reference was to the Ku Klux Klan, known since the Civil War as "the invisible empire of the South."

The Klan became an issue at the 1924 Democratic convention. Liberal, urban forces behind New York Governor Al Smith wanted to denounce the Klan by name in the party platform; agrarian Democrats behind Wilson's son-in-law, W. G. McAdoo, took a more ambivalent attitude toward the extremists, not wishing to alienate the rural vote where the Klan was strongest. As Barry Goldwater did forty years later with EXTREMISM, McAdoo took the key phrase of his opposition, gave it a twist, and flung it back; playing on the "invisible empire" description of the Klan, he spoke of "the sinister, unscrupulous invisible government which has its seat in the citadel of privilege and finance in New York City." With William Jennings Bryan's support, McAdoo won the battle against naming the Klan in the platform by a single convention vote. But the bitterness of this issue, as well as that of the League of Nations, brought forth a moderate dark horse, and John W. Davis was selected as the nominee.

The phrase touches a responsive chord in the minds of people already suspicious of faraway federal government. In the early sixties, ardently anti-Communist Dallas newsletter writer Dan Smoot published a book about the Council on Foreign Relations, titled *The Invisible Government*, which preceded the better-selling Wise-Ross book of the same title.

See DIRTY TRICKS; CIA-ESE.

in your hands A Lincoln construction used by John Kennedy; an oratorical device of involvement.

From Lincoln's first inaugural: "In your hands, my dissatisfied fellow countrymen, and not in mine, is the momentous issue of civil war."

From Kennedy's inaugural: "In your hands, my fellow citizens, more than mine, will rest the final success or failure of our course."

Irish Mafia The Bostonians of Irish descent who were John Kennedy's earliest and closest political aides.

According to Theodore Sorensen, a Nebraskan with no known Irish blood, *Irish Mafia* was a "newspaper designation bitterly resented by its designees when first published." Stewart Alsop probably printed it first, but by the time the Kennedy Administration took office in January 1961, Irish Mafia was a smart "in" phrase. Among the group's prominent members were Kenneth O'Donnell, who became Kennedy's appointments secretary; Lawrence O'Brien, chief congressional liaison and later Democratic National Chairman; and David Powers, a general White House factotum.

Another group, drawn primarily from the academic world typified by McGeorge Bundy, Kennedy's assistant for national security affairs, was often contrasted with the practical politicians of the O'Donnell-O'Brien group. Pierre Salinger, who by background belonged to neither camp, said stories of power struggles between the EGG-HEADS and the Mafia "would arouse JFK to profane anger."

The inference that the Kennedy clan leaned heavily on power plotters hardly blended with the idealistic NEW FRONTIER image. Even worse was the connotation of gangsterism. The original Mafia—a Sicilian slang word of disputed origin—consisted of primitive racketeers. When an Italian-American group objected in the seventies to what they felt was an ethnic slur, the word was avoided by many law officers.

Although the first use in politics of the word was to compare the most useful qualities of a mob hierarchy to those of men surrounding a President, and to salute the loyalty, dedication, background, and toughness common to both, the jocular tone of the phrase was jolted by revelations in 1975 that the "real" Mafia may have been used by the "Irish Mafia"—or at least the CIA, with Kennedy knowledge—to carry out an assassination attempt against Fidel Castro.

In 1964 political writers showed their nonpartisanship by dubbing Barry Goldwater's Republican coterie from home the "Arizona Mafia." A subsequent article in the New York *Herald Tribune* about English governesses in the U.S. was entitled "The Nanny Mafia." By 1978 the "real" Mafia cloud had passed, and the men in the Carter Administration—Georgians Joseph L. "Jody" Powell, Hamilton Jordan, Griffin Bell, Robert Lipshutz, and others—were often called the "Georgia Mafia" or "Magnolia Mafia." Ronald Reagan's entourage included Ed Meese, William Clark, and Martin Anderson, dubbed part of the "California Mafia." George H.W. Bush, from both Maine and Texas, had no Mafia, and the Clinton early cadre went by FOB (Friends of Bill) rather than the "Arkansas Mafia." The younger Bush circle was called "the Bushies."

iron curtain A barrier to communication between peoples, lowered to permit a regime to operate in a society isolated from outside criticism.

This was one of the two great figures of speech in the generation following World War II (for the other, see COLD WAR). It was popularized by Winston Churchill, who had used it several times before deciding to use it strongly in a speech at Fulton, Missouri, on March 5, 1946: "From Stettin in the Baltic to Trieste in the Adriatic, an iron curtain has descended across the continent. Behind that line lie all the capitals of the ancient states of central and eastern Europe.... The safety of the world, ladies and gentlemen, requires a new unity in Europe from which no nation should be permanently outcast." That meant West Germany.

The forum Churchill chose was an unexpected one. The president of tiny Westminster College at Fulton wrote to alumnus General Harry Vaughan, President Truman's military aide, inviting Churchill to speak at the college during a forthcoming trip to the United States. Truman endorsed the idea and passed it on to Churchill, who replied that he had something he would like to say.

The "iron curtain speech" of Churchill marked the end of a peaceful honeymoon with Soviet Russia that had existed in the minds of many Americans after World War II. It became the symbol of Soviet oppression, and the rallying cry for the Western European military organization that came to be NATO.

Phrase detectives—principally Ignace Feuerlicht, writing in *American Speech* quarterly—tracked down a variety of previous uses. It began as a theatrical phrase. A theater in Lyons, France, introduced a curtain in the eighteenth century to prevent the spread of fire, and in 1794 the Drury Lane Theatre in London did the same. Throughout Europe, *iron curtain* was the name for the fireproof curtain in theaters, and the Earl of Munster, writing of travels in India, used it as a metaphor in 1819: "As if an iron curtain had dropped between us and the Avenging Angel, the deaths diminished."

H. G. Wells used it in 1904 in *The Food of the Gods* as a metaphor for enforced privacy; American author George W. Creel in *A Mechanistic View of War and Peace* in 1915 described France as a "nation of forty million with a deep-rooted grievance, and an iron curtain at its frontier." The London *Times Literary Supplement* recalled a 1920 use by Viscountess Snowden in her account of a visit to Russia after the war: "We were behind the 'iron curtain' at last!"

German militarists liked the phrase. Writing in 1923, Walther Nicolai, who served as intelligence chief of the German General Staff during World War I, used the metaphor about a news blockade the wartime allies had planned to impose upon Germany: "It became clear that in case of war, the enemy would shut off Germany from the outside world as with an iron curtain."

Hitler's minister of finance, Ludwig Schwerin von Krosigk, was credited with the phrase as well; Nazi propaganda minister Joseph Goebbels used it often, as in this Reuters dispatch appearing in the Manchester *Guardian* in February 1945: "If the German people lay down their arms, the whole of Eastern and Southern Europe,

together with the Reich, will come under Russian occupation. Behind an iron curtain mass butcheries of people would begin."

On May 12, 1945, Churchill wired Truman: "An iron curtain is drawn down upon their frontier. We do not know what is going on behind." In his memoirs, Churchill called this "the iron curtain telegram." Ten months later, he popularized the term at Fulton, Missouri.

A predecessor to the *iron curtain* was the *cordon sanitaire*, which was drawn around western Russia at the end of World War I in an early attempt at CONTAINMENT of Communism; the *Wall of China* has often been used as a figure of speech saying "Keep out" in international language, later echoed by the *Berlin Wall* (see WALL, POLITICAL SYMBOL OF); and the French military establishment was denounced during World War II for its "Maginot Line thinking."

One of the longest-lived derivatives of the metaphor was *bamboo curtain*, describing the inward outlook of Communist China. Others included *Jim Crow curtain*, coined by Adam Clayton Powell; the *sand curtain* (between the Arabs and Israel); the *marble curtain* (between newsmen and the government), a coinage of Senator Hubert Humphrey; *cobweb curtain* (separating the English press from the royal court); and a *lace curtain* (the closing of New England to Russian tourists), coined by *Pravda*, its unconscious humor noted by some Irish-Americans.

irrational exuberance Mindless euphoria, excessive optimism.

Irrational exuberance rattled investors when uttered by Federal Reserve Board Chairman Alan Greenspan during the course of a speech on "The Challenge of Central Banking in a Democratic Society" before the American Enterprise Institute in Washington, D.C., in December 1996. Greenspan employed the phrase in a rhetorical question: "How do we know when irrational exuberance has unduly escalated asset values which then become the subject of unexpected and prolonged contractions as they have in Japan over the past decade?" The question was buried fourteen pages deep into the speech and might not have been noticed right away, but the speech was televised live by C-SPAN. Traders interpreted Greenspan's words as meaning he thought stocks were overvalued and that the Federal Reserve might respond by raising U.S. interest rates, which would affect markets everywhere.

They reacted immediately: In Tokyo, where the stock exchange was open as Greenspan spoke, prices plunged 3.2%. Reverberations continued through the world's time zones. When the New York Stock Exchange opened on the morning after, the Dow Jones average plunged 145 points, or about 2%, within 30 minutes of trading (prices later recovered somewhat and Wall Street closed down only 55 points at the end of the day).

"It wasn't that I wanted to stand up and shout, 'The stock market is overvalued and it will lead to no good,'" he recalled in his 2007 memoir. "I didn't believe that. But I thought it important to put the issue on the table." He added that "the concept of exuberance came to me in the bathtub."

Greenspan's utterance quickly became a catchphrase. Yale economist Robert Shiller adopted *Irrational Exuberance* as the title of a book, published with eerily prescient timing in March of 2000, just as the dot–com bubble burst with a loud pop: the Nasdaq composite index dived from 5,000 to 2,000 within a matter of months—and kept going down, reaching a low of 1114.11 in October of 2002. Because of the book title and because Shiller had testified before Greenspan and the Federal Reserve Board on December 3, two days before Greenspan's speech, and had lunch with him that day, some people speculated that Shiller was the original source of *irrational exuberance*. He declined the honor of coiner, however, noting that Greenspan was quoted as referring to the "over-exuberance" of the financial community in an article in *Fortune* in 1959, long before he became chairman of the Fed.

Transferring the phrase to a political context, John Derbyshire wrote in the *National Review* in 2005, at a time when "my pals on the neo-Right" were still optimistic about the course of events in Iraq, that "they all have the phrase 'there are many things that could still go wrong' set up as a macro on their word processors, but let me tell you, in private they are pretty darn cheerful. The phrase 'irrational exuberance' comes to mind." In the original, financial sense, referring to China's equity exchanges, which appear to have "more in common with casinos than markets," William Pesek of *Bloomberg News* observed in 2007 that "To say that 'irrational exuberance' has crept into China would make Alan Greenspan's catchphrase seem like an understatement."

"I see" construction A favorite device of speechwriters, outlining a vision of the future punctuated with "I see."

Orator Robert G. Ingersoll, who coined the "Plumed Knight" title for candidate James Blaine, offered an example of this highly effective technique in 1876:

> I see our country filled with happy homes. ...
> I see a world where thrones have crumbled. ...
> I see a world without a slave. ...
> I see a world at peace ... a world where labor reaps its full reward. ...
> I see a world without the beggar's outstretched palm ... the piteous wail of want. ...
> and, as I look, life lengthens, joy deepens, love canopies the earth; and over all, in the great dome, shines the eternal star of human hope.

When Samuel Rosenman prepared a speech for FDR's inaugural in 1937, he used the "I see" repetition in a reportorial, rather than visionary, sense: "I see tens of millions of its citizens" denied the "necessities of life"; "I see millions denied education ..." See ONE-THIRD OF A NATION.

Judge Rosenman and playwright Robert E. Sherwood collaborated on an FDR speech in 1940 that used the "I see" construction in its visionary sense:

> I see an America where factory workers are not discarded after they reach their prime. ...
> I see an America whose rivers and valleys and lakes ... are protected as the rightful heritage of all the people ...
> I see an America where small business really has a chance to flourish and grow.
> I see an America of great cultural and educational opportunity for all its people.

I see an America where the income from the land shall be implemented and protected. ...

I see an America devoted to our freedom ... a people confident in strength because their body and their spirit are secure and unafraid.

Toward the close of his 1952 campaign, Adlai Stevenson outlined his own vision:

I see an America where no man fears to think as he pleases, or say what he thinks.

I see an America where slums and tenements have vanished and children are raised in decency and self-respect.

I see an America where men and women have leisure from toil—leisure to cultivate the resources of the spirit.

I see an America where no man is another's master—where no man's mind is dark with fear.

I see an America at peace with the world.

I see an America as the horizon of human hopes. This is our design for the American cathedral ...

Variations of this construction include "I look forward to" and Martin Luther King Jr.'s "I HAVE A DREAM." Stevenson used the "I look forward" structure in a Los Angeles speech on the American future in 1952; John Kennedy used it in 1963, a month before his assassination:

I look forward to a great future for America, a future in which our country will match its military strength with our moral restraint, its wealth with our wisdom, its power with our purpose.

I look forward to an America which will not be afraid of grace and beauty ...

I look forward to an America which commands respect throughout the world not only for its strength but for its civilization as well. And I look forward to a world which will be safe not only for democracy and diversity but also for personal distinction.

Preparing his acceptance speech at the 1968 Republican convention, Richard Nixon reviewed all the foregoing research submitted by the author, and offered his own vision of America in the year 2000:

I see a day when Americans are once again proud of their flag. ... I see a day when the President of the United States is respected and his office is honored because it is worthy of respect and worthy of honor. ... I see a day when we will again have freedom from fear in America and freedom from fear in the world. I see a day

when our nation is at peace and the world is at peace and everyone on earth—those who hope, those who aspire, those who crave liberty—will look to America as the shining example of hopes realized and dreams achieved.

In what press secretary Joseph L. Powell described as an "ambitious new text," candidate Jimmy Carter incorporated a passage by speechwriter Patrick Anderson in May 1976: "I see an America that has turned its back on scandals and shame ... I see an America that does not spy on its own citizens ..." Will the construction be used again in some acceptance speech or inaugural address? We'll see.

In rhetoric, the Greek-based term for repeated beginnings is *anaphora*. See VISION OF AMERICA; VISION THING; PERORATION.

I shall go to Korea A pledge to confront a problem directly and personally; promise of a hands-on approach to ending a long war.

Dwight Eisenhower introduced this phrase in a statement made in Detroit during his first presidential campaign. Although General Omar Bradley had testified to the Senate in 1951 that widening the Korean conflict "would involve us in the WRONG WAR, at the wrong place, at the wrong time and with the wrong enemy," the conflict did escalate, and in October 1952 truce talks were indefinitely postponed. Eisenhower, however, promised action in his stump speech, pledging, "I shall go to Korea."

This phrase was adopted by the Democrats in the 1992 election. Bill Clinton reminded listeners at the Democratic National Convention in New Orleans: "President Eisenhower didn't complain that the Korean problem was a problem he inherited. He said, 'Vote for me. I will [*sic*] go to Korea.'"

Implicit, but calculated to be not explicit, in the Eisenhower formulation was a promise to end the Korean war (or "conflict," as it was legally called, conducted under UN auspices). Nixon, campaigning in 1968 against Hubert Humphrey in the midst of the Vietnam war, said he would "end the war and win the peace" but never committed to a "SECRET PLAN." Democratic candidates for the 2008 nomination differed mainly in the time it would take to end the U.S. military mission in Iraq but at first were reluctant to open themselves to a charge of CUT AND RUN; several promised that if President Bush did not end U.S. involvement in that war, the next president surely would.

is is, meaning of A profound semantic question that became emblematic of President Bill Clinton's supple, subtle, and sometimes evasive use of language.

The occasion was Clinton's testimony via closed-circuit television to a grand jury on August 17, 1998, about his sexual relationship with White House intern Monica Lewinsky. One of Special Counsel Kenneth Starr's interrogators asked Clinton why he had not corrected his lawyer at a court hearing the previous January when the lawyer denied everything, asserting that "There is absolutely no sex of any kind, in any manner, shape or form."

"It depends on what the meaning of the word 'is' is," Clinton replied.

What the president had in mind was that the relationship with Ms. Lewinsky had ended some months before the January hearing. As he went on to say, parsing the meaning of *is:* "If the—if he—if *is* means 'is, and never has been,' that is not—that is one thing. If it means 'there is none,' that was a completely true statement."

Is is the present tense of the verb *be*, the past tense of which is *was*. Clinton, trained in the law's fine language distinctions, explained, "Now, if someone had asked me on that day, 'are you having any kind of sexual relations with Ms. Lewinsky?'—that is, asked me a question in the present tense—I would have said no. And it would have been completely true." As it happened, when asked under oath and later by interviewers if he *had* (past tense, not *was having*) a sexual relationship, Clinton replied, "there's no sexual relationship," with his elided *s* capable of being construed as either *is* or *was*. Because no questioner thought to clarify whether his "there's" meant "there is" or "there was," he could truthfully claim he had told the literal truth—that no sexual

relationship was being carried on between them at that moment.

Nobody knows whether he planned the obfuscation in advance or thought of it afterward; either way, to the general public his hair-splitting was too legalistic by half, reminiscent of his excuse in 1992 of having smoked marijuana in his youth "but I didn't inhale." Clinton's reply may also have been true in the sense that the meaning of *sexual relations* had been defined very narrowly in terms of a checklist of body parts for the purposes of the January court hearing.

Such legalisms could not save Clinton from impeachment proceedings—or in the court of public opinion. Hours after testifying on August 17, the president admitted on national TV that he had misled everyone, "even my wife," saying: "I did have a relationship with Ms. Lewinsky that was not appropriate." As if recognizing that "not appropriate" would be taken as no less euphemistic than the evasive "mistakes were made," Clinton set aside all such footwork with the admission "In fact, it was wrong."

After his impeachment by the House, he was acquitted by the Senate, served out his second term, and regained his popularity in his ex-presidency. However, *the meaning of "is" is*, even more than his startling "the era of big government is over," remains a memorable part of his legacy.

See also WHITEWATER.

Islamofascism Epithet for militant Muslim enemies of the United States, popularized by American conservatives in the wake of the 9/11 attacks.

Andrew Sullivan, senior editor of *The New Republic*, referred in *The Wall Street Journal* on Oct. 4, 2001, to "Osama bin Laden and the Islamo-fascism of the Taliban." Marking the first anniversary of the attacks, former Secretary of Education William Bennett noted that many young Americans "don't know the greatness that is America, and if they do, they haven't been taught about the evils of the world, the evils of tyranny most relevantly represented by Islamo-fascism." Other early users of the term included Stephen Schwartz, executive director of the Center for Islamic Pluralism, and Christopher Hitchens, who writes for *Vanity Fair* and other magazines as well as the paperless *Slate*. Hitchens also employed the variants "theocratic fascism" and "fascism with an Islamic face." (The latter was a play on Susan Sontag's characterization of the declaration of martial law in Poland in 1981 as "fascism with a human face," in turn based on the 1968 "Prague spring" theme "Communism with a human face.")

Maxime Rodinson, a French Marxist, has been credited with coining *Islamofascism* in connection with the Iranian revolution of 1978. The earliest example of the word in print that I have found comes from an article by the journalist and scholar Malise Ruthven in the London *Independent* of Sept. 8, 1990: "Authoritarian government, not to say 'Islamo-fascism,' is the rule rather than the exception from Morocco to Pakistan."

President George W. Bush in 2006 said that the foiling of a plot in Britain to blow up airliners headed for the U.S. was "a stark reminder that this nation is at war with Islamic fascists." Almost immediately, however, White House aides began having doubts about aptness of the epithet. Michael Gerson, Bush's chief speechwriter at the time, recalled to *Newsweek*: "There was a conscious desire not to use just one definitive word, because there wasn't a perfect word."

The difficulty was the many faces of the enemy: Al Qaeda, ex-Baathists, the Taliban, Hezbollah, Hamas, the Egyptian Muslim Brotherhood, and Shia and Wahhabi groups that detested each other almost as much as they hated the U.S., along with copycat killers who had little in the way of organizational ties. The Taliban, meanwhile, attempted to create a theocratic state but were not fascist in the historical sense of that word. Nor did anyone in the White House want to take the next logical step of applying *Islamofascist* to the governments of such allies as Pakistan and Saudi Arabia.

Nevertheless, *Islamofascism* may have staying power: useful for broadly defining terrorists who profess a religious mission while embracing totalitarian methods, the second part of the word helps separate them from devout Muslims who regard terrorism as a perversion of their religion.

President George W. Bush, straining to be fair to Muslims generally, declined to make a final choice among the possible labels: "Some call this evil Islamic radicalism; others, militant jihadism; still others, Islamofascism. Whatever it's called, this ideology is very different from the religion of Islam."

See also INSURGENT; JIHADIST; 9/11; WAR ON TERROR.

ism A political, social, or economic belief or system; as a suffix, a way of converting names or ordinary descriptive words into broad labels.

In pragmatic America, dogma (whether right or wrong) has always been suspect. ("Let sleeping dogmas lie.") Oswald Garrison Villard, summarizing Calvin Coolidge's appeal to businessmen during the 1924 campaign, said, "He is just what the country needs, a quiet, simple, unobtrusive man, with no *isms* and no desire for reform."

The word goes back to the seventeenth century. In a work published pseudonymously in 1680, the *Vision of Purgatory*: "He was the great Hieroglyphick of Jesuitism, Puritanism, Quaquerism, and of all Isms from Schism."

Ism can be attached to almost anything for the sake of a catchword, either to defend or attack. During William McKinley's Administration, Secretary of War Russell Alger became a controversial figure because of the conduct of his department during the Spanish-American War. "Algerism" became a short-lived but lively topic of conversation and target for political shafts. Senator Joseph McCarthy died in 1957, but MCCARTHYISM remains a key word in a defense against GUILT BY ASSOCIATION or as a counterattack after charges of disloyalty.

Capitalism, militarism, pacifism, nationalism, AMERICANISM, and scores of other *isms* are part of political discourse, although the meaning of any one term varies widely, depending on the ideology of the user and the context of the use. Charles de Gaulle's concept of nationalism, for instance, differed widely from that of a leader of a former

French colony in Africa. The British diplomat Sir Andrew Cohen observed in 1958: "To campaign against colonialism is like barking up a tree that has already been cut down."

Quincy Wright noted in 1954 that social scientists have "long deplored" such terms because they are "highly sentimentalized, ambiguous, controversial, and changeable." He conceded it is impossible to "give precise definition to these words or to substitute other words with no connotation in the popular vocabulary."

Three of the leading political epithets today are RACISM, SEXISM, and *age-ism*, as DEFEATISM is facing off against *triumphalism* and the hitherto unassailable *patriotism* is being challenged by *exceptionalism*, the objection to the idea that America is in a class by itself.

isolationism The theory that America's national interest is best served by a minimum of involvement in foreign affairs and alliances.

Isolationism became a major issue in American politics and a fixture in the American political vocabulary in the post–World War I fight over whether the United States should join the League of Nations. Woodrow Wilson, the preeminent pro-League advocate, castigated those who would have the U.S. retreat into "sullen and selfish isolation." Warren Harding responded: "We seek no part in directing the destinies of the world." Harding prevailed, and the country entered its last period of separation from international power politics, although even during the 1920s it participated in arms-control conferences.

The rise of Nazism in Germany and the Spanish Civil War once again made isolationism versus internationalism a major domestic issue here. Throughout most of the '30s the country's traditional preference for separation from Europe—what Thomas Jefferson called "the exterminating havoc of one-quarter of the globe"—continued at least nominally in force. Franklin Roosevelt, whose name was to become identified with internationalism, said in 1936: "We are not isolationists except insofar as we seek to isolate ourselves completely from

war. ... If we face the choice of profits [from munitions exports] or peace, the nation will answer—must answer—'we choose peace.'" But by 1941 the United States had become the ARSENAL OF DEMOCRACY, and Pearl Harbor ended the isolationists' sway. Senator Arthur Vandenberg, one of the many Republican leaders who abandoned isolation, watched German V-rockets assaulting London in 1944 and asked, "How can there be any immunity or isolation when men can devise weapons like that?"

After World War II, with relatively little dissent at home, successive administrations kept the U.S. in the mainstream of world affairs. But a variation of the old dispute arose when American defense of South Vietnam became bloody and costly. Lyndon Johnson's Administration was accused, in effect, of extending internationalism beyond the bounds of prudence. Many of his most vituperative critics were liberals who had favored earlier foreign intervention. Defenders of the Vietnam commitment charged the dissenters with "neo-isolationism." The liberal historian Henry Steele Commager responded that too much U.S. military activity abroad was leading the country into "intellectual and moral isolationism." For the isolationist-interventionist dispute about the second Iraq war, see STAY THE COURSE and CUT AND RUN.

Isolationist has outlasted *America-firster* as an attack word; those so labeled attack *interventionists* as *warmongers*, while *interventionists* prefer to be called *internationalists* or more recently *globalists* with a "freedom agenda." A word occasionally used as a synonym for isolationist is *peacemonger*. Objectively, the antonym of *isolationism* is *internationalism;* isolationists prefer to denounce *interventionism* and *adventurism*.

See ENTANGLING ALLIANCES; GO IT ALONE.

Israel lobby See CHINA LOBBY.

issues, the Important but dull subjects, treated rationally, which most candidates solemnly promise to campaign upon; a promise usually honored in the breach.

"I intend to campaign on the issues," a candidate frequently announces, and that pledge is dutifully reported as "So-and-so pledged an issue-oriented campaign." The candidate who proclaims his fealty to *the issues* usually refuses to ENGAGE IN PERSONALITIES, which is what interests most voters.

Real issues run the gamut from *gut issue* to *burning issue* to SOCIAL ISSUE and the recurring BREAD-AND-BUTTER ISSUE; but *the issues* is gaining a do-good, bogus-intellectual connotation.

The phrase was popularized in politics by Senator William E. Borah in the campaign of 1928. On March 10 of that year he charged that the Republican National Committee had accepted over a quarter-million dollars from oil magnate Harry Sinclair, adding that "the people are baffled and discouraged because they cannot get the issues squarely and fairly presented." He then delivered a quotable line: "Give the people issues, and you will not have to sell your souls for campaign funds."

In 1972, after presidential candidate George McGovern dropped Senator Thomas Eagleton from the ticket, a *New York Times* editorial adjured the Democratic team to address "itself vigorously to the real issues," which caused one of its columnists, Russell Baker, to comment:

The odd thing about Senator McGovern's Vice Presidential entr'acte was the amount of noise from the press urging that the Vice Presidential crisis be disposed of quickly so that the campaign could proceed to deal with the issues—sometimes called "the real issues." Reviewing Presidential campaigns back into the nineteen-fifties, we are led to suspect that the press people who wanted to move on to these "real issues" were trying to cheat us of what will probably be our one opportunity to perceive Mr. McGovern as he might actually behave in the White House.

In 1977, after a campaign in which he had been accused of being "fuzzy on the issues," President Jimmy Carter told reporter John Sherwood of *The Washington Star* that he felt a kinship with successful congressional campaigners: "We're all fuzzy on the issues. That's proven by the fact that we did get elected. The advantage of being a presidential candidate is that you have a much broader range of issues on which to be fuzzy."

The issues is becoming an issue in itself. Richard Reeves, speculating about a possible 1980 Democratic primary race between Jimmy Carter and California Governor Jerry Brown, wrote in *The Washington Monthly*: "Since both can afford pollsters, Carter and Brown will not be that far apart on what the *New Republic* calls 'issues.'" Tom Bethell seized on this line in *Harper's* (January 1978):

There at last were the issues—the Issues—being referred to within ironical quotation marks. As indeed they should be, if it is true that candidates' (or incumbents') positions are now determined by the findings of pollsters rather than by the principles of officeholders or -seekers. If this is so, then "the issues" have in an important sense disappeared and fully deserve their quotation marks, because they are no longer the object of decision on the part of "decision-makers" in Washington...thus the Issues have become mere ornaments, the wearing of which would inevitably attract such a careful student of style as *Women's Wear Daily*.

The noun *issue* by 2002 had gone beyond vogue status and by 2006 became a thundering cliché, pushing aside *matter, subject, affair, debate, difficulty,* and *bone of contention*, and was giving *problem* a big problem.

In addition to the above cross-references, see CHARACTER ISSUE; LITMUS TEST; PARAMOUNT ISSUE; MAGNET ISSUE; WEDGE ISSUE; HOT BUTTON.

itch to run A yearning for elective office, used most often as a *presidential itch*; a tingling early symptom of POTOMAC FEVER that sometimes turns into a raging PRESIDENTIAL FEVER.

Rutherford B. Hayes, Governor of Ohio, wrote to a correspondent in 1871: "If I thought there was the slightest danger of so obscure a personage as I being attacked with that wretched mania, an itching for the White House, I would beg for the prayers of your church for my deliverance." Five years later he was off and running, winning the presidency despite losing the popular vote to Democrat Samuel Tilden in one of the most disputed elections in U.S. history; as a result, he became known as "His Fraudulency," and said as he departed the capital in 1881: "Nobody ever left the presidency with less regret." However, he did withdraw federal troops from the South and left behind this aphorism: "He serves his party best who serves his country best."

The itch-to-run expression is common in English politics as well. Alfred Austin, poet laureate of England at the turn of the twentieth century, wrote:

You want a seat! Then boldly sate your itch;
Be very radical, and very rich.

item veto See RIDER.

It's the economy, stupid! Formulaic reminder of central campaign goal; purpose in replacing the incumbent.

James Carville, his sobriquet "the ragin' Cajun"—Bill Clinton's main political strategist in the 1992 election—placed a sign over his desk in the Little Rock headquarters: "It's the Economy, Stupid!" For a campaigner fixed on a need for a central theme, the sign encapsulated a pointed response to the question "What is the campaign about?"

After the Clinton victory in 1992, the formula of noun-plus-*Stupid!* became a focus for writers of political headlines. Ethan H. Siegal of Prudential Securities offered the financial-newsletter headline "It's the Deficit, Stupid!" The headline above a David Twersky column in *The Forward* was "The Mideast, Stupid!"

From the Latin *stupere*, "to be stunned," *stupid* is frequently used in direct address. In 1964, *Kiss Me, Stupid* was the title of a movie directed by Billy Wilder. In the '70s, advertisers were told to use "the KISS formula," which stood for "Keep It Simple, Stupid!" Howard Barbanel, an adman, wrote the author in 1993: "The 'stupid' part refers to the one doing either the copywriting or the selling—as a warning to that person not to be tempted to attempt wedging 'War and Peace' into a 2×4 ad or a 15-second spot."

The jocular nature of the imperative takes out the sting of insult; the reader of the notice knows he is merely being urged to keep the central issue in focus.

-ize suffix See VIETNAMIZATION.

J

Jacobins See INTELLECTUAL-IN-RESIDENCE.

janissary See HENCHMAN; SATRAP.

Janus words See OVERSIGHT; TABLE.

jawboning The use of presidential admonition as a tool of INCOMES POLICY.

"The jawbone method" was the phrase used by Walter Heller, chairman of the Council of Economic Advisers in 1962, to describe GUIDELINES set down to restrain prices and wages. The most vivid example of this technique was the confrontation between President Kennedy and the steel industry (see S.O.B.).

When the guidelines began to break down in 1965, the word *jawboning* gained a connotation of ineffective protest.

President Nixon flatly told the Cabinet Committee on Economic Policy in early 1969: "I'm against jawboning." In economic speeches, he said the economy needed "more backbone, not more jawbone." (His speechwriter had been boning up on skeletal metaphors.) Even after his announcement of a new economic policy on August 15, 1971, the President retained his distaste for the ineffective connotation of the word; in September, describing the phase of policy that would follow the wage-price freeze, he told a press conference, "you cannot have jawboning that is effective without teeth," a metaphor too far.

Jimmy Carter, as president, preferred the phrase *moral suasion*, and assigned Robert Strauss, a former Democratic National Chairman, to the job of jawboning business and labor in 1978. The word has fallen into disuse as monetary policy controlled by the Federal Reserve (more than fiscal policy controlled by the president and Congress) is seen as the main determiner of inflation. One word like *firming* spoken by the Fed chairman in regard to interest rates beats all the jawboning the White House can do.

The word *jawboning* invites the citation of Samson's boast (Judges 15:16) "With the jawbone of an ass...have I slain a thousand men." Winston Churchill's remark at a 1954 White House luncheon: "To jaw-jaw is always better than to war-war."

jihadist A holy warrior—or unholy terrorist, depending on one's point of view.

A classified national intelligence study, parts of which were released by Pres. George W. Bush in 2006, stated: "The Iraq conflict has become the 'cause celebre' for jihadists, breeding a deep resentment of U.S. involvement in the Muslim world and cultivating supporters for the global jihadist movement." Writing in *The Washington Post* in 2007, Richard Perle, hardline strategist, blamed the CIA for not anticipating the terrorist attacks on the United States on Sept. 11, 2001: "The greatest intelligence failure of the past two decades was the CIA's failure to understand and sound an alarm at the rise of jihadist fundamentalism."

Jihadist is a term Pres. Bush employed after 9/11 in an effort to put a name and face on the enemy. Others included *evildoers*, *Islamic extremists* or *radicals*, ISLAMO-FASCISTS, and *Al Qaeda suiciders*. None of them were very satisfactory. *Evildoers* was a powerful reminder for those who know the Bible of Psalm 27 ("When evildoers come upon me to devour my flesh"), but the term also had an overly dramatic ring to it; references to *Islam* risked tarring all Muslims with guilt by association; and *Al Qaeda* was one of several enemies in Iraq.

As for *jihadist*, it presented semantic difficulties. For most English-speakers, the foreign word was too unfamiliar to register as a label. Muslims, meanwhile, objected that *jihad* evoked the historical stereotype of fanatic warriors imposing Islam by the sword. (This impression was reinforced by Saddam Hussein's pre-war call for *jihad* against "wicked Americans" should they attack Iraq.) Deriving from the

Arabic *jahada*, "to strive or struggle," the term can be read to apply to spiritual as well as armed struggles. It has had different meanings at different times to different Muslim sects, and some have claimed that it did not necessarily call for bloodshed, but to most Americans it means terrorist war without the "holy."

In September 1990, more than a decade prior to the 9/11 attacks, *Los Angeles Times* columnist John Dart presented the non-bellicose definition: "Many American Muslims cringe at reports from the Middle East of calls for *jihad*, an Arabic word translated 'holy war.' They dislike the English translation. In Islam, the word 'holy' applies only to Allah. And the word 'jihad'—literally 'striving'—primarily describes spiritual and intellectual efforts to become better Muslims and to spread the faith through peaceful means, Muslim scholars say."

See INSURGENT; ISLAMOFASCISM; WAR ON TERROR.

Jim Crow Laws and customs that discriminate against, segregate, or otherwise humiliate African-Americans.

"I was offered the Ambassadorship to Liberia once," said Ralph Bunche, after becoming Undersecretary of the United Nations in 1960, "when that post was earmarked for a Negro. I told them I wouldn't take a Jim Crow job."

At the Republican convention in San Francisco in 1964, a band of black demonstrators marched in front of the Cow Palace shouting and clapping "Jim Crow [clap, clap]—must go!"

A crow is notoriously black. A Kentucky plantation song, sung early in the eighteenth century, coined the name for a dance, or jig:

First on the heel tap,
den on de toe,
Ebery time I wheel about
I jump Jim Crow.

In 1829, entertainer Thomas Dartmouth Rice blacked his face and "jumped Jim Crow" in a Louisville theater. Soon after, the name became synonymous with *Negro*, and around 1840 the segregated car on the Boston Railroad became known as the "Jim Crow." In 1841 the abolitionist *Liberator*

told of the indignity to black editor and later diplomat Frederick Douglass: "The conductor ... ordered Douglass to leave, and to take his seat in the forward car; meaning the 'Jim Crow,' though he felt ashamed to call it by that name."

President Truman took a major step in ending Jim Crow practices by desegregating the armed services. "Experience on the front has proved," the World War I artillery officer wrote, "that the morale of troops is strengthened where Jim Crow practices are not imposed." With great pride, Truman recounted the reaction of Southern Democrats to his insistence on a strong civil rights plank in the 1948 Democratic platform. As South Carolina Governor J. Strom Thurmond walked out of the national convention with his followers, a reporter pointed out to him, "Truman is only following the platform that Roosevelt advocated." Thurmond replied, "I agree, but Truman really *means* it."

The legality of Jim Crow was crushed by the Supreme Court desegregation decision of 1954 (see WITH ALL DELIBERATE SPEED). The most dramatic challenge to Jim Crow customs as well as laws came with the FREEDOM RIDERS in the South in 1961. With education and transportation desegregated, Negroes made housing their next target. Although Lester Maddox won a narrow victory in Georgia in the 1966 race for governor on a slogan of "Your Home Is Your Castle—Protect It," his segregationist ardor cooled somewhat after election day as blacks began to register in greater numbers. In a profile of Senator Strom Thurmond, Republican of South Carolina, *The Washington Post* commented in 1993: "He always kept the voters of South Carolina first on his agenda; when the Voting Rights Act of 1965 guaranteed blacks the vote, he dumped segregation for egalitarianism faster than you can say 'Jim Crow.'"

For other developments in the lexicon of civil rights, see SEGREGATION; BUSING; RACISM; BLACK, POLITICAL USE OF.

jingoism Shrill, aggressive posturing by SUPERPATRIOTS; chauvinism.

In a Venezuelan boundary dispute between Great Britain and the U. S. in 1895, New York

Police Board chief Theodore Roosevelt warned: "We will settle the Venezuelan question in Canada. Canada would surely be conquered, and once wrested from England it would never be restored." To Senator Henry Cabot Lodge, Roosevelt said, "This country needs a war," but added that "the bankers, brokers and Anglomaniacs generally" seemed to favor 'PEACE AT ANY PRICE.' "

Horrified, President Charles William Eliot of Harvard asked whether anything could be more offensive "than this doctrine of Jingoism, this chip-on-the-shoulder attitude of a ruffian and a bully," and added that both Roosevelt and Lodge were "degenerated sons of Harvard." (Roosevelt became more restrained in later years, his best-known remark beginning with "Speak softly …")

The doctrine of *jingoism* that Eliot referred to, along with Roosevelt's peace-at-any-price remark, came from the English parliamentary battle in 1876, with Gladstone on one side facing Queen Victoria and Disraeli on the other. The issue was intervention in Turkey over alleged persecution of Christians there. Gladstone held that Britain should support the Christian minorities against the Turks, threatening to bundle the Turks out of Europe "bag and baggage." Disraeli and the Queen felt it was all a plot by the Russians to expand at the expense of Turkey. When Disraeli threatened the Russians with war if they did not halt the flow of "volunteers" into Turkey, this refrain was heard in the music halls of London:

We don't want to fight,
but by Jingo, if we do,
We've got the ships,
we've got the men,
We've got the money, too!

Jingoism quickly became a synonym for bellicose threats and national cockiness. Disraeli was initially forced into neutrality, but when Russia invaded Turkey in 1878, he sent in the British fleet and helped arrange what he called a PEACE WITH HONOR.

In more recent times, *jingoism* was a charge leveled at U.S. participation in the war in Vietnam. In answer, McGeorge Bundy wrote that the American people "have refused to give support to easy wrong answers at either extreme. Open opposition has flourished. There has been less jingoism than in any previous war in our history." In 1978, opponents of the Panama Canal treaties, who charged GIVEAWAY, were denounced as "jingoes," but in the torrent of criticism aimed at the conduct of the war to establish democratic government in Iraq, *jingoism* was seldom used.

The synonym is SUPERPATRIOTS, or *chauvinists*, from the French *Chauvin*, the name of a semi-mythical Napoleonic veteran mocked as an over-the-top patriot in plays such as Scribe's 1821 *Le Soldat laboureur*. Academic synonyms are *unilateralist* and *triumphalist*.

Winston Churchill wrote in *My Early Life*: "I have always been against the pacifists during the quarrel, and against the Jingoes at its close."

job seeks the man A philosophy of attaining high office believed in by the fatalistic, the idealistic, or the lazy.

A paradox exists in the minds of most American voters. They expect a candidate for high office to be mildly reluctant at first, as "the office seeks the man"; then, with the possibility implanted, he expects the candidate to hungrily seek the office. The man must not try too hard at first; he must not fail to try his hardest toward the end. Many a politician has played "hard to get" a little too long, the possibility of his candidacy does not take root, and he is dismissed with his acquiescence unspoken. (See MAN ON HORSEBACK.)

President Harry Truman, in a passage about "luck" in his memoirs, observed:

> If a man starts out to make himself President, he hardly ever arrives. Henry Clay is an outstanding example. He was so sure he would be President that he twice refused the vice-presidency, and in both cases he would have succeeded to the highest office because of the death of the President. James G. Blaine was another such man. And I was convinced … that Thomas E. Dewey was another whose determined efforts to make himself President would never materialize.

Richard Nixon took the same fatalistic view: "I have a theory," he said in 1958, "that in the United States those who seek the Presidency never win it. Circumstances rather than a man's ambition determine the result. If he is the right man for the right time, he will be chosen." This did not remain his opinion.

Adlai Stevenson, subject of a rare genuine draft in 1952, appeared to many to have overplayed reluctance and humility. In his acceptance speech, he reminded the delegates, "I would not seek your nomination for the presidency because the burdens of that office stagger the imagination…its potential…smothers exultation and converts vanity to prayer." Many politicians felt he made the right speech at the wrong moment.

The concept of "the job seeks the man" applies less to lesser offices than president. In the case of Supreme Court Justice, however, it applies most of all. When Governor Abraham Ribicoff of Connecticut, a strong and early Kennedy supporter, was asked if he had hopes for the High Court, he replied, "He who does not seek is often found. The one thing you should never seek is the Supreme Court."

Columnist Clayton Fritchey wrote in 1967 about the way California Governor Ronald Reagan ducked the question of national candidacy: "When asked about White House aspirations, he declined to be drawn out because, as he reminded the reporters, in this country 'The Office seeks the man,' not the other way around." He added: "Like Lola, what The Office wants, The Office gets. Ask Eisenhower. The General fled to Paris in 1952 and tried to hide out in NATO, but it didn't work…. It's time somebody seeks The Office instead of vice versa."

In this expression, *job* and *office* are used interchangeably; *job*, the more recent usage, seems to be ascendant. With the emergence of women candidates for every level of office, the aphorism—in this dictionary for its historic interest—is doomed unless its final word becomes *person*.

Joe Smith A fictional stand-in; surprise star of the 1956 Republican convention.

After Harold Stassen's effort to replace Richard Nixon as the Republican nominee for vice president proved abortive (see KINGMAKER), the nomination was a foregone conclusion. Speaker Joseph Martin,

convention chairman, had been tipped off by Interior Secretary Fred Seaton of Nebraska that "a misguided and recalcitrant Nebraska delegate" was going to put Seaton's name in nomination, using that as a wedge to make a nominating speech. In that proposed speech, National Chairman Len Hall suspected some alarming things were to be said about President Eisenhower's health; Hall urged Martin to avoid giving the Nebraska delegate, Terry Carpenter, a chance to speak.

When Nebraska was reached on the roll call, the head of the delegation said that Carpenter wanted the floor. "Who does he desire to nominate?" asked Martin, probably out of order. The Nebraskan did not know. Martin explained that the reason he was asking was that he had a note from "a distinguished son of Nebraska" (Seaton) stating he wanted no part of being nominated. This robbed Carpenter of his candidate to "dump Nixon," but he thought fast and came up with a fictional nominee.

"Mr. Chairman," he called out, "we are going to nominate Joe Smith."

"Joe who?"

"Joe Smith!" Amid a roar of laughter in the otherwise cut-and-dried convention, suddenly awakened reporters raced to the Nebraska delegation. Martin thundered the classic order of the day: "Take your Joe Smith and get outa here!"

See CHARLIE REGAN.

John Bull See UNCLE SAM.

John Q. Public The mythical average man, or MAN IN THE STREET; often cartooned as bespectacled, long-suffering, clad in a barrel, but eternally optimistic.

In the fifteenth century his name was *Everyman*, hero of English and Dutch morality plays; when Death called him, he asked his friends Beauty, Kindred, and Worldly Goods to go along. They turned him down, and only one—Good Deeds—accompanied Everyman to heaven. See EVERY MAN A KING.

In the Progressive movement of the nineteenth century, John Q. was *The Man of Good Will*; William Graham Sumner called him *the forgotten man* (not to be confused with FDR's FORGOTTEN MAN who lived "on the bottom of the economic pyramid"); and Woodrow Wilson idealized him as *the man on the make* from "out of the unknown homes" who was the hope of America. Wilson's aim was to set up a government "where the average man, the plain man, the common man, the ignorant man, the unaccomplished man, the poor man had a voice equal to the voice of anybody else in the settlement of the common affairs, an ideal never before realized in the history of the world."

John Q. Public made his appearance on the sports pages of the *New York Evening Mail* in 1922: "John Q. Public Tells Views on the Giants." William Allen White, editor of the *Emporia Gazette*, took the side of the consumer in a 1937 speech: "We are all the children of John Q. Public, and our interests as members of the consuming public are after all our chief end and objective as citizens of our democracy. ... If labor insists," he warned, "upon maintaining its class lines of bitter intransigent hostility to all capital, the American middle class—old John Q. Public and his heirs and assigns— will not support labor."

He signs specimen checks under the name of *John Doe* and *Richard Roe;* his wife, *Jane Doe,* signs specimen subscription orders for her favorite magazines. To a younger set, he has a glazed expression that asks, "What— me worry?" and answers to *Alfred E. Newman.* In other incarnations, he appears as *Joe Zilch* and *Joe Blow.* In China he is known as *Old Hundred Names.* Theatergoers know him as *Littlechap,* who cries, "Stop the world—I want to get off!" Only the Devil himself (Satan, Mephisto, Scratch, Old Nick, Lucifer, etc.) has more aliases.

John is the most common first name, with the "Q" added to give a distinctive, humorously dignified fillip; the last name has genuine built-in dignity, its Latin root *populus,* "people," influenced by *pubes,* "adult."

Robert Bendiner wrote in 1960 about the political diminutives—"*little man, common man, small businessman, small farmer,* and the like. In an election year, we seem to have an enormous population of midgets. The candidate's immediate audience, how-

ever, is never made up of these wee folk; it is made up of *the great people of this great state.* That's you. The little people are your relatives and neighbors."

The trouble with the foregoing monickers for the average person is that they are all male. All of the above presumed "man embraced the woman," as in *mankind.* However, many women felt left out by the terminology; enter *humankind* or the older *humanity. Time* magazine took this into account in renaming its annual cover "*Person* of the Year." A sense of equality and justice demands a personification that is sexless; Jane Q. Public, Everywoman, Jane Doe, even a beer-loving Josephine Sixpack are strained and obviously derivative and do not solve the problem.

That explains the rise of *the little guy. The little woman* has a patronizing connotation; *the little people,* as the above Bendiner quotation notes, suggests midgets or Lilliputians. However, *guy,* which used to be male (*guys* and *gals*), in the 1990s gained a neutral status: *you guys* is used by both sexes about men or women, evidence of a new inclusiveness or embrace of vagueness.

The little guy has an early citation in a 1926 *Port Arthur* (Tex.) *News:* "Why send this *little guy* to jail when the higher up is getting off by graft and bribery?" In current politics, women who embrace populism are enlisted in the army of *the little guy.* See COMMON MAN, CENTURY OF THE.

Johnson treatment The "LBJ brand," or style of presidency; in a narrow sense, the technique of badgering, domineering, dickering, and overpowering that President Johnson was widely reputed to use in person-to-person persuasion.

Jack Bell, AP White House correspondent, called his book about the President *The Johnson Treatment,* subtitled "How Lyndon B. Johnson Took Over the Presidency and Made It His Own."

The Treatment, as it was familiarly known, was described by a recipient, Texas Lieutenant Governor Ben Ramsey, in explaining to Governor Allan Shivers in 1956 why he suddenly switched his support on a matter from Shivers to Johnson: "Lyndon got me by the lapels and put his face on top of mine and talked and talked and talked. I figured it was either getting drowned or joining."

The Johnson treatment was an all-stops-out display of pressure, cajolery, threats, promises of quid pro quo, and refusal to take no for an answer. Rowland Evans and Robert Novak described this scene of the persuasion of Senator Richard Russell to become a member of the Warren Commission on the assassination of President Kennedy: "In a conversation lasting most of an hour, Johnson unleashed The Treatment, dormant now for three years. Emotionally, he recalled their long, intimate association. He appealed to Russell as his friend, and he appealed as the President of the United States. 'If you say no,' Johnson said, 'I'll have you drafted.' Russell accepted, and the Commission was complete."

Used in its general sense, the Johnson treatment was synonymous with his presidential style. The word *style* was almost always used admiringly in regard to Kennedy, derisively regarding Johnson and most presidents since, excepting Reagan; those who liked Johnson's style used the Western metaphor, *brand*. Harvard professor Theodore Levitt made the case in favor of The Treatment in the *Harvard Business Review*:

At best Johnson gets pejorative praise, summarized in tasteless references to the "Johnson Treatment"—the endless telephone calls, implied threats, stubborn push, pleading entreaties, back-room quid pro quos... The Johnson Treatment is nothing more or less than his practice of taking business and other opponents, or potential opponents, into his private and genuine confidence, to talk comfortably about the problems of our people, not intellectually about the issues of our times.

Criticized for his "swagger," George W. Bush told a GOP convention, "In Texas, we call it 'walkin.' "

journalese At the BACKGROUNDERS held by AUTHORITATIVE SOURCES, which can be MEDIA EVENTS in themselves, members of the FOURTH ESTATE—evoking the public's RIGHT TO KNOW—refuse to settle for NO COMMENT or OFF THE RECORD. Instead, reporters, protected by a LID and on a NOT FOR ATTRIBUTION basis, eschew any CHILLING EFFECT and probe the SOURCES

for material for their TICK-TOCKS and KEEPERS, sometimes seeking SOUND BITES to enliven MEGOS with the technique of RULE OUT.

Meanwhile, some PUNDITS and other BIG-FEET—eager for LEAKS but suspicious of PLANTS and scornful of handouts—REPORT-EDLY write such infuriating DOPE STORIES, THINK PIECES, and THUMBSUCKERS that they REPORTEDLY wind up on the ZOO PLANE.

juice Political power.

Among the many slang senses of *juice* (liquor, gasoline, hot money) is "electrical current," which is the metaphoric base of this political term that surfaced in the '70s. To be able to apply "juice" is to be able to flip the switch that generates great political power.

Reporter Nicholas Horrock wrote in *The New York Times* in 1977 of a plan proposed by the Director of Central Intelligence, Admiral Stansfield Turner, to take over "line authority" of intelligence agencies currently under the Defense Department: "But reportedly, Vice President Mondale... opposed the plan on the ground that it would have placed too much of what in Washington is called 'juice' at the admiral's fingertips."

When a surprise roll-call vote overturned an expected voice-vote approval of cargo-preference legislation in 1977, *The Washington Post* reported the bitter comment of an aide to House Merchant Marine Chairman John Murphy: "We got juiced."

The word appeared to be squeezing out CLOUT, but was short-circuited by the attention paid to the trial for murder of O.J. Simpson, whose nickname was "Juice" because "OJ" is a way of ordering orange juice.

junket See NONPOLITICAL TRIP; FACT-FINDING TRIP.

junketeering gumshoes Derisive description of a European fact-finding tour taken by two members of Senator Joseph McCarthy's subcommittee staff.

Roy M. Cohn and G. David Schine visited U.S. Information Service libraries in Europe during 1954, and recommended that certain anti-American books be removed from the taxpayer-supported shelves. Cohn informed the author it was Theodore Kaghan, at the U.S. High Commissioner's office in Germany, who coined the phrase.

"It turned out to be one of the most publicized journeys of the decade," wrote Cohn in 1968, characterizing the trip as a "colossal mistake. What we failed to foresee was the propaganda uses to which our critics would put the journey. David Schine and I unwittingly handed Joe McCarthy's enemies a perfect opportunity to spread the tale that a couple of young, inexperienced clowns were bustling about Europe, ordering State Department officials around, burning books, creating chaos wherever they went, and disrupting foreign relations."

Junket and *junketeer* carry connotations of *joyride*, a vacation at public (or anyone else's) expense. Congressmen called these NONPOLITICAL TRIPS, inspection tours, or FACT-FINDING TRIPS by a *Codel*, short for *congressional delegation*; critics call them *junkets*. When a business firm or tourist board invites newsmen on a junket, it is so labeled; some newspapers insist on paying the equivalent air fare to the destination.

Gumshoe has a long history. The present word for the item it originally identified is *sneaker*—a canvas shoe with rubber sole and heel used most often in sports. Because the wearer can move most quietly, the gumshoe became synonymous with stealth. See PUSSYFOOTING. Martin Van Buren, who had acquired a certain reputation for wiliness, was accused of "rowing to his object with muffled oars" and "making his way to the White House in gumshoes." *Gumshoe campaign* was used at the turn of the century, especially in the Midwest, to describe a quiet campaign; currently the word is slang for "detective," used often as a verb.

Kaghan's skillful combination of the two words made it an effective derogation of McCarthy's investigators, and led to the BOOKBURNER speech by Eisenhower.

Junketeering remains a sneering participle. "Lawmakers are back in session tomorrow after an exhausting week of junketeering," wrote the *Sacramento Bee* in the spring of 2007. "We can't wait to see their slide shows."

junta A small group, usually military, that rules a country after a coup d'état.

This Spanish word, meaning "council" or "meeting," was popularized by its 1808 use to describe the groups formed in Spain during the Peninsular War against Napoleon. In Latin America, the noun has been used frequently; it usually denotes a council coming into power as the result of force or revolution and often includes military leaders.

The word comes from the Latin *juncta*, a past participle of the verb *jungere*, "to join." (In the sense of a self-appointed ruling committee after a coup, the spelling *junto* may also be used, although *junta* is the earlier spelling.) When a group that seizes power is not predominantly military, it is called a CABAL.

Junta is almost always used pejoratively, as the group has by definition come to power through undemocratic means. In Myanmar, also known as Burma, Aung San Suu Kyi, the Nobel laureate whose National League for Democracy won an election in 1990, has since been imprisoned by a military clique that is universally called a *junta*. The word is pronounced "HOON-ta" in the United States, after the Spanish pronunciation, and Anglicized as "JUN-ta" in Britain.

just and lasting peace A Lincoln coinage about the Civil War, used in regard to the settlement of almost every war since then.

The phrase comes from Lincoln's second inaugural address, along with "bind up the nation's wounds" and "with malice toward none": "to do all which may achieve and cherish a just and lasting peace among ourselves, and with all nations."

President Eisenhower, in his statement in Geneva in 1955, departed slightly from the text to refer to "a just and durable peace," but returned to report to the American people that "we will make constantly brighter the lamp that will one day guide us to our goal—a just and lasting peace."

"Bad" peaces are usually described as *uneasy* or *shaky;* "good" peaces are referred to as *peace with justice* or PEACE WITH HONOR. The overriding ideal, however, appears to be permanence; the Chartist petition of 1828 in England called for the universal suffrage that would bring "true and lasting peace."

just war See WAR OF NATIONAL LIBERATION.

K

K Street See BELTWAY BANDITS.

kangaroo ticket One in which the vice presidential candidate has greater political appeal than the presidential candidate.

Unnamed friends of Treasury Secretary John F. Connally were described by R. W. Apple in *The New York Times* in 1971 as saying he would run for vice president in 1972 if asked by President Nixon, but joked that one condition would be that "he would insist that the Nixon-Connally partnership be advertised as a 'kangaroo ticket.'"

The phrase was tracked by lexicographer Grant Barrett to an 1848 usage in the *Zanesville* (Ohio) *Courier*: "We may say of this ticket, thus formed, as some one said in 1844, when the Baltimore Convention nominated Silas Wright as Vice President with James K. Polk, that it is a 'kangaroo ticket, with all its strength in its hind legs.'" It was repeated often, as in 1932, when some thought that John Nance Garner, the Democratic vice presidential nominee (the hindquarters in this analogy), had more spring than Franklin D. Roosevelt (the forequarters). In 1992, Paul Greenberg of the *Arkansas Democrat-Gazette* wrote, "Clinton-Gore may yet turn out to be a kangaroo ticket a la Dukakis-Bentsen: stronger in the hind legs."

The kangaroo, a herbivorous, leaping marsupial mammal native to Australia, has made other contributions to American slang. It has been used as a variant of *rump convention*, because it has a muscular posterior; in an issue of the *Sonora Democrat* in Santa Rosa, California, in 1868, *kangaroo convention* was used in a way that indicated previous coinage.

A *kangaroo court* is an irregular tribunal, such as a trial by prisoners in a jail, or a minor court in a frontier jurisdiction; the military tribunals set up after 9/11 in the U.S. base at Guantanamo Bay, Cuba, were so described in 2001 by the author. *Kangaroo closure* occurs when a chairman or speaker selects only those amendments of a bill he is interested in as subject to debate. In underworld lingo, a *kangaroo* is a shoplifter with capacious pockets.

K_1C_2 The Republican campaign symbol combining the three key issues of 1952: Korea (and the Democrats' inability to end the war), Communism (SOFT ON), and Corruption (the MESS IN WASHINGTON).

Combinations of numbers and letters resembling chemical or mathematical formulas are catchy political devices for bumper stickers. In 1964, the Goldwater campaign used $AuH_2O = 1964$. In 1972, Republican Senator Hugh Scott branded Senator George McGovern, about to be selected the Democratic presidential nominee, "the 3A candidate," standing for "acid, abortion, and amnesty." In the new millennium, G3 was an insider signal for the use of GOD, GUNS, AND GAYS.

keeper A news story held for use at a more newsworthy time.

This journalistic term can be used to describe an innocent delay of a story until a more propitious moment, or a manipulative delay of a story until it can do the most damage.

"It is largely in the executive offices of the printed press and the networks that slanting the news and its editorial evaluation is to be found," wrote Arthur Krock, former Washington correspondent and later conservative columnist of *The New York Times*, on page 229 of his 1971 book, *The Consent of the Governed*, in a chapter on "The Power of the Press." "Important in the process are: the placement of the news by which it can be minimized or magnified; and holding back news stories called 'keepers' for publication on a date when they will have the stronger impact in forming public opinion aligned with the editorial policy of the newspaper concerned."

keister The buttocks.

President Ronald Reagan in 1983 popularized the old euphemism, expressing his ire at the disclosure of his private conversations by saying, "I've had it up to my keister."

Pronounced "KEE-ster," with its variant spelling *keester*, the word is of uncertain origin, but may have come from the German *Kiste*, "chest." Its earliest English meaning is "suitcase, satchel," particularly in criminal slang for "burglar's tool-bag"; in The *National Police Gazette* of 1881 was a listing of New York con artists including "Keister Bob."

The journal *American Speech*, listing in a 1931 glossary the current sense, reported two meanings for the word: "*Keister*, a satchel; also what one sits on." By 1983, the term *ass* no longer needed a euphemism, except in *The New York Times*, though it is still often avoided as a vulgarism, in which case it is replaced by *buttocks* or by the jocular use of *butt, rear end, fanny*, and the bookish *posterior*. See C.Y.A., in which one's posterior is covered for posterity.

key aide See STAFFER.

kinder and gentler nation A wish for the nation's future; a vision of a peaceful America.

Vice President George Herbert Walker Bush used the modifiers *kinder* and *gentler* in his speech accepting the presidential nomination speech at the 1988 Republican National Convention in New Orleans: "But where is it written that we must act if we do not care, as if we're not moved? Well, I am moved. I want a kinder and gentler nation." (See THOUSAND POINTS OF LIGHT.) The adjectives were chosen by the speechwriter Peggy Noonan to express Bush's vision for the post-Reagan era in America.

Bush repeated the phrase in his Inaugural Address, and the words became identified with him, sometimes with a sarcastic twist, more often taking him at his word. Former First Lady Nancy Reagan's reportedly acerbic comment: "Kinder and gentler than whom?"

Readers, however, sought literary sources of the phrase from Tolstoy to Thomas Mann, and collocations of the adjectives that predate the Bush usage. Bruno Stein, director of the Institute of Labor Relations at New York University, found this comment made by the defense attorney Clarence Darrow about the labor leader Eugene V. Debs: "There may have lived somewhere a kindlier, gentler, more generous man than Eugene Debs, but I have not known him."

Kingfish Self-proclaimed nickname of Huey Long, governor and later senator from Louisiana, assassinated in 1935.

The nickname was drawn from "Kingfish of the Lodge," a likeably pompous African-American character on the popular "Amos 'n Andy" radio program of the '30s. Long's choice of the name showed a good instinct for self-deprecating humor that was to become fashionable a generation later. His son, Russell Long, managed to live down the nickname "Princefish," and became one of the powers of the Senate.

"Share the Wealth" and "EVERY MAN A KING" were two of Long's short slogans.

kingmaker One who places another in a position of power when, for reasons of personality, circumstance, or preference, he cannot or will not place himself there.

"In elective governments," wrote English royalist Roger L'Estrange in the time of Cromwell, "there is a tacit covenant that the king of their own making shall make his makers princes." Richard Neville, 16th Earl of Warwick, is known in English history as "the Kingmaker"; he gained his sobriquet during the Wars of the Roses by helping Edward IV depose Henry VI in 1461, then restoring Henry to the throne in 1470. He figures prominently in Shakespeare's *Henry VI*, Parts 2 and 3.

Rarely do kingmakers serve their sovereigns without expectation of reward. Theodore Roosevelt passed the mantle of the presidency to his personal choice, William Howard Taft, and was convinced he acted with the purest altruism. But when Taft wrote Roosevelt immediately after the election that "you and my brother Charlie" made him President, the estrangement began. Roosevelt wondered to a friend what "brother Charlie" had to do with it, and soon was taking umbrage at what he felt were slights by the new President.

The most famous American kingmakers were Henry Clay, who delivered the swing vote necessary to elect John Quincy Adams and received the post of Secretary of State in return, enraging the Jackson men ("Bargain and Corruption" was their slogan); Mark Hanna, the Cleveland industrialist who masterminded and financed William McKinley's election; and Harry Daugherty, who spotted Warren Harding, a handsome, small-town newspaper editor in Ohio, and helped him up the ladder through the SMOKE-FILLED ROOM (in which Daugherty was not present) to the White House. Years later Daugherty said of Harding: "I found him sunning himself like a turtle on a log, and I pushed him into the water."

However he exaggerates his own importance, the manipulative politician knows that he is dispensable after power is achieved by his candidate. Since kings tend to resent playing the statue Galatea to its sculptor Pygmalion, the wise counselor admits only to having "helped."

Most recently, television advisers have been given Warwick's sobriquet. In an article on advisers Jerry Rafshoon and David Garth, opposed in the 1977 New York mayoral campaign, reporter Joseph Lelyveld described Rafshoon's national reputation as the man who helped "create" Jimmy Carter: "When the votes were in, [Carter] sent his media man a lightly ironic note that hangs now above the fancy new desk in Rafshoon's fancy new office, a block from the White House. 'I'll always be grateful,' the note says, 'that I was able to contribute in a small way to the victory of [the] Rafshoon agency.'"

Mr. Garth, who was Mayor John Lindsay's media adviser, had this quotation on his wall, from Niccolò Machiavelli: "Whoever causes another to become powerful is ruined, because he creates such power either with skill or with force; both these factors are viewed with suspicion by the one who has become powerful."

The term has been applied to foreign political figures as well as to Americans.

According to the December 3, 1990, *New Republic*, "[Lech Walesa] happily played kingmaker, choosing Mazowiecki, his longtime adviser, as prime minister."

The term remains in current use. Karl Rove was described by George W. Bush as "the architect" of his election victories; partisan Democrats called him "Bush's brain." When he retired as resident White House GURU in 2007, Australia's *Daily Telegraph* headlined: "Rove the kingmaker is jumping ship."

See GRAY EMINENCE; POWER BEHIND THE THRONE; POWER BROKERS.

kiss of death Unwelcome support from an unpopular source, sometimes engineered by the opposition.

Occasionally, unpopular organizations move in Machiavellian ways, publicly supporting the candidate they most want to defeat. More often, they will quietly pass the word to their members to support a candidate they would like to see elected and then scrupulously avoid making any public statements in his support that might embarrass him.

Governor Al Smith of New York popularized the phrase in its political context in 1926, when he called William Randolph Hearst's support of his opponent, Ogden Mills, "the kiss of death."

Walter Lippmann discussed the technique in 1936: "Thus it has recently been said that Senator Borah received 'the kiss of death' when Dr. Townsend gave him his blessing. Governor Landon has received the kiss of death because Mr. Hearst is for him. Senator Vandenberg has received the kiss of death because someone took it into his head to say that Mr. Hoover is for him. ... Colonel Knox has been repeatedly kissed to death because certain not too savory Illinois machine politicians are for him ..."

The phrase is derived from the kiss of Judas and the betrayal of Christ. It is also described as coming from a gangland custom said to have begun in Sicily. The code of the criminal organizations of southern Italy is called *omertà*, implying absolute prohibition of cooperation with state authorities; "kiss of death" in Italian is *bacio della morte*.

"In the mobs," wrote Russell Baker, "a kiss from the boss is tantamount to arriving at the office one morning and finding your rug gone. When [Joseph] Valachi got the kiss and noted that Johnny Dio was oddly anxious to have him step into the privacy of the showers, Valachi concluded that he was a 'dead duck' and defected."

Coming down the center aisle of the House of Representatives to give the 2005 State of the Union address, President Bush shook hands with and embraced many members of Congress. One who got a big hug and a touching of cheeks was Connecticut Democratic senator Joseph Lieberman, a strong supporter of the war in Iraq despite its waning support in the polls. The following year, Lieberman was challenged in the Democratic senatorial primary in Connecticut by an ardent anti-war liberal with substantial funds and the enthusiastic backing of activists and bloggers locally and around the nation. Their most stinging ad was a picture of "the kiss"—a picture and papier-mâché sculpture that dramatized the degree of support by Lieberman of the man most Democrats angrily opposed. The anti-anti-war *Weekly Standard*'s worried headline as voting approached was "Kiss of Death?" Lieberman lost the Democratic primary but ran as an independent and went on to defeat his Republican and Democratic challengers in the general election.

kitchen cabinet Informal advisers to the President who, while holding only minor offices themselves—or none at all—may exert more influence on policy than the real cabinet because of their close personal relations with the Chief Executive.

Early in his first Administration, Andrew Jackson for a time suspended formal cabinet deliberations. His enemies accused him of substituting the judgment of five of his friends—two editors and three minor Treasury Department officials—for that of the regular department heads, especially in directing the attack against the United States Bank. Despite their presumed influence, it was no compliment to be called a member of the kitchen cabinet. Said Davy Crockett in 1834: "I might easily have been

mistaken for one of the Kitchen Cabinet, I looked so much like a ghost."

Presidents before and after Jackson were similarly charged. Thomas Jefferson was accused of forming "an invisible, inscrutable, unconstitutional cabinet" that dealt in "back-stairs influence." Jackson's frontier coterie was the first designated as the "kitchen" cabinet, presumably because of his and their reputation for unpolished manners. But the kitchenites had their defenders. The *Washington Globe* described them in 1838 as "men fresh from the ranks of the people, acquainted with their wants and understanding the current of their opinions."

The term began to lose its sting after Jackson's time and today is rarely used by itself. But because most presidents do have circles of personal friends, the phrase has developed variants. Theodore Roosevelt had his "tennis cabinet." Jonathan Daniels refers to Warren Harding's "poker cabinet." Herbert Hoover had an exercise-loving "medicine ball cabinet." Even governors could play the game: in writing of New York's Alfred Smith, Ed Flynn mentions the "golfing cabinet."

Harry Truman pretended to organize a facetious "kitchen cabinet" consisting of a Secretary for Inflation, Secretary of Reaction, Secretary for Columnists, and Secretary of Semantics ("to furnish me with 40- to 50-dollar words"). More than most modern Presidents, Truman was accused of relying too much on the advice of longtime friends (see GOVERNMENT BY CRONY). John F. Kennedy later observed: "Congressmen are always advising Presidents to get rid of presidential advisers. That's one of the most constant threads that run through American history, and Presidents ordinarily do not pay attention."

When it became known in 1977 that President Carter's Special Trade Representative, Robert Strauss, was becoming the most listened-to adviser in the President's cabinet, the Texan was asked when he expected to move his office into the White House. "You don't have to be inside the kitchen," he replied, "to be a member of the kitchen cabinet." He went on to become a member of the kitchen cabinet of his fellow Texan George H.W. Bush—without losing his Democratic connections. (It was Strauss who began one of his rousing, amusing talks with "Before I begin this speech, there is something I want to say …")

kitchen debate The verbal sparring match between Vice President Nixon and Soviet Chairman Nikita Khrushchev in the "typical American home" at the U.S. exhibition in Moscow in 1959.

There were two debates that day. At the RCA color television exhibit, Khrushchev unexpectedly attacked U.S. policy before the cameras, with the Vice President parrying the remarks, trying to be the good American-exhibition host. By the time the Russian leader strolled out of the studio, however, it was clear that this was only the opening round, which went to the determinedly aggressive Khrushchev; the main bout would be elsewhere.

The author, then a press agent publicizing the "typical American home" exhibit, enlisted the aid of Nixon's military aide, Major Don Hughes, in arranging for a mixup in the flow of the crowd, trapping the leaders in the ranch-house exhibit. Nixon felt that an American kitchen was a suitable forum for a comeback in debate, to discuss the standard of living and the variety of choice available to American working people.

In *Six Crises*, Nixon wrote: "The conversation began innocently enough. We discussed the relative merits of washing machines. Then I decided that this was as good a place as any to answer the charges that had been made in the Soviet press, that only 'the rich' in the United States could afford such a house as this. I made the point that this was a typical house in the United States, costing $14,000, which could be paid over twenty-five or thirty years. Most U.S. veterans of World War II have bought houses like this, in the $10,000 to $15,000 range, I told him, adding that most any steelworker could buy one."

Khrushchev retorted, "We too can find steelworkers and peasants who can pay $14,000 for a flat." He accused American builders of planning obsolescence—building a house to last only twenty years—while Soviets build for generations. He made a sarcastic point: "If an American citizen does not have dollars, he has the right to buy this house or sleep on the pavement at night."

The debate was accompanied by jabbing fingers and lapel-grabbings. Nixon tried to end it with a light touch: "Isn't it better to be talking about the relative merits of our washing machines than the relative strength of our rockets?" But Khrushchev, with the world press crowded around, pressed ahead: "Yes, that's the kind of competition we want, but your generals say we must compete in rockets. … We are strong, we can beat you." Nixon came back hard behind a pointed finger, in a picture caught, with Khrushchev blinking in surprise, by Elliot Erwitt of Magnum: "You are strong and we are strong. … For us to argue who is the stronger misses the point. If war comes, we both lose."

The AP photographer, Hans Von Nolde, was blocked by guards and lobbed his camera to the press agent in the kitchen, who took the other famous picture of the two leaders in debate transmitted by AP Wirefoto, though he had to include a Russian bureaucrat who pushed his way into the scene in what turned out to be Leonid Brezhnev's first publicity break.

To the observers in the kitchen, Khrushchev appeared to be using, rather than losing, his temper, and Nixon played off that, firm but not unfriendly. After a discussion about threats and ultimatums, Nixon broke off the debate with a light remark and Khrushchev picked up the cue, thanking the refrigerator demonstrator "for letting us use her kitchen for our argument."

The event was initially dubbed the "Sokolniki Summit" (after Sokolniki Park, in which the exhibition was held) by Harrison Salisbury of the *New York Times*. However, Salisbury was accompanied in the kitchen by an American press agent (the author) who assured the Russian guards the reporter was a "refrigerator demonstrator." The press agent, whose job it was to publicize the house and kitchen rather than the Russian park, told other reporters about the "kitchen conference." Salisbury, repaying the flack for his access to the guarded kitchen, adopted the phrase in briefing other reporters, and it is still recalled as the "kitchen debate" or "kitchen conference."

klong Stomach-churning dismay at a personal crisis caused by one's own thoughtlessness.

Senator George McGovern's 1972 presidential campaign manager, Frank Mankiewicz, who coined the term, defined *klong* as "a sudden rush of shit to the heart."

Klongs are divided into the *petit klong*, which can be the dismayed realization of a candidate taking a nap on a couch at headquarters that he invited a dozen major contributors to dinner at his house beginning an hour ago and he has no excuse, and the *grand klong*, which comes to a politically ambitious prosecutor who prepares and publicizes a case and brings it to fruition one day after the statute of limitations has run out.

knee-jerk liberal An unthinking pseudo-intellectual; an attack phrase on one who gives automatic support to causes favored by the political left.

In current usage, a PROFESSIONAL liberal is the most uncommitted, a FLAMING LIBERAL is the most militant, and a *knee-jerk liberal* the most automatic. There is also a large crowd of *proud liberals* who have taken to calling themselves PROGRESSIVES. For answering accusations aimed at conservatives, see HIDEBOUND; NEANDERTHAL WING; ROCK-RIBBED; MOSSBACK.

Knee-jerk is among the most descriptive and least pedantic medical words coined in the past century. Sir Ernest Gowers, a giant of linguistics who edited the second edition of Fowler's *Modern English Usage*, told of its origin in *Plain Words* (1948): "Some seventy years ago a promising young neurologist made a discovery that necessitated the addition of a new word to the English vocabulary. He insisted that this should be *knee-jerk*, and *knee-jerk* it has remained, in spite of the efforts of *patellar reflex* to dislodge it. He was my father; so perhaps I have inherited a prejudice in favor of homemade words."

knock on the door See RAP IN THE NIGHT.

know-nothings A political faction, active during the 1850s, which opposed immigration and sought anti-Catholic measures; in the twenty-first century, an accusation of bigotry.

The Know-Nothings sprang from splinter groups that had several names, such as the Order of the Star-Spangled Banner, the American Party, and the Native American Party (leading to a nickname "Sams," after Uncle Sam). They were widely described as Know-Nothings because they refused to tell outsiders of their activities. The Cleveland *Plain Dealer* revealed the routine in 1854: "When one Know Nothing wishes to recognize another, he closes one eye, makes an O with his thumb and forefinger and places his nose through it, which, interpreted, reads eye-nose-O—'I know nothing.'"

One of the party's key publicists was Anna Ella Carroll, an unrecognized military strategist who helped the candidacy of Millard Fillmore. Although the party had some successes in the 1854 elections, it soon broke up because of internal disputes. Its members joined other parties, but to be accused of having been associated with the Know-Nothings was a political liability. This led Abraham Lincoln to say in 1855: "I am not a Know-Nothing. How could I be? How can anyone who abhors the oppression of negroes, be in favor of degrading classes of white people?" (Note: *Negro* was not at that time capitalized; current usage requires it, even as most U.S. blacks prefer *African-American*.)

Although the Know-Nothing party disintegrated, its spirit lived on in such organizations as the American Protective Association and the Ku Klux Klan. The phrase is still used occasionally to describe REACTIONARIES, SUPERPATRIOTS, and other residents of the extreme right, as when *Time* magazine described George Wallace as seeking to run for President in 1968 "under a neo-Know Nothing banner."

The historian Eric Goldman, who as a Johnson aide tried and failed to bring together the White House and the academic or intellectual community, passed this judgment on the conduct of both camps at an ill-fated arts festival, in his *The Tragedy of Lyndon Johnson* (1969): "I had seen a President reacting with arrogant know-nothingism, and influential figures in the cultural world reacting with an equally arrogant know-it-allness."

With an estimated 12 million immigrants living illegally in the U.S., and with their children born here legal U.S. citizens under the Constitution, immigration became a major issue in the twenty-first century's first decade. An immigration law passed in 1986, signed by President Reagan, which gave most illegal immigrants in the U.S. the "green cards" of permanent residency did not stop the influx. Proposals in 2007 ranged from a fence along the border between Mexico and the U.S., with an increased force to patrol the border and sanctions on employers who hired the "*ilegales,*" to a form of waiting time and "earned citizenship" that opponents called a thinly disguised form of *amnesty,* a word that polled as unpopular.

"America's New Know-Nothings" was the headline over a column by Fareed Zakaria, editor of *Newsweek International.* He recalled a 1996 statement by Rudy Giuliani: "You look back at the Chinese Exclusionary Act, or the Know-Nothing movement— these were movements that encouraged Americans to fear foreigners, to fear something that is different and to stop immigration." Although President George W. Bush and other Republicans supported a bipartisan border-enforcement-plus-earned-citizenship compromise for "guest workers" and their families put forward by Senators John McCain and Edward Kennedy, the columnist charged that the Republican party Giuliani was campaigning to lead "is becoming the modern incarnation of the Know-Nothings."

See THIRD-PARTY MOVEMENT; UN-AMERICAN; YAHOO; AMNESTY.

kooks, nuts and Extremists; far-right or far-left wingers; distinguished by hate campaigns, occasional scruffiness, and unconventional political behavior.

Gook was a slur used by American soldiers to describe any Asian, friend or foe;

it should not be confused with *kook,* which made its appearance in the late '50s as teenage slang to replace *drip* or *jerk* and later to compete with *dork.* As an adjective, *kooky* described far-out behavior, changing to *kicky* in the mid-'60s regarding mini-skirted clothes with op-art and pop-art patterns, and to *kinky* in the '70s as a description of taboo sex habits.

Politically, *nuts and kooks* came into popularity as a derogation of the more extreme supporters of Senator Barry Goldwater before his nomination in 1964. Goldwater himself used the word, according to publisher John S. Knight in a post-convention interview: "He [Goldwater] remarked with a wry smile that some of the 'kooks' supporting him are convinced that the concept of metropolitan government is the handiwork of the Communist Party."

The Goldwater managers did what they could to discourage demonstrations of the "kooks," since they were a source of embarrassment easily exploited by the Democrats. Reported Theodore White at the 1964 convention: "There is not, and was not, anywhere in the entire high command, in the brains trust or in the organizational structure of the Goldwater campaign, anyone who remotely qualified for the title 'kook.' Nor was there evident any 'kook' on the floor. But the 'kooks' dominated the galleries, hating and screaming and reveling in their own frenzy."

In the late '60s the word *kooks* (along with *beats* and *potheads*) was applied less to right-wingers and more to members of the NEW LEFT, especially those who burned draft cards and participated in antiwar demonstrations. *Nuts* is a more general term, of longer history and more current usage. According to the historian William Manchester (who presumably heard it from either Jacqueline Kennedy or Kenneth O'Donnell), President Kennedy, on his way to Dallas in 1963, looked at a virulently anti-Kennedy advertisement in the *Dallas News* and commented, "We're heading into nut country today." See LUNATIC FRINGE.

A different meaning of *nut* is found in campaign financing: *the nut* is the basic amount needed to get a campaign started.

In its sense of "a crazy" there has been a tendency to use *nut* as a self-mocking characterization, meaning "enthusiast." Many who object strongly to the intrusiveness of both governmental and private snooping into personal lives call themselves *privacy nuts*. (We also describe ourselves as "First Amendment *Freaks*.")

Koreagate See -GATE CONSTRUCTION.

Kremlinologist A Western observer who interprets the intricate workings of the Russian government.

Syracuse University political science professor Harry Schwartz wrote in 1967: "The recent shift in the leadership of the Soviet secret police, perhaps the most sensitive single post in the Moscow bureaucracy, has given Kremlinologists around the world a shot in the arm. From Washington to Beijing the effort to analyze the meaning of the change and its impact on the future of Soviet leadership is now in high gear."

Before the breakup of the Soviet Union, specialists in Russian affairs studied the play of news in *Pravda* and *Izvestia*, examined photographs of Communist leaders on Lenin's Tomb reviewing troops on May Day to see who stood closest to the top man, and sifted reports of travelers to the Soviet Union. According to *Time* magazine, "in an office of the U.S. embassy in Bonn, a rotund Sovietologist digests a stack of reports that may originate from any one of a thousand sources—a barber in East Berlin, a whore-house madam in Vienna ..." Soviet leaders treated the interpretations of foreign pundits with much the same disdain as U.S. officials looked askance at predictions by specialists on Washington matters. (In a kind of back-formation, Soviet analyst of U.S. affairs Georgi Arbatov was described as an "Americanologist.") Said Khrushchev in 1955 of the Western interpretation of Soviet attitudes: "They pay little attention to what we say and prefer to read tea leaves."

The Russian tea leaves were easier to read with the emergence of Mikhail Gorbachev (see GLASNOST), and for a brief time after his replacement by Boris Yeltsin, Russians had their first taste of press freedom. With the collapse of the Soviet Union, the previous era's word—*Sovietologist*—no longer applied. *Kremlinology* was practiced domestically; no longer did it mean THUMBSUCKING from afar, with analysts from the outside looking into what Churchill in 1939 had called "a riddle wrapped in a mystery inside an enigma." However, the era of Vladimir Putin, Yeltsin's chosen successor, marked a return to media suppression and one-party rule, and Kremlinology became again a rich academic-diplomatic field.

The counterpart term for Chinese Communists is *Beijingologist*. See CHINA WATCHERS.

Ku Klux Klan See INVISIBLE GOVERNMENT.

Kumbaya moment See BIPARTISAN.

L

labels Oversimplified identification of ideological position; universally deplored by politicians unwilling to be pigeonholed.

FDR positioned himself "a little left of center" (see LEFT WING, RIGHT WING; LIBERAL) but once told a press conference about appointees: "If we have the right kind of people, the party label does not mean so much."

Party labels are readily accepted by political figures in those areas where that party's registration dominates, but it has become popular to denounce ideological labels. In his 1960 State of the Union message, Dwight Eisenhower said: "We live, moreover, in a storm of semantic disorder in which old labels no longer faithfully describe. Police states are called 'people's democracies.' Armed conquest of free people is called 'liberation.' Such slippery slogans make difficult the problem of communicating true faiths, facts and beliefs ..."

Six years earlier, however, President Eisenhower had tried to come to grips with ideological labels in a well-known statement: "When it comes down to dealing with the relationships between the human in this country and his government, the people in this administration believe in being what I think we would normally call liberal, and when we deal with the economic affairs of this country, we believe in being conservative." (See Adlai Stevenson's riposte in DYNAMIC CONSERVATISM.)

Judging by his popularity, Eisenhower was able to solve a dilemma that had long been plaguing Republicans. More Americans considered themselves "liberal" than "conservative," and the Republicans are more closely identified with conservatism, often placing them in an electoral bind. Thomas E. Dewey was frank to admit it: "One of the standard weapons of party conflict both between conventions and during campaigns is the effort to pin labels on individuals or movements, attractive or sinister, depending upon the point of view. On the whole, the Democratic party in recent years has been the more successful in this use of semantics." That changed under Reagan, and Republicans worry that it may have changed back under the younger Bush.

Then-Senator Lyndon Johnson adopted a few labels and rejected labeling in a 1958 statement of his political philosophy:

> I am a free man, an American, a United States Senator, and a Democrat, in that order.
>
> I am also a liberal, a conservative, a Texan, a taxpayer, a rancher, a businessman, a consumer, a parent, a voter, and not as young as I used to be nor as old as I expect to be—and I am all these things in no fixed order ...
>
> I am not able—nor even the least interested in trying—to define my political philosophy by the choice of a one-word or two-word label.

Sometimes a label is useful: Bill Clinton in 1992 wanted to be known as a "new Democrat," to differentiate himself from the liberal, losing Democrats; in the same way, George W. Bush liked the label "COMPASSIONATE CONSERVATIVE." But the reasons for political squirming when it comes to most ideological labeling are these: (1) A label excludes more voters than it includes, and no politician wants to say "I am not one of you" to a large portion of the electorate. (2) Although in one area one label may predominate, politicians are ambitious; acceptance of a label may preclude advancement. (3) A label is simplistic, and thoughtful people reject its rigidity. See PRESIDENT OF ALL THE PEOPLE.

ladies in tennis shoes See LITTLE OLD LADIES IN TENNIS SHOES.

lame duck An officeholder whose power is diminished because he is soon to leave office as a result of defeat or statutory limitation.

During the 1920s this venerable phrase was modernized and widely publicized by the campaign for the "lame-duck amendment," which in 1933 was finally ratified as the Twentieth Amendment to the Constitution. Previously the incoming president was forced to wait until March to assume office while the old Congress—some of whose members had been retired at the last election—met in December and held nominal legislative powers until March.

The system today brings November's winners into office in January, thus halving the difficult lame-duck period for the outgoing administration and, in the absence of an emergency, eliminating the lame-duck session of Congress. Franklin D. Roosevelt's New Deal was the first beneficiary of the change, but not until after the historic HUNDRED DAYS had to be deferred by the last application of the old schedule. Said Rexford Tugwell, a member of the BRAIN TRUST: "The old stretch of four months, devised for a country without rapid transportation, was a dangerous hiatus in the [Depression] circumstances of 1932–33."

Lame duck, originally an eighteenth-century import from Britain meaning a bankrupt businessman, was used in the 1830s to label politically bankrupt politicians. In 1910, *The Nation* described Election Day casualties hoping for better days as "lame ducks in the sense that they have been winged, but hope to preen their plumage again." Today it is often used contemptuously, as when a mayor, governor, or President makes "lame-duck appointments" by rewarding supporters with judicial or commission posts during his last days in office.

The *Washington Post* columnist Sebastian Mallaby wrote in September 2006 that British Prime Minister Tony Blair "became a political eunuch last week … Blair's forced promise to step down reduces America's most faithful friend to lame-duck status." See EUNUCH RULE.

In late summer of 2007, after White House Chief of Staff Josh Bolten told appointees to leave at that point or to commit to staying the remainder of George W. Bush's second term—and both chief political strategist Karl Rove and embattled Attorney General Alberto Gonzales resigned—a spate of articles and TV commentaries appeared discussing Bush's "lame-duck status." Press aide Tony Fratto disputed the notion: "The

term 'lame duck' is for dime-store political scientists," demonstrating "a misunderstanding of the power of the presidency, and a miscalculation of the energy and intentions of this president." *The Wall Street Journal* editorialized: "even a 'lame duck' President still retains his powers under the Constitution and will be more effective if he's willing to use them." (*Dime-store*, a shortening of *five and ten cent store*, has been made obsolete by inflation.)

This particular fowl has an honored position in American slang. In addition to *lame duck*, there is *sitting duck* (vulnerable), *queer duck* (odd), *dead duck* (finished), and *ducky* (great, unless used scornfully). See Walter Reuther's use of "If it quacks like a duck" in PROVERBS AND AXIOMS, POLITICAL. For other business-financial metaphors in politics, see POLITICAL CAPITAL.

landslide A resounding victory; one in which the opposition is "buried." ("Snowed under" is better suited for an AVALANCHE.)

In its natural-disaster sense, the word made its appearance about 1838, and headline writers began applying it politically a few years later. (For usage differentiation from *tidal wave, prairie fire*, etc., see DISASTER METAPHORS.)

Alfred M. Landon, "the Coolidge of the West," sported an optimistic slogan in 1936: "Land Landon with a Landslide!" A landslide it was—Roosevelt carried 46 states with 523 electoral votes, Landon 2 states with 8.

The electoral college system makes landslides look more severe than they are. Landon managed to get 16 million votes to Roosevelt's 27 million—37 percent of the popular vote looks a little better than 1.5 percent of the electoral vote.

When Lyndon Johnson squeaked through a senatorial election in Texas—a post–Election Day correction gave him a majority of 87 votes out of almost a million cast—he was dubbed "Landslide Lyndon." The phrase was used again, minus the sarcasm, in the presidential election of 1964—Johnson carried 61 percent of the popular vote. This was not quite as high as Roosevelt's 63 percent in 1936 or Harding's 64 percent in 1920, but it was enough to qualify as a genuine landslide. Before those, the great landslides were Andrew Jackson in 1828 and 1832; U.S. Grant in 1872; Theodore Roosevelt in 1904.

Senator Henry Jackson made a unique use of the word after his New York State Democratic primary victory in April 1976. Against a sizable field, including Jimmy Carter, Senator Jackson won a plurality but fell short of his hoped-for 50 percent of the total vote. Reminded that he had predicted a landslide, he replied, "We got a landslide, but we missed a majority."

After the resounding election defeat of George McGovern in 1972, Senator Thomas Eagleton—who was forced to quit the Democratic ticket when it was revealed he had a history of mental illness—dismissed the episode involving him as merely "one rock in a landslide." Five years later Senator McGovern wrote: "Perhaps that is true, but landslides begin with a single rock."

land war in Asia See LET ASIANS FIGHT ASIANS; WRONG WAR.

last hurrah The final, usually losing, exit of a politician, especially one who has had a boisterous career.

The phrase was popularized by Edwin O'Connor, who used it as the title for his 1956 novel, *The Last Hurrah,* loosely based on the life of Boston Mayor James Curley, showing the calculations and compromises—as well as the rapport with his constituency—of an Irish politician in Massachusetts in the first third of the twentieth century.

The title was based on the "hurrah boys," name of the Andrew Jackson enthusiasts in 1828 and 1832, which then became the phrase for any noisy supporter in a campaign filled with HOOPLA. "When General Jackson was first brought before the public," wrote the *Ohio State Journal* in 1828, "his admirers…earned for the pains, the appropriate name of 'hurra boys.'"

George William Curtis, editor of *Harper's* magazine, told this story in a collection of speeches published in 1894:

An anti-Jackson partisan fell into the water, and, when nearly drowned, was seized by the hand and drawn to the surface, while his excited rescuer, delighted to save him, expressed his joy in the familiar phrase, "Hurrah for Jackson!" "What d'you say?" asked the drowning man thickly, but not so far gone that he could not hear the obnoxious name… "Hurrah for Jackson!" replied the other. "No, I'll be darned if I'll be saved by a hurrah-for-Jackson man" said the first, shaking off his hand and sinking back into the water.

The word *hurrah* is a seventeenth-century derivation from *huzza,* an imitative sound expressing joy and enthusiasm. In current use, *the last hurrah*—while usually connoting farewell after defeat—sometimes refers to a final win as well. The *National Observer,* after the 1966 New York gubernatorial election, titled an article "The Almost Perfect Political Campaign," with the subtitle "Nelson Rockefeller's Last Hurrah." It was not. And columnists Evans and Novak wrote in the spring of 1977: "Although even staunch Reaganites believe he is too old for anything other than a KINGMAKER's role in 1980, he has by no means ruled out a last hurrah."

late unpleasantness See EUPHEMISMS, POLITICAL.

laundered money Funds passed through a foreign account to conceal illegitimate origins.

The corrupt sense of *launder* was popularized in the 1973 Watergate hearings, as $200,000 in contributions was sent to Mexico and later used to finance illegal Nixon campaign operations.

The word had previously been used in this sense to describe the way "hot money"— that is, gambling profits or undeclared funds from foreign sources—was legitimized before re-entering the country. Metaphorically, the money laundry was used to "cool" rather than "clean" the money, as in this citation in the *San Francisco Call-Bulletin* of June 3, 1935, supplied the author by the late lexicographer Peter Tamony: "There is not a hot money passer in America who will 'wash' this money exchanging it for 'cool' currency—unless it is offered him at such a tremendous discount that he can afford to hold it for years, if necessary, before attempting to pass it." Tamony speculated: "As the mob/syndicate took over in Cuba in the decades preceding Fidel Castro, circa 1959, it is probable the *washing/laundering* was done there until Mexico became handy again fifteen years ago."

The locution was used in 1977 to describe the contributions of South Korean lobbyist Tongsun Park, who was said to use various cultural foundations as means of "laundering" funds for passage to U.S. congressmen, and in the 1990 prosecution of Panamanian strongman Manuel Noriega.

laundry ticket Jocular symbol of the popularity of an individual candidate who does not need organization support to win.

Franklin Roosevelt wanted the strongest possible Democratic candidate to succeed him as governor of New York, thereby helping him to carry the state in his race for president in 1932. Former Governor and presidential nominee Al Smith, although by now a bitter enemy of FDR, united with him in supporting Herbert Lehman, then Lieutenant Governor, but Tammany leader John Curry opposed Lehman. At the state convention, just an hour before the balloting, both Smith and Roosevelt threatened to denounce Curry on the floor if Lehman was not nominated. What's more, added Smith, he personally would run for mayor and "take the town away" from Curry and Tammany.

"On what ticket?" Curry sneered, with some logic.

"Hell," replied Smith, supremely confident of his power with New York voters, "on a Chinese-laundry ticket."

A related phrase, *laundry list*, has a different meaning: "a long, soporific list of items in a speech," or "a series of patronage requests by a political supporter after a successful campaign."

law and order Stress on repression of violence; regarded by many civil rights supporters in the '60s to be CODE WORDS for repression of the rights of blacks.

Some candidates, while not going so far as to oppose integration and civil rights legislation, sought to appeal to the anti-black BACKLASH by stressing *law and order* and urging control of CRIME IN THE STREETS. Advocates of the rights of African-Americans, who could not argue against the ideal of law and order, instead concentrated their fire on the code-word concept, charging this was part of Senator Goldwater's 1964 SOUTHERN STRATEGY aimed at winning anti-integration votes in the South without blatantly appealing to racist feelings.

An editorial in *The Insurgent*, a publication of the W. E. B. DuBois Clubs (a far-left group), argued: "the law is built to defend the white power structure. 'Order' means keeping people 'in their place.'"

However, many who did not intend to attack what they considered legitimate black aspirations also felt strongly about urban violence, which reached a peak during riots in Detroit and Newark in the LONG HOT SUMMER of 1967. But they found it difficult to stress *law and order* without being attacked in turn for using the same phraseology as the subtle racists.

With the mood of the nation turning against violent demonstrations and riots in the mid-sixties, the "code word" counterattack generally failed, and those espousing *law and order*—for whatever motives, sincere or not—found the issue effective.

The ability to cope with a breakdown in law and order was the quality that projected Calvin Coolidge on the national political scene. Massachusetts Governor Coolidge met the crisis of the Boston police strike of 1919 with the statement "There is no right to strike against the public safety by anybody, anywhere, anytime." He was nominated in 1920 for Vice President on the Harding ticket after a convention demonstration with "Law and Order" banners waving.

"Thus Coolidge, who was no rabble-rouser," wrote his biographer, Donald McCoy, in 1966, "had become the uncrowned king of the rabble-rousers and the Saint George of the innocently frightened. He who had given little thought to Marxism had become the champion of the anti-Marxists. He who had often been labor's friend had become a hero of antilabor forces. He who had not wanted to become involved had become deeply involved. He who had been the last in acting had become the first in receiving credit."

The phrase reaches further back into American political history. In the first half of the nineteenth century, Rhode Island was governed under a Colonial charter with a property qualification so high that less than one third of its citizens could vote. A Suffrage Party was formed by Thomas Dorr, which led to "Dorr's Rebellion" in 1842. The political group opposing suffrage called itself the "Law and Order Party."

The phrase became the title of a popular television dramatic series, with thespian-politico Fred Dalton Thompson a featured player. It gave him name and face recognition in his quest for the GOP nomination in the presidential campaign of 2008.

leader See BOSS, BOSSISM; SACHEM; SATRAP; BIG-WIG; MUCKEY-MUCKS; MOVERS AND SHAKERS.

leak Disclosure of information, usually concerning government or political activity, through unofficial channels, by what those embarrassed or exposed by such disclosure consider improper means.

The Latin saying *plenus rimarum sum*, "I am full of leaks," was chosen by Francis Bacon, who became Lord Chancellor of England in 1618, having confessed to taking bribes and spending four days imprisoned in the Tower of London: "As for Cabinet Councils, it may be their motto, *plenus rimarum sum*. One futile person, that maketh it his glory to tell, will do more hurt than many that know it their duty to conceal."

Lexicographers in the U.S. have kept their eyes on this term, both noun and verb, for a long time. In 1832 Noah Webster defined *to leak out* as "to escape privately from confinement or secrecy; as a fact or report," and G. W. Matsell in his 1859 *Vocabulum* defined *to leak* as "to impart a secret." One of the earliest sensational leaks occurred in 1844, when Senator Benjamin Tappan of Ohio gave a copy of the still-secret treaty of annexation with Texas to the *New York Evening Post*, causing an uproar; Tappan admitted his part in it and was censured.

The commonest leaks are those sprung by middle-echelon officials in order to get publicity for themselves or their agencies: an official tips off one reporter or a small group in advance of a general announcement in the hope that the exclusivity will get the story better coverage than it would otherwise enjoy.

Franklin Roosevelt complained bitterly about a number of leaks, including one about Henry Morgenthau's controversial plan (later shelved) to strip Germany of all industry after World War II. In 1955 Dwight Eisenhower said: "I have been plagued by inexplicable, undiscovered leaks in this government." President Johnson was accused of corking leaks by changing his plans or his nominees once information had come out prematurely.

The *courtesy leak* is used when an official owes a reporter a favor—or would like the journalist to owe him a favor—and uses information as a form of currency. However, while a courtesy leak makes the leakees happy, some in the scooped media think morosely of revenge.

The *authorized leak* is a disclosure given with attribution such as "informed sources" and "government officials." In this case the insider wishes to see something in print or broadcast but would rather not be on the record as formally committed to a particular policy or view. See TRIAL BALLOON; NOT FOR ATTRIBUTION. Some argue that the press should not allow itself to be used in this way. Others justify the practice by pointing out that news BACKGROUNDERS—the sessions at which such information is conveyed—are better than news blackouts.

Authorized leaks have been known to backfire. In one of his first informal meetings with the press, Defense Secretary Robert McNamara disclosed that there really was no MISSILE GAP. This flatly contradicted an important point made during the Kennedy campaign, much to the embarrassment of the new Kennedy Administration.

During the Nixon years, the author, one of the White House speechwriters, was authorized by the president to leak the contents of a forthcoming welfare reform speech;

Nixon said, "otherwise it'll never get in the papers." In so doing, I said to Henry Brandon of the London *Times* over my telephone "Want a leak? Here's what the president will say tomorrow about welfare reform." However, the FBI had a "national-security wiretap" on Brandon's home phone—one of 18 such taps of reporters and White House aides—which resulted in the tapping of my phone for six weeks.

An obsession with leaks led indirectly to Richard Nixon's downfall. In May of 1969 Nixon, Attorney General John Mitchell, and National Security Adviser Henry Kissinger determined to crack down on "national security leaks," using the FBI to conduct a series of wiretaps; when J. Edgar Hoover turned reluctant to pursue this technique, a Kissinger aide—David Young—was assigned to a leak-plugging unit that he later dubbed the PLUMBERS.

The most massive leak in U.S. history was the Pentagon Papers, a trove of files given by former national security consultant Daniel Ellsberg to *The New York Times*, which caused the Nixon Administration to go to court seeking to enjoin publication. The suppression effort failed; for a generation, that case and the subsequent leaks of Watergate information to *Washington Post* reporters Bob Woodward and Carl Bernstein by the disgruntled FBI official Mark Felt—identified only as "Deep Throat," his identity protected until his death three decades later—made heroes of those engaged in the practice of leaking and of publishing information embarrassing to the government (or in the eyes of officials, damaging to the national interest).

Director of Central Intelligence Stansfield Turner wrote in 1977 that our society should "trust the judgment of its public servants regarding what should and should not be withheld from the public." Daniel Schorr, a journalist who had obtained more than his share of leaks during his tenure at CBS, CNN, and National Public Radio, wrote in reply: "The awareness that 'secrets' may leak tends to have a healthful, ombudsman effect in government, making covert operators ask themselves how their plans would look if they were exposed. In balance, this nation has probably been harmed much less by undue exposure than by undue secrecy." Richard Neustadt, professor of government at Harvard, agreed: "The class of confidential communication commonly called 'leaks' play, in my opinion, a vital role in the functioning of our democracy. A leak is, in essence, an appeal to public opinion. Leaks generally do not occur in dictatorships."

Not all presidents were infuriated by leaks. When Ronald Reagan, mildly irritated at a disclosure, said, "I've had it up to my keister with leaks," the interest was his euphemistic usage of *keister*—the buttocks—rather than the leaks.

A generation later, Schorr examined the term's usage for the lexicographer: "Originally, when information 'leaked,' it was thought of as an accidental seepage—a lost document, a chauffeur's unwary anecdote, loose lips in the Pentagon. Today, when information 'is leaked,' it is a witting (if sometimes witless) action. One leaks (active) to float or sink an idea, aggrandize self ... or derogate an opponent." See PLANT; BACKGROUNDER; WHISTLEBLOWER; for the effects on First Amendment protections of a heavily publicized three-year hunt for a leaker who had confessed to inadvertent leakage early on, see CONFIDENTIAL SOURCE.

lebensraum Literally, "living space," or "enough room to live in"; an excuse for territorial expansion.

The word, spelled with a capital L in German, is attributed to the Swedish political scientist Rudolf Kjellen, who was a student of Freidrich Ratzel, and appropriated by a German geographer, Dr. Karl Haushofer, to describe what he considered to be Germany's needs and, therefore, rights. An English phrase, *land-hunger*, had been used earlier to describe the state of a nation whose population has expanded too rapidly for its territory to support.

The Nazis used *lebensraum* to mean that because Germany was crowded—"limited to the absurd idea of 500,000 square kilometers," wrote Adolf Hitler in *Mein Kampf*—and the fertile portions of Russia were occupied by inferior beings, thus Germany, as home of the "master race," had the right to take the geographical areas it wanted by war.

In 1942, during a visit to Washington by Winston Churchill, Franklin Roosevelt made a speech that greatly impressed the British prime minister, especially the line "The world is too small to provide adequate 'living room' for both Hitler and God." Churchill told FDR, "Whoever wrote that sentence, I'd like to take with me to England." The President did not reply; the speechwriter, famed dramatist Robert E. Sherwood, was too valuable to him.

After World War II a German novelist told reporter John Gunther what impressed him most about the U.S.: "Space. *Lebensraum.* The impression that no crisis can be really severe or permanent in this country because people are free to move around so much."

The word has been used by ENVIRONMENTALISTS to project some of the troubles of the world of the future. In the June 1955 *Fortune* magazine, the poly-mathematician John von Neumann wrote:

> In the first half of this century the accelerating industrial revolution encountered an absolute limitation—not on technological progress as such, but on an essential safety factor. This safety factor … was essentially a matter of geographical and political Lebensraum: an ever broader geographical scope for technological activities, combined with an ever broader political integration of the world. Within this expanding framework it was possible to accommodate the major tensions created by technological progress.
>
> Now this safety mechanism is being sharply inhibited; literally and figuratively, we are running out of room.

The *Los Angeles Times* reported in 1993 on Hungary's right-wing leader István Csurka: "Despite the political uproar that has ensued since publication of an August essay replete with anti-Semitic overtones, Csurka insists he speaks for many Hungarians and has no regrets about anything he has said, including his use of the Nazi term lebensraum—living space—in his call for expanding the borders." See PLACE IN THE SUN.

The word is in current use as a frequent excuse for GENOCIDE. Reporting in 2006 on the mass killing by the Janjaweed tribesmen in Sudan's Darfur region, Nicholas Kristof of *The New York Times* wrote: "As in Rwanda or even during the Holocaust, racist ideologies sometimes disguise greed, insecurity and other pathologies. Indeed, one of the genocide's aims is to drive away African tribes to achieve what Hitler called Lebensraum: 'living space' for nomadic Arabs and their camels."

left field, left coast A figurative location slightly less remote than Siberia; out of the ordinary; out of touch; far out.

When used as a place of origin, as in *out of left field*, the phrase was picked up by politicians and meteorologists as a slang equivalent of "far-fetched; off the wall." When a professor of atmospheric science predicted a dry spell in the Northeast, Robert Harnack, a meteorologist at Rutgers, ridiculed that forecast as being "completely out of left field."

Baseball's left field was the place of far-outedness by the late 1950s. The phrase *out in left field* came to have two meanings: "removed from the ordinary; unconventional" and "out of contact with reality, out of touch." A 1960 *New York Times* report on the state of U.S. scientific research used the phrase in the first sense: "if this country is to compete with Europe and Japan, engineers and scientists must start taking risks 'way out in left field.' "

The second meaning is illustrated in a 1959 *Time* magazine article, also in a science context: "The virus theory of cancer causation long seemed to be far out in left field, but growing knowledge tends to link it with other anti-cancer plays."

Sports fans differ on the reasoning behind the metaphor. Some suggest that left fielders play farther out to get the power balls hit by right-handed players. Others note that in most of the older, asymmetrical ballparks—Yankee Stadium, Ebbets Field, Forbes Field among others—left field was deeper than right field. That gave left-handed batters an advantage because distances to right-field fences were shorter.

The phrase has only peripheral connection to the political left. A more ideological use of *left* that emerged in the 1990s, as the State of California moved more solidly into the Democratic column, is *Left Coast*. That was also influenced by the map of the U.S., where the West Coast appears on the left. *The Boston Globe*'s John Aloysius Farrell observed that much depended on California's voters in the 1992 election: "now the residents of the Left Coast are being asked to shoulder what may be the most onerous burden of all: the presidential hopes of the Democratic Party." After the Democrats won and Bill Clinton assumed office, *The Denver Post* noted that the President "swayed to the left coast and invited gays into the military."

The term has become so closely with the Golden State, and the state of its culture, that it should be treated as a proper noun and capitalized, as in a *Los Angeles Times* guide to the geographic origins of guests at a Conga Room party during the 2000 Democratic National Convention: "If she was wearing a revealing top, a short, tight micro-mini and strappy stilettos, if she had a come-hither look, she was definitely Left Coast."

left wing, right wing The ideological spectrum; reading from left to right, radical, liberal, centrist or moderate, conservative, reactionary.

The presiding officers of the French National Assembly seated the radicals at the *côté gauche* (left side), the moderates in the center directly in front, and the conservative nobles on the right. Like so many political terms, the "wings" derived from military use, with the use of "left wing" of an army traceable to 1707.

The left-wing–right-wing spectrum is not a straight bar; the relationships are better explained by considering it as a kind of horseshoe. An extreme leftist, socialist or Communist, has more in common with an extreme reactionary, or fascist, than either has with the MODERATE, CENTRIST, or MIDDLE OF THE ROADER.

Franklin Roosevelt established his position in a 1944 press conference when reporter May Craig asked him if he was going "left or right politically." He replied, "I am going down the whole line a little left of center." See LABELS. Another reporter asked about recent appointments of conservatives. FDR said, "I have got a lot of people in the Administration—oh, I know some of them are extreme right and extreme left, and everything else.... Just think, the crowd here in this room—my gracious, you will find every opinion between left and extreme right."

Sociologist C. Wright Mills, who coined NEW LEFT, defined the *right* as "celebrating society as it is: a going concern," and *to be left* as "to connect up with cultural and political criticism."

One on the left is called: RED, *pink*, PINKO, (PARLOR PINK is leftist in theory only), *commie*, *bomb-thrower*, COMSYMP, FELLOW TRAVELER, *ultraleft*.

One on the right is called RADICAL RIGHT, DIEHARD, MOSSBACK, *Bourbon*, *bitterender*, *ultrarightist*, OLD FOGY, *standpatter* (see STAND PAT), LITTLE OLD LADIES IN TENNIS SHOES, and TROGLODYTIC.

CENTRISTS and MODERATES are: ON THE FENCE, STRADDLERS, MIDDLE OF THE ROADERS, OPPORTUNISTS, and ALL THINGS TO ALL MEN, though they claim to be the MAINSTREAM.

Winging nuance: those on the left resent being called "left-wingers" more than those on the right resent being called "right-wingers." Lefties are more likely to say "we on the left" and righties more likely to say "we right-wingers."

let Asians fight Asians A recurrent proposal to replace American troops with allied Asian troops in warfare in the Far East.

In the 1952 presidential campaign, Dwight Eisenhower held that the U.S. commitment of ground troops might be curtailed, the men replaced by South Korean troops. "If there must be a war there," he is reported to have said, "let it be Asians against Asians." A few days before the election, as Stevenson realized the efficacy of Eisenhower's "I SHALL GO TO KOREA" promise, the Democratic candidate attacked the General's Asian suggestion: "'Let Asians fight Asians' is the authentic voice of a resurgent isolationist. In 1939 the Republican Old Guard, faced with the menace of the Nazi world, was content to say 'Let Europeans fight Europeans,' ignoring completely the fact that the menace of Nazism was a menace to Americans ..."

The thought has a genuine appeal, similar to the fervent desire to avoid a "land war in Asia." In 1964, President Lyndon Johnson said: "We are not about to send American boys nine or ten thousand miles away from home to do what Asian boys should be doing for themselves."

See VIETNAMIZATION. For a similar word pattern, see LET [WHOMEVER] BE [WHOMEVER]; also see I AM THE LAW.

let me make one thing perfectly clear See POINTER PHRASES.

let sleeping dogmas lie See UNLEASH CHIANG.

let's look at the record A rousing appeal to reason by presidential candidate Alfred E. Smith.

The New York governor began using "Let's look at the record" in his 1928 campaign for president against Herbert Hoover. See WHISPERING CAMPAIGN.

The phrase was used both as a defense and an attack phrase in its early days, though in recent years it has become a bromide mainly used in attacks on the opposition record. "As Al Smith used to say, 'Let's look at the record'" has been used so often that it elicits yawns from generations who never heard of Al Smith. For a reminder of other contributions by this source, see BALONEY; DOVES; LAUNDRY TICKET; KISS OF DEATH; LULU; and SANTA CLAUS, NOBODY SHOOTS AT. For a vicious attack on a record from a different source, see TWENTY YEARS OF TREASON.

A modern form of calling for a look at the record was Ronald Reagan's line in his 1980 debate with President Jimmy Carter, directed to the TV audience: "Are you better off than you were four years ago?"

let's talk sense See DIALOGUE.

let the dust settle See WATCHFUL WAITING.

let them eat cake The height of political patronization; an attack phrase against economic suggestions that do not directly benefit the LITTLE MAN.

This famous "quotation" is supposed to be one of the examples of hauteur by Marie Antoinette that helped bring about the French Revolution. She never said it.

The first reference appears in the sixth book of Jean-Jacques Rousseau's *Confessions*, written about 1767, two or three years before Marie Antoinette's arrival in France: "At length I recollected the thoughtless saying of a great princess, who, on being informed that the country people had no bread, replied, 'Let them eat cake.'" Nearly a quarter of a millennium later, the "great princess"—Rousseau's BACKGROUND source—has still not been identified.

The remark (in French, *qu'ils mangent de la brioche*) is still used to signify unconcern with the needs of most people. When Vice President Agnew delivered a keynote address at a National Governors' Conference in 1971 that included a defense of the profit motive, it was denounced by an anonymous Democratic spokesman as "Marie Antoinette economics."

In 1991, the Senate fell one vote short of overriding the elder George Bush's veto of extending unemployment benefits. The *Seattle Times*, identifying Washington's Senator Slade Gordon as the only Northwest Senator to vote with the President, headlined the article "Let Them Eat Cake."

"let us continue" Lyndon Johnson's exhortation as he stepped into the presidency after the death of John F. Kennedy.

Five days after the Kennedy assassination, President Johnson told a joint session of Congress: "On the twentieth day of January in 1961, John F. Kennedy told his countrymen that our national work would not be finished 'in the first thousand days, nor in the life of this Administration, nor even perhaps in our lifetime on this planet. But,' he said, 'let us begin.' Today, in this moment of new resolve, I would say to all my fellow Americans, let us continue."

The words were written by Kennedy speechwriter Ted Sorensen (probably quoting a speech on which he worked), but the President's Texas accent grated on the nerves of some of the former president's greatest admirers—the pronunciation of "continya" was later mocked. (Kennedy and Johnson were the only two presidents up to that point in the twentieth century to have strongly regional accents.)

The choice of the phrase, however, was apt, recalling the early words of Kennedy's and updating them, thereby gracefully acknowledging another's leadership while asserting a leadership of one's own.

Author John Dos Passos had written of the need for this kind of reaching back and establishing the sense of continuity: "In times of change and danger when there is a quicksand of fear under man's reasoning, a sense of continuity with generations gone before can stretch like a lifeline across the scary present."

By 1967 the context of solemnity in which Johnson had used the phrase was long forgotten, and columnist Russell Baker wrote: "It is curious that we let beloved old phrases expire and trundle off the Old Phrases' Burying Ground without even noticing that they have left us ... what about 'Let Us Continue!'? Gone, simply gone, and all unnoticed. Can it mean that somewhere back there, without noticing it, we stopped continuing?"

let [whomever] be [whomever] A call for a return to basic character or ideology; a slogan urging the removal of soothing overlays or excessive handling from a political leader.

The phrase, now most often identified with Ronald Reagan, was not new with that President.

In 1648, Sir Francis Nethersole wrote, "Let bygans be bygans." (Wordplay on this cliche about "bygones" came from Meg Greenfield, the *Washington Post* editorialist; when Bhagwan Shree Rajneesh was arrested for wrongdoing, she suggested, "Let Bhagwans be Bhagwans.") The formulaic usage on national character, however, comes from a 1938 poem by Langston Hughes titled "Let America Be America Again," which says, "O, let America be America again— / The land that never has been yet— / And yet must be— / The land where everyman is free."

Other nations have been inserted into the formulaic phrase. In January 1982, a broadcast of the United States Information Agency being aimed at Soviet imperialists took the theme of "Let Poland Be Poland." But the expression probably reached its heights during Reagan's Presidency. At a final White House briefing of the Reagan Administration, Marlin Fitzwater was asked whether the staff knew of any plans for a final Presidential speech, and he responded, "Let the staff be staff, and let Reagan be Reagan."

It returned in 1993. Senator David L. Boren, Democrat of Oklahoma, convened a meeting of conservative Democrats to balance the left wing of the Party in negotiations with the new President. Said Senator Boren, "We want to let Clinton be Clinton."

level playing field Equity in competition; equality of opportunity.

The *American Banker* used the phrase in a 1979 article about the Oregon Bankers Association: "Mr. Brawner said the Oregon B.A. welcomed 'any and all competition, on a level playing field,' a metaphor the association has used frequently in arguments for 'competitive equality.'" In 1986, the same newspaper elaborated: "When bankers talk about a 'level playing field,' they usually mean that similar financial services firms should be subject to the same 'game rules.'"

President Reagan picked up the term in a 1986 speech against tariffs: "If the United States can trade with other nations on a level playing field, we can outproduce, outcompete and outsell anybody, anywhere in the world." Speaking out against protectionists in 1986, Republican Senator Bob Packwood of Oregon added, "That's their idea of a level playing field—a legislative advantage."

Origin of the phrase is uncertain—the playing fields of Eton have been mentioned as a source, but the image of a flat surface for equality in battle has roots as old as the Bible. As the servants of Benhadad, king of Syria, tell their leader about the army of Israel: "Their gods are gods of the hills; therefore they were stronger than we; but let us fight against them in the plain, and surely we shall be stronger than they" (1 Kings 20:23).

Levelers, however, have their critics. "Sir, your levelers wish to level *down* as far as themselves," said Samuel Johnson in 1763, "but they cannot bear leveling *up* to themselves."

levels See GOBBLEDYGOOK.

leverage Indirect pressure that can be brought to bear on politicians, particularly delegates at conventions.

The "delegate book" that each serious presidential candidate brings to an open convention includes data on each man's social and business background, as well as his political leanings. This book is for the purpose of "getting to him"—finding some Achilles' heel that makes him receptive to the candidate.

A typical question before the convention, while the delegate book is leafed through, is "What kind of leverage do we have on this one?" In other words, is the delegate's best friend, wife, employer, most important customer, school chum, banker, country club president—anyone in a position to exert pressure—a crowbar to pry that delegate's support away from another candidate?

The process may be as old as balloting. Daniel Manning, Grover Cleveland's manager in the 1884 MUGWUMP campaign, gave these instructions to William C. Hudson, who was to open the Cleveland headquarters at Chicago for the convention: "Now, I want you to devote yourself to these doubtful men. Find out the conditions surrounding them, the influences political, commercial and moral. ... We must subject them to pressure, but first we must learn the sort of pressure that should be applied."

Financial leverage is the use of borrowing power; political leverage is the use of financial or personal pressure. See FEET TO THE FIRE.

liberal Currently one who believes in more government action to meet individual needs; originally one who resisted government encroachment on individual liberties.

In the classic sense the word described those of the emerging middle classes in France and Great Britain who wanted to throw off the rules the dominant aristocracy had made to cement its own control.

During the 1920s the meaning changed to describe those who believed a certain amount of governmental action was necessary to protect the people's "real" freedoms as opposed to their purely legal—and not necessarily existent—freedoms.

This philosophical about-face led former New York Governor Thomas Dewey to say, after using the original definition, "Two hundred years later, the transmutation of the word, as the alchemist would say, has become one of the wonders of our time."

In U.S. politics the word was used by George Washington to indicate a person of generosity or broad-mindedness, as he expressed distaste for those who would deprive Catholics and Jews of their rights.

The word became part of the American vocabulary in that earlier meaning during a rump convention of Republicans dissatisfied with the presidency of Ulysses S. Grant, at Cincinnati in 1872. German-born Carl Schurz, who chaired the convention, used the word often. So did the leading journalist-thinker of the rebellion, Edwin L. Godkin of *The Nation*, who began his career in England. The short-lived party born of the convention was called the Liberal Republican party.

The word acquired significance during the presidency of Franklin D. Roosevelt, who gave it a centrist cast during the campaign for his first term: "say that civilization is a tree which, as it grows, continually produces rot and dead wood. The radical says: 'Cut it down.' The conservative says: 'Don't touch it.' The liberal compromises: 'Let's prune, so that we lose neither the old trunk nor the new branches.'"

Liberalism takes criticism from both right and left, leading to various terms of opprobrium. See LEFT WING, RIGHT WING. Herbert Hoover in a magazine article referred to "fuzzy-minded totalitarian liberals who believe that their creeping collectivism can be adopted without destroying personal liberty and representative government."

To its opponents, *liberalism* and *liberals* seem to call out for qualifying adjectives expressing contempt. Barry Goldwater, trying to combat the popularity of President Johnson with businessmen, told a U.S. Chamber of Commerce conference, "If you think President Johnson is going to give you any better attention than you have got, you're very, very mistaken. If he's a conservative," said the senator, "I'm a screaming liberal."

Sometimes even liberals cannot avoid the temptation to assault the term. Adlai Stevenson, quoting an uncertain source, once described a liberal as "one who has both feet firmly planted in the air." Columnist Heywood Broun, who came to consider himself a radical, wrote: "A liberal is a man who leaves a room when a fight begins," a definition adopted by militant Saul Alinsky.

The word has fallen on hard times. In the 1976 presidential primaries, Representative Morris Udall told columnist David Broder: "When a word takes on connotations you don't like, it's time to change the LABEL." Henceforth, Udall said—though he would think of himself as a liberal—he would use the word *progressive* instead because the word *liberal* was "associated with abortion, drugs, busing and big-spending wasteful government." Two generations later, as Udall surmised, *progressive* has become the chosen self-identification of the left.

Daniel Patrick Moynihan, the sociologist, Nixon domestic policy adviser, Democratic Senator from New York, and prolific author, put the serious and profound difference between liberal and conservative political philosophies in a pair of sentences: "The central conservative truth is that it is culture, not politics, that determines the success of a society. The central liberal truth is that politics can change a culture and save it from itself."

Adjectives giving a pejorative cast to the honorable old word include LIMOUSINE, *double-domed, screaming,* KNEE-JERK, *professional,* BLEEDING HEART; also see PINKO; PARLOR PINK; NEW LEFT; COMMITTED; EGGHEAD. For liberal ripostes, see CONSERVATIVE; MOSSBACK; ROCK-RIBBED; DINOSAUR WING.

liberation of captive peoples The promise of the Republican platform of 1952 and subsequently of the Eisenhower Administration that the U.S. would help the people of the countries under Communist rule gain their freedom.

The 1952 platform was meant to cast aspersions on any "secret agreements" made at Yalta by Roosevelt, Stalin, and Churchill. Russian power, combined with the vague wording of the Yalta agreement, had led to the seizure of most of Eastern and Central Europe by Communist factions, dominated by the Soviet Union.

In the Republican platform, Yalta was condemned as aiding "Communist enslavements." The plank went on: "United States policy, as one of its peaceful purposes, looks happily forward to the genuine independence of those captive peoples." General Eisenhower amplified this in an address during the campaign to the American Legion in which, after reciting the litany of Communist-dominated nations, he said: "We can never rest—and we must so inform all the world, including the Kremlin—that until the enslaved nations of the world have in the fullness of freedom the right to choose their own path, that then, and then only, can we say that there is a possible way of living peacefully and permanently with Communism in the world."

In reply, Democratic candidate Adlai Stevenson warned of the dangers such words created. He said to a predominantly Polish audience on Labor Day of 1952: "the cruel grip of Soviet tyranny upon your friends and relatives cannot be loosened by loose talk or idle threats. It cannot be loosened by awakening false hopes which might stimulate intemperate action that would only lead your brothers to the execution squads ..."

President Eisenhower's biographer, Robert J. Donovan, and the long-time State Department trouble-shooter, Robert Murphy, both insisted that the liberation referred to was to come only by peaceful means; John Foster Dulles told a Senate committee that "liberation does not mean a war of liberation."

This was not clear to restive elements in Communist-dominated ("enslaved") countries, many of whom were convinced that American troops would come to the aid of the Hungarian people when they staged their uprising in 1956. In the U.S., the abortive Hungarian revolt marked the beginning of the end of the "liberation of captive peoples" as a political phrase, and it soon went the way of UNLEASH CHIANG.

In a 1976 televised debate with Jimmy Carter, President Ford refused to recognize the dominance of East European nations by the Soviet Union, which was widely interpreted as a foreign-policy gaffe.

Liberation was a noble World War II word that came to mean the acquisition of booty (as in "liberating" a wine cellar, subject of a famous cartoon by Bill Mauldin showing Willie and Joe amid hundreds of broken wine bottles, furious at "those atrocity-committin' skunks!"). It was also frequently used in Communist terminology; see WAR OF NATIONAL LIBERATION.

It was adopted by small terrorist groups in the U.S. (the "Symbionese Liberation Army," which kidnapped Patricia Hearst) and large groups abroad (the Palestine Liberation Organization). The term also has been embraced by extremists within the animal rights and environmental movements. ALF (Animal Liberation Front) and ELF (Earth Liberation Front) have engaged in vandalism and other aggressive tactics. FBI director Louis J. Freeh testified in Senate hearings in May of 2001—not four months before 9/11—that "Eight of the terrorist incidents occurring in the United States during 1999 have been attributed to either ALF or ELF." The Department of Homeland Security cited ALF as a terrorist threat in 2005.

lid A White House assurance to journalists of newsmaking inactivity.

Political reporters need to know not only when news is breaking, but when news will not be breaking—so they can plan their lives accordingly. This need to know when there is nothing to know has led to the invention of the pressroom *lid*, the signal to reporters that no news is scheduled for distribution, or press conference planned, until an announced time when the lid ends. Reporters can use this promise of suspended animation to protect themselves while they cover other stories, or sun themselves on PEBBLE BEACH, secure that they will not be caught napping—unless an emergency arises, at which point all lids are off.

The word is taken from "The lid's off," a turn-of-the-century expression for no-holds-barred activity. "Commissioner of Police McAdoo," wrote the Philadelphia *Public Ledger* in 1904, "has taken frequent occasions to deny that the 'lid' was off, to use the slang definition of a lax police administration."

In modern political-press parlance, a lid may be *soft* ("Probably nothing happening, but stick around") to *hard* ("I'm going home, too").

For examples of other forms of "masterly inactivity," see WATCHFUL WAITING.

life is unfair The apologia for economic or social inequity; a gentle shrugging-off of egalitarian demands.

In a press conference on March 21, 1962, President John F. Kennedy was asked about demonstrations by army reservists who—having "done their time" in the armed forces—resented being mobilized to fight in the Vietnam war. After observing that the calling up of the reservists had "strengthened the foreign policy of the United States," he extemporized in a more philosophical vein:

> There is always inequity in life. Some men are killed in a war and some men are wounded, and some men never leave the country, and some men are stationed in the Antarctic and some are stationed in San Francisco. It's very hard in military or in personal life to assure complete equality. Life is unfair …

The phrase did not at first appear to fit in the ringing, high-minded Kennedy rhetoric; it gained an overtone of fatalism after his assassination.

President Carter, in a press conference on July 12, 1977, used the same argument (with a rough approximation of the phrase) in handling a question about the Supreme Court decision that the federal government was not obligated to provide money for abortions for women who cannot afford them. "There are many things in life that are not fair," the President replied, "that wealthy people can afford and poor people can't. But I don't believe that the federal government should take action to try to make these opportunities exactly equal, particularly when there is a moral factor involved."

The unintended evocation of John Kennedy's remark was widely noted, and reinforced journalistic usage of the phrase. *Washington Post* columnist George Will, writing about the Panama Canal treaty negotiated by Ambassador Sol Linowitz, observed: "Carter inherited the negotiations, and the general shape of the outcome. The fight for ratification will diminish his popularity, and defeat—a real possibility— would diminish his stature. It isn't fair, but as has been said, life is unfair."

The term continues to be used in labeling inequities or unfairness. The *Cook Political Report* wrote in 1991: "In the 'life is unfair' category, the population loss in New Jersey has clearly been in the heavily Democratic city of Newark, but it appears that the state's lost seat will be a Republican one."

lift of a driving dream Nixonian vision of the impetus of idealism.

At the Highway Hotel in Concord, New Hampshire, on February 3, 1968, Richard Nixon made the first speech of his second presidential campaign, beginning with "The finest hours in our nation's history have been triumphs of the American spirit. We now are engaged in a great test of that spirit."

The use of a Churchill phrase—"finest hours"—and the use of the Lincolnian construction "We are now engaged in a great" reflected the candidate's dual purposes: to rally and to heal. The centerpiece of the speech, written by Ray Price, was this line: "What America needs most today is what it once had, but has lost: the lift of a driving dream."

Correspondent Nancy Dickerson, interviewing the President with other network commentators on January 4, 1971, brought up the earliest use of the phrase and observed "many people have failed to perceive 'the lift of a driving dream.'" Nixon replied in part: "Before we can really get the lift of a driving dream, we have to get rid of some of the nightmares we inherited …" After the Watergate revelations had driven Nixon to resignation, his successor, Gerald Ford, evoked the same image in his first speech and most memorable line: "Our long national nightmare is over."

One would think that this phrase would disappear from the political language as the Nixon presidency recedes in memory, but Ray Price's phrase may have staying power independent of memories of its speaker. "It is unclear whether Carter, the problem-solver," wrote Hedrick Smith in 1978, "understands that his greatest shortcoming so far has been his failure to rouse the nation with the lift of a driving dream … he has not used the White House effectively as a BULLY PULPIT."

lightning may strike The wish of the dark-horse or long-shot candidate; the possibility of a sudden shift in fortune that may nominate a man for major office.

In the California primary before the 1964 Republican nomination, Rockefeller supporters looked in vain for help from other liberals and middle-of-the-roaders in the campaign against Barry Goldwater. "It's understandable," said Nelson Rockefeller, four days before Goldwater's narrow victory. "All of them are available for the nomination and hoping that lightning will strike."

The phrase has been in use, in its precise meaning today, for at least a century. R. W. Thornton's *American Glossary* has this definition: "The lightning is said to strike, when a person or a place gains sudden and unexpected fame, notoriety, or good fortune. Not in the dictionaries." He offers this example from the *Congressional Record* of 1879: "Mr. Sparks: I wish to suggest to the gentleman from Iowa that in districts near his own the lightning has been striking."

"Mr. Price: Oh, no…no danger of that kind of lightning in my district."

A vivid use of the phrase was made by magazine publisher and parachutist Bernarr Macfadden in 1936. Alva Johnson reported that Macfadden was bilked of a quarter of a million dollars by a group that convinced him he had a chance for the presidency against FDR. "If lightning strikes," the eccentric publisher announced, "it will find me a willing victim."

lightweight A hollow public figure behind an impressive facade; a good-looking politician lacking either intellect, grasp of administrative detail, or guts.

Lightweight is an attack word, often as cruel and hard to shake as *loser*, usually accompanied with "he just doesn't have it." See STRAW MAN. The opposite—*heavyweight*—often refers to political aides who carry prestige and authority. "We need a heavyweight to operate on the top level."

Classic definition of a lightweight, attributed in 1960 to Brooklyn Republican leader John Crews about New York Mayor Robert Wagner: "He's light enough to do a tap dance on a charlotte russe." (Another pastry metaphor was used by newswoman Louise Lamprey in 1897, in a remark later attributed to Theodore Roosevelt: "President McKinley has no more backbone than a chocolate eclair.")

The word's political use can be traced back to 1809 and an allusion to "lightweight princes." In 1882 New York Congressman S. S. Cox said on the House floor, "I never took my friend from New Jersey [George Robeson] to be a lightweight in any regard."

In boxing, a lightweight can be an excellent fighter, even a champion; not so in politics. In the political arena, weight categories do not exist to protect the light from the heavy, and the fastest lightweight is easily taken by the slowest heavyweight. Other boxing terms used in politics include ARENA, HAT IN THE RING, *throw in the towel, take off the gloves, hit below the belt, on the ropes.* Wrestling terms include *eye-gouging* and *no holds barred.*

Synonyms are *airhead*, a locution imputing vacuousness rather than lack of seriousness, usually aimed at women, and *empty suits*, for lightweight male politicians. See HEFT, POLITICAL.

like ugly on an ape Thoroughly; inescapably; without moderation.

The elder George Bush popularized this dialect term during the 1988 Presidential campaign: "I knew the minute I said 'CARD-CARRYING member of the A.C.L.U.' a couple of your best columnists would jump all over me, like ugly on an ape."

Seven years earlier, Bush had used the phrase in a vice presidential statement reported by United Press International: "The Vice President said Russia pounced on the neutron-bomb decision 'like ugly on [an] ape,' but the Soviet Union's reaction was 'thoroughly expected.'"

Variations of the phrase have ranged from *like white on rice* to Jimmy Carter's *like a duck on a June bug.* The simile *ugly as a hairless monkey* was used in Margaret Mitchell's novel *Gone With the Wind.* The equating of primates with ugliness can be tracked back as far as William Dampier's report in his 1699 *Voyages and Descriptions*: "The Monkies that are in these Parts are the ugliest I ever saw."

Ugly as an absolute (an adjective used as a noun) dates back to the early nineteenth century. In 1835, the American humorist Augustus Longstreet wrote in *Georgia Scenes* that "I want to get in the breed of them sort o' men to drive ugly out of my kin folks."

The phrase *like ugly on ape*, without the article *an*, was a favorite saying of the character Festus Haggen, played by Ken Curtis, on the TV western *Gunsmoke* in the mid-1960s.

Bush, however, told the British interviewer David Frost of an earlier source in Texas for *like ugly on an ape*: "That's all over the oil fields. I got it in Odessa in 1948—that's when it started, I guess."

limited modified hangout See WATERGATE WORDS.

limited war A military conflict in which the goal is defined as short of total victory and in which one or both combatants may use less than full military resources.

Limited war, a variant of TOTAL WAR, became a common phrase—and a politically contentious one—during the Korean conflict. The Truman Administration called its intervention to save South Korea from its northern Communist invaders a POLICE ACTION rather than actual war and described its strategy as "limited warfare." The diplomatic rationale for circumlocution was clear: Washington wanted to keep Beijing and Moscow out of the fighting and did not want to intensify the battle either rhetorically or militarily. General Douglas MacArthur could not live with the restrictions, and Truman finally dismissed him as commander. See NO SUBSTITUTE FOR VICTORY; NO-WIN POLICY.

The Truman-MacArthur showdown and the frustrations of fighting an indecisive war under unusual conditions in a remote land set the issue. The goal of total victory and unconditional surrender in World War II was so fresh in the national consciousness that many forgot, as historian Samuel Eliot Morison pointed out, that "limited war is also in the American tradition." We had fought such wars with Great Britain, Spain, and Mexico. Nonetheless, when the Eisenhower Administration took office, Defense Secretary Charles Wilson said: "We can't afford to fight limited wars. We can only afford to fight a big war, and if there is one, that is the kind it will be."

As a result of this policy decision, the American military establishment during the 1950s emphasized strategic nuclear weapons at what critics said was the expense of conventional forces. But the change was temporary. Secretary of State John Foster Dulles acknowledged that the country had to be flexible enough in its arsenal to inflict less than MASSIVE RETALIATION.

While still a senator, John Kennedy insisted that "limited brushfire war," rather than all-out nuclear conflict, was the more likely threat. As President, Kennedy favored "balanced forces" and "flexible response" and had the military reorganized along these lines. Two generations later, criticism of the second Iraq war labeled it a "war of choice," rather than one of necessity. See PEACE WITHOUT VICTORY.

limits to growth See ENVIRONMENTALIST.

limousine liberal One who takes up hunger as a cause but never felt a pang; who will talk at length about the public school system but sends his children to private schools.

Mario Procaccino used this scornful phrase in New York City's mayoral campaign of 1969, casting aspersions of hypocrisy at John Lindsay's followers on the Upper East Side of Manhattan—the SILK STOCKING district. "Proc" was disdained by opponents who passed along BLOOPERS like "I want every kid in New York to have the same chance I did—to come up the hard way."

His "limousine liberal" was a phrase that stung, however, alliteratively caricaturing people of relative wealth who felt that the downtrodden should have more—but at the expense of the lower middle class. Race as well as class was of course a factor in this; it was an attack on white elitists who spoke out for open housing and had no fear of blacks moving into the expensive apartment next to them.

Of course, there has never been a need for a man to be poor to believe in liberal ideas, and some aristocrats—FDR, for example—did more for the indigent "one-third of a nation" than did any member of that third. Thus, in its broadest sense, the application was unfair. In a narrower sense, however, it had substance, as brought out by Tom Wolfe in *New York* magazine, who dissected "radical chic"—the sponsorship of groups like the Black Panthers by some of New York's cultural elite.

Both terms had a sobering effect on many old-line liberals who had to take into consideration the needs and votes of hardhats, often homeowners and people not poor enough for welfare.

Scorn at hypocrisy is offered in international affairs as well. Egyptian President Anwar el-Sadat, rejecting radical Arab criticism after his 1977 visit to Israel, said, "Those militants in nightclubs are going about while the real militants are there in jail in Israel." The "nightclub militant" is a metaphoric cousin of the "limousine liberal." See PARLOR PINK.

Lindley Rule See NOT FOR ATTRIBUTION.

linkage A global negotiating strategy holding that progress on one front is necessary to, or strongly helpful to, progress on other fronts.

The word was used by Dr. Henry Kissinger, President Nixon's national security adviser, in a background briefing on February 6, 1969, explaining what the President had said in a press conference about not wanting to dissociate arms control from political issues. "To take the question of linkage between the political and the strategic environment," said Kissinger, "the President would like to deal with the problem of peace on the entire front in which peace is challenged and not only on the military one."

Linkage was intended to describe a tie between nuclear-arms talks and discussions of political tensions; in the public mind, however, it came to mean a PACKAGE DEAL in geographic terms—that is, the U.S. would agree to reduce tensions in an area where the Soviets wanted such reduction, in return for détente in another part of the world where superpower interests were in conflict.

Ironically, the word was used by U.S. diplomats in the mid-'60s to object to the Soviets' connection of U.S. bombing of North Vietnam to détente elsewhere. The popularizer of the term—originally, in the sense of tying foreign affairs to domestic concerns—was James Rosenau, then professor of international relations at Rutgers, who titled a 1968 collection of essays *Linkage Politics*.

The word surfaced again in the Carter Administration, as National Security Adviser Zbigniew Brzezinski sought to establish a linkage between Soviet desire for arms control with Soviet support of Cuban troops in Africa, but has since fallen into desuetude.

lion and the fox Combination of strength and craftiness.

Niccolò Machiavelli wrote in *The Prince*:

A prince must imitate the fox and the lion, for the lion cannot protect himself from traps, and the fox cannot defend himself from wolves. ... a prudent ruler ought not to keep faith when by so doing it would be against his interest.

This view of morality is the essence of "Machiavellianism." James MacGregor Burns, popularizing the metaphor in his 1956 book, *Roosevelt: The Lion and the Fox*, wrote: "To the idealists who cautioned him he responded again and again that gaining power—winning elections—was the first, indispensable task. He would use the tricks of the fox to serve the purposes of the lion."

The phrase crops up in political columns. On the death of former German Chancellor Konrad Adenauer in 1967, columnist Max Lerner wrote: "Konrad Adenauer had considerable of the lion in him, and even more of the fox—a combination, as Machiavelli was one of the first to see, that gives a man a galloping advantage in politics."

In 2007, columnist Dominic Odipo in the Kenyan *East Africa News* wrote, "John F. Kennedy was a lion in the making who, nonetheless, had fox-like qualities of cunningness, caution and fear of groups. Richard Nixon was all fox."

liquidity crisis See ECONOMIC JARGON.

litmus test A subject used as an indicator of a candidate's ideological purity.

This phrase made its appearance in the mid-seventies to fill the need for a description of topics that separated the committed from the CENTRISTS, or the TRUE BELIEVERS from the OPPORTUNISTS.

One *litmus test* was a Republican's position on the Panama Canal treaties of 1977: supporters of Ronald Reagan said it would determine whether a candidate could get the 1980 presidential nomination. A Democratic litmus test was the Humphrey-Hawkins bill to reduce unemployment, and a Republican litmus test was opposition to the campaign for an Equal Rights Amendment for women.

In discussing the sale of war planes to Saudi Arabia in 1978, Mr. Reagan told this writer: "It isn't a litmus-test issue"—that is, conservatives could differ without having it considered a test of ideological virtue.

Professional politicians, to whom winning is the paramount issue, take pains to avoid the litmus. "Whatever Republican disunity may develop," wrote reporter Adam Clymer in 1978, "the party is doing one thing right, and that is not squabbling much in 1978. The party's right and middle (it has no real left) distrust each other, but they are working hard at electing Republicans without resorting to litmus-test issues." In 2007, the *Los Angeles Times* headlined: "GOP Candidates Face Litmus Test: Tax Cuts."

The phrase is often applied to the selection of Supreme Court justices. That litmus test is their opinions about abortion.

Under the headline "Reid sets Iraq Litmus Test," the Capitol Hill newspaper *The Hill* reported in 2007 that Senate Majority Leader Harry Reid "offered a unique litmus test for Democrats seeking a strongly anti-war supplemental." One was a bill giving the Democrats' strongest anti-war critics a symbolic victory, sure to draw a presidential veto; the other a bill including waivers that Mr. Bush would sign. The test was militancy versus practicality; Bush prevailed.

The phrase comes from the organic dye that turns blue in alkaline solutions, red in acid. See SWITCHER.

little group of willful men A small, powerful clique disposed (in its opponent's view) to put its own interests above the public's.

During the post–World War I debate over U.S. entry into the League of Nations, Woodrow Wilson characterized the opposition—centered in the Republican Senate leadership—as stubborn obstructionists. Later writers attributed "little group of wilful men" to Wilson as his theme during the League dispute.

In fact, Wilson coined it just before rather than after the war in a speech attacking roughly the same group of Senate isolationists after their successful filibuster killing his bill to allow the arming of merchant vessels. "A little group of wilful men," Wilson said on March 4, 1917, "representing no opinion but their own, has rendered the great government of the United States helpless and contemptible."

Wilson's "little group" is often misquoted as a "little band," as that phrase has often been applied to valiant fighters against superior forces. It is reminiscent of a group of three hundred Thebans who fought in the fourth century B.C., were annihilated at Chaeronea, and became known to history as "the Sacred Band."

Despite the rather specialized Wilsonian use of "little group," later Presidents borrowed the idea in fights of their own. It became a favorite political gambit to portray oneself as the public's defender against predatory oligarchs and power brokers. Franklin D. Roosevelt answered conservative critics of his economic policy in 1941 by saying: "Beware of that small group of selfish men who would clip the wings of the American eagle in order to feather their own nests." John F. Kennedy, in his 1962 confrontation with the steel industry over prices, attacked "a tiny handful of steel executives whose pursuit of private power and profit exceeds their sense of public responsibility."

Vice President Spiro Agnew, in his campaign supporting Republican congressional candidates in 1970, chose *band* over *group*, but deliberately used the rhythm of the Wilson sentence to recall senatorial obstructionism: "Will a little band of radical-liberals, with no constituency but each other, succeed in frustrating the will of the new majority of the American people?"

little left of center See LEFT WING, RIGHT WING.

little man, the See JOHN Q. PUBLIC.

little old ladies in tennis shoes Characterization of female right-wing extremists.

Columnist Robert Novak informs the author that the phrase was coined in 1961 by Stanley Mosk, then the Democratic Attorney General of California, in a report on right-wing activity.

The expression was one of many attacking Senator Barry Goldwater's campaign for the Republican nomination in 1963 and

1964. Republican liberals, members of what Goldwater supporters called the Eastern Establishment (Goldwater: "We ought to saw off the Eastern seaboard and float it out to sea"), denounced the conservative champion as the captive of the John Birch Society and other extremist groups, which included "nuts and kooks" (see KOOKS, NUTS AND). Among these were a resolute, intensely dedicated women's group—Western (or at least not Eastern urban), unsophisticated, often white-haired and wearing rimless eyeglasses. They were called "the little old ladies in tennis shoes" with considerable disdain. However, their doorbell-ringing helped upset the Rockefeller forces in the crucial California primary.

Ronald Reagan, campaigning for governor of California in 1966 and recognizing the backlash against the sexism and ageism implicit in the phrase, joked about the charge of ultraconservative support by addressing audiences occasionally as "Gentlemen—and 'little ladies in tennis shoes' ..."

When in 1992 the Smithsonian Institution decided to license four antique American quilts for reproduction in China, a spokeswoman for the national quilt community objected. "We are not little ladies in tennis shoes. This is a billion-dollar-a-year industry and this institution ... is cutting our throats having these quilts made offshore for rock-bottom prices."

The tennis-shoes metaphor can be contrasted with the SILK STOCKING metaphor; other political uses of foot coverings include "the heel of a dictator" and Adlai Stevenson's "hole in the shoe" symbol, as well as JUNKETEERING GUMSHOES.

Editors of *The New Yorker* have frequently pointed out that they were not editing their magazine for "the old ladies in Dubuque." In *Here at The New Yorker* Brendan Gill wrote that the founder-editor, Harold Ross, launched the publication "with the stipulation that it was *not* to be edited for the old lady in Dubuque." The phrase came to mean a low common denominator of taste, and is used patronizingly. There may be a relationship between the ladies in Dubuque (Iowa) and those in tennis shoes (anywhere).

little tin box Symbol of graft; a hiding place for money.

Thomas M. Farley (no relation to James A.) was sheriff of New York County in the early thirties, and a Tammany SACHEM. In his investigation of corruption that led to the resignation of Mayor James Walker, Judge Samuel Seabury discovered that Farley had deposited $396,000 in his bank account over a six-year period. In that time, his total salary had been $90,000. Seabury's interrogation of Farley led to the coinage of the phrase.

Q: "Where did you keep these moneys that you had saved?"
A: "In a safe deposit box at home in the house."
Q: "Whereabouts at home in the house?"
A: "In a big safe."
Q: "In a little box in a big safe?"
A: "In a big box in a big safe."
Q: "And, Sheriff, was this big box that was safely kept in the big safe a tin box or a wooden box?"
A: "A tin box." [It turned out that Farley's bank deposits, year after year, came from this tin box, which seemed to generate cash all by itself.]
Q: "Kind of a magic box, wasn't it, Sheriff?"
A: "It was a wonderful box."

In 1959 a musical based on Mayor La Guardia's life titled *Fiorello!* was produced by Harold Prince. One of the hit songs was "A Little Tin Box" by Jerry Bock and Sheldon Harnick:

Mister X, May we ask you a question?
It's amazing, is it not?
That the City pays you slightly less than fifty bucks a week
Yet you've purchased a private yacht.
I am positive Your Honor must be joking
Any working man could do what I have done.
For a month or two I simply gave up smoking
And I put my extra pennies one by one
Into a little tin box, a little tin box.
There's a cushion for life's rude shocks,
There is faith, hope and charity,
Hard won prosperity,
*In a little tin box.**

The word's meaning was inverted in 1971 by Abraham Beame, then comptroller and later Mayor of the City of New York, who used it to refer to the container for sealed bids by banks for city financing. "The ritual of unlocking the city's 'little tin box' and then unsealing the bids," said Beame, "got under way at 11:03 A.M. yesterday." In this sense, the box is a symbol of financial fairness and rectitude.

The original sense, however, continues. In 1989, *The Washington Post* reported on Oliver North's testimony in the Iran-contra scandal: "North's account of a little tin box, containing $15,000 and stapled to his closet floor, 'echoed,' as the prosecutor noted in his sentencing recommendations, 'the flimsy lies offered by corrupt municipal officials in the days of Tammany Hall.'"

There is no connection between the *little tin box* in New York and the *loose box* of British usage, which refers to the seats set aside for Edward VII's mistresses at his coronation, in turn taken from an enclosure for horses that permits them to move about without tethering.

living wage Enough earnings to pay for necessities and a little more; a frequent promise of politicians seeking votes of workers.

This has its roots in *living price*, or the price at which a businessman can make a profit and thereby earn his living. Congressman John Lind of Minnesota said in the House in 1890: "Things are at a standstill. We have plenty to sell but no buyers at 'living' prices."

Father Coughlin, "the radio priest" of the '30s who later became a bitter isolationist and anti-Semite, was an ardent supporter of Roosevelt in the early New Deal days, calling for currency inflation, nationalization of the banks, and "a living annual wage."

Living wages were contrasted with *starvation wages*; both terms fell into disuse with the accent on *fringe benefits* and a *guaranteed annual wage* and health entitlements. For a related usage, see HIGH COST OF LIVING.

lobby As a verb, to attempt, as a private citizen or group, to influence governmental decisions and particularly legislative votes; as a noun, a group organized for this purpose.

The practice of lobbying is doubtless as old as the practice of legislating, but the term did not come into vogue until the mid-seventeenth century, when the large anteroom near England's House of Commons floor became known as the *lobby*. The word is akin to the Old High German *lauba*, meaning "a shelter of foliage"; when adopted into English, it came to mean "a covered walk or passageway." The lobby was a public room, and thus one in which Members of Parliament could be approached by special pleaders, with or without protective foliage.

In the early nineteenth century those who lobbied were called *lobbiers* in the U.S., later *lobbyists*. In England a *lobbyist* came to mean a reporter covering the Commons, while a *lobby-agent* meant one who urged particular measures.

But in the U.S. during the politically venal 1800s, lobbying and lobbyists earned a bad name that their professional descendants today, no matter how pure in motive and high-minded the cause, have yet to expunge. See BELTWAY BANDITS.

To Walt Whitman, *lobbiers* were among the "lousy combings and born freedom sellers of the earth." Dennis Tilden Lynch, writing of New York State politics circa 1820, said that "corruption has erected her court.... Her throne is the lobby."

In such low repute were lobbyists—universally considered buyers-up of votes and sellers-out of the public welfare—that to be branded one was an almost automatic disqualification for public office. Mark Hanna was William McKinley's political strong man and an intimate as well. But it is said that when Hanna pressed a particular appointment on McKinley, the President replied, "Mark, I would do anything in the world for you, but I cannot put a man in my cabinet who is known as a lobbyist." By this time lobbyists were considered so numerous and powerful that they were sometimes referred to collectively as the Third House of Congress.

Lobbying has grown more diverse. The federal government and some of the states have imposed legislative restrictions in an attempt to end the more blatant abuses. Most lobbyists now operate openly as registered advocates for their employers and clients, appearing before legislative committees and regulatory agency proceedings, where they are often useful in supplying information on complex issues.

When a reporter asked President Harry Truman in 1948, "Would you be against lobbyists who are working for your program?" the President replied, "We probably wouldn't call those people lobbyists. We would call them citizens appearing in the public interest."

For a derogation of pressure groups in international affairs, see CHINA LOBBY; for a melancholy view of lobbyists, see POCATELLO, YOU CAN'T GO BACK TO.

lobby terms See NOT FOR ATTRIBUTION.

lockbox A symbolic budgetary container for reserving funds for particular purposes.

In his first debate with Texas Governor George W. Bush in the 2000 presidential campaign, Vice President Al Gore popularized the metaphoric use of an old term: "I will put Medicare and Social Security in a lockbox and protect them," said the Democratic candidate in his opening statement. He drove home the usage repeatedly: "I will put Medicare in an iron-clad lockbox and prevent the money from being used for anything other than Medicare," later adding: "I think we need to put Medicare and Social Security in a lockbox. The governor will not put Medicare in a lockbox. I don't think it should be used as a piggy bank for other programs." (A child's *piggy bank* can be easily broken into; an adult's *lockbox* is more secure.)

Gore's proposal was made at a time when the federal government had multi-billion-dollar surpluses in both the Social Security and Medicare accounts, with more money being paid annually into the programs than was being disbursed. Gore's idea was that Social Security and Medicare should be separated in the *lockbox* from the rest of the government's budget, thus preventing

Congress from using the surpluses, as it had in the past, to pay day-to-day expenses of other programs or to fund PORK BARREL projects. Any lockbox funds not spent on Medicare and Social Security, in Gore's proposal, could be used only for retiring the national debt.

Gore did not invent the budgetary lockbox. The device was first proposed by GOP legislators in reaction to Pres. Bill Clinton's puissant slogan, enunciated in his 1998 State of the Union address, to "Save Social Security First." Clinton's aim was to forestall the Republicans from using budget surpluses of the late 1990s for tax cuts. House Republicans, not wanting to be accused of doing this, and at the same time not wanting to see the surplus funds used for enlarging other governmental programs or creating new ones, enacted what they called the "Social Security and Medicare Safe Deposit Act of 1999." The *Washington Post* termed this "a phony lockbox" because the lock could be picked relatively easily in an emergency by a majority vote in the House and 60 votes in the Senate. The author of the House legislation, Rep. Wally Herger (R-Calif.), responded: "While one may argue about the effectiveness of this lockbox, the political reality is that the House-passed lockbox may be the best chance to make real progress toward protecting the Social Security surplus from further raids." The Republican-controlled Senate passed similar legislation.

After George W. Bush was elected president, taxes were cut, national-security spending rose largely on account of 9/11, the surpluses that he had inherited from the Clinton years rapidly disappeared, and the idea of reserving funds in a lockbox became academic—and also the subject of wry jokes. Gore said to Florida Democrats in 2002: "I won't say I told you so, but if anyone is in the market for a 'never-been-used' lockbox, they should see me afterwards." Delivering a mock State of the Union address on the TV show *Saturday Night Live* in 2006, Gore orated: "There are some of you who would like to spend our money on some made-up war. To you I say, 'what

part of "lockbox" don't you understand?'"
And when Gore won an Academy Award in
2007 for his documentary film about GLOBAL
WARMING, *An Inconvenient Truth*, wags suggested that he keep his Oscar in—what
else?—a *lockbox*.

log cabin Humble origins which, when
part of a candidate's personal history, are
presumed to be worth many votes (now
used mostly in a humorous vein).

When the Whigs nominated William
Henry Harrison for President in 1840, one
of his detractors observed that if someone gave Harrison a supply of hard cider,
a small pension, and his choice of how to
spend his time, the old hero of Indian fighting would sit contentedly by his log cabin
the rest of his days. At that point Harrison
owned some 2,000 acres of farmland and a
mansion built around the old cabin, but his
friends seized on the cider-cabin remark
after it was printed in the *Baltimore Republic* as a way of emphasizing their man's ple-
bian past. Harrison himself campaigned
from a log cabin built on a wagon bed that
had a seemingly bottomless cider barrel
attached. The crowds loved it.

Complained a Democrat: "We defend
the policy of the administration; the Whigs
answer 'log cabin.' We urge the honesty,
sagacity, statesmanship of Van Buren; the
Whigs answer that Harrison is a poor man."
Harrison won in what became known as
the "Log Cabin and Hard Cider" campaign.
See BANNER DISTRICT.

As a specific prop, the log cabin remained
a Harrison monopoly, but rare is the candidate or incumbent who fails to point out his
close relations with the common man, to the
public's apparent approval. From Lincoln's
log cabin to Harry Truman's haberdashery
store, the lean yesterdays of presidents are
milestones of political folklore—all the
more so in this era when personal wealth
and political success are hardly unrelated.
John Nance Garner, a two-term Vice President under Franklin D. Roosevelt, said in
1959, "That log house [in which he was
born] did me more good in politics than
anything I ever said."

logorrhea See FOOT-IN-MOUTH DISEASE.

logrolling Mutual aid among politicians,
especially legislators who must vote on
many items of economic importance in
individual states and districts.

H. L. Mencken traced the use of *logrolling* back to 1820. Hans Sperber and Travis
Trittschuh tracked down derisive newspaper comments of "great log rolling captains" in politics to 1809.

In the *Apocolocyntosis*, written early in
the first century A.D. and attributed to Sen-
eca, Hercules urges the gods to deify the
Emperor Claudius. The Latin *Deinde tu si
quid volueris, in vicem faciam* translates:
"And then if you may desire something, I
would reciprocate."

Among settlers in the wilderness, cooperation in handling logs for land clearing
and construction was a force overriding
any differences among neighbors. So too in
politics. "If you will vote for my interest,"
said Congressman B. F. Butler in 1870, "I
will vote for yours. That is how these tariffs
are log-rolled through."

Reformers have inveighed against the
practice as assiduously as practitioners
have pursued it. In 1871 *The New York
Times* complained of Republicans who
established "corrupt alliances with the
enemy in the way of log rolling legislation." In 1967 *Time* magazine, cataloging
the problems of the Post Office—then an
institution as afflicted by bad politics as any
in the country—noted "construction programs pressured on the one side by budget
vagaries and on the other by congressional
log rolling."

The classic description of the theory of
logrolling is attributed to Simon Cameron,
Pennsylvania politician who served as Lincoln's first Secretary of War: "You scratch
my back and I'll scratch yours."

loneliest job in the world Description of
the presidency, emphasizing its "awesome
burdens."

It is a wonder that there are any applicants.

Thomas Jefferson, who served first as
vice president, said: "The second office of

this government is honorable and easy, the first is a splendid misery." Andrew Jackson called the presidency "a situation of dignified slavery." The term of office has been likened to a term in jail by George Washington, who felt like "a culprit, going to the place of his execution." Warren Harding said, "This White House is a prison. I can't get away from the men who dog my footsteps. I am in jail." Harry Truman agreed; returning from a pre-breakfast stroll, he sighed and told a reporter, "There is the big white jail."

He wrote in his memoirs: "To be President of the United States is to be lonely, very lonely at times of great decisions."

"My God," said James Garfield two months after taking office, "what is there in this place that a man should ever want to get into it?" James Buchanan called it "a crown of thorns."

Several presidents thought it a ruiner of friendships. Grover Cleveland wrote: "Henceforth, I can have no friends...I must face the difficulties of a new official life almost alone." John F. Kennedy, who enjoyed the presidency, agreed that it "is not a very good place to make new friends." Old friendships are often strained. General Omar Bradley had called Dwight Eisenhower "Ike" for forty years; when he properly addressed him as "Mr. President," Eisenhower felt a twinge of isolation. He wrote: "His salutation put me on notice: from then onward, for as long as I held the office, I would...be separated from all others, including my oldest and best friends. I would be far more alone now than when commanding the Allied Forces ..."

Wendell Willkie asked FDR why he kept Harry Hopkins so close to him. FDR replied, "Someday you may well be sitting here where I am now as President of the United States. And when you are, you'll be looking at that door over there and knowing that practically everybody who walks through it wants something out of you. You'll learn what a lonely job this is, and you'll discover the need for somebody like Harry Hopkins who asks for nothing except to serve you."

Of all the burdens of the presidency, loneliness is the one complaint that threads through the writings of the occupants of the White House. William Howard Taft summed it up to Woodrow Wilson on the latter's inauguration day: "I'm glad to be going—this is the loneliest place in the world."

In 1977, *National Journal* overturned the oxymoron of splendid misery (which may have been Jefferson's reworking of Goethe's phrase, "radiant misery"): "We can thank Carter for exposing the myth of the 'splendid misery' of the Presidency. He recently told a group of editors that he enjoys being President. 'It is a fairly pleasant life,' he said." The columnist Mary McGrory further contested the validity of this phrase; in 1990, she wrote, "The term 'splendid misery' underwent considerable erosion during the Reagan years. Ronald Reagan seemed to enjoy himself most of the time. But Reagan was St. Sebastian compared to George [H.W.] Bush, for whom every day in the Oval Office is Christmas. The President's palpable delight in being where he always wanted to be has not waned in the 15 months since he took office."

Both Bill Clinton and George W. Bush found the job exhilarating in the first term, much less so—more lonely—in the second. Same with George Washington.

loner Politician who "goes his own way," "keeps his own counsel"; used pejoratively, as one who will not mix or take good advice.

Probably derived from *lone wolf* or *Lone Ranger*, the word is applied to those who reject the camaraderie of political life, and on the policy level, who know enough (or think they do) to arrive at conclusions on issues independent of advisers. A *loner* is not necessarily a maverick; he may not oppose the organization, but he does not give the organization a sense of participation in his decisions and his future.

Chicago Democratic Boss Jake Arvey assessed Senator Paul Douglas' beginnings in politics this way: "Paul was a 'loner' in Chicago politics. He was an alderman and somewhat of a stormy petrel. ... I knew Paul Douglas was thinking about maybe running for Mayor. The indications were that if he did run, he would make the race as an independent Democrat. This was in line with Douglas' history of being a 'loner.'" Arvey talked Douglas out of running for mayor and into running for senator, with Adlai Stevenson running on the same ticket for governor. "In neither case," Arvey continued, "were these men 'developed' in the sense that they came out of the organization. Stevenson was a political unknown about to break on the public consciousness; Douglas had made himself in politics by bucking the organization on many important issues." Though each man was, in a different way, a *loner*, the organization used and was used by them.

Although Henry Kissinger once described himself to Italian interviewer Oriana Fallaci as a kind of lonely cowboy on the international scene—evoking the "Lone Ranger" image, which was followed by hoots of derision from critics—a loner's reputation is not one that political figures usually seek. Joan Mondale, when her husband was Vice President, used the word and its current antonym, *team player* (which, during the Watergate hearings, temporarily gained a negative connotation), in a comment about her husband: "He is very much a team player, not a loner." See MAVERICK.

long hot summer A threat of violence in urban ghettos, when summer heat shortens tempers and crowds gather out of doors.

The phrase began as the title of a 1958 movie based on a number of works by William Faulkner; a television series based on the characters, also titled *The Long Hot Summer*, ran on the ABC-TV network in 1965.

Michigan Governor George Romney, who was to face a riot in Detroit that required federal troops to quell, predicted with prescience in April 1967 that the U.S. faced not only long hot summers at home but "the equally forbidding prospect of a long, hot century" throughout the world. In June 1967, before the riots of Newark and Detroit, Martin Luther King, Jr. said: "Everyone is worrying about the long hot summer with its threat of riots. We had a long cold winter when little was done about the conditions that create riots."

Faulkner's phrase was an apt turnaround of an earlier image that connected unrest with winter. *The Winter of Our Discontent* was a 1961 book by John Steinbeck, its title taken from a Shakespearean pun in *Richard III*: "Now is the winter of our discontent / Made glorious summer by this son of York."

President Kennedy used a seasonal image in a remark at the conclusion of the frigid 1961 Vienna meeting with Khrushchev: "It's going to be a cold winter."

long war See WAR ON TERROR.

loose box See LITTLE TIN BOX.

loser, show me a good In full: "Show me a good loser, and I'll show you a loser" was a saying favored by President Richard M. Nixon, proud of his ability to come back from two consecutive, seemingly irreversible defeats.

The quote comes from the world of sports. Fred R. Shapiro, editor of *The Yale Book of Quotations*, credits it to Boston Celtics coach Arnold "Red" Auerbach on the basis of a 1965 citation in the *Mansfield (Ohio) News Journal*. Others credit Notre Dame football coach Knute Rockne, who seems to have said something similar in the 1920s: "Show me a good and gracious loser, and I'll show you a failure."

Writing about his days as a football player at California's Whittier College, from which he graduated in 1934, Nixon recalled in *RN*, his 1978 memoir, that "Show me a good loser, etc." was a maxim of the team's coach, Wallace Newman. (Another Newman maxim: "When you lose, get mad—but get mad at yourself, not your opponent.") Nixon wrote that he was no great shakes as a player, never getting into a game until it "was already safely won or hopelessly lost," but remembered "Chief" Newman (the coach was an American Indian) with affection: "I think that I admired him more and learned more from him than from any man I have ever known aside from my father.... He drilled into me a competitive spirit and the determination to come back after you have been knocked down or after you lose."

Another politician who had no love of losing was Rep. Morris Udall, who observed, after placing second to Jimmy Carter in New Hampshire's 1976 Democratic presidential primary: "The people have spoken—the bastards!" See CAN'T-WIN TECHNIQUE.

loved for the enemies he made Innocence by dissociation; a campaign cry of Grover Cleveland supporters in 1884.

Grover Cleveland, mayor of Buffalo and later governor of New York, did not work well with the SACHEMS of Tammany Hall. While this caused him some difficulty in his home state, he was able to play up the opposition of Tammany leaders as an asset in the campaign for the Democratic nomination. With Samuel Tilden ill and declaring himself out of the running, Cleveland was the leading candidate. In a seconding speech, Governor Edward S. Bragg of Wisconsin electrified the delegates with "They love him most for the enemies he has made." (Senator Joseph McCarthy used the same slogan in a full-page ad in the Milwaukee *Journal* in 1952, as he ran for a second term; New York Mayor Robert F. Wagner was to make the same turning-on-Tammany appeal running for his third term in 1961.)

Franklin D. Roosevelt knew how to exploit the appeal of enmity from an unpopular source. In a Madison Square Garden speech bringing his 1936 campaign to a climax, he zeroed in on the enemy: "financial monopoly, speculation, reckless banking, class antagonism, sectionalism, war profiteering." In a hard voice he said: "Never before in all our history have these forces been so united against one candidate as they stand today. They are unanimous in their *hate* for me—and I welcome their hatred."

Presidents have taken private reassurance from the source of attacks as well. When Harry Truman fired Secretary of Commerce Henry Wallace, he incurred the wrath of the far-left wing. Writing to his mother, the President observed: "Well, now he's out, and the crackpots are having conniption fits. I'm glad they are. It convinces me I'm right."

love feast Humorous exaggeration of a friendly meeting, especially one that could have revealed tensions and bitterness but ends amicably.

The phrase was originally religious, to describe the *agape*, or love feast, among early Christians—an informal dinner, with songs and prayers, prevalent in the first two centuries of Christianity. Suspicions of bacchanalian zeal were voiced early, as the Book of Jude warned of "blemishes on your love feasts"; Pope Paul in 1967 disapproved of changes in the celebration of the Eucharist, following reports of experiments in the liturgy that included mass at home accompanied by modern music, with non-Catholics participating. "Such masses," reported the *The New York Times*, "are frequently thought of as imitations of the 'agape,' or love feast, common in the early church, and the emphasis is on the close fellowship of small numbers of believers."

Colonel Edward House set up a luncheon for Franklin Roosevelt and Massachusetts Democratic leaders in 1932 to discourage Al Smith. Ralph Martin wrote in *Ballots and Bandwagons*: "Uninvited to this 'love feast,' promoted by Colonel House, [former Boston Mayor James] Curley not only showed up with Roosevelt, but invited his own press and newsreel people."

The religious phrase was probably introduced into politics by Mark Twain and Charles Dudley Warner in 1873, in the novel *The Gilded Age*, a story about the politics of Reconstruction. The newspaper in their fictional Washington, D.C., is so much the supporter of the corrupt status quo that it is called the *Daily Love-Feast*. A more restrained form is "mutual admiration society."

low profile Self-denigration to reduce vulnerability; abhorrence of the vivid or dramatic in public posture.

A low profile is one step short of a PASSION FOR ANONYMITY; one who maintains the creative crouch gets some public exposure, but does not invite attack. It is normally used to describe the low-keyed approach of an individual, but can also be used to characterize an administration.

The meaning of the expression was best captured in John F. Kennedy's advice to his speechwriter, Ted Sorensen: "Stay out of sight and you stay out of trouble." The phrase remained in active use. Presidential assistant Leonard Garment told the author in early 1970, "I've kept my profile so low for so long, I've got a permanent backache." It has achieved a certain linguistic universality. "In last year's election campaign," wrote *The Wall Street Journal* in 1977 about Canadian separatists, "unlike previous contests, the Parti Quebecois kept what its strategists called '*le low profile*' on the independence issue."

This figure of political speech probably has a military origin; in tank warfare, a vehicle with a low profile is less readily identified through binoculars and presents less of a target for artillery. *The Third Barnhart Dictionary of New English* dates the term to 1964 as a translation of the Japanese *teishisei*, from *tei*, "low," and *shisei*, "posture," which was the motto for the Hayato Ikeda cabinet of 1960–64.

In 2007, just after having provoked a controversy in denying that the Japanese military had forced "comfort women" into sexual slavery during World War II, Japan's Prime Minister Shinzo Abe came to Washington on a visit described as "almost exclusively behind the curtains." The *Los Angeles Times* came up with an apt headline: "Japanese leader to keep a low profile in U.S."

low road See HIGH ROAD ... LOW ROAD.

loyal opposition The sometimes uncomfortable position of the political opposition in a republican form of government, endowing the responsibility to oppose with patriotic motives.

In eighteenth-century Britain, when political parties were first being formed, the term was meant to indicate that the party in opposition, like the party in power, was true to the Crown—in fact, loyal—but felt that the best interests of the nation would be served by different policies. It is officially used to describe the party out of power in Great Britain, as "His (Her) Majesty's Loyal Opposition."

In the U.S. it was popularized by Wendell Willkie in a radio speech delivered several days after he and the Republican party had been defeated by President Roosevelt in November 1940.

Willkie spoke of the war already under way in Europe, and of the calls by some for a coalition cabinet of Democrats and Republicans. He rejected such a cabinet (though FDR had already enlisted Republicans Frank Knox and Henry Stimson) and described what he considered to be the role of the Republican party: "A vital element in the balanced operation of democracy is a strong, alert and watchful opposition ... I say: 'Your function during the next four years is that of the loyal opposition.' ... Let us not, therefore, fall into the partisan error of opposing things just for the sake of opposition. Ours must not be an opposition against—it must be an opposition for—an opposition for a strong America ..."

Republican leader Joe Martin, who would excoriate Willkie three months later for backing away from his anti-war rhetoric on the stump (see CAMPAIGN ORATORY), was with him on this: "Willkie got off on the right foot with the whole country, Republicans included, with his 'Loyal Opposition' speech." Martin's praise did not come easy, for the "duty" of the opposition was still felt by many to oppose, and not to cooperate.

That principle had long been articulated. Winston Churchill told of his father, Lord Randolph Churchill, quoting an early-nineteenth-century politician as saying bluntly: "The duty of an Opposition is to oppose." (What Edward Stanley, 14th Earl of Derby, said in the House of Commons in 1841 was "to quote Mr. Tierney, a great Whig authority, 'The duty of an Opposition [is] very simple ... to oppose everything, and propose nothing.'" The "editing of history" has snipped off the last four words, which make the aphorism a little over-the-top.)

In his years as Senate Majority Leader, Lyndon Johnson established himself as a Democratic leader who was frequently prepared to support legislation desired by the Republican Administration of Dwight D. Eisenhower. He expressed his philosophy to fellow Democrats at a Senate conference early in 1953: "I have never agreed with the statement that it is 'the business of the opposition to oppose.' I do not believe that the American people have sent us here merely to obstruct."

But there are those who still subscribe to the Tierney theory. Fred Vinson, Supreme Court Chief Justice from 1946 to 1953, told the story of a Kentucky politician who was asked whom he was going to support in a primary election. The politician's answer: "I don't know yet. I'm waiting to see what the opposition does, so I can take the other side."

Loyal opposition appears to be an oxymoron (a phrase made memorable by the jarring juxtaposition of contradictory words); however, the adjective *loyal* runs not to the political opposition currently in power, but to the government itself. More clashing oxymorons are *profitless prosperity*, UNTHINKABLE THOUGHTS, and WAGING PEACE. As a member of the loyal opposition, Churchill in 1936 flung a handful of oxymorons at the government of Stanley Baldwin: "So they go on in strange paradox, decided only to be undecided, resolved to be irresolute, adamant for drift, solid for fluidity, all-powerful to be impotent."

A member of the Canadian opposition, René Lévesque of the secession-minded Parti Québécois, in 1978 threw an oxymoron at a plan by Prime Minister Pierre Trudeau, calling it "profoundly insignificant."

loyalty oath A pledge of fealty to a government; more specifically in recent years, a promise of abstinence from subversive activities or merely opposing causes.

Modern concern with loyalty oaths started soon after World War II. Charges of Communist infiltration of the American government became the biggest domestic issue of the late '40s and early '50s. Although President Harry Truman sometimes scoffed at it (see RED HERRING), he also issued an Executive Order in 1947—called the "loyalty order"—which prescribed security procedures for the executive branch. The issue arises periodically after wars and upheavals. The "red menace" after World War I also made the country security-conscious, and loyalty oaths had a brief vogue.

Another form of loyalty oath is often required by a political party of its convention delegates; it is a pledge to abide by the decision of the convention and not to BOLT if dissatisfied. Columnist Arthur Krock wrote: "Without the discipline which was enforced by the 'loyalty' requirement at the Democratic Convention of 1964, a political party as such loses its identity as a responsible group accountable to the people."

During the Civil War, Congress enacted legislation that required Confederate sympathizers to take the *ironclad oath* if they wished to regain their civil rights. No former rebel could hold important public office, for instance, without swearing his opposition to the Confederate cause. Sometimes called the *amnesty oath* in the North, it was more often termed the "damn nasty oath" in the South.

In *Andrew Johnson and Reconstruction*, Eric McKitrick wrote of the Southern girl who was brought before a Union captain and told she had to swear an oath of loyalty to the Union. "The girl refused on the grounds that it was wrong to swear an oath—her church forbade it, her mother told her that no lady ever swore. The captain insisted that she swear the oath and the girl finally agreed, saying: 'I will swear an oath, but it will be forever on your conscience. Damn all you Yankees to hell! There, Captain, I swore my oath!' " See AMERICANISM; AMNESTY; KNOW-NOTHINGS.

lulu Payment made to legislators "in lieu of" expenses.

Instead of requiring a detailed accounting of expenditures from its legislators, New York State set a fixed fee to be paid them "in lieu of" (in place of) expenses; if the legislators could skimp on the outlay, the leftover money was theirs to keep. Governor Al Smith named them "lulus," a play on the word *lieu* and the meaning of the girl's name in old slang as "a whopping mistake."

Lulu is in current, but northeastern regional, use; attacks on the expense system are made periodically, but the word more often chosen nationally is PERKS, emoluments ranging from free parking, box seats, and subsidized haircuts to extensive trips abroad by "codels" (congressional delegations). *Perks* is a clip and alteration of *perquisites*, rooted in the medieval "acquisition other than by inheritance"; a euphemism is sometimes *benefits*, privileges granted "in lieu of" salary increases. See WALKING AROUND MONEY.

lumpenproletariat See PROLETARIAT.

lunatic fringe Extremists, with a connotation of nutty views but not violent behavior; a derogation of persons or groups with political views far to the left or right of the MAINSTREAM.

The emergence of militant right-wingers and professional anti-Communists since the 1940s revived *lunatic fringe*. In one of his last campaign speeches, Franklin Roosevelt in 1944 attacked "labor baiters, bigots and some politicians who use the term Communism loosely." This "fear propaganda," he said, had been used by fascist blackshirts, Nazi brownshirts, and "in this country by the silver shirts and those on the lunatic fringe." Since then the term has been most frequently applied to "extremism" or the RADICAL RIGHT.

It was not always so. According to Fred Shapiro, editor of *The Yale Book of Quotations*, the phrase had an early debut in *Oliver Optic's Magazine* in 1874: "'The girls!' exclaimed Miss Lizzie, lifting her eyebrows till they met the 'lunatic fringe' of hair which straggled uncurled down her forehead." *The Washington Post* in 1880 described a dandy from Atlanta with "hair cut lunatic fringe, coat cut heart shape" and "a diamond the size of a walnut in his left ear."

Though the phrase continued to be used early in the twentieth century to describe outlandish clothes or hairstyles, Theodore Roosevelt gave it currency in its political sense in October 1913, when he wrote in the magazine *Outlook* about modern art: "Every reform movement has a lunatic fringe." Although a progressive and a reformer himself, Roosevelt said he was talking about "the votaries of any forward movement." Evenhandedly, he wrote: "I am always having to fight the silly reactionaries and the inert, fatuous creatures who will not think seriously; and on the other hand to try to exercise some control over the lunatic fringe among the reformers."

A Calgary correspondent wrote to advice columnist Ann Landers in 1992: "Every minority has its lunatic fringe, extremists and nut cases who impede progress, block acceptance and make life hard for everybody."

When a collocation has been in the language for a century, it tends to get clipped. Of late, *fringe* has been used often as a shortening of the two-word mother phrase. In his column in *National Review* in 2007, Mark Steyn wrote: "I get a gazillion e-mails a day saying: 'Well, if the death of Europe is really happening, how come no one else is talking about it except you and a few other fringe wackos?'"

In current usage, labeling from near right to far right goes *rightist, far rightist,* REACTIONARY, *ultrarightist,* MOSSBACK, *paleoconservative,* DINOSAUR WING, *Neanderthal,* TROGLODYTIC, and *lunatic fringe.* Also see LITTLE OLD LADIES IN TENNIS SHOES; KOOKS, NUTS AND. For the fringe on the other end of the spectrum, or scarf, *lunatic* lent itself to the alliterative *loony left*; also see RED; PINKO; BLEEDING HEARTS; KNEE-JERK LIBERAL; EGGHEAD.

lunching him out See ADVANCE MAN.

M

macaca See BLOOPER.

machine politics The election of officials and the passage of legislation through the power of an organization created for political action.

The phrase is derogatory because it suggests that the interests of the organization are placed before those of the general public; also, a machine is bloodless, needing to be "well oiled."

Machine politics in the United States is (I construe *politics* as singular) identified with big cities: The Vare organization in Philadelphia (Republican) and the Kelly-Nash machine in Chicago (Democratic) are examples of machine politics in the classic sense, but the beginnings of urban organization politics can be tracked back to Tammany (see TAMMANY TIGER). Theodore Roosevelt, a politician of substantial skill, wrote that "Van Buren was the first product of what are now called 'machine politics' put into the Presidential chair. The people at large would never have thought of him for President of their own accord; but he had become Jackson's political legatee."

The creation of the first political machine in the U.S. at the end of the eighteenth century in New York has often been credited to Aaron Burr, Jefferson's Vice President and rival. His political acumen was praised by those who won the right to vote through his political manipulations, and damned by those, led by Alexander Hamilton, whose careers had prospered from a franchise based on possession of property.

The word *machine* in the political sense is believed by Mencken to have been Burr's invention, though it did not come into general use until after the Civil War. It generally means "strict organization, with rewards going to those who observe its disciplines and traditions." Discipline is central. Edward Flynn, the Bronx County Democratic leader who became a national figure in the Roosevelt era, wrote: "the

so-called 'independent' voter is foolish to assume that a political machine is run solely on good will, or patronage. For it is not only a machine; it is an army. And in any organization as in any army, there must be discipline."

The charge against machines is that they are undemocratic and invariably encourage corruption. One answer is in primary elections in which candidates for office may be selected directly by the voters who register for one political party or the other. But the primary system often means selection of the best-known candidate, or the one supported by the organization leadership who can use "troops" to turn out the vote.

To the reformer or INSURGENT, the machine is dominated by a BOSS and consists of his HENCHMEN and their "dupes"; to a regular, the machine is headed by a "leader" and consists of ACTIVISTS and "public-spirited citizens." To a blogger, connections through a website create the soul of a new machine.

In Japan, the word for political machine is *jiban*, literal translation "foundation." See BASE.

machinery of government Metaphor to show complexity of interrelationships within public administration.

"I think we have more machinery of government than is necessary," wrote Thomas Jefferson in 1824. He might have seen the phrase in Edward Gibbon's *Decline and Fall of the Roman Empire*, written between 1776 and 1788: "The nice and artificial machinery of government was out of joint."

Geared to press the *panic button* at the first *feedback* from *machine politicos*, government planners *mesh* their thinking to get *traction* for their programs to *spark* action, *engineering* their budgets so as to ignore *start-up* costs, and *mechanically* warn those *automatons* and *cogs* whose *machinations* might throw *monkey wrenches* into the *works* that *counterpro-*

ductive people usually get the *shaft*. See INOPERATIVE; WHEELS WITHIN WHEELS.

President William Howard Taft listened in wonderment to an adviser who spoke of "the machinery of government" and said later to a friend, "You know…he really thinks it *is* machinery."

In 1969 a White House aide told President Nixon he would relay a request "to the appropriate mechanism." The President proceeded to reminisce to the author about a visit he had made to Poland in 1959:

> There was a steel mill on the itinerary. The Polish diplomat who was my escort officer—a brilliant fellow—turned me over to the plant manager for the usual guided tour. The manager was especially proud of the new machinery in the plant, and he told me all about what it cost and how it speeded up the process. He got a little impatient when I stopped to shake hands with the workers around whatever machine he was showing off. In the car on the way back from the mill, the diplomat said something I've always remembered. "It's not hard to find men who understand machinery," he said. "Our trouble is we don't have enough men who understand men."

In 1978 the metaphor was just as cranked up as ever. "Carter's an engineering officer, a protege of Admiral [Hyman] Rickover," said the President's Energy Secretary, James Schlesinger, to reporter Hedrick Smith. "Rickover has to know how every single engine or pump works. Carter is that way. He looks upon government as machinery to be improved, to be lubricated."

Madison Avenue techniques The other side's gimmicky, slick use of the communications media to play on emotions, contrasted with your own forthright use of modern marketing methods to "get the message to the people."

The phrase *Madison Avenue*, in its present sense descriptive of the advertising community, was born in 1944, when an article in *The New Republic* describing advertising's contribution to the war effort was signed "Madison Avenue." "The avenue," as columnists soon called it, covered agencies on Park, Third, and Fifth avenues in New York City as well.

Madison Avenue techniques was a phrase used to derogate the "hidden persuaders" (author Vance Packard's term) who are "SELLING CANDIDATES LIKE SOAP"—neatly packaged, making popular appeals in catchy phrases, always new, ever-improved.

These techniques can be startlingly successful in politics. In Picoazá, a town of 4,000 in Ecuador, the producer of Pulvapies, a foot powder, tied in to the local campaign for mayor with the following slogan: "Vote for any candidate, but if you want well-being and hygiene, vote for Pulvapies." Well-being and hygiene turned out to be gut issues in Picoazá, and the human candidates were chagrined when the voters chose Pulvapies, the foot powder, over the human candidates for mayor. "Cynics may feel," editorialized *The Wall Street Journal*, "the ensuing result reflects on the literacy of Ecuadorans, but we're not so sure. There are times in this enlightened land when the citizenry would welcome a chance to vote for a ticket that promised, not PIE IN THE SKY, but something down to earth and believable." See MEDIA EVENT.

Mae West hold See BLUE SLIP.

Mafia See IRISH MAFIA.

magnet issue A topic offering a politician a vote-attracting stance to create a coalition on a common problem.

"A 'magnet' issue," explained John J. Pitney Jr. in 1993, assistant professor of government at Claremont McKenna College in California, "is a positive policy stand that attracts voter support and inspires people to take part in politics." Examples include some of FDR's vote-attracting issues of the Democratic Party in the 1930s, including Social Security, workers' rights, and the creation of jobs.

The antonym of magnet issue is WEDGE ISSUE. "Wedge issues make powerful weapons," Pitney instructed, "but they cannot alone sustain a realignment of the electorate. Disrupting and discrediting the opposition is not the same as creating loyalty to one's own side. That task requires 'magnet' issues."

The metaphor is strong. Francis Bacon wrote in his 1620 Latin work *Novum Organum* about three major discoveries, "namely, printing, gunpowder, and the mariner's needle [i.e., magnet]. For these three have changed the whole face and state of things throughout the world." See also BREAD-AND-BUTTER ISSUE; HOT BUTTON; ISSUES, THE; PARAMOUNT ISSUE; POCKETBOOK ISSUE.

Magnolia Mafia See IRISH MAFIA; SMELL OF MAGNOLIAS.

maiden speech A first speech by an oratorical virgin in a legislative body.

Probably the best-known example was a fiasco. Benjamin Disraeli, destined to be Prime Minister of Great Britain twice and to enter the House of Lords as the Earl of Beaconsfield, was at the time he first secured a seat in the House of Commons merely an ambitious young man of thirty-two. His maiden speech to that body was badly received; in fact, so raucous was the laughter of the members that Disraeli was forced to take his seat, his speech unfinished. His parting words were: "The time will come when you shall hear me."

The Senate of the United States, which likes to think of itself as the world's greatest deliberative body, long had a tradition that new senators did not deliver their virgin speech-making efforts until they had sat through a congressional session in silence. This rule was discarded with the election of men already nationally prominent to that body; for example, the maiden speeches of men like Robert Kennedy of New York and Edward Brooke of Massachusetts, and in a later generation Hillary Clinton of New York and Barack Obama of Illinois, delivered shortly after having taken their places in the Senate, were given careful attention all over the nation. In Great Britain, however, Winston Churchill called Sir Alan Herbert's maiden effort "a brazen hussy of a speech."

mainstream The central current of a political doctrine or an electorate.

Mainstream—or variations thereof—has long appealed to writers and statesmen as the watery equivalent of the broad MIDDLE OF THE ROAD. A Japanese proverb notes that "one man can stand still in a flowing stream, but not in a world of men." In 1792, Mary Wollstonecraft wrote in *A Vindication of the Rights of Woman*, a seminal feminist work: "In every age there has been a stream of popular opinion that has carried all before it, and given a family character, as it were, to the century."

John F. Kennedy often used the mainstream image, or byplays on it. He told the historian James MacGregor Burns: "Some people have their liberalism 'made' by the time they reach their late 20s. I didn't. I was caught in cross-currents and eddies. It was only later that I got into the stream of things." Addressing the Irish Parliament in Dublin on June 28, 1963, he returned to the image: "Ireland is moving in the mainstream of current world events. Your destiny lies not as a peaceful island in a sea of trouble but as a maker and shaper of world peace."

No modern politician used the word more often, however, than New York's Governor Nelson Rockefeller. "The mainstream of American political thought and action" was one of his favorite phrases. Speechwriter Hugh Morrow recalled that Rockefeller's first use of the term was in a statement released July 14, 1963:

it has now become crystal clear that the vociferous and well-drilled extremist elements boring within the Party utterly reject these fundamental principles of our heritage. They are, in fact, embarked on a determined and ruthless effort to take over the Party, its platform and its candidates on their own terms... wholly alien to the broad middle course that accommodates the mainstream of Republican principle.

See BORING FROM WITHIN.

At the 1964 Republican presidential convention in San Francisco's Cow Palace, Rockefeller supporters, in a futile effort to halt Barry Goldwater's drive for the nomination, unfurled a 30-foot canvas banner urging Republicans: "Stay in the Mainstream." (The author was among the unfurlers.) But the delegates' votes were not there; as the old English proverb states, "the stream cannot rise above its source."

In politics, mainstreams meander. After the Goldwater debacle, the influence of the "hard right" softened; with Nixon, the mainstream moved toward détente in foreign affairs and progressive policies domestically, leading to a 1972 reelection landslide. Post-Watergate, the GOP mainstream was subterranean. As the final year of President Gerald Ford's presidency began in 1976, Christopher Lydon of *The New York Times* saw partisanship dissolving: "the independent stream through the center of American politics has now widened to a river, about 40% of the electorate ... And it is within the fluid and independent middle that analysts search for currents that could shape new parties, realign the old ones or extend the history of erosion in a new 'post-partisan' era." See BIPARTISAN.

Surveying the Democratic center, George F. Will used the term in a 1986 column: "Senators Howard Metzenbaum and Edward Kennedy, whose liberalism is even more pronounced than the liberalism rejected by 93 states in the last two [Reagan] elections, are not exactly a Lewis and Clark team you would send exploring to locate the American mainstream." However, the Democratic mainstream began moving toward the center, progressive on taxation and entitlements, multilateral in foreign affairs, culminating in Bill Clinton's victory in 1992 and resounding reelection in 1996 (see TRIANGULATION and IT'S THE ECONOMY, STUPID!).

The word's major use both in and out of politics in the Internet era came with its switch from a noun to an apposite modifier in the phrase *mainstream media*, often used with more than a hint of derogation. The rising bloggers took up a phrase that had been coined in 1985 by Ralph Nader, then the director of the Corporate Accountability Research Group and in 1996 and 2000 a splinter-party candidate for president: "In recent years," said Nader, "corporate criminal activity has spilled onto the pages and screens of the *mainstream media*."

The phrase was taken up by many members of the new media that substituted its own, often quite personal, webcasting for the previous communications dominance of broadcast and cable networks and major newspaper and magazine publishing. In the usage of the Internet generation, the modifier *mainstream* carried an old-fashioned, almost quaint, connotation, as distinct from its earlier political meaning of "centrist." Bloggers, as is their wont, soon initialized the phrase, which now appears both in print and on the Web as MSM.

See DON'T CHANGE HORSES; EXTREMISM; BIPARTISAN.

majority rule See ONE MAN, ONE VOTE.

make my day A dare; anticipated delight at an action that will permit a powerful reaction.

In *Sudden Impact*, a 1983 movie starring Clint Eastwood as Dirty Harry, a violent vigilante cop, the law officer aims his gun at a hostage-taker brandishing his own weapon and snarls, "Go ahead, make my day." The phrase was a challenge to the felon to resist arrest, providing the officer with the chance to kill him, an act that would presumably give the cop pleasure.

Speaking to a conference of business executives in Washington on March 13, 1985, President Ronald Reagan used the imperative phrase in a jocular fashion: "I have my veto pen drawn and ready for any tax increase that Congress might even think of sending up. And I have only one thing to say to the tax increasers: Go ahead, make my day."

Washington Post columnist Mary McGrory wrote: "At last a slogan for the second term of Ronald Reagan ... a shade more genteel than 'Drop dead,' which is what it really means." More accurately, in political parlance, it means "give me the chance to respond devastatingly."

At the 1988 Republican National Convention, George H.W. Bush used a variation of the phrase in accepting the presidential nomination: "There are actually those who claim that I don't always communicate in the clearest, most concise way. But I dare them to keep it up. Go ahead, make my 24-hour time period."

make the world safe for democracy A rallying phrase as America entered World

War I, which acquired a hollow sound after that war and is currently used to derogate idealistic intervention.

President Woodrow Wilson's phrase was: "The world must be made safe for democracy." His speech, delivered before Congress on April 2, 1917, went on to disclaim any "selfish ends" on the part of the U.S.

Had it not been for one man, however, Wilson's phrase might never have caught on. Senator John Sharp Williams of Mississippi, a good orator himself, but at this time aged and almost deaf, was leaning forward, concentrating intently on the speech. When Wilson said, "The world must be made safe for democracy," he began slowly—and alone—to clap, continuing until others joined him. This underlined for the reporters in the press gallery that a phrase had been turned.

The construction has been played upon in a sarcastic manner, as in this official statement in the '60s by Kenya's ruling party, the African National Union: "America's presence [in Vietnam] is not in the interests of the people. It is there to make the Far East safe for Coca-Cola."

President Nixon in 1971 varied the phrase: "By his example, Woodrow Wilson helped make the world safe for idealism." But it is still used with a note of skepticism. In a 1992 commentary on American foreign policy, *The San Francisco Chronicle* asked, "Should America be the world's policeman, intervening in hot spots to make the world safe for democracy?" See POLICEMAN OF THE WORLD; WAR TO END WARS.

malefactors of great wealth The irresponsible rich; an early attack phrase on Big Business.

Annoyed by continued attacks on him as the destroyer of business and the author of the Panic of 1907, Theodore Roosevelt declared in a speech at Provincetown, Mass., on August 20, 1907, that the economic trouble had been caused, at least in part, by "ruthless and determined men" hiding "behind the breastworks of corporate organization." He added: "It may well be that the determination of the government to punish certain malefactors

of great wealth has been responsible for something of the trouble, at least to the extent of having caused these men to bring about as much financial stress as they can in order to discredit the policy of the government."

For Franklin D. Roosevelt, ECONOMIC ROYALISTS and "plutocrats" were latter-day equivalents of his cousin's famous "malefactors."

Words like *malefactor* and *infamy*, rarely used but immediately understood, give solemnity and significance to a phrase. *Malefactor* (directly from the Latin for *evil-doer*) is used less frequently than its opposite, *benefactor* (good-doer), and it made TR's phrase successful. As president, George W. Bush embraced the English translation of malefactor, *evil-doer*.

Ma, Ma, where's Pa? See SMEAR.

managed news Information generated and distributed by the government in such a way as to give government interest priority over candor.

News management surfaced in October and November 1962 along with the Russian offensive missiles in Cuba to give a name to one of the oldest truisms in the relations of government officials and journalists. Long before he was president, John F. Kennedy warned an aide about the press: "Always remember that their interests and ours ultimately conflict." To the reporter, news is the publication of information that will interest and enlighten the reader. To the official, it is news that will advance or destroy his or her political future.

Newspapers, magazines, and broadcasters harped on "news management" as soon as the worst of the missile crisis was over, with much justification. There had been some fibbing in high places. Assistant Defense Secretary Arthur Sylvester later talked about the "government's right, if necessary, to lie" and of news as "weaponry." Reporters were barred from ships on blockade duty around Cuba. The White House made requests about self-censorship but refused to impose official censorship. Sylvester in the Pentagon and his counterpart Robert Manning in the State Department imposed requirements irksome to reporters that all interviews be either monitored or reported to an official's superior.

Some critics of these policies recalled Nazi propaganda minister Joseph Goebbels' statement: "During a war, news should be given out for instruction rather than for information." However, the policies were not new in the U.S. Pierre Salinger, who as Kennedy's press secretary had to take much criticism for news management, pointed out that the very phrase was invented to describe not his activities but those of his predecessor under Dwight Eisenhower, James Hagerty. The author was James Reston of *The New York Times*, concerned about Hagerty's "management of the news."

It was paradoxical that such concern about "news management" arose during the Kennedy Administration. Kennedy himself was adept at his press relations and had enjoyed generally favorable coverage. Yet he had his share of scrapes, as when he banned the *New York Herald Tribune* from the White House for its too-vigorous coverage of the Billy Sol Estes case. When asked in the spring of 1962 how he liked the press, Kennedy half-joked: "Well, I'm reading it more and enjoying it less."

The Cuban missile crisis, however, was unique in the grayness of its status between war and peace. The government was groping for a solution by trying to keep all factors—including information—in fine balance. Douglass Cater later wrote: "Certainly news is bound to be regarded as a weapon by officials who are involved in struggles of statecraft. But they are foolish if they expect to say so out loud and get away with it."

Managed does not always have a manipulative connotation. In the 1990s, *managed competition* was a description of a health care system, and *managed trade* was a euphemism for "industrial policy," or more government control of trade.

See MEDIA EVENT; PROPAGANDA.

mandate The authority to carry out a program conferred on an elected official; especially strong after a LANDSLIDE victory.

Before the midterm elections in 1918, Woodrow Wilson appealed to the nation for a "mandate" to carry out his policies in the form of a Democratic Congress. He did not get one, and later he hit on the idea of a "Senatorial mandate." Wilson's unusual notion was to have those senators who opposed him on such issues as the League of Nations resign, then run in a special election. If they won a clear mandate, Wilson said, he would appoint one of the opposition leaders—perhaps Henry Cabot Lodge—as Secretary of State. Then he and his vice president would resign, automatically making the Republican Secretary of State the new president—under the Succession Act as it then worked. The notion went nowhere.

An interesting use of the word occurred during the British general election in the midst of the worldwide depression of the 1930s. A coalition government was then in power, and it asked voters for a "doctor's mandate"—one that would prescribe the proper treatment for the country's ills.

In the U.S., the TWO-PARTY SYSTEM has helped ensure the transfer of mandates at frequent intervals. Thus, in 1936, Franklin Roosevelt noted that "it will never be possible for any length of time for any group of the American people, either by reason of wealth or learning or inheritance or economic power, to retain any mandate, any permanent authority to arrogate to itself the political control of American public life." Dwight Eisenhower, who was elected after twenty years of Democratic control of the White House, titled the first volume of his memoirs *Mandate for Change*.

How many votes constitute a mandate? In the U.S. system, the winner need receive only one electoral vote more than the loser. A political saying is "'Close' counts in horseshoes and hand grenades—but not in politics." In his first inaugural address, FDR interpreted his sizable victory as "a mandate [for] direct, vigorous action." John F. Kennedy, on the other hand, won narrowly, yet did not shrink from acting for that reason. "The fact remains that he won," wrote Theodore Sorensen, "and on the day after election, and every day thereafter, he rejected the argument that the country had given him no mandate. Every election has a winner and a loser, he said in effect. The margin is narrow, but the responsibility is clear. There may be difficulties with the Congress, but a margin of only one vote would still be a mandate."

Nonetheless, the closeness of his victory over Nixon often acted as a brake. "Kennedy had very little leverage," wrote Arthur Schlesinger, Jr. He had been elected "by the slimmest of margins; no one could possibly claim his victory as a mandate for radical change."

In 1955 Walter Lippmann described how a mandate may be achieved by means other than electoral. "Political ideas acquire operative force in human affairs when…they acquire legitimacy, when they have the title of being right which binds men's consciences. Then they possess, as the Confucian doctrine has it, 'the mandate of heaven.'"

Five months after he won reelection by 3.5 million votes in 2004, George W. Bush drew fire from Leon Panetta, President Clinton's second-term chief of staff. "He has really burned up whatever mandate he had from that last election. You can't just SLAM-DUNK issues in Washington. You can't just say 'This is what I want done' and by mandate get it done." See POLITICAL CAPITAL

manifest destiny The doctrine that it was the duty and fate of the U.S. to expand to the Pacific coast—and beyond.

One of the earliest uses of the phrase is attributed to Andrew Jackson. In 1824, Jackson described the U.S. as "a country manifestly called by the Almighty to a destiny which Greece and Rome, in the days of their pride, might have envied."

An enthusiastic promoter of the concept was John O'Sullivan, an American diplomat and journalist. In 1839 O'Sullivan wrote: "In its magnificent domain of space and time, the nation of many nations is destined to manifest to mankind the excellence of divine principles." Six years later an unsigned editorial in the expansionist journal *The United States Magazine and Democratic Review* noted that certain foreign governments were trying to prevent the U.S. annexation of Texas and spoke of "our manifest destiny to overspread the continent allotted by Providence for the free development of our yearly multiplying millions." O'Sullivan was the author of the editorial.

In a congressional debate on the U.S. treaty with Great Britain settling the borders of Oregon in January 1846, Massachusetts Representative Robert C. Winthrop declared that it was "the right of our manifest destiny to spread over this whole continent." James Gordon Bennett wrote in a *New York Herald* editorial in 1865: "It is our manifest destiny to lead and rule all other nations." The doctrine disturbed some Americans. In his *Journals*, Ralph Waldo Emerson wrote in 1865: "That word, 'manifest destiny,' which is profanely used, signifies the sense all men have of the prodigious energy and opportunity lying idle here."

It did not lie idle for long. In 1898 President William McKinley told George Cortelyou, an aide, "We need Hawaii just as much and a good deal more than we did California. It is manifest destiny." McKinley's critics saw in this attitude an imperialistic "greed of conquest," but Hawaii was annexed in July 1898. Former President Grover Cleveland, who never cared much for the idea, wrote to a friend at the time: "Hawaii is ours. As I look back upon the first steps in this miserable business and as I contemplate the means used to complete the outrage, I am ashamed of the whole affair."

man in the street The average person, of normal intelligence and middle-class values, who could also be a woman and indoors.

The phrase was popularized by Ralph Waldo Emerson, in his 1841 essay "On Self-Reliance," regarding the spiritually debilitating effect of civilization on man: "A Greenwich nautical almanac he has, and so being sure of the information when he wants it, the man in the street does not know a star in the sky." (For a parallel metaphor in *Pilgrim's Progress*, see MUCKRAKER.)

Lord Bryce, in *The American Commonwealth*, used "man in the cars"—presumably using public transportation—in 1888 in a sense that holds up well today as a condemnation of how too many people form their opinions:

one need only try the experiment of talking to that representative of public opinion whom the Americans call "the man in the cars" to realize how uniform opinion is among all classes of people, how little there is of that individuality in the ideas of each individual which they would have if he had formed them for himself, how little solidity and substance there is in the political or social ideas of nineteen persons out of every twenty. These ideas, when examined, mostly resolve themselves into two or three prejudices and aversions, two or three prepossessions for a particular leader or section of a party, two or three phrases or catchwords suggesting or embodying arguments which the man who repeats them has not analyzed.

Theodore Roosevelt used the phrase in a 1900 letter, also in derogation of the public's short-term view: "But the man in the street naturally does not look as far ahead as this." The phrase has atrophied, largely because of the tendency to drop *man* in favor of *person*; this has been overcome in the LITTLE MAN. Also see JOHN Q. PUBLIC.

man of the people Public figure identified with humble origins and usually a POPULIST philosophy.

"The President will not be a man of the people," warned Founder James Wilson in 1787, "but the minion of the Senate." Wilson held that the senatorial veto of presidential appointments would cripple the office of Chief Executive, but the Constitutional Convention disagreed. See ADVICE AND CONSENT.

The meaning of the phrase was narrowed to nonaristocrats with the emergence of Andrew Jackson, whose background and manner were far more plebeian than those of Washington, the Adamses, Jefferson, Madison, or Monroe. As Harry Truman assessed him: "Jackson was recognized as the 'man of the people'—an advocate of the liberal interpretation of democracy as practised by Jefferson."

In current use, the phrase has dropped most of the "humble origin" connota-

tion and is concerned more with a man who identifies himself with the needs and aspirations of the common man. Thus, a wealthy politician—Franklin Roosevelt, for example—could be classed "a man of the people" even to the extent of being a TRAITOR TO HIS CLASS.

Rich candidates still seem to feel a need, however, to prove that even if they are well-off, they are still "regular guys"—witness supporters of Adlai Stevenson making much of a photo showing him with a hole in his shoe. When Wendell Willkie pointed out his middle-class Hoosier origins, Harold Ickes nailed him with BAREFOOT BOY FROM WALL STREET. Democratic presidential candidate George McGovern, campaigning in New York City in 1972, led a crowd of reporters and camera operators into a delicatessen in the Lower East Side and loudly ordered "a kosher hot dog and a glass of milk." (His handlers had failed to brief him beforehand that mixing meat and dairy products was not kosher.)

man on horseback A military figure with political potential; or a would-be dictator; or any strong, authoritarian leader.

The idea, though not the phrase, appeared in a scaffold statement by English rebel Richard Rumbold, hanged in 1685: "I never would believe that Providence had sent a few men into the world, ready booted and spurred to ride, and millions ready saddled and bridled to be ridden."

The phrase was introduced to American politics by General Caleb Cushing, who described to a group of Maine Democrats assembled in Bangor on January 11, 1860, what the impending civil strife would mean to the nation: "cruel war, war at home; and in the perspective distance, a man on horseback with a drawn sword in his hand, some Atlantic Caesar, or Cromwell, or Napoleon."

In France in 1885, the "Opportunist" Republicans sought support from the Radicals, and General Georges Boulanger was named Minister of War the next January. He liked to ride at the head of military parades and made a striking figure astride his mount, becoming known as "the man on horseback" and hoping to win votes in the parliamentary election of 1889; however, believing he was to be arrested for subversive activities, he fled to Brussels and his "movement" fell apart as centrist Opportunists gained strength.

The predecessor phrase, with the same metaphor, is *on a high horse.* Shakespeare had Marc Antony say of Julius Caesar that he "sits high on all people's hearts," and the Reverend John Brown, in a letter to David Garrick dated October 27, 1765, complained of Dr. Samuel Johnson's criticism of Shakespeare: "Altogether upon the high horse, and blustering about Imperial Tragedy!"

Etymologist Hans Sperber concluded that the phrase was drawn from the "solitary horseman" appearing in six books by a popular novelist of the period, G. P. R. James.

Lincoln professed not to be concerned about the chances of a military dictatorship. In a letter to General Joseph Hooker, a bombastic officer who had said the nation needed a dictator, Lincoln wrote: "Only those Generals who gain successes can set up dictators. What I now ask of you is military success, and I will risk the dictatorship."

General George B. McClellan, true to General Cushing's prophecy, did turn out to be the Democratic nominee of 1864, losing to Lincoln by only 400,000 votes out of 4,000,000. But the *man on horseback* phrase was first applied to a presidential candidate in Ulysses S. Grant's 1868 campaign, and "Vote as You Shot" was a slogan of veterans' groups for many years after the Civil War.

Military men who made it to the top in U.S. history include George Washington, Andrew Jackson, William Henry Harrison, Zachary Taylor, U.S. Grant, Theodore Roosevelt (as a "Rough Rider," he is on the edge of this category), and Dwight D. Eisenhower. Generals who lost presidential bids were Lewis Cass in 1848, Winfield Scott in 1852, McClellan in 1864, and Winfield Scott Hancock in 1880. In addition, Admiral George Dewey, General Leonard Wood, and General Douglas MacArthur awaited lightning that never struck.

Eisenhower, for one, was disturbed by the "man on horseback" image. Sought by both parties for the 1948 nomination, he declared: "The necessary and wise subordination of the military to civil power will be best sustained ... when lifelong professional soldiers, in the absence of some obvious and overriding reasons, abstain from seeking high political office."

In 1961 E. M. Dealey, chairman of the board of *The Dallas Morning News,* said in an angry letter to President John Kennedy that "we need a man on horseback to lead this nation, and many people in Texas and the Southwest think that you are riding Caroline's bicycle."

Kennedy replied indirectly in a Los Angeles speech, referring not to his daughter Caroline but to those "voices of extremism" who "look suspiciously at their neighbors and their leaders. They call for a 'man on horseback' because they do not trust the people ... they object quite rightly to politics intruding on the military—but they are very anxious for the military to engage in their kind of politics."

man on the wedding cake Derisive characterization of Republican presidential candidate Thomas E. Dewey in 1944.

Coinage has long been in vociferous dispute. In the first edition of this dictionary in 1968, the author tentatively wrote: "Though columnist Walter Winchell was often credited with the coinage ... Harold Ickes, FDR's Secretary of the Interior, was possibly the author."

Winchell promptly took issue:

> From page 250 of a new book about the new language of politics: "'Man on the wedding cake' (a characterization of Republican candidate Thomas E. Dewey in 1944) was often credited to Walter Winchell, but Harold Ickes, FDR's Secretary of the Interior, was possibly the author." But Mr. Ickes wasn't. Alice Longworth and many others were credited with its coinage. "Dewey, the Little Man On The Wedding Cake" was auth'd by "Paul Revere, II" in "P.M.," a New York pro-Democrat newspaper.... Mr. Paul Revere, II was not the name-de-ploom of Harold Ickes, but of WW, then under contract to the New York Mirror, which was pro-Dewey. (Catch on?)

New York Post columnist Leonard Lyons, who delighted in disputing Winchell, wrote that "WW" was misinformed. "The fact is Ethel Barrymore created the line. I printed the story November 3, 1944, quoting Mrs. Longworth: 'Ethel Barrymore said that, and she's mad as hell because I've been getting credit for it.'"

The *Los Angeles Times* offered another possible coiner of the expression in 1988: "If playwright Clare Boothe Luce called Dewey 'the little man on the wedding cake,' Dukakis is the little man on the Massachusetts regional development brochure."

Because Mrs. Alice Roosevelt Longworth, daughter of Theodore Roosevelt and grande dame of Washington society, was obviously a central figure in the case, the author sent her a query, and received this reply:

> Thanks for your letter. I did *not* coin the phrase "little man on the wedding cake." The first time I heard it Mrs. Flandrau remarked "Dewey looks like the bridegroom on the wedding cake." I thought it frightfully funny and quoted it to everyone. Then it began to be attributed to me. To everyone who asked if I originated it, I said no and told just what I have written here, though I did admit that "I gave it currency."

Thus, it can be stated with some assurance that the phrase was coined in 1944 by either Walter Winchell, Ethel Barrymore, or author Grace Flandrau, probably not Harold Ickes, and was given currency by Mrs. Longworth. Additional claims will be met with suspicion.

Four years later Mrs. Longworth peppered candidate Dewey with "You can't make a soufflé rise twice" and "You have to know Dewey really well to dislike him thoroughly." (She is also credited with the devastating "weaned on a pickle" characterization of President Coolidge, which she attributed to her doctor in her 1933 autobiography. None of her victims fired back, because Teddy's daughter was a distinguished lady, very old and frail, and her retort could kill you.)

Governor Dewey was short, mustachioed, and held himself stiffly erect; calling him "the little man on top of the wedding cake" was as inspired as it was cruel. Walter Winchell added insult to this injury with "He's the only man able to walk under a bed

without hitting his head." Dewey was also young for a presidential candidate, which was not implied in the wedding-cake reference; Ickes completed the description when the New York governor formally announced his candidacy by commenting, "Dewey has thrown his diaper in the ring."

The phrase returned during the 1992 presidential campaign. *National Journal* commented in September 1992, "Though in many ways Clinton is a much more formidable candidate personally than was Dewey, who was often derided as 'the little man on the wedding cake,' vulnerabilities that surfaced during the primaries could jeopardize his prospects. ..."

The author followed up his exchange of correspondence with Mrs. Longworth by taking tea at her Massachusetts Avenue home, where she pointed to a large cushion on which was sewn in petit-point, "If you have nothing good to say about anybody, come sit by me."

Maoism The militant philosophy of Mao Zedong, especially as redefined by the split in the Chinese Communist hierarchy in the mid-sixties.

Probably the best-selling book in the world in 1966 was "the little red book," containing quotations from the speeches and writings of Mao, read as scripture by his followers and brandished at demonstrations.

Traditionally, after the revolutionaries come the pragmatists—politicians with a zeal to administer rather than overthrow. In China this evolution was interrupted by the desire of the architect of the Communist revolution to recapture its revolutionary, fiercely doctrinaire spirit. Mao tried to rekindle the spirit of the generation of the Long March in his Red Guards, young men who formed the cadres that launched the CULTURAL REVOLUTION.

Maoism's book of quotations, like most scripture, was written to permit widely varying interpretations. "The Maoists," wrote Columbia professor Doak Barnett, "can appeal to certain writings which emphasize the need for revolutionary radicalism and self-sacrifice; while the anti-Maoists can stress others, which prescribe pragmatic realism and the need to adapt policy to reality."

Maoism taught "uninterrupted revolution" and the overriding role of the human will in history: "Nothing in the world is difficult for one who sets his mind to it." The indoctrinated revolutionary character of the people is essential: "An army without culture [revolutionary zeal] is a dull-witted army, and a dull-witted army cannot defeat the enemy."

Philosophies or techniques named after powerful leaders rarely last. We still speak of Jeffersonian democracy and Churchillian prose, but the ISM-ized names—Stalinism, Gaullism, Titoism, and Maoism—faded not long after the deaths of their authors. *Marxism-Leninism*, however, seems assured of a place in the political lexicon.

March on Washington A civil rights rally held in Washington, D.C., in August 1963; the largest demonstration to that date in the city's history.

Its purpose, in the words of its initial proposer, labor leader A. Philip Randolph, was to give voice to "a great moral protest against racial bias." Randolph had proposed such a march twenty years earlier to President Franklin D. Roosevelt as a protest against discrimination against Negroes, as they were then identified, in war industries. The president had used a series of protest meetings in several of the larger American cities as an excuse to issue his Executive Order No. 8802, designed to end such discrimination. That 1943 march never was held.

The Democratic president in the White House in 1963, John F. Kennedy, did not look forward at first to the realization of Mr. Randolph's proposal. One reason for Kennedy's early lack of enthusiasm was his fear that a march, ending at the Capitol as originally intended, would make it appear the Congress was being besieged and thus would have a negative effect on the civil rights bill then being considered.

When the plan was changed to a demonstration around the Lincoln Memorial, JFK gave it his public support. In a mid-July

news conference he said he understood it would be "a peaceful assembly calling for a redress of grievances" and added, "I think that's in the great tradition." He had no choice.

The march had received so much nationwide publicity that it would seriously jeopardize the civil rights legislation (1) if the number of those attending did not exceed the promised one hundred thousand and (2) if there was any violence. Both dangers were overcome. The march, as organized by civil rights leader Bayard Rustin, brought almost a quarter of a million people to the rallying point at the Washington Monument. When the area around the monument was almost completely filled with people, the demonstrators quietly walked down to the Lincoln Memorial, where several civil rights leaders addressed them. See I HAVE A DREAM. At nightfall the demonstrators departed for their home cities. In contrast to the Bonus March of 1932, when the participants rioted and terrified the capital, this March on Washington had been a powerfully moving and peaceful event.

In current use, although a *march* implies military organization and discipline, it has become less "militant" than a demonstration. The pejoration of *demonstration* was shown in a statement made by an FBI agent in a crowd of several hundred lawmen at the arraignment of former FBI officials in April 1978: "This is not a 'demonstration.' This is a show of support."

Martin, Barton and Fish A campaign catchphrase made effective by the use of rhyme and rhythm in encapsulating the names of opponents.

Working in 1940 on a speech for Franklin Roosevelt in his campaign to be the first U.S. president elected to a third term, Judge Samuel I. Rosenman and dramatist Robert E. Sherwood wanted to mention the Republican party's opposition to moves for preparedness. In the first draft they cited GOP Congressmen Bruce Barton and Hamilton Fish of New York and Joseph Martin of Massachusetts, in that order.

Rosenman recalled in *Working With Roosevelt*:

We sat around—I remember we were writing in my apartment in New York City—working on that paragraph. Then as we read those names, we almost simultaneously hit on the more euphonious and rhythmic sequence of Martin, Barton and Fish. We said nothing about it when we handed the draft to the President, wondering whether he would catch it as he read the sentence aloud. He did. The very first time he read it, his eyes twinkled; and he grinned from ear to ear.... He repeated it several times and indicated by swinging his finger in cadence how effective it would be with audiences.

In his own memoirs, *My First 50 Years in Politics*, Martin noted that the line followed the meter of "Wynken, Blynken, and Nod." Though he wrote that "I felt no particular resentment over it," Martin did tell FDR that it was "a bit unfair" to blame the GOP alone for the sad state of U.S. military preparedness. As for the famous phrase, Martin declared that "Roosevelt's attack lent a new bond to our friendship. Afterward, whenever we three would meet one another here and there we used to refer to ourselves as 'members of the firm.'"

massive retaliation National strategy to meet foreign military assault with nuclear attack.

Eisenhower's Secretary of State, John Foster Dulles, said in a speech on January 12, 1954, to the Council on Foreign Relations: "Local defense must be reinforced by the further deterrent of massive retaliatory power." The last three words were immediately changed in coverage to "massive retaliation," and American policy had a forceful label.

The Eisenhower Administration had been in office for a year when Dulles made the speech and had already begun to de-emphasize "conventional" or nonnuclear strength while stressing the nuclear. Defense Secretary Charles Wilson had already foreclosed post-Korea LIMITED WAR and spoke out for a "BIGGER BANG FOR A BUCK." And five days before Dulles' speech, Eisenhower himself in his State of the Union address had stressed the need for "massive capability to strike back" against any aggression.

But the phrase crystallized the policy, presaging generations of long-range bombers, nuclear submarines, and missiles—and strategic controversy as well. General Maxwell Taylor, Army Chief of Staff, left the service furious that the Army's role was being reduced and wrote an angry book, *The Uncertain Trumpet*, calling massive retaliation a "great fallacy."

As soon as the Kennedy Administration took office, General Taylor was recalled from retirement and eventually installed as Chairman of the Joint Chiefs of Staff. Robert McNamara became Defense Secretary. After one week in office McNamara reported: "A strategy of massive nuclear retaliation... [is] believed by few of our friends and none of our enemies." Conventional forces were emphasized, and the bywords became "flexible response" and "measured response."

The adjective *massive*—as used in "massive aid to the cities"—became a vogue word in the liberal lexicon during the '60s, along with *decent, obscene, unacceptable, root cause*, and *human needs*. In the '90s, *massive* gave way in usage to *awesome*.

masterly inactivity See WATCHFUL WAITING.

maverick One who is unorthodox in his political views and disdainful of party loyalty, who "bears no man's brand."

Maverick drifted into the political vocabulary around the turn of the century; *McClure's Magazine* mentioned the occasional appearance of a "maverick legislator." The simplicity and aptness of the metaphor made it both durable and universally understood.

Like *boycott, bloomer, cardigan*, and *sandwich*, this is an eponymous word, taken from a person's name. Samuel Maverick, son of an Anglican minister in England, settled in Massachusetts about 1624 and became noted for his hospitality; later an inn, Maverick House in Boston, was named after him and became a well-known political hangout. His direct descendant, Samuel

Augustus Maverick, established himself as a Texas rancher in the mid-1800s and became known for his unbranded calves.

J. David Stern, author of *Maverick Publisher*, advised the author of one theory behind this practice: "Old man Maverick, Texas cattleman of the 1840s, refused to brand his cattle because it was cruelty to animals. His neighbors said he was a hypocrite, liar, and thief, because Maverick's policy allowed him to claim all unbranded cattle on the range. Lawsuits were followed by bloody battles, and brought a new word to our language."

Maverick's descendants included Maury Maverick senior and junior, both Texas congressmen. The younger, while showing John F. Kennedy around the Alamo, was asked by the president where the back door was located. He replied, "There is no back door, that's why they were all heroes." The maverick Maverick lost his next election.

Theodore Roosevelt wrote in 1887 for the edification of Eastern tenderfeet: "Unbranded animals are called mavericks, and when found on the round-up are either branded by the owner of the range … or else are sold for the benefit of the association."

Ten years later TR was back in New York himself, winning his reputation as a maverick on the political range. When Cousin Franklin ran for vice president in 1920 on the Democratic ticket, TR's son, Theodore Jr., was tapped by the Republicans to dispel the idea that FDR was son or political heir to the recently deceased former president. "He's a maverick," said young Theodore about FDR. "He doesn't have the brand of our family."

Despite this pejorative use, independence—and hence *maverick* status—has traditionally been considered a virtue, especially at election time. Many of the nation's most successful politicians, going back to Andrew Jackson, were mavericks at some stage. Russell Baker wrote Estes Kefauver's epitaph: "From Harry Truman in the White House down through the bull-roasting-and-clambake crowd, the party professionals despised him. He was a maverick." In American politics, one who wins many

enemies among the pros often wins many friends among the more numerous laymen; thus it is often more difficult for a maverick to get nominated than elected.

The political figure in the new millennium most often identified as a maverick has been Senator John McCain (called early in life a "scamp" by his mother), even though he strongly supported his former rival George W. Bush in 2004. True to form, he risked his political future in 2007 by going against public opinion polls to speak in favor of a "surge" of troops to avert defeat in Iraq.

See LONER; MUGWUMP.

mayoralty See HIZZONER; DEAD END.

McCarthyism The approach with which the late Senator Joseph R. McCarthy won fame as a Communist-hunter, now applied to any investigation that flouts the rights of individuals in pursuit of its ends.

"Tail Gunner Joe" McCarthy, as his supporters called him, burst into prominence after a speech in Wheeling, W.V., on February 9, 1950.

> While I cannot take the time to name all of the men in the State Department who have been named as members of the Communist Party and members of a spy ring, I have here in my hand a list of 205 that were known to the Secretary of State as being members of the Communist Party and who nevertheless are still working and shaping the policy of the State Department.

Over the next four years the free-swinging accusations, the announcements and press releases timed to catch newspapers on deadline, and the McCarthy manner during hearings (see POINT OF ORDER) became intensely familiar and controversial. His many followers were convinced that he succeeded in alerting the nation to the danger of internal subversion.

Probably the first to tag a pejorative *ism* to his name was the *Washington Post* cartoonist Herblock (Herbert Block), who in March 1950 showed "McCarthyism" crudely lettered on a tar barrel that rested precariously on a tower made up of buckets of tar. Said President Harry Truman: "A powerful group of men in the Republican

Party is now determined to rise to power through a method of conduct as hostile to American ideals as anything we have ever seen. This method has come to be known as McCarthyism."

In *The Fourth Branch of Government*, the liberal Douglass Cater noted that "McCarthyism's greatest threat was not to individual liberty or even to the orderly conduct of government. It corrupted the power to communicate, which is indispensable to men living in a civilized society."

McCarthy, a Republican, was a particularly painful problem for the first Republican Administration in twenty years. When a White House aide drafted a strong anti-McCarthy statement, President Eisenhower rejected it, saying, "I will not get in the gutter with *that* guy." The President made it clear much later, however, how he had felt about the senator's tactics. "McCarthyism," he wrote in his memoirs, "took its toll on many individuals and on the nation. No one was safe from charges recklessly made from inside the walls of Congressional immunity. Teachers, government employees, and even ministers became vulnerable...The cost was often tragic."

When McCarthy attacked the Protestant clergy and the U.S. Army early in 1954, Eisenhower abandoned some of his restraint. He denounced the Senator as one who tried "to set himself above the laws of our land" and "to override orders of the President." On December 2, 1954, the Senate condemned McCarthy. Many wondered why the word *censure* was avoided; the reason was that he still had a following among those who suspected Communist infiltration in high places, some of which turned out to be true. His political influence faded quickly thereafter; he died in 1957.

The issue of McCarthyism plagued John F. Kennedy during his 1960 campaign for the presidency. As a senatorial candidate in 1952, Kennedy had gone out of his way to avoid antagonizing McCarthy. "Hell," he later explained to his aide, historian Arthur Schlesinger, Jr., "half my voters in Massachusetts look on McCarthy as a hero." McCarthy did not enter Massachusetts to campaign against Kennedy, and as colum-

nist Emmet John Hughes wrote, if JFK's "view of Joe McCarthy had been publicly and candidly more critical, at a time when such courage counted, he almost certainly would not have reached the White House in 1960."

In the 1968 primary campaign, liberal Democratic Senator Eugene McCarthy of Minnesota wryly labeled the attacks on his patriotism by President Johnson's supporters as "McCarthyism."

The word resurfaced during the 1991 hearings to confirm Clarence Thomas as a Supreme Court Justice. Thomas, who testified in the same Senate room where the Army-McCarthy hearings took place in 1954, denounced "interest groups [and] hate-mongers" for using tactics "far more dangerous than McCarthyism"; he pointed out that, unlike interest groups and staff aides, "At least McCarthy was elected." After Anita Hill's testimony alleging sexual harassment, a columnist accused Senator Alan K. Simpson of using McCarthy-like tactics at the hearings. Simpson replied, "Accusing someone of McCarthyism is a McCarthyist tactic itself."

The charge was repeated during the 1992 presidential and vice presidential debates, when Bill Clinton and Al Gore criticized the Bush campaign for questioning Clinton's patriotism and his visit to Moscow as a student at Oxford. See CHARACTER ASSASSIN; JUNKETEERING GUMSHOES; PHILIPPIC; PROFILES IN COURAGE.

measures, not men An alternative phrase for GOVERNMENT OF LAWS, NOT OF MEN and RULE OF LAW.

The inbuilt distrust of rulers and the desire to see rights guaranteed in writing underlies the concept of "measures, not men," a phrase coined by Philip Stanhope, 4th Earl of Chesterfield, in a March 6, 1742, letter. Picked up by Oliver Goldsmith ("Measures, not men, have always been my mark") and later by Edmund Burke, it was attacked by George Canning (later a Prime Minister) in the House of Commons in 1801:

"Away with the cant of 'Measures, not men!'—the idle supposition that it is the harness and not the horses that draw the chariot along," said Canning. "If the comparison must be made, if the distinction must be taken, men are everything, measures comparatively nothing."

Canning, who had the courage to blast the fine-sounding phrase, was associated with it in history not as its denouncer, but as its author; the New York *World* in 1874, warned: "There is danger in the blind following of Canning's maxim, 'Measures, not men.'" Obviously, there is danger in a politician's head-on attack of a favorite phrase.

In modern times the idea is best remembered in the form given it by John Adams in his draft of the Massachusetts Constitution in 1778: "In the government of the Commonwealth of Massachusetts the legislature, executive, and judicial power shall be placed in separate departments, to the end that it might be a GOVERNMENT OF LAWS, NOT OF MEN."

media A slightly sinister or clinical word for "the press," often used with an intent to convey a manipulative or mechanistic connotation.

As Dwight Eisenhower discovered in the roar of approval that followed his 1964 comment deriding "sensation-seeking columnists and commentators," considerable public sentiment is directed against the press by both the public and the self-critical media, old and new. That latent hostility was dramatized by the reaction to a speech by Vice President Spiro Agnew in Des Moines in 1970 lacing into INSTANT ANALYSIS and other presumed sins.

In the nineteenth century, *media* (plural *mediae*) was a term in phonetics to describe an intermediate sound between the tenues and the aspirates, and in biology for a middle membrane of an artery. In this usage, it is a Latin feminine singular. Of course, it is also the plural of *medium*, and the first famous use of that word in the sense of communications was by Lord Francis Bacon in 1605: "But yet is not of necessitie, that Cognitions bee expressed by the Medium of Wordes." Another sense, that of an intervening substance, was used by Burton in his 1621 *Anatomy of Melancholy*: "To the Sight three things are required, the

Object, the Organ and the Medium." In 1850, the *Princeton Review* wrote proudly: "Our periodicals are now the media of influence. They form and mould the community."

Mass medium came into the language in a 1923 article by S. M. Fechheimer in N. T. Praigg's *Advertising & Selling*, where he also used the plural: "Class appeal in mass media." In 1927, *American Speech* noted that it had "finally decided to allot a definite media to each member," and in 1929 E. O. Hughes wrote in an advertising magazine: "The advertising media to which reference will be made … are newspapers, journals, magazines and such-like printed publications."

J. S. Huxley took a benign view of the emerging word and industry in 1946: "The media of mass communication—the somewhat cumbrous title (commonly abbreviated to 'Mass Media') proposed for agencies, such as the radio, the cinema and the popular press, which are capable of the mass dissemination of word or image.… The use of the mass media to foster education, science and culture … Regarded from this angle, the mass media fall into the same general category as the libraries and museums—that of servicing agencies for man's higher activities."

Political advertising had much to do with the change in attitude toward the word from a neutral conveyor of information to a manipulator of minds. As television and its use rose in importance in politics, so did the *media adviser* (see SELLING CANDIDATES LIKE SOAP). In the '60s, concern for the changing of opinion by television spot advertising increased with its effectiveness, and "media manipulation" became worrisome to many.

In the early '70s the phrase *news media* began to gain in frequency of use, which married the fear of advertising with some doubts about the credibility of the purveyors of information. This was exploited by those who believed that too much power was concentrated in "an unelected elite" from too few news organizations.

The press itself extended the use of the word, dividing into *electronic media* and *print media*, discussing *media campaigns*, MEDIA EVENTS (or PSEUDO-EVENTS), and *media hype* (for too much promotion and attention). In May 1973 *The New York Times*'s "Winners and Sinners" sheet, sent to editorial employees and interested outsiders, complained: "Media…there is no need to overwork the word, which we and everybody else have been doing. Twice in one sentence is a little too much: 'It would appear counterproductive for the Administration to continue to attack the media at a time when it has, in effect, accepted media accounts of the Watergate case' (April 24). Try words like 'journalism,' 'the press,' 'broadcasting,' 'news accounts,' 'newspapers.' "

The word is plural, like *data*, and takes a plural verb. "Media" *is* a word, but the media *are* thousands of newspapers and magazines, television broadcast and cable stations, and the hundreds of thousands of websites, faxes, text messaging and blogs that have replaced printing presses and mimeograph machines, all covering the words of political leaders blasting "the media." See MSM, initialese for *mainstream media*, which was coined by Ralph Nader in 1985, under MAINSTREAM.

media adviser See KINGMAKER.

media event An occasion so stage-managed for wide coverage that the coverage gets more coverage than the occasion.

For the background to this phrase, see PSEUDO-EVENT. *Pseudo* has been replaced by *media*, but the word *media* frequently acquires the phoniness of *pseudo*. People who are concerned about the manipulation of public opinion, including many in the *press* (a more likable term for *news media*, and the word used in the First Amendment), tend to derogate any occasion that appears to be arranged for maximum publicity.

A second meaning of *media event* is an occasion that is important not in itself, but in how the media interpret it. On January 30, 1976, the night of Jimmy Carter's victory in the Iowa presidential caucus, CBS News correspondent Roger Mudd told anchorman Walter Cronkite: "The English [meaning "twist," later becoming SPIN] that is applied to these results is going to be applied by the

media and the politicians themselves. It's not exactly the precise figures that will be important, it's whether the media and the politicians agree that this man won and this man lost."

Joseph Lelyveld, a reporter and later executive editor of *The New York Times*, who was covering the coverage, wrote: "That was a working definition of a 'media event': an occasion on which the discussion overwhelms and finally obscures the fragile reality that gives rise to it."

That was the sophisticated definition; most references are rooted in *pseudo-event*, coined in 1962 by the historian Daniel Boorstin, about an occasion planned for coverage, like an interview or a "photo-opportunity." A media event does not "break" spontaneously, like a news event; instead, it is an occasion planned to make news or to "hype" an unimportant story. When Carter Attorney General Griffin Bell held a much-heralded briefing of congressmen about the Justice Department's investigation into payoffs by South Korean businessman Tongsun Park, Representative Patricia Schroeder (D-Colo.) said, "This was a big P.R. media event. I feel gypped. I feel like a co-conspirator in a cover-up."

Hype, as used above, also *media hype*, means "investing a minor occurrence with spurious importance," from the euphoric kick one gets from an injection of a narcotic with a hypodermic needle.

medical metaphors
Speech doctors and political pundits take advantage of medical tropes. In 1967, a *New York Post* editorialist was able to pack five medical words into a single sentence: "After *consultation* with his political *doctors*, Governor Romney of Michigan has resolved to refrain from further comment in the near future on Vietnam; this self-imposed *quarantine* may help arrest his *virulent* attack of FOOT-IN-MOUTH DISEASE."

That affliction of cattle should not be confused with *logorrhea*, which means "oratorical excess; speaking on and on past the point of no interest." To apologize in advance for a long speech and to avoid the appearance of verbal diarrhea, politicians often use the self-depreciating line, a favorite of Hubert Humphrey: "This reminds me of the little girl who claimed she knew how to spell 'banana' but she didn't know when to stop." See BODY POLITIC.

Medicare Health insurance for the elderly paid for by the federal government.

The creation of this word shows how a resistant bureaucracy crumbles before a mighty coinage; as such it is worthy of detailed examination.

In his "economic bill of rights," FDR had called for "the right to adequate medical care and the opportunity to achieve and enjoy good health." In 1943 the Wagner-Murray-Dingell bill providing compulsory health insurance was proposed; this, along with some other Truman health proposals, was attacked as "socialized medicine" and defeated.

The word *medicare* cropped up in early 1956. It was the name applied to the Dependents Medical Care Program of the Department of Defense, probably used first by Jerry Gross, editor of the *Washington Report on Medical Sciences*. The original program called for medical care of dependents of armed services personnel, but the word outgrew this narrow use in the mid-'50s.

Defense Department officials were troubled by the term, which newspapers began to apply both to plans for general medical care and for assistance to the elderly, then being discussed as part of the Social Security program. Dr. Frank Berry, senior medical adviser to the Assistant Secretary of Defense for Manpower, wrote to Abraham Ribicoff, President Kennedy's first Secretary of Health, Education and Welfare, about the confusing overlap in the use of the term. On April 27, 1961, Secretary Ribicoff made one of the most short-lived semantic stands of the decade: "This will acknowledge your letter of April 7 concerning the use of the term 'Medicare.' I am sure that we have no intention of using this term in connection with any present or planned programs to be administered by this Department." (Compare this with Churchill's resistance to INFRASTRUCTURE.)

The scene shifts from Defense to HEW. Wallace Kendall, an information officer, informed the author:

In 1964 and early 1965, we in social security were trying as hard as we could to discourage use of the term "medicare" in connection with the limited program of hospital insurance for older people which was under consideration in Congress. HR-1 and earlier Administration bills would have provided only hospital insurance, not medical insurance, and for this reason we thought "medicare" would be a misleading term.

After the medical insurance part was added in Congress and Public Law 89–97 was passed, the law had been called "the medicare law" in so many newspaper articles and radio-TV broadcasts that it was impossible for us to avoid using it. At this point, I called Colonel McKenzie to find out whether or not the Department of Defense would object.

Kendall kept a record of his August 12, 1965, conversation with Lt. Col. Vernon McKenzie, in the office of the Assistant Secretary of Defense, which McKenzie corroborates:

When the term was first introduced the Dept. of Defense intended to use it as a specific and meaningful term and they went so far as to register use of the term with the copyright office in the Library of Congress. Col. McKenzie told me that this gave them no legal rights to use of the term; it simply established the fact that they were using it in a certain sense at a certain time. Several private insurance companies later tried using the term, and in at least one case the Dept. of Defense wrote to the company and pointed out that the term was a registered one with a specific meaning within the Dept. of Defense. I gather that the companies stopped selling "Medicare" policies after receiving these letters from the Dept.

After a while, however, Col. McKenzie and other officers in the Dept. of Defense began to realize that the term was causing confusion instead of clearing it up. Some people used it to mean the entire program of medical care within the Dept. of Defense both for active duty military personnel and their dependents and retired people. Others used it to refer to all kinds of medical care for the dependents of people on active duty. A third group used it to mean only the care of dependents in civilian hospitals. These confusing factors…all combined to cause Col. McKenzie to stop using the term "Medicare" in his own work about two years ago ... it seemed to him that the term *Eldercare* would have been a much more accurate term for the social security bill as it finally passed the House. He had also thought about the term *Fedicare* but he said that there was a certain logic of events that seems to be requiring the Social Security Administration to use the term "Medicare" for the bill now under consideration.

Col. McKenzie said that he has never done anything official about halting the use of the term "Medicare" in the Dept. of Defense but he will now give some thought to the idea of recommending that the military bow out and not use the term any further in order to clear the way for its use by the Social Security Administration.

Who in the Department of Defense had the foresight to register the use of the word with the copyright office?

Paul I. Robinson, M.D., was the major general in charge of the Dependents Medical Care Program from 1956 to 1958 and was later chief medical director of the Metropolitan Life Insurance Company. He credits the late Jerry Gross with the word's coinage, and points out that Gross's further sponsorship of *eldercare* was more descriptive. As to the decision to protect the use of the word legally, Dr. Robinson recalls: "Soon after the word began being used early in 1956, I received a call from a man who was making a patent medicine for acne, which he called 'Medicare.' He told me to tell the Defense department to cut it out. I called the Judge Advocate General to tell him of this, and he said not to worry about it." Immediately afterward, the government copyrighted its use of the name.

State governments adopted such versions as *medicaid* and *medi-Cal*, and a tax-credit plan is *medicredit*. In the '60s, *medi-* was almost as popular a prefix as *mini-*, but in the generation that followed, the less colorful *health insurance* became the generic term. Soon after the Clinton administration took office, a plan to substantially change Medicare was put forward, led by the First Lady, which envisioned wider coverage under a much greater government participation; proponents called it "reform," opponents denounced it as "Hillarycare" and it was withdrawn. In 2002, a prescription drug benefit was proposed to be added to Medicare; for that controversy, see DOUGHNUT HOLE.

MEGO Rhetorical soporific; the acronym for "My Eyes Glaze Over."

This useful term is newsmagazine lingo. Like *violin piece* (a mood-setter) and TICK-TOCK (a chronological account), it was introduced to the author in 1969 by Mel Elfin, Washington bureau chief of *Newsweek*. "A MEGO is something that is both undeniably important and paralyzingly dull," Elfin explained. "Latin American policy is a MEGO. Petrodollars is a MEGO. I'm falling asleep explaining this to you."

melting pot The process by which immigrants become Americanized; a nation that assimilates all nationalities and cultures.

The phrase originated in *The Melting Pot*, a turn-of-the-century play by Israel Zangwill, and was quickly accepted as expressing a sense of pride in America's tradition of immigration, alongside Emma Lazarus' poem containing "Give me your tired, your poor ..." A predecessor phrase was "Asylum of the Oppressed of Every Nation," from the 1856 Democratic platform.

However, the big-city politician who takes the phrase seriously is soon disabused. Nathan Glazer and Daniel P. Moynihan pointed out in their study of ethnic patterns in New York City, *Beyond the Melting Pot*, that the Italian, Irish, Jewish, Negro, and Puerto Rican communities of New York were more separate than similar. Ticket-balancing and ethnic appeals are still important to the big-city vote-getter. "New York City is not a melting pot," Governor Thomas E. Dewey told reporter John Gunther in 1947, "it's a boiling pot." President John F. Kennedy, in a 1963 civil rights message, called the denial of equal access to public accommodations "a daily insult which has no place in a country proud of its heritage—the heritage of the melting pot, of equal rights, of one nation and one people."

The melting-pot theory held that immigrants would become "Americanized" and assimilated into the general society, but the existence of persistent patterns of social, cultural, and educational life within large cities shows that this theory did not materialize. A more realistic approach, called *cultural pluralism*, is now current, treating the American system more as a salad bowl than a melting pot. "If the 'melting pot' had completed its work," wrote the British observer Henry Fairlie in 1974, "there would be no 'ethnics.'" See ETHNICS.

In an article in the *Honolulu Advertiser* headed "Hawaii's imperfect melting pot a big influence on young Obama" about Senator Barack Obama on the eve of his 2007 declaration of candidacy for president, reporter Johnny Brannon noted: "Like his Kenyan father, who became the first African graduate of the University of Hawaii, Obama saw flaws in the state's *melting pot* mythology. Obama's father, also named Barack, had found decades earlier that people from similar ethnic backgrounds often tended to stick together in Hawaii, co-existing with the group rather than mixing freely."

mending fences See FENCE MENDING.

men of thought People (not only men) who live the life of the mind; frequently contrasted with "men of action."

The phrase "men of thought and men of action" was popularized by Woodrow Wilson, but the concept of the tension between the two types has a long history. British essayist William Hazlitt, in an essay "On Thought and Action," observed: "Thought depends on the habitual exercise of the speculative facilities; action, on the determination of the will. The one assigns reasons for things, the other puts causes to act." Personally, he disclaimed the ability to act: "I...had rather write one of these Essays than have to seal a letter." (E-mail changed all that.)

Historian Thomas Babington Macaulay, noting the criticism of men of action, explained: "A politician must often talk and act before he has thought and read. He may be very ill-informed respecting a question...but speak he must; and if he is a man of talents, tact, and intrepidity, he soon finds that, even under such circum-

stances, it is possible to speak successfully." Thomas Carlyle was another man of thought who admired action: "The end of man is an action, and not a thought, though it were the noblest."

Although John Galsworthy held that "a man of action, forced into a state of thought, is unhappy until he can get out of it," Theodore Roosevelt, a man with credentials in both areas, disagreed: "Power undirected by high purpose spells calamity; and high purpose by itself is utterly useless if the power to put it into effect is lacking."

Men of action also describe men of thought with the same respect. Argentine dictator Juan Perón said in 1950: "The Peronist movement needs men of action, but it also requires preachers of the doctrine."

John F. Kennedy, early in 1960, hoped "to reopen the channels of communication between the world of thought and the seat of power," and did much to activate thinkers. Richard Nixon, in a 1966 speech on academic freedom, pointed out that "Woodrow Wilson's distinction between men of thought and men of action can no longer be made. The man of thought who will not act is ineffective; the man of action who will not think is dangerous."

For praise of dreamers, see MOVERS AND SHAKERS; for derogation of intellectuals, see EGGHEAD.

mentor See RABBI.

merchants of death Armament manufacturers or brokers; more recently, sellers of firearms by mail or over the counter to minors or incompetents.

The phrase comes from the title of a 1934 book by H. C. Engelbrecht and F. C. Hanighen, one of many exposes in the '20s and '30s attempting to prove that the causes of war were economic.

Businessmen have often been suspected of being *profiteers*, a word based on the *privateers*, free-lance pirates in the service of a nation but not officially part of its navy. Thomas Jefferson observed in a letter in 1814 that "merchants have no country." The German House of Krupp was most commonly identified as the "merchants of death." The "captains of industry" celebrated by Thomas Carlyle became the MALEFACTORS OF GREAT WEALTH of Theodore Roosevelt and the ECONOMIC ROYALISTS denounced by Franklin Roosevelt.

Interventionists have often been accused of economic motives. Vermont ("the Granite State") Senator Redfield Proctor, after the sinking of the battleship *Maine*, made a speech supporting President McKinley's policy of disputing Cuba with Spain. Speaker Thomas B. Reed dismissed the marble king's remarks with: "A war will make a large market for gravestones." Each of the U.S. wars in the Persian Gulf was initially denounced as a "war for oil."

One Swedish explosives manufacturer was particularly sensitive to characterizations that later became phrased as "merchant of death." Alfred B. Nobel, who invented dynamite by combining nitroglycerine with more stable elements, established a will that made his name synonymous with peace rather than death.

After the Kennedy assassination in 1963, attempts were made to limit the sale of firearms through the mail, which was Lee Harvey Oswald's method of purchase of a gun. The efforts were resisted by the National Rifle Association, quoting the Constitution: "the right of the people to keep and bear arms shall not be abridged." Proponents of "gun control" countered by quoting the words in the Second Amendment preceding those: "A well-regulated militia being necessary to the security of a free State ..." holding that the right belonged to a well-regulated militia and not to individuals.

A new use of *merchants of death* sprang up to describe sellers of guns to incompetents, minors, and those likely to participate in race riots. The "gun lobby" countered with "guns don't kill people, people kill people." The issue did not break along the usual liberal-conservative lines; an East-West division surfaced, along with the fear of single women living alone who felt safer with a gun in their night-table or auto glove compartment.

The man most frequently pointed at as a nuclear *merchant of death* is Dr. A.Q. Khan

of Pakistan. In an interview with Japanese news agency Kyodo in 2005, President Pervez Musharraf confirmed that Dr. Khan provided centrifuge machines and their designs to North Korea: "Yes, he passed centrifuges, parts and complete. I do not exactly remember the number." The year before, Khan confessed to supplying nuclear technology to North Korea, Libya, and Iran, but he was a hero to Pakistanis for making that nation a nuclear power and was pardoned by Musharraf. Former Prime Minister Benazir Bhutto, in exile in London, charged that Khan was a scapegoat: "We believe that A.Q. Khan was asked to fall on a sword in order to save other more powerful people and in exchange he was pardoned and was also allowed to keep the $400 million too." Upon her return to Pakistan to campaign in late 2007, Bhutto was assassinated.

See "God, guns and gays" under ALLITERATION.

mere size is no sin See CURSE OF BIGNESS.

mess in Washington Specifically the 1952 Republican campaign characterization of cronyism and corruption in the late Truman era; generally, the way the "Outs," of whatever party, always see conditions in the capital under the "INS."

"It was the 'mess in Washington,' that, more than any other single factor, caused President Truman's image to fade as his term drew to a close," wrote Cabell Phillips in *The Truman Presidency*. There was, he added, a "climate in which a handful of cheats, frauds and simple fourflushers in the government managed to spray the tint of corruption across his second Administration." By 1952 Truman's popularity was down to 26 percent in public opinion polls; a half-century later, he was to be embraced by many historians as "near-great." This major reassessment of Truman was profoundly noted by George W. Bush, whose popularity plunged to near-Truman levels late in his war-torn second term. A winner of a 2006 Medal of Freedom was the historian David McCullough, whose perceptive biography of Truman was read—and reread—by Bush.

General Harry H. Vaughan, the President's friend and military aide, became the focus of the charges. A Senate investigating subcommittee reported that FIVE PERCENT-ERS who hung around the Defense Department, the War Assets Administration, and the Reconstruction Finance Corporation relied on Vaughan's friendship to steer contracts and projects their way. Though the subcommittee found no evidence of direct payoffs, it noted that Vaughan became the channel for some generous contributions to the Democratic party and himself received a deep-freeze from the grateful client of a friend. The deep-freeze (see INFLUENCE PEDDLER) came to symbolize the "mess."

Talk of a "mess" irked Truman. In his memoirs he noted that Adlai Stevenson, campaigning in Oregon in 1952 under the Democratic banner, said he would clean up "the mess in Washington." Wrote Truman: "I wondered if he had been taken in by the Republican fraudulent build-up of flyspecks on our Washington windows into a big blot or 'mess.' For several years the Republican opposition had tried to make a case against the Administration, only to find that the Administration was always alert in rooting out corruption or bad practices wherever they existed."

Though Dwight Eisenhower's speechwriter, Emmet John Hughes, said that he wanted to shun the mess phrase as "petty, self-righteous and extravagant," other advisers urged him to use it. He did. As Eisenhower wrote in his memoirs, the furor over Richard Nixon's campaign fund in 1952 was especially welcome to the Democrats "because of the emphasis we had been putting on the 'mess in Washington' ... so much evidence of woeful negligence and apparent crookedness had turned up ... that I had again and again talked about the need for an Administration that would renew Americans' faith in the government."

As a phrase, *the mess* is no newcomer to Washington: when Theodore Roosevelt was being urged to seek the presidency again in 1912, he resisted at first, saying, "I'm not in the running and I'm not going to be dragged into it. Taft created the mess and let Taft take his spanking for it." He changed his mind, ran as an independent, split the Republican support for William Howard Taft, and Democrat Woodrow Wilson won.

The *White House mess* is a restaurant in the basement, with *mess* based on the Navy term for food service area. Walter Shapiro of *Esquire* described that area during the Clinton Administration as "a restaurant, not a management philosophy."

me, too Copycat campaigning; a derogation of the adoption of the other side's stands; most often applied by conservatives to MODERATE Republicans.

The phrase first became current when Thomas C. Platt of New York resigned as senator in 1881, following the lead set by his colleague, Senator Roscoe Conkling, after a dispute with President Garfield over patronage appointments in the Empire State. A cartoon showed Platt as a small boy sticking out of Conkling's pocket, with a card labeled "Me, too!" tied to one of his hands.

Campaigning for a second term in 1936, Franklin Roosevelt ridiculed Republicans for "me-too" speeches in which they endorsed his goals but attacked his methods:

> let me warn the nation against the smooth evasion which says—"we believe in social security; we believe in work for the unemployed; we believe in saving homes. Cross our hearts and hope to die, we believe in all these things; but we do not like the way the present Administration is doing them. Just turn them over to us. We will do all of them—we will do more of them—we will do them better; and, most important of all, the doing of them will not cost anybody anything."

In 1940 the *New York Daily News* labeled FDR's opponent "Me-Too Willkie," complaining: "Instead of a knockdown and drag-out political fight, this is getting to be a LOVE FEAST." Socialist candidate Norman Thomas said of Wendell Willkie: "He agreed with Roosevelt's entire program of social reform—and said it was leading to disaster."

Ever since, the *me-too* label (hyphenated when used as a compound adjective) has been pinned on Republicans considered insufficiently conservative. In 1948, after New York's Governor Thomas E. Dewey won the presidential nomination, the Chicago *Tribune* protested: "For the third time, a Republican convention fell under vicious influences and nominated a 'me-too' candidate who conducted a 'me-too' campaign." President Harry Truman derided Dewey's promises during a Pittsburgh speech on October 23, 1948: "The candidate says, 'Me, too.' But the Republican record still says, 'We're against it.' These two phrases, 'me, too' and 'we're against it,' sum up the whole Republican campaign."

Defending liberal Republicans pinned with the *me-too* label, Dewey noted during a 1950 series of lectures at Princeton: "There are some loud voices in the Republican Party denouncing all the platforms and nominees with the epithet 'me too.' The complaint and the epithet largely originated with those who hold isolationist or extremely conservative views, or both. As for myself, and I believe most of the members of the Republican Party, we refuse to be against the Ten Commandments just because the Democrats say they are for them."

Barry Goldwater, the least "me-tooish" GOP candidate in a generation, campaigned in 1964 on the slogan "A CHOICE, NOT AN ECHO," and suffered one of the worst drubbings in the party's history. In a 1993 column about GOP resistance to the health care proposal submitted by Hillary Rodham Clinton, then the First Lady, Evans and Novak wrote: "After two years in which Republicans either kept silent or said 'Me too,' the White House is determined to win passage this year. ..." It did not.

After the Democratic congressional sweep in 2006, based largely on disapproval of the Bush Administration's conduct of the war in Iraq, a reader of the *Concord* (N.H.) *Monitor* wrote the editor about that state's two GOP senators: "Gregg and Sununu, who have been strong 'stay the course' advocates in Iraq ... are now the 'me-too' duo and jumping over to the can't-win side." The following year, this headline appeared in *The Politico*, a Capitol Hill newspaper: "GOP Conservatives Push 'RINOs' To Become

More Right-Minded." The acronym stands of "Republicans In Name Only."

In a quasi-intellectual attack on trendy alienation, the author tried out the neologism "anomie-tooism" in his column, but it never caught on. The best non-political use of the phrase was by Geraldine Stutz, head of the chic Henri Bendel store for three decades; when asked to explain the difference between fashion and style, she replied, "Fashion says 'Me, too' and style says 'Only me.'" See ROAD TO DEFEAT; BIG TENT.

Metroamerican See MIDDLE AMERICA.

Mickey Mouse See HUMPTY DUMPTY.

Middle America Payers of most of the taxes, holders of most of the values, electors of most of the candidates.

Columnist Joseph Kraft coined the term in a piece on June 23, 1968: "For two years before that," he informed the author, "I had been beating around the term, talking about ordinary Americans, middle-class Americans, Americans who were not young or poor or black and that kind of thing. My focus on that group was stimulated in 1967 by a Labor Department study of living costs for people in the $7,000 to $10,000 income bracket in the major cities. It showed that their requirements were outrunning their earnings and I was struck by the fact and have been writing about it ever since."

A variety of phrases have been coined in recent years to replace the several facets of JOHN Q. PUBLIC:

Un-young, un-poor, and un-black is a *statistical* concept, according to Richard Scammon, who used it in response to a question in early 1968. Someone who is none of the three is not necessarily conservative; as Scammon put it, a left-winger who commands high legal fees and is fifty or so is neither poor, young, nor black.

Middle America is primarily an *economic* concept, as Kraft used it, showing the conflict between the middle class and the classes above and below, though the phrase is sometimes used to mean a state of mind or region of the country. *Middle American,* derived from Kraft's phrase, also dates back to 1968. In 1983, *Business Week* used the term to describe reporter Harrison Salisbury as "a quintessential Middle American, born and raised in Minnesota and a registered Republican." This recalls novelist Herman Melville's usage in his 1851 masterpiece *Moby-Dick:* "The unread, unsophisticated Protestant of the Middle American States."

The SILENT MAJORITY is a *social* concept, referring to those who uphold traditional morality, and who resent the attention given by the media to the demonstrators and noisemakers. The FORGOTTEN MAN is the predecessor phrase for Silent Majority, and is interchangeable with it; an antonym for both, coined by historian Eric Goldman in 1969, is the *Metroamerican*, who is youthful, wealthy, educated, public-spirited, ambivalent, and, as the coiner put it, "liberal but without ideology ... flexible, pragmatic, and a devotee of the ironic edge."

The GREAT UNWASHED, a *class* concept, has fallen into disuse, even though television sets and computers outnumber bathtubs in America. See HEARTLAND.

middle of the road The place where most U.S. national political candidates, Democratic and Republican, make their stand or take their straddle; the land equivalent of the MAINSTREAM.

"The objective of a nominating convention," Henry L. Stoddard wrote in his 1938 book *It Costs to Be President*, "is not a candidate who is strongest in states certain to be carried by his party, but one who is likely to be the strongest in those states in which party prospects are weakest—in other words, a middle-of-the-road man."

At the turn of the century the term characterized Populists who opposed joining the Democratic party. An 1892 POPULIST campaign song went:

Side tracks are rough, and they're hard to walk,
Keep in the middle of the road:
Though we haven't got time to stop and talk,
We keep in the middle of the road.

To some, though, it seemed a barren place. "I am a middle-of-the-road man," said Populist James Baird Weaver in 1894, "but I don't propose to lie down across it so no one can get over me. Nothing grows in the middle of the road."

German politician August Bebel, speaking to a congress of the German Social-Democratic party in Dresden in 1903, echoed the theme denigrating the center: "The field of politics always presents the same struggle. There are the Right and the Left, and in the middle is the Swamp. The Swamp is made up of the know-nothings, of them who are without ideas, of them who are always with the majority."

Nonetheless, a U.S. president who departs from the middle will find himself in dangerous territory. "Missouri friends represented Mr. Truman as a 'middle-of-the-road' man on all current political and economic issues," complained conservative columnist Arthur Krock in September 1945, "but the 'middle of the road' was way off to one side." Texas radio commentator Jim Hightower, a Democrat, titled a 1997 book *There's Nothing in the Middle of the Road but Yellow Stripes and Dead Armadillos.* See BASE.

Eisenhower firmly planted his feet in the middle in a 1949 Labor Day speech in St. Louis. "The path to America's future," he said, "lies down the middle of the road between the unfettered power of concentrated wealth ... and the unbridled power of statism or partisan interests." Robert Frost, the poet, took issue with the metaphor: "The middle of the road is where the white line is—and that's the worst place to drive." But "Ike" never lost that conviction. In October 1963, three years out of office and irritated at LABELS, he wrote: "People talk about the middle of the road as though it were unacceptable. Actually, all human problems, excepting morals, come into the gray areas. Things are not all black and white. There have to be compromises. The middle of the road is all of the usable surface. The extremes, right and left, are in the gutters."

See CENTRIST; MAINSTREAM; OPPORTUNIST; PRESIDENT OF ALL THE PEOPLE.

midterm election See OFF YEAR.

military-industrial complex A combination of forces that, left unchecked, it was feared might soon control the U.S. economy and foreign policy.

Dwight Eisenhower, who had been a military man and whose best friends were industrialists, startled the nation with his farewell address on January 17, 1961, warning of the danger of military-industrial power. Speechwriters Malcolm Moos and Ralph Williams had drafted the speech for Eisenhower and are credited with having submitted the famous passage. An early draft warned of a "military-industrial-scientific complex," but science adviser James Killian persuaded the president to omit "science."

Until World War II, the president said, the U.S. had no permanent armaments industry.

> But … we can no longer risk emergency improvisation of national defense. We have been compelled to create a permanent armaments industry of vast proportions. Added to this, three and a half million men and women are directly engaged in the defense establishment. … Now this conjunction of an immense military establishment and a large arms industry is new in the American experience …
>
> In the councils of Government, we must guard against the acquisition of unwarranted influence, whether sought or unsought, by the military-industrial complex. The potential for the disastrous rise of misplaced power exists and will persist.

Asked about this statement at a press conference a few days afterward, he added that he was thinking not so much of a willful abuse of power, but of "an almost insidious penetration of our own minds that the only thing this country is engaged in is weaponry and missiles—and I'll tell you we can't afford that."

Columnist Walter Lippmann, who had grown increasingly critical of Eisenhower's presidency, called his farewell address "in the great tradition. Washington made the theme of his farewell address a warning against allowing the influence of foreign governments to invade our political life. That was then the menace to the civilian power. Now Eisenhower, speaking from his experience and looking ahead, is concerned with a contemporary threat to the supremacy of the civilian power."

Political scientist Harold Lasswell had coined a term in 1941 on this subject. In *The Garrison State* he warned: "The military men who dominate a modern technical society will be very different from the officers of history and tradition. It is probable that the specialists on violence will include in their training a large degree of expertness in many of the skills that we have traditionally accepted as part of modern civilian management." See WHIZ KIDS.

The concept of restraining the military is at least as old as Cicero, who said in 60 B.C.: "Let the soldier yield to the civilian." Woodrow Wilson, preparing for war, insisted "one thing that this country never will endure is a system that can be called militarism. … Men who are in charge of edged tools and bidden to prepare them for exact and scientific use grow very impatient if they are not permitted to use them."

But the danger pointed out by Eisenhower was more subtle than militarism, or civilian control of the military. He recognized that there was no line of demarcation between "civilian" and "military" in the modern defense establishment, where huge companies depended on defense contracts. He held that these companies, through their economic impact on an area, had political power of their own that contributed to military appropriation decisions, building a vicious circle or "complex."

When President Bill Clinton introduced his economic program to Congress in February 1993, Hillary Rodham Clinton was seated between Federal Reserve Board chairman Alan Greenspan and John Sculley, chief executive officer of Apple Computer. Wrote *Newsday*, "Sculley's prominence symbolizes a fact of life in Washington: Through personal contacts and lobbying groups large and small, computer-related industries—Big Silicon—now wield the kind of clout once held by Big Steel, Detroit or the military-industrial complex."

military metaphors

Soon after the *opening gun* of the CAMPAIGN, the STANDARD-BEARER was denounced as a HATCHETMAN, an OLD FOGY and a *flash in the pan* by the LEFT WING, and it appeared to DIEHARDS that the old WAR-HORSE'S BOOM was a *lost cause*; but the MAN ON HORSEBACK turned out to be a GOOD SOLDIER, and the TROOPS—from PALACE GUARD to OLD GUARD to the FIFTH COLUMN in the *enemy camp—closed ranks*, ignored the SMOKESCREEN, and did not hesitate to wave the BLOODY SHIRT; the CALCULATED RISK of the BANNER DISTRICTS was *saluted* at a victory RALLY, with the SPOILS divided by a TASK FORCE at *campaign headquarters* before the new Administration's first HUNDRED DAYS.

Of the military phrases above so often used in politics, the not-so-obvious are *hatchetman* (who cleared the woods for General Washington's troops), *flash in the pan* (a cannon charge that misfires), *spoils* (originally of war), *left wing* (of a military front), *hundred days* (Napoleon's final campaign), and *old fogy* (originally a Scottish term for "an invalid or garrison soldier"). The others appear elsewhere under individual entries. Also see FIELD EXPEDIENT; FIGHTING THE PROBLEM; HOLD THE LINE; LOW PROFILE; ON THE POINT; SHOCK AND AWE.

Military images appear in international diplomacy (ARSENAL OF DEMOCRACY), and words born in hot and cold wars are used in politics (FIFTH COLUMN; EYEBALL TO EYEBALL); in return, politicians create phrases for warriors (BIGGER BANG FOR THE BUCK; OVERKILL).

In the application of metaphor to politics, only SPORTS METAPHORS (particularly racing) compare to the military. WAR-GAMING WORDS will direct the reader to words created for military-political use, and PENTAGONESE to military jargon.

Even SLOGAN comes from a Scottish war cry. See RANK AND FILE.

milk for Hottentots See HOTTENTOTS, MILK FOR.

ministry of all the talents See HACK.

mink coats See INFLUENCE PEDDLER.

mishmash Confusion; meaningless material.

An English word in use for five centuries, *mishmash* is particularly applicable in pol-

itics to describe the confused nature of a policy or speech.

Mishmash suggests a picture of lumpy, gray porridge, tasteless and not especially nourishing. Its meaning can be illustrated in the following communication from an attaché of the Soviet embassy in Washington, D.C.: Haydon Burns, a governor of Florida, misaddressed an invitation to Soviet Foreign Minister Andrei Gromyko as "Ambassador to the United Nations," asking him to speak at a lecture series in Florida. By the time an answer was forthcoming, a new governor had replaced Burns; this is the text of the letter the Soviets sent Governor Claude R. Kirk:

Dear Sir:

Sometime ago, we received a letter signed by the Honorable Haydon Burns with the kind invitation to visit the place and speak before Daytona Beach Open Forum. We apologize for an unfortunate delay in answering the letter since there was some mishmash in it.

Andrei Gromyko whom the letter was applied to as "Ambassador to the United Nations" is the USSR Foreign Minister in the course of the last ten years. ...

Besides that, any speaker of our Embassy is not able to participate as this particular place is restricted to travel by Soviet citizens.

A second communication, published in *The Groucho Letters*, was to Governor William Scranton of Pennsylvania in 1964 and illustrates a belief that the word *mishmash* has a Yiddish derivation:

Dear Sir:

If you contemplate campaigning in any more Jewish neighborhoods, I suggest you learn how to pronounce "mishmash." It is not pronounced "mash" as you said on "Meet the Press," but rather as though it were spelled MOSH.

Sincerely yours,

Groucho Marx.

The author wrote the first draft of this entry under the impression that the word did indeed have a Yiddish derivation; one of his editors sent it back with proof from the *OED* that the word was English, and the entry was accordingly revised. However, when a copy editor saw the revision, she penciled a note in the margin paraphrasing the punch line of an old Jewish joke: "Funny, it doesn't *look* English." She backed up her doubts with a copy of the Groucho letter.

Under this usage pressure, the first editor returned the manuscript to the author with the following note: "Here we go again on mishmash. The word is *not* Yiddish. However, the pronunciation of the word, as if *mishmosh*, is probably due to Yiddish influence in certain regions in the U.S. Perhaps it would be a good idea to add a short sentence of explanation: it's not Yiddish but maybe the pronunciation *-mosh* is due to Yiddish influence—though this pronunciation is not that of the majority of Americans."

Note to Oxford University Press: *print as is*. This entry is enough of a mishmash (pronounced mishmosh) already.

missile gap A Kennedy charge that U.S. missile production lagged behind Soviet production; a hot issue in the 1960 presidential campaign, it was soon afterward coolly dismissed as nonexistent by the new Administration.

The Eisenhower Administration decided in the late 1950s not to invest heavily in intercontinental ballistic missiles, on the grounds that they were technologically inadequate; Defense Secretary Neil McElroy was charged by Democrats in Congress with planning a "missile gap." General James Gavin resigned from the Army in 1958 with a blast at the "missile lag." The charge became a key point in the 1960 Kennedy campaign (along with "the prestige gap") but was dismissed by the new Defense Secretary, Robert McNamara, soon after his appointment by Kennedy.

Arthur Schlesinger, Jr., later frankly labeled it a "fake issue"; Ted Sorensen, taking the most charitable view, wrote: "Kennedy's error in 1960 on the 'missile gap' had been the result of the public's being informed TOO LITTLE AND TOO LATE—even after the facts were certain—about a danger which he had in good faith overstated."

For other phrases spawned by this phrase, see GAP; CREDIBILITY GAP.

mistakes were made A passive-evasive way of acknowledging error while distancing the speaker from responsibility for it.

Politicians have had frequent occasion to lean on this crutch, a linguistic construction creatively described by William Schneider, at the American Enterprise Institute, as the *past exonerative*.

President Ronald Reagan took general responsibility in his 1987 State of the Union address for selling weapons to Iran in order to obtain the release of hostages, but sidestepped the rest of the Iran-contra scandal (using profits from the arms sales in an effort to overthrow the government of Nicaragua), saying, "we did not achieve what we wished, and serious mistakes were made in trying to do so." Lt. Col. Oliver North, convicted of ordering the destruction of documents in trying to conceal this activity, had his conviction overturned because Congress had given him limited immunity. The bemedaled Marine said later: "I'm not ashamed of it. People say 'Mistakes were made.' But I'll also tell you lives were saved."

President Bill Clinton resorted to the same passive, impersonal admission in January of 1998, replying to questions about improper Democratic party fundraising activities with the bland "Mistakes were made here by people who did it either deliberately or inadvertently." In March of 2007, Attorney General Alberto Gonzales tried to defuse complaints about the firing of eight U.S. prosecutors, saying: "I acknowledge that mistakes were made here."

The unapologetic apology can be softened even further by prefacing it with a hypothetical "if." Anonymous aides to Secretary of State Condoleezza Rice denied in 2005 that she had admitted to German Chancellor Angela Merkel that the U.S. had abducted a German citizen by mistake. Instead, they insisted that Ms. Rice "had said only that if mistakes were made, they would be corrected."

A blame-spreading refinement is to cast the apology in the more distant present perfect tense. PLO leader Yasir Arafat took this tack when fending off criticisms in 2004 by Palestinian legislators, conceding that "Some mistakes have been made by our institutions." Connecticut's ex-governor John Rowland downplayed his admission of guilt to a federal corruption charge the same way, telling the press that "Obviously mistakes have been made throughout the last few years, and I accept responsibility for those."

A skillful further refinement is the subordinate-clause admission or error, compounding passivity and present-perfection with a conditional "whatever," as in this sentence of a George W. Bush speech urging Americans weary of war in the fall of 2006 to STAY THE COURSE: "Whatever mistakes have been made in Iraq, the worst mistake would be to think that if we pulled out, the terrorists would leave us alone."

The artful dodge of the impersonal apology has roots. President Ulysses S. Grant, fondly remembered by grammarians for his activist self-description, "I am a verb," appended a note to his final annual report to Congress on December 5, 1876, acknowledging the scandals that had plagued his two terms in office with the words, "Mistakes have been made, as all can see and I admit."

A disarmingly honest way of admitting error was shown by New York Mayor Fiorello La Guardia, criticized in the 1940s for closing the elite Townsend Harris High School: "I don't make many mistakes, but when I make one it's a beaut!" It takes the wind out of the sails of criticism.

When the lexicographer admonished a political figure for using the much-ridiculed "mistakes were made," he replied, not for attribution, "lessons were learned."

See Winston Churchill on mistakes under GAP.

misunderestimate See BLOOPER.

moderate An adjective positioning a liberal slightly to the right, and a conservative slightly to the left, especially when they resist the label of *centrist* or *middle-of-the-roader*.

President Eisenhower began using the noun *moderation* in cabinet meetings in late 1954, just after the midterm elections. A year later Adlai Stevenson told a fundraising dinner in Chicago: "I agree that moderation is the spirit of the times. But we best take care lest we confuse moderation for mediocrity, or settle for half answers to hard problems. ... Moderation, yes! Stagnation, no!" At the same dinner New York Governor Averell Harriman, a potential foe of Stevenson's for the 1956 Democratic nomination and eager to be identified as a liberal, disagreed: "There is no such word as 'moderation' in the Democratic vocabulary."

Senator Lyndon Johnson, however, on December 12, 1955, declared, "I have always thought of myself as one who has been a moderate in approaching problems." Joseph Rauh, chairman of Americans for Democratic Action, suggested, "It would make sense to try to figure out what Eisenhower moderation is versus Johnson moderation, if indeed there is a difference."

Moderate as a noun established itself as "centrist," though as an adjective modifying liberal or conservative, it meant "not rootin'-tootin.'" Relatively quiescent during the Kennedy years, the word reappeared strongly in the Rockefeller-Goldwater fight for the Republican nomination of 1964. Rockefeller National Campaign Director John A. Wells, an attorney who had managed Jacob Javits' landslide victory for the Senate in 1962, urged that Rockefeller use *moderate* rather than *liberal* in describing his philosophy in the New Hampshire primary, in the hope of capturing mildly conservative voters who might not identify with "Mr. Conservative," Barry Goldwater. *Moderate* and MAINSTREAM became the bywords of the stop-Goldwater movement, and *moderate* appears to have become a permanent label. Conservatives see through it. In describing Illinois Senator Charles Percy as "a sort of in-between Republican," columnist William F. Buckley Jr. added: "I resist the word 'moderate' because it is a base-stealing word for the benefit of GOP liberals."

Both as adjective and noun, it has had a long history in politics. In his essay "Of Faction," written in 1597, Francis Bacon sent this message to partisans today: "it is often seen, that a few that are stiff, do tire out a great number that are more moderate." Robert Clive, in a hot parliamentary debate in 1773, exclaimed, "By God, Mr. Chairman, at this moment I stand astonished at my own moderation!" In 1875 Leon Gambetta, who was to become Premier of France, told the Assembly, "Moderation is the reason of politics."

A year before being elected president, Abraham Lincoln, not the leading candidate for the Republican nomination, wrote an answer to a letter from Thomas Corwin that had said, "I was sorry to hear from you that a moderate man on our side would lose Illinois by 50,000." Lincoln replied, in a letter he marked "confidential," on October 9, 1859, that he did not mean that Illinois should have "an extreme anti-slavery candidate," but that since slavery was "the living issue of the day," the Republican candidate should be one "who does not hesitate to declare slavery a wrong... I did say at Cincinnati, that a candidate who shall turn up his nose at the Republican cause, can not carry Illinois, by 50,000; but I do not consider such a man , as 'a moderate man *on our side*.' I understand such men as not being on our side at all ..." As these citations show, the meaning of *moderate* and *moderation* has been a source of extreme controversy through most of U.S. political history.

See ME, TOO; MIDDLE OF THE ROAD.

modern Republicanism An approach to politics "liberal in human affairs, conservative in fiscal affairs"; an attempt to give a more progressive label to the GOP.

In 1955 Arthur Larson, then Under Secretary of Labor and a former dean of the University of Pittsburgh Law School, wrote *A Republican Looks at His Party*, which President Eisenhower endorsed as having "expressed my philosophy of government as well as I have seen it in a book of that size."

Though Larson wrote mainly of a "new" Republicanism, his liberal approach was dubbed "modern," and he was attacked by conservatives—Republicans and Democrats alike—when he was appointed to head the U.S. Information Agency. Conservative journalist George Sokolsky complained that the Republican party under

Eisenhower "has gone so modern that it is indistinguishable from the New Deal."

As the 1956 Eisenhower landslide rolled in on election night, the President told Richard Nixon what he planned to discuss on the air after Stevenson's concession. "I think I'll talk about Modern Republicanism." He formally used the phrase for the first time that night: "Modern Republicanism, as I have said time and again, is to follow the Lincoln dictum of what government is for, and then to do it within the concept of competitive economy, sound fiscal arrangement and a sound dollar." (Eisenhower was referring to this comment of Lincoln's: "The legitimate object of government is to do for a community of people whatever they need to have done, but cannot do at all, or cannot so well do, for themselves—in their separate, and individual capacities. In all that the people can individually do as well for themselves, government ought not to interfere.")

Though Eisenhower's Administration was marked by its breadth of support, the *modern Republican* phrase was curiously divisive. It implicitly labeled traditionalists as "OLD FOGY." In the '60s it was used only occasionally, with the "moderns" adopting the more conciliatory *moderate Republican*, and in the '70s NEOCONSERVATIVE. See MAINSTREAM; MODERATE; ME, TOO.

modified limited hangout See WATERGATE WORDS.

mollycoddle As a verb, "to pamper"—a charge made by opponents of many social welfare benefits that recipients are being treated with undue solicitude, to the detriment of working taxpayers; as a noun, "a weakling."

Said John Jay Chapman, an American writer and critic, in *Practical Agitation* in 1900: "In a martial age the reformer is called a *mollycoddle*; in a commercial age, an *incompetent*, a disturber of values; in a fanatical age, a *heretic*. If an agitator is not reviled, he is a *quack*."

In politics, the word is most closely associated with Theodore Roosevelt, who espoused "the strenuous life." In his autobiography he referred to those who opposed the building of battleships and the fortification of the Panama Canal as "the large mollycoddle vote, people who are soft physically and morally."

Like MOSSBACK and SNOLLYGOSTER, it was one of President Harry Truman's favorite Americanisms. "I wasn't going to go down in history," he promised toward the end of his term, "like Pierce or Buchanan or Chester Arthur or Benjamin Harrison—he was one of the most mediocre Presidents we ever had. I wasn't going to be one of your arm-rolling cheek-kissing mollycoddles!"

The colorful old slang term still pops up around the English-speaking world. The *Times of India* in 2006 reported favorably on a U.S. editorialist warning of "the dangers of mollycoddling Pakistan's leadership."

-monger A suffix meaning "peddler of," used to create derogatory phrases.

Ever since the sixteenth century, *monger*—an Anglo-Saxon word for "trader"—has had a connotation of petty, disreputable trafficking. Although *ironmongers* and *fishmongers* carried on respectable enough businesses, as once did *warmongers* (originally a word for a mercenary soldier), *boroughmongers* were wealthy landowners in England who sold representation of the ROTTEN BOROUGHS and helped give the suffix a bad name. Pimps were called *whoremongers*, and Mark Twain's hero in the 1889 *A Connecticut Yankee in King Arthur's Court* derogated knights as "lummoxes" and "*suspicion-mongers.*"

-Monger has been particularly used to describe people who pass along damaging information: *gossipmongers, rumormongers.* One who warns of imminent danger is sometimes attacked as a *panicmonger,* or more seriously as a *warmonger.* See TRIGGER-HAPPY. The author titled a novel about an early U.S. muckraker *Scandalmonger.*

As with other phrases using the idea of war (see WAGING PEACE), a turnaround has taken place and those who speak against containment or intervention have been labeled *peacemongers.*

Monroe Doctrine See DOCTRINES.

moonbat A knee-jerk liberal, short for *barking moonbat;* a derogation by knee-jerk conservatives—or *wing nuts,* as they, in turn, are derided by *moonbats.*

From a 2006 profile in *The Washington Post* of NBC's White House correspondent, David Gregory: "At Free Republic, another conservative site, a poster said: 'This barking moonbat is just mad because he realizes there is no way to turn this into a "Get Bush" or even "Get Cheney" scandal.'" Vinay Menon, slamming a reality TV show, *Wanted Ted or Alive,* in the *Toronto Star* in 2006, put the insult in flavorful context: "The show is not for everybody. Specifically, vegans, liberals, gun-control advocates, vegetarians, pansies, evolutionists, elites, sophisticates, urban snobs, atheists, treehuggers, feminists, Germans, useful idiots, moonbats, multiculturalists, and profanity-averse viewers are advised to proceed with caution."

Moonbat was introduced as an epithet by Perry de Haviland in 1999 and popularized in the blogosphere, starting in 2002, on de Haviland's libertarian Web site, Samizdata (see SAMIZDAT). De Haviland has rejected the suggestion that *moonbat* was inspired by the surname of George Monbiot, a pro-environmental columnist for the Manchester (U.K.) *Guardian.* "I coined the term long before George came onto my radar," he wrote in a 2006 e-mail message. "I rendered the term as 'Barking Moonbat' as part of a conversation I was having with some friends about how when certain topics appear in the media or on the internet, some people start howling just like wolves reflexively at the visual stimuli. However as wolves seems too noble a connotation, I started to describe the reflex as 'the Barking Moonbat reflex.'"

De Haviland thought of *moonbat* as an "ecumenical" term of abuse, applicable equally to "dogmatists of any ilk, left, right, or libertarian," but coiners cannot be choosers. In practice, righties took over *moonbat,* using it as a club for beating lefties exclusively. The *moon* part is key. On account of its changing phases, earth's satellite has long been associated with instability—with insanity in general, and with the "loony left" in particular. (*Loony* comes from *luna*, Latin for "moon"; see LUNATIC FRINGE.) *Chicago Sun-Times* columnist Mike Royko played upon the association in 1979 when he referred to California governor Jerry Brown as "Governor Moonbeam." The label stuck because of Brown's perceived eccentricities, but Royko took it all back in a 1991 column, saying that he had thought at the time it was an "amusing phrase" but "if he had to do it over again, he sure as hell wouldn't."

Moonbat had prior, nonpolitical incarnations. Aviation buffs adopted it as the nickname of an experimental nighttime fighter, the XP-67, developed by McDonnell Aircraft during World War II. Only one of the planes was ever built and it was not called the *Moonbat* at the time. The name came later, popularized by aviation buffs, according to Lawrence Merritt, archivist and historian for Boeing. "The plane had an unusual body. ... Some folks thought it looked like a bat and it was supposed to fly at night. That's where they must have dreamed up *Moonbat*," said Merritt. The earliest example of the name in his files come from a December 1973 article in *Wings Magazine*, entitled "It Must Have Been 'Moonbat'" (a play on a lyric in the 1934 pop hit "Moonglow").

Still earlier, Robert Heinlein used *moonbat* in two sci-fi short stories, "Space Jockey" and "The Black Pits of Luna," published in 1947 and 1948, respectively. In the first, *Moonbat* is the name of a landing craft employed in a three-stage voyage (anticipating the multi-stage Apollo missions) to the moon. In the second, a tour guide on the moon also serves as scoutmaster of the *Moonbat Patrol.*

Moonbat's companion in infamy is *wingnut,* not to be confused with the *wing nut* for fastening screws, the *Wingnut* who was a fan of *The West Wing* TV series or who roots for the Detroit Red Wings hockey team, the exotic *Caucasian Wing-nut* tree, or Robert "Wingnut" Weaver, the surfer who starred in the 1994 documentary *The Endless Summer II.*

Like *moonbat*, the political *wingnut* is an abbreviation of a longer term, in this case *right-wing nut*, where *nut*, as slang for the head, has long been used to refer to a person who is silly, stupid, crazy, or simply *nutty.* The shortened *wingnut* is especially popular among bloggers, who delight in abbreviation and who do not always use it in a strictly pejorative sense. Matt Drudge, of The Drudge Report, told *The Washington Post* in May of 1999 why he regularly checked conservative websites: "I get to see how my story is playing among the wing nuts. This tells me it is going to be a huge radio thing."

The original *right-wing nut* is of considerable antiquity, dating at least to the 1960s, well before the blogosphere emerged to fan the fringes. Early examples come from letters to newspapers. Edward Cowan referred in a letter to *The Austin* (Tex.) *Statesman* on Nov. 1, 1962, to "the emergence within our borders of right-wing nut-groups which preach a diplomacy of cloak-and-dagger and a politics of apocalypse." John Lewis complained to the *Modesto* (Calif.) *Bee and News-Herald* on Oct. 15, 1965, that the newspaper's editorials cast too wide a net: "I am, by being a conservative, automatically a neo-Fascist, right-wing nut and a fanatic."

Today, the long and short forms coexist amicably in print. Scripps Howard columnist Dale McFeathers used the long form in 2002, reporting that his e-mail on the subject of bias in the press was "split 50–50 between those who think I'm a pinko traitor and those who think I'm a right-wing nut." *Slate* went with the short form in a December 2003 headline for an article on a Supreme Court case: "The Wing Nut's Revenge: A Conspiracy Theorist Has His Day in Court." The anonymous headline writer picked up on reporter Dahlia Lithwick's observation that during oral arguments Justice Antonin Scalia is "never afraid to call a wing nut a wing nut."

The presumed *wing nut* in this case was a California lawyer who wanted to obtain death-scene photos of Vince Foster, the Deputy White House Counsel, who committed suicide in 1993. The legal issue was whether the right of privacy extended after death under the Freedom of Information Act to Foster's family. Scalia joined in the unanimous opinion that it did.

moonlighting Working for a second source of income; in politics, doing private work for pay at night while on the public payroll during the day.

The word originally applied to the nighttime raids of poverty-stricken Irishmen in the 1880s, to punish unpopular tenants or prevent payments of rents. The concept of working for a second employer after putting in a full day elsewhere was called *smooting* in England at that time, and it was prohibited by the trade unions, which wanted to spread the work to as many different members as possible.

A political issue is occasionally raised as to whether police officers and fire fighters should be allowed to supplement their pay by taking a second job during off-hours. Opponents argue that moonlighting drains the worker's stamina for his civic job; and they claim it leads to conflict of interest in the case of white-collar public workers or officials.

See DOUBLE DIPPING.

moral equivalent of war Fervor without destructiveness; an acknowledgment of man's psychological need for the martial arts, with a recommendation that the need be satisfied through peaceful challenges.

William James, in an essay entitled "The Moral Equivalent of War," published in a leaflet of the American Association for International Conciliation in February 1910 (and later that year in *McClure's Magazine*), wrote: "So long as anti-militarists propose no substitute for war's disciplinary function, no *moral equivalent of war*, analogous, as one might say, to the mechanical equivalent of heat, so long they fail to realize the full inwardness of the situation."

Four U.S. wars later, President Jimmy Carter used the James phrase in his address to the nation on April 19, 1977. He pictured an energy crisis as "the greatest challenge that our country will face in our lifetimes," adding: "Our decision about energy will test the character of the American people and the ability of the President and the Congress to govern this nation. This difficult effort will be the 'moral equivalent of war'—except that we will be uniting our

efforts to build and not to destroy." (His writers felt that the last phrase, although redundant, was necessary to stress that the President was not advocating any kind of "shooting" war.)

A committee of economists supporting the oil industry blazed back in a full-page ad: "Congress has been told that it must rush to pass Mr. Carter's current energy plan. 'This is the moral equivalent of war.' And what is that? William James, from whom President Carter borrowed the phrase, defined 'the moral equivalent of war' as nonmartial suffering, something which involves 'discomfort and annoyance, hunger and wet, pain and cold, squalor and filth.' We do not believe that the American people deserve to have 'discomfort, pain, squalor, etc.' imposed upon them by their government."

Charles Krauthammer of *The Washington Post* wrote in February 1993 on President Clinton's call for economic sacrifice: "It shows in the vast disproportion between the size of the threat posed by the deficit and the magnitude of the sacrifice Clinton is asking of the American people to meet it. As usual with these kinds of summons to the moral equivalent of war—Bush on drugs, Carter on energy—a pop-gun is produced to fight it."

The lofty James phrase received its cruelest blow from the columnist Russell Baker, who took to using its feline acronym: MEOW.

moratorium An officially declared stoppage or delay; applied to politics, a truce.

The sonorous *moratorium*, invariably attached to the verb *declare* with the same cement that binds *doctrine* to *enunciate*, stems from the Latin for "delay" but has a more majestic connotation. In 1931 Herbert Hoover called for a one-year moratorium on war-debt payments, and this "debt holiday" was called the *Hoover moratorium*. When Lyndon Johnson traveled to a conference of Asian leaders just before the off-year elections of 1966, Richard Nixon ordered his aides to "declare a moratorium on foreign-policy criticism" while he was gone, for fear of appearing to undercut the president abroad on the business of all the people.

When political figures want to tell their friends to shut up while they try to settle a sticky situation, they find it more polite to "request a moratorium." Ted Sorensen wrote that civil rights leaders in 1963 "were angry at the Kennedys for requesting a moratorium on demonstrations while an agreement was worked out ..."

Early in the 1992 presidential primary campaign, the term was used by Democratic candidate Paul Tsongas: "This morning, I call for a moratorium, a kind of nonaggression pact between the candidates. Let's start talking about what we stand for. Let's have a positive program, and let's end this negative advertising ..."

In 1993, J.P. Mackley used the word in a *Washington Post* piece on the war in Bosnia: "Even the Russians, whose historical support for Serbia has worried Western negotiators, could not object to an equal opportunity moratorium on artillery fire."

NBC correspondent Herbert Kaplow, chafing at candidate Richard Nixon's declaration of a moratorium on Vietnam discussions at the start of the 1968 campaign, suggested to this Nixon speechwriter: "You ought to hold your next rally in a huge moratorium."

morning in America Upbeat political message leading to victory; or, derision at unfounded or fuzzy optimism about the country's future.

Ronald Reagan's message of fresh optimism began in his second presidential campaign. A 28-second commercial for his reelection showed idyllic scenes of America—people going to work, a bride in a wedding gown, a child admiring the flag—accompanied by reminders of low inflation and interest rates, with a reassuring voiceover saying "It's morning again in America."

The 1984 campaign's glowing and effective message was paraphrased by the liberal columnist Anthony Lewis of *The New York Times* in his reading of Reagan: "the sense that he feels good and that we should." Within three years, however, as a result of the Iran-contra scandal and the usual "second term blues," the optimistic message was turned against Republicans and voiced in *The Washington Post* in 1987 as a concern that conservatives must "finally realize that it is not 'morning in America' anymore."

By 1993, the phrase was being satirized as an ideal of undue optimism. The former Democratic Senator Gary Hart wrote about the Reagan years: "The orgy was fun, at least for some, while it lasted. But it carried some bitter costs, The champagne has gone flat. It is no longer 'morning in America.'"

The memorable advertising message produced for Reagan had historical resonance. A leader of the American Revolution, Samuel Adams, exclaimed on April 19, 1775, when he first heard the gunfire at Lexington, "What a glorious morning this is."

mossback A reactionary; one who furiously resists progress of any kind.

The word is derived from a sea creature so ancient that it has moss or seaweed growing on its back. During the Civil War it was used to describe those who fled to the swamps and forests to evade the draft; in the 1870s the word was given a political meaning as a Northern counterpart to a Southern "Bourbon (i.e., conservative) Democrat."

Emporia Gazette editor William Allen White, in his famed "What's the Matter with Kansas?" editorial in 1896, thundered: "We have an old moss-back Jacksonian who snorts and howls because there is a bathtub in the State House; we are running that old jay for Governor."

Pennsylvania Congressman J. C. Sibley drew a typical word picture in 1900: "Primitive man lived in caverns, clothed himself with skins, and ate his meat raw, sitting on his haunches; and there has never occurred a change for the higher and better forms of life without arousing the hostility of some old mossback, conservative hunker[s], who will prate of those fairer and better days of old, when their grandfathers swung by their tails from the limbs of the trees."

Will Rogers told defeated Democratic candidate Al Smith in 1929: "taken out from under the influence of a lot of these old Mossbacks, you are a pretty progressive fellow, Al, and with you and this fellow Roosevelt as a kind of nucleus, I think we can, with the help of some Progressive young Democratic governors and senators and congressmen, make this thing into a Party, instead of a Memory."

The word was relatively dormant during the thirties and early forties, but President Harry Truman gave it new life in the 1948 campaign. In the Far West he charged that the Republican party's domination by "eastern mossbacks" would stifle the economy of the West. Throughout the country, he denounced the Republican chairmen of Senate and House committees as "a bunch of mossbacks."

One of the lines that best describes a mossback was leveled at House Speaker "Uncle Joe" Cannon: "If he had been present at Creation, he would have voted for Chaos." See DO-NOTHING CONGRESS.

In 1992 President George H.W. Bush complained that he had extended a "hand of friendship" to Congress at the start of his presidency "and these old mossbacks bit it off." Long Island's *Newsday* reported a year later that "Clinton joined … Richard Nixon in toasting [Strom] Thurmond's inspiring 90-year journey from racist Democratic segregationist to mossback Republican obstructionist." See DO-NOTHING CONGRESS; TROGLODYTIC.

most favored nation Not, as the phrase implies, preferred or special treatment in trade but an assurance that economic relations will be "equal to that of the most favored nation."

The essence of MFN is that "nobody else gets a better deal." The idea appears in the commercial treaty that Oliver Cromwell, Lord Protector of England, negotiated with Sweden in 1654 that won recognition of his commonwealth: people of either confederate "shall have and possess in the countries, lands, dominions and kingdoms of the other as full and ample privileges, and as many exemptions, immunities and liberties, as any foreigner doth or shall possess in the dominions and kingdoms of the said confederate."

Cromwell got this idea from the Turkish "capitulations": extraterritorial privileges granted in the twelfth century by Byzantium's successors to the Italian city-states. The *OED*'s earliest example comes from a *History of England* (1758) by Tobias Smollett, better remembered as a novelist: "The same privileges that France granted to the most favoured nation." A typical treaty phrasing can be found in a 1905 British-Rumanian pact: "the commerce, navigation and industry of each country shall be placed, in all respects, on the footing of the most favoured nation."

The underlying idea behind MFN, as it came to be called in the '60s, is "a fair field with no favor": any special privileges demanded by one nation, and agreed to by another, then become available to all. That is the "unconditional" MFN, guaranteeing equal treatment without any reciprocal strings attached. The founders of the U.S., however, recognizing that their new nation was a newcomer to world commerce, and faced with English, French, and Spanish attempts to exclude the newcomer from their overseas possessions, came up with a new wrinkle on the hoary clause: the "conditional" MFN. Only if other nations permitted access to their markets would the U.S. permit access to its own.

That conditional principle can be found in the first U.S. trade treaty, concluded with France, in July of 1778. The idea was to make trade reciprocal and dependent upon receipt of equal treatment. Secretary of State John Quincy Adams wrote in 1818 that such reciprocity could not confer special treatment on any one nation: "If any such advantage is granted for an equivalent, other nations can have no right to claim its enjoyment, even though entitled to be treated as the most favored nation, unless by the reciprocal grant of the same equivalent." (Curiously, Adams' sobriquet was "Old Man Eloquent.")

After World War I, however, the U.S.—which originated the conditional most-favored-nation clause—found it no longer useful, since the condition allowed other countries to discriminate against U.S. exports. "By offering complete and nondiscriminatory treatment," reads a 1974 staff study by the Senate Finance Committee, "the United States sought to obtain the same treatment from other countries... Authority for the U.S. to offer unconditional MFN was included in the Tariff Act of 1922... The Trade Agreements Act of 1934 included an unconditional MFN provision and made it a requirement of United States domestic law." From this open policy flowed the U.S. participation in the international General Agreement on Tariffs and Trade (GATT), which puts MFN in its first provision of Article 1.

The cold war turned U.S. policy around again. In 1951, Congress directed President Truman to withdraw MFN status from Communist countries. He did so, excepting only Tito's Yugoslavia. When, in 1972, détente became the order of the day, another switch in MFN was sought: Nixon Administration trade experts, led by Peter Flanigan, lobbied to remove this barrier. The verbal approach Flanigan used was not to seek to make the Soviet Union "a most favored nation" (implying special favors to Russia, in the untutored mind) but "to end trade discrimination" (*discrimination* was a word most people were accustomed to being against).

However, when the U.S.S.R. began to levy exit fees on emigrants, Senator Henry Jackson led Congress into forbidding the extension of most-favored-nation status to "non-market economy" nations which deny their citizens the right to emigrate; the Jackson-Vanik amendment to the Trade Act of 1974 enshrined the principle in law. (See QUIET DIPLOMACY.) For decades afterward, this became important in Sino-American relations, as successive Administrations used MFN to goad China into human rights improvements, especially in Tibet.

Evidence that the 250-year-old phrase had permanently entered the language could be found in a 1978 *Newsweek* magazine cover story on the entertainment industry, which defined a Hollywood "Most Favored Nation Clause" as "a contractual promise to a star who signs early that no latecomer will get a better deal."

mother of all battles An epic confrontation.

As U.S.-led coalition forces began gathering for the 1991 invasion of Iraq, Saddam Hussein's Revolutionary Command Council issued a warning on Sept. 21, 1990: "Let everyone understand that this battle is going to become the mother of all battles."

The threat, from the Arabic *umm al-ma'arik*, "mother of battles," an example of *umm al-* "mother of" used figuratively to mean major, best, or greatest of a type, which spawned a host of variations. Many of them were coined with tongue in cheek in view of the quick collapse of the Iraqi army (the Desert Storm campaign lasted just 43 days—Jan. 17 to Feb. 28). Among them: *mother of all briefings*, Gen. Norman Schwarzkopf's televised briefing at the war's conclusion; *mother of all Bushes*, Barbara Bush, so-called by her husband, Pres. George H. W. Bush; and *mother of all covers*, a *Vanity Fair* magazine cover featuring a nude and very pregnant actress Demi Moore.

The expression has proven resilient. Contemplating future Supreme Court confirmation hearings, Gary Bauer, president of American Values, a conservative group, said in 2006: "The next vacancy, depending on who it is, will really be the mother of all battles." The phrase also makes an eye-catching headline. For example, the on-line magazine *Salon* used "The mother of all battles" as the head for a story in 2005 about protests against the second Iraq war. Another variation on the theme is *mother of all clichés*, meaning the expression *mother of all battles*.

mountaintop, take him to the A private promise, made prior to a convention, of high appointive office or a place on the ticket, in return for delegate support.

This phrase rarely appears in print but is current usage in spoken negotiations. "Take him to the mountaintop" implies, first, complete privacy in dealing—unbugged, unwitnessed conversation, promises made that would be denied if repeated. Second, the *mountaintop* offers a pulse-quickening view of the vista below, glimpses of far horizons that persuade the man with the delegates to come across and stay across.

In December 1967, Drew Pearson and Jack Anderson wrote that Senator Eugene McCarthy entered Democratic primaries opposing Lyndon Johnson because "McCarthy is bitter at the man who, he thinks, took him up on the mountain to the Vice Presidency, then pushed him off into the Atlantic City breakers."

The phrase appears as "take him up the mountain" and "take him on the mountaintop," as well as "take him to the mountaintop."

Mountaintop also appears in labor relations, as "now we have to get them down off the mountaintop." In early stages of negotiations, a labor leader often makes unrealistic demands, fully expecting to scale them down for a settlement. However, his rank and file becomes enamored of items like a four-day week and other "asking prices," and the union leader at settlement time has to bring his own men "down off the mountaintop."

The phrase originates in the temptation of Christ (Matthew 4:8–9): "the devil taketh him up into an exceeding high mountain, and sheweth him all the kingdoms of the world and the glory of them; and saith unto him, All these things will I give thee, if thou wilt fall down and worship me." The stern, get-thee-behind-me response of Jesus led later political tempters to be both more specific and more successful.

Movement, the Self-description by adherents to a cause.

In the nineteenth century, the word was adopted by believers in the *progressive* tradition; in the early twentieth century, "the movement" was organized *labor*; in the second half of the century, it was the word that held together advocates for *civil rights* for blacks, moving into a self-description of advocates of feminism and abortion rights in the *women's movement*; in the '60s, the word was self-applied both to the NEW LEFTISTS as well as "TRUE BELIEVER conservatives."

In *The New Radicals* (1966), Paul Jacobs and Saul Landau defined the phrase for the New Left:

Those in The Movement feel that modern American liberals have substituted empty rhetoric for significant content, obscured the principles of justice by administrative bureaucracy, sacrificed human values for efficiency, and hypocritically justified a brutal attempt to establish American hegemony over the world with sterile anti-Communism...To those in The Movement the new technologies of automation and cybernation, with their computers and memory-bank machines, are instruments of alienation, depersonalizing human relations to a frightening degree.

The amorphous radical Movement of the '60s appeared to many Americans to have adopted the techniques of previous movements (sit-ins, protests, demonstrations, strikes) without their direction or national leadership. But many of its leaders were anti-leadership. Tom Hayden warned of "maintaining a dependency on fixed leaders, who inevitably develop interests in maintaining the organization (or themselves) and lose touch with the immediate aspirations of the rank and file." Stokely Carmichael of SNCC, trying to avoid the taint of leadership, assumed the title of "field hand."

Commentary magazine editor Norman Podhoretz told television interviewer Ben Wattenberg in June 1978: "The movement with a capital M, as it used to be called, was made up of a kind of a political arm and a cultural arm. The political arm was called the NEW LEFT, the cultural arm was called the counterculture...I think it disappeared because it won. Its critique of American society and institutions came to be widely accepted by people who were not themselves members of that movement...You see an ominous growth of neo-isolationist sentiment...the idea that the United States is not a benevolent force in world affairs but a malevolent force." (Podhoretz, along with Irving Kristol, were fathers of NEO-CONSERVATISM, which was and is an ISM—an intellectual mindset and policy center—but rarely presumes to be a Movement.)

The labor movement, the civil rights movement, and the women's movement (see SEXISM) had more clear-cut goals, and were readier to organize and communicate their needs to the general public, to lobby for change in law and business opportunity; in many ways they succeeded in changing

American domestic policy and culture. Gays and lesbians, in "coming out of the closet" to assert their demands not just for tolerance but for equal rights and approval, describe themselves more often as a *community* than a *movement*.

When capitalized as *the Movement* or used as the modifier for a given cause, it is the members' way of separating their cause from all others. When used as an attributive noun, acting as a modifier, *movement* is not capitalized. "The two Republicans polling best at present," wrote Tod Lindberg in *The Washington Times* in 2006, "are both outliers with respect to the party's activist, conservative base. They are John McCain and Rudy Giuliani. Mr. McCain is a maverick with a long record as a thorn in the side of those who consider themselves 'movement' conservatives on issues ranging from campaign finance reform to immigration."

For the past generation, the commentator and occasional candidate Pat Buchanan has referred to his right-wing supporters as "movement conservatives" (also often called "social conservatives"), harking back to the Goldwater days and to some extent the Reagan era to distinguish them from NEOCONSERVATIVES. Paul Wolfowitz, a leading neocon at the Defense Department described as the "intellectual architect" of REGIME CHANGE in Iraq in 2002, was driven from his office as head of the World Bank in 2007 in what *The Wall Street Journal* believed was a case of vengeance by Europeans angry at U.S. war leadership combined with a bank bureaucracy upset at his anti-corruption demands. Sam Tanenhaus wrote in *The New York Times* that "Mr. Wolfowitz was not a 'movement conservative.' He did not inveigh against the sins of 'secular liberalism' or homosexuals and the American Civil Liberties Union ... But after 9/11, neoconservatives and evangelicals found common cause in their shared belief in American exceptionalism and in the idea that the country's values could be exported abroad."

Neocons advocate "extending freedom" and defending human rights, making them both interventionist and idealistic in foreign affairs; *movement conservatives* are more interested in restraining government power except in policing. Both movement and non-movement conservatives look askance at *libertarian conservatives*, who—in advocating privacy in an era gripped by the primacy of security—see themselves as more of a principled splinter group than a movement.

movers and shakers Opinion leaders; influentials, especially those who are political or economic activists.

Mass-communications theorists like Columbia professor Paul I. Lazarsfeld hold that there is a "two-step flow" of most communication: from source, to opinion leader in that idea's category, to the great number of people.

Movers and shakers is applied to both the source group and the transmitting opinion leaders; a strict definition would narrow it down to those who decide policy, develop new ideas, and—most important—make it happen.

The historian Clinton Rossiter explained the self-image of Democratic voters: "They delight in the whole sweep of American history, certain that they have been the 'movers and shakers' and their opponents, whether Federalists or Whigs or Republicans, the 'stick-in-the-muds.'"

The economist Walter Heller used the phrase to describe how Lyndon Johnson sought to achieve consensus, using both private meetings and public pronouncements: "this method combines Presidential persuasion and education of hundreds of the country's 'movers and shakers' *in person* in small White House meetings ... with public persuasion of millions of citizens by performance under the resulting policies and legislation."

The phrase was coined by nineteenth-century English poet Arthur O'Shaughnessy:

We are the music-makers,
And we are the dreamers of dreams ...
Yet we are the movers and shakers
Of the world forever, it seems.

The phrase is often used with a faint note of derision at those who believe themselves to be powerful. See MUCKEY-MUCKS.

moving the goalposts Changing the rules in the middle of the game; allowing an unfair advantage.

As an accusation of unfairness, *moving the goalposts* comes from the language of games. Peter Stothard, while United States editor of *The Times* of London, defined the expression: "This term is British and means 'changing the terms of a debate or a conflict after it's been started.' I expect it's more from children's playing, where the sticks marking the goal can be moved, than from organized football [what Americans call "soccer"]. It's a very common term now, both in politics and in social conversation. A child, for instance, who's been told to keep his room clean for an extra 50 pence a week, and then doesn't get the extra money, may say, 'Hey, you've moved the goalposts.'"

Use of the term is always condemnatory. The elder President Bush played with the phrase in a 1990 talk about his criteria for trade with South Africa: "These conditions are clear-cut and are not open to reinterpretation, and I do not believe in moving the goalposts."

Mr. Clean See BOY SCOUT.

Mr. Dooley See DOOLEY, MR.; SUPREME COURT FOLLOWS THE ELECTION RETURNS; BEANBAG.

Mr. Nice Guy Everybody's friend; a practitioner of the politics of pacification.

"Nice guys finish last" is remembered as the dictum of Brooklyn Dodger baseball manager Leo Durocher in the 1940s, and to a degree this has application to modern politics. ("Nice guys finish seventh" was probably closer to what he said, but "Leo the Lip" accepted the revision of history in the 1975 title of his book. Ralph Keyes, in his book of misquotations, says the actual quote was "The nice guys are all over there. In seventh place.")

Writing about Senator Edmund Muskie in October 1971, columnist David Broder pointed out: "Tagged as a cautious, cool Mr. Nice Guy by most observers, the Maine Senator has turned into a deliberately hard-nosed, independent character, often seeming to go out of his way to demonstrate he is his own man."

Nice guy, as in "Mr. Nice Guy," connotes weakness, while *good guy* has an aura of moral strength (see GOOD FIGHT). In 1978, a *Washington Post* article about government officials who found the demands of the political life too demanding was headlined "Good Guys Bow Out." A Clinton aide was quoted in a 1993 *Wall Street Journal* story about dealing with Congress: "No More Mr. Nice Guy."

The expression is current and is traveling: "The new prime minister of Malaysia, Abdullah Badawi," reported Jane Perlez in the *International Herald Tribune* in 2003, "is popularly known here as 'Mr. Nice Guy,' an endearment that could hardly be conferred on … his volatile predecessor."

In his 2007 memoir, columnist Robert Novak—a dour man who revels in his devilish sobriquet of "the Prince of Darkness"—recounted an episode in covering the ill-fated 1972 McGovern campaign. The press secretary denied him a seat on the plane that carried the traveling press, assigning the scowling media BIGFOOT instead to the ZOO PLANE. This was insultingly *infra dig* because it relegated him to the aircraft carrying the technicians and camera crews derogated by elite journalists as "the animals." Novak, trying to be ironic, told the McGovern press aide, Dick Dougherty: "I get the message and I'm telling you: from now on, no more Mr. Nice Guy." The phrase had been popularized by a joke current in the mid-'50s. Hiding out in South America, the story went, Hitler deputy Martin Bormann sought to convince his former chief to return to Germany and take over a neo-Fascist movement. Reluctantly Adolf Hitler agreed to make a comeback, warning, "But this time—no more Mr. Nice Guy."

See BOY SCOUT.

Mr. Republican A sobriquet for the recognized embodiment of party leader; usually unhelpful in a general election.

Putting *Mr.* before a generic word and applying the name to an individual locks up that area—but may also lock a man inside that area. Senator Robert A. Taft of

Ohio was "Mr. Republican" in 1952, but it only served to emphasize the "CAN'T WIN" charge, since Democratic votes are needed for a Republican nominee to win. Similarly, Barry Goldwater was styled "Mr. Conservative," which focused and dramatized his specific strength, but limited his appeal.

Richard Nixon, in his introduction of Goldwater at the 1964 Republican convention—traditionally punctuated by the oratorical phrase "THE MAN WHO"—sought to overcome the "Mr." problem in a progression of phrases: "He is the man who earned and proudly carries the title of Mr. Conservative. He is the man who, by the action of this Convention, is now Mr. Republican. And he is the man who, after the greatest campaign in history, will be Mr. President—Barry Goldwater."

Mr. X A sinister figure who cannot be named; or, the nom de plume of diplomat George Kennan.

Sometimes identified by his nom de guerre, "Mr. Big," the mysterious *Mr. X* occasionally appears as a character in the last few days of an election campaign.

In the New York City mayoralty race of 1953, Manhattan Borough President Robert F. Wagner, Jr., choice of the regular Democrats, was being overshadowed in the press by independent Democrat Rudolph Halley, former chief counsel of the Kefauver crime-investigating committee. A Wagner backer was given some anti-racketeering information damaging to local Republicans, but with not enough proof to substantiate a charge against a specific individual. He passed the information to the candidate, who alluded to it in a "Who is Mr. X?" broadcast—capturing the headlines and the curiosity of the voters during the final weekend of the campaign. Wagner was elected.

The danger of any "Mr. X" charge is in mistiming; it must come toward the very end of a campaign, or else voters begin demanding that the speaker answer his own question or shut up. Mishandled, it can also appear to be a desperate last-minute ruse, which it usually is.

This is an extension of a technique New York Mayor James J. Walker used as a way to infuriate Fiorello La Guardia, whom he defeated decisively in 1929 despite a variety of scandal charges against the Walker administration. "The question I would like to ask Mr. La Guardia," Walker would say solemnly in many of his speeches, "is: What was he doing in Providence on a certain day in 1926?" Of course, Walker had no evidence La Guardia had ever been in Providence, or if he had been, what he was doing there. It succeeded in needling his opponent.

In foreign affairs, "Mr. X" was a well-known figure. George F. Kennan, a U.S. State Department policy planner in 1947, wrote a long memorandum to his superiors urging a new, tougher policy toward Communist expansionary aims. Part of the memo was printed in *Foreign Affairs* quarterly under the title "Sources of Soviet Conduct," signed by "X." (See CONTAINMENT.) Kennan later surfaced as one of the United States' chief planners on Soviet affairs and a DOVE on many issues.

muckey-mucks (muck-a-mucks) High officials; big shots; term of derision for party leaders by party workers.

The expression is still often heard as *high muck-a-muck* because of its probable derivation from Chinook jargon, *hiu* (plenty) *muckamuck* (food); hence, one who has plenty to eat, or a man of power, a big wheel.

The *Democratic State Journal* of Sacramento, California, in 1856 wrote: "The professors—the high 'Muck-a-Mucks'—tried fusion, and produced confusion." A comic-strip character in the *Chicago Tribune* in 1947 said, "They's a high-mucky-muck in th' radio business vacationin' here, so we gotta be good."

Synonyms are PARTY ELDERS, the INNER CLUB, POWER BROKERS, BOSSES. Oldest is BIGWIG, traced in Farmer and Henley's slang dictionary to 1703. For other American Indian (or as many prefer, Native American) expressions in politics, see SACHEM; TAMMANY TIGER; GREAT WHITE FATHER; MUGWUMP; RAINMAKER.

muckraker A journalist who searches through the activities of public organizations seeking to expose conduct contrary to the public interest or damaging to a public figure.

While still used to describe investigative reporters, gossip columnists, and intrepid bloggers (see SWIFT BOAT SPOT), the term reached its greatest popularity in the days of the crusading magazines between 1903 and 1909.

Theodore Roosevelt first used it in its present meaning at a time when he was suspected of being antibusiness by the businessmen who formed an important part of his own Republican party. Articles exposing shady activities in business had already shocked the public when President Roosevelt, first in an off-the-record Gridiron Club speech and later in a speech at the laying of the cornerstone for the new House of Representatives Office Building on April 14, 1906, warned that this kind of antibusiness journalism could go too far. Roosevelt said, "the men with the muckrakes are often indispensable to the well being of society; but only if they know when to stop raking the muck, and to look upward to the celestial crown above them, to the crown of worthy endeavor. There are beautiful things above and round about them; and if they gradually grow to feel that the whole world is nothing but muck, their power of usefulness is gone."

Roosevelt's reference was to the Man with the Muck Rake in John Bunyan's *Pilgrim's Progress*, written in jail in 1675, about the man who could never look any way but down; when offered a celestial crown, he refused to gaze upward and continued to rake the filth on the floor.

"TR" was repeating a phrase he had found successful at the Gridiron Club dinner of March 17, 1906. Then he had used it more strenuously to describe men who attacked those who had acquired means merely because of wealth "but [who] were prepared to condone crimes of great brutality, including murder, if those committing them can obtain the support of powerful labor organizations."

Muckraker was not completely new to politics; as early as 1871 it was used to describe the ambitious politician who rakes in muck, hoping to come up with valuable ammunition.

Mr. Roosevelt's version caught on immediately. One of the most famous—though least virulent—of the school, Ray Stannard Baker, was hailed by a friend on the street almost immediately after the speech with the cheery salutation, "Hello, Muckraker." Baker said he didn't know what was meant at the moment but was quickly educated.

Lincoln Steffens, whose articles in *McClure's Magazine* made him the leader of the school, wrote in his autobiography: "I did not intend to be a muckraker. I did not know that I was one till President Roosevelt picked the name out of Bunyan's 'Pilgrim's Progress' and pinned it on us and even then he said that he did not mean me." He and others such as Baker and Ida Tarbell, did not long resent the word. According to historian Mark Sullivan, "all the writers of exposure accepted the epithet that was meant for some of them, and in the eyes of most of the public, 'muckraker' became a term of approval."

For a short time the pages of *McClure's*, *Collier's*, *The American Magazine*, *Cosmopolitan*, and others were rife with stories of misconduct, previously sheltered from public exposure. In its day, when the exposés in the popular magazines came weekly, a favorite muckraker story was of the wealthy Alaskan miner who walked into a magazine office demanding a crusade. Said the editor, "You certainly are a progressive, aren't you?" "Progressive!" the miner roared. "I'm a full-fledged INSURGENT. Why, man, I subscribe to thirteen magazines!"

Today's muckrakers prefer the term *investigative reporter*. The breed was criticized by Bert Lance, President Carter's first Director of the Office of Management and Budget, who had been driven from office by press criticism of his financial affairs (with the author leading the pack). Lance cautioned the American Society of Newspaper Editors in April 1978 that censorship could follow press irresponsibility: "The press has always had its share of professional cynics, as quite properly it should. But that once healthy dash of cynicism appears to have become a pervasive and destructive cynicism, another sad legacy of Vietnam and Watergate.

"Along with this unhealthy climate of suspicion," said the Georgian, "is a change in the standards governing publication of allegation, rumor and gossip, and an intense post-Watergate competition among investigative reporters." Then he added a "snapper," as it is called in the trade: "There are more muck*rakers* around these days than muck*makers*."

mudslinging Wild, unsubstantiated charges; a word, like "SMEAR," used to turn an attack back on the attacker.

"Calumniate! Calumniate! Some of it will always stick," advised Beaumarchais in *The Barber of Seville* in 1775. This was based on Latin advice, *Fortiter calumniare, aliquid adhaerebit*, or "Throw plenty of dirt and some of it will be sure to stick."

Sometime after the Civil War, *dirt-throwing* picked up some water to become *mud-throwing*, *mud-gunning*, and the word that gained preeminence, *mudslinging*. The *New York Tribune* in 1876 disagreed with the Latin dictum: "Mud doesn't stick to Mr. Blaine any better than it does to Mr. Bristow. The slander peddlers are having a bad season." The word was so well entrenched by 1878 that the *Tribune* could refer to it obliquely, as "the dredging machine was set at work again yesterday, and brought up a small load of sediment from the dirty stream of Louisiana politics."

Bruce Felknor, of the Fair Campaign Practices Committee in the '60s, classified six presidential campaigns as "spectacularly dirty": Jackson's first election, Lincoln's second, the Hayes-Tilden debacle, Cleveland's first election, Theodore Roosevelt's third campaign, and the Hoover-Smith clash of 1928. Harry Truman agreed on the last, recalling: "Al Smith was given the nomination, and that set off the most vicious anti-Catholic, anti-Jewish, anti-Negro movement that we have ever had in any political campaign…there was more slander and mudslinging going on than at any time I can remember."

Mudslinging and *dirty politics* are obviously from the same source. "I was told repeatedly not to enter politics," said then-Governor Nelson Rockefeller, "that politics is a 'dirty' business.… Politics is the lifeblood of democracy. To call politics 'dirty' is to call democracy 'dirty.'"

Adlai Stevenson in 1954 combined a couple of earthy metaphors to put together a Confucianist epigram: "He who slings mud generally loses ground."

mugwump Bolter; MAVERICK.

Anyone who bolted his political party was a *mugwump*, especially those Republicans who refused to support the presidential candidacy of James Blaine in 1884. The true mugwump went a step further and gave his support to the Democratic nominee, Grover Cleveland of New York.

Early use of the word was by John Eliot in his *Indian Bible*, published in 1663 in Massachusett, an Algonquian language, in which the word *mugquomp* is used to denote a chief or another individual of high rank. See SACHEM.

In 1884 it was popularized politically by the New York *Sun* and quickly became common political parlance. The Republicans had met in convention and picked Blaine as their candidate. Many figures of stature (though not much influence) in the party decided they could not accept a man they felt was so corrupt. They met June 7, 1884, in Boston and decided to support Grover Cleveland. The *Sun* jeered at them as "Little Mugwumps," meaning little men attempting to be big chiefs. Little they were not: their ranks sparkled with such names as President Eliot of Harvard, Carl Schurz, Charles Francis Adams, and George William Curtis.

The *little*, in fact, was soon dropped; the term *mugwump* persisted and, indeed, those so labeled soon accepted and even affected the description after Admiral Horace Porter defined a *mugwump* as "a person educated beyond his intellect."

Mugwumpery or *mugwumpism* has persisted both here and in Great Britain to describe bolters, though most usually the term has been applied to independent Republicans.

Political lexicographers have always felt obligated to report that a mugwump was described by the *Blue Earth* (Minn.) *Post* in the early 1930s as "a sort of bird that sits on a fence with his mug on one side and his wump on the other."

Theodore Roosevelt, who was persuaded to adopt party regularity in 1884 by Henry Cabot Lodge of Massachusetts, called mugwumps "dudes"; they had also been reviled as "pharisees." Roosevelt professed contempt for mugwumps through the years—right up to the time he bolted the Republican party and ran for the presidency as an independent in 1912.

multilateralism Policy of creating alliances of three or more nations, as contrasted with agreement between just two nations (*bilateralism*) or a single nation taking action on its own (UNILATERALISM).

Multilateral has been applied to relations between nations since the mid-nineteenth century, but *multilateralism* is a much newer phenomenon, at least by that name. The oldest example of the term in the *OED* is from a 1928 report in the *Glasgow Herald* on negotiations that led to the Kellogg-Briand pact to outlaw war: "M. [Aristide] Briand insisted specifically on the term 'war of aggression' after first talking generically of all war. The reason was the transformation of bilateralism into multilateralism."

The distinctions between *multilateralism*, *bilateralism*, and UNILATERALISM depend on context. Columnist Christopher Hitchens parsed the exceedingly fine differences in an essay on "Multilateralism and Unilateralism," in *Slate* in 2002:

If the United States had supported the Czech proposal, then that proposal would have automatically ceased to be unilateral and become, just like that, bilateral or (since bilateral carries the implication of two contrasting parties) well on its way to becoming multilateral. That's if you forget that multilateral means "many-sided," whereas the recruitment of more nations or forces to any one "side" means that the cause may remain "one-sided" but has at least succeeded in attracting multiparty or multiple-country support.

Conservatives tend to have a visceral distrust of *multilateralism*, thinking that American freedom of action should not be restrained unduly by the wishes of other nations, while liberal internationalists generally bemoan *unilateralism*, believing that in the long run the U.S. needs allies to succeed. Both terms are employed frequently as epithets when attacking the opposition, and neither side displays much consistency in following the policies usually attributed to them.

For example, Vice President George H. W. Bush, while campaigning for the presidency in 1988, mocked the Democratic candidate, Massachusetts governor Michael Dukakis, for stressing the importance of multilateral alliances: " 'Multilateralism' seems to be my opponent's answer to Soviet aggression in the Western Hemisphere." After being elected, however, Mr. Bush put on a virtuoso display of *multilateralism*, proclaiming a NEW WORLD ORDER and assembling a grand coalition of nations to defeat Iraq in the first Gulf War. (Because the U.S. clearly dominated the coalition, Michael Lind in *The New Republic* classed this as this *ersatz multilateralism*.)

The elder Bush's successor, Bill Clinton, also was attacked for relying on *multilateralism*. Writing in *Foreign Affairs* in 1994, Paul Wolfowitz, then Dean of the Paul H. Nitze School of Advanced International Studies at Johns Hopkins University, asserted: "Clinton has been too wedded to two tools of diplomacy: multilateralism and peacekeeping. Neither is as important as is currently fashionable to think."

Soon Clinton's first Secretary of State, Warren Christopher, began qualifying the administration's devotion to *multilateralism*, declaring in a speech in January of 1995: "When our vital interests are at stake, we must be prepared to act alone. Our willingness to do so is often the key to effective joint action. The recent debate between the proponents of unilateral and multilateral action assumes a false choice. Multilateralism is a means, not an end."

Christopher's successor as Secretary of State, Madeleine Albright, sought to put some rhetorical spine in the policy by calling it *assertive multilateralism*. That did not catch on, nor did former Senator Gary Hart's alliterative *enlightened engagement.*

Clinton's successor, George W. Bush, began his first administration in 2001 on a distinctly unilateral note, pulling out of the Kyoto accord on GLOBAL WARMING. The President rejected the *unilateralist* label, telling the press following a meeting of NATO leaders that year: "Unilateralists don't come around the table to listen to others. ... Unilateralists don't ask opinions of world leaders." The President caught everyone's attention in his 2004 State of the Union Address when he declared in *unilateralist* vein: "America will never seek a permission slip to defend the security of our people," but in practice catchwords of his administration fluctuated between *consultation* (multi) and *leadership* (uni).

Nicholas Burns, a foreign service officer and U.S. permanent representative to the North Atlantic Council, put it this way in 2004 at a workshop in Berlin on global security: "Americans have an obligation to reject unilateralism and to work instead to preserve the great multilateral institutions such as NATO that are so important to our common future. For the U.S., President Bush and Secretary [of State Colin] Powell have emphasized repeatedly our commitment to 'effective multilateralism.'" (*Assertive* was replaced by *effective.*)

In essence, most people in a democratic great power expect strong leadership from their elected leaders—but not too much, and not over too many strong objections—unless a vital national interest is involved.

multipolar world A world view beyond Russian-American superpower competition; a global strategic vision recognizing several different centers of power.

The simpler adjective *bipolar* dates back to 1810; its use in twentieth-century politics was to indicate two opposed centers of power, the U.S. and the U.S.S.R. As early as 1859, however, *multipolar* was coined to describe the possibility of "having several poles," though this put a strain on the metaphor. In political usage, the newer adjective

acknowledged more than two centers of power, as in "a multipolar world."

In 1980, Alexander Haig spoke with *The Washington Post* about the Soviet threat. The newspaper paraphrased parts of General Haig's comments, reporting, "The bipolar world of the early postwar years has given way to a complex multipolar world with 'three competitive centers of Marxist influence—one in Moscow, one in Peking and one in the revolutionary Third World.'"

Haig's mentor, Henry Kissinger, helped popularize the expression. In a 1992 column about the possibilities of peaceful coexistence in the Middle East, Dr. Kissinger wrote, "The readiness to run military risks in faraway countries will diminish in a multipolar world in which doctrines of collective security and U.N. actions rule the day."

Political commentators also considered the effect of this phrase on the 1992 presidential election. A *Newsday* editorial during the campaign suggested that "The demise of the communist threat and the emergence of a multipolar world has left the G.O.P. without one of its central organizing principles."

Munich analogy Symbol of a place of appeasement leading to war.

Cities that are the scene of a great event, when they are not major capitals that are the scene of too many other great occasions, are often identified with the meaning of that event.

Yalta was the scene of the last meeting of Roosevelt, Churchill, and Stalin toward the end of World War II. "Another Yalta" has come to be used as a warning against gullibility in dealings with Communist leaders.

Guernica, a small city in Spain, was bombed by German aircraft in support of the Franco forces in April 1937; its obliteration came to mean ruthless attacks against defenseless cities.

Sarajevo, now the capital of Bosnia and Herzegovina, was the scene on June 28, 1914, of the assassination of the Austrian Archduke Ferdinand, which history texts dubbed "one of the immediate (but not underlying) causes of the World War."

"Another Sarajevo" means a spark that ignites a major conflict. This was recalled during the city's siege as Serbian forces sought to drive out Muslim Bosnians after the breakup of Yugoslavia in 1992–93.

Munich was the scene of an agreement between British Prime Minister Neville Chamberlain, French Premier Edouard Daladier, Hitler, and Mussolini on September 30, 1938, granting Germany the Czech territory of the Sudetenland as well as its defense border. The Czechs were not present at their "sellout." Today, "another Munich" means an agreement that appeases an aggressor at the expense of a weak nation and only leads to greater war later.

Writer Bernard Fall, killed in Vietnam in 1967, wrote a year earlier: "If Munich is not a good example of how to settle the Vietnamese conflict, neither is Guernica, or Sarajevo."

See PEACE FOR OUR TIME; VIETNAM SYNDROME.

murder board A panel that subjects an individual or proposal to harsh questioning as a dress rehearsal prior to formal presentation or a news conference.

Murder board is encountered most frequently today in connection with nominations to the United States Supreme Court. Referring to the role of Assistant Attorney General Rachel Brand in the hearing on the nomination of Samuel Alito to the Court in 2006, *The Washington Post* reported: "She's a rising star in administration legal circles who was trusted to run all three 'murder boards' (the practice hearings)—for Chief Justice Roberts, Harriet Miers, and Alito." Nominees for other offices, up to and including the presidency, also are subjected to *murder boards*. Telling how Texas Governor George W. Bush got ready for his first debate in 2000 with Vice President Al Gore, the *Post* reported: "Bush's final preparations included a 'murder board' session where he was peppered with questions."

The term is of military origin. It has been dated to 1944 in reference to a panel that questioned WAC officer candidates. Within the military, the usage was broadened to include groups of instructors who passed on the abilities of would-be instructors by asking the kinds of tough questions that students would ask in actual classes. The *murder board* test was adapted in other ways. In "Internet Marketing and Public Speaking: The Murder Board Practice," Larry Tracy recalled: "When I ran the Defense Intelligence Agency's (DIA) briefing team, we had three Murder Boards before the daily briefing to the Chairman of the Joint Chiefs of Staff.... By the time my briefer or I was standing in front of the Chairman, those intense sessions provided the right answers to virtually any conceivable question the Chairman was likely to ask."

Concepts as well as people may undergo *murder boards*. Robert E. Watkins told *The New York Times* in 1980 that the Grumman Political Action Committee used a 15-member "murder board" to determine which candidates to support and how much to donate to each: "It's like any budgetary process within the company. You have to justify the money."

Considerable efforts may be made by *murder boards* to simulate actual conditions. Speaking of business practice, Larry Tracy wrote: The 'Murder Board' audience should be encouraged to ask the toughest, most realistic questions, and the entire session should be audio and/or video-taped. You can then review your performance. Look for distracting body language, listen for annoying vocal patterns. Place yourself in the position of your prospective audience. Would you 'buy' what that person on screen is 'selling?' "

The author participated in a *murder board* at Camp David in August 1971 preparing then Treasury Secretary John Connally to deal with hostile media questioning after the surprise economic speech combating inflation containing what the Japanese called the *Nixon shokku*: imposing wage and price controls, imposing an import tax, and upending the international monetary system by ending the convertibility of the dollar into gold. Having written the speech, it fell to me to lead the tough questioning, trying to trap the Secretary with arcane points, until he glared at me and said, "You're pretty good on the questions, Safire—how are you on the answer to that one?" I did not have the answer, but the economist Herbert Stein did, and Connally went into the news conference well primed by the *murder board*.

musical metaphors
"For if the trumpet give an uncertain sound, who shall prepare himself to the battle?" (I Corinthians 14:8). This Biblical musical metaphor has occasionally been applied to political leadership; former Army Chief of Staff General Maxwell Taylor used it as the title of a book, *The Uncertain Trumpet*, attacking the downgrading of conventional army units in the fifties.

The Defense Secretary who later worked closely with Taylor, Robert McNamara (see WHIZ KIDS), became the subject of a musical metaphor. "McNamara's Band," the nickname for his organization, was taken from a turn-of-the-century song beginning "My name is McNamara, I'm the leader of the band ..."

New York Mayor Fiorello La Guardia orchestrated his administration with sirens chasing fire engines and explosions of temper against "TINHORN gamblers and two-bit politicians." One night at Radio City Music Hall, listening to the organist at intermission, "the Little Flower" explained his theory of administration to his City Council president and protégé, Newbold Morris: "Newbold, that's how our city must be run. Like that organist, you must keep both hands on the keyboard and both feet on the pedals—and never let go!"

A celestial harp was used subtly and skillfully by Abraham Lincoln as a metaphor in his first inaugural address, perhaps the best metaphor of any kind used by any U.S. president: "The mystic chords of memory, stretching from every battlefield and every land, will yet swell the chorus of the Union when again touched, as surely they will be, by the better angels of our nature." The composition of this passage, originally suggested by Secretary of State William Seward, is described in the Prolegomenon to this dictionary.

Playing on President Clinton's ability to play a musical instrument, a pundit in 1993 criticized his "uncertain saxophone."

must list See HIT LIST.

mutual and balanced See CODE WORDS.

muzzle To censor; to stifle criticism; an attack word on an attempt to present a united front.

Journalists have applied the word to the requirement by Eisenhower and subsequent administrations that all policy speeches by military men be approved by the government and changed or suppressed if they differ materially with official policy.

An early example occurred during the first week in office of President Kennedy. The Soviets were holding several American fliers whose reconnaissance plane had been shot down near Russian waters. Negotiations for their return were in progress. The Chief of Naval Operations, Admiral Arleigh Burke, voluntarily submitted a speech that had a strong anti-Soviet tone. When the speech was toned down and that fact became known, the President was accused of "muzzling" the military.

Kennedy replied: "If a well-known, high-ranking military figure makes a speech which affects foreign policy or possibly military policy, I think that the people and the countries abroad have a right to expect that that speech represents the opinion of the national government. ... The purpose of the review ... is to make sure that ... government speaks with one voice."

An investigation by a senatorial committee headed by Senator Strom Thurmond sought to equate the policy with censorship and being SOFT ON COMMUNISM. The committee received encouragement from a statement made by former President Eisenhower, who somewhat deplored a similar policy of speech review required during his two terms, saying that "after mature consideration" he now felt the policy should be dropped. Columnist Walter Lippmann believed otherwise, writing that "the talkativeness of American military men, most of them reading speeches written by professional speech writers who are paid by the government, is an international scandal."

The word has long been used in a political context. In 1880, *Harper's Weekly* described a "unit rule" (see GAG RULE) as "a muzzle and gag unworthy of honorable men."

The case is often made that the public has a RIGHT TO KNOW the differences of opinion within the military establishment; Administration officials feel that a general's overt lobbying for a change in policy encroaches on civilian control of the military.

Despite "the word" from the White House, generals and admirals—usually retired, but occasionally on active duty—find a way to leak their points of view to correspondents they trust. As George W. Bush discovered when a group of retired military officers spoke out against the conduct of the war in Iraq, a muzzle prevents a dog from biting and barking, but not from growling.

my (use of possessive pronoun) Used as in "my ambassador," either a slip of the tongue leading to an attack for royalist tendencies, or a deliberate presidential effort to undercut the State Department.

In the campaign of 1940, Franklin Roosevelt referred to Joseph P. Kennedy, Ambassador to the Court of St. James's, as "my ambassador," a phrase which the Republicans promptly pounced on as proof of his dictatorial ambitions in their "no third term" drive. Similarly, in 1966, Lyndon Johnson played into Republican hands with a reference to "my Congress," giving Richard Nixon an opportunity to flay the "do-anything Congress," a play on Harry Truman's DO-NOTHING CONGRESS.

Abraham Lincoln was attacked in 1858 for his use of "I" in speeches. The *Burlington Gazette* wrote, "he is known all over Suckerdom by the name of 'the Perpendicular pronoun.'" (On *Suckerdom*: Illinois was nicknamed "the Sucker State," its residents known as "suckers." This fell into disuse for various reasons.) But President Andrew Johnson drew the most fire on the subject—the *Cleveland Press* made a count of personal and possessive pronouns in an 1866 Johnson speech: "This humble individual, one; myself, two; me, nine; my, 28; I, 69. That's not much, only 109 allusions to himself in a 15 minute speech... President Johnson is a my-ty man."

Although John F. Kennedy did not refer to "my" ambassadors in any speech, Arthur Schlesinger, Jr., made this point: "He felt this [the State Department] in some particular sense 'his' department... in the relationship between the President and the ambassadors, there had been, it is true, a slippage since Roosevelt's day. Roosevelt regarded them correctly as 'my' ambassadors and encouraged them to supplement their reports to the State Department by personal communication with him." Ambassadors like Kenneth Galbraith in India and George Kennan in Yugoslavia often communicated directly with President Kennedy.

Dwight Eisenhower, a team player, consciously avoided the possessive pronoun. "I don't believe," wrote reporter Robert Donovan, "that Eisenhower has ever used the expression 'my administration' or 'my cabinet.' He speaks of *the* Cabinet or *the* administration." A speech General Eisenhower made in 1945 in New York City at a dinner in his honor as a war hero suggests that his selection or rejection of the personal pronoun had always been deliberate: "You have great hospitals in your city that are filled with wounded men. I call them 'my wounded men'; they came back from my theatre. I don't want to see any more of them there, ever."

my friends FDR's use of a salutation to establish quickly a personal bond between himself and his audience.

Running for the New York State Senate in 1910, Franklin Roosevelt admired the way his fellow campaigner, Richard Connell, running for U.S. congressman in that area, established quick rapport with his listeners. FDR copied Connell's "My friends" for that and subsequent campaigns, but the phrase became identified with him because of the lilt of his pronunciation and the special requirement for warmth in radio addresses. No longer was the audience "vast" and "out there"; most listeners were in small groups in their own living rooms, and FDR pressed the intimacy with frequent use of "you and I know ..."

Roosevelt probably did not know of the trouble the phrase caused for one of his predecessors as governor of New York, Horatio Seymour. When, trying to calm a group of draft rioters at City Hall in 1863, he opened his remarks with "My friends," Republicans attacked him for being unduly friendly to those "COPPERHEADS" who opposed the Civil War.

Salutations are dismissed as mere formalities by most speakers, which (as Seymour discovered) is a mistake. Abraham Lincoln chose his salutations with great care: to the citizens of Springfield, Illinois, upon his departure, he used "My friends," because many of them were his lifelong friends and neighbors; at Gettysburg he used no salutation at all, appropriate in that atmosphere of solemnity; in his inaugural addresses he said "Fellow countrymen," which, along with "My countrymen," was long traditional for inaugurals. Not any more; to avoid sexism, it has become *my fellow Americans* or *fellow citizens*. Even before that, however, *fellow countrymen* came under fire for its redundancy.

In 1781 John Witherspoon, president of Princeton (and coiner of AMERICANISM in its sense of "a word peculiarly American") unsuccessfully made the case against "fellow countrymen" as a salutation, decrying its "very frequent use in America. It has been heard in public orations from men of the first character, and may be daily seen in newspaper publications. It is an evident tautology, for the last word expresses fully the meaning of both. If you open any dictionary you will find the word *countryman* signifies one born in the same country. You may say fellow citizens, fellow soldiers, fellow subjects, fellow Christians, but not fellow countrymen."

Napoleon gave a martial ring to his addresses and messages to his troops: a simple, forceful "Soldiers!" By contrast, the Selective Service system bureaucratically addressed its soldiers-to-be with a ludicrous "Greeting" (not "Greetings," but a draftee became known as one who "got his greetings").

Lenin made "Comrades" famous to the point where all Communists were called, often derisively, comrades.

Chief Tecumseh addressed General "Tippecanoe" Harrison with a translation of a dignified American Indian greeting: "Friend and Brother." Members of the American labor movement address letters to each other as "Dear Sir and Brother," harking back to more fraternal times.

Jefferson chose "Friends and fellow citizens," and both William Howard Taft and John F. Kennedy preferred "Fellow citizens," with Harry Truman and Dwight Eisenhower leaning toward "My fellow Americans." During the 1940 campaign, Republican nominee Wendell Willkie made "fellow Americans" his own, rasping out his hoarse "Feller Amurrricans ..."

The most effective "example" of the use of a salutation as a weapon is supposedly the opening of Franklin Roosevelt's speech to the Daughters of the American Revolution following a dispute about the DAR's emphasis on white Anglo-Saxon lineage. FDR did *not* begin his speech, as legend has it, with "Fellow immigrants." The closest he came to this was a line in his speech to the DAR of April 21, 1938: "Remember, remember always, that all of us, and you and I especially, are descended from immigrants and revolutionists."

myth Frozen point of view attacked by John Kennedy; later, ironically, used to describe the aura of legend around Kennedy.

"Myths Respecting American Government" was the title of a speech given by President John F. Kennedy at Yale University, June 11, 1962. "Mythology distracts us everywhere—in government as in business, in politics as in economics, in foreign affairs as in domestic policy." In considering the "myth and reality in our national economy," he said that the dialogue between business and government was "clogged by illusion and platitude," adding, "For the great enemy of the truth is very often not the lie—deliberate, contrived and dishonest—but the myth, persistent, persuasive and unrealistic. Too often we hold fast to the clichés of our forebears. We subject all facts to a prefabricated set of interpretations. We enjoy the comfort of opinion without the discomfort of thought."

Senator J. William Fulbright picked up the "myth and reality" theme in a foreign-affairs context two years later: "We are clinging to old myths in the face of new realities, and we are seeking to escape the contradictions by narrowing the permissible bounds of public discussion, by relegating an increasing number of ideas and viewpoints to a growing category of 'UNTHINKABLE THOUGHTS.'" "Included among the "old myths" in this speech (which became expanded into a book titled *Old Myths and New Realities*) were U.S. policies regarding Cuba, Panama, and Vietnam.

Critics of Kennedy also liked the *myth* phraseology. Author Victor Lasky published a scathing attack on Kennedy in 1963 titled *JFK: The Man and the Myth*. The book was climbing on the best-seller lists until November, when it was withdrawn after the assassination, not to be marketed again for nearly fifteen years. With the martyrdom of a youthful president, the Kennedy mystique or image did soon achieve near-mythic proportions. The liberal columnist Tom Wicker refused to go along:

> For my part, I reject the myth…I refuse to believe that any but a particular light went out…Above all, in Kennedy's case or any other, I refuse to deny the harsh reality of death—that life goes on anyway, not unchanged, for the death of any man must diminish the sum of humanity, but undaunted, unabated in all its glory and misery. That is the meaning of the "ghastly futility" at Dallas. That is what the Kennedy myth distorts.

N

nabob See NATTERING NABOBS OF NEGATIVISM.

nation of shopkeepers Derisive description of England; meant to imply small-minded, business-dominated, greedy people.

Earliest known use was not in a pejorative sense. Josiah Tucker, Dean of Gloucester Cathedral (1712–68), wrote in 1763: "What is true of a Shop-keeper is true of a Shop-keeping nation."

The phrase was given currency in 1776 by Adam Smith in *The Wealth of Nations:* "To found a great empire for the sole purpose of raising up a people of customers may at first sight appear a project fit only for a nation of shopkeepers. It is, however, a project altogether unfit for a nation of shopkeepers; but extremely fit for a nation whose Government is influenced by shopkeepers."

The phrase was probably already in current usage when Smith used it; on August 1, 1776, American revolutionary Samuel Adams reportedly said in Philadelphia: "Men who content themselves with the semblance of truth and a display of words talk much of our obligations to Great Britain for protection. Had she a single eye to our advantage? A nation of shopkeepers are very seldom so disinterested. Let us not be so amused with words; the extension of commerce was her object."

The phrase became secure in the political lexicon when it was attributed to Napoleon Bonaparte by his physician in exile on St. Helena, Barry O'Meara: *"L'Angleterre est une nation de boutiquiers"* ("England is a nation of shopkeepers").

Does the phrase apply to the United Kingdom today? Dr. Tim Leunig, lecturer in economic history at the London School of Economics, did a study of business growth and decline within Yellow Pages classifications from 1992 to 2002. He found that greengrocers had dropped by 59%, butchers 40%, and hardware retailers 34%. While these traditional "shopkeep-ers" were down, he found that purveyors of "lifestyle classifications" had boomed; these included aromatherapy, cosmetic surgery and services, weight control, saunas, and sunbeds. "The areas of growth," concluded Dr. Leunig, "are things that make us feel better about ourselves." Headline on the school's press release: "The UK is a nation of shopkeepers no longer."

nattering nabobs of negativism An updated version of a denunciation of pessimists as PROPHETS OF GLOOM AND DOOM.

In the congressional campaigns of 1970, alliteration was one device Vice President Spiro T. Agnew used to call attention to his speeches. "Pusillanimous pussyfoot-ers" and "vicars of vacillation" were his targets, and the phrases had a ring that reporters could not ignore. After the fascinated response to the first few speeches, the looked-for alliteration was delivered tongue-in-cheek, culminating in a display of oratorical pyrotechnics in San Diego on September 11, 1970. Working with the Vice President on that speech, this writer offered a choice of alliterations about naysaying to parallel the Stevenson "gloom and doom" phrase, but the VP chose to go with both: "In the United States today, we have more than our share of the nattering nabobs of negativism. They have formed their own 4-H Club—the 'hopeless, hysterical hypo-chondriacs of history.'"

As intended, the line got a laugh from the audience, but was taken seriously by James Reston of *The New York Times*, a frequent tennis partner of Agnew, who called it "the worst example of alliteration in American history." (See Harding's "not nostrums but normalcy, not revolution but restoration, not agitation but adjustment…not experiment but equipoise …" under ALLITERATION.) Columnist William F. Buckley Jr. picked it up to apply to the British Prime Minister's problems over the sale of arms to South

Africa: "Heath's point was that he has not been elected Her Majesty's first minister in order to take orders on matters affecting English security from nattering nabobs of negativism."

In the construction of the phrase, the outlook—*negativism*—was the key word. A practitioner of that outlook, beginning with *n*, was added next; *nabob* is from an Urdu word for "governor," and the word in English has come to mean a self-important potentate, carrying a jocular connotation. (See John Adams' 1776 use under SACHEM.) *Nattering*, the offbeat adjective that made the phrase memorable, was the last to be found, and its meaning of "complaining" was disputed by columnist Stewart Alsop, the author's pundit-mentor, who believed the word was of British origin and meant "chattering," as in CHATTERING CLASSES, a derogation of the hyperarticulate media, academic, and think-tank types known in the U.S. as "talking heads."

The reason this entry is written with such dreary authority is that this lexicographer was the coiner, while serving as a speechwriter-on-loan from the President to Mr. Agnew in the fall of 1970. The unwritten Speechwriters' Code of the Judson Welliver Society of Former White House Speechwriters, which frowns on writers who claim their clients' prose as their own, is suspended in this case because the disgraced former Vice President publicly ascribed the phrase to this writer; it requires me to deny repeatedly authorship of other Agnevian gems such as "effete corps of impudent snobs" (see EFFETE SNOBS), "When you've seen one slum, you've seen 'em all," and INSTANT ANALYSIS.

The phrase was later used self-mockingly and aimed derisively at politicians who whine about negative treatment in the media. From the *Washington Star* of December 20, 1977: "Ray Blanton, the Tennessee governor who's constantly being castigated by political rivals as well as those nattering nabobs of negativism, the media . . . says he's not going to answer reporters' questions any longer 'unless you report the positive side.'"

The phrase helped repopularize *nabob*, and the word—one cut below a *nizam* in Urdu—is now synonymous with SATRAP,

PANJANDRUM, POOH-BAH, high MUCKEY-MUCKS and other members of the POWER ELITE. But some writers have to be different: in *The New York Times Magazine* in 1978, humorist S. J. Perelman used the original Urdu word—*nawab*—in a description of the patrons of Manhattan's "21" Club:

> Here congregated tycoon and political nawab, screen idol and press overlord, rock star and capo of capos, secure in the knowledge that no losers were present. Here the illuminati rubbed elbows with the cognoscenti, publishers rubbed knees with nascent lady novelists, male dress designers rubbed thighs and spat at each other like cats. The drumfire of epigrams and the bray of egotism were rising to sawmill pitch . . .

The technique of dismissing doomsayers with alliteration goes on: President Clinton in 1993 denounced the "preachers of pessimism." In 2006, Victor Gold, who had been Spiro Agnew's press secretary, noted a use of the n-n-n phrase in *The New Yorker*, and wrote to the editor: "While the phrase was indeed coined by William Safire during Agnew's 1970 mid-term campaign, it referred not to the Administration's press critics but to Democratic members of the U.S. Senate, specifically Senators Kennedy, Fulbright, and Montoya, with Larry O'Brien, then the D.N.C. chairman, thrown in to complete the '4-H Club—the hopeless, hysterical hypochondriacs of history.'"

natural rights Freedoms inherent in humanhood; the birthright of autonomous individuals, which can be extended to government for purposes of the protection and development of society.

This term from Western philosophy, sometimes expressed in the singular, entered the political vocabulary in a 1689 translation of a treatise by the Dutch philosopher Baruch Spinoza: "In Democratical Government, no man so transfers his own Natural Right to another, as for ever after to be excluded from consultation, but only transfers it upon the major part of the Society, of which he still makes one."

The ancient idea, known to the Greeks, was further developed by John Locke and Jean-Jacques Rousseau. It became a central part of Thomas Jefferson's philosophy, expressed as *unalienable rights* (which some stylists believed should be *inalienable rights*), including "life, liberty and the pursuit of happiness" in the Declaration of Independence.

Thomas Paine enlarged upon the theme, further enumerating these privileges in his 1791 tract on *The Rights of Man*: "the natural and imprescriptible rights of man; and these rights are liberty, property, security, and resistance of oppression." These were in contradistinction to the "divine right of kings."

THIRD WORLD countries have asserted natural rights as well, often in the sense of entitlement to the earth's resources and the technological wealth of industrialized nations. *National Journal* stated in a 1977 commentary on nuclear energy: "Many developing countries regard the possession of the world's most advanced technology as their natural right."

Still current in democratic debate, the phrase (both singular and plural) was used by Senator Gordon J. Humphrey, a conservative from New Hampshire, in a 1989 statement on freedom of speech: The Bill of Rights, he said, protects "the natural right to speak one's mind, however offensive that may be to the hearer.... It is a precious right, this binding the power of government so it cannot begin to interfere in the natural rights of any human being."

The subject arose during the controversial Senate Judiciary Committee hearings in 1991 on the nomination of Clarence Thomas to the Supreme Court. "One of the more curious displays of cultural illiteracy," editorialized *The New York Times*, despite its opposition to the Thomas nomination, "has been the consternation and bafflement created by Judge Clarence Thomas's expressions of esteem for 'natural law.' For some of the critics, it was as though the man had let slip a reference to torture by thumbscrews." The liberal Harvard Law Professor Laurence Tribe came back with this: "My objection is not necessarily to 'natural law' thinking, which I agree has a venerable history and much to commend it. My concern is with how Judge Thomas deploys

natural-law approaches. He lavishes praise on an essay [by Lewis Lehrman] that uses 'natural law' to insist that all abortions must be outlawed as murder because the fetus has 'natural rights.'" In his hearings, Judge Thomas defused the issue by saying, "My interest in exploring natural law and natural rights was purely in the context of political theory."

See HUMAN RIGHTS.

Neanderthal wing See DINOSAUR WING.

negative advertising See DAISY SPOT; -BASH-ING; SWIFT BOAT SPOT.

neoconservativism A political philosophy that rejects the utopianism and egalitarianism espoused in liberalism, but departs from conservatism by embracing collective insurance and cash payments to the needy; a philosophy that takes modern democratic capitalism to be exemplary and exportable, with the active furtherance of freedom abroad to be the best course in most cases.

Neoconservatism (the word triumphed over "the new conservatism") was spawned in the pages of a quarterly, *The Public Interest*, edited by Irving Kristol and Daniel Bell, published by Warren Manshel, and frequently contributed to by Daniel Patrick Moynihan and Seymour Martin Lipset. These former liberals were troubled by the failures of Lyndon Johnson's "Great Society" and dismayed at the way political orders throughout the world—especially the social democracies—were becoming statist and simultaneously less stable. When Keynesian economics began to fail to contain inflation, neoconservatives felt the economic basis for social democracy as it has been practiced began to erode. The last straw for many of the lifelong Democrats was the strident discontent of the youthful counterculture of the sixties, which made liberal elders uncomfortable with the culture that produced it.

As it became fashionable all along the political spectrum to be alienated by "big government," that cultural chasm between NEW LEFT and "old" left widened: many of the former liberals could not stomach what they saw as the social permissiveness, national self-flagellation and rejection of individual responsibility so often espoused by the inheritors of liberalism.

What distinguished neoconservatism from the "old" conservatism? The novel feature of the new conservatism is a relaxed attitude toward collective responsibility: "A welfare state, properly conceived," wrote Irving Kristol in *The American Spectator* in 1977, "can be an integral part of a conservative society." Such a statement is heresy to traditional conservatives; they hold that conservatism teaches that statism leads to a repression of individuality. But Kristol plunged ahead: "It is antisocialist, of course... but it is not upset by the fact that in a populous, complex, and affluent society, people may prefer to purchase certain goods and services collectively rather than individually... People will always want security as much as they want liberty, and the nineteenth-century liberal-individualist notion that life for all of us should be an enterprise at continual risk is doctrinaire fantasy."

Kristol, his wife Gertrude Himmelfarb, and their son William (founder and editor of *The Weekly Standard*, more politically partisan than the forerunning *Public Interest*) saw liberal institutions such as Social Security to be bulwarks against further socialization. Many of their intellectual followers hope the effect of their movement will be to remove utopian dreams from practical government. To the socialists (who want to center more power in the state), as well as to the "old" conservatives (who want to place more reliance on the individual), neoconservatives say that the system the U.S. has now evolved—while not, in Voltaire's phrase, "the best of all possible worlds"—is the best of all available worlds, and well worth not only defending but extending.

An early use of the term was by James Schall in *Time* magazine on August 23, 1971: "Judaism and Christianity have always placed primacy in man. Now this primacy is attacked by what I call the neoconservative ecological approach to life." Senator Moynihan recalled to the author that it was Michael Harrington, writer on poverty, who popularized the term at about that time in its present context.

In foreign policy, most neoconservatives from liberal cultural backgrounds parted company with their longtime colleagues on dealing with the threat of world Communism. They drew ideological fire from accomodationist friends as they aligned themselves with Ronald Reagan HARD-LINERS. After the Soviet Union collapsed after being, in the neocon view, economically stressed by the U.S. arms buildup and encouragement of dissidents, the neocons were in the policy ascendancy.

After Iraqi dictator Saddam Hussein invaded Kuwait, threatening pan-Arab conquest and endangering world oil supplies, neocons applauded George H.W. Bush's "line in the sand" and the end of the VIETNAM SYNDROME; the fact that many neocon leaders were Jews led to angry accusations from some on the far right as well as the far left that they put Israel's interests first (see AMEN CORNER). In 2002, when most intelligence reports indicated that Saddam was preparing a comeback with associations with Al Qaeda, suspected development of weapons of mass destruction, and mounting human rights abuses within Iraq, neoconservatives in think tanks and the media were in the forefront of those supporting President George W. Bush's argument for REGIME CHANGE. However, as the expected similarly short conflict became "the long war," public anger at the conduct of the war tarnished the neoconservative, idealistic "freedom agenda"; REALISM was soon in the public-policy saddle, and in 2006 war-weariness was a primary cause of the change in the majorities in House and Senate. The national debate then centered on the Administration's plan to STAY THE COURSE, a phrase reviled by the anti-war majority, versus CUT AND RUN, a counterattack phrase by neocons and other HAWKS opposing withdrawal as a form of surrender.

Among political journalists, the word is now almost always clipped to *neo-cons*, often without the hyphen—more a description of the articulators of the embattled foreign policy than of the policy itself. The clipped version, *neocon*, is often taken to be synonymous with "rightwing hawk." In the opening stages in 2007 of the Democratic presidential primary season, Senator Barack Obama, who made a point of having opposed the Iraq war from the start, was widely seen as a liberal dove; when criticized for this as being "naïve" by Hillary Clinton, he sternly took aim at Pakistan's president: "If we have actionable intelligence about high-value terrorist targets and President Musharraf will not act, we will." The gleeful *Wall Street Journal* editorial headline: "Barack Obama, Neocon."

nepotism See DYNASTY.

nervous Nellies The easily upset; President Lyndon Johnson's characterization of some critics of his Vietnam policy.

In old American slang, the word *nervous* acquired the connotation of cowardly; "nervous in the service," Army slang, meant a psychological disorder leading to a medical discharge—a "Section 8"—as well as a milder impatience or "itchiness." The term was introduced into politics during the 1923 Senate conformation as Ambassador to Great Britain of Frank Kellogg, who later served Calvin Coolidge as Secretary of State; an Ohio newspaper welcomed "the chastening to which Ambassador Designate Kellogg, known as 'Nervous Nellie,' will be subjected in the Senate by Messrs La Follette, Shipstead et al ..."

On May 17, 1966, President Johnson spoke of "some Nervous Nellies and some who will become frustrated and bothered and break ranks under the strain. And some will turn on their own leaders and their own country, and on our own fighting men." LBJ's repeated use of "some" differentiated between "Nervous Nellies" and other dissenters, but the catchphrase was so strong that many critics of the policy soon used it as though Johnson had so labeled all anti-involvement or anti-escalation forces. A year later, the President added fuel to the fire with a remark about "cussers and doubters."

"Nervous Nellies" was parodied so often by opponents of the war in Vietnam that it became part of the Johnson Adminis-

tration lore, and was included in a satiric song by joyful journalists in a Gridiron Club revue. To the tune of "A Wand'ring Minstrel, I," a reporter portraying Henry Kissinger sang:

A wandering merchant, I
Who deals in confrontation
Detente and consternation
And schemes that mystify.
Bismarck and Metternich
and me and Machiavelli
I'm not a Nervous Nelly ...

In a taped conversation with Richard Nixon during the late stages of the Vietnam war, Rep. Gerald Ford said he was not among the "sunshine soldiers and summer patriots," a slightly garbled version of Thomas Paine's "summer soldiers and sunshine patriots" who did not shrink from service to their country. In May 1992, an anonymous White House aide was quoted on the faltering start of the elder Bush's re-election campaign: "It's Nervous Nellies that get unnerved this early in the game and depart from the track you're on." During the second Iraq war, members of President George W. Bush's Administration avoided the term with its boomeranging connotation, and instead denounced "DEFEATISTS" who would "CUT AND RUN."

The collocation is not limited to politics. A 2007 *Washington Post* piece about opposite methods of preparing for a vacation trip began, "I never thought of myself as a travel wuss" and was headlined "Nervous Nellie vs. Mr. Wing-It." A related term, *Nice Nellie*, is slang for "prude." (*Wuss*, a play on *puss*, is a vaginal vulgarity.)

netroots Liberal wing of the blogosphere, as contrasted with the slower developing conservative *Rightroots*.

"You've heard the story," observed Perry Bacon, Jr., in *Time* magazine in September 2006: "the Netroots, the Democratic Party's equivalent of a punk garage band—edgy, loud and antiauthoritarian—are suddenly on the verge of the big time. The gang of liberal bloggers and online activists who helped raise millions of dollars for Howard Dean's presidential campaign two years ago are now said to be Democratic KINGMAKERS."

Netroots, a portmanteau of *Internet* and *grassroots*, was popularized by Jerome Armstrong, on his blog, MyDD, starting Dec. 18, 2002, when he went to work on Vermont governor Howard Dean's presidential campaign. He headed his entry that day: "Netroots for Dean in 2004." In his 2006 book, *Crashing the Gate: Netroots, Grassroots, and the Rise of People-Powered Politics*, co-authored with Markos Moulitsas, Armstrong claims credit for coining the term.

Actually, Armstrong re-invented *netroots*, not knowing that it had been used a decade before. The earliest example that I have found is in a Jan. 15, 1993, message on the newsgroup bit.listserv.words-l. Apparently complaining about a shake-up at the University of California at San Diego, "rmcdonell" (identified by etymologist Ben Zimmer as Robert McDonell, a student at UCSD in the early '90s) wrote: "Too bad there's no netroots organization that can demand more than keyboard accountability from those who claim to be acting on behalf of the 'greater good' when they do things like this."

Armstrong insists that *netroots* does not have a political coloration: "The term netroots is ideologically and politically neutral." Most observers differ. While the *netroots* in 2007 may total less than six million people (*Time*'s estimate), a small number in national political terms, the sheer volume of their postings appeared to push Democratic candidates leftward. *Time*'s early assessment: "Moderate Democrats say it with remorse, conservatives with glee, but the conventional wisdom is bipartisan: progressive bloggers are pushing the Democratic Party so far to the left that it will have no chance of capturing the presidency in 2008."

GRASSROOTS started off in politics as a populist term, however, associated with the "Bull Moose" convention of 1912 and Theodore Roosevelt's break with the Republican Party. Today, *grassroots* is neutral. Over time, *netroots* also may gravitate toward the center.

neutralist A nation that refused alignment with either Communist bloc or Western bloc, acting as mediator between, or beneficiary of, both.

Laotian Premier Souvanna Phouma defined the art of being a neutralist in 1961: "I am a good friend to Communists abroad but I do not like them at home." *Neutral*—applied to Sweden and Switzerland during World War II—differed from *neutralist*, *uncommitted*, or *nonaligned* nation. In the U.S., *neutral* is considered merely "non-belligerent," but *neutralist* (a term most Americans used with a pejorative connotation) was a nation that did not understand the threat of world Communism, or that cooperated with the U.S. only when it suited its immediate interests and was not a good "ally" in a pinch.

That was a far cry from Woodrow Wilson's explanation of U.S. neutrality in 1915: "The basis of neutrality is not indifference; it is not self-interest. The basis of neutrality is sympathy for mankind. It is fairness, it is good will, at bottom. It is impartiality of spirit and of judgment."

About the same time, Italy's Benito Mussolini was saying: "Neutrals never dominate events. They always sink. Blood alone moves the wheels of history."

Neutralism was sometimes called "the THIRD WAY" in 1957, until its replacement by THIRD WORLD. (The former resurfaced in Britain in the 1990s as Labor's domestic-policy slogan.) When superpower confrontation ended in the early '90s, the end of the COLD WAR sent *neutralism* into the deep freeze.

neutrality See SCRAP OF PAPER.

never again See HOLOCAUST.

never lost a war or won a peace A frequent criticism, by the "out" party, of peace negotiations

Will Rogers' lugubrious assessment of U.S. postwar diplomacy in the decade after World War I: "The United States has never lost a war or won a peace." See WINNING THE PEACE.

The point of view simultaneously carries a banner of patriotism and a partisan lance leveled at the bungling peacemakers who "sold out" our national interests.

Some Republicans bitterly attacked Woodrow Wilson for advocating U.S. entry into the League of Nations. After World War II, Republicans were suspicious of "secret agreements" purportedly made with Joseph Stalin at Yalta by President Roosevelt.

Thomas E. Dewey made the debatable point in 1950:

> During the First World War we said we wanted nothing for ourselves and nothing is what we got. In the Second World War again we said we wanted nothing and again nothing is what we got. At other times in our history we have known what we wanted and got it. Consider the War of 1812. The actual hostilities were indecisive and often humiliating for us. But at the peace conference which produced the Treaty of Ghent, the United States won a very advantageous frontier with Canada and all the other national objects for which we had fought. That was a war we did not win but we won the peace.

There is substance to the observation that the U.S. has been more successful in warmaking than peacemaking. Canadian Prime Minister Lester Pearson, in receiving the Nobel Peace Prize in 1957, gave one reason: "The grim fact is that we prepare for war like precocious giants and for peace like retarded pygmies."

new, political use of No word stands out like *new* in the framing of themes for political movements.

Clement Laird Vallandigham, Ohio Democrat banished to the Confederacy during the Civil War for his dissent as a COPPERHEAD, in 1871 stirred his party with his NEW DEPARTURE: "It is not a New Departure but a Return: the restoration of the Democratic party once more to the ancient platform of Progress and Reform." Despite the disclaimer, the phrase caught on and helped rejuvenate the staggered Democrats.

Theodore Roosevelt, known for the SQUARE DEAL, also pressed his NEW NATIONALISM in 1912: "This New Nationalism regards the executive power as the steward of the public welfare." Woodrow Wilson followed by entitling the collection of his campaign speeches "the NEW FREEDOM," taken from this line: "And the day is at hand when it shall be realized on this consecrated soil—a New

Freedom—a Liberty widened and deepened to match the broadened life of man in America ..." Roosevelt, as the "Bull Moose" independent candidate, knew a good slogan when he heard one, and quickly tried to put it down: " 'The New Freedom' is nothing whatever but the right of the strong to prey on the weak."

The Wilson phrase clicked, and spawned a wide range of others: the New Poetry, the New History, the New Art, the New Democracy, the New Woman—"the new anything," wrote historian Eric Goldman, "so long as it was new and gave an intoxicating sense of freedom."

As Adolf Hitler was talking of a *New Order*, Franklin Roosevelt was expounding the NEW DEAL, in the campaign of 1960 John F. Kennedy talked of a NEW FRONTIER, and Edmund Muskie in 1972 called for a *New Beginning*. Adlai Stevenson captured that theme in a 1956 address: "There is a *New America* every morning when we wake up. ... The New America is the sum of many small changes—a new subdivision here, a new school there, a new industry where there had been swampland—changes that add up to a broad transformation of our lives ..."

In President Jimmy Carter's inaugural address, he invoked a "new spirit" several times, but the time was evidently not ripe for the phrase. Ronald Reagan called for a "new beginning"; George Bush had some success with NEW WORLD ORDER, but that was promptly parodied as "new world disorder" as local wars broke out. Bill Clinton, described as a "New Democrat," used "New Covenant" nine times in his Inaugural address, but that phrase, with its biblical connotation, never got off the ground.

See GREAT, POLITICAL USE OF.

new American revolution See REVOLUTION OF RISING EXPECTATIONS.

new broom See SPOILS SYSTEM; CLEAN SWEEP.

new class The technical and managerial elite.

Communist doctrine taught that with the destruction of capitalism, a classless society would emerge. That did not happen in the Soviet Union; what emerged instead was a bureaucracy of party and government which substituted power and perquisites for money, and enabled an elite to enjoy luxuries that capitalists use money to buy.

The phrase was coined by Yugoslav Communist Milovan Djilas, in his 1957 book *The New Class: An Analysis of the Communist System*. Djilas, harassed and jailed by Marshal Tito, held that "the new class, the bureaucracy, or more accurately the political bureaucracy, has all the characteristics of earlier ones ... the Party makes the class, but the class grows as a result and uses the Party as a basis. The class grows stronger, while the Party grows weaker; this is the inescapable fate of every Communist party in power." The same could be said of the oligarchy-KGB complex that emerged after Russia's brief moment of post-Soviet democracy.

In the early '70s, Professor Irving Kristol and other NEOCONSERVATIVES used the phrase to describe the academic-technical-governmental-foundation elite that sought to represent and to help, but not be a part of, the working class in the U.S.

A related term is TECHNOCRAT, a backformation from *technocracy*, an intellectual movement in the early '30s that argued for the replacement of consumer-dominated capitalism with an economic system that gave its priority to production at capacity. Because of its similarity to *bureaucrat*, with the lowering of public regard for that occupation, the word *technocrat* gained a mechanical and bloodless connotation. In the '70s Zbigniew Brzezinski, who became Jimmy Carter's National Security Adviser, coined "the technitronic age" to herald the new society ahead, but that phrase never caught on.

Well-educated managers and students of the newest *new class*—whether technocrats, computer geeks, Microsoft-Google-Yahoo entrepreneurs, or members of the academic CHARLES RIVER GANG—are sometimes distrusted by "privacy nuts" and throwbacks to nineteenth-century Luddites worried about machines and computers having too much to do with their personal lives.

New Deal Franklin D. Roosevelt's program, enunciated in his acceptance speech at the 1932 Democratic convention; since divided into First New Deal (1933–35) and Second (1935–37).

"I pledge you," Roosevelt told the convention, "I pledge myself, to a new deal for the American people. Let us all here assembled constitute ourselves prophets of a new order of competence and of courage. This is more than a political campaign; it is a call to arms. Give me your help, not to win votes alone, but to win in this crusade to restore America to its own people."

This brief peroration, drafted by Samuel Rosenman, offered commentators four possibilities for a slogan: "new order," which became known as Adolf Hitler's program; "CRUSADE," which became Dwight Eisenhower's theme; "call to arms," which was never picked up by anybody; and "new deal."

On the day of the speech, cartoonist Rollin Kirby drew a sketch of a man leaning on a hoe, looking bewildered but hopeful, watching an airplane flying overhead labeled "New Deal." This was an indication to the Roosevelt forces and the Democratic National Committee that they had an exciting catchphrase. (Cartoonists can do much to propagate a phrase; see MCCARTHYISM.)

"I had not the slightest idea that it would take hold the way it did," wrote Rosenman later, "nor did the Governor [Roosevelt] when he read and revised what I had written. In fact, he attached no importance to the two monosyllables.... Some have said that it was intended to be a combination of the SQUARE DEAL of President Theodore Roosevelt and the NEW FREEDOM of President Woodrow Wilson. There was no such intention when it was written or when it was delivered ... when I handed him the scrap of paper on which the few paragraphs had been written he said that he thought they were all right as a peroration.... It was simply one of those phrases that catch public fancy and survive—short, concise, and yet comprehensive enough to cover a great many different concepts."

Other versions of the origin exist. Both Judge Rosenman and Professor Raymond Moley reviewed some of the Roosevelt entries in this book, and in this case, these were Professor Moley's comments to the lexicographer:

You will find an account of the preparation of the acceptance speech on pages 23–27 inclusive in my "After Seven Years." When Rosenman says that he wrote it he is in error. The expression "new deal" was in the draft which I left at Albany with Roosevelt. What happened at Albany was not the rewriting of the speech but a rearrangement of it in a somewhat shortened version. If you will look at the exhibit opposite page 14 in my book you will see where the expression appeared first. I merely put this in to carry out the rhythm of the sentences at that point.

Of course, I have in my possession the original drafts before Rosenman and Roosevelt worked on them in Albany and some of the original drafts have Roosevelt's notations on them. I was not aware that this would be the slogan of the campaign. It was a phrase that would have occurred to almost anyone, and it certainly did not come from the book written by Stuart Chase, for I had not seen the book at that time.

The first person who spotted the importance of the phrase was Herbert Bayard Swope, who wrote a letter to me immediately after the speech was delivered, saying that it should be pulled out and made the keynote of the campaign. I don't know about Rollin Kirby's cartoon. Later Roosevelt allowed the New Deal legend to be embellished by pointing to Mark Twain's Connecticut Yankee, who said that "when six men out of a thousand crack the whip over their fellows' backs, then what the other nine hundred ninety four dupes need is a new deal."

See CARD METAPHORS.

British reporters pointed out that "A New Deal for Everyone" was David Lloyd George's campaign slogan in 1919, one year before FDR ran unsuccessfully for vice president. Other phrase hunters came up with a few lines from a Woodrow Wilson speech on October 24, 1910: "If it is reorganization, a new deal and a change you are seeking, it is HOBSON'S CHOICE. I am sorry for you, but it is really vote for me or not vote at all." Robert La Follette had written in his 1912 autobiography that his Committee of 100 "believe that the time has come for a new deal," and Carl Schurz had used it several times in the previous century, as in this 1871 citation that puts the phrase in quotation marks: "There were the spoils ahead, with the prospect of a 'new deal.'" The humorist Petroleum V. Nasby wrote a year after Lincoln's assassination: "Wilkes Booth's ghost came in, and wanted to know what he wuz to hev in the new deal, 'for,' sed he, 'ef't hadn't been for me, where'd yoo all hev bin?'" And Nicholas Biddle, head of the Bank of the U.S., received a letter in Andrew Jackson's day calling for "a new bank and a New Deal." Further search seems unrewarding.

Around the time the speech was delivered, Stuart Chase had written an article in *The New Republic* titled "A New Deal for America," which Rosenman does not recall ever having seen. Suffice it to say the phrase was in the air and meant little until it was given the context of the man, time, and place. Indeed, "time and place" without the significant source meant nothing; on that same day and from that same rostrum, speaking several hours before Roosevelt, John McDuffie of Alabama nominated John Nance Garner for Vice President with the words: "There is a demand for a new deal in the management of the affairs of the American people."

The phrase was promptly parodied as "New Dole," "Raw Deal," and even "Jew Deal"; a generation later, Adlai Stevenson characterized Dwight Eisenhower's cabinet, made up mostly of businessmen, as "The Big Deal," and George Romney called Lyndon Johnson's administration "The Fast Deal." See DEAL.

Columnist Russell Baker wrote the lexicographer after publication of the first edition of this dictionary about another possible source for the term:

The phrase is used several times by Henry James in "The Princess Casamassima" (1886), which I believe is Henry's only political novel. Reading the book, I became conscious of "new deal" recurring in the characters' discussion of the revolutionary political future they anticipate. In Chapter 34, for example, the Princess— an uptown dilettante of revolution—says, "I'm one of those who believe that a great new deal is destined to take place and that it can't make things worse than they are already."

I note your earlier reference from Petroleum Nasby in 1866, but James's coming up with it in London 20 years later makes me wonder if the phrase was a political commonplace among political malcontents in the late nineteenth century. James had no first-hand experience of political people when he set out to write "The Princess," so in his thorough manner spent a lot of time eavesdropping in workingmen's hangouts and talking to people who were involved in politics, to familiarize himself with the lingo.

new departure A recurrent phrase urging a fresh approach, based on a nautical metaphor. See SHIP OF STATE.

Senator John C. Calhoun of South Carolina used *new departure* frequently in the 1830s: "My aim is fixed, to take a fresh start, a new departure on the States Rights Republican tack." *Tack* is a sailing term; Massachusetts Senator Henry Wilson, one of the founders of the Republican party, picked it up in 1871 in an *Atlantic Monthly* article titled "New Departure of the Republican Party," and sailed on further: "the new under-currents in the popular mind ... have driven and drifted the ship of state from its former course, and rendered necessary new observations, new calculations and a new departure." Also in that year, Clement Laird Vallandigham, a COPPERHEAD briefly banished by Lincoln to the Confederacy during the Civil War, popularized the phrase in seeking a reorientation of the Democratic party in Ohio in 1871.

At the same time, Republican Henry Wilson was selected by Ulysses S. Grant to run as his Vice President in his second term, opposing the Liberal Republican-Democratic coalition headed by Horace Greeley. Thus both sides in the campaign of 1872 were hammering away at their own *new departure*, successfully preventing that nautical theme from gaining political identity.

new economics Political economic thought stemming from the school of John Maynard Keynes, holding that government fiscal and monetary policy can help end depressions and stimulate orderly economic growth.

Lord Keynes's publication in 1936 of the *General Theory of Employment, Interest and Money*—followed by Alvin Hansen's "translation" into understandable English and application to the U.S. economy, in turn

followed by Paul Samuelson's "neoclassical synthesis" combining the Keynes position with some classical economic theory—resulted in a startling approach to managing a nation's business.

Keynes and his followers, dubbed "new economists" in the late '50s, sought new ways to provide full employment and a high annual growth rate at a minimum cost to the stability of prices and the balance of trade. The concept of "pump-priming," used in the '30s, was vastly expanded, and the startling idea of reducing deficits by reducing, rather than increasing, taxes at certain stages was introduced. In what was probably the last stand of the old-line economists, Eisenhower Treasury Secretary George Humphrey said in 1957 about government spending during business declines, "I don't think you can spend yourself rich."

The increase in revenues after the 1964 tax cut, proposed during the Kennedy Administration (which stimulated business and thereby increased the amount of tax revenues received), probably provided the breakthrough for *new economics* in the councils of government. A large question remained: If the new thinking could stimulate the economy out of recessions, could it restrain the economy from inflation?

A key word in the new economist's vocabulary was TRADE-OFF. Former chairman of the Council of Economic Advisers Walter Heller explained:

The political economist typically thinks in terms of *trade-offs*—for example, the trade-off between jobs and inflation, the problem at which we pitch our Phillips Curves (relating the behavior of prices to the behavior of unemployment); the trade-off between international payments equilibrium and internal expansion, for which monetary policy did the twist (pushing short-term interest rates up to discourage the outflow of volatile funds, while holding long-term rates down to encourage capital spending); the trade-off between price-wage stability and unfettered markets, for which we erected the wage-price guideposts (providing guides to noninflationary wage and price behavior).

The new economics marked the entry of "the Respectable Professors of the Dismal Science," in Thomas Carlyle's phrase, into the top level of government planning. John R. Commons, whose "progressive individualism" was a controversial economic approach at the turn of the twentieth century, believed that "the place of the economist is that of adviser to the leaders, if they want him, and not that of propagandist to the masses." But which economist to trust? That was a question agonizingly expressed by Warren G. Harding: "I know somewhere there is an economist who knows the truth, but I don't know where to find him and haven't the sense to know and trust him when I find him. God, what a job!"

John F. Kennedy tried to take some of the controversial sting out of the new economics by making it appear to be simple good business management: "What is at stake in our economic decisions today is, not some grand warfare of rival ideologies which will sweep the country with passion, but the practical management of a modern economy."

Herbert Stein, chairman of the Council of Economic Advisers in the early '70s, wrote:

Now we come to the New Economics of 1993. Of course, it is not entirely new. Even good old President Eisenhower in 1958, before we were all Keynesians, talked about the possible use of "a little needle" to stimulate the economy. Every president since, except Ronald Reagan, has proposed a stimulus package when the economy was slack . .

What is new about Mr. Clinton's New Economics is the degree to which it is willing to intervene in the market. This is seen in the talk about managed international trade, in proposals for price controls in the healthy industry and in numerous plans for "targeting" investment…they seem to have a centrality in the 1993 New Economics that they have not had before …

In a 1996 addendum to his classic *Fiscal Revolution in America*, Dr. Stein wrote what he thought was new in the New Economics since its emergence in the Kennedy era: "What was probably new was the belief, which reached its peak in the early 1960s, that economic science had provided commands that politics would and should obey. That belief has now disappeared."

new face A candidate unscarred by previous major contests, unencumbered by known positions, offering politicians and voters a fresh choice.

A striking example of *new faces* on the national scene was the choice offered Republicans at their 1940 convention: Robert A. Taft, elected senator from Ohio just two years before; Thomas E. Dewey, who had recently been defeated in his first race to be governor of New York; and Wendell L. Willkie, a businessman who had never run for public office. That year the newest face (Willkie's) won; in 1944 Dewey's face was no longer new, but won; in 1948 Dewey's face was the "oldest" by virtue of his previous election defeat, and won the nomination again, only to lose to Truman's old face.

The desire for a new face—"untarred by the brush of defeat"—is perennial at national conventions, but is usually at its peak long before the convention meets. The balance sheet of every well-known candidate includes liabilities: enemies made in previous contests, a possible lost election and a CAN'T-WIN aura, perhaps a haunting record on what has become an embarrassing issue, and often a contempt-breeding familiarity with his voice and his personality. Because the presence of some new and mysterious candidate like a William Jennings Bryan in 1896 or a Dwight Eisenhower in 1952 is a thrilling uncertainty, the appeal of a new face in an "out" party is understandable.

As the Brookings Institution pointed out in 1960, "the limitations of well-known candidates are likely to be about as well understood as their potentialities. But both limitations and potentialities of less-known men can only be guessed at—unless the testing process before the convention is sufficient to bring out evidence."

Among political professionals, suspicion about a new face's "trustworthiness"—i.e., willingness to work with a party—usually increases as convention time approaches, and media demand becomes more insistent for specific stands on controversial issues. These combined forces can lessen the appeal of a new face, reminding delegates of the security of an "old face"—one less likely to blunder on the campaign trail, one who understands their local political problems, and above all, one whose victory will mean victory for themselves.

In May of 2007, the *Chicago Sun-Times* reported that "[Barack] Obama's supporters waited for hours outside the theatre in a line that stretched down the block. Many of them said he represented a fresh start and a new face."

The phrase itself was popularized in the Broadway theater by Leonard Sillman, who began producing a series of "New Faces" revues in 1934. The countervailing phrase, used occasionally about the sudden rise of Jimmy Carter to the national scene in 1976, is the title of a 1948 novel by Harold Robbins: *Never Love a Stranger*.

See TIME FOR A CHANGE.

New Federalism A political approach that sought to wed the sometimes conflicting need for national action with the desire for greater local participation.

The phrase was coined, and the idea expounded, in a speech to the nation by President Nixon on August 8, 1969. "After a third of a century of power flowing from the people and the States to Washington it is time for a New Federalism in which power, funds and responsibility will flow from Washington to the States and to the people." (See CREATIVE FEDERALISM; POWER TO THE PEOPLE.)

Revenue sharing (see TAX SHARING)—the no-strings return to the states of some taxes collected by the federal government—was a step in the direction of decentralization and devolution of power, which the president developed with a much more heavily funded proposal the next year; on the other hand, the proposed welfare reform (see WORKFARE) was a step toward centralization. To explain this seeming anomaly, the President encouraged his aides to do some thinking and writing on the subject.

That brought forth memoranda from "Publius" (this writer) and "Cato" (Tom Charles Huston, an outspoken conservative who later gained notoriety as author of a scheme of counterespionage known as "the Huston Plan").

Wrote Publius in January of 1970, in "New Federalist Paper #1":

We like the blessings of strong central government: a clear direction toward social goals, a willingness to counteract economic freezings and overheatings, a single voice in world affairs. But we are repelled by centralization's side effects: ineffective administration that breeds resentment, inflexible bureaucracy that breeds alienation.

We also like the blessings of decentralization or "home rule," with its respect for diversity, its ready response to local demands, its personality tailored to its constituents. But we are repelled by frequent local unwillingness or inability to meet human needs.

Do we have to choose one way or the other—centralization or decentralization—taking the bitter with whatever we consider the sweet? Many think not, and have spent the past year working out a synthesis of the most desirable in both central government and home rule. It has been called "The New Federalism."... The purpose of the New Federalism is not to wrap liberal principles in conservative clothing, or vice versa; the purpose is to come to grips with a paradox: a need for *both* national unity and local diversity; a need to protect *both* individual equality at the national level and individual uniqueness at the local level; and a need to *both* establish national goals and decentralize government services.

Replied Cato the following month:

At the heart of New Publius' contrived synthesis is this simple proposition: while decision-making must be nationalized, administration should be decentralized...he simply brushes aside States rights as a constitutional guarantee; he, New Publius, declares (the Constitution of the United States notwithstanding) that States rights have now become rights of first refusal. Perhaps one should give him the benefit of the doubt and assume that in his eagerness to replace the melting pot with the salad bowl he has inadvertently mixed apples with oranges. If, for example, New Publius is simply saying that within the scope of legitimate federal authority Congress may choose to give the States first option on the administration of a federal program, such a statement is unobjectionable. If, however, New Publius is saying that once the Federal Government determines that a problem—any problem—exists and decides that something should be done about it, the States have the first option to take action and if they refuse, the Federal Government may rightly act on its own—if this be his argument, then not only is it objectionable, it is revolutionary.

These two schools of thought contended, on varying levels and in many ways, throughout the next year; in the 1971 State of the Union message, President Nixon espoused much of the philosophy described in the Publius memorandum. Soon afterward, a syndicated cartoon by Jim Berry appeared showing the president writing at his desk and one aide saying to another, "he's going to change the terminology of the New Federalism and wants to know who's in charge of catch phrases."

New Freedom The slogan used by Woodrow Wilson in the presidential campaign of 1912.

Wilson believed with Louis Brandeis, who had won fame as a trust buster and whom he would later appoint to the Supreme Court, that the greatest enemies of the American people were not only the dominance of trusts but the growth in size of powerful corporations. He felt that the only instrument that could and should do something to curtail this was the federal government.

His New Freedom called for government intervention to safeguard the democratic rights of small business against the industrial behemoths. Wilson described it as "a revival of the power of the people, the beginning of an age of thoughtful reconstruction, that makes our thought hark back to the great age in which democracy was set up in America." See CURSE OF BIGNESS.

Wilson's belief that bigness was dangerous brought him into direct conflict with Theodore Roosevelt, an independent candidate whose run was splitting the Republican vote. Former President Roosevelt, an early believer in defining an administration's political philosophy with a slogan—"SQUARE DEAL"—had a new slogan of his own, "the NEW NATIONALISM." The growth of successful enterprise, with a certain necessary minimum of regulation, was perfectly natural from Roosevelt's point of view, and late in life the former trustbuster found little reprehensible in trusts.

On this subject Wilson drew the issue: "I take my stand absolutely, where every progressive ought to take his stand, on the proposition that private monopoly is indefensible and intolerable."

His writings and speeches of the campaign were gathered in a 1913 book titled *The New Freedom*. More important to his reelection victory in 1916 was his slogan "He Kept Us Out of War."

New Frontier Style adopted by the Kennedy Administration.

"A new frontier had been discovered," a hard-driving presidential candidate told a crowd in West Middlesex, Pennsylvania, "the frontier of invention and new wants. Under our American way of life, men with courage and imagination were free to occupy this new frontier and develop it. They built a greater America."

The candidate was Alf Landon, the date August 22, 1936. The Kansas governor used the phrase several times in his campaign against Roosevelt, but he could not make too much of it, since *New Frontiers* was the title of a book that had been published two years before by Henry A. Wallace.

In 1951 Walter Prescott Webb wrote a pessimistic piece in the *Atlantic Monthly* decrying the boosterism of those who "speak of new frontiers," adding: "The businessman sees a business frontier in the customers he has not yet reached… The social worker sees a human frontier among the suffering people whose woes he has not alleviated … If you watch these peddlers of substitute frontiers, you will find that nearly everyone wants you to buy something, give something, or believe in something… They are all fallacies, these new frontiers, and they are pernicious in proportion to their plausibility and respectability."

Of course, previous usages can be found of almost any famous phrase in the English language (see NEW DEAL; GREAT SOCIETY); the memorable usage was by John F. Kennedy, accepting the Democratic nomination in the Los Angeles Coliseum in 1960: "we stand today on the edge of a new frontier—the frontier of the 1960s, a frontier of unknown opportunities and perils, a frontier of unfulfilled hopes and threats. ... The new frontier of which I speak is not a set of promises—it is a set of challenges. It sums up not what I intend to offer the American people, but what I intend to ask of them."

Who suggested the phrase to Kennedy? Arthur Schlesinger, Jr., recounted in *A Thousand Days* that he had given a speech himself a few months before titled "New Frontiers of American Liberalism." Reporter David Wise credited Walt Whitman Rostow, then an MIT economic historian, with suggesting the phrase to Kennedy at a Boston cocktail party a month before the nomination; later both Rostow and Max Freedman, Washington correspondent for the Manchester *Guardian,* are supposed to have submitted separate drafts of the acceptance speech, each containing the "New Frontier" theme.

However, a Kennedy intimate, speaking "not for attribution," told the lexicographer that neither Freedman nor Rostow submitted any material for this particular speech. He added that rough draft material was solicited from many sources, including Professor Allan Nevins of Columbia, but that the term itself was in none of them.

W.W. Rostow, on the record and in writing, informed me:

> Your puzzlement about the origins of "The New Frontier" leads me to set down the following extremely minor footnote to history, as I remember it.
>
> Early in the Kennedy Administration, David Wise wrote a piece for the *New York Herald-Tribune* asserting that I had provided J.F.K. with "Let's get this country moving again" and "The New Frontier." I called and told Wise I had, indeed, given J.F.K. the first of those phrases but not The New Frontier. After I had gone on for some time in this vein, he asked: "Are you finished?" He then said: "First, the President of the United States said the phrase came from you; second, he showed me a speech draft of yours containing the phrase; third, he told me it came from your book, 'The Stages of Economic Growth.'" I subsided and, indeed, found three references to the new frontier theme in "The Stages," which I had forgotten.

Then Max Freedman sent a letter to the *Herald-Tribune* saying that Ted Sorensen had used the phrase in a draft of his for Kennedy. When the question has been raised with me occasionally, I have responded that it is wholly possible Freedman was correct; the phrase may well have been in the air at the time; and the issue is trivial because the working politician alone deserves whatever credit there may be in such phrases because he alone takes the responsibility and risk of using them.

The origin here was probably similar to NOTHING TO FEAR BUT FEAR ITSELF, when Louis Howe—probably—picked it up from a newspaper advertisement and suggested it to FDR.

The phrase *new frontier* was in the air in early 1960. For example, the U.S. Chamber of Commerce appointed a Committee on New Frontiers in Technology in April of that year, with the name chosen months before that. "The Chamber would not have adopted this name if it had been already used by and identified with Mr. Kennedy," the secretary of that conservative group wrote the author. After Kennedy made the phrase his own, the Chamber ruefully changed the name of its "new frontiers" committee to the more pedestrian "Committee on Science and Technology."

In his memoir *Kennedy*, Ted Sorensen, who prepared the acceptance speech for the candidate, takes a defensive stance: "the basic concept of the New Frontier— and the term itself—were new to this speech. I know of no outsider who suggested that expression, although the theme of the Frontier was contained in more than one draft. Kennedy generally shrank from slogans, and would use this one sparingly, but he liked the idea of a successor to the New Deal and Fair Deal."

Thus Kennedy popularized and made his own, probably at Sorensen's suggestion, a phrase that was "around."

New Left A deliberately leaderless grouping that broke with traditional liberals in the 1960s.

This movement, begun in England in 1957 by young radicals who rejected the "old" liberal philosophy, was joined in the next decade by pacifists and civil rights militants, who opposed the war in Asia and the "power structure" that they believed robbed them of their freedom and individuality.

Sociologist C. Wright Mills is credited with the coinage of the phrase in the late '50s. In England, two university periodicals merged in 1959 to form the *New Left Review*, staffed mainly by disenchanted young Marxists. At that time in the U.S., a group calling itself SLATE was formed at the University of California's Berkeley campus, and a similar student political party was formed in Chicago. The young intellectuals adopted new vocabularies and new forms to contrast with the "liberal establishment" they felt no longer met their needs. See MOVEMENT, THE.

Mills wrote in 1960: "If there is to be a politics of a New Left, what needs to be analyzed is the structure of institutions, the foundation of policies. In this sense, both in its criticisms and in its proposals, our work is necessarily structural—and so, for us, just now—utopian." His followers seized upon this rationale for their emphasis on questions over answers, their apparent negativism and lack of a program.

In later use, it encompassed the antibureaucracy, alienated groups who dissociated themselves from the liberals of the "old" left.

From the point of view of Democrats and longtime liberals, the New Left represented a splintering of support, an embarrassment and an affront implicit in the name that made them the "old" left. Many conservatives derided it as a collection of Vietniks and far-out radicals, with whom no communication was possible, overlooking the common ground possible in a mutual distaste for strong, centralized government.

new look A change in defense strategy in 1953, as the Korean War ended, de-emphasizing "conventional" forces and relying more on nuclear deterrents. See BIGGER BANG FOR A BUCK.

The phrase came from the fashion world, where it was used in 1947 to describe the Paris-inspired change to dramatically lower hemlines and softer details after the austere fashions of wartime. The phrase fitted a reassessment of the nation's defense attire.

Defense's *new look* appealed to those who wanted a reduction in total defense spending, and who felt that our preparation for nontotal "brushfire" wars diminished our threat of nuclear retaliation. It was opposed by many Army generals who agreed with retiring Chief of Staff Matthew Ridgway in assailing the "overemphasis" on air power and MASSIVE RETALIATION.

In his memoirs, General Eisenhower traced both the coinage and what he felt was an overreaction:

At about the time of the change-over in the Joint Chiefs of Staff, active fighting in Korea ended. This fact, along with the epochal developments which were transpiring in nuclear armaments, occasioned what Admiral [Arthur] Radford described in a talk late in the year as a "New Look" [at the Press Club, Washington, December 14, 1953]. It happened that this term had a definite place in the parlance of the day; it had been coined to describe noticeable changes in the style of women's dresses (not entirely an improvement, some men felt). Thus the tag "New Look" probably suggested to many minds a picture of a far more radical change in the composition of our armed forces than was truly the case.

New Nationalism Theodore Roosevelt's progressive program of 1910, designed to lead the Republican party toward more liberal paths.

The former president was stamping about Africa in 1910, bored and regretting not having sought a third term. His friend, Judge Learned Hand, sent him a book by Herbert Croly, *The Promise of America*, which differed from the Jeffersonian ideal of the least government being the best government, and restated and extended much of Roosevelt's own thought. On his return, TR invited Croly to tea in Oyster Bay and promptly took over the program; the phrase *new nationalism* probably came from Croly as well.

In a speech at Osawatomie, Kansas, the former president said: "The New Nationalism puts the national need before sectional or personal advantage. ... This New Nationalism regards the executive power as the steward of the public welfare. It demands of the judiciary that it shall be interested primarily in human welfare rather than in property, just as it demands that the representative body shall represent all the people rather than any one class or section of the people."

Elihu Root shrugged it off with "The only real objection I see to it is calling it 'new,'" but many other Republicans considered it heresy. Two years later, in the Wilson-Taft-Roosevelt "Bull Moose" campaign of 1912, Woodrow Wilson adopted most of the principles expressed by the "New Nationalism" with the exception of an attitude toward trusts, which TR felt were good if properly supervised and Wilson felt were the embodiment of evil. Wilson called his own program "the NEW FREEDOM"; President William Howard Taft was the only candidate running with nothing "new."

Ironically, ten years after Roosevelt introduced the term, Warren G. Harding—apostle of "normalcy"—declared Roosevelt's Osawatomie speech the basis of his platform, but he did not later become known as a proponent of a strong central government.

new world order An ideal of cooperation and peace among nations.

Alfred, Lord Tennyson pointed to this phrase in his 1842 poem "Morte d'Arthur," in which the dying King Arthur says, "The old order changeth, yielding place to new."

The elder George Bush used the phrase in an August 1990 news conference: "As I look at the countries that are chipping in here now, I think we do have a chance at a new world order." He repeated it a month later in urging the United Nations General Assembly to work against chemical and biological weapons: "It is in our hands to leave these dark machines behind, in the dark ages where they belong, and to press forward to cap a historic movement toward a new world order, and a long era of peace."

During his 1991 State of the Union Message, Bush called upon all nations "to fulfill the long-held promise of a new world order—where brutality will go unre-

warded and aggression will meet collective resistance."

Earlier uses of *new world order* have been less supportive of worldwide unity. Malcolm X commented in his 1965 *Autobiography* (written with Alex Haley): "Let us face reality. We can see in the United Nations a new world order being shaped, along color lines—an alliance among the non-white nations."

Various sources for the phrase have been suggested, from the 1970s New World Information and Communications Order, a Unesco-sponsored plan, to the Latin phrase on the back of dollar bills: *Novus Ordo Seclorum*, "A New Order for the Ages."

Without *world*, the phrase *new order* conjures images of *die neue Ordnung*, Hitler's description of a National Socialist regime in Europe. That phrase, however, was also used in that era by Franklin Delano Roosevelt at the 1932 Democratic National Convention: "Let us all here assembled constitute ourselves prophets of a new order of competence and of courage."

In 1993, President William Jefferson Clinton returned part of the phrase to its poetic origin in his inaugural address: "Today, as the old order passes, the new world is more free but less stable."

See NEW, POLITICAL USE OF, and MULTILATERALISM.

nickel-and-diming See BUTTONHOLE.

nicknames Derisive or laudatory sobriquets that popularize or stigmatize a politician.

Chief executives and other famous politicians of the U.S. have usually welcomed nicknames, some of them still familiar: "Father of His Country" for Washington; "Honest Abe" for Lincoln; "Old Hickory" for Jackson; "The Little Giant" for Stephen A. Douglas.

Not every schoolchild introduced to our history is informed that Washington, in his lifetime, was often referred to as "The Stepfather of His Country" and "The Old Fox." Lincoln was derided by Confederates and Northern Democrats alike as "The Baboon" and his wife Mary as "The She-Wolf." U.S.

Grant, observed H.L. Mencken, "because he was always the soldier more than the politician, escaped with nothing worse than 'The Butcher,' but his successors got it hot and heavy."

Hayes was "The Fraud" as well as "The Hero of '77"; Arthur was "The Dude" and "America's First Gentleman"; Cleveland, "The Stuffed Prophet" and "Perpetual Candidate"; Theodore Roosevelt was "Bull Moose," "MAN ON HORSEBACK," and "Teddy the Meddler." (MR. DOOLEY, referring to Teddy Roosevelt as "Tiddy," was told not to be disrespectful; he retorted that he was not being disrespectful, he was being affectionate.)

Wilson was "The Phrasemaker" and "The Schoolmaster." Coolidge was "Silent Cal."

Franklin Roosevelt was known variously as "Boss," "Houdini in the White House," "Sphinx," "Squire of Hyde Park," and "THAT MAN IN THE WHITE HOUSE."

Nicknames are often borrowed and transferred: "Great Commoner" (Pitt the Elder) was applied to Henry Clay and later to William Jennings Bryan; "Bald Eagle of Foggy Bottom" (Robert Lovett in his State Department days) came from "The Bald Eagle of Rhode Island," Tristram Burges (1770–1853), a member of Congress.

New York's Mayor John Lindsay was known as "Mr. Clean" and "Batman." President Truman enjoyed "Give 'Em Hell Harry" but not "High-Tax Harry." President Eisenhower was simply "Ike." Nixon was "Tricky Dick." With Franklin Roosevelt, John Kennedy, and Lyndon Johnson, presidential initials became popular. President Johnson was both LBJ and "Big Daddy." James Earl Carter, Jr., was the first to formally adopt the informal style with "Jimmy." Ronald Reagan was called "The Great Communicator," while the elder George Bush had no sobriquet but did have a nickname given by his children: "Poppy." Bill Clinton, though saddled with "Slick Willie" by detractors, liked to be known as "The Comeback Kid." George W. Bush, known for his skill in nicknaming others, picked up his own nickname, based on the Texas pronunciation of his middle initial, as "Dubya."

The *nick* in nickname comes not from the variety of characterizations given

the Devil (Old Nick) but from the Middle English *eke*, meaning "something added, an extension," or (as a verb) "to increase or lengthen" (still used, with the meaning "get with great effort," in phrases like *eke out a living*) and *an ekename* became *a nickname*, or an extra surname applied in jest or familiarity.

See INITIALS, PRESIDENTIAL; SOBRIQUETS.

nightmare is over See GOVERNMENT OF LAWS, NOT OF MEN; LIFT OF A DRIVING DREAM.

night mayor A city official of whatever rank assigned to remain at City Hall or tour the city on official business during the night hours.

Begun by the administration of John Lindsay of New York in 1966, the program was intended to publicize the wide-awake, round-the-clock officials and give them an opportunity to make surprise inspections that often resulted in newspaper photos.

The practice derived from the military CQ (charge of quarters) and OD (officer of the day, or on duty) who is responsible for any decisions requiring immediate attention when ordinary authority is off duty; a journalistic term for that is *night editor*.

The phrase was coined by James J. Walker, who served as a sparkling, beloved mayor of New York, habitué of nightclubs, who resigned in 1932 as a result of Samuel Seabury's investigation of municipal corruption: "Some folks call me the 'night mayor' of New York."

night of the long knives A time of purge; a savage, surprise attack by one's supposed friends.

"It was no secret that this time the revolution would have to be bloody," Adolf Hitler told the Reichstag meeting at the Kroll Opera House on July 13, 1934, explaining the events of the weekend of June 29 to July 2; "when we spoke of it, we called it 'The Night of the Long Knives' [*die Nacht der langen Messer*]."

"In every time and place," Hitler continued, "rebels have been killed...I ordered the leaders of the guilty shot. I also ordered the abscesses caused by our internal and external poisons cauterized until the living flesh was burned."

In the summer of 1934 Hitler was Chancellor, his rise to power helped by the Brown Shirts headed by Ernst Roehm. But the leaders of Germany's regular army were worried about Roehm and the private Nazi militia, who were calling for a "second revolution" to overthrow the military and industrial elite in Germany. Hitler made a deal to enhance his power in government while wiping out his undisciplined former comrades, and personally directed Heinrich Himmler and Reinhard Heydrich of the Gestapo, and their boss, Hermann Goering, to arrest and execute eighty-three of the leaders of the storm troopers. After that weekend, Hitler's power was unchallenged.

The *night*, then, was originally supposed to be a time of revolution conceived by Hitler, Roehm, and the early Nazis; to its planners the phrase denoted an entire weekend of purge and the elimination of an obstacle to complete power. Ironically, the *night* that took place eliminated one of the men who had planned it, and turned the "second revolution" into an internal purge.

Today, the phrase is an example of the use of catastrophic terms to describe far less bloody developments, like *massacre* for extensive firings. In *Time* magazine's 1978 obituary of Charles Chaplin, Stefan Kanfer wrote: "Let a man rise in show business, even to so stratospheric a level as The Tramp's, and there comes an evening of the Long Knives.... he became embroiled in a series of affairs ... after the war, he could no longer be saved from his enemies."

In 2006, when the reformist prime minister of Japan, Junichiro Koizumi, stirred political retribution from his conservative opposition, the *Singapore Times* headlined: "Night of the Long Knives in Japan; conservatives are out to get Koizumi supporters."

See PURGE and PUTSCH; for other Nazi-era terms, see FINAL SOLUTION; HOLOCAUST; and MUNICH ANALOGY.

-nik suffix As in the derisive terms *beatnik*, *peacenik*, *Vietnik*, and others. Suggests youth, scruffiness, beardedness, and irresponsibility.

A 1963 *New York Times* headline read: "'BEATNIK' TROUBLES LEXICOGRAPHER." The lede: "Dr. Charles Talbot Onions ... celebrated his 90th birthday here recently worrying about the word 'beatnik.'" Those who "knew their Onions" worried as well; was it a neologism that would last, deserving a place in a dictionary—or a "nonce word" that struts and frets its hour on the tips of tongues and then is heard no more? (And *lede* is the spelling of the noun *lead* in journalese.)

The popularization of the suffix *-nik* probably started with Al Capp, creator of the *Li'l Abner* comic strip, who developed a subseries in the country of "Lower Slobbovia," a land of ice, wolves, and miserable people who spoke a combination of English, Russian, and Yiddish. "Leettle Noodnik" (from the Yiddish *nudnik*, "tedious fellow" or "dope") was one of the characters. The suffix is of Russian origin; *-nik* when added to stems of Russian words means "one who."

-nik crashed like a meteorite into the English language with the launching of the Soviet *Sputnik* (from *iskustvennyi sputnik zemli*, "artificial satellite," literally "fellow traveler of the earth") on October 4, 1957. When a second satellite, containing a dog, was launched on November 4, several newspapers tagged it a "muttnik," and the fad of the *-nik* construction was launched as well.

There were *no-goodniks* and *far-outniks*, *beatniks*, and *sickniks*. Even the typical suburban home shown at the 1959 U.S. exhibition in Moscow—not split-level, but with a walkway splitting it—was dubbed the *Splitnik*, its name coined with inordinate pride by its press agent, the author. After some flirtation with *peacenik*, public fancy in 1958 appeared to settle on *beatnik*, bottomed on the *beat generation*, novelist Jack Kerouac's switch on Gertrude Stein's *lost generation*.

Columnist Herb Caen coined the term in the *San Francisco Chronicle* in 1958: "*Look* magazine, preparing a picture spread on S.F.'s Beat Generation (oh, no, not AGAIN!) hosted a party in a No. beach house for 50 Beatniks." The term was active as a derogation of young people who let their hair grow and refused to work, to be replaced in the late sixties by *hippie*, a somewhat different subculture.

Time and *Newsweek* turned *beatnik* to *Vietnik* in October 1965, as the war in Vietnam because more divisive at home, and the pejorative connotation of *beatnik*—lazy, irresponsible—was transferred to a derogatory term for war protesters.

In the mid-seventies the suffix was returned to its country of origin, by way of giving an English word a Russian flavor. A headline in the *New York Times* letters section in June 1977 read: "Robert Toth Explains Refuseniks' Role." A *refusenik* was a Soviet citizen, often Jewish, who was refused permission to emigrate. In Israel, supporters of the Likud coalition of the right were called *Likudniks*.

NIMBY "Not in my back yard"; refusal to allow unpleasant or dangerous projects to be moved into one's own neighborhood.

The five-letter acronym, pronounced "NIM-bee," first appeared in print in a 1980 report in *The Christian Science Monitor*: "A secure landfill anywhere near them is anathema to most Americans today. It's an attitude referred to in the trade as NIMBY—'not in my backyard.'"

By 1986, this expression of intolerance was gaining international acceptance. *The Times* of London described a politician who became "a convert to the Nimby...principle. A chief whip who thinks that nuclear waste is too dangerous for his constituency will find it hard to persuade other Tory MPs that it is safe for theirs."

Current use of the acronym is primarily as a noun, often attributively as in *the nimby syndrome*, and the plural form may be *nimbys* or sometimes *nimbies*. *The Nation* reported in 1991 on "prisons, sanitation works and other 'NIMBYs'"; this noun is also used for any protestor of such projects. From the acronym has come the noun *nimbyism*, a 1989 term for the practice of opposing local facilities for disagreeable projects.

Coinage has been attributed to Walton Rodger of the American Nuclear Society, who used the term as early as 1980 to deride protesters who campaigned against nuclear facilities near their homes.

9/11 Collective term for the suicide attacks on Sept. 11, 2001.

Islamic terrorists, led by Mohammed Atta, from a wealthy Saudi family, and inspired by Osama bin Laden, destroyed the twin towers of the World Trade Center in New York City and damaged the Pentagon in Arlington, Va., by crashing three hijacked airliners into them, killing about 3,000 people. A fourth airliner, United Flight 93, never reached its target, presumably the Capitol or White House, after courageous passengers and crew tried to regain control of the plane, causing it to crash in a field in rural Pennsylvania.

9/11 is a metonym—a word or phrase substituted for another. (*Oval Office* for President is another example.) In this instance, creation of a shorthand term probably was inevitable, given the complicated nature of the event (a sequence of attacks on three buildings in two cities) and its traumatic psychological impact as well as physical significance.

People groped for several weeks for a way to describe what had happened. New York Mayor Rudolph Giuliani referred to the "attack" or "massive attack." President George W. Bush spoke of "acts of war" and "mass murder." Three weeks afterward, on Oct. 3, *The Wall Street Journal* reported: "In daily conversations, many people are resorting to an assortment of vague monikers to describe the events: 'the terrorist attacks,' 'the events of Sept. 11,' 'the bombing,' 'the tragedy.' or simply 'it.'"

The date was employed in different forms within a matter of days to denote the attacks. Some referred to the events of 9-11-01 or simply to Sept. 11. The United Way established a September 11th Fund for disaster relief, while the International Association of Fire Fighters set up a 9-11 fund for New York City fire fighters. *The New York Times* used 9/11, which came to be the accepted style for referring to the attacks, as early as Sept. 12, headlining an Op-Ed piece by Bill Keller "America's Emergency Line: 9/11."

The coincidence of the date of the attacks with the national 911 emergency telephone number made the metonym as memorable as the comparable Pearl Harbor for the Japanese air raid on Dec. 7, 1941, that precipitated U.S. entry into World War II.

9/11 is an Americanism not picked up by the rest of the English-speaking world because U.S. usage puts the number of the month ahead of the number of the day; from Britain to Australia, 9/11 signifies not the 11th day of September but the 9th day of November. Writers outside the U.S. refer to "the attacks of 11 September 2001" or "the World Trade Center attack" (which leaves out the crash into the Pentagon and Flight 93).

Why the numeration 9/11 and not Sept. 11, when we still remember Dec. 7 and not 12/7? That is primarily because numbering has gripped this generation, as Americans stay open "24/7," not "around the clock all week long"; secondarily, the rhyming 7/11 is central to a game played with dice and subsequently was the name adopted by the 7-Eleven chain of convenience stores. "The compact and catchy rhythm of 9/11 makes it memorable," Steven Poole, a correspondent for *The Guardian* observed to the author. "If the attacks had occurred on the 23rd of November, I don't think we would still hear people saying 'eleven twenty-three' or see '11/23' written. Too many syllables; not catchy enough. The chance homology with the U.S. emergency telephone number gives it an extra *frisson*, too."

Although terrorist attacks had taken place years before on U.S. embassies and the destroyer USS *Cole*, this stunning surprise, followed almost immediately by sweeping national-security legislation, was seen as the beginning of the WAR ON TERROR.

nine old men A derogation of the nine justices of the Supreme Court, a majority of whom blocked Franklin Roosevelt's programs in the mid-'30s.

The average age of the Supreme Court members in 1936 was seventy-one. Throughout his first term, Roosevelt had no opportunity to make a single appointment. "Chance and the disinclination of the individuals to leave the Supreme Bench," said Roosevelt, "have now given us a Court in which five Justices will be over 75 years of age before next June and one over 70."

FDR came up with a plan to bring the Court out of what he called "the horse and buggy age." He proposed that for every Supreme Court justice who failed to quit the bench within six months after reaching his seventieth birthday Congress empower the President to appoint a new justice up to a total of six.

Roosevelt had overreached himself; his plan was denounced as court-packing, and he found himself on the defensive. "If by that phrase 'packing the Court' it is charged," he said, "that I wish to place on the bench spineless puppets who would disregard the law and would decide specific cases as I wished them to be decided, I make this answer: that no President fit for his office would appoint, and no Senate of honorable men fit for their office would confirm, that kind of appointee to the Supreme Court."

Roosevelt's plan died in committee on July 22, 1937; however, the President's purpose was served when the Court began to show its shifting position. Justice Owen Roberts threw the balance of power to the liberals, and the Court soon upheld a minimum-wage law for women, a National Labor Relations Act, and the Social Security Act.

"By the time the Court recessed for the summer," wrote Judge Samuel Rosenman, one of FDR's speechwriters, "it was obvious that the liberal dissenting views of the minority in 1935 and 1936 had in large measure become the majority views of the Court. As a contemporary wag put it: 'A switch in time saved nine.'"

The phrase *nine old men* was coined by Drew Pearson and Robert S. Allen in a 1936 book dealing with the Court, and was further made famous by a characterization of them as a kind of chorus line in the 1937 Rodgers-Hart musical, *I'd Rather Be Right*.

Since that time, attacks on the age of Supreme Court justices or senators have been rare. The Latin word *senator* is based on *senex*, "old man," the root of *senile*.

Cruel joke on the subject in the 1980s: at a dinner with the other eight Supreme Court justices, the youngest justice was asked by a waiter: "Your meat course?"

"Roast beef."

"And what about the vegetables?"

Answer: "They'll have to order for themselves."

nitty-gritty Detail work; difficult minutiae to be handled by staffers after strategy has been decided higher up.

"SNCC's resources for nitty-gritty organizing—" wrote *The New Republic* in 1967, "and perhaps its will to work in a low key over a long period of time—are thin."

This expression of Southern origin is in common current use, and one can speculate on its derivation: *nit* means the egg of a louse, something tiny and distasteful; *nit-picking*, or fault-finding, uses *nit* in a sense of something small or detailed. (Shakespeare's *Taming of the Shrew*: "Thou flea! thou nit, thou winter-cricket, thou!")

Grit is rooted in sand or dust, and later in coarse meal (as *hominy grits*); as a verb, it means to grind in sand, and to "grit one's teeth." Thus, the rhyming words mean to take tiny details (*nitty*) and grind them carefully (*gritty*). Speculation aside, somebody probably thought of it in a flash of inspiration, as with other rhyming compounds like *willy-nilly* (willing or not) and *helter-skelter* (probably onomatopoeic). These are reduplicated or ricochet words; a political FLIP-FLOP is called a gradational compound.

Nixon Doctrine A foreign policy that sought to maintain U.S. involvement in the affairs of the world, in a way that required allies to bear the manpower burden of their own defense.

In his November 3, 1969, SILENT MAJORITY speech, President Nixon first used the phrase publicly: "Let me briefly explain what has been described as the Nixon Doctrine." (Somewhat self-conscious about using the phrase with his name in it, he toned it down with "what has been described as." Needless to say, he wanted it described exactly that way. It had been called the "Guam

doctrine," because it had been issued on background on that island, but as H.R. Haldeman pointed out to me, "nobody elected Guam.")

These were the three principles of the doctrine set forth in that speech:

First, the United States will keep all of its treaty commitments. Second, we shall provide a shield if a nuclear power threatens the freedom of a nation allied with us or of a nation whose survival we consider vital to our security. Third, in cases involving other types of aggression, we shall furnish military and economic assistance when requested in accordance with our treaty commitments. But we shall look to the nation directly threatened to assume the primary responsibility of providing the manpower for its defense.

When it comes to doctrines, one does not have to be doctrinaire. At a meeting in the White House's Roosevelt Room in 1970, as U.S. troops in Vietnam made a foray into Cambodia, the author asked Henry Kissinger, "Doesn't this fly in the face of the Nixon Doctrine?" The National Security Adviser replied heatedly: "We wrote the goddam Doctrine, we can change it!"

The doctrine first presented at Guam was in a BACKGROUNDER, not for specific attribution, and Nixon could not correctly say he had "announced" it there. The operative verb, appropriate for DOCTRINES generally, is *enunciated*.

noble experiment Now-sarcastic characterization of Prohibition, based on a phrase of Herbert Hoover's.

President Hoover wrote Senator William E. Borah on February 28, 1928, of "a great social and economic experiment, noble in motive and far-reaching in purpose." But there were 327 murders in Chicago alone in one Prohibition year, and not a single conviction for murder that year; the "wets" quoted Isaiah (24:11): "There is a crying for wine in the streets; all joy is darkened, the mirth of the land is gone."

Hoover is best remembered for phrases he nearly said, or claimed he did not originate, or denied having said at all. He did not say CHICKEN IN EVERY POT; he said he did not originate RUGGED INDIVIDUALISM; and as seen here, he did not quite say *noble experiment*—just "experiment, noble in motive," where the noble modifies the motive and not the experiment. And he certainly did not name the collection of Depression shacks "Hoovervilles."

Noble experiment is applied now to hopelessly lost causes. Its predecessor phrase was *Holy Experiment*, English Quaker William Penn's term for his 1682 colony of Pennsylvania. That experiment was successful.

nobody drowned at Watergate A slogan used by Nixon partisans to express resentment at what they believed was a double standard of political morality.

In the early stages of the Watergate scandal, many of the President's supporters believed that the break-in at Democratic headquarters was little more than had been described by press secretary Ron Ziegler: a "third-rate burglary." To them, the COVER-UP that aroused such widespread indignation was similar to the attempts made by Senator Edward F. Kennedy in 1969 to seal information at an inquest in Edgartown, Mass., following "the Chappaquiddick incident."

At Chappaquiddick, a young woman named Mary Jo Kopechne had died when a car Senator Kennedy was driving plunged into a river. Some diehard Nixon supporters, claiming that Senator Kennedy was not subjected to the same rigorous examination that a non-Kennedy would have been under similar circumstances, suggested that the loss of life in the Chappaquiddick incident made it more worthy of investigation than the Watergate break-in. Hence the phrase "nobody drowned at Watergate," which was in the air some months before *The Wall Street Journal* quoted Secretary of Agriculture Earl Butz repeating it in 1974.

A twist on the attempt to show hypocrisy came in 1978 when Georgia supporters of banker Bert Lance believed he was being unfairly hounded out of his job (by the author) as Jimmy Carter's Director of the Office of Management and Budget for minor irregularities committed when he ran a bank in Calhoun, Georgia. Their resentment took the form of a bumper sticker reported to be on a car in southern Georgia: "Nobody Drowned at the Calhoun Bank."

no comment An outdated, pretentious phrase to ward off a reporter's query, now used by political novices with no skill at fencing.

When the expression was fairly fresh, Winston Churchill used it with zest. After a White House meeting with President Truman in 1946, he evaded questions with: "I think 'No comment' is a splendid expression. I got it from Sumner Welles."

Before making that discovery, Churchill—early in his career—used a form of excruciating euphemism to avoid a position. When asked, in 1906, if the British government was condoning slavery of Chinese laborers in South Africa, he replied, "It could not, in the opinion of His Majesty's Government, be classified as slavery in the extreme acceptance of the word without some risk of terminological inexactitude."

Before he was a candidate for president, Franklin Roosevelt said he knew the value of "sitting tight, sawing wood and keeping my mouth shut"; his cousin Theodore had once written: "what is needed for me is to follow the advice given by the New Bedford whaling captain to his mate when he told that all he wanted from him was silence and damn little of that."

At press conferences FDR's favorite evasive action was "That's an IFFY QUESTION." Grover Cleveland was much more blunt; once, when asked something he preferred not to answer, he glared at the reporter and said, "Young man, that is an issue too big to be brought up in a brief interview that is drawing rapidly to a close."

Best known for his taciturnity was "Silent Cal" Coolidge, who answered critics with a mild "I have noticed that nothing I never said ever did me any harm." President Lyndon Johnson, when pressed, avoided the words "No comment," substituting something like "I don't have anything to say about that at this time." He passed along advice given him by former House Speaker Sam Rayburn: "You don't have to explain what you don't say."

Another riposte is to challenge the basis or the phraseology of the question or to play tricks with language: At his first press conference as head of the Council of Economic Advisers, Walter Heller listened to a reporter object to a lack of cost estimates of the Administration's anti-recession program. "The inference will be drawn," said the reporter, "that you don't care very much about how much they'll cost." Heller snapped back with a smile: "That may be the inference, but not the implication."

Diplomats, when they must say nothing, must say it nicely to reporters; Harold Macmillan said of the post of Foreign Secretary, "He is forever poised between a cliché and an indiscretion." U.N. Secretary General Dag Hammarskjöld phrased his "No comment" as "I never discuss discussions."

Tammany chieftain Charles Murphy advised young mayor-to-be James Walker: "Most of the troubles of the world could be avoided if men opened their minds instead of their mouths." A century earlier, banker Nicholas Biddle told party managers to pass the word to "Tippecanoe" Harrison: "Let him say not one single word about his principles, or his creed—let him say nothing—promise nothing. Let no committee, no convention—no town meeting ever extract from him a single word about what he thinks or what he will do hereafter. Let the use of pen and ink be wholly forbidden."

The reason for Biddle's advice was explained by Alexis de Tocqueville in *Democracy in America*: "The general interest of a party frequently demands that members belonging to it should not speak on great questions which they understand imperfectly; that they should speak but little on those minor questions which impede the great ones; lastly, and for the most part, that they should not speak at all. To keep silence is the most useful service that an indifferent spokesman can render to the Commonwealth."

John Selden, who served in Parliament in the seventeenth century, observed: "Wise men say nothing in dangerous times." Three centuries later, physicist Albert Einstein reduced this advice—and that of Tammany boss Murphy—to the following formula:

"If A equals success, then the formula is A equals X plus Y plus Z. X is work. Y is play. Z is keep your mouth shut."

Charles de Gaulle put it this way in *The Edge of the Sword*: "There can be no power without mystery. There must always be a 'something' which others cannot altogether fathom, which puzzles them, stirs them, and rivets their attention.... Nothing more enhances authority than silence. It is the crowning virtue of the strong, the refuge of the weak, the modesty of the proud, the pride of the humble, the prudence of the wise, and the sense of fools."

-nomics The economic policies of or economic theory of.

This combining form first became popular in 1969, with the formation of *Nixonomics* to indicate Nixon's economic policies. Inside the White House, it was propagated by speechwriters to put the presidential brand on a subject turgid to many; outside, it was popularized by the columnists Rowland Evans and Robert Novak.

Its ease of formation is based on the final *n* in Nixon's name; the lack of a final *n* in the names of Ford and Carter accounts for the rare usage of *Fordonomics* and *Carternomics*.

More popular was *Reaganomics*, again with the suffix easily combining with the *n* that ended Reagan's name. Two years after the 1980 Republican presidential primary campaigns, in which George H.W. Bush had derided Reagan's supply-side theories as "voodoo economics," Urban League president John Jacob said that Reaganomics "is giving voodoo a bad name."

The same combining form, which joins with the final *n* without repeating the letter, produced *Clintonomics*. Both Bushes had no such luck.

nonpaper A tentative diplomatic proposal committed to paper but not committing a government; so described as to be deniable as "unofficial" without requiring an official denial.

Writing in *The Christian Science Monitor* in 1980, Joseph Joffe, a leading West German columnist, suggested that Willy

Brandt may have been a go-between in a dispute between the U.S. and the Soviet Union. He reported that "Soviet Ambassador Semyonov did deliver a 'nonpaper' (diplomatic jargon for an unofficial message) that hinted at a message of mediation."

The phrase continues to require parenthetical definition. *Washington Post* foreign-affairs columnist Jim Hoagland revealed a communication between the Iranian diplomat Ali Larijani and the European Union negotiator Javier Solana about a plan to resolve the dispute regarding U.N. opposition to Iranian uranium enrichment. "A diplomatic device known as a nonpaper (so its existence can be denied) and dated Oct.1, 2006, describes a 'gentlemen's agreement' by the two diplomats to use the proposal 'to help open the way to negotiations.'" Evidently the journalist had seen the nonpaper, or had it read to him, and telephoned the U.N. official in Berlin to dig further: "Solana affably but deftly warded off questions about the nonpaper," Hoagland reported, and then quoted him in adding what is the perfect definition of the term: "Nothing has been agreed. Nothing has been put forward in formal terms."

nonpartisan Without apparent thought of party politics.

In current usage, *bipartisan* means the cooperative efforts of both parties in an area usually the scene of party disagreement; *nonpartisan* (or, as Senator Arthur Vandenberg preferred, *unpartisan*) means areas of civic or patriotic interest where party or ideological difference never arises. The meaning corresponds to the prefixes: two-party, no-party.

The phrase most closely associated with nonpartisan is ABOVE POLITICS; with bipartisan, WATER'S EDGE.

Pleas for nonpartisanship stem from George Washington's farewell address deploring the "baneful effects of the spirit of party," Madison shaking his head at "faction," and Jefferson stating flatly, "If I could not go to Heaven but with a party, I would not go there at all."

When FDR in 1939 called for "cooperation…without trace of partisanship,"

speechwriter Samuel Rosenman properly called it "a plea for nonpartisanship in the form of bipartisanship."

Denunciations of partisanship and of party connection have been prevalent throughout U.S. history, particularly by weaker candidates who felt the need to assert their independence. Zachary Taylor, for example, whose long military COATTAILS helped popularize that expression, took no controversial positions as a Whig in 1848: "If elected, I would not be the mere president of a party. I would endeavor to act independent of party domination. I should feel bound to administer the government untrammeled by party schemes." Taylor won, but the Whigs lost Congress.

Nonpartisanship is also called for by leaders of a party under attack, with some reason, for corruption. Charles Evans Hughes, a tower of integrity in the Harding Administration, said as scandals like Teapot Dome began to be exposed: "Neither political party has a monopoly of virtue or of rascality. Let wrong be exposed and punished, but let no partisan Pecksniffs affect a 'holier-than-thou' attitude. Guilt is personal and knows no party." Adlai Stevenson, fighting off the Truman-era MESS IN WASHINGTON charge in 1952, used Hughes's statement to no avail.

Rarely if ever do public figures stand foursquare in favor of partisanship, though all will speak up for the TWO-PARTY SYSTEM, another way of saying almost the same thing. Bronx Democratic boss Ed Flynn got to the heart of the matter: "There is no such thing as nonpartisanship. If there were, there would be no need for elections. The phrase 'nonpartisanship' has a high moral tone. It is used by men running for public office to attract votes, but deep down in their hearts these men know that it is only a word without real meaning. There is, and always must be, honest disagreement. All of us have our likes and dislikes. And that is the genesis of partisanship." See PARTISAN; PRESIDENT OF ALL THE PEOPLE.

nonpolitical trip Tongue-in-cheek term for a political tour, or "swing around the circle," made to appear "nonpolitical" for strategic or fund-raising reasons.

When an officeholder travels on official business, the public pays his way; on an admittedly politically motivated journey, he must get his party or his supporters to finance him. In the case of presidents, the very appearance of acting as president is more potent than any purely or frankly "political" act; therefore, presidential press secretaries straight-facedly announce "nonpolitical" trips that must, whether intended or not, have strong political overtones. (For a similar construction, see FACT-FINDING TRIP.)

Washington attorney Clark Clifford, appointed Defense Secretary in 1968 and an adviser to Democratic candidates and presidents for a generation, wrote a campaign memo to Harry Truman in 1948 that charted one portion of what was to be a stunning upset:

Since he is President, he cannot be conspicuously active politically until well after the convention. So a President who is also a candidate must resort to subterfuge. He cannot sit silent; he must be in the limelight.... He must resort to the kind of trip Roosevelt made famous in the 1940 campaign—the inspection tour.... No matter how much the opposition and the press pointed out the political overtones of those trips, the people paid little attention, for what they saw was the Head of State performing his duties.

Manchester *Guardian* correspondent Alistair Cooke wrote of a 1964 campaign tour of Lyndon Johnson's: "on this 'nonpolitical,' two-day 9000-mile trip, somebody saw to it that 10,000 people turned up in Great Falls, Montana, 25,000 in Blaine, Washington, that he paid a swift courtesy call on the Mormon Church in Salt Lake City, and that he touched down at Seattle, Portland, and Sacramento, the political power stations of the West Coast."

It is hard to get passionate about this practice, especially since Thomas Jefferson and James Madison visited New York in 1791 for political reasons, blandly letting it be known they were looking for wildflowers and a rare species of butterfly in the Hudson Valley. John F. Kennedy, early in the 1960 primaries, referred to this excuse and added, "But I'm not looking for butterflies. I'm looking for votes."

nonstarter A doomed proposal; one that fails to develop or to make progress.

In British horse-racing jargon, a horse entered in a race but withdrawn before the start is called a *nonstarter*; the American term is a *scratch*. From horse racing, the British term was extended into business usage. In the 1970s, it was in frequent use by Washington Foreign Service Officers, and the word's diplomatic pedigree goes back decades.

Michael Stoil of Arlington, Virginia, provided the lexicographer a British Foreign Office memo dated February 12, 1918. The unprophetic writer of the memo discusses three potential winners in the struggle for control of Russia at the end of World War I: "The Ukrainian Rada [nationalist parliament] was certainly a bad horse to back, Cossack [the Don Cossacks were at the time uneasily allied with General Denikin's anti-Bolshevik army] is almost a non-starter, but Bolshevik would be the worst horse of the lot on which to lay our money, although we may run him as a pacemaker."

For other racing metaphors, see BOLT; DARK HORSE; SHOO-IN.

nonviolence A technique of bringing about social change through peaceful though dramatic demonstrations.

The word is most closely associated with Mohandas K. Gandhi as "the first article of my faith." But the Mahatma's method of "passive resistance" was improved upon by leaders of the civil rights movement in the U.S. in the early 1960s.

The Reverend Martin Luther King, Jr., called 1961 "a year of the victory of the nonviolent method; although blood flowed, not one drop was drawn by a Negro from his adversary." In Birmingham, Alabama, in 1963, King and his followers were criticized by clergymen of that city for provoking violence. In "Letter from a Birmingham Jail" King answered that criticism: "Is not this like condemning the robbed man because his possession of money precipitated the evil act of robbery?" He added: "I have tried to stand between these two forces saying that we need not follow the 'do-nothingism' of the complacent or the hatred and despair of the black nationalist. There is the more excellent way of love and nonviolent protest. I'm grateful to God that, through the Negro church, the dimension of nonviolence entered our struggle. If this philosophy had not emerged I am convinced that by now many streets of the South would be flowing with floods of blood."

By the mid-'60s, however, the word was used to mock black leaders unable to moderate their own extremists. Though the Student Nonviolent Coordinating Committee had nonviolence in its title, it became an anachronism to SNCC leaders like H. "Rap" Brown, who called in 1967 "for less rooting and more shooting."

no problem 1. easy; 2. yes; 3. you're welcome; 4. the situation is being handled.

This expression of approval has joined *O.K.* among the most famous Americanisms in global use.

The Russian equivalent of the term is *nyet problemy*. A similar Russian term, *normalno* (from the same Latin root as English *normal*), expresses the idea without offering the same degree of assurance.

Print citations for *no problem* date back to the early 1960s. In 1963, the journal *American Speech* used it to gloss another, slangier synonym: " 'No sweat' means 'no problem.' " The overuse of the expression, however, has led to its inclusion in the title of Christine Ammer's dictionary of clichés: *Have a Nice Day—No Problem!*

Out of this expression has come another one bordering on a cliché: *to have a problem with* (something), meaning "to find (it) unacceptable, disagreeable, unwelcome, etc." It is often used positively, as in "I don't have a problem with that." But equally often, and especially among outspoken feminists, it serves as an aggressive (or defensive) verbal tactic, as in this passage in a 1992 issue of *People* magazine: "Evander Holyfield, who'll defend his heavyweight title this week, loosens up with ballet exercises. You got a problem with that?"

For at least a generation, *no problem* was a frequent response to "Thank you," replacing "you're welcome," though at the turn of the millennium that old acknowledgment

of gratitude was in turn replaced by "Thank *you*."

normalcy Period of retrenchment, of stability; the promise of President Warren G. Harding.

"Not heroism but healing, not nostrums but normalcy" was the campaign theme of Ohio publisher Warren Harding in 1920, running with Coolidge against Cox and Roosevelt. For the rest of the quotation, see ALLITERATION; for variations, see CATCHWORD.

"After a diet of strong occasions," wrote political scientist Harold Laski in 1940, "a nation, like an individual, turns naturally to the chance of a quiet time. 'Normalcy' is always certain to be popular after crises." Wrote Eisenhower in his 1963 memoir *Mandate for Change*: "Twice in this century the United States, at the end of a war, had celebrated the victory, brought the troops back home, and with relief and hope tried to return to 'normalcy.' "

Harding's use of the word might have been a mistake; "If 'normalcy' is ever to become an accepted word," wrote the British historian G.N. Clark in 1929, "it will presumably be because the late President Harding did not know any better." Such condescension was widespread; many were sure the intended word was written "normality" and fluffed by the speaker. However, the word became a symbol for not only a campaign but an era. The much-abused Harding (whose talent for alliteration led to his popularization of FOUNDING FATHERS) was defended on the charge of error by no less an authority than H. B. Woolf, editorial director of G. & C. Merriam Company, who wrote in 1972: "It is true that Harding's use of *normalcy* subjected him to considerable criticism, but he defended himself by pointing out he found it in the dictionary. (See the [*New York*] *Times* for July 21, 1920.) The word dates from at least 1857, and it is an entry in the 1864, 1890, and 1909 editions of the Merriam-Webster Unabridged."

James McCawley, the great linguistics professor at the U. of Chicago, wrote the author in 1992: "You express puzzlement that *normalcy* caught on and some other neologisms didn't. One reason that the use of normalcy in Harding's address was so catchy is that with that form of the word the alliteration is between two syllables that bear the primary stress (no'strums, no'rmalcy) whereas if Harding had said norma'lity instead, the alliteration would have been on a syllable of that word that had only secondary stress." (It is unlikely that Harding—or his "literary clerk," Judson Welliver, the first fulltime White House speechwriter—thought that through in creating the alliterative passage, but now we know why *normalcy* caught on.)

In a less sloganeering way, Harding returned to the theme that elected him in his inaugural address: "Our supreme task is the resumption of our onward, normal way…the normal balances have been impaired, the channels of distribution have been clogged, the relations of labor and management have been strained…we must strive to normalcy to reach stability."

In 1993, the term was used in *The Washington Post* to describe the situation in Mogadishu, Somalia: "The fragile calm that gave a semblance of normalcy to this ravaged city burst apart today as rampaging mobs shouted for American troops to leave, pelted U.S. and U.N. forces with rocks and looted the Egyptian and French embassies."

A comparison of the frequency of usage in the Google search engine in 2007 shows about two million citations for *normality* and one and a half million for *normalcy*. The alternative usage encouraged by Harding (see OHIO GANG), who won the election in 1920, is closing in on *normality* and may yet win this one, too.

normalization See VIETNAMIZATION.

nose count Informal, often secret, survey of a likely vote within a relatively small but representative group, frequently in Congress.

Drawn from the verb phrase *to count noses*, a more colorful equivalent of *to count heads*, this noun phrase is sometimes hyphenated; it is turned into a gerund as *nose-counting*.

The description began in the 1930s with the sense of a calculation of numerical size. *Life* magazine reported in 1938: "in London

peace-yearning Prime Minister Chamberlain again tried to quarantine the Spanish war by proposing a nose-count and withdrawal of foreign troops."

By 1960, the term was being applied to that decade's census. The *Times* of London commented in September 1960 that "There was much talk just then of the coming 'Nose Count' over the U.S.A. which was one way of making their census sound more personal and pointed." A decade later, *Business Week*, printing the phrase as a one-word compound, referred to the census as "the decennial nosecount."

The term's sense has been narrowed in political usage to the estimation of the outcome of a close vote. A *Christian Science Monitor* article on Western voters in 1986 acknowledged that "a nose count along party lines may be meaningless in much of the region, where party ties tend to be weaker than in the East or the South."

In current use, it is applied most often to assessments of strength within legislatures or caucuses; to be successful as a majority or minority leader in the House or Senate, one must be known as a good *nose-counter*.

no substitute for victory The rallying cry of General of the Army Douglas MacArthur, in his address to Congress of April 19, 1951, following his removal from command in the Far East by President Truman.

Said MacArthur, a superb orator in the old-fashioned manner:

> I know war as few other men now living know it, and nothing to me is more revolting. I have long advocated its complete abolition, as its very destructiveness on both friend and foe has rendered it useless as a means of settling international disputes. …
>
> But once [war] was forced upon us, there is no other alternative than to apply every available means to bring it to a swift end. War's very object is victory, not prolonged indecision.
>
> In war there can be no substitute for victory.

This statement put him into conflict with another theory of war that had been gradually evolving: that it is possible to wage deliberately controlled, LIMITED WAR for an objective short of total victory.

The statement should be considered in the context of the times. General MacArthur had ruled Japan since World War II as something of a proconsul, neither brooking nor being offered much interference. He had conducted the Korean conflict in much the same spirit. But he had been refused permission to turn the 600,000 Chinese Nationalist troops on Formosa loose against the mainland with American logistical support. (See UNLEASH CHIANG.) He had been denied the large numbers of reinforcements he had demanded and refused permission to send bombers against enemy bases north of the Yalu River, the border between North Korea and China.

The General's pressure led President Truman and his advisers to consider MacArthur's removal. When the General wrote a letter to Republican House Minority Leader Joseph Martin, which he read in the House of Representatives, Truman determined to replace his Far East Commander. The recall came hastily when it became known that the *Chicago Tribune*, a paper friendly to the General's views, was about to break the story.

The immediate result was a furor in which personalities, strategies, and constitutional positions were intermixed. A senatorial investigation was begun by those friendly to the General's views, but the course of the investigation ran eventually in the Administration's favor.

The conflicting theses were stated in May 1951 when Senator Leverett Saltonstall quoted from a speech by Dean Rusk, then Assistant Secretary of State, who formulated the core of the limited-war concept: "What we are trying to do is to maintain peace and security without a general war. We are saying to the aggressors, 'You will not be allowed to get away with your crime. You must stop it.' At the same time we are trying to prevent a general conflagration which would consume the very things we are now trying to defend."

General MacArthur totally rejected the new theory. "I think," he said, "that introduces into the military sphere a political control such as I have not known in my life or have ever studied." See NO-WIN POLICY; OLD SOLDIERS NEVER DIE.

no-tax pledge A promise to take future taxation "off the table"; because it binds a winning candidate's hands, it is often considered the last resort of one running behind.

This draconian "contract" often makes a re-election campaign a nightmare for the politician who signs it. The "Taxpayer Protection Pledge" was designed by Grover Norquist, who formed Americans for Tax Reform, a Washington-based lobbying group. The pledge for gubernatorial candidates reads: "I (fill in the blank) pledge to the taxpayers of (fill in the blank) and all the people of this State, that I will oppose and veto any and all efforts to increase taxes." Those who signed it and were forced by a legislature, a referendum, a budget law or an attack of fiscal conscience to break the pledge were inscribed in a "Hall of Shame."

The *Cincinnati Post* in 2007 viewed it as a sign of weakness. "It's an admission that a candidate is so desperate for election that he or she is willing to cede autonomy over tax policy—one of the most important aspects of governing—to an unelected, unaccountable special interest group in Washington."

Early in his campaign for the Republican nomination for president in 2008, former Arkansas governor Mike Huckabee, accused of having raised taxes as governor, told a conservative gathering he was leaning toward signing the no-tax pledge. Mr. Norquist said such candidates would, by so doing, redeem their previous taxation apostasy. "It's called 'secondary virginity,'" he said. "It's a big movement in high school and also available for politicians."

That phrase, along with *neovirginity* and *retroactive virginity*, surfaced in the mid-1980s to assure teenagers who had the experience of sexual intercourse that it was possible to regain high moral status by promising not to repeat that act until marriage. It gave some new impetus to abstinence, and, Norquist apparently hoped, would do the same for fallen politicians.

See READ MY LIPS.

not for attribution An agreement between journalist and news source to use information with the clear understanding that the source's identity would not be revealed.

Not for attribution should not be confused with OFF THE RECORD, when the information is given with the understanding that it will not be used at all, or with *on background*, where a source's general position or political interest may be indicated but the source's name will not be used.

Until late 1971 (when *Washington Post* editors began to object to "collusion" between government and press) the Washington press corps had generally accepted the Lindley Rule, named after journalist Ernest K. Lindley, enabling the President to discuss affairs of the day with reporters without either being quoted or referred to at all. In an article in the *Columbia Journalism Review* titled "The President Nonspeaks," Ben Bagdikian wrote: "Under the Lindley Rules...no meeting took place so far as the public is concerned. If reporters want to use something the nonspeaker has said at the nonmeeting, they must paraphrase the nonspeaker and attribute his ideas to their own intuition or some nameless source." See BACKGROUNDER; TRIAL BALLOON; PLANT.

Lindley, in 1968 a Special Assistant to Secretary of State Dean Rusk, informed the lexicographer (for attribution):

The Lindley Rule was laid down early in the Truman Administration to enable high ranking officials to discuss important matters—especially those involving international and military affairs—without being quoted or referred to in any way. It was, and is, a rule of no attribution—thus differing from the usual "background rule" permitting attribution to "official sources" or "U.S. officials," etc. Thus the paragraph you quote from Bagdikian is not quite correct—attribution to a "nameless source" is not permitted under the Lindley Rule.

The point is a fine one, but there can be no arguing with Hoyle himself: *not for attribution* means the newsman must take responsibility for the statement without hinting where it came from. This is also called *deep background*. The British use *on lobby terms* for the same technique, from the *lobby journalist* who picks up his news outside legislative halls.

In 1992, the D.C. newspaper *Roll Call* wrote of foreign policy discussed "by some advisors to Clinton (in not-for-attribution conversations)." Howard Kurtz in *The Washington Post* recalled a precedent in the previous administration: "And don't forget how James Baker led a charmed media life by feeding not-for-attribution tidbits to key reporters."

The tactic was used by the campaign of Sen. Barack Obama (D-Ill.) when taking on Sen. Hillary Rodham Clinton (D-N.Y.) during their contest for the Democratic presidential nomination in 2007. After Sen. Clinton released personal financial information in June, the Obama campaign circulated to news organizations what *The New York Times* called "a scathing analysis" on "what it demanded to be a not-for-attribution basis." In this instance, the Clinton campaign replied by ripping off the veil. Frustrated by Obama's effort to present himself as not engaging in conventional attack politics, the Clinton campaign obtained a copy of the document and provided it on a *for attribution* basis to the *Times*. A spokesperson for Obama then admitted the campaign's responsibility for disseminating the document, but declined to explain the reason for not wanting initially to be connected with it.

See also AUTHORITATIVE SOURCES; BACKGROUNDER; CHILLING EFFECT; OFF THE RECORD; SOURCES.

nothing to fear but fear itself As-remembered phrase of Franklin Roosevelt's, from the opening of his first inaugural address, March 4, 1933.

In an early draft, FDR was to say, "This is no occasion of soft speaking or for the raising of false hopes." The newly elected president crossed out that line and substituted the more positive statement:

This is preeminently the time to speak the truth, the whole truth, frankly and boldly. Nor need we shrink from honestly facing conditions in our country today. This great nation will endure as it has endured, will revive and will prosper.

So, first of all, let me assert my firm belief that the only thing we have to fear is fear itself—nameless, unreasoning, unjustified terror which paralyzes needed efforts to convert retreat into advance.

Who wrote it? This was the subject of heated controversy among Roosevelt intimates. The copy of the first draft of the speech, in Roosevelt's handwriting, and with a cover note from FDR attesting to its composition at Hyde Park, February 27, 1933, from 9 P.M. to 1:30 A.M., does not contain the famous opening. "The final draft," wrote Samuel I. Rosenman, who edited the Roosevelt public papers, "was typed on March 3.... In that last draft the ... 'fear' sentence had been inserted. The way it was changed was typical of what the President could do with a speech—even in the great rush ..."

Rosenman never asked Roosevelt where the "fear" sentence came from, and did not notice until after FDR's death that it was not in the first draft. He speculated: "It bears a striking resemblance to a statement about fear written by Henry David Thoreau: 'Nothing is so much to be feared as fear.' Eleanor Roosevelt has told me that one of her friends had given the President a copy of some of Thoreau's writings shortly before the day of inauguration, and that it was in his suite at the hotel while this speech was being polished."

In *FDR: The Lion and the Fox*, historian James MacGregor Burns puts that speculation in such a way that the reader can only draw one conclusion: "In his hotel room Roosevelt worked over the speech. Nearby was a copy of Thoreau, with the words, 'Nothing is so much to be feared as fear.'"

Brain truster Raymond Moley dismissed all that. He stated without equivocation in 1966 that Louis Howe wrote the "fear" line, and that Howe got the idea from a newspaper ad that featured the quote a few weeks before. "I was in Roosevelt's Mayflower suite," Moley wrote this lexicographer, "I saw no books there. Nor was I familiar with Thoreau. I had been with Roosevelt more than a year and never heard him mention Thoreau.... And Howe, whose reading—which his asthma-provoked insomnia required—was confined exclusively to detective stories and newspapers, may never have heard of Thoreau."

Moley's history thus marches to the beat of a different drummer: he was with FDR at Hyde Park on the night of February 27, and submitted a draft of the inaugural to him. "He read over my draft carefully and then said that he had better write out the text himself because if Louis Howe (who was expected the next morning) failed to see a draft in his (Roosevelt's) handwriting, he would 'have a fit.'" Presumably FDR wanted to conceal from Howe the fact that he had a ghostwriter. After Roosevelt copied out the speech, Moley says he tossed his own first draft into the fire. "Then, in the morning, as had been anticipated, Howe got his hand into the composition. He proceeded to redictate the draft, adding ... a first paragraph.... I do clearly remember that the phrase appeared in a department store's newspaper advertisement some time earlier in February. I assume that Howe, an inveterate newspaper reader, saw it too.... To Howe's everlasting credit, he realized that the expression fully fitted the occasion."

The who-wrote-it controversy is dwelt on in some length here because it illustrates (1) the difficulty of pinning down the originator of a phrase, and (2) the relative unimportance of the writer as compared to the speaker and the forum. The message was in the ad, assuming Moley's recollection is correct, but who cared? Who even noticed, besides the gnomelike Howe who had the ear of the President-elect? The phrase did not belong to Howe, nor to the advertising copywriter, nor to all those who had used it previously (including Sir Francis Bacon, who said "Nothing is to be feared but fear," and Epictetus, Cicero, Burke, William James, and others). It was Roosevelt's phrase, and it might have rated only a modest mention in a news story had it not been spoken in a momentous inaugural address.

In current memory of the phrase, *nothing* takes precedence over FDR's *the only thing*, as in a 1968 cartoon by Mahood in the *Times* of London showing Dean Rusk reading a newspaper to a worried Lyndon Johnson: "Apart from Kennedy, McCarthy, Nixon, the Viet Nam war, the Senate Foreign Relations Committee and the price of gold, you have nothing to fear but fear itself."

In 2007, *The Washington Times* reported that "political fear still hovers over any legislation that touches on the fight against terrorism, which, for Democrats, may be the new THIRD RAIL of politics.... 'Republicans care more about catching Democrats than catching terrorists,' said Rep. Rahm Emanuel (Ill.), chairman of the House Democratic Caucus. 'They have spent years taking Roosevelt's notion that we have nothing to fear but fear itself and given us nothing but fear.'"

not too much zeal See GUNG HO.

November Republicans Voters who register in the Democratic party to participate in its primary but who intend to vote Republican in the general election.

This began as a Texas expression. Since the Democratic party long dominated Texas politics on the local level, many voters who wished to have a voice in the selection of a candidate for sheriff would register Democratic. But their voting habits in the general election, especially on the national scene, run to the opposite party—hence, *November Republicans*.

Democratic leaders also suspected that some shrewd Republicans registered as Democrats so as to choose a weak candidate for the Republican to run against. See CROSSOVER VOTE.

novus ordo seclorum See UNITED WE STAND; NEW WORLD ORDER.

no-win policy Attack phrase on what is considered an overly cautious military effort, leading not to victory but to stalemate.

The phrase illustrates the exasperation felt by many people at LIMITED WARFARE. General Douglas MacArthur (see NO SUBSTITUTE FOR VICTORY) told the Republican convention in 1952: "It is fatal to enter any war without the will to win it."

But the fact that the newly chosen Eisenhower was a Republican, a former general with an overwhelming reputation for military judgment, and had promised vaguely "I SHALL GO TO KOREA," muted the hardliners' attacks on the lack of a "victory plan" against Communism.

Barry Goldwater's biography was titled *Victory Is His Flight Plan*. Moderates and liberals had difficulty finding phrases that counseled patience and firmness without provocation. "In the face of right-wing attacks," wrote sociologist David Riesman, "the administration denies that it is pursuing a 'no-win' policy; it argues instead that it is just as combative, only more clever or roundabout."

Bayard Rustin, organizer of the March on Washington, made the phrase part of the civil rights lexicon: he charged Negro radicals who rejected the help of white liberals with having a "no-win" attitude, seeking shock with no legislative or social goal. "My quarrel with the no-win tendency," Rustin wrote in the February 1965 *Commentary* magazine, "parallels my quarrel with the moderates outside the movement. As the latter lack the vision or the will for fundamental change, the former lack a realistic strategy for achieving it. For such a strategy they substitute militancy. But militancy is a matter of posture and volume and not of effect."

The turnaround of the phrase came in 1977 when *The Washington Star* carried a headline: "On the Middle East, Carter Lucks into a 'No-Lose' Position." A *Washington Post* headline in 1989 presented a synonym for that optimism: "Win-Win for the Rich."

now is the time ... for all good men to come to the aid of the party. A typewriter exercise and not a political slogan.

Charles E. Weller, a court reporter in Milwaukee in 1867, devised the sentence to cover most of the keys on the typewriter, a new invention by his friend Christopher Latham Sholes. It has about as much political significance as "the quick brown fox jumps over the lazy dog," which is much more useful, since it covers all 26 letters in the alphabet, compared to Weller's 18.

With the virtual demise of typewriters and rise of computers, *key in* has largely replaced the verb *type*.

nuclear option Mock-alarming name for a tactic to prevent filibusters on judicial nominations.

Frustrated by successful maneuvers of the Democratic minority to prevent votes on a number of President George W. Bush's nominees for federal judgeships (tactics used previously by Republicans to prevent votes on many of President Bill Clinton's nominations), Republicans threatened in March of 2005 to bypass Senate Rule No. 22, which requires 60 votes to end a filibuster, and instead cut them off with a simple 51-vote majority. The end-run around Rule 22 would not apply to filibusters on legislation, just those on judicial nominations.

Proponents of the *nuclear option* argued that judicial nominations could be excepted from the usual rule because the Senate's constitutional duty to provide ADVICE AND CONSENT required a regular vote that could not be blocked by the minority.

The metaphoric *nuclear option* drew on the nearly UNTHINKABLE THOUGHTS of military strategists. The phrase was coined in the March 1962 issue of the *American Political Science Review:* "The strategic nuclear option was a policy for which both the weapons and a doctrine existed." During the 1972 campaign, President Nixon charged that his opponent, Senator George McGovern, would so weaken the nation's conventional forces that the U.S. would be left "with only a nuclear option."

Credit for first calling the Republican legislative tactic a *nuclear option* was given to Mississippi Republican Trent Lott. (The tactic itself was first suggested by Alaska Republican Ted Stevens in February of 2003, according to *The Washington Post;* GOP aides referred to it then as "the Hulk," after the muscle-bound comic-book character depicted on the necktie that Stevens was wearing at the time.) Democrats quickly turned the radioactive metaphor back on the Republicans, asserting that they were getting ready to "go nuclear" or "detonate a bomb" on the Senate floor. Not wishing to appear so bellicose, Senator Lott told this columnist: "I don't recall being the first to use the word 'nuclear.' This is a matter of the rules of the Senate, which sets its own rules. I prefer calling it the 'constitutional option.' The other side is acting like we're going to blow the place up."

Legislative Armageddon was avoided in 2005 by a compromise that allowed votes on some judgeships to go forward in return for a promise not to exercise the *nuclear option.* See GANG OF FOURTEEN.

nuclear freeze See FREEZE.

nuclear proliferation The growth in the number of nations that possess atomic or hydrogen bombs.

The mouth-filling phrase is a constant challenge to speakers. Atomic jargoneers say that when the possession of atomic weapons *diffuses* among many nations, the result of scientific information's *dissemination*, what takes place is nuclear *proliferation.*

Proliferation comes from a Latin root meaning "offspring," and was mainly used in biology to denote division of cells or budding of plants. Adlai Stevenson was an early political user of the word in his 1949 inaugural address as governor of Illinois, describing the process by which state departments mushroomed into large bureaucracies. As U.S. Ambassador to the U.N., Stevenson used the word often, as in a 1964 broadcast about Soviet attitudes: "They, too, want to insure the world against the proliferation of nuclear weapons."

President Kennedy had said much the same thing, using a smaller word: "The struggle against nuclear spread is as much in the Soviet interest as our own." The word *spread* means the same in this case, is far easier to handle and understand, and was often used later by Senator Robert Kennedy. However, the subject is momentous, and *proliferate*—though rooted in reproduction—is properly ominous.

nuclear trigger See FINGER ON THE BUTTON; TRIGGER-HAPPY; TRIPWIRE.

numbers game The misleading use of statistics in political argument.

"Figures don't lie, but liars figure" is an expression often applied to those who play the numbers game. An effective attack phrase against those who marshal sound or unsound statistical arguments, *numbers game* connotes gambling (the *numbers racket*).

When the White House in 1954 announced that 2,427 SECURITY RISKS had been removed from their jobs since the Eisenhower administration took office, Adlai Stevenson dubbed it a "numbers game," pointing out that this figure included many who had resigned their posts unaware that they had ever been considered "risks."

"Through two political campaigns," wrote Cabell Phillips in *The Truman Administration*, referring to 1954 and 1956, "Republican party spokesmen played an avid 'numbers game' with the monthly statistics of the Loyalty Review Board to demonstrate the GOP's prowess in cleaning out the Communists left behind by the Democrats. The totals were made to look impressive by lumping voluntary resignations with dismissals. When this bit of chicanery was exposed by the press, the 'numbers game' fell into disuse."

A similar expression is *crowdsmanship*, the technique of inducing a police official to overestimate to reporters the number of people in a rally crowd. A cooperative cop can turn a meager airport turnout (adding the pilot and crew, innocent bystanders and the reporters and police themselves) into "a few hundred enthusiastic supporters, despite the threatening weather." Some policemen try to be scientific, estimating crowds by figuring two square feet per person; others have been known to straight-facedly explain, "I get down on my haunches, count the feet, and divide by two."

For an updated expression of the numbers game, see FUZZY MATH.

nut-cutting A slang allusion to political castration: the denial of favors and the removal of power; or, painful attention to details requiring decision.

To "get down to the nut-cutting" means to abandon broad policy discussion and deal with hard specifics of PATRONAGE and PECKING ORDER. The phrase was inadvertently used by Richard Nixon publicly at the end of the 1968 campaign in its second sense of detail work, "brass tacks" or "NITTY-GRITTY," causing his staff in the television control booth to plunge their faces into their hands. Other taboo expressions with the same metaphoric source used in and out of politics include *ballbuster* (a slave-driving boss, or a particularly difficult problem) and *by the short hairs* (to have another in circumstances where control is an easy matter).

See HANG TOUGH.

nuts and kooks See KOOKS, NUTS AND.

O

obsolete political terms

anxious seat (potential candidate, probable loser)

backstairs influence (manipulation by hidden supporters)

barnacle (hanger-on)

bashaw (high-ranking politician, from Turkish *pasha*)

big bug (replaced by *big shot*, *big wheel*)

black-and-tans (pro-Negro Southern Republicans)

bogus baby (bad legislation)

bottle holder (adviser, from boxing)

buffalo hunt (cover for territorial acquisitions)

bullwhacker (tough political boss)

candle-box returns (phony votes)

come-outer (bolter)

crawfish (back out of a firm position)

cuttlefish (obscure an issue, confuse)

dirt eater (Southerner favoring Union)

doughface (Northerner favoring slavery)

fat-frying (fund solicitation)

fire eaters (Southern secessionists)

floater (swing voter)

forty thieves (politicians in control of finances)

fugleman (henchman)

half-breed (splinter group, antiregular)

heroite (Jackson supporter)

hewgag (clarion call for action)

hunker (conservative Democrat)

leg treasurer (official who absconds with money)

loaves and fishes (spoils, plums)

Loco Foco (anti-Tammany, hard-money Democrats)

mucker (reformer)

off horse (disgruntled politician)

organ grinder (partisan newspaperman)

pap (government handouts)

persimmon (plum)

rag baby (greenback Democrat)

regulators (vigilantes)

ring (derogatory, political organization)

rooster (Democratic symbol)

Salt River (place of political defeat)

scratcher (split ticket voter)

shrieker (noisy abolition supporter)

soap (graft)

still hunt (undercover investigation)

straight-outs (Democrats who tend to bolt)

subsoil (secretly laying the groundwork)

Sunday School (civil service reformers)

swing around the circle (tour the country)

taffy (phony promises)

tin pan (a caucus)

trimmer (opportunist)

wide-awakes (independent Republican clubs)

wire worker (small-time political manager)

young scratcher (antimachine Republican)

obstruction of justice See COVER-UP; SMOKING GUN; STONEWALLING.

-ocracy Combining form for "government" or "power."

This suffix is most often seen in *democracy*, a noun first found in English in the 1500s and ultimately derived from the Greek *demos*, "people," and *kratos*, "power." For a follower or advocate of such power, the combining form is *-crat* or *-ocrat*, as in *democrat*.

Many nouns have been formed using the *-cracy* suffix, usually connected to the root word by the vowel *o*:

intellocracy: This term designates the rule by philosophers and great thinkers of Paris in the mid-twentieth century. As the critic John Sturrock wrote in *The New York Times Book Review* in early 1993, "Once Paris had, not common intellectuals, but *intellocrats*, hardened professionals of abstraction whose job it was to direct the thoughts of their fellow citizens, particularly along the sinuous paths of political correctness.... The old-style French intellocracy died a sumptuous death in 1980 with Jean-Paul Sartre."

kakistocracy: Meaning "government by the worst citizens," this negative term dates back to 1829.

kleptocracy: From the same first root as *kleptomania*, this word means "rule by thieves." It appeared in an 1819 comment on "titular ornaments, common to the Spanish kleptocracy" and was later applied to the Panamanian regime of Manuel Noriega.

meritocracy: A 1958 coinage, this term refers to advancement by merit, either in government with leaders selected by intellectual ability or in schools with advancement according to achievement.

mobocracy: This 1754 creation means "rule by the mob." (*Mob* itself is a shortening of the Latin *mobile vulgus*, "inconstant crowd.")

monocracy: For "rule by a single person," this word dates back to 1651.

plutocracy: "Government by the wealthy" is the definition of this 1652 noun, formed from the Greek *ploutos*, "wealth."

punditocracy: This term is based on *pundit*, from the Sanskrit *pandita*, "learned," now applied to scholars and opinion-givers. An October 1992 piece by David Von Drehle in *The Washington Post* is headlined "Punditocracy Faces Dizzying Spin Cycle," and the reporter satirizes talk-show political commentary by suggesting, "Normally, the punditocracy needs at least a day or two to calcify spontaneous reactions into Conventional Wisdom (C.W.). But with debates scheduled for Oct. 11, 13, 15 and 19, there may not be enough time for the orderly formation of groupthink."

technocracy: Coined during World War I, this term refers to a society managed by technical experts.

theocracy: Using *theo-*, a Greek-based prefix for "God," this 1622 formation refers to any system of government based on divine or religious rules, including any whose leaders are considered to be guided by God. It gained currency after the 9/11 attacks to describe the Taliban in Afghanistan and the mullahs in Iran. See THEOCON.

October surprise Last-minute disruption before an election; unexpected political stunt, revelation, or diplomatic maneuver that could affect an election's outcome.

The prospect of an October surprise by the opposition, planned or not, worries politicians. In 1980, Reagan campaign manager William Casey told this Washington columnist of his suspicion that Democrats supporting the reelection of Jimmy Carter, trailing in the polls, would pull a fast one at the last minute. GOP vice presidential can-

didate George H.W. Bush soon promoted the term in a 1980 campaign statement: "All I know is there's a concern, not just with us but I think generally amongst the electorate, well, this Carter's a politically tough fellow, he'll do anything to get reelected, and let's be prepared for some October surprise."

The Iran-contra controversy, however, turned the attack phrase (as well as a variant, *October fix*) back on the Republicans. For a decade after the '80 campaign, Carter aides charged that Reagan-Bush intermediaries influenced the Ayatollah Khomeini's followers to delay releasing American hostages until after the 1980 election. A congressional investigation found no evidence of such a plot.

By 1991, the noun phrase was being applied to any controversial or unpleasant event in October. *U.S. News & World Report* commented in October 1991 that "The big investment story currently unfolding is not in stocks, where the financial press is fanning fears that another nasty October surprise could lie in store. It's in the fixed-income markets—bonds."

office seeks the man See JOB SEEKS THE MAN.

officialese Government jargon, intended to impress, conceal, or confuse; often the result of writing with scissors and pastepot.

Early among the words ending with the *-ese* suffix was *legalese*, presumably coined by an exasperated layman who could not make sense out of a legal opinion or the warning on a bottle or disclosure statement. However, legalese often has the virtue of eliminating ambiguity, and should be read more as a mathematical equation than as prose, anything herein to the contrary notwithstanding.

Commercialese is a clean-prose movement aimed at killing the use in business correspondence of *ult.*, *inst.*, *per*, and *enclosed please find*.

Gamalielese was H. L. Mencken's word for BLOVIATION by President Warren Gamaliel Harding.

Circumlocution has been around since the sixteenth century but was most memorably used by Charles Dickens in *Little Dorrit* to describe the lofty pretension of *officialese*: "The Circumlocution Office was (as everybody knows without being told) the most important Department under Government."

GOBBLEDYGOOK was coined by Texas Congressman Maury Maverick the younger, and Milton Smith coined its synonym BAFFLEGAB.

CIA-ESE's coinage, although unclassified, is unknown. Its jocular synonym *spookspeak* was a "boosted coinage" by the author on the analogy of George Orwell's *Newspeak*.

For examples, see the capitalized entries above and PENTAGONESE, which includes examples of *diplolingo*, and COMMUNIST TERMINOLOGY.

official family The appointees of a Chief Executive of nation, state, or city, especially those of national importance or who work closely with him or her.

In listing the Secret Service code names in use in November 1963, Kennedy biographer William Manchester grouped the *first family* (Lancer, Lace, Lyric, and Lark—the President, wife, daughter, and son), the *vice-presidential group* (Volunteer, Victoria, Velvet, Venus, Vigilant—the Vice President, wife, two daughters, and aide) and the *official family*: the President's personal secretary, press secretary, military aide, Air Force aide, naval aide, and a White House assistant—all with code names beginning with W—as well as the President's physician and the Secretary of State.

Current usage of *official family* is looser than KITCHEN CABINET, BRAIN TRUST, or (whatever-) MAFIA. It does cover all cabinet officials, the secretary of the cabinet if there is one, White House Chief of Staff, ranking assistants to the President, his legal counsel, heads of the National Security, Economic, and Domestic councils, speechwriters, and whoever the president wants to call "Counselor." It often applies to appointees down to Assistant Secretaries, but at that point the line blurs. It seems not to include the Joint Chiefs of Staff, the FBI Director, or the Intelligence czar, who are presumed to be nonpolitical. A regional director of HUD whom the President is never likely to

meet and does not know is equivalent to a second cousin once removed: a member of the family in a formal sense, but one whose passing is not mourned unless an inheritance is involved.

Walter Lippmann in 1942 considered those in the official family to be those "participating in the action," as in this passage denouncing publicity men and ghostwriters, whose role the columnist dismissed as cosmetic:

> The address of a President should be an event and not a lecture or a public reading, and the decision about when he should speak and what needs saying can be wisely made, not by supposed experts on public opinion, but only by men participating in the action he is going to talk about. There is all the difference in the world between being assisted by his official family and being assisted by GHOST WRITERS.

President Grover Cleveland, preparing to bolt the Democratic party in 1896 over the issue of "free silver" being drawn by candidate William Jennings Bryan, used the phrase in a letter to his Secretary of the Interior, Hoke Smith: "You know how free my association with my official family has been." Smith had said: "While I shall not accept the platform, I must support the nominees of the Chicago Convention." Cleveland told his official family man: "It seems to me like straining at a gnat and swallowing a camel."

off the record In its strict sense, not for publication or dissemination in any way; information for a reporter's private knowledge and guidance only. In loose, unprofessional usage, "don't say where you got this."

Although H. L. Mencken attributed the coinage of this heavily used phrase to Al Smith, he probably confused it with "LET'S LOOK AT THE RECORD"; Mitford Mathews in his *Dictionary of Americanisms* traces *on the record* to 1900, but none of the dictionaries pinpoint the origin of *off the record*.

It probably stemmed from FDR's press conferences in the '30s, which had these categories of answers: *direct quotation* when specifically permitted; *indirect quotation*, but directly attributable to the

President, as "The President said that he …"; *background information* (see NOT FOR ATTRIBUTION; BACKGROUNDER) that could not reveal the President as a source; and *off the record*, information that could not be used at all. Wrote Douglass Cater: "Roosevelt played the various categories with tremendous skill, keeping the correspondents informed even when it did not suit his purpose to inform the public."

Charles Hurd, a White House correspondent during the early '30s, wrote:

the press conference reached, prior to 1941, a preeminent place in our system of government. It did bring into the language, unfortunately, the phrase "off the record." Soon everyone, from the divorcee being interviewed by the society columnist in the Blue Angel to the ward heeler talking to a police reporter, was preceding answers to inquiries with the phrase "off the record," thinking thereby to make their words sound more important—and more likely to be printed.

Perhaps FDR took the term from Harold L. Ickes, who became his Secretary of the Interior. In 1933, Ickes wrote, "He met and answered every question, although in some instances his answers were off the record."

The new weapon occasionally backfired; Ambassador to Great Britain Joseph P. Kennedy gave what he claimed was an off-the-record interview to a *Boston Globe* reporter, who promptly printed Kennedy's thoughts about the King's speech impediment, the Queen's housewifely appearance, Churchill's fondness for brandy, and the notes he kept getting from Eleanor Roosevelt asking him "to have some little Susie Glotz to tea at the Embassy." At that point Kennedy's political future in his own right was finished.

Off the record can be abused by reporters who break the confidence, to the embarrassment of the source; by sources who are embarrassed about their own on-the-record comment, and while not willing to lie about not having said it are willing to claim they said it off the record; and by sources compromising journalists by giving them information "off the record" that they would soon be able to find out elsewhere, thereby temporarily blocking them from publishing their story.

Used before a noun as a modifier, the phrase should be hyphenated. *The Cook Political Report* wrote in 1990 about "numerous 'off-the-record' conversations with reliable non-party committee sources."

See NO COMMENT; SOURCES.

off the reservation Remaining nominally within a party, but refusing to support the party's candidate.

In current use, *off the reservation* is one step short of TAKING A WALK—supporting the other party's candidate—and two steps short of an outright, bridge-burning BOLT—switching to the other party permanently.

Former President Harry Truman explained in his memoirs: "The South's opposition to [Democrat] Al Smith gave Hoover many southern states, and he won by a comfortable margin. In the general election two years later, however, almost all the people who were running for office in the south and had supported [Republican] Hoover were defeated. That was the price they had to pay for going 'off the reservation' in 1928." In Truman's usage, the phrase included those who actively supported the opposition candidate; most politicians consider outright support of the opposition to be the act of a turncoat, more than a shade stronger than "off the reservation."

The phrase first surfaced in *The Atlanta Constitution* in 1909. The metaphor is rooted in traders' lingo, referring to Indian reservations in the days when unscrupulous whites would trade "firewater" for goods, and *off the reservation* was a lonely and dangerous place for an aboriginal American to be.

off-year Description of congressional or state elections that take place in the middle of a presidential term, where the number of registered voters who vote is always lower than in years that feature a national race.

This compound adjective is in a state of semantic flux; the above definition is under challenge by a competing usage. *Off-year* used to mean "halfway through a presidential term," as in this 1954 use by Eisenhower: he told a press conference halfway through his first term that he did not think a President should intervene "too intensively and directly in off-year Congressional elections," but rather create an "umbrella of accomplishment" under which congressional candidates of his party could run.

In recent years, however, *midterm* is increasingly taken to mean "halfway through a presidential term," while *off-year* is sometimes, but no longer usually, taken to be a synonym for that. Candidates for mayor and other local offices, as well as some governors, run in odd-numbered years between congressional elections, but until the late 1980s there had been no special expression for these way-off years. In those odd-numbered years, when elections for mainly local offices take place, the awkward term *off-off year* emerged (probably bottomed on the theatrical designation of small houses farther from the Times Square "theater district" than well-established off-Broadway houses as *off-off Broadway*).

"The irony is that the attack commercial," reported *The Wall Street Journal* in 1989, when voter turnout plummeted to 48%, "has come of age in an off-off election year with only a few contests scattered across the country."

A reluctance to campaign at midterm is a characteristic of presidents, who often assign that task to their vice presidents; traditionally, the party in control of the White House loses seats in Congress in elections held in the middle of a presidential term.

In *midterm* elections, the average reduction of House seats held by the party in power in the White House ranges from twenty to forty, depending on how far back one wishes to start and whether one chooses all midterms or comparable first or second terms. The Republicans did badly at Eisenhower's midterms, but well at Nixon's; the Democrats did well under Kennedy, badly under Johnson. At the middle of the second term of a president, the party in power in the White House is especially vulnerable; Republicans in 2006 lost their majority in both houses of Congress in the wake of the low popularity of George W. Bush caused by the Iraq war, exacerbated by corruption scandals involving Republican congressmen.

Both major parties are concerned with what Lynn Sweet of the *Chicago Sun-Times* referred to as "drop-off voters" in the D.C. newspaper *The Hill*: "Drop-off voters from 2004 are a sought-after micro-target for Democrats in 2006." She quoted Rep. Rahm Emanuel, an Illinois Democrat heading that party's midterm (formerly *off-year*) House efforts, saying, "The entire focus of our effort...is to focus on those people who do vote presidential but don't vote in non-presidential years." Within a week, the paper was headlined "Dems hunt for drop-off voters." See TURNOUT.

Ohio gang See SMOKE-FILLED ROOM.

old bull An influential senior member of Congress; used in pejoration by YOUNG TURKS, and sometimes in amused self-deprecation by a politically secure OLD FOGY.

Rebellious House Democrats in 1985 deposed 80-year-old Rep. Melvin Price as chairman of its Armed Services Committee and replaced him with Wisconsin Democrat Les Aspin, the first time in a decade that an ouster of such magnitude had taken place. "It's like the animals," observed Rep. Claude Pepper, at 84 the oldest member of Congress. "When the old bull weakens, the young bull comes up and starts running him off."

In 1995, the *Rocky Mountain News* noted that "Old bull conservatives, typically from Midwestern small towns, were once a large majority of House Republicans; now they number about 75 of the 230." The characterization is bipartisan: in 2003, the *Washington Post* headlined a David Broder column "'Old Bull' Democrats Frustrate House GOP." In 2006, Stephen Moore observed in *The Wall Street Journal* that Governor Mark Sanford of South Carolina "may be the only politician in America under assault for governing as a fiscal tightwad...some of his most formidable adversaries are the old bull politicians in his own party."

The phrase is usually applied to elected officials, a synonym of the "College of Cardinals," a name given to members of the House Appropriations committee. However, some appointed members of an administration are criticized with the phrase, as was William J. Casey, first a Nixon campaign aide and later a Reagan campaign manager, appointed after Reagan's 1980 victory to be Director of Central Intelligence. "Casey, the old bull who'd led Reagan's presidential campaign," opined *The Boston Globe* in 1987, "lied routinely to Congress ..."

The lexicographer asked the profoundly experienced Casey about that usage. He recounted a story that he believed to be the source of the expression: "An old bull and a young bull were standing high on a hill overlooking a verdant valley. As a herd of cows entered the field below, the young bull got all excited and said 'Let's paw the ground and snort loudly and then race down the hill and service a couple of them beautiful cows.' And the old bull replied, 'Let's not paw the ground. No snorting at all. Let's just walk slowly down the hill—and service 'em all.'"

Old China Hands Western journalists or diplomats, often the children of missionaries, who spent years in China.

Author Pearl Buck and Time, Inc. founder Henry Luce, both children of missionaries to China, were the best-known *Old China Hands*. Authors Edgar Snow and Alice Tinsdale Hobart were included in this category, along with diplomats John Davies and John Service, who were attacked as Communist FELLOW TRAVELERS in the fifties.

"The prime time of Old China Hands," wrote Nym Wales, pseudonym of Helen Foster Snow (wife of Edgar Snow), "was in the thirties. ... There are still a few Old Hands living in China, notably Anna Louise Strong, now in her eighties [died in 1970, buried in China], whose first book described the 1927 revolution and who still sends out a newsletter favoring Mao and the Red Guards. ... Living in China is always a searing experience; the letter 'C' remains branded on every China Hand."

China Hand differs from CHINA WATCHER: *hand* connotes previous residence, *watcher* (or *Beijingologist*) connotes observation from outside.

old Europe Western European nations; originally and specifically, France and Germany, whose leaders opposed the U.S. plan to attack Iraq in 2003.

Secretary of Defense Donald Rumsfeld, who had served as U.S. Ambassador to NATO in the early '70s, characterized France and Germany as "old Europe" at a briefing for the foreign press in Washington two months before the U.S.-led invasion of Iraq. Questioned by a Dutch correspondent about lack of public support for the impending war in France, Germany, and other European countries, including his own, Rumsfeld replied: "You're thinking of Europe as Germany and France. I think that's old Europe. If you look at the entire NATO Europe today, the center of gravity is shifting to the east."

Rumsfeld's distinction between the traditionally dominant powers of western Europe and the nations to the east—formerly part of the Soviet bloc but in the process of becoming NATO members and gaining European influence as he spoke—fed existing anti-American sentiment in Germany and France. One of the more measured responses came from the German defense minister, Volker Ruehe: "Rumsfeld is not exactly a diplomat and it is not very wise to say something like that." Roselyne Bachelot, French environment minister, expostulated, "If you knew what I felt like telling Mr. Rumsfeld—" and added that Rumsfeld was talking "Cambronne's word," this being a French euphemism for *merde*; translation in OLD GUARD.

Rumsfeld was not aware of it, but he did not coin the phrase. (*Old Europe* "just popped into my head," he told this columnist at a subsequent conference of mainly hardline European leaders in Munich.) Karl Marx and Friedrich Engels employed it in the opening of *The Communist Manifesto*, published in German in 1848, on the eve of that year's revolutionary upheavals throughout much of Europe, and first translated into English two years later. The *Manifesto*'s initial image grabs the attention: "A specter is haunting Europe—the specter of communism. All the powers of old Europe have entered into a holy alliance to exorcise this specter." For Marx and Engels, "old" Europe meant the *anciens régimes* of Russia, Prussia, and Austria. (The 1850 English version, by Helen Macfarlane, began, "A frightful hobgoblin stalks throughout Europe. We are haunted by a ghost, the ghost of communism. All the Powers of the Past have joined in a holy crusade to lay this ghost to rest ..." The famous "specter" translation, which also renders "des alten Europa" accurately as "old Europe," is the 1888 one by Samuel Moore in collaboration with Engels, who had a good knowledge of English and may well have contributed to the striking first line.)

Rumsfeld's casual comment led Spanish Prime Minister José Luis Rodríguez Zapatero to reassure the leaders of Germany and France in a Madrid meeting in 2004 that "the old Europe is brand new." Rumsfeld tried to smooth ruffled European feathers with humor. He began a speech at the above-noted conference in Munich in early 2005 by saying: "When I first mentioned that I might be traveling in France and Germany it raised some eyebrows.... One wag said it ought to be an interesting trip after all that has been said. I thought for a moment and then I replied: 'Oh, that was the old Rumsfeld.'"

His most profound line dealt with the limitations of military intelligence: "There are known unknowns ... things that we know we don't know. But there are also unknown unknowns ... things we don't know we don't know."

old fogy A REACTIONARY; in the bureaucratic sense, a time-server burdened with the barnacles of backwardness.

The word may have a military origin. *Fogy* was originally a Scottish term for "an invalid or garrison soldier" or "a man advanced in life." (There is a theory that this derives from "an increase of pay due to length of service," but the *OED* has this sense as "U.S. colloq.," attested only from 1881.)

William Makepeace Thackeray used it in *The Book of Snobs*, published in *Punch* in 1846–47: "the honest, rosy old fogies, the mouldy old dandies, the waist-belts and glossy wigs and tight cravats of these most

raucous and respectable men." *The John-Donkey*, an American imitator of *Punch*, gave it a political twist a year later in an article titled "The Political Old Fogy."

Kentucky Rep. John Cabell Breckenridge, later James Buchanan's Vice President and then a candidate against Lincoln in 1860, said in 1852: "their principles are denounced in the cant language of the day as 'old fogyism,' and themselves as 'old fogies' ... wholly incompetent to fathom the ideas or control the policy of this generation."

Current meaning has not changed. In 1967 *The New Republic*'s "TRB" (Richard Strout) wrote: "When the House repeatedly backed an amendment for direct election of senators and the Senate refused to act, the threat of a constitutional convention finally brought the old fogeys around."

As can be seen above, there are several ways to spell the noun in the phrase; currently, *fogy* and *fogys* compete with *fogey*, *fogies*, and *fogeys*.

Youthful conservatives are occasionally referred to as *Young Fogys*, but elderly reformers are not called *Old Turks*. See OLD BULL.

Old Guard Hard-core loyalist; strongly conservative Republican.

Very few represent themselves as being members of the Old Guard, since it now has the connotation of HIDEBOUND and stodgy; it is most often an epithet used by liberals against conservatives, or by reformers against regulars. Among Republicans, the party's wings in the 1880s were the Stalwarts vs. the Half-Breeds; in the 1900s the Regulars vs. the Progressives; in the '50s, the Old Guard vs. the Modern Republicans, or (as characterized by liberal Republicans) extremists vs. moderates, or (as characterized by conservatives) ME-TOOers vs. "real" Republicans, and more recently, NEOCONS vs. MOVEMENT conservatives.

When the Old Guard is used in its broadest sense—an entrenched conservative faction in either party, loyal to its traditions—its opposing faction is often called the YOUNG TURKS, which, because it can include women, has outlasted ANGRY YOUNG

MEN. The righties refer to the lefties as RINOs—"Republicans In Name Only."

Most Old Fogies and Guardsmen are derided as "implacable." The conservative humorist Vic Gold, writing under the pseudonym "Ernst Angst" in his 1969 book *So You Want to Be a Liberal*, defined "implacable" as "*hard-line, old guard, last ditch.* Pertaining to Non-Liberal zealotry, as distinguished from *principled*, the approved description of Liberal implacability."

When the Republican platform in 1944 "accepted the purposes" of the National Labor Relations Act, the Social Security Act, and other New Deal legislation, Franklin Roosevelt solemnly read the Republican plank to a Democratic audience and commented: "The whole purpose of Republican oratory these days seems to be to switch labels.... Can the Old Guard pass itself off as the New Deal? I think not."

Adlai Stevenson, just before his first defeat in 1952, said, "It is a tragedy that the Old Guard has succeeded in doing what Hitler's best general could never do: they have captured Eisenhower."

The expression was used politically in the U.S. as early as 1844. "The Old Guard knows how to die," quoted the *Ohio State Journal*, "but the Old Guard does not know how to surrender. So said Napoleon on a celebrated occasion. So will all the Whigs say ... we have gallant Whig champions and a glorious cause: 'The Old Guard will never surrender!'" (The Whig Henry Clay lost to the Democrat James Polk; after the subsequent defeat by Democrat Zachary Taylor, the Whigs surrendered.)

Source of the term was Napoleon's *Old Guard*, his most loyal troops. Count Pierre-Jacques-Étienne Cambronne, who was captured at the Battle of Waterloo, supposedly said about them: "The Guard dies, but never surrenders." According to French writer Édouard Fournier in 1859, the remark was invented by a reporter named Rougemont; Count Cambronne went to his grave denying he ever said it. The count is remembered today by a monument erected to him in Nantes, upon which is inscribed: "The Guard dies, but never surrenders." This following story

may be counter-apocryphal, but the count's response to a surrender demand was really supposed to have been *"Merde!"*, the expletive for excrement now known in France as *le mot de Cambronne*. There are reports that Cambronne insisted he'd said "Merde." (See OLD EUROPE.)

The Old Guard became identified with the Republican party in 1880 by advocates of a third term for Ulysses Grant. "Three hundred and six of them," wrote Don Chidsey, "stood on the burning deck when all but them had fled. One, Chauncey I. Filley, went so far as to have 306 Grant medals struck, and he distributed these: they bore not only the much publicized number, but also the words 'The Old Guard,' and thereby gave Republican reactionaries ... a new title."

Young Americans for Freedom, a conservative group, gave the diehard phrase a fresh fillip in the '70s by naming their magazine *The New Guard*. The older expression, however, continues to be used. South Carolina Governor Carroll Campbell told the Republican National Convention in Houston in 1992, "George [H.W.] Bush is working hard to keep this country moving by changing the tax-and-spend philosophy of the old guard in Congress." And the French-based phrase, mixed in with political Americanisms, was used in 2007 by the columnist Joceline Tan in the *Malaysia Star*: "The grouses of the old guard are wide-ranging ... they are upset about toning down the Islamic State agenda and uncomfortable with the YOUNG TURKS who were blown in by the so-called WINDS OF CHANGE."

old pro One richly experienced in politics, regardless of age; the highest accolade among professionals.

Not to be confused with PARTY ELDERS, *old pros* may be found among: (1) officeholders who "know the ropes" and "where the bodies are buried"; (2) self-proclaimed "amateurs," who can be depended upon to run citizens' movements in a sound professional manner every few years; (3) party professionals adept at a NOSE COUNT who can be distinguished from the "three *h*'s" who populate campaign headquarters—HACK, HENCHMAN, and *hanger-on*.

Old pros on different sides of the political fence know of one another, and are sometimes acquainted, but seldom know one another well. This contrasts with opposition-party elected officials, who come to know and often like one another because of their daily contact and need for striking compromises. To them, Shakespeare's words about lawyers apply: "Adversaries…in law strive mightily, but eat and drink as friends."

Professional campaign managers, however, often make it a point to honor their respected foes by not socializing with them. Julius C. C. Edelstein, New York Mayor Robert F. Wagner's executive assistant and campaign planner, once explained why he never met John A. Wells, an eminent attorney who often managed major Republican campaigns in New York. Edelstein told the author a story about a college student in Chicago in the 1920s:

The student had made contact with a gang of mobsters and asked if he could observe some of their activities for his course in criminology. The mobsters were strangely delighted by the prospect of a "perfesser" studying their habits, and they took him under their wing. One day the student inquired why the gang had to import out-of-state torpedoes to kill off rival hoodlums. Didn't the gang have its own able trigger men?

The gangsters explained that the local hoodlums, in all the rival gangs, had grown up together in the same neighborhood. When one was assigned to rub out another, he just couldn't pull the trigger—friendship and sentiment stood in the way. So they had to hire guns from out of town to do the job that only a stranger could do.

Now, I wouldn't say that campaign managers are quite like torpedoes. But a man who manages a political campaign is in the hottest end of politics, and he is often called on to strike hard for his candidate with no thought of personal consideration.

Edelstein added: "That's why Jack Wells and I are not likely to meet." They never did.

old soldiers never die Sentimental touch introduced by General Douglas MacArthur at the conclusion of his speech in 1951, after having been relieved of command by President Truman.

MacArthur, who favored "hot pursuit" of Communist aircraft into China, was relieved by President Truman, who felt he was insubordinate and trying to dictate rather than carry out policy decided upon by civilians. Upon his return, MacArthur spoke to a joint meeting of Congress (not a joint session; only presidents address joint sessions):

I still remember the refrain of one of the most popular barracks ballads of that day which proclaimed most proudly that old soldiers never die; they just fade away. And like the old soldier in that ballad, I now close my military career and just fade away, an old soldier who tried to do his duty as God gave him the sight to see that duty.

The last few words, overlooked in the rush to look up and issue a recording of "Old Soldiers Never Die," were reminiscent of a phrase in Lincoln's second inaugural: "with firmness in the right, as God gives us to see the right …" See NO SUBSTITUTE FOR VICTORY.

old-time religion Conservative economics.

Herbert Stein, chairman of the Council of Economic Advisers in 1972–73, frequently referred to "that old-time religion" in discussing economic politics to eliminate or restrain inflation. Dr. Stein liked the phrase because conservative economics, like some fundamentalist religious worship, has been honored more with lip service than with church attendance.

The phrase is used usually but not always with a derisive cast. "Discipline and patience are required," wrote Tilford Gaines in a 1974 bank newsletter, "if the 'old-time religion' is to work, and there is every reason to hope that it will."

The expression was first popularized in the '40s by bandleader Phil Harris' rendition of "(Give Me That) Old Time Religion."

old wine in new bottles A derogatory characterization of negotiating proposals presented in a fresh form but holding to the previous position.

At the Paris peace talks on September 17, 1970, the North Vietnamese and Viet Cong delegations presented an eight-point plan for ending the war that U.S. Ambassador David E. K. Bruce promptly labeled "old wine in new bottles."

This vivid figure of speech made the U.S. delegation's point more dramatically than any ordinary diplomatic rejection as "nothing new." The phrase became part of the language of diplomacy, and later in 1970, when Henry Kissinger, President Nixon's National Security Adviser, was going over the language of a U.S. proposal for a standstill cease-fire and immediate prisoner exchange, and this writer did not seem impressed with its likelihood of acceptance, he protested: "It's new wine."

When the Communists presented another proposal nearly a year later, the reporter Marilyn Berger wrote: "There appeared to be a determined U.S. effort, however, not to dismiss the Communists' seven-point plan in the way the chief U.S. negotiator at the Paris peace talks [Ambassador Bruce] turned aside the last Communist proposal as 'old wine in new bottles.'"

In 1968 the National Advisory Commission on Civil Disorders—the Kerner Commission, its staff headed by Washington attorney David Ginsburg—reported that "What is new about Black Power is phraseology rather than substance...the rhetoric is different, but the ideas are remarkably similar." The heading for that section of its report was "Old Wine in New Bottles."

A much earlier use was remarked by the novelist Herman Melville, who noted in a diary during a European tour in 1849 that he had been given a book by Dr. Augustus Gardner entitled *Old Wine in New Bottles, or Spare Hours of a Student in Paris*.

The expression is current in international commentary. Steve Hurst of Cable News Network remarked of Boris Yeltsin's leadership of Russia in 1992, "President Yeltsin has offered a power-sharing compromise that to most smacks of old wine in new bottles."

The phrase is a switch on a line in the Gospel according to St. Matthew (9:17), in which Jesus says: "Neither do men put new wine into old bottles; else the bottles break, and the wine runneth out, and the bottles perish: but they put new wine into new bottles, and both are preserved." In

biblical times, bottles were made of leather, and used bottles could not bear the fermentation strain of new wine; the parable means that the old Law of the Hebrew religion could not encompass the new spirit of Christ's gospel.

Thus, in the original use, *new wine in old bottles* was destructive; in current use, *old wine in new bottles* is deceptive.

No wine is so old that a pun cannot be uncorked: on May 19, 1976, strategist Stanley Hoffmann scoffed at Secretary of State Henry Kissinger's attempt to put a good face on Franco-American relations with an Op-Ed piece titled "Old Whine, New Bottles."

oleaginous lingo See BUNK; WEASEL WORDS.

ombudsman An official intermediary between citizen and government or other large organization to counteract accusations of delay, error, injustice, and impersonality of bureaucracy.

The word comes from Swedish, a derivative of the Old Swedish *umboth*, meaning "commission, order." In modern Swedish, an *ombudsman* can be any kind of agent, from commercial representative to member of Parliament (Riksdag), but the worldwide meaning of the term is taken from what Swedes call the "JO": *Riksdagens Justitieombudsman*, Parliamentary Commissioner for Justice.

The office was started in Sweden in 1809, has been adopted in varying forms by other countries, and has aroused worldwide interest as the complexity of government administration grows. In 1967 the State of Hawaii adopted an Ombudsman Act: "the Ombudsman may establish procedures for receiving and processing complaints, conducting investigations, and reporting his findings" without regard to "the finality of any administrative act." The crucial point in his powers is the right to look into "unreasonable, unfair, oppressive, or unnecessarily discriminatory" acts by government officials "*even though* in accordance with law" (italics in the act).

"A key characteristic of the Ombudsman," writes Professor Stanley Anderson of the University of California, "is his accessibility to the public. Anyone may file a complaint simply by writing a letter. This is especially important to those deprived of their freedom in jails, hospitals, sanitoria, etc." A similar function is provided by the military in the U.S. in its office of Inspector General, which overlooks "channels" in its investigations.

The argument against ombudsmen is that they take over functions that properly should be handled by mayors, district attorneys, and other elected officials; if these officials are not responsive to legitimate citizen complaints, goes the criticism, they should be replaced, not second-guessed or circumvented.

Media organizations have begun to designate intermediaries between editors and readers. When *The New York Times* did so, it avoided the foreign word and chose the name *public editor*. (There is not yet a "private" editor.) Some journalists refer to media ombudsmen as "shooflies," a slang term used by some police officers about members of internal departmental units investigating accusations of police brutality.

omnibus bill See PACKAGE DEAL.

on all fours See UP TO SPEED.

one glass of water doctrine See DOCTRINES.

one-house bill Legislation intended for grandstanding only, not for passage into law.

Lobbyists in state capitals often work on one-house bills: getting passage in the state senate or assembly with the tacit assurance that the bill will be killed in the other house. The lobbyist can then show his client proof of some success without disturbing the status quo. (See FETCHER BILL.)

Another meaning has to do with divided legislatures, when one house is Democratic and the other Republican, and the passage of the bill is not venal but equally hopeless, unless it can be tied to another "one-house bill" and a deal struck.

one-idea parties See IDEAS.

one man, one vote A slogan urging reapportionment of legislatures so that each legislator represents approximately the same number of people; now modified to "one person, one vote."

Peter Straus, owner of New York radio station WMCA, brought the lawsuit that resulted in the Supreme Court decision setting forth the principle of *one man, one vote*. He told the author in 1968:

> We wanted to do a radio spot campaign to back up our editorials about reapportionment. But how do you get anybody excited about anything sounding as dull as "reapportionment"? We needed a phrase, a handle, that would make this issue come to life. Digging through the literature on the subject, one of our writers came across "one man, one vote." We used it, and we hit it hard.

The Supreme Court in 1963 had already picked up the phrase in its decision in *Gray v. Sanders* to forbid a state from electing governors or senators by the county unit system, but modified the slogan to include women voters: "The conception of political equality from the Declaration of Independence, to Lincoln's Gettysburg Address, to the Fifteenth, Seventeenth and Nineteenth Amendments can mean only one thing—one person, one vote."

In a subsequent decision, the Court held: "While it may not be possible to draw congressional districts with mathematical precision, that is no excuse for ignoring our Constitution's plain objective of making equal representation for equal numbers of people the fundamental goal for the House of Representatives." On June 15, 1964, the Court capped the series of decisions with an order to apportion both houses of all state legislatures on the basis of population only.

Because the U.S. Senate is not elected on the basis of population, opposition to the Court's decisions could be expected to be articulated there. Senator Everett Dirksen (R-Ill.), then Minority Leader, called attention to some of the points made in dissent by Justice Harlan: "Legislators can represent their electors only by speaking for their interests—economic, social, political—many of which do reflect the place where electors live," and thus geographic area, as well as population, should be represented.

"By focusing exclusively on numbers … the Court deals in abstractions which will be recognized even by the politically unsophisticated to have little relevance to the realities of political life."

One effect was the transfer of power from rural to urban areas, and the slogan did much to crystallize that issue. Wrote the conservative columnist Arthur Krock: "The one-man, one-vote principle on which the Supreme Court ruling is based has the quality of those political slogans which appeal to the strong streak of idealism in the American people."

The phrase was coined in England early in the nineteenth century in a different context: Major John Cartwright (1740–1824), a radical Member of the House of Commons, called "the Father of Reform," led the fight against "plural voting" with the slogan "one man, one vote." At that time it was possible for a man to cast two ballots, one on the basis of his residence and the other a "business" or "university" qualification. The House of Lords rejected bills passed by the House of Commons on this subject for more than a century; in 1948 the Representation of the People Act finally abolished the right to exercise more than one vote in a parliamentary election.

Both slogan and issue resurfaced in the mid-seventies, as international pressure was applied to the white leadership of Rhodesia and South Africa to allow "majority rule," which many blacks saw as the end of intolerable repression by whites and which many whites took to be revolution by the blacks. A 1977 dispatch to the London *Daily Telegraph* from Salisbury, Rhodesia, read: "The Rhodesian Government will accept the principle of 'one man, one vote' only if there are adequate safeguards written into a new constitution …" That newspaper's conservative columnist, Peregrine Worsthorne, held that "this theory can mean nothing less than a whole great continent's return to primitive savagery." It turned out he was mistaken.

As sexual equality in language gained in the 1980s, the phrase was edited to the Supreme Court's prescient "one *person*, one vote." The original use, however, remains;

in 1993, *The Boston Globe* opined about the war in former Yugoslavia: "As bestial as the Serbs have been, it is too late to bring back the vision of a unitary, one-man, one-vote state that the Bosnian government hoped for."

one-party press An accusation that the news media favors one political party, and as a result denies the opposition equal or fair coverage.

Andrew Jackson's supporters called any newspaper who opposed their man "the kennel press." In that tradition, Harry Truman wrote, "As far as I was concerned, they had sold out to the SPECIAL INTERESTS, and that is why I referred to them in my campaign speeches as the 'kept press and paid radio.' " Truman reminded his staff that since 1800, the press had played an important role in thirty-six elections: eighteen times behind the winner, eighteen times behind the loser. "That was the clearest proof I needed that I had nothing to fear regarding the influence of the newspapers …"

Although abolitionist Wendell Phillips had been certain "we live under a government of men and morning newspapers," Democratic candidates in more recent times found press opposition did not ensure defeat. In 1936 FDR told Samuel Rosenman: "Wait till October comes around when we really get a chance to tell the people the facts—which they're not getting now from their newspapers." Harold Ickes confided to his diary that "the outstanding thing about the campaign was the lack of influence of the newspapers … the very bitterness of the assault upon the President by the newspapers reacted in his favor."

At that same time, in Britain, Prime Minister Stanley Baldwin was making much the same discovery. The combined attack of Lord Beaverbrook and Lord Rothermere, the press peers, together with the denunciations of Winston Churchill, did not succeed in destroying Baldwin's leadership of the Conservative party. "It disclosed," wrote historian R. J. Minney, "that the influence of the popular press was by no means as wide and effective as had been imagined." Baldwin suffered in silence, then finally lashed back: "What the proprietorship of these papers is aiming at is power, and power without responsibility—the prerogative of the harlot throughout the ages."

Adlai Stevenson popularized the phrase *one-party press* in 1952 in a speech to newspapermen of Portland, Oregon:

> the overwhelming majority of the press is just against Democrats. And it is against Democrats, so far as I can see, not after a sober and considered review of the alternatives, but automatically, as dogs are against cats. As soon as a newspaper—I speak of the great majority, not of the enlightened ten per cent—sees a Democratic candidate it is filled with an unconquerable yen to chase him up an alley.... I am in favor of a two-party system in politics. And I think we have a pretty healthy two-party system at this moment. But I am in favor of a two-party system in our press too. And I am, frankly, considerably concerned when I see the extent to which we are developing a one-party press in a two-party country.

Democrats are not the only ones to suffer from what they feel is slanted treatment from the press. Richard M. Nixon, in what he promised would be his "last press conference" after his unsuccessful race for the governorship of California in 1962, bitterly reminded the reporters covering his campaign of the press's responsibility to "put one lonely reporter on the campaign who will report what the candidate says now and then." See FAIR AND BALANCED. Eleven years later, in his farewell to the White House staff, the new ex-president passed along some hard-earned advice that could well be considered by his successors: "Those who hate you don't win unless you hate them—and then you destroy yourself."

one-party rule Charge made by candidates of a minority party in areas where the majority is entrenched; a system that often leads to inefficiency and sometimes to corruption.

Depending on demography and voting patterns, Republicans and Democrats alike join in denouncing *one-party rule*. See SOLID SOUTH. Its opposite is the TWO-PARTY SYSTEM, and its predecessor phrase was probably *one-man power*, used to attack Andrew Jackson and his followers, who favored a strong executive branch.

Congressman (later Speaker of the House) Thomas B. Reed said in 1880: "The best system is to have one party govern and the other party watch." This was an excellent argument against coalition and in favor of the two-party system—provided the parties changed places from time to time. In 1994, Republicans became the majority in Congress for the first time since 1954, and checked a Democratic president; in 2006, Democrats became the majority during the administration of a Republican president, and became a balancing force. In both cases, this pleased those who liked CHECKS AND BALANCES and displeased those worried about GRIDLOCK.

one-term president If said about an incumbent, a charge of weakness and vulnerability; if said about a past occupant of an office, a cool and cruelly accurate account.

The first noted use of the phrase was by Jacob Brinkerhoff, a two-term congressman from Ohio, on the House floor January 13, 1845: "The North had been taunted with the fact that it never had any but one-term presidents, democratic or federal."

Dwight Eisenhower used the phrase in 1968 about Richard Nixon, in a way that imputed courage to the one-termer: "I think Dick's going to be elected President but I think he's going to be a one-term President. I think he's really going to fight inflation, and that will kill him politically." Nixon must have remembered the phrase: in a line he added to the speech he made on April 30, 1970, announcing an incursion into Cambodia, he said: "I would rather be a one-term President and do what I believe is right than to be a two-term President at the cost of seeing America become a second-rate power ..." See I'D RATHER BE RIGHT.

New York Times columnist Tom Wicker used the phrase in a column headed "One Term for Carter" in 1977: "People who think and talk about politics are beginning to ask each other openly: 'Is Jimmy Carter a one-term President?' The question may seem strange and premature, when the man has been in office less than a year; yet it has a certain validity." Six months later, an editorial in the *Times* began: "The story is told in Washington of two Senators. Senator A says, 'Carter is beginning to look like a one-term President.' Senator B replies, 'Yes, but when does it begin?'"

The question of a one-term presidency was posed early in the Administrations of Reagan (two terms), the elder Bush (one) and Clinton and the younger Bush (two), usually after the HONEYMOON PERIOD ended and ratings dropped. One rarely hears the question asked positively: Will the incumbent be a two-term President?

one-third of a nation FDR's memorable phrase calling the nation's attention to the extent of poverty within.

There was probably more revising and rewriting of President Roosevelt's second inaugural address of January 20, 1937, than any other major Roosevelt speech. Thomas Corcoran, Stanley High, Donald Richberg, and Samuel Rosenman submitted drafts and made changes. FDR insisted on a human treatment of the statistics. "I see tens of millions of its citizens" denied the "necessities of life"; "I see millions denied education, recreation, and the opportunity to better their lot and the lot of their children"; and there followed several other examples of what "I see."

Rosenman had written in an early draft a summation of the "I see's" with a final "I see." He recalls: "I do not remember nor is there a record of what that summation of mine was, for the President rubbed out all I had written in pencil after that final I see and after a moment's reflection substituted in his own hand his summation: 'I see one-third of a nation ill-housed, ill-clad, ill-nourished.'" See "I SEE" CONSTRUCTION.

The fraction as a phrasemaking device, particularly in regard to the poorest segment of society, had been successful before. Said Winston Churchill in 1950:

I remember in Victorian days anxious talks about "the submerged tenth" (that part of our people who had not shared in the progress of the age) and then later on in the old Liberal period (the grand old Liberal period) we spoke of "going back to bring the rearguard in." The main army we said had reached the camping-ground in all its strength and victory, and we should now, in duty and compassion, go back to pick up the stragglers and those who had fallen by the way and bring them in.

See WAR ON POVERTY.

one world Internationalist Republican philosophy of Wendell Willkie, expressed after his defeat by FDR in 1940.

After his campaign, Willkie made a 31,000-mile trip to the Soviet Union, the Middle East, Africa, and China. In Chungking, he called on the Allies to recognize that World War II was not "a simple tactical problem for task forces. It is also a war for men's minds."

On his return he reported to Americans that the U.S. had a vast "reservoir of good will" that was being drained because our war aims were not being articulated. "The United States has lost moral force," he said after U.S. dealings with Admiral Darlan of Vichy France upset liberals, "and by it, we may lose the peace...I hate this false finagling with expediency..."

Willkie put these thoughts in a 1941 book titled *One World*. To Willkie, *one world* meant a peace founded without regard to a nation's size, wealth, power, or the color of its citizens. "Our western world and our presumed supremacy are now on trial. Our boasting and our big talk leave Asia cold. Men and women in Russia and China and in the Middle East are...coming to know that many of the decisions about the future of the world lie in their hands."

After the explosion in 1945 of the first atomic bomb, a group of scientists put forth a statement headed "One World or None." Radio commentator Elmer Davis asked: "Has it occurred to them that if their one world turned out to be totalitarian and obscurantist, we might better have no world at all?" See BETTER RED THAN DEAD.

Willkie's *One World* sold two million copies within two years in the U.S. "Bookleggers" in China (a play on "bootleggers" who smuggled liquor in the legs of their boots) ignored the copyright and published it under a title that translates: "Within Four Seas, All Are Brothers." (When the lexicographer's sympathetic but not sycophantic memoir about Nixon, *Before the Fall*, was published in 1975, bookleggers in the Far East reprinted it in Chinese, ignoring the copyright; when I told Nixon about that, he shrugged and uncharacteristically came up with a pun: "Better read than dead.") Curiously, Willkie's title—apparently familiar in China—resurfaced a half-century later, when the Communist capitalists in Beijing adopted a slogan for the 2008 Olympics: "One World, One Dream."

only President we've got See PRESIDENT OF ALL THE PEOPLE.

only thing we have to fear See NOTHING TO FEAR BUT FEAR ITSELF.

on message Focused on the main selling point; coordinated with a central political theme.

In SPINMEISTER lingo, to be *on message* is to agree to concentrate on the one or two *gut issues* that ignite a campaign. When a candidate or his supporters stray *off the message*, voter interest supposedly erodes—not because the strategy is mistaken, say the message-makers, but because too many necessary subjects on the public plate make it difficult for those uncomfortable with complexity to digest.

The phrase, a shortening of *on the message*, is associated with James Carville, chief Clinton political strategist in 1992 (see IT'S THE ECONOMY, STUPID!), and appeared that year in *The Dallas Morning News*. The idea is rooted in the "Unique Selling Proposition," a theory of advertising espoused by Ted Bates in the 1960s: to pick out a unique quality that sets a product off from others on the shelf and then concentrate on selling that quality.

In April of 2004, Fred Barnes of *The Weekly Standard* covered a George W. Bush press conference in which "you could see why he drives the press crazy. No matter what they asked, his answer was invariably the same: We're STAYING THE COURSE in Iraq…He was heroically on message,

relentlessly repetitive, but effective in his own way." Months later, after the Democratic convention of 2004 that nominated Senator John Kerry, *Nation* columnist Jonathan Schell, disappointed in the failure of party leaders to take a strong position against the war in Iraq, posted a column on AlterNet headlined "Peace is Not On-Message" and noting that the most anti-war delegate, Rep. Dennis Kucinich, had said in sadness, "Peace is *off-message*." (Two years later, when a sex scandal involving a Republican congressman's suggestive emails to congressional pages appalled many in the party's conservative "base," the *Newsweek* headline was "Off Message.")

British Prime Minister Tony Blair understood the importance of political focus exemplified by the domestic approach taken first by Bill Clinton, then by George W. Bush: like those U.S. presidents, the British "New Labour" leader sought a THIRD WAY between the "hard" free-market right and the "soft" statist-entitlement left. As Blair's political star was finally falling in 2006, largely because of his support of President Bush's resolve to succeed in Iraq, *Washington Post* columnist Sebastian Mallaby wrote of Blair that "His can-do optimism, his relentlessly *on-message* spin, his frank love of the camera: All would have been unremarkable in an American pol, but all challenged the British tradition…He was even more upbeat than Americans."

The extreme of staying relentlessly attuned to "bumper-sticker issues" invites media resentment of *message control*. "In more than an hour of conversation with me and Lally Weymouth of *Newsweek*," wrote David Ignatius in *The Washington Post* in 2006, Iranian president Mahmoud Ahmadinejad "didn't deviate from his script…This is a man adept at message control."

A similar phrase is *on the model*. This term points to the "fit"—cultural and ideological, as well as in terms of age, dress, and degree of enthusiasm—of an individual within a campaign organization. It usually is posed as a question by staffers feeling threatened by older or offbeat types who might not fit in a preconceived mold: "Is he *on the model*?" means "Is he one of us?"

For the closest metaphorical synonym, which mushroomed in the 1980s with the rise of the evangelical movement's activism in politics and is in active use throughout the English-speaking world, see PAGE, ON THE SAME, from which all are "singing from the same hymn-book."

on the point The vulnerable position of being in the lead of a group of candidates; the exposed status of the FRONT RUNNER.

The derivation is from military terminology: the member of a squad of soldiers who "takes the point" (often a volunteer, or a more experienced member of the squad) moves out ahead of his comrades and, as the scout, is the one in greatest danger. In an ambush, the experienced ambushing force will allow the scout to penetrate, in order to entrap the entire squad; for this reason, the squad is instructed to be spread wide enough so that the last two men of the wedge are far enough back to avert capture or killing, and can warn the main force. The men at the ends of the inverted "V" (farthest from the *point man* in the middle front) are called the *getaway men*, a phrase not yet adopted by politics.

The candidate *on the point* is the object of "Stop (Whoever)" movements by coalitions of other candidates, and the man whose every misstep is given greatest play by the press. Colorado Governor John Love was asked by a reporter what he thought of the attacks being made in 1967 on then Republican front runner George Romney. He replied: "It's a hard place to live, out there on the point."

In 1977 President Carter's Ambassador to the United Nations, Andrew Young, who had stirred controversy when he hinted at a forthcoming improvement of relations with Cuba, and who created a furor when he said Cuban forces in Angola were "a force for stability" in Africa, agreed on a television panel interview to a description of himself as "a point man"—that is, one who goes out in front of events and takes the heat. A *Washington Post* editorial disagreed: "To toss off personal opinions—or (in Young's words) to play 'point man'—and then be repudiated is to lose a certain part of one's

claim on another government's or the public's attention: to lose effectiveness." That year *National Journal* titled a piece about California Congressman James Corman "The House Point Man on Welfare."

A synonym is *cutting edge*, as in this *New York Times* editorial from 1977: "Secretary Califano has become the cutting edge of the Government's affirmative action drive." In the late 1980s, *on the cusp*, a phrase describing the points of a crescent moon, took over the *cutting edge*.

Mixing horseracing and military metaphors is common practice in political oratory. A *front runner* (racing) is *on the point* (military); a *campaign* (origin military) can be a *horse race* (turf); there can be a *boom* (military cannon origin) for a *dark horse* (racing); a TV *blitz* (World War II) in the *home stretch* (last two weeks, racing), as the two *camps* (military) come *down to the wire* (racing) with the *standard-bearers* (military) in a *dead heat* (racing), and the *right wing* (military) threatening to *bolt* (racing). See MILITARY METAPHORS.

open convention A political convention that begins with no single candidate nearing a majority, now becoming a fond memory.

"I don't think any one candidate has enough votes to win," said California Governor Earl Warren on the eve of the 1948 Republican convention. "As long as that prevails it's a wide-open convention."

In 1956, former President Harry Truman let it be known that he favored an open Democratic convention, thereby helping block Adlai Stevenson from "locking everything up" before the convention began. New York Governor Averell Harriman announced he was "for Stevenson" but not necessarily "for him for president." ("What does he think I'm running for," asked Stevenson, "county coroner?") Truman supported Harriman, but Stevenson was able to overcome that challenge as well as Senator Estes Kefauver's.

At that point, Stevenson in turn announced that he favored an "open convention" in the choice of a vice-presidential nominee. The delegates, who couldn't remember a previous opportunity to choose a vice president freely, almost went for Senator John F. Kennedy, but chose Senator Kefauver.

At the 1960 convention Harry Truman didn't feel that John Kennedy "was ready" and again called for an "open convention." Senator Kennedy told an aide: "Mr. Truman regards an open convention as one which studies all the candidates, reviews their records and then takes his advice."

The phrase is understood by those interested in politics wherever English is a first or second language. Syed Mansoor Hussain of the Pakistan *Daily Times* noted in 2007 that "much wheeling-dealings is to be expected if there is indeed an open convention in the U.S."

As state caucuses and primary elections gained importance in the winnowing-out of candidacies, national political conventions, far from being open, have become a form of nominee coronation aimed at achieving a public-opinion CONVENTION BOUNCE as the official campaign begins.

The anything-can-happen meaning of *open* is probably rooted in gambling terminology: a *wide-open* town is one in which gambling, as well as prostitution, is permitted. For the usage of *open* convention compared with *rigged* or *locked up* convention, see BROKERED CONVENTION.

open covenants President Woodrow Wilson's rejection of agreements containing secret codicils.

His Fourteen Points included: "Open covenants of peace, openly arrived at, after which there shall be no private international understandings of any kind, but diplomacy shall proceed always frankly and in the public view."

France's Clemenceau, Britain's Lloyd George, and others were dismayed at Wilson's apparent naiveté because "in the public view" seemed to mean "no confidential discussions," without which diplomacy could hardly be done. To correct this impression, Wilson sent his closest adviser, Colonel Edward House, to explain to world leaders what he meant before armistice negotiations began. House used a memorandum, approved by Wilson, on this point:

The purpose is clearly to prohibit treaties, sections of treaties or understandings that are secret. The phrase "openly arrived at" need not cause difficulty. In fact, the President explained to the Senate last winter that his intention was not to exclude confidential diplomatic negotiations involving delicate matters, but to insist that nothing which occurs in the course of such confidential negotiations shall be binding unless it appears in the final covenant made public to the world.

In effect, Wilson's high-sounding words—which had an appeal to millions who were curious about what went on behind the scenes at international conferences—had a meaning to Wilson that required confidential explanation. Columnist Walter Lippmann wrote in 1932: "great masses of people cannot negotiate. They can no more negotiate than they can make love or write books or invent. They can approve or disapprove the results, but if they participate in the negotiation itself they merely shout themselves hoarse and fall into a hopeless deadlock."

At the end of World War II, Republicans were able to use "open covenants" against Wilson's Democratic successors. In his "Equal Justice Under Law" speech attacking the war-crimes trials of Nazi leaders that he believed to be based on ex post facto law, Senator Robert A. Taft clearly set up the line about secret agreements: "The Atlantic Charter professed a belief in liberty and justice for all nations, but at Teheran, at Yalta, at Moscow, we forgot law and justice. Nothing could be further from a RULE OF LAW than the making of secret agreements distributing the territory of the earth in accordance with power and expediency."

Open covenants, as used today, still requires explanation. It means "no secret agreements," but does not obviate "necessary private discussions" and as much as says "forget that part about 'openly arrived at.'" Lippmann in 1961 made the point:

By open diplomacy, which only too often means loud-mouthed diplomacy, we can do little to assuage, indeed much to exacerbate these crises. For then one side or the other has to back down if there is to be any accommodation. But in quiet diplomacy, there is no loss of face if a country backs away from an extreme position which has proved to be untenable. For this reason, QUIET DIPLOMACY is for the time being the hope of the world.

The word *covenant* rather than *treaty* or *agreement* appealed to Wilson. The Covenant of the League of Nations was his phrasing, chosen because he liked the Biblical solemnity of the word. It recalled "The Solemn League and Covenant" of 1643, unifying religious practice in England, Scotland, and Ireland. Abolitionist leader William Lloyd Garrison liked the word too, in 1831 calling a U.S. Constitution that permitted slavery a "Covenant with Death and an Agreement with Hell," which became a slogan for the Massachusetts Anti-Slavery Society.

In his 1993 Inaugural address, Bill Clinton used *New Covenant* nine times, but the phrase was not picked up as the style of his Administration.

See PITILESS PUBLICITY; QUIET DIPLOMACY.

Open Door Policy A diplomatic position at the turn of the twentieth century that called for all important trading nations to have equal trading rights with the Chinese government, with all respecting that country's territorial integrity.

Goaded by the British government, President William McKinley's Secretary of State, John Hay, acted at a time when it looked as though every powerful nation was about to fall on the hapless Chinese government and tear away both concessions and territory. This supported neither British nor American interests. Britain already had rich concessions in the Yangtze Valley; the U.S., though it wanted to share the Chinese market, was not prepared to fight for it.

China in these last days of the Manchu Empire had been soundly defeated in a short but decisive war waged against her by Japan. Only the combined disapproval of all the Western nations currently involved in China in 1895 had prevented imperial Japan from slicing off chunks of the prostrate Celestial Empire. At British insistence, Hay sent a series of notes to the concerned powers, which included Italy, Japan, and France, as well as Britain and the U.S., asking for assurances that existing treaties would be observed with China. He announced in September 1899 that all had concurred. However, the Boxer Rebellion and the Russo-Japanese War of 1904–05 resulted in further encroachments on China, largely by Japan.

The U.S. continued to talk of the *Open Door* and used the $25 million forced from China as reparations after the Boxer Rebellion to educate young Chinese in America. For some time, successive Chinese governments felt friendly to the U.S. as the least voracious of all the nations that were busily involved in taking away the country's wealth.

In current usage, diplomats refuse to *close the door* on negotiations.

open shop See CLOSED SHOP; RIGHT TO WORK.

open-skies proposal President Eisenhower's suggestion at the 1954 Geneva Convention to permit unlimited aerial photography of the U.S. and the Soviet Union.

Eisenhower laid the proposal before Premier Bulganin and Communist party chief Khrushchev:

I propose…to give each other a complete blueprint of our military establishments, from beginning to end, from one end of our countries to the other…to provide within our countries facilities for aerial photography to the other country—we to provide the facilities within our country, ample facilities for aerial reconnaissance, where you can make all the pictures you choose and take them to your own country to study; you to provide exactly the same facilities for us and…by this step to convince the world that we are providing as between ourselves against the possibility of great surprise attack …

When the Soviets showed no inclination to accept this proposal, the U.S. proceeded to open up the Russian skies unilaterally and secretly with high-altitude U-2 flights. When a U-2 was shot down and the incident broke up a summit conference, the U.S. State Department took pains to point out that the flights had begun immediately after the Soviet rejection of our *open skies* proposal.

Senator Lyndon Johnson, who frequently built phrases on top of other phrases, added in 1957: "We must create a new world policy. Not just of 'open skies'—but of open eyes, ears, and minds, for all peoples of the world. I call for the 'open curtain.' Let truth flow through it freely. Let ideas cleanse evil just as fresh air cleanses the poisoned, stagnant mass of a long-closed cavern."

Satellite photography later opened the skies with no need for agreements; though some blotting-out of military installations still takes place, Internet access through Google Earth and other programs makes aerial surveillance more open than Eisenhower and Khrushchev dreamed of in 1954.

open society A social order in which the people are granted a RIGHT TO KNOW and to speak out as opposed to the *closed society* of a totalitarian state, in which secrecy is predominant.

The phrase achieved common political usage in the fifties, especially after the OPEN-SKIES PROPOSAL by President Eisenhower in 1954; there was another flurry of usage after the U-2 incident in 1959 when it was explained that the U.S. was an *open society* and needed to find ways to explain the goings-on in *closed societies*.

Dwight Eisenhower coined one of his best metaphors around the subject of an open society in a draft for a speech that was never delivered. Had the President been permitted to visit the Soviet Union, he would have delivered a speech in Leningrad on May 12, 1960, about Soviet-American relations that used these words:

When I was a boy, we put blinders on horses so they would not shy in fright of a scarecrow, a shadow, a rabbit. But today we human beings deliberately put blinders on ourselves, not to avoid the sight of frightful things, but to ignore a central fact of human existence …

I mean that all of us too much live in ignorance of our neighbors; or, when we take off our blinders, view them through the contortionist spectacles of propaganda.

And we will continue that way—forever fearful, forever suspicious—until we convince our-

selves that the only way to peace is through the mutually open society. Then, at long last, seeing our human neighbors as they really are, we shall come to realize that we need no more fear them than the horse the rabbit.

The phrase is often used in discussions seeking to explain the necessity of (or deploring the actions of) the Central Intelligence Agency. Walter Lippmann wrote in 1967 about covert CIA support of student groups: "black propaganda, secret interventions, intrigue and subornation are incompatible with our open society. They are the methods of a totalitarian state and without a totalitarian environment of secrecy and terror, they are unworkable. This most unpleasant and embarrassing affair is the proof than an open society cannot act successfully like a totalitarian society."

Said President Johnson soon after, about the bad press he was getting: "There is something about our open society that gives the play to what went wrong instead of what went right." Defense Secretary Robert A. Lovett looked at the problem another way: "I cannot escape the feeling that, as a government, we tend to talk too much. To be sure, we are an open society, but we give the impression of being unbuttoned."

After the phrase was in common use, a new meaning was introduced as part of the language of the civil rights movement. *Open* instead of meaning "nonsecret" was defined as "available to all," as in *open occupancy* or *open housing*. *Ebony* magazine quoted Dr. Leo K. Bishop in this context: "In two decades the Jews and the Roman Catholics have moved into the open society of the United States, and the Negroes will make it too."

operation A labeling device for a military action within a war or less than a war.

With only Congress able to declare a war, lesser military actions have required different terms. Harry Truman preferred *police action*, and the 1950s witnessed the Korean *conflict*.

When the United States engaged in military activity in Panama in late 1989, White House officials could argue that *invasion* was too harsh a word, because the elected government of Panama invited the action. The State Department suggested *consented intervention*, but the action became widely known by the name conceived by Pentagon public affairs specialists: "Operation Just Cause."

Operation, first found in English in Chaucer's 1391 *Treatise on the Astrolabe*, is from French, ultimately based on the Latin *opus*, meaning "work, effort." The word was applied to a surgical procedure by 1425, and it offers a sense of clinical detachment in labeling a military action short of war.

Operation Overlord was Churchill's name for the invasion of the continent in World War II, and many other secret projects in the planning stage received similarly obscure titles to conceal their objectives.

In recent years, the word has been used to precede descriptive or selling titles: the American action to stop Iraq from invading Saudi Arabia in 1991 was called *Desert Shield*, with the name changed to *Desert Storm* as the action changed to drive Iraq out of Kuwait. Famine relief in Somalia, requiring military assistance, was dubbed *Operation Restore Hope*. In 2003, *Enduring Freedom* was the name for the Afghanistan operation and *Iraqi Freedom* for the war in Iraq.

opinion leader A person or organization with the position, expertise, or facilities to influence the convictions of others.

An obvious "influential" might be a newspaper. In 1859 John Stuart Mill wrote in regret: "The mass do not now take their opinions from dignitaries in church or state, from ostensible leaders, or from books. Their thinking is done for them by men much like themselves, addressing them or speaking in their name, on the spur of the moment, through the newspapers."

Congressman Robert La Follette, seeking a second term against the opposition of the regular leaders of the Republican party in Wisconsin, devised a technique for reaching those he considered opinion leaders. Before the 1886 elections, he had the voter list broken down into townships. He then sent such a list to a supporter in that partic-ular area, requesting the names of any of the local men considered to be people whose names had local leadership significance. To these people, he regularly sent accounts of his congressional actions and copies of his speeches. The rudimentary system worked; despite continued party opposition he was renominated and reelected.

Columbia University behavioral scientist Paul Lazarsfeld led the way to the formulation of the *opinion leader*. His theory of the "two-step flow of communication" held that the general public did not take its opinions directly from either the mass or class media; instead, these messages were filtered through a layer of respected activists. These opinion leaders, however, do not lead in all categories. For example, a sophisticated woman may be an opinion leader in matters of fashion, but she may be a follower of a gregarious housewife in marketing matters, and both these leaders may be followers of a League of Women Voters president in political affairs.

The power of the personally known opinion leader began to be diluted by the increase in the mass media of bylined commentary and more recently by the rise of strongly opinionated bloggers. Political candidates have used email as well as legions of paid and volunteer canvassers to affect voters' opinions "over the heads" of neighborhood opinion leaders.

opinion of mankind See WORLD OPINION.

opium of the people A metaphor by Karl Marx about religion, used against Marxism and Communism by God-fearing critics for more than a century.

"Religion is the sigh of the oppressed creature," wrote Marx in 1844, in his *Critique of the Hegelian Philosophy of Right*, "the feeling of a heartless world, just as it is the spirit of unspiritual conditions. It is the Opium of the People." The German phrase *Opium des Volkes* can be translated *opium of the people* or *opiate of the people*; the former gets almost three times more usage.

Although Marx went on to stress the point—"the first requisite for the people's happiness is the abolition of religion"—

Communist leaders in countries with strong religious traditions tried to water down the metaphor. "Marx's position is widely misunderstood," wrote the Socialist Labor party's official organ in 1959. "When the essay was written, opium was used in Europe almost exclusively for relieving pain.... Marx was using the word 'opium' in this sense and not in the sense that religion is a stupefier deliberately administered to the people by agents of the ruling class."

As president of Columbia University in 1950, Dwight Eisenhower made a typical attack on the "Godlessness" of Communism, using Marx's vivid phrase against him: "Hundreds of millions behind the Iron Curtain are daily drilled in the slogan: 'There is no God, and religion is an opiate.' But not all the people within the Soviet accept this fallacy; and some day they will educate their rulers, or change them."

Clare Boothe Luce played with the phrase in 1955, calling Communism "the opiate of the intellectuals... but no cure, except as a guillotine might be called a cure for a case of dandruff." A creative turnaround was in a 1967 editorial in the *Suffolk* (L.I.) *Sun* about the LSD prophet, Dr. Timothy Leary, "who hopes to make opiates the religion of the people."

opportunist One who sacrifices principle to expediency; a frequent attack word used against ambitious or fast-rising political figures.

The word grew popular in the political lexicon in the '50s, although columnist Arthur Krock accused Senator Robert Taft of playing "obvious or even opportunist politics" in 1946.

One who is attacked as an opportunist is usually (1) on the way up, (2) in the public eye, and/or (3) controversial. As an attack word, *ambitious* was losing its sting because ambition pervades politics and in some degree is a necessary trait. The predecessor word, now obsolete, was *trimmer*, from one who trims his sails to capture the prevailing breeze.

An opportunist, in current usage, is one who changes his position to comply with what is presently popular (see ALL THINGS TO ALL MEN). Britain's Harold Wilson attacked Harold Macmillan: "Cynical opportunism in place of leadership, an appeal to cupidity rather than to the moral purpose of the nation."

Contrariwise, one who sticks to a single position can be attacked as "inflexible, MOSS-BACKED, unwilling to meet new situations with new solutions." The most common defense of one who has radically switched his position (Arthur Vandenberg on isolationism, Lyndon Johnson on civil rights, John Edwards on the war in Iraq) is that the individual has "matured," or "been man enough to admit a mistake," or has become "pragmatic." See FLIP-FLOP.

In 404 B.C. a member of the Athenian oligarchy named Theramenes was nicknamed *Cothurnus*, which was a sandal that could be worn on either foot, because he was considered an opportunist. From this came the expression "He wears the sandals of Theramenes," not to be trusted. Cobham Brewer in his *Dictionary of Phrase and Fable* quoted the proverb "He blew hot and cold with the same breath."

In 1597 Francis Bacon pointed to an example of opportunism still practiced today: "It is commonly seen, that men once placed, take in with the contrary faction to that by which they enter; thinking, belike, that they have the first sure, and now are ready for a new purchase."

Republicans in 1967 were surprised when Michigan Governor George Romney called fellow Republican, Illinois Senator Charles Percy, an opportunist; he later backed off and explained that he meant that Percy understood timing, that he knew how to seize an opportunity. This is a positive sense the word may one day gain, but neither was nor is current usage. (His son, Mitt Romney, a candidate for the Republican nomination in 2008, switched his position on abortion rights and was criticized by rivals for opportunism.)

The word is rooted is the Latin *ob*, "before," and *portus*, "harbor," and bears a relation to the man who keeps hoping his ship will come in. According to former Nixon speechwriter Benjamin Stein, writing in *Esquire* in 1977, Henry Kissinger assessed President Carter's national security adviser, Zbigniew Brzezinski, with the wistful tone of one whose ship had come and gone: "He's a bit of an opportunist."

No publication ever gave the idea more of a metaphoric blast than the *Liberation Army Daily*, published in Beijing. After the overthrow of the radical "Gang of Four," the army paper attacked a group of unnamed opportunists who had not been swept from power by Chairman Mao's successor, Hua Guofeng: "The main features of those who follow the wind are steering the boat according to which way the wind blows and the advocacy of opportunism. Their color changes when they hear the wind, and they sell their soul at a discount. Speculation has become their habit, and they treat any woman who gives them milk as their mother ... They are like grass growing atop a wall, bending with the wind. They are as changeable as clouds and rain. Their necks function like ball bearings and their waists like spring bands, and wind gauges are planted on their heads."

This dazzling display of anti-opportunistic rhetoric was reprinted in the *People's Daily* on January 6, 1978, in the same space where—only two years before—a similar attack on opportunists had been launched by those later labeled the "Gang of Four." See CULTURAL REVOLUTION.

The adjective and noun are as pejorative as the related word *opportunity* is politically sacrosanct. A talent show televised in Britain in the 1960s was titled *Opportunity Knocks*; in 2004, Labour's Deputy Prime Minister John Prescott derided David Cameron, new leader of the Conservative opposition, with "Opportunism knocks." See CENTRIST.

opposition research See DIRTY TRICKS; HARDBALL.

options Choices; alternatives.

In a sophisticated political sense, the existence of a number of options offers freedom to maneuver; as options are narrowed, the decision-maker loses leverage on his adversaries because his chances for TRADE-OFFS are decreased, and the element of surprise is lessened. See NEW ECONOMICS.

President Lyndon Johnson was often quoted as insisting on "keeping my options open." The word *open*, in this sense, is used to mean "not narrowed by elimination." Whenever Franklin Roosevelt asked Congress for discretionary authority in legislation, he called it "room to turn around." It has since been expressed as *wriggle room*.

The word became the vogue in Washington in the '60s, probably from war-gaming vocabulary. The doctrine of flexible response and a decision about which weapons systems to develop depend largely on what—and how many—options are available.

This is a far cry from George Washington's use of the word: "There is an option left to the United States of America, whether they will be respectable and prosperous, or contemptible and miserable, as a nation." More often, the option is between the lesser of two evils; as entertainer Maurice Chevalier said on reaching seventy-two: "Old age isn't so bad when you consider the alternative."

In the early '70s, as a result of National Security Adviser Henry Kissinger's use of the term in backgrounders, *Option Three* became synonymous with compromise. In a choice of five options, option three is nicely situated between extremes, and is the easiest to choose; an *option three philosophy* is not conducive to bold leadership. This was satirized using "preventive war" as option one and "abject surrender" as option five.

As a verb, *opt* has gained academic popularity, despite connoting a more impulsive selection than the thoughtful *choose*. Bergen Evans used it precisely in *Comfortable Words*: "Confronted with a choice between *choose* and *opt*, my impulse is to opt for *choose*."

opt out See -OUT CONSTRUCTION.

other body An arch reference by a member of the Senate to the House, and vice versa.

Both houses in a bicameral legislature are jealous of their prerogatives; in the U.S., "the other body" is a way for a legislator to refer to the Senate or the House of Representatives without appearing to pay it too much respect; in current use, the pronunciation attempts to reproduce the "sound" of quotation marks.

The phrase originated in a rule of the British Houses of Parliament which states that a member of one house may make no reference to the proceedings of the other, a vestige of the days when rivalry between the House of Commons and the House of Lords could have led to a constitutional crisis. To get around the old custom, British politicians call their other body "another place."

out of context See QUOTED OUT OF CONTEXT; DEFOLIATE.

out of pocket See UP TO SPEED.

out of the loop Not informed; outside the circuit of news or information; maliciously or providentially ignored.

The elder George Bush popularized this phrase by insisting that in 1985 he was not involved in Iran-contra discussions or arms-for-hostages negotiations during the Reagan Administration, thereby distancing himself from the arms-for-contras scandal. On January 1, 1987, then Vice President Bush said of decisions by the National Security Council: "I'm not trying to jump sideways on this, but I think it is important to have the facts. And the facts are that the Vice President is not in the decision-making loop. He does not have to sign off on decisions, is sometimes overlooked, although not on purpose by the N.S.C. bureaucracy."

The phrase, however, was not limited to Bush. In 1986, a White House aide was quoted as saying about the former chief of staff Donald Regan: "A lot of the people he cut out of the loop are gunning for him."

Possible origins of the *loop* phrase range from electrical circuitry and computer processing to a term for a conference or network (the *Big Ten Loop*), all figurative or extended uses of the literal sense of "a circle formed with a rope." The circular *loop* has been used since the turn of the twentieth century to refer to the railway built around Chicago's business district

by Charles Tyson Yerkes; the area itself became known as *the Loop*.

The antonymic phrase, *in the loop*, means "well-informed; among those consulted," often implying a tight circle. Hedrick Smith used the phrase as a test of insiderness in his 1988 book *The Power Game: How Washington Works*, under the heading "Are You in the Loop?" Recently, "In the Loop" was the title of a column by Al Kamen on the Federal page of *The Washington Post*.

out party See INS AND OUTS.

out to lunch See UP TO SPEED.

Oval Office The formal office of the President of the United States; by extension, the center of executive power.

In his 1931 biography of General Leonard Wood, Hermann Hagedorn wrote of his visit to the White House during the Woodrow Wilson presidency: "Wilson was in his oval office, standing near the door of the Cabinet room as Wood was announced."

A headline on page 16 in the *Washington Post* of July 6, 1934, read: "President's New Oval Office/Carefully Planned for Beauty—FDR." The story predicted that the West Wing of the White House would have "a main floor unchanged except for filling in the clothes yard …"

According to the January 1935 issue of *Building Modernization*, the expansion of space from 15,000 to 40,000 feet "was accomplished by filling in the old 'drying yard'—a lattice-inclosed square adjacent to the old laundry once used for drying presidential wash. In its place along the side portico, opening on a rose garden, is the office of the President and his personal staff." The office was described as "oval in shape and besides the fact that it is almost always flooded with southern sun, its chief feature is its large bay made up of a series of steel sash windows of immense proportion."

Perhaps because it is one of several oval rooms in the White House, including the Diplomatic Reception Room and the "Yellow Room" on the second floor of the residence, the Oval Office did not get capitalized and used to symbolize the seat of power through several administrations. When Harry Truman gave his farewell address from his office on January 15, 1953, he said: "This is the President's Office in the West Wing of the White House." Dwight Eisenhower used "West Wing" to mean the center of action during his Presidency and in his book *Mandate for Change*.

Although Jack Valenti told the author that he often heard "The President's oval office" used by White House aides in the Johnson Presidency, the phrase did not come into the general language until Nixon's term. Among White House assistants who were my colleagues, *Oval Office*—capitalized, and without *the President's* in front of it—was a phrase used to suggest decision-making by the President without using his name.

The phrase was speeded into wide public use as a result of Watergate: The earliest Merriam-Webster citation is an October 19, 1972, article by Robert Semple Jr. in *The New York Times*, followed eight months later by a report that "Mr [Egil] Krogh told him [John Dean] that the order for the break-in came 'from the Oval Office.'" In his 2007 memoir, *Integrity*, Krogh reaffirmed that usage: "This pressure had come directly from the Oval Office."

That notion—of executive power being more a function of a place than a person, making the presidency less personally accountable—was behind the early internal use of *Oval Office*, and later led to its popularization.

Lexicographers report a rush of citations late in 1974 and 1975; the White House Historical Association, which in previous editions of its guide referred to "the President's Office," switched in 1973.

Oval Office, in its initial caps, seems to be the only Watergate-era word that carries no unpleasant connotation into the present. Soon after the election of Jimmy Carter, Leslie Gelb wrote: "A crisis like another Middle East war, saber-rattling by Moscow, the embrace of the foreign policy bureaucracy and the enormous complexity of issues and pressures when viewed from the Oval Office could consign the most ardently believed campaign rhetoric to oblivion."

The phrase has become a neutral reference to the Presidency; similarly, *the West Wing* refers to the President's Senior staff and *the East Wing* to the First Lady's offices until 1993, when Hillary Rodham Clinton chose to locate her office in the West Wing.

overexposure The worry in the minds of public figures that continuous publicity leads to public boredom.

Kennedy biographers are fond of quoting a passage from this letter by Franklin Roosevelt to Ray Stannard Baker, dated March 20, 1935, that had earlier been quoted by Richard Neustadt in *Presidential Power*:

> I know…you will be sympathetic to the point of view that the public psychology and, for that matter, individual psychology, cannot, because of human weakness, be attuned for long periods of time to a constant repetition of the highest note in the scale…Whereas in this country there is a free and sensational press, people tire of seeing the same name, day after day, in the important headlines of the papers, and the same voice, night after night, over the radio…if I had tried [in 1935] to keep up the pace of 1933 and 1934, the inevitable histrionics of the new actors, Long and Coughlin and Johnson, would have turned the eyes of the audience away from the main drama itself …

That highest-note-in-the-scale theory has become a kind of credo of political mass communications. "I do not believe it is possible," wrote Ted Sorensen loyally, "to 'overexpose' a President like Kennedy." Then he became pragmatic, to use a word popular in the Kennedy era: "Nevertheless he could not, with any effectiveness, go on the air to denounce Big Steel, or announce a Cuban quarantine, or deliver some momentous message, every month of the year.… As a commander saves his biggest guns for the biggest battles, so Kennedy limited his direct national appeals to situations of sufficient importance to demand it and sufficiently fluid to be helped by it."

Eisenhower press secretary James Hagerty felt sufficiently confident of the magnetism of Eisenhower's presence to permit—for the first time—the filming of presidential press conferences, despite the danger of "overexposure." Kennedy extended this to live coverage and more frequent conferences; Lyndon Johnson, early in his Administration, made a great many television appearances to "put his stamp" on the presidency. As Arthur Krock wrote: "He does not share the fear of some friends that he is taking too heavy a toll of his incredible energy, and has already incurred whatever political peril there may be in 'overexposure.'" By 1967, however, Johnson made it a point to say and appear less.

Krock's successor as the Washington correspondent of *The New York Times*, James "Scotty" Reston, applied the exposure yardstick with a photography metaphor to Senator Robert Kennedy in 1967, after a Kennedy dispute with FBI Director J. Edgar Hoover over wiretapping and Kennedy's handling of *The Death of a President*, historian William Manchester's book on the assassination. (Jacqueline Kennedy had withdrawn her approval of the book written with her cooperation lest it harm Robert Kennedy's bid for the Democratic presidential nomination.) "Publicity is not the same thing as power," wrote Reston about RFK, "and while it is often useful to a rising politician, it can sometimes be the opposite…He is better known now, but he looks a little underdeveloped and overexposed."

See PEAKING.

overkill Application of a surfeit of power; more nuclear destruction capable of being inflicted than is needed to kill an enemy's entire population.

"In describing the aftermath of a war," Hudson Institute operations analyst Herman Kahn wrote coolly in 1960, "it is not particularly illuminating to use such words as 'intolerable,' 'catastrophic,' 'total destruction,' 'annihilating retaliation,' and so on. Such words would be useful only if it were really true that in a modern war all possible targets would be overkilled by factors of five or ten, as many people have assumed." After coining the word, he advocated a shelter program that would, he thought, cut U.S. casualties from eighty million down to forty million. See UNTHINKABLE THOUGHTS.

U.S. strategic planners picked up the word in explaining their policy of "limited deterrence," which held that if the U.S. had enough nuclear weapons to inflict "unacceptable" damage to an enemy, any further expenditure on weapons would only be for "overkill" and a waste of money.

One of the charms of political language is its ability to absorb colorful words, no matter how shocking or bloody the concept. Writing about the ovation given Robert Kennedy at the 1964 Democratic convention, political columnists Rowland Evans and Robert Novak observed: "It brought second thoughts to the politicians who had accused Johnson of overkill in deploying the powers of the Presidency on The Bobby Problem."

In a 1969 speech, William McChesney Martin, then chairman of the Federal Reserve Board, showed how the word could be used in an economic context as well. He described a conversation he had with President Johnson in 1965, in which he pointed out that increased expenditures required higher taxes to avert inflation. "I remember him saying to me, 'Well, yes, I think so too, but we can't do it now. We'd risk overkill.' That was the first time I'd heard that expression used, but I've heard it plenty over the years since, when all the while the economy—and inflationary pressures as well—were burgeoning."

When the litigious "Minister Mentor" Lee Kwan Yew challenged the opposition Workers' party to sue the Singapore government in 2006, the *Straits Times* gently chided the old authoritarian: "Political firmness must be distinguished from political overkill."

oversight Presumed vigilance of a government operation by a congressional committee.

In a working paper for the House Select Committee on Committees, Walter Oleszek wrote in June 1973: "A result of this expansion [of administrative agencies since the New Deal] has been an enlargement of

Congress' oversight function, a traditional legislative function that philosopher John Stuart Mill considered as the most important responsibility of a legislature."

This "oversight function" of the U.S. Congress is relatively new, first formally authorized by Section 136 of the Legislative Reorganization Act of 1946: "To assist the Congress in appraising the administration of the laws and developing such amendments or related legislation as it may deem necessary, each standing committee of the Senate and the House shall exercise continuous watchfulness of the execution by the administrative agencies concerned of any laws, the subject matter of which is within the jurisdiction of such committee ..."

"Continuous watchfulness," Congressmen felt, was too vague, or too time-consuming; in 1970 this was changed to "legislative review." In practice, the investigative part of "oversight" was largely neglected by Congress, which was more interested during the '50s and '60s in legislative reach—adding to the laws regulating commerce or creating new agencies.

However, with the CIA revelations of the Senate Select Committee on Intelligence in 1975, it became apparent that Congress had been remiss in its obligation to act as a check on actions of the executive branch, especially in the intelligence area.

The word *oversight* became voguish in the mid-'70s, not only as an accusation of lack of previous vigilance but as a means of extending congressional power. A related term, *accountability*, has a positive connotation, while *monitoring* often carries an intrusive, pejorative tone.

Ted Sorensen, the Kennedy speechwriter who was resisted by the Senate in 1977 as nominee to be Director of Central Intelligence, wrote wryly: "The word 'oversight' has two meanings, and they chose the wrong one." The other is "mistake; omission." Another: *overview*. While *oversight* implies some modicum of control, *overview* denotes perspective, or a survey conducted with Olympian detachment. The latter has good lineage: "Too bitter is thy jest," says the King in Shakespeare's *Love's Labour's Lost*, written in 1588. "Are we betrayed thus to thy overview?"

oxymoron See LOYAL OPPOSITION; SPLENDID MISERY; UNTHINKABLE THOUGHTS; WAGING PEACE; WITH ALL DELIBERATE SPEED.

P

package deal An omnibus bill, often containing something for everybody; a compromise that enables an executive to get legislation he wants in return for agreeing to sign legislation he has opposed.

Running for reelection as governor of California in 1950, Earl Warren stressed his nonpartisanship, resisting efforts to get him to support any other Republican on the ticket, including Richard Nixon for senator: "I have no present intention of endorsing candidates for other offices in the November 7 election. We are all running independent campaigns. I've never believed in package deals. I believe the public is entitled to make its own selection and I'm just interested in one campaign—my own." It was not a snub that Nixon forgot.

This is a merchandising expression, referring to the two-for-the-price-of-one sales appeals, or the inclusion of a tube of toothpaste in the same package with a toothbrush. In an early Eisenhower cabinet meeting, it was pointed out that conservatives resisted a negotiated peace in Korea because they felt it might lead to recognition of Red China. Defense Secretary Charles E. Wilson, former head of General Motors, popped up with: "Is there any possibility for a package deal? Maybe we could recognize Red China and get the Far East issues settled." As Sherman Adams recalled later, "Eisenhower managed to control himself." Emmett Hughes commented, "Quite a few cabinet meetings were jerked to quivering attention by such remarks." (In retrospect, "Engine Charlie" was more prescient than his more sophisticated colleagues.)

The President explained that such a quid pro quo was not feasible; the phrase *package deal* was not used again in cabinet meetings. However, in his 1957 message to Congress on mutual security, Eisenhower put together a series of foreign operations recommendations into "one vital parcel which we must not neglect."

Fifty years later, Dick Polman of *The Philadelphia Inquirer* remembered: "The Clintons want to party like it's 1992. Back at the dawn of their excellent adventure, Hillary would tell voters that she and her husband were a package deal, two for the price of one."

The older term, *omnibus bill*, dates back to the 1850s and is based on the French term for a public conveyance, *voiture omnibus*, "vehicle for everybody." The *omnibus bill* sweeps together a little of everything. *Time* magazine in late 1992 cited President-elect Bill Clinton's use of the term: "On legislative strategy, Clinton said he would emulate, of all people, Ronald Reagan and pack 'a whole lot of changes into omnibus bills.... The fewer votes [in Congress] you have, the better off you are."

In 2007, cartoonist Tom Toles drew a politician wrapped in a bundle for mailing, with one observer saying, "He's understandably reluctant to talk about his bundlers," and another replying, "And he really hates the term 'package deal.'" See BUNDLING; CHRISTMAS TREE BILL; LINKAGE.

packing the galleries Placing the supporters of one candidate at a national convention in the galleries to the exclusion of others, in the hope of stampeding the delegates.

"We want Willkie! We want Willkie!" The thunderous demand from the galleries at the 1940 Republican convention heartened many a Wendell Willkie supporter among the delegations on the floor, and convinced many waverers that a bandwagon was rolling.

The floor manager for Senator Robert A. Taft, R. B. Creager, stormed up to the platform with a complaint to Chairman Joe Martin: When Taft supporters showed up for their gallery seats, they had found them already occupied by Willkie fans who were using counterfeit tickets. (For counterfeiting instructions, see SPONTANEOUS DEMONSTRATION.)

"It was an open scandal," Martin admitted later, "that several hundred counterfeit tickets had been printed and given to a Willkie claque who filled the best seats in the gallery to the exclusion of holders of bona fide tickets." Creager wanted to be recognized in order to denounce the tactics, but Martin talked him out of it. "We had no evidence in hand…we weren't even sure that we could distinguish the counterfeit tickets from the real ones, so skillfully were the former printed."

As the hollering continued, Martin banged his gavel: "I regret to have to admonish those in the galleries to be quiet, and to remind them that they are the guests of this convention …" A voice was heard to shout, "Guests, hell—we *are* the convention!"

After Willkie was nominated, Taft men insisted that the packing of the galleries had "put over" Willkie. Roscoe Drummond, then a *Christian Science Monitor* correspondent, disagreed: "Willkie was no more 'put over' on the Republican convention than Babe Ruth was 'put over' on the New York Yankees."

Willkie's gallery-packing was in the grand tradition of the first candidate of the Republican party to be elected. According to historian Carl Sandburg, Lincoln supporter Ward Lamon had been to the printers of tickets for seats to the Republican convention held in Chicago's Wigwam in 1860: "Young men worked nearly a whole night signing the names of convention officers to counterfeit seat tickets so that the next day Lincoln men could jam the hall and leave no seats for the Seward shouters."

page, on the same To be in agreement, to be working together, to swell the chorus that is "singing from the same hymn book."

Following the 2006 midterm elections that gave Democrats control of the House of Representatives, John Murtha (D-Pa.) expressed reservations about some aspects of the program of the new Speaker of the House, Nancy Pelosi (D-Calif.). As columnist Jim Shea of the *Hartford Courant* put it: "Murtha was also quoted this past week as calling [Pelosi's] ethics reform plan 'total crap,' which is not what you categorize as being on the same page as the boss."

On the same page, a euphemism for "lockstep," is a phrase dated only to 1965 in the *OED*. It is synonymous with *sing from the same hymn book* (also *sing the same song* or *tune*, or *from the same hymn sheet*) and is related to *preaching to the choir*. The *preaching* and *singing* phrases have been dated to the mid-nineteenth century, but probably were around for many years before being committed to writing. The London *Times* noted in 1857 that "It is an old saying that to preach to the converted is a useless office, and I might add that to preach to the unconvertible is a thankless office." A hundred and fifty years later, *The Washington Times* headlined an editorial about former vice president Al Gore's scheduled testimony to House and Senate panels run by "climate-panicked Democrats": "Al Gore to preach to the choir."

The different clichés may be embellished in different ways. Ron Charles, of *The Washington Post*, cast a jaundiced eye on a 2007 collection of writings intended to show "the spiritual possibilities within the realm of housekeeping," saying: "These poems and essays are lovely, but most of them are preaching to the choir—whose robes, you'd better believe, have been washed in holy water and ironed with the rock of salvation." A 1989 Op-Ed column in *The Washington Post* about the first President Bush's programs noted: "Education is another area in which Bush and the conservatives are singing from the same hymn book, if not always in the same key." See ON MESSAGE.

A subtle distinction was made by an anonymous aide to President Ronald Reagan, as quoted in *Newsweek* in 1981: " 'We didn't exactly woodshed them,' a Reagan man said, 'but we did let them know it's time to sing from the same sheet of music.' " For more about the function of that outbuilding in American politics, see WOODSHED, TAKE HIM TO THE.

paid his dues See CARD-CARRYING.

pairing An agreement between two legislators, in disagreement about an upcoming vote, that neither will be present at the voting; thus, each is on record without the necessity of appearance.

When supporters of John F. Kennedy explained that their candidate was seriously ill at the time of the McCarthy censure, liberal Democrats refused to accept the excuse because, they argued, "the Senator could have been paired against McCarthy."

The system is a useful device when absence is caused by illness or other important official business; similarly, it is an alibi-ruiner. However, Ralph Waldo Emerson made a case against the idea in the nineteenth century:

> What a vicious practice is this of our politicians at Washington pairing off! as if one man who votes wrong, going away, could excuse you, who mean to vote right, for going away; or as if your presence did not tell in more ways than in your vote. Suppose the three hundred heroes at Thermopylae had paired off with three hundred Persians: would it have been all the same to Greece, and to history?

palace guard Attack phrase on a leader's inner circle from one who has been excluded; those who protect or "insulate" a president, taking an undue share of power.

"Either make up your minds," Eisenhower chief of staff Sherman Adams said to two department heads in some dispute, "or else tell me and I will do it. We must not bother the President with this. He is trying to keep the world from war." Adams (see ABOMINABLE NO-MAN) was denounced by Senator Joseph McCarthy for heading a "palace guard," usurping power by "insulating" the chief executive from decisions properly only his.

From the point of view of one unable to reach the leader's ear, the sin of the palace guard is insulation. F. Clifton White, who organized the "Draft Goldwater" movement only to find himself frozen out when Goldwater was nominated, said nothing against the candidate but was bitter about what he termed "the tight little coterie that insulated him from all other Republicans."

According to Lyndon Johnson, House Speaker Sam Rayburn told Harry Truman soon after Truman became president: "Harry, they'll try to put you behind a wall down here. There will be people who will surround you and cut you off from any ideas but theirs. They'll try to make you think that the President is the smartest man in the world. And, Harry, you know he ain't and I know he ain't."

James Farley broke with FDR in 1940, when he thought there was a possibility of a presidential nomination for himself. Of those days, he wrote: "Housing Administrator Nathan Straus brought me word that the White House 'palace guard' realized the anti-Catholic campaign against me had failed ..." Earlier, when Farley was a member of that guard, he explained the political subtlety behind the willingness of Louis Howe, FDR's closest adviser, to permit Farley to be close to Roosevelt: "The reason Louis had faith in me and trusted me was that he knew I didn't want to get between him and Roosevelt. In other words, Louis didn't have anything I wanted, see?"

A good political campaign appears to "stay loose," to avoid the strict lines of authority that discourage influential supporters from reaching the candidate or his manager. If the circle of men around a candidate freezes into a few familiar faces, there is a tendency for those men to identify too closely with the candidate and an understandable reluctance of others to try to "break in."

The idea of the *palace guard* probably comes from the Praetorian Guard, an imperial bodyguard established by the Emperor Augustus which, under later Roman emperors, assumed considerable power of its own. In 1791 James Madison warned that the "stockjobbers will become the praetorian band of the Government, at once its tool and its tyrant." Around "King Andrew" Jackson's time, the White House was referred to as "the palace," a usage William Leggett objected to in 1837: "The word 'palace' ... as applied to the President's house is entirely out of place ..."

The phrase was applied to the Nixon senior staff by Dan Rather and Gary Paul Gates in a 1971 book of that title; because of the Germanic origin of some of the key aides' names (Haldeman, Ehrlichman, Kissinger, Ziegler), the Nixon palace guard was also known as the *Berlin wall*.

In the Carter Administration, the number of Georgians on the staff (Joseph Powell, Hamilton Jordan, Robert Lipshutz, Stuart Eizenstat) led to the occasional use of the *Magnolia Mafia*. (See IRISH MAFIA.) Carter cabinet secretary Jack Watson insisted: "The White House staff will not be a palace guard giving commands to the rest of government." Asked why he had placed a stern call to a cabinet member, Watson replied, "He will constantly need a presidential perspective on issues, and the White House staff has to give him that perspective." The Reagan palace guard was headed by Nancy Reagan, who brought down White House Chief of Staff Don Regan; the Clinton by Hillary Rodham Clinton.

The use of *palace guard* can be stretched to cover any group suspected of protecting presidential reputation, as a synonym for *sycophancy*. An anonymous blogger in 2007 wrote of George W. Bush: "I've never met him and suspect he can be as amicable in person as members of the White House Palace Guard…oops!… I mean White House press corps say he is. But he has clearly taken our nation to war on the basis of lies …"

In the synonymy of high staff, *palace guard* is a mild term of reproof to the circle of advisers that must be near a President or governor; *inner circle* (see INNER CLUB) is a term of respect or awe; KITCHEN CABINET is a group of trusted, unofficial advisers on policy; *coterie* implies trailing admirers or circle of cronies; *retinue* is critical of the number of people who travel with the executive; *clique* is definitely pejorative, connoting snobbism; *mafia* (see IRISH MAFIA) imputes fierce loyalty, often used in admiration mixed with a dash of fear; OFFICIAL FAMILY is a wide-ranging roster of appointees and imputes no criticism; *set*, as in the *Cliveden Set* in wartime England, or the *Georgetown cocktail party set*, is snobbish with a sinister overlay; *privy council*, used by Franklin Roosevelt, never caught on in the U.S., and his BRAIN TRUST connoted professors: "the back door to the White House can only be opened with a Phi Beta Kappa key."

panjandrum Mock title for a self-appointed big shot; a more intellectual form of MUCKEY-MUCK or POOH-BAH.

In a 1977 book review by the cultural writer John Leonard, the mouth-filling word was used in its intended meaning: "As we might expect from Mr. [Ben] Wattenberg—coauthor of 'The Real Majority,' adviser to Senator Henry Jackson, panjandrum of the 'centrist' Coalition for a Democratic Majority and public-television personality—'Against All Enemies' has more on its mind than mere entertainment."

Panjandrum was a word concocted by playwright Samuel Foote sometime in the latter half of the eighteenth century as part of a passage to test the memory of a character who claimed to be able to repeat anything after having once heard it: "And there were present the Picninnies, and the Joblillies, and the Garyulies, and the Grand Panjandrum himself, with the little round button at top."

In his 1997 book, *Right in the Old Gazoo: A Lifetime of Scrapping with the Press*, Wyoming senator Alan K. Simpson wrote, "I have appointed myself the chairman, High Panjandrum, Grand Inquisitor—and sole member—of a grievance committee of my own making." The historian Arthur Schlesinger Jr. referred to newspaper columnists as "panjandrums of the opinion mafia."

paper the file See CYA.

paper tiger False ferocity; exaggerated danger; in diplomacy, a blustering nation with no real strength.

"All reactionaries," Mao Zedong told correspondent Anna Louise Strong in 1946, "are paper tigers. In appearance, the reactionaries are terrifying, but in reality they are not so powerful."

On other occasions Mao said of imperialists and feudalists: "Look! were these not living, iron tigers, real tigers? But in the end they changed into paper tigers, dead tigers, bean-curd tigers." And of the threat of nuclear destruction: "The atom bomb is a paper tiger which the U.S. reactionaries use to scare people. It looks terrible, but in fact it isn't."

Paper is a word used to symbolize the name of a thing rather than the thing itself; a picture of a cow drawn on paper cannot be milked, nor can a picture of a tiger on paper harm the viewer. Hence, *paper blockade*, declared but not enforced; *paper profits*, real but unrealized; and *to paper the house*, to distribute free tickets to give the illusion of a sellout crowd.

Tiger metaphors have long stalked politics. *Riding the tiger* is an ancient image, used in 1936 by Winston Churchill: "Dictators ride to and from upon tigers from which they dare not dismount. And the tigers are getting hungry." A Tammany chieftain is said to have mounted a tiger's head on an old fire engine to rally his voters, and Thomas Nast locked in the image of a hungry TAMMANY TIGER in a cartoon.

paradigm shift The idea that a shift in perception causes inventive changes throughout; used in politics as a call for reinventing and reorganizing government, not enlarging it.

Historian Thomas Kuhn introduced this term in his 1962 book, *The Structure of Scientific Revolutions*, explaining the force of scientific change. He explored how old assumptions have historically been replaced by new paradigms, as in the shift from thinking that the sun revolves around the earth. Kuhn's point—that a new paradigm can lead to drastic change—led to the movement for rethinking, or "reinventing," government.

The key word, *paradigm*, offers such synonyms as *model, example, pattern, archetype*. In 1984, *Paradigm Shift* was the title of a book by Robert L. Humphrey on the teaching of universal values.

In 1992, David Osborne and Ted Gaebler applied the idea of a paradigm shift to politics when they wrote *Reinventing Government*. The verb *reinvent* had been popularized in recent usage by the 1985 book *Re-Inventing the Corporation*, by John Naisbitt and Patricia Aburdene. Specifically, the reinventing of government calls for new ways to help the poor and middle class without the problems created by bureaucracy.

James P. Pinkerton, a George H.W. Bush aide for policy planning, picked up and popularized Kuhn's term in his "New Paradigm" memoranda in 1990, creating a New Paradigm Society to attract speakers like Osborne. At Pinkerton's urging, President Bush touched on the subject in an April 1990 speech: "When old centralized bureaucratic systems are crumbling, the time has come for yet another paradigm." This formulation, substituting "yet another paradigm" (acronym: YAP) for "the new paradigm," did not lend itself to clarion calling; critical of the idea, Richard Darman, Bush's budget director, who remembered Depression-era song titles, wryly commented that the concept would be dismissed with "Brother, can you spare a paradigm?"

The "reinventing government" and "new paradigm" ideas found a welcome at the Progressive Policy Institute in Washington, where Will Marshall brought them to the attention of Arkansas Governor Bill Clinton. After Clinton's election in 1992, Pinkerton wrote in *The Washington Post:* "Maybe it *will* take a Democrat to 'reinvent' our oxidized, barnacled Ozymandias of a government. But if Clinton fails, a reinvented Republican Party will be waiting in the wings."

A similar phrase, *tipping point*, was a borrowing from physics by the sociologist Morton Grodzins in an early '60s study of sudden "white flight" from neighborhoods increasingly occupied by blacks. The phrase caught the public fancy in 2000 as the title of a book by Malcolm Gladwell. "It's that ideas and behavior and messages and products sometimes behave just like outbreaks of infectious disease. They are social epidemics," Gladwell explained. "As human beings, we always expect everyday change to happen slowly and steadily, and for there to be some relationship between cause and effect. And when there isn't—when crime drops dramatically in New York for no apparent reason, or when a movie made on a shoestring budget ends up making hundreds of millions of dollars—we're surprised. I'm saying, don't be surprised. This is the way social epidemics work."

parallel construction See TURNAROUNDS; CONTRAPUNTAL CONSTRUCTION.

paramount issue The overriding concern on the minds of voters in a campaign.

The phrase was popularized by William Jennings Bryan about "free silver," and has had a steady use since. Michigan Governor George Romney called Vietnam the "paramount issue" of 1967 (see UNTHINKABLE THOUGHTS). *Paramount issue* implies importance, for rational discussion, such as continuance of a long war; BURNING QUESTION is more emotional discussion from entrenched positions, as on abortion rights; *gut issue* is one which is not so much discussed as it is felt, as resentment about immigrant groups or fear of social change or same-sex marriage; POCKETBOOK ISSUE is the fear of inflation or recession. In recent years, TOPIC A has been in use to define the subject that leads news coverage and is at the tip of many tongues.

Before an issue can become paramount, it must (1) be drawn so as to show a difference between parties or ideologies, (2) show voters that the issue-drawing party's side is close to their own, and (3) hit home—have a direct impact on a voter's life.

The word *paramount*, originally a preposition meaning "above," was applied to the Chinese leader Deng Xiaoping, after he refused to keep a title while still retaining power. Western reporters gave him the title "paramount leader."

parity The price at which a farmer maintains his purchasing power.

Parity and *price supports* are used interchangeably, further confusing a farm program that most urban Americans do not try to understand.

Parity, like *par* and *peer*, is from a Latin root meaning "equal." In agricultural policy, it is the price established by government statisticians that will bring the farmer a return equal to a previously favorable base period. The *parity price* gives the farmer a fair return on his investment in comparison with his costs.

To make sure the farmer was adequately paid for his goods, government price supports were begun; this meant that the federal government promised a farmer to purchase his crop at 90 percent of the parity price—provided the farmer planted only on those acres fixed by the government. As Dwight Eisenhower explained it: "At harvest time, if the market price had fallen below the support price … a farmer could get a loan from the government, with his crops as collateral, for the full support price. If the market price then rose above the support price, the farmer paid the government back; if not, he kept the loan, and the government took his crop."

The program had been denounced in the New Deal's early days as "a program of scarcity in a hungry land" and mock tears were shed for "little pigs not born" because of the element of the plan that restrained production. Republicans in the '60s pressed a program of "flexible price supports," with farmers compensated at between 75 percent and 90 percent of the parity price, depending on scarcity and timing.

Politically, the issue has always been hot, with both parties attacking the other's position as the one that stimulates overproduction, causes huge surpluses, helps the big farming combines but not the "family farm," and does not help rural America gain its share of national prosperity. Secretaries of Agriculture since Henry Wallace have been centers of political controversy, with *parity* the incendiary word.

In a different sense, the word is in active use in strategic arms control. As the Soviet Union approached (and in some respects outstripped) the United States in the ability to conduct nuclear war, a word was needed to change the desired American posture from continued "superiority." In 1969, "sufficiency" was discussed, but "parity" persevered. ("Equality" would have been misleading, since each superpower led in certain categories and trailed in others.) Nixon speechwriters, distressed that the President could no longer say "America must remain number one" in strategic arms, found their answer in a ringing but accurate "America must be second to none," a positive way of presenting parity.

park-bench orator A private citizen outspoken about public affairs, especially in places of public assembly.

The picture of a person seated, spouting opinions with no responsibility for their consequences if undertaken, is also expressed by ARMCHAIR STRATEGIST. However, *park-bench orator* has a more benign connotation, and is less noisy than *soapbox orator*, especially since Bernard Baruch made a park bench in Lafayette Park, opposite the White House, his headquarters when in Washington. In his later years, he would sit bundled in a heavy overcoat holding conferences with important government officials and newsmen. "His bench," wrote biographer Margaret Coit, "to which mail was duly addressed and delivered, was just off dead center of the park, near the end of the equestrian statue of Andrew Jackson. It was four feet six inches long, just enough to accommodate Baruch and one average-sized Cabinet officer." The bench sits there today, with a bronze plaque nearby identifying it as "the Bernard M. Baruch Bench of Inspiration," and it has been used by at least one Washington pundit as an unbugged, publicly private place to meet and interview White House aides.

The studious lack of ostentation was ostentatious in itself, but the ELDER STATESMAN's stature was such that he could carry it off. Two generations earlier, Baruch had taken the edge off what had been a dirty word by telling the Pujo Committee that his occupation was "speculator" and then defining the need for speculators in the making of markets (much as hedge-fund and private equity managers did a half-century later). In his old age, Baruch did much the same to rehabilitate the phrase *park-bench orator*, despite its metaphoric contradiction: one usually orates from a stump or soapbox, not a bench.

Occasional continued use is illustrated in this 1967 *Wall Street Journal* item: "[defining Communism]...A pastime for park-bench orators and intense collegians has rather suddenly blown into an important Congressional debate ..."

parlor pink Socialite socialist; in the past, an attack word on a leftist or FELLOW TRAVELER who limited political radicalism to cocktail-party discussions.

Theodore Roosevelt was the coiner of the "parlor" end in a Minneapolis speech, September 28, 1917: "The parlor pacifist, the white-handed or sissy type of pacifist, represents decadence, represents the rotting out of the virile virtues among people who typify the unlovely, senile side of civilization. The rough-neck pacifist, on the contrary, is a mere belated savage who has not been educated to the virtues of national patriotism."

A year later, in a magazine article, Roosevelt applied the noun-become-adjective to the left as "parlor bolshevism." See PROFESSIONAL.

Since Bolsheviks were "reds," their sympathizers were called *pinks*, or *pinkos*, especially from the '30s through the '50s; the alliteration of the Roosevelt adjective and the noun locked up the phrase as *parlor pink*.

The phrase outlived the use of the word *parlor* in American speech. With changes in housing, the parlor—a small formal sitting room for guests—became merged into a general living room, den, or dining area. As the room was designed out of houses and apartments, the word *parlor*—based on the French verb *parler*, "to speak"—atrophied, except for its political use in this phrase, and in invitations from spiders to flies. The phrase was replaced for a generation by *radical chic*, a coinage of journalist Tom Wolfe. In France, it is *la gauche de salon*. See PINKO; RED; FELLOW TRAVELER; LEFT WING, RIGHT WING; LIMOUSINE LIBERAL.

partisan Praised as basic to the TWO-PARTY SYSTEM, the adversary mode of arriving at clean, effective government; attacked as introducing unnecessary strife, placing party advantage above the public interest.

The dispute about the pros and cons of partisan political activity can be illustrated by the following quotations, only some of which are familiar.

George Washington: "The alternate domination of one faction over another, sharpened by the spirit of revenge natural to party dissension, which in different ages and countries has perpetrated the most horrid enormities, is itself a frightful despotism."

Joseph Addison in *The Spectator*: "There is nothing so bad for the face as party zeal. It gives an ill-natured cast to the eye, and a disagreeable sourness to the look. ... I never knew a party-woman that kept her beauty for a twelve-month."

On the other hand, John Stuart Mill: "A party of order or stability, and a party of progress or reform, are both necessary elements of a healthy state of political life."

Graham Wallas (see GREAT SOCIETY): "Something is required simpler and more permanent, something which can be loved and trusted, and which can be recognized at successive elections as being the same thing that was loved and trusted before; and a party is such a thing."

In the past century, statesmen like Woodrow Wilson felt free to say, "The trouble with the Republican Party is that it has not had a new idea in thirty years," and Dwight Eisenhower, who was ABOVE POLITICS, was not above referring to Democrats in high office as "too big for their britches and too small for their jobs."

The object of that last crack, Harry Truman, enjoyed the heat of the kitchen: "There never was a non-partisan in politics. A man cannot be a non-partisan and be effective in a political party. When he's in any party he's partisan—he's got to be. The only way a man can act as a non-partisan is when he is in office, either as President or head of a state or country or city." See IF YOU CAN'T STAND THE HEAT ...

Truman is regarded by many as the example of HAPPY WARRIOR partisanship in the twentieth century, just as Andrew Jackson came to be the focus of partisan attack and support in the formative years of the American party system. (It is true that Jackson wrote President Monroe in 1818, "Now is the time to exterminate the monster called party spirit," but that can be dismissed as a burst of reformist exuberance and is never quoted at Democratic Jackson Day dinners.)

In his preliminary notes for *Profiles in Courage*, John F. Kennedy wrote of Senator Robert A. Taft: "He was partisan in the sense that Harry Truman was—they both had the happy gift of seeing things in bright shades. It is the politicians who see things in similar shades that have a depressing and worrisome time of it."

In 1971, at the dedication of the Johnson Library, President Nixon applied a phrase of Albert Beveridge's to Lyndon Johnson: "a partisan of principle." In retirement to San Clemente, elder statesman Nixon told the author, "I'm no longer a partisan." See NON-PARTISAN; BIPARTISAN; FUSION.

party See TWO-PARTY SYSTEM.

party elders The "Grand Old Men"—and now women—of a party, venerated for their age, presumed sagacity, length of party service, and present or past political power.

Politicians of a certain age, survivors of campaigns past, are occasionally turned to for mediation because they have no political ambitions of their own. In the deadlock of the 1920 Republican convention, a group of what historian Mark Sullivan called the "party elders" gathered to resolve the impasse between General Leonard Wood and Governor Frank Lowden. See SMOKE-FILLED ROOM; OVAL OFFICE. Seven senior senators were in the group, and one of them, Henry Cabot Lodge, put forth the name of Warren G. Harding, a newspaper publisher without enemies, who was chosen. Harry Daugherty, Harding's prime mover who was not present at the meeting, referred to the elders as "the Sanhedrin of the Solemn Senators" (a reference to the Sanhedrin, or supreme council, of Jews in ancient Jerusalem).

Party elder is probably derived from *church elder*, and from the Council of Elders who "appealed" to Napoleon to lead France after the excesses of its revolution. The phrase is more partisan than "ELDER STATESMAN," though in the case of former Presidents Harry Truman and Herbert Hoover, each was a party elder and elder statesman simultaneously. General Eisenhower, who had remained ABOVE POLITICS, was considered only an elder statesman and not a party elder.

The phrase is current more in written political analysis than in political talk. In a 2006 piece with a Boston dateline by David Shribman, editor of the *Pittsburgh Post-Gazette*, the headline was "Massachusetts Party Elders Put the Kibosh on Negative Ads." His lead: "The party elders are watching… In the long war against negative advertisements in politics, there has never been anything quite like the board of elders the Democrats have set up as they work to win back the governor's office on Beacon Hill …"

A *party elder* is not to be confused with an OLD PRO, which refers to political experience and not to age. A person under 40 can be referred to as an *old pro*, but white hair has been a requirement for party elders, with the exception of veterans like Speaker Sam Rayburn, who was bald.

ABC's George Stephanopoulos, a former Clinton aide, when asked in late 2000 about the defeated Al Gore's chances for a comeback in 2004 in light of anger at his campaign by some Democratic party elders, told *Newsweek*'s Fareed Zakaria: "What party elders think is irrelevant because there is no party anymore. Those who style themselves as 'elders' are just old pols looking for something to do."

party emblems Identifying symbols at the top of a ballot, originally as a signal to illiterate voters, now used as a kind of trademark.

At the time of the Jackson Administration, the Democratic party emblem was a hickory pole and broom—"a new broom sweeps clean" was a slogan (see CLEAN SWEEP)—which was replaced in the 1840s by a rooster. Legend has it that a Democratic leader named Chapman had a reputation for crowing like a gamecock. When the Democrats won, an expression arose: "Tell Chapman to Crow." In 1842 and 1844, after Democratic victories over the Whigs, the rooster became the usual party emblem.

Republicans in the 1850s and 1860s needed a counterpart. While Democrats were being urged to "vote for the big chick," Republicans were told to "vote for the bird on the dollar," an eagle. In the 1950s,

however, with the "white rooster" closely identified with segregation in the South, Democrats there dropped the emblem and replaced it with a variety of others, most often a star.

Minor parties have used the torch and the scale of justice (mainly Socialist), the Liberty Bell (Liberal party), or the arm and hammer (labor parties); the Prohibitionists always featured the fountain.

Party emblems differ from party symbols. See ELEPHANT, REPUBLICAN; DONKEY, DEMOCRATIC.

National emblems differ from national symbols (John Bull of England, Marianne of France, UNCLE SAM of the U.S.). For America's national emblem, see BALD EAGLE. Other national emblems include the lion of England (see TWISTING THE LION'S TAIL); the cock, as well as the fleur-de-lis, of France; the double-headed eagle of Austria; and the black eagle of Prussia.

party faithful Rank-and-file regulars; hardcore voters and soft-touch contributors.

The originally militant implication of *faithful*, taken from its religious usage, appears now to be used of the long-suffering, often overlooked regulars taken for granted by politicians who spend their time wooing the SWING VOTER.

"The party faithful distrust Mr. Schwarzenegger," wrote Britain's *Economist* magazine about California's Republican Governor in 2007, "for the same reason that most Californians like him. Last year he began to work closely with the Democrats who dominate the state legislature." A badge worn by some of the faithful at the state GOP convention scorned "RINOs," an acronym for "Republicans In Name Only."

A wistfulness permeates today's use of the phrase, as if the faithful's hope for ultimate reward is far in the future. *The faithful* is a cliché in the reportage of fundraising functions, where "eight hundred of the party faithful turned out to munch rubber chicken and listen to …"

REGULAR, with its military origin, implies militant fidelity; *faithful*, with its religious origin, implies mystic, spiritual fidelity; RANK AND FILE, from military via labor, implies fidelity to orders from above but not on high; TROOPS, military, are more disciplined than rank-and-file, and will go out and ring doorbells.

With the rise of the "religious right" of social conservatives, *party faithful* gained a double meaning. See BASE; RELIGIOUS METAPHORS.

party line Official position of a political organization.

This phrase has several political meanings: (1) the principles or position set down by an authoritarian political organization, to be adhered to at lower levels without deviation or, worse, revision; (2) the line or column on a ballot, voting machine, or touchscreen displaying the party's nominees (when the display is horizontal, the word *row* is gaining preference over *line*), and (3) in the plural, the lines of demarcation between parties, which regulars do not cross but issues often do.

The *OED*'s first citation is from Thomas Hart Benton's 1854 memoir *Thirty Years' View*: "Look at the vote in the Senate upon the adoption of the resolution, also as clearly defined by a party line as any party question can ever be expected to be."

"Each Communist is entitled to his opinion," said Nikita Khrushchev in 1963 to the party's Central Committee, "but when the Party adopts a decision, maps out a general line, then all Party members toe the line and do what has been worked out by the collective thinking and will of the party." (Some spell *toe the line*—placing one's foot on the starting line—as *tow the line*, which means "drag a line behind"; this is revisionism.)

Because *party line* was popularized in Communist terminology, most Americans use it sweepingly, as Communists use *general line*; thus, the "general line of the transition period" in China was a broad directive to Communist cadres to place themselves in strategic positions "in a state of readiness." Later, more specific lines set more immediate targets for takeover and national indoctrination. In the U.S., specific Communist party lines zigzagged before World War II as the Soviet Union first reached an accommodation with, and later fought, Nazi Germany.

The phrase was then adopted in the U.S. as an ironic description of Democratic and Republican positions on specific issues. When Defense Secretary Robert McNamara insisted on military officers clearing all speeches with his office, there were objections to the establishment of "a military party line." See MUZZLE; HUNDRED FLOWERS.

In the second sense of "a position on the ballot," a party with a poor comparative registration in an area likes to play down its Democratic or Republican designation, and urges voters to "Vote Row A All the Way"; individual candidates trying to deemphasize their party affiliation advertise "the next to the last name on Line C."

The third sense was illustrated by Wendell Willkie's call in his 1940 acceptance speech: "Party lines are down; nothing could make that clearer than the nomination by the Republicans of a liberal Democrat who changed his party affiliation because he found democracy in the Republican party and not in the New Deal."

In discussing the Republican choice of Eisenhower over Taft in 1952, Harry Truman used the phrase in that context: "The Republicans, being a minority party, knew they had to borrow strength from the Democratic and independent vote. Their only hope of gaining such strength was to find a candidate whose appeal to the voters would cut across party lines."

At Senate hearings in 2006 on the Bush nomination of Samuel Alito for the Supreme Court, Judiciary Chairman Arlen Specter (R.-Pa) said the opposition by Democrats in his panel "says more about the Senate than the nominee ... People who have voted for [Chief Justice John G.] Roberts don't want to cross party lines twice."

party loyalty The ability to support a candidate of an IDEOLOGY not one's own against another party's candidate who does espouse one's own ideology, in the belief that only by "closing ranks" now can your faction come to party power in the future.

"Sometimes party loyalty asks too much," said John F. Kennedy to a Democratic friend, excusing him for supporting Republican Leverett Saltonstall for senator of Massachusetts. But JFK also hinted that if he was reelected in 1964, he would not be too kindly disposed to those in the Democratic party who had thwarted his programs or had opposed him personally. "We can make loyalty to the ticket the test in 1964," he said in 1962, "and then we can deal with those who failed to support the ticket."

The argument against party loyalty is usually founded on "principle": a liberal Democrat finds it sticks in his craw to support a conservative Democrat against a liberal Republican, and vice versa for both parties. Yet this overlooks the nature of the TWO-PARTY SYSTEM in America; the two parties are not ideologically divided, as in England where Labour faces the Conservatives. The BIG TENT of each American party includes factions within of the left and right, struggling for dominance or working for compromise.

When one faction wins, it naturally expects its opposing faction to support the majority choice against the other party. If discipline breaks and the minority faction bolts, it surrenders its right to the loyalty of the opposite faction in the next election. Thus, the bolters see their "principle" temporarily upheld as the other party wins, but they are not likely to ever gain control of a united party that can win.

Party loyalty can be attacked as blind and unprincipled, but to those who view politics as a practical route to the position of power that can make principles operative, party loyalty is essential. That is what Benjamin Disraeli was getting at when he said: "Damn principles! Stick to your party." See BOLT.

party of privilege Frequent Democratic characterization of the Republican party.

The Democratic platform of 1908 dispensed with subtleties and the gray areas of party overlapping: "The Democratic party is the champion of equal rights and opportunities to all; the Republican party is the party of privilege and private monopoly."

As if this were not a wide enough gulf, the platform went on: "The Democratic party listens to the voice of the whole people and gauges progress by the prosperity and advancement of the average man; the Republican party is subservient to the comparatively few who are the beneficiaries of governmental favoritism."

The Republican nominee in 1908, William Howard Taft, won handily, but the emerging phrase was to plague Republicans for years to come. Calvin Coolidge did his best to knock it down. "The governments of the past," he said in 1924, "could fairly be characterized as devices for maintaining in perpetuity the place and position of certain privileged classes...The Government of the United States is a device for maintaining in perpetuity the rights of the people, with the ultimate extinction of all privileged classes."

But not even Coolidge sounding like Lenin could alter the stereotype that was forming in the mind of most of the American electorate. Political scientist Clinton Rossiter put it bluntly: "Most men recognize the Republicans as the party of the upper and upper-middle classes and the Democrats as the party of the lower and lower-middle classes. The short title for the former classes is 'the rich,' for the latter 'the poor.'"

In phraseology applied to parties, Democrats have been fairly successful in tagging Republicans as the "party of privilege" and styling themselves as the PARTY OF THE PEOPLE. For a partial offset, see WAR PARTY. Also see VESTED INTERESTS.

party of the people Democratic party's characterization of itself.

"Our party is the party of the people," wrote Democrat Grover Cleveland in 1896, "because in its care for the welfare of all our countrymen it resists dangerous schemes born of discontent...reinforced by the insidious aid of private selfishness ..."

In that year William Jennings Bryan, whose "dangerous scheme" of free silver caused Cleveland to bolt, asked in his "Cross of Gold" speech: "Upon which side will the Democratic party fight: upon the side of 'the idle holders of idle capital' or upon the side of 'the struggling masses?'... The sympathies of the Democratic party...are on the side of the struggling masses who have ever been the foundation of the Democratic party." See TRICKLE-DOWN THEORY.

Renegade and embittered Republicans helped Democrats seal their slogan throughout the twentieth century. In the Bull Moose campaign of 1912, the Theodore Roosevelt campaign against President Taft included this challenge: "Let us find out whether the Republican party is the party of the plain people; or whether it is the party of the bosses and the sinister interests of special privilege." Democrat Woodrow Wilson, echoing these sentiments, was able to defeat the divided Republicans. After the Dewey upset by Truman in 1948, liberal Republican Russell Davenport, a top Willkie campaign aide in 1940, complained: "The theme of the last sixteen years (which must now become twenty years) has been—the Republican party versus the people. And the people have won."

Truman in 1948, and Adlai Stevenson in both of his campaigns, did not neglect the populist theme that had been absorbed by the Democrats. Said Stevenson: "the Democratic Party is the people's party, not the labor party, not the farmer's party, not the employer's party—it is the party of no one because it is the party of everyone."

Lyndon Johnson, using orthography that would have appealed to Noah Webster and George Bernard Shaw, spelled it out in 1966: "The people... P-E-E-P-U-L ..."

party unity The vital ingredient to winning an election, when dissident factions accept the majority decision and unite behind the nominee, grumbling only in private.

American parties have no monopoly on the desire for party unity. "This democratic method of resolving contradictions among the people," wrote Mao Zedong in 1957, "was epitomized in 1942 in the formula 'unity, criticism, unity.'... It means starting from the desire for unity, resolving contradictions through criticism or struggle and arriving at a new unity on a new basis."

The argument for national unity can be applied to parties. When Lincoln asked,

"The Union, is it a marriage bond or a free-love arrangement?" or when Jefferson ameliorated dissension with "every difference of opinion is not a difference of principle," the point was made that splitting was losing.

The Democratic party prides itself on its ability to split wide apart in primaries and come together in time for elections. "No, sir, th' dimycratic party aint on speakin' terms with itsilf," said Mr. DOOLEY to Mr. Hennessey. "Whin ye see two men with white neckties go into a sthreet car an' set in opposite corners while wan mutthers 'Thraiter' an' th' other hisses 'Miscreent' ye can bet they're two dimmycratic leaders thryin' to reunite th' gran' ol' party."

Party harmony is used almost interchangeably with *party unity*: James Garfield nominated John Sherman "in the interests of party harmony," and Henry Clay, after a nomination defeat was certain, said, "If my name creates any obstacle to Union and Harmony, away with it, and concentrate upon some individual more acceptable to all branches of the opposition."

However, party *harmony* is milder than party *unity*, which is militant; party *loyalty* is the spirit that results in party *regularity*, which in turn is the key to party *unity*. See SURRENDER ON MORNINGSIDE HEIGHTS.

passion for anonymity A willingness to submerge one's identity for the benefit of a public figure; a passion that often passes as the price of memoirs rises.

Franklin Roosevelt took the phrase from Louis Brownlow, who was chairman of his Committee on Administrative Management in 1936–37. Brownlow was thinking of men like Harry Hopkins and Felix Frankfurter; the Reorganization Act of 1939 permitted the President to add six assistants to his staff, each with what Brownlow had described as a "passion for anonymity."

Historian Eric Goldman directed the author to the source of the phrase. Brownlow, who entitled his 1958 autobiography *A Passion for Anonymity*, credits it to Welsh politician Tom Jones, who served as private secretary to three British Prime Ministers: David Lloyd George, Ramsay MacDonald, and Stanley Baldwin. Brownlow related

Jones's comments in 1939 about the need for one key aide:

Being both a Welshman and a veteran of many parliamentary and ministerial battles, he was inclined to put the emphasis on the man rather than on the institution and, therefore, talked more about Sir Maurice Hankey than he did about the Cabinet secretariat. Then he asked me if I would take a message to President Roosevelt for him, a mission which I gladly undertook. The message was this: "Tell the President that the way to solve his problem is to find that one man who would turn out to be another Maurice Hankey, a man possessed of high competence, great physical vigor, and a passion for anonymity." Later, when we rejected the one-man idea and proposed, among other new aids recommended for the President, six administrative assistants, we used Tom Jones's language to describe their qualifications.

During his second term FDR chose assistants less colorful than in his first. "The later careers of Moley, Tugwell, and Hugh Johnson," wrote Samuel Rosenman, "indicate that there is something about administrative power along the Potomac that excludes the concept of anonymous helpfulness which was the basis of the success of the original BRAIN TRUST."

President John F. Kennedy, in speaking of assistant Kenneth O'Donnell, sketched the qualities he wanted in a White House aide: "He has good nerves and a good memory. He has a passion for anonymity. He is always optimistic." Ted Sorensen wrote that "while few of us had a 'passion for anonymity,' most of us had a preference in that direction." President Kennedy told him to turn down requests for speeches and magazine profiles: "Every man that's ever held a job like yours—Sherman Adams, Harry Hopkins, House, all the rest—has ended up in the [Sorensen substituted a blank for the next word]. Congress was down on them or the President was hurt by them or somebody was mad at them. The best way to stay out of trouble is to stay out of sight."

The ability to stay out of sight is invaluable, of course, to members of what came to be called the INVISIBLE GOVERNMENT, the Central Intelligence Agency. As might be expected, CIA chief Allen Dulles told Con-

gress of the kind of men he was trying to recruit: "The agency should be directed by a relatively small but elite corps of men with a passion for anonymity." Years later, as angry CIA operatives published books, they were denounced by old hands as having a "passion for notoriety."

paternalism See GREAT WHITE FATHER.

patronage Governmental appointments made so as to increase political strength.

"Dear Tit: The bearer understands addition, division and silence. Appoint him! Your friend, Bill." According to Charles Ledyard Norton, writing his *Political Americanisms* in 1890, these "qualifications of a successful lobbyist or unscrupulous political worker" first appeared in the New York *Sun* of March 15, 1872, in a letter alleged to have been written by W. H. Kemble, then State Treasurer of Pennsylvania, to T. J. Coffey of Washington, introducing G. O. Evans. This may be legend; the source of "addition, division and silence" has also been given as New York Boss William Marcy Tweed and Pennsylvania Boss Matthew Quay.

The dispensing of patronage, long considered a necessary ingredient in political life—sometimes called "the mothers' milk of politics"—has always been described by Presidents as an odious task. Thomas Jefferson said: "No duty the President had to perform was so trying as to put the right man in the right place." Andrew Johnson tried to defend himself: "Congress, factious, domineering, tyrannical Congress has undertaken to poison the minds of the American people, and create a feeling against me in consequence of the manner in which I have distributed the public patronage."

Dwight Eisenhower came out of a cabinet meeting on October 9, 1953, in a bad temper. "Everything seems to have been patronage this morning," he said as he left. That was because the power of appointment has always invited the charge, and carries with it the stigma, of favoritism, nepotism, and dishonesty. "Our present mayor," said a Boston clergyman about John ("Honey Fitz") Fitzgerald in 1906, "has the distinction of appointing more saloon keepers and bartenders to public office than any previous mayor."

Woodrow Wilson in 1913 took a high-minded view and refused to allow political considerations to dictate appointments. Wilson told Albert S. Burleson, his Postmaster General and dispenser of patronage, "On appointments I am not going to advise with reactionary or STANDPAT Senators or Representatives." Burleson quietly pointed out that this would mean "the defeat of the measures of reform that you have next to your heart. The little offices don't amount to anything. They are inconsequential. It doesn't amount to a damn who is postmaster at Paducah, Kentucky. But these little offices mean a great deal to the Senators and Representatives in Congress. ... If they are turned down, they will hate you and will not vote for anything you want. It is human nature." Wilson gave in.

Rarely do politicians articulate a defense of patronage. Tammany leader Edward Costikyan, who was forced by his reform associates to rename his "Patronage Committee" the "Government Appointments Committee," wrote:

> How does one secure good government with good people, and strengthen a political party through the use of the power to appoint people to government office? This is the basic problem in dealing with "patronage," and it is one which our mythology prevents us from dealing with effectively. ... The basic lesson I quickly learned was that a political leader cannot afford to insult his supporters by rewarding his opponents.

The opprobrium connected with patronage, and its association with phrases like SPOILS SYSTEM, TURKEY FARM, and the "power of public plunder," did not originate with politics. Originally, *patronage* meant the protection of the rights of the Church. The *OED* traces the word back to 1395: "A newe couetous bisshop of Rome ... wole ... make voide fre elecciouns and ordenauncis of the clergie of oure rewme [i.e., realm] bi title of patronage ... which eleccions and ordenauncis of patronagis camen forth of seculer lordis." Following its defense-of-religion use, the word became associated with the patronage of authors and artists

by the Church and the nobility. "Patron of the arts" stems from this.

The effect of the patronage of either kind on the morale of the receiver was observed by Cardinal Wolsey in Shakespeare's *Henry VIII*: "O, how wretched is that poor man that hangs on princes' favours."

In 1976 the U.S. Supreme Court, in *Elrod, Sheriff et al. v. Burns et al.*, held that the practice of patronage dismissals in a sheriff's office violated the First and Fourteenth Amendments. In the majority opinion, Justice William Brennan wrote: "More recent times have witnessed a strong decline in [patronage's] use, particularly with respect to public employment. Indeed, only decades after Andrew Jackson's administration, strong discontent with the corruption and inefficiency of the patronage system of public employment eventuated in the Pendleton Act (1883), the foundation of modern civil service. And on the state and local levels, merit systems have increasingly displaced the practice."

In a footnote, the Court cited *To the Victor* (1971), a book by Martin Tolchin and Susan Tolchin, as expert in modern patronage, and its authors supply the lexicographer their 2008 definition: "The traditional view had been that patronage referred only to jobs. We defined patronage—after consultation with scores of politicians who said that they were not pressed for jobs but for many other governmental favors—as the disbursement of the discretionary favors of government in exchange for political support." The purpose of such disbursement was best described by Chicago boss Jacob Arvey: "Politics is the art of putting people under obligation to you."

pax Americana "American peace"; praised as the welcome assumption of the burden of peacekeeping, or criticized as one-superpower hegemony of the United States.

This phrase is based on the Latin *pax Romana*, "Roman peace," the two centuries of peace in the Roman Empire beginning with the reign of Augustus. The word *pax*, "peace" (personified in Roman myth as Pax, the goddess of peace), is related to the verb *pacisci*, meaning "to make a bargain or pact," and it was applied by Pliny the Elder to the extended period of peaceful rule by the Roman empire.

From *pax Romana* came *pax Britannica* in the nineteenth century, describing the peace that Britain imposed on hostile nations. A use of the 1894 phrase *pax Americana* by the writer Richard Raine in 1967 dutifully noted the derivation: "The whole Western world…is living under…a Pax Americana, just as the world once lived in peace under a Pax Britannica."

Michael T. Klare, writing in *The Nation* in 1991 about Operation Desert Storm, described a second phase of this peace: "The cold war era, which ended with the tearing down of the Berlin wall, was characterized by U.S. supremacy in the military, economic and political spheres—Pax Americana I. The gulf conflict inaugurates a new era characterized by continuing U.S. military supremacy accompanied by neither economic nor political strength—Pax Americana II."

The elder George Bush, in a 1992 speech to the United Nations General Assembly, sought to dissociate the U.S. from the exclusive responsibility of global policing as well as from the attendant resentment: "We seek a Pax Universalis, built upon shared responsibilities and aspirations." In 1993, the novelist John Le Carré predicted, "With the clamps of the Cold War removed, old feuds are going to flare up everywhere. A Pax Americana of some kind is inevitable." (See POLICEMAN OF THE WORLD.) Fifteen years later, as success appeared possible in Iraq, Fouad Ajami wrote in *The Wall Street Journal*: "from Egypt to Kuwait and Bahrain, a Pax Americana anchors the order of the region. In Iraq, the Pax Americana, hitherto based in Sunni Arab lands, has acquired a new footing in a Shiite-led country, and this is the true source of Arab agitation."

pay as you go Withholding taxes from income as it is received, rather than requiring payment later; centuries ago, the way to a balanced budget.

"It is incumbent on every generation," Thomas Jefferson wrote a friend in 1820,

"to pay its own debts as it goes—a principle which, if acted on, would save one-half the wars of the world." The phrase had earlier occurred as an aphorism in *Poor Richard's Almanack* by Benjamin Franklin.

The phrase has had a long economic-political application. Thurlow Weed, a journalist who later became a power in the Republican party, wrote in 1839 about the construction of the Erie Canal: "The Democracy proclaimed itself in favor of the 'pay as you go' policy." John Randolph of Roanoke cried in Congress, "I have found the Philosopher's Stone! It is contained in four words: Pay-as-you-go!"

The phrase continued to mean a policy of balanced budgets until 1943, with the adoption of the withholding tax, espoused by Beardsley Ruml, chairman of R.H. Macy. Subsequently, with the adoption of the estimated tax, U.S. policy on taxation policy extended *pay as you go* to anticipated income—prepare to pay as you expect to go—and not just past wages, dividends, and capital gains.

The practice reduces the payer's pain of the annual tax "bite," and the principle was long taken to be conservative, although in 2006 it was seen by some anti-tax advocates as a liberal scheme: Cal Thomas, a conservative columnist, wrote in *The Washington Times* after the midterm defeat of Republicans in 2006 that "Democrats will try to raise taxes (they call it 'pay as you go') …"

For short, it has come to be called *paygo*: former House Republican leader Richard Armey opined that "*Paygo* was first concocted by Richard Darman, George H.W. Bush's budget director, as part of the 1990 budget deal that raised taxes in hopes of reining in the deficit…at Darman's urging, George H.W. Bush broke his famous 1988 campaign promise and signed on to a deficit reduction package that increased taxes and instituted paygo. The economy tanked, the deficit ballooned and the GOP suffered an electoral rout in 1992." (See READ MY LIPS.)

Democrats Roger Altman and Alan Blinder wrote that in the 110th Congress, "Nancy Pelosi has promised to restore pay-as-you-go financing…the new Congress should bring back *paygo* immediately."

peace See FULL GENERATION OF PEACE; JUST AND LASTING PEACE.

peace at any price A slogan formerly used in earnest, now an attack phrase on those considered appeasers.

The idea of a *price* to be paid for peace probably stemmed from the *price* for liberty. "Eternal vigilance is the price of liberty" is the "quotation" developed out of a 1790 remark by Irish lawyer John Philpot Curran: "The condition upon which God hath given liberty to man is eternal vigilance."

In 1645, Britain's Lord Digby wrote of "the Kingdom's quiet, at any price to the King, to the Church, and to the faithfulest of his party." Edward Hyde, Earl of Clarendon, wrote in his 1647 *History of the Rebellion and Civil Wars in England:* "That [Lord Falkland] was so enamoured on peace, that he would have been glad the king should have bought it at any price." English poet Arthur H. Clough attributed the first political use of *peace at any price* to French poet and Minister of Foreign Affairs in 1848 Alphonse de Lamartine, although the historian Thomas Arnold wrote in 1823 in his *History of Rome* of Hannibal's probable intent in "purchasing peace at any price." Lord Avebury, in *The Use of Life*, in 1849 turned the phrase into a hyphenated compound modifier: "Though not a 'peace-at-any-price' man, I am not ashamed to say I am a peace-at-almost-any-price man."

In 1856 in the U.S., the phrase was used without sarcasm as the rallying cry of the KNOW-NOTHINGS behind former President Millard Fillmore, who ran behind James Buchanan and John Frémont. "Peace at any price—peace and union" was the slogan of those willing to pay the price of slavery to avoid civil war.

A strangely familiar "quotation of the day" appeared in *The New York Times* in January 1959, attributed to Admiral Arthur W. Radford: "The things that will destroy America are prosperity at any price, peace at any price, safety first instead of duty first, the love of soft living and the get-rich-quick

feeling of living." The quotation, with the substitution of "life" for "living" at the end, is from Theodore Roosevelt, who also liked to inveigh against the "professional pacifists, the peace-at-any-price, nonresistance, universal arbitration people" who he felt were "seeking to Chinafy this country."

President Woodrow Wilson told an Iowa audience in 1916: "There is a price which is too great to pay for peace, and that price can be put in one word. One cannot pay the price of self-respect."

Senator William Borah, in 1919, attacked Woodrow Wilson's peace treaty and League of Nations with "Would you purchase peace at the cost of any part of our independence?" In 1937 Harold Macmillan urged England to "settle with Germany now, or coerce her now. But don't let us purchase an uncertain peace at a terrible price to be paid later."

The idea of peace having a high price, worth paying, but not going so far as "any" price remains a current political metaphor. At the height of the Cuban missile crisis, President Kennedy said on television: "The cost of freedom is always high, but Americans have always paid it." Bernard Baruch, urging the United Nations to adopt a plan for atomic weapons control in 1946, gave the phrase an added dimension: "The solution will require apparent sacrifice in pride and in position, but better pain as the price of peace than death as the price of war."

In 1991, George H.W. Bush repeated the phrase in remarks about America's stance against Iraq, which had invaded Kuwait and threatened the world's oil supply: "APPEASEMENT—peace at any price—was never an answer."

peace bloc See BLOC.

Peace Corps A 1960 Kennedy campaign phrase and idea appealing to youthful idealism, which was translated into a "signature" program after the campaign.

Senator Hubert Humphrey, along with Senator Richard Neuberger and Congressman Henry Reuss, had proposed several ideas in the late fifties for sending voluntary technical assistance workers overseas.

Senator Humphrey provided the author with this background:

> Congressman Henry S. Reuss of Wisconsin played a very important role in a government-sponsored youth service corps. After a visit to Cambodia in 1957, he created the Point Four Youth Corps which he submitted to the House of Representatives early in 1960, calling for a study on his proposal. The study was eventually assigned to the University of Colorado Research Foundation and put under the general direction of Dr. Maurice Albertson. The Albertson report was completed in May 1961. Much of the concrete planning of the present Peace Corps was based on it.
>
> On June 15, 1960, while I was a Senator, I introduced the "Works for Peace" bill. This bill differed from that of Congressman Reuss' in that instead of asking for a study of the Peace Corps, it asked for the Peace Corps itself. President Kennedy took the Peace Corps idea and continued to call it by that name.

After pointing out its origin in Humphrey's work, Arthur Schlesinger, Jr., added:

> General James Gavin urged a similar plan on Kennedy. Kennedy himself advanced the idea a little tentatively during the campaign—it was mid-October and two in the morning—to an audience of students at the University of Michigan. The response was unexpectedly warm.... Later, in California, Kennedy called for the establishment of a peace corps, broadening it from Humphrey's original conception to include women as well as men and older people as well as young.

Ted Sorensen, however, played down Humphrey's contribution in his recollection of the origin: "The Peace Corps proposal, for example, was based on the Mormon and other voluntary religious service efforts, on an editorial Kennedy had read years earlier, on a speech by General Gavin, on a luncheon I had with a Philadelphia businessman, on the suggestions of his academic advisors, on legislation previously introduced and on the written response to a spontaneous latenight challenge he issued to Michigan students."

General Gavin, in response to the author's query, reports that his idea germinated at an October 18, 1960, meeting of a committee of the U.S. Chamber of Commerce.

The more I thought about it, the more I became convinced that the country should organize something like a Peace Corps.

I returned to Arthur D. Little, Inc., and discussed it with some of my colleagues. One of them wrote a memo to me recommending the title, "Peace Corps." I personally was a bit reluctant to use the "Corps" because of its military connotation.

Several days later, I addressed a group of educators in Miami, Florida, on Thursday, October 27, and advanced the idea of a Peace Corps to them. A bit to my surprise they greeted my idea with great enthusiasm and applause.... The Governor-Elect of Florida suggested that I should call John F. Kennedy and urge him to adopt the idea.

I returned to Wellesley on Friday, October 28, and got in touch with Mr. Kennedy by phone. He asked me to send him a brief memo on the subject to San Francisco. I wrote the paper over the weekend and referred to the undertaking as the "Peace Corps." Mr. Kennedy spoke on it in San Francisco the following Wednesday, urging the adoption of such a program.

Who, then, "coined" Peace Corps? Humphrey probably coined the phrase, if you define coinage as "first use." General Gavin and his aide at Arthur D. Little "coined" it, if you define coinage as setting up the concept and suggesting the label. John F. Kennedy "coined" it, if you define coinage as making a phrase famous.

Ideas generated in the heat of a campaign rarely see the light of election day (heat and light metaphors may be mixed). To the surprise of many politicians, this suggestion of Gavin's did.

peace feeler A diplomatic probe, real or imagined, to end hostilities.

A *feeler* has long been defined as a remark or proposal put forth to ascertain the attitudes of others. Colloquially, to *feel out* means to subtly find out another's opinion or disposition.

Peace feeler came strongly into the political terminology during the war in Vietnam, as the U.S. sought some receptivity to negotiations by the North Vietnamese government. In 1966, the Johnson administration was criticized for ignoring peace feelers supposedly extended through the United Nations. When Robert Kennedy traveled abroad in 1967, a controversy arose as to whether a peace feeler was extended to him. A Bill Mauldin cartoon showed Senator Kennedy arriving home with a snake-like vine twitching behind him; he asked, "Can I help it if a peace feeler followed me home?"

Lyndon Johnson gave the phrase the presidential seal on March 15, 1967, in a speech to the Tennessee legislature. "We have just lived through another flurry of 'peace feelers.'" In that context, the phrase carried a connotation of vain hopes, of illusory approaches.

When a tape recorded in 2006 had Osama bin Laden saying, "We don't mind offering you a long-term truce," Victor Davis Hanson of the Hoover Institution wrote in *The Washington Times*: "The winning side does not ask for a reprieve. Losing autocrats—whether the officers of the German army in the summer of 1918 or Hitler's cadre in the spring of 1945—always 'don't mind' sending out peace feelers in the 11th hour to salvage their power before they lose it for good."

peace for our time British Prime Minister Neville Chamberlain's optimistic prediction after negotiations with Hitler before World War II; now used derisively.

Chamberlain returned from the Munich Conference on September 30, 1938, convinced that his concessions to Hitler dismembering Czechoslovakia had paved the way to peace. For a fuller discussion, see MUNICH ANALOGY; SELLOUT.

Paraphrasing a remark of Disraeli's (see PEACE WITH HONOR), Chamberlain said, "My good friends: This is the second time in our history that there has come back from Germany to Downing Street peace with honor. I believe it is peace for our time."

The phrase is often misquoted as "Peace *in* our time," perhaps because it appears in that form in Morning Prayer: "Give peace in our time, O Lord." When Senator Orrin Hatch (R-Utah) rose in April 2007 to oppose the bill that Democratic majorities in both houses of Congress had passed to tie the funding of the war in Iraq to a specific timetable for withdrawal, he called the legislation—certain to draw a presidential veto—"the worst case of capitulation to appeasement since Neville Chamberlain spoke the words 'peace in our time.'"

peaceful coexistence As seen in the U.S., a proposal for fair competition of ideologies ("live and let live"); as long expressed in the U.S.S.R., a program for evolutionary triumph over capitalism.

In 1920, V.I. Lenin reportedly told an interviewer: "Our plans in Asia? The same as in Europe: peaceful coexistence with the peoples, with the workers and peasants of all nations."

On June 30, 1954, President Dwight Eisenhower was asked at a news conference: "Mr. President, what are the possibilities for peaceful coexistence between Soviet Russia and Communist China, on the one hand, and the non-Communist nations on the other?" He replied in part:

> For a long, long time, everybody in the United States had urged that we attempt to reach a proper basis for peaceful coexistence. We had found, though, an aggressive attitude on the part of the other side that had made such an accomplishment or consummation not easy to reach. In other words, there had to be good faith on both sides. Moreover, we had to make certain that peaceful coexistence did not mean APPEASEMENT. ... We have got to find ways of living together.

The phrase had its greatest impact when Nikita Khrushchev made it the subject of a speech on January 6, 1961, just before a new American President—John F. Kennedy—was to be inaugurated. Khrushchev's definition: "the policy of peaceful coexistence, as regards its social content, is a form of intense economic, political, and ideological struggle of the proletariat against the aggressive forces of imperialism in the international arena."

This was in line with Russian policy enunciated by Lenin: "International imperialism disposing of the might of capital cannot coexist with the Soviet Republic. Conflict is unavoidable"—a far cry from his soothing statement at the beginning of this entry. However, in October of 1961 the Communist line appeared to change.

In the *Programme of the Communist Party of the Soviet Union* a switch back to a softer line was evident: "Peaceful coexistence of the socialist and capitalist countries is an objective necessity for the development of human society. War cannot and must not serve as a means of settling international disputes … The policy of peaceful coexistence is in accord with the vital interests of all mankind, except the big monopoly magnates and the militarists."

The zigzags in the PARTY LINE confused many Americans who were under the impression that "peaceful coexistence" meant "live and let live." Barry Goldwater warned in 1961, "Nor is there such a thing as peaceful coexistence." In 1963 John F. Kennedy urged "peaceful cooperation" at the U.N., and a year later U.N. Ambassador Adlai Stevenson defended coexistence as the alternative to "coextinction."

Thus, the phrase means—in the words of Humpty Dumpty—"whatever I choose it to mean."

In the 1990s, as the existence of the Soviet Union ended, the phrase was used beyond U.S.-Russian relations. *The Washington Post* reported in 1993 on the Pope's visit to Africa: "In Benin and Uganda, John Paul stressed peaceful coexistence between Muslims and Christians. … 'The way of those who believe in God and want to serve him is not that of domination; it is the way of peace.'"

peacenik See -NIK SUFFIX.

peace process Negotiations to end armed conflict; the sometimes seemingly interminable business of reaching agreement to end or at least reduce hostilities.

As early as 1975, this alliterative phrase was in use in Middle East coverage. *The Economist* noted that some diplomats claimed "to have no idea where Mr. Kissinger's piecemeal peace process is leading."

In December 1977, *The Washington Post* paraphrased the words of a Damascus newspaper, *Tishrin*, under the control of the Syrian government, which called for Anwar Sadat's resignation after the Begin/Sadat summit: "The only important result of the summit was that Egypt and Israel succeeded in alienating the Palestine Liberation Organization from the peace process."

The Washington Post helped popularize the noun phrase. A 1979 article asserted that "prospects dimmed for Palestine Liberation Organization contacts with the United States and participation in the U.S.-sponsored peace process." Six years later, the same paper commented on terrorism, "The Achille Lauro affair deals Yasir Arafat out of the Mideast peace process, for his Palestine Liberation Organization was using the talks as a cloak for terror against Israel."

The phrase appeared in 1990, when *Newsday* covered a speech by Gov. Mario L. Cuomo supporting Israel. According to *Newsday,* "The governor charged that 'the exigencies of the political moment' had prompted the United States to open a dialogue with the Palestine Liberation Organization and to follow a peace process that he said 'is turning out to be unworkable because it depends on assurances of peace from people still committed to the destruction of Israel.'"

This term emphasizes a continuing movement or progress toward conflict resolution. In April 1993, *The Washington Post* reported the warning of Hanan Ashrawi, spokeswoman for the Palestinian delegates to the current round of talks, about a recent rise in violence: "I don't want to be the voice of gloom and doom. … But certainly if this round fails, it's not that the peace process is dead, but it's that you're unleashing forces that are the opposite of the peace process."

The "process" launched with the Oslo agreement and signed by Israeli Prime Minister Yitzhak Rabin and PLO Chairman Yasir Arafat on the White House lawn on Sept. 13, 1993, raised high hopes that were dashed by two *intifadas* and the demand by Arafat of a "right of return" of Palestinians to Israel that would have changed the character of the Jewish state, followed by the election in 2006 of a Hamas government in Gaza that refused to recognize Israel's right even to exist.

See PROCESS.

peace scare See WAGING PEACE.

peace with honor A wartime leader's excuse for not concluding a peace; or, an explanation to a leader's people that the peace concluded was a good one; or, an assertion that an end to war would not or does not mean surrender.

The earliest use was negative: in 49 B.C. Cicero wrote *turpi pace*, or "peace with dishonor." Burton Stevenson, in his book of proverbs, maxims, and phrases, traced the early uses of "peace with honor": Theobald, Count of Champagne, in a letter to Louis the Great in 1125; Shakespeare's *Coriolanus* ("We have made peace / with no less honour to the Antiates / than shame to the Romans"); Sir Kenelm Digby's letter to Lord Bristol in 1625; and Edmund Burke's *Conciliation with America* in 1775.

Honor became closely associated with *peace* over the years, always increasing the difficulty of negotiations. In 1864, "peace with dishonor" was thrown by Lincoln Republicans against the Democratic platform that claimed the Civil War had been a failure and called for peace talks.

The phrase is best remembered and occasionally quoted today because of its use by Benjamin Disraeli, Lord Beaconsfield, Queen Victoria's Prime Minister, in 1878. When the Russians forced the Turks to a "dishonorable" peace in the Treaty of San Stefano, Great Britain intervened and demanded a European Congress; fearing war with England, the Russians agreed, and Disraeli traveled to Berlin to negotiate. He forced Russia to give back Macedonia to the Turks, and came away with Cyprus for England in the bargain. He said on his return: "Lord Salisbury and myself have brought you back peace—but a peace I hope with honor, which may satisfy our sovereign and tend to the welfare of the country."

Disraeli was a hero; but England was soon involved in a war in Afghanistan and another against the Zulus in South Africa, a crop failure led to a recession, and Disraeli was turned out of office eighteen months after his "peace with honor."

In more recent times, the phrase has been used along with "peace without surrender" and "no reward for aggression."

peace without victory A Wilsonian phrase urging a limitation to the objectives of World War I and a peace settlement not so harsh to any side as to bring about a future war.

Coming as it did from a neutral U.S. early in 1917, Woodrow Wilson's proposal did not set well with leaders of France and England who were fighting a war against Germany: "it must be a peace without victory.... The world must be made safe for democracy." See MAKE THE WORLD SAFE FOR DEMOCRACY.

Like "TOO PROUD TO FIGHT," Wilson's "peace without victory" was greeted with disdain in America as well. He had just won a close election over Charles Evans Hughes, and Wilson's slogan in 1916 had been "He Kept Us Out of War," but the nation was closely divided and memories of Theodore Roosevelt's "Big Stick" were still green.

When unrestricted submarine warfare brought the U.S. into the conflict later in 1917, "peace without victory" was forgotten in the enthusiasm and fury of war. The traditional American demand for "unconditional surrender" was recalled (the War of 1812 was always forgotten), and Wilson's "Fourteen Points" as a basis for a peace treaty were taken with a grain of salt by other Allied leaders.

In World War II, unconditional surrender was again the goal, and Churchill's "V" sign assured the allies that peace would indeed come with victory. Not until the Korean War did the idea of LIMITED WAR appear, and that was countered by General Douglas MacArthur's statement that there was "NO SUBSTITUTE FOR VICTORY" and denunciations of a "NO-WIN POLICY."

However, most Americans in the late '60s were ready to accept "peace without victory" in South Vietnam, as they did in Korea, provided an "honorable solution" could be found. Senator J. William Fulbright touched a sensitive nerve in *The Arrogance of Power*:

When we talk about the freedom of South Vietnam, we may be thinking about how disagreeable it would be to accept a solution short of victory; we may be thinking about how our pride would be injured if we settled for less than we set out to achieve; we may be thinking about our reputation as a great power, fearing that a compromise settlement would shame us before the world, marking us as a second-rate people with flagging courage and determination.

Wilson's phrase, *peace without victory*, was not used by DOVES in their argument, perhaps because the compromise they were willing to accept was more of a peace without defeat; it turned out to be peace with defeat, leading to the VIETNAM SYNDROME. For recent attempts to counter the "without victory" appeal, see STAY THE COURSE and CUT AND RUN.

peaking A campaigning technique that seeks to bring a crescendo to its climax in the forty-eight hours before Election Day.

The presidential primary campaigns for the election of 2008 began to be reported in 2006, with the pace picking up for what media pundits and pollsters decided in 2007 was the "first tier" of candidates: Hillary Clinton, Barack Obama, John Edwards, and Bill Richardson for the Democrats, and John McCain, Rudy Giuliani, Mitt Romney, and Fred Thompson for the Republicans, with Al Gore and Mike Bloomberg hot question marks. "Because this year's presidential campaign started so early," wrote Blake Fontenay in the Memphis (Tenn.) *Commercial Appeal*, "some candidates run the risk of peaking too soon or running out of money." He reported that local politicians believed that such "peaking too soon" was a trap that former Tennessee Senator Thompson, the latest starter, could avoid.

Franklin Roosevelt pointed out the difficulty of maintaining the "highest note on the scale" (see OVEREXPOSURE); a candidate who "peaks" too early usually finds it impossible to regain the momentum of his campaigning. (For a discussion of the opposite type of strategy, see FLAT-OUT.)

The word was probably first used by pollsters, or those studying the popularity charts submitted by pollsters. Graphically, a line showing a rise and fall in voters' attitudes toward a candidate forms a peak.

The term was popularized during the Nixon-Kennedy campaign of 1960, with Nixon strategy calling for a steady rise in activity and intensity *peaking* once about three weeks before Election Day, and then again just before the final decision. Kennedy strategy called for a "flat-out campaign," sometimes called an "all-out scramble," starting from the beginning. The closeness of the contest left unresolved the question of which strategy was "best." Many politicians feel the wisest strategy is the one that best fits the nature and stamina of the individual candidate.

Peaking was long identified with Nixon. Democratic Congressman Michael J. Kirwan writes that the Nixon-Brown race for governor of California in 1962 "contrasted the so-called 'peaking' campaign techniques followed by Nixon to the 'all-out scramble' technique of Brown." D. E. Butler and Anthony King, in *The British General Election of 1964*, wrote:

> Like Mr. Richard Nixon in America, Mr. Wilson believed in the need to "phase" his campaign carefully in order to avoid "wearying" the electorate. He was haunted by the belief that Mr. Gaitskell had lost in 1959 partly because his campaign had "peaked" too early; Labour had drawn ahead mid-way through the campaign only to fall behind in the closing stages.

Peaking is regarded as a more sophisticated technique than flat-out campaigning, or scrambling, and is usually given more thought by those who start out slightly ahead. Underdogs are best advised to run HELL-BENT FOR ELECTION. When Republican Norbert Tiemann ran against Val Peterson in a 1966 primary for governor of Nebraska, he put in 600 appearances over 65,000 miles and edged out the favored Peterson by 15,000 votes. "We paced him just right," said Tiemann's campaign manager, David Pierson. "When election day came, we figured he was just about 14 hours away from total collapse."

When President Nixon announced in 1971 that Henry Kissinger had secretly arranged for his historic visit to China, a puckish speechwriter, worried about the reaction of U.S. conservatives, asked, "Peking too soon?"

peanut politician An insignificant political hack.

The word *peanut* has had a long history as a synonym for *insignificant*. "I know them—a set of peanut agitators," said Representative Mike Walsh of New York on May 19, 1854. Three decades later, the *peanut* modifier was attached to the word *politics*. An editorialist in the New York *Mail and Express* in 1887 inveighed: "If the Governor would consent not to play peanut politics . ." But politicians are careful not to offend any interest group. Another congressman told the House in 1894: "It would be gross disrespect to a great commercial product of several States in this Union for me to denounce the course pursued by this Administration ... as 'peanut politics.' "

The peanut at one time had a lowdown, dirty connotation, as writers pointed out that a peanut (which is the seed of a vegetable and not a nut) grows and ripens underground. Big spenders habitually refer to small sums as *peanuts*, giving rise to the demeaning sense of the attributive noun. However, another derivation is suggested in an 1880 book by Al G. Field: "Those from the West Side chewed tobacco. All ate peanuts. Special appropriations were requested by John Ward, city hall janitor, to remove the peanut hulls after each talk fest. And thus it was that peanut politics and peanut politicians came to be known in Columbus [Ohio]. Peanut politics, like all infections, spread until the whole political system became affected."

In World War II, to show his contempt for Generalissimo Chiang Kai-shek, General Joseph Stilwell gave him the code name "Peanut." Because President Jimmy Carter was a peanut warehouseman, it was natural to assume the phrase would be thrown at him, although his campaign workers countered the derogation by proudly using peanuts in rallies and giving out small packages of peanuts in lieu of buttons. The most frequent use of the metaphor was by those leaving his Administration, who would say, "I'm tired of working for peanuts."

In 1993, Representative Dick Armey of Texas wrote the lexicographer about a wasteful government program:

Under the Agriculture Department's peanut program, a person needs a license from the government—known as a peanut quota—to grow and sell peanuts inside the United States. This protects a Southern peanut grower monopoly, prevents wide competition and artificially boosts the price of peanuts. As a result, every American family pays more for peanut butter and other basic foods using peanuts. Think of it as a miniature OPEC for peanuts.

Though the slang sense of *peanut* is "trifling," the eating of peanuts can be habitforming. According to a 2006 book by the reporter Bob Woodward about the Bush administration's trials after Baathist-terrorist insurgency took hold in Iraq, Henry Kissinger gave the Bush speechwriter Michael Gerson a copy of what he called "the salted peanut memo" written in the Vietnam era, in which Kissinger had warned that "withdrawal of troops will become like salted peanuts to the American public; the more U.S. troops come home, the more will be demanded."

pebble beach Gravel area along driveway to the West Wing of the White House, a far cry literally as well as metaphorically from the famed California golf course of the same name.

TV correspondents deliver their "standup" reports from cameras that are set up on *pebble beach*. The camera operators and other broadcast technicians who spend long hours in tents and often in inclement weather are often derogated by snootier members of the electronic media. See STIR UP THE ANIMALS and ZOO PLANE.

peckerwood See REDNECK.

pecking order Unofficial hierarchy; status of aides to a chief executive of city, state, or nation, or within a government department. Emerges when no "table of organization" is provided.

Like a linguistic Inspector Javert, Professor Porter G. Perrin of the University of Washington followed the origin and development of this phrase from its technical inception to its modern political use. His evidence, along with other contributions to *American Speech* magazine, is summarized here. During and following World War I, a

Norwegian zoologist-psychologist named Thorleif Schjelderup-Ebbe made some remarkable studies of the social organization of birds, particularly hens. Because of the nature of his subject, he had to develop a group of compound nouns beginning with *Hack*, "peck," including *Hackordning*, or "peck order."

University of Chicago zoologist W. C. Allee explained Schjelderup-Ebbe's findings in the U.S.:

> He recognized a so-called peck-order in which the animal highest in the order pecks and is not pecked in return while that at the extreme bottom of the order is pecked without pecking in return. The social order is indicated by the giving and receiving of pecks, or by reaction to threats of pecking; and hence the social hierarchy among birds is frequently referred to as the peck-order.

A minor government official would do well to study this followup comment by Mark A. May in a 1929 psychology text: "It seems that the bird which is despot over only a few shows its annoyance at the pecks to which it itself is exposed by especially furious pecking, while the birds that rank high in the pecking order, and so are seldom pecked, are more reasonable."

Professor Allee saw the political possibilities: "I pass over the possibilities of studying the peck-order in women's clubs, faculty groups, families or churches... we may be able to work out an adequate control even for the prestige problems of the international peck-order."

Novelist Aldous Huxley, who liked to turn scientific theory to use in fiction dealing with social experiments, picked up the idea in *Point Counter Point*. Anthropologist Margaret Mead used the phrase in a 1942 book, *And Keep Your Powder Dry*. That year, poet W. H. Auden used the phrase in its original sense in "Nones": "the smug hens, / Passing close by in their pecking order ..."

Then the Alsop brothers, Joseph and Stewart, got hold of it in 1954, using it four times that year in their syndicated column and magazine articles, from a straightforward "in the Washington officialdom, a secretaryless official is at the very bottom of the pecking order" to a less intelligible "Prediction was the by-word, with a number of variables used in multiple regression equations determining the pecking order in the status hierarchy." (Explain that to Schjelderup-Ebbe!)

Professor Perrin concluded:

> This brief case history of *pecking order* illustrates the typical progress of words from specialized to general usage, and in addition suggests: (1) that this particular word is definitely established in English and now runs the full range of usage from gobbledygook to poetry; (2) that, when it is used of human beings, its connotation is generally dyslogistic [unfavorable]; and (3) that once acquired, pecking order tends to be habit forming.

When President Bill Clinton urged reporters to "ignore this who's up, who's down stuff" in his White House's *pecking order*, nobody did.

peerless leader Ironic description of a precinct captain or local boss.

The "Peerless Leader" in American history was William Jennings Bryan, three times nominated for president by the Democratic Party. Along with "The Great Commoner," a sobriquet that had been applied to William Pitt the Elder and later to Henry Clay and Thaddeus Stevens, Bryan was given the sobriquet of *peerless leader*, which later was the title of a 1929 biography of him by Paxton Hibben. (Opponents termed the ticket of Bryan and Arthur Sewall "Brine and Swill.")

Because of the rhyme, the phrase is often rendered "fearless leader" (a Helen Gray Cone poem called Pickett's men at Gettysburg "peerless, fearless, an army's flower"). The pomposity of the phrase has led to its sarcastic use today.

Pekingologist (new style, **Beijingologist**) See CHINA WATCHERS; KREMLINOLOGIST.

Pentagonese Military-industrial jargon designed to provide its users with a convenient linguistic shorthand that sometimes serves to obfuscate the obvious, or to lend a sense of importance to routine communications.

In common with other jargon, *Pentagonese*—a word that had entered the language by 1950—is used not only within "Fort Fumble" but also throughout the U.S. military establishment. A sample: Within certain *parameters* (range of possibilities, not perimeter), there exist *options* (choices) for *tradeoffs* (trades) that will *maximize* (strengthen) the *software* (thinking) to *escalate* (raise) *the state of the art* (what can be done now). Many of these terms have become *embedded* in the general language, about which we should all have a *situational awareness* (know what's going on).

As *Newsweek* noted in 1967, nuclear weapons "unleashed a fallout of acronyms, neologisms, euphemisms and technical jargon," and the development of antiballistic missiles "has produced a second generation of Strangelovisms." Among the additions to Pentagonese: *megadeaths*, for millions of deaths; *credible deterrent*, a defense that needn't be effective as long as the enemy thinks it is; *preferential defense*, protecting some areas but not others; *rippled attack*, sending missiles in salvos to trick an enemy into using defensive missiles on the first few waves, leaving no defense for later waves.

Officials in the Pentagon popularized, or in some cases invented, scores of other words, from *cost-efficiency* to *quantification* (a reference to Robert McNamara's reliance on facts and figures) and *spasm* (meaning a reflexive response to an enemy attack, real or imagined). Weapons made obsolete by the end of the Cold War have been *overtaken by events*. Something that goes against common sense is described in Pentagonese as *counterintuitive*.

A kissing cousin of Pentagonese is State Departmentese, or *diplolingo*. The historian and Kennedy aide Arthur Schlesinger, Jr., wrote in *A Thousand Days*:

> The intellectual exhaustion of the Foreign Service expressed itself in the poverty of the official rhetoric. In meetings the men from State would talk in a bureaucratic patois borrowed in large part from the Department of Defense. We would be exhorted to *zero in* on *the purpose of the drill* (or of the *exercise* or *operation*), to *crank in* this and *phase out* that, to *pinpoint* a

viable policy and, behind it, a *fallback position*, to ignore the *flak* from competing government bureaus or from the Communists, to refrain from *nit-picking* and never to be *counterproductive*. Once we were *seized of the problem*, preferably in as *hard-nosed* a manner as possible, we would review *options*, discuss *overall* objectives, seek *breakthroughs*, consider *crash programs*, *staff out* policies—doing all these things preferably *meaningfully* and *in depth* until we were ready to *finalize* our deliberations, *sign on to* or *sign off on* a conclusion (I could never discover the distinction, if any, between these two locutions), and *implement* a decision.

(Italics mine. To finalize approval, see CHOP.)

Words that achieved vogue status in the '60s and have not in the past half-century been dislodged by ridicule or overuse can be seen in a list compiled in 1968 by Malcolm McLean in the *Foreign Service Journal*, based on a survey made at the National War College by Marine Colonel Ralph Spanjer. Lecturers were clocked as to the number of times they used Pentagonese; these were the most frequently used bits of jargon: *quid pro quo*, *pragmatic*, *vis-à-vis*, *caveat*, *per se*, *viable*, *dialogue*, *ambivalence*, *xenophobia*, *scenario*, *charisma*, *academician*, *thrust*, *escalate*, *exacerbate*, *expertise*, *dichotomy*, *low silhouette*, *hegemony*, *quantum jump*, *cost effective*, *flexible response*, *proliferation*, *rapprochement*, *counterproductive*, *détente*.

Less frequently used, but mentioned in the survey, were *boggle*, *simplistic*, *in-house*, *time frame*, *pluralistic*, *poly-centrisms*, *infrastructure*, *real world*, *bipolar*, *confrontation*.

Herman Melville, author of *Moby-Dick* and other novels, wrote: "A man of true science uses but few hard words, and those only when none other will answer his purpose; whereas the smatterer in science thinks that by mouthing hard words he proves that he understands hard things." Pentagonians who do not want to openly disagree say that they *non-concur*.

See OPTIONS; ESCALATION; UNFLAPPABLE; SCENARIO; FALLBACK POSITION; SHOCK AND AWE; VIETNAM LINGO; WHIZ KIDS; FALLOUT; INFRASTRUCTURE; WAR-GAMING WORDS.

Pentagon Papers See RIGHT TO KNOW; LEAK.

people of color Members of all racial groups except Caucasians; people of mixed race; nonwhites.

In the late eighteenth century, French-speaking colonies used *gens de couleur libres*, "free people of color." In the "I have a dream" speech at the Lincoln Memorial in August 1963, the Rev. Martin Luther King Jr. revived the phrase in speaking of American "citizens of color."

Colored people, often shortened to "the colored," was long used by whites to mean "people of racially mixed ancestry." That term, first expressed as "coloured countenances" by the historian John Speed in 1611, is now considered a slur, while *people of color* is often used proudly as a self-description.

Black replaced the newly pejorative *colored people*, except in the name of the National Association for the Advancement of Colored People. James Williams, an N.A.A.C.P. spokesman, explained, "Times change and terms change. Racial designations go through phases; at one time 'Negro' was accepted, at an earlier time 'colored' and so on. This organization has been in existence for 80 years, and the initials N.A.A.C.P. are part of the American vocabulary, firmly embedded in the national consciousness, and we feel it would not be to our benefit to change our name."

People of color, when used by whites, generally connotes respect. The term includes all nonwhites, however, and should not be considered a synonym for *blacks* or *African-Americans* (see HYPHENATED AMERICAN). In careful political and journalistic style, *African-American* is preferred in first usage, with *black* acceptable in second reference or in space-saving headlines.

The emergence of Tiger Woods in golf and Barack Obama in politics led to the category "mixed heritage."

people's democracy A phrase with a redundant root adopted by Communists to differentiate between "their" democracy and "capitalists'" democracy.

Though the political glorification of the word *people* is best known in the close of the Gettysburg Address, *people's party* and *people's ticket* were familiar phrases throughout the nineteenth century. In China, the Manchu dynasty was overthrown in 1911 by forces whose ideological leader was Dr. Sun Yat-sen; among his "Three Principles of the People" was a "Principle of People's Democracy," a long-range plan to be started by the revolutionary leaders.

Later in the twentieth century, Communist governments adopted the style of "people's republics," and Communist terminology used "people's democracies" as a generic phrase for Communist or Communist-dominated nations.

In a good twist on the phrase, the New York Stock Exchange in the early '50s began publicizing "people's capitalism" to dramatize the degree of stock ownership in the U.S. The Exchange recognized the Communist capture of the word *people*, and by combining it with the word most often attacked by Communists put forth a useful counterphrase to "Wall Street warmongers."

People's Republic of China See CULTURAL REVOLUTION; GREAT LEAP FORWARD; HUNDRED FLOWERS; MAOISM.

perennial candidate Attack phrase on one who has tried and failed before.

Republican Harold Stassen was the man most often identified as a "perennial candidate" in recent memory; in the previous century, the honor belonged first to Grover Cleveland (the "perpetual candidate") and then to thrice-defeated William Jennings Bryan.

Said Stassen in 1967: "I suppose there is a lot of misunderstanding about me. People try to understand me as seeking office. Actually it's not the office itself. Not at all. It's the office in relation to what I'm trying to do, what I'm seeking. I want a progressive Republican Party."

A similar attack was launched by President Lyndon Johnson in 1966 on Richard Nixon, labeling him a CHRONIC CAMPAIGNER. The effect, contrary to Johnson's intention, was to focus attention on Nixon in the closing weeks of the midterm elections, helping him help Republican candidates win back 47 House seats and positioning him to win the GOP presidential nomination two years later.

perestroika Russian for "restructuring"; the reconstruction or revision of the Soviet political system.

The Russian term entered the English language in the mid-1980s with Gorbachevian reforms. "If words can define an era," wrote Celestine Bohlen of *The Washington Post* in 1986, "then perestroika is the catchword here before Tuesday's opening of the Communist Party Congress as Soviet leader Mikhail Gorbachev enters a decisive phase of his leadership."

Pronounced "per-uh-STROY-kuh," the noun has a literal meaning of "rebuilding" and was popularized as the term for political and economic changes in what was then the Soviet Union. Its prominence was underscored by the title of Gorbachev's 1987 book, *Perestroika: New Thinking for Our Country and Our World*. A *New York Times* feature on that book enumerated elements of that restructuring: "He has slightly opened the emigration spigot, given greater freedom to question the party and the government, and faced up to the severe economic difficulties that restrain Soviet military expenditures and force a new look at Afghanistan." However, he tried to maintain the Soviet Communist politico-economic system, wheezing under the strain of an arms race, and soon fell to a clique led by Boris Yeltsin.

This buzzword is similar to, but not synonymous with, the Russian *peredyshka*, the "breathing space" or "respite" that marked Lenin's secret policy to strengthen Bolshevism. In 1987, *U.S. News & World Report* quoted John Erickson, a Western authority on Soviet military activity, about the similarity of these terms. "We must be careful," Erickson said, "that *perestroika* doesn't turn out to mean *peredyshka*." (See COMMUNIST TERMINOLOGY.)

perks Clipped form of *perquisites*; the delicious trappings of power; the cherry on the sundae of public service.

Michael Satchell in *The Washington Star* in January 1977 wrote:

> Perks! ... hundreds of public servants enjoy the perquisites of power, the freebies, privileges, emoluments and prestige that go along with the job, that make life at the office a little nicer, that stamp the individual as a favored employe. Perks! For politicians, Cabinet officers and ranking career bureaucrats, they mean limousines, government jets and even boats to get you from A to B with a corps of chauffeurs, military aides, escort officers, staff assistants, coat holders and Filipino Navy stewards to make sure the steaks are rare, the martinis cold, the trip smooth and trouble-free.

Originally a Briticism, the word took hold firmly in coverage of American officialdom. In the '60s, *with perks* was most frequently a description of "fringe benefits" available to corporate officers. Politicians' perks—especially limousine service—came under attack in the mid-seventies, led by Senator William Proxmire's harassment of Pentagon officials whose salaries were supplemented by extra, untaxed services. President Carter, sensitive to the anti-Washington, anti–big shot feeling of most taxpayers, did away with many of the frills enjoyed previously by the White House staff, but these soon returned.

Perks are not inexpensive trappings; a car and driver in effect nearly doubles many government officials' after-tax salaries. The new interest in the subject saves the taxpayer sizable amounts, although it is not so much the money as the principle: if the voter has to pay for his haircut, then why, he wonders, should his congressman get one free? The system that used to permit the local cop on the beat to swipe an apple from the vendor, as a right of his job, now frowns on—and even threatens to tax—some of the extra income that is taken in the form of service. Voter irritation with these perks—exacerbated by a check-kiting House banking scandal in 1991—was exploited by Ross Perot in his Independent campaign the following year.

Perks cover a range of presumed rights, including *freebies*, which are small gifts or costless tickets; *annie oaklies*, which are always tickets or passes; and *junkets*, which are not always entirely official trips (see JUNKETEERING GUMSHOES). *Perquisite* is not related to *perky*, which comes from the verb "to perch," but is rooted in the Latin *quaerere*, "to seek"—thus, a *query* about a *perk* digs for its own root. See LULU.

peroration The stirring conclusion of an address, exhorting or uplifting the audience; in political slang, the ZINGER or *snapper*.

"Perorations usually add nothing to the context of the speech," wrote Samuel Rosenman, who wrote many for FDR, "they are more inspirational than informative. Every oration needs one, however, and a well-written peroration can clinch an argument or inspire confidence or lift morale."

In the peroration of his 1932 acceptance address FDR introduced *New Deal*: "I pledge you, I pledge myself, to a new deal for the American people." (For the dispute over who wrote it, see NEW DEAL.) The most stirring peroration was at the conclusion of Lincoln's second inaugural address, beginning "With malice toward none ..."

A well-prepared, well-delivered speech without a peroration dribbles off and leaves an audience unsatisfied. Simple, clear English prose, the stuff of good speeches, is difficult to make soar; there cannot be many thrilling moments or high notes in any speech, and if there is to be one, the place where the audience will remember it most is at the end. Reminder: a reference to God's help is expected, especially on solemn occasions.

"His enthusiasm kindles as he advances," wrote Edmund Burke of a good orator, "and when he arrives at his peroration it is in full blaze." Here is a peroration (the closing of Woodrow Wilson's first inaugural) that includes a disclaimer of pride, an element of suspense, a question, a challenge, a summons to the audience to help, a reference to the Deity, and a promise of success:

This is not a day of triumph; it is a day of dedication. Here muster, not the forces of party, but the forces of humanity. Men's hearts wait upon us; men's lives hang in the balance; men's hopes call upon us to say what we will do. Who shall live up to the great trust? Who dares fail to try? I summon all honest men, all patriotic, all forward-looking men, to my side. God helping me, I will not fail them, if they will but counsel and sustain me!

In Shakespeare's time, *peroration* meant an overblown, flowery speech ("What means this passionate discourse? This peroration with such circumstance"); over four centuries, it has come to mean the conclusion or wrap-up of a speech, where some passion is permitted to flower and to signal to a seated audience that the moment has come to rise to its feet. See I SEE CONSTRUCTION.

personally obnoxious Verbal signal that calls down the wrath of "senatorial courtesy"; the Senate then refuses to confirm an appointment opposed by a senator from the state affected.

Senatorial courtesy, or *courtesy of the Senate*, is the gun; *personally obnoxious*, or the less vigorous *personally objectionable*, is the trigger. The system was explained by *Harper's Weekly* in 1870: "Senator Fowler of Tennessee claimed the right which the courtesy of the Senate affords every member of vetoing the appointment of any postmaster in the place of his residence who is not agreeable to him." Ten years later the magazine defined the phrase in more political terms: "The courtesy of the Senate is an exceedingly smooth phrase. It means control of patronage."

President Woodrow Wilson first attempted to fight this system, then gave way. See PATRONAGE. His closest adviser, Colonel Edward House, and Treasury Secretary William McAdoo, both Democrats from New York, sought to break Tammany's power by dispensing patronage to reformers. Senator James O'Gorman of New York, while not closely allied with Tammany, saw this as an effort to build a New York machine that might be a danger to him. He warned the President that such appointments would be *personally obnoxious* to him, and they were not made.

Dwight Eisenhower ran into the same problem when he started making presidential appointments in 1953. He planned to name Val Peterson, a former Nebraska governor, as ambassador to India, but Nebraska Senators Hugh Butler and Dwight

Griswold—longtime political enemies of Peterson—said no. "They informed me," wrote Eisenhower, "that if I should send his name to the Senate they would find it necessary to state on the Senate floor that he was 'personally objectionable'; the Senate has normally honored such an announcement." The President appointed Peterson to several other jobs not requiring Senate approval, and ultimately—after the two senators were gone—as ambassador to Denmark. But the initial rejection bothered him. "I believe that the custom of allowing one disgruntled senator to block an appointment by the phrase 'personally objectionable' is unjustified and should be disavowed by the Senate."

As the Peterson episode illustrates, there has been a tendency to replace *obnoxious* with *objectionable*, a much milder word. This is a shame, as *obnoxious*—rooted in the Latin *noxa*, "injury," and now a synonym for *odious*—so well describes the true feeling of the dissenting senator.

For a form of reasonableness in Senatorial blockage, see "Mae West hold" under BLUE SLIP.

phantom coinage See BACKLASH; ESCALATION; MEDICARE.

Philippic Diatribe; tirade; vitriolic attack.

"Forensic Philippics" was FDR's description of some of the Supreme Court decisions striking down New Deal measures. See NINE OLD MEN. The word comes from the three orations of Demosthenes, rousing his fellow Athenians to resist Philip of Macedon; subsequently, the orations of Cicero against Mark Antony were also called *Philippics*.

Dwight Eisenhower was urged by many friends to ENGAGE IN PERSONALITIES with Senator Joseph McCarthy, using the prestige of the presidency to condemn his methods. In this unpublished letter to his early political supporter, broadcaster John R. ("Tex") McCrary, President Eisenhower wrote on December 4, 1954:

I would not, under any circumstances, glorify—or at least publicize—such an individual by attempting a Presidential Philippic, with him as the target. When any individual or any

idea goes completely outside the realm of logic and of reason, I doubt that elimination can be achieved through argument! In fact, it is only the persistent and senseless publicity he has achieved that has made the matter of any concern to our people. My own reaction to this whole messy business has been to uphold Americanism and preach fairness, justice and decency... If young or old want a President who will indulge in billingsgate—and demean the office as it has been demeaned before—they'll have to find another.

philosophy See IDEOLOGY.

phony war The period of relative inaction by military units after the fall of Poland in the fall of 1939 and the German attack on Norway and Denmark in the spring of 1940; also called a *sitzkrieg*.

Sitzkrieg, literally "sitting war," was of course a play on *blitzkrieg*, "lightning war." To some Americans, the desultory warfare in this period showed that Britain and France did not really want to fight, but simply entered the war grudgingly, committed as they were to the defense of Poland; these critics also held that Hitler wanted no war with France and Great Britain. Senator William Edgar Borah of Kansas, a Republican who had opposed President Wilson on the Versailles Treaty, was a strong critic of FDR's domestic New Deal and foreign policy as well; he was among the first, possibly the first, user of the phrase, as reported in the September 30, 1939, issue of *The Nation*: "Senator Borah talks about a 'phony' war and contemplates with democratic disgust the intrenched power of the British Empire."

The London *News-Chronicle* on January 19, 1940, headlined: "This is Not a Phoney War: Paris Envoy." The story explained that *phoney* was "American slang, anglicized about 1920." (British spelling is with an *e*; the American spelling at the start was both with and without an *e*, but is now running more than 3-to-1 *phony*.)

French Premier Paul Reynaud used the phrase in English during his French-language radio speech on April 3, 1940: "'*Il faut en finir*'; tel fut, dès le début, le refrain qu'on entendit. Et cela signifie qu'il aura *pas de* 'phony peace' *après une guerre qui n'est nullement une* 'phony war.'" ("'It must be finished'; that is the constant theme heard since the beginning. And that means that there will not be any 'phony peace' after a war which is by no means a 'phony war.'")

During this time Neville Chamberlain continued as prime minister of England. When the British fleet was repulsed trying to land troops in Norway, he came under heavy criticism in Parliament. On May 9, 1940, he asked Winston Churchill to join his government; Churchill refused. After the German invasion of Holland and Belgium on May 10, Chamberlain agreed to turn over the reins completely to Churchill. There was no more talk of "phony war" or of weak leadership in Great Britain.

According to Eric Partridge, *phoney* can be traced back to 1781 when "the ring-dropping game, one of the old everlastings for fooling the credulous, was known as the *fawney rig*, the *fawney trick, fawney* being an English attempt at the Irish *fáinne*, a finger ring."

In the early '80s, *The Washington Post* wrote of Poland that "there is still an atmosphere of 'phony war.' The weapons remain the old ones of political rhetoric, resolutions, verbal ultimatums and threatening allusions."

photo op See SOUND BITE.

phrasemaker One who captures the essence of an issue in a few highly quotable, soundbite-able, bumper-stickable words.

Sloganeer, which now has acquired a pejorative connotation, is the closest synonym. *Ghostwriters*, *speechwriters*, and *research assistants* who prepare speeches may be *phrasemakers* or they may not. If not, a *speech doctor* may be called in to "punch up" the prose. For a discussion of usage, see GHOSTWRITER.

A phrasemaker is similar to a "play doctor" who is called in to add lines and sharpen the scenes of another playwright. He or she should be capable of taking an ordinary speech and adding a news lead in the form of inflammable words or a stunning new

thought in quotable form. The phrasemaker should also have the old-fashioned PASSION FOR ANONYMITY; although the public has come to accept the idea of a public figure employing a speechwriter, a provocative phrase must seem to "belong" to the public figure and not be attributable to a manipulator with a bumper sticker in mind, at least not for the life of an administration.

President Eisenhower called an early assistant of his, Emmet Hughes, "a writer with a talent for phrasemaking." Other presidents, notably Abraham Lincoln and Theodore Roosevelt, had a genius for phrasemaking. In politics, however, every talent is attackable; among Woodrow Wilson's nicknames were "schoolmaster in politics," "coiner of WEASEL WORDS," "professor"—and equally damning, "phrasemaker."

How is a phrase made? If original inspiration is lacking, *boosting*—a play on a previous phrase—can save the day. This word-substitution in a familiar phrase is a frequent technique: in the congressional campaign of 1966, the Republican decision was to attack President Johnson on the subject of inflation. Possibilities: "Johnson Inflation," "Johnson Dollars Buy Less." Neither very catchy, and the word *inflation* is rather abstract. However, *the high cost of living* was a well-known and well-understood phrase, and it offered a minor boosting possibility. Hence, "the High Cost of Johnson" was used and served its purpose, although it never became a part of the language. A second booster was more effective: "Johnson's War on Poverty has now become a War on Prosperity."

Seminal phrases are rare: for coinages, see MEDICARE; COLD WAR; for emphasis using contrast, see CONTRAPUNTAL PHRASES; for adaptation, see TURNAROUNDS; for poetic imagery, see THOUSAND POINTS OF LIGHT; for the most useful phrasemaking word, see NEW, POLITICAL USE OF.

pie in the sky Mockery of liberal or populist promises.

In the vocabulary of rhetorical counterattack—"empty promises," "cruel demagoguery," "callous vote-buying"—none has been more durable than "pie in the sky." In the face of this withering return fire, even the word *promise* has disappeared from campaign oratory, supplanted by the more solemn *pledge*.

The origin of *pie in the sky* was supplied the author by labor-lore specialist Archie Green, a professor of English at Ohio State University. The phrase was coined around 1910 in "The Preacher and the Slave," a composition by the legendary labor hero Joe Hill, which became part of the widely distributed *Little Red Songbook* of the Industrial Workers of the World (the I.W.W., or "Wobblies"):

You will eat, bye and bye,
In that glorious land above the sky;
Work and pray, live on hay
You'll get pie in the sky when you die.

Professor Green rightly called this phrase "the most significant Wobbly contribution to the American vocabulary." Conservative speakers have been seizing on it for denunciation for a century.

An example is in a cartoon by Auth for the Philadelphia *Inquirer* in November 1977: people in line for unemployment benefits are shown looking skyward at a vision of a pie labeled "Humphrey-Hawkins," a bill designed to bring down the rate of unemployment in the U.S. And after Larry Flynt, publisher of the raunchy *Hustler* magazine, announced his spiritual rebirth in 1978 thanks to an airborne conversion by Ruth Carter Stapleton, *The Washington Post* headlined a feature "Piety in the Sky." See CAMPAIGN ORATORY. For a don't-you-believe-it lexicon, see BALONEY and FREE LUNCH (food is often associated with the metaphors for disbelief). For a holiday flavor, see SANTA CLAUS, NOBODY SHOOTS AT.

pinko Epithet for anyone in a spectrum ranging from quite liberal to near-Communist, but most often aimed at FELLOW TRAVELERS.

Pinko, pink, and the more effete PARLOR PINK were often used against Democratic candidates in the late '40s and '50s. Just as Republicans after the Civil War said, "Not all Democrats were rebels, but all rebels were Democrats," some conservatives a century later used "Not all Democrats are pinkos, but all pinkos are Democrats."

Those who found communism "a god that failed" and those who changed their minds about fellow-traveling were the foremost users of the contemptuous word. When the CIO purged its membership in 1949 of the United Electrical Workers Union because of their Communist party links, former pinko Michael J. Quill, colorful boss of the Transport Workers Union, lashed out at the "pinks, punks and parasites."

In 1926, when *Time* magazine was popularizing the Homeric adjective ("Berkshire-cradled," "Beethoven-locked," "Yankee-shrewd"), its editors were fond of "pinko-liberal" and "pinko-political." (See PUNDIT for other *Time* coinages, a favorite pastime of admen and cinemoppets.)

As Communism's red star faded, pink was embraced by feminist groups as an identifying color. Code Pink was formed in 2002 as a woman-run organization to protest the war in Iraq.

pipeline, in the On its way; in the process of being developed, but not ready for public disclosure; or, inertia in action.

Government officials answer complaints of inaction with the oily assurance that work is *in the pipeline*. The phrase was popular in the White House in the early '70s, sometimes carrying a connotation of inexorability: once some proposal got in the pipeline, it could not be stopped, and any attempts to sidetrack it were met with "That train has left the station."

A subtlety of this phrase is in the understanding that not everything in political affairs is cause-and-effect, and that often an event comes about not by virtue of its apparent cause, but because it had already been "in the pipeline." When a project is cut off, it may continue for years because funds to support it were "in the pipeline."

Another meaning of *pipeline* is "channel of information," usually surreptitious, as "we have a pipeline into the Joint Chiefs."

pissant One who is a stickler for detail; a derogation of a too-technical minor functionary.

In a 1977 *New Republic* piece on former Defense Secretary James Schlesinger, who had been named by President Carter to be his energy chief, Eliot Marshall wrote: "He began his career in the Nixon administration in 1969 as a second-rung functionary in what was then the gritty Bureau of the Budget. As one departing cabinet aide put it, he began as a mere 'pissant'… His worldly skills are sometimes referred to as his 'practical sense,' or his appreciation of detail. It explains why he once was considered a pissant."

The word can be used as an adjective ("every pissant line in the Budget") and is now usually written as a solid word. The Associated Press opined in 1989, "When is the attorney general going to stop trying to stage-manage every little pissant development in this department that has political advantage, and authorize his people to talk to us candidly if not on background?"

Pissant is just what it sounds like, *piss* plus *ant* (named from what the *OED* calls "the urinous smell of an anthill"). An earlier word for the same creature, using a different term for "ant," is *pismire*, first found in Chaucer's "Summoner's Tale," written in 1395: "He is as angry as a pissemyre."

For another derogation of low-level bureaucrats, See ANKLE-BITERS.

pissing post See POWER BASE.

pit-bull politics Brutal campaigning by ATTACK DOGS.

This slur on dogs uses the generic term *pit bull*, which is not a breed but a cross between a bulldog and a terrier. (The United Kennel Club does recognize the *American pit bull terrier*, but the larger American Kennel Club recognizes a similar dog which it calls the *American Staffordshire terrier*.)

The term *pit bull* comes from pit fighting, in which animals are forced into bloody confrontations, a brutal activity that has drawn mean-spirited spectators for centuries and in 2007 disgraced a celebrated pro football player. During Shakespeare's time, the Globe Theatre faced competition from the Bear Garden, featuring fights between dogs and chained bears; England outlawed those fights in 1835.

On rare occasion, the term *pit bull* is applied to humans admiringly as a label connoting courage: In the 1988 presidential campaign, the elder George Bush referred to himself and his running mate, Dan Quayle, as "a couple of pit bulls"—and they won. But more often the compound noun, usually hyphenated when used attributively, is pejorative: *Time* magazine labeled the campaign that year "pit-bull politics."

In 2006, under the headline "Pit-bull Politics," the Bergen (N.J.) *Record* wrote about the race for senator: "The contest between Thomas Kean Jr. and Robert Menendez is already in full pit-bull mode, and it's only June. The attacks are nasty and personal and unusually vitriolic, even by New Jersey standards."

pitiless publicity The purifying power of the public gaze on the operations of government, where secrecy can breed corruption; now also the encroachment on privacy by reporters seeking sensation.

Woodrow Wilson used the phrase often in his New Jersey gubernatorial campaign of 1910 and in the presidential campaign of 1912 against Taft and Roosevelt. He took it from Ralph Waldo Emerson's use in *The Conduct of Life*: "As gaslight is found to be the best nocturnal police, so the universe protects itself by pitiless publicity."

In the 1912 campaign, Wilson explained: "Publicity is one of the purifying elements of politics. Nothing checks all the bad practices of politics like public exposure. An Irishman, seen digging around the wall of a house, was asked what he was doing. He answered, 'Faith, I am letting the dark out of the cellar.' Now, that's exactly what we want to do."

True to his pledge of welcoming *pitiless publicity*, Wilson inaugurated the regular presidential press conference after he took office. At the first, he told reporters: "A large part of the success of public affairs depends on the newspapermen—not so much the editorial writers, because we can live down what they say, as upon the news writers, because news is the atmosphere of public affairs."

The same concern for shining a beam of publicity in the dark corners of diplomacy led to his expression "OPEN COVENANTS, openly arrived at"; but just as he modified that position to include confidential discussions, in his later years in office he withdrew from the regular press conference routine.

A related phrase, "the white light of publicity"—the same metaphor as "letting the dark out"—was coined a few years later by writer Theodore F. MacManus in a 1915 *Saturday Evening Post* article: "In every field of human endeavor, he that is first must perpetually live in the white light of publicity."

The word *publicity* has a Janus-like double image today. In the Wilsonian sense, it is regarded as a good thing, calling politicians immediately to account for almost every action. Joseph Pulitzer told his editors at the New York *World* in 1895: "Publicity, *publicity*, PUBLICITY, is the greatest moral factor and force on our public life."

Contrariwise, the press agent (now *media representative*) is often scorned as he inveigles "free publicity" for his "publicity hound" client, either through "cheap stunts" or the manipulative devices of "hidden persuasion." For this reason, people in the field often shy away from the phrase *publicity agent* or even the word *publicist*, which once meant a person dedicated to the affairs of the public, and adopt *public relations counsel* or *public affairs officer*. To them, publicity—getting space in the press and time on the air for the client's product or principle—is a single arrow in the large quiver of public relations techniques.

As a result of this double image, *pitiless publicity* in current usage is something the public not only gets the benefit of, but which it is constantly subjected to. The phrase is also used to express concern with too-zealous reporters and photographers who invade privacy, particularly in the coverage of tragedies.

place in the sun Justification for expansion and conquest.

Kaiser Wilhelm II, speaking at Hamburg on August 27, 1911, laid the basis for Germany's claim to territorial growth: "No one can dispute with us the place in the sun that is our due."

"Place in the sun" became a German rallying cry during World War I and during the rise of Hitler. The Nazis, however, preferred LEBENSRAUM, "living room."

The Kaiser's phrase can be found in the 1727 translation of the *Pensées* of Blaise Pascal: "This Dog's mine, said the poor Child: this is my place, in the Sun. From so petty a beginning, we can trace the Tyranny and Usurpation of the whole Earth."

plant As a verb, to induce a reporter to ask a question at a press conference; as a noun, a news story released to a single reporter which benefits the person leaking the story; or, an individual placed in an opposition camp.

Anthony Leviero, a Washington correspondent of *The New York Times*, broke an exclusive story in 1951 about the details of the Truman-MacArthur conference on Wake Island. Following MacArthur's dismissal (see OLD SOLDIERS NEVER DIE) it occurred to the reporter that the assumption about total agreement between Truman and MacArthur at Wake might have been false, and that the Administration might be ready to release the document to refute MacArthur's charges.

Leviero pointed out how he went after the news in a memo, and added:

> This disposes of the stories about a "plant," although I or any other Washington correspondent would gladly accept a planted authentic document. ... A final word on the claims of discomfited rivals that this was an Administration "plant." Without conceding the story came from the White House, I can say that never in more than three years of covering the place did a member of the President's staff offer me a story. But I often scored by asking at the right time.

In current political usage, a LEAK is usually deliberate (as in Daniel Ellsberg's massive leak of the Pentagon Papers to the *Times*), sometimes inadvertent (as in Undersecretary of State Richard Armitage's offhand mention to columnist Robert Novak of the CIA operative Valerie Plame Wilson's recommendation to send her husband to Niger to check out a tip about the sale of uranium ore to Saddam Hussein). A *plant* is always deliberate, and connotes "control" of the reporter's story; an *exclusive* has a more legitimate ring, although reporters left out are envious; a *scoop* is dated slang for what is now a *beat*, which carries the least stigma of deliberate origination by the source, and usually means the reporter dug out the information by his own enterprise.

Question-planting in the U.S. is always surreptitious, and reported use embarrassed Hillary Clinton in the 2008 primaries. But French President Charles de Gaulle practiced it openly, according to former Kennedy press secretary Pierre Salinger: "His aides plant every question in advance with pro-Administration reporters, and *Le Président* carefully rehearses the answers."

platform Ideally, the published party standards to which the wise and honest voters can repair; in practice, a list of principles and positions designed to attract most and offend least, important mainly in the work it gives a convention to do other than crown a candidate preselected by voters in primaries.

Francis Bacon, in 1623: "The wisdom of a lawmaker consisteth not only in a platform of justice, but in the application thereof." In most early use in the U.S., the word related to the principles of a church, taken from the French word for ground plan of a building. Since the word also came to mean a raised area from which a person could speak, its metaphoric use in politics married both senses. Like STUMP and HUSTINGS, a place to stand soon was allied to a place to take a stand.

As early as 1803, the Massachusetts *Spy* was writing about "The Platform of Federalism," but it was William Lloyd Garrison in his antislavery *Liberator* who would popularize the term; in 1844 the first national party platforms were adopted, and by 1848 the word was a political standby.

The word *plank* was a natural derivative: in the 1848 *Bigelow Papers*, one line of

doggerel read: "They kin' o' slipt the planks frum out th' old platform one by one / An' made it gradooally noo, 'fore folks know'd wut wuz done."

In current use, a party platform is taken with great seriousness at a convention, since it enables many compromises to be made and gives appointment plums to many factional leaders, but is soon forgotten in the campaign. A frequent saying, of obscure origin, is that "A platform is not something to stand on, but something to run on," soon followed by "A platform is what you start by running on and end by running from."

playing politics Placing partisan gain above the public interest; more mildly, adeptly embarrassing a political opponent.

While it is laudable to *participate in* politics, and stimulating to *talk* politics, it is considered reprehensible to *play* politics.

Notwithstanding Frank R. Kent's book title, *The Great Game of Politics*, when politics is *played* rather than engaged in, the gambling verb casts suspicion on the otherwise innocent noun *politics*. Walter Lippmann wrote in 1955 that "a political figure must never in so many words admit that in order to gain votes he sacrificed the public good, that he played 'politics.'"

Warnings about *playing politics* have been popular with presidents; Herbert Hoover in 1930 in connection with unemployment relief said, "They are playing politics at the expense of human misery"—a charge that was to be repeated a generation later as "playing politics with poverty." Franklin Roosevelt, in his MARTIN, BARTON AND FISH speech before the election of 1940, cautioned Republicans about "playing politics with national defense," and Dwight Eisenhower in 1954 applied it to White House–Capitol Hill relations in words that might have been used by Bill Clinton in 1995 or George W. Bush in 2007, when majorities in Congress shifted: "History shows that when the Executive and Legislative Branches are politically in conflict, politics in Washington runs riot.... The public good goes begging while politics is played for politics' sake."

A middle ground between the praiseworthy *participate in politics* and the accusatory *playing politics* appears to be the turning of the noun *politics* into verb or participle: *to politic* and *politicking* have the neutral connotation of "campaigning."

For allusions to political activity as gambling, see CARD METAPHORS; as a sport, see SPORTS METAPHORS.

play in Peoria An assessment of what will appeal to the folks in the HEARTLAND, usually taken to be patronizing.

Some White House aides excuse cornball gestures by a politically savvy president with a shrug and "It'll go over well in the boonies," or—in the Nixon Administration—"It'll play in Peoria."

Columnist Russell Baker disparaged the language of Nixon aides in a June 9, 1973, essay: "If the Administration's critics (Eastern liberal intellectuals, 'establishmentarians,' 'elitists') complained that they could not understand the language, much less the name of the game, the Nixon men had a standard rebuttal. 'It will play in Peoria,' they said."

The phrase has a hucksteresque quality (see SELLING CANDIDATES LIKE SOAP) derived from its metaphor of politics as a performance; it originated in vaudeville during the 1920s, as entertainers discussed how an act would be received in the hinterland. *The Saturday Evening Post* noted in 1949 that "more are resentful of the implication that 'Peoria' is synonymous with 'hick town.'" However, the Peoria Area Convention and Visitors Bureau proudly asserted in 2006 that "as national test marketers have found, Peoria is a microcosm of America herself. 'To play in Peoria' is not only an old term from vaudeville, but a catch phrase used today to measure the thoughts and habits of the typical American."

Its political coiner was John Ehrlichman, an Assistant to President Nixon and head of his Domestic Council. Ehrlichman, after his release from prison as a result of the Watergate scandals, informed the author: "'Play in Peoria' appeared in a *Wall Street Journal* story after I'd run the school for advance men in New York City in 1968. I used the expression there." Why Peoria? "Onomato-

poeia was the only reason for Peoria, I suppose. And it personified—exemplified—a place, removed from the media centers on the coasts, where the national verdict is cast, according to Nixon doctrine." (Ehrlichman, a literate lawyer who also contributed TWISTING SLOWLY, SLOWLY IN THE WIND to the political lexicon, probably meant alliteration, the repetition of initial sounds, usually consonants, in two or more words; onomatopoeia is the coining of words that imitate sounds, like *bang* and *buzz*.)

Everett Dirksen (R-Ill.), then Senate Minority Leader, did not like the put-down implicit in the phrase, as if Peoria were not cosmopolitan. In 1969, reminiscing about his youth to the author, he gave the connotation attributed to Peoria a wholly different note: "I was born in Pekin, Illinois. A lovely town, kind of on the quiet side. But for those young rakes who wanted excitement—not too far away were the bright lights of Peoria."

House Speaker Tip O'Neill offered a rhyming variant in his 1986 attack on Reagan White House trade policy with South Africa, then under pressure to abandon its policy of apartheid: "Mr. President, your brand of trade policy may play in Pretoria, but it won't play in Peoria."

ploy An artful device aimed at deception; a maneuver of indirection to achieve an objective without revealing the ultimate goal.

This old Scottish word, probably a derivative of *employ* and meaning "escapade" or "merry mischief" to Highland clans, gained in political usage in the 1960s, stimulated by the popularity of Stephen Potter's frequent use in his "one-upmanship" series.

Another possible derivation of *ploy* comes from the military *deploy*; in infantry terminology, a *ploy* is a means used to diminish the front exposed to the enemy, or to form a column from a line.

Ted Sorensen referred to a diplomatic ploy in discussing the many "inside" accounts of the Kennedy Administration's handling of the Cuban missile crisis in 1962: "Much information has been written about this series of meetings, about who said what, and about such terms as 'hawks and doves,' 'think tank,' 'Ex Comm' and 'Trollope ploy' which I never heard used at the time."

The "Trollope ploy" stems from the nineteenth-century romantic novels of Anthony Trollope, in which the heroine interprets—or deliberately misinterprets—her beau's squeeze of her hand as a proposal of marriage. In the Cuban missile crisis, it was suggested that the most recent communication from Khrushchev be ignored, and the U.S. make its reply to an earlier communication as if the most recent message had not been received. "It was Robert Kennedy," wrote Roger Hilsman in 1967's *To Move a Nation*, "who conceived a brilliant diplomatic maneuver—later dubbed 'The Trollope Ploy' ..."

The word has political promise, because of its alliteration with *politics* (a "political ploy"), the degeneration of *gimmick* into so wide a variety of meanings as to make it useless, and the lack of color in *device* or *maneuver*. The word it competes with is *gambit*, which comes from an opening chess move sacrificing a pawn to improve position and which became a diplomatic word for a concession to begin discussions.

plum, political An appointive job, especially a sinecure; PATRONAGE.

"Shaking the plum tree" is attributed to Matthew Stanley Quay, political boss of Pennsylvania in 1885 and later U.S. senator.

The idea of plums falling from a fruitful political tree is evident in this reply by presidential candidate William Howard Taft in 1908 to a query by editor William Allen White about how Taft got started so young: "I always had my plate the right side up when offices were falling."

The meaning has remained unchanged. Raymond Moley, writing in *Newsweek* in 1967 about Postmaster General Lawrence O'Brien's plans to remove the "political plum tree" from the U.S. postal system by turning it into a nonprofit corporation, reminisced: "Starry-eyed idealists have long since deplored the use of government jobs, contracts and favors as rewards for political service. But they fail to realize that keeping the plum tree is not a happy lot."

The predecessor word, no longer used in politics, was *persimmon. Plum* is current. A published list of appointive positions, avidly perused by supporters of a winning candidate the day after election, is informally called "the Plum Book." After Bill Clinton's presidential victory in 1992, the *Washington Post* reported, "Some of the biggest plums to be doled out by the Democrats are the 94 U.S. marshal's jobs around the country."

plumber One who investigates and seeks to plug up leaks of information; originally, the inept crew of wrongdoers who undertook that task in the Nixon Administration.

Room 16, in the basement of the Old Executive Office Building across West Executive Avenue from the White House, was assigned to G. Gordon Liddy and David Young in 1970. One of their overt jobs was to track terrorist groups, at home and abroad, and to inform White House staffers of means to avoid letter-bombs and other dangers. Another, less spoken about, part of their job was to find out who was leaking what information to the press, an activity that fascinated the President and Henry Kissinger.

Liddy later went on to fame and prison as one of the leaders of the Watergate break-in; Young did not get involved in those illegal matters. His contribution to history, however, was the sign he drew and placed on the door of Room 16: "The Plumbers." After the Watergate break-ins were exposed, all eavesdropping operations—from the seventeen FBI wiretaps of newsmen and White House aides to the bungled attempts by agents hired by the Plumbers—were widely publicized, culminating with disclosure of clandestine break-ins and other abridgments of Fourth Amendment protections committed by the FBI and CIA in previous administrations.

When people spoke of the Plumbers in the late '70s, it was usually applied to the Special Investigation Unit, headed by Howard E. Hunt and G. Gordon Liddy, that was pressed into action in 1971, after the publication of the Pentagon Papers. The most famous bungled target of the Plumbers was the office of Daniel Ellsberg's psychiatrist, in a search for material that could be used to discredit the leaker of the secret history of the Vietnam war.

The author visited the basement of the Old Executive Office Building years later to see who occupied the old "plumbers' office." The door was walled up; there was no longer a Room 16.

See *black bag jobs* under CIA-ESE; and the word from which *plumbers* sprang, LEAK.

plumed knight See THE MAN WHO; STALWART.

plump To give active support; to strive for the election of another without reservation.

An obscure meaning of the word *plump* is "cluster," or group; to vote as a BLOC, or using a group's votes in a cumulative manner, was known as *to vote plump*. John Adams used it in that way in 1776: "New Jersey has dethroned Franklin, and in a letter, which is just come to my hand from indisputable authority, I am told that the delegates from that county 'will vote plump.'"

The word *plumping* came to have opposite meanings on the same subject in England and the U.S.: "One of the English election phrases for which there is no equivalent in the United States," wrote the New York *Tribune* in 1880, "is 'plumping.' Whenever [an English] constituency returns two members, each voter can give one vote each to any two candidates but he cannot give his two votes to any one candidate. If he chooses he can give one vote to only one candidate, and this is termed 'plumping.'" In 1904, in the U.S., *Weber's Weekly* showed how the word came to mean the opposite of the English word: "The practice of casting three votes for one candidate has come to be known as 'plumping.' By 'plumping' the minority may concentrate its votes."

This is the same as cumulative voting, practiced in some publicly owned corporations in the U.S., where a number of votes for a slate of directors can be lumped together to be cast for a single director,

encouraging minority representation on the Board.

In current use, the verb *plump* has lost its clustering connotation, and means "advocate"; a *Financial Times* writer in 2006 noted, "If you asked the average member of the European elite when world affairs began to take a turn for worse, my guess is that many of them would plump not for 9/11, but instead for the moment when the U.S. Supreme Court ruled that George W. Bush had won the 2000 presidential election." In political terms, it has come to mean "to express or solicit support for a candidate." Australia's *Sunday Herald Sun*, after an interview with American real estate tycoon Donald Trump in 2007, used rhyme in its headline: "Trump Dumps on Bush, Plumps for Hillary."

In its verb form, it is sometimes confused with STUMP.

Pocatello, you can't go back to A wistful but not melancholy expression about the loss of hometown roots by those who flower in Washington, D.C.

"This is one case in which you can cite your source with confidence," Jonathan Daniels, once the press secretary to FDR and in 1978 the editor emeritus of the Raleigh *News and Observer*, wrote the author. "It was invented by Dick [Oregon Senator Richard L.] Neuberger and myself in 1943 or 1944." He had recounted the origin of the phrase in his 1946 book *Frontier on the Potomac*, which I shorten here:

Neuberger had just come back to Washington from Alaska and was telling me about the cold up there and the state of his kidneys.

"There's Worth Clark," he said suddenly. [Clark had been a senator from Idaho.]

"Is he living here now since he was defeated?" I asked. ...

"Yes," said Dick, "I think he is practicing with Tommy Corcoran... You know, somebody ought to write an article, 'You Can't Go Back to Pocatello.'... That's his home town. It's a big town for Idaho. Oh, I guess twenty thousand people."

"Why can't he go back?"

"They just can't. They come down here to the Senate or something. Then they get beat. It isn't easy to go back and practice local law and lead local lives."

"It is not only the little towns it's hard to go back to," I said.

And while we watched, big Jim Watson, of Indiana, walked across the room. Nobody noticed him. He had been Republican majority leader of the Senate under Hoover. He was an old man, eighty, I guessed. He had been defeated, too, but he was in Washington still.

"You can't go back to Pocatello," I said.

… You couldn't tell in the big dining room who hadn't gone back but had stayed as bureaucrats on the other side of the street. The lobby and the government were laughing together. The only difference would be which picked up the check. And suddenly the big, wicked lobbyists seemed, above the noise of people eating and talking on expense accounts that auditors far away would approve and the Bureau of Internal Revenue might pass, less wicked than sad.

In current use, the phrase is an insider's alternative to POTOMAC FEVER and is usually changed to "They never go back to Pocatello." In a 1975 editorial the now-defunct *Washington Star* referred to the bittersweet line as evidence that the much-condemned Washington atmosphere was not all bad: "Whatever its drawbacks—and we acknowledge some—the number of politicians who come here and 'never go back to Pocatello' would indicate that the Nation's Capital is a pretty good place after all."

pocketbook issue A voter's concern with what is happening to his income and its buying power.

"The great mass of the people," Boston politician Martin Lomasney discovered, "are interested in only three things—food, clothing and shelter."

In the midst of depression or inflation, pocketbook issues take precedence over more esoteric, philosophical appeals, and can exert a greater influence than personalities. Republicans in 1966 decided to make pocketbook issues their theme; a piece of literature distributed in several areas of the nation was a long paper in the shape of a supermarket cashier's tape, with comparative food prices on it and a denunciation of "Johnson INFLATION." This could be consid-

ered fair play, as "Hoover depression" had been a Democratic approach to pocketbook issues for a generation.

Pocketbook issue is synonymous with BREAD-AND-BUTTER ISSUE. AFL-CIO President George Meany said of the 1970 congressional race: "The gut issue is going to be the pocketbook issue." In 1993, *The Cook Political Report* reported, "Pocketbook issues dominate voters' broadly minds, and they worry about the middle class being squeezed and about the deficit." In March of 2007, as the war in Iraq dominated the news, the *Sarasota* (Florida) *Herald Tribune* reported the hopes of Republicans for 2008: "Pocketbook issues take center stage; lawmakers hope fattening wallets will win voters' hearts." See PARAMOUNT ISSUE; ISSUES, THE; IT'S THE ECONOMY, STUPID!

pocket veto On bills passed within ten days of congressional adjournment, the ability of the president to effectively veto by withholding his signature.

The U.S. president may retain a bill for ten days before either signing or vetoing it. If, during that time, Congress adjourns, the president will have vetoed it merely by "putting it in his pocket."

In practical terms, this means that the president need not give reasons for vetoing the bill, which is why the term originally applied was *silent veto*; such a rejection cannot be overridden by a two-thirds vote of Congress because it is no longer in session.

President Andrew Jackson brought the pocketing practice into full flower. "The silent veto," wrote Senator Daniel Webster, "is, I believe, the exclusive adoption of the present administration.… In an internal improvement bill of a former session, and in the State interest bill, we have had the silent veto, or refusal without reasons." The Ohio *Statesman* headlined "Pocket Vetoes" in 1842.

Abraham Lincoln, at odds with Rep. Thaddeus Stevens about the severity to be shown the South after the Civil War, gave the pocket veto a new twist. He let it be known that he was not going to sign the harsh Wade-Davis bill, and that a *pocket veto* would take effect; however, instead of refusing to give his reasons, he issued a proclamation to show which parts of the legislation he would accept. But the Radicals were in no mood for conciliation. Thaddeus Stevens exploded: "What an infamous proclamation! The idea of pocketing a bill and then issuing a proclamation as to how far he will conform to it ..."

In effect, the ten-day rule gives the president the power to accept or reject legislation passed in the last ten days of any session; congressional leaders try to get important bills through before the president gets this uncheckable power.

The word *veto* comes from the Latin, meaning "I forbid." Louis XVI and Marie Antoinette were called "Monsieur and Madame Veto" by the Jacobins, because of abuse of the veto power given him in 1791 by the Constituent Assembly.

The origin of *pocket* as a synonym for *suppress* was given the author by Senator Edward Kennedy, who referred to the word in an April 1977 *Virginia Law Review* article. In Shakespeare's *The Tempest*, Antonio asks: "If but one of his pockets could speak, would it not say he lies?" Sebastian replies: "Ay, or very falsely pocket up his report."

Podunk See SOUTH SUCCOTASH.

pointer phrases Speechwriters' term for verbal signals that underscore essential points in a speech.

"Let me make one thing perfectly clear," Richard Nixon liked to say. He stopped using the phrase, just as John Kennedy stopped using the word *vigor* when it became the target of impressionists' parody. *Quite clear, crystal clear*, and even plain, unadorned *clear* became taboo words in the lexicon of those working with Nixon on speeches.

A speaker who uses a pointer phrase is consciously trying to help his audience understand his message. Writers of manifestos have an edge: A reader of written prose can skip back to catch an important point, but the listener cannot. The technique appears an oversimplification when transcribed to text for reading, but

is a helpful device for the listener whose attention tends to wander. When this writer included a pointer phrase—"make no mistake about it"—in an early draft for a Nixon speech, the President crossed it out with the comment, "Leave this out of the text—if it comes naturally for me to say it, I will."

Here are some other pointer phrases in frequent use today: *My point is this, Let me be quite blunt, It all comes down to this, In plain words, In a nutshell, Cutting to the chase, Let's face it, The most important thing to remember is this.*

In the use of pointer phrases, the most important thing to remember is this: when any particular phrase is used to excess, it becomes an object of ridicule. A cartoon by Gardner in *The Washington Star* in 1971, soon after the announcement of President Nixon's plan to travel to China, showed Secretary William Rogers bursting into the State Department's translation division to ask: "How do you say 'Let me make one thing perfectly clear' in Chinese?"

Point Four Program See CONTAINMENT.

point man See ON THE POINT.

point of order Cry of interruption made famous by Senator Joseph McCarthy in 1954.

"Our counsel, Mr. [Ray] Jenkins," said temporary chairman Karl Mundt of the Senate Subcommittee on Investigations, "will now call the first witness—"

"A point of order, Mr. Chairman," said Senator McCarthy at the televised Army-McCarthy hearings. "May I raise a point of order?"

The senator's insistent use of the parliamentary device had schoolchildren repeating a phrase that had been limited to formal debates and congressional hearings. It marked the high point—and the beginning of the decline—of the senator's "era." See MCCARTHYISM. Eric Goldman wrote: "The children stopped saying 'Point of order, point of order.' The housewives went back to 'I Love Lucy.' A different subject was filling conversations."

The phrase became the title of a film documentary and articles posthumously blasting the senator, who was censured by the Senate in 1954 and died in 1957. Though he did not always use the device for determining a breach of the rules, here is why he was able to get the floor from the chairman whenever he chose, from *Robert's Rules of Order*:

> While it is the duty of the presiding officer to enforce the rules, members might differ from the Chair as to whether the rules are being violated or the Chair might have noticed a violation of the rules. In either case, the member who thinks there is breach of the rules has the right to raise the question as to whether they are being violated, and this is called raising a question of order or making a point of order. The point of order must be made at the time the breach of order occurs.

In the House of Commons in 1978, visitors protesting the presence of British troops in Northern Ireland threw three bags of manure at the legislators. One Member responded, "Politics is a dirty business," and another called for "a point of ordure."

The parliamentary objection, while useful in maintaining debate discipline, is subject to abuse, as many felt in the McCarthy era. The *Houston Chronicle*, in a May 2007 article by Janet Elliott of its Austin bureau, had this lead:

> It's become the phrase of the session, striking terror in the hearts of lawmakers when directed against their bills: "Mr. Speaker, I'd like to raise a point of order against further consideration of this bill." Used time and again, including Monday night against a bill to shield journalists' confidential sources, the parliamentary procedure is defended by many as a legitimate tool to kill legislation. But some House members say it's gotten out of control, turned into a gotcha game used as often for personal animosity as for philosophical reasons.

point with pride ... view with alarm
Clichés associated with national party platforms.

A classic party platform has been said to include at least these five elements:

1. "pointing with pride" at past accomplishments;
2. "viewing with alarm" the blundering record of the opposition;
3. firm positions on issues long since resolved;

4. ambivalent positions on current issues;
5. one nervously taken stand on a controversial matter.

In 1878, *The Nation* used the phrase in connection with one Republican platform: "Besides 'pointing with pride,' the remainder of the platform approves of 'temperance among the people' and the navigation laws, and exposes the evil designs of the Democrats." Fourteen years later, the same magazine drove home its alliterative phrase: "The Republican Convention in the Portland (Me.) district ... adopted a platform which 'points with pride' to the McKinley Law."

The phrases are often used today in the full knowledge that they are clichés, most often with the same irony and quotation marks as used a century ago. Anyone using them seriously is considered a blowhard.

pol Short for politician.

Use of this shortened form indicates a spurious familiarity with politics. It is an inexperienced reformer's kind of word, resented by those who do not resent *politician*; the user tries to insinuate himself into the political world by using a word that he does not know is disliked by insiders.

Fletcher Knebel, reporter and novelist, put his finger on it in 1964: " 'Pol' is to politician what 'cop' is to policeman."

polarize To accentuate the differences within a party or an electorate; to drive those ordinarily in agreement on many positions to extremes of disagreement.

In optics, to *polarize* means to affect light waves so that they vibrate in a definite pattern, and an obsolete metaphorical sense of the word was "to set a trend." But politics preferred the sense that has remained current, "to concentrate forces or interests into opposing or conflicting positions."

In California in 1946, moderate Democrat Will Rogers, Jr., campaigned against strongly liberal former Congressman Ellis Patterson for the Democratic nomination to the Senate. "The battle between Rogers and Patterson," said Democratic candidate for Governor Robert Kenny, "polarized the party. It was the one highly emotional issue and it became a touchstone. Nothing else mattered to the partisans of the two men. … They just didn't give a damn."

Polarization within a party, when struggles in primary elections split it into wings, often results in the defection of the losers in the general election; because of that, it is resisted by the party leadership. When Vermont Governor Howard Dean in 2004 announced he represented "the Democratic wing of the Democratic party," he had a good line, an original *netroots* organization, and a bad nomination strategy; the body of the party, not the wings, came together behind Massachusetts Senator John Kerry. To smooth over internal policy differences, the cliché used is "There are many more areas in which we agree than disagree." See ELEVENTH COMMANDMENT; SURRENDER ON MORNINGSIDE HEIGHTS.

In 1948 the Democratic party polarized to the point of dropping off both ends: Dixiecrats followed Strom Thurmond while ultraliberals followed Henry Wallace, leaving Harry Truman with just enough of a center to win. In 1964 the ideological split between Goldwater and Rockefeller polarized the Republican party, leaving very little middle at all, and this kind of polarization—when, in the poet Yeats's phrase, "the center cannot hold"—led to the Lyndon Johnson landslide.

Within an entire electorate, a little polarization is not a dangerous thing; indeed, it adds spice to political life and moves the pendulum of policy left and right. "Politics of its nature is about polar competition," wrote Daniel Henninger in *The Wall Street Journal* in 2007. "Opposed ideas *should* compete for public support. Withdraw all possibility of contact or crossover, however, and 'politics' becomes just a word that euphemizes national alienation. That, effectively, is what we have now."

In foreign policy tracts of the seventies, and especially in the writings of Carter National Security Adviser Zbigniew Brzezinski, the term *bipolar* was used to signify a world dominated by the opposition of two superpowers, in contrast to *multipolar*, where power centers included China, the West European bloc, and the THIRD WORLD.

A personal experience with the word: as a White House speechwriter on loan to Vice President Agnew during the 1970 midterm elections, after having contributed such phrases as NATTERING NABOBS OF NEGATIVISM to his robust oratory in San Diego, I raced back to Washington to be in my seat in temple for Yom Kippur services just in time to hear the rabbi admonish the congregation "not to let our country to be divided and polarized by those who use the technique of alliteration." Israeli Ambassador Yitzhak Rabin, seated nearby, caught my eye and indicated he would have a chat with the rabbi after the services.

A play on the word came from the literary agent Morton Janklow's comment in 2007, as public opinion surveys affected the emphasis on issues by many candidates: "Poll-arized: political determination of positions of principle based on public opinion polls." See LITMUS TEST.

police action Diplomatic euphemism for a war conducted under United Nations auspices; specifically, the Korean war.

When North Korean forces invaded South Korea in 1950, the Soviet delegate was in the midst of a boycott of U.N. Security Council sessions; this astounding lack of communication between Communist allies made it possible, with no Soviet delegate present to cast a veto, for the U.S. to get through a resolution providing a U.N. umbrella for our decision to intervene. Thus, U.S. troops could serve with some others as "United Nations forces" in Korea.

The phrase, like RED HERRING, was placed in President Harry Truman's mouth by a journalist. At his first press conference after the North Korean attack, a reporter asked: "are we or are we not at war?"

"We are not at war," Truman replied positively, and gave journalists the unusual (at the time) permission to quote him directly, adding that the U.S. was only trying to suppress a "bandit raid" on the Republic of Korea.

"Would it be correct," asked another reporter, "to call this a police action under the United Nations?" Truman said yes, that was what the action amounted to. Headline writers took this as "Truman Calls Intervention 'Police Action,'" which associated the President closely with the phrase.

Since the president was so definite in his statement that this was not a war, and since no declaration of war was ever made, legislative attorneys drawing up bills to make veterans of the not-a-war eligible for benefits called it the *Korean Conflict*. Similarly, a later war's legislative evasion became the *Vietnam Era*. The second war in Iraq became subsumed in the unofficial WAR ON TERROR.

police brutality See CIVILIAN REVIEW.

policeman of the world Attack phrase on America's assumption of responsibility for, or global leadership of, action to guard human rights or allies' national borders.

Benjamin Harrison, who had lost the popular vote but won the presidency in 1888, served as the 23rd president for the four years between the administrations of Grover Cleveland. On May 3, 1898, former president Harrison told the Indiana National Guard that the Spanish-American war was "a war for humanity ... for the oppressed of another race. We could not escape this conflict ... We dare not say that we have God's commission to deliver the oppressed the world around. To the distant Armenians we could send only the succor of a faith that overcomes death, and the alleviations which the nurse and the commissary give. But the oppressed Cubans and their starving women and children are knocking at our doors; their cries penetrate our slumbers."

The following year, on July 4, 1899, he sharpened that phrase in a speech in Paris, saying that the U.S. "had let it be known that she reprobated cruelty and persecution, but she has not felt that she had a commission to police the world." Intervention nearby, yes; far overseas, no. On Sept. 6, 1904, *The Washington Post* reported that Harrison "in a public address" declared: "We hold no commission from God to police the world."

President Theodore Roosevelt, in his message to Congress on December 6, 1904, went further: he claimed the duty of the U.S. was to exercise an "internal police power" throughout the Western hemisphere because "chronic wrongdoing, or an impotence which results in a general loosening of the ties of civilized society, may ... ultimately require intervention by some civilized nation." This became known as Roosevelt's corollary to the Monroe Doctrine.

With the adoption of a policy of CONTAINMENT of Communist expansion early in the 1950s, Roosevelt's corollary was extended throughout the world. Critics of this policy took the position that the United Nations, not the U.S., was properly charged with the responsibility for keeping world peace; moreover, they held, this policy was escalating wars rather than keeping the peace. Supporters of the *world policeman* idea, while rejecting the phrase as slanted to their opponents' arguments, believed the Soviet veto made the U.N. ineffective in halting aggression; in the vacuum, the U.S. had to step in on the basis of its own long-range self-interest, as well as the Wilsonian ideal of preserving the self-determination of nations.

Senator J. William Fulbright, after quoting Abraham Lincoln's use of the Biblical phrase "judge not that ye be not judged," said: "The United States must decide which of the two sides of its national character is to predominate—the humanism of Lincoln or the arrogance of those who would make America the world's policeman." In the latter half of his sentence, the Foreign Relations Committee chairman (later to lead senatorial opposition to the Vietnam war) was referring to Theodore Roosevelt, but his sense of new reality kept him from attacking a well-loved old myth.

Speaking in Montreal in May 1966, Defense Secretary Robert McNamara surprised and delighted DOVES with "neither conscience nor sanity, itself, suggests that the United States is, should, or could be the Global Gendarme." Without credit to President Harrison, he assured the Canadians that "The United States has no mandate from on high to police the world, and no inclination to do so ..."

For a time, rhetorical goalposts switched. Hawkish Secretary of State Dean Rusk felt obliged to say a year later that our efforts to pursue peace "does not mean that we are the world's policeman. It does not mean that we aspire to a PAX AMERICANA." This was a play on *pax Britannica*, meaning the peace imposed upon the world by the power of the British Empire.

Dovish George Ball, former Undersecretary of State who served Lyndon Johnson as the leading internal dissenter on the escalation of the Vietnam war, objected to the use of what had become a cliché, in *Foreign Affairs* magazine (July 1969): "man is still so bedeviled by greed and passion that force and authority must be ever at hand if he is not to blow the world up. So, unhappy as may be the policeman's lot, if we do not walk his thankless beat, who will?"

After the first Persian Gulf war, as the "VIETNAM SYNDROME" of avoiding foreign military involvement was supposedly overcome, the incongruity was stark: adherents to a muscular, interventionist foreign policy—to avoid appearing bellicose—tended to disclaim any interest in being the world's policeman. At the same time, multipolar policymakers—to avoid accusations of being weak or isolationist—also shied away from Harrison's famous formulation.

A decade later, however, as the second Gulf war lengthened in Iraq and war-weariness took hold among many in the U.S., the use of *world policeman* in derogation returned. Saudi Arabia's King Abdullah bin Abdul Aziz al-Saud, whose kingdom was preserved by the U.S. in the first Gulf War, told *Time* magazine in 2002, "America is a friend, but America cannot be the sole policeman in the world."

police state See TOTALITARIAN.

policy wonk *A grimly serious scholar of the tedious side of public affairs; stiff staffer steeped in study.*

In the 1992 election, both Bill Clinton and Al Gore were known to delight in the minutiae of program development, causing Meg Greenfield of *Newsweek* to refer to them as "tough, ambitious, leadership-minded policy wonks."

Wonk is nautical slang for "cadet," but there is no clear relation between the terms.

Sports Illustrated in 1962 wrote: "A wonk, sometimes called a 'turkey' or a 'lunch,' roughly corresponds to the 'meatball' of a decade ago." The suggestion that wonk may be "*know* spelled backward" may be dismissed as folk etymology.

In the 1984 Presidential election, Sidney Blumenthal of *The New Republic* used the academic slang politically, referring to Walter Mondale's "thralldom to the policy wonks and wise men of the Washington establishment." In 2007, Senator Hillary Clinton, presenting her concerns about healthcare costs to an audience of medical professionals at George Washington University, having been described in the local media as "a battle-scarred participant in the 1993 health-care overhaul failure," made a self-deprecating comment about not getting "overly wonky," using the adjective derived in 1978 from the noun.

political animal *What Man is reputed to be; usually employed with open—or grudging—admiration.*

Aristotle said it in his *Politics*: "Man is by nature a political animal" (meaning a creature of the *polis*, or "city-state"). Some have since complained that man is too much so, but George Bernard Shaw was not among them. "It is very doubtful whether Man is enough of a political animal," GBS noted in a speech in New York on April 11, 1933, "to produce a good, sensible, serious and efficient constitution. All the evidence is against it."

The term was often applied to Lyndon Johnson. Writing on May 24, 1964, *New York Times* columnist Arthur Krock noted: "The most political animal to occupy the White House since Andrew Jackson, if not since the creation of the Federal Government, has just completed the first six months of his presidency."

Winston Churchill in 1942 classified animals as air, sea, and land, and assigned allies their proper roles: "We were sea animals, and the United States are to a large extent ocean animals. The Russians are land animals. Happily, we are all three air animals." If the accent is placed on the second word—as political *animal*—the phrase can become an epithet. *Newsweek* in 1967: "Mrs. Lenore Romney became so upset when the governor [George Romney] angrily denounced the President as a 'political animal' that her eyes filled with tears." In 1978 House Speaker Thomas P. "Tip" O'Neill denounced a Republican prosecutor, David Marston, as "nothing but a Republican political animal." The Republican leader, John Rhodes, made a point of taking offense.

See STIR UP THE ANIMALS; for canine metaphors, see ATTACK DOG; BIRD DOG ... KENNEL DOG; PIT-BULL POLITICS.

political capital, to make To take unfair partisan advantage; capital is used in the sense of considering political prestige, notoriety, and influence as "property."

"I tell you," said Senate Majority Leader Lyndon Johnson in the debate on the 1957 civil rights bill, "out of whatever experience I have, that there is no political capital in this issue. Nothing lasting, nothing enduring has ever been born from hatred and prejudice—except more hatred and prejudice." In voting for civil rights legislation for the first time in his life, Senator Johnson was determined to make the civil rights bill his own, and it served to add to his *political capital* as a national, rather than sectional, leader.

The phrase was used in America in an 1842 issue of the Ohio *Statesman*: "the attempt of the whigs ... to make 'political capital,' as was avowed by whig members, fizzles out." The use of quotation marks indicates the phrase was used earlier than that, and the June 2007 revision of the *OED* adds this 1818 citation from the autobiography of Lady Morgan, a popular Irish novelist and patriot (who became famous under her maiden name, Sydney Owenson, before marrying Sir Charles Morgan, an English physician): "They all turn *moi, pauvre chétive*, into political capital in the fund of Illiberals." (At the time, *illiberal* meant "ill-bred, uncouth, with no liberal culture." The French phrase means "poor puny me"—Lady Morgan was less than four feet seven inches tall.)

Adlai Stevenson in 1952 tried to blunt the SOFT ON COMMUNISM issue this way: "It is never necessary to call a man a Communist to make political capital. Those of us who have undertaken to practice the ancient but imperfect art of government will always make enough mistakes to keep our critics well supplied with standard ammunition. There is no need for poison gas."

A year after that election, Eisenhower Attorney General Herbert Brownell charged that Harry Dexter White, a Truman Assistant Secretary of the Treasury, was "a Russian spy." Eisenhower recalled later: "The central point in this case was this shocking FBI evidence, but a host of partisan critics chose to ignore this and to attack the Attorney General for 'trying to make capital' out of incontrovertible evidence."

To expend political capital is considered laudable, as presidential popularity is best used to further policy goals. Two days after his reelection victory in 2004, President Bush told a news conference he had earned plenty of "political capital, and now I intend to spend it." His immediate goal was to reform the Social Security system. In March of 2006, asked what became of his political capital, he replied, "I'd say I'm spending that capital on the war. Social Security—it didn't get done." Robert Dalleck, a presidential historian, said in 2005 that Bush's Iraq-war travails reminded him of FDR overreaching in trying to "pack" the Supreme Court (see NINE OLD MEN). "Second terms are treacherous, and presidents enter a minefield where they really must shepherd their credibility and political capital."

Business has not contributed nearly as many metaphors to politics as religion, sports, or the military. *Stock* is occasionally used, as in this 1836 *Scioto Gazette* comment: "The rapid advance of Jackson stock in the political market presented too splendid a speculation to be eluded by such jobbers as the house of Van Buren & Company" and the 1876 Cleveland *Leader*'s headline, "Hayes Stock Is Strong." LAME DUCK is the best-known borrowing from finance, with *gravy train, angel, blue sky laws*, and BOOM AND BUST used often. Up-and-coming politicians are considered *hot properties*.

political football, to make a To thrust a social, national security, or otherwise ostensibly non-political matter into partisan politics.

"Smart of the Belfast Free Press," wrote the *Bangor* (Maine) *Whig and Courier* in 1857, "is laboring with all his might to keep the temperance question as a political football."

This phrase continues to have a lively usage throughout the English-speaking world as an admonition to leave political considerations out of the discussion of issues that should be ABOVE POLITICS. The bioethicist Sigrid Fry-Revere of the libertarian Cato Institute wrote in the *Los Angeles Times* in 2006 that "when stem cell research is not a political football, less time and money is wasted on campaigns, bureaucracy and litigation." In Britain the same year, Tory leader David Cameron said, "we must not allow the security of this country to become a political football either between the parties or within the parties," which was reported in the *Evening Standard* as "a blistering attack on the leading contenders for the Labour crown by accusing them of using national security as a political football."

A person can consider himself a political football, unfairly put upon by those would profit by castigating him. In 1953, as an armed forces correspondent, the author taped an interview with Charles "Lucky" Luciano—a Mafioso usually identified as "the international vice overlord" in tabloids—at the Hotel Vesuvio in Naples, Italy. He had been released from a U.S. jail and deported to Italy at the behest of New York prosecutor and later Governor Thomas E. Dewey. I asked Luciano if his release had been a reward for getting the Mafia to keep the New York docks safe from Nazi saboteurs during World War II, and he brushed off the question with a laconic "I been a political football."

politically correct Conforming to liberal or far-left thought on sexual, racial and environmental issues.

Politically correct began in the 1970s as an assertion of liberal or progressive activists. The earliest known use of the term was in an essay by Toni Cade (later Toni Cade Bambara) in her 1970 anthology *The Black Woman*: "A man cannot be politically correct and a chauvinist too." It was later used in a December 1975 statement by Karen DeCrow, then president of the National Organization for Women, who said that NOW was taking the "intellectually and politically correct direction."

The adjectival phrase, frequently abbreviated to *p.c.* by conservatives attacking regimentation in language and thought by "conformist" liberal academics, became a controversial expression on college campuses in the early '80s. Senator Daniel P. Moynihan sent the author a note enclosing a cartoon drawn by his son, John, and published in the Wesleyan *Argus* in 1982 using *politically correct.*

In November of 1933, the *Christian Science Monitor* reported, "The results of a recent investigation of the knowledge of 65,000 Soviet pupils are candidly summed up in the official newspaper, Izvestia, in the following terms: 'Bad grammar, abundance of mistakes in spelling, … superficial and often politically incorrect information in civics and social sciences.'" The *OED* reports that the phrase was used again in a 1939 *New Republic* magazine: "It isn't just because of rapidly shifting times and attitudes—going back to 'Lives of a Bengal Lancer' almost five years afterward, you will find it just as politically incorrect and marvelous as ever."

In *A Century of New Words*, John Ayto tracked the phrase back to 1793, when John Wilson heard someone give a toast to "the United States." He said, "'The people of the United States' is the toast given. This is not politically correct."

The popularization of the Communist phrase came with Maoist "correct thinking." Chairman Mao Zedong titled a 1963 thought "Where Do Correct Ideas Come From?" He answered his own question: "They come from social practice, and from it alone." Correct thinking, "the disciplined acceptance of a party line," led to the definition of the adjective *correct* as "reflecting the views of the group." The noun equivalent of this phrase is *political correctness* (also abbreviated to *p.c.*), and one who is not politically correct (from the p.c. standpoint) is dubbed *politically incorrect.*

The phrase soon became jokingly used in other combinations, and *environmental correctness, morally correct, patriotically correct,* and even *nutritionally correct* and *sartorially incorrect* found their way into print.

Attempts to police language, with terms such as *feminine* and *codger* labeled "objectionable," led to parody: at the 1992 Democratic National Convention in New York, a handout for *The Official Politically Correct Dictionary and Handbook* recommended replacing *ballot-box stuffing* with "nontraditional voting," *cliché* with "previously enjoyed sound bite," and *sore loser* with "equanimity-deprived individual with temporarily unmet career objectives." However, some discriminatory words deserved correction: *fireman* was replaced by *firefighter, policeman* and *lawman* with *police officer,* and *mailman* with *postal worker. Mankind,* always intended to encompass women, is now better expressed as *humanity.*

To a different order of magnitude of political incorrectness: in 2007, when a popular radio star, Don Imus, used the slur "nappy-headed hos" (whores with the kind of frizzy hairdos chosen by some African-American women) regarding a champion women's basketball team, reaction was intense and advertisers caused the broadcaster and his producer to be fired. Columnist Daniel Henninger of *The Wall Street Journal* briefly reviewed the history of such reactions: "Don Imus…the Duke lacrosse team, Jimmy the Greek, the kid who yelled 'water buffalo' at Penn, Howard Cosell, Jon Stewart, Chief Illiniwek, Jackie Mason and 'South Park' all have in common only one thing: They have not been Politically Correct." He added "the annihilation of Harvard President Larry Summers" for suggesting the possibility that women are underrepresented in science and engineering because more men than women "are four standard deviations above the mean." The p.c. reaction to the Imus slur, however,

had an effect on the use of slurs by hip-hop artists, and a move to discourage the proliferation of "n, b, and h words" on the air. Imus, chastened, found another job.

See THOUGHT POLICE.

political miracle An upset or comeback.

"Barring a political miracle," wrote *Time* magazine in 1948 about the Dewey-Warren combination heavily favored to swamp President Truman, "it was the kind of ticket that could not fail to sweep the Republican party back into power." See EAT CROW.

Four years later, a WRITE-IN campaign was begun in Eisenhower's behalf by a citizens' group in Minnesota, just after his New Hampshire primary victory over Robert Taft. Professionals warned Eisenhower against it, feeling its likely failure would slow down the bandwagon. Bradshaw Mintener, state chairman of "Minnesotans for Eisenhower," appealed to the voters for "a political miracle." As the surprised General commented later: "It appeared to have happened: more than one hundred thousand people wrote in varying versions of my name."

In California in 2006, Governor Arnold Schwarzenegger—having been rebuked by voters the year before on four referenda he tried to put across—changed his political spots, stopped calling Democratic state legislators "girlie-men," and abandoned efforts to cut benefits for teachers, nurses, and police. The result of his reelection campaign brought this headline from the Indo-Asian News Service: "Schwarzenegger works political miracle in California."

The adjective *political* seems to have a particular affinity for the nouns *miracle, upheaval,* and *tsunami.* Taking any unpopular stand, or one that used to be unpopular and still gives the illusion of courage in opposing it, is called POLITICAL SUICIDE by tut-tutters; keeping one's "political cool" means refusing to overreact in adversity or triumph.

political similes See LIKE UGLY ON AN APE.

political suicide An obviously unpopular action, likely to result in defeat at the polls;

or, an action so obviously against popular opinion as to redound to the political figure's benefit.

These suicides, like the report of Mark Twain's death, are usually exaggerations. Actions unpopular on their face can be taken as evidence of courage; it may appear to some commentators as "political suicide" to question or oppose automatic increases in funds for education, but some governors who take this controversial step find they may stay alive by proving they have made a "white elephant" more efficient, or held the line on taxes, or whatever the other side of the coin enables them to say.

The phrase, sometimes expressed as "political hara-kiri" (often mispronounced "Harry Carey"), does not mean taking one's own political life deliberately; it means, rather, taking an action that some other people feel will lead to political oblivion. In that second sense, the word was used by Woodrow Wilson in a letter to Bernard Baruch in 1916 early in the presidential campaign against Republican Charles Evans Hughes, and in 1964 could have been applied to Lyndon Johnson's strategy: "I am inclined to follow the course suggested by a friend," noted President Wilson, "who says that he has always followed the rule never to murder a man who is committing suicide."

politician One who engages in a career either in government or in a political party on a full-time, usually professional, basis.

In most countries the practice of politics is considered a respectable profession, worthy of this 1770 definition by English parliamentarian Thomas Burke: "It is the business of the speculative philosopher to mark the proper ends of government. It is the business of the politician, who is the philosopher in action, to find out proper means towards those ends, and to employ them with effect."

That was a far cry from the derogation in Shakespeare's *Richard III*: "meerly a politician, and studied only his owne ends." In 1879 Sir George Campbell reported to his countrymen that "the word 'politician' is used in a bad sense in America as applied

to people who … are skilled in the area of 'wirepulling.'" In the U.S. the politician has been looked upon with suspicion from the first, because the colonists felt themselves misunderstood and mistreated by a government in London (in which they were not represented) that inflicted on them such distasteful regulations as the various Acts of Trade and the Stamp Act. President George Washington expressed the feeling of most of his countrymen when in his Farewell Address he referred to "the mere politicians."

Artemus Ward, Lincoln's favorite humorist, said: "I am not a politician, and my other habits are good."

In more recent times, the practice of politics in this country has become more than acceptable, and a growing number of men and women are prepared even to accept the appellation without wincing. One who bore the badge proudly was former President Harry Truman, who told the Reciprocity Club in 1958: "A politician is a man who understands government, and it takes a politician to run a government. A statesman is a politician who's been dead ten or fifteen years."

A professional politician's image is similar to that of the professional soldier: patronized in peacetime, lionized in wartime. Between campaigns, the politician is an embarrassment and a pest to many government officials; at campaign time, he is leader, guide, and confidant.

In current usage, a *public figure* is a celebrity; a *political figure* is an officeholder or likely candidate; a *professional politician* is usually a technician without ideology; a POL is one of *the boys in the backroom*; a GOFER is the lowest political functionary; a *political expert* or *political observer* is sometimes a journalist's fiction for quoting himself without appearing to do so; and an OLD PRO knows enough ropes to hang himself.

politics of A framework for titles, to suit all speech and punditry purposes.

In the 1949 English edition of his book *The Vital Center*, the title used by Arthur Schlesinger, Jr., was *The Politics of Freedom*.

He informed the author that titles like *The Strategy of Terror* by Edmund Taylor might have inspired his frequent use of this construction. Schlesinger followed this with *The Politics of Upheaval* in 1957, and *The Politics of Hope* in 1962. In the 1968 presidential campaign, Hubert Humphrey tried out "the politics of joy," and in 1970 Senator Edward Kennedy denounced Vice President Agnew's "politics of fear." In 1992, the call by the "hard right" of the Republican Party to launch a "cultural war" against homosexuals and abortion-rights activists was denounced by GOP moderates as the "politics of exclusion."

First Lady Hillary Clinton spoke in 1993 of "the politics of meaning," a phrase from writer Michael Lerner, which she said had to be "thought through on various planes," adding, "We need a new politics of meaning. We need a new ethos of individual responsibility and caring." Her husband, the president, accused of an affair with the intern Monica Lewinsky, deplored "the politics of personal destruction."

Fourteen years later, as Senator Hillary Clinton's fellow Democratic candidates for the presidential nomination concentrated their fire on the front runner, causing her to equivocate on some issues, a spokesman for the Clinton campaign returned to the favored construction, complaining of "the politics of piling-on."

On the politics of anything: the word *politics* is construed as singular, as in "Politics is fun," but when it is used to denote a set of beliefs, the plural takes over, as "My politics are nobody's business."

pollster One who measures public opinion, especially with an eye to predicting election results.

"A pinch of probably is worth a pound of perhaps," wrote the humorist James Thurber. The politician's desperation for reassurance combined with a journalist's curiosity led to the rise of public opinion polling, a technique in use in the U.S. since the Adams-Jackson-Clay-Crawford presidential race of 1824.

The word *poll* comes from the Middle English *polle*, meaning "top of the head," the part that showed when heads were being counted. Today, a *poll tax* is a head tax; the *polls* are where the heads are counted; and a *poll* is a counting of a sampling of heads, selected at random or by prearrangement, to reflect the opinion of a given populace. Dr. Elmo Roper and Dr. George Gallup were the leaders in the field for many years, establishing their profession in the 1930s, blossoming after the debacle of the *Literary Digest* poll of 1936. See STRAW POLL.

Pollster is a relatively new word, coined in *Time* magazine in 1939 to describe Gallup as the "punditical pollster of public opinion." It was popularized in—and especially after—the Truman upset of Dewey in 1948. Wrote *Time*, wrong as any, afterward: "The press ... had failed to do its own doorbell-ringing and bush-beating, it had delegated its journalist's job to the pollsters." The *-ster* suffix is slightly jazzy (*jokester, trickster, hipster*) and not at all scientific; many people in the survey business resisted it at first but now put up with it. Dr. Roper informed the author:

> To the best of my memory, the first time the word *pollster* was ever applied to me was in the summer of 1944, but—again according to my memory—it didn't achieve anything like its present currency until the campaign of 1948. Since we have always tried to do something above and beyond a mere nose counting job—seeking always for the reasons *why* people were going to do whatever it was they were about to do—I have always preferred to be called a "public opinion analyst." But the press—in its normal omniscience—apparently needs a shorter phrase and I haven't ever developed what might be called an active resentment against the word *pollster* ... Our organization has never used the word *poll*. When we started the first published poll, we insisted on calling it "The Fortune Survey."

Time drove home its coinage in 1939 commenting on FDR's popularity: "Gallup pollsters reported that 43 percent of the voters want Mr. Roosevelt to run again." In the 1992 presidential election, *The Washington Post* wrote of the three-way race by Bush, Clinton and Perot: "As a consequence, some pollsters say, election results may be much different than the findings of election-eve weekend polls."

At century's end, *exit polling*—asking voters how they had voted as they came out of the polling places—fell into disrepute because the results were leaked to radio, TV, and blogs before the polls closed, or because many voters (who felt their ballot was their secret) freely lied to pollsters. But the business of polling is undeterred by politicians running behind who claim "the only poll that counts is on Election Day," or by the manipulations of *push polling*, the abuse of the business to implant opinions in the guise of measuring them. In a 2006 *New York Times Magazine* article on the advanced techniques of Ken Mehlman, chairman of the Republican National Committee, Adam Nagourney wrote, "Mehlman's chairmanship has become an argument for the notion that the garrulous and instinctual political boss may be all but obsolete in this age of supersophisticated polling, data mining, niche marketing and microtargeting." See DEPTH POLLING; TRIAL HEAT; and for *push polling*, DIRTY TRICKS.

pollution See ENVIRONMENTALIST.

poodle See THIRD WAY.

pooh-bah Big shot; pompous functionary.

A huffing and puffing sound surrounds the word, imitative of the "high MUCKEY-MUCKS" it derogates.

When the "McGovern Victory Special" rolled in June of 1972, Haynes Johnson wrote in *The Washington Post*: "They all climbed aboard that train today; movie stars, jocks, beautiful people, old politicians, new politicians, erstwhile Kennedy and McCarthy followers, big pooh-bahs of the press and other assorted people on the make."

When President Jimmy Carter nominated the former Kennedy aide Theodore Sorensen to be Director of Central Intelligence, columnist Joseph Kraft supported him: "He is an avowedly political man, not the kind of antiseptic pooh-bah usually picked to build public confidence." (Antiseptic pooh-bahs usually do better facing Senate inquisitors, most pooh-bahs of the press believe. See BIG FOOT.)

The politico-cultural columnist Frank Rich, a consistent Bush Administration critic, wrote in 2007 on the death of Jerry Falwell, the Moral Majority founder: "The Karl Rove theory that Republicans cannot survive without pandering to the religious-right pooh-bahs is yet another piece of Bush dogma lying in ruins …" At the same time, *The Washington Post* reported that Senator John McCain refused to act discouraged about low presidential poll ratings: "Most of the pooh-bahs have quit. Now he's alone again, without a big entourage or media scrum, and he likes it."

Although the onomatopoeic compound is sometimes thought to be derived from A. A. Milne's *Winnie-the-Pooh*, Pooh-bear is not the source. The complete derivation is given in this answer to the author's query by Stuart Berg Flexner, who was coauthor of the *Dictionary of American Slang*:

> *Pooh-Bah* was first heard the night of March 14, 1885, when Gilbert & Sullivan's "The Mikado" opened (in London's Savoy Theatre, the one Richard D'Oyly Carte built for their operas). Pooh-Bah was the name of the pompous bureaucrat holding many offices and titles…the one who informs the Lord High Executioner Ko-Ko that he must execute someone within a month or lose his office, Ko-Ko eventually reporting that he has executed Nanki-Poo (the son of the Mikado traveling in disguise) who has fallen in love with Yum-Yum.
>
> W. S. Gilbert loved these cute/humorous names…Pooh-Bah merely comes from his combining the two negative exclamations *pooh!* plus *bah!*, typical put-downs from a typical bureaucrat.
>
> By the 1890s the English were using the name Pooh-Bah in a general way, to mean any pompous person with a lot of bureaucratic offices and titles (the English almost always retain the capital P and B though we don't).

King Taufa'ahau Tupou IV, the 300-pound monarch of Tonga (an island group between New Zealand and Samoa), presided over the Independence Day of his nation happily, and liked to say in the '60s: "I'm a bit of a Pooh-Bah, you know, except that I don't cut off any heads."

See BOSS; SACHEM; PANJANDRUM.

popular front Name adopted by many radical movements, including the cooperating Communist and socialist forces in Europe during the 1930s.

This phrase is often capitalized when referring to the specific movement combining radicals, Communists, and socialists; this international alliance began in 1935, spreading from France and Spain to Chile as a result of the new policy of collaborating with non-Communist socialists introduced by the Comintern in 1934.

In French, where the term first appeared, the term is *front populaire*; in Spanish, *frente popular*. In English, *popular front* (first found in 1936) has produced various related forms.

Although the European movement lost effectiveness after 1938, the phrase resurfaced in recent political struggles in the Middle East. For example, George Habash has led the Popular Front for the Liberation of Palestine, as well as guerrilla fighters of the Rejection Front.

populist Attuned to the needs of "the people"; now used with a connotation of old-fashioned radicalism; a liberalism rooted deeply in U.S. history.

Lyndon Johnson was called by friendly writers a political leader "in the old populist tradition." When Jimmy Carter inveighed against favoritism (and the Nixon pardon) in his 1976 acceptance speech with "I see no reason why big-shot crooks should go free, while the poor ones go to jail"—that, too, was described as *populist*.

The word is used today with a small *p* as a reminder of the theories rather than the structure of the Populist or "People's party" (see PARTY OF THE PEOPLE), which was a political party of a radical nature that won substantial backing in the U.S. at the end of the nineteenth century.

A populist economic policy in recent years is one that features a call to "soak the rich." That phrase, according to columnist Joe Klein, dates back to the early 1930s; he cites Thomas Kessner's book *Fiorello H. La Guardia and the Making of Modern New York*, which states that on March 10, 1932, the Congressman from New York blasted a tax bill in the House and added his own advice: "I am simply going to say, 'Soak the rich.'" An alliteration-appreciative *New York Times* writer (quoting Horatio in *Hamlet*) denounced him for those "wild and whirling words."

In the nineteenth century, periodic sharp economic declines and a widespread belief that the federal government was dominated by large money interests inimical to both the farmer and the mechanic led to some informal alliances between these groups and socialists. In 1890 a state party calling itself the People's party was founded in Kansas. In that same year, various Farmer's Alliance groups, founded largely to fight the railroads, scored heavily in the South and the West; there, candidates advocating new economic legislation favored by the Alliances were elected in five senatorial, six gubernatorial, and 46 congressional races.

These state and local victories led to the organization of a national Populist party in 1891. At its convention in Omaha it demanded, among other things, public ownership of the railroads and the telegraph and telephone systems, direct election of U.S. senators, a graduated income tax, and cheaper money. The delegates, coming predominantly from the farmers' organizations and the Knights of Labor, wrote a radical platform calling for "a permanent and perpetual...union of the labor forces of the United States.... The interests of rural and civic [urban] labor are the same, their enemies are identical.... We believe that the time has come when the railroad corporations will either own the people, or the people must own the railroads."

Other planks were no more friendly to capitalists. When the Populist candidate, General James B. Weaver, won 22 electoral-college and 1,029,846 popular votes in the 1892 election, many people, including some considered liberals, were fearful of impending revolution.

Watching Populist congressmen in action, novelist Hamlin Garland foresaw "a great periodic upheaval similar to that of '61. Everywhere as I went through the aisles of the House, I saw and heard it...the House is a smouldering volcano." A woman announced she was going to Europe "to spend my money before those crazy people take it."

The party lingered until 1908, but most of its members had returned to the Democratic fold by then, and the word is used now by politicians who want to identify with "the little guy," who can be found under JOHN Q. PUBLIC. The word *populist* is also used internationally, as in *Maclean's* 1983 assessment of leadership in the Philippines: "Even the Communist Party expressed the belief that Aquino had a unique populist approach." In 1993, *New York* magazine media columnist Edwin Diamond described Bill Clinton's use of televised town halls and appearances of many national and local talk shows as "electronic populism."

Democrat John Edwards, former Senator from North Carolina, son of a mill worker who became a leading trial lawyer, ran first for vice president in 2004 on the theme of "the two Americas," rich and poor, which had a decidedly populist edge, and in the primaries aiming toward 2008 with emphasis on healthcare, alleviating poverty, and asserting his mistake in supporting the invasion of Iraq, staking a position to the left of most other "first-tier" candidates. "Today's most prominent Democratic candidates," wrote columnist David Brooks, "are more Mines and Mills than Towns and Gowns."

pork barrel The public treasury, into which politicians consumed by prospects of reelection dip for "pork," or funds for local projects.

The classic example of the *pork barrel* is the Rivers and Harbors bill, a piece of legislation that provides morsels for scores of congressmen in the form of appropriations for dams and piers, highways and bridges.

The trope is derived from the pre–Civil War practice of periodically distributing salt pork to the slaves from huge barrels. A story by E. E. Hale called "The Children of the Public," which appeared in an 1863 issue of *Frank Leslie's Illustrated Newspaper*, helped popularize the term. In Chapter I, entitled "The Pork Barrel," Hale wrote: "We find that, when an extraordinary contingency arises in life, as just now in ours,

we have only to go to our pork barrel, and the fish rises to our hook or spear." By the 1870s, congressmen were regularly referring to "pork," and in 1919 C. C. Maxey vividly made the analogy in the *National Municipal Review*: "Oftentimes the eagerness of the slaves would result in a rush upon the pork barrel, in which each would strive to grab as much as possible for himself. Members of Congress in the stampede to get their local appropriation items into the omnibus river and harbor bills behaved so much like Negro slaves rushing the pork barrel, that these bills were facetiously styled 'pork barrel' bills."

Labor "skates"—a fond old-time term for union historians—remember the use of the term *pork-chopper* in the '30s meaning "full-time union leader" or "holder of a political patronage job." *Time* magazine noted in 1948 that one New York politician "fished in Tammany's pork barrel for 28 years to bring improvement to 'me people.'" In a Baltimore speech on inflation in 1952, Adlai Stevenson pledged "no pork-barreling while our economy is in its present condition." Former Senator Paul H. Douglas (D-Ill.) called pork-barrelers "drunkards who shout for temperance in the intervals between cocktails." See DELIVER.

The practice of channeling federal or state tax revenues to local projects is defended as a means of making certain that improvements in the nation's infrastructure are directed by local authorities reflecting the needs of local voters rather than "Washington bureaucrats." More often, the porcine image is invoked as an attack on a system that is later embraced by the successful attacker. Recent attacks using other symbols can be found under EARMARK and BRIDGE TO NOWHERE. Arizona Republican representative Jeff Flake, asking "And we wonder why we were beaten like a rented mule on Tuesday?" after the 2006 elections, answered, "Pork-barrel earmarks, or 'member projects' (as we preferred to call them so as not to offend our own sensibilities) greatly multiplied under Republican rule. The Democrats were happy as long as enough crumbs fell from the Republican appropriators' table."

position paper A statement of policy on an issue in a campaign, for guidance of speechwriters and supporting speakers; in diplomacy, an *aide-mémoire* at an international conference.

Before any major campaign begins, bright young lawyers are brought in to work on *position papers*. They check past speeches by the candidate on the subject to be careful of inconsistency, draft the latest "new ideas" that have been bruited about on the subject, farm out research to academicians at THINK TANKS specializing in the area. Papers are then drawn up on subjects like urban renewal, agricultural policy, air and water pollution, transportation, crime, and housing; in more local campaigns, on "home rule" and traffic congestion; and in national campaigns, on foreign affairs and broad themes of social welfare.

The position papers are useful in briefing a candidate on areas he or she knows little about and getting a briefing from candidates on areas they have definite ideas about. They are usually packaged in a loose-leaf folder and made available to the writers and headquarters staff; in abridged form they may be sent to canvassers to equip them with answers to questions likely to be asked when they ring their doorbells.

A position paper is detailed, including a background statement of position; it should not be confused with a *brief*. When Adlai Stevenson said in 1952, "each day their statement of position moves in like a new fog bank," he was deriding sweeping Republican policy pronouncements, not detailed papers.

In diplomacy, a WHITE PAPER is a formal report issued by a government to define its policy, while a *position paper* is a private guide to its diplomats. "A full-scale international conference involves difficult and intricate preparation," wrote Dwight Eisenhower; "'position papers'—documents on all conceivable issues, setting forth the position the government intends to present at the meeting—have to be carefully written and approved." He added sharply: "Position papers can be written only after a chief executive has decided precisely what his position is to be."

One-page position papers, prepared as answers to anticipated press-conference questions, make up a president's "black BRIEFING BOOK."

poster See SNIPE.

Potomac fever The proximity to power that turns a PASSION FOR ANONYMITY into a yearning for notoriety.

An ordinary human being whose statements have been ignored or merely tolerated all his life will, upon taking a job in Washington, D.C., find his statements quoted and his picture appearing in media all over the world. The sensation that follows, often linked with the drinking of "heady wine," is euphoric; men who have always decried "personal publicity" find it necessary, after their appointment, to utilize the avenues of mass communication to get across their agency's message.

"The rivalry for the attention and support of Congress," wrote Harry Truman in his memoirs, "was, in part, responsible for many news leaks. 'Potomac fever,' too, creates a great desire on the part of people to see their names in print."

Named for the river that flows through Washington, Potomac fever has several symptoms. In 1988, the *Los Angeles Times* quoted a White House veteran on the sickness: "We called it Potomac fever. Because people treat you like a star if you work in the White House, it's easy to start behaving like one. You're mentioned in talk shows and written about in books. Before long some start to feel as if they actually are a little President."

Even the President may be susceptible; early in the Clinton Administration, Rep. Dick Armey (R-Tex.) said on *Meet the Press*: "It strikes me that what I've seen in the President is the first, worst, most definitive case of Potomac fever that I've watched in this town."

A similar disease, contracted before arrival in Washington, or a virulent strain contracted while in Washington on a senatorial level, is PRESIDENTIAL FEVER, transmitted by the PRESIDENTIAL BUG. Related to this illness is *Hill fever*, which afflicts those in proximity to congressional power on Capitol Hill. See POCATELLO, YOU CAN'T GO BACK TO.

potted plant Symbol of a mute, helpless object, used in assertions of the right to object or oversee.

Washington attorney Brandan Sullivan, counsel to Lt. Col. Oliver North, objected frequently to questions being put to his client at a Senate hearing into the Iran-contra scandal in 1987. Told by Chairman Daniel Inouye to let North object for himself if he wished to do so, the attorney snapped, "What am I, a potted plant? I'm here as a lawyer; that's my job."

A *potted plant* is a living thing that stands mute. The phrase has since been used to describe refusals to remain silent or reluctance to engage in debate. When Secretary of State Colin Powell decided to boycott the U.N. conference on racism that was certain to condemn Israel on behalf of Palestinian Arabs with no mention of worse abuses of human rights by many other nations, Harold Koh, a Clinton administration human-rights official, told the *PBS News Hour* he believed Powell should go to Darfur and speak out: "He's not a potted plant. This is moment for engaged diplomacy."

Regarding the oversight function, soon after Democrats took control of Congress in 2007 and began a series of investigations into Bush Administration activities, the new House majority leader, Steny Hoyer, said "The days of see no evil, hear no evil and speak no evil are over … The United States Congress will no longer be a potted plant or signer of blank checks." A few months later, *The Wall Street Journal* noted that Senator Hillary Clinton had told the AP that, if elected president, she would make her husband a roving ambassador to the world. This should concern, wrote the *Journal*, "those aspiring to be Secretary of State, Treasury and Defense, who'd likely serve as potted plants in the shade of these two dominant personalities."

"Potted plants get little respect," complained a 2007 Web posting from the Earth-Scholars Research Group. "Indeed, most people think of them as passive, trivial, dispensable, a nuisance to tend, and purely decorative. One cannot even assume indoor potted plants are alive, given how easily today's artificial ('silk') potted plants can deceive the untrained eye!"

Sullivan's "What am I, a potted plant?" has, in the political language, replaced the earlier general protest, "What am I, chopped liver?"

Pottery Barn Rule You break it, you own it.

While pledging to support the planned war on Iraq, Secretary of State Colin L. Powell cautioned President George W. Bush during a meeting on Jan. 13, 2003, that military victory would bring its own problems. "You know," he told the president, "you're going to be owning this place?" Bob Woodward, who first reported the conversation, presumably sourced to Powell, in *Plan of Attack* (2004), added that Powell and his second in command, Deputy Secretary of State Richard Armitage, referred privately to "You break it, you own it" as "the Pottery Barn rule."

The *Pottery Barn rule* was in keeping with Powell's penchant for rules and maxims. In his 1995 memoir, *My American Journey*, he included sayings that he had kept on his desk in the Pentagon when he was chairman of the Joint Chiefs of Staff. Among them: "It ain't as bad as you think. It will look better in the morning"; "Be careful what you choose. You may get it"; and "Perpetual optimism is a force multiplier."

The Pottery Barn home-furnishings chain was not happy with the rule that Woodward publicized, protesting that it did not charge customers for accidental breakage. Powell apologized during an appearance on Larry King's CNN television program, saying, "We know that your corporate policy is that if you break it accidentally, then you don't have to pay for it." And he passed the buck in a jocular way, noting that he had picked up the "rule" from speeches by *New York Times* columnist Tom Friedman, "so it is Tom Friedman's fault."

Some etymologies are easier to track down than others: In this case, all the lexicographer had to do was to walk ten steps down the hall to the office of his *Times* colleague in column. Tom readily admitted responsibility. He had called it "the pottery store rule" when making the point in a column on Feb. 12, 2003, that the United States was responsible for rebuilding Iraq, but had often used "Pottery Barn" before the war and in speeches. He also absolved the company. "I made up the whole thing," he said. "I just remembered the phrase from the china shop—'You break it, you own it.' That was in my head for years." And he added:

"I was a little surprised to see Powell as being quoted as telling that to the president. I was also pleased. I only wish the president had paid attention."

See also PROVERBS AND AXIOMS, POLITICAL; RUMSFELD'S RULES.

potus/flotus Acronyms for, respectively, *President of the United States* (pronounced POE-tus) and *First Lady of the United States* (pronounced FLOE-tus, not FLOT-tus, to rhyme with *potus*).

Potus has been used for many years among White House staffers and Secret Service agents to refer to the President, while *flotus* for the FIRST LADY (a quasi-official title initially applied to Mary Todd Lincoln) is relatively recent. As a Clinton White House aide, Brian Bailey, noted in 1994 in connection with the collection of names of potential donors to political campaigns: "POTUS and FLOTUS have expressed interest in having these names added to the database." When the First Couple are away from Washington, they are said to be either in *CONUS* (the continental United States) or *OCONUS* (outside the continental United States).

Potus was devised in 1879 by Walter P. Phillips, then a telegraph operator for the United Press Association, as part of a shorthand code for expressions that frequently appeared in news reports. The code consisted of hundreds of abbreviations for reducing the number of dots and dashes that had to be transmitted, among them: *ckx* for "committed suicide," *fapib* for "filed a petition in bankruptcy," *mu* for "murder," and *xn* for "constitution." It also included numbers: *73* stood for "best regards," and

30, meaning "end of message," is still used by some nostalgic reporters to mark the end of a news story.

Reminiscing about his days a telegraph operator in the 1880s and '90s, Clarence Vincent told the *Oakland* (Calif.) *Tribune* in 1941 that before the code was introduced "we had to tap out each letter so that the term 'President of the United States' took quite a little time. Under the Phillips code one merely tapped out 'POTUS.'" The oldest example of the term found so far in the popular press comes from the *Fort Wayne* (Ind.) *News* of Feb. 25, 1903: "This is the way a message is sent on the wire: T potus, ixs, wi km to Kevy... This jargon conveys the following information: The president of the United States, it is said, will communicate to King Edward VII ..."

By the 1950s, *Potus* was employed by those who surround the President and travel in his wake. In 1958, *The Gettysburg* (Pa.) *Times* reported that a ham, or amateur, radio operator in Houston, Tex., heard another ham signing off with the call letters W3WTE. The Houston ham, a Southern Pacific Railroad electrician, "immediately called this station and found himself talking to POTUS.... The man at W3WTE was Dwight D. Eisenhower himself," then aboard a train bound for Washington.

Subsequent administrations embraced the usage. This lexicographer first noticed the acronym in 1969 on the extension of a five-line telephone along the back wall of the cabinet room in the West Wing. When the button next to the *POTUS* label lit up, people jumped. As a novelist, the lexicographer later helped popularize the term beyond the White House. In the 1977 novel *Full Disclosure*, the fictional President's inamorata-photographer felt awkward addressing the Chief Executive by his first name. At the same time, "Mr. President" seemed overly formal on intimate occasions. She solved the problem by adopting *potus* as a pet name for her lover.

By 1983, the frequency with which *potus* was cropping up in the press led an editorial writer for *The New York Times* to protest: "Is no Washington name exempt from shorthand? The chief magistrate responsible for executing the laws is sometimes called the *Potus* (President of the United States). The nine men who interpret them are often the *Scotus*. The people who enact them are still, for better or for worse, the Congress." This editorial elicited an amused letter from Justice Sandra Day O'Connor, who suggested that the *Times* might update its files, since the *Scotus* now included the *Fwotsc*, as The First Woman on the Supreme Court termed herself. The *Times* editorialist might have added *Codel*, the inside acronym for a *congressional delegation*, usually on a mission abroad.

The *potus* has been known to use the acronym when referring to himself. A few days after George W. Bush briefly choked on a pretzel in 2002, he sent reporters on Air Force One a large bag of pretzels with the advice, scribbled on the bag in black marker, "From POTUS—Chew slowly."

power base A politician's foundation of support, usually his home district or state.

A favorite axiom of Democrat Jim Farley, FDR's Postmaster General and political adviser, was this: "The most important lesson for a politician to learn is that he must always be sure he can carry his own precinct."

De Tocqueville took note of this phenomenon in his *Democracy in America*. In aristocracies, he wrote, a member of the legislature "is rarely in strict dependence on his constituents." But in the United States,

a representative is never sure of his supporters, and, if they forsake him, he is left without a resource.... The seeds of his fortune, therefore, are sown in his own neighborhood; from that nook of earth he must start, to raise himself to command the people and to influence the destinies of the world. Thus it is natural that in democratic countries the members of political assemblies should think more of their constituents than of their party, while in aristocracies they think more of their party than of their constituents.

The importance of preserving this base of power has other effects. "There is nothing quite like a Curley or Hague or Crump or even a De Sapio in other countries that have well-developed party systems," wrote Clinton Rossiter in 1960 in *Parties and Politics in America*. "To be a real boss, and not just a flunky, a politician must have his own base of power and immunity from external discipline, if not from internal revolt."

Not even presidents are immune from this requirement. Charles Hurd, in *When the New Deal Was Young and Gay*, notes that "all Presidents have had permanent residences that they maintained during their periods in office, partly out of sentiment and partly in order to maintain political 'roots.' "

The term *pissing post* is occasionally used to refer to one's power base, or home district, or political *pied-à-terre*. The author's attention was drawn to this phrase by Professor Edward Banfield of Harvard, who reported its use in Cook County, Illinois, as a "trivial base."

A surprise loss in his home district in Greenwich Village to Ed Koch (later Mayor of New York) toppled Tammany leader Carmine De Sapio from his position as the most powerful Democrat in New York State. For a method of maintaining communications in one's power base, see FENCE MENDING; BACKER. For the clip of this phrase that is in rampant current use, see BASE.

power behind the throne Unofficial adviser of great influence; used to attack an administration when the President is popular.

William Pitt the Elder coined it in 1770: "there is something behind the throne greater than the King himself." Black (then *negro*, not yet capitalized) leader Frederick Douglass echoed it toward the end of the Civil War, but in a benevolent sense: "we are not to be saved by the captain, at this time, but by the crew. We are not to be saved by Abraham Lincoln, but by the power behind the throne, greater than throne itself."

Woodrow Wilson had his Colonel Edward House, FDR his Louis Howe and later Harry Hopkins, Eisenhower his Sherman Adams, Clinton his Hillary, Bush the younger his Karl Rove. In modern usage, GOVERNMENT

BY CRONY and KITCHEN CABINET are mildest in terms of extralegal influence; *power behind the throne* is more severe, PALACE GUARD and GRAY EMINENCE more sinister, RUSTLING BEHIND THE JALOUSIES indicative of womanly influence, and *Svengali* or *Rasputin* imply complete control from behind the scenes.

power brokers Those who control a bloc and can DELIVER its support; or, middlemen trusted by disparate forces who can help bring about a coalition.

Though the president of the U.S. may exercise great power, he "is endowed with far greater responsibility than authority," wrote Douglass Cater in *Power in Washington*. "To make his office operable, the President often finds himself serving as broker among the power groups rather than as banker drawing on his own limited reserves of power."

Broker is from Old North French *brokeor*, or broacher, "one who taps wine casks (in order to sell the wine at retail)." The broker eventually turned into a middleman, handling anything from marriages to mutual funds.

Bismarck was known as the "honest broker" at the Berlin Conference of 1878 after the Russo-Turkish War because all the powers involved won new territories except Germany. But the German Chancellor had achieved an important objective for Germany: the continued isolation of France. At the turn of the century Senator Nelson Aldrich, the Rhode Island Republican, was known as "Morgan's floor broker in the Senate."

During his mayoral campaign and often after he was elected, former Republican John Lindsay spoke scornfully, and often despairingly, of the *power brokers* (a phrase coined and popularized by Theodore White in his series of making-of-the-president books) who ran New York behind the scenes. A less detrimental reference appeared in *Newsweek* magazine in 1967. Discussing how critics of the Vietnam war boycotted a 1965 art festival sponsored by the White House, the magazine quoted an anonymous Johnson Administration official: "Presidents deal with power. Power is real. Power is not pretty. And I guess these people don't understand power brokers like they do art brokers."

The collocation was further sealed in the political lexicon in 1974 as the title of Robert Caro's Pulitzer Prize–winning biography of New York's Robert Moses. Such brokerage as does go on takes place in the *corridors of power*, evoking images of transactions made while walking to and from the *center of power*. British novelist C. P. Snow coined the "corridors" in a 1956 novel called *Homecomings* and used the phrase as the title of a later novel. In his pursuit of the 2008 GOP presidential nomination, former Arkansas governor Mike Huckabee charged that "the Wall street-to-Washington axis, *this corridor of power*, is absolutely, frantically against me." That recalled Bill Clinton's first speech from the Oval Office in 1993 lambasting "those who profited from the status quo. ... Many have already lined the corridors of power with high-priced lobbyists."

Teddy White's coinage continues to be used, in international contexts as well. When the Shiite parliamentary leader Abdul Aziz al-Hakim visited the White House in December of 2006, CBS reported: "President Bush told a key Iraqi power broker that he is not satisfied with the progress of efforts to stop the sharp escalation of violence."

power corrupts A charge usually made by Outs against Ins to persuade voters that it's TIME FOR A CHANGE.

In a speech in the House of Lords in 1770, William Pitt the Elder declared: "Unlimited power is apt to corrupt the minds of those who possess it." That observation, while possibly original, did not quite sing. Sir John Acton later amended it to the more forceful: "Power tends to corrupt; absolute power corrupts absolutely." In loose quotation, the Acton qualifiers tend to be removed absolutely, leaving only "power corrupts."

Lord Acton's famous maxim was quoted frequently when Franklin Roosevelt was being chided for trying to pack the Supreme Court. (See NINE OLD MEN.) John F. Kennedy also touched on the idea; honoring Robert Frost at Amherst College in October 1963,

President Kennedy said: "When power leads man toward arrogance, poetry reminds him of his limitations. When power narrows the area of man's concern, poetry reminds him of the richness and diversity of existence. When power corrupts, poetry cleanses."

Some see politics as an inevitable sullier of souls. In a 1945 essay on "The Evil of Politics and the Ethics of Evil," Hans Morgenthau wrote: "Only the greatest dissenters of the age have been clearly aware of this necessary evilness of the political act. A great non-liberal thinker writing in the liberal age, such as Lord Acton, will find that 'power corrupts ... absolute power corrupts absolutely,' or he will, like Jacob Burckhardt, see in politics the 'absolute evil'; or, like Emerson, in force 'a practical lie' and corruption in every state."

Others have been less gloomy. "Power does not corrupt men," George Bernard Shaw wrote. "Fools, however, if they get in a position of power, corrupt power." In *The Short Reign of Pippin IV*, novelist John Steinbeck wrote: "The King said: 'Power does not corrupt. Fear corrupts, perhaps the fear of a loss of power.'" See ARROGANCE OF POWER.

power curve The speeded-up, forced march of events, requiring leadership to keep up or be trampled on; the onrushing flow of the news.

To be *behind the power curve* is to risk crashing; to be *ahead (or in front) of the power curve* is to be on top of the situation or in control of events.

In early 1977, an aide to Jimmy Carter used the negative phrase to refer to a colleague uninformed about the latest decisions: "He's behind the power curve on this." In 1980, the campaigning George H.W. Bush told a *Time* reporter, who'd asked him about his low ratings, "You're behind the power curve. You haven't been to Iowa with me, or across the top of New Hampshire to see the improvement."

Asked in 2005 about the U.N. investigation into the murder of former Lebanese prime minister Rafiq Hariri, Syrian president Bashar Assad promised that the killer would be punished as a traitor. Columnist

David Ignatius wrote, "That sounds like a man trying to get ahead of the power curve."

Although the term has been used since the 1930s as a statistics-graph test for alternatives, the political use of *power curve* is based on the related aeronautics usage (see PUSHING THE ENVELOPE). Curves developed by mathematicians and engineers were used to indicate the performance limits of an aircraft, representing its speed, altitude, and other factors. In 1975, *Aviation Week and Space Technology* reported on "a STOL aircraft's tendency to operate on the back side of the power curve."

Aeronautics still uses the phrase. In 1993, the *Houston Chronicle* quoted Eugene Kranz, director of mission operations for the Johnson Space Center: "The hardware is moving from design to development and test. We have to stay ahead of the power curve."

power elite A charge that there exists an interlocking directorate of moneymen, politicians, and military men who shape national policy no matter who is elected.

The phrase was the title of a 1956 book by sociologist C. Wright Mills, who held that "neither professional party politicians, nor professional bureaucrats are now at the centers of decision. These centers are occupied by the political directorate of the power elite." Mills said this elite was composed of the "political directorate," the "corporate rich," and the "ascendant military," who formed "over-lapping cliques [which] share decisions having at least national consequences. Insofar as national events are decided, the power elite are those who decide them."

Journalist (later presidential aide) Douglass Cater disagreed, calling Mills's theory "too pat to be convincing." He argued that "it would be difficult to document the thesis that an elite really rules on matters of national consequence ... the growth of giant organizations has not brought cumulatively greater power to the individuals who head them.... The swaggering tycoons of business and labor unions no longer exist to dictate their demands to the subservient politicians.... Mills' concept of a sinister and cynical power elite hardly seems applicable to decision-making in Washington today."

As Mills argued in the '50s that a power elite kept intellectuals and liberals out of the decision-making process, conservative journalist William F. Buckley Jr. was arguing that an "establishment" of intellectuals and liberal politicians was freezing out the prudent, businesslike conservative who understood the American system best.

Mills's theory received an unexpected boost from Dwight Eisenhower in his farewell address. See MILITARY-INDUSTRIAL COMPLEX.

Elite, from the French for "(that which is) chosen," has always referred to the socially select; in this sense, it was widely popularized by a radio program of the '30s and '40s, *Duffy's Tavern,* "where de elite meet t'eat." The *intellectual elite,* as broadcaster "Tex" McCrary used to say, "looks down on the power elite with the utmost envy." The *jet set* and *Beautiful People* phrases are passé, though the *glitterati,* decked out in *bling,* sometimes meet on press junkets. The *mandarinate* is no longer used; much power in Congress is in the hands of the appropriations *cardinals.* The *media elite* have been demoted to the *mainstream media,* though *media biggie* still waggishly describes the potentates of punditry.

See ELITISM.

power grab Attempt to assume authority, or to jockey for new control; in extreme cases, a prelude to a coup; an attack phrase on insurgents.

This is a curious collocation because those who denounce a *power grab* do not call themselves *power holders* from whom power is grabbed. Consequently, it is most often used by supporters once removed from the seat of power, with the implication that the reason the insurgents want power is not for the opportunity to render public service, but to have it for power's sake or to use it for their own selfish ends.

The phrase, along with CARPETBAGGER, was used often against Robert Kennedy in his successful campaign against incumbent

Senator Kenneth Keating in 1964. Since both candidates were liberals, there was little ideological argument; Keating, to overcome Kennedy's fame and name, played on his opponent's reputation for ruthlessness. This particular thrust reached its high, or low, point when a small boy appeared at a Kennedy rally carrying a sign: "Don't use *me* in your cynical power grab."

Grab is a classic political Americanism. The opponents of the Embargo Act of 1807 spelled the word backwards and called it the "O Grab Me" Act, because they felt it favored the agricultural interests of the South over the shipping and commercial interests of New England. Railroad tycoons were attacked as *land grabbers* for the way they bought valuable land from the government at low prices, often by laying original track in serpentine patterns to pick up added acreage.

The *salary grab* was the best-known use of the word before *power grab.* Congress in 1873 raised the president's salary from $25,000 to $50,000, gave raises to many other federal officials and judges, and increased a congressman's own draw from $5,000 to $7,500. This might have gone through with mild public criticism had not the raises been made retroactive to the start of the Congress then sitting. The "salary grab" became an issue, and the next Congress cut back all salaries except those of the president and Supreme Court.

The venerable usage is current. When the new Speaker of the House, Nancy Pelosi, led a delegation of Democrats to the Middle East in 2007 despite the disapproval of the Bush Administration, many Republicans believed she was exceeding her authority by trying to conduct foreign affairs, traditionally a province of the president. A column in the conservative *Washington Times* was headlined "Pelosi's Power Grab," and the columnist, Barry Casselman, concluded, "Who's in charge of the executive branch? The speaker or the president of the United States? The only way to settle it is to impeach the imposter, whoever she or he may be."

powerhouse Place of influence or action.

In New York City, "The Powerhouse" was a nickname of the Catholic Archdiocese of New York, in recognition of the political and economic power inherent in the Church.

In an article on the Archdiocese in the *World Journal Tribune* in 1967, just before that newspaper's demise, the Church leadership was described as operating "out of the south wing of the old Whitelaw Reid mansion on the east side of Madison Avenue between 50th and 51st Streets...The press and some laymen refer knowingly to the Archdiocesan Chancery offices as *The Powerhouse*. The clergy, and others who have business there, call it simply 'Madison Avenue.'"

In a more general sense, the word is used to describe a place of action and turbulence. "Originally installed in the predominantly feminine East Wing," wrote the *New York Times Magazine* of the shifting position of the INTELLECTUAL-IN-RESIDENCE at the White House, "[John P.] Roche took just two months to become the first academic in recent White House history to be allowed into the powerhouse setting of the West Wing." In the Clinton Administration, First Lady Hillary Rodham Clinton chose to work in the West Wing's "powerhouse setting."

power to tax ...the power to destroy.

"An unlimited power to tax involves, necessarily, the power to destroy," argued Daniel Webster before the U.S. Supreme Court in 1819. The case was the landmark *McCullough v. Maryland*, when the state of Maryland sought to tax a branch of the new Bank of the United States. The issue was federal supremacy of the young nation's monetary system, which sought to curtail the issuance of currency by state banks.

Chief Justice John Marshall, writing the Court's decision, agreed "that the power to tax involves the power to destroy; that the power to destroy may defeat and render useless the power to create... [the states] have no power, by taxation or otherwise, to retard, impede, burden or in any manner control the operations of the constitutional laws enacted by Congress." The classic phrase is usually attributed to Marshall rather than Webster in a miscarriage

of coinage. In another decision in 1930, Justice Oliver Wendell Holmes wrote: "The power to tax is not the power to destroy while this court sits."

The phrase has current usage in attacks on the very institution it originally defended: the federal government and its tax policies. Arguing against a federal tax increase for 1967, economist Pierre Rinfret said: "The power to tax is the power to destroy, and a tax increase at this time would destroy our economic growth." SUPPLY-SIDE economists in the 1980s took the position that any tax increase damaged economic growth.

power to the people Slogan of dissident groups, especially the Black Panthers in the '60s.

"All power to the Soviets!" was a battle cry of the Bolsheviks during the Russian Revolution. In the 1960s, advocates of "participatory democracy" like Tom Hayden of Students for a Democratic Society were calling for a transfer of power to the "people," whom they were able to identify as themselves. Power became a vogue word of the civil rights movement (see BLACK POWER), later parodied as Irish Power and ultimately, for elderly people, Geezer Power.

"Power to the People!" shouted with clenched fist raised in a mock fascist salute, was publicized as a Black Panther slogan at a meeting under the leadership of Bobby Seale in Oakland, California, on July 19, 1969. Earl Caldwell of *The New York Times* reported:

> They came with long hair and in faded old Army field jackets, in bulky sweaters and in worn and ragged levis. Most of them were white; some were youthful hippies. The majority were students, and they came off the campuses fired with what they called revolutionary fervor. "Power to the people," they shouted. "Power to the people." They made it a chant and they used it again and again. When they did, their arms shot into the air with their fists clenched.

Slightly modified, the slogan reemerged in Asia. "That phrase was adopted by Cory Aquino in the Philippines," wrote Jack Cushman, "when she courageously stepped in after her husband's assassination in 1983. I still have a yellow (Laban Party color) T-shirt emblazoned with people power and another with a picture of a tank with a flower in the barrel."

In 2004, standing in Kiev's frigid Independence Square and making a political statement with an orange scarf around her neck, the 16-year-old Tatiana Fedurchuk said of the "Orange Revolution" reversing a fraudulent election in Ukraine: "This is a victory for people power."

practical politics To some, a euphemism for cynical or dishonest dealing; to others, a coming to grips with the reality of people's prejudices and foibles.

"Practical politics," wrote historian Henry Adams in 1906, "consists in ignoring facts." The phrase was in current use at the time, having been popularized by British Prime Minister Gladstone in his "bag and baggage" speech of 1877, dismissing the Turks as "out of the range of practical politics." Before that, Richard Steele wrote in a 1709 *Tatler*: "He can … distinguish between Chimærical and Practical Politicks."

A century before Gladstone, Edmund Burke's letter to the Sheriffs of Bristol made a case for practicality in politics: "I was persuaded that government was a practical thing, made for the happiness of mankind, and not to furnish out a spectacle of uniformity to gratify the schemes of visionary politicians. Our business was to rule, not to wrangle; and it would have been a poor compensation that we had triumphed in a dispute, whilst we lost an empire."

Thomas Jefferson, a student of Burke, surprised his friends with his willingness to occasionally set idealism firmly aside. "What is practicable must often control what is pure theory, and the habits of the governed determine in a great degree what is practicable." He considered his own Louisiana Purchase unconstitutional, but he told Congress the agreement with Napoleon must be ratified, "casting behind them Metaphysical subtleties."

The dual meaning of the phrase was evident in 1890, when Charles Ledyard Norton defined *practical politics* in *Political Americanisms*: "The minor details of party management, including practises that are corrupt and criminal, as well as those that are legitimate and honorable. The phrase in this sense was in common colloquial use in 1875."

Theodore Roosevelt, fighting his protégé, President William Howard Taft, for the Republican nomination in 1912, was offered a deal on delegates that might have won him the nomination, but he turned it down unless all "stolen" delegates were purged. See THOU SHALT NOT STEAL. After Taft had won, the former president was asked why he had been so rigid. The reply defined a practical politician as applying to one who might cut a few corners but who would not do anything basically dishonest: "Yes, I am a practical politician," said Roosevelt, "and I have played the game. But that was something different. … It had gone far beyond the mere question of expediency or political shrewdness. It was a fundamental question of morality."

Teddy's cousin Franklin Roosevelt was often accused of compromising his ideals and gave this Lincoln example to a group of young people questioning him about it: "Lincoln was one of those unfortunate people called a 'politician' but he was a politician who was practical enough to get a great many things for this country. He was a sad man because he couldn't get it all at once. And nobody can." FDR was also fond of quoting Grover Cleveland's practical remark: "We are faced with a condition and not a theory."

In the Eisenhower years, the word *practical* was used for "cynical," though it fell short of "dishonest." In his memoirs, Eisenhower told of the amazement of party leaders when he told them he was determined to redeem every one of the 1952 Republican platform's provisions. "More than once I was to hear this view derided by 'practical politicians' who laughed off platforms as traps to catch voters. But whenever they expressed these cynical conclusions to me, they invariably encountered a rebuff that left them a bit embarrassed."

Correspondent Arthur Krock, after the election of the Kennedy-Johnson ticket in 1960, used the word in the same sense as Eisenhower had used it: "Rarely had there been an instance of more cynical 'practical' politics than the choice of Johnson to run on a platform pledging him to major policies and legislation he has steadfastly opposed."

Ever since the Kennedy years, *pragmatic* has been used by political leaders who thought of themselves as "problem-solvers." Although is rooted in "affairs of state," its meaning became close to "practical" with a modern flavor, and is now lodged between *dogmatic* and *principled*.

See REALPOLITIK.

prairie fire See WHIRLWIND CAMPAIGN; DISASTER METAPHORS.

pranks See HARDBALL; DIRTY TRICKS.

praxis See REVOLUTIONARY PRAXIS.

prebuttal A rebuttal to a speech not yet given; a preemptive response.

Al Gore has been credited with the coinage of *prebuttal* early in the 1996 presidential campaign. In an article on the "Clinton the War Room" (see WAR ROOM), Dan Balz wrote in *The Washington Post*: "President Clinton's White House and campaign team have been drawing favorable reviews for their rapid response operation and penchant for picking off issues before Senate Majority Leader [and Republican presidential candidate] Robert J. Dole ... even gets his TelePrompTer warmed up. Vice President Gore calls it 'prebuttal.'"

In an age of ever-shortening news cycles, the tactic, and the term, quickly caught on. Referring to an instant poll, or "prepoll," just before President George W. Bush's 2003 State of the Union address, columnist Ellen Goodman of the *Boston Globe* noted: "Prepoll is a word that I invented to match prebuttal, the word just created to describe a reply to a speech that hasn't yet been delivered."

The usefulness of *prebuttal* also was recognized across the Atlantic. The *Yorkshire* (U.K.) *Post* in 2001: "So it was off to the Conservative Central Office yesterday for a New Labour-style 'prebuttal' on next week's Pre-Budget Report statement from Gordon Brown."

The new word—rooted in the Old French *bouter*, "to strike or thrust"—in turn inspired variants of its own, as observed in *The Denver Post* in 2004: "Opponents this year are tenaciously rebutting candidates' speeches and positions even before they are uttered. 'We call it the "prebut,"' said Jennifer Duffy, an analyst with the Cook Political Report.... Another tactic is a response to comments that weren't made. Call it the postbuttal."

Prebuttals today come fast and furious. Pres. George W. Bush's speech on Jan. 10, 2007, announcing a troop "surge," or escalation, in Iraq, was preceded by a wave of *prebuttals*. First, Sen. Ted Kennedy (D-Mass.) *prebutted* the president's address, then White House Bush counselor Dan Bartlett rebutted Kennedy. *The Washington Post*'s Dana Milbank recapped the ensuing sequence:

> Kennedy ... scheduled a news conference in the Senate press gallery to rebut Bartlett's rebuttal of Kennedy's prebuttal. By then, however, the prebuttals were everywhere.
>
> Senator majority leader Harry Reid (D-Nev.) alone issued three written prebuttals of the Bush speech and one orally in the White House driveway. ...
>
> Sen. Robert Menendez (D-N.J.) ... announced that he was issuing his prebuttal in the form of a "radio actuality and a direct-to-camera interview." Rep. Louise Slaughter (D-N.Y.) also offered an "audio" option with her written prebuttal. Sen. Gordon Smith (R-Ore.) was busy prebutting Bush on MSNBC, while Sen. Sam Brownback (R-Kan.) released his prebuttal from Baghdad.

The White House, fearing it was losing the battle to the *prebutters*, scheduled a briefing in advance of the president's speech. Thus, the preemptive pre-prebuttals created a time warp, in effect, in which the president ordered his aides to preempt him.

The "buttal war" shows no signs of deescalation. The expectation of a prebuttal often forces the speechmaker to anticipate the counterarguments likely to be made before the speech, and to send supporters to talk shows and blogs to preempt the preempters. In the case of the Bush speech cited above, which was entitled "The Way

Forward in Iraq," the *Post* headline was "'Prebutters' Ensure Debate Over 'Way Forward' is Backward."

The new word is part of a prefixation vogue. In law enforcement, *reactive* spawned *proactive*; in Hollywood, *sequel* led to *prequel*. As the motto from Shakespeare's *The Tempest* and favored by historians reads, "What's past is prologue."

precinct captain A local commander of political TROOPS, equivalent to a sergeant in an infantry platoon; one who is called on to DELIVER the vote.

"In the old Tammany days," writes former Tammany leader Ed Costikyan, "a political captaincy was a much-prized honor.... Such a captain...would build up a following among his voters loyal to both his party, his leader, and to him. Ultimately several hundred people would follow his direction on election day, and vote for whichever candidates he told them to."

While the position still carries some local respect, the function has changed. The captain's job now calls for education and persuasion of voters by precinct leaders and their canvassers (see CANVASS) who might not be well acquainted with their target voters. With the welfare function of the local political organization taken over by the government, the captain's service function has been reduced to steering constituents through the maze of government machinery to get "what you might not realize you're entitled to."

With voters increasingly concerned with the campaigns for major office that they see, hear, and read about in mass media, the precinct captain's job is to point out the importance of local campaigns for minor offices, on websites and by email, using the "top of the ticket" to help the rest of the party's slate.

Many political leaders at the top level recognize the importance of providing COATTAILS for local precinct workers to cling to, in return for turning out the vote for the major candidate on Election Day. That was why Mayor Edward Kelly of Chicago said in 1940: "Roosevelt is the greatest precinct captain I've ever known. He's made

the job of our workers easy." (See HYMIE'S FERRYBOAT.)

preemptive strike See PREVENTIVE WAR.

preference poll See TRIAL HEAT.

presence Diplomatic word for "showing the flag"; particularly, a United Nations force on the scene to avert or end hostilities.

Traditionally, a great power would send a naval squadron to a trouble spot within its SPHERE OF INFLUENCE to remind the locals of the power the squadron symbolized. This is now considered heavy-handed. Modern diplomacy requires the dispatch of military advisers or an economic mission to establish a *presence* underscoring the power's commitment in the area. A specific *military presence* differs from the old-fashioned *showing the flag* by the continuity of the assignment—an extended stay rather than a brief display.

The usage has a United Nations origin. In November of 1958, British troops left Jordan; despite inter-Arab "good neighbor" pledges, King Hussein's country was not expected to remain independent. U.N. Secretary-General Dag Hammarskjöld sent a thirty-man mission to Jordan headed by Pier Spinelli, Italian chief of the U.N. European office in Geneva. Spinelli's mission established what came to be called "U.N. presence" in Amman, Jordan, providing a steadying effect in the area by virtue of evidence of continuing U.N. interest.

Wrote Andrew Boyd of *The Economist*: "Hammarskjöld also proposed to appoint a 'high-level' representative at U.N. headquarters who could visit the various Arab countries as required for 'diplomatic actions.' But this official (at once nicknamed 'the absent presence') was never appointed; the Secretary-General found things going smoothly enough to dispense with the idea."

The U.N. presence was applied to all U.N. peacekeeping efforts "in the field" as in the Congo and the Gaza Strip. The idea was to keep the great powers out of small wars that could, with Soviet or U.S. intervention, become world wars. When Secretary-General U Thant quickly acceded to Egyptian demand for the withdrawal of the U.N. force in 1967, he was sharply criticized in the aftermath of the Arab-Israeli conflict.

By that time the usage had spread to non-U.N. bodies. The U.S. Sixth Fleet in the Mediterranean was "the U.S. presence" and the British Colony at Hong Kong was called "the threatened Western presence on China's border." But a part of the word's effectiveness is its vagueness—a presence can be a visiting diplomat, an aircraft carrier, a permanent military base, or a force of troops. Hammarskjöld, author of the idea, liked the flexibility of the term and insisted on what he called "a completely pragmatic" view: "There is a U.N. presence wherever the U.N. is present."

Presidential bug A mythical insect whose bite results in PRESIDENTIAL FEVER; breeds best where the opposition has been swamped, or in an atmosphere charged with power.

The phrase may have originated with Abraham Lincoln's "chin fly" story, told to Henry Raymond, editor of *The New York Times*. Lincoln's Treasury Secretary, Salmon P. Chase, was often critical of the President because, it was widely believed, he wanted the top job himself. Raymond quoted Lincoln:

> you were brought up on a farm, were you not? Then you know what a chin fly is. My brother and I…were once plowing corn on a Kentucky farm, I was driving the horse, and he holding the plough. The horse was lazy but on one occasion rushed across the field so that I, with my long legs, could scarcely keep pace with him. On reaching the end of the furrow, I found an enormous chin fly fastened upon him, and knocked him off. My brother asked me what I did that for. I told him I didn't want the old horse bitten in that way. "Why," said my brother, "that's all that made him go!" Now if Mr. C[hase] has a presidential chin fly biting him. I'm not going to knock him off, if it will only make his department go.

The only trouble with this story is that Lincoln's brother died before young Abe was old enough to plow. Maybe Lincoln was exaggerating. See POTOMAC FEVER; ITCH TO RUN.

Presidential fever A raging desire for the top job, accompanied by the "sweating out" of delegates' decisions.

New York Governor Al Smith said in 1924: "A plague on all individuals who would like to be president!" This particular plague is called *presidential fever*, and was so termed at least as far back as 1858, when abolitionist clergyman Theodore Parker wrote: "The Land Fever is more contagious than the Presidential Fever, and equally fatal to the moral powers."

Leading up to his final SHERMAN STATEMENT, General William Tecumseh Sherman said in 1879: "I am not now, and do not intend to get, infected with the presidential fever." Five years later he phrased it slightly differently, as "infested with the poison of presidential aspiration."

In 1879, in tandem with Sherman, Republican James Garfield of Ohio was feverishly making notes in his diary. On February 8: "I have so long and so often seen the evil effect of the Presidential fever upon my associates and friends that I am determined it shall not seize me. In almost every case it impairs if it does not destroy the usefulness of its victim." The following April, two months before the convention: "I long ago made the resolution that I would never permit the Presidential fever to get lodgment in my brain. I think it is the one office a man should not set his heart upon." When Grant and Blaine were deadlocked, Garfield's name came up, the fever rose, and he became the twentieth president.

Presidential initials See INITIALS, PRESIDENTIAL.

Presidential seal See BALD EAGLE.

Presidential timber See TIMBER, PRESIDENTIAL.

President of all the people The expressed desire of presidents, especially after a divisive campaign, to represent a unified nation, not limited to any blocs, groups, or partisans that elected them.

It should go without saying that the President of the United States, as chief of state, is president of all the people, including those in opposition or who did not vote at all. Yet there is a nagging doubt in the minds of most presidents that they do indeed lead everybody; this concern has led each president to press the idea and many to express it in the phrase.

The first president to use it in the now familiar way was James K. Polk, in his 1845 inaugural address: "Although in our country the Chief Magistrate must almost of necessity be chosen by a party and stand pledged to its principles and measures, yet in his official action he should not be the President of a part only, but of the whole people of the United States." Since the idea was not to extend authority over those who did not vote for him, but to recognize and show respect for the right to dissent, Polk added eloquently: "He should not be unmindful that our fellow-citizens who have differed with him in opinion are entitled to the full and free exercise of their opinions and judgments, and that the rights of all are entitled to respect and regard."

The publicist Herbert Bayard Swope wrote Franklin Roosevelt in 1936 that his strategy should be "to be firm without being ferocious; to be kindly rather than cold; to be hopeful instead of pessimistic; to be human rather than to be economic; to be insistent upon every man having a chance, and above all, to make yourself appear to be the President of *all* the people …"

President Harry Truman, like Polk, used "whole people" rather than "all the people": "As the President came to be elected by the whole people, he became responsible to the whole people. I used to say the only lobbyist the whole people had in Washington was the President of the United States."

Dwight Eisenhower used the phrase in his memoirs: "The man in the White House, I believe, should think of himself as President of all the people."

Eisenhower succeeded more than most in achieving a recognition of leadership by almost all Americans. Arthur Schlesinger, Jr., wrote about Eisenhower's successor, John Fitzgerald Kennedy: "it seemed that Kennedy suffered from the illusion so common to new Presidents (even Roosevelt had it till 1935) that he, unlike any of his predecessors, could really be President of all the people and achieve his purpose without pain or trauma …"

President Kennedy, however, took the idea a step forward: "For each President, we must remember, is the President not only of all who live, but, in a very real sense, of all who have yet to live. His responsibility is not only to those who elected him but also to those who will elect his successors for decades to come."

Lyndon Baines Johnson, who sought to become identified with the term CONSENSUS, used the phrase in 1964 and again often: "As long as I am President, this Government will not set one group against another—but will build a creative partnership between business and labor, farm areas and urban centers, consumer and producer. This is what I mean when I choose to be a President of all the people." (A joke during the 1964 campaign was: "If Johnson loses more than eight states, he will refuse to serve because he wants to be 'President of all the people.'")

In the mid-'60s, as Lyndon Johnson's popularity fell, a related phrase came to the fore: the "only president we've got," from a frequent remark along those lines by Johnson. In the '70s, when former Director of Central Intelligence Richard Helms said, "I have one president at a time. I only work for you," the single-president theme was accentuated.

President Polk's phrase has traveled. After a close, hard-fought campaign between left and right in France in 2007, Nicolas Sarkozy, the son of Hungarian immigrants elected president, took care to point out that his was not a victory of one France against another: "I will be the president of all the French."

pressing the flesh Handshaking; physical contact between candidate and voter from gentle squeezing of the arm to an all-out hug.

The phrase, which first appeared in 1918, was politically popularized by Lyndon Johnson in 1960. "I just want to tell you how happy I am that you would come here and howdy and shake hands with us this morning," the vice-presidential candidate told small crowds at whistlestops. "You make us feel so wonderful to come out here and look us in the eye and give us a chance to press the flesh with you."

In that Kennedy-Johnson presidential campaign, a pickpocket in a Los Angeles crowd was reported to have groped inexpertly for someone's wallet and found himself, instead, shaking the hand of the Democratic candidate for president. John F. Kennedy's grandfather, "Honey Fitz" Fitzgerald, was supposed to have perfected the art of the "Irish Switch": a technique of shaking one voter's hand while talking to a second voter, simultaneously smiling and winking at a third.

G. Mennen "Soapy" Williams, running for governor of Michigan, felt it was necessary to grasp the hands of at least two thousand voters a day. A *Detroit Free Press* reporter chronicled his method of working an auto plant in Flint at the time of a shift change, with hundreds of men streaming in and out:

> Williams was standing in a familiar position, straddling the two stairways the men must take for entering the plant. Perhaps one man in 75 would try to slip by the Governor without shaking his hand. He couldn't get away with it. Williams would quickly spot him veering away and give chase. Two or three quick steps and his long legs would be planted firmly in the man's path. He would reach out, grab the man's hand, pump it once and say: "Nice to see you." Then he would smile proudly and step back in front of the two staircases, one foot blocking each.

Senator William Proxmire of Wisconsin, who estimated that he shook approximately 300,000 hands a year, had a formula for avoiding "politician's grip": Avert knuckle-crunching by shoving your hand into the voter's hand right up against the thumb. President Harry Truman's receiving-line technique was to use the handshake to pull the guest along and deposit him with the next person on the line.

Politicians agree that *pressing the flesh* requires concentration on the crowd, even when "Irish Switching." Wendell Willkie broke this rule while campaigning in Rushville, Indiana, in 1940, and absent-mindedly shook hands with his own wife. When she protested, he apologized: "Gosh, Billie. Excuse me, I was thinking."

Senator Robert Kennedy often leaned across a platform and reached out with both hands to touch the outstretched hands, thereby covering more people than individual handshakes; Governor Nelson Rockefeller liked to backslap and squeeze arms with his familiar "Hiya, fella" and millionaire-mocking "Thanks a thousand."

In an era of television campaigning, the necessity of physical contact is still with us; white candidates in black areas are especially told by their managers of the need to "press the flesh" and "lay on the hands" so as not to appear unwilling to be in close touch. In the Clinton-Gore Administration, flesh-pressing escalated to bear-hugging. George W. Bush, walking down the aisle of the House of Representatives on his way to give the State of Union address, stopped to handshake, touch, and gently punch the shoulders of many political figures; a picture of him embracing Democratic Senator Joe Lieberman, captioned "the Kiss," was used against the senator in a 2006 primary challenge.

George Washington, as general and president, made clear to all that he did not want anybody to touch him.

press secretary See GHOSTWRITER.

pressure group Attack phrase on a lobbying organization or bloc advancing its own cause.

Political parties gain broad power over short periods; pressure groups seek narrow power over long periods. Just as organized labor "punishes its enemies and rewards its friends," *pressure groups* work inside the political system to promote their causes on a continuing basis no matter who is in power. The origin and usage of the term are explained in a 1924 issue of the *Nebraska State Journal* (cited in the March 2007 revision of the *OED*): "Wayne B. Wheeler, general counsel of the anti-saloon league, is credited with coining the expressive term of 'pressure groups' in connection with national legislation and the formation of public opinion. A 'pressure group' is made up of a larger or smaller body of citizens who know exactly what they want and have enough energy to press their claims."

James Madison, in *The Federalist* Number 10, defined *faction* as we now use *pressure group*: "a number of citizens, whether amounting to a majority or minority of the whole, who are united and actuated by some common impulse of passion, or of interest, adverse to the rights of other citizens, or to the permanent and aggregate interests of the community."

Although in Madison's view factions could operate for good or evil, the phrase *pressure group* has a bad connotation. Dwight Eisenhower, describing Henry Cabot Lodge's plea to him to campaign for President in 1952, said the former senator painted the possibility of "at least a partial reversal of the trend toward centralization in government, irresponsible spending, and catering to pressure groups …"

The common denominator in any definition of pressure groups is *interest*; if the interest is *special* or *vested*, the pressure is imputed to be selfish or even venal, but if the interest is *public*, the pressure is benevolent. "We call them 'interest groups' when we are feeling clinical," wrote historian Clinton Rossiter, "'pressure groups' when we are feeling critical, and 'lobbies' when we are watching them at work in our fifty-one capitals." See VESTED INTERESTS; LOBBY; BLOC.

preventive war An attack aimed at destroying a prospective enemy before he can launch an attack of his own.

On November 20, 1948, pacifist Bertrand Russell approached the subject in this way: "Either we must have a war against Russia before she has the atom bomb," he told an audience at the Westminster School, "or we will have to lie down and let them govern us." Once Moscow acquired nuclear weapons, Lord Russell became more disposed to lying down. See BETTER RED THAN DEAD.

Others have argued for decades that preventive war might be preferable to a devastating sneak attack—presumably from any nation with weapons of mass destruction—in the future. There was some talk of it when mainland China threatened the

offshore islands of Quemoy and Matsu in 1955 and again in 1958. During the Berlin crisis in 1961, John F. Kennedy told an interviewer that "a clear attack on Western Europe" might require the U.S. to use nuclear weapons first. As Theodore Sorensen wrote in *Kennedy*, "others read 'preventive war' or 'preemptive strike' overtones into this, but it was in fact longstanding policy and depended on an initial attack by the Soviets."

In the semanticist Mario Pei's *Language of the Specialists*, Robert E. Hunter noted that a first strike must be directed against enemy nuclear systems or else it will leave the attacker open to terrible retaliation:

> A first-strike strategy might be adopted where an attacker has a vulnerable force, and must strike first (i.e. before being struck) if at all; where an attacker wishes to achieve "victory" through surprise attack, particularly against a strategically inferior nation (preventive war); where an attacker wishes to preempt a threatened enemy attack; or where a strategically inferior nation wishes to bring about catalytic war involving other powers.

Herman Kahn, in *Thinking About the Unthinkable* (see UNTHINKABLE THOUGHTS), noted: "Almost all authorities agree that at present the advantages of striking first are so great that, should there seem to be a high probability that the other side is actually attacking, it might be better to risk the certainty of a relatively small retaliatory strike, rather than the high probability of a much more destructive first blow."

Preventive war is still a phrase looked on with revulsion by most Americans; *preemptive strike*, however, lost much of its pejorative connotation when it was used to describe Israel's thrust against the Arabs following Gamal Abdul Nasser's closing of the Gulf of Aqaba in 1967, and its SURGICAL STRIKE against the Iraqi Osirak nuclear reactor in 1981.

The NATO threat to take military action against the Serbs in Kosovo prevented the necessity of preventive war, but the unforeseen bloody consequences of REGIME CHANGE in Iraq in 2002 soured many on what was derogated as a mistaken "war of choice"; the counterargument was that if the war on terror were not carried aggressively to the enemy in the Mideast, it would have to be fought defensively in the U.S. homeland.

The WAR ON TERROR is a form of preventive war, waged to deny terrorist groups the ability to inflict horrendous casualties, but without a national base they present few specific targets for MASSIVE RETALIATION or a preventive "first strike."

primary An intraparty election to select candidates for a forthcoming general election.

The *closed primary* is restricted to registered members of a particular party. In an *open primary*, voters may cross lines, regardless of their party affiliation, to vote for candidates of another party. See CROSS-OVER VOTE.

Designed to give a party's rank and file a greater voice in the choice of national candidates (and of convention delegates as well), the primary began appearing in the early nineteenth century. H.L. Mencken traces one to New York City in 1827. In the early twentieth century, the presidential-preference primary was launched by the progressive Republicans of the Middle West who wanted to reduce the influence of state party machines in the nomination of candidates. As governor of Wisconsin in 1901, Robert La Follette promoted a direct-primary bill. By 1916 both Republicans and Democrats chose a majority of their national convention delegates by this method. It lost ground for a time, but in the early '70s more states saw political and publicity advantages in holding them.

Their importance was hotly disputed. In 1952 Senator Estes Kefauver of Tennessee won most of the preferential primaries he entered, but Adlai Stevenson won the Democratic nomination nonetheless. Stevenson considered the presidential primary "almost a useless institution." In 1958 he described it as confusing and time-consuming, and added, "Finally, it is terribly expensive; it's exhausting physically; you burn up yourself, you burn up your ammunition, you burn up your means. I think that it's a very, very questionable method of selecting Presidential candidates and actually it

never does. All it does is destroy some candidates." But it did get John F. Kennedy on the road to nomination in 1960, it provides a "shakedown cruise" for a campaign staff, and it settles arguments about vote-getting ability with some finality. By 1976 Jimmy Carter proved that the winner of most of the early primaries could gain an unstoppable momentum for nomination.

After generations in which the primary election in New Hampshire and the caucus system of selecting delegates in Iowa dominated the political landscape in the four or five months before the national conventions, state party organizations in some heavily populated states demanded a larger role in the selection of nominees. In 2006, a race to the front of the line began with New Hampshire making clear it would be first no matter how early on the calendar its polling would have to be. Threats from both the Republican and Democratic national committees to rescind the credentials of some or all of the delegates, or aimed at candidates who campaigned in states in defiance of national committee wishes, met with resistance from legislatures in crucial states like California and Florida. Political scientists, pundits, and fundraisers for long-shot candidates, as well as assorted GOO-GOOS, bewailed the hugely expensive two-year campaign that loomed. The experiment of 2008 could be seen as a new way to test the stamina of candidates and increase the turnout of voters—or as a lesson in the political danger of sustained voter boredom. See CATTLE SHOW; CONVENTION BOUNCE.

priorities See REORDERING PRIORITIES.

privileged sanctuary Base from which attacks can be made without reprisal.

General Douglas MacArthur transferred the phrase from the religious or bird-refuge sense to the military-political in a communiqué, on November 6, 1950, after Chinese Communist "volunteers" entered the Korean war:

> In the face of this victory of United Nations arms the Communists committed one of the most offensive acts of international lawlessness of

historic record by moving without any notice of belligerency elements of alien Communist forces across the Yalu River into North Korea and massing a great concentration of possible reinforcing divisions with adequate supply behind the privileged sanctuary of the adjacent Manchurian border.

Nine days later President Harry Truman stated: "United Nations forces are now being attacked from the safety of a privileged sanctuary."

Since that time, the phrase has appeared in hawkish statements whenever a nonbelligerent provided airfields or supplies for belligerents, where a nation at war could not permit "hot pursuit" by planes or troops without enlarging the war.

The words have been married at least since 1788, when Edward Gibbon wrote *The Decline and Fall of the Roman Empire*: "The ancient privilege of sanctuary was transferred to the Christian temples."

Right of asylum, almost synonymous in one sense, is considerably different in political usage, meaning the protection granted by one state to an individual citizen of another. Oddly, the "right" of asylum is more of a privilege, and the "privilege" of sanctuary is more of a right.

In 1970 President Nixon ordered U.S. troops into Cambodia to counter a North Vietnamese invasion after a pro-Western government overthrew a neutralist regime. Explaining this move to the American people on television, he said: "For the past five years...North Vietnam has occupied military sanctuaries all along the Cambodian frontier with South Vietnam...neither the United States nor South Vietnam has moved against those enemy sanctuaries because we did not wish to violate the territory of a neutral nation."

The operation, which Nixon carefully labeled an "incursion" (signifying "temporary") rather than an "invasion," tacitly approved of by the leaders of Cambodia, caused sharp protests in the U.S. and a major increase in opposition to the war in Vietnam. Anthony Lewis suggested this definition in his column in *The New York Times:* "Privileged sanctuary: Area where the enemy can rest and regroup in safety.

See Laos, Cambodia. Do not see Thailand, Hawaii, or other base and recreation areas for American forces."

privy council See BRAIN TRUST.

probe See WITCH HUNT; WHITEWASH.

problem See NO PROBLEM.

procedural safeguard See RED TAPE.

process, the The majesty of the machinery; the inexorable procedures of government; more broadly, the American way of self-government.

"I realize that, in our democratic process," said Office of Management and Budget Director Bert Lance in July 1977, "government officials at times come under public and political scrutiny. That is part of the process."

Process came into vogue in the mid-'70s, a clipped form of both *democratic process* and DECISION-MAKING PROCESS, the historic *due process* and the nascent PEACE PROCESS, as well as a partial replacement for "the SYSTEM" in its positive sense. A favorite word of the Carter White House, it reflected President Carter's interest in the management of the workings of government. Vice President Walter Mondale, assessing President Carter's first year in office to a group of reporters at the end of 1977, put the best face on the presidential fascination with details down to the scheduling of the tennis court: "Now he has had a year's experience. He has seen this process work first hand. He is anxious that in succeeding years that what he has learned about that process permits him to better schedule and pace his proposals."

Meanwhile, in the office of the Governor of California, an aide described Democrat Edmund "Jerry" Brown's approach to *Washington Post* columnist David Broder, who had been asking about "a core of policy" in Governor Brown's philosophy: "No, I see a particular kind of process reflected in the way the place operates and in the people who are here. He really does want a lot of dialogue. But no consistent philosophy. It drives a lot of people nuts when he quotes Gandhi: 'the means are the ends in process.' Sometimes it drives me nuts, too." See MACHINERY OF GOVERNMENT.

professional An experienced, cool political operative; or in a second sense, one who protests too much his allegiance to a cause.

For the definition of the first sense, see OLD PRO. For the second sense, the adjective turns completely around: a *professional liberal* or *professional intellectual* is one who poses as a liberal or intellectual but does not accept responsibility for the work of promoting a cause.

In the same way, a *professional Irishman* is a politician who cultivates his brogue and acts in such a way as to appear to be the very model of what he thinks other Irish-Americans expect an Irishman to be, in an effort to identify with what may no longer be a voting bloc.

In 1918 Theodore Roosevelt used the derogatory sense as it is used today: "Prominent, although not always powerful, among the latter are the professional intellectuals, who vary from the soft-handed, noisily self-assertive frequenters of frowsy restaurants to the sissy socialists, the pink tea and parlor Bolshevists ..." See PARLOR PINK.

One occasional use of the term today is not political: "professional virgin" is a frustrated suitor's epithet.

In the first sense of *professional*, the antonym is *amateur*; in the second sense, the antonym is *authentic*.

profiles in courage Those who brave ignominy or loss of office by daring to take unpopular positions, in a phrase popularized by a 1955 book of that title by Senator John F. Kennedy.

"Richard Nixon etched his profile in political courage," wrote columnist Murray Kempton in 1966, "by mentioning the word 'Rockefeller' in Syracuse." This was a sardonic comment about Nixon's strong support of Rockefeller's gubernatorial candidacy in what was then a strongly conservative Republican area of upstate New York. But the *profiles in courage* phrase is frequently used without irony (evoking memories of the assassinated President) whenever any act that will offend voters is undertaken by a political figure.

That was the point of Kennedy's analysis of the crucial moment in the lives of eight American politicians, mostly senators: "It may take courage to battle one's President, one's party or the overwhelming sentiment of one's nation; but these do not compare, it seems to me, to the courage required of the Senator defying the angry power of the very constituents who control his future."

This particular point was flung back at Kennedy, who had remained silent on MCCARTHYISM, by Mrs. Eleanor Roosevelt: "I feel that I would hesitate to place the difficult decisions that the next president will have to make with someone who understands what courage is and admires it, but has not quite the independence to have it." After blasts like these, a friend suggested to Kennedy that he had paid a price for giving his book that title. "Yes," he replied, "but I didn't have a chapter in it on myself." See POLITICAL SUICIDE.

progressive A movement of social protest and economic reforms; an adjective now offering an alternative to those reluctant to be labeled LIBERAL.

The late nineteenth century brought the first great progressive surge to the U.S. Russell B. Nye wrote in *Midwestern Progressive Politics*:

> Spreading outward after 1870, diminishing in force as it encountered increased resistance from adjacent and politically different areas, the so-called Midwestern spirit of "progressivism" (or "insurgency" or "radicalism") became a real force in American political life. The Grangers, the Populists, the "progressives," the "insurgents," the Non-Partisan Leaguers, even the Socialists represented phases of this movement.

Progressivism reached high tide in the first decade of the twentieth century. The "Wisconsin idea," a progressive experiment, bore fruit in Robert La Follette's governorship at the beginning of the century. In 1912 the GOP split into progressive and conservative factions, with Theodore Roosevelt in his independent "Bull Moose" campaign leading the progressives.

The word retains its attraction. For a time during and after World War II, it was preempted by the far-left followers of Henry Wallace, but its frequent use by Republicans—especially in the Theodore Roosevelt context—has restored its luster. In a 1948 essay titled "What Is Liberalism?" Earl Warren, Republican, then governor of California and later Chief Justice of the United States, wrote:

> I would divide people into three groups—reactionary, progressive and radical. I particularly like the term "progressive," not necessarily as a party label, but as a conception...It is distinguishable from both reaction and radicalism, because neither of these philosophies makes for real progress. The reactionary, concerned only with his own position, and indifferent to the welfare of others, would resist progress regardless of changed conditions or human need. The radical does not want to see progress because he hopes that our democratic institutions will fail and that he will be able to take over with some form of alien tyranny.

Similarly, President Lyndon Johnson, in a March 16, 1964, interview, said, "I want to be progressive without getting both feet off the ground at the same time.... If I had to place a label on myself, I would want to be a progressive who is prudent." Housing and Urban Development Secretary George Romney said on several occasions: "I'm as conservative as the Constitution, as liberal as Lincoln and as progressive as Theodore Roosevelt."

In 1989, the Progressive Policy Institute was formed, a THINK TANK for liberal-centrist ideas that attracted Governor Bill Clinton and had an impact on the domestic policies of his subsequent presidency. See TRIANGULATION. Former Democratic senator Gary Hart in 1993 described the word *progressive* as "a point not on, but above, the liberal-conservative spectrum." In recent years, liberals unhappy with the label *liberal* have identified themselves as *progressive*.

proletariat The lowest class in society; or, the industrial working class.

From the Latin *proletarius*, a member of the lowest social class in Roman society, the word entered the English language from French in the nineteenth century. The earliest *OED* citation is from an 1847 issue of *The Daguerreotype* (a Boston "magazine of foreign literature and science"): "The proletariat, which has not morally and physically any thing to lose, has allied itself to this revolutionary tendency...[*Note*] This word, which has lately become familiar to all readers of German and French literature, signifies the lowest and poorest classes, those in fact who are totally destitute of property." Karl Marx defined "proletariat" in a critique (written in 1843 but unpublished during his lifetime) of Hegel's *Philosophy of Right*: "It is not the naturally arising poor but the artificially impoverished, not the human masses mechanically oppressed by the gravity of society but the masses resulting from the drastic dissolution of society, mainly of the middle estate, that form the proletariat, although, as is easily understood, the naturally arising poor and the Germanic serfs gradually join its ranks."

Marx's solution to proletarian poverty was never more forthrightly stated than in the conclusion of the *Communist Manifesto*: "The proletarians have nothing to lose but their chains. They have a world to win. Workingmen of all countries unite!" (The last sentence is often translated: "Workers of the world, unite!")

Communist dogma holds that "the dictatorship of the proletariat" lies just beyond bourgeois rule. Returning to Russia in 1917 to prepare for the Bolshevik takeover, Lenin wrote in his April Theses: "The peculiarity of the present moment in Russia consists in the transition from the first stage of the Revolution, which gave power to the bourgeoisie because of the insufficient class-consciousness and organization of the proletariat, to the second stage, which must give power to the proletariat, and the poorer peasantry."

Joseph Stalin described proletarian rule in hard terms: "The dictatorship of the proletariat is the domination of the proletariat over the bourgeoisie, untrammeled by law and based on violence and enjoying the sympathy and support of the toiling and exploited masses."

Walter Lippmann, in a column called "How Liberty is Lost," urged the West in 1938 to avoid creating the conditions for a revolution in the name of the proletariat:

> The greatest evil of the modern world is the reduction of the people to a proletarian level by destroying their savings, by depriving them of private property, by making them the helpless employees of a private monopoly or of government monopoly.... The experience of Europe shows clearly that when a nation becomes proletarian, the result is not, as the Communists taught, a dictatorship by the proletariat but a dictatorship over the proletariat.

Lumpenproletariat, a German word coined by Marx and dressing the lowest class in rags, is occasionally used for emphasis or out of affectation. *Proletarian* is sometimes clipped to *prole,* as in Anthony Burgess's political novel set in a dystopia, *A Clockwork Orange.*

promises See CAMPAIGN ORATORY; PIE IN THE SKY.

propaganda Attack word on an adversary's ideas and publicity techniques.

Your side *disseminates information, deals with the issues, communicates the facts, publicizes the truth, gets the message to the people*; the other side *engages in* PSEUDO-EVENTS, *puffery, deliberate distortion, the* BIG LIE, SMOKE SCREENS, *media hype* and *propaganda.*

In two centuries, the word has traveled from religion to war to politics. The ninth edition of the *Encyclopaedia Britannica* (1875) has an archbishop covering the subject, pointing out its derivation in Pope Gregory XIII's commission of cardinals *de propaganda fide* in the sixteenth century. In *Britannica*'s fourteenth edition (1929), the article concerned itself with war propaganda.

Senator Daniel Webster, speaking about the revolution in Greece in 1824, helped the word enter the political vocabulary in its adjectival form, using the phrase "emanation of a crusading or propagandist spirit." President Millard Fillmore said in 1852 that the founders of the U.S. knew that "it was not possible for this nation to become a 'propagandist' of free principles without

arraying against it the combined powers of Europe."

The religious usage became limited in the nineteenth century, replaced by the political. The English *Fraser's Magazine* in 1844 wrote that "we did not fight to propagandize monarchical principles," and W. T. Brande's 1843 *Dictionary of Science, Literature, and Art* gave a definition that is current: "Derived from this celebrated society [for the propagation of the faith] the name *propaganda* is applied in modern political language as a term of reproach to secret associations for the spread of opinions and principles which are viewed by most governments with horror and aversion."

The transmutation of the word from evangelism to sinister political persuasion is not surprising: the word continues to carry its meaning of persuasion by faith rather than by fact. The sinister connotation was emphasized by books on war propaganda after World War I, with titles like *Atrocity Propaganda 1914–1918* and *Spreading Germs of Hate.*

Nazi Minister of Propaganda Paul Joseph Goebbels, however, raised the word and the art to an instrument of national policy and blackened its name forever. In 1923, he said, "It is the absolute right of the State to supervise the formation of public opinion," and in 1943 wrote in his diary: "Not every item of news should be published: rather must those who control news policies endeavor to make every item of news serve a certain purpose." See MANAGED NEWS.

In the U.S., *white propaganda* meant the selection of favorable items for persuasion, and *black propaganda* (jokingly called "impropaganda") the spreading of lies and false rumors. To dissociate our techniques from those of the Nazis, *psychological warfare* was a useful term. Publicist Leo J. Margolin added "paper bullets" in a book title, a phrase from Shakespeare's *Much Ado About Nothing.* A tried-and untrue technique of black propaganda is *disinformation,* "misinformation deliberately spread."

Despite occasional efforts to insist the word is neutral—that there can be "good" propaganda—current usage is definitely pejorative. Charges of "Communist propaganda" and "imperialist propaganda" were traded for three generations, making this word (because of its Latin root and bad connotation) one of the few that mean the same to both Communists and anti-Communists.

While all this has been going on, the Society for the Propagation of the Faith continues its work, and visitors to St. Peter's Basilica in Rome continue to stroll up the *via Propaganda*.

prophets of gloom and doom See GLOOM AND DOOM.

protectionism See GRASS WILL GROW IN THE STREETS.

protest vote A ballot cast for a candidate who stands little chance of winning, thereby registering a voter's dissatisfaction with the other candidates.

Eugene Debs, who served a term in jail for his opposition to World War I, polled 920,000 votes on the Socialist ticket in 1920. At least half of these were non-Socialists who "threw their vote away" on Debs; they were disillusioned with Woodrow Wilson's wartime administration and the new Democratic ticket—James Cox and Franklin Roosevelt—but were unwilling to vote for Republican Warren Harding. See DON'T WASTE YOUR VOTE.

"Vote 'No' for President" was a button worn during the 1964 and 1972 campaigns. A more sardonic message on a 1972 button, expressing dissatisfaction with vice presidential candidates, was "Agnew and Eagleton—Nobody's Perfect." (See BUTTONS, CAMPAIGN.) A voter unhappy with the choice in the TWO-PARTY SYSTEM has three choices: to pick the lesser of the two evils, to stay home, or to cast a protest vote. Whenever there is a third candidate in the field, he or she is likely to rate higher in public-opinion polls than the final vote reflects. That is because most voters talk about protest during a campaign, but when it comes to the final moment in the voting booth, revert to party or choose the candidate with a chance whom they dislike least.

Protest voting reached its apogee in 1992 as third-party candidate Ross Perot, well-financed, running against two-party GRIDLOCK, and given the chance to participate in major television debates, won nearly 20 percent of the popular vote. Four years later, denied debate participation, he did poorly. A cartoon showed this columnist in a rowboat shooting a popgun at a battleship, with Perot on its bridge screaming "Incoming!"

proverbs and axioms, political
A fish rots from the head first. Michael Dukakis in 1988 called this "an old Greek saying" in attacking Reagan Administration ethics.

Any party that takes credit for the rain must not be surprised if its opponents blame it for the drought. Dwight Morrow.

Don't get mad, get even, vaguely attributed to "the Kennedy mafia." Followed by *Don't get mad. Don't get even. Just get elected. THEN get even.* Bill Clinton's political strategist James Carville (for more Carville wisdom, see IT'S THE ECONOMY, STUPID!).

Don't just do something, stand there! Adlai Stevenson in 1956 on Eisenhower's domestic policy; used in 1970 in objection to government meddling by Nixon Labor Secretary George Shultz.

Don't look past the next election or you might not get past the next election. Former president Bill Clinton to CNN in 2005.

Don't roll up your pants legs before you get to the stream. Congressman Emanuel Celler (D-N.Y.).

Don't sell America short. Attributed in the 1890s to John Pierpont Morgan, based on the stock market technique used by investors who believe a stock will decline.

Every man has his price. Punchy version of a comment in the House of Commons in 1734 by Robert Walpole: "I know the price of every man in this House."

Few die and none resign. A shortening of a passage in an 1801 letter of the newly elected President Thomas Jefferson, whose few replacements were criticized by his political opponents: "If a due participation of office is a matter of right, how are vacancies to be obtained? Those by death are few; by resignation none."

Forgive but never forget. Attributed to John F. Kennedy by Ted Sorensen in a 1968 television interview.

GO FIGHT CITY HALL (resigned version); *You can't fight City Hall* (helpless version).

How you stand depends on where you sit. Attributed to former Bureau of the Budget employee Rufus E. Miles, by University of Chicago professor Arnold Weber.

I don't care what the papers say about me as long as they spell my name right. Attributed to Tammany leader "Big Tim" Sullivan.

If it ain't broke, don't fix it. Bert Lance, President Carter's Director of the Office of Management and Budget, on government reorganization, from what he called "an old Southern saying."

IF YOU CAN'T STAND THE HEAT, get out of the kitchen. A favorite adage of Harry Truman's.

If it walks like a duck, and quacks like a duck, then it just may be a duck. (On how to tell a Communist, attributed to labor leader Walter Reuther. Among many variations of this phrase is a 1993 use in *Variety*: "What smells like a skunk and looks like a skunk. ...")

If you don't go to other people's funerals, they won't go to yours. (Put positively, this proverb suggests that if you do go to other people's funerals, they will attend yours— as ghosts, presumably. Attribution perhaps by a ghostwriter.)

If you have an elephant on a string, and the elephant starts to run—better let him run. Attributed to Lincoln.

If you want a friend in Washington, buy a dog. Attributed (frequently, but without evidence) to Harry Truman.

In politics a man must learn to rise above principle. No attribution found for this, or its more recent version: *We'll doublecross that bridge when we come to it.*

Never hold discussions with the monkey when the organ grinder is in the room. Attributed to Winston Churchill, replying to a query from the British ambassador in Rome as to whether he should raise a question with Mussolini or with Count Ciano, his Foreign Minister.

Never murder a man who is committing suicide. Woodrow Wilson. See POLITICAL SUICIDE.

NOBODY SHOOTS AT SANTA CLAUS.

No man ever went broke underestimating the intelligence of the American voter. H. L. Mencken.

ROOT, HOG, OR DIE.

Show me a good loser, and I'll show you a loser. Attributed to Knute Rockne, the Notre Dame football coach. See LOSER.

Speak softly and always carry a big stick. The saying is always identified with Theodore Roosevelt, but he attributed it in this manner: "I have always been fond of the West African proverb ..."

The basic maxim of democracy should always be: Turn the rascals out. Arthur Schlesinger Jr. attributes this saying to Charles A. Dana in 1872. Theodore Dreiser, in his 1914 political novel, *The Titan*, wrote "there could be but one thing left—an appeal to the voters of the city to turn the rascals out."

The dogs may bark, but the caravan moves on forever. "Middle East adage" cited in regard to media critics by *U.S. News & World Report* publisher Mortimer Zuckerman.

The duty of an Opposition is to oppose. Attributed by Lord Derby to a Whig named Tierney. See DISH THE WHIGS.

THE JOB SEEKS THE MAN.

Ticker tape ain't spaghetti. New York Mayor Fiorello La Guardia.

To the victor belong the spoils of the enemy. William Marcy. See SPOILS SYSTEM.

Watch what we do, not what we say. Attorney General John Mitchell.

When a fellow says it hain't the money but the principle of the thing, it's th' money. *Indianapolis News* columnist Frank McKinney Hubbard, 1926. Updated by Senator Dale Bumpers in the impeachment trial of Bill Clinton: *When somebody says "It's not about sex"—it's about sex.*

Whenever you have to start explaining— you're in trouble. Barber Conable (R-N.Y.).

When the going gets tough, the tough get going. Attributed to John Mitchell by Jeb Magruder during the Watergate hearings; earlier attribution to Joseph P. Kennedy.

This has been satirized on T-shirts by substituting "shopping" for the final "going."

When the water reaches the upper deck, follow the rats. Attributed to FDR's Secretary of the Navy Claude Swanson.

You can get a lot more done with a kind word and a gun, than with a kind word alone. Gangster Al Capone, quoted jocularly by economist Walter Heller, in connection with wage and price controls.

YOU CAN'T BEAT SOMEBODY WITH NOBODY.

You can't make a soufflé rise twice. Alice Roosevelt Longworth, on Thomas E. Dewey's second presidential campaign.

You scratch my back, I'll scratch yours. Attributed to Pennsylvania politician Simon Cameron, Lincoln's first War Secretary.

Your opponent can't talk when he has your fist in his mouth. Bill Clinton, quoted in February 2007 in *Slate* magazine by John Dickerson.

proximity talks See QUIET DIPLOMACY; SHUTTLE DIPLOMACY.

proxy war Great-power hostility expressed through client states.

"The first case of a proxy war between China and the Soviet Union" was the way National Security Adviser Zbigniew Brzezinski described the fighting between Vietnam and Cambodia that resulted in a break of relations on New Year's Eve of 1978. He cautioned that the two nations had a tradition of enmity, "but the larger international dimension of the conflict speaks for itself."

Cambodian Communists had the support of the People's Republic of China, while the Soviet Union supported Vietnam. Tass, the official Soviet news agency, wanted no part of a *proxy war* and charged Mr. Carter's aide with trying to "palm off the desired as reality" and attempting to "whip up animosity between the peoples of China and the Soviet Union."

The phrase may be rooted in *proxy fight*, an attempt to get control of a corporate management through a contest for stockholders' proxy votes. *Proxy war* has also been taken to mean both "localized conflict" with outside sponsors and "brush-fire war" (a war likely to spread quickly unless put out).

psephology The study of elections and voting behavior.

In their 1970 book *The Real Majority: An Extraordinary Examination of the American Electorate*, Richard M. Scammon and Ben J. Wattenberg popularized the 1952 word and provided the etymology: "from the Greek *psephos*, or pebble. The derivation comes from the ancient Greek custom of voting by dropping colored pebbles into the equivalent of our ballot box."

The authors had a significant impact on the 1970 congressional elections with their argument that "the social issue" was becoming decisive—that voters were most concerned with unrest, alienation, drugs, crime, and changing morality rather than the traditional BREAD-AND-BUTTER ISSUE. Candidates of both parties made much of the "social issue," and not until late in the campaign did Democrats take advantage of the economic issue, which Republicans had feared most all along.

Time magazine credited the coinage of *psephology* to writer Michael Demarest in its 1964 election issue, but an *OED* citation from 1952 credits R.B. McCallum for its invention.

pseudo-event Contrived news; a happening that is made to take place for the purpose of the coverage it will get, or centered on people famous for being well known.

The phrase is Dr. Daniel Boorstin's, coined in *The Image; or, What Happened to the American Dream?* Historian Boorstin, later Librarian of Congress, held that American life has become unreal, based on illusion and images, with heroes replaced by celebrities. The manufactured "event"—a headquarters opening, a press conference for the dissemination of nothing much, a staged picture of a ribbon-cutting or "topping out" ceremony—have taken the place of much real news, designed to manipulate and promote rather than inform. As Boorstin put it, a pseudo-event "is not a train wreck or an earthquake, but an interview."

A predecessor phrase was *pseudo-statement*, used by I. A. Richards in his 1926 *Science and Poetry*: "A pseudo-statement is a form of words which is justified entirely by its effect in releasing or organizing our impulses and attitudes...a statement, on the other hand, is justified by its truth."

Reporter Richard Rovere described Senator Joseph McCarthy's skillful use of the press:

> He knew how to get into the news even on those rare occasions when invention failed him and he had no un-facts to give out. For example, he invented the morning press conference called for the purpose of announcing an afternoon press conference.... This would gain him a headline in the afternoon papers: "New McCarthy Revelations Awaited in Capital." Afternoon would come, and if McCarthy had something, he would give it out, but often enough he had nothing...He would simply say that he wasn't quite ready, that he was having difficulty in getting some of the "documents" he needed or that a "witness" was proving elusive. Morning headlines: "Delay Seen in McCarthy Case—Mystery Witness Being Sought."

Why are Americans prone to a diet of pseudo-events? Because, wrote Boorstin, "Pseudo-events are more sociable.... Their occurrence is planned for our convenience."

Boston University political scientist Murray B. Levin, in an analysis of the Edward Kennedy–Edward McCormack Massachusetts Democratic senatorial primary in 1962, suggested that "Edward Kennedy's rise to power and subsequent political stardom, and that of many other candidates, was based partly on...Kennedy's ability to pay for the services of men expert in the business of creating and selling pseudo-events."

The concept of the *pseudo-event* overdramatizes the degree of successful manipulation in American commercial and political affairs; a surprising and newsworthy position taken in an interview is not rendered counterfeit by the fact that it was arranged for maximum coverage. But the idea and the phrase are helpful in both planning for and watching out for *pseudo-events*.

In the 1972 campaign for the Democratic presidential nomination, several candidates announced their intention to formally announce their candidacy later. That pseudo-event was followed a generation later with candor and self-mockery by Senator John McCain and others in announcing the announcement of their 2008 candidacies for president.

The phrase is being replaced by MEDIA EVENT.

public interest, convenience and necessity Phrase (often shortened as PICON) binding broadcasters to a degree of public-service programming, as they act as licensees of the public airwaves (cable transmission differs).

The phrase has traveled a long legal road. PICON's predecessor can be found in the Interstate Commerce Act of 1887, as "public convenience and necessity." Before that, in 1876, the Supreme Court permitted regulation of prices in a "business affected with a public interest." A new word was slipped into the phrase in the Radio Act of 1927, Public Law 632: "Public convenience, interest or necessity." In 1934, when the Communications Act was passed, an unknown legislator apparently felt that "public convenience" sounded too much like a toilet, and switched the words around to their present "public interest, convenience and necessity."

Speaking to a group of broadcasters while he was still a senator, John F. Kennedy said: "Will the politician's desire for reelection—and the broadcaster's desire for rating—cause both to flatter every public whim and prejudice—to seek the lowest common denominator of appeal—to put public opinion at all times ahead of the public interest? For myself, I reject that view of politics, and I urge you to reject that view of broadcasting."

In current usage, *public interest* has become a useful antonym to VESTED INTERESTS and "special, selfish interest." Franklin Roosevelt used it in his 1936 annual message to Congress, appealing from "the clamor of many private and selfish interests, yes, an appeal from the clamor of partisan interest, to the ideal of the public interest."

The phrase can be traced back over four centuries to Richard Cosin's 1591 *An Apologie for Sundrie Proceedings by Jurisdiction Ecclesiasticall*: "Now the publike interest … is chiefly shewed by procuring common tranquillity and repose of the subiect."

Who determines the public interest? Often the "public" member of a board or commission, who serves with an industry member and perhaps a labor member. But the public, writes sociologist C. Wright Mills, "consists of the unidentified and the nonpartisan in a world of defined and partisan interests.… What the 'public' stands for, accordingly, is often a vagueness of policy (called 'openmindedness'), a lack of involvement in public affairs (known as 'reasonableness') and a professional disinterest (known as 'tolerance')."

public office is a public trust Phrase popularized by Grover Cleveland, used today in charges of graft or calls for codes of ethics for public officials.

"When a man assumes a public trust," Thomas Jefferson remarked to Baron von Humboldt in 1807, "he should consider himself as public property."

Other political figures and writers began to mold this into a useful phrase. Henry Clay in 1829: "Government is a trust, and the officers of the government are trustees; and both the trust and the trustees are created for the benefit of the people."

Senator John C. Calhoun, in 1835, began a paragraph: "So long as offices were considered as public trusts, to be conferred on the honest, the faithful, and capable, for the common good, and not for the benefit or gain of the incumbent or his party …" By 1872 Senator Charles Sumner was observing, "The phrase, 'public office is a public trust' has of late become common property."

The Democratic national platform in 1876 muddied up the phrase as follows: "Presidents, vice-presidents, judges, senators, representatives, cabinet officers—these and all others in authority are the people's servants. Their offices are not a private perquisite; they are a public trust."

W. C. Hudson, a newsman working for Grover Cleveland in the campaign of 1884, was looking for a phrase to embody integrity in government. He recalled the 1876 platform statement, and found in previous Cleveland speeches statements like "Public officials are the trustees of the people" and "We are the trustees and agents of our fellow citizens, holding their funds in sacred trust." Hudson felt all this provided the basis for a slogan and wrote in his 1911 *Random Recollections of an Old Political Reporter*:

> I went at the making of one.… Public Office is a Public Trust was the result.… It was the dogmatic form of what he had expressed with greater elucidation. …
>
> I took it to the Governor for his inspection. His eye at once went to the top line and pointing to it, he asked:
>
> "Where the deuce did I say that?"
>
> "You've said it a dozen times publicly, but not in those few words," I replied.
>
> "That's so," he said. "That's what I believe. That's what I've said a little better because more fully."
>
> "But this has the merit of brevity," I persisted, "and that is what is required here. The question is, Will you stand for this form?"
>
> "Oh, yes," replied the Governor. "That's what I believe. I'll stand for it and make it my own."

Hudson later learned that the slogan had predated his coinage but insisted he had never been aware of an earlier use when he showed it to Cleveland. The phrase was accepted and used by everyone except Cleveland; as his biographer, Robert McElroy, pointed out: " … throughout the campaign, and throughout the remainder of his life, Grover Cleveland continued to express this, his most cherished conviction, not in the words of Hudson's brilliant slogan, but in ponderous phrases of his own which he persisted in considering better because longer."

Campaigning against Herbert Hoover in 1932, Franklin D. Roosevelt gave the phrase a twist: "Private economic power … is a public trust." Adlai Stevenson, in 1952, extended the idea of public office to those (like his opponent, General Eisenhower) who hold public confidence: "A man who has the confidence of the public has a public trust not to abuse that confidence for any ends, let alone his own."

public trough, feeding at the The practice of politicians and their hangers-on of fattening themselves on public funds; in current jocular use.

An article in the *New York Tribune* in 1881 noted that "the Republican Party is tired of bossism, quarrels about patronage, slavery to the machine, and the statesmanship of the feed trough." The word *troughman* (pronounced "troff-man") was also used to describe a politician who spoons funds from government treasuries—that is, from the public trough. *The Nation* in 1904 wrote that grafters included "a number of lesser persons spoken of as 'troughsmen.' These used to be called 'henchmen,' then 'heelers,' but the newer word may be accepted without cavil."

The conservative columnist R. Emmett Tyrrell Jr. wrote in *The Washington Times* in 2006 that "most of our federal legislators want another stint at what the Democrats call 'public service,' a euphemism for what all reasonable observers call the 'public trough.'"

A variation of the trough is the *public crib*. In his *Thirty Years' View*, Senator Thomas Hart Benton wrote: "They have no other view than to get one elected who will enable them to eat out of the public crib."

Still another variation, though one less redolent of corruption and the spoils system, is *public teat*. Here the image is warmer, connoting a more paternalistic—or maternalistic—government, and is used less by critics than by politicians in a spirit of camaraderie. Perhaps this is because the image of a hog hungrily munching his garbage or a piglet rooting at its mother is too strong for criticism, crossing over into an area of mild irony. A politician often greets a friend who has just been elected or reappointed with "Still on the public teat?"

The phrase has Biblical roots, recalling how the Prodigal Son, at his nadir, ate from a trough with the swine. *Emporia Gazette* editor William Allen White referred to the story when, in the 1920s, he rejected a friend's suggestion that he write a biography of Warren G. Harding. "It isn't Harding's story," said White of the late President and the scandal that followed his death, "it is the story of his times, the story of the Prodigal Son, our democracy that turned away from the things of the spirit, got its share of the patrimony ruthlessly, and went out and lived riotously and ended it by feeding among the swine."

See ROSIE SCENARIO.

pull-aside A mini-*démarche*; a planned but low-key diplomatic approach.

This snippet of diplolingo has few printed citations but was drawn to the attention of the author in 1993 by Clifford Wharton, then Deputy Secretary of State. When, in conversation, Mr. Wharton said of a contact with a foreign counterpart, "It was just a pull-aside," he then defined the term as "a contact made at a reception or similar informal gathering for a specific diplomatic purpose."

The *Business Mirror* of the Philippines reported in 2006 on "the hoopla on the 'pull-aside'" between President George W. Bush and Philippines President Gloria Arroyo at the APEC summit in Hanoi that year, when Bush, who had been cool after the withdrawal of Filipino troops from the coalition in Iraq, pulled up a chair next to her and said, "Let's have our meeting here."

Coined on the analogy of *drop-by* (a brief appearance by a political figure to show respect but not commitment), this verb-based noun is more calculated than a chance meeting, less formal than an approach. A *pull-aside* is usually but not always planned; its utility lies in its apparent spontaneity, requiring no advance notification of the other side, and it is begun with taking the target diplomat's arm and saying something like "Step over here where we can talk." It is more overt than an intelligence agent's *brush pass*, defined in CIA-ESE under *gap, in the*.

pump-priming Using federal funds to stimulate the economy, usually during a recession or depression.

The *OED* quotes the 1882 definition of *to prime a pump* from John Ogilvie's *Imperial Dictionary*: "to pour water down the tube with the view of saturating the sucker, so causing it to swell, and act effectually in bringing up water." (The word *sucker* is used there in its literal, not figurative sense, such as in "Saturate that sucker!")

The phrase became popular during Franklin Roosevelt's presidency, when vast expenditures for the Public Works and Works Progress Administrations were characterized as *pump-priming*. "Most revolutionary of all," wrote Charles Hurd in *When the New Deal Was Young and Gay*, "was the theory that when business slackens, the government should spend money—even if it has to go into debt—to 'prime the pump' of the economy." During the 1937–38 recession, FDR said: "The things we had done, which at that time were largely a monetary and pump-priming policy for two years and a half, had brought the expected result, perfectly definitely." He blamed the recession on a drop in *pump-priming* caused by congressional economizers and the Supreme Court's nullification of several of his agencies.

The economic practice, its critics point out, can be overdone. In 1722, the *New-England Courant* pointed out: "No covetous Person will use more Water to fetch the Pump, than he designs to pump out again."

The phrase is punnable. A 1978 *New York Times* editorial on the plan of President Carter's media adviser, Gerald Rafshoon, to restore some imperial trappings to the presidency, was headlined: "Priming the Pomp." See TRICKLE-DOWN THEORY.

pundit A serious political analyst or self-important sage, usually syndicated in print media, a regular on a talking-head telecast or cable panel program, or with an influential weblog.

A *New York Times* editorial of 1921 admired the writing style of President Warren G. Harding: "[He] is not writing for the superfine weighers of verbs and adjectives, but for the men and women who see in his expressions their own ideas, and are truly happy to meet them … [it] is a good style, let the pundits rage about it as they will."

In his column about the press in *The Village Voice*, Alexander Cockburn wrote in 1976: "The use of the word 'governance,' incidentally, is the sure mark of a pundit; the other favored word is 'polity.'"

Mark Cocker presented in his 1993 book about travel writing this view of the term's historical usage in espionage: "From the 1860's onwards British intelligence officers had used another strategy to fill some of the political and geographical blanks on the map of their northern borders. Agents, drawn from the Himalayan communities under Indian control and resembling Tibetans in appearance, crossed the mountains disguised as pilgrims. These Asian spies, known collectively as the Pundits, were able to travel extensively in trans-Himalayan regions, even as far as Mongolia, and brought back an enormous quantity of intelligence. The Pundits' work involved enormous risks."

The word lends itself to spoofing, since its first syllable is about word play. *Time* magazine in the fall of 1977 headed an article about this conservative columnist: "Punder on the Right."

Pundit comes from a Sanskrit word for "learned man." In the late nineteenth century a group of Yale undergraduates founded a club called the Pundits, sponsored by William Lyon Phelps. When Yaleman Henry R. Luce started *Time* in 1923, he recalled the term and began applying it, as a courtesy title, to playwright Thornton Wilder and columnist Walter Lippmann. (Also to the American discourse contributed *Time*: *tycoon, moppet, socialite, cinemactor,* and *adman,* as well as the weird, backward construction of this sentence, long ago abandoned after years of parody.)

The term is widely and often mockingly applied to almost any member of the media—what President Eisenhower derided as "sensation-seeking columnists and commentators." However, the sensation sought by putative pundits is longheadedness: *The Washington Post* wrote in 1992 of "the real heavyweights—the pundits, the network stars, the interpreters and analyzers of political tea leaves." In a 2006 note to the author about current use of the word FIASCO, the *Post* reporter and TV commentator Dana Priest observed that "I've seen the word pop up in punditville …"

punt and pray See SPORTS METAPHORS.

puppet (government) A nation or individual controlled by another; a SATELLITE.

Just before the off-year elections of 1966, Defense Secretary Robert McNamara went to the LBJ Ranch in Texas to appear at a press conference with President Johnson. After he made an optimistic report on the progress of the war in Vietnam, Richard Nixon said he had demeaned his office and called him a "Charlie McCarthy," referring to the dummy created by ventriloquist Edgar Bergen that was popular in the heyday of network radio. (Johnson later labeled Nixon a CHRONIC CAMPAIGNER.)

Puppetry is a hand-fashioned political metaphor. Political satire was part of the Punch and Judy shows of the seventeenth century in England; *Punch*, a satiric British magazine first published in 1841, took its name from the lead character; and "pleased as Punch" comes from the satisfaction the character took in the effects of his mischief.

In 1670 Baruch Spinoza used the figure of speech in his *Writings on Political Philosophy*: "the object of government is not to change men from rational beings into beasts or puppets, but to enable them to develop their minds and bodies in security, and to employ their reason unshackled …" John Adams in 1775 warned of American subjugation in which "we should be little better than puppets, danced on the wires of the cabinets of Europe."

Puppet government achieved its popularity as a phrase in World War II, when conquering Nazi forces set up local civilian regimes (see QUISLING); however, when Communist-dominated regimes were set up in Eastern Europe after the war, they were mainly referred to as *satellites* or *captive nations*. In return, Communist speakers used *puppet* to refer to small nations supporting the Western position. However, domination of small states is not so easy as it seems. According to McGeorge Bundy, former Kennedy and Johnson national security aide, "Anyone who thinks that the lines of influence from Washington are like so many strings to so many puppets has never sat at the pulling end."

A synonym for *puppet*, with a more contemptuous connotation, is *stooge*. Among bloggers on the Internet, the adoption of a false persona to conceal one's identity is known as a *sock puppet*, after a rudimentary hand puppet using a sock. "The use of sock puppets," declared Harvard Professor of Internet Governance and Regulation Jonathan Zittrain in 2006, "is one of the graver transgressions you can make online."

purge To forcibly eliminate opposition within a party; to retaliate for party irregularity or governmental disloyalty.

"Pride's Purge," as it came to be called, was the ejection in 1648 of ninety-six Presbyterian Members of Parliament by Colonel Thomas Pride in the Cromwell era. In modern history, the term was most often associated with the bloody crackdowns of the Communists. As Thomas Dewey said in his 1950 lectures at Princeton: "In the Soviet Union and its satellites today the purge is both the instrument of change and the means of securing the leadership in undisputed control."

When leaders get the urge to purge, the NIGHT OF THE LONG KNIVES is recalled: on the weekend of June 29 to July 2, 1934, Adolf Hitler and Heinrich Himmler's Black Shirts pounced on eighty-three followers of Ernst Roehm's Brown Shirts and killed them all, establishing Hitler's complete control of the Nazi movement.

The bloodless *purge*, however, has also been used as an instrument of party politics in the U.S. In 1870, after the Senate defeated President Grant's attempted annexation of Santo Domingo, a party-wide purge followed. "Grant showed vindictive traits," wrote Matthew Josephson in *The Politicos*, and there was much "cutting off of political heads."

One victim was Carl Schurz, the transplanted German liberal who had fled to the U.S. after the abortive 1848 Revolution and later became a U.S. senator from Missouri. After refusing to back Grant on the annexation, Schurz found the White House door closed to him and complained to a friend: "Grant has read me out of the Republican Party." See READ OUT OF THE PARTY.

In the 1938 midterm election, Franklin Roosevelt tried to purge those congressmen who consistently torpedoed his programs—particularly three Democratic senators. All three won reelection.

Dwight Eisenhower on several occasions resisted the temptation to attempt a purge. When Senator Ralph Flanders of Vermont launched his censure effort against Senator Joseph McCarthy, Republican Majority Leader William Knowland resisted and indirectly warned Ike against trying to punish him for it. As Ike wrote in *Mandate for Change*: "Sensing my sympathy with Senator Flanders' action, he [Knowland] cited President Franklin Roosevelt's efforts to 'purge' Senators he did not like. I told him that I would not be trapped into any purging action."

When in 2006 Democrats in Connecticut sought to deny renomination to Senator Joseph Lieberman as punishment for his support of the Bush policy in Iraq, the blogger Barry Casselman wrote: "Bill Clinton, the shrewdest Democratic political figure of recent times, has called the move to purge Lieberman 'the nuttiest idea I ever heard.'" The purge succeeded in denying the senator the Democratic line on the ballot, but he ran as an independent, won handily, and returned to the Senate unpurged.

pushing the envelope Reaching beyond boundaries; stretching or exceeding the known limits.

This phrase pushed its way into print in the July 3, 1978, issue of *Aviation Week & Space Technology*. An aircraft designed for sea-level operation was being tested for higher flight: "The aircraft's altitude envelope must be expanded to permit a ferry flight across the nation. NASA pilots were to push the envelope to 10,000 feet."

Tom Wolfe popularized this aeronautics term in 1979 in *The Right Stuff*, a book about the character and values of astronauts. "The 'envelope' was a flight-test term referring to the limits of a particular aircraft's performance," Wolfe wrote, "how tight a turn it could make at such-and-such a speed, and so on. 'Pushing the outside,' probing the outer limits, of the envelope seemed to be the great challenge and satisfaction of flight test."

In 1988, Tom Wolfe told the lexicographer: "I first heard the phrase in 1972, among test pilots who later became astronauts. They were speaking of the performance capabilities of an airplane as an envelope, as if there were a boundary. Why they chose 'envelope,' I don't know, but if you get outside the envelope, you're in trouble." His conjecture is that the test-pilot use started at the Patuxent River Naval Air Station in Maryland during the 1940s.

Envelope, however, is a much older noun in math and science. Alexander H. Flax of the National Academy of Engineering informs the author: "Usage of the term envelope in science and engineering goes back at least to the mid-nineteenth century. In mathematics the envelope is the outer boundary of a related family of curves."

As early as 1901, the aeronautical noun *envelope* was in use to mean "the gas or air container of a balloon or airship." The magazine *Scientific American* explained in that year: "The balloon is inflated with hydrogen, and in order to maintain at all times a tension on the envelope—that is to say, perfect inflation—a compensating balloon filled with air is placed in the interior." The *Journal of the Royal Aeronautics Society* in 1944 extended the sense of a balloon's inflation to indicate optimum performance of any aircraft: "Tests at other heights can then be confined to what are termed 'envelope' conditions; that is, the engine conditions which will give the maximum economy at any given speed."

The *Dictionary of Military Terms* stretches the noun's definition further: "The three-dimensional space that is within range, altitude and deflection reach of a weapon, particularly an air defense weapon." This term, related to the French verb *envelopper* ("to wrap completely"), has been Anglicized in pronunciation to "EN-ve-lope." The verb *push*, as in "You're pushing it," extends the sense of envelope conditions, to suggest moving beyond current limits into untested areas.

The full phrase *pushing the envelope* is used widely, describing daring activity from politics to standup comedy, but the space use continues. In *U.S. News & World Report* in 1986, William Broyles Jr. wrote of Christa McAuliffe, the schoolteacher who was a member of the doomed space shuttle *Challenger* crew, as "pushing out the envelope of the planet."

push poll See DIRTY TRICKS.

pussyfooting Sidestepping an issue; being mealy-mouthed; failing to tread where angels fear to tread.

This was the sobriquet of W. E. "Pussyfoot" Johnson, an ardent advocate of Prohibition, who was so named because of his stealthy, unrelenting, catlike approach to revenue-evaders in the Indian Territory. "Special Agent Johnson," wrote the *Muskogee* (Georgia) *Democrat* in 1907, "he of the 'Panther' tread, has resented the action of the peddlers of bogus beer and had them all indicted by the Grand Jury. It is evidently *lèse majesté* to sue a velvet-shod emissary of Uncle Sam's Booze Department."

The word probably began with a note of sneakiness: earliest noted reference was in a *Scribner's Magazine* of 1893, about men who "were beginning to walk pussy-footed and shy at shadows"; *The Atlanta Constitution* later spotted Theodore Roosevelt's Vice President, Charles Warren Fairbanks, "pussyfooting it around Washington."

Pussyfooting has lost its stealthy connotation and has acquired a meaning of evasion of hard issues. James Farley wrote in 1932: "We Democrats must meet the issue fairly, without any pussyfooting." Wendell Willkie in 1944: "I'm getting pretty sick of the pussyfooters who try to catch the WPA and the National Association of Manufacturers with the same kind of talk." In a speech written by Pat Buchanan, Vice President Spiro

Agnew in 1970 alliteratively denounced the "pusillanimous pussyfooters."

Pussyfoot today has a more cautious, fearful connotation than STRADDLE or ON THE FENCE, works harder at evasion than *sidestep*, is less blatant than *to carry water on both shoulders*, is less investigative than *gumshoe* (see JUNKETEERING GUMSHOE), and is not as Machiavellian as being ALL THINGS TO ALL MEN. See CREEP.

putsch An attempted coup.

A *rebellion* is a *revolution* that failed; a *putsch* is a rebellion that was not considered a serious threat.

Adolf Hitler's Beer Hall Putsch took place on November 8, 1923, as the National Socialists, with General Ludendorff as a front, attempted to force the leaders of Bavaria to form a new government under Hitler. "The putsch," wrote William L. Shirer, "even though it was a fiasco, made Hitler a national figure and, in the eyes of many, a patriot and a hero. Nazi propaganda soon transformed it into one of the great legends of the movement." Hitler, tried for treason, was sentenced to five years, serving nine months during which he dictated *Mein Kampf* to Rudolf Hess.

Because of its Nazi association, *putsch* is used now as an attack word on INSURGENTS in any political situation. In 1991, the plot by hard-line communists against Mikhail Gorbachev was described by some as a "failed coup." Like the French *coup*, the German word means "blow or thrust"; *putsch*, however, adds a Nazi beer-hall connotation and suggests a clumsy attempt rather than a quick success.

A think tank in Washington passed along "speculation that Gorbachev may not have been quite the innocent victim of the putsch," adding, "whether one buys the 'Potemkin coup' theory or not." (That coup is named for Grigori Potemkin, Catherine II's adviser and lover, who supposedly built fake villages along the Dnieper River to fool the Empress about regional development. *Potemkin village* is still the term used for an imposing but phony facade intended to disguise a shabby condition. *Potemkin* to mean "phony" was also used in "Potemkin coup" to speculate wildly that Mikhail

Gorbachev may have orchestrated his own victimization.)

Among the puns to come out of the failed takeover in Moscow (that subsequently led to the emergence of Boris Yeltsin) was Leon Wieseltier's headline in *The New Republic* of "When Putsch Comes to Shove," along with the lawyer Leonard Garment's description of the bungling plotters as "the Coup Klutz Clan."

puzzle palace See PENTAGONESE.

quagmire Any situation or a position that appears to be unwinnable as well as difficult to exit; specifically, a seemingly interminable foreign conflict.

Quagmire is employed frequently as an attack term by opponents of U.S. military engagements abroad. The power of the epithet derives from its association with the long conflict in Vietnam; see VIETNAM SYNDROME.

Criticizing a critic of the war in Iraq in 2003, David Gelernter wrote in the *Los Angeles Times* in 2005: "Sen. Edward M. Kennedy [D-Mass.] has announced that the Iraq war 'has been consistently and grossly mismanaged' and our troops 'are now in a seemingly intractable quagmire.' Quagmire is not a state of war but a state of mind. ... The U.S. has been stuck in countless potential quagmires in many wars. Each time, we could have announced 'this is a quagmire and we're going home.' Thank God we didn't—usually."

Quagmire also was used with reference to Iraq during the first Gulf war. *The Washington Post* editorialized in March of 1991: "Already there is talk of a 'quagmire' in Iraq. It's an evocative metaphor taken from Vietnam." Later that year, the *National Review* dismissed the idea that "the U.S. must avoid the 'quagmire' of a civil war in Iraq. Use of the word 'quagmire'—one of the first symptoms of the VIETNAM SYN-DROME—has become an obstacle to rational thought on foreign policy."

A 1994 comment by Dick Cheney, then Defense Secretary, defending the decision by George H.W. Bush not to go on to Baghdad, was picked up by opponents of the Iraq war in 2007 and became a favorite of bloggers around the world: "Once you got to Iraq and took it over, took down Saddam Hussein's government, then what are you going to put in its place? ... It's a quagmire if you go that far and try to take over Iraq."

The term also has been applied to conflicts by other nations in other places, among them the Russian war in Afghanistan between 1979 and 1989 and the involvements of Jordan and Syria in the "Lebanese quagmire."

The Vietnam *quagmire* was epitomized by the title of David Halberstam's 1965 book, *The Making of a Quagmire*. A review of the book that year by United Press International began: "The 'quagmire' described by *New York Times* correspondent Halberstam is the mess of United States involvement in Vietnam. No international undertaking short of full-scale war has brought Americans more trouble or frustration over a long period." Arthur M. Schlesinger, Jr., referred to the domestic impact of the war in passing in *The Washington Post* in 1988: "There has not been a liberal administration in Washington since the Great Society vanished into the Vietnam quagmire in 1966."

Dated in the *OED* to the late sixteenth century in the sense of a piece of ground that is too soft to support the weight of men or large animals, the word's meaning was extended by the eighteenth century from actual bogs to metaphoric ones, meaning positions or situations generally that are easier to stumble into than extricate oneself from. Richard Brinsley Sheridan wrote in his 1775 play, *The Rivals:* "I have followed Cupid's Jack-a-lantern, and find myself in a quagmire at last."

Though now linked closely in the public mind with Vietnam and used frequently in criticism of the conduct of the second Iraq war, the political application of *quagmire* predates those wars by many years. The AP reported in 1951 a charge by the national chairman of the Democratic Party, William M. Boyle, Jr., that Republicans are "reluctant to aid Europe, but they are enthusiastic about getting us mired down in the military quagmire of China, where a decisive world victory could never be won."

In 1900, Mark Twain deployed the term in the current sense in an interview with the New York *World*. Asked for his opinion on events in the Philippines, which the U.S. had liberated from Spain only to face an insurrection by native Filipinos, Twain declared: "But now—why, we have got into a mess, a quagmire from which each fresh step renders the difficulty of extrication immensely greater."

See CUT AND RUN and EXIT STRATEGY.

quality of life The pursuit of happiness unsullied by the drawbacks of modern life; excellence of environment, idealistically reaching beyond an improved standard of living.

The first known use is by English novelist J.B. Priestly, writing in his 1943 *Daylight on Saturday* of "the plans already...maturing that would give all our citizens more security, better opportunities, and a nobler quality of life."

Democratic candidate Adlai Stevenson used the phrases *quality of life* and *quality of living* frequently in the campaign of 1956. His source was probably TV commentator Eric Sevareid, who answered this writer's query: "Long ago, I think in '56, I wrote a radio broadcast for a Sunday series we called 'Newsmakers' about the nature of Adlai Stevenson. I put in the phrase 'the quality of life' to try to describe his approach to the national condition as it differed from the stock New Deal approach which, it seemed to me, was pretty directly concerned with more quantities for every group. He read the script later, on an airplane trip; twice, in notes to me, he expressed gratitude for the phrase. He used it often in his speeches."

Stevenson, however, did not elevate the phrase to slogan status. Arthur Schlesinger, Jr. recognized its potential and helped popularize it in the intellectual community. In 1955 he wrote a memorandum comparing the "quantitative liberalism of the thirties" to the necessary "qualitative liberalism" of the future, as the needs of people in a depression change in a time of affluence. This memo was published in *The Reporter* magazine in the spring of 1956.

When conservation and pollution in the mid-'60s became transfigured into "the environment" and a new political cause, the *quality of life* phrase was born again—this time to stress the other-than-material needs of the AFFLUENT SOCIETY.

The phrase is now an unassailable political cliché, indispensable to environmentalists, useful as shorthand for orators appealing to youthful voters turned off by promises of a higher standard of living. New York Traffic Commissioner Samuel I. Schwartz used the phrase as a hyphenated modifier in 1984: "As more and more citizens begin to demand a reduction in quality-of-life infractions—such as running red lights—you'll see a return to the time when police stringently enforced laws."

A related cliché is *lifestyle*, sociologese for "way of life." That word was coined by psychologist Alfred Adler in 1929. Vice President Agnew in 1970 castigated the drug culture as "a lifestyle that has neither life nor style."

Quality of life, so well established as a generalized national and personal goal, is overdue for a TURNAROUND, but proponents of zero population growth have yet to denounce "the quantity of life."

See ENVIRONMENTALIST.

quarantine Euphemism for *blockade*, when that word is too belligerent.

The health of the BODY POLITIC has long been a rich vein of metaphor for politicians. Jefferson talked of "the disease of liberty" and Lincoln of "the scourge of war." In the fall of 1937 Franklin Roosevelt wanted to speak out against Hitler and Mussolini; Norman Davis of the State Department drafted a speech that included the phrase "war is contagion." Harold Ickes told Roosevelt that a neighborhood had a right to "quarantine" itself against threatened infection; according to the Interior Secretary, FDR jotted down the word and said he would use it sometime.

"When an epidemic of physical disease starts to spread," FDR said in Chicago, "the community approves and joins in a quarantine of the patients in order to protect the health of the community against the spread of the disease." How to stop this "epidemic of world lawlessness"? He avoided *blockade*— a hostile action to isolate, usually considered an act of war—as well as the milder *sanction*.

The next day, reporters led by Ernest K. Lindley (see "Lindley Rule," under NOT FOR ATTRIBUTION) tried to pin him down. How did a quarantine fit in with a policy of neutrality laid down by act of Congress? "I can't give you any clue to it," the President parried, "you will just have to invent one." How about sanctions? "Sanctions is a terrible word. They are right out the window." Is a quarantine a sanction? "No. I said don't talk about sanctions." A reporter said, "This is no longer neutrality." Roosevelt replied, "On the contrary, it might be a stronger neutrality."

By the time John F. Kennedy was faced with the threat of Russian missiles installed in Cuba, the word *quarantine* was installed in the American political lexicon as a kind of stern but peaceful act risking dangerous involvement in a good cause. Kennedy, according to his aide Roger Hilsman, "again repeated his preference for a blockade and at this time supplied the word quarantine to describe it. This was a phrase with obvious political advantages both at home, where it was reminiscent of President Roosevelt's 'quarantining the aggressors' speech, and abroad, where it struck a less belligerent note than the word blockade."

Sanction, a "Janus word" (one with opposite meanings, like the noun *oversight* and the verb *table*) is in *quarantine*'s neighborhood as a method of coercion short of war. *The Washington Post* reported in 1992: "In Germany, Chancellor Helmut Kohl told television interviewers that the West should escalate its sanctions against Serbia into a complete blockade to throttle the Serb military campaign in Bosnia." Not sanctions but threat of military force by NATO nations stopped the Kosovo bloodshed.

Subsequently, diplomatic and economic sanctions were applied to such nations as Iraq, Iran, North Korea, Zimbabwe, and Myanmar (Burma), usually with limited success. They worked on Libya in 2003. Unless supported by a nation's neighbors and key customers, sanctions are merely a way of expressing high moral dudgeon.

quick and the dead, the The living contrasted with the dead; phrase used to dramatically pose the choice of mankind in the nuclear age.

"My fellow CITIZENS OF THE WORLD," said Bernard Baruch on June 14, 1946, to a U.N. meeting in New York's Hunter College gymnasium, "we are here to make a choice between the quick and the dead. ... Behind the black portent of the new atomic age lies a hope which, seized upon with faith, can work our salvation. ... We must elect World Peace or World Destruction."

The Baruch phrase about life and death might have been the work of his publicist and friend, Herbert Bayard Swope, who said it was; however, while Baruch freely credited his "COLD WAR" phrase to Swope, he would never credit the former New York *World* editor with "the quick and the dead."

The phrase occurs twice in the Bible (Acts 10:42, 1 Peter 4:5) in the context of Judgment Day. In Shakespeare's *Hamlet*, Laertes leaped into his sister Ophelia's grave saying, "Now pile your dust upon the quick and dead ..."

quick fix A snap solution; the foolhardiness of expecting minor treatment to solve a major problem.

President George H.W. Bush suggested a drug-lingo origin of this term, perhaps unintentionally, in a 1991 comment on indictments of Libyan terrorists. He said the charges were not "some quick hit, quick fix on trying to find the answer."

Hit, now a slang term for "assassination," has been slang since 1949 for the instant rush of gratification felt by a narcotics user. Since 1867, the term *fix-up* was used for a shot of liquor or, more recently, of dope. The current use of *to get a fix* for drug usage began in the 1930s with *to get a fix-up*.

By the mid-1970s, *quick fix* was being applied in politics. Its connotation is almost always negative. In a Christmas 1976 issue, *National Observer* reported on conflicting advice for President-elect Jimmy Carter: "On the one hand, he is urged to make quick-fix tax cuts and get the economy moving." In 1980, when Carter ran unsuccessfully for a second term, he derided Ronald Reagan for "fantasy goals of strength without sacrifice, the irresponsible advocacy of short-cut economics and quick-fix defense policy."

quiet diplomacy Behind-the-scenes efforts, held to be more effective in achieving desired ends than attempts to publicly embarrass another nation into acceding to the first nation's wishes.

"Through quiet diplomacy," Secretary of State Henry Kissinger said in 1976, "this [Ford] Administration has brought about the release or parole of hundreds of thousands of prisoners throughout the world and mitigated repressive conditions in numerous countries. But we have seldom publicized our specific successes."

Kissinger was derogating the Jackson-Vanik amendment to trade legislation that had long tied MOST FAVORED NATION treatment to Soviet emigration policies. He sought to counter Jackson-Vanik's argument against *quiet diplomacy*: that without public pressure, neither the U.S. government nor the Soviets, with whom it was seeking DÉTENTE, would enter into any talks at all to protect human rights.

Democrat Jimmy Carter, campaigning against Ford in 1976, firmly allied himself with the forces in favor of human rights publicly sought; after his election, he tempered his rhetoric considerably. "The shift in President Carter's human-rights campaign from shrill publicity to quiet diplomacy," wrote columnists Evans and Novak in October 1977, "has cost him a powerful cutting edge for domestic politics, but quiet diplomacy...may be having a more productive impact on Moscow than the headlines of early 1977."

Senator Daniel P. Moynihan (D-N.Y.), one of the earliest spokesmen for the human rights campaign, was having none of that backsliding: "It is entirely correct to say that 'quiet diplomacy' is effective in obtaining concessions from totalitarian regimes with respect to particular individuals who need our help. But the result of proceeding in this fashion is that the democracies accommodate the dictators. The dictators let the occasional prisoner out of jail in return for our silence about those jails."

In 2007, after Palestinians had elected Hamas, an organization that did not recognize Israel's right to exist, and negotiations stalled, U.S. Secretary of State Condoleezza

Rice held what she called "parallel communications...a bilateral approach in which I talk in parallel to the parties from a common approach." This one-at-a-time mediation avoided the danger of highly publicized failure at summit conferences. David Ignatius noted in the *Washington Post* that "in Kissinger's day, such meetings were called 'proximity talks.'" See SHUTTLE DIPLOMACY.

For 1961 usage, possibly coinage, by Walter Lippman, see OPEN COVENANTS. See also HUMAN RIGHTS; LINKAGE; MOST FAVORED NATION; SAMIZDAT. For a 1967 usage of *quiet diplomacy*, see SUMMITRY.

quisling A collaborator with the enemy; a traitor; one who cooperates with a foreign country in the overthrow of the government of his own, and especially one who then serves in a PUPPET GOVERNMENT.

The example of Major Vidkun Quisling, head of the Nazi party in Norway and of that country's puppet government during World War II, spawned the eponymous word. Norway executed him for treason at war's end in 1945.

On April 15, 1940, the London *Times* reported that: "Comment in the Press urges that there should be unremitting vigilance also against possible 'Quislings' inside the country [sc. Sweden]." The *OED* also cites another *Times* use a week later: "There seem to have been no Quislings, partly because it was unnecessary to 'quisle' in a country which, as the Nazis have always said 'could be taken by telephone.'"

On May 22 the Manchester *Evening News* wrote: "Major Quisling, the betrayer of Norway, has given us one of the first new words of the war." In the U.S., *Time* magazine's issue of May 24 dropped the capitalization: "South America becomes very quisling conscious." The London *Star*, on July 10, explained why the word caught on: "The Norwegian traitor was cursed with a name which by its very sound conveyed all the odious, greasy wickedness of the man." The Manchester *Guardian* wondered on October 19: "So far the most significant and valuable addition in this war has been Quisling. Will there be a verb, to quisle?" Briefly, there was—as noted, *The Times* had already used the verb on Apr. 22—but it never caught on.

Eponymy is the use of a person's name as a word. Other people whose names have become words include Captain Charles Cunningham Boycott, a land agent in County Mayo, Ireland; Miss Amelia Bloomer, American feminist; British General Henry S. Shrapnel; and a seventeenth-century English hangman named Derrick. Eponymy in politics includes GERRYMANDER, SOLON, SHERMAN STATEMENT, ROORBACK, and the verb *Hooverize*, meaning to conserve food, stemming from Herbert Hoover's relief activities in World War I. Best known is MAVERICK. Once removed from eponymy are phrases like *to pull a Perot* ("to start a third party, to BOLT") and *another Stassen* (a PERENNIAL CANDIDATE).

quota The number permitted or required; in civil rights terminology, government-set numerical standards to require admission or employment of African-Americans and other minorities to compensate for past discrimination.

The word is based on Latin *quota pars* meaning "how great a part," from *quot*, "How many?" In the first half of this century, the political use of this word was concerned with immigration policy (how many should be let into the U.S. from which other nations) or with discrimination against Jews and Catholics (how many should be allowed into medical schools, country clubs, corporations).

In the civil rights backlash of the 1970s, the word *quota*—like BUSING—became politically sensitive, as many who had been proponents of civil rights for blacks in theory did not like the practice; they believed it abridged civil rights for whites. When black activists sought a form of reparations for past prejudice, on the grounds that special preference was due to enable them to enter the "mainstream" of American life, this was attacked as *reverse discrimination*; the argument was made that the Constitution must remain "color-blind" or the courts would be filled with pleas for preference by every minority and ethnic group, undermining the tradition of the MELTING POT.

The critical words in the issue were *affirmative action, goals, quotas,* and *reverse discrimination.*

Affirmative action, as a phrase, was employed during the Eisenhower Administration; former Nixon and Reagan Cabinet member George Shultz tells the author he recalls that it was being used in the 1955 White House Conference on Equal Job Opportunity. Before that, the *OED* has a *New York Times* citation from 1935: "If...the Board shall be of the opinion that any person...has engaged or is engaging in any such unfair labor practice, then the Board shall...issue...an order requiring such person...to take such affirmative action, including reinstatement of employees with or without back pay, as will effect the policies of this Act." This was quoting the Wagner Act of 1935. Evidence that this phrase was bubbling up through the bureaucracy was its official use, six weeks into the Kennedy Administration, in Executive Order 10925 (March 1961): "The contractor will take affirmative action to ensure that applicants are employed, and that employees are treated, during employment, without regard to their race, creed, color or national origin." These actions came to mean providing remedial education or compensatory training, making certain that testing did not incorporate forms of discrimination, and aggressive recruiting—in other words, sincerely trying to find, and hire or admit, qualified blacks.

Goals are numerical targets, set to put a specific criterion before a school or employer or union, which can be achieved through *affirmative action* on agreed "timetables." If good-faith efforts are made to provide equal opportunity, failure to reach the goal would not trigger a government penalty such as cancellation of contracts.

Quotas do not permit of explanations: if the number set by population percentages is not met, penalties ensue; this rigidity can result in the hiring or admission of minority applicants less qualified than other applicants, primarily on the basis of race, and the charge of reverse discrimination.

In *Regents of the University of California v. Allan Bakke,* decided on June 28, 1978, Justice

Lewis Powell, writing for the Supreme Court, swept aside the differences between "goals" and "quotas"—at least as applied in that case—as "semantic distinction beside the point." The point was that nobody could be denied admission to a college specifically by virtue of his race; Bakke, who was white and had claimed "reverse discrimination," won entry. At the same time, the Court held that "race or ethnic background may be deemed a 'plus' in a particular applicant's file"—in other words, that race could be taken into consideration provided it was not the only element in the admissions decision.

Twenty-five years after *Bakke*, the High Court again sought to strike a balance: The majority approved the University of Michigan law school's use of race in admissions that involved "highly individualized, holistic review" of applicants, but in the same 2003 case disallowed the undergraduate admissions plan granting preferences based only on race. Justice Sandra Day O'Connor expected that a generation hence, "the use of race preferences will no longer be necessary."

In June 2007, after Justice Samuel Alito had replaced the "swing" vote of the retired O'Connor, the Court ruled that public school systems in Seattle and Louisville, Ky., cannot adopt desegregation plans that take explicit account of a student's race. The decision by Chief Justice John G. Roberts Jr. for the Court held that the landmark *Brown v. Board of Education* decision of 1954, which forbade segregation of children on the basis of race, did not mean that school districts could use "racial classifications designed to include rather than exclude." Roberts wrote: "The way to stop discrimination on the basis of race is to stop discriminating on the basis of race." (This recalled to some the dictum of Justice Hugo Black regarding the First Amendment: "No law means no law.") However, the "swing voter" in the majority of this 5–4 decision, Justice Anthony Kennedy, objected to Roberts' "all-too-unyielding insistence that race cannot be a factor" when a school's program to achieve racial diversity was sufficiently "narrowly tailored." That suggested that the constitutional debate over quotas—and the need for, or undue reliance on, affirmative action to make education "color blind"—was far from over.

See SEPARATE BUT EQUAL.

quoted out of context A defensive charge that one's words have been quoted in such a way as to twist the original meaning of the statement.

During the French Revolution, Jean-Paul Marat was arrested and tried by the Convention for alleged outrages against that assembly in 1793. In his successful defense, he said: "I demand a consecutive reading … for it is not by garbling and mutilating passages that the ideas of an author are to be learnt, it is by reading the context that their meaning may be judged of."

In the 1944 presidential campaign, Franklin Roosevelt was irritated at Thomas E. Dewey's jabs at FDR's "promise" not to campaign "in the usual sense" when he accepted the Democratic nomination. He planned to use the following passage in a speech:

> In accepting the nomination in this campaign I said: "I will not campaign, in the usual sense, for the office."
>
> Apparently the Republican campaign orators came to the conclusion that meant that they were free to say anything they wanted without contradiction. … But in their habit of tearing sentences from their context, which they seem to do in their campaign speeches with great facility, they decided to overlook what I said in the same paragraph. It was this: "I shall, however, feel free to report to the people the facts about matters of concern to them and especially to correct any misrepresentations."
>
> So last week, I exposed their misrepresentations.

Speechwriter Samuel Rosenman felt this was intemperate and out of character, and FDR agreed not to use it. Instead, he made the point obliquely: "I am quoting history to you. I am going by the record. And I am giving you the whole story and not merely a phrase here and a half a phrase there." There was an outburst of laughter at that point and the master orator promptly scrapped the rest of the line, which was "picked out of context in such a way that they distort the facts." Instead, the president said: "In my reading copy there's another half-sentence. You've got the point and I'm not going to use it."

During the debate in 1954 on a Senate resolution to censure Wisconsin Senator Joseph McCarthy, Senator Samuel J. Ervin Jr. (D-N.C.) told the Senate:

> I now know that the lifting of statements out of context is a typical McCarthy technique ... practiced by a preacher in North Carolina about 75 years ago. At that time, the women had a habit of wearing their hair in top knots. This preacher deplored that habit. As a consequence, he preached a ripsnorting sermon one morning on the text "Top Knot Come Down." At the conclusion of his sermon an irate woman, wearing a very pronounced top knot, told the preacher that no such text could be found in the Bible.
>
> The preacher thereupon opened the Scriptures to the 17th verse of the 24th chapter of Matthew and pointed to the words: "Let him which is on the housetop not come down to take anything out of his house." Any practitioner of the McCarthy technique of lifting things out of context can readily find the text "top knot come down" in this verse.

R

rabbi Sponsor, or sage adviser; mentor.

When given a unique political sense, this word has no religious or spiritual significance. In political relationships, a *rabbi* is primarily a sponsor or protector, although there is a second meaning of mentor or teacher. "Who's his rabbi?" is a question often asked by wary hatchetmen before cutting loose at a target.

When a speechwriter escaping the White House in 1973 asked *Newsweek* pundit Stewart Alsop to "be my rabbi" in giving advice about which newspaper offer to accept, Alsop—a self-described "confirmed WASP"—delightedly signed all future correspondence with his new colleague in journalism "Your rabbi, Stew."

Dating back to the 1950s in New York police slang, *rabbi* was used in a 1989 CNN commentary on the troubled savings and loan associations: "Ninety percent of the S & L's that are in trouble have no political rabbi."

Rabbi is derived from Hebrew for "my master." Its eponymous synonym, *mentor*, comes from ancient Greek, where it is the name of the teacher and adviser of young Telemachus, the son of Odysseus.

A more frequently used term equivalent to *mentor*, becoming a cliché, is *guru*, from the Indian "holy man" or "teacher," rooted in the Sanskrit for "weighty." The term began to lose its religious connotation in 1940 when H. G. Wells wrote in *Babes in the Darkling Wood*, "I ask you, Stella, as your teacher, as your Guru, so to speak, not to say a word more about it." In 1949, Arthur Koestler used it in *The God That Failed* as "My self-confidence as a *Guru* had gone."

By 2007, the AP was reporting that "Democrats, armed with subpoenas for President Bush's guru Karl Rove and other top aides, are pressing the White House ..." In political usage, *guru* is for outsiders, *rabbi* for insiders.

racial balance See BUSING.

racism Originally, an assumption that an individual's abilities and potential were determined by his biological race, and that some races were inherently superior to others; now, a political-diplomatic accusation of harboring or practicing such theories.

"This word [racism]," wrote Harvard Professor J. Anton De Haas in November 1938, "has come into use the last six months, both in Europe and this country ... Since so much has been said about conflicting *isms*, it is only natural that a form was chosen which suggested some kind of undesirable character." In fact, *racism* came into use two years earlier; in his 1936 book *The Coming American Fascism*, Lawrence Dennis wrote, "If ... it be assumed that one of our values should be a type of racism which excludes certain races from citizenship, then the plan of execution should provide for the annihilation, deportation, or sterilization of the excluded races."

Racism, a shortening of *racialism*, was at first directed against Jews. In the nineteenth century, anti-Semites who foresaw a secular age in which religion might not be such a popular rallying force against Jews put forward the idea of Jewishness being less a religion than a race. Adolf Hitler, with his "master race" ideology, turned theory into savage practice.

The lexicographer Anne Soukhanov informs the author: "Citations for *racism* ran very heavy from the late 1930s through the late 1940s; most of them referred to fascism. Then they thinned out until the late 1950s, when references to U.S. (and, in particular, to Southern) racism began to build up. The citations seemed to peak for that sense in the Sixties."

Meg Greenfield, in her *Newsweek* column in 1975, agreed: "US Ambassador [to the U.N.] Daniel P. Moynihan observes that the term 'racism' only became a fixture of official General Assembly prose sometime in the mid- to late 1960s. The same is true of official prose in this country. I remember being astonished in 1968 by the abandon with which the Kerner commission, appointed by President Johnson to study the causes of civil disorder in our cities, stigmatized vast segments of the American population with the charge of 'white racism.'"

Curiously, the term that had originally characterized (and derogated) attacks on Jews—and then became associated with racism directed at African-Americans—returned as an attack on Jews when the U.N. General Assembly in 1975, dominated by a Soviet-Arab-African coalition, passed a resolution condemning Zionism as a form of racism.

Ambassador Moynihan, who had been an academic expert and author on the subject of ethnicity and race, was quietly seething at the hypocrisy on display just one generation past the predations of the Nazi racial doctrines. He told his U.N. colleagues: "The term derives from relatively new doctrines—all of them discredited—concerning the human population of the world, to the effect that there are significant biological differences among clearly identifiable groups, and that these differences establish, in effect, different levels of humanity." Vigorously opposing the anti-Semitic resolution on behalf of the United States, Moynihan declared that "today we have drained the word *racism* of its meaning…The United States of America declares that it does not acknowledge, it will not abide by, it will never acquiesce in this infamous act."

Seymour Martin Lipset, writing in the October 1977 *American Spectator*, was pessimistic: "The racism and ethnic tension that have been potent aspects of human experience from ancient days down to the present continue as strong or stronger than ever…the story of people's hatred of each other for reasons of ancestry, culture, religion, race or language is far from over."

Fifteen years after the passage of what was called in the U.N. "Z equals R," President George H.W. Bush reminded the U.N. General Assembly that "to equate Zionism with the intolerable sin of racism is to twist history." Assistant Secretary of State John Bolton (later to become a Moynihan successor at the U.N. in the younger Bush's administration) led a campaign to overturn the vote considered by many Jews around the world to be an abomination. Although the U.S. initiative was opposed by supporters of Palestinian Arabs, on December 16, 1991, by an overwhelming vote of 111 to 25, the U.N. nullified its 1975 resolution.

In the campaign for the 2008 Democratic presidential nomination, the emergence of Senator Barack Obama as a credible "first tier" candidate raised the question—not racist in intent, but dealing with the fact of racism—of whether a "person of color" was electable. Unexpectedly, some African-American leaders wondered if Obama—with a black Kenyan father and white American mother—was "black enough," that is, closely identified with political issues of longstanding concern to blacks.

This raised a separate semantic question, of "acting black"—that is, appearing to be the stereotype of what many whites expected of blacks. The North Carolina editor Aleta Payne wrote in *The Washington Post* in 2007, under a headline reading "No, My Son Doesn't 'Act Black,'" about music videos and rap lyrics "that paint a picture of African-Americans as loud, rude, undereducated, oversexed…hip-hop wannabes…or its inverse, what Sen. Barack Obama has called 'the slander that a black youth with a book is acting white.'"

radical chic See LIMOUSINE LIBERAL; PARLOR PINK.

radical right Attack phrase on right-wing EXTREMISTS, especially on an angry segment that believes treason motivates many of the government's leaders.

Prince Klemens von Metternich, who put the stamp of reaction on the Congress of Vienna in 1814, coined a predecessor phrase—"white radicals"—to define the activists of the far right, counterbalancing the "red radicals" of the left. And attorney Clarence Darrow, who defended a teacher's right to discuss evolution at the Scopes "monkey trial," liked to refer to the Catholic hierarchy as "the right wing of the right wing." (Howard Dean identified himself in 2004 as representing "the Democratic wing of the Democratic party.")

Telford Taylor, a prosecutor at the Nuremberg war-crimes trials, is credited with the coinage of "radical right" in the foreword to his 1954 book, *Grand Inquest*. Sociologist Daniel Bell picked up the phrase one year later in his *The New American Right*, which he updated and retitled *The Radical Right* in 1963. Bell defined the group as a melange of

soured patricians ... whose emotional stake lay in a vanishing image of muscular America defying a decadent Europe ... the "new rich"—the automobile dealers, real-estate manipulators, oil wildcatters—who needed the psychological assurance that they, like their forebears, had earned their own wealth, rather than accumulated it through government aid, and who feared that "taxes" would rob them of that wealth; the rising middle-class strata of the ethnic groups, the Irish and the Germans, who sought to prove their Americanism, the Germans particularly because of the implied taint of disloyalty during World War II; and finally, unique in American cultural history, a small group of intellectuals, many of them cankered ex-Communists, who, pivoting on McCarthy, opened up an attack on liberalism in general.

Writers who use this attack phrase are unanimous in their denunciation of the far right. Alan Barth, writing in 1961:

They are commonly called "Rightist"—a term which connotes conservatism. But in sober truth there is nothing conservative about them. They are much more in a rage to destroy than a fervor to conserve.... Sometimes they are referred to as the "radical Right." But the fact is that there is nothing radical about them ... They are fundamentally and temperamentally "aginners." And perhaps the commonest characteristic among them is anger.

The appeal of the phrase was the application of the adjective *radical*, previously associated with the revolutionary left, to the activist right. In 1970, Renata Adler carried this forward with a book titled *The Radical Middle*, picked up by Canadian Prime Minister Pierre Trudeau in 1978: "We are a party of the extreme center, the radical middle." That urgently ultra-centrist label was attached to supporters of the maverick presidential candidate Ross Perot in his surprisingly high-percentage showing in 1992.

A long step short of *radical* right is *hard* right, as followers of the television panelist and occasional protest candidate Pat Buchanan were called in 1993. See BIRCHER;

EXTREMISM; KOOKS, NUTS AND; LITTLE OLD LADIES IN TENNIS SHOES; REACTIONARY.

rainmaker A lawyer, lobbyist or public relations executive capable of making political manna fall on the client.

This apt term showered down on the political lexicon in 1968 when new trans-Pacific airline routes were to be awarded, and a half-dozen of President Johnson's former political associates were retained by individual airlines to lobby for their interests. David Hoffman of *The Washington Post* wrote: "Among airline men, corporate officials and consultants with high political contacts are referred to as 'rainmakers.' Half in jest and half in jealousy, airline men say the so-called rainmakers can precipitate new route awards for companies that employ them."

Former Attorney General John Mitchell gave a sophisticated definition of the term during his first trial in April 1974 (the one in which he was acquitted). Mitchell said that a New Jersey Republican leader approached him on behalf of financier Robert Vesco, and asked him to set up a meeting with William J. Casey, then chairman of the Securities and Exchange Commission. Casey was on vacation and the meeting was never arranged, but that did not stop the rainmaking politician from claiming he almost did it. According to Mitchell: "Rainmaking is a situation where an individual who is trying to obtain a favor for a client does things for the record that never happened."

The term is current. The *Los Angeles Times* reported in a 2006 profile of a corrupt lobbyist: "[Jack] Abramoff was drawn back into politics in 1994 when the GOP takeover of Congress created opportunities for a talented rainmaker."

The word, in its original sense, is associated with the aboriginal Americans. The earliest use of the word in print found so far is in *Adair's Indians*, in 1775: "When the ground is parched, their rain-makers (as they are commonly termed) are to mediate for the beloved red people, with the bountiful holy Spirit of fire." Two centuries later, cloud-seeding operations proved somewhat more reliable, but in both literal and political senses, the *rainmaker* often takes the credit for rain that was already on the way. See FIVE PERCENTER; INFLUENCE PEDDLER; LOBBY.

rally As a noun, an event to stimulate and channel enthusiasm; as a verb, to enlist support.

"Rally round the flag" is tenuously attributed to General Andrew Jackson at the Battle of New Orleans, but it illustrates the military use of the word, from the French *rallier*, to re-ally or join again, to reassemble scattered troops to fight again. Poet Robert Burns warned of repercussions "ere we permit a foreign foe, / On British ground to rally."

The military phrase was given a political interpretation in the campaign for a military hero, William Henry ("Tippecanoe") Harrison. "If Pennsylvania should adopt him as her candidate," wrote the *Scioto Gazette* in 1835, "the west will rally around the Old Pioneer." Abolitionist Wendell Phillips followed an extension of the word in *The Liberator* in 1844: "until slavery be abolished, the watchword, the rallying-cry, the motto on the banner of the American Anti-Slavery Society shall by 'No Union With Slave Holders!'"

The political rally, as practiced today, can be a *streetcorner rally*, one of many brief appearances by the candidate on a city-wide tour, providing an event for local supporters to organize in a neighborhood; a *headquarters rally* or *kick-off rally* to "open" a headquarters largely for the benefit of camera crews; a COFFEE-KLATSCH gathering of supporters in a home but nevertheless a rally of sorts; a *virtual rally*, organized and promoted on the Internet; and the all-stops-out, ring-a-ding, HOOPLA-filled *Garden rally* (after Madison Square Garden in New York) or *major rally*, also called the *wind-up rally*, at the end of a state or national campaign, bringing in celebrities, raising funds by charging admission to a section of the best seats, generating publicity and enthusiasm.

A great rally can change the course of politics. General Dwight Eisenhower, who had been resisting the importunings of politicians of both parties to run for president, wrote General Lucius Clay from Supreme Headquarters, Allied Powers Europe in early 1952: "My attitude has undergone a quite significant change since viewing the movie of the Madison Square Garden show." This "show" was a rally organized by a group of political amateurs—led by New York broadcasters Tex McCrary and Jinx Falkenburg, with political backing from Senator Henry Cabot Lodge—that filled the 18,000-seat Garden with an enthusiastic crowd singing a new Irving Berlin song, "I Like Ike," joined by Clark Gable, Humphrey Bogart and Lauren Bacall, calling for Eisenhower to come home and take the nomination away from the expected GOP nominee, Senator Robert A. Taft. Until then, Eisenhower had been doubtful of the grassroots support that professional Republicans, including Thomas Dewey, assured him would appear if he came home to campaign. But the kinescope of the Garden rally, flown to his Paris SHAPE headquarters and presented by the aviatrix Jacqueline Cochran, moved him.

Eisenhower wrote to McCrary on February 20, 1952: "it would be idle as well as false for me to attempt to deny that I am deeply touched by the obvious energy and conviction that you devoted to the Garden effort and by the extraordinary enthusiasm shown by the great crowd of Americans who gathered there." McCrary told several of us (as Tex's radio producer, I was pressed into my first political experience at age 23 as the rally's chief of staff) that Cochran flew back to relay this message from the General to the leaders of the Eisenhower Bandwagon Committee: "Go back and tell them I'll do it."

See BALLYHOO; BANDWAGON; HOOPLA; SPONTANEOUS DEMONSTRATION.

rank and file The broad range of party members; the TROOPS, more active than the average voter registered with a party.

Former New York Governor Al Smith, making a late effort to get the Democratic nomination in 1932, stated that "it would be wiser … not to instruct delegates to the convention in favor of any candidate." This ploy was aimed at eroding delegate strength already pledged to Franklin Roosevelt. FDR immediately objected to "the kind of national convention which became merely a trading post for a handful of powerful leaders, and where the nomination itself had nothing to do with the popular choice of the rank and file of the party itself. ... The rank and file of the party should be heard." See POWER BROKERS.

In Congress, the rank-and-file members are all those not in the leadership, and who are reminded in words attributed to long-time House Speaker Sam Rayburn, "those who go along, get along." The phrase, now most often used in the labor movement, is from the military, where *rank and file* means the whole body of enlisted men, including corporals but sometimes excepting sergeants. See MILITARY METAPHORS.

rap in the night Symbol for police state that rules by fear; a heart-clutching sound, preliminary to arrest or search.

The crash of gun butts on the door in the dead of night is a device to strike terror into a populace. Night-time is chosen because the resident is startled out of sleep, and a fear of the dark is added to the fear of authority. The Gestapo made it a kind of trademark. In some cases, night is chosen to avoid publicity.

"The clearest way to show what the rule of law means to us in everyday life," said Dwight Eisenhower in 1958, "is to recall what has happened when there is no rule of law. The dread knock on the door in the middle of the night ..."

This became a political issue in the U.S. in 1962 following an increase in the price of steel. President John F. Kennedy put pressure on the steel companies to roll back their increase, which he believed to be unjustified and inflationary. As part of this pressure, Attorney General Robert Kennedy asked the Federal Bureau of Investigation to check into newspaper reports of remarks made by Bethlehem Steel executives at a stockholders meeting. "Unhappily," wrote Arthur Schlesinger, Jr., "though the instruction went to the FBI in the afternoon, it was apparently passed on to Philadelphia by Pony Express, for the reporter involved was not called till three the next morning. The FBI's postmidnight rap on the door caused a furor."

That *rap in the night* was used against Robert Kennedy in his 1964 senatorial campaign as an indication of his ruthlessness;

it was also phrased as "rap on the door" and "knock in the night." This helps explain why political canvassers are told by their leaders not to ring doorbells or knock on doors after 9:00 P.M.

The expression fell into disuse, perhaps temporarily, when *rap* music became popular in the late 1980s.

rather be right See I'D RATHER BE RIGHT.

rattle the cage Attempt by a political figure to break out of the restraints imposed on him by his staff.

This phrase is an arrogation of importance by political staffers who jokingly speak of themselves as zookeepers of gorillas that must be protected from their own rampages.

When Nixon special counsel Charles Colson arranged a night out at the Kennedy Center for Richard Nixon to conform to a sudden presidential whim, he was dressed down by chief of staff H. R. Haldeman in these terms: "You could have put the President's life in jeopardy. The Secret Service wasn't prepared." Asked what to do when the President expressed a desire for an unscheduled public appearance, Colson writes he was told: "Just tell him he can't go, that's all. He rattles his cage all the time. You can't let him out."

A second meaning, when the keeper rather than the gorilla is doing the rattling, is "to warn," as in this *Wall Street Journal* use in 1977: "A congressional staffer recalls that a lobbyist for the American Israel Public Affairs Committee, after noting that a friendly congressman wasn't on hand for a key vote, ordered the congressman's aide to 'get up there and rattle his cage and get him down here.'"

The metaphor of center of power as prison is not new: Harry Truman referred to the place he worked as "a big white jail."

A related metaphor is *run the traps*. A hunter will check his traps in the morning to see what, if any, animals were caught; a reporter will *run the traps* of his sources to check out a story.

raw meat See RED MEAT; STIR UP THE ANIMALS.

reached Bought off; corrupted.

A public official may be *approached* with no implication of wrongdoing on anyone's part; when *spoken to*, the implication is often that he is neutralized or partially persuaded pending a final decision; when he has been *reached*, however, the implied message is that he has been bought and sold.

California Attorney General Earl Warren, launching a gambling investigation in 1939, used the word in its current meaning: "It is impossible to open a big, notorious gambling operation without buying off public officials. Every time you see such a place, you can be sure they are paying off someone for the privilege to operate. This does not necessarily mean a sheriff or a District Attorney or a chief of police is being reached. Most often, it is someone higher up."

The question "Can he be reached?" or "Is he reachable?" is occasionally answered with another word, taken from Chicago gangland investigations and in turn from the Hindu caste system: *untouchable*. See GRAFT; BOODLE; BAGMAN.

reactionary One who believes in returning to governmental and economic conditions of an earlier time; often an attack word on a conservative.

The word was originally applied to the conservative groups who opposed the French Revolution's extremists. The conservative columnist and linguist H. L. Mencken wrote that the word, first used as a religious term, was adopted in J. A. Froude's *History of England* in 1858, "in the current sense of a political conservative reactionary. ... It is now used to designate any opponent of a new device to save humanity."

Populists and Democratic supporters of William Jennings Bryan popularized it in this country, but as early as 1868 *Harper's Weekly* used *reaction* to describe the Democrats who met in their party's national convention in Ohio: "the resuscitation of every notorious COPPERHEAD to control the government is the beautiful PLUM which 'the great reaction' offers the country."

The political use of the noun goes back to the eighteenth century, reports the *OED*. Arthur Young, in his 1792 *Travels* [in France] *during the Years 1787, 1788 and 1789*, writes: "A most curious political combination, which seems to shew, that ... where evils are of the most alarming tendency, there is a re-action, an under-current, that works against the apparent tide, and brings relief."

President Franklin Roosevelt defined it in a 1939 radio speech: "A reactionary is a somnambulist walking backward." (Curious, that he didn't use the simpler word *sleepwalker*.) Six years later, Herbert Hoover, accustomed to the label, wrote: "If it be 'reactionary' to be for free men then I shall be proud of that title for my remaining days." Communist China's Chairman Mao Zedong wrote in *On People's Democratic Dictatorship*: "Reactionaries must be deprived of the right to voice their opinions. Only the people have that right."

Like LIBERAL, MIDDLE OF THE ROADER, CENTRIST, and CONSERVATIVE, *reactionary*—and its counterpart on the left, *radical*—is a subjective label shifting in meaning with each labeler. However, left-wingers are more likely to be proud of the title *radical* than right-wingers of the label *reactionary*. In the late '70s, some ultraconservatives—picking up on the growing use of NEOCONSERVATIVE—called themselves "neoreactionaries." It did not catch on.

Forces of reaction is often used as an alternate to the adjective, and *fossilized thinking* and DINOSAUR WING shore up the antediluvian picture of the word. See EXTREMIST; HIDEBOUND; MOSSBACK; OLD FOGY; OLD GUARD; RADICAL RIGHT. A proud self-description by some on the farthest right is "I'm to the right of Attila the Hun," a reference to a fifth-century barbarian leader who led an austere life on the banks of the Danube, twice attacked the Roman empire to increase its taxes to him, and was said by some to have been killed on his wedding night by his bride, Ildico.

read my lips Pay close attention; make no mistake about what I say.

When the elder George Bush was first nominated to the Presidency, he told the 1988 Republican National Convention in New Orleans during his acceptance speech:

"Congress will push me to raise taxes, and I'll say no, and they'll push, and I'll say no, and they'll push again. And I'll say to them: 'Read my lips. No new taxes.'"

This imperative phrase comes from rock music, not the usual source of metaphors in Republican speeches. In 1978, the singer Tim Curry used the phrase to title an album (which did not include a 1957 song with that title by Joe Greene). Curry recalls getting the phrase from a recording engineer of Italian-American descent: "I would say to him, 'We got it that time,' and he would say, 'Read my lips—we didn't.' That phrase arrested me." He defined the expression as "Listen and listen very hard, because I want you to hear what I've got to say."

Sports figures picked up the term. A football coach, Mike ("Read My Lips") Ditka of the Chicago Bears, got the nickname by emphasizing spoken orders.

Political usage began when Elisabeth Bumiller, then of *The Washington Post*, reported a tense exchange concerning aircraft for the hostages released by Iran in 1981. Joseph Canzeri, a Reagan aide, was told by a State Department official that the aircraft were unavailable, committed elsewhere. Canzeri replied, "Read my lips—these are English words. Uncommit them."

In 1987, Senator Albert Gore questioned Under Secretary of Defense Fred Ikle about the Midgetman missile. Interpreting Ikle's lukewarm response, Gore said, "You're saying, 'Read my lips, cut the money.' Your message is clear."

Its use by George H.W. Bush the following year in the speech written by Peggy Noonan led to its use against him after he compromised with the Democratic Congress in 1990 and agreed to a tax increase. At first, it plagued him with conservatives; later, it was taken up by Democrats as evidence of Mr. Bush's willingness to break a promise.

Five years later, the Clinton-Gore campaign issued faxes quoting Bush's 1988 statement of "no new taxes" and his 1992 comment on "no more tax increases," followed by spokesman Marlin Fitzwater's qualification, "It wasn't a pledge, no." George Stephanopoulos, Clinton's communications director, based his response on a proverb attributed to labor leader Walter Reuther on how to tell a Communist (see PROVERBS AND AXIOMS, POLITICAL): "If it walks like a duck, and quacks like a duck, then it just may be a duck." Commented Stephanopoulus, "If it looks like 'read my lips,' sounds like 'read my lips' and reads like 'read my lips,' it's 'read my lips.'"

readout Report to the media; public reciting of information about a meeting.

Marlin Fitzwater, Press Secretary to George H.W. Bush, popularized this noun. A 1990 transcript of a White House press briefing began, "Welcome to the pre-brief—or *readout*, excuse me—on the visit of President Ben Ali of Tunisia."

Asked by the lexicographer about the usage, Fitzwater replied, "*Readout* is a colloquial conjunction of two separate expressions. The first is 'to read your notes,' which is what we do in reporting to the press about a meeting we attended. The second part, the *out* part, may be from 'to speak out,' as in telling the press about what happened."

Fitzwater dated the term back to the early Reagan Administration. "I've heard it since I got here in 1983," he said, providing a definition: "A readout is a report on what happened at a meeting."

Its source is computerese. The hyphenated form has a primary sense of "the transfer of data from a storage medium."

Pete Cottrell of the University of Maryland's computer science department refines the meaning: "*Readout* refers to instrument panels or video displays. It's human interface with the machine conveying information, as opposed to *printout*, which is the output of the machine that you can carry away in your hand."

Unlike a *handout*, a *readout* requires no printed form. Instead, it is a public reciting of information that allows reporters to take notes or, when permitted, to broadcast pictures.

read out of the party Declared *persona non grata* by party leaders, usually after a BOLT.

The situation is similar to a dismissed employee grumbling, "You can't fire me, I quit." When a party leader or public figure within the party commits some unpardonable sin (like supporting the opposition or engaging in a romantic relationship with a known journalist), he or she has in effect deserted; any metaphoric expunging of the miscreant's name from the party rolls simply vents the spleen of the party leadership deserted. It makes no difference, except to make it more difficult for the bolter to return.

Nobody actually "reads" anybody out of a party; if a man says he is a Democrat, he's a Democrat, no matter what Democratic leaders say or how many Republicans he votes for. The phrase is merely a way of showing party disapproval.

Like PARTY ELDERS, the origin is in the Church. As the *Guidebook in the Administration of the Discipline of the Methodist Episcopal Church* states: "It is made the duty of the 'official minister or preacher' at every quarterly meeting to read the names of those who have been excluded from the Church during the preceding quarter.... When persons are thus read out of the society by the official minister," etc.

Political use was evident in 1840, when the *Logansport* (Indiana) *Herald* wrote: "If their candidates in expectancy are guilty of the unpardonable sin of telling the truth... they're immediately read out of the party."

When Republican Frank Knox, GOP presidential nominee Alfred Landon's running mate in 1936, accepted a Cabinet post in the Roosevelt Administration, Republican National Chairman John Hamilton professed to *read him out*. When Earl Warren, who had turned down the offer to be Thomas E. Dewey's running mate in 1944, was asked to run with Dewey in 1948, he felt he had to accept. "If he did turn Dewey down," wrote Warren biographer Leo Katcher, "he would be reading himself out of politics."

See PURGE. For another term formed from the same verb phrase, see READOUT.

Reaganomics See -NOMICS.

realism Originally a foreign policy that emphasized stability between superpowers and minimized confrontation to promote democracy; later, a much different policy opposing military intervention abroad as naively idealistic and against the national interest.

In a 2006 *Washington Post* column titled "This Is Realism?" Charles Krauthammer led with "Now that the 'realists' have ridden into town gleefully consigning the Bush doctrine to the ash heap of history, everyone has discovered the notion of interests, as if it were some new idea thought up by James Baker and the Iraq Study Group." Contrariwise, Tom Ricks wrote in the same paper: "The Iraq Study Group report might well be titled 'The Realist Manifesto,'" a repudiation of the Bush administration's diplomatic and military approach now being challenged by recommendations stemming from "the 'realist' school of foreign policy."

In a 2007 essay in *Time* magazine headlined "The Return of the Realists," Walter Isaacson noted that "the doctrine of realism, or its Prussian-accented cousin realpolitik, emphasizes a hard-nosed focus on clearly defined national interests, such as economic or security goals, pursued with a pragmatic calculation of commitments and resources. Idealism, on the other hand, emphasizes moral values and ideals, such as spreading democracy."

Pragmatism was the word that proponents of realism preferred in the Nixon Administration to define the opening to Communist China and détente with the Soviet Union, as well as a tolerance for authoritarian (a euphemism for "dictatorial") leaders like Lee Kwan Yew of Singapore who were on our side in the Cold War (see S.O.B.)

The old realism of the 1960s and '70s coined "the balance of terror," glorified "strategic stability" with its "mutual assured destruction," and derided President Woodrow Wilson's dream of a "WAR TO END WARS" that would "MAKE THE WORLD SAFE FOR DEMOCRACY" as hopelessly idealistic and naïve—that is, not pragmatic.

In the 1980s, however, under Ronald Reagan, it was the word *realism*'s turn to take a hit: the lexical pendulum swung toward evocation of America as a "CITY ON A HILL," an embrace of human-rights rhetoric, and the moral denunciation of an EVIL EMPIRE. Crusading idealism was in vogue and amoral realism was passé.

But not for long. In the elder Bush's term of 1989–93, *stability* became the byword and paramount goal of diplomacy, and the idea of realism (though not yet the word) began to make a comeback. It peaked in the senior Bush's 1991 visit to Kiev, just as the Soviet Union showed signs of coming apart in the Baltics and Ukrainians sought their freedom from Moscow rule. Brent Scowcroft, a retired general who had been a longtime Kissinger aide in the Nixon era, helped write a stability-first speech for President George H. W. Bush on a visit to Kiev that urged Ukrainians to stay within the Soviet Union and direly warning of "suicidal nationalism." This caused a right-wing opinionmonger at *The New York Times* to label the outburst of realism "Chicken Kiev" (and the elder Bush has not spoken to the author since).

As word and policy, *realism* had its ups and down through the two Clinton terms, 1993 through 2000. But in the first term of Bush II, the "old" realism of Kissinger and Scowcroft was battered by what the historian Robert Kagan called "Americans' belief in the possibility of global transformation—the 'messianic' impulse." President Bush called it his "freedom agenda."

Public impatience grew with "the long, hard slog" in Iraq, however, and that fresh stock of Wilsonian idealism—reborn in the Reagan years and reborn yet again in the younger Bush's administration—fell into disrepute, not only in liberal and academic circles and among antiwar activists but as reflected in public opinion polls and Democratic victory in the 2006 congressional elections. *Realism* came back into oratorical vogue; the headline in an August 2007 *National Observer* read "Hot Policy Wonks for the Democrats: the New Realists." Subhead: "Neo-Liberalism is Passe, Anti-Idealogues Surge. Kind of Scowcrofty."

"We are all realists now." That was the lede of George Packer's article in an April 2007 issue of *The New Yorker*. "Iraq has turned conservatives and liberals alike," Packer wrote, "into cold-eyed believers in a foreign policy that narrowly calculates national interest without much concern for what goes on inside other countries." Unexpectedly in a magazine with unabashed Bush-bashing credentials, Packer offered a sobering note to triumphalist realists: "At some point events will remind Americans that currently discredited concepts such as humanitarian intervention and nation-building have a lot to do with national security—that they originated as necessary evils to prevent greater evils. But, for now, Kissingerism is king."

That equated *realism* with Kissingerism, synonymy that "Henry the K" (who supported the Iraq war) surely considered insufficiently nuanced, and reminded the "new" realists that they had to dissociate themselves from the "old" realism.

See REALPOLITIK.

realpolitik Scientific-sounding power politics; international diplomacy based on strength rather than appeals to morality and world opinion.

The coiner was German writer Ludwig von Rochau, in his 1853 *Grundsätze der Realpolitik* ("Fundamentals of Realpolitik"), attacking what he felt were the unrealistic policies of the German Liberals. "The term was particularly applied to Bismarck's policy during and after the years of German unification," writes Professor Donald Cameron Watt in the *Fontana Dictionary of Modern Thought*, "and is to be distinguished from a policy of selfish self-interest or from a ruthless reliance on naked power."

"Historians may argue for years," wrote *Time* magazine about the brief Israeli-Arab war in 1967 (dubbed the "blintzkrieg"), "over who actually fired the first shot.... But the *Realpolitik* of Israel's overwhelming triumph has rendered the question largely academic."

In 1939, after the Soviets had signed a nonaggression pact with the Nazis, American Communists were forced to do a sharp zigzag in their party line, causing *The Nation* magazine to scoff at their dialectics. A clergyman wrote a letter to *The Nation*'s editor patiently explaining that Stalin was only fighting for the life of his regime, adding: "I would suggest that you leave the morals of the situation to us parsons and concentrate yourselves upon the realities in terms of Realpolitik."

The German word is pronounced "re-AL-pol-i-teek"; in Europe, it continues to mean "power politics," but in the U.S. the word is used to mean "the realities of politics," which puts it closer to PRACTICAL POLITICS. See QUIET DIPLOMACY; REALISM; WORLD OPINION.

reapportionment See ONE MAN, ONE VOTE.

recession A decline in economic or business activity.

A recession can be *temporary, deep, nationwide, rolling,* or *regional.* According to some economists, a deep recession can become a depression; according to others, recessions are normal parts of a recurring rise and fall of economic activity. A combined recession and INFLATION, involving both rising unemployment and rising prices, is often called STAGFLATION. A colloquial word for a recession is *slump*; if mild, a *downturn,* slowdown or DIP, which if repeated becomes a *double dip.*

The first use of *recession* in print is recorded in the *OED* in an article in *The Economist* of November 2, 1929, shortly after the stock market crash of October 1929. "The material prosperity of the United States," declared *The Economist,* "is too firmly based, in our opinion, for a revival in industrial activity—even if we have to face an immediate recession of some magnitude—to be long delayed." The "immediate recession" was of *some* magnitude—it lasted ten years and was called the Great Depression.

The prolonged recession plaguing the George H.W. Bush Administration after the boom of the 1980s was a leading cause of the Republican defeat in 1992 and the election of Bill Clinton, whose mandate to stimulate the economy was encapsulated in the slogan, "IT'S THE ECONOMY, STUPID!"

When Alfred Kahn, Jimmy Carter's economic adviser, was forbidden to use the word *recession* lest he be a source of gloom, he substituted the word *banana.*

reclama Appeal; objection to a decision or a request for review.

A popular term in late 1980s spookspeak, *reclama* began as a clipped form of the noun *reclamation,* based on the verb *reclaim.* All are rooted in the Latin verb *clamare,* "to cry out," by way of a French verb *reclamer,* meaning "to complain, object." Pronunciation: "re-CLAM-uh."

Aviation Week & Space Technology showed military use of the term in 1975: "Navy and Army officials are now in the process of preparing reclamas on the ... aerial scout helicopters." The same publication used the word six years later, when an angry defense official protested that there was "zero time available to ... accept reclamas from the services."

The *Naval Terms Dictionary* in 1978 defined the noun as "a request to superior authority to reconsider its decision or its proposed action."

Diplomats picked up the expression from the military. James R. Schlesinger, formerly Director of Central Intelligence and Secretary of Defense, wrote in *Foreign Affairs* magazine in 1986 that Prime Minister Margaret Thatcher "appeared at Camp David to deliver a reclama on Reykjavik."

By the mid-1980s, political use of the word appeared. In 1984, Secretary of State George P. Shultz discussed the difference between business and government: "In business you had to be very careful when you told somebody that's working for you to do something, because the chances were very high that he'd do it. In Government you didn't have to worry about that, because if he didn't like it, there'd be a reclama."

The noun was used in 1989 when Secretary of Defense Richard B. Cheney requested that Brent Scowcroft, the national security adviser, review a request. Scowcroft was overheard complaining, "Cheney had done a reclama."

Like its synonyms *appeal* and *review,* the word *reclama* is now equally acceptable in political lingo as noun or verb. Another member of the National Security Council turned the noun into a verb during a 1989 meeting with the elder George Bush: "I'd like to reclama that."

red Color originally symbolizing radicalism and anarchy, later identified with Communism.

Les républicains rouges, so called for their red caps and occasional willingness to dip their hands in the blood of their victims and then wave them in demonstrations, gave the anarchistic tinge to the color associated till then with magic and the Church.

This did not occur, as popularly assumed, during France's Revolution of 1789 and the "Reign of Terror" that followed; the "red Republicans" earned their nickname in the insurrection of June 1848, which led to the establishment of the short-lived Second Republic. The red flag, however, which had been used in the Roman Empire as a call to arms, was taken up in the 1789 Revolution. German revolutionaries in the mid-nineteenth century called themselves *rote Republikaner*, and the Cleveland *Plain Dealer* in 1856 made an interesting comparison: "They call themselves 'Red Republicans,' indicating by that name their bloody and revolutionary purposes. They have found congenial spirits in a party in this country called 'BLACK REPUBLICANS.' "

A character in *Uncle Tom's Cabin*, the 1852 novel by Harriet Beecher Stowe, warned that "the masses are to rise, and the under class become the upper one." The answer was, "That's one of your red republican humbugs, Augustine!" At the same time, the specter of Communism was haunting Europe, in the Marx-Engels word picture, and the timing was perfect for the color and the cause to come together. Red was the color adopted by the Communist party in the twentieth century. PINKO and PARLOR PINK are obvious derivatives; BLEEDING HEART might have an association. See COLOR METAPHORS.

redheaded Eskimo bill Extremely limited focus in legislation; a bill narrowly targeted to benefit an individual or corporation.

The Washington Post provides a 1986 citation for this phrase, found almost as rarely in print as its intended beneficiaries are in life. At that time, the Maryland state legislature was considering a tax credit for gasohol, delivering a tax break for a specific petroleum company. Delegate Mary Boergers of Montgomery County, who was in favor of the bill, commented, "It's a redheaded Eskimo," an image that *Post* writer Tom Kenworthy defined as "legislative parlance for a narrowly constructed bill that applies to only one person or company."

It used to be thought that the word *Eskimo* (many Eskimos, especially in Canada, prefer to be called *Inuit*, meaning "people") was from an Algonquian word for "eaters of raw flesh," but linguists now consider it more likely that it meant "snowshoe-netter." (See http://alt-usage-english. org/excerpts/fxeskimo.html for details.) Among the distinguishing physical characteristics of Eskimos is their straight black hair, emphasizing the rarity of finding a "redheaded Eskimo."

Kenworthy reported another use of legislature lingo in the use of *snake bill*, applied by some Maryland delegates to similarly self-interested legislation. Lawrence LaMotte, a Baltimore County Democrat, defined *snake* as "a 'simple' bill, usually very short, which eliminates vast quantities of existing law." But not always short: Delegate Gerard F. Devlin, another Maryland Democrat, explained the image of the word, negative even in the Bible, as "a bill where the hidden meaning is disguised in a forest of verbiage."

red herring A political diversion; a side issue that draws attention away from the main issue.

A herring, cured with saltpeter and slowly smoked, turns red; its delicious taste led to the English expression "neither fish nor flesh nor good red herring," which has been around at least since the sixteenth century. Dragged across a trail, however, the strong smell irritates the nostrils of tracking dogs and throws them off the scent of their prey.

An early political use was by Alfred E. Smith, Governor of New York, the first Catholic candidate for president, campaigning in Oklahoma City in 1928: "The cry of Tammany Hall is nothing more nor less than a red herring that is pulled across the trail in order to throw us off the scent ... but it has grown to a proportion that compels me to let the country know that at least I know what's behind it; it's nothing more nor less than my religion." See WHISPERING CAMPAIGN.

For a phrase to explode into an issue, it needs both forum and context. President Harry Truman's first use of it had the forum of his acceptance speech to the Democratic convention in July 1948, but the room was not gas-filled when the match was struck: "I am going to call Congress back and ask them to pass laws to halt rising prices, to meet the housing crisis—which they say they are for in their platform. ... They are going to try to dodge their responsibility. They are going to drag all the red herrings they can across this campaign ..."

The phrase that caught attention in that speech was his call-back day, "which out in Missouri we call 'Turnip Day,'" and *red herring* made little impression at the time because there was no double meaning to *red*. But during the special session of Congress, the House Un-American Activities Committee found two witnesses who unfolded a spectacular tale of Communist intrigue at high government levels. Elizabeth Bentley and Whittaker Chambers started labeling "spy" and "collaborator" such officials as Lauchlin Currie, ex-White House aide; William T. Remington of the Department of Commerce; and the State Department's Alger Hiss.

One month later, in this inflammable context, a reporter reached back to Truman's convention-speech red-herring phrase and asked, "Mr. President, do you think that the Capitol Hill spy scare is a 'red herring' to divert public attention from inflation?" Truman took the bait and replied, "Yes, I do." He read a prepared statement saying the hearings "are serving no useful purpose," and ad-libbed the phrase from the reporter's question at the end: "And they are simply a 'red herring' to keep from doing what they ought to do." The shrewd reporter asked for permission to quote him directly on the concluding remark, and Truman agreed.

Now the phrase had its context and its second meaning—red Communism. Republicans attacked Truman on it, but the issue had not yet ripened—Hiss had not yet been convicted of perjury. Four years later, however, as the 1952 Eisenhower-Stevenson contest picked up steam, "SOFT ON COMMUNISM" was an issue and *red herring* was its

shibboleth. Eisenhower, stung by Stevenson's wit, asked, "Is it funny when evidence was discovered that there are Communists in government and we get the cold comfort of the reply, 'red herring'?"

Thus, Truman's first use of the phrase, which passed unnoticed in his "Turnip Day" speech, gave him confidence to accept a reporter's use of it a few weeks later; in the meantime, however, the context and meaning had changed enough to make the use of the phrase a major blunder that haunted Democratic candidates for years. As Senator Robert Taft's wife Martha summed up: "To err is Truman." (For another case of a politician falling into a reportorial trap, see INOPERATIVE.)

Though still in use, the phrase has lost its soft-on-communism coloration. Some Democrats in 2006, seeking an issue that was not the hot potato of the Iraq war, attacked Wal-Mart for not providing enough health insurance for its employees. The economics columnist Robert J. Samuelson concluded that the company selected as a corporate villain "though tempting as a symbol, is mostly a diversion from weightier issues where what politicians do really matters." *The Washington Post* headlined his article "Wal-Mart as Red Herring."

redlining Delineating an area as a slum in which mortgage financing is not available, thereby speeding its decline.

"Redlining," wrote U.S. District Court Judge David Porter in 1976, "contributes to the decay of our cities." A *Washington Post* editorial added:

> It is a self-fulfilling prophecy. When the first signs of blight or impending racial or economic change appear, some lending institutions, anticipating a drop in market value, draw an imaginary red line around the endangered neighborhood and make no further investments within it. This usually makes it impossible for responsible and credit-worthy people to buy homes and for landlords to make improvements in the "redlined" neighborhood.

Since many urban slums are inhabited largely by blacks, the practice has been attacked as RACISM, and the Connecticut House of Representatives passed a bill prohibiting banks from refusing mortgages on grounds of geographic decline. The California Association of Realtors defined *redlining* in October 1976 as "the practice of denying the availability of home financing without regard to the credit worthiness of the individual or the soundness of the structure," a definition that implies disapproval.

The word crossed into diplomatic usage when Israelis told Syrian leaders in 1976 not to cross a "red line" in Lebanon, close to the Lebanese-Israeli border. This recalled the rhyming *deadline*, which originated in Civil War prison camps as a limit beyond which a prisoner could not walk.

red meat Also "raw meat"; material in a speech designed to elicit applause and shouts of approval from the BASE in the audience.

This has to do with HOT-BUTTON issues: "Let's give 'em some red meat" is an instruction to deal with matters that will make a crowd, like a lion, roar its approval. Vice President Spiro Agnew in 1970 would often ask his speechwriters, "Got some red meat in this to stir 'em up?" When Bush press secretary Tony Snow broke precedent by giving political fundraising speeches in 2006, he explained, "These aren't red-meat speeches. I'm staying out of the bare-knuckle stuff."

"We're already deep into the red-meat season," wrote Joel Auerbach in a June 2007 *Washington Post* article deploring the brutally long primary campaign and headed "Feeding Frenzy: Red Meat Season," illustrated by a large slab of beef and subheaded "The Base Likes It Bloody. The Candidates Dish It Up. Do the Rest of Us Have to Swallow It?" He wrote: "This is the season of the marginal candidate whose voice rises higher and higher until it threatens to reach a pitch that only a dog could hear." That was DOG-WHISTLE POLITICS. "We'll be on this red-meat diet so long it may kill us."

It won't kill political junkies or sought-after pundits and pollsters; they lap it up as much as the "bases." Newspaper editor Bill Keller told CBS that he was only a little surprised by the level of criticisms the newspaper was getting. "It's an election year. Beating up on *The New York Times* is red meat for the conservative base." See STIR UP THE ANIMALS; WEDGE ISSUE.

redneck A bigoted rural white, especially Southern; used as an attack word on Southern conservatives or segregationists, though sometimes adopted self-mockingly.

The invaluable *Dictionary of American Regional English* (DARE) defines it as "a derogatory term for a White person perceived as ignorant, narrow-minded, boorish, or racist." An 1893 citation explains the source: "men who work in the field, as a matter of course, generally have their skin burned red by the sun, and especially is this true of the back of their necks." The word came to mean "poor white" or "white trash" in some usages, the "backwoods vote" in others. The stereotype is of a white racist resenting blacks, and the irony is that the use of the stereotype also reflects anti-white racism.

The word belongs in the political lexicon: an 1891 manuscript citation reads, "Primary on the 25th. And the 'rednecks' will be there. And the 'Yaller-heels' will be there also. And the 'hayseeds' and the 'gray dillers,' they'll be there, too." Albert Kirwan's book on Mississippi politics from 1876 to 1925 was titled *Revolt of the Rednecks*. In his 1946 novel *All the King's Men*, about Southern politics, Robert Penn Warren included a line: "Mason County is red-neck country and they don't like niggers ..." In 1967, Florida Governor Claude R. Kirk told *The Saturday Evening Post*, "Look, I'm not one of these red-necked governors like Lester Maddox."

The noun *redneck* can also be used as an adjective, though some copy editors prefer to dress it up as *rednecked*. *Red-necked*, hyphenated, means "angry," contrary to the *Post* transcription of the word Kirk used; it probably derives from the flush of blood to the neck and face in a moment of fury, and is only tangentially related to *redneck*, through a connection possible in the red-faced anger of a bigot. George Wallace, campaigning in 1968, described some of his followers as *peapickers*, *peckerwoods*, and *woolhats*. Semanticist Mario Pei suggested that "these are evidently to be taken as complimentary replacements for less flattering terms, such as 'redneck' and 'cracker.'"

In current usage, *prejudiced* is genteel, more concerned with religion than race; *dis-*

criminatory legalistic; *bigoted* blunt; *biased* mild; *anti-Negro* outdated; and *redneck* descriptive of a person the speaker thinks is ignorant, rustic, and anti-Northern.

In the 1977 *Redneck Power: The Wit and Wisdom of Billy Carter*, the President's brother was quoted as drawing the distinction between the complimentary *good ole boy* and the derogatory *redneck*: "Well, a good ole boy…is somebody that rides around in a pick-up truck—which I do—and drinks beer and puts 'em in a litter bag. A redneck's one that rides around in a truck and drinks beer and throws 'em out the window." See BUBBA FACTOR.

red state/blue state Republican state/ Democratic state and, by extension, culturally conservative states (red) vs. more liberal ones (blue).

The association of red with the Republican and blue with the Democratic parties stems from the election-eve maps shown on TV and produced in newspapers able to print in color. The present color code is relatively new, however. During the presidential campaigns of 1992 and 1996, most media outlets used blue for states that voted Republican and red for those that went Democratic. Thus, foreseeing a Democratic victory three weeks prior to the 1992 election, *The Boston Globe*'s David Nyhan wrote on Oct. 15: "But when the anchormen turn to their electronic tote boards election night and the red states for Clinton start swamping the blue states for Bush, this will be a strange night for me."

Those colors switched parties throughout the '90s, depending on media preference, but became firmly fixed in the 2000 Bush-Gore election. On NBC's *Today Show* during the week before the election, *Meet the Press* moderator-interviewer Tim Russert led host Matt Lauer through a potential political alignment of the states, based on a graphic first used on the cable network MS-NBC. Russert asked himself aloud how George W. Bush would "get the remaining 61 electoral 'red states,' if you will?"

Most of us willed. On election night, the lexicographer, present with Russert in the NBC studio as an analyst, noticed the frequent use of *red state* and *blue state* to substitute for the party names, and recalls pitying viewers with only black-and-white sets. Russert disclaims coinage, as the red-blue graphic was becoming familiar both on television and in color print in newspapers and magazines, but he was the leading popularizer as the blue-Democrat, red-Republican assignment took hold nationally that night.

This arrangement is likely to last a long time, having been imprinted indelibly on the public psyche by the closeness of the elections of 2000 and 2004; by the starkness of the geographic divisions, with essentially contiguous blocks of color (red states in the south and middle portion of the nation, blue states along the coasts and in the upper Midwest); and by the minimal amount of change in the red-blue groupings from 2000 to 2004, with only three states (New Mexico, Iowa, and New Hampshire) switching camps between the two elections. The extraordinary amount of time that people had to ponder the maps in 2000, from Nov. 7, when voters went to the polls, to Dec. 8, when the U.S. Supreme Court halted recounts, awarding victory to George W. Bush, may also have helped fix the association of red with Republican and blue with Democratic.

The red vs. blue division mirrors the winner-take-all provisions in forty-eight states and the District of Columbia that the presidential candidate who wins a plurality at the polls gets all the state's electoral votes. (Nebraska and Maine are exceptions to the winner-take-all rule.) The graphic display masks deeper differences, however, since contests in many states can be close, with sizable minorities losing to barely larger majorities. Many red states contain deep pockets of blue (typically the more urban areas), while most blue states include red regions (generally the outer suburbs and rural areas). Thus, political consultant James Carville characterized Pennsylvania as "Philadelphia and Pittsburgh, with Alabama in between."

Closely divided states usually are described as *battleground states*, a locution popularized by Nixon campaign manager

John Mitchell in 1968 in rejecting the Goldwater SOUTHERN STRATEGY. Since then *battleground* has been joined by *swing states* (see SWING VOTER), or, a newer term, *purple states*. As noted in the Cleveland *Plain Dealer* in early 2004: "In Washington, pundits talk of red states (Republican), blue states (Democratic), and purple states, which are blue states getting redder." Or vice versa. Barry Dill, a political consultant and lobbyist in Phoenix, Arizona, told the *Sacramento Bee* in 2005 that Latino voters could have an effect on his state's reddish complexion: "There are blue and there are red states, right? Well, we're a purple state."

The present red vs. blue alignment has lasted long enough for the two colors to become shorthand for conservative values vs. liberal ones. Thus, cultural critic Frank Rich contended in 2004 that "it's blue America, not red, that is inexorably winning the culture war," while his fellow *New York Times* columnist, Maureen Dowd, said of her own conservative family members that same year: "They're beyond red—more like crimson."

The rendering of Republican states as red is ironic, considering the historic associations of that color with revolution: "Red ruin, and the breaking up of laws," as Tennyson put it in the *Idylls of the King*. French revolutionaries in the 1780s sported red cockades, while "Red Republicans" sought to overthrow European governments in the revolutions of 1848. See RED. Reporting on the turmoil in France that year, the London *Times* wrote of "the *red* Republic, as the Ultras there call themselves, against the *blue*—colours being used to designate the parties as much in provincial France as in our counties in England." And red went on to become the color of socialism and Communism. Unhappily for Republicans, red also is a symbol of debt—"to be in the red," a saying that derives from the old banking practice of using red ink for overdrawn accounts.

Blue for Democrats is slightly more appropriate than red for Republicans. Historically, it was one of the traditional colors of the Scottish Presbyterians or Whigs, who adopted it in opposition to the scarlet of royalty. But less happily for the Democrats, the Whiggish blue may also have inspired our much-maligned BLUE LAWS, first described as such in 1781 by the Rev. Samuel Peters in his *General History of Connecticut*. At the Democratic National Convention in 2004, the soon-to-be-elected Senator from Illinois, Barack Obama, made a favorable impression on the partisan gathering with his nonpartisan theme: "The pundits like to slice and dice our country into red states and blue states: red states for Republicans, blue states for Democrats," he said. "But I've got news for them, too. We worship an awesome God in the blue states, and don't like federal agents poking around our libraries in the red states."

red tape Bureaucratic sluggishness; unnecessary paperwork; administrative delay.

"Steel Pipes and Red Tape Don't Mix," advertised the British steel industry in 1964, warning voters that a vote for Labour was a vote for nationalization of their industry, with all the bureaucracy it was expected to entail. In 2006, the *Financial Times* (London) headlined a plan of Britain's then Chancellor of the Exchequer Gordon Brown "Brown Seeks 25% Cut in Red Tape"; one year later, after he had become Prime Minister, *The Daily Telegraph* headlined "Brown Pledge to Cut Red Tape Rings Hollow." The tape triumphed again.

Red tape as a method for securing legal and official documents is mentioned in Maryland Laws of 1696–1715. Official documents in England were tied with a string or tape of a reddish color, and many lawyers followed the practice in packaging their briefs.

Early in the nineteenth century, Washington Irving used the phrase in "His brain was little better than red tape and parchment." A popularizer was the English historian Thomas Carlyle, who wrote in 1840: "Keep your red-tape clerks, your influentialities, your important businesses." A decade later, in *Latter-Day Pamphlets*, he described a politician as "little other than a redtape Talking-machine, and unhappy Bag of Parliamentary Eloquence." A passage from *Little Dorrit* by Charles Dickens, written in 1857, added to the lexicon of governmental turgidity: "Whatever was required to be done, the Circumlocution Office was beforehand with all the departments in the art of perceiving how not to do it."

The phrase *red tape*, along with BUREAU-CRACY, is a convenient weapon for citizens frustrated by what might be the delay of sensible administrative review, or what may be, in Shakespeare's phrase, "the law's delay, the insolence of office." *Washington red tape* and the need to *go through channels* called for the creation of *expediters* in World War II, whose job was to *cut through the red tape* and *open up bottlenecks* in war production.

Endless paperpushing depresses the most industrious; the late rocket scientist Wernher von Braun said in 1958: "We can lick gravity, but sometimes the paperwork is overwhelming."

A rare defense of red tape was made in 1977 by Herbert Kaufman of the Brookings Institution: "One person's red tape may be another's treasured procedural safeguard...We are ambivalent about the appropriate trade-offs between discretion and constraint, each of us demanding the former for ourselves and the latter for our neighbors...Accepting red tape as an ineradicable foe is not to give up the fight, but to join battle on the only terms that offer any hope of success." Kaufman enlivened the pages of his iconoclastic tract with a cartoon by Lichty: "Gentlemen, the bad news is the company is in a state of bankruptcy...the good news is we have complied with federal rules and regulations."

reform The creation of a temporarily organized opposition to an administration or party hierarchy based upon its corruption, assumption of privilege, or, in some cases, its refusal to share power with those espousing reform.

Reformers, often capable of defeating those in power, are less successful in maintaining themselves on top. This was bemoaned by Lincoln Steffens, who wrote: "It is an emotional gratification to go out with the crowd and 'smash something.' This is nothing but revolt, and even monarchies have uprisings to the credit of their

subjects. But revolt is not reform and one revolutionary administration is not good government."

Steffens was writing about an attempt by a reform mayor, Seth Low, to win reelection in 1903; the Tammany motto was: "To Hell with reform." Tammany won.

Professional politicians have always had disdain for reform movements and reformers. Tammany Mayor John F. Hyland told the Civil Service Reform Association in 1918: "We have had all the reform that we want in this city for some time to come." Another New York mayor, Jimmy Walker, quipped: "A reformer is a guy who rides through a sewer in a glass-bottomed boat."

Reformers have taken abuse from more distinguished sources. Speaker of the House Thomas Reed wrote his own sardonic definition of reform in 1902: "An indefinable something is to be done, in a way nobody knows how, at a time nobody knows when, that will accomplish nobody knows what..."

George Washington Plunkitt, of Tammany Hall, expressed his own conviction that reform will always fail: "The fact is that a reformer can't last in politics. He can make a show for awhile, but he always comes down like a rocket. Politics is as much a regular business as the grocery or the dry-goods or the drug business. You've got to be trained up to it or you're sure to fail."

Enthusiasm, moral fervor, and a conviction that reform will save the city, state, nation, and world is a hallmark of the genuine reformer, but to the philosopher George Santayana, it was all spurious. In *The Life of Reason* (1905) he wrote: "A thousand reforms have left the world as corrupt as ever, for each successful reform has founded a new institution, and this institution has bred its new and congenial abuses."

Such disdainful references to reform are easy to find, but the intermittent movement is a vital part of any political system. Those associated with reform movements need not be stereotyped as "goo-goos," the nickname of New York's Good Government Clubs of the 1890s. Mrs. Eleanor Roosevelt, retired Senator Herbert Lehman, and former

Air Force Secretary Thomas K. Finletter were the tough, politically savvy leaders of the reform movement in New York in the late fifties and early sixties.

Columnist Murray Kempton gave an insight into the steel behind Mrs. Roosevelt's charm in quoting a remark she made to congressional candidate and novelist Gore Vidal, who had introduced former Tammany leader Carmine de Sapio at a dinner. "The dear old lady," wrote Kempton, "gazed across those hills ennobled by our history and said sweetly, 'I told Carmine that I would get him after what he did to Franklin [Jr.] at the 1954 state convention.'"

The word became a euphemism for any planned revision in law in the '60s and '70s. When the Hatch Act (protecting government employees from political influence from their superiors at election time) was attacked as unfairly limiting the political activity of appointees, the suggested return to the old ways was called "reform reform."

"Mr. Carter wants 'legal and judicial reform,'" wrote columnist James J. Kilpatrick in February 1978. "He wants 'criminal code reform.' He wants 'wiretap reform.' He wants 'mining law reform.' He wants 'a series of reforms'…'long-needed reforms'…'to reform the sewage treatment construction grant program'…In times past, Presidents have regularly asked that various programs be enlarged, expanded, strengthened, enhanced, improved or even reorganized, but this is not Mr. Carter's approach. Politically, he is the inheritor of Luther, Calvin and Knox. Reform! My own thought," concluded Kilpatrick, "is that reform is like garlic in the dressing: a little bit, as every cook knows, goes a very long way."

American political writers, at a loss to describe the scrambled spectrum of Russian politics after the fall of Communism, called the followers of Boris Yeltsin *reformers.*

Those who try to upset party leadership always call themselves *reformers*; the entrenched leadership prefers to call them INSURGENTS.

refusenik See -NIK SUFFIX.

regime See ADMINISTRATION.

regime change Replacement of one government by another, especially a hostile foreign one by a presumably friendlier one, either by overt or covert means.

"It is the stated policy of this government to have regime change. And it hasn't changed. And we'll use all the tools at our disposal," declared President George W. Bush at a White House press conference on July 9, 2002. The "stated policy" had been made plain in the Iraq Liberation Act of 1998, signed into law by President Bill Clinton. *The New York Times* reported on a mission of Mr. Clinton's Secretary of State in 1999: "On every stop on her quick trip to moderate Arab states, Secretary of State Madeleine K. Albright explained the Administration's goal for Iraq: regime change."

The 1998 Iraq Liberation Act, while providing for transfer of surplus military equipment to Iraqi groups (especially Kurdish) opposed to Saddam Hussein, along with other assistance, specifically precluded the use of U.S. armed forces; it also urged the president to call upon the United Nations to establish an international war crimes tribunal for prosecuting Saddam and other Iraqi officials.

"Regime change allows a state to solve its problems with another state by removing the offensive regime there and replacing it with a less offensive one," wrote Richard N. Haass, president of the Council of Foreign Relations, in an article on "Regime Change and Its Limits," in *Foreign Affairs*, in 2005. "Using regime change as a policy panacea is nothing new," Haass continued. "The Roosevelt administration ultimately chose to deal with Germany and Japan through a policy of regime change, seeking not simply to defeat them on the battlefield and reverse their conquests but to continue war until the regimes in Berlin and Tokyo were ousted and something much better was firmly ensconced."

Dated to 1925 in the *OED*, *regime change* has been pursued in various ways over the years. As reported in *International Security* in 1990: "The U.S. government tacitly acknowledged that the struggle to promote regime change [in Nicaragua] had shifted from the military to the political-electoral terrain."

Regime is a pejorative term, commonly used to denigrate an opposing government. As noted in 1978 in *[MORE]*, a publication for journalists: "If *Time* makes a regressive contribution to literary language, it nonetheless does so with enormous care. Socialists not only plan, they 'concoct'; they rarely have governments, they have 'regimes.'" The negative connotations of *regime* are in keeping with its etymology, from the Latin *regere,* "to rule," making it an inherently more authoritarian term than *government,* from Latin *gubernare,* "to guide or steer (a ship)."

Regime change became a catchphrase in the late 1990s. Reporting on the release of a home video version of Andrew Lloyd Webber's musical *Cats* in 1998, the *Los Angeles Times* quoted producer Gary Lucchesi: "Universal wanted to do it [as an animated feature], but then there were three regime changes at Universal."

Stickers proclaiming "Regime Change Begins at Home" later blossomed on the bumpers of those who strongly opposed the war in Iraq. It was the Bush Administration that was the target of a paid death notice in *The New York Times* that began: "Leipziger—Arthur F. Age 82. On November 2, 2004, still hoping for a regime change."

regular The party-designated candidate in a primary, as opposed to the insurgent; or a loyal party voter, the basic individual element of the "core constituency," usually a member of a local organization.

In a primary fight within a party for a specific nomination or for local party leadership, the Ins proudly display "Regular Democratic [or Republican] Candidate" on their posters and literature; the Outs, who cannot very well call themselves "irregulars," usually choose "Independent Republican Candidate" or "Reform Democratic Candidate." See INS AND OUTS.

Most politicians today use a yardstick of willingness to vote in a primary as a test of "regularity": if a voter registers with a party at a general election, he is a registered Democrat (or Republican), but if he takes the trouble to turn out at a primary—and about three out of ten do in a contest—he may be considered a regular—that is, if he votes for the "Ins."

A *regular* is more active than a *registered voter,* less active than a *party worker.* Though a regular is usually a PARTISAN, a partisan is not necessarily a regular. The regular vote is the hardcore strength of any party on Election Day, which usually needs to be supplemented by the independent or SWING VOTE for victory.

See MILITARY METAPHORS; BASE.

reign of terror See TERRORIST.

religious issue See WHISPERING CAMPAIGN; UNPACK; REVERSE BIGOTRY; BAILEY MEMORANDUM; RED HERRING; THEOCON.

religious metaphors
All the following political expressions have religious derivations, some not so obvious, that are covered under their separate entries:

ALL THINGS TO ALL MEN
BLEEDING HEARTS
BORN AGAIN
BULLY PULPIT
CRUSADE
CULT OF PERSONALITY
GRAY EMINENCE
HELLBENT FOR ELECTION
LOVE FEAST
OPEN CONVENANTS
PARTY ELDERS
PARTY FAITHFULL
PATRONAGE
PUBLIC TROUGH
QUICK AND THE DEAD, THE
READ OUT OF THE PARTY
ROOT AND BRANCH
SANTA CLAUS, NOBODY SHOOTS AT
WITCH HUNT

Used in politics, but not primarily political phrases, are *Bible belt* (a coinage of H. L. Mencken); *holier than thou* (a coinage of Ezekiel); *side of the angels* (Disraeli opposing Darwin's evolution theory); *sacred cow* (from the Hindus).

rendezvous with destiny Fated to be great.

FDR told the 1936 Democratic convention: "There is a mysterious cycle in human events. To some generations much is given. Of other generations much is expected. This generation of Americans has a rendezvous with destiny."

Historian Frank Freidel, who used the phrase as the subtitle of his biography of FDR, credited it to one of Roosevelt's speechwriters, Raymond Moley; others say FDR aide Thomas Corcoran suggested it to the President. Poetic and effective, it stimulated strong reaction. The conservative columnist and linguist H. L. Mencken warned soon after the speech that "The Rooseveltian 'rendezvous with destiny' will turn out, in November, to be a rendezvous with a bouncer." (Republican nominee Alf Landon was defeated in a landslide.)

Thomas E. Dewey, seeking the Republican nomination in 1940 that ultimately went to Wendell Willkie, tried another substitution: "The President has said we have a 'rendezvous with destiny.' We seem to be on our way toward a rendezvous with despair."

Why was the word *rendezvous* chosen rather than "date with destiny" or "appointment with destiny"? Perhaps because the previous generation of Americans had a "rendezvous with death," in the phrase of U.S. poet Alan Seeger, killed while fighting with the French army in 1916:

But I've a rendezvous with Death
At midnight in some flaming town,
When spring trips north again this year,
And I to my pledged word am true,
I shall not fail that rendezvous.

This poem had an effect on a later president. Arthur Schlesinger, Jr., wrote of John F. Kennedy: "On Cape Cod, in October, 1953, when he returned from his wedding trip, he had read his young wife what he said was his favorite poem. She learned it for him by heart, and he used to love to have her say it. It was Alan Seeger's 'I Have a Rendezvous with Death.'"

President Lyndon B. Johnson was intrigued by "this generation of Americans," the beginning of FDR's rendezvous-with-destiny phrase. In his 1964 campaign, he said that Barry Goldwater offered a "doctrine that plays loosely with human destiny, and this generation of Americans will have no part of it." (In the same campaign, the actor

Ronald Reagan, in his speech on television supporting Goldwater—"*The* Speech," as it was quickly called, as it launched his political career—melded the FDR quote with a Lincoln quote about the last best hope of Earth: "You and I have a rendezvous with destiny. We will preserve for our children this, the last best hope of man on Earth—or will sentence them to take the last step into a thousand years of darkness.") LBJ's "this generation" allusion to FDR's "rendezvous with destiny" was subtle; however in a Nashville, Tennessee, speech on March 16, 1967, Johnson edited FDR's construction into mediocrity: "This generation of Americans is making its imprint on history."

rendition Seizure and transport of a suspected terrorist to a foreign country for custody and interrogation; in full, *extraordinary rendition*.

The modern meaning flows from *rendition*'s original sense of surrendering a place or person, as in, from *The Encyclopaedia Britannica*'s 1860 edition, "The rendition of fugitive slaves by the Northern States." Howard Safir (no relation to the author), former New York City police commissioner, recalled using the term in the current sense when he was a U.S. Marshal in the late 1970s. "It's when we would go overseas and kidnap fugitives and bring them back to the U.S. We called it 'extraordinary rendition' because, although it was legal under U.S. law, it was not always legal under the law of the country in which the fugitive was residing."

Renditions became much more controversial after knowledge became public that the CIA had begun conducting them in the wake of 9/11. The AP defined the term in 2004 as "the covert practice of expelling suspects to countries known to use torture to extract information." The CIA disputed this, saying the purpose of rendition was to transfer suspects to nations where interrogators speak their dialects and can develop cultural intimacy. George Tenet, Director of Central Intelligence, told the 9/11 Commission that "disruptions, rendition, and sensitive collection activities no doubt saved lives." Officials in various European nations complained that their laws were broken, launched investigations, and began issuing arrest warrants and indictments of Americans, many of them CIA officers; Bush administration officials and intelligence sources, both active and retired and usually speaking not for attribution, insisted that "harsh" interrogation techniques had led to the aborting of terrorist plots and saved lives. Revelation in 2007 of Justice Department documents conflicting with White House statements denying approval of torture and CIA destruction of tapes—especially in the light of rendition of some prisoners—were a source of embarrassment to the Bush Administration.

See CIA-ESE.

reordering priorities Putting first things first, though what is first to the reorderer is not always first to the reorderee.

This phrase achieved the status of a thundering cliché in the late '60s, when debate began about limiting the size of U.S. defense and space expenditures and redirecting those resources to "meet human needs." Though not the coiner, John Gardner, first at the National Urban Coalition and later at Common Cause, was identified with the phrase.

Top priority was heavily used in World War II, and *high priority* became bureaucratese subsequently. In calling for change, the participle used is never *changing* or *reorganizing*; it is occasionally *resetting* or *reassessing*, but most frequently *reordering*. The word usually appears near another vogue term, *agenda*.

With the relish experienced by soldiers who capture enemy guns and turn them around, the conservative writer of the preamble to the lengthy 1972 budget message of President Nixon "put the story in the lead": "*To the Congress of the United States:* In the 1971 budget, America's priorities were quietly but dramatically reordered: for the first time in twenty years, we spent more to meet human needs than we spent on defense."

reportedly A leading WEASEL WORD in journalism; a modifier that uses the prevalence of repetition to impute truth.

Alleged, a word whose roots may be linked with *litigate*, has long been used to avert libel litigation; the word has since become such a transparent, though often ineffective, libel-ducker that newsmen now prefer *charged with* or *accused of*, with some official source credited.

Less precise than *alleged* is *reported* or *reportedly*, which is a form of the gossipy *they're saying*; it implies "nobody has been sued using this before, so here goes." In Communist terminology, the preferred construction of such a blithe assumption was "as is well known."

When *New Yorker* profilist Geoffrey Hellman died, Alden Whitman of *The New York Times* wrote in an obituary that Hellman "feuded fiercely" with his colleagues on the magazine. "One such feud was with Brendan Gill...the two were reportedly not on speaking terms." Mr. Gill blazed back in a letter to the editor: "Certainly he and I never had a feud. Moreover, having adjacent offices at the magazine, we spoke almost daily up to the time he fell ill, and we often lunched together. It is a fact that as an old friend of Geoffrey's I was one of the last of his colleagues to be granted the privilege of visiting him as he lay dying. So much for 'reportedly'—a word that has little to recommend its use in write-ups of the distressed living and the defenseless dying."

President Carter's Attorney General, Griffin Bell, put it this way in 1977, justifying his practice of correcting journalistic errors: "Once information is published, it is likely to be reprinted by journalists yet unborn unless a denial has been posted in neon at Times Square." This has since been ameliorated somewhat by adding corrections to articles stored in electronic archives.

For a list of other terms which will be used by journalists yet unborn, see JOURNALESE.

republican As a noun, a political party in the U.S. whose center of gravity is more conservative, more resistant to radical change, than the more liberal party with which it creatively contends. See DEMOCRAT, noun, a back-formation from *democracy*, a member of a political party favoring greater government action than its conservative opposition does to direct and promote the welfare of the people in the republic it often governs.

John Adams worried about the word *Republican* in 1790: "all good government is and must be republican. But, at the same time, you can or will agree with me, that there is not in lexicography a more fraudulent word.... Are we not, my friend, in danger of rendering the word *republican* unpopular in this country by an indiscreet, indeterminate, and equivocal use of it?"

Thomas Jefferson, who used the word as an antonym for *monarchic* all his life, disagreed in 1816: "of the import of the term *republic*, instead of saying, as has been said, 'that it may mean anything or nothing,' we may say with truth and meaning, that governments are more or less republican as they have more or less of the element of popular election and control in their composition ..."

Jefferson's party became known as the Republicans; he preferred it to "anti-Federalists" and sought to turn the tables by referring to his opposition as "the anti-republicans."

Hans Sperber and Travis Trittschuh pointed out in the *Dictionary of American Political Terms* that "since the Constitution guarantees to every state a republican form of government, it would seem that republican from the beginning had every chance of becoming a unifying not a partisan word." The Jeffersonian party became known as the Democratic-Republicans, and their opposition as the National Republicans, because of this unifying sense of the word in its form-of-government meaning (as defined above).

In the Jacksonian era, the word's previous bipartisan use led both parties, beginning to take more adversarial positions after the Era of Good Feeling, to drop it completely. Democratic-Republicans became Democrats; National Republicans became Whigs.

As the Whig party fell apart, the term *Republican* began to be bandied about, probably around 1852. In 1854 A. E. Bovay wrote to *New York Tribune* editor Horace Greeley: "Urge them to forget previous political names and organization, and to band together under the name I sug-

gested to you at Lovejoy's Hotel in 1852, while Scott was being nominated. I mean the name *Republican*." About the same time, Greeley wrote a friend regarding the formation of an antislavery party: "Call it Republican—no prefix, no suffix, but plain Republican." At Jackson, Michigan, in July 1854, the party was organized and chose that name, picking John C. Frémont as its first presidential candidate in 1856 with the slogan "Free Soil, Free Men, Frémont."

To differentiate: a *republic* is a form of government in which the people exercise their power through elected representatives, while a *democracy* is a government where the people exercise their powers directly *or* through elected representatives.

revanchism A policy or movement to regain territory lost either in war or through treaties signed under duress.

The word is rooted in the French *revanche*, meaning "revenge," which first appeared in English as an ironic use of the French noun. Queen Victoria wrote in an 1858 letter, "She never allows a word to be said against Leopold who in revanche is much kinder to her than he was."

Using the derivative adjective *revanchist*, a political sense was added by 1889 and used in 1926 in *The Scots Observer*: "It is France's policy [toward Germany] that the sores be kept open even if they give a handle to Monarchist revanchists."

Following World War II, Soviet writers applied *revanchist* to Germans who sought reunification of their country, and *revanchism* to the movement for such a reunification as a means of redressing Germany's defeat in the war.

"German Nazism marched under the standards of revanchism," Foreign Minister Eduard A. Shevardnadze told the United Nations in 1989. "Now ... the forces of revanchism are again becoming active and are seeking to revise and destroy the postwar realities in Europe."

Pronounced with the "vanch" of *revanchism* rhyming with *ranch*, the term is never self-applied, because it suggests no higher motive to policy than getting even. A scholarly synonym is *irredentism*, from the Italian word for "unredeemed"; this term was used by Italian politicians in the nineteenth century who sought to incorporate regions like Trieste (*Italia irredenta*) into the mother country. Wags like to urge superpatriots to "see your irredentist twice a year."

revenue sharing See TAX SHARING.

reverse bigotry The technique of crying "foul" to solidify a racial or religious group behind the candidate supposedly being fouled.

Democratic Congressman Abraham Ribicoff, running for governor of Connecticut in 1954 against John Davis Lodge, said, "Nowhere except in the Democratic party could a boy named Abe Ribicoff be nominated for governor of this state." In his 1966 *America's Political Dynasties*, Stephen Hess wrote: "The Republicans charged that this was a form of reverse bigotry: Ribicoff, in reply, justified his statement by citing some stories from New York newspapers as evidence that his opponents were conducting an undercover smear campaign against him."

In the 1960 presidential campaign, many Republicans took pains not to raise the "religious issue" against Sen. John F. Kennedy, lest it backfire against them with conservative Catholics, but Nixon chairman Len Hall and campaign director Bob Finch were convinced that Kennedy was deliberately raising it at every opportunity in cities with large Catholic populations. Portions of his eloquent speech to the Houston ministers, pleading for no prejudice in the campaign, were rebroadcast often in major cities where—Nixon campaigners were convinced—many regular Republicans who were Catholics were persuaded to switch to one of "their own" who was being unfairly attacked because of his religion. They described this device as "reverse bigotry." See BAILEY MEMORANDUM.

Reverse bigotry is a charge almost as hotly denied as bigotry. It applies to racial as well as religious appeals. When the House of Representatives in 1967 denied a seat to Congressman Adam Clayton Powell of New York because of his contempt-of-court citations and improprieties with committee funds, he claimed that his skin color was the reason for the censure. Black activist James Meredith decided to challenge Powell in an election, then changed his mind under pressure from civil rights leaders. "There won't be any election in the contested sense," observed the *Miami Herald*. "Adam Clayton Powell's appeal to reverse bigotry has seen to that."

When less anger is involved, the practice of favoring nonwhites is called *reverse discrimination*. For related words and phrases, see WHISPERING CAMPAIGN and QUOTA.

In the synonymy of racial, religious or sexual hatred, *intolerance* and *bias* are the mildest terms of disapprobation; *discrimination* adds a note of action against a group; *prejudice* deals mainly with religion as *racism* does with race, *homophobia* with sex, and *zealot* with politics. The most severe and all-encompassing charge is *bigotry*; the only time that word was successfully modified was in George W. Bush's criticism during the 2000 campaign of "the soft bigotry of low expectations."

revisionism Originally, a neutral 1890s term describing Marxists who thought revolution was unnecessary; later, a Communist charge that the accused seeks to alter basic tenets of Marxism-Leninism.

In COMMUNIST TERMINOLOGY, *deviationism* is internal criticism or refusal to recognize the official party line at any given moment; *revisionism* is a far more serious charge, as explained in the *Political Dictionary*, published in Moscow in 1958: "A tendency in the workers' movement which, to please the bourgeoisie, seeks to debase, emasculate, destroy Marxism by means of revision, that is, reconsideration, distortion, and denial of its fundamental tenets.… Contemporary revisionism seeks to defame the teaching of Marxism-Leninism …"

Communists recognized revisionism as carrying the seeds of self-destruction (and the source of that cliché can be found in BODY POLITIC). Nikita Khrushchev said on January 6, 1961: "We must always keep our powder dry and wage implacable war on revisionism which tries to wipe out the revolutionary essence of Marxism-Leninism, whitewash modern capitalism, undermine the solidarity of the Communist movement, and encourage Communist Parties to go their separate national ways."

Those who were charged with *deviationism* and *revisionism* replied that their accusers were afflicted with *dogmatism*— a sin that, according to the 1961 party program, hinders "a correct appraisal of the changing situation and the use of new opportunities for the benefit of the working class and all democratic forces." Another defense was a countercharge of *sectarianism*, which according to one source "gives birth to striving to quit the masses and to enclose oneself in a narrow circle, and throttles down the initiative of the toiling masses."

Thus, *revisionists* and the milder *deviationists* stood on one side, with *dogmatists* and the milder *sectarians* on the other. In 1964, Communists in China began issuing polemics saying that the Soviet Union was led by revisionists: "The revisionists are producing their own opposites and will be buried by them."

The Chinese charge could not be more serious in terms of Communist philosophy. Chairman Mao Zedong had said in 1957: "The revisionists deny the differences between socialism and capitalism, between the dictatorship of the proletariat and the dictatorship of the bourgeoisie. What they advocate is in fact not the socialist line but the capitalist line. In present circumstances, revisionism is more pernicious than dogmatism."

In the -ISM crossfire, the Chinese in the '60s and '70s added HEGEMONISM to their charge of Soviet revisionism, which meant that the Soviets were not only corrupting the Marx-Engels ideal, but also seeking to impose their corruption on China.

revolutionary praxis Practical activity or action for overthrowing the existing political system.

Praxis, "action based on will," comes from the Greek for "doing, acting, practice" (its plural is *praxes*). Sir Philip Sidney was first to use the term in English, in his 1586 treatise on poetry: "For as Aristotle sayth, it is not *Gnosis* [knowledge], but *Praxis* must be the fruit." Bishop Robert Lowth used the now obsolete sense of "collection of examples to serve for practice" in his 1762 *Short Introduction to the English Grammar*, in the heading "A Praxis, or Example of Grammatical Resolution"; modern grammarians contrast *praxis* (speech as action) with *lexis* (speech as meaning).

Political philosophers and historians defined the term in the nineteenth century as "practical activity." Count August von Cieszkowski used this definition in 1838, and Karl Marx soon followed. In his *Dictionary of Political Thought*, Roger Scruton explained that revolutionary praxis "sustains itself without ideology, since it is directed to the essential nature of social reality."

In recent decades, the phrase had been largely limited to discussions of religion and politics in Latin America. Michael Novak wrote in *The New York Times Magazine* in 1984, "Liberation theology says that truth lies in revolutionary praxis." In *National Review* in 1986, Richard John Neuhaus suggested that a reporter at the 1985 Roman Catholic Synod of Bishops missed its deepest meaning because he "had come to cover hot issues, such as revolutionary praxis and women's ordination."

In 1989, paradoxically, the Marxist sense was revitalized by students demonstrating for democracy in Tiananmen Square in Beijing. Their call for *revolutionary praxis* merged two antithetical senses: the capitalist "practicality" and the revolutionary "action."

revolution of rising expectations Unrest caused by extravagant promises; or, the constructive desire for change based on an optimistic view of society's future; or, the increased demand for a high standard of living that comes when the media bring evidence of others' affluence into poor people's homes.

"Reflections on the Revolution of Rising Expectations" was the title of a 1949 speech by U.S. diplomat Harlan Cleveland.

Fifteen years later, in a speech to the U.N., Cleveland asserted his coinage claim: "The phrase has since been attributed to nearly every literate American of our time, but I think this was the first time that phrase saw the light of day." He titled his U.N. speech "The Evolution of Rising Responsibilities."

When Theodore Sorensen was asked to list the qualifications of a USIA director to President-elect John F. Kennedy, one of the key points was: "should comprehend the 'revolution of rising expectations' throughout the world, and its impact on U.S. foreign policy." In 1968, London's *The Economist* titled a review of Gunnar Myrdal's *Asian Drama: An Inquiry into the Poverty of Nations* "The Revolution of Falling Expectation?"

Revolution, a slashing political word, was somewhat defanged by this phrase, and the process has continued in recent years. When violent protesters preached revolution in the late sixties and early seventies, their word was preempted, and thereby softened, by Establishment figures. "The American Revolution is a continuing one," said industrialist David J. Mahoney, upon taking the chairmanship of the American Revolution Bicentennial Commission in 1970, "a peaceful revolution in a system capable of managing change."

In his 1971 State of the Union address, President Nixon labeled his revenue sharing, welfare reform, and government reorganization plans "a New American Revolution." (The author, pushing hard for this phrase within the Nixon speechwriting staff, had to drop it hurriedly upon learning that its initials—N.A.R.—were those of Nelson Aldrich Rockefeller, and would result in some derision.)

Semantically, *revolution* means "violent change" and *evolution* "peaceful change," but the assumption of the word *revolution* by those opposed to violence has taken out a lot of the sting; it is a good example of how a democratic system can counter a threat by absorbing its terminology. In a similar way, President Johnson's use of WE SHALL OVERCOME and President Nixon's evocation of the new-leftist POWER TO THE PEOPLE (in connection with REVENUE SHARING) drowned out the original users of the phrases with the System's echoes.

In July of 2000, in a speech to the NAACP, Republican presidential candidate George W. Bush paralleled Cleveland's famous phrase with his most felicitous line, promising to confront "another form of bias—the soft bigotry of low expectations."

revolving door See BELTWAY BANDITS; HONEST GRAFT

rhetoric Originally, the study of persuasive presentation of argument, as in speeches; now, bombast, soaring oratory.

Several forces combined to give a pejorative cast to a word once honored by Aristotle. "DEEDS, NOT WORDS" was a favorite saying of Eisenhower's; "lower our voices" was urged by Nixon in his inaugural; and with the escalation of ESCALATION, the phrase "de-escalate the rhetoric" was aimed at political speakers who liked to provide partisan audiences with RED MEAT. Rhetoric was associated with expansive promises; when delivery fell short of promise, emptiness insinuated itself into the definition of *rhetoric*.

In a 1968 column, Art Buchwald conducted an imaginary interview with a man "manufacturing" political rhetoric as if it were bunting and buttons:

"What item has been moving the best?"

"'Law and Order' has been the biggest seller this year. We can't even keep the law and order rhetoric in stock. The minute it's put out on the counter, it's grabbed up."

"What else is selling?"

"'Peace at Home and Abroad' is a very big item. I don't think there's a politician running for office this year who hasn't brought at least one. 'The Crisis of the Cities' is also moving very well, but the one that really surprised us was 'A Piece of the Action.' We made a few samples, and before we knew it, everybody was using it to describe what the minorities wanted. ...

"Another big surprise is our 'Erosion' kit. It comes in a set: 'Erosion of the Cities,' 'Erosion of the Dollar,' 'Erosion of Moral Values,' and 'Erosion of America's Prestige Abroad.'"

Rhetoric, as a word, is now most often demeaned by those who admired the effective and inspiring use of language by FDR, Adlai Stevenson, John F. Kennedy, and

Ronald Reagan. In denouncing its use, Hubert Humphrey in 1968 used a little himself: "It is time to have done with the language of promise; to have done with the language of excess, of exaggeration. It is time not to carry more sail by way of rhetoric than the ship of state in fact can carry."

In connotation, *rhetoric* has fallen to the depths of *oratory*. See BLOVIATE; CAMPAIGN ORATORY; PERORATION; TROT OUT THE GHOSTS; VISION OF AMERICA.

rhyme, political use of

The device of rhyme can make phrases memorable, as in the American GLOOM AND DOOM and the British description of a price-and-wage-control policy, *squeeze and freeze.*

It may also be used subtly, appearing to be more rhythm than rhyme, as an oratorical device, as in this speech by President Kennedy to the U.N. in 1961: "We prefer world law, in an age of self-determination, to world war in the age of mass extermination." The cadence of Jimmy Carter's "a dis*grace* to the human *race*," about the tax system, was rhetorically effective.

Or rhyme can be used with a kind of lighthearted determination, as in Churchill's "Better jaw-jaw than war-war," or his playful message to FDR prior to the Yalta Conference in 1945: "No more let us falter. From Malta to Yalta. Let nobody alter."

For political use of poetic construction, see MARTIN, BARTON AND FISH; for poems that spawned political phrases, see CRADLE AND THE GRAVE; MOVERS AND SHAKERS; STROKE OF THE PEN; TWEEDLEDUM AND TWEEDLEDEE.

rich man's war, poor man's fight Protest against inequities in military conscription.

The slogan appears to have originated in the Confederacy in 1861, as a protest against laws favoring wealthy plantation owners; it was then picked up in the North and used in the New York draft riots of 1863. At the time, it was possible for a wealthy man to put up cash to have a "substitute" serve in his stead.

Resentment about who does the financing and who does the fighting exists between allies as well; some Britons in 1940 said, "America will fight to the last drop of English blood," and American isolationists turned the phrase around to use against the British.

Regarding student deferments during the Vietnam war, University of Chicago sociologist Morris Janowitz pointed out in *Trans-action* magazine that "a young man's chances of serving in the armed forces are decreased to the extent that he applies his energies to extending his education beyond four years of college." Obviously, this slanted student deferments toward wealthier students who could afford postgraduate education.

During the Korean conflict, the casualty rate of the lowest income groups was four times higher than that of the highest income groups, and black casualties—considering their proportion to the population—was twice as high as white. The Rev. Martin Luther King, Jr., an opponent of U.S. involvement in Vietnam, spoke out often in 1967 about what some African-American leaders were calling a "white man's war, a black man's fight." "There are twice as many Negroes in combat in Vietnam," said Dr. King, "and twice as many died in action in proportion to their number in the population as whites." Others countered that black reenlistments ran three times higher than white, accounting for the higher proportion in military service. The surrebuttal was that black reenlistments were high because career opportunities outside the service were almost nonexistent for blacks. In subsequent military conflicts, large and small, the absence of a draft did much to dampen the charge that only the poor and the black were being called on to fight; the better-paid "all-volunteer army" offering educational opportunities acted as a leveler, and less as a source of resentment.

In 1966, black leader Floyd McKissick was able to make a quadruple historical racial reference when he said that the war in Vietnam was "a way of drafting black men to go fight yellow men in order to protect this land that the white men stole from the red men."

rider A clause added to a bill often beside the point of the legislation.

A bill passed by a legislative body must be signed by a Chief Executive to become a law; in most cases, an "item veto" is not permitted, and the President, governor, or mayor must accept it all or reject it all. Riders are tacked on to unrelated legislation for two reasons: (1) an objectionable rider, sure to be vetoed, is added so as to force a veto of the entire bill the rider-sponsoring legislator is trying to "bring down"; (2) a provision that, on its own, would likely be vetoed is added to vital appropriations legislation so as to "slip past" the Chief Executive.

Said President Roosevelt in 1938: "I want you to know that I completely agree with your criticism of legislative 'riders' on tax and appropriation bills. Regardless of the merits or demerits of any such 'riders'—and I do not enter that phase of the discussion at the moment—the manifest fact remains that this practice robs the Executive of legitimate and essential freedom of action in dealing with legislation."

During his second term, George W. Bush found a partial solution to this in his increased, and highly controversial, practice of adding "signing statements" to bills that he signed into law, indicating that he would not carry out portions of them that he considered unconstitutional.

Charles Ledyard Norton, the pioneer lexicographer of political Americanisms, offered a fanciful derivation of the word in 1890: "In common speech, a rider is the top rail of a zig-zag fence. Such a fence is 'staked and ridered' when stakes are driven in the angles and a rider laid across them. A rider is not an essential part of a fence, nor of a bill, but it adds considerably to the effectiveness of both."

In fact, the *OED* traces the expression back in English jurisprudence to 1669: "That which is certified shall be annexed to the Record, and is called a Rider-roll."

When riders get out of hand, the resulting bill is derided as a CHRISTMAS TREE BILL. Elliot Richardson, then Secretary of Health, Education and Welfare, said in 1970: "Until I became Secretary, I had never heard 'Christmas tree' used as a transitive verb." Alan Otten of the *Wall Street Journal* explained:

"On Capitol Hill, the practice of tagging a host of special-interest amendments to a popular bill is known as 'Christmas-treeing' the bill." See EARMARK.

rif To discharge from a government job; or, to eliminate a job category or slot in such a way as to make it difficult for the employee to stay.

"I thought you'd be interested in a word that has entered the Albany argot as a result of Governor [Hugh] Carey's budget cutbacks," reporter Paul Hoffman wrote the author in 1977, "—the verb *to rif*, usually used in past tense, as 'I've been riffed,' or 'He was riffed.' Meaning to lose one's job as the result of a Reduction in Force." Hugh Rawson recalls encountering the term, an acronym for *Reduction in Force*, in the U.S. Army in the late '50s.

To *rif* became a '60s Washington verb that has spread to state capitals. The term is usually heard during the transition between Administrations, and is a euphemism intended to make coolly impersonal what is usually a personal or political decision. Spelled both RIF and (to be sure it is pronounced as a single word) "riff," the verb was included in Merriam-Webster's *New International Dictionary* (3rd edition) with its first citation from 1953. After nearly three generations, it is fair to assume the transition from initialese to acronym has been made.

See ACRONYMS, POLITICAL; HIT LIST.

rigged convention See BROKERED CONVENTION; OPEN CONVENTION.

right to know An interpretation of the First Amendment that free-speech advocates say justifies investigations into official and personal conduct; sometimes requires balance with a right to privacy and constitutional right to fair trial.

Arthur Hays Sulzberger, then publisher of *The New York Times*, stated the underlying case in 1956: "The crux is not the publisher's 'freedom to print'; it is rather, the citizens' 'right to know.'"

Ten years later, columnist Max Lerner took a different view, in connection with

Jacqueline Kennedy's successful effort to edit material she had given in confidence to author William Manchester:

> Clearly there are limits on such a right. We have no right to know about top-secret documents which have not yet been declassified.... Nor have we a right to know private things, even about public officials or their families against their wishes. Thus the right to know is circumscribed by public policy, by taste, by codes of fairness, by the right of privacy.
>
> More important than the right to know is the right to publish.
>
> This too, is a limited right—limited by the obscenity statutes, by libel laws, by judicial interpretations of both. But the right to publish becomes a precious right when there are unwarranted censorship efforts to prevent publication.

The phrase *right to know* is not in the Constitution; many consider it the underpinning of the First Amendment's "Congress shall make no law ... abridging the freedom of speech or of the press" (and expressed in Justice Hugo Black's absolutist aphorism, "'No law' means no law"). In the 1960s, controversy grew over the issue called "free press vs. fair trial." The Supreme Court held in 1966 that Dr. Samuel Sheppard had been denied his right to a fair trial—that is, by a jury unprejudiced by information obtained outside the courtroom—because of the press campaign against him.

The public's *right to know*, shouldering its way among other established rights, often resists widespread support, especially when parts of the public resent the adversarial approach taken by "the media" (a less admired term than "the press") toward an elected administration. When journalists are jailed for contempt of court for refusing to reveal a CONFIDENTIAL SOURCE, prosecutors argue that the needs of discovering leakers outweigh the claimed First Amendment protection; journalists assert that such an undermining by prosecutors of traditional means of newsgathering makes it impossible for them to keep the public informed, which they maintain is the public's "right."

In 1971 *The New York Times* published selections from a secret 47-volume study of the origins of the Vietnam war, labeled "Vietnam Archive" but which promptly became known as the Pentagon Papers. After the series began, the government moved to enjoin publication; the Supreme Court ultimately upheld the right of the *Times* and other newspapers to publish the documents (taking their chances on subsequent prosecution). This decision also made clear that under circumstances presenting a clear danger to lives or an overriding national interest, the courts could uphold the government's ability to prevent public disclosure.

Soviet dissident and author Alexander Solzhenitsyn (see GULAG) turned the phrase around in a cultural rather than legal context at a Harvard commencement address in June of 1978: "People also have a right *not* to know, and it is a much more valuable one. The right not to have their divine souls stuffed with gossip, nonsense, vain talk. A person who works, who leads a meaningful life, does not need this excessive flow of information." Cartoonist Edward Sorel mocked this view in *Esquire* magazine with a drawing of well-to-do flag wavers marching under the banner of "Americans for a Closed Society."

The controversy recalled to some writers George Washington's complaint in 1777 suggesting journalists in wartime exercise self-restraint: "It is much to be wished that our Printers were more discreet in many of their Publications. We see almost in every Paper, Proclamations or accounts transmitted by the Enemy, of an injurious nature. If some hint or caution could be given them on the subject, it might be of material Service." General William Tecumseh Sherman went much further. He arrested one of Horace Greeley's correspondents covering the Civil War for the New York *Herald*, charged him with spying, and would have shot him were it not for President Lincoln's intervention. Upon hearing that three other correspondents covering a battle were killed by artillery, General Sherman observed, "Good, now we shall have news from Hell before breakfast." See CHILLING EFFECT.

right to work A movement to stop making union membership a requirement for employment.

Management has won the battle of semantics with organized labor while labor has won the more substantive victories. *Right to work* is a management slogan that has been adopted as the generic term for anti–compulsory-union legislation, which labor refers to as "union-busting laws." Management's term for a factory that will employ only a union member is CLOSED SHOP, connoting the shutting-out of workers who refuse to join a union, while its term for no such requirement is *open shop*, where workers may or may not be union members; a *union shop* is one where a worker can refuse to join but must pay dues. (A rough ratio of usage on search engines is *closed* 6, *open* 5, *union* 4.)

Popularization of *right to work* belongs to Socialist leader Eugene V. Debs: "Every man has the inalienable right to work." Ralph Waldo Emerson, in his essay on politics, said, "A man has a right to be employed," and in the first half of the nineteenth century, the phrase was *the right to labor*. French social scientist François Fourier originated the idea in his 1808 *Theory of the Four Movements*, which included *le droit du travail* (in German, *das Recht auf Arbeit*). In Franklin Roosevelt's 1944 campaign, the most vital part of his "economic bill of rights" was "the right of a useful and remunerative job," though he hastened to add, "I believe that private enterprise can give full employment to our people."

In all those cases, the *right to work* meant "the opportunity to make a living must be given to all."

Early use of the phrase in its present meaning was in a 1912 Bernard Partridge cartoon—"the Right to Work"—in *Punch*. John Bull is saying sternly to a striker: "I can't make you work if you won't; but if this man wants to, I can make you let him. And I will."

The same turnaround—taking a negative or defensive position and fashioning it into a positive slogan—was used by opponents of abortion in the seventies, who changed their appellation from "anti-abortion" to "right to life." This was soon countered by the proponents of abortion rights with the "right to choose."

right wing See CONSERVATIVE; LEFT WING, RIGHT WING; REACTIONARY.

ripper bill Action of a legislature to emasculate, or *rip out*, power held by a lower body or administrative agency dominated by the opposite party.

"Some of the warmest arguments in the legislature," wrote Al Smith, ex-governor of New York, in 1929, "occurred over what were called 'ripper' bills. The party in power would legislate their opponents out of office."

By "Special Acts," state legislatures would set up municipal charters, grant franchises, transfer powers between state agencies, and restrict or expand the powers of governors. A state legislature controlled by one party can *rip* the charter of a city controlled by the other party, and thus elicit demands for HOME RULE; by this means, party leaders can also punish reform elements in their own party.

rising tide lifts all boats The idea that general prosperity is best for individual welfare.

John F. Kennedy repeatedly sounded the optimistic note that "a rising tide lifts all the boats," suggesting that good times for all will be beneficial to each. In his June 1963 address in Frankfurt, he said: "As they say on my own Cape Cod, a rising tide lifts all the boats. And a partnership, by definition, serves both partners, without domination or unfair advantage."

Joan Payne, a researcher at the John F. Kennedy Presidential Library in Boston, found an earlier use. Speaking in Newcastle, Pennsylvania, on October 15, 1960, then-Senator Kennedy said in campaigning that "The country is tied together, and a rising tide lifts all the boats."

Ted Sorensen, the Kennedy speechwriter and in many policy and prose ways alter ego, informed the author in 1993: "As Legislative Assistant to Senator John F. Kennedy, 1953–1961, I often received material from a regional chamber of commerce–type organization called 'The New England Council.' I was favorably struck by the motto set forth on its letterhead: 'The rising tide lifts all the boats,' and not surprisingly it found its way into J.F.K.'s speeches."

Since the brief Kennedy era, however, the expression is often balanced by a second clause that adds a note of caution, lest the optimism seem undue. An economist is quoted in a 1987 issue of *National Journal* on the budgetary problems in government after a boom: "In a sense, the rising tide lifts all boats. The falling tide in the Defense Department puts ships in the sand selectively."

Nine years before, Vernon Jordan, a black leader, had used the same rhetorical technique before an audience: "There are those who believe, in John F. Kennedy's phrase, that a rising tide lifts all boats. But we must remind them that a rising tide only lifts those boats in the water, and black people are in the drydock of this economy."

Liberals use the *rising tide* line in a positive sense; they deride the same general watery trope on economics as TRICKLE-DOWN THEORY when used by conservatives.

road to defeat Conservative Republican charge that ME-TOO policies, stolen from liberals, have failed to get them elected.

Senator Everett Dirksen stood at the rostrum in the Chicago Stockyards International Amphitheater at the 1952 Republican convention and waved a finger at twice-defeated New York Governor Thomas E. Dewey, now supporting Dwight Eisenhower against Senator Robert A. Taft.

"We followed you before," Dirksen intoned in his mellifluous voice, "and you took us down the road to defeat."

Taft supporters rose and booed Dewey; the New York delegation returned the jeers, and hecklers shouted at the speaker and each other. Dirksen, who had brought the latent resentment to a head with his "road to defeat" charge, promptly reversed his field and said innocently: "This is no place for Republicans to be booing any other Republican."

Dirksen was able to live down the divisive statement and become Senate Minority Leader, but Goldwater supporters frequently recalled the remark in the 1964 primary fight against Nelson Rockefeller.

The political-road metaphor, sometimes paved with good intentions, is well traveled. The MIDDLE OF THE ROAD is favored on the campaign trail, and HIGH ROAD . . . LOW ROAD is referred to by politicians with sights set on Pennsylvania Avenue who decry GUTTER FLYERS and MADISON AVENUE TECHNIQUES as efforts to confuse the MAN IN THE STREET.

robocall A prerecorded telephone call sent by an automatic-dialing computer to a selected list of recipients; also called *phone spam.*

Robocalls may be placed to hundreds of thousands of telephone numbers and designed to reach particular demographic groups by sex, age, income, and political affiliation. The technique, first used for promoting causes or products, was reported in *Forbes* magazine in January of 2001: "The next message on your answering machine is as likely to come from a rock star or a politician as from your Uncle Seymour. Broadcast phone messaging called a phone blast or robocall is popular because at 8 cents a call, it is cheap advertising. . . . For now the messages are novel enough that people listen to them. Not for long. Last year hundreds of millions of prerecorded sales pitches clogged answering machines."

A sample message, this one from retired general Norman Schwarzkopf in support of George W. Bush's presidential candidacy in 2000: "The fighting in the Middle East, the terrorist attack on the U.S.S. Cole has [sic] caused me great concern." (The "sic" is courtesy of *Forbes*, alert to the general's need for subject-verb agreement.)

Political campaign strategists soon realized that *robocalls* could be used to attack as well as promote. During the 2006 midterm elections, the GOP launched *robocall* campaigns in at least 53 competitive House races, according to AP reporter Philip Elliott. Many calls began in a deceptive way, opening with words to the effect: "Hello, I am calling with information about So-and-So," referring to the Democratic candidate, then went on to criticize that person. People who hung up quickly on the automated call were left thinking that message was paid for by the Democrat, and felt harassed when the call was repeated again and again. The intent of the calls obviously was to annoy recipients into not voting for the Democrat. A number of complaints were lodged with the FCC, whose rules specify that prerecorded messages must begin by stating "clearly the identity of the business, individual, or other entity that is responsible for initiating the call."

Neither party had a monopoly on the technique. In Connecticut's 4th District, for instance, the spokeswoman for the Democratic candidate told the AP that the campaign had been "a victim of 'constant pummeling,' including robocalls that begin with a recorded voice saying, 'I'd like to talk to you about Diane Farrell.'" For his part, the Republican candidate, and eventual winner, Rep. Christopher Shays, said that he had survived more than 20 robocall campaigns, including one that attempted to link his position on stem-cell research to that of religious extremists. In a letter to local newspapers, Shays asserted that "These calls are at best misleading and often blatantly wrong."

(The DIRTY TRICK of annoying voters by pretending to represent the opposing candidate was used by sneaky young Republican women who handed out buttons at the Democratic convention nominating Jimmy Carter that read "Cuties for Carter," infuriating feminists.)

Robocall is a blend of *robot* and telephone *call*. The former was popularized by Karel Čapek's 1920 play *R.U.R.*, featuring Rossum's Universal Robots, first produced in English in 1923. Čapek's brother Josef coined the word when Karel told him of the idea for the play but said he didn't know what to call the artificial workers. It is based on the Czech *robota*, meaning "forced labor" or "servitude." (When computers were first issued to *New York Times* columnists in the '80s, the password assigned to the author was *Capek*. Asked why, the semantically savvy technician issuing the passwords replied, "who else would know the coiner of *robot*?" At *The Washington Post*, the password issued to the columnist Meg Greenfield, who insisted she would never remember her password, was "Password.")

rock and a hard place, between a To be in difficulty; in recent usage, to be faced with either a moral dilemma or a HOBSON'S CHOICE.

Nixon domestic council director John Ehrlichman used this phrase in testifying before the Senate Watergate committee; it was common parlance in the White House in the early '70s and became a vogue phrase in politics in the mid-'70s.

With the emphasis on *hard*, the phrase seems to suggest that the choice faced is between a rock and a substance even harder than a rock. The meaning is similar to "between the devil and the deep blue sea."

In the *American Thesaurus of Slang* (1953), Lester Berrey and Melvin Van den Bark place the phrase under the entry for "bewildered; perplexed; baffled" and include it with *against the wall, flummoxed*, and *hot and bothered*, although the last has a connotation of "sexually aroused."

In 1921 B. H. Lehman, writing in the American Dialect Society's *Dialect Notes* about words used in California, gave a different interpretation. "To be between a rock and a hard place" is defined as "to be bankrupt." Professor Lehman reported the phrase "common in Arizona in recent panics, sporadic in California."

The expression has a Western flavor, and many of the aides in the Nixon White House were Westerners; it is likely that they popularized it in a media center like Washington, much as the Japanese word HONCHO was picked up in California and blossomed in the District of Columbia.

The phrase is a colloquial updating of the classic *between Scylla and Charybdis*, an allusion to Homer's *Odyssey*, in which Ulysses has to sail between Scylla, a monstrous rock, and Charybdis, a raging whirlpool.

In current use, the phrase's meaning of "confusion" seems to have atrophied; it is generally used now to mean "to be in big trouble," or "deep doo-doo," and carries a special meaning of being torn by a moral choice.

In the 1970s, *Washington Post* editorial writer Meg Greenfield told the author she had been toying with, but decided against, the notion of titling an editorial about Afghanistan "Between Iraq and a Hard Place." Others picked up the pun in the '90s and have been using it ever since.

rock-ribbed Inflexible, used by a critic; steadfast, staunch, used by a friend.

Alliteration has helped assure *rock-ribbed* to be as closely associated with conservative Republicans as DYED-IN-THE-WOOL is with loyal Democrats. Poet William Cullen Bryant, in "Thanatopsis," wrote of "The hills / Rock-ribbed and ancient as the sun," which Senator Andrew Johnson quoted in a political context in 1861, as the Civil War loomed: "we stand immovable upon our basis, as on our own native mountains—presenting their craggy brows, their unexplored caverns, their summits, 'rock-ribbed and ancient as the sun'—we stand speaking peace, association and concert to a distracted Republic."

This hyphenated adjective often has a shifting pronunciation. If the noun does not follow, the emphasis is on the second word, as "He is rock-*ribbed*," but if the noun follows, the emphasis is on the first word, as "He is a *rock*-ribbed Republican."

roorback A fictitious slander, an outrageous lie intended to smear a political figure during the final stages of a campaign.

"A roorback!" expostulated *New York Times* columnist James Reston to the author, denouncing a false story about presidential candidate Jimmy Carter during the 1976 campaign. "Scotty" was unable to find the word in any of the college dictionaries and came charging into my office next to his to dig it up in my 13-volume *OED*, which revealed the following:

As election day drew near in 1844, the *Ithaca* (N.Y.) *Chronicle* printed what it purported to be a portion of *A Tour Through the Western and Southern States* by a "Baron Roorback," stating that Democratic candidate James K. Polk had bought forty-three slaves and branded his initials on their shoulders. Other newspapers picked up the story, which later turned out to be a forgery by an Ithaca abolitionist.

The name can be applied to any last-minute smear, and is one reason responsible

journalists are leery of breaking damaging stories on the day before election. See GUTTER FLYER; SMEAR.

root and branch In the entirety; from bottom to top, from beginning to end; the spatial equivalent of *24/7*.

The modern popularization comes from Supreme Court Justice William J. Brennan Jr., in the 1968 decision of *Green v. County School Board of New Kent County, Virginia*. Justice Brennan delivered the opinion of the Supreme Court against the segregation policies of that Virginia county's school system, and later wrote the author:

It's the decision that abandoned the "all deliberate speed" standard, which had been adopted in the second *Brown* decision, *Brown v. Board of Education*, decided May 31, 1955. The pertinent quote from that opinion directs the district courts to enter orders "as are necessary and proper to admit to public schools on a racially nondiscriminatory basis with all deliberate speed."

Green discarded this approach, holding that "the burden on a school board today is to come forward with a plan that promises realistically to work, and promises realistically to work *now*."

A search by Fred R. Shapiro of the *Yale Book of Quotations* yielded the full use of *root and branch* in the 1968 *Green* decision. Justice Brennan wrote then: "School boards such as the respondent then operating state-compelled dual systems were nevertheless clearly charged with the affirmative duty to take whatever steps might be necessary to convert to a unitary system in which racial discrimination would be eliminated root and branch."

The phrase took root. In a July 1992 environmental hearing on Capitol Hill, William K. Reilly, administrator of the Environmental Protection Agency, responded to questions about unethical practices of environmental contractors by saying, "I think we are going after the problem root and branch."

The lexicographer Sol Steinmetz found the source of the phrase in the King James version (1611) of the Hebrew Bible, from Malachi, last of the Prophets, 4:1, directly quoting the Lord of Hosts about the fate of the arrogant and the evildoers: "The day that cometh shall burn them up…that it shall leave them neither root nor branch." See WITH ALL DELIBERATE SPEED.

root, hog, or die A political proverb meaning "work for your office, or leave it."

In lean years, a hungry hog must learn to root in the ground for his food or starve. This proverb probably had nonpolitical origins, but it was popularized early in the Andrew Jackson era.

The weekly Springfield, Ohio, *Tippecanoe Calumet and War Club* in 1836 spelled out the SPOILS SYSTEM agreement of the Jacksonians: "Root, hog, or die—work for your office, or leave it—support the party, right or wrong—are the terms of the agreement."

The original spoils-system connotation has worn off, and the current occasional use is now a rough exhortation to get out and campaign.

See PROVERBS AND AXIOMS, POLITICAL.

Rose Garden rubbish Supposedly ad-lib remarks made by the President on minor occasions, usually prepared in talking-point form by the most junior of White House speechwriters.

Political leaders are expected to make "appropriate remarks" at informal ceremonies, and often wish to have ideas submitted in advance, around which they can extemporize. Because many of these ceremonies occur in places like the White House Rose Garden, the phrase *Rose Garden rubbish* was coined by the Lyndon Johnson speechwriting staff to derogate the job of preparing the seemingly off-the-cuff appropriatenesses. In 1966, *The Wall Street Journal* reported that presidential assistant Robert Kintner "has also taken over [Jack] Valenti's assignment of riding herd on what White House men call the 'rose garden rubbish'—the more-or-less routine speeches ground out for the President to give to assorted groups in the White House rose garden." Peter Benchley, a junior speechwriter who later gained fame as the author of the novel *Jaws*, popularized the term in a *Life* magazine article.

The phrase is too self-critical or arrogant to be used officially around the White House; presidential remarks are hardly considered "rubbish" to those visitors to whom they are directed. In the Nixon era, the task was referred to by the President with a musical metaphor: "Grace notes."

John McDonald, one of the junior Nixon speechwriters in 1972, wrote an open letter to the Jimmy Carter speechwriters in the *Washington Post* in 1977, cautioning them that not all presidential prose was earthshaking or even important: "You're not yet acutely familiar with Rose Garden Rubbish—but you soon will be. Why is the President delighted that Miss Teenage America is calling on him? What does he say to the head of the American Dental Association? What does he tell someone who is off to deliver two musk oxen to the People's Republic of China?…these are all real items and the President can't wing them—somebody has to develop some background suggestions for lines of credible commentary. Don't look around—you're it."

The outdoor area near the Oval Office—a small lawn surrounded by flower beds, with magnolia trees in the corners—is called the Rose Garden, though it contains few rose bushes. White House gardeners informed the author, who turned out his share of the talking-point "rubbish," that they rarely put red rose plants in because they consider dark colors "heavy" for a garden. That is the sort of fact a speechwriter would provide to a president who was welcoming a delegation of horticulturists.

Rosie Scenario Overly optimistic projections of economic growth and incoming revenues, designed to present budgets as approaching balance.

This phrase borrows the word SCENARIO from film jargon for a script outline, and is bottomed on the 1970s usage *best-case scenario*, in turn derived from the 1964 *worst-case scenario*, both of which have been used more recently in horrific computer war games. The modifier plays on the adjective *rosy*, as in the optimism of the mid-nineteenth-century phrase about "seeing through rose-colored glasses" and the girl's nickname "Rosie" for Rosemary. The full name, Rosie Scenario, serves as a personification of hope.

A 1985 *Washington Post* piece extended the metaphor, suggesting a title for a possible book by budget director David Stockman: "How Rosie Scenario Fell Off Her Trojan Horse When It, Too, Stopped to Feed at the Public Trough." One political take on George H. W. Bush's election in 1988 was that "It means 'Rosie Scenario' assumptions on economic growth and interest rates."

The term is also used in lowercase as a common noun, and is finding its way out of economic jargon into general political use. In 1992, the *Chicago Tribune* used the lowercase phrase in discussing the Democrats' hope that Ross Perot's candidacy would help Bill Clinton to "win, or failing that, throw the election into the Democrat-controlled House of Representatives. Oh, what a rosie scenario, Democrat-style."

rubber-chicken circuit The interminable series of public luncheons and dinners which are an inescapable part of campaigning, fund-raising, and officeholding.

"Rubber" chicken is tough; so is campaigning. Robert Phelps of *The New York Times* described in 1964 the stamina needed by a presidential candidate: "The candidate must be capable of covering up to 200,000 miles by air, ingesting 600 chicken dinners, delivering 2,500 speeches, clasping hands with a million persons and smiling gaily while being smacked with 10 tons of confetti." Another reporter in 1967 wrote of George Wallace's presidential campaign: "his political advance men soon discovered that the baked chicken and green pea circuit was not only willing, but often eager, to have him as a speaker."

FAT CATS at $1,000-a-plate affairs get steak or roast beef and rissolé potatoes (why always rissolé potatoes?), but at non-fund-raising affairs, where the purpose is to meet the candidate and $50 covers the cost of the function, chicken is *de rigueur*. Candidates are expected to make appearances sitting on the dais of several functions per evening, many philanthropic or civic, at which they make nonpolitical remarks and make a pass at their plates. (Speakers must eat lightly; nobody wants to belch while addressing an audience.)

The result is often a combination of mental and physical malnutrition, brought on by distaste for hotel food in general and chicken in particular. "When the dinners run out," said presidential candidate John F. Kennedy in 1960, "the luncheons begin, and when the luncheons run out, the breakfasts begin. We may all meet next week to get the campaign out of the red with a midnight brunch at eighty-five dollars a person—and I will be there."

According to restaurateur George Lang, the rubberization of chicken requires (1) a miscalculation of timing by the organizing committee, allowing the juices of the chicken to congeal while the dais is being introduced; (2) a chef whose oven is too hot; and (3) a food buyer with a sharp eye for stringy birds. A practiced rubberizer cooks the chicken hours before the function and reheats it for serving; "when this is not possible," says Lang, "a tender roast chicken can be made quite rubbery by exposure to a steam table for a few minutes." *The Washington Post* described such affairs mercilessly: "By and large, the 'testimonial dinner' is a political fraud, a gastronomical affront, an ethical outrage, a colossal bore, an insufferable social disaster and financial shakedown."

A counterpart in England is *function fish*. In the U.S., the key to the phrase is "circuit": *baked (or roast) chicken circuit, roast beef circuit, chicken-and-mashed-potatoes circuit* are among the many variations. The phrase, first tasted in Canada in 1959, derives from vaudeville use, when performers were booked into a chain, or *circuit*, of theaters, emerging exhausted from the tour; the word's treadmill connotation has carried over into politics. For the frozen expression of the faces at the head table, see WAXWORKS.

rubber stamp A legislature or a public figure taking orders from a political leader, or dominated by orders from higher up.

Congressional Democrats in 2007, after a dozen years in the minority, chose to honor their leader, Rep. Nancy Pelosi, with the House Speakership after she capitalized on the sinking popularity of President Bush by running against "the rubber-stamp Congress."

The campaign phrase had 70-year-old roots. "They centered all their powers in the Executive," Herbert Hoover reported Al Smith as saying in 1936 about the previous two Congresses, "and that is the reason why you read in the newspapers reference to Congress as 'the rubber-stamp Congress.'"

In 1967, former FDR brain truster Raymond Moley disagreed. "The seventy-third Congress [in 1936] was no 'rubber stamp.' Its leadership was rich in talent and experience. The concept of an assembly line from the White House to the Congress cannot be sustained by the facts."

Theodore Roosevelt's biographer, William Thayer, used the phrase in 1919, as an exhortation William Howard Taft (long dominated by Roosevelt) might have heard: "Be your own President; don't be anybody's man or rubber stamp." Edward Conrad Smith, in his 1924 *Dictionary of American Politics*, wrote: "the term was first used to characterize several members of President Wilson's cabinet who seemed to have practically no influence on the conduct of affairs."

On a television program in 1962, Harvard Law Professor Mark DeWolfe Howe objected to Ted Kennedy's candidacy for senator from Massachusetts: "Seeking an office in the United States Senate, while his brother is in the White House, seems to me to represent a total misunderstanding of the responsibilities of a United States Senator. To have a rubber-stamp Senator is to me an offense against the whole tradition that there should be a separation of powers in our government."

In Huey Long's heyday, the Louisiana state legislature was known as "Huey's trained seals." As senator, Long ran the state through the supremely acquiescent Governor O. K. Allen, about whom Huey's brother Earl once said, "A leaf blew in the window of Allen's office one day and fell on his desk. He signed it."

rugged individualism Herbert Hoover's philosophy of economic freedom, equal opportunity, and personal initiative, as opposed to what he considered paternalistic government.

Toward the close of his successful 1928 campaign against Democrat Al Smith, Herbert Hoover spoke in New York on October 22, determined, as he recalled years later, to "draw the issue of the American system, as opposed to all forms of collectivism." He sketched the background of the necessary government involvement in the economy in World War I, then posed the peacetime dilemma: "We are challenged with a peacetime choice between the American system of rugged individualism and a European philosophy of diametrically opposed doctrines—doctrines of paternalism and state socialism."

Six years after the phrase became a part of the American political lexicon, Hoover disclaimed coinage: "While I can make no claim for having introduced the term 'rugged individualism,' I should be proud to have invented it. It has been used by American leaders for over a half-century in eulogy of those God-fearing men and women of honesty whose stamina and character and fearless assertion of rights led them to make their own way in life."

At the time and for many years afterward, opponents of Hoover used the phrase with a sneer. Socialist Norman Thomas, two weeks after the speech was delivered, used the phrase as his text: "Mr. Hoover calls his capitalism 'rugged individualism' and professes to find some peculiar virtue in the wasteful and chaotic mismanagement of coal, in our frantic real-estate speculation …"

In 1936, Franklin Roosevelt—up for the first of three reelections—was too cagey to tackle individualism head-on at the Democratic convention. His reference was oblique: "I believe in individualism … up to the point where the individualist starts to operate at the expense of society."

The association of Hoover with the phrase, however, enabled FDR to make it a target in a campaign speech:

> I know how the knees of all of our *rugged individualists* were trembling four years ago and how their hearts fluttered. They came to Washington in great numbers. Washington did not

look like a dangerous bureaucracy to them then. Oh, no! It looked like an emergency hospital. ... And now most of the patients seem to be doing very nicely. Some of them are even well enough to throw their crutches at the doctor.

As Hoover-hatred abated, the use of *rugged individualism* lost some of its sarcasm, and came to be regarded by most as a quaint evocation of the simple virtues of America's early days. But President Harry S. Truman chose to run against Hoover as well as Dewey in 1948: "Many of you remember 1932. ... Out here on Eighth Avenue veterans were selling apples. Ragged individualism, I suppose that's what you would call it."

rule of law The rubric used to attack the assumption of extralegal authority or "inherent power" by the Executive; the assertion that a nation's leaders must abide by a written constitution or unwritten common law.

Though Tom Paine had said a century before that we stood as a nation "where the law is king," the phrase was popularized by A. V. Dicey, in his 1885 *Introduction to the Law of the Constitution*. In his definition, the *rule of law* in England meant that ordinary courts determined every man's legal rights and liabilities; that executive officers had less arbitrary power and more limited discretion than in other European countries; and that government officials could be brought to court for wrongs done even under the cloak of official authority.

In the U.S., this idea is more frequently expressed as GOVERNMENT OF LAWS, NOT OF MEN. Although the maxim "Necessity knows no law" is sometimes used as a justification for emergency actions, most politicians concede that—when the emergency is over—the extralegal acts are not to be condoned. (*Extralegal* is a forgiving euphemism for *illegal*, which in turn is less severe than *unlawful*.)

Historian J. G. Randall, in his 1926 classic *Constitutional Problems under Lincoln*, wrote of Civil War repression: "Instead of the 'rule of law' prevailing, as Dicey defined it, men were imprisoned outside the law and independent of the courts; and governmental officers were given a privileged place above the law and made immune from penalties for wrongs committed ... Legally, the

Civil War stands out as an eccentric period, a time when constitutional restraints did not fully operate and when the 'rule of law' largely broke down." See MEASURES, NOT MEN; HIGHER LAW.

rule or ruin See GAG RULE.

rule out To deny the existence of even a remote possibility.

The use of a question that begins "Are you ruling out ..." is a sign of journalistic desperation. On dull news days, reporters are forced to ask a question that gives them a weak lead either way it is answered.

The only story more tenuous than "The President today ruled out any chance of [whatever]" is "The President today refused to rule out consideration of [whatever]."

The rule-out question gained popularity in the late 60s, especially at press conferences of White House press secretary Ronald Ziegler. An attempt is made occasionally to blunt the surefire either-way story with an odd use of language: "I'm not ruling it out, but that doesn't mean I'm ruling it in."

rum, Romanism and rebellion See EXTREMISM.

rump session A gathering of dissidents; or, a legislative body that refuses to disband according to law.

"It is not fit that you should sit here any longer!" shouted Oliver Cromwell to the "Rump Parliament." "You shall now give place to better men." After England's Second Civil War of 1648, Cromwell's Colonel Thomas Pride ejected ninety-six Presbyterian members from Parliament who were suspected of dealings with the defeated King Charles ("Pride's PURGE"), and the remaining sixty were known as the *Rump*.

The word *rump* is from a Scandinavian word for the hindquarters of an animal, its meaning crossing over to "remnant" or "tail end."

The word was popularized in the U.S. around the time of our own Civil War. In 1860 Stephen Douglas was called the candidate of a "rump convention," and Congress in Reconstruction days was called a "rump

Congress" by Democrats and Southerners who felt it did not represent all the states and was therefore in unlawful session. The most famous *rump convention* was Theodore Roosevelt's "Bull Moose" split-off from the Republicans in 1912.

In current use, *rump* is used with *caucus, convention, session,* and *meeting,* usually connoting a sorehead minority that cannot lose gracefully.

Rumsfeld's Rules A set of pithy guidelines for survival in the bureaucratic jungle of Washington, D.C. and, by extension, in corporations and other organizations.

Donald H. Rumsfeld began assembling aphorisms for success in the late 1950s when he was a congressional aide, and gradually enlarged his collection of rules, reflections, and quotations as the trajectory of his career took him to higher offices: congressman from Illinois, assistant to President Nixon, ambassador to NATO, Ford White House chief of staff, corporate CEO, and two tours as Secretary of Defense. Mr. Rumsfeld printed his rules for the first time in 1974 and copyrighted them in 1988. In 2001, shortly after George W. Bush appointed him to his second term as Secretary of Defense, he had the rules, then numbering 154, posted on the Pentagon's website. A sampling:

Learn to say "I don't know." If used when appropriate, it will be often.

If you foul up, tell the president and correct it fast. Delay only compounds mistakes.

Don't play president—you're not. The constitution provides for only one president. Don't forget it.

Don't forget that the fifty or so invitations you receive a week are sent not because those people are just dying to see you, but because of the position you hold. If you don't believe me, ask one of your predecessors how fast they stop.

Don't say "the White House wants." Buildings can't want.

If in doubt, don't.

It is easier to get into something than out of it. [He was reminded of this as the war in Iraq, which he dubbed a part of "the long war" against terrorism, dragged on.]

Be able to resign. It will improve your value to the president and do wonders for your per-

formance. [As calls for his resignation grew during George W. Bush's beleaguered second term, Rumsfeld's supporters amended this to "Be willing *not* to resign"; his resignation was accepted after the Republican midterm defeat in 2006.]

Remember: A's hire A's and B's hire C's.

Control your time. If you're working off your in-box, you're working off the priorities of others.

Late in 2007, lunching with a longtime friend, the former Defense Secretary recalled the aphorism often attributed to Harry Truman—"If you want a friend in Washington, D.C., get a dog"—and added Rumsfeld's Corollary: "Better make it a small dog, because it may turn on you also."

See also POTTERY BARN RULE; PROVERBS AND AXIOMS, POLITICAL; SHOCK AND AWE.

run between the raindrops Dodge repeated attacks or problems; race to escape trouble.

This vivid word picture suggests the need to keep moving to avoid attacks. The term surfaced during the Supreme Court confirmation hearings for Judge David Souter, nominated by George H.W. Bush in 1990. Senator Arlen Specter, Republican of Pennsylvania, announced his intentions to confirm the candidate, adding, "During these hearings, Judge Souter really had to run between the raindrops in a veritable hurricane." The nominee, who had not left much of a paper trail in the law, was surely agile; once on the High Court, he turned out to be far more liberal than any of the Republicans suspected.

The movement in the metaphor—popularized in song and book titles—is in contrast to the forced lack of movement in a similar but not synonymous phrase about being in trouble, between a ROCK AND A HARD PLACE.

running against Washington Representing oneself as a political outsider; seeking power by making the most of not having been in national power.

Arguing against government excess and bureaucratic gridlock, politicians who cast themselves deliberately as outsiders are said to be "running against Washington."

The phrase became popular during the 1970s when Jimmy Carter presented himself as a newcomer to INSIDE-THE-BELTWAY politics, a candidate apparently unbeholden to established interest groups and the existing power structure. Within two years of his election, however, he found that the phrase could be turned against his Administration. *National Journal* commented in 1978, "After running against Washington, the Carter White House was obliged to turn to a quintessential Washington pol for a crucial job."

Bill Clinton repeated the winning strategy in 1992, attacking Republicans who "have gotten away with running against Washington, and they are the Washington insiders. They are the people that have to take responsibility for not making this government work."

The center of power that is under attack may change, but the phrase retains its meaning. A Soviet studies specialist commented in 1990 on the possibility that Gorbachev would eventually run for president in a popular election: "He will try to run against Moscow, just as someone else won by running against Washington." The Russian wisely chose not to.

running dogs See FELLOW TRAVELER.

running for the exercise Going through the motions of campaigning in a hopeless cause.

Asked in February 1976 who he thought his most likely Democratic opponent would be, President Ford told reporters he thought all along it would be Senator Hubert Humphrey "—and I think all the rest of them are running for the exercise." (It turned out that Georgia Governor Jimmy Carter was not.)

When candidates enlist in a seemingly impossible campaign, they enter a self-hypnotic experience that soon magnifies a *remote possibility* into an *outside chance* into a probability of *making a good showing* into a *good bet for an upset* into an *unexpectedly strong closer*. They point out that they are not *running for the exercise*; in early stages, their friends think they are.

running like a dry creek One of the watery political metaphors, describing a campaigner who is not surging as hard as supporters would like.

Nineteen newspapers of the Scripps-Howard chain ran a front-page editorial in 1952, six weeks after Eisenhower was nominated, declaring, "Ike is running like a dry creek." This was just after he half-heartedly defended General George C. Marshall against criticism by Senator William Jenner of Indiana, concluding, "Maybe he made some mistakes. I don't know about that." The editorial said that the General sounded like "just another ME-TOO candidate" and criticized him for not "coming out swinging. ... If Ike doesn't know [about Marshall], he had better find out. We still cling to the hope that ... he will hit hard. If he doesn't, he may as well concede defeat."

The phrase appears to be of Western origin and is in current use. In Eisenhower's case, of course, the *dry creek* spilled into a *torrent* and a *flood* of votes, a *tidal wave* of support, as he received *thunderous* ovations and a *shower* of contributions, *snowing under* his opponent and establishing his *don't-rock-the-boat* position in the *mainstream*. For other watery metaphors, see TRICKLE-DOWN THEORY; PUMP-PRIMING.

running mate A candidate on the same ticket, for a lower office; most often used in connection with the vice-presidential nominee.

"Governor Marshall bears the highest reputation," said Woodrow Wilson on July 4, 1912, "and I feel honored by having him as a running mate." This may be the first recorded use of the phrase by a presidential nominee, though the racing term had been in use in 1900. "Men of all parties," wrote the *Review of Reviews* in that year, "will admit that Mr. [Elihu] Root's name would add positive strength, and that a better man could hardly be selected as Mr. McKinley's 'running mate.'"

In horse racing, a single stable will often enter more than one horse in a race, with one of the lesser horses used as a pacesetter and called a *running mate*. This second or third horse usually vanishes into obscurity. Vice President Hubert Humphrey, reminiscing in 1966 about the 1964 campaign against the Goldwater-Miller ticket: "To this day I have a great deal of respect for Barry Goldwater and his running mate, what's-his-name." (This was soon followed by a satiric song by Tom Lehrer, "I Wonder What Happened to Hubert.")

When the running mate is stronger or better-known than the candidate for the top job, the result is called a KANGAROO TICKET, its hindquarters stronger than its front legs.

running metaphors An American *runs* for election; a Briton *stands* for election; a French candidate *se presente*, "presents oneself," for election. The English metaphor may be based on a trial, with the candidate standing for election as one would "stand trial"; the French is on competing presentations; the American metaphor is that of a race.

Run has a place in a variety of political expressions, its usage traceable to Alexander Hamilton in 1792. See RUN SCARED; RUNNING MATE; FRONT RUNNER. The Ohio *State Journal* in 1840 pointed out that "General Harrison constantly *runs* ahead of his ticket." A campaign is most frequently compared to a race in which an easy victory is *winning in a walk*. Former Interior Secretary Harold Ickes, referring to a poor speech at the Gridiron Club by Senator John Bricker in 1946, said, "Before his speech ... Bricker thought he was running for the Republican nomination for President. Now he is not only walking, he is limping ..."

run scared An admonition to avoid complacency; to run as if a good chance to lose existed, despite indications of likely victory.

"I expect to win running like a singed cat," said Adlai Stevenson in 1952. Dwight Eisenhower in 1956, who had less reason to campaign aggressively, said, "I believe when you are in any contest you should work like there is—to the very last minute—a chance to lose it. This is battle, this is politics, this is anything."

The candidate whose polls show him behind needs no advice to run scared; he does so automatically. The phrase is directed in particular to the candidate who is in the position of Thomas E. Dewey in 1948, considered a SHOO-IN. Hindsighted politicians now say Dewey should have *run scared*—conducted a more aggressive, fighting campaign—but the fact was that the Dewey managers did run scared, at the behest of party leaders—scared of saying anything that would "rock the boat," fearful of making a mistake that would give Truman an opening. See STIR UP THE ANIMALS.

run the traps See RATTLE THE CAGE.

rustling behind the jalousies Intervention in political affairs by the candidate's wife.

John A. Wells, a New York attorney who managed campaigns for such Republicans as Nelson Rockefeller, Jacob Javits, Louis Lefkowitz, and others, once agreed to manage a political campaign provided, as he put it to Senator Javits, "there is no rustling behind the jalousies." His condition was met: the candidate's wife Marian, noted for her outspoken opinions about overly tight scheduling of the candidate's time, was almost silenced on that score for the duration.

The phrase is not as strong as POWER BEHIND THE THRONE or GRAY EMINENCE; its reference, up to now, has been primarily feminine. A *jalousie* is a slatted screen, providing concealment without stopping whispered confidences.

S

sachem A party leader.

"Take me to your leader," a bromide used in dealing with fictional beings in jungles or on other planets, is reflected in the first recorded use of *sachem*: "They brought us to their Sachim," the 1622 *Journal of the Plantation at Plymouth* records, "very personable, gentle, courteous, and fayre conditioned." (A political joke based on this construction is the pseudo-Indian grafter's request: "Lead me to your taker.") The word is from Narragansett, an Algonquian language, meaning "sagamore" or "party chief," and was used by the leaders of New York's Tammany Hall as early as 1876.

John Adams, in 1776, wrote of "The patricians, the sachems, the nabobs...[who] sigh, moan and fret." The braves and warriors of the Tammany political organization named their leader the *Grand Sachem*, who presided over meetings held at the *wigwam*; today, political leadership meetings are sometimes termed *powwows*.

The word is not used currently by politicians, but is frequently used—along with SATRAP—by political columnists and reporters. For other aboriginal American words in politics, see MUCKEY-MUCKS; MUGWUMP; CAUCUS; RAINMAKER.

safe Applied to a politician, reliable; applied to a district or constituency, taken for granted.

In James Russell Lowell's *Bigelow Papers* of 1862, a character says, "Long 'z ye sift out 'safe' canderdates thet no one aint afeared on." Lincoln Steffens wrote in a 1905 issue of *McClure's* magazine: "The gubernatorial chair [in Rhode Island] never had amounted to much more than an empty honor for 'safe men.'"

In its political use, *safe* means REGULAR and not likely to BOLT. Mencken defined it as "not radical," but a radical can be safe to other radicals if he is not likely to turn conservative. When presidential candidates total up likely delegate support, the categories are "safe," "shaky," and "leaning away."

"They don't concede [Harold] Stassen one chance in a million," wrote John Gunther in 1947, "they know that the better the prospects of Republican victory in 1948, the less are Stassen's own chances for the nomination—since, if victory is certain, there is no temptation to choose any but the 'safest' candidate." In 1952 Eisenhower was not nearly as ideologically safe to delegates as "Mr. Republican," Senator Robert A. Taft, but after twenty years out of office they preferred a safe bet for election to a safe candidate.

safety net Social welfare programs or assistance to protect the needy.

This favorite catchphrase of the Reagan Administration was built on the circus metaphor of a net to catch falling trapeze artists or high-wire performers.

Reagan and his spokesmen added the adjective *social*. David A. Stockman, his director of the Office of Management and Budget (whose sobriquet was "the blow-dried Grim Reaper"), defined the three-word phrase in early 1981: "A social safety net encompasses the long-range programs of basic income security, most of which were established in the New Deal 50 years ago and are now widely accepted. This includes basic Social Security and Medicare, unemployment compensation, the two components of what we call welfare (Aid for Families with Dependent Children, and Supplemental Security Income), and basic veteran's benefits."

This metaphor for welfare may have started in the 1970s, specifically in editorials by Jude Wanniski for *The Wall Street Journal*. He told the lexicographer: "The safety-net idea that I used applied to the international banking system—that is, there would be an international lender of last resort that would serve as a safety net for third-world loans in the event of international turmoil. I always liked the idea of a safety net. When I got to that chapter in the Jack Kemp book, I held on to that metaphor."

That book is *An American Renaissance*, written in 1979. Kemp wrote:

Americans have two complementary desires. They want an open, promising ladder of opportunity. And they want a safety net of social services to catch and comfort those less fortunate than themselves.... Yet because people want this safety net in place, it doesn't follow that they therefore want it filled up with sufferers. Least of all do they want their assistance to seduce others into habits of dependency.

The net metaphor predates that usage.

The earliest citation I have is from a speech by Winston Churchill on October 8, 1951:

The difference between our outlook and the Socialist outlook on life is the difference between the ladder and the queue.... We ask: "What happens if anyone slips out of his place in the queue?" "Ah!" say the Socialists. "Our officials—and we have plenty of them—come and put him back in it. ..." And then they come back at us and say: "... What is your answer to what happens if anyone slips off the ladder?" Our reply is: "We shall have a good net. ..."

salami tactics Little by little, one slice at a time; gradualism.

The columnist Stewart Alsop wrote in *Newsweek* in 1969: "It remains to be seen just how far the Russians and their Czech and Slovak stooges will have to go in order to complete the process of re-scaring the people. One theory is that press censorship, secret-police pressure, and salami tactics will do the trick. Alexander Dubcek will certainly not be the last of the liberals to fall victim to the salami knife."

Two years later, in his syndicated column, Stew's brother Joseph Alsop denounced "the orgy of public hypocrisy touched off by the *Times*'s collection of stolen Pentagon documents," pointing out that the two men whose advice was taken by President Johnson were Dean Rusk and Ambassador Llewellyn Thompson: "Both of them pressed strongly for the salami-slicing approach—for 'gradualism' as they called it."

In their *Dictionary of Modern Thought*, Alan Bullock and Oliver Stallybrass credit the coinage to Mátyás Rákosi of the Hungarian Communist party, who in 1945 described how he came to power by getting his opposition to slice off its right wing, then its centrists, until only those collaborating with Communists remained in power. *Time* magazine reported from Budapest in 1947: "Rakosi has eaten the last of the salami."

The redolent metaphor is current and international. In an April 2005 *Turkish Daily News* Mehmet Ögütçü wrote, "we easily become the 'victims' of successfully deployed 'salami tactics.' Consider where we have ended up regarding the Iraqi/Kurdistan issue, where once we had demarcated 'red lines' that cannot be crossed ..." The columnist explained the figure of speech to readers: "Drop a frog into boiling water and it will immediately jump out. Heat the water up gradually from cold and the frog will take no action—with fatal consequences. Cut one thin slice of salami at generous intervals and few will notice its disappearance."

For another meaty political metaphor, see BALONEY.

SALT Acronym for *Strategic Arms Limitation Talks*, begun in November 1969, between the Soviet Union and the U.S. Most often used redundantly, as *SALT talks*. Followed in the early 1980s by START, Strategic Arms Reduction Talks.

According to John Newhouse, in his 1973 *Cold Dawn: The Story of SALT*, the man who invented the acronym *SALT* is Robert Martin, who was a low-level staffer in the State Department's Bureau of Political-Military Affairs. Newhouse wrote:

In the Spring of 1968, when the prospect of talks suddenly brightened, bureaucrats began having to write cables about limiting strategic arms. Any combination of words labeling the process was inevitably cumbersome. Martin, who was then a member of the political section of the U.S. Nato mission in Brussels, finally gave up and concocted SALT. His ambassador, Harlan Cleveland, resisted the term for a while; so did a number of Washington officials, finding it too cute. ACDA [the Arms Control and Disarmament Agency] disliked it. The issue arose at a meeting of senior officials; the CIA finally insisted on formal adoption of SALT because its filing system was already being organized around the term.

Robert Martin confirms this. Reached in 1978 at the U.S. embassy in Tehran, where he was counselor for Political-Military Affairs, he responded: "The acronym SALT is one that I developed in order to save…some of that precious commodity—time…The initial reaction, both in Brussels and Washington, was negative. Harlan Cleveland, my Ambassador at USNATO, kept scratching it out, insisting that the four words be spelled out…he did not view the acronym as being sufficiently formal and serious for the exercise that the U.S. proposed to begin."

As sometimes happens, the man who resisted the term got credit for it. A German newspaper reported Cleveland (coiner of REVOLUTION OF RISING EXPECTATIONS) to be the author of the acronym. "He sent me a marvelous letter," writes Martin, "expressing delight at the credit being heaped upon him for something he had so belittled originally; yet further proof, he pointed out, that the Chiefs get all of the credit while the poor blighters in the trenches do all the work."

Limitations is used, but Martin shoots the plural down: "As created, it was singular, and for the purist it remains so." How did the acronym translate during negotiations? "Even the Soviets who work on SALT use the term when speaking Russian."

The vocabulary of nuclear warfare causes some shudders (see UNTHINKABLE THOUGHTS), and in one case deliberately mocked itself: the acronym for "Mutual Assured Destruction" is MAD. See BARGAINING CHIP.

salutations See MY FRIENDS.

samizdat The underground press that planted the seeds of freedom in the former Soviet Union.

"By *samizdat*," wrote *Time* in 1970, "Russians endlessly retype and clandestinely circulate the work of such banned writers as Alexander Solzhenitsyn."

Samizdat is the hand-to-hand distribution of manuscripts—handwritten, typed, mimeographed, or photocopied—of works that Soviet printing houses refused to handle. The Solzhenitsyn novel *August 1914* had an epilogue to its foreign edition noting that the book could not be published in the U.S.S.R. "except in samizdat."

The word comes from the Russian *sam*, "self," plus the first part of *izdatelstvo*, "publishing," and was probably coined as a pun on *Gosizdat*, the State Publishing House in Moscow. Vladimir Bukovsky had a nice definition in his 1978 autobiographical novel *To Build a Castle*: "write myself, edit myself, censor myself, publish myself, distribute myself, go to jail for it myself."

The mid-'60s birth of the word coincided with the beginning of recognition outside the U.S.S.R. that an organized opposition was operating within the Soviet regime. The word was first used in an official Soviet publication, the weekly magazine *Ogonyok*, in September 1971, in a story about dissident physicist Dmitri Mikheyev, defining the word as "in effect, anti-Soviet."

Soviet expert Harry Schwartz noted soon afterward that the spread of unofficial publications raised the question of whether a "zone of tolerance" had been created in the U.S.S.R. for illegal publication of dissent, providing a safety valve for political malcontents.

Through the '70s, that tolerance waxed and waned; after Solzhenitsyn's departure for the West, Soviet physicist Andrei Sakharov became the best-known dissenter, his positions made known by samizdat. In time a similar word—*tamizdat*, "published over there"—came to cover publication abroad, with copies smuggled back into the U.S.S.R. By the late '70s *samizdat* came to mean the material of dissent as well as its system of distribution. In the 1980s, one reason given for the absence of personal computers in Soviet cities—a restriction that held back Russian technological skills—was that they might provide dissenters with "instant samizdat."

Following the dissolution of the Soviet Union, the term was used in historical contexts and occasionally as a word adopted by English to mean "underground press." By 2007, Hendrick Hertzberg reported in the *New Yorker* that details of Saddam Hussein's execution beyond the official videotape were vividly disseminated "via cell-phone-camera samizdat, jerky and noisy. "Later that year, the Russian word was used by the *Los Angeles Times* reporting the leaking of copies of music albums via the Internet worrisome to industry executives but "for more indie-minded artists, though, this sort of samizdat circulation of their work has become a valuable, even crucial marketing tool ... " Samizdat has been absorbed into English meaning "unofficial, daring, perhaps illegal distribution of information and entertainment."

See HUMAN RIGHTS; MOST FAVORED NATION; QUIET DIPLOMACY.

sanctions See QUARANTINE.

sandbag To attack from behind; treat duplicitously by feigning friendship or weakness.

The elder George Bush helped introduce this usage: "We feel we were sandbagged," the candidate said after a 1980 primary, repeating the verb used by his New Hampshire campaign manager.

Six years later, Secretary of State George P. Shultz referred to the term during a lunch with Turkish officials who complained about United States quotas on Turkish imports: "Do you have a word in your language called *sandbag*?" Shultz asked. "I have been brought here in order to have a nice luncheon and get hit behind the ear." *The Wall Street Journal* explained the Secretary's usage in card-playing terms: "The word means to entice someone into putting money into a poker pot—either by not betting yourself or by betting only a small amount—and then raising back with a large bet later."

At the turn of the twentieth century, Farmer and Henley's slang dictionary referred to the noun *sandbag* as coming from thieves' argot, defined as "a large sausagelike bag of sand dealing a heavy blow that leaves no mark." The American use of

the verb has been specifically limited to the sense of "to hit from behind."

San Francisco Democrat See BLAME AMERICA FIRST.

sanitize Of a document, to delete damaging statements; of a person, to make innocent by association.

"The President has moved in seven months," wrote John Osborne about Jimmy Carter in *The New Republic* in 1977, "from thought of opening Cabinet meetings to the press, to maybe releasing edited transcripts of Cabinet discussions, to having a White House press officer attend meetings and afterward give reporters a sanitized account."

In that usage, to *sanitize* is to make palatable, or less embarrassing. The cleanliness metaphor—removing political dirt—is obvious, as in the Nixon instruction given to H. R. Haldeman to "clean up the tapes," that is, to remove the material that might raise doubts or eyebrows.

A less obvious meaning is to remain in place after a scandal affecting one's colleagues, thereby proving one's absence of taint. Many Nixon appointees asked to be kept on in the first year of the Ford Administration in order to be thus "sanitized."

Sometimes the word carries a political sting. Members of the House committee investigating the CIA (the "Pike Committee") objected in 1975 to the lack of cooperation they received from the intelligence agency. In the report, which was published in the *Village Voice* by CBS correspondent Daniel Schorr after the House decided to suppress it, the committee report stated: "We were given heavily 'sanitized' pieces of paper. 'Sanitized' was merely a euphemism for blank sheets of paper."

Ordinarily the word is only mildly pejorative, as sanitization is taken to be the customary manner of protecting insiders from publication of their indiscreet or unduly frank observations.

The extreme of sanitizing is *shredding*, the confetti-like product of the electric paper shredder; for a more venal or deceptive form of avoiding detection see LAUNDERED MONEY.

Santa Claus, nobody shoots at Proverb about the political folly of attacking government entitlements.

Former Governor Alfred E. Smith, in a press conference in New York late in 1933, said, "No sane local official who has hung up an empty stocking over the municipal fireplace is going to shoot Santa Claus just before a hard Christmas." In 1936, when Smith, the embittered 1928 Democratic presidential candidate, was campaigning against Roosevelt, he shortened the point to a simple "nobody shoots at Santa Claus."

Barry Goldwater, campaigning for the Republican presidential nomination in 1964, told the Economic Club of New York: "It is my chore to ask you to consider the toughest proposition ever faced by believers in the free-enterprise system: the need for a frontal attack against Santa Claus— not the Santa Claus of the holiday season, of course, but the Santa Claus of the FREE LUNCH, the government handout, the Santa Claus of something-for-nothing and something-for-everyone."

Another man to take aim at the popular symbol of Christmas was Orville Freeman, campaigning for a fourth term as governor of Minnesota. According to economist Walter Heller, Freeman went around the state telling people frankly that the services they wanted could only be paid for with higher taxes—that, in his phrase, "There ain't no Santa Claus." He lost.

A synonym for *Santa Claus* is *tooth fairy*, after the practice of telling a child that if a recently extracted tooth is placed under the pillow at night, a fairy will come and replace the lost tooth with a coin. *Tooth fairy*, meaning "a story told to gullible children," carries the same connotation of suspended reality as the cheerful ho-ho figure with the welcoming lap, though Santa retains an exclusive franchise for government largesse.

USC economics professor Arthur B. Laffer, who provided the intellectual underpinning for the TAX REVOLT in California in 1978 and subsequently was a leading advocate of SUPPLY-SIDE economics, wrote in the July 1978 *AEI Economist*: "In the absence of the 'tooth fairy' the resources spent by the government are the total tax burden on the economy's productive sector."

In the don't-you-believe-it lexicon, BALONEY is the harshest denunciation; PIE IN THE SKY is severe, but fondly archaic; FREE LUNCH is usually limited to economic affairs; *tooth fairy* requires the most childlike belief; *Santa Claus* and *Uncle Sugar* are most closely associated with government benefits. Not too far afield is a Goldilocks economy—"not too hot, not too cold, but just right," as in perfect porridge.

satellite A state formally independent but in fact subordinate to a hegemonic power; occasionally, an official under the domination of another.

To Americans before the demise of the Soviet Union, satellites included the states of Eastern Europe as well as Cuba, whose economy depended on Soviet largesse. Senator Thruston Morton of Kentucky, urging the adoption of a consular treaty with these countries in 1967, hoped that it would lead to changes in "the so-called satellite countries." However, many Americans with ethnic roots in Eastern European nations preferred the phrase *captive nations*. When President Gerald Ford, in a televised debate with challenger Jimmy Carter in 1976, refused to admit those nations were under Soviet domination, that was considered a major BLOOPER.

Satellite is of Middle French origin, meaning "attendant" or "follower," applied to those sycophants who fawned on French princes. Its pejorative meaning of subservience traveled to the U.S.; in the 1852 novel *Uncle Tom's Cabin*, Harriet Beecher Stowe's cruel Simon Legree "encouraged his two black satellites to a kind of coarse familiarity with him." The word has retained its political sense: Charles de Gaulle characterized the removal of Western Europe from what he considered American domination as "desatellization." See PUPPET.

The word gained a sense of planetary "follower" in astronomy, and the senses merged on occasion as Soviet spokesmen denounced nations "in the U.S. orbit." Later, with the advent of communications and spy satellites orbiting the Earth, *satellite diplo-*

macy came to mean the conduct of global affairs on live television transmitted by satellite. (For related terms, see DIPLOMACY.)

satrap Minor party official.

This imperial word has had a rough time in politics. Originally from the Old Persian *xshathrapavan*, "protector of the imperium," used by Persian provincial governors, the word *satrap* in the U.S. became associated in English with the unpopular military governors of the South during Reconstruction.

President Andrew Johnson popularized the word in 1866: "I could have remained at the capital with fifty or sixty millions of appropriations... with my satraps and dependents in every township." In the off-year election that followed in 1866, this was used against him in a campaign flyer: "Mr. Johnson said that, with forty or fifty millions of dollars placed at his disposal, under the Freedmen's Bureau bill, with his satraps scattered throughout the land, he could make himself a dictator.... Satraps, you know, are Turkish officers who are liable to lose their heads by the scimitar if they do anything to displease the Sultan." In 1876 the New York *World* linked "the miserable scallawag and oppressive black satrap."

The word has continued its use as a minor official inclined to officiousness, although John Gunther in his *Inside U.S.A.* called the older brother of Missouri boss Thomas Pendergast "a satrap of considerable eminence." In 2007, Jaime Daremblum in the online Daily Standard was concerned about "an oil supply largely controlled by unsavory characters like Venezuela's Hugo Chavez and the Middle East's satraps."

In current use, BOSS, SACHEM, *leader* are on the top level, with *satrap*, HENCHMAN, HATCHETMAN, and *functionary* below, and TROOPS, *braves*, FAITHFUL, *workers*, RANK AND FILE at the bottom. POOH-BAH, MUCKEY-MUCK, and PANJANDRUM are spoofs of *big shots*.

Another word associated with the Turkish sultans occasionally used in politics is *janissary*, Turkish slave-soldiers dating back to the fourteenth century, whose 1826 uprising ended in their massacre. An FDR clique in the '40s was called "the Janissariat," a play on the Russian *commissariat*.

Saturday Night Massacre The events of the evening of October 20, 1973, when the two top officials of the Department of Justice refused to fire the Watergate Special Prosecutor, and were swept out along with him, leading to a public-opinion FIRESTORM.

Nixon chief of staff Alexander Haig told Attorney General Elliot Richardson to dismiss Special Prosecutor Archibald Cox, who had been pressing hard for subpoenaed White House tapes. Richardson, with tears in his eyes (as Haig later told the author), demurred; he had promised the Senate, as part of his confirmation, he would not fire the Special Prosecutor for any reason other than malfeasance. Haig then called Deputy AG William Ruckelshaus, replacing Richardson as the nation's top law enforcement officer; when Ruckelshaus declined, he reported Haig to have said: "Your commander-in-chief has given you an order. You have no alternative." Ruckelshaus said he did, and resigned. Haig then reached the Solicitor General, Robert Bork, third in the Justice hierarchy, who believed that there was a constitutional requirement that somebody in charge of the Justice Department carry out a legal order from the nation's elected leader. Bork intended to fire Cox and then resign, but he was persuaded to stay on, which some senators held against him in subsequent confirmation hearings for his Supreme Court nomination. (See the eponymous verb BORK.)

At 8:25 P.M., press secretary Ron Ziegler told reporters in the White House briefing room that the three officials had been removed and the Special Prosecutor's office "abolished." At 9:05, FBI agents took positions inside the Special Prosecution Force offices at 1425 K Street on orders from Haig, who had heard that members of Cox's staff had been removing files for several days (which Cox aide Richard Ben-Veniste later confirmed as true in his Watergate memoirs).

"There was blood all over the floor," said White House aide Leonard Garment to this writer and others during that weekend, and the blood image—as a "massacre"—quickly took hold. By Monday the *Saturday Night Massacre* had become a phrase locked into WATERGATE terminology.

Massacre has long been a sloganizing word: the *Boston Massacre*, on the night of March 5, 1770, led to the celebration of Massacre Day in Boston until 1783, when the celebration was switched to the Fourth of July. Fans of gangland movies recall the *St. Valentine's Day Massacre*. As with many terms of catastrophe or bloodshed, the word *massacre* has been absorbed into politics to denote bloodless coups, and is used ironically: when Admiral Stansfield Turner began dismissing 800 members of the CIA's clandestine branch in late October 1977, the laid-off agents and operatives called it the "Halloween Massacre."

Saturday night, before nearly everybody's day off, has a festive, sometimes lonely or violent connotation. In his 1978 book *With Nixon*, speechwriter Ray Price compared the angry television commentaries of that crucial weekend in 1973 to "Saturday-Night Specials, the television equivalent of those cheap but lethal handguns that have given Saturday night a bad name."

scalawag Rascal; an archaic political epithet, now as mild as *scamp*.

"A scapegrace" was how *scalawag* was defined in the 1848 *Bartlett's Dictionary of Americanisms*. *Harper's Monthly* in 1868 said that "Southern men who side with the Republican Party are called 'Scalliwags.'" The spelling varies, but the term, by the end of the Civil War, was used by Southerners to describe other whites from their own region who helped the Northern officials get established throughout the former Confederate states and who were answerable primarily to the radical Republican faction then dominant in Congress.

In 1865 the *Washington Morning Chronicle's* correspondent wrote that "Whenever a white man appears to vote [in Alabama] every one of these infuriated devils … set up a yell calling him 'white negro,' 'low trash,' 'Scalawag.'" The distinction between *scalawag* and CARPETBAGGER was that the latter was of Northern origin.

The word possibly derives from an old Scottish word, *scurryvaig*; another theory is that its origin can be traced to *Scalloway*, a Scottish island famed for its small Shetland ponies. An 1804 citation (from the *Dictionary of the Scots Language*) for the Scots word from the poet Robert Couper: "Vile scurryvaig, why did ye steal / The remnant o' my swine!"

A quote from Isaac Kelso's 1863 book *The Stars and Bars: Or, The Reign of Terror in Missouri* suggests that early in the Civil War it was used as a term of general, not necessarily political, contempt: "companies of armed men, gangs of ruffians, gentlemen and scallawags … white trash and black trash, were pouring into town from every quarter."

The Reconstruction word has returned to its earlier meaning. *Scalawag* now means a rascal, scapegrace, one who is never up to any good, rather than a Southerner intent on grinding down his own kind. See COPPERHEAD.

scenario Military-diplomatic jargon for a possible course of action, its extremes modified as "best-case" or "worst-case."

Arthur Schlesinger, Jr., wrote of Ambassador Averell Harriman:

> He believed in giving good men their head. When long, detailed instructions would come across his desk intended for ambassadors in the field—"scenarios," in the jargon, designed to deprive envoys abroad of all discretion—Harriman, before clearing the message, liked to add a liberating introductory sentence: "For your guidance, you may wish to consider the following."

Scenario is a theatrical word used in wargaming to mean the manner in which military action is expected to develop.

White House correspondent Max Frankel wrote in 1967 of the extrapolation of likelihoods in "peace games" that go on within warring governments: "Both are regularly confronted, it seems, by 'scenarios' to step up the war, to step down the war or, in various ways, to interrupt the war—all presented as the quickest way to conclude the war."

Three decades later, looking forward to the 2008 Olympic games in China, James Mann wrote in the *Los Angeles Times* that it is possible to envision three scenarios for China. One can be called the Soothing Scenario: that China's authoritarian political system is bound to open up…another scenario holds that China is so fundamentally unstable that it is headed for some sort of political cataclysm or economic nosedive, or both. Call this the Upheaval Scenario…the third scenario…holds that China will remain an authoritarian regime over the long term…perhaps the most likely.

See PENTAGONESE; ROSIE SCENARIO; WAR-GAMING WORDS.

scorched earth A policy of destruction in defeat; destroying one's own supplies and possessions to prevent the supply or enrichment of an invading enemy.

In the spring of 1992, Democratic national chairman Ronald H. Brown denounced what he called candidate Jerry Brown's "scorched earth policy" of attacks on Bill Clinton's character and record.

This figurative use of the phrase is rooted in reports of Joseph Stalin's orders to his armies during World War II to destroy grain or supplies that would have gone to the invading Germans. In his broadcast of July 3, 1941, Stalin announced, "All valuable property, including nonferrous metals, grain and fuel, which cannot be withdrawn must without fail be destroyed."

His words were promptly designated a *scorched-earth policy* because that vivid phrase had been used in the Sino-Japanese war of the 1930s, in which the Chinese *jiaotu* (*zhengce*) was used for "scorched earth (policy)." A *Times* of London reporter wrote in 1937: "The populace…are still disturbed…by wild rumors of a 'scorched earth policy' of burning the city before the Japanese enter." The literal meaning of the smoldering term has not been extinguished. A Mideast report of the first Persian Gulf war in *The Washington Post* in 1993 mentioned "the few trees that survived Iraq's scorched-earth policy."

Recent use of the phrase is mainly figurative. During the presidential campaign of 1992, the term resurfaced in a description of Ross Perot's "draconian" economic plan; according to the *Los Angeles Times*, "His own scorched-earth approach…is

commonly dismissed as beyond the pale of public acceptance." After Bush's defeat, *The Boston Globe* commented in early 1993 that "the President has not undertaken a 'scorched earth' policy by releasing a flood of controversial actions, as some critics had feared." In 2007, the conservative *Washington Times* editorialized that the "partisan gunslingers" like Rep. Rahm Emanuel (D-Ill.), architect of the 2006 Democratic takeback of control of the House of Representatives, had "a scorched-earth plan to take back the White House."

scrap of paper Attack phrase on a treaty; cavalier treatment of a written diplomatic agreement.

On August 4, 1914, Germany's Chancellor Theobald von Bethmann-Hollweg said to Great Britain's ambassador Sir Edward Goschen at their final interview: "Just for a word—neutrality, a word which in wartime has so often been disregarded—just for a scrap of paper Great Britain is going to make war." The "scrap of paper" was Britain's treaty with Belgium guaranteeing that nation's neutrality. When Belgium was attacked, the British were true to their written guarantee.

"In and ever since 1914," wrote Eric Partridge in *Usage and Abusage*, "one totalitarian state has sneered at the validity of a *scrap of paper*. Bethmann-Hollweg's famous phrase…caused Lord Samuel, in 1937, to say that, 'under stress, treaties may become mere scraps of paper.'"

The phrase has currency in writing about international affairs, especially in connection with the phrase "honoring our commitments." A similar phrase on another subject is "STROKE OF A PEN."

Seal of the President See BALD EAGLE.

secondary virginity See NO-TAX PLEDGE.

second-class citizen One deprived of rights, especially voting rights, and particularly an African-American.

"The Constitution does not provide for first and second class citizens," wrote Wendell Willkie in *An American Program*.

A generation later, Dwight Eisenhower used the phrase several times, but historian Samuel Eliot Morison commented: "It was all very well for President Eisenhower to declare, 'There must be no second-class citizens in this country'—there were, and still are."

Oddly, before the Civil War there was no definition of the term *citizen of the United States*. Each state determined federal citizenship, until the Fourteenth Amendment stated that "all persons born or naturalized in the United States, and subject to the jurisdiction thereof, are citizens of the United States and of the States wherein they reside." The "and subject to the jurisdiction thereof" clause was inserted to deny citizenship to children of foreign ambassadors and to American Indians.

In the post-bellum reaction against Reconstruction, blacks were denied the right to vote by impossible "literacy tests," poll taxes, and direct intimidation. Congress in 1957 passed a civil rights law, the first since 1875, to protect the Negro's right to vote, adding other legislation in later years to strengthen it.

As a result, in the '60s *second-class citizen* lost much of its voting-rights meaning and was applied to those to whom education and economic benefits were denied.

Second-class became a phrase to be avoided generally; transportation companies with *first-class* accommodations offered "coach," "tourist," "economy," "club," "business," "executive" (even "royal coach" and "deluxe economy") in an effort to get away from "second-class." The only area where the phrase has had a happy sound is in the postal service, as publishers sought "second-class mailing privileges," in effect a subsidy of distribution costs.

secret agreements See OPEN COVENANTS; GRAND DESIGN.

secret plan Implied but unannounced intentions; suggested suspicion of a political proposal that has been prepared but not released.

This noun phrase, variously considered artful or sinister, dates to early 1968 and

Richard Nixon's first successful presidential campaign. During the weeks before the New Hampshire primary, in a speech about the fighting in Vietnam, the candidate promised to "end the war and win the peace in the Pacific"—a phrase appealing to a general public desire but avoiding any specific proposal. Supporters of Michigan Governor George Romney, also a presidential aspirant, raised Nixon's words to the level of a "plan," and the Governor found his campaign theme in repeatedly asked throughout the New Hampshire primary campaign, "Where is your secret plan?" (Romney may have taken the phrase, not in quotation marks, from coverage by United Press International reporter Milt Benjamin.)

Nixon was then repeatedly quoted as having said, "I have a secret plan to end the war," which he had never said. After the election victory over Democratic nominee Hubert Humphrey, when the *New York Times* columnist Anthony Lewis used this false quotation, the lexicographer (author of the "end the war and win the peace" phrase, who had been taken into the White House as a Nixon speechwriter) offered to buy the columnist a lunch if he could come up with the citation. When Lewis, after an assiduous quotation hunt, could not find any direct citation, he honorably stopped using the line.

The expression resurfaced during Ronald Reagan's reelection campaign. When Democrats charged in 1984 that Reagan had a "secret plan" to raise taxes after the election, the President said he had "no plans" to raise taxes. Because "no plans" often means "plans not yet ready to be announced," candidate Walter Mondale's accusation led Reagan to promise that he would raise taxes only as "a last resort." Mondale himself had been the target of the same charge during the Democratic primaries from Senator John Glenn, who criticized his undue wariness: "To be so cautious that your platform consists of secret plans to be revealed after the elections," said Glenn, "—to be that cautious is not leadership, it's politics." A headline over that story caught the former astronaut's catchphrase: "Glenn Says Rival Has 'Secret Plans.'"

The phrase was familiar enough to parody. Wayne Stayskal, a cartoonist for *The Tampa Tribune*, depicted a housewife responding to a political pollster: "I'm a registered Democrat...but I've got a secret plan to vote Republican."

Like the urban myth of crocodiles in the sewers, the non-quotation never seems to go away: "Senate Democrats...recognized that the party out of the White House doesn't need a detailed strategy for ending a war, just a general sense of direction," wrote Jonathan Alter in *Newsweek* in 2006. "When Richard Nixon was asked how he would end the Vietnam War in 1968, he said he had a 'secret plan'—and got away with it."

Rick Beyer, author of *The Greatest Stories Never Told*, informs the author:

In 1972, I was 16 years old and working for the McGovern campaign in Rhode Island. I was given a button that said "Remember Oct. 9th." I was told that when someone asked with the button meant, I should tell them that October 9th, 1968, was the day that Richard Nixon had announced he had a "secret plan to win the war" in Vietnam. After we spoke yesterday [in 2006] I glanced at some of the articles in the NY Times archive from October 10th, 1968. One of them had some mention of Nixon refusing to give details about what he would do concerning Vietnam, but alas, no mention of a "secret plan."

(George Romney began charging Nixon with claiming a "secret plan" in February of 1968.)

secular humanism Philosophy of humanistic values or practice of good behavior independent of religion, a frequent target of those strongly religious.

Although secular humanists are sometimes equated with "ethical atheists," many humanists are agnostics, and others belong to organized religions. The disagreement about definition has led to varied use of the phrase, often as a euphemism for "atheism" or as an attack phrase to impugn an opponent's faith in God.

Michael J. Rosenberg, editor of *Near East Report*, offered this definition in 1985: "Secular humanist has become the new label

employed to indict anyone who opposes school prayer, believes in education or disagrees with the religious right's views on abortion." The evangelist James Kennedy defined secular humanism as a "godless, atheistic, evolutionary, amoral, collectivist, socialistic, communistic religion" that poses a threat to schoolchildren.

The source of the term may be a 1933 religious work, according to Merriam-Webster's citation files. William G. Peck used the noun phrase in *The Social Implications of the Oxford Movement*, commenting, "In face of this secular humanism, the return of the Oxford leaders to Catholic doctrine and practice necessarily signified a criticism of the secular standpoint, and the provision of a positive alternative."

As the usagist Jacques Barzun has pointed out, the label has become "a description turned into a tautology," because "humanism by itself is secular, since it makes man and his concerns primary—man the measure, instead of God."

security risk A person considered likely to commit anything from an indiscretion to an act of espionage that may harm the safety of the U.S.

The expression was popularized during what is loosely termed "the McCarthy era" (see MCCARTHYISM) when the Wisconsin senator charged that the State Department was harboring hundreds of *security risks*. The phrase broadly covered those who could easily be blackmailed (alcoholics and homosexuals), those who had Communist associations or belonged to groups considered subversive by the Justice Department, and those whose close relatives' associations might compromise them.

Attorney General Herbert Brownell charged in 1954 that the Truman Administration harbored a Treasury Department official, Harry Dexter White, who was "a known traitor." Some 2,427 "security risks" were removed from government service in two years, the White House announced, drawing a charge from Adlai Stevenson that it was participating in a NUMBERS GAME.

America's best-known "security risk" was atomic scientist J. Robert Oppenheimer.

He contested the suspension of his secret "Q" clearance before a board set up by the Atomic Energy Commission, which decided he had "fundamental defects of character" because of his "associations" and his nonconforming attitude toward his sworn official obligations. The criteria were set up in the McMahon Act, the commission's regulations, and a White House directive of April 1953.

Testifying on Oppenheimer's behalf before the board, former High Commissioner for Germany John J. McCloy pointed out that scientists like Oppenheimer were needed, and that if anything was done "to dampen their fervor ... to that extent the security of the United States is impaired ... a security risk in reverse." See REVERSE BIGOTRY.

When a journalist labeled two State Department employees as "well-known security risks" in a press-conference question, President Kennedy flared in anger, saying he believed the men could carry out their assignments "without detriment to the interests of the United States, and I hope without detriment to their characters by your question."

See LOYALTY OATH.

segregation Attack word on what was the doctrine of SEPARATE BUT EQUAL facilities; the enforced separation of races in fields such as education, housing, and social and economic affairs.

Proponents of what is now described as *segregation* preferred the word *separation*, as used in the Supreme Court decision in *Plessy v. Ferguson* in 1896: "Laws permitting, and even requiring, their separation in places where they are liable to be brought into contact do not necessarily imply the inferiority of one race to the other ..." Some proponents accepted the word and defended the practice, as did Judge Thomas P. Brady before the Commonwealth Club of California in 1957: "Segregation in the South is a way of life. ... It is the means whereby we live in social peace, order and security."

Opponents of separation adopted the words *segregation* and *integration*, making them a part of the vocabulary as confrontational terms, joining the issue that was ultimately resolved in their favor by the Supreme Court in 1954.

A new word for extreme segregation, popularized by South African Prime Minister Daniel F. Malan, appeared in English in 1947: *apartheid*. It was derived from the Dutch *apart* (same meaning as English) and *heid* (-hood), or "apartness," the state of being totally segregated. The word was adopted in the U.S. only as a policy to denounce. Wrote South African author Alan Paton in 1960: "'Segregation' is such an active word that it suggests someone is trying to segregate somebody else. So the word 'apartheid' was introduced. Now it has such a stench in the nostrils of the world, they are referring to 'autogenous development.'"

In its slang form, the word is *segged*— with a hard *g*—for *segregated*, *desegged* for *desegregated*, which for a time was preferred over *integrated*. In an Alabama primary early in his career, George Wallace said he had been "out-segged" by a more extreme opponent and vowed never to let that happen again; later in life, with the rise of black voting in that state, he relented.

The sale of houses to blacks in formerly all-white neighborhoods is attacked as "blockbusting," taken from the World War II bombing term.

See BUSING TO ACHIEVE RACIAL BALANCE; CIVIL RIGHTS; FREEDOM RIDERS; JIM CROW; QUOTA; RACISM; SEPARATE BUT EQUAL; SIT-IN; WITH ALL DELIBERATE SPEED.

self-appointed See SNEER WORDS.

self-determination The right of a people in an area, or citizens of a nation, to assert their political status and choose their form of government.

The phrase *national self-determination* is associated with President Woodrow Wilson and is generally considered to be one of the most important of his Fourteen Points, although it was not one of them at all. Wilson called later for a fairly traditional nationalism based largely on language and common cultural heritage, with boundaries drawn on that basis and the people within them free to choose their own leadership.

The idea had wide appeal at the close of World War I; the Versailles settlement, to the surprise of skeptics, largely succeeded in achieving Wilson's self-determination aim. Winston Churchill, in 1929, wrote: "Probably less than 3 per cent of the European population are now living under Governments whose nationality they repudiate ..."

Churchill and Franklin Roosevelt included "self-determination" in the 1941 Atlantic Charter. Three years before, in a speech at the Sportpalast in Berlin, Adolf Hitler made Czechoslovakia his "last territorial demand" and scathingly derided Wilson's idea: "In 1918 Central Europe was torn up and reshaped by some foolish or crazy so-called statesmen under the slogan 'self-determination and the right of nations.'... To this, Czechoslovakia owed its existence." Hitler spoke of the oppression of the German-speaking people of that state and then sharply reversed his rhetorical field: "at last, nearly twenty years after, Mr. Wilson's right of self-determination for the 3,500,000 [Germans] must be enforced and we shall not just look on any longer."

The issue of self-determination surfaced strongly, often violently, after the breakup of the Soviet Union began in the Baltics. Critics of the desire of ethnic groups to secede from established states called their actions "dismemberment," and in a 1991 visit to Kiev President George H.W. Bush urged Ukrainians not to succumb to "suicidal nationalism" by withdrawing from the Soviet Union. A vituperative right-wing columnist denounced this speech under a headline he wrote that read "Chicken Kiev" and Mr. Bush has not talked to me since.

sell-by date See "TRUTH-IN" CONSTRUCTION.

selling candidates like soap A charge that MADISON AVENUE TECHNIQUES are being used in an appeal to emotion

The company that advertises most is Procter & Gamble, manufacturer, among many other things, of Ivory Soap. Successful soap-selling is thus a hallmark of excellence in the advertising world.

In 1919, with World War I ended, Major General Leonard Wood wanted the Republican nomination for president the following year. He had been denied a combat command in Europe by the U.S. commander, General "Black Jack" Pershing, who considered him insubordinate, and according to Hermann Hagedorn, Wood's biographer in 1931, President Woodrow Wilson detested him. See OVAL OFFICE.

General Wood's financial backer was Colonel William C. Procter, who was accused of spending $1,750,000 in seeking the 1920 nomination for Wood. (It ultimately went to Warren G. Harding; see SMOKE-FILLED ROOM.) In a lawsuit brought by Procter to recover some of the money, a New York lawyer named Henry Satterlee was deposed, and his sworn testimony revealed the rudiments of a technique never before used in politics.

According to the deponent, Col. Procter—a descendant of the founder of Procter and Gamble—had asserted that the day of the torchlight procession was over, and the time had arrived for up-to-date business methods. "Mr. Procter said he had not been active in politics before, at least not in a national campaign," Satterlee swore, "but that he had some experience in business and was very familiar with the methods of reaching the people in the homes of the country. It took money to reach them. His idea was, he said, that in these days, to use a commercial expression, it was necessary to 'sell' the candidate to the people."

The *New York Times* account of the trial, filed from Chicago on Sept. 25, 1926, reported: "Mr. Satterlee deposed that Colonel Procter's idea was to 'sell' the candidate to the public just as if he were an unknown, new proprietary article, a useful appliance, or an invention. Particularly, in view of the number of women that were to be added to the electorate at the election, the candidate would have to be made known—his name, his face and his qualities." The newspaper's headline read: "Charges 'Selling' of Wood like Soap."

The discovery of this lexicographic revelation was serendipitous. The author was researching the early use of *Oval Office* as the synecdoche for "the President," found a usage in the Wood biography (see OVAL OFFICE), and followed the Wood clippings to the soap story, which he is 99 and 44/100 percent certain has never before been recounted in advertising histories. Such are the frissons of satisfaction that come to etymologists.

Admen have long been active in politics. Bruce Barton, of Batten, Barton, Durstine & Osborn, was the congressman immortalized by FDR's MARTIN, BARTON AND FISH; Chester Bowles, of Benton & Bowles, served as a Kennedy State Department official; his partner, William Benton, was senator from Connecticut. But it is the adman behind the scenes in every political campaign that is most often criticized, with the gibes sometimes written by the admen on the other side. See KINGMAKER.

Since an attack on the Eisenhower spot television campaign was part of Adlai Stevenson's message in 1952, the phrase was used often in that campaign. A typical Stevenson use:

> Man does not live by words alone, despite the fact that sometimes he has to eat them. Alas, in this world he sometimes, or perhaps too often, lives by CATCHWORDS. SLOGANS are normally designed to get action without reflection. This one, "TIME FOR A CHANGE," fits these specifications admirably. This may not be too serious when all that is at stake is whether to buy one cake of soap or another, but I don't think it furnishes a sound basis for deciding a national election.

Soap has many uses in politics. In the 1880 Republican campaign it was used as a code word for money in dispatches, was deciphered, and for many years meant funny money, or graft; it is now obsolete. *Soft soap* is a soothing, ingratiating string of platitudes, and *soapbox* has an origin similar to STUMP: a makeshift platform used by street-corner speakers, with a connotation of use by blowhards or extremists.

That does it for *soap*'s role in the political language, though it should be added that a candidate overwhelmingly defeated is said to have "taken a bath."

sellout Betrayal; attack word on a political compromise.

A weak political party that supports an opposition party's candidate in return for patronage is said to *sell out*; in its simplest sense, a politician who takes graft sells out his constituents.

The phrase has been traced to 1857, when the *Lawrence* (Kansas) *Republican* wrote about a rival: "If the *Times* has not been 'sold out' to the Border Ruffian party, it looks very much as if it had been 'chartered.'" In O. Henry's 1906 story, "Trimmed Lamp," a cynical character says, "When I sell out it's not going to be on any bargain day."

Soon after he became President, Harry Truman demanded that the Russians invite anti-Communist Poles into the Polish government as his price for admission of Poland into the United Nations. The Russians made a small gesture in this direction in 1945 and agreed to drop their objection to the admission of Argentina. When the U.S. agreed to the deal, anti-Communist Poles charged this was "the great sellout."

Previously the best-known diplomatic use of the phrase occurred after the Munich conference of 1938, when British Prime Minister Neville Chamberlain was charged with "selling Czechoslovakia down the river," a phrase with its origins in American slavery. The charge was raised again as Serbians took over Bosnia in 1993 until NATO, with the U.S. as the prime mover, forced them to retreat. See MUNICH ANALOGY.

sell us the rope See USEFUL IDIOTS OF THE WEST.

senatorial courtesy See BLUE SLIP; PERSONALLY OBNOXIOUS.

send them a message A plea to vote symbolically for a candidate who is given little chance to win but whose votes will be seen as endorsement for a different point of view; a way for voters to protest policies of the party in power.

"The average voter," wrote *Washington Post* reporter and analyst David Broder, "sees a great gulf between himself—struggling with the family budget, problems in his kids' schools, the uncertainties of his job and the threats to his neighborhood—and the politicians in power, who act as if they have it made, which they probably do. It is that sense of distance—and of indifference from the top—that George Wallace exploited with his brilliant slogan, 'Send Them a Message.' "

That was the mood presidential candidate Jimmy Carter sought to capture in his campaign for the 1976 Democratic nomination, which began in earnest in 1974. Like Wallace, he talked the LITTLE MAN's language, even spoke in the same accent, but was able to dissociate himself from the Wallace "segregation forever" stigma. Carter avoided the RACIST "message," but was "running against Washington," exploiting the resentment at unfeeling bureaucrats, or musclebound government.

A frequent form of the phrase today is "send the President a message." In 1992, The *Chicago Tribune* wrote of Pat Buchanan's strong finish against President Bush in the New Hampshire primary as an "appeal to conservatives who want to send the President a message."

Columnist Ruth Marcus noted in 2007 that New Hampshire voters in the primary of 2004 "fixated on electability. They weren't so much swept away by John F. Kerry as calculating that he had the best chance of winning. Their hearts may have been with Howard Dean and his antiwar stance, but their heads were with Kerry and his pragmatic pitch: 'Don't just send them a message. Send them a president.' "

See DIME'S WORTH OF DIFFERENCE.

senior citizen See EUPHEMISMS, POLITICAL.

separate but equal The phrase at the heart of the civil rights dispute, posing the question: Can separate facilities ever be equal?

Justice Henry B. Brown, speaking for the majority of the Supreme Court in the 1896 case of *Plessy v. Ferguson*, found that "separate but equal accommodations" satisfied the demands of the Fourteenth Amendment, adding: "We consider the underlying fallacy of the plaintiff's argument to consist in the assumption that the enforced separation of the two races stamps the colored

race with a badge of inferiority. If this be so, it is not by reason of anything found in the act, but solely because the colored race chooses to put that construction upon it."

John Marshall Harlan, in dissent, wrote: "If evils will result from the commingling of the two races upon public highways established for the benefit of all, they will be infinitely less than those that will surely come from state legislation regulating the enjoyment of civil rights upon the basis of race. The thin disguise of 'equal' accommodations for passengers in railroad coaches will not mislead any one, nor atone for the wrong this day done ..."

The doctrine was reversed in a series of decisions of the Warren Court in 1954, the most famous of which was handed down on May 11: "We conclude that in the field of public education the doctrine of 'separate but equal' has no place. Separate educational facilities are inherently unequal." And on May 17: "Does segregation of children in public schools solely on the basis of race, even though the physical facilities and other 'tangible' factors may be equal, deprive the children of the minority group of equal education opportunities? We believe that it does.... We conclude that in the field of public education the doctrine of 'separate but equal' has no place."

A similar phrase, with *and* instead of *but*, appears in the Declaration of Independence, where this nation dissolved its bonds with Great Britain "to assume among the powers of the earth, the separate and equal station to which the Laws of Nature and of Nature's God entitle them."

See QUOTA; SEGREGATION; SEPARATISM.

set See COMMUNITY.

seven dwarfs See CATTLE SHOW.

sexism Gender-engendered bias; a condemnation, usually made by women, of discrimination on account of sex.

The above definition gingerly avoids sexism. Alma Trinor, a feminist and lexicographer with the *American Heritage Dictionary* in 1973, noted that the word *spokeswoman*, which a rival lexicographer defined as "a female spokesman," was better defined as "a woman who speaks on behalf of another or others." She also pointed out that an early edition of this dictionary "includes: the average man; the common man; the man in the street; the man of the people; the man who; one man, one vote. At this rate, how will women ever get into politics?" Her point: "I find that the word 'man' in its extended senses is the most overworked noun in the language, and it is a word that most definitely excludes women, no matter what dictionaries say to the contrary."

Her complaint was prescient; by the turn of the millennium, *man* and *mankind* were being replaced in phrases by *person* and *humankind* or *humanity*—and not just by sexism-sensitive politicians. However, the entries she listed in this dictionary are still here for their historical content as well as current usage, though updated to reflect discomfort with some of the usages. Resistance continues to the substitution of *spokesperson* for *spokesman*, but newspaper *women's pages* are now the *style section*, and *policemen, firemen,* and *workingmen* are now properly *police officers, firefighters,* and *workers.*

In 2007, radio commentator and interviewer Don Imus adopted some hip-hop vernacular to refer to a group of black women basketball champions as "nappyheaded ho's" referring to their hairstyle and using *ho* as a slang term for "whore." His combination of slurs against women who are black caused a firestorm of protest, resulting in his firing for a time from his programs and criticism of—and soulsearching by—hip-hop and rap artists who had been using such terms, along with the derogation *bitch,* for years.

See CONSCIOUSNESS-RAISING; WOMEN'S LIB.

shadow cabinet (government) A formal organization of leaders of the main party out of power, to take issue with policies followed by their counterparts in government.

The system is British, and is drawn from the rarely used meaning of *shadow* as "image, reflection." Whenever a party loses power and becomes the LOYAL OPPOSITION, the specialists in the various departments—who have often served as ministers in the previous government—form a cabinet-out-of-power and sit on the "front bench" of their party in Parliament. "The 'front bench' is more closely in touch with the members on the back benches when the party is in Opposition," writes Sir Ivor Jennings, "than when it is in office."

See BACKBENCHER.

Each member of the shadow cabinet contributes expert knowledge to the prompt criticism of the government ministry he or she observes; the public understands that is the person chosen in advance by the opposition as likely to head that ministry if the party wins the forthcoming election.

Advantages of the shadow cabinet system are that it provides quick, expert rebuttals to government decisions; a certain order to the party position; a coherence to the overall party program, often with a series of specific alternatives. Disadvantages are that too much party discipline leads to rigidity and that young leaders find it difficult to advance through the party hierarchy.

Why hasn't it been adopted in the U.S.? Probably because the TWO-PARTY SYSTEM in America differs sharply from the mainly two-party (or two-and-a-half-party) system in England. There, the parties differ on ideology; here, the parties are in many ways closer in ideology—see TRIANGULATION—with a conservative-liberal split within each party, although POLARIZATION has modified that in recent years. It is difficult to reach a party consensus in the U.S., as convention platform fights indicate, and the TITULAR LEADER of the party out of power in the U.S. has no real authority to speak for the party or to appoint "shadow" ministers. (See the above entry for the reason that term is losing frequency in use.)

The closest Americans came to having a *shadow cabinet* was in 1948, when Thomas E. Dewey, considered a SHOO-IN to defeat President Truman, chose several advisers who were widely understood to become cabinet appointees after his victory; John Foster Dulles, when he spoke on foreign affairs, was referred to as "Dewey's likely Secretary of State." In 2004, it was widely assumed in the media that Richard Holbrooke would be Democratic nominee John Kerry's choice for State, though the candidate did not confirm it. Candidates running against SITTING PRESIDENTS have avoided picking cabinets in advance, lest it look presumptuous.

share the wealth See EVERY MAN A KING.

sharp elbows Pushiness or assertiveness; the ability to protect political turf or to encroach on that of others.

Thomas Carlyle paved the way for this noun phrase. The British essayist wrote in 1838: "No man lives without jostling and being jostled; in all ways he has to elbow himself through the world, giving and receiving offence."

In slang, to *bend the elbow* has long been used as a term for drinking. Francis Grose's 1785 *Dictionary of the Vulgar Tongue* defined *elbow shaker* as "a gamester, one who rattles Sir Hugh's bones—i.e., the dice"; the same reference work included *elbow grease* as "labor" and *elbow room* as "sufficient space to act in." In early-twentieth-century slang, a cop was known as an *elbow*, synecdoche for the body part used to pass quickly through a crowd during a chase.

International politics picked up the sharpened image by 1980. A Bonn politician was censured that year for describing a German candidate as "a man with razor blades on his elbows."

The term's connotation, however, has changed. At one time, having sharp elbows was not a compliment, as the German usage shows. Michael Barone of *The Washington Post* wrote in 1984, "This campaign shows that Mondale, far from being a patsy, is a politician with elbows." Nowadays, *sharp elbows* may be needed to show a candidate's macho, or aggressive, side.

sheep in sheep's clothing See INVECTIVE.

Sherman statement Irrevocable declaration of non-candidacy; frequently used term, infrequently taken action.

Conservative Republican leader Charles Halleck was disconsolate after a talk with Senator Barry Goldwater in early 1963 about the possibility of a Goldwater candidacy. "He was throwing cold water on the whole idea," Halleck told F. Clifton White, who was to organize the draft-Goldwater movement, "and he was throwing it by the bucketful—with ice cubes in it." "At least," replied White, "he didn't pull a Sherman on us."

Issuing a Sherman statement—"pulling a Sherman"—is the extreme of nonavailability. General William Tecumseh Sherman, Civil War Union hero second only to U. S. Grant, wired John B. Henderson, chairman of the Republican National Convention in Chicago on June 5, 1884: "I will not accept if nominated, and will not serve if elected." The directness of this statement has been corrupted by usage into a slightly more cadenced and definitive "If nominated I will not accept; if elected I will not serve."

This early shaping of Sherman's statement was prophetic; hopeful supporters of genuinely reluctant public figures always seek to find loopholes in declarations of no interest.

When President Harry Truman was considered a sure loser in 1948, some Democrats turned to Justice William O. Douglas, who affected a horsewrangler's drawl in reply, "I never was a-running.' I ain't a-runnin,' and I ain't goin' tuh."

In that year, Dwight Eisenhower issued a whole series of Sherman statements. To a young reporter at a Pentagon press conference: "Look, son, I cannot conceive of any circumstance that could draw out of me permission to consider me for any political post from dogcatcher to Grand High Supreme King of the Universe."

Can a Sherman statement be taken literally—would any man turn down a firm nomination? There is vice presidential precedent: one man did say no after formal nomination. Silas Wright, senator and later governor of New York, was nominated as James W. Polk's running mate in 1844 by the Democrats. Angry at Martin Van Buren's defeat, he telegraphed the convention: "I am not and cannot under any circumstances be a candidate before your convention for that office," and he was hastily replaced.

While politicians will take a Sherman statement as evidence of a genuine "no," nobody takes it literally; the man might not campaign, but he would serve. Consider the dialogue between James Farley and FDR in 1940, when Farley—who wanted the nomination himself—tried to persuade the President not to run for a third term. "What would you do in my place?" the President asked, according to Farley. "Exactly what General Sherman did many years ago," Farley replied, "issue a statement saying I would refuse to run if nominated and would not serve if elected." FDR said: "Jim, if nominated and elected, I could not in these times refuse to take the inaugural oath, even if I knew I would be dead within thirty days." (He died four years and nearly three months after his third inaugural oath.)

The cadence of the Sherman phrase is so familiar that it can be used as the basis for parody. When it was important in 1969 for Henry Kissinger to gain a reputation as a "secret swinger" to create a Dr. Strangelove reputation and provide cover for secret trips, he would appeal to White House wags and their friends (Richard Moore, television producer Paul Keyes, and this writer) for lines making that point. An opportunity arose when a picture appeared in many newspapers of Dr. Kissinger at a cocktail party with feminist leader Gloria Steinem, who scotched gossip rumors with an icy mock-statement: "I am not now, and have never been, a friend of Henry Kissinger's." The writers huddled, and Kissinger went before a Washington Press Club dinner to recall that rejection, and to add: "But she did not say that if nominated, she would not run"—long, pregnant pause—"or if elected, she would not serve."

sherpa A skilled Himalayan guide; or, diplomat who assists in preparing for summit meetings.

This word entered diplomatic lingo in a *New York Times* account of a Khrushchev-Eisenhower meeting in July 1955: "There was an array of experts—Sherpa guides, as one British wit put it—behind the mountaineers at the summit."

Sherpa, capitalized, refers to a member of a Tibetan people who live on the southern slopes of the Himalayas in Nepal. The Sherpas are famed for mountain-climbing abilities and guiding others through the dangerous ascensions; Sherpa Tenzing Norgay became famous in 1953 for assisting Sir Edmund Hillary's team in the first conquest of Mount Everest.

See SUMMITRY.

ship of state A nation, particularly in regard to its diplomacy.

Sailors always refer to ships as "she"; this expression might be the cause of the use of the feminine reference to nations, as "America will defend her national interests." The description of a nation as a vessel on a course can be traced in English to a 1675 translation of Machiavelli and can be found in ancient Greek poetry.

Lincoln liked the metaphor. "If we do not make common cause," he said in 1861, "to save the good old ship of the Union on this voyage, nobody will have the chance to pilot her on another voyage." Grover Cleveland in 1894 agreed: "The Ship of Democracy, which has weathered all storms, may sink through the mutiny of those on board." In more recent times, when candidate Thomas E. Dewey in 1948 said, "We need a rudder to our ship of state and a firm hand on the tiller," Republican Joe Martin shrugged, "Sounds good and brings the applause. But promises nothing."

The metaphor offers a tool for criticism; an 1883 reference in the *Congressional Record* says, "Twenty percent of the employees in all Departments in the City of Washington … are really barnacles upon the ship of state."

Most dramatic use of the metaphor was in a message from President Franklin Roosevelt, given to defeated Republican candidate Wendell Willkie in 1941 to take to Winston Churchill, quoting an 1849 poem by Henry Wadsworth Longfellow:

Thou, too, sail on, O Ship of State!
Sail on, O Union, strong and great!
Humanity with all its fears,
With all the hopes of future years,
Is hanging breathless on thy fate!

Other nautical metaphors in politics include Sir Walter Scott's "sea of upturned faces" and Lord Acton's maxim, "The ship exists for the sake of the passengers." *Groundswells* lead to *tides of support.* George Shultz, Director of the Office of Management and Budget, concluded a 1971 economic speech with the nautical reference: "Those of you familiar with sailing know what a telltale is—a strip of cloth tied to a mast to show which way the wind is blowing. A captain has the choice of steering his ship by the telltale, following the prevailing winds, or to steer by the compass. In a democracy, you must keep your eye on the telltale, but you must set your course by the compass…The voice from the bridge says, 'Steady as you go.'"

On March 20, 1969, Senator Everett Dirksen delivered a speech drafted by this writer, who vaguely recalled the Dewey usage, and included the line: "Around the world there is the feeling that there is a firm hand on the rudder of our ship of state." A letter to the editor of the *Washington Post* observed: "When I am on the high seas, I would like my skipper to keep a firm hand on the tiller, and to leave that rudder alone. Any skipper with a firm hand on the rudder is likely to be in water way over his head." This convinced one speechwriter that ship metaphors are best left to sailors. See NEW DEPARTURE.

shirtsleeve diplomacy Informal, plainspeaking international relations, contrasted with the diplomatic niceties of *striped-pants diplomacy.*

The phrase has a pleasantly hardworking connotation, from the expression *roll up one's sleeves* (to get to work). Earlier use of the phrase suggested that American ambassadors were chosen as a result of political contributions, and their demeanor was boorish compared to the conservative mannerisms of diplomats of nations steeped in international affairs. London's *Pall Mall Gazette*, reporting in 1908 on American customs, wrote: "The Congressmen have a preference for what they picturesquely describe as 'Shirt-sleeve Ambassadors'—men who they think will labor for their country's interests and scorn social fascinations."

John Hay, a Lincoln secretary who became Theodore Roosevelt's Secretary of State, was probably the first diplomat associated with the phrase. Wrote the *Cyclopaedia of American Government* in 1914: "Shirt Sleeve Diplomacy. A title which has been given to some of the diplomacy of recent years which has disregarded much of the circumlocution and indirectness of earlier practice and has stated clearly the purpose of the negotiation and the methods by which a state proposed to attain the purpose. This term has been particularly applied to the diplomacy of the United States from the late years of the nineteenth century."

Wealth and social standing are supposed to inhibit the willingness to work in shirtsleeves (to deal informally, directly, often harshly). Columbia University president Nicholas Murray Butler referred to "a society like ours of which it is truly said to be often but three generations 'from shirtsleeves to shirtsleeves.'"

For a different type of diplomat, see COOKIE PUSHER.

shock and awe A military doctrine featuring air strikes on such a huge scale as to cause an adversary to be demoralized and lose the will to resist.

The doctrine of *shock and awe*, much discussed during the run-up to invasion of Iraq in 2003, was developed at the National Defense University by Harlan K. Ullman and James Wade. The object of *shock and awe*, as outlined in their 1996 book with that title, is to achieve *rapid dominance.* The authors contrasted *shock and awe* with the prevailing strategic doctrines of "dominant battlefield awareness," "dominant maneuver," and "overwhelming and decisive force" (often called the Powell doctrine, after General Colin Powell). Where prevailing doctrines had required assembling a half-million troops over a six-month period prior to the start of the Gulf war of 1991, Ullman and Wade argued that "Rapid Dominance and its attendant focus on 'Shock and Awe'" would produce victory more quickly and at less cost by relying on a massive assault using precision-guided weapons.

The opening aerial bombardment of Iraq, as large as it was, did not fulfill Ullman's requirements for *shock and awe*. "The current campaign does not appear to correspond to what we envisioned," said Ullman that April, two weeks after the war began.

Fighting in Iraq continued long after Saddam was overthrown. *Shock and awe*, even if applied as proposed in theory, had its limits. Ullman and Wade recognized this possibility in the second chapter of their book: "there are certainly situations such as guerilla war ... where most means of employing force to obtain Shock and Awe may simply prove inapplicable."

Within weeks of the war's start more than a dozen companies applied for trademarks on *shock and awe* to market a variety of products, among them fireworks, energy drinks, and lingerie. Sony, for one, had quick second thoughts. Less than a month after the war began it announced that it was withdrawing its application to use *shock and awe* on one of its video games, saying the attempt to capitalize on the phrase was "an exercise of regrettable bad judgment." Ullman, asked in May of 2003, by the host of an Australian radio program, *The World Today*, if he wished that he had tried to trademark the term himself said he had "absolutely no regrets because I suspect that the marketing value will be somewhere between slim and none."

After President Bush charged during the midterm election campaign of 2006 that "the party of F.D.R. and the party of Harry Truman has become the party of CUT AND RUN," Democratic Rep. Rahm Emanuel, adept at plays on words, slammed back with the way the administration had "gone from *shock and awe* to an American public *shocked* at how *awful* the situation in Iraq is."

shoo-in A sure winner; one who can only be defeated by a POLITICAL MIRACLE.

Like FRONT RUNNER, BOLT, DARK HORSE, and many others, the metaphor is taken from racing, but this one has a fraudulent back-

ground. When jockeys form a "ring" and bet on a single horse, they hold back their own mounts and "chase in" or "shoo in" the horse selected to be the winner. *Racing Maxims and Methods of "Pittsburgh Phil,"* published in 1908, points out: "There were many times presumably that 'Tod' would win through such manipulations, being 'shooed in,' as it were." In the 1935 *The Underworld Speaks*, A. J. Pollack defines *shoo-in* as "a horse race in which the winner is the only horse trying."

To *shoo* is a colloquialism meaning "gently to urge a person or animal to go in a desired direction." First recorded around the turn of the twentieth century, *shoo-in*—minus its crooked connotation, now only meaning "sure thing"—began to be used politically in the '40s. "Taft Appears to Be Shoo-In for Top Senate G.O.P. Job" headlined the *San Francisco News* in 1948, and *Life* magazine predicted, "Dewey looks like a shoo-in for the presidency."

The word was sufficiently secured in the political lexicon in 1967 to rate a TURNAROUND. *The Wall Street Journal* called the candidate hopelessly running against popular Congressman Adam Clayton Powell in New York's Harlem "a shoo-out."

shoot from the hip See TRIGGER-HAPPY.

shooting war See COLD WAR.

short list Finalists under consideration; narrowed group of contenders for appointive office.

From British English, *short list* first appeared in print in *Contemporary English: A Personal Speech Record*, a 1927 book by William E. Collinson. "Selection committees to University posts first familiarized me with the meaning of the short list" suggested earlier use of the phrase. Britain's *The Economist* trans-Atlanticized the expression, which is now often hyphenated in verb form ("she's been short-listed"), and some dictionaries are making the open compound a solid word on the analogy of *blacklist*. The two-word phrase, however, parallels WATCH LIST, *wait list*, a politician's *wish list*, or a *laundry list* of desired goals. See HIT LIST.

Synonyms for somebody who's short-listed are inexact: *contender* suggests active soliciting of an office, *competitor* is even more active, and *finalist* carries a beauty-contest connotation. The antonym of *short list* is not "long list," but rather "everybody else remotely available."

Political usage of the phrase became popular during the 1988 presidential campaign. At the Republican National Convention, Alexander M. Haig Jr. described the Democratic ticket as "blind as a bat…hanging upside down in dark, damp caves up to its navel in guano," prompting convention chairman Robert H. Michel to remark about the tough language, "That's probably why Al Haig is not on the short list for Vice President." That same year the Associated Press identified Senator Charles S. Robb (D-Va.) as being "on most short lists of potential Presidential candidates in 1992 or 1996."

The phrase offers itself for spoofing. A *New Yorker* cartoon by James Stevenson depicts a woman asking her husband, "How come you're never on anybody's short list?" See ENEMIES LIST.

showing the flag See PRESENCE.

shredding See SANITIZE.

shrimps whistle A variant of a Russian figure of speech indicating a day never to come.

When Russian Premier Nikita Khrushchev heard a Western suggestion in 1955 that the Soviet Union's fidelity to Communism might fade with the years, he replied, in the usual translation, "Those who wait for that must wait until a shrimp learns to whistle." The Russian expression is actually *kogda rak svistnet*, "when the crawfish whistles."

The image became a favorite of editorial writers doing pieces on PEACEFUL COEXISTENCE. *The New York Times*, suggesting in 1967 that Rhodesian Prime Minister Ian Smith surprise the world by making progress toward majority rule, wrote: "A move so contrary to Mr. Smith's every act since entering public life would confound African experts around the world. Shrimps, in Mr. Khrushchev's colorful expression, would surely whistle."

The nearest American expressions are "until the cows come home" or "until hell freezes over."

shuttle diplomacy Negotiations assisted by a middleman hurrying between capitals by jet plane; in particular, the Kissinger peace attempts after the 1973 Arab-Israeli war.

"At week's end," wrote *Time* on March 4, 1974, "Kissinger was to return…to the Middle East for another round of 'shuttle diplomacy'—this time to Damascus, Jerusalem and Cairo." Three months later, the magazine had dropped quotation marks and extended the metaphor: "The only possible accomplishment left for Henry Hercules is for him to become an astronaut, and then maybe he could be the first space-shuttle diplomat."

The word *shuttle* might have been introduced to diplomacy by talk of NASA's *space shuttle*, which in turn came into the language from the Eastern Airlines Boston–New York–Washington shuttle, which probably had its origin in New York's Grand Central Station–Times Square subway shuttle. All these transportation metaphors are extensions of the weaving *shuttle* that shoots the thread of the woof between the threads of the warp.

Coinage is claimed by Joseph Sisco, former Assistant Secretary of State: "On the first trip that Henry Kissinger took to the Middle East after the Yom Kippur war, I remember saying to Marvin Kalb and Ted Koppel, 'Welcome to *shuttle diplomacy*.' " (Sisco also tells the author, "I was the one who coined *proximity talks*. It was in 1970 or '71, the time of the meetings between the Israelis and Egyptians. Indirect talks had not worked, and direct talks were not then feasible. So we used the 'Rhodes formula': they stayed in separate hotel suites in the Waldorf Astoria in New York, and the Americans would shuttle back and forth.") In 2000, Alexander Vershbow, Foreign Service Officer speaking for the National Security Council, defined *proximity talks* as "the buzzword for this notion of shuttling, but within one site."

Diplomacy has long been a convenient word with which to conclude a new phrase.

From DOLLAR DIPLOMACY to GUNBOAT DIPLOMACY, the phrasemaking progressed to *ping-pong diplomacy* regarding the Chinese, QUIET DIPLOMACY, and *satellite diplomacy*, which, for a time, overshadowed "shuttle diplomacy."

See STEP-BY-STEP DIPLOMACY.

sick man of Europe Originally Turkey; applied in modern times to whatever European nation is in political or economic trouble.

"To make an alliance with Turkey," writer François Chateaubriand quoted a diplomat in 1807, "is the same as putting your arms around a corpse to make it stand up." This echoed the judgment of Sir Thomas Roe, British ambassador in Constantinople almost two centuries earlier, who said the Ottoman Empire had "the body of a sick old man who tried to appear healthy, although his end was near." In 1853 Russian Czar Nicholas I told British Ambassador Sir George Seymour, "We have on our hands a sick man—a very sick man," and Turkey was tagged throughout the remainder of the nineteenth century "the sick man of Europe."

The patient changes, but the phrase lingers on. Australian editor Colin Bingham wrote in 1967: "For years after the Second World War, France was frequently described as 'the sick man of Europe,' but by 1966 the United Kingdom's economic difficulties prompted a transient application of the epithet to Britain." The phrase is used to illustrate the opposite meaning of its early coinage: what the subject is not. "Perception is that Germany is the 'sick man of Europe,'" observed the *Financial Times* in 2005, "but it is still the most powerful economy in Europe."

side of the angels The right or acceptable moral viewpoint; purity of motive.

"Is man an ape or an angel?" asked Benjamin Disraeli rhetorically in 1864 at the Oxford Diocesan Conference. He was concerned about the impact of Charles Darwin's theory of evolution on religion in England. His answer was unequivocal: "I, my lord, am on the side of the angels. I repudiate with indignation and abhorrence those newfangled theories."

In 1989, an economist told Federal News Service about a budget fight: "Neither side is on the side of the angels; neither side is pure in the sense of what they want to do." *Newsday* continued the term's popularization in 1992. Reporting on a Republican judge in Texas, *Newsday* wrote that his battle with extremist party members placed him "on the side of the angels, from the national party's viewpoint."

The phrase, and public sentiment about evolution theory, was evolving toward complete acceptance until believers in "intelligent design" (a phrase coined in 1847 but given new life as "neo-creationism" or "neo-creo")—that some spiritual force had to be responsible for the mind-boggling complexity of life—introduced a fresh round of controversy, though not among most scientists, in 2002.

A variant of the phrase was suggested by New York Governor Mario Cuomo, appearing on *This Week With David Brinkley* in late 1991. Asked about his plan for "an investment-led recovery," Cuomo responded, "I'm trying to stay with the angels."

sign off on Approve; specifically, to initial one's endorsement.

"If you want to make sure the President will sign off on something," Carter White House aide Stuart Eizenstat told *New Times* writer Robert Shrum in July 1977, "the best way is to get Bert [Lance] to agree."

This off-again, on-again locution became popular in government in the '60s. (See the Arthur Schlesinger, Jr., puzzlement in PENTAGONESE.) Seeking tacit approval is *running it past* an official, but nailing down that approval is inducing him to *sign off on* it. (In radio parlance, to *sign off* is to go off the air; the noun *signoff* is the conclusion of a broadcast day with an announcement including the call letters, or *sign*, of the station.) In its political sense, one can extrapolate to the meaning of *sign off* as termination, or final approval—in the sense that the BUCK STOPS HERE, at the top executive's desk. But why the *on*? One may speculate that if to *sign off* is taken to mean "to approve," then the *on* refers to the placement of initials on a document.

The awkwardness of the locution does not bother those fluent in bureaucratese. At the end of 1977 President Carter proudly announced: "I've signed off on the budget." Similar to the military *endorse*, the phrase has replaced *clear with* as a verb that helps a bureaucrat share responsibility. See CHOP; CLEAR IT WITH SIDNEY; CYA.

An element of "accountability," a favored Washington term among members of the Out party, is connected with the phrase. Elizabeth Drew, writing in *The New Yorker* in 1978 about National Security Adviser Zbigniew Brzezinski, pointed to a debate within the Carter Administration about accountability in the President's executive order on intelligence oversight: "The executive order requires that the President must 'sign off' on any activity of any importance. Brzezinski is known to believe that the President should have broad flexibility, including 'deniability'—that is, it should be possible to carry out operations in a way that would enable the President to deny he knew about them."

The vogue use of *on*—as in *add on*, or even the Americanization of the British *early on*—is ongoing.

silent majority The remarkable legion of the unremarked, whose individual opinions are not colorful or different enough to make news, but whose collective opinion, when crystallized, can make history.

The voices of the Vietnam dissenters were relatively muted during the first nine months of the Nixon presidency, but in October 1969 an anti-war "moratorium" was organized, featuring a march on Washington, D.C., with more strident demonstrations planned the following month.

In the midst of this rebirth of demonstrations, President Nixon made a televised address, in prime time, to counter the mounting dissent. The November 3 "silent majority" speech had a strong effect on public opinion, buying time for his "Vietnamization" program. The anti-war demonstrations did not make important news

again until the incursion into neighboring Cambodia six months later.

"If a vocal minority," the President warned, "however fervent its cause, prevails over reason and the will of the majority, this Nation has no future as a free society. Let historians not record that when America was the most powerful nation in the world we passed on the other side of the road and allowed the last hopes for peace and freedom of millions of people to be suffocated by the forces of totalitarianism. And so tonight—to you, the great silent majority of my fellow Americans—I ask for your support."

Nixon, who wrote this speech with no help from his speechwriters, was not consciously "making a phrase." The words were not capitalized, nor was the phrase repeated, but it did fill a need for a description of all the people who were not demonstrating, and was promptly taken up by the media.

Though the phrase officially came into the political language on November 3, 1969, it had of course been used previously, and Nixon had used the thought many times. In a radio speech during the primary campaign, on May 16, 1968, he referred to "the silent center, the millions of people in the middle of the American political spectrum who do not demonstrate, who do not picket or protest loudly.... We must remember that all the center is not silent, and all who are silent are not center. But a great many 'quiet Americans' have become committed to answers to social problems that preserve personal freedom."

John F. Kennedy wrote in *Profiles in Courage* in 1956: "They were not all right or all conservatives or all liberals. Some of them may have been representing the actual sentiments of the silent majority of their constituents in opposition to the screams of a vocal minority, but most of them were not."

Previous usage of almost any famous phrase can be found. In Plautus' *Trinummus, ad plures penetrare*—"to join the great majority"—is used as a euphemism for dying, similar to the modern *passed away*. The September 1874 issue of *Harper's New*

Monthly Magazine had an article entitled "The Silent Majority" about burial customs around the world. Supreme Court Justice John Marshall Harlan spoke on Dec. 9, 1902, of "great captains on both sides of our Civil War [who] have long ago passed over to the silent majority, leaving the memory of their splendid courage."

Vice President Spiro Agnew used the phrase in its non-lugubrious sense on May 9, 1969: "It is time for America's silent majority to stand up for its rights, and let us remember the American majority includes every minority. America's silent majority is bewildered by irrational protest ..." During that spring of 1969, the journalist Theodore White reflected on the paradoxes that marked the previous election year: "Never have America's leading cultural media, its university thinkers, its influence makers been more intrigued by experiment and change; but in no election have the mute masses more completely separated themselves from such leadership and thinking. Mr. Nixon's problem is to interpret what the silent people think, and govern the country against the grain of what its more important thinkers think."

Six months later, as White predicted, Nixon rallied "the silent majority." In the late seventies the phrase carried the opprobrium generally accorded Nixon-Agnew utterances, but its users were careful to deride the INSIDE-THE-BELTWAY phrasemakers rather than the group described. In 1993, Frank Luntz, a Republican pollster, gave his opinion to *The Boston Globe* about the Clinton tax plans: "Now that silent majority is about to scream and reject the tax increases. These people think they've already sacrificed and can't do it anymore." See MIDDLE AMERICA; GREAT UNWASHED.

silent vote The unmeasurables, who may or may not turn out.

Different meanings: (1) a sector of the public unhappy with the sameness of both parties, which can be turned out only by offering a CHOICE, NOT AN ECHO; (2) a sector that remains "undecided" to pollsters, for such reasons as religious preference, bigotry, BACKLASH, or actual indecision, and

remains a mystery until Election Day; (3) the wistfully hoped-for vote that was simply never cast. See STAY-AT-HOMES; TURNOUT.

"In the next election," the *Cincinnati Campaigner* predicted in 1848, "the silent vote for Van Buren will be immense." The former president, running on a third-party ticket, picked up only one-tenth of the vote cast. "The silent vote, as it is called," editorialized *The New York Times* in 1880, "is what will tell in November." This is usually a fairly safe prediction. In that case, James Garfield squeaked past Democrat Winfield Scott Hancock with 10,000 votes out of 10 million cast, with a "silent vote"—possibly costing Hancock the election—going to the Greenback splinter party.

The phrase is most often used today by apologists for candidates who are far behind in the public opinion polls; workers for Goldwater in 1964 cheered themselves up with the assurance that an enormous *silent vote* would appear on Election Day. In 2006, Republican senator Rick Santorum of Pennsylvania told a rally on election eve, "I do believe that there's a silent vote, and that we've got a lot of those people out there who are going to be coming out because we've given them a reason." He lost decisively, but nobody blames a trailing candidate for trying to inspirit the troops.

Of those people old enough to vote for president, almost half do not. Conservatives have long claimed this vote is essentially conservative; others say these potential voters are simply apathetic, illiterate, ill or infirm, or have moved too recently to qualify, and are of all political persuasions. The story is told about the campaign manager who was asked what was the most significant element in failing to turn out support—voter ignorance or apathy? He replied, "I don't know and I don't care."

silk stocking Wealthy; originally used to derogate the upper class, now only as descriptive of a high-income area.

The phrase can be found in the writings of Jefferson against the well-to-do Federalists ("the Gores and the Pickerings will find their levees crowded with silk stocking gentry, but no yeomanry; an army of officers without soldiers") and Lincoln ("They came not like 'the silk stocking gentry' as they are called by their opponents; but as farmers, mechanics, etc.").

In the era of knee britches and silk hose, only the wealthy could afford silk stockings. Over the years, *kid glove politics*, *swallow-tail politician*, and *ruffled shirt* appeared as synonyms, but *silk stocking* outwore them all, and is similar to *lace curtain* (as opposed to *shanty*), used to describe the social classes of Irish-Americans. Louis Howe said he had originally sized up Franklin Roosevelt as a "spoiled, silkpants sort of guy."

The best-known use of the phrase in its current sense was popularized by Theodore Roosevelt: "I was a Republican from the 'silk stocking' district, the wealthiest district in New York." The *New York Post* wrote in 1903 of "the 'silk stocking' quarter—the middle reaches of Manhattan, between 14th and 96th Street." But it is used generically as well. "In as chairman," wrote *Time* magazine in 1948, "went 47-year-old Hugh Scott, Jr., a three-term congressman from a suburban Philadelphia 'silk stocking' district."

similes, political See LIKE UGLY ON AN APE.

single-issue politics Reduction of a campaign or election to a single question.

This approach to politics attempts to project a single issue like war, abortion, taxes or immigration as the determining factor in an election, excluding all other considerations. Such a narrowing of focus, however, draws the criticism that single-issue politics is capable of limiting a general election to a referendum on a specific issue.

Timothy Clark wrote in *National Journal* in 1978, "In an era of single-issue politics and highly organized lobbying, it will be difficult for Congress to restrain itself to the degree necessary to meet Carter's goal." That same year, T. R. Reid of *The Washington Post* commented, "The rampant apathy towards the primary may also stem from the voters' concentration on single-issue politics."

A decade later, the term was applied to political events other than campaigns or elections. After the Senate rejected Robert Bork as a Supreme Court nominee in 1987, Ronald Reagan derogated the confirmation process as "a spectacle of misrepresentation and single-issue politics."

R. W. Apple Jr. of *The New York Times* revived the charge in a 1992 commentary on the elder George Bush's Presidency: "Less welcome is the harsh political fact that pragmatists have trouble building constituencies, especially in this era of single-issue politics." See ISSUES, THE.

sinners' roll See HIT LIST.

sit-in A technique of demonstration launched by civil rights activists in 1960 to dramatize segregation in the South.

Four black youths from North Carolina Agricultural and Technical College entered the F. W. Woolworth store in Greensboro, North Carolina, on February 1, 1960, and sat down at the "white" lunch counter. "It is regrettable," said Mayor William G. Enloe of Raleigh as the sit-ins spread throughout the state, "that some of our young Negro students would risk endangering Raleigh's friendly and cooperative race relations by seeking to change a long-standing custom in a manner that is all but destined to fail."

The sit-ins, at first dismissed as a college fad, were destined to bring into prominence the Congress of Racial Equality (CORE) and to change the pattern of SEGREGATION throughout the South.

The "-in" construction quickly caught on, leading to *kneel-ins* and *pray-ins* in the early '60s, *teach-ins* in 1965 (first organized in Michigan by Students for a Democratic Society), and subsequently *love-ins*, *be-ins*, *eat-ins*, etc. It may be related to union labor's *sit-down strikes* of the '30s.

John Kennedy, campaigning for president in September 1960, caught the significance of the sit-ins and turned a phrase about them: "He [the president] must exert the great moral and educational force of his office to bring about equal access to public facilities, from churches to lunchcounters, and support the rights of every American to stand up for his rights, even if he must sit down for them."

As the "-in's" proliferated in the '60s, and the original civil rights connotation was diluted by the "hippies," Clark Kerr, ousted president of the University of California, predicted in 1967: "The sit-in will gradually join the coonskin coat as an interesting symbol of a student age retreating into history." But the hyphenated word is not routed; an AP dispatch in March 2007 read "War protesters end sit-in at California congresswoman's office."

The former meaning of the phrase *to sit in* was "to have a place as a player of a game," especially of cards, and although it remains a colloquialism, the meaning has been traced by the *OED* to 1599.

See FREEDOM RIDERS.

Sit Room The White House Situation Room.

The basement conference room in the White House, not far from the White House Mess, isn't called "the Crisis Center," because the Administration does not want to cause too much excitement whenever the room is used. A crisis-management team, however, does meet in this communications center, often chaired by the vice president.

McGeorge Bundy was John F. Kennedy's national security adviser in 1961, when the Situation Room was named, later shortened to *Sit Room.* "I don't think we met down there during the Cuban missile crisis," Bundy told the lexicographer in 1992; neither he nor Ted Sorensen recalls why the room received the name, presumably given for the type of *situation* (a euphemism for *crisis*) to be handled from that basement room.

George M. Elsey, a speechwriter for Harry Truman, offered the author this background on predecessor phrases:

The first such was William McKinley's War Room, a small chamber on the southeast corner of the second floor of the Executive Mansion. When I was first assigned to the White House as a young Naval Reserve officer in April 1942, the Executive Clerk was Rudolph Forster, who had been in presidential service since McKinley's

day. He had lively tales of the maps and the telegraph equipment emplaced there, bringing McKinley flash news on the Spanish-American war.

F.D.R. fell in love with Winston Churchill's "Map Room" installed on the second floor of the White House during Churchill's December 1941 visit. After his guest's departure, F.D.R. ordered a Map Room of his own, to be placed on the ground floor, easily accessible to him as it was directly across the corridor from the elevator. The room is still, 50 years later, known as the Map Room and is so designated on all descriptive material about the White House.

The cramped basement space is almost always a disappointment to first-time visitors, many of whom expect to see the giant television screens depicted in doomsday movies. The meeting room's shortened form, *Sit Room,* is now prevalent. When George H.W. Bush visited Maine in 1991, a reporter asked him about a possible release of hostages in the Mideast: "Any hopeful signs on the situation?" Bush replied, "Just talked to the sit room and ... no new developments overnight at all."

See also WAR ROOM.

sitting on the fence See FENCE, ON THE.

sitting president A president in office; the power of incumbency in achieving renomination or reelection.

The phrase derives from a *sitting monarch,* whose throne is a seat of power, and from a *sitting hen,* whose inactivity conceals a procreative purpose whose success is announced with loud clucking. A judge is *sitting* when court is in session, and *sitting judges* (those holding judicial office, whether court is in or out of session) are rarely considered as candidates; Alton B. Parker was the only one to run for president.

Harry Truman put it this way: "When the President is sitting in the White House, the National Convention of his party has never gone against his recommendations in the choice of a candidate or in the formation of a platform on which that convention is to operate." In his memoirs, the former president pointed out how sitting president Theodore Roosevelt in 1908 could dictate the choice of his successor, William Howard Taft; but in 1912, with all his popularity, Roosevelt could not take the nomination away from the incumbent Taft. He did not add that he, Truman, as a sitting president, found it simple to designate Adlai Stevenson as his choice in 1952, but in 1956, no longer a sitting president, he was unable to deliver for Averell Harriman.

For a time in the mid-'60s, there was talk of Senator Robert Kennedy challenging President Lyndon B. Johnson for the 1968 presidential nomination, which was dismissed by Kennedy associates as "impossible against a sitting President." After a strong showing by Senator Eugene McCarthy in the New Hampshire primary, Kennedy changed his mind and made his move, which ended with his assassination. Ronald Reagan's 1976 challenge to President Gerald Ford made the presidential seat more insecure; in 1978, as Jimmy Carter slipped in polls, pundits fanned talk of a challenge to him in the 1980 primaries by California Governor Edmund "Jerry" Brown.

Florida Governor Claude Kirk, warning Republicans against overconfidence when Lyndon Johnson was thought likely to seek reelection, told a press conference: "A sitting president is never a sitting duck." See INCUMBENT.

sitzkrieg See PHONY WAR.

sixty million jobs See HOTTENTOTS, MILK FOR.

skunk at the garden party A rigidly proper ethicist, seen as undesirable in a gathering of broad-minded pragmatists; or, a single problem that has the potential to vex or annoy.

Into the midst of a group of elegantly dressed partygoers strolls a small animal capable of causing an enormous stink; after a horrified silence comes a panic that leads to havoc.

This anti-elitist trope appears usually in the negative: "I don't want to be the skunk at the garden party, but. ..." *Skunk* comes from the Algonquian name of the animal and was used figuratively by 1840, along with *polecat*, to label a low or contemptible person.

This animal's use in invective has been popular in American rhetoric. Senator Charles Sumner, an abolitionist in the "bloody Kansas" debate of 1856, was violently beaten after euphemistically referring to another Senator as "the noisome, squat and nameless animal." In recent positive usage, a secret laboratory or experimental division is known as the *skunk works*, based on cartoonist Al Capp's "Skonk Works" in the comic strip *Li'l Abner*, which ran from 1934 through 1977.

The term *garden party* is first found in print in Anthony Trollope's 1869 novel *Phineas Finn*: "The Duke's garden party was becoming a mere ball."

Skunk at the garden party, however, is much more recent. The *Dictionary of American Regional English* (DARE) reports that the image was Wisconsin usage in the early '70s, with printed references beginning in politics during the '80s. Representative Pat Schroeder of Colorado said in 1987, "In 1984, I was the skunk in the garden party who said we women have to run like men do." In the 1988 presidential primary, former Arizona Governor Bruce Babbitt withdrew from the race and commented that Gary Hart, Jesse Jackson, and he "were sort of skunks at the garden party, always saying 'This debate is supposed to be about something' and raking our fingers down the chalkboard."

slam dunk A sure thing; decisive, without a doubt.

Originally a basketball term, *slam dunk* became tinged with irony when employed in nonsporting contexts as a result of its initial, misguided political usage.

At a meeting in the White House on December 21, 2002, President George W. Bush asked George Tenet, Director of Central Intelligence, about evidence that Saddam Hussein possessed weapons of mass destruction. Tenet replied with the vivid metaphor: "It's a slam dunk case." The conversation, first reported by Bob Woodward in his 2004 book *Plan of Attack*, was confirmed by the second-highest authority, Vice President Dick Cheney, on *Meet the Press* in 2006: "George Tenet sat in the Oval Office and the president of the United States asked him directly—he said, 'George, how good is the case against Saddam on weapons of mass destruction?' The director of the C.I.A. said, 'It's a slam dunk, Mr. President, it's a slam dunk.'"

The late Los Angeles Lakers announcer Chick Hearn is credited with coining *slam dunk*, successor to the *stuff shot*. (He also produced *slam dunk*'s diametric opposite, *air ball*.) Hearn was inspired by the way L.A. Laker center, Wilt Chamberlain, all 7 foot, 1 inch of him, reached above the rim of the basket, then jammed the ball through with an unstoppable shot. Other players "improved" upon the feat, grabbing the rim on the way down, often shattering glass backboards in the process, and bringing games to a halt until the backboards could be replaced.

The print media soon picked up on the sportscaster's term. The *Long Beach* (Calif.) *Press-Telegram* noted in its account of a Laker contest in January of 1969: "Chamberlain, with help from Elgin Baylor, turned the game into a rout. ... The big guy first made a free throw, then a slam dunk." The *OED*'s earliest example comes from 1976, when Tom Wicker, of *The New York Times*, fondly characterized Rep. Morris Udall (D-Ariz.) as "The only one-eyed candidate who would know how to put in a slamdunk on a New York playground." (The verb *dunk*, akin to *dip*, means "to briefly immerse in liquid" or, in naval lingo, "to sink." Thus, one *sinks a basket* by dipping, or dunking, the ball down into it.)

After the long search for weapons of mass destruction in Iraq proved fruitless, the *slam dunk* metaphor bounced off the rhetorical rim. It began to be employed off the basketball court with tongue in cheek or in a negative manner, as in "Beware of Slam-Dunks in the Bond Market."

Tenet parsed his language in his 2007 memoir, *At the Center of the Storm*, contending that his *slam dunk* remark was misinterpreted. The decision to invade Iraq already had been made, according to Tenet's recollection of the meeting, when he said the president asked if there was some way to "add punch" to the public presentation of the case for going to war. "I told the president," Tenet wrote in his memoir, "that strengthening the public presentation was a 'slam dunk,'" a phrase that was later taken completely out of context." Promoting the book on CBS's *60 Minutes*, he added that—contrary to Bob Woodward's account—he did not "jump up from the couch" to make that point. Woodward responded to *The New Yorker*, "He's fried about 'slam dunk' ... I say he rose from the couch—look at the '60 Minutes' interview—he does it all the time." Other memoirs with passages focusing on that usage in that meeting are likely to follow.

slate A list of candidates, presented as a "package"; hopefully, take-one-take-all.

TAMMANY boss Charles Murphy reelected his candidate for mayor, George B. McClellan, Jr., in 1906 and promptly submitted a list of names for patronage. McClellan, backed up by New York Governor Charles Evans Hughes, proceeded to fire some Tammany men who already had jobs and turned down most of Murphy's suggestions. When asked by McClellan to supply some more acceptable alternatives, Murphy snapped: "That's my slate. Take it or leave it. I got no other candidates." The Tammany boss won.

The name, in use since 1842, is taken from the material used in school blackboards; a slate on which students write offers the convenience of easy erasure, something often needed in assembling political teams.

The word acquired a special meaning for the New Left in the late '50s, when a group of students at the University of California at Berkeley submitted a "Slate of Candidates" to run the student government. As they became involved in a wider field, organizing demonstrations against the House Un-American Activities Committee, the group continued to be known as SLATE. The word has since become the name of an online magazine. See TICKET.

sleaze factor Sustained ethical trimming; a pattern of seeming petty corruption among a political figure's official family.

Columnist Gerald Nachman put the term within quote marks in 1977, indicating its freshness: "The overall 'sleaze factor' was determined by interviewing 100 citizens—some with raunchy minds, others without a nasty thought in their head—to find the community's average prurient person." It entered politics during the next decade. "Public perceptions may lump all 535 House and Senate members together in a great ball of sleaze," noted *The Washington Post* in 1980, "but in the real world of Capitol Hill it is not that way."

Sleaze, a noun attested since the early 1950s, is a back-formation from *sleazy*, an adjective of unknown origin, though it has often been connected with Silesia, a region in Central Europe. A flimsy cloth woven there was named *Sleasie Holland*, but the word—in the sense of flimsy and unsubstantial—is found earlier than the name of the cloth.

In 1980, a vituperative right-wing columnist, accusing friends and relatives of Jimmy Carter of unethical behavior, titled a diatribe "The Politics of Sleaze." (He had already escalated some foolish connections with Libya by the president's brother Billy to the level of "Billygate.") Bert Lance, a longtime Carter ally also under fire, subsequently came up with a memorable riposte: "There's more muck*rakin'* than there is muck*makin'*.") See MUCKRAKER.

Laurence Barrett of *Time* magazine used *sleaze factor* as a chapter title in his 1983 book *Gambling With History*. In the inevitable political turnabout, Democrats seized upon that term in 1984 to characterize a pattern of small scandals during the Reagan Administration. A reporter commented to Ronald Reagan at a presidential press conference in early 1984, "More than a dozen members of your Administration have left under some sort of a cloud, and this is what the Democrats are calling 'the sleaze factor.'" Reagan responded, "I reject the use of the word 'sleaze.'" In *The Christian Science Monitor* in March 1984, the term was used in quotation marks: "Asked about the 'sleaze factor' in the campaign, Senator George McGovern told reporters … that he expected to see more mention of it." A day later, Walter Mondale said at a news conference that the factor to unite the Democrats in the 1984 campaign "will be the 'sleaze factor' in this Administration," because almost every week "another rotten apple falls from the tree."

Derivative derogations are *sleazeball* and *sleazebag*, coined on the analogy of *scum*. Reagan's ability to deflect the charges was nicknamed "the Teflon factor." (See TEFLON-COATED PRESIDENCY.) For a predecessor phrase, see HONEST GRAFT.

sleeper An amendment slipped into a bill to nullify or alter its intent; or, a piece of legislation whose significance is not realized until after it has been passed.

The political derivation is from both horse racing and cards. In racing, a *sleeper* is a horse that had been held back in previous races to build up its odds, and then allowed to go full speed in a race on which its owner had bet heavily. (For another fraudulent racing scheme turned into a political expression, see SHOO-IN.) In cards, the 1866 *American Hoyle* states: "A bet [in faro] is said to be a sleeper, when the owner has forgotten it, when it becomes public property, any one having a right to take it." See CARD METAPHORS.

The denunciation of *sleeper amendments* is difficult and embarrassing, since it usually includes an admission that the denouncer was not awake enough to catch the legislation when originally offered. *Sleeper* has generally replaced the previous slang word—*joker*. For a *sleeper issue*, one which assumes surprising importance in a campaign, see RIGHT TO WORK.

In spookspeak, it means "an agent long in place but not yet activated." A 1995 novel by the lexicographer about such a character was titled *Sleeper Spy*. Just after the 9/11 attacks on the World Trade Center and Pentagon, *The Christian Science Monitor* on September 24, 2001 quoted an investigator into the movements of Mohammed Atta and his al-Qaeda terrorist cell saying, "They were pretty effective sleeper agents. They were here for some time …" (For more spookspeak, see CIA-ESE.)

sleeping giant Unrealized source of great power; untapped or potential force.

This term may be derived from the plight of the title character in Jonathan Swift's 1726 novel *Gulliver's Travels*, in which Gulliver visits the land of Lilliput, where the tiny inhabitants tie down the giant while he is asleep.

Respectfully Quoted, a collection of quotations published by the Library of Congress, tracks the term to a 1970 motion picture, *Tora! Tora! Tora!* In the film Isoroku Yamamoto, a Japanese admiral in World War II, says, "I fear all we have done is to awaken a sleeping giant and fill him with a terrible resolve." The attributed remark, however, has no printed evidence to support Yamamoto's use. At any rate, the phrase is far older than that. In a 1909 article titled "Why China Sleeps," by Lieut. Lyman Gotten: "We often hear China compared to a sleeping giant that dreams not of his own dormant strength, nor knows how to use that strength were it realized." This followed by two years an article about China by Dr. Griffith John: "The railway, the telegraph, the imperial postal service and other western inventions and appliances have been invading the land of the hitherto sleeping giant."

In 1978, the columnist Vermont Royster offered another possible source nearly a century earlier in *The Wall Street Journal*: "'China is a sickly, sleeping giant. But when she awakes the world will tremble.' For over a century and a half that prophecy—attributed to Napoleon by Lord Amherst who visited him at St. Helena on his way back from China in 1816—has remained unfulfilled."

Implicit in this expression is the idea that the sleeping giant will soon assert a previously unused power. By the 1970s, the term was applied metaphorically to any potential powerhouse of political force. In 1977, a *Washington Post* article referred to the ethnic diversity of voters in the District of Columbia; a District candidate commented that the city's Hispanic community "is a sleeping giant no more." In 1992, the *Los Angeles Times* quoted Oscar Gonzales, a California activist, as saying, "There is the realization that this could be a WATERSHED year, the awakening of the sleeping giant," adding, "The sleeping giant is the vast potential Chicano bloc in Ventura County."

Ronald Reagan applied the term to the United States in 1980. On the eve of his election to the Presidency, Reagan sent America's allies a message: "At last the sleeping giant stirs and is filled with a resolve—a resolve that we will win together a struggle for world peace, our struggle for the human spirit."

slime See SMEAR.

slogan Rallying cry; catchphrase; a brief message that crystallizes an idea, defines an issue, the best of which thrill, exhort, and inspire.

Good slogans have rhyme, rhythm, or alliteration to make them memorable; great slogans may have none of these, but touch a chord of memory, release pent-up hatreds, or stir men's better natures.

It is in the nature of slogans to appeal to emotions, slipping past rational argument. "Men suppose that reason has command over their words," wrote Francis Bacon in his 1620 *Novum Organum*, "still it happens that words in return exercise authority on reason."

Themes recur in sloganeering. Many of the following have separate entries in this book, but here are some common denominators.

There are slogans that are essentially *promissory*: Reconstruction's Forty Acres and a Mule (which dwindled to Three Acres and a Cow, taken from British radical agrarian Jesse Collings by American populists); The Full Dinner Pail; Every Man a King; $2 a Day and Roast Beef; I Shall Go to Korea; He Can Do More for Massachusetts; Peace and Prosperity.

Other slogans are primarily *warnings*: Don't Let Them Take It Away; Coolidge or Chaos; Hoover and Happiness, or Smith and Soup Houses; You Never Had It So Good; Save the American Way of Life; No Third Term; Let's Keep What We've Got; Your Home Is Your Castle—Protect It.

Calls for *change* have been effective: Had Enough?; Turn the Rascals Out; Time for a Change; Let's Get America Moving Again.

Overtly *rational* slogans have failed: Let's Look at the Record; Let's Talk Sense to the American People; Experience Counts; as has one overtly *anti-rational*: In Your Heart You Know He's Right.

Challenge is an effective slogan technique: Fifty-Four Forty or Fight; Freedom Now.

Appeals to *gratitude* seem weak, but have worked: One Good Term Deserves Another; Keep Him on the Job; He Kept Us Out of War.

Evocative: A Country Fit for Heroes; General Taylor Never Surrenders; Vote as You Shot; Remember the Maine; Remember Pearl Harbor.

Alliterative slogans abound: Ban the Bomb; Beat the Bosses; Love That Lyndon; Rum, Romanism, and Rebellion; Tippecanoe and Tyler Too; Wilson's Wisdom Wins Without War; Win with Willkie.

So do *rhyming* slogans: I Like Ike; Jim Crow Must Go; All the Way with LBJ; In Hoover We Trusted, Now We Are Busted; The Grin Will Win.

Symbolic: Log Cabin and Hard Cider; I Am as Strong as a Bull Moose.

Punning: Keep Cool with Coolidge; Land a Job with Landon; (and Franklin Pierce won despite) We Polked You in 1844, We Shall Pierce You in 1852.

Slogans have been *frantic*: Anything to Beat Grant; *sardonic:* Make Love, Not War; Draft Beer, Not Students; *vicious:* Elect a Leader Not a Lover; Twenty Years of Treason; *meaningless:* Nixon's the One; and *questioning*: Why Not the Best?

In his 1960 campaign John F. Kennedy gave a general review of slogans, including the names of programs as slogans: "The Democratic party's candidates in this century never ran on slogans like 'Stand Pat with McKinley,' 'Return to Normalcy with Harding,' 'Keep Cool with Coolidge,' and 'Two Chickens in Every Pot with Hoover.' I don't know what Dewey's slogan was because he never worked it out.... Our slogans have meaning. Woodrow Wilson's New Freedom, Franklin Roosevelt's New Deal, Harry Truman's Fair Deal, and today, we stand on the threshold of a New Frontier."

The knack of turning a phrase was explained by Theodore Roosevelt to his young aide, Lieutenant Douglas MacArthur, in 1906. MacArthur had asked the President to what he attributed his popularity, and Roosevelt replied, "To put into words what is in their hearts and minds but not in their mouths." ("Hearts and minds" later became a slogan of sorts, as what had to be won in Vietnam.)

Some see sloganeering as a danger. "Slogans are both exciting and comforting," said educator James Bryant Conant in 1934, "but they are also powerful opiates for the conscience: some of mankind's most terrible misdeeds have been committed under the spell of certain magic words or phrases." Examples of this category include: Workers of the World, Unite; *Mare Nostrum*; Tomorrow the World.

Sir Ernest Gowers in the second edition of Fowler's *Modern English Usage* defines slogans as "those catchwords with which in the modern world politicians, ideologists, and advertisers try to excite our emotions and atrophy our minds." The word itself comes from the Gaelic *sluagh-ghairm*, from *sluagh*, "army," and *gairm*, "yell," the army-shout or war cry of the Scottish Highlanders, and has been in use, according to the *OED*, since 1513. An early American political use occurs in *Harper's Weekly* in 1854: "As party bitterness has died away ... let us take up the old slogan: Hurrah for Jackson!"

Good sloganeering advice was provided by University of Wisconsin professor Robert T. Oliver in the February 1937 issue of *American Speech*: "The party out of power would do well to mass its attack behind one or two key phrases. Thus it will gain the same concentration that advertisers seek with their reiteration of They satisfy! Not a cough in a carload! Ask the man who owns one! In the use of slogans, it would appear, the chief poverty is riches. The force of vivid impression through which slogans operate is vitiated when there are too many."

And then there are *facetious* slogans: "Support Mental Health or I'll Kill You" appeared on buttons, but a candidate for local office in Washington, D.C., won on

"Dog Litter—An Issue You Can't Sidestep." See CATCHWORD.

sloganeer See GHOST-WRITER.

slow-walk To delay deliberately, with an eye to letting the matter fade away in the mists of bureaucracy.

The way to get a memo or decision paper on up to the decision-maker and then on to the executor is to ignore channels and to *hand-carry* it, or *walk it through*. But if the purpose is otherwise—to delay until its idea is presented by another or until it is overtaken by events—then the verb is to *slow-walk* it, a fresh locution for *dragging a foot*.

Democrats in Congress early in 2007 passed a bill calling for the withdrawal of troops under a timetable that they knew was certain to draw a veto from President Bush. The liberal magazine *The American Prospect* wrote, "Some Democrats are willing to force the confrontation by *slow-walking* revisions of the bill after the veto."

On another front at the same time, the Bush administration was resisting requests from Congress for internal e-mails and sworn testimony by Justice Department officials and White House counsel about the dismissal of eight U.S. Attorneys; Democrats believed they could embarrass the president by showing the firing had political motivations. White House Counsel Fred Fielding, a veteran lawyer in the Nixon and Reagan administrations (considered a "grown-up" even by Democratic partisans), delayed responding in writing to several Senate and House letters of inquiry, instead meeting informally with lawmakers of all stripes to work out an accommodation averting a constitutional impasse. "The White House may be *slow-walking* this," wrote Ruth Marcus in *The Washington Post*, "because it wants to wait for the make-or-break testimony of Attorney General Alberto Gonzales ..." (The slow-walking was to no avail; his testimony broke rather than made the A.G.'s tenure.)

Origin may be in the Tennessee Walking Horse, which has three gaits: a flat or slow walk, a running walk, and a canter. The term was used in its current sense in a 1973 decision of the U.S. Court of Appeals for the Sixth Circuit concerning testimony in a labor dispute that "many of the men were simply standing around and were purposely 'slow-walking' the project ... to stretch out the term of employment."

slumlor A landlord who realizes unconscionable profits on crowded slum dwellings, packing in tenants and withholding money for maintenance.

The word appeared in 1953; an early citation is from a 1957 *New York Times Magazine*: "The landlord had bitterly protested to the Buildings Commissioner that he was not a 'slumlord' and avowed that he was ready to put the building in condition if he could get a guarantee that it would stay that way; otherwise he had no alternative but to demolish it." *Barron's* magazine in 1960: "To prevent the enrichment of slumlords, for example, the General Accounting Office, in fixing property values, would rule out all income earned in defiance of local ordinances."

Slumlords defend themselves by claiming that tenants overcrowd their facilities without their permission, and that vandalism is the cause of most of the complaints. This cuts no ice with campaigning candidates; a typical picture in this genre was Mayor Robert F. Wagner of New York touring a slum dwelling and coming face to face with a large rat.

Landlords, particularly absentee, have traditionally been unpopular. Dean Jonathan Swift inveighed against the English landlords of Ireland in the early eighteenth century, and this comment by Richard Hildreth in his 1836 novel *The Slave; or, Memoirs of Archy Moore* was typical of complaints against Southern plantation owners before the Civil War: "The absentee aristocracy congregates in Charleston, or dapples and astonishes the cities and watering places of the North by its profuse extravagance and reckless dissipation. The plantations are left to the sole management of overseers."

Slumlord is a word born with its time out of joint. The word was created by the substitution of the *land* in *landlord* with *slum*, which was slang for "room" (possibly from *slumber*) in the early nineteenth century, later coming to mean "poverty-stricken neighborhood." But as *slumlord* was being coined, so were euphemisms for *slum*. Linguistic renewal replaced that run-down word with *culturally deprived environment, urban ghetto*, or *inner city*, making *slumlord* a word in dire need of relocation.

slumpflation See ECONOMIC JARGON.

slush fund A collection of money for pay-offs, or for personal use without proper accounting.

"Is Dodd Dead?" went the political question early in 1967, a play on "Is God Dead?" which had been memorably featured on a 1966 *Time* magazine cover. As a result of an exposé by columnists Drew Pearson and Jack Anderson, Connecticut Senator Thomas Dodd was censured by the Senate for personal use of funds collected ostensibly for campaigning purposes.

Though *slush fund* was used often in Dodd's hearings, the meaning of the phrase is usually narrowed to a specific fund. Richard Nixon was accused by Democrats of having a slush fund in 1952, which he defended in the CHECKERS SPEECH, concurrently releasing contributors, amounts, and purposes. Soon afterward Adlai Stevenson was discovered by Republicans to have a fund as Illinois governor for supplementing the salaries of state employees. Since neither fund had a nefarious purpose, the furor soon died down.

The word may be derived from the Norwegian *slask*, with the same meaning. Naval vessels would sell the slush and other refuse on board; the proceeds went into a fund to purchase sundries for the crew. Later this practice was extended to war-damaged equipment as well, and to military as well as naval refuse and equipment. "The polite Commissary informed us," wrote the *Rio Abajo Press* of Albuquerque in 1864, "that they received twelve dollars a barrel for the [coffee] grounds, and thus added materially to the 'slush fund.'"

The first political use found was in 1874. Connecticut Congressman S. W. Kellogg,

referring to a $5 million appropriation administered by the Treasury Secretary, said: "It was a matter of economy and good judgment...to consolidate all these offices into one bill, and dispense with what has been received out of...the 'slush fund.'... We have had this 'slush fund' since 1866...although during Andrew Johnson's administration that 'slush fund' was five or six times larger than it ever has been since."

Congressman Champ Clark used the term in 1894 in the sense of a campaign fund gathered for propaganda purposes, as he defended President Grover Cleveland, who "was not elected in 1888 because you had got the 'fat fried' out of your manufacturers; because of pious John Wanamaker and $400,000 of campaign slush funds. ..." See FAT CAT.

What gives *slush fund* its sinister meaning is its lack of accountability: money goes into a pot and is ladled out without public scrutiny. From the original "fringe benefit" connotation in naval vessels, the phrase has gained a thieving image, as in this 1924 comparison of chicanery by Will Rogers: "If I was running for office I would rather have two friends in the counting room than a Republican slush fund behind me."

smear As a verb, (1) to slander, or (2) to bribe; as a noun, (1) a malicious lie, or (2) a payment.

"I know this will not be the last of the smears," said vice presidential candidate Richard Nixon in 1952, at the conclusion of his television defense of the "Nixon fund" in his CHECKERS SPEECH. "In spite of my explanation tonight, other smears will be made.... And the purpose of the smears, I know, is this: to silence me, to make me let up."

Both the word and the political device are ancient. The word comes from Old English *smeoru*, "grease," a close relative of Old Norse *smjör*, "butter." As a verb, one of its meanings is "to besmirch or pollute," and that sense—of tainting a reputation—is its most common political meaning.

A second political meaning—"to bribe"—comes from the use of GREASE as money for graft. This is usually pronounced *schmear*, perhaps because of the German cognate

Schmiere, "grease," or its Yiddish equivalent *shmir,* "smear," which appears in the frequent breakfast order "a bagel with a *schmear* (of cream cheese)."

"Be thou as chaste as ice, as pure as snow," Hamlet told Ophelia, "thou shalt not escape calumny." (The noun *calumny* means "false and malicious charges"; when stooped to by a columnist, it can be called *columny.*) An attack on a reputation can be labeled pretentiously as "impugning integrity." A more legalistic mind uses *slander* (spoken) or *libel* (written). A recent label, implying systematic smearing, is CHARACTER ASSASSINATION.

Peggy Eaton, wife of Andrew Jackson's Secretary of War, was ostracized by Washington society for supposedly living with her husband-to-be before her first husband committed suicide, and the President accurately diagnosed the attack on the young woman as "a plot by Clay and Calhoun to separate Eaton and me." The lady herself put it quaintly: "It was the designs of politics that led to the slander of my fair frame …"

Fathering a bastard, which can one of the dirtiest of smears if untrue, was used unsuccessfully against Grover Cleveland, who admitted he supported a child born out of wedlock; a campaign song against him was "Ma, Ma, where's my Pa?," answered after his victory with "Gone to the White House, ha-ha-ha."

Smear was popularized during the latter part of the Hoover Administration, when Democrats blamed Herbert Hoover for breadlines; President Hoover charged that Charlie Michelson, a former New York *World* reporter acting as head of the Democratic National Committee's publicity department, "came out of the smear department of yellow journalism." John J. Raskob, Chairman of the Democratic National Committee in 1932, taunted the Republicans on their "smear" charge: "Upon consulting the dictionary," he told the national convention, "we found a definition of the word 'smear' to mean, 'to prepare a dead body with sacred oils before burial.'"

Republicans in 1936 continued to complain about the "Smear Department of the New Deal," but in the next decade the use of the word became bipartisan. In political terminology, it was a useful antonym to *whitewash:* Harry Truman wrote that his senatorial investigating committee "was not going to be used for either a whitewash or a smear in any matter before it but was to be used to obtain facts." Senator Margaret Chase Smith, in her 1950 "Declaration of Conscience" aimed at Senator Joseph McCarthy, said: "The American people are sick and tired of being afraid to speak their minds lest they be politically smeared as 'Communist' or 'Fascist.' The American people are sick and tired of seeing innocent people smeared and guilty people whitewashed."

The spring and summer of 1960 was a high point, or low point, of smearing. John F. Kennedy's West Virginia primary campaign featured a smear by Kennedy supporter Franklin D. Roosevelt, Jr., suggesting that Senator Hubert Humphrey had been a draft dodger; the Lyndon Johnson forces, led by Texas Governor John Connally (injured when Kennedy was assassinated three years later), accused Kennedy's father, Ambassador Joseph P. Kennedy, of harboring anti-Semitic sentiments during World War II.

Can the truth be a smear? The Johnson supporters claimed that John Kennedy was a victim of Addison's disease, requiring regular cortisone treatment. The Kennedy doctors admitted only "a mild adrenal deficiency," but an article in the *Journal of the American Medical Association* in 1967 substantiated the original charge. Nevertheless, many politicians consider the original attack a smear; while truth may be a legal defense against libel, the spreading of a damaging story about a candidate—even if true—can be considered a smear. Most journalists, as well as supporters of the person whose reputation suffers from such exposure, do not agree with that; however, a *Chicago Tribune* editorial at the end of 1992 lectured Republicans about appointments by President-elect Clinton: "What we ought not to have is an obfuscating cloud of smear and slander and distortion."

Recently, another noun-turned-verb has provided writers with a more emphatic synonym: to *slime*, going back to an Indo-European root that is also the source of *slippery* and *slick*. In the 2006 controversy pitting Senator John McCain against President George W. Bush over what the Administration called "aggressive" or "harsh" interrogation of terrorism suspects, including the simulation of drowning known as "waterboarding," a *Wall Street Journal* editorial defended Justice Department lawyers Jay Bybee and John Yoo for having been "slimed as 'pro-torture' for grappling with these issues in the past." A predecessor word was ROORBACK; also see DIRTY TRICKS and GUTTER FLYER.

smell of magnolias The occasional political burden of being a Southerner in a national campaign; contrariwise, Southern charm exercised with great political finesse in the South.

"Johnson the candidate," wrote *Life* magazine in 1956 about the candidacy of Senator Lyndon Johnson of Texas, "has grave and probably decisive drawbacks as he, despite the hopes of his supporters, well knows. He has little support in organized labor. He 'smells of magnolias,' i.e., is a Southerner."

Though the phrase seldom appears in print, it has a lively political usage, as do "magnolia talk"—an intimate, richly accented, we-have-the-same-roots seduction—and "smell of magnolias," the fragrance that causes Southern conservatives to sigh and Northern liberals to sniff.

When Richard Nixon impressed the Republican platform committee in 1960 with the need to adopt a strong civil rights plank, a Southern lady from Louisiana told reporter Theodore White, "I know what you Northerners think. But we've lost Louisiana, I tell you, we've lost Louisiana. Lyndon Johnson's going to come across the border now and talk 'magnolia' to them and they'll vote Democratic and we could have had Louisiana, we could have had it." See CORN PONE.

In the presidential campaign of 1976, the presence of a Southerner, Jimmy Carter, at the top of the Democratic ticket led to a new use of the *magnolia* metaphor: unfriendly writers referred to his strong-willed but soft-spoken wife, Rosalynn Carter, as "the steel magnolia." In April 1978, *Time* magazine referred to the group of Georgians working in the White House as the "magnolia mafia."

smoke and mirrors Illusion; use of deception for manipulation of public opinion.

Columnist Jimmy Breslin coined the term in a 1975 book, *How the Good Guys Finally Won*, about House Speaker Tip O'Neill's participation in the removal of Richard Nixon from the presidency. Quoting Thomas Hobbes's "The reputation of power is power," Breslin opined that political power is primarily an illusion: "Mirrors and blue smoke, beautiful blue smoke rolling over the surface of highly polished mirrors, first a thin veil of blue smoke, then a thick cloud that suddenly dissolves into wisps of blue smoke, the mirrors catching it all, bouncing it back and forth. If somebody tells you how to look, there can be seen in the smoke great, magnificent shapes, castles and kingdoms, and maybe they can be yours."

Breslin added that the operator of an illusion begins to believe in it himself, "at the same time knowing that what he is believing in is mirrors and blue smoke."

In usage, Breslin's phrase was inverted as *blue smoke and mirrors*, with the color often clipped. Using the stage metaphor of a magician's act, in which a girl is produced from nowhere with a puff of smoke and sometimes with deceptive mirrors, it became political jargon by the late 1970s. Bill Peterson wrote in *The Washington Post* in 1979 about a STRAW POLL showing George H.W. Bush as the winner of the Republican nomination for president: "The victory was fleeting, meaningless except in the blue smoke and mirror world of politics."

Jack Germond and Jules Witcover used the phrase to title their 1981 book, *Blue Smoke and Mirrors: How Reagan Won and Why Carter Lost the Election of 1980*. Reagan himself used the term, with its extended magician metaphor, to describe the budget process: "wink and blink and smoke and mirrors, and pulling rabbits out of hats."

During the 1987 Iran-contra hearings, Senate counsel Arthur L. Liman asked former national security adviser Robert C. McFarlane about support given the Nicaraguan resistance after Congress had cut off aid. Replied McFarlane, "Basically it was smoke and mirrors." The *blue* returned in 2005 as liberal columnist Tom Oliphant denounced the response to Hurricane Katrina as "just more federal government blue smoke and mirrors leaving millions of people to beg each year for budgetary table scraps."

smoke-filled room A place of political intrigue and chicanery, where candidates were selected by party bosses in cigar-chewing session.

This sinister phrase is usually attributed to Harry Daugherty, an Ohio Republican who supported Senator Warren Harding for the party's presidential candidacy. Daugherty sensed that the two best-known candidates, General Leonard Wood and Governor Frank Lowden of Illinois, would start off with almost equal support. "The convention will be deadlocked," Daugherty is quoted as having said, "and after the other candidates have gone their limit, some twelve or fifteen men, worn out and bleary-eyed for lack of sleep, will sit down about two o'clock in the morning, around a table in a smoke-filled room in some hotel and decide the nomination. When that time comes, Harding will be selected."

Daugherty later denied having said any such thing, calling "The Fable of the Senatorial Clique" an "amazing yarn." But William Allen White, editor of the *Emporia Gazette* and a respected Republican figure, corroborated the Daugherty prediction. A story filed at 5 A.M. on June 12, 1920, by Associated Press reporter Kirke Simpson, led off with the words "Harding of Ohio was chosen by a group of men in a smoke-filled room early today as Republican candidate for President." Newsmen call this "putting the story in the lede." (The spelling *lede* is preferred by journalists to avoid confusion with the *lead* once used in setting type.)

Present in Colonel George Harvey's room at the Blackstone Hotel that night were some of the most respected political figures

in the U.S.: Senators Wadsworth, Calder, Smoot, Watson, McCormick, and Lodge, along with Joe Grundy, a political boss who later became a senator. Not present were most of those later to become known as "the Ohio gang."

Historian Mark Sullivan, curious about the birth of a famous saying, elicited a letter from New Yorker Charles E. Hilles, who (Sullivan wrote) "was present at, so to speak, the obstetrical bedside of this verbal birth." The first-hand Hilles account:

> Daugherty was hastily packing his bag in a Waldorf Astoria Hotel room when two reporters called. He expressed regret that he had not time for an interview. One of the reporters persisted…he said that he presumed that as Daugherty could not support by an authentic table of delegates his boast that Harding would be the nominee, it followed that Daugherty must expect to win by manipulation—probably in some back room of a hotel with a small group of political managers reduced to pulp by the inevitable vigil and travail.
>
> The reporter went on to say to Daugherty that he presumed the conferees would be expected to surrender at 2 A.M. in a smoke-filled room. Daugherty, unaffected by the taunt, retorted carelessly, "Make it 2:11."

(For similar tales of phrases planted by reporters, see RED HERRING and INOPERATIVE.)

Harry Truman pointed out that "the 'smoke-filled room' was nothing new but Harding's nomination dramatized the tag and made it stick." That kind of session was bound to happen, wrote Thomas E. Dewey, "where there are enough strong candidates to prevent anyone from getting a majority and there is a stalemate."

The era of air-conditioned hotel rooms has blown away most of the literal meaning, but the symbolism makes the phrase current and useful. Carmine de Sapio, Tammany leader in the '50s, had an eye ailment that made it impossible for him to endure cigarette smoke. In tagging him with a "bossism" charge, his opponents continued to charge him with "operating in a smoke-filled room."

smoke screen Disguising intentions or evading issues by creating a diversion or giving a deliberately false impression.

British Prime Minister Harold Wilson attacked a London newspaper, the *Daily Express*, for revealing government secrets in 1967, despite a special commission's findings that the paper was innocent of the charges. Speaking in the House of Commons, a Conservative leader, Reginald Maudling, said of Mr. Wilson, "It is one of his most unlovable characteristics that he is never prepared to admit he is wrong. On the frequent occasions when he is, he tries to escape by throwing up a smokescreen."

The term has long been in active use in American politics as well. A 1940 cartoon in the *Rochester* (N.Y.) *Times-Union* shows a Democratic donkey flying an airplane that is putting down a smoke screen around various articles labeled "Taxes," "Extravagance," "Third term," "Public debt."

The derivation of *smoke screen* is naval, from the days when destroyers would dash at high speeds between an enemy fleet and their own, laying down large quantities of black smoke to conceal the movements and intentions of their own vessels. Later, airplanes were sometimes used to accomplish the same aims on the battlefield.

In Japanese politics, a more poetic phrase is used to describe the effort to evade an issue by creating a diversion. Translated literally, it is "throwing up cherry blossoms."

smoking gun Incontrovertible evidence: the proof of guilt that precipitates resignations.

"The chaplain stood with a smoking pistol in his hand," wrote A. Conan Doyle in his 1893 Sherlock Holmes story "The 'Gloria Scott.'" Such a stance is generally considered suggestive of obvious (sometimes too obvious) guilt.

During the Watergate investigation, Nixon defenders insisted that while much impropriety could be observed, no proof of presidential obstruction of justice—no "smoking gun"—had been found. Then, on the release of the June 23, 1972, tape, H. R. Haldeman was shown to have said to the President that "the FBI is not under control" and that the CIA could be used to block the FBI investigation. When Haldeman said, "And you seem to think the thing to do is to get them, the FBI, to stop?," the President replied, "Right, fine."

Representative Barber Conable, a conservative Republican, said that the evidence on the June 23 tape "looked like a smoking gun." The term, which had been "in the air" for months, was widely quoted. Within days the President resigned, and the simile's incontrovertible-evidence meaning was reinforced.

The term did not die with Watergate. Covering former Governor Marvin Mandel's corruption trial in Maryland, reporter Jerry Oppenheimer wrote in *The Washington Star* in 1977: "While no 'smoking gun' of new damaging evidence is expected to be introduced by the government, knowledgeable observers of the case believe that the 'morality of Maryland politics' in general will stand trial."

In 1992, the term resurfaced when David Shaw of the *Los Angeles Times* was quoted by *The Boston Globe* on the campaign style of Ross Perot: "Unless there's a real smoking gun that the press comes up with, I think that he might be able to manipulate anti-press feelings in the public and turn attacks on him to his advantage."

Condoleezza Rice, then national security adviser, gave the phrase an ominous twist when she justified the approaching war with Iraq in an interview in September 2002 with CNN's Wolf Blitzer, saying: "The problem here is that there will always be some uncertainty about how quickly he [Saddam Hussein] can acquire nuclear weapons. But we don't want the smoking gun to become a mushroom cloud." Hans Blix, the chief United Nations weapons inspector, picked up the metaphor, declaring the following January: "The absence of smoking guns which we have had so far … is no guarantee that prohibited stocks or activities could not exist at other sites." White House press secretary Ari Fleischer commented: "The problem with guns that are hidden is that you can't see their smoke." Despite intensive post-invasion searches, however, no *smoking guns* were found. See WATERGATE WORDS.

snake bill See RED-HEADED ESKIMO BILL.

snake in the tunnel An agreement that one nation's exchange rates will fluctuate within a narrower band than other nations' rates; an attempt to give some limited flexibility to fixed exchange rates, opposed by free-marketers who want an unrestricted "float."

This is as good a metaphor as the "invisible hand" (Adam Smith's phrase) of the "dismal science" (Thomas Carlyle's phrase) of economics has ever crafted, and is remembered more for the vividness of its image than the longevity of its practice. The word-picture combines the evil lurking in "snake in the grass" with the hope implicit in "light at the end of the tunnel." When this lexicographer went to Professor Herbert Stein, who served as a member, and later Chairman, of the Council of Economic Advisers during the early '70s when the snake was in the tunnel, the answer received went more to the way all catch phrases are born than to the serious business of politico-economic etymology. The droll Dr. Stein recounted:

> It seems that one day in 1972, at a reception following a meeting of the Group of 10 in Paris, Dr. Karl Schiller, German Minister of Economics and Finance, found that the cream cheese had been spread on the lox, instead of vice versa. *"Diese snack ist in eine tummul!"* he exclaimed, meaning, of course, that the snack was mixed up.
>
> The information director of the Group of 10, who was British, thought Schiller had said that the snack is in the *tunnel*, the underground passage connecting the Chateau de la Muette with the OECD office building. At a press briefing later, when asked what Dr. Schiller's opinion was, he quoted Schiller as saying that "the snack is in the tunnel."
>
> A stringer for the *Wall Street Journal* misunderstood and cabled to New York that Schiller had said, "The *snake* is in the tunnel." And so it all began.

"This story," concluded the eminent economist, "while uninteresting, is also unauthenticated." Coming finally to the object of the author's query, he added: "However, I do have it on good authority that the expression was coined by Dr. Schiller."

Reached in West Germany, and responding in all seriousness, Dr. Schiller recalled the birth of the expression in Brussels at the end of 1970. "The meaning was quite simple," he wrote in March 1978. "At the time, we still had a fixed par value system and it was decided to agree on a narrower margin in the actual exchange rates between EEC countries as a preparatory step towards an economic and monetary union in Europe (Werner Plan)... this situation created the so-called 'Tunnel' within which the European exchange rates, i.e., the 'snake,' moved.

"Now that we have a joint floating of the currencies of some European countries against the dollar," Dr. Schiller explained, "we speak of the Snake only as a group consisting of some EEC member and some non-member counties. The Tunnel has, so to speak, disappeared."

Thus, for the reader who wants a straight-faced explanation of the expression, what economists needed was a metaphor for a long, narrow band in which Common Market countries' currencies could go up or down by 1 1/8 percent (the snake) while they could vary twice that much up or down against the U.S. dollar (the tunnel)—like a nervous arm in a sleeve, or a wriggling snake in a tunnel.

More important, however, is an understanding of Dr. Stein's points: that folk etymology is easily born, even in economics, and that in multilingual international conferences, much flavor is gained, rather than lost, in translation and transmission.

The metaphor is now primarily used in historical contexts. *Institutional Investor* wrote in 1992: "The so-called 'snake in the tunnel' concept didn't last long, and market pressures caused Europe in 1973 to abandon efforts to keep any limits against the highly volatile dollar."

sneer words Adjectives that cast aspersions on high-sounding nouns, or are used as a defense against entrapment by loaded phrases.

Self- is the prefix of the most frequently used sneer words—followed by *appointed, styled, proclaimed* and *anointed*—used to modify *guardian*, *protector*, and *watchdog* of the public interest.

So-called is often used as a defensive adjective, when a shining phrase has been adopted generically by the opposition. Western diplomats used "so-called 'People's republic'" to show they don't really believe that the people run the republic; Russians speaking English used the compound adjective, pronounced as "succolt," as often as the favored introductory phrase, *as is well known.*

"Called," "purported" and "said to be" are not limited to English in its aspersion-casting sense; Charles de Gaulle scornfully referred to the United Nations as "*Les nations dites unies.*" American labor union leaders opposing RIGHT TO WORK laws acknowledge that the slanted phrase has become generic, and refer to "so-called right-to-work laws, which are really union-busting laws …"

A curled lip can be used in spoken English to show derision, but the use of quotation marks creates the same effect in written prose, as "My opponent 'forgot' to say" or "This entry 'neglects' to mention …" A 2006 parody of the excessive use of quotation marks to cast aspersion was supplied by the *Washington Post* television critic Tom Shales, reviewing "one of those 'sensitive' family dramas that virtually require 'sensitive' to be put in 'quotes' when one 'talks' about 'it.'"

"Quote-unquote" preceding the noun to be sneered at has been gaining in popularity, sometimes accompanied by a wiggling of two fingers on each hand next to the speaker's ears to add a visual dimension on television. In print, however, to follow the sneer word by putting quotation marks around the noun it modifies, though intended to add emphasis, is redundant.

snipe As a noun, a candidate's poster slapped up on "free space" such as fences, walls, telephone poles; as a verb, to post such advertising clandestinely.

This splendid little word has long been overlooked in political etymology. A *snipe* is a small bird with a long bill, akin to a woodcock; a *snipe hunt* is an elaborate practical joke in which the victim is left in a lonely field at night holding a sack and a tennis racket, one origin of the phrase *left holding the bag*; a *snipe* is also a fool, or a contemptible person, as in Churchill's "bloodthirsty guttersnipe" reference to Hitler; and it has been used to mean "cigarette" and "cigar butt," as well as "a member of a railroad section gang." No link has been found to bring these meanings together.

In its current political use, a *snipe* is a poster. An explanation was given in *The Relations Explosion*, a 1963 book by this writer: "In almost every city, there is an organization well acquainted with building superintendents and construction crews, which will put up a candidate's snipes for a fee. The plastering-up is done in the dead of night, with no questions asked, but never covers up the snipes of the opposing candidate, for whom the same snipers also work. Amateur snipers soon see their posters covered or disfigured with beards and mustaches."

In China, *dazibao*, or big-character posters, are an effective propaganda tool, sometimes posted by angry students or supporters of disgraced officials. This form of communication occasionally reflects the genuine feelings of a minority.

In Japan, a term for reputation or prestige is *kamban;* its literal translation is "poster, signboard" (or "snipe"). In Britain, Americans are often puzzled by the prevalence of posters apparently threatening a mysterious individual: "Bill Stickers Will Be Prosecuted."

snollygoster An unprincipled politician; according to Harry Truman, "a man born out of wedlock."

President Truman revived this obsolete Americanism in a 1952 Labor Day speech at Parkersburg, W. Va., twitting politicians who pray in public to win votes. The replating of a fanciful term coined during or prior to the Civil War sent reporters to the *Dictionary of American Regional English*, where an entry from the *Columbus Dispatch* in 1895 quoted a Georgia editor's definition: "A snollygoster is a fellow who wants office, regardless of party, platform or principles, and who, whenever he wins, gets there by the sheer force of monumental talknophical assumnancy [sic]."

The Baltimore *Sun* in 1952 ran an editorial headed "Snolly and Snally" suggesting that the word along with the similar-sounding *snallygaster* came from the German *schnelle Geister,* or "Wild Host," which it defined as "birds of prey that terrorize man" and compared such a bird to an "ostentatious, vociferous politico."

Senator Charles Mathias supplied the author with "information about the Maryland Snallygaster which is apparently a different species from the Missouri Snollygoster mentioned in your 'Language of Politics'...as you will see, the Maryland Snallygaster was a crude and cruel beast employed against black voters." Senator Mathias enclosed a copy of an article that appeared in the *Valley Register* on March 5, 1909, intended to frighten black voters who intended to go to the polls. The headline was: "Emmitsburg Saw the Great Snallygaster / It Ate a Coal Bin Empty and Then Spit Fire / Looked Like a 'Coonscooper.'"

Merriam-Webster's *Third New International Dictionary* uses the Maryland "a" spelling, and after calling the word "perhaps a modification of Pennsylvania German *schnelle geeschter,* literally, quick spirits" defines it as "a mythical nocturnal creature that is reported chiefly from rural Maryland, is reputed to be part reptile and part bird, and is said to prey on poultry and children."

Presidential use of an obscure political term gives it currency and enriches the vocabulary; for other once-obsolete terms that made it back, see CARPETBAGGER and MERCHANTS OF DEATH; for ones that did not, see OBSOLETE POLITICAL TERMS.

soak the rich See POPULIST.

s.o.b. Abbreviation for *son of a bitch,* an appellation which creates a furor whenever the public learns that a president of the United States has used it.

The dictator of Nicaragua, President Anastasio Somoza García, was scheduled to visit President Franklin Roosevelt in Washington, D.C., in 1939. *Time* magazine reported in 1948 that FDR had been briefed on the visit by Sumner Welles, then Undersecretary of State: "To prime President Roosevelt for the visit, Sumner Welles sent him a long, solemn memorandum about Somoza and Nicaragua. According to a story told around Washington, Roosevelt read the memo right through, wisecracked 'As a Nicaraguan might say, he's a sonofabitch, but he's ours.'" That quotation must be considered apocryphal because there is no source attributed other than "a story told," and the article in *Time* was unsigned, as all were during that period of anonymous "group journalism."

However, FDR's possible remark is frequently cited as an example of REALISM in diplomacy. In November of 2007, the U.K.'s *Daily Telegraph* criticized the British and American governments' unwillingness to make a complete break with the President of Pakistan, who had just fired his nation's Chief Justice and declared emergency rule. In an editorial titled "Bankrupt relationship," the writer reached back to the phrase made diplomatically unforgettable by its use of a possessive adjective: "The struggle against terrorism is provoking a reaction familiar from the Cold War...In the old parlance, General Pervez Musharraf is 'our sonofabitch.'" The newspaper later printed a response about that "old parlance" from Pakistan's press minister that showed it had not lost its sting: "The language used for the President of Pakistan in your leading article is offensive and flouts the norms of decent journalism."

President Harry Truman's military aide, Major General Harry Vaughan, was criticized by columnist Drew Pearson for accepting a medal from Argentine dictator Juan Perón. On February 22, 1949, in Arlington, Va., where Vaughan was being given another award by the Reserve Officers Association, President Truman expressed his feelings: "I am just as fond of and just as loyal to my military aide as I am to the high brass, and want you to distinctly understand that any s.o.b. who thinks he can cause any one of these people to be discharged by me by some smart aleck statement over the air or in the paper has got another think coming."

White House stenographer Jack Romagna changed *s.o.b.* to "anyone" in the official transcript, but most newspapers quoted Truman verbatim. The *Christian Science Monitor* simply said "He used a vulgar abbreviation," but the *Chicago Tribune* felt it necessary to explain that "s.o.b. is an abbreviation for a vulgar expression casting reflection on a person's parentage." The *Indianapolis Star* added, "The phrase, freely translated, means male offspring of a female canine." Drew Pearson himself capitalized on the attack by urging his listeners and readers to become "Sons of Brotherhood."

During the Eisenhower years the use of the epithet and its abbreviation appeared to subside in politics. The phrase had even had a heroic connotation, from Marine Sergeant Daniel Daly's coinage of a World War I battle cry at Belleau Wood: "Come on, you sons of bitches! Do you want to live forever?" Frederick the Great made a similar statement at Kolin, June 18, 1757, hurling at his retreating troops, "*Ihr Racker, wollt ihr denn ewig leben?*" ("You rascals, do you want to live forever?"—to which a fleeing and ill-paid grenadier is said to have responded, "Fritz, for eight groschen we've done enough today!").

The phrase made a political comeback in connection with the steel-price rise and rollback in 1962. After U.S. Steel chairman Roger Blough had left the President's office, John F. Kennedy was widely reported to have said: "My father always told me that all businessmen were sons of bitches." This time, however, the furor was less over the President's choice of language (it was in private conversation) but on whether he actually said "all businessmen," which Kennedy denied.

Thus, current use indicates that the phrase is politically acceptable when used by anyone in private conversation; it is considered tasteless when used by public officials in public; and it shocks when used publicly by a president.

sobriquets Terms of affection or derision used interchangeably with the names of famous men. More grandiose than a nickname.

Tracing the line of American presidents: *The Father of His Country*, or the *American Fabius*, was succeeded by the *Colossus of Independence*, sometimes called the *Machiavelli of Massachusetts*, and followed by the *Sage of Monticello*, or *Long Tom*.

The *Father of the Constitution* was next, and then the *Last of the Cocked Hats*, author of the famous Doctrine. *Old Man Eloquent* (son of *Colossus*) gave way to *Old Hickory* (*King Andrew* to his enemies), and then his protégé (we're up to Martin Van Buren now) *The Little Magician*, or *Wizard of Kinderhook. Tippecanoe* died in office, making way for the *Accidental President* (Tyler), then *Young Hickory* (Polk) who died and was succeeded by *Old Rough and Ready* (Taylor). The *American Louis Philippe* (Fillmore) succeeded him, followed by *Purse*—just a play on the name Pierce—and then the *Old Public Functionary*, or *Bachelor President* (Buchanan).

Father Abraham came next (called by some the *Illinois Baboon*), with *Sir Veto* (Johnson), *Unconditional Surrender* (Grant), *President de Facto* (Tilden supporters wouldn't concede that "Rutherfraud" Hayes was *de jure*), the *Dark Horse* (Garfield), replaced after his assassination by the *First Gentleman of This Land* (Arthur), taking us up to Cleveland, the *Man of Destiny* or *Stuffed Prophet*. *Grandpa's Grandson* was Benjamin Harrison (Tippecanoe was the Grandfather), and he ushered in *Prosperity's Advance Agent* (McKinley), succeeded at his death by his Vice President, the *Rough Rider* (T.R.), and then by William Howard Taft, who was not blessed with an outstanding sobriquet.

The *Phrasemaker*, or *Professor* (Wilson), was followed by Harding (no sobriquet), then *Silent Cal, The Chief, That Man in the White House*, and *Give-'Em-Hell Harry*. Sobriquets paled for a time—Ike, JFK, LBJ—but came back with *Tricky Dick* until fading again with Ford and Carter. Ronald Reagan was called the *Great Communicator*; he liked to say "I wasn't a great communicator, but I communicated great things." The elder Bush was belatedly known as "41"—the 41st president, as distinguished from his son, the 43rd—and Bill Clinton styled himself the *Comeback Kid*. The younger Bush was known by his middle initial, pronounced with a Texas accent, *Dubya*.

Tom Braden, in a 1971 column, bemoaned the disappearance of the sobriquet:

> Our people have gradually and unconsciously deprived themselves of the romance which once accompanied the nation's business ... How much more fun, how much more romantic. ... Imagine a candidate for President whom people referred to as "The Plumed Knight,"—which was the way the followers of James C. Blaine talked about their leader. And after Bryan, Czar Reed was speaker of the House, Blackjack Pershing was leader of American forces in World War I, Fighting Bob La Follette was to run for President on the Progressive ticket and silent Cal Coolidge was to win. ... But why has the sobriquet gone? ... maybe we are lacking in that pride in being American, which caused us to sprinkle our politics with characters like Old Rough and Ready, Tippecanoe, Fuss and Feathers, and the Little Giant. Or for that matter, Honest Abe? The new standard is cool and polite, and correct, and not much fun.

so-called See SNEER WORDS.

soccer mom Assumed to be a married, white, suburban resident, driver of a sport-utility vehicle or minivan (large enough for a team of young soccer players), and embodying the values and concerns of many female voters.

The *soccer mom* became a political player in the run-up to the 1996 presidential election. Ellen Goodman, of *The Boston Globe*, noted in her column that September: "The icon of the 1994 campaign was the 'Angry White Male.' The icon of the 1996 campaign is the 'Stressed Out Soccer Mom.'" Under the headline "Suburbs Soccer Moms, Fleeing the G.O.P., Are Much Sought," *The New York Times* reported in early October: "If the catch phrase that emerged from the Republican sweep in the 1994 elections was 'angry white men,' then what will it be this election season? ... In fact, the white suburban women ... who are fast becoming the most sought-after voters of the campaign season are already known in campaign circles by a different

name that is only now gaining currency: soccer moms."

Pat Harrison, a Republican Party worker from Arlington, Va., believed that "The phrase started in 1976, when women were first starting to enter the work force in droves and had to sacrifice to participate in their children's extracurricular activities." The earliest written citations come from 1982. The *Springfield* (Mass.) *Morning Union* reported that year: "The Soccer moms and the boys and girls raise $5,000 to $8,000 annually through door-to-door sales of candy." Such treasuries can be tempting, as indicated by a second 1982 example, an AP dispatch from Palmer, Mass.: "A judge has found a husband guilty of looting $3,150 from the treasury of the Soccer Moms booster club in Ludlow headed by his wife."

For all the talk of soccer moms in 1996, they made little difference in the election. Pat Schroeder, then a Democratic Representative from Colorado, and a onetime soccer mom herself, characterized *soccer mom* as "one of the most overused terms in America." Ellen Goodman noted after the election: "Suburban, married moms with kids at home were never more than 6 percent of the voters." Moreover, according to exit polls, they voted the same way as female voters generally: 54% to 37% for Bill Clinton (Bob Dole won the male vote, 44% to 43%). For the first time men alone would have elected a different candidate than women. See *gender gap* in GAP.

For the 2008 election, the "dream demographic" may have changed. "Soccer moms were the coveted voting bloc that helped bring President Bill Clinton into power," noted Chris Rovzar in the New York *Daily News*. "This time around, it's the 22% of voters who are never-married women ... between 18 and 44, mobile ... Single Anxious Females—and Hillary has already begun courting their precious vote."

socialism See CREEPING SOCIALISM.

social issue See PSEPHOLOGY.

soft bigotry See REVOLUTION OF RISING EXPECTATIONS.

soft landing Economic slowdown without a full recession; slowed growth of the economy that succeeds in averting inflation.

Astronautics provided the term in the 1950s. In an article on lunar exploration, *The Times* of London reported on March 28, 1958, that "Next (in difficulty) would be a 'soft' (controlled) landing by an unmanned vehicle." That year's *Proceedings of the Lunar and Planetary Exploration Colloquium* repeated the phrase: "With a soft landing on the moon, one might put down a payload of 225 to 800 pounds."

In the '70s, the phrase transferred from space use to economic jargon. *Newsweek* reported in September 1973, "Even if the President succeeds in pulling in the rampaging economy for a soft landing, of course, the arrival will be nonetheless bumpy for many."

By the late '80s, this economic usage was a favorite expression of the Federal Reserve. Robert T. Parry, president of the Federal Reserve Bank of San Francisco, commented in the summer of 1989 that balanced growth "enhances the prospect that we can achieve a soft landing," defining that phrase as "a needed slowdown without a recession.... The goal is to have the economy grow at a slow rate relative to its potential to cause the rate of inflation to come down." A 1989 newsletter from the Federal Reserve Bank of Cleveland offered the headline "How Soft a Landing?"

Caroline A. Baum, a Treasury market commentator, explained, "Economists turned to a nonsocial science like aeronautics for a term that would adequately describe a maneuver designed to land the economy softly without inflicting damage on itself or its payload." *Soft landing* is used in contrast to the stark *crash landing*.

Other fields have been lifting the same space term. In 1985, a commodities dealer hoped "to organize a soft landing for tin." In 1989, an Israeli scientist said, "We have provided a soft landing for a certain number of immigrants," and a *Financial Times* wine critic complained about some sparkling wines, wishing "to arrange a soft landing back into real wine at some point."

soft money See HARD MONEY.

soft on Communism Attack phrase used by those convinced that the United States was in danger from internal Communist subversion, later aimed at accommodationists who did not agree with a HARD LINE posture abroad.

The charge was most often heard during the peak of Senator Joseph McCarthy's influence. The Soviet Union had acquired nuclear weapons and increasingly efficient rockets, a legitimate cause for American concern. In a series of trials and hearings, seemingly respectable and in several cases high-ranking U.S. officials were accused of having been involved in espionage on behalf of Russia. Truman's thoughtless defense of the phrase RED HERRING made the charge more potent.

The case that gave most ammunition to those making the "soft on Communism" charge was that of Alger Hiss, who had held a series of high governmental posts, including working with the U.S. delegation to the Yalta conference. Hiss's denials under oath led to his conviction for perjury. In 1952, Democratic presidential candidate Adlai Stevenson was attacked by Republicans for having made a deposition saying that Alger Hiss's reputation was good. Stevenson said, "My testimony in the Hiss case no more shows softness towards Communism than the testimony of these Republican leaders (Taft, Bricker, and Joe Martin) shows softness towards corruption."

President Harry Truman, belatedly recognizing the public appeal of the attack, said, "The most brazen lie of the century has been fabricated by reckless demagogues among the Republicans to the effect that Democrats were soft on Communism." He added that the Stevenson forces had made a serious tactical error in allowing themselves to be put on the defensive in the campaign by the *soft on Communism* charges.

After the Cold War ended, *soft on* remained a combining form used by the right against the left. Bill Clinton was accused in 1993 of being "soft on Saddam Hussein" and in 2006, President George W. Bush charged that Democrats "talk tough on terror, but when the votes are counted, their softer side comes out." This was headlined in *The*

Washington Post as "Bush Calls Democrats 'Softer' on Terrorists." When President Bush, at a nadir of his popularity in the summer of 2007, warned that any Democratic failure to give him authority for international wiretapping might result in a terrorist attack on the U.S., the anti-war activists backed off and passed the legislation he wanted. Senator Barack Obama was candid about the reason: "Everybody was afraid they might be branded as soft on terrorism."

Solid South The supposedly monolithic vote of the Southern states for the Democratic party, used now more in the breach than in the observance.

Southerners knew after the Civil War that (1) Lincoln and his BLACK REPUBLICANS freed the slaves, and (2) the CARPETBAGGERS and SCALAWAGS descended on them during Reconstruction under a Republican regime. Not surprisingly, the Democratic party had an appeal for white Southerners, who had the vote.

The phrase *Solid South* was popularized by General John Singleton Mosby, a cavalry leader (Mosby's Rangers) on the staff of Confederate General J. E. B. Stuart. Mosby, with his impeccable Southern credentials, startled his Southern friends by coming out in 1876 for Republican Rutherford B. Hayes against Democrat Samuel Tilden. In a widely publicized letter, he wrote: "Suppose Hayes is elected with a solid South against him—what are you going to do then?"

Though this phrase had been used by House Speaker Schuyler Colfax in 1858, Mosby's use—in the context of a Southerner fighting against the solidity of the South—gave it political excitement. "The Solid South," reported *Harper's Weekly* immediately afterward, "is the Southern Democracy seeking domination of the United States through the machinery of the Democratic party."

The phrase delighted Republicans; coined by a renegade Democrat, it helped Republicans slightly in the South and strongly in the North. The *New York Tribune* got the origin wrong, but the result right: "The claim of a 'solid South' is likely to do the Democrats fully as much harm as good. They origi-

nated the expression, and the Republicans are using it with great force against them."

In *The Century Magazine*, Edward Clark wrote:

> The Solid South … came into vogue during the Hayes-Tilden canvass of 1876. The Democratic tidal wave in the elections of 1874 had shown a powerful, if not irresistible, drift toward Democracy in all the then lately reconstructed States, as well as in their sisters on the old borderline which had also maintained slavery, but which had not gone into the rebellion. The alliterative term commended itself to the Republican stump speakers and newspaper organs as a happy catch-word, and the idea which underlay it was impressive enough to arrest the attention of the whole country.

Thomas E. Dewey made the same point in 1950: "The only danger nationally has been that one party might become too strong, or able to use the enormous new powers of government to perpetuate itself in office, as is the case in politically lop-sided, machine-dominated cities or in the 'Solid South.' "

Through the years, the South remained solid for the Democratic party, but in 1928, when Democrat Al Smith was the candidate, his Catholicism and support of Prohibition repeal defeated him in Texas, Florida, Tennessee, and Virginia. All four of those states went for Republican Dwight Eisenhower in 1952 and 1956, and all but Texas for Nixon in 1960. In 1964 the "deep" South was almost solid again, but this time for Republican Barry Goldwater in a vote attributed to the BACKLASH over black civil rights gains. See SOUTHERN STRATEGY.

Tension between Northern Democratic liberals and Southern Democratic conservatives led to an open break in 1948. Governor Strom Thurmond of South Carolina led a delegation of six Democratic governors to a tense meeting at Democratic National Headquarters in Washington, demanding withdrawal of "the highly controversial civil rights legislation." Turned down, they issued a joint statement: "The present leadership of the Democratic party will soon realize that the South is no longer 'in the bag.' " Thurmond ran as a third-party candidate to punish Truman (see DIXIECRAT) and later became a Republican.

The political tradition of the "new South" is a far cry from the situation described in an anecdote used by Harry Dent in his 1978 book *The Prodigal South Returns to Power*: "In 1924 Senator Coleman L. Blease, Democrat of South Carolina, was alarmed to learn that Republican Calvin Coolidge had won 1,123 of 50,131 votes cast in South Carolina in the presidential race. 'I do not know where he got them,' Blease supposedly said. 'I was astonished to know they were cast and shocked to know they were counted.'"

Today the phrase is used mainly by commentators showing that the "solid" South has turned fluid.

Solon Headlinese for legislator; originally meant "wise statesman," now used ironically.

A headline writer who uses "Solons Probe" rather than "Legislators Investigate" saves eleven letters, providing space for two more clichés. Neither *solon* nor *probe* is used in the spoken political language.

Solon, an economist and early Attic poet, was an aristocratic Athenian born about 640 B.C. and referred to by Plato in the *Symposium* as "the revered father of Athenian laws." For other eponymous words in politics, see GERRYMANDER; MAVERICK; PHILIPPIC; QUISLING.

sons of the wild jackass Political irregulars inclined to vote against the party line, especially liberal Republicans; also, reformers in general.

John Hay, later Secretary of State, used *wild ass* in the sense of "unreasonable reformer" in an 1890 letter to Theodore Roosevelt: "You have already shown that a man may be absolutely honest and yet practical; a reformer by instinct and a wise politician; brave, bold, and uncompromising, and yet not a wild ass of the desert." Hay had been a Lincoln secretary and was probably aware of the phrase "wild asses of the desert" in the Book of Job, 24:5.

William Jennings Bryan suggested in 1896 that reforming asses occasionally kicked each other's heads in: "I remember that a few years ago a Populist in Congress stated that the small burros that run wild upon the prairies of South America form a group, when attacked by a ferocious animal, and, putting their heads together and their feet on the outside of the circle, protect themselves from the enemy. But he added that the advocates of reforms sometimes showed less discretion, and turning their heads toward the enemy, kicked each other." (A century later, squabbles within a party were described as "a firing squad lined up in a circle.")

The wild asses of reform or independence were popularized when Republicans in the '20s included a number of Westerners who were indifferent to party discipline. Since they were politically akin to the Populists of an earlier generation, the liberal Westerners tended to look upon the more conservative Eastern portion of the party with suspicion as "lackeys of Wall Street." Senator George H. Moses of New Hampshire, lamenting the alliance between these Republicans and liberal Democrats, which blocked the higher tariffs the GOP leadership wanted, said on the Senate floor in 1924: "Mournfully, I prophesy that the program of these sons of the wild jackass who now control the Senate will probably go forward to complete consummation."

Senator Moses later said his inspiration came from the Old Testament, Jeremiah 14:6: "And the wild asses did stand in the high places, they snuffed up the wind like dragons."

sop to Cerberus See SWEETHEART.

sound bite Snappy recorded snippet.

The presidential campaign of 1988 was characterized by the headline over a David Gergen essay in *U.S. News & World Report*: "The Politics of Sound Bites."

The phrase refers to clips of quick quotations or memorable words on news broadcasts. The earliest print citation is a piece by Sandy Kyle Bain in *The Washington Post* on June 22, 1980. That article described the coaching of candidates on television by William Rhatican: "Remember that any editor watching needs a concise, 30-second sound bite. Anything more than that, you're losing them."

Rhatican told the lexicographer that "the phrase was in the air. I used it in a lecture I gave in the mid-'70s advising political candidates on the use of television: if you wander all over the place in your statements, you won't provide pithy sound bites for TV."

Daniel Schorr, senior news analyst for National Public Radio, dates its use back to the early 1960s when he worked at CBS News. "It came out of the editing room, in the days before videotape," he recalls. "When the producer saw the excerpt he wanted, he'd tell the film editor, 'Take that bite'; out of longer interviews, the bite would be 30 to 45 seconds."

Often the phrase is used to derogate the superficiality of the quick takes—down to an average of eight seconds in the early '90s—of TV and radio news. Reporter Roger Mudd denounced the presidential campaign of 1984 as a mixture of "sound bites and photo opportunities." (The latter term, since shortened to *photo op*, meaning "an event staged for photographs," was a Ron Ziegler coinage during the Nixon Administration.) Both of these media-politics phrases, however, may also be used without a pejorative connotation. After the vice presidential debate in 1988 when Senator Lloyd Bentsen stunned Dan Quayle with "you're no Jack Kennedy" (see YOU'RE NO JACK KENNEDY), Jeff Greenfield of ABC called that riposte "the biggest sound bite of the night."

sources A word used by reporters who want to show they are not originating some information to identify people who are passing on the information but do not want their identity known.

During the "impeachment summer" of 1974, *New York Times* Washington bureau chief Clifton Daniel, concerned about the overuse of anonymous tips in the news columns, posted a memo to his staff:

"Sources" has become a discredited word in our business. Let's stop using it.

Sources are people (or pieces of paper). We should identify them whenever possible. When we cannot identify them, we should describe them as fully and accurately as circumstances permit. We should never misrepresent them— as, for example, by pluralizing a single source.

If we cannot identify or describe a source but have absolute confidence in it, we can use information from that source without attribution. A phrase such as "reliably reported" is better than "sources said." If we don't have confidence in a source, we should not use the information, whether attributable or not.

Sources are usually described as "reliable," sometimes as "usually reliable," never as "an unreliable source." Since the Daniel memo, the phrase "who asked that his name not be used" has been used more frequently. Reporters at the *Times* were also urged to locate sources, as in "an FBI source" or "an Administration source," which sometimes indicates the possible bias at the point of origin. "Sources close to the investigation" are usually police or prosecution.

The noun has been turned into a verb as well: a story that is not *sourced* is considered *unsourced*—that is, either speculative or obtained on "deep background."

See AUTHORITATIVE SOURCES; CHILLING EFFECT.

Southern strategy An attack phrase attributing RACIST or at least political motives toward any position taken on desegregation or BUSING that would be well received by most Southern whites.

In the summer of 1963, the conservative weekly *National Review* published a map showing how Senator Barry Goldwater could win the 1964 election, which included a sweep of the Deep South. In answer to the author's query in 1971, the magazine's publisher, William Rusher, disclaimed coinage of the phrase itself and added:

I would guess that it goes back to some point in the early 1960s at which the liberals finally became aware of the strategy by which the Goldwater forces proposed to win the nomination and the election of 1964. It seems to me much more likely that the term "Southern strategy" was invented by the liberals and fastened by them upon the strategy, since the pejorative implication was that the Goldwater forces were preparing to turn their backs upon the blacks and sell out to southern bigotry. (From our standpoint, of course, the correct term would have been "Southern-Midwestern-Western strategy," since that was what we really had in mind—a coalition of these three against the dominant Northeast; but obviously such a term would have been too cumbersome.)

Somewhat testily, Senator Goldwater nailed down the coinage in a letter to *Business Week* in October 1971:

> The first writer to use the term "southern strategy" was Joe Alsop, after his visit to my office back in the 1950s. At that time I was chairman of the Senate Campaign Committee and had conducted a very in-depth survey of voting trends in the U.S. for President Eisenhower. This survey showed that the only areas in the whole United States where the Republican Party had been making gains were in the Southwest. For that reason we decided to put more emphasis on that part of the nation, where Republicans historically had not done well.
>
> That is the so-called "Southern strategy." It has nothing to do with busing, integration, or any other of the so-called closely held concepts of the Southerner. The South began to move into Republican ranks because of the influx of new and younger businessmen from the North who were basically Republican. And they were aided by young Southern Democrats who were sick and tired of the Democratic stranglehold on the South and switched over to the Republican Party. Nowhere in any platform adopted by the Republican Party since I can remember can there be found any thing aimed directly at the South which could be indicative of some strategy employed by the Republican party that the Republican Party does not employ elsewhere.

Goldwater did carry the Deep South (and only those five states) in the Johnson landslide, giving the phrase a "losing" connotation, as not only a racist strategy, but a politically mistaken one.

In the 1968 presidential campaign, when Nixon's Southern manager, Howard "Bo" Callaway, called for support from voters leaning toward George Wallace, Ward Just wrote in *The Washington Post* that some Republicans "are worried lest Nixon pursue a 'Southern strategy' in his election campaign that would compromise potential support among minority groups and moderates in the North."

Nixon managers let it be known that their 1968 strategy centered on the "battleground" states: California, New Jersey, Pennsylvania, Ohio, Illinois, Michigan, and Texas, only one of which—Texas—was

below the Mason-Dixon line. Don Irwin of the *Los Angeles Times* wrote on July 14, 1968: "Richard M. Nixon's avowed determination to concentrate on voters in large industrial states if he wins the Republican presidential nomination tells much about the election campaign he has in mind. It appears to bar revival of the all-out 'Southern strategy' that proved so disastrous for the GOP in 1964."

It would have been foolish of Nixon to adopt the losing strategy that much of the press had attributed to Goldwater; he did not, and won. However, alliterative phrases die hard. At the Gridiron Dinner spoofing the Nixon Administration in 1970, the hit song of the evening was sung to the tune of "Rock-a-Bye Your Baby with a Dixie Melody":

> *Rock-a-bye the voters with a Southern strategy;*
> *Don't you fuss; we won't bus children in ol'*
> *Dixie!*
> *We'll put George Wallace in decline*
> *Below the Mason-Dixon line ...*
> *A zillion Southern votes we will deliver;*
> *Move Washington down on the Swanee River!*
> *Rockabye with Ol' Massa Nixon and his Dixie*
> *strategy!*

To practical politicians, any strategy that wins one region at the expense of all others is nonsense; however, any national election strategy that seeks to include Southern support is attacked as a *Southern strategy* because it helps the attacker disaffect the opposition's support elsewhere.

Although Georgian Jimmy Carter swept the South in 1976 (excepting Virginia), his strategy was never considered to be "Southern"; he won that region primarily because that was where he came from.

The phrase is firmly fixed in the political lexicon not as a viable strategy, but as a charge of deviousness and discrimination. See SOLID SOUTH.

South Succotash Put-down of rural area; indication of a place's remoteness.

In 1982, President Reagan questioned media coverage of unemployment: "Is it news that some fellow in South Succotash someplace has just been laid off—that he should be interviewed nationwide?"

The alliterative collocation uses a direction (South) to modify the place name, further suggesting remoteness from a center of activity. The name itself comes from the Narragansett *msickquatash,* meaning "ear of corn," and refers to a dish originally made of corn and beans (sometimes with meat), now usually a mixture of corn and lima beans.

In 1991, a Democratic Policy Committee report offered a partisan comparison of the approaches of Democrats and Republicans in helping the unemployed; the report's title was "South Succotash Revisited."

Although there is a Succotash Point in Rhode Island, Reagan's *South Succotash* used a fictional name for his derogation of remote areas. Earlier uses of this technique include *Podunk,* or *East Jesus,* or as LBJ aide Liz Carpenter preferred, *Resume Speed, Texas.*

special interests See VESTED INTERESTS.

special relationship Historical ties between two countries with common values and interests; atypical or exclusionary connection justifying favored treatment.

This term was applied to ties between Britain and the United States at the time of World War II by Prime Minister Winston Churchill, who told the House of Commons on November 7, 1945, "We should not abandon our *special relationship* with the United States and Canada about the atomic bomb." The following March, when Churchill delivered his IRON CURTAIN speech at Westminster College in Fulton, Missouri, he repeated the phrase: "Neither the sure prevention of war nor the continuous rise of world organization will be gained without what I have called the fraternal association of the English-speaking peoples. This means a *special relationship* between the British Commonwealth and Empire and the United States of America."

The pairing with *special* has been noted as a point of contention for countries not part of this relationship. In *The New Yorker* in 1991, John Newhouse wrote of France's "view of Britain as unwilling to put its role in Europe ahead of a *special relationship*

with Washington." The term has also been applied to other pairings, some of which include the United States. *Time* magazine reported in 1991 about an American-Israeli connection, which had suffered under the elder Bush: "If he means what he says, Bush has initiated a fundamental change in America's 'special relationship' with Israel." This breach was healed when the two nations' leaders were Ariel Sharon and George W. Bush.

Other connections may bypass the United States. Abdul Hamid Sharif, Jordan's envoy to the U.S., commented in 1977, "Gaza used to be under Egyptian administration, and there is a *special relationship* between all the Arab countries and the Palestinians." The most frequent usage of the phrase, though, still refers to the British/American connection. Henry Brandon of London's *Sunday Times* used the term as the title of his memoirs in 1988.

Not everybody agreed that the U.K./U.S. special relationship is necessarily positive. As early as 1981, in fact, a *Washington Post* column by Philip Geyelin questioned the connection: "This supposedly 'special relationship' is not so much a tradition as it is a sometime thing, evoked for particular purposes at particularly propitious times. One thinks of the pen-pal relationship between Winston Churchill and Franklin Roosevelt; one forgets Suez, or John F. Kennedy being taken neatly to the cleaners in the matter of the Skybolt missile at Nassau by his good friend Harold Macmillan, or Lyndon Johnson upbraiding the British over the sale of buses to Cuba."

On the other side of the Atlantic, a 1992 editorial in Britain's *Independent* stated, "The special relationship between this country and the United States is at its worst when the American authorities demonstrate arrogance and insensitivity and their British counterparts are supine."

In 2006, after the second Iraq war caused George W. Bush's popularity to plummet in Britain along with that of Prime Minister Tony Blair, David Cameron, leader of the Tory opposition in Parliament, said, "we should be solid but not slavish in our friendship with America."

speechwriter One who writes speeches on assignment; for differentiation between *ghost, wordsmith, research assistant,* and *press secretary,* see GHOSTWRITER.

Robert Smith, who had done a creditable job as Secretary of the Navy under Thomas Jefferson, faced a problem when he was promoted to Secretary of State by the new President, James Madison: Smith was no writer. Wisely, he accepted the ghostwriting services of the best writer in the federal employ at the time: President Madison.

The President did not consider it menial work; Jefferson and Hamilton and he had helped Washington in the preparation of his Farewell Address, which stands out over most of the first president's prose. Washington had asked them to look over his version, which he asked be "curtailed, if too verbose; and relieved of all tautology, not necessary to enforce the ideas in the original or quoted part. My wish is, that the whole may appear in a plain stile; and be handed to the public in an honest; unaffected; simple garb."

Judge Samuel Rosenman, who worked on speeches with FDR, justified a presidential speechwriter's existence on the basis that "there just is not enough time in a president's day" to handle the chore. Some point out that Abraham Lincoln served in a busy era, wrote his own speeches, and turned out some of the best in the English language. But Lincoln, it is argued, had a knack for it; the presidency has grown in complexity; chief executives—even senators and congressmen—should not take time from their busy schedules to labor over a speech, certainly not its first draft. And since presidential words carry such import, why not get a great writer to put them down in the clearest, most inspirational way?

The columnist and author Walter Lippmann in 1942 was having none of this. In a column entitled "Something Off My Chest," he wrote:

A public man can and needs to be supplied with material and advice and criticism in preparing an important address. But no one can write an authentic speech for another man; it is as impossible as writing his love letters for him or saying his prayers for him. When he speaks to the people, he and not someone else must speak. For it is much more important that he could be genuine, and it is infinitely more persuasive, than that he be bright, clever, ingenious, entertaining, eloquent, or even grammatical.

It is, moreover, a delusion, fostered into an inferiority complex among executives by professional writers, that in an age of specialists some are called to act and some are called to find the right words for men of action to use. The truth is that anyone who knows what he is doing can say what he is doing, and anyone who knows what he thinks can say what he thinks. Those who cannot speak for themselves are, with very rare exceptions, not very sure of what they are doing and of what they mean. The sooner they are found out the better.

Lippmann's view did not prevail; the public does not frown on a president having speechwriters, indeed has come to expect a president to work from others' drafts. The idea of a speechwriter's assignment, in most people's minds, is one gently sold by every top-level speechwriter: to discuss the speech ideas with the public figure, reflect his point of view clearly and in organized fashion, to submit extra phrases and slogans for the top man's consideration, and to rewrite according to the speaker's wishes. This is sometimes what happens.

Who were the modern speechwriters for presidents? Here is a compilation with names listed alphabetically and not in order of importance, to avoid brickbats from friends and colleagues. It does not include others who occasionally contributed speeches in whole or part, or suggested themes or edited speeches but whose responsibilities were not primarily speechwriting.

FDR's became well known: editor Stanley High, Professor Raymond Moley, lawyer Donald Richberg, Judge Samuel Rosenman, and dramatist Robert E. Sherwood, were among them.

Truman's writers were almost anonymous: Clark Clifford, George Elsey, Ken Hechler, William Hillman, Milton Kayle, Charles J. Murphy, and Rosenman contributed from time to time.

Dwight Eisenhower used Stephen Benedict, William Ewald, Bryce Harlow, Gabriel Hauge, Stephen Hess, Emmet Hughes,

Robert Kieve, Arthur Larson, Kevin McCann, and Malcolm Moos, among others.

With Kennedy, writers became famous again: Myer Feldman, John Galbraith, Richard Goodwin, Arthur Schlesinger, Jr., and Ted Sorensen were already well known or became so.

Lyndon Johnson began with Kennedy holdovers, and soon found journalist Horace Busby, Joseph Califano, Douglass Cater, Ervin Duggan, Harry McPherson, Harry Middleton, and Ben Wattenberg, with Jack Valenti both writing and editing.

The Nixon writing and research operation was headed by editor James Keogh for two years, with Raymond K. Price replacing him. The senior writers, along with Price, were William Safire and Patrick Buchanan. Other writers included John Andrews, William Gavin, David Gergen, Lee Huebner, Noel Koch, Tex Lezar, and John McLaughlin, with researchers Ceil Bellinger and Anne Morgan.

Gerald Ford's speechwriters were Aram Bakshian (who returned with Reagan), David Boorstin, Patrick Butler, Milton (not the economist) Friedman, Robert Hartman, humorist Bob Orben, and Paul Theis.

Jimmy Carter employed the services of Bernard Aronson, Jerome Doolittle, James Fallows, Hendrik Hertzberg, Christopher Matthews, Achsah Nesmith, Walter Shapiro, Griffin Smith, and Gordon Stewart.

Ronald Reagan writers were Anthony Dolan, Bentley Elliott, Joshua Gilder, Clark Judge, Peggy Noonan (returning with the elder Bush), Landon Parvin, John Podhoretz, Peter Robinson, and Dana Rohrabacher.

George H.W. Bush writers were Mary Kate Cary, Andrew Ferguson, Dan McGroarty, Edward McNally, Curt Smith, and Anthony Snow.

Bill Clinton had Don Baer, Anthony Blinken, Robert Boorstin, Carolyn Curiel, Terry Edmonds, Paul Glastris, David Kusnet, Jonathan Prince, Jeff Shesol, Jordan Tamagni, and Michael Waldman.

George W. Bush ("Bush 43") writers include David Frum, Michael Gerson, Jonathan Horn, Matt Latimer, John McConnell, William McGurn, Chris Michel, Noam Neusner, Matthew Scully, and Marc Theissen.

All those named above who are still living are members of the Judson Welliver Society, a Washington-based association of former White House speechwriters. (The Bush 43 writers, not yet "former," are candidate-members.) The Society, formed in the '80s by Harlow, Clifford, Sorensen, Valenti, and the author (dubbed "foundering president"), was named after the writer who held the title "literary clerk" for Presidents Harding and Coolidge. Mr. Welliver was the first full-time White House speechwriter (and never received credit for the reputation for eloquence held by "Silent Cal").

One question nags public figures employing speechwriters: writers are dangerous, because they publish—will this or that speechwriter kiss and tell? Emmet Hughes, who enjoyed Eisenhower's confidence and did much campaign speechwriting, infuriated Republicans later with what they considered a too-revealing book, *The Ordeal of Power*; Ted Sorensen, John Kennedy's alter ego of the written word, respected many confidences in his 1965 memoirs and was criticized for being too discreet; his 2008 memoir supplemented it. At the first meeting of the Nixon campaign team for the 1968 race, the candidate introduced the author to the original cadre, only half in jest, with "and watch what you say—he's a writer."

spellbinder An orator capable of fascinating and even persuading an audience, at least temporarily; also, a speech of that type.

This is based on *spellbound*, which means "fascinated, enthralled" in the way a cobra is spellbound by a fakir's flute. Its political debut occurred in the 1888 presidential campaign. The *New York Tribune* wrote: "A big and successful dinner was given at Delmonico's by the Republican Orators—'Spellbinders'—who worked during the recent campaign." The Republican STUMP speakers were widely publicized during that race between Grover Cleveland and Benjamin Harrison (which the Republican, Harrison, narrowly won); William Cassius Goodloe was quoted in 1888 as pointing to one and remarking, "Here comes another of the spellbinders!"

The word is current, though the practice is not; historian Eric Goldman termed General Omar Bradley as "the last man anyone would pick for a spellbinder" in Bradley's surprisingly effective attack on General MacArthur's Korean strategy in 1951. See WRONG WAR.

A gripping speech is a *spellbinder*; a rousing speech is a STEMWINDER; a low blow, or a bodyguard, is a *sidewinder*; an influential but crude or dishonest politician is a *highbinder*, as in this 1920 use by Emporia, Kansas *Gazette* editor William A. White: "a lot of old high-binder standpatters who haven't had an idea since the fall of Babylon ..."

spend and spend A New Deal philosophy, attributed to Harry Hopkins, emphasizing the vote-getting potential of federal projects.

Hopkins, who after Louis Howe's death became FDR's closest aide, is supposed to have said to theatrical producer Max Gordon at the Empire Race Track in New York in August 1938: "We will spend and spend, and tax and tax, and elect and elect."

Others in Gordon's box that day denied having heard any such thing; Hopkins denied it; that left Gordon, who had passed the remark to a columnist, out on a limb. He had not realized how the phrase could be used against his friend Hopkins, but he could not call it back. The theatrical producer was in this dilemma for forty years, and it bothered him. When reached on the telephone by the author before he died in 1978, Gordon said—as if reading from a small card in his desk blotter—"I have absolutely nothing whatsoever to say about the incident, thank you and goodbye."

Whether or not Hopkins said it (and on the basis of Gordon's refusal to recant, my judgment is that Hopkins did say it) the phrase has been used to attack BIG GOVERNMENT as having raised the PORK BARREL to national policy.

Jonathan Daniels wrote in 1966 of the Tennessee Valley Authority: "As the most damned New Dealer, Harry Hopkins had little to do with its building, yet ... it loomed as the embodiment of his supposed philosophy 'spend and spend, tax and tax, elect and elect.'"

The phrase is often remembered in this form: tax, tax, tax—spend, spend, spend—elect, elect, elect. A 1967 cartoon by Hesse of the *St. Louis Globe-Democrat* showed President Johnson groping in an empty bag for dollars saying, "Like I say—tax, tax—spend, spe ..."

When the most liberal of Senate Republicans, Lincoln Chafee of Rhode Island, was challenged in a 2006 primary by Stephen Laffey, a most conservative Republican mayor, the Chafee defenders—seeking to hold a GOP seat in a strongly Democratic state—attacked the rightwing challenger in TV spots with a compound adjective inverting two-thirds of the phrase, as "tax-and-spend Steve Laffey." The unorthodox attack on an anti-tax, anti-spending challenger worked; Chafee won the Republican nomination (but lost the general election).

spending cap Limit on spending; maximum allowance for expenses.

John K. Inglehart reported in *National Journal* in 1977 that "A little-noticed aspect of the [Carter] Administration's proposal would impose an annual spending cap of $2.5 billion on hospital facilities."

Such a limitation may be expressed either as an actual amount ("$2.5 billion") or as a percentage ("a 2 percent spending cap"). The phrase, using a metaphorical sense of *cap* as "a cover or top," comes from the image of *capping* an oil well. Fred Mish, editor of Merriam-Webster, told the author of its possible first usage: "We have a somewhat ambiguous citation from *The Wall Street Journal* of May 22, 1972, applying the term to a 'rule' (perhaps a Federal regulation) which limited the extent to which certain companies could raise their prices at that time."

The term became one of George H.W. Bush's campaign pledges during his unsuccessful reelection bid. A *New York Times* report in August 1992: "Mr. Bush favors a Constitutional amendment requiring a balanced budget and says he would put a spending cap on 'mandatory programs.'"

Bill Clinton helped popularize the term soon after his election: "We stayed below the spending caps approved by this Congress, including the Republicans." Not only spending is subject to the possible imposition of *caps*; soon after, *The Washington Post* asserted the possibility of medical-cost controls: "Health Care Price Caps Considered," as an element in what critics soon labeled "Hillarycare," which resurfaced in her campaign for president in 2007–08.

sphere of influence An economically undeveloped or militarily weak area under the domination of a great power, usually with the agreement or tacit acceptance of other great powers.

Winston Churchill could remember the Anglo-Russian agreement of 1907 dividing Persia into separate spheres of influence— the North for Russia, the South for England; the phrase came naturally to him in 1946, in his IRON CURTAIN speech at Fulton, Mo.: "Warsaw, Berlin, Prague, Vienna, Budapest, Belgrade, Bucharest and Sofia, all these famous cities and the populations around them lie in what I might call the Soviet sphere, and all are subject, in one form or another, not only to Soviet influence but to a very high and in some cases increasing measure of control from Moscow."

The diplomatic phrase, coined in 1885 and best described by Merriam-Webster's *New International Dictionary* (2nd edition) as "regions more or less under the control of a nation, but not constituting a formally recognized protectorate or suzerainty," has been used along with *sphere of interest*, *sphere of action*, *field of operations*, and *zone of influence* for more than a century. In 1993, former Prime Minister Margaret Thatcher said that the war in Bosnia may be beyond our "sphere of interest" but is within our "sphere of conscience."

spin Deliberate shading of news perception; attempted control of political reaction.

Beginning as a verb meaning "to whirl," by the '50s *spin* also meant "to deceive," perhaps based on *to spin a yarn*. Functional shift occurred in the nineteenth cen-

tury, turning the verb into the noun *spin*, used for the curve or twist put upon a ball in cricket (in billiards, that spin is known as *English*), just as pitchers nowadays put a *spin* on baseballs. Like its synonym *twist*, *spin* is now both a verb and a noun.

Spin entered the political lexicon in the late '70s. Referring to the Carter administration, *The New Yorker* reported on January 15, 1979: "The White House aides are growing concerned that there may indeed be a fight tomorrow over the budget resolution, and they won't rule out the possibility that they might lose; they are even beginning to try to figure out what 'spin' to put on it for the press in that event." The quotes around the term suggest that it was relatively new at the time.

By the 1984 presidential campaign, *spin* inspired the phrase *spin doctor*. A *New York Times* editorial in that year commented on the televising of presidential debates: "Tonight at about 9:30, seconds after the Reagan-Mondale debate ends, a bazaar will suddenly materialize in the press room. ... A dozen men in good suits and women in silk dresses will circulate smoothly among the reporters, spouting confident opinions. They won't be just press agents trying to impart a favorable spin to a routine release. They'll be the Spin Doctors, senior advisers to the candidates."

Four days after its first print appearance, *spin doctor* was lowercased and defined by Elisabeth Bumiller in *The Washington Post:* "the advisers who talk to reporters and try to put their own spin, or analysis, on the story."

Spin doctor may be based on the slang sense of the verb *doctor*, as in illegally *doctoring* records; the noun phrase was built on the analogy of *play doctor*, a writer who fixes an ailing script. An earlier German term that may have led to the political *spin doctor* is *Kopfverdreher*, which literally means "head turner" and figuratively suggests "mind bender."

Spin terms have spun several derivatives, from *spin control* by *spin doctors* or SPINMEISTERS who have formed a *spin patrol* operating in an area called *spin valley*.

spinmeister A disparaging term for an expert at presenting negative facts in the most positive possible way.

Spinmeister surfaced shortly after the synonymous *spin doctor* (see SPIN). The oldest example in the *OED* comes from *Newsweek* in 1986: "The spinmeisters can't take all the credit for the burst of patriotic solidarity." The *-meister* suffix (from the Yiddish *meyster*, "master") has been attached to many words over the years, always with negative impact. Among them: *hypemeister, jargonmeister, newsmeister, perkmeister* (one who dispenses favors and patronage in political organizations), and, the closest parallel to *spinmeister* and perhaps partly an inspiration for it, *schlockmeister*, where *schlock* (probably from the German *Schlacke*, "dregs, dross") applies to cheap or shoddy goods of all sorts, including information. For example, from James Michael Ullman's 1965 novel, *Good Night, Irene:* "Public relations, an elastic term that encompasses everything from crude schlockmeisters operating out of phone booths to high-powered representatives of billion-dollar corporations."

The title of *spinmeister* has been awarded to a wide variety of personages, including political consultants, staffers, publicists, pundits, press secretaries, and office-holders, from the president on down. Calvin Trillin entitled one of his "deadline poems" for *The Nation* in 2006 "'Mushroom Cloud' Rice, The Icy Spinmeister, Tries Again." This was an allusion to Secretary of State Condoleezza Rice's 2002 likening of Saddam Hussein's suspected nuclear weapons program to a smoking gun that could turn into a mushroom cloud.

In using the word applied to women, *spinmeister* is practically required, since the grammatically logical alternative for a female spinner of *spin* would be *spinster*, a term that was once gender-neutral but which has been applied mainly to unmarried women, pejoratively "old maids," for the last several centuries. See also SMOKING GUN.

spirit of The aura of hope surrounding summit meetings, born of the chance that reasonable negotiators can lessen the threat of war.

The Spirit of '76 was a favorite name for newspapers just after the American Revolution. On September 13, 1808, a Richmond, Virginia, journal was issued under that name; in Goshen, New York, the *Orange County Patriot; or, The Spirit of Seventy-Six* started five months later. The phrase was frequently used as a colorful masthead for political campaign newspapers, but made its greatest impact as the title of a painting of a boy, an old man, and a Continental Army soldier by Archibald Willard in 1876 shown at the Philadelphia Centennial Exhibition. (The painting now hangs in the Marblehead, Mass., town hall.)

In its international relations sense, *spirit of* was originated by President Eisenhower at the Geneva Conference of 1955. On July 15, before he left for Geneva, Eisenhower warned "as long as this spirit that has prevailed up to now continues to prevail in the world, we cannot expose our rights, our privileges, our homes, our wives, our children to the risk which would come to an unarmed country." Three days later, at the conference, he said, "We are here in response to the peaceful aspirations of mankind to start the kind of discussions which will inject a new spirit into our diplomacy ..." On his return, he continued to summon that spirit in a July 25 speech: "if we can change the spirit in which these conferences are conducted we will have taken the greatest step toward peace ..."

By August 25 the word had caught on enough for him to title a speech to the American Bar Association "The Spirit of Geneva," making this point:

Whether or not such a spirit as this will thrive through the combined intelligence and understanding of men, or will shrivel in the greed and ruthlessness of some, is for the future to tell. But one thing is certain. This spirit and the goals we seek could never have been achieved by violence or when men and nations confronted each other with hearts filled with fear and hatred. At Geneva we strove to help establish this spirit.

British Prime Minister Anthony Eden returned home with what he called "this simple message to the world: it has reduced the danger of war." Foreign Minister Harold Macmillan, who had gleefully said, "there ain't gonna be any war," discovered at a Foreign Ministers' conference three months later that the Soviet attitude had hardened; "once more we are back in the strange nightmare where men use the same words to mean different things." But Macmillan remained optimistic: "The Geneva spirit if it is anything is an inward spirit. Its light is not bright today. It burns low. But it burns."

What Eisenhower had heralded as "evidence of a new friendliness in the world" proved illusory. Soviet activity in the Middle East late in 1955 added to the disenchantment. The next spirit to be conjured was *the spirit of Camp David,* scene of another Khrushchev-Eisenhower meeting in 1959. Camp David is a presidential mountain retreat, called "Shangri-La" by FDR. (That name was taken from FDR's evasive reply when asked where U.S. aircraft that attacked Tokyo early in World War II were based. FDR took the mythical name from a James Hilton novel; Eisenhower renamed the camp after his grandson.) Pictures of the two world leaders strolling through the rustic setting raised hopes once more, quickly dashed by the abortive Paris summit conference and the incident of the downed U-2 reconnaissance plane.

A spirit-haunted President Kennedy met Khrushchev in Vienna in 1961. The new President, wrote Ted Sorensen, "wanted no one to think that the surface cordiality in Vienna justified any notion of a new 'Spirit of Geneva, 1955,' or 'Spirit of Camp David, 1959.' But he may have 'over-managed' the news. His private briefings of the press were so grim, while Khrushchev in public appeared so cheerful, that a legend soon arose that Vienna had been a traumatic, shattering experience, that Khrushchev had bullied and browbeaten the President and that Kennedy was depressed and disheartened."

Meeting in Glassboro, New Jersey, in the aftermath of the Arab-Israeli war of 1967, President Johnson and Soviet Premier Alexei Kosygin met in a world atmosphere that no longer took its spirits straight. Wrote the *Times* of London: "Atmospherics, of course, tend to be transient. The spirit of Geneva and the spirit of Camp David were short-lived."

Thus the use of *spirit of* changed from hope to derision, or at least suspicion and more recently back toward hope. The Soviet Union, in the late '70s, often complained that the Carter campaign for HUMAN RIGHTS endangered the "spirit of DÉTENTE."

That skeptical attitude was that of Hotspur's, in Shakespeare's *Henry IV,* Part I, who replied to Glendower's boast that he could "call spirits from the vasty deep" with "Why, so can I, or so can any man; But will they come when you do call for them?"

See SUMMITRY.

splendid misery See LONELIEST JOB IN THE WORLD.

splinter group A dissident faction that splits away from a larger group; if it forms a party, it becomes a *splinter party.*

"When you get too big a majority," House Speaker Sam Rayburn used to say, "you're immediately in trouble." This became known as "Rayburn's Law," growing out of the Speaker's difficulty in keeping his Democratic majority in line during FDR's second term. "Mr. Sam" felt that lopsided majorities had a way of producing splinter parties and factions along regional, ethnic, or economic lines.

Wooden metaphors abound in politics: PRESIDENTIAL TIMBER, PLATFORM, *plank,* and *splinter* the least significant of them all.

More than several splinter groups or parties produce a *multiparty system* (as against the TWO-PARTY SYSTEM) and often produce a weak government; the expression "always falling, never fallen" referred to the tendency of French governments to fall as factions bickered, though the French Republic went on. In postwar France, the political return of Charles de Gaulle fused many of the parties of the center and the right; the General himself called one of the smaller splinter groups "that party with six members and seven tendencies!"

In the 1972 presidential campaign, McGovern manager Frank Mankiewicz went to a Reform Democratic club on the West Side of Manhattan to instill enthusiasm for his candidate. After several hours with the articulate, highly splintered group, he came out and said, playing on an old lyric, "Every little meaning has a movement all its own."

See BOLT; THIRD-PARTY MOVEMENT.

split ticket A ballot cast by a voter choosing individual candidates without regard for party slates.

A party regular will vote a *straight ticket*; an independent is more likely to vote a *split ticket*, choosing a candidate for governor from one party, a senator from another, an assemblyman possibly from a third.

The candidate at the top of the ticket is expected to discourage ticket splitting (see COATTAILS); a candidate's strength is sometimes measured in terms of how many of the opposing party regulars he can get to split their tickets and "cross over" to vote for him or her. However, it is considered disloyal to appeal to voters to vote a split ticket—in effect, this urges voters to cast their ballots against a candidate's running mates. For this reason, separate committees are formed, called "Democrats for [some Republican]" and vice versa, or "Independents for —."

The expression is found in an 1846 biography of Martin Van Buren: "I was reproached by you for having voted a 'split ticket.'" In 1904 the *New York Post* patiently explained to voters: "To vote a split ticket, which is one for candidates of different parties, the voter should make a cross mark before the name of every candidate for whom he wishes to vote."

Political scientist Clinton Rossiter pointed out in 1960 that the American electorate was tending toward greater reliance on issues and personalities, less on party affiliation. "Thanks to the looseness of legal definitions of party affiliation, to the fact that most of us are called upon to vote several times a year, and to the multiplicity of choices to be made in any one election, we enjoy unusual opportunities to be inconstant and even wayward; and every study made of this subject in recent years confirms the suspicion, with which our politicians must live bravely, that we seize these opportunities gaily. If ticket splitting is our privilege, ticket splitting is our delight."

For other types of tickets, see LAUNDRY TICKET and BALANCED TICKET; for a look at those most likely to split, see SWING VOTER; for the most selective of all, see BULLET VOTE.

spoiler A candidate with no realistic hope of winning, but capable of splitting another's vote, thereby lessening a potential winner's chances.

Rarely is a candidate defeated for a nomination so vindictive as to run in the general election solely to ruin the chances of the nominee who defeated him. It is not smart politics, as it throws away the chance of toppling the chosen nominee another day. More often, a third-party motive is (1) to provide a place for a PROTEST VOTE on a matter of principle, (2) to build a third party into a balance-of-power situation, or (3) the self-hypnosis of a long-shot chance of winning.

In *Tigers of Tammany* Alfred Connable and Edward Silverfarb wrote in 1967 of the fight between the "Barnburners" and the "Hunkers" in 1848; when the conservative Hunkers won, nominating Michigan Democratic Senator Lewis Cass, the antislavery Barnburners bolted and joined the Free Soilers to nominate Martin Van Buren. "Martin Van Buren's last political act was to run on principle and thereby doom to defeat the party which he had once unified... Tammany's allegiance was split... Van Buren was the 'spoiler' in a three-way race."

National Review editor William F. Buckley ran for mayor of New York in 1965 on the Conservative ticket against Republican-Liberal John Lindsay and Democrat Abraham Beame. His purpose was not to win (when asked what he would do in that eventuality, Buckley replied, "Demand a recount") but to build the Conservative party in New York State as a threat to Republicans ready to nominate too-MODERATE candidates. He was dubbed a "spoiler" by supporters of Lindsay, who later became a Democrat.

Conservative Republicans after Senator Barry Goldwater's overwhelming defeat in 1964 placed a portion of the blame on Governor Nelson Rockefeller, whose primary battles had placed the TRIGGER-HAPPY tag on Goldwater. Conservative Congressman John M. Ashbrook of Ohio said of Rockefeller in 1967: "he's a great administrator and has a fine personality. But the heart of the problem is his party posture—he's a spoiler." Ashbrook went on to challenge President Nixon in the 1972 Republican primaries; his party-splitting effort did not spoil the subsequent Nixon landslide of 61% of the popular vote; of the 53 U.S. presidential elections since Washington ran unopposed, this was matched only by Harding in 1920, FDR in 1936 and LBJ in 1964.

The colorful billionaire Ross Perot was not often called a spoiler in 1992 because he drew support from voters in both major parties as well as independents, because his "great sucking sound" criticism of loss of jobs to Mexico had a nativist appeal, and because in the summer he led the elder Bush and Clinton in opinion polls. His 19% showing in the popular vote was the highest since former president Theodore Roosevelt's 1912 campaign as an independent "Bull Moose." (TR outpolled his fellow Republican, William Howard Taft, thereby making possible the victory of Democrat Woodrow Wilson; that qualifies "Teddy" to be the leading spoiler in American politics.)

Ralph Nader, a name to which the informal title "consumer advocate" is riveted, was denounced as a spoiler by Democrats in 2004 because he drew three million votes that supporters of John Kerry thought would mostly go to their candidate. Asked by the author in 2004 for his definition of a spoiler, Nader offered a choice of three: (1) "A spoiler is any candidate who refuses to believe that the two largest parties own all the voters in America"; (2) "any candidate who is perceived as drawing votes away from a Democrat so long as this candidate is not a Republican"; and, with apologies to Ambrose Bierce, (3) "A spoiler is any person who dares to exercise his or her First Amendment rights *inside* the electoral arena but *outside* the two-party duopoly."

When rumors spread in the fall of 2007 that New York City's billionaire mayor Mike Bloomberg—a Democrat-turned-Republican-turned-Independent—might be a third-party candidate for president, a worried fundraiser for Hillary Clinton was quoted saying, "I don't think Mike Bloomberg wants his legacy to be that of a spoiler."

spoils system Staffing the government by awarding the fruits of party victory to loyal partisans; opposite of *merit system*.

The first political use found so far in the U.S. was in 1812, in the Massachusetts House of Representatives: "The weaker members of the party would be overlooked ... whilst the more powerful would disagree in the division of the spoils."

"The country is treated as a conquered province," said Congressman J. S. Johnson in 1830, objecting to the political appointments of Democrat Andrew Jackson, "and the offices distributed among the victors, as the spoils of the war."

Two years later, Senator William Marcy of New York, defending President Jackson's appointment of Martin Van Buren as ambassador to Great Britain from an attack by Senator Henry Clay, gave the phrase greater currency: "The politicians of New York are not as fastidious as some gentlemen are as to disclosing the principles on which they act. They boldly preach what they practice ... If they are successful, they claim, as a matter of right, the advantages of success. They see nothing wrong in the rule, that 'to the victor belong the spoils of the enemy.'"

Clay turned the "rule" into a weapon against the Democrats in 1840: "If we acted on the avowed and acknowledged principle of our opponents, 'that the spoils belong to the victors,' we should indeed be unworthy of the support of the people."

Marcy, who served later as governor of New York, Secretary of War and Secretary of State, is remembered mainly with scorn because of the popularization of the phrase. His reputation was further besmirched much later when a Tammany politician named Richard Tweed was said (falsely) to have named his son after the distinguished American statesman, and William

Marcy Tweed—and his "ring"—became the essence of bossism.

The word *spoils*, in its sense of Roman plunder, was used in the Bible as the Israelites were told, "Ye shall spoil the Egyptians," an instruction carried out in 1967, and in Shakespeare: "Are all thy conquests, glories, triumphs, spoils, shrunk to this small measure?"

Jackson's Administration increased the use of patronage started by Jefferson, and historians like to quote a quite uncharacteristic 1818 letter from Jackson, then a General, to Jefferson's protégé, President James Monroe: "By selecting characters most conspicuous for their probity, virtue, capacity and firmness without regard to party…you will acquire for yourself a name as imperishable as monumental marble." When President Jackson was queried later about this letter by one of his private secretaries, he replied, "We are never too old to learn."

Jackson was not the spoilsman he was made out to be; despite the "new broom" and the CLEAN SWEEP, only about 9 percent of federal officeholders were removed in his first year of office, and less than 20 percent of all previously appointed officeholders were removed on political grounds during his entire two terms. (President Benjamin Harrison changed 31,000 out of 55,000 local postmasters within one year.)

The spoils system became the target of civil service reformers, aided by statements like this made by Tammany boss Richard Croker after the election of Thomas Gilroy as mayor of New York in 1893: "You may say for me that offices will be held by politicians." Carl Schurz ripped into the system a year later: "The spoils system, that practice which turns public offices, high and low, from public trusts into objects of prey and booty for the victorious party, may without extravagance of language be called one of the greatest criminals in our history, if not the greatest."

In modern political usage, *spoils* is used mainly for historical purposes; the more benign PATRONAGE has replaced it in regard to appointments. The nature of spoils has changed as well; today, favoritism toward certain defense companies, franchises granted large contributors, discretion shown in the failure to prosecute possible antitrust cases, the placement of bond issues and insurance policies through FAT CAT supporters, and "revolving-door" employment to friendly officials add up to a much more lucrative version of spoils than the primitive fruits of an earlier day.

Political leaders now meet to *slice the pie* rather than *divide the spoils*; RIPPER BILLS are a help in placing power in party hands, and DESERVING DEMOCRATS is a phrase now only used by Republicans.

In his 1922 novel *The Beautiful and Damned*, F. Scott Fitzgerald coined an apt turnaround: "The victor belongs to the spoils."

spokesman See BACKGROUNDER.

spontaneous demonstration A carefully planned, organized, and routed march around the crowded hall at a national convention by delegates to demonstrate support of a candidacy.

At the "Bull Moose" party convention in 1912, according to historian George E. Mowry,

Fifteen thousand people roared their welcome [to Theodore Roosevelt]. For 52 minutes, wildly waving red bandanas, they cheered him as they had never cheered anyone else. Here were no claques, no artificial demonstration sustained by artificial devices. None were needed. Men and women simply stood on their feet for an hour because they liked him and believed in him. When Roosevelt himself finally sought to stop the demonstration, the crowd once more broke into song.

In the 1940 Republican convention, the balconies were "packed" with Willkie supporters; their overpowering "We Want Willkie" chant, cued by the candidate's campaign managers, helped sway the convention delegates away from Taft. Ever since, tickets have been carefully allocated to prevent a recurrence. See PACKING THE GALLERIES.

In the 1964 Republican convention at San Francisco's Cow Palace, these were the ground rules laid down by the Republican

National Committee for spontaneous demonstrations:

1. Goldwater and Scranton demonstrations to last 22 minutes before gaveling; Rockefeller 11 minutes; all others as long as they like up to 11 minutes. 2. No more than 200 outside demonstrators permitted inside the hall, inclusive of candidate's band, and they must exit at end of demonstration. Twelve-piece National Committee band available for all demonstrations. 3. Only those signs and banners carried by 200 demonstrators permitted; no "stashing" inside hall beforehand; delegates could also carry in signs. 4. Parade route carefully delineated, not to obscure television cameras inside hall. 5. No "drops" of balloons from ceiling.

In practice, each of these rules was deliberately broken by each candidate. Tickets were counterfeited by Goldwater and Scranton forces; Rockefeller had lent most of his convention staff to Scranton, and—as floor manager of that skeleton crew—the author purchased the counterfeit tickets for an extra hundred Rockefeller demonstrators from the other two camps (from the Goldwater group at $3 each, from Scranton managers at $5 each). Ticket takers at the gate would collect tickets from incoming demonstrators and sell them to floor managers, who would toss them over the fence to more demonstrators.

Each group had a secret cache of signs, banners, and noisemakers hidden inside the Cow Palace; the Goldwater managers infuriated the Scranton men by springing a "drop" of gold confetti instead of balloons, staying within the letter of the rules.

The only truly spontaneous demonstration was for Senator Hiram Fong of Hawaii, whose small parade was joined by many delegates who felt like a walk around the hall and could hardly be criticized for paying tribute to the first non-Caucasian placed in nomination.

After one losing candidate's demonstration, the floor manager was given the supreme accolade by the campaign manager: "I watched it on television, and you couldn't tell it from the real thing."

"A convention feels about demonstrations somewhat like the big man who had a small wife who was in the habit of beating him," wrote William Jennings Bryan. "When asked why he permitted it, he replied that it seemed to please her and did not hurt him." See VOICE FROM THE SEWER.

spook A ghostwriter; or, a professional spy or intelligence agency analyst.

Speechwriters occasionally refer to themselves as *spooks*, derived from a synonym for ghostwriter. Also used as a verb, to *spook* a book; when given credit on the cover, the ghost is known as an *as-told-to*.

From the phantomlike operations of its covert agents, *spook* is a friendly, bantering name for spy. In a 1967 story on the Director of the Central Intelligence Agency, *Time* magazine wrote: "Dick Helms has been, in Washington parlance, a 'spook' for nearly 25 years."

After reporter Seymour Hersh in 1975 revealed spying on American citizens by the CIA (usurping the FBI role in internal security) and a Senate select committee chaired by Frank Church reported on its investigation, the term lost its madcap, likable, breezy quality and absorbed much of the disapproval directed at the intelligence agency. A controversy arose in 1977 over the use of journalists as "cover" by the CIA, which *The New York Times* denounced: "American readers have a right to assurance that the journalists they trust for information are not in any sense accountable to unseen paymasters." This was countered by an editorial entitled "The Spooks and the Press" in *The Washington Star* approvingly quoting former columnist Joseph Alsop: "I've done things for [the CIA] when I thought they were the right thing to do. I call it doing my duty as a citizen." His view, which would endanger reporters working in totalitarian or autocratic countries, is not shared by most journalists. See CIA-ESE.

spookspeak The language of espionage; for a brush pass of the lexicon, see CIA-ESE.

sports metaphors

Shakespeare recognized the value of a sports metaphor in politics; King Henry V exhorted his troops before Harfleur: "I see you stand like greyhounds in the slips, straining upon the start. The game's afoot …"

It has been afoot ever since, given impetus by the probably apocryphal Duke of Wellington quote, "The battle of Waterloo was won on the playing fields of Eton." Football is especially well represented: "Politics is like football," John F. Kennedy passed along an aphorism to Pierre Salinger, "If you see daylight, go through the hole." Woodrow Wilson put it more formally: "I have always in my own thought summed up individual liberty, and business liberty, and every other kind of liberty, in the phrase that is common in the sporting world, 'A free field and no favor.'" Soon after taking office in 1933, FDR claimed his Administration had made some "ten-yard gains, but it is a long field." Truman-campaign strategist Clark Clifford said after the 1948 victory, "We were on our own 20-yard line. We had to be bold. If we kept plugging away in moderate terms, the best we could have done would have been to reach midfield when the gun went off. So we had to throw long passes ..."

Truman, during that campaign (see GIVE 'EM HELL), used a legendary horse to rally his dispirited troops. Citation, one of the great racing thoroughbreds, would lay back at the start of a race and come on with a rush at the end. "I am trying to do in politics what Citation has done in the horse races. I propose at the finish line on November 2 to come out ahead ..."

FDR brushed off occasional failures with "I have no expectation of making a hit every time I come to bat," and Sherman Adams dismissed the first Russian Sputnik with a refusal to become engaged in "an outer-space basketball game."

Winston Churchill, defending the Speaker of the House of Commons in 1951, observed: "In these hard party fights under democratic conditions, as in football matches and the like, there are moments when the umpire gets a very rough time."

Political commentators use sports metaphors as well, occasionally mixing them. Theodore White, in *The Making of the President 1964*, wrote: "Like aging prize-fighters, short of wind and stiffening of muscle, the Southerners were left with no resource but cunning; and cunning told them to delay, day by day, hour by hour, until somewhere, somehow, there might be a turning of national sentiment. It was the strategy, said someone, of 'punt and pray.'"

Sports metaphors relate closely to many people, which is why politicians spend the time to create them; at other times, they are tossed off without thinking because they are already a part of the language. After a Kennedy aide appeared on NBC's television news interview program *Meet the Press*, the President called to say, "They never laid a glove on you." It is the classic remark of a trainer to a prizefighter who has been belted all over the ring.

Ron Nessen, President Ford's press secretary, wrote in 1978 that a favorite White House expression in the Ford years was "Welcome to the NFL"—a term used by announcers for the National Football League when a rookie received his first savage, bone-rattling tackle.

For boxing metaphors, see HAT IN THE RING and ARENA; for racing metaphors, see DARK HORSE. For more football, see FOOTBALL, POLITICAL and GAME PLAN; for baseball, see HARDBALL; for basketball, FULL-COURT PRESS and SLAM DUNK.

sputnik See -NIK suffix.

square deal Theodore Roosevelt's campaign slogan, originally directed against the trusts; also, honest dealing (see CARD METAPHORS).

"We demand that big business give people a square deal," said President Roosevelt in 1901, urging government curbs on the new U.S. Steel Corporation. He took the issue to the people in a tour, urging his "square deal"—a phrase Lincoln Steffens claimed to have suggested—adding, "We do not wish to destroy corporations, but we do wish to make them subserve the public good." Campaigning for election, he hammered it home: "If elected, I shall see to it that every man has a square deal, no more and no less."

He continued to use the phrase, but the emphasis changed with the years. In 1910 he told a conservative Kansas audience:

> I stand for the square deal. But when I say that I am for the square deal, I mean not merely that I stand for fair play under the present rules of the game, but that I stand for having those rules changed so as to work for a more substantial

equality of opportunity and of reward for equally good service. One word of warning, which, I think, is hardly necessary in Kansas. When I say I want a square deal for the poor man, I do not mean that I want a square deal for the man who remains poor because he has not got the energy to work for himself.

Every man's phrase can be used against him. William Howard Taft, under strenuous attack from his former sponsor, said in 1912: "Mr. Roosevelt prides himself in being a true sportsman.... The maxim which he has exalted above all others is that every man is entitled to a square deal.... Is he giving me a square deal?"

The Square Deal was followed by the NEW DEAL of Franklin Roosevelt and the FAIR DEAL of Harry Truman; returning to its square form, it was used by Wendell Willkie against FDR in 1940.

The phrase has lost most of its Roosevelt association and reverted to mean simply "honest dealing," as it had when Mark Twain used it in *Life on the Mississippi* in 1883: "Thought I had better give him a square deal." In this general form it was used in 1893 by Missouri Congressman Champ Clark ("What I want is a square deal and a 'divy' all around"), and by Louisiana Senator Huey Long in 1932 thanking columnist Claude Bowers for a friendly piece: "As a rule, I don't care a damn what any crooked newspaperman says about me, because they're mostly goddam liars; but you gave me a square deal and I want to thank you for it."

stab in the back Treachery; or, withholding expected support.

"On this 10th day of June, 1940," said Franklin Roosevelt, "the hand that held the dagger has struck it into the back of its neighbor." When Mussolini's Italy attacked France, French Premier Paul Reynaud had cabled FDR asking for help, using the phrase "stab in the back." When a draft of the President's speech was submitted by the State Department, FDR inserted his version of the phrase but was dissuaded from using it by Sumner Welles. Other Democratic political leaders suggested this phrase might alienate the Italian-American vote in the coming election. However, on his way to the University of Virginia at Charlottesville, FDR wrote it in again and used it.

His successor, Harry Truman, used the same word-picture in a more partisan sense. Addressing 75,000 farmers and their families in Dexter, Iowa, in the 1948 campaign, Truman attacked: "The Republican Congress has already stuck a pitchfork in the farmer's back. They have already done their best to keep price supports from working... when you have to sell your grain below the support price because you have no place to store it, you can thank this same Republican Congress." Truman's use of the phrase annoyed Earl Warren, campaigning as Dewey's running mate: "Restraint is not easy when the President accuses Republicans of sticking a pitchfork into the backs of our farmers."

A familiar reflex to military disaster is the *Dolchstoss in den Rücken*, or *Dolchstosslegende*, which Prussian officers used to explain their 1918 defeat; Hitler revived the charge in the '30s, blaming Germany's defeat on Jews. Historian Seymour Martin Lipset held in 1955 that the radical right was using this same kind of alibi for the loss of Eastern Europe, China, and Indochina: "The theory that these events occurred because we were 'stabbed in the back' by a 'hidden force' is much more palatable than admitting that the Communists have stronger political assets than we do."

FDR probably did not realize how apt the phrase was, or how sensitive the Germans would be to that figure of speech. In the medieval legend of the *Nibelungenlied* the hero, Siegfried—tired from being pursued, stopping to drink from a spring—was murdered by a man thrusting a spear into his back, spawning the *Dolchstosslegende* and making Germans culturally aware of the duplicity of a stab in the back. To Americans, a similar episode is the shooting of the outlaw Jesse James.

staffer A full-time member of a public figure's headquarters group.

In military terminology, there is a distinction between *line* and *staff*—between combat command and headquarters command.

In government, *line* came to mean executive departments and *staff* the White House staff; though the staff started to grow in the Roosevelt years, the term *staffer* became prevalent in the Eisenhower years. *New York Times* style does not yet accept its use.

The PECKING ORDER: *counselor* carries the most prestige; *strategist* gets the most respect; *adviser* is close-in but not as operational as an *assistant*; a *staffer* follows (with a connotation of permanence); and an *aide* usually brings up the rear, though *aide* can be used to refer to all of the above, and journalists often try to unlock secrets by calling staffers "key aides." At the bottom is the GOFER.

As a verb, to *staff out* means to solicit a variety of views on a recommendation before submission to the decision maker.

stagflation See ECONOMIC JARGON; INFLATION.

stalking horse A decoy; a candidate put forward to split a vote or deadlock a convention, concealing another candidate's plan.

In hunting, a *stalking horse* is used to conceal a sportsman stalking game, allowing the hunter to creep up close to his quarry; from this the expression, used in print since 1519, has come to mean a person put forward to mislead. "He uses his folly like a stalking horse," wrote Shakespeare in *As You Like It*, "and under the presentation of that he shoots his wit."

Political writers and politicians have used it freely for over a century. *Niles' Register*, in 1846, said: "The 54–40 Doctrine is a mere stalking horse." In 1866 *Harper's Weekly* wrote of President Andrew Johnson: "He must know that they would willingly use him as a wedge to split the Union party, as a stalking horse to their own purposes, as a springboard to leap into power." In 1872 Rep. Hamilton Fish called Horace Greeley "the stalking horse of the secessionists."

In 1971 columnist Marianne Means wrote: "Senator George McGovern is plagued by this problem more than the other candidates. He has been accused of being a [Edward] Kennedy stalking horse, sent out merely to soften up Muskie and divide the field until an eventual Kennedy blitz occurs."

The *Los Angeles Times* wrote in 1990 about opposition to Nicaraguan President Violeta Barrios de Chamorro: "Sandinista candidates…used their economic battles with the United States to wage a nationalist campaign against Chamorro's American-financed coalition, calling her a stalking horse for yanqui imperialism."

That meaning of "sham candidacy" turned up in a London *Sunday Times* report by Sarah Baxter in June of 2007 as former Tennessee Senator Fred Thompson prepared to announce he was running for the Republican nomination: "Until the start of the year Thompson was quietly raising money for McCain's 2008 campaign. When the rumour spread that he might join the race himself, there was talk that he would serve as a stalking horse who would ultimately direct his supporters to back McCain." The headline: "Et tu, Fred: friend who stabbed McCain."

See SPOILER; STRAW MAN.

stalwart An unwavering party REGULAR; a staunch supporter.

James G. Blaine ("The Plumed Knight") of Maine, wrote *The Boston Herald* in 1877: "the Boston Press no more represents the stalwart Republican feeling of New England on the pending issues than the same press did when it demanded the enforcement of the Fugitive Slave law in 1851." Commented *The Nation* four years later: "The epithet 'Stalwart' as applied to a class of politicians was first used by Mr. Blaine in 1877 to designate those Republicans who were unwilling to give up hostility and distrust of the South as a political motive."

Blaine used the adjective *stalwart* as an accolade; more often, it had served as an epithet. This was because Republicans had divided into two factions: "Stalwarts," regulars who opposed Blaine, and "Half Breeds," independents who supported him. Blaine was in the position of having his own word appropriated by the opposition. The "Stalwarts," led by N.Y. Senator Roscoe Conkling, organized the "Home Guard" behind General U.S. Grant at the Republican convention; the "Half Breeds" pressed for Blaine. In the deadlock, DARK

HORSE James Garfield won the nomination and election.

Blaine was an avid reader of Sir Walter Scott, who frequently used *stalwart*. The Scottish word (the English equivalent was *stalworth*), from Old English "serviceable," means "steadfast"— which stalwarts are to a party. (*Half-breed* is now a slur; persons partly white and partly of color—Senator Barack Obama, golf champion Tiger Woods—are identified as "of mixed heritage.")

Current use of *stalwart* has dropped the anti-Southern connotation, retaining the loyal-party-worker meaning. Dwight Eisenhower, in his memoirs, wrote of Senator Robert A. Taft: "In some things I found him unexpectedly 'liberal,' specifically in his attitudes on old-age pensions, school aid, and public housing—attitudes, incidentally, which were miles away from those of some self-described 'Taft stalwarts.'"

Stalwart Democrats are called DYED-IN-THE-WOOL, BRASS COLLAR, and YELLOW DOG; and stalwart Republicans are ROCK-RIBBED.

stampede As a noun, panic-stricken decision on the part of delegates to jump on a bandwagon as it gathers speed; as a verb, to stimulate such a movement.

President William McKinley, looking over the field of candidates for his second-term running mate, told Senator Joseph B. Foraker, "I hope you will not allow the convention to be stampeded to Roosevelt for Vice President." That was Foraker's recollection; true or not about Theodore Roosevelt, the current use of the word is unchanged.

The Mexican Spanish word is *estampida*, meaning "a sudden, thundering rush of frightened cattle." *The New York Times* used a political application in June 1876: "It is well known that many nominations, both in State and national conventions, have been made by what is known as stampedes. A candidate runs ahead of all competitors, but while yet far short of the required number of votes some county or State which has not kept tally supposes the plurality man to be nominated, and wishing to be on the winning side changes to him."

Though the noun is most closely identified with the action of conventioneers, the verb has frequent use in relation to ideas or movements rather than people. Candidate Thomas E. Dewey in 1948, sounding like an incumbent: "Ours is a magnificent land. Every part of it. Don't let anybody frighten you or try to stampede you into believing America is finished." Dwight Eisenhower, in his 1963 memoir *Mandate for Change*: "Stories written with the purpose of damaging the reputation of a candidate have been a SLEAZY feature of many political campaigns. I resolved not to let such a story stampede me." See BANDWAGON.

standard-bearer The candidate at the top of the ticket, who carries the nomination of his party as his *standard*.

From a French word meaning "banner," a *standard* is carried by a leader, as on a flagship. George Washington gave it an early use in America by calling on the delegates to the Constitutional Convention in Philadelphia to "raise a standard to which the wise and honest can repair."

The New York Herald in 1848 wrote: "It is on the old platform of principles, and for the good old cause, that the new standard-bearer is to be chosen." For a time, the phrase applied to the vice presidential candidate as well. "The national convention," recorded the *Congressional Record*, "summoned Garret A. Hobart to be standard-bearer with William McKinley." The president–vice president team is still referred to as *standard-bearers*, but the vice president individually is *a*, and never *the* standard-bearer.

At the Democratic convention of 1884, Daniel Lockwood rose to nominate Grover Cleveland, asking the delegates "to go to the independent and Democratic voters of the country, to go to the young men of the country, the new blood of the country, and present the name of Grover Cleveland as your standard bearer."

The word, despite its archaic tone, is in current use. Theodore White on the 1964 campaign: "So many major Republican candidates avoided their standard-bearer whenever he entered their states that it was an act of grace when Charles Percy appeared in the late afternoon of Goldwater's second day in Illinois for three joint whistle-stop appearances."

In a 1975 column, a political hypocrite was denounced as a "double standard bearer." See BANNER DISTRICT; MILITARY METAPHORS.

stand in the doorway To resist symbolically; to make a dramatic show of opposition.

Governor George C. Wallace promised to "stand in the doorway" to block the admission of two black students into the University of Alabama on June 13, 1963. This phrase became a symbol of Southern resistance to school integration, much as "he should have taken her by the hand" was a much-used criticism of Eisenhower's refusal to make a dramatic personal gesture at Little Rock, Arkansas.

Wallace, making good his pledge, stood in the doorway of the university administration building at Tuscaloosa and blocked the entry of the two students and federal marshals. President Kennedy promptly federalized part of the Alabama National Guard, which soon arrived on campus. His symbolic show of resistance recorded by cameramen, Wallace retreated and the students were registered.

Both the *take her by the hand* and *stand in the doorway* expressions were used by Kennedy aide Ted Sorensen: "There were recurring suggestions that the President should personally appear in Birmingham and take a Negro child by the hand into a school or lunch counter. But that suggestion badly confused the physical presence of the President with the official presence of his powers. It would have demeaned the dignity of the office by relying on the same kind of dramatic stunt and physical contest that was staged by those Southern governors who 'stood in the doorway.'"

Andrew Kopkind reported in *The New Republic* in 1967 that California Governor Ronald Reagan sought early in his administration to cut funds spent on education and then funds allocated for mental hospitals.

"First Reagan stood in the school-house door," he quoted an economist as saying, "then he stood in the nut-house door." As pressures built up, Reagan restored the cuts and retreated from the doorways.

stand pat Put positively, to adhere to a position, to refuse to waver; put negatively, to accept the status quo, to freeze.

"We will stand pat!" Senator Mark Hanna, the foremost McKinley supporter, was supposed to have said in 1900; this has led to the mistaken assumption that "Stand Pat with McKinley" was a slogan in that election.

Mark Hanna did give a new political meaning to the poker expression but not until 1902. Hans Sperber and Travis Trittschuh found the September 28, 1902, Cleveland *Plain Dealer* report on a Hanna speech the preceding day at Akron. Said Hanna: "About a year ago it was my privilege to attend the opening meeting of the Republican party, and after thinking and looking over the situation, I came to the conclusion—'Let well enough alone.' That was the whole chapter: that is all there was in the campaign of interest to you. Now I say stand pat."

The *Plain Dealer* article went on to explain what Hanna meant:

> The player "stands pat" when he declines to discard from his hand, and draw other cards, and the supposed earning quality of such a hand is superior to that of three aces. According to the rules of the game it is perfectly honest, however, for a player to hold a pat hand when it has little or no value, and if successful in scaring his opponents into laying down their hands he wins the bank or "pot." This is, we are informed, called a "bluff." Thus it will be seen that Dr. Hanna in his Akron speech invented a singularly appropriate figure of political speech.

Obviously the senator was needled after using this expression; politicians were considered too distinguished to be familiar with poker terminology. "When I told the people 'stand pat,'" Hanna told the Cincinnati *Enquirer* five days later, "it was merely to use a familiar saying to express the situation. I have been told that this is a phrase used in the game of poker; but everybody understands it just the same."

The *Enquirer* kept tongue in cheek: "Senator Hanna probably got the suggestion of his 'stand pat' speech from some fellow who played poker; but the Senator didn't know that, of course."

Although Hanna popularized the expression (apparently in 1902, casting doubt on its use in the 1900 McKinley campaign), he was not the first to use it politically. Speaker Joseph G. ("Uncle Joe") Cannon used the expression in the House in 1896 regarding adherence to high tariffs. The *Congressional Record* of February 28, 1896, reported the following exchange:

J. G. Cannon:—That proposition was fought bitterly in the House; but the Senate *stood*, if the gentlemen will allow me the expression, *pat*... and they had their own way, because no bill can pass without an agreement between the two houses.

G. L. Johnson of Calif.:—I understand the explanation made by the gentleman from Illinois, with the single exception of some technical, abstruse term which he used, but which I suppose is well understood in Illinois, though unfamiliar in California. I will ask the gentlemen however why should not the House "stand pat" as the Senate did?

Mr. Cannon:—Oh no: It was invented in California and put into the dictionary there.

After being popularized by Hanna, *stand pat* and *standpatter* came to mean REACTIONARY. Progressive Robert La Follette equated the two words in a comment on Calvin Coolidge's first message to Congress: "It was an able, concise and frank presentation of the stand-pat, reactionary theory of government." This criticism could not have come as a surprise to Coolidge, who had given the following advice to political leaders of Massachusetts when he became Governor there ten years before:

Expect to be called a standpatter, but don't be a standpatter. Expect to be called a demagogue, but don't be a demagogue. Don't hesitate to be as revolutionary as science. Don't hesitate to be as reactionary as the multiplication table. Don't expect to build up the weak by pulling down the strong. Don't hurry to legislate. Give administration a chance to catch up with legislation.

In his 1960 campaign John F. Kennedy scorned "Stand Pat with McKinley" as an example of Republican reaction. Richard Nixon learned in that campaign that a political phrase could have an embarrassing double meaning. He countered Kennedy's "Let's get America moving again" with his own "America cannot stand pat." When his wife, Pat Nixon, looked surprised, he hurriedly changed that line in subsequent appearances to "America cannot stand still."

Arthur Schlesinger, Jr., turned it into a one-word -ISM with a *Wall Street Journal* piece in 1978 entitled "Carter's Retreats into Standpattism."

star wars Space-based defense; positioning of military equipment in orbit around the Earth to shoot down attacking missiles.

On March 23, 1983, Ronald Reagan surprised the arms-control establishment—which had always thought in terms of "mutual assured destruction" (MAD), or deterrence only by threat of MASSIVE RETALIATION—by calling for a new approach "to counter the awesome Soviet missile threat with measures that are defensive." He asked: "What if free people could live secure in the knowledge that their security did not rest upon the threat of instant U.S. retaliation to deter a Soviet attack, that we could intercept and destroy strategic ballistic missiles before they reached our own soil or that of our allies?"

That idea, seen by opponents as both expensive and potentially destabilizing to the balance of terror, immediately became identified as Reagan's "star wars" proposal. The derisive name came from the title of the hit 1977 film by George Lucas, whose science-fiction vision of rebels against the empire contributed another image to Reaganese (see EVIL EMPIRE). The President protested the nicknaming, saying, "I wish whoever coined that expression would take it back again, because it gives a false impression of what it is we're talking about."

Pentagon officials suggested Strategic Defense Initiative, abbreviated S.D.I., and in 1985 Reagan attempted to interject the redundant "security shield" in his second Inaugural address. (One presidential adviser, fearing the shield was less than promised, complained that they were "up the laser river.")

Although the derisive nickname *star wars* stuck, the need for an alternative to "mutual assured destruction (MAD)" saw the funding for an anti-missile program, though substantially different from the original Reagan plan, continue into the Clinton Administration. In May 1993, Secretary of Defense Les Aspin announced the end of SDI (Strategic Defense Initiative), and *The Washington Post* headlined the story "'Star Wars' Is Declared Dead." By 2006, with North Korea clearly in possession of nuclear devices as well as long-range missiles, the program was continued at the Department of Defense under the unromantic name of the Missile Defense Agency.

State Department-ese See PENTAGONESE.

State of the Union The name of the information and recommendations—presented in the form of a written message or a speech—that the president of the U.S. is constitutionally required to deliver.

"He shall from time to time give to the Congress information of the state of the union," mandates Article II, Section 3 of the U.S. Constitution, "and recommend to their consideration such measures as he shall judge necessary and expedient."

The term "from time to time" is fairly loose; it was George Washington, in 1790, who established the precedent of annual messages, and when Washington established a precedent, it tended to stick. (His two-term precedent was broken by Franklin Roosevelt, who trounced Wendell Willkie, one of whose slogans was "No third term"—see DON'T CHANGE HORSES—but the two-term precedent was made law by the 22nd Amendment, ratified in 1951. Another Washington precedent is "So help me God" spoken at the end of the Inaugural Oath, which is not in the Constitution, but has been said loud and clear by the choice of almost all inaugurees.)

The message—called the "S.O.U." by the White House aides who draft it—was delivered in person to a joint session of Congress by Washington and John Adams,

but not by Thomas Jefferson in 1801, who believed that such pomp smacked too much of British royalism—and perhaps because he was more of a writer than a speaker. Not until Woodrow Wilson in 1913 did a president again deliver the annual message orally. Harding and Coolidge subsequently declined, but FDR reinstated the Washington precedent (though Roosevelt's last, in 1945, was a radio summation of his written State of the Union message).

As World War II loomed, FDR's Jan. 6, 1941 message, which became known as "the FOUR FREEDOMS speech," contained the constitutional phrase itself but did not try to encapsulate the Union's state in a single word: "Therefore, as your President, performing my constitutional duty to 'give to the Congress information of the state of the Union,' I find it unhappily necessary to report that the future and the safety of our country and of our democracy are overwhelmingly involved in events far beyond our borders."

The word that is today listened for, however, and the one that speechwriters labor longest over, is the adjective that follows the traditional "The state of the Union is —." Harry Truman, in his two oral messages, chose "good" and "continues to be good." Eisenhower liked the long form: "continues to vindicate the wisdom of the principles on which this republic is founded." Kennedy gave it uplift and scope: "the State of this old but youthful Union, in the 175th year of its life, is good." The wartime Lyndon Johnson chose "challenged." Nixon in 1973, perhaps discerning great personal trouble ahead, used "basic" as a qualifier in saying "the basic state of our Union is sound and full of promise."

Jerry Ford broke the pattern with "I must say to you that the state of the union is not good," later in his presidency saying, "we have a 'more perfect union' than when my stewardship began." Jimmy Carter stuck three times to "sound." Ronald Reagan looked ahead: "In the near future the state of the union and the economy will be better— much better." George H.W. Bush chose "sound," later "strong," and a lyrical flight: "the state of the Union is the union of each of us, one to the other—the sum of our friendships, marriages, families and communities." Clinton chose "strong," then "stronger" and "the strongest it has ever been." The younger Bush also liked that word: "Our nation is at war, our economy is in recession and the civilized world faced unprecedented dangers. Yet the state of our union has never been stronger."

states rights Democrats See DIXIECRAT.

stay-at-homes Those eligible to vote who do not.

"They are not radical," wrote sociologist C. Wright Mills in excoriation, "not liberal, not reactionary. They are inactionary. They are out of it. If we accept the Greek's definition of the idiot as an altogether private man, then we must conclude that many American citizens are now idiots."

Political pollsters call them the "politically inert." Hopeful (and usually mistaken) politicians lagging in the polls call them the SILENT VOTE.

In 1948 President Harry Truman castigated those Democrats he considered responsible for the DO-NOTHING CONGRESS who, "because they stayed at home and did not vote last year, got just the kind of Congress they deserve." Political scientist Sam Lubell, analyzing that Truman-Dewey election, came up with a surprising observation: "Far from costing Dewey the election, the [Democratic] stay-at-homes may have saved him almost as crushing a defeat as Landon suffered in 1936."

Overcoming the ennui of stay-at-homes is likely to remain an unreached goal of campaigners. A more subtle approach, playing on their guilt, was made by poet Ogden Nash:

> *They have such refined and delicate palates*
> *That they can discover no one worthy of their*
> *   ballots,*
> *And then when someone terrible gets elected*
> *They say, There, that's just what I expected!*

The problem of stay-at-homes plagues both parties and is not limited to this country or this time. British political philosopher Edmund Burke is frequently quoted as having written: "The only thing necessary for the triumph of evil is for good men to do nothing." (The closest anybody has found to this in his extensive writings is "When bad men combine, the good must associate; else they will fall, one by one …") And the French have a saying: *"Qui s'excuse, s'accuse."* See TURNOUT.

staying bought Constancy in corruption.

Simon Cameron, Lincoln's first Secretary of War, who was later censured by Congress for remarkably lax administration, defined "an honest politician" as "one who, when he's bought, stays bought." That was widely attributed to him but there is no hard evidence that he was the one who originated it.

The phrase reappeared and was made part of the political language after the campaign of 1904. Although the Democrats put up Judge Alton B. Parker, a gilt-edged conservative, Republican Theodore Roosevelt was able to attract financial support from Morgan, Rockefeller, Depew, Frick, Harriman, and other industrial and financial titans. Judge Parker accused Roosevelt of having blackmailed the financial giants, promising them immunity from trustbusting if they contributed heavily.

At least one, Henry Clay Frick—Andrew Carnegie's man for many years—felt he had been given commitments in return for his donation to Roosevelt. "He got down on his knees before us," Frick was reported to have angrily claimed. "We bought the son of a bitch and then he did not stay bought!"

stay the course Stirring call for unwavering resolve and persistence in policy.

"I was able to assure them," said President George W. Bush, after spending Thanksgiving of 2003 with U.S. troops at Baghdad airport, "that we were going to stay the course and get the job done."

For supporters of the war in Iraq, *stay the course* had the rhetorical advantage of boxing in those who opposed it as all too ready to CUT AND RUN. Speaking for the Democratic opposition, Rep. John Murtha tried to change the terms of the debate, telling Tim Russert on *Meet the Press* in

June of 2006 that "'stay the course' is 'stay and pay.'" James A. Baker III, Republican co-chairman of the bipartisan Iraq Study Group, sought a middle ground, saying in an interview with ABC News on October 8, 2006: "Our commission believes that there are alternatives between the stated alternatives... of 'stay the course' and 'cut and run.'"

Three days later, Mr. Bush began to back away from the muscular metaphor: "The characterization of, you know, 'it's stay the course' is about a quarter right. 'Stay the course' means keep doing what you're doing. My attitude is, don't do what you're doing if it's not working—change. 'Stay the course' also means don't leave before the job is done." The following January, when announcing his decision to change commanders and add 20,000 additional troops in Iraq, the president stopped using the verb *stay* and said his new "surge" strategy would "change America's course."

Stay the course has a political history. Ronald Reagan employed the phrase frequently when discussing the economic difficulties prevalent in the late Carter years (high inflation, soaring interest rates, and unemployment) that bedeviled his first few years in office. Transmitting his budget for Fiscal Year 1983 to Congress in February, 1982, he said: "Our task is to persevere; to stay the course; to shun retreat; to weather the temporary dislocations and pressures that must inevitably accompany the restoration of national economic, fiscal, and military health." Later that year, at a pre-election rally for Texas Republicans in Irving, he said: "Unless we have the courage to stay on course and lick inflation for good, we'll never have lasting recovery.... Well, I intend to stay the course."

Stay the course is of particular linguistic interest for having reversed its meaning during the past two centuries. The original senses of *stay*, going back to the sixteenth century, revolved around the ideas of coming to a halt or stop; in law, a *stay* remains an order not to proceed. The protagonist of Christopher Marlowe's *Doctor Faustus* (c. 1588) was not persevering with unflagging determination when "Hee stayed his course, and so returned home." Edgar Allan Poe also used the phrase in the sense of "to stop or check the course (of something)," writing in *King Pest the First* (1835): "But it lay not in the power of images, or sensations... to stay the course of men."

The modern sense of the phrase arose among sportsmen in the second half of the nineteenth century. Early examples refer to the ability of oarsmen and thoroughbred horses to hold out to the ends of their respective races. In 1879 the London *Times* said of a racehorse of suspect abilities: "Jockeys who have ridden him think that he cannot stay the course." The reversal in the phrase's meaning was shown by Winston Churchill, who said in 1948 that "America is like a great and powerful horse, pulling all the rest of the world up the hill to peace and prosperity.... But sometimes I ask myself... will America stay the course?"

In January of 2007, as President Bush decided to "surge" U.S. troops to pacify Baghdad and change the dynamic of the war in Iraq, Senator Ted Kennedy in his call for redeployment—in effect, withdrawal—sought to tie President Bush's previous use of the phrase to a similar presidential exhortation in the Vietnam era:

> Listen to this comment from a high-ranking American official: "It became clear that if we were prepared to stay the course, we could help to lay the cornerstone for a diverse and independent Asia.... If we faltered, the forces of chaos would scent victory and decades of strife and aggression would stretch endlessly before us. The choice was clear. We would stay the course. And we shall stay the course."
>
> That is not President Bush speaking. It is President Lyndon Johnson, forty years ago, ordering a hundred thousand more American soldiers to Vietnam.

See SURGE.

steamroller Rough tactics used by those in control of a political party to overpower those who disagree with them.

The steamroller began to roll at the Republican convention in June 1908. The word was probably first used in this country by a newsman in Chicago, Oswald F. Schuette of the *Inter Ocean*, about the Roosevelt-Taft supporters within the Republican National Committee in disposing of those who protested against the seating at the convention of slates of Taft delegates from Alabama and Arkansas.

Turnabout was called unfair play in 1912 when the Roosevelt supporters at the Republican convention complained that their Southern slates were being *steamrollered* by a Taft-dominated Republican National Committee.

The word had already been used in international politics some years earlier. In 1902 *Munsey's Magazine* said of Russia: "She sought to achieve her end by means of the 'steam roller' of the concert of Europe."

In 1932 Franklin D. Roosevelt forces surrendered their plan to get the Democratic convention to give up the hoary two-thirds rule on the selection of candidates; it had become obvious they could not win the fight. Candidate Roosevelt wrote the convention acknowledging that asking for revision at that time might be considered unfair by some and saying: "I decline to permit either myself or my friends to be open to the accusation of poor sportsmanship, or to use the methods which could be called, even falsely, those of a steamroller ..."

In 1956, knowing his nomination was a certainty, President Eisenhower wired his aide, Sherman Adams, that he must "guard against steamrollering, no matter what the proposition is." He remembered 1952, and the charge made by Ike's supporters against Senator Robert Taft for trying that technique. See THOU SHALT NOT STEAL.

Steamrollering is often defined by those who have been defeated as "using overwhelming strength unfairly, or even illegally." Senator Robert La Follette wrote in his autobiography: "Whether one is on top of or under the steamroller influences somewhat one's point of view."

stemwinder An orator, or a speech, capable of rousing a crowd.

A stemwinding speech, like a stirring stump speech, is intended for delivery at large rallies, where roars of approval add to its effectiveness. The whirling image of the word pictures the orator "winding up"

and flinging stimulating words and phrases. In current political usage, the word is used to describe a loud, partisan speech, either approvingly or mockingly. Its opposite is a low-key, reasonable-sounding, "sincere" speech, best used on television to reach people at home.

The word is derived from the stemwinding watch or clock, which was a major advance in timepieces patented in 1866. It soon became the word for modernity and excellence: "Ain't he a stem-winder" can be traced to 1892, and short-story writer O. Henry used it in 1902 in that sense: "There's a new bank examiner over at the First, and he's a stem-winder." Dictionaries of slang at the turn of the century included the word's meaning as "the best of its kind; a keyless watch, at the time a new and exquisite improvement."

Though its usage in timepieces is archaic (battery power has replaced the need to wind by hand), the word is actively used in politics. Often one quality of a vice presidential candidate is his ability to deliver stemwinders, while the presidential candidate delivers less partisan, ABOVE POLITICS speeches. For comparative usage, see SPELLBINDER.

step-by-step diplomacy A policy to proceed cautiously, seeking bilateral agreements, often in stages, rather than a comprehensive solution.

Garry Wills, in a 1975 *New York Review of Books*, covered some of the vocabulary of Mideast diplomacy in a sentence: "For a country with scholar-rulers, Israel's debates live to an extraordinary degree on slogans: one side's 'step by step' is the other's 'SALAMI TACTICS,' just as a friend's 'piece of peace' is a foe's 'intangible for tangibles.'"

The phrase was associated in 1974 with Secretary of State Henry Kissinger's SHUTTLE DIPLOMACY; but reporter David Zuckerman found a 1953 quotation by Secretary of State John Foster Dulles, pledging that the U.S. would help bring about "a step-by-step reduction of tensions in the area and the conclusion of an ultimate peace."

On September 20, 1977, Moshe Dayan, Israeli Foreign Minister in Menachem Begin's government, told a group of Washington reporters that "step by step is dead," and defined the phrase as "a piece of land for a piece of peace." However, Israel soon became uncomfortable with President Carter's plans for a "comprehensive" settlement at a Geneva conference, fearing a veto over Arab moderation by Arab radicals and the Soviet Union. When Egyptian President Anwar el-Sadat made his dramatic visit to Jerusalem in 1977, talk of direct dealings between Israel and Egypt dominated the Mideast, and "step-by-step"—though never generating the same enthusiasm as when it was first expressed—did not seem such a bad approach to a solution.

Step-by-step was at first totally identified with Kissinger, although it was originally an Israeli idea, adopted—as Kissinger noted—after "every attempt to discuss a comprehensive solution failed." The phrase was in the title of a book about Kissinger by Israeli Matti Golan: *The Secret Conversations of Henry Kissinger: Step by Step in the Middle East.*

To dissociate himself from the author of the previous policy, Carter's National Security Adviser Zbigniew Brzezinski referred to an approach of "concentric circles." See SHUTTLE DIPLOMACY.

steppingstone Springboard to higher office; used to show ambition, demeaning the office held at the time.

Harry Truman offered the vice presidential nomination in 1948 to Supreme Court Justice William O. Douglas. He considered the offer for a weekend, and then called the President: "I am very sorry, but I have decided not to get into politics. I do not think I should use the Court as a steppingstone."

The only judges to run for president were Alton B. Parker in 1904 and Charles Evans Hughes in 1916; John F. Kennedy once jotted in a notebook: "No congressional leader of the very first rank save James Madison has been elected Pres.,—and apart from Polk, Garfield, McKinley and Truman no parliamentarians of the 2nd rank."

Certainly, House Speakers had tried. Henry Clay in 1824, James Blaine in 1876, Champ Clark in 1912, John Garner in 1932, all tried and failed; only James Polk succeeded. Thirteen men who had served as senators made it, but only one—Harding—made it directly from the Senate in the twentieth century, before the election of 1960, when for the first time two senators (Kennedy and Johnson) ran on the same ticket, against two former senators (Nixon and Lodge).

This was not what Thomas Jefferson had foreseen. "Congress is the great commanding theatre of this nation," he wrote William Wirt in 1808, "and the threshold to whatever department of office a man is qualified to enter." But the best steppingstones to the presidency have been the governor's chair and the vice presidency. Senator Henry Cabot Lodge at the turn of the century said that the vice presidency should not be looked on with disdain by great men, but should be desired by "our most ambitious men ... as a stepping stone to higher office." Theodore Roosevelt, on the other hand, called it "a steppingstone ... to oblivion."

The cabinet, especially in our early history, was an excellent steppingstone (nine made it), when the steppingstone was the State Department; in the twentieth century, Taft of the War Department and Hoover of the Commerce Department became Chief Executive. President Nixon used to say "Every Cabinet should have one potential president in it"; his preference was Treasury Secretary John Connally, a longtime Texas Democrat.

In current usage the word is often employed to attack a candidate for having his sights set on greater things than the office he is currently running for. This attack was potent in California, as William Knowland discovered, but New Yorkers in 2006 voted to vote to reelect a senator—Hillary Clinton—knowing she was likely to run for president. Only a generation before, critics of Michigan Governor George Romney, a Mormon, and later of the born-again candidate Jimmy Carter, seizing on what they considered an overly devout nature, spread a joke that their target was "only seeking the White House as a steppingstone."

still hunt See BIRD DOG ... KENNEL DOG.

stir up the animals Start an unwanted controversy; take a position that needlessly incurs criticism.

Reviewing Governor Thomas E. Dewey's disastrous 1948 campaign strategy, Dewey's (later Eisenhower's) press secretary James Hagerty said: "The main campaign worry was not to rock the boat. While Governor Dewey set the strategy, he was greatly influenced by the state chairmen and local leaders. They kept saying, telegraphing, and writing that the campaign had to be kept on a low level, that there was no need to stir up the animals."

This zoo or circus metaphor refers to the commotion caused by sleeping denizens when wakened. *The animals* is a half-jocular, half-derisive reference to a lower order of life; news reporters frequently call television technicians by that name, which is never appreciated. (See ZOO PLANE.) For a closely related expression, see RED MEAT.

stonewalling A policy based on saying "NO COMMENT" and HANGING TOUGH.

As transcribed from the Nixon tapes, White House counsel John Dean assured the President on February 28, 1973: "We are stonewalling totally."

Mr. Nixon picked up the word, which was in widening use, and at a subsequent meeting said, "I want you all to stonewall it, let them plead the Fifth Amendment, cover up or anything else ..." The first two instructions are not suggesting criminal behavior; for review of the third, see COVER-UP.

Several witnesses before the Senate Watergate Committee attributed the word *stonewalling* to John Mitchell. During an interrogation in which the former Attorney General volunteered nothing, Senator Lowell Weicker (R-Conn.) asked if his testimony was "an exercise in stonewalling." Mitchell assumed an attitude of wonderment and replied, "I don't know that term. Is that a Yankee term from Connecticut?"

The word's roots had heroic, if defensive, connotations. On July 21, 1861, at the First Battle of Bull Run, Confederate General Thomas Jonathan Jackson held his position and earned his sobriquet when a soldier was said to have cried, "There stands Jackson like a stone wall—rally behind the Virginians!"

As a verb, it comes from Australian cricket slang, meaning to block balls persistently, playing only on the defensive. In the sense of obstruction as a strategy, the word was transferred to the business and political worlds in that region; the *Victorian Hansard* in 1876 asked "whether the six members constituted 'the stone wall' which was to oppose all progress?"

A related second meaning is to delay, filibuster, or stall. James Reston wrote in *The New York Times* in 1961 that the Kennedy Administration was "stonewalling for time in order to close the missile gap ..."

To *stonewall* is to impede an inquiry, usually through silence, sometimes through delay, and is not as pejorative as COVER-UP, which is a layman's term that can mean obstruction of justice. The word now appears to be firmly fixed in the political lexicon; in a letter to the author at the *Times* from federal prison dated July 23, 1977, former Attorney General Mitchell wrote: "Please keep after the establishment and make them account. You should continue to have a field day with Koreagate. Sooner or later they will have to quit stonewalling and get on with the fireworks."

Richard L. Berke of the *Times* used the term in a 1993 article on campaign reform: "Though President Clinton has vowed to change how candidates get elected by pushing through a campaign finance reform package, the passage of a serious bill anytime soon is far from assured. Congress has its reasons for stonewalling. And so, after all, may the President." An AP dispatch from Tehran in June 2007 shows how the word can be used and understood around the world: "Iran has pledged to end years of stonewalling and provide answers on past suspicious activities to the UN nuclear monitoring agency."

straddle See FENCE, ON THE.

straight arrow A person beyond moral reproach; a model of uprightness or, when used derisively, uptightness.

A noun phrase to label somebody who is without vice, *straight arrow* uses a sixteenth-century sense of the adjective *straight*: "honest." The simile "straight as a shingle" led to the variant "straight as an arrow," now shortened to two words, hyphenated when used as a compound adjective.

A popular radio drama of the late 1940s took the eponymous title *Straight Arrow*; its hero was named for his skill in archery as well as for his moral outlook. In 1967, Jann Wenner of *Rolling Stone* magazine selected Straight Arrow as the name of his publishing house, explaining that his choice was a term for "square dealing." The counterculture use in the 1960s led to a connotation of Boy Scout probity, sometimes disparaged as rigidity. (See BOY SCOUT, which also covers the use of *Mr. Clean*, the name of a household detergent also applied to straight arrows.)

In 1969, *Time* magazine reported, "The new eco-activists include groups as straight-arrow as the Girl Scouts." In 1979, "A 'Straight Arrow' Quits the Pentagon" headlined an article about Stanley Resor, who was described as a "'straight-arrow' public servant who simply got 'frozen out' by a bureaucracy whose power games he had no taste for."

Straight Talk Express Name of John McCain's campaign bus, used in the Republican presidential primaries of 2000 and revived for the primaries leading up to the 2008 election.

The name capitalized on the Arizona senator's unusual (for a politician) free-wheeling, plain-spoken, what-you-see-is-what-you-get image. As CNN reported in February 2000 on McCain's swing through South Carolina: "Life aboard the Straight Talk Express could only be described as stream-of-consciousness … in an era where candidates restrict their appearances before the press and stage-craft every move, McCain has opted for a difference media strategy: All McCain, all of the time.… No subject is off-the-record."

Seven years later, CBS News led into a story about McCain's travels through two early-primary states, Iowa and New Hampshire: "John McCain fired up the 'Straight Talk Express' bus from his first presidential campaign.… He chatted with reporters nonstop inside the plush blue tour bus emblazoned with a 'Straight Talk Express' logo and McCain's campaign web site."

The vehicle's name inevitably inspired such embellishments as "The Straight Talk Express Turns Right" (after McCain hired several of George W. Bush's political operatives who had trashed him in 2000) and "Has the Straight Talk Express Stalled?" (when momentum of his campaign slowed in the spring of 2007; a "no surrender" theme helped him regain it). The phrase also was extended to other politicians. *New York* magazine headlined a 2007 article about Rudy Giuliani's occasionally overly frank, off-the-cuff responses to questions on the campaign trail: "Too-Straight-Talk Express."

Straight talk in the sense of plain speaking is dated to 1900 in the *OED*, appearing initially in a political context. From the *Westminster Gazette* of Sept. 1 of that year: "One candidate … is already consoling himself in advance with the thought of the Straight Talks he will give the … deputations that are certain to descend upon him."

straight ticket See TICKET; SPLIT TICKET.

strange bedfellows Enemies forced by circumstances to work together; members of an unlikely alliance, often attacked as an UNHOLY ALLIANCE.

"True it is," wrote Charles Dudley Warner in 1850, "that politics makes strange bedfellows." Warner, editor of the *Hartford* (Conn.) *Courant*, was co-author with Mark Twain of *The Gilded Age*; he might have taken the expression from Edward George Bulwer-Lytton's novel *The Caxtons*, published in 1849, which contained the phrase "Poverty has strange bedfellows."

The source for both was Act II, scene 2 of Shakespeare's *The Tempest*, when a storm drives Trinculo to seek shelter under a gabardine sheet with Caliban, whom he regards as a monster: "There is no other shelter hereabout: misery acquaints a man with strange bedfellows. I will here shroud till the dregs of the storm be past."

In current usage, both misery and poverty have given way to politics as the excuse for strange bedfellows. Historian Mark Sullivan titled a chapter "Strange Bedfellows" when he wrote in his 1930 *Our Times* about the cooperation between Senator "Pitchfork Ben" Tillman and his arch-enemy, Theodore Roosevelt, on a bill to end rate preferences on railroads.

The most dramatic strange bedfellow in modern times was Joseph Stalin. When the Soviet Union signed a nonaggression pact with anti-Communist Germany in 1939, later following Hitler's invasion of Poland with an invasion of his own from the east, British cartoonist David Low presented the paradox in all its absurdity: the two leaders bowing to each other over the smoking ruins of Poland, Hitler saying to Stalin, "The scum of the earth, I believe?" and Stalin courteously replying, "The bloody assassin of the workers, I presume?"

After Russia was attacked by Germany, Stalin became Churchill's strange bedfellow. When the British Prime Minister was asked how he could say anything good about the Communist dictator, he replied, "If Hitler invaded Hell, I would make at least a favourable reference to the Devil in the House of Commons."

The latent double meaning of the phrase surfaced in the House of Representatives in the '30s. Former House Speaker Joe Martin recalled a member shouting, "I say to you, Mr. Speaker, that politics makes strange bedfellows. Especially since women got into 'em."

straw man (man of straw) A weakling; one who is all façade, no substance; also, a false issue or phony candidate set up to distract and draw attack.

"Condemn me if you will," said President William Howard Taft in 1912, under savage attack from the man who made him president and who now wanted the job back, "but condemn me by other witnesses than Theodore Roosevelt. I was a man of straw; but I have been a man of straw long enough.

Every man who has blood in his body, and who has been misrepresented as I have … is forced to fight."

A man of straw—one who looks like a man but is stuffed with straw—comes from the farmer's scarecrow, and from its military use as a false target set up to draw enemy fire. The phrase was used by Taft in the sense of LIGHTWEIGHT; in the following use, the synonym would be STALKING HORSE:

Columnist Clayton Fritchey wrote with some sarcasm in 1967 that "The Fearless Ninetieth [Congress] … has shown once more that it wears no strawman's collar" by enacting a bill against race riots "which is aimed at the strawman of the mythical 'outside agitator.'"

A similar but more profound term is *hollow man*. The quality of bloodlessness equates *straw* and *hollow*, as in this use by Jersey City Democratic leader Frank Hague about Governor Franklin Roosevelt: "a weather vane, beautiful against the sky, shining and resplendent, built of hollow brass." "The Hollow Men" is a poem by T. S. Eliot, the title of which is said by some analysts to characterize the postwar politicians of the Western world. The poem concludes: "This is the way the world ends / Not with a bang but a whimper." Historian Samuel Eliot Morison wrote: "Congress, too, was full of hollow men. William E. Borah, perpetual senator from Idaho, was the most pretentious and the emptiest, although he looked more like a statesman than any senator since Daniel Webster. Borah would support any liberal bill with great rumbling oratory, yet in the end vote with the regular Republicans. Senator Norris said of him, 'He fights until he sees the whites of their eyes.'" See TURNAROUNDS.

"The key word here again is responsibility," said a *Washington Post* editorial in 1993, using the term in discussing broadcast practices. "When Howard Stern and his supporters whine about First Amendment rights, they set up their straw man."

The phrase itself can be tracked to English proverbs popular in the early seventeenth century: "A man of straw is worth a woman of gold" and "A man of straw eats a servant of steel."

An African-affairs scholar, Sue Cott Wunderman, informs the author that the phrase has an independent West African parallel. Tribes were reluctant to have their real chiefs deal with French colonial officials. William Foltz points out in *From French West Africa to the Mali Federation*: "Usually a younger man or an elder of inferior caste or status was put up by the people themselves as a 'straw chief' to deal with the conqueror, but beneath the dignity of the tribesman really in charge."

The most recent reincarnation of the straw, or hollow, man is "an empty suit." See CHARLIE REGAN.

straw poll (straw vote) Originally an informal survey of a small group to determine opinion; now becoming a term for a scientific, large-scale poll based on the theory of a random sample.

"Ballads, bon mots, anecdotes, give us better insight into the depths of past centuries than grave and voluminous chronicles," wrote Ralph Waldo Emerson in his *Journals*. "'A Straw,' says Selden, 'thrown up into the air will show how the wind sits, which cannot be learned by casting up a stone.'"

Emerson was right in the point he was making, though he took some liberties with the quotation from John Selden (1584–1654), who wrote, "Take a straw and throw it up into the Air,—you may see by that which way the Wind is, which you shall not do by casting up a stone. More solid things do not show the Complexion of the times so well, as Ballads and Libels." However, an earlier use of a similar phrase can be found in Shakespeare's *Merchant of Venice*, Act I, scene 1: "I should be still / Plucking the grass to know where sits the wind."

A *straw* is metaphorically weighty (the last straw can break a camel's back), necessary (you can't make bricks without it), empty (STRAW MAN), and not so powerful (a *straw boss* is a foreman who can give orders but carries no executive responsibility).

A *straw in the wind*, probably derived from Selden's usage, is a rough indication or portent, similar to a "cloud no bigger than a man's hand" (1 Kings 18:44) on the horizon.

The term *straw vote* is traced to the *Cleveland Leader* in 1866, with indications that it had been used long before: "A straw vote taken on a Toledo train yesterday resulted as follows: [Andrew] Johnson 12, Congress, 47." Surveys had often been taken on river steamboats, and *steamboat vote* was a predecessor phrase that was considered "a straw," as in this item in *Old Zack*, an 1848 campaign weekly supporting Zachary Taylor: "Straws.—For a while the Locofoco papers ventured to publish steamboat votes…A vote was taken on the Steamer Fairmount on her trip to Pittsburg.—This is the vote: Taylor 75, Cass 37, Van Buren 4."

Most modern public-opinion surveys create a panel of voters, based on age, previous voting record, location, socioeconomic background, ethnic group, and so on, hoping to build a cross section of the actual population makeup. However, straw polls—if they gather enough straws, or votes—can reflect the attitudes of the population of an area if they adhere rigidly to a "random sample" and not just those easiest to reach or passing by a certain corner.

Strength of a big straw poll is in the size of its sample, and the fact that most people do *not* change their vote in the final two weeks; weakness of such polling is that some people *do* change their minds, which can be decisive in a "squeaker," and the pollsters are stuck with straws carefully gathered in a final go-around that begins several weeks before Election Day. The pre-caucus "straw poll" taken in Ames, Iowa, by each party is not a scientific measurement at all, but a test of organizational strength; see CATTLE SHOW.

When the poll shows a candidate behind, his supporters say with O. Henry in a 1913 story: "A straw vote only shows which way the hot air blows."

See POLLSTER; DEPTH POLLING; TRIAL HEAT.

street money See WALKING-AROUND MONEY.

street smarts Savvy; cunning; intuitive understanding of the way the urban voter will react.

To *have the smarts* is to be mentally sharp; the specific *street smarts* is a political insider's term, meaning sensitivity to opinions at the grassroots, gained by experience, without benefit of polls.

In 1972, reporter Paul Hoffman wrote: "Street smarts—in New York City, Wagner, Lefkowitz and Javits have it, Rockefeller and Lindsay do not."

Beyond politics, the phrase is used to mean an understanding of the ways of the real world. In a 1972 article on the rock group the Rolling Stones, *Time* reported: "the Stones from the start based their appeal partly on their reputation as delinquents. They were always too shaggy, too street smart ..."

In the Southern U.S., new-products marketer Phyllis Bishop reported in 1997 that a variant phrase with the same meaning is *street sense*.

Street as an attributive noun modifying *smarts* (synonymous with *mother wit*) does not have the same meaning as in *the Arab street*, based on a rough guess at public opinion expressed in public demonstrations.

strict constructionist In law, one who tends to interpret the Constitution literally, as meaning exactly what it says and no more, much as a fundamentalist interprets the Bible; in politics, one who feels that judges in their broad interpretation of the law have been encroaching on the lawmaking function of the legislative branch.

The *Congressional Globe*, in 1841, defined a *strict constructionist* as "a Pharisee's Pharisee." In 1850 a Pennsylvania congressman named Chandler explained the breed to his House colleagues in this way: "You remember the anecdote of the youngster who received an admonition from his father that it was time to be steady, make some money and take a wife. 'Why, sir,' said he, 'I like the money-making, but whose wife shall I take?' He was a strict constructionist."

"We need more strict constructionists on the highest court of the United States," said Richard Nixon in a law-and-order speech in 1968, reprising a theme he had made frequently during the campaign. The emphasis was on the "strict."

The phrase connoted hard-line judges who would not hamstring law enforcement officials with pettifogging procedural complaints. It connoted something else as well—judges who would not let their own social beliefs carry them into the lawmaking region reserved to Congress. Many lawyers believe that such usage confusingly encompasses two different doctrines: one of *strict construction*, and the other of *judicial restraint*.

In law, according to Bouvier's *Law Dictionary*, "A *strict* construction is one which limits the application of the provisions of the instrument or agreement to cases clearly described by the words used. It is called, also, literal. A *liberal* construction is one by which the letter is enlarged or restrained so as more effectually to accomplish the end in view. It is called, also, equitable."

While most strict constructionists are also believers in judicial restraint, it has been possible to abandon judicial restraint in pursuit of strict construction.

Historically, the *construction*, or interpretation, of the Constitution is the United States' longest-lived controversy. Soon after the document was written, public opinion was divided between the "strict constructionists" (the Democrat-Republicans behind Thomas Jefferson) and the "loose constructionists" (the Federalists, favoring a strong central government, behind Hamilton).

Chief Justice John Marshall made a case for loose construction in *McCulloch v. Maryland*: "Let the end be legitimate, let it be within the scope of the Constitution, and all means which are appropriate, which are plainly adapted to that end, which are not prohibited, but consist with the letter and spirit of the Constitution, are constitutional." (However, Marshall also wrote, in *Marbury v. Madison*, that the Constitution is "committed to writing" so that its "limits may not be mistaken or forgotten.")

While the phrase *strict construction* has a general appeal to conservatives because of the word *strict*, another word came along in a 1980 article in the *Boston University Law Review* by A. Boyce Brest: "By 'originalism' I mean the familiar approach to constitutional adjudication that accords binding authority to the text of the Constitution or the intentions of its adopters." Foremost and most articulate advocate of originalism (or textualism, literalism, or the new strict constructionism) has been Justice Antonin Scalia.

Ironically, Justice Hugo Black, an ardent New Dealer named to the High Court by FDR in 1937—whose liberal opinions often made him the target of many who considered themselves strict constructionists—was such a strict constructionist on the First and Fourteenth Amendments that he was described as not just a literalist but an absolutist. Justice Black liked to pull a copy of the Constitution out of his pocket, point to the words in the First Amendment that read "Congress shall make no law … abridging the freedom of speech or of the press" and say, " 'No law' means *no law.*"

strike a blow for freedom A pleasant drink in a politician's office, accompanied by informal political discussion; a legislative code phrase.

"On a hot afternoon in 1958," wrote Rowland Evans and Robert Novak in 1966, "Speaker Sam Rayburn's 'BOARD OF EDUCATION' met in his offices, as it did almost every day after work to 'strike a blow for freedom'—good political talk accompanied by good whiskey."

The phrase is especially used among Texans and effectively confuses outsiders; when Texas Congressman Olin E. Teague invited the author to "strike a blow for freedom" one evening in 1963, about the last thing expected was a glass of Early Times bourbon along with a general discussion of the political scene.

New York *Daily News* columnist Ted Lewis, who covered Washington for United Press in the early '30s, attributes coinage to Vice President John Nance Garner. He informed the author: "Garner called it 'striking a blow for liberty.' He was a stingy man with the liquor, though—he could strike a blow with a thimbleful."

A similar phrase has long existed in England. To a tavernkeeper, an *Act of Parliament* is a small (which means weak) beer, stemming from an ancient require-ment that landlords billeting soldiers had to provide five pints of small beer free to each—"by Act of Parliament." The *strike a blow for freedom* phrase is sufficiently pretentious to make it useful for an ironic twist, even to the extent of giving it a meaning of enjoying a straight shot of whisky.

However, some political leaders still use the phrase in the original context. Said Rhodesian Prime Minister Ian Smith in 1965 as he broke from Great Britain: "We have struck a blow for the preservation of justice, civilization, and Christianity; and in the spirit of this belief we have this day assumed our sovereign independence." Thirteen years later he acquiesced in majority rule by blacks, which they felt was more of a "blow for freedom."

In 2003, Rep. Lynn Woolsey said of a California constituent, jailed by China for his activities in a movement disapproved by Beijing authorities, "We must continue Falun Gong's struggle for freedom in China, and in so doing, we will strike a blow for freedom everywhere."

strike force See TASK FORCE.

striped-pants diplomacy See SHIRTSLEEVE DIPLOMACY; COOKIE-PUSHER.

stroke As a verb, to persuade soothingly, or to hold in line with murmured reassurances; as a noun, influence.

When White House officials are concerned with a legislator's possible defection on a vote, instructions are passed to the congressman's colleagues or to lobbyists to *stroke* him (from the image of caressing the raised hackles of an angry or frightened animal).

The noun form, less frequently used, has a different meaning: a person with *stroke* is one with CLOUT; the metaphor is possibly from golf or tennis. When the author used this definition in a 1975 column, Meridyth Senes of Wynnewood, Pa., wrote: "If anything, 'stroke' … would have derived more from the street phrase 'different strokes for different folks,' with its obvious sexual connotation." Her suggestion that *stroke* as a verb has to do with the rhythm of intercourse is not far-fetched: in Navy slang, to *stroke around* is to wander about, looking for company, similar to the old Air Force term *strafing the Strasse*. Significantly, to *stroke* in auto-racing argot means to mill the crankshaft for a longer plunge.

Russell Baker of *The New York Times* in 1978 compared *stroking* favorably to another form of presidential persuasion, JAWBONING: "President Nixon, revolted by such direct methods, preferred what he called 'stroking,' a process of jawboning so sweet to the strokee's earbones that the victim fell into a hypnotic state in which he could be deboned without realizing it."

stroke of a pen By executive order; action that can be taken by a chief executive without legislative action.

Candidate John F. Kennedy said in 1960 that the president could end discrimination in federally financed housing with a "stroke of the pen," a phrase that was then current with civil rights leaders impatient with Eisenhower. When Kennedy, as president, delayed taking such action himself, Martin Luther King, Jr., called on him to "give segregation its death blow through a stroke of the pen," and disenchanted civil rights advocates began sending pens to the White House as a not-so-subtle reminder.

Typical prose use is in this passage from a 1966 book by Raymond Moley: "The closing of the banks was the anesthetic before the major operation. A proclamation that had been considered for weeks, assured of authority under the law, required merely the stroke of a White House pen. The hard part lay ahead."

In 1971 Leonard Woodcock, president of the United Automobile Workers, objected to a wage-price freeze in these words: "If this Administration thinks that just by issuing an edict, by the stroke of a pen, they can tear up contracts, they are saying to us they want war. If they want war, they can have war."

An early political use was by stockbroker-poet Edmund Clarence Stedman (1833–1908) in his 1862 poem titled "Wanted—A Man":

Give us a man of God's own mould
Born to marshal his fellow-men;
One whose fame is not bought and sold
At the stroke of a politician's pen.

stump As a noun, the campaign trail; as a verb, to exhort informally, usually outdoors, in a campaign.

After listening to a speech by President Harding in 1921, H. L. Mencken wrote: "The stump speech, put into cold type, maketh the judicious to grieve. But roared from an actual stump, with arms flying and eyes flashing and the old flag overhead, it is certainly and brilliantly effective."

To achieve a dominating posture, a frontier speechmaker would use a convenient tree stump as a platform. The earliest reference clearly shows the origin; Ann Maury, in her 1716 *Memoirs of a Huguenot Family*, wrote, "I went down to the Saponey Indian town. There is in the center of the circle a great stump of a tree. I asked the reason they left it standing, and they informed me that it was for one of their head men to stand upon when he had anything of consequence to relate to them, so that being raised, he might the better be heard."

By 1838 it was part of the American political vocabulary. *The New York Herald* tells of the Speaker of the House, James K. Polk, "Stumping it about the State of Tennessee." And the *Hamilton* (Ohio) *Intelligencer* was editorializing sniffily about this innovation which it was quite certain would not last: "'Stumping it' is a new game for candidates for Governor in Ohio, and we very much doubt whether the 'Experiment' will be sanctioned by a dignified people."

As with other apt phrases, this one was picked up across the ocean, sometimes in exalted circles. Prime Minister Gladstone displeased Queen Victoria by campaigning for a broadening of the eligible electorate in a tour through Scotland while she was staying at her Balmoral residence in the same area. Her Majesty's secretary, General Ponsonby, noted "his constant speeches at every station.... The Queen is utterly disgusted with his stump oratory—so unworthy of his position—almost under her very nose."

Others have defined *stump* oratory in the same vein, as bombastic, even inflammatory; generally the word is accepted today in its original sense of taking the candidate in person to the people, and no candidate can afford to let even the most televised and net-rooted campaign go by without ostentatiously *taking to the stump*. See HUSTINGS; STEMWINDER.

Another sense of *stump*, as a verb, is to pose a question that the person asked cannot answer. It is fanciful to suppose that this is connected with embarrassed stump speakers.

See THE SPEECH.

suaviter in modo See EGGHEAD.

sucking sound See SPOILER.

sufficiency See PARITY.

summitry The art of dealing at the top level; the notion that diplomacy can best be practiced by face-to-face meeting of world leaders.

Winston Churchill, unhappy with the international impasse in 1950 that his friend Bernard Baruch had described as the COLD WAR, recalled the wartime meetings with Stalin and Roosevelt and issued a call for a "parley at the summit."

Immediately, diplomats around the world pointed out that such a meeting would bring about little of substance, that the hopes of the world would be raised and dashed, and that many months of intricate preplanning on lower levels would be necessary before any decisions could be made as to what would be discussed.

Churchill dismissed all this. "This conference should not be overhung by a ponderous or rigid agenda or led into mazes of technical details, zealously contested by hordes of experts and officials drawn up in a vast cumbrous array."

As a rule, foreign ministers resist summit conferences, on the theory that world problems are too complex to be left to world leaders and the world is led to expect too much; what's more, the second echelon is left to fight over what was said, meant, and

not meant. "Conferences at the top level are always courteous," career diplomat Averell Harriman said in 1955. "Name-calling is left to the foreign ministers."

Turning a careful phrase in 1959, Senator John Kennedy said, "It is far better that we meet at the summit than at the brink." As president, he had a rough session at the summit with Khrushchev in 1961. But, wrote Sorensen, "The Soviet leader also made clear his belief in summitry. If the heads of state cannot resolve problems, how can officials at a lower level? He liked as much personal contact as possible, he said, no matter how able one's ambassadors might be—just as natural love is better than love through interpreters."

A question that always arises in debating the use of summitry is: How much freedom of action does a world leader have? How bound is he by past policy, and how much leeway does his Politburo or Congress or public opinion at home give him? The quiet style of Alexei Kosygin led this question to be asked in 1967 before the summit conference with Lyndon Johnson at Glassboro, New Jersey. This meeting was arranged hurriedly, during a trip to the UN to debate the Arab-Israeli war, proving that the need for extended advance preparation was not as overwhelming as it seemed. Though the conference was fringed with warnings not to expect much, and indeed did not produce much, President Johnson expressed this attitude afterward: "It does help a lot to sit down and look at a man right in the eye and try to reason with him, particularly if he is trying to reason with you." See COME NOW, AND LET US REASON TOGETHER.

In *Present at the Creation* Dean Acheson wrote in 1970 that summitry could be traced back to the early sixteenth century, but that in only two cases was it clearly successful: the meetings at Münster and Osnabrück in 1648 that ended the Thirty Years' War with the Peace of Westphalia, and the Congress of Vienna in 1814. Summits have "all too often been a gamble, the experience nerve-wracking and the results unsatisfactory," wrote the former Secretary of State, and quoted advice given to Woodrow Wilson's aide, Colonel Edward House, on the eve of

Wilson's journey to Europe: "The moment President Wilson sits at the council table with these prime ministers and foreign secretaries," the adviser said, "he has lost all the power that comes from distance and detachment...he becomes merely a negotiator dealing with other negotiators."

Acheson added a metaphor familiar to football fans: "When a chief of state or head of government makes a fumble, the goal line is open behind him." (One does not "make" a fumble, however; one fumbles.)

In a nondiplomatic context, the best-known uses of the word *summit* were Napoleon's "Soldiers, from the summits of the pyramids, forty centuries look down upon you" and Edmund Burke's eulogy of Charles James Fox, quoted by John Kennedy as the keynote in *Profiles in Courage*, and recalled by his acolytes after the Cuban missile crisis of 1962: "He may live long, he may do much. But here is the summit. He never can exceed what he does this day."

sunset law A provision in a bill shutting off a program on a specific date, requiring a fresh authorization in the future. Senator Hillary Clinton in May 2007 joined in offering a bill that would "*sunset* the 2002 authorization of military operations in Iraq," reported *The Washington Post*. "Clinton's endorsement of the *sunset* legislation represents a significant escalation in her opposition to the White House on war policy."

The technique, and the phrase, began in Colorado over three decades before. Rosalie Schiff of Colorado Common Cause answered the author's query:

The phrase "sunset law" was coined by Craig Barnes, a member of our Board of Directors, at an Issues committee meeting in May 1975. Mr. Barnes coined the term to describe a process whereby agencies would terminate periodically unless they could justify their continued existence. Since affirmative legislative action would be required for continued life, should an agency fail to prove a public need for its existence, the "sun would set" on said agency. The two-fold purpose of Sunset is to require more public accountability from these agencies

and to reduce the proliferation and growth of bureaucracy.

The idea behind the mechanism was expressed in *Go East, Young Man* by Supreme Court Justice William O. Douglas:

The great creative work of a federal agency must be done in the first decade of its existence if it is to be done at all. After that it is likely to become a prison of bureaucracy and of the inertia demanded by the Establishment of any respected agency. That is why I told FDR over and over again that every agency he created should be abolished in ten years. And since he might not be around to dissolve it, he should insert in the basic charter of the agency a provision for its termination. Roosevelt would always roar with delight at that suggestion, and of course never did do anything about it.

Because administrative agencies often tend, after a while, to identify with the interests they are supposed to administer or regulate, the idea of incorporating a termination date appealed to many Colorado liberals, while conservatives could be expected to be for any antibureaucratic measure.

The cutoff idea was embraced by candidate Jimmy Carter in his 1976 campaign, as the legislative counter-part of his administrative zero-base budgeting. However, the sun sometimes sets on a colorful coinage: the bill he put forward to require new budget authority every five years was titled "The Program Evaluation Act of 1977."

sunshine laws Measures to force the conduct of public business in public.

"Publicity is justly commended," wrote Supreme Court Justice Louis D. Brandeis, "as a remedy for social and industrial disease. Sunlight is said to be the best disinfectant and electric light the most efficient policeman."

The Florida Sunshine Act was first proposed in 1961; while it was being debated for six years, five other states— Arkansas, Indiana, Nebraska, New Jersey, and New Mexico—enacted open-meeting laws. The Florida act directed "All meetings...at which official acts are to be taken are declared to be public meetings open to the public at all times, and no resolution, rule, regulation or formal action shall be considered binding except as taken or made at such meeting."

In proposing similar legislation on the national level, Florida Senator Lawton Chiles wrote in 1974: "Experience under the sunshine law has shown that the open meeting principle does not hamper public business operations, but rather increases public confidence in government… Closed doors are not necessary to sound resolution of conflicting views and interests."

Many legislators who do not like to derogate open meetings publicly disagree privately: in the horse trading that goes on in closed committee sessions, they hold, sensible compromises are reached that could not be struck in the harsh light of PITILESS PUBLICITY. Although the Freedom of Information Act has made much material in the executive branch, other than the White House, available to citizens, Congress has been unwilling to provide such access to its own files and deliberations. In states with sunshine laws, it is charged, much of the public business is done in advance of open meetings—in secret, making the "open" meeting a charade.

Despite the criticism of impracticality, and the derision long leveled at OPEN COVENANTS, openly arrived at, the pressure toward "government in the sunshine" has helped the trend toward more public disclosure of governmental activities. Florida, the "sunshine state," remains in the forefront: "One of Charlie Crist's first acts as governor," noted the *St. Petersburg Times* in 2007, "was to publicly embrace the value of government in the sunshine."

superpatriots Flag-waving extremists; attack phrase on those who protest too much their love of country.

"I don't think the United States needs super-patriots," wrote President Eisenhower in 1962. "We need patriotism, honestly practiced by all of us, and we don't need these people that are more patriotic than you or anybody else."

Carl Schurz defined "mock patriotism" as "the kind of sentiment which leads a man to say with Decatur, 'Our country, right or wrong.'" (G. K. Chesterton undermined "my country, right or wrong" with a toast to "my mother, drunk or sober.") Dr. Samuel Johnson found plain—not even super—patriotism "the last refuge of a scoundrel." Some are more charitable. Adlai Stevenson, writing of the McCarthy era: "We have survived it. We shall survive John Birchism and all the rest of the super patriots—but only at the price of perpetual and truly patriotic vigilance."

The fashion in "super" words—from *supercolossal* to *superduper* and *superpower*—was set by George Bernard Shaw. Nietzsche's *Übermensch* had been translated as "Overman" or "Beyondman"; Shaw coined *Superman*, who later left politics to become a comic strip "man of steel." *Superstar* became a familiar word of the sixties in both show business and sports, and *superpower* an appellation in world politics. The *OED* cites William T. R. Fox's 1944 *Super-Powers*: "There will be 'world powers' and 'regional powers'. These world powers we shall call 'super-powers', in order to distinguish them from the other powers… whose interests are great in only a single theater of power conflict."

"We will never become a superpower," Chinese Premier Zhou Enlai promised the Canadian Broadcasting Company in 1971; "we are opposed to the power politics of the big powers." Though Zhou used the term pejoratively, as leaders of non-superpowers occasionally do, the word is more generally used neutrally in reference to the U.S. and (formerly) the Soviet Union.

A synonymous prefix, *ultra*, is also used politically. There are *ultraconservatives* and *ultraliberals*; although there are *superpatriots*, there are no *supertraitors*. By the turn of the 21st century, *mega* had superseded, or megaseded, both *super* and *ultra* as the superlative prefix of choice.

Conservative satirist Vic Gold spoofed the fashion of denigrating patriotic fervor as "superpatriotism" by titling a fictitious work *Paul Revere and the Superpatriotic Tradition in American History*. See KOOKS, NUTS AND; LITTLE OLD LADIES IN TENNIS SHOES; TURN-AROUNDS.

supply side Economic policy that emphasizes the use of tax cuts to give incentives for increasing investment and creating jobs, aimed thereby to increase total national taxable income.

Sometimes criticized as *Reaganomics* (see -NOMICS), *supply side* economics stresses marginal tax cuts and was named in 1976 by the economist Herbert Stein, who had been chairman of the Council of Economic Advisers late in the Nixon administration. This alliterative phrase is hyphenated when used to modify economics or policy. Early printed use occurred in a 1976 headline in *The Wall Street Journal*: "Supply-Side Fiscalism."

Stein wrote in 1996 that the idea "antedated Nixon," an allusion to the Kennedy tax-cut proposals. The economics writer Jude Wanniski coined the agent noun *supply-sider*.

In a 1980 essay in *The Wall Street Journal*, Stein wrote about "Some 'Supply-Side' Propositions," concluding, "Supply-side economics may yet prove to be the irritant which, like the grain of sand in the oyster shell, produces a pearl of new economic wisdom. But up to this point the pearl has not appeared." Later in the decade, it appeared in full necklace form: *supply side* was the theory articulated by and most closely associated with the economist Arthur Laffer, who sketched the *Laffer curve* on a cocktail napkin to illustrate its effect; it was also taken up and espoused by Rep. Jack Kemp during his brief 1988 campaign for the presidency.

Although George H.W. Bush had once denounced this policy (see VOODOO ECONOMICS), the *Chicago Tribune* reported during his 1992 campaign against challenger Bill Clinton that "President Bush is returning to the supply-side economic program of Ronald Reagan in promising across-the-board tax cuts and spending reductions to lift the economy out of the most prolonged economic slump since the 1930's."

With the economy booming in early 2007, Senator John McCain attracted conservative support by embracing the continuation of the Bush tax cuts and urging greater spending restraint; a Robert Novak column was given the *Washington Post* headline "Born Again Supply-Sider?"

See also FLAT TAX.

Supreme Court follows the election returns A view that the supposedly dispassionate and disinterested Supreme Court bench usually reflects the current political scene.

This bit of irreverence was the work of Finley Peter Dunne's "Mr. DOOLEY." America's war against Spain had just been concluded. The majority of Congress, swept up by a new feeling of America's MANIFEST DESTINY, had approved the taking of the Philippines and of Puerto Rico from Spain. Puerto Rico was not part of the U.S., yet our government claimed the right to collect taxes and to levy tariffs among its people. The Democratic party, in convention in 1900, had contended that wherever U.S. sovereignty extended, the people of that area gained the rights and protection of the U.S. Constitution; in the phrase of the day, "We hold that the Constitution follows the flag." The Democrats lost.

The Supreme Court labored until it came up with a fuzzy doctrine: territories like Puerto Rico weren't exactly foreign, since the U.S. had acquired them; on the other hand, they weren't really domestic, either, so the U.S. government did have the right to levy taxes on these unrepresented people. This, more or less, agreed with the position of the winning Republicans.

All of which drew from Mr. Dooley the caustic comment, "No matter whether th' Constitution follows th' flag or not, th' Supreme Coort follows th' iliction returns."

Chief Justice Hughes once said, "We are under a Constitution, but the Constitution is what the judges say it is." Life tenure enables justices to resist the passions of the moment, but by and large, the members of the Court reflect their time, the evolving culture, and the judgments of the populace, giving some support to Dunne's gibe. See DOOLEY, MR.; NINE OLD MEN; STRICT CONSTRUCTIONIST.

surge Military term for sharp increase in troop strength to overwhelm an enemy; specifically, the use of that strategy to make possible the defeat of the insurgency in Iraq in 2007.

The verb rooted in the Latin *surgere*, "to rise," its primary sense "to billow suddenly, as in a great wave," was used by President Bush in August 2004 about Pentagon plans to move U.S. troops to new locations outside Europe "so they can *surge* quickly to deal with unexpected threats."

With casualties mounting in Iraq in December of 2006, and with American public displeasure expressed in a resounding midterm political defeat by Democrats who were calling for quick withdrawal of the 130,000 U.S. troops, President Bush did the unexpected: To quell the sectarian and terrorist warfare, he ordered a "surge" of an additional 30,000 to the crucial area of Baghdad and its environs, which began in February under a new commander, General David Petraeus, who employed a new counterinsurgency strategy.

The troop strength reached the "surge" level in June 2007, and the tide appeared to turn; by year's end, key Sunni tribal leaders turned on al-Qaeda, enemy attacks declined by nearly two-thirds and official Iraqi security forces increased by 110,000. At home, "purge the surge" headlines stopped; war opponents in Congress charging QUAGMIRE were unable to cut appropriations or force an immediate EXIT STRATEGY. Their criticism continued of the Iraqi government's inability to get its rival factions to match the military progress, but anti-war fervor was lessened in 2008 Democratic primaries as U.S. troop withdrawals were predicted to below "surge" levels. Bush was frequently said to have "found his Grant" in General Petraeus, a reference to President Lincoln's opportune promotion of General Ulysses Grant.

For comparison of Bush's "surge" to LBJ's Vietnam ESCALATION, see Senator Edward Kennedy's speech under STAY THE COURSE.

surgical strike Attack designed to destroy a military facility with a minimum of civilian deaths; a narrowly focused action executed quickly and precisely.

The phrase was popularized in 1981, when Israeli bombers obliterated a plant near Baghdad where the Iraqi dictator Saddam Hussein was about to go onstream with a facility processing nuclear fuel. *Surgical strike* reappeared during the spring of 1986, when the United States mounted a bombing raid on Qaddafi forces in Libya.

Its origins, however, were at least two decades earlier. "Following a conversation with President Kennedy," Murray Marder wrote in a 1981 *Washington Post* article, "the late Stewart Alsop wrote in 'The Saturday Evening Post' that 'a surgical strike' against China's gaseous diffusion plant at Lop Nor was under serious consideration."

Theodore Sorensen wrote in his 1964 memoir, *Kennedy*, about White House discussions of an attack on Cuba: "The idea of American planes suddenly and swiftly eliminating the missile complex with conventional bombs in a matter of minutes—a so-called 'surgical' strike—had appeal to almost everyone first considering the matter."

To counter *surgical strikes*, secret nuclear facilities, as in North Korea and Iran, are widely scattered and placed deep underground, which led to the development of bombs known as "bunker busters."

surrender on Morningside Heights A party-unity conference between Eisenhower and Taft after the bruising fight for the 1952 nomination, which Democrats tried vainly to exploit.

Like the Nixon-Rockefeller COMPACT OF FIFTH AVENUE in 1960, the meeting between Dwight Eisenhower and Robert A. Taft in 1952 was an attempt at unifying a party that was immediately characterized as a SELLOUT by the opposition party, as well as by some disgruntled Republican liberals.

The meeting took place on September 12, 1952, at 60 Morningside Drive in New York City, Eisenhower's residence as president of Columbia University. Earlier, Taft had let it be known from his post-convention vacation retreat in Murray Bay, Canada, that his price for active support of the ticket would be some written assurances on policy. This Democrats called "the ultimatum of Murray Bay," but it did not catch on; Adlai Stevenson's characterization of the meeting as "the surrender on Morningside Heights," considering the General's military background, had greater appeal.

A statement issued after the meeting had a strong Taft flavor. They had agreed that an issue at home was "liberty against CREEP-ING SOCIALIZATION" and Taft added, "General Eisenhower emphatically agrees with me in the proposal to reduce drastically overall expenses.... General Eisenhower has also told me that he believes strongly in our system of Constitutional limitations on Government power and that he abhors the left-wing theory that the Executive had unlimited powers.... General Eisenhower has also told me that he believes in the basic principles of the Taft-Hartley Law, its protection of the people and the freedom of the union members themselves against the arbitrary use of power by big business or big labor, and is opposed to its repeal ..." He concluded, "It is fair to say that our differences are differences of degree."

Stevenson slammed away at the meeting throughout the campaign: "I wonder what happened to all those declarations of undying principle we heard from both sides while they were calling each other nasty names in Chicago.... It looks as if Taft lost the nomination but won the nominee ... when he walked out of the General's house in New York with the surrender in writing I have never seen such a contented smile since the cat swallowed the canary ... part of the price of the embrace on Morningside Heights has been to lay no affirmative program before this nation for its approval."

Eisenhower recalled: "Some journalists and the Democratic nominee, however, seemed to think that here was raw drama. The opposition saw in this meeting a great 'surrender on Morningside Heights.' The fact was that Senator Taft and I had agreed emphatically on the need for fiscal sanity in the government, as on most other issues, long before the breakfast talk."

This was one of the classic minuets of politics. A savage primary is followed by a sullen requirement for assurances; these are then given at a sweetness-and-light unity meeting or LOVE FEAST; this is then attacked and derided by the opposition which tries to keep the primary split from healing; that attack is then pooh-poohed by the unifying candidates. The French analysis of this type of activity was given by the novelist and editor Alphonse Karr in his magazine *Les guêpes* (Jan. 1849): *"Plus ça change, plus c'est la même chose"*—the more things change, the more they stay the same.

surrogate candidate See ADVANCE MAN.

swap horses See DON'T CHANGE HORSES.

sweetheart Shorter than arm's length; collusive.

In labor terminology, a *sweetheart contract* is one in which a union leader makes an unfavorable settlement for his fellow employees and then takes an emolument from management on the side.

The adjective has crossed into political parlance without the illegal meaning, but with the implicit charge of favoritism. Columnist Tom Wicker used the word in 1977 in its most modestly pejorative sense: "The Administration's broader anti-inflation policy is based on a vague, soft, sweetheart reliance on business voluntarism ..."

In business, a *sweetener* is an acceptable extra incentive to close a deal; in politics, such sweetness strikes a sour note. In diplomacy, a *sop to Cerberus* is a minor appeasement, based on the bribe of cake dipped in honey a visitor to Hades must give the three-headed dog guarding passage across the river Styx.

swift boat spot Television commercial that attacked the war record of the Democratic candidate for president in 2004, Sen. John Kerry.

The *swift boat spot* was produced by a group called Swift Boat Veterans for Truth. Initially aired in a few swing states in August of 2004, and widely disseminated through the blogosphere, the commercial featured statements by men who had served with Lt. Kerry in 1968 and 1969 on the fast, 50-foot aluminum boats that patrolled coastal waterways in Vietnam. The veterans claimed that Kerry had lied about his service, including the injuries for which he received silver and bronze stars as well as three Purple Hearts.

Though independent of the Republican Party, the Swift Boat group had strong ties to it. Financing came largely from a major donor to the Republican Party, Bob J. Perry, a Houston home builder. John E. O'Neill, one of the group's prime movers and co-author of a book attacking Kerry, *Unfit to Command*, had led another group in 1971, Vietnam Veterans for a Just Peace, in an effort to neutralize Kerry's public opposition to the war after he returned home from it.

Kerry defenders charged that claims in the *swift boat spot* were contradicted by Navy records and by other veterans who served with Kerry, including all the members of his own boat crew, but the ad inspired a great deal of press coverage damaging his presidential campaign in part because he was slow to respond to it.

The name of the naval craft soon turned into a verb. Nine months after Bush's reelection, referring in August 2005 to attacks on Cindy Sheehan—who protested the war in Iraq with a well-covered vigil beside the road leading to President Bush's ranch in Crawford, Tex.—columnist Frank Rich wrote in *The New York Times:* "Once Ms. Sheehan could no longer be ignored, the Swift Boating began. Character assassination is the [White House political strategist] Karl Rove tactic of choice, eagerly mimicked by media surrogates."

Countering this later in 2005, criticizing Kerry's post-election criticisms of Bush, the electronic magazine *Slate* headlined a column by John Dickerson, "Kerry Swift-Boats Bush." In an article on the coming 2006 mid-term election, Jonathan Allen reported in the Capitol Hill newspaper, *The Hill:* "Democrats vowed again yesterday not to get 'swift-boated.'"

Not everyone considered *swift-boating* to be pejorative. A former Navy SEAL, Larry Bailey, who organized Vets for Truth to oppose the reelection in 2006 of Rep. John Murtha (D-Penn.), who was urging withdrawal of U.S. troops from Iraq, told *Army Times:* "I totally approve of what the Swift Boat guys did in 2004 and would love to have been a part of that." Bailey's website defined *swift-boating* as "exposing the lies, deceit and fraud of self-glorifying public officials or candidates for office who exaggerate their military service by lying about their feats of heroism and combat wounds."

A minor lexical mystery is the origin of name of the *Swift* boat. Douglas Brinkley asserted in his biography of Kerry, *Tour of Duty*, that it arose as an acronym for "Shallow Water Inshore Fast Tactical Craft." Use of all-capitals in an early reference to the boats in *The Wall Street Journal*, of Feb. 16, 1966 supports that theory: "At sea, a 50-foot U.S. Navy patrol vessel, known as a SWIFT boat, was destroyed by an underwater mine in the Gulf of Siam."

Those who were there disagree. Rear Adm. Roy F. Hoffmann (Ret.), chairman of Swift Boat Veterans for Truth and commander of Swift boats and Coast Guard Cutters in Vietnam, told the lexicographer that the manufacturer, Stewart Seacraft, named the different boats it produced for seabirds—a *swift* in this instance (though the swift is closer to a hummingbird than a seabird). The owner of Stewart Seacraft, F. W. Stewart, reportedly said the name came from an admiral's comment during a demonstration of the boats that they were "swift."

Long after the election-time furor of charge and counter-charge, the noun's transmutation into a verb became its leading form, as *swift-boating, to swift-boat*, and *to be swift-boated*, for "angry charges that a candidate's claimed record is false."

See also BORKING and DAISY SPOT.

swing around the circle See NON-POLITICAL TRIP.

swing voter One who votes for the person, not the party; the independent vote that often *swings* elections one way or the other.

Over recent decades, some political scientists have estimated that not more than

60 percent of the American electorate is partisan and regular in its voting habits. As personalities and issues have become more significant than party affiliation, the size of the swing vote has grown. Pollster Samuel Lubell noted in 1959 that the electorate "seems to have undergone a curious quickening of its voting reflexes" in elections since 1948, making it "easier to shift the party allegiance of the American voter."

A half-century later, in 2006, it had not changed much: under a *Washington Post* headline reading "Partied Out," an editor of the *Hotline* on the Internet noted that "Consistently, about 30 percent of U.S. voters tell pollsters they don't belong to a party... These non-affiliated voters tend to be less fiscally liberal than the Democratic mean and less socially conservative than the Republican mean."

What has changed in the new millennium, some analysts believe, is the emphasis the parties have given to turning out their BASE, deepening, solidifying, and energizing that core constituency—at the expense of going after the fickle *swing voter*. This was a strategy often attributed to the Bush adviser (*guru* was the word most often used) Karl Rove.

After the Democratic takeover of majority control of both houses of Congress in 2006, the AP headline read "Republicans hold on to base, learn they can't win without the center." The *Albuquerque Journal* agreed: "Swing Voters Pull Politics Back to Center." The swing voter, it seemed obvious by the results, had swung left, if only propelled largely by dissatisfaction with the Iraq war.

However, in *The American Prospect*, a Democratic magazine, Mark Schmitt wrote against the grain: "I doubt that Karl Rove's insight was that 'there are no swing voters.' There are always swing voters. What Rove discovered was that it might not be as much of a waste of time and money as previously thought to go after people who hadn't voted—and, therefore, one could worry less about the electoral middle. He was right—there was a vast untapped potential vote out there—and his insight was so radical and disruptive that it dominated politics

for the five years that it took Democrats to understand it. But like a hedge fund genius with a brilliant strategy, he took it too far, didn't recognize its limits, and never diversified his portfolio."

Swing vote and *swing voter* are not used to any extent in Britain, where an obsolete American expression, *floater*, often defines the independent group. In the U.S., *floater* enjoyed its greatest popularity in 1888, when the Treasurer of the Republican National Committee, W. W. Dudley, was charged with recommending to the Indiana state committee that they secure "floaters in blocks of five." This was construed to mean the purchase of votes wholesale; politicians in ancient Greece dealt out bribes to voters in "blocks of ten."

Claudian, a Latin poet of the fourth century, wrote of *mobile...vulgus* ("the fickle crowd"), which led to the pejorative English word *mob*. The German poet Johann Wolfgang von Goethe came up with a simile that explains one reason for the growth of the swing vote: "In politics, as on the sickbed, people toss from one side to the other, thinking they will be more comfortable."

switcher Registered voter in one party seen to be likely to "split his ticket," or to cross over entirely, on the basis of having done so before.

Pollster Oliver Quayle included a "switcher analysis" in most of his surveys of the voting complexion of an area. These are voters who have crossed party lines in previous elections, indicating a lack of deep party commitment and a likely source of votes for an attractive opposition candidate.

Independents and SWING VOTERS have no party alliances; *switchers* do, if only nominal.

Adlai Stevenson told a story in 1952 about "the little boy who asked his father what a 'convert' was, and the father—evidently a politically minded father—said, 'Well, son, if a Republican becomes a Democrat, he is a convert.' And what, asked the boy, is a Democrat who becomes a Republican? With a scowl his father said, 'Why, he's a traitor, of course.'"

A *switcher issue* is one that presses an internal HOT BUTTON and causes a fiercely committed voter to abandon all other patterns and preferences. See SPLIT TICKET.

sympathizer See COMSYMP.

syntax, presidential See EISENHOWER SYNTAX.

system, the The political structure, not to be despised when it works for you.

Originally *the System* was a phrase accompanied by a sneer, synonymous with *City Hall* or *the Establishment* or *the bureaucracy*. After the Watergate scandal and Nixon's forced resignation, the phrase "the system works" came into wide use, and the word *system* took on a glow as a protector of individual rights.

That nonpejorative use of the System was, in turn, parodied. In the January 1977 *American Spectator*, conservative editor R. Emmett Tyrrell disparaged the Carter election victory as having been the result of a bored electorate: "The voice was faint: 27.5 percent of the people said Jimmy, 26 percent said Jerry, and a whopping 46.5 percent said *yecch*. The system works!"

Although the phrase was used in a positive sense, it had not lost its overtone of entrenched-authority-to-be-opposed. In 1978, when Philadelphia U.S. Attorney David Marston, a Republican, was fired with an explanation from Democratic Attorney General Griffin Bell that "we have a system," Marston retorted, "I don't agree with that. They had a 'system' too in Philadelphia before I got there and I didn't accept that system." In the sense used by Marston, "the system" was a matrix of official corruption and mob influence. Nearly three decades later, the practice of replacing U.S. Attorneys with political allies came under fire as "politicizing justice" but was defended by the Republican Bush administration as the normal workings of the system. See SPOILS SYSTEM.

A Yiddish question, translated into English, expresses a wonderment at the sometimes illogical workings of government: "Is this a system?"

As the *System* replaced the *Establishment*, it has been overtaken in some ways by the PROCESS, which is not capitalized; see that entry for differences, and AMERICAN SYSTEM for origins.

T

table 1. propose for discussion; 2. postpone discussion.

Like *sanction* and *cleave*, the verb *table* is an example of antilogy, a "Janus" word—named after the Roman god of beginnings, with two faces depicted as looking in opposite directions—describing a word that holds opposite meanings.

This verb began in British English in the eighteenth century with the sense of "to bring up for consideration or discussion." The earliest *OED* citation for this legislative sense is in the 1718 correspondence of the Scottish theologian Robert Wodrow: "Another act was passed...that all appeals should be brought up and tabled before the Bills, within three days after the Assembly sit down." Its source is the phrase *upon the table*, from 1646 in the meaning "under consideration."

In American usage, however, the verb *table* took the opposite meaning, "to put away or postpone discussion," a synonym of the verb *shelve*. The verb is first attested in that sense in the mid-nineteenth century, but a 1744 citation for the noun suggests that it had the meaning earlier. This sense of "delay" was commented on by London's *Daily Telegraph* in 1866: "To table a resolution has nearly the same effect in America as the order to read a bill 'this day six months' has in England."

Letting a proposal *lie on the table* led to this sense of postponing indefinitely. The *Archives of New Jersey* showed this political delaying tactic as early as 1744: "The House of Representatives...would not commit it [a bill] but ordered it to lie on the table."

Confusion still exists about the dual meanings, particularly when an American politician uses the primarily British sense. On *The MacNeil/Lehrer NewsHour* in 1985, Georgia Senator Sam Nunn said of a U.S./Soviet summit, "The good news from the Soviets is that at last they are tabling something." His audience did not know whether they were considering it or killing it. See UP-OR-DOWN VOTE.

take a walk Leave the party after a dispute.

The phrase entered the political language with the embittered Al Smith's comment after the renomination of FDR in 1936: "I guess I'll have to take a walk." Democrats lashed back at him with his own symbol: "The brown derby has gone high hat."

Those who BOLT—a racing term—are called MUGWUMPS—an American Indian term—and *soreheads*, from the expression "mad as a bear with a sore head." An Albany (N.Y.) *Weekly Argus* correspondent wrote in 1848: "I have just returned from a ringed, striped, and speckled 'sore-head' demonstration at Sharon Springs," about the formation of the Free Soil party.

Bolters have been denounced by party regulars as determined to "rule or ruin." To *take a walk* and to *change stripes* is to make an (almost) irrevocable decision to *cross the street* to the other party; however, to *sit it out* or to *go fishing* means to remain within the party without supporting—but not publicly rejecting—its candidate in a particular election. To go OFF THE RESERVATION is to take a short, temporary walk, opposing a candidate of one's own party with the intention of returning to the fold after the election.

take her by the hand See STAND IN THE DOORWAY.

taken a bath See SELLING CANDIDATES LIKE SOAP.

talking points A list of reminders to speakers of the essential points of a proposal or an argument; a phrase often derogated by the opposition as "marching orders," simplistic selling points to be followed by supporters in lockstep.

Talking points may be designed to highlight parts of a message for public consumption as well as to ensure that different spokespeople will say the same thing. Referring to tax and spending proposals by President George W. Bush, the

AP reported in 2001: "In talking points distributed on Capitol Hill, administration officials emphasized Bush proposals that could have been made by a moderate Democrat." In 2006, columnist Marc Humbert discussed the jockeying between Andrew Cuomo and Mark Green for the Democratic nomination for attorney general of New York State: "A sample of just how the Cuomo-Green battle could play out came when the *New York Post* reported Tuesday on a 'talking points' memo prepared by the Green campaign for use by campaign surrogates."

Politicians of all persuasions have relied on *talking points* for many decades. Getting ready for brief talks (see ROSE GARDEN RUBBISH), President Nixon would often tell his speechwriters: "Never mind preparing formal remarks for this bunch, just give me a page of talking points." He referred to other brief lines with a musical metaphor as *grace notes*, as contrasted with prosaic *talking points*.

In the singular, the phrase has a long political history: *The Indiana Democrat* (of Indiana County, Pennsylvania) advised Republican leaders in 1901 to tell Pres. Theodore Roosevelt "that while reciprocity [in trade with Cuba] is excellent as 'a talking point' it will not 'go' with the Senate."

The phrase arose in a business context, where *talking points* were part of a sales pitch. In 1862, with the Civil War raging, the Finkle & Lyon Sewing Machine Co. of New York boasted of its machines in an ad in *The Indiana Democrat:* "We prefer such a reputation to one based merely on 'talking points,' as they are technically called in the trade." Sinclair Lewis satirized the protagonist of his 1929 novel *Babbitt* as "a broker who had Vision and who understood Talking Points, Strategic Values, Key Situations, Underappraisals, and the Psychology of Salesmanship."

The pejorative connotations of puffery linger on. "Please check your facts before calling in your Republican talking points," demanded Joe Landers in a letter to the Doylestown, Pa., *Intelligencer* in 2004. On a conservative weblog, RedState, Mike D., from South Carolina, dismissed a Democratic congressional candidate's publica-

tion: "The 'news' articles were all standard MOONBAT talking points."

A mock-reverent phrase is *singing from the same hymn book*. See ON MESSAGE.

Tammany Tiger Symbol of big-city machines.

The Society of Tammany was a fraternal organization that controlled the New York Democratic party from the middle of the nineteenth century to the middle of the twentieth: often corrupt, sometimes effective, it was the prototype of all urban political machines in the U.S. and remains the best known today.

In its heyday, the motto of its leadership might well have been the remark made by Tammany leader George Washington Plunkitt: "I seen my opportunities and I took 'em."

The organization was founded in 1789 by New Yorkers who thought they saw a dangerous drift toward aristocracy in the popularity among the wealthier and the well-born of such societies as St. Andrew's. The Society, named after a Delaware chief famed for his sagacity—Chief Tammany, or more likely, Tamanend—dedicated itself to the defense of democracy. At the beginning of the nineteenth century, with Aaron Burr's help, it became the most efficient political organization of the day.

Legend has it that the tiger symbol came from a stuffed tiger's head on the front of a fire engine used by Tammany in parades. Cartoonist Thomas Nast popularized the tiger symbol in his attacks on the Tweed Ring, which is believed to have stolen anywhere from $200 to $300 million, a large sum in that era. Those who thought Nast's attacks and the subsequent exposures meant the end of Tammany were mistaken. "Honest John" Kelly took over, creating the classic structure of absolute, unquestioning autocracy which was inherited by Richard Croker and later by Charles Murphy.

Reformers were in continual battle with Tammany; nearby boroughs were determined to keep their minions out. In 1876 R. G. Ingersoll said, "Tammany Hall bears the same relation to a penitentiary as a Sunday-school to the church." And in Brooklyn, the motto was: "The Tiger shall not cross the Bridge."

In modern times, Carmine de Sapio did much to reform the autocratic system—and cause his own downfall—by bringing about the direct election of district leaders by the RANK AND FILE. His successors have tried to stress the name "New York County Democratic Organization," as if Tammany were not the name of the club. Cartoonists, however, have too much invested in the tiger to let it die. Although the tiger of Tammany, as drawn on most editorial pages, has lost much of its ferocity and usually appears battered and bandaged, it is still alive.

See SACHEM; PAPER TIGER.

tantamount to election As much as elected.

There must be an unwritten law prohibiting the use of the following: "Nomination in that solidly partisan district is the *equivalent* of election," or "being nominated there is *as much as* being elected." *Equivalent to, as much as, the same as, equal to, amounts to*—all are crushed under the heel of the political cliché, *tantamount to election*.

In 1993, the *Chicago Tribune* wrote of local primaries: "In both elections, victory in the primary is tantamount to election in April." In 2005, the *New York Observer* observed that veteran District Attorney Robert Morgenthau "faces a real contest for the Democratic Party nomination, which is tantamount to election in Manhattan."

Once the tanta is mounted, Election Day is taken to be a mere formality; the political pundit's bromide rides triumphantly into the jungle of jargon. An election-night parlor game is to count the number of times "tantamount to election" is used on television, a competition more rewarding to the viewer than seeing who calls the winners first on the basis of leaked exit polls or the earliest, scattered returns.

The key word is from the Anglo-French *tant*, "so much," and *amunter*, "amount," meaning "to amount to as much." Only ridicule can break up such a rigidly stereotyped phrase; for the foreseeable future, *tantamount* will remain as close to *election* as *unmitigated* remains wedded to *gall* and *inextricably* to *linked*.

taps and bugs Electronic eavesdropping equipment.

Tap, short for *wiretap*, means an intercept placed on a telephone; a *bug* is a tiny transmitter designed to send conversations to a receiver elsewhere. To be *wired* means to be outfitted with a "bug" so as to transmit a conversation to a receiver out of sight. Confusion is caused when a "bug" is used in a "tap"—by placing a transmitter in a telephone, the conversation is effectively tapped, though no wire intercept is made. To *have a tap in* does not necessarily mean to have a wiretap monitoring somebody; frequently the phrase means to have nonelectronic access to a leaker, the meaning taken from the way sap is tapped from a tree.

Lexicographer Peter Tamony found an early use of the word in Civil War literature, referring to a telegraph wire. "Tapping the wires at Lebanon Junction," ran an account of Morgan's raid of 1863, "we learned from intercepted despatches that the garrison at Louisville was much alarmed, and in expectation of immediate attack."

In 1878, two years after Alexander Graham Bell invented the telephone, George B. Prescott warned in *The Speaking Telephone, Talking Phonograph, and Other Novelties*: "The observations made in the course of these experiments convinced those present that the telephone presents facilities for the dangerous practice of tapping the wire, which may make it useful or dangerous, according as it is used for proper or improper purposes."

Mr. Tamony wrote the author:

Telephone wiretapping, according to the New York police, dates from 1895 when a former employee of the N.Y. Telephone company walked into headquarters to suggest the possibilities of such information gathering and surveillance. However, another story bases such methods from a chance discovery of the "Extension telephone" in a home by a telephone company employee in 1909, this man becoming the "King of the Wiretappers" in the service of the U.S. government from 1920 to 1949. During World War I, eavesdropping was widely encouraged, the government tapping thousands of lines from a central office switchboard set up in the N.Y. Customs House. Whenever a suspected alien lifted his receiver a light flashed, and a stenographer recorded the conversation.

The author, whose home telephone was tapped on White House orders by the FBI in 1969, later obtained the order from one agent to another for "technical surveillance," which was the government euphemism for wiretapping. Searching for earlier political use, the author was directed to William Roscoe Thayer's biography of Theodore Roosevelt, written in 1919, in the section about the Republican convention in Chicago in 1912: "Roosevelt had not intended to appear at the Convention, but when he discovered that the long distance telephone from Chicago to Oyster Bay, by which his managers conferred with him, was being tapped, he changed his mind."

The term *bugged*, in the sense of "electronically overheard," came into use around World War One, first cited in 1919. In A. J. Pollock's 1935 *The Underworld Speaks* an entry reads: "Bugged, a room in which a dictaphone has been installed by the police." Speculated Mr. Tamony: "As anything that impeded a criminal process was a nuisance, a *bugbear*, calculated to drive a burglar crazy, or bugs, these perhaps are the basis of the allusion to sound detection and wiring." For a different etymology of BUG, see that entry.

Modern bugging technology, financed by the National Security Agency (NSA does not stand for "no such agency"), has of course refined eavesdropping (a word derived from the eaves of a roof, from which water dropped about a foot away from the wall, and in that "eavesdrop" stood a listener to what was going on inside). The author was having lunch a few years ago with a former KGB agent who, when asked about a Russian "mole" in the CIA, asked to see my cellphone. I showed him that it was turned off, that it could not send a signal. He opened it, took out the battery, nodded toward a minivan across the street, and said "now they cannot hear until they re-set their equipment. We have a few minutes to talk."

task force Committee assigned a military name to give the illusion of vigor.

The appointment of a committee has long been an effective political gambit to avoid direct action, but by the 1950s many people began to bridle at overuse of the word: "another committee" became a derisive term implying delay, unfiled reports, and meandering discussion leading down blind alleys.

Television commentator Richard Harkness took note of this prevalent attitude in 1960. "When it comes to facing up to serious problems," he wrote, "each candidate will pledge to appoint a committee. And what is a committee? A group of the unwilling, picked from the unfit, to do the unnecessary. But it all sounds great in a campaign speech." See BLUE-RIBBON PANEL.

President John F. Kennedy fulfilled promises to appoint many supporters to committees, but avoided the static word. Within two weeks after his election, he dictated a memorandum to his aides on Latin America ("Who should chair the task force—what about Berle?") and Africa ("We should set up a similar task force …") and foreign aid ("We should set up a task force on the distribution of our agricultural surpluses abroad …").

As *task force* began to lose its force, Northwestern U. linguistics professor Thomas Pyles was able to use a string of space-age clichés in a single intelligible sentence: "*Task force* and *breakthrough* are attractive additions to the vocabulary of those who are geared to the space age, who spearhead drives, set target dates, make spot checks, give rundowns and fill-ins—in short, of those who take an overall view …"

In the Justice Department, a committee of lawyers set up in a region to combat organized crime is called a *strike force*—like *task force*, a naval term. In the Clinton White House, which resisted military metaphors, the preferred term was WORKING GROUP.

tax and tax See SPEND AND SPEND.

tax revolt A movement to roll back rapidly increasing property taxes; more generally, an uprising of middle-class taxpayers against having to pay for the rise in the cost of government.

Who shall be taxed how much has always been a most sensitive political subject.

Senator Russell Long of Louisiana liked to recite this doggerel: "Don't tax you, don't tax me, tax that feller behind the tree." Liberals, sensing voter discontent about the rise in taxes in the '70s, concentrated on the unfairness of the tax system: "tax inequities." In this way, they sought to channel the resentment along populist lines: the reason our tax system is "a disgrace to the human race," as candidate Jimmy Carter put it, was that "the rich" were getting through the tax "loopholes" that the wealthy liked to call "incentives." See THREE-MARTINI LUNCH.

The phrase *taxpayer's revolt* was originally popularized around this unfairness idea. In 1968 Joseph Barr—longtime Undersecretary of the Treasury, appointed to the top job in President Johnson's final months in office—created a stir by testifying to Congress that more than 240 people who earned over a quarter-million dollars were paying no taxes, thanks to the "loopholes" in the tax system. He predicted that such inequity would cause a "taxpayer's revolt."

The Nixon Administration, in its 1969 tax-reform act, worked out a "minimum tax" schedule that made it difficult for the wealthy to completely avoid tax payments, but failed to tie income to inflation; this caused resentment in the middle class after the millenium, requiring a congressional "patch."

However, what ultimately caused the "tax revolt" of 1978 was not so much resentment at unfairness by the poor, who paid little or no taxes, as anger by middle-class taxpayers at the rising level of their taxation. Many felt their taxes provided too much welfare for the nonworking.

"Tax-bracket creep" was one element: with a DOUBLE DIGIT inflation, these middle-income taxpayers found themselves pushed into higher tax brackets on the same purchasing power. In the state of California, soaring property taxes were the trigger: as property assessments rose, many retired homeowners—whose income was fixed, or who were living on savings whose value was being eroded by inflation—were forced to move to cheaper neighborhoods, which seemed to them the antithesis of the American dream.

A movement to lower the tax rates substantially and permanently had been brewing in the mid-seventies. Arthur Laffer, a USC economist, interested Congressman Jack Kemp (R-N.Y.) and others in the "Laffer curve," a chart showing the relationship between tax rates and revenue production: his theory was that current high tax rates depressed incentive and growth, thereby lowering tax revenues and defeating its own purpose.

That approach provided the philosophical framework for a drive to cut tax rates that would otherwise be suspect as "irresponsible." In June of 1978, despite the united opposition of California Governor Edmund G. Brown and most of the press and political leadership in that state, Proposition 13—the Jarvis-Gann initiative to reduce property taxes to 1 percent of market value—passed by a 2-to-1 landslide. Howard Jarvis, a veteran tax lobbyist, appeared on the cover of *Time*, and both that magazine and *Newsweek* featured the same phrase on their covers: "Tax Revolt!"

"The cry of pain from voters," grumbled *The New York Times* editorially, "has made tax cutting a new political credo. And the theory offered by the Laffer Curve makes the idea even more seductive...unfortunately, with inflation running close to 10 percent, the Federal Government cannot afford to cut taxes ..."

Which was the way of FISCAL INTEGRITY: holding down the deficits by maintaining tax rates? Or cutting taxes on the theory that this would ultimately increase revenues, a seeming anomaly that had taken place under President Kennedy in the early '60s? In the "tax revolt" (the preferred shortening of "taxpayer's revolt"), liberals, worried about a cut in services to the poor, were surprised to find some economic conservatives willing to take the chance of high short-term deficits. They suspected rightly that these conservatives would call for a cut in government spending if the deficit stayed too high too long.

Thus the original "revolt" over tax *unfairness* did not place; instead, the voters in California rebelled against the high *levels* of taxation. Many national political leaders saw this as evidence that voters wanted to SEND THEM A MESSAGE: more than tax reform, what was wanted was tax reduction, which was given the votes during the Reagan Administration.

The "revolt" was put down during the first Bush Administration (see READ MY LIPS) and lost ground through the prosperous Clinton years, but the low-tax-rate philosophy manifested itself in the younger Bush's terms—despite high deficits driven by his unwillingness to veto costly domestic entitlement legislation passed in a Republican Congress at a time of sharply increased wartime defense spending.

Paradoxically, the Alternative Minimum Tax, put in place in the Nixon years to prevent the rich from escaping income taxation by using legal "loopholes," was transformed by a generation of inflation into a headache for the middle class and became an issue in the 2008 campaign.

tax sharing Collection of revenues by the federal government, returned directly to the state governments without federal control of state expenditures.

Grants-in-aid from the federal government to the states include close supervision of spending. The special attraction to states of *tax sharing* is that it eliminates federal control of the way federally collected money is spent, while removing from states the political stigma of tax collection.

Walter Heller, first Kennedy's and then Johnson's chairman of the Council of Economic Advisers, began to promote the plan in 1964. As the economy produced greater tax revenues, he reasoned, the extra money could be used for increased federal spending (and further undesirable centralization) *or* tax reduction (not likely) *or* reduction of the national debt (deflationary and least likely of all). A fourth alternative could be the return of a portion of the federal tax revenues to the states for expenditures as they saw fit.

Heller took as his text a White House press release promising exploration of new "methods of channeling federal revenues to states and localities which will reinforce their independence while enlarging their capacity to serve their citizens." Republicans in Congress and in the state capitols took the idea to heart. They pointed to the cost efficiency of collection, and more important to the renewal of supervision of spending by "government closest to the people"—i.e., the states and localities, where Republicans traditionally fared better than on the national level.

Richard Nixon preferred the term "revenue sharing" and made it the keystone of his "New American Revolution"—the method by which he proposed to "reverse the flow of power in this country." Democrats in Congress, seeing this as a diminution of their power, refused to share the President's enthusiasm, and passed a bill for a limited amount of string-free aid to states.

Twenty years later, when President Bill Clinton proposed a form of revenue sharing in an economic stimulus bill, Republicans described it as pork (see PORK BARREL) and successfully blocked it.

teach-in See SIT-IN.

technocrat A scientist or engineer in a position of power, making policy in areas supposedly too complicated for the lay public to judge.

"How unlike Stalin and Khrushchev," wrote the *Saturday Evening Post* during Alexei Kosygin's first visit to the U.S. in 1967, "is the quiet, rather dour technocrat Kosygin."

Technocracy was a movement that enjoyed a brief vogue in California early in the Depression. Coined in 1919 by William Henry Smyth in a call for a rule by technicians, it was popularized by disciples of Thorstein Veblen, using his 1921 book *The Engineers and the Price System* as their guide. The movement urged that government be placed in the hands of scientists and engineers ("But Herbert Hoover was an engineer" was one criticism by Democrats who blamed Hoover for the Depression); the end of the profit system; the application of all modern techniques and discoveries to the alleviation of human want; a working-age span from twenty-five years to forty-five years; and a much shorter work year.

Historian Robert Glass Cleland described technocracy as "a strange mixture ... of scientific principles, mumbo jumbo, and skillful publicity." Its successor was "Utopianism," for which Cleland had a new recipe: "a goulash of technocracy, State Socialism, the Ku Klux Klan, Populism, Pacifism, Evangelism and Voodoo." (Slogans were "End Poverty in California" and "Thirty Dollars Every Thursday.")

After a period of disuse, *technocrat* came back into use in the 1950s to describe members of the MILITARY-INDUSTRIAL COMPLEX who expend huge sums for weapons systems. As with most words ending in *-crat*, it is mildly pejorative: though *democrat* is good, *autocrat, aristocrat, bureaucrat* (see BUREAUCRACY), and *technocrat* are suspect.

The underlying suspicion of technocrats was expressed by Harold Macmillan in 1950: "Fearing the weakness of democracy men have often sought safety in technocrats. There is nothing new in this. It is as old as Plato. But frankly the idea is not attractive to the British. ... We have not overthrown the divine right of kings to fall down before the divine right of experts."

See NEW CLASS.

Teflon-coated presidency A president's ability to deflect charges of sleaze or corruption aimed at his administration.

Rep. Patricia Schroeder (D-Col.) first used the phrase in the summer of 1983 to refer to Ronald Reagan's ability to overcome charges of corruption in his Administration.

Noting that Teflon allows eggs to slide easily out of a frying pan, Representative Schroeder told the House: "Mr. Speaker, after carefully watching Ronald Reagan, he is attempting a great breakthrough in political technology—he has been perfecting the Teflon-coated Presidency." (The DuPont trade name *Teflon* comes from polytetrafluoroethylene, a coating bonded to metal pans to keep food from sticking; the trademark was registered in 1945.)

Influenced by SLEAZE FACTOR, an attack by Reagan administration critics, the *Teflon* phrase took on the parallel form: Tim Carrington wrote in *The Wall Street Journal* in 1984 about "the *Teflon factor*, which refers to the President's apparent political immunity to most of his aides' mistakes or misdeeds. ... Ronald Reagan's ability to deflect embarrassment seems nothing short of uncanny."

The antonym of this term uses another product name, in *Velcro Presidency*. That phrase, from the name *Velcro* (trademarked in 1960 and based on the French phrase *velours croché* "hooked velvet") for a fabric tape with adhesive qualities, provided the label for criticism that stuck to the elder Bush's administration.

tennis shoes See LITTLE OLD LADIES IN TENNIS SHOES.

terminological inexactitude See NO COMMENT.

terrorism Persuasion by fear; the intimidation of society by a small group, using as its weapon that society's repugnance at the murder of innocents.

Terrorisme originated with the Jacobins of the French Revolution. *Le Néologiste Français* (published in 1796) claimed that the extremists had coined the term about themselves and used it proudly, but soon after the "reign of terror," the word was a term of abuse with a connotation of criminality. In 1795 British statesman Edmund Burke had written of "thousands of those hell hounds called terrorists" that afflicted the French people.

Although it temporarily had a secondary meaning of ALARMIST, the word *terrorist* traveled from the particular Jacobins to a system using fear of sudden and unexpectable violence to coerce others into obedience, or—in modern times—to trigger such official repression as to encourage revolution.

The names of sects employing terrorism have become synonyms for violence or irrationality. In A.D. 70, the *zealots* in Palestine had a group called the *sicarii*, or "dagger men," who attacked crowds on holidays; in the eleventh century, the *assassins* (from Arabic *hashshashin*, "hashish users") roamed Persia and Syria, killing political leaders systematically, always with a dagger as a part of a sacramental act; in the nineteenth century, the *thugs* (from Hindi *thag*, pronounced "tug") in India always strangled their political victims with a silk tie.

In his 1977 book *Terrorism*, Walter Laqueur focused on the dilemma that faces the targets of political fear: "Concessions may be advisable in some exceptional cases; consistent conciliation of terrorism on the other hand is bound to claim a higher toll in human life in the long run than resisting it … societies facing a determined terrorist onslaught will opt for a hard-line policy in any case." The question that faces all students of terrorism: What to do when a terrorist group builds or acquires a nuclear weapon, even as rudimentary as a "dirty bomb," and the means of its delivery?

The American use of the word was traced by Sperber and Trittschuh to the June 1858 *Atlantic Monthly*: "Every form of terrorism [in Kansas], to which tyrants all alike instinctively resort to disarm resistance to their will, was launched at the property, the lives, and the happiness of the defenceless settlers." Stephen Dodson has found an earlier use by Rep. Philemon Bliss of Ohio in May 1856, in a speech also dealing with Kansas and slavery: "The discordances of Abolitionism, Free-Soilism, and Republicanism, are not permitted to disturb the reign of free-loveism, barbarism, and terrorism." Three years after the Civil War ended, *Harper's Weekly* headed an article about Democratic tactics to win Southern elections as "Political terrorism."

Words that describe terrorists reflect the bias of the describer. *Bomb thrower*, once a description of the bearded, wild-eyed anarchists of the 1890s, is now a term of amused contempt; *partisan* connotes an irregular army unit, with a positive connotation lingering from the anti-Nazi partisans of Yugoslavia; *guerrilla* is often positive, a hit-and-run defender of land against an invader, with the word used in Wellington's dispatches from the Peninsula campaign;

commando is usually a self-description by a force striking in secret, and though it dates to the eighteenth century, it is colored favorably by its use for shock troops in Great Britain in World War II; *skyjacker* is a 1961 American neologism based on *hijacker*, and is usually taken to mean a single deranged person unless further modified; *freedom fighter* is the most laudatory of descriptions, with a value judgment clear in the word itself, first found in a John Lehmann poem of 1942: "Their freedom-fighters staining red the snow."

Only the appellation *terrorist* is rejected by users of terror; the word is unqualifiedly negative, even though the philosophy can be construed to be—in the words of Wilhelm Weitling, one of the first German Communists—"founding the kingdom of heaven by unleashing the forces of hell."

In an effort to appear unbiased in the '90s, Reuters news agency dropped the use of *terrorist* in reporting Arab bomb attacks against Israeli civilians, preferring *gunmen* and *militants*, which drew criticism as unduly neutral from other journalists when the targets were civilians in schools and hospitals. After the attacks of 9/11 brought terrorism home to the U.S., there was less reluctance to call a terrorist a terrorist.

A difficult choice is when a legitimate political activist must be treated as a potential terrorist. At the 2004 Republican convention in New York City, 1,800 protesters were arrested and many fingerprinted by the city's police department, countering what had been announced as a "day of Chaos." Stung by charges by civil liberties groups that this infringed on freedom of speech, the Department released files to justify that the arrest of 1,800 out of a crowd of 800,000 demonstrators was the lowest arrest-to-crowd ratio of any political gathering.

The journalist Judith Miller, who paid her First Amendment dues with 85 days in jail (see CONFIDENTIAL SOURCES), writing in *The Wall Street Journal* in 2007, concluded, "I also want the NYPD to have the tools and programs to protect the city from terrorist attacks. If that means scanning the Internet and sending plainclothes officers to public meetings to learn about planned actions that might turn violent, or be infiltrated and taken over by violent dissidents, so be it."

See WAR ON TERROR; INSURGENTS.

testimonial dinners See RUBBER-CHICKEN CIRCUIT.

that man in the White House A denunciation of Franklin Roosevelt by those too furious with him to even mention his name; now, an exasperated reference to any president.

FDR, hailed by Democrats in 1936 as "The Gallant Leader" and "The Gideon of Democracy," was called by Republicans "The New Deal Caesar," "The Raw Dealocrat," "The American Dictator," "The Feather-Duster of Dutchess County," "Kangaroosevelt," "Franklin Deficit Roosevelt," and most often "That Man in the White House."

The humorist Frank Sullivan, collecting clichés for *The New Yorker* in the early days of the New Deal, headed his list with "That Madman in the White House" and "That Fellow Down in Washington," who was admonished, "You can't spend your way out of a Depression" and "Our children's children will be paying." Jokes of the time were "There's only six Dwarfs now ... Dopey's in the White House" and "Why is a WPA worker like King Solomon? ... He takes his pick and goes to bed."

Many commuter lines had what some of their riders called "Assassination Specials"; Robert Bendiner reported: "the President of the United States was referred to by the kindlier passengers as 'That Man,' a designation useful for those who didn't want to be nasty in front of children and who couldn't bear to pronounce the dread name." When the famed hostess Elsa Maxwell threw a "Pet Hates Ball," guests were warned not to come dressed as "that man" with a cigarette holder because the ball would be jammed with imitation Roosevelts.

Like many epithets, it was soon adopted in an affectionate manner by the target's supporters. When Bronx Democratic leader Ed Flynn accepted the post of national chairman, he went home to break the news to his wife that they would have to move to Washington. "That silly grin on your face," Mrs.

Flynn said to him before he said anything, "tells me 'that man' has talked you into it."

The phrase did not vanish with Roosevelt. It is now used occasionally to refer to any president who must accept criticism with the job. Political scientist Richard Neustadt wrote in 1960 that the public's "unreality" was an unseen enemy of the prestige and power of any president: "the groundless hopes, the unexpected happenings, the unaccepted outcomes that members of their public feel in daily life and relate, somehow, anyhow, to That Man in the White House."

See TRAITOR TO HIS CLASS.

the man who The nominee; the person proposed for a nomination.

Until Hillary Clinton launched her campaign in 2007, speculation about a party designee usually included the phrase "Who will be 'the man who'?" The phrase is taken from bombastic nomination speeches; since the nominator or seconder knows that the signal for a long, loud demonstration will be mention of the name of the person being proposed, he usually refrains from giving the signal until the end of the nominating speech; of course, the audience knows who "the man who" is.

Until 1876, nominations at national political conventions were mercifully brief: in the 1860 Republican convention, Abraham Lincoln was put in nomination by Norman B. Judd of Illinois with a single sentence.

The oratorical dam burst in 1876 with the nomination of James G. Blaine by the Republicans. Robert G. Ingersoll of Illinois gave Blaine the title of "The Plumed Knight" in this classic *man-who*:

Our country ... asks for a man who has the audacity of genius; asks for a man who is the grandest combination of heart, conscience and brain beneath her flag ...

Like an armed warrior, like a plumed knight, James G. Blaine marched down the halls of the American Congress and threw his shining lance full and fair against the brazen foreheads of the defamers of our country and the maligners of his honor ...

Gentlemen of the convention ... Illinois nominates for the next president of the United States that prince of parliamentarians, that leader of leaders, James G. Blaine!

The Man (without the *who*) is a reference of blacks to white men; of staffers to their leader; and in Washington, D.C., of politicians and journalists to the President. It is not considered sexist, and could easily be adapted—actually, with great dramatic effect—to "the woman who."

themeless pudding Unfocused discussion; speech or campaign lacking originality, punch or clear purpose.

Winston Churchill introduced this metaphor in response to an unpalatable dish set before him: "Take away this pudding—it has no theme." His biographer, Sir Martin Gilbert, informs the lexicographer that "This is an exact quotation."

In covering one of Ronald Reagan's early presidential speeches, this usually supportive columnist turned Churchill's well-known remark into a noun phrase: "The themeless pudding called this year's State of the Union address was a series of banalities intended to ingratiate the President with his political opposition." Richard Cohen of *The Washington Post* picked up my compressed quotation in a comment on the 1988 Bush-Dukakis contest: "The current campaign is a themeless pudding."

By 1992, Churchill's bland-flavored trope was part of the vocabulary of political pointlessness. Helen Dewar of *The Washington Post* proposed a recipe for policy proposals: "Democrats have always had more of a domestic agenda than [the elder] Bush. But it tended to resemble a themeless pudding—a dash of transportation, a pinch of energy and a big dollop from the pork barrel." The columnist Charles Krauthammer panned Bill Clinton's 2004 autobiography as "a wild MISHMASH of remembrance, anecdote, appointment calendar and political payback. This themeless pudding of a million small things is just what you would expect from a president who once gave a Saturday radio address on school uniforms."

theocon One who advocates shaping governmental policy by religious belief.

Theocon was introduced into politics with tongue at least partly in cheek, its first known appearance in print coming in the April 17, 1989, issue of *Newsweek*. The term appeared there as part of a list of *Cons* (*NeoCons*, *EconoCons*, and *Genghis Cons*, among them) that accompanied an article headlined "A Pocket Guide to the Right." The term lay dormant, however, until Jacob Heilbrunn used it in an article entitled "Neocon v. Theocon," in the December 30, 1996, issue of *The New Republic*.

Heilbrunn thought at the time that he had coined *theocon*. "We were inordinately proud of it when we came up with it," he told the lexicographer. Heilbrunn devised the term (intended to echo *theocracy*) to distinguish NEOCONSERVATIVES—*neocons*, as they usually are known today—from fellow conservatives who were edging into what he regarded as religious zealotry. Heilbrunn wrote:

> Now challenging the neocons is an equally small (and equally ambitious, and equally disputatious) group of what might be called theocons—mostly Catholic intellectuals who are attempting to construct a Christian theory of politics that directly threatens the entire neoconservative philosophy.... The neoconservatives believe that America is special because it was founded on an idea—a commitment to the rights of man embodied in the Declaration of Independence—not in ethnic or religious affiliations. The theocons, too, argue that America is rooted in an idea, but they believe that idea is Christianity.

Heilbrunn's piece popularized the term, which continues to be used frequently, as in the title of a 2006 book by Damon Linker: *The Theocons: Secular America Under Siege*. Those so categorized do not appreciate the label. Writing in *The Wall Street Journal* in 2006, Ross Douthat suggested that "perhaps it's time for religious conservatives to stop complaining about the term 'theoconservative'... and accept it with a wink and a grin, as the kind of backhanded compliment that any successful movement earns from its opponents." (Precedent: NEOCONSERVATIVE was not intended as a compliment when popularized by the Socialist writer Michael Harrington.)

Douthat went on to argue that "contemporary 'theoconservatism' is best understood as an heir to America's long line of Christ-haunted reforms—the abolitionists and the populists, the progressives and the suffragettes, the civil-rights crusaders and even the anti-war activisms of the middle 1960s. ... More broadly, it means finding a rhetorical mode that is moral without being moralistic, religious without being sectarian—and finding a new generation of leaders who are more articulate and less polarizing than the last."

A related noun is *theocrat*, from *theocracy*, used by the Jewish historian Josephus to mean "the government of God himself." In modern politics, it is generally used pejoratively, especially directed at governments under the control of religious leaders as in Iran, or for a time Afghanistan. When Georgia Governor Jimmy Carter entered the national scene to campaign for the presidency in 1976, he excited many evangelicals in the U.S. with his forthright self-identification as "born again." The liberal theologian Albert Outler was angered, arguing that religious conservatives or fundamentalists "want a society ruled by those who know what the Word of God is. The technical name for that is 'theocracy,' and their Napoleon, whether he likes it or not, is Jimmy Carter." Michael Gerson, the former speechwriter for George W. Bush, wrote in late 2007 that "It was perhaps the only time that Jimmy Carter has been compared to Napoleon. And the American theocracy did not arrive—though the charge has been made again and again in the decades since."

there you go again A homespun dismissal that suggests one's opponent is purveying misleading or erroneous information.

Ronald Reagan popularized this apparently amiable put-down in his October debate with Jimmy Carter during the 1980 presidential campaign. When Carter tried to paint Reagan as a warmonger—likely to be TRIGGER-HAPPY in the event of a nuclear confrontation—Reagan began his denial of the charge by saying, "Now there you go again, Mr. President," implying that Mr. Carter was in the habit of misleading the public.

At the time, *The Washington Post* offered a baseball analogy: "Softballer Jimmy Carter served up a fat pitch that gave Reagan a chance to knock it out of the ballpark and then plaster an engaging Irish grin on his face and hold it determinedly in place until the TV cameras had made a 'freeze frame' of it. ... He was just a nice, good-humored, friendly, peace-loving fellow who kept saying, patiently and politely, 'Now there you go again, Mr. President.'"

During the 1992 Bush-Clinton campaign, when the Senate's Republican Minority Leader Bob Dole did not support the GOP attacks on independent candidate Ross Perot, Michael Kramer of *Time* magazine compressed the quotation into a compound modifier: "While Dole's stance was unwelcome, there was only the slightest there-he-goes-again headshaking at the White House, for everyone knows that Dole is a special case."

The political power of a folksily dismissive phrase should not be underestimated. The pollster Lou Harris recalled the 1980 election for The *Boston Globe* in 1992: "Reagan was behind until October 10 and the debate, when he said to Carter, 'There you go again.'"

the **speech** With *the* emphasized, pronounced as "thee"; the standard stump speech developed during a campaign, compressing all the best issues and punch lines into a single adaptable package.

When *the* speech begins, reporters roll up their eyes and put away their pencils; they have heard it a hundred times. It contains the applause-pulling and laugh-getting lines of a dozen other speeches made in the same campaign by the same candidate. The difference is that it is not a television speech, with the necessity for new material; it is this particular candidate's particular gospel, refined to a rhythm comfortable for him, edited by practice and crowd reaction, punching away at the issues with pet phrases ("that do-nothing Eightieth Congress. ... I think we have to get America moving again...that's your money he's spending, not his ... it's time for a new direction ...").

A half-dozen writers may write speeches, but nobody, not even the candidate, writes what politicians call *the* speech. It seems to evolve by itself, and is carried around like sourdough to mix in with local jokes, timely references to newsbreaks and deferences to local party politicians.

When a candidate does not have his own *the* speech by the end of a campaign, he has not figured out in his own mind what the campaign was really about.

In 1993, a *Washington Post* editorial stated: "If President Clinton continues to encounter difficulties in his fight over the budget, you can count on hearing more about welfare reform. That's because Mr. Clinton, first as a candidate and then as President, has always trotted out his excellent talk about welfare whenever he's run into political trouble. That's fine, but the next time he gives 'the speech,' he ought to be closer to achieving something real."

thinking about the unthinkable See UNTHINKABLE THOUGHTS.

think piece See BACKGROUNDER; DOPE STORY; THUMBSUCKER.

think tank The human brain; or a group of advisers; or, specifically, a research organization or policy institute developing plans and projects often for government and defense-connected industries.

Harry Truman, on his eightieth birthday in 1964, used the phrase in its original sense of "brain," hoping to live until ninety, but only "if the old think-tank is working."

The phrase enjoyed a brief period as substitute for BRAIN TRUST as politicians turned to colleges for TASK FORCES of academicians to provide new approaches to solving new and old problems. This meaning was superseded with the emergence of the RAND Corporation, the Hudson Institute, and similar institutions, where physical and social scientists can exercise and socialize in pleasant surroundings while doing profound research and planning on government or commercial assignments.

RAND, an acronym for *Research and Development*, was set up in 1946 by Air Force General "Hap" Arnold. (Some say the name came from "random sample," which the firm used in its early research days.) He recognized the need for scientists to work in civilian surroundings, but wanted to keep their brainpower available to the military establishment. "Observers impressed with the high-level intellectual atmosphere at RAND," the *Ramparts* magazine editor Sol Stern wrote, "have often referred to the Corporation as 'a university without students.' It would be more accurate to say that RAND, like other think tanks, has become a kind of halfway house between the university and the Department of Defense."

In a week-long series of articles on "U.S. Think Tanks: $2-Billion Industry," *New York Times* reporter Richard Reeves wrote in June 1967: "Although the term is used arbitrarily, the think tanks have one thing in common: all are groups of men with impressive credentials who conduct interdisciplinary research."

In politics as well as science, the necessity for solitude and time to figure out plans and programs in the midst of hectic campaigns is always a problem, and many politicians envy the scientists at *think tanks* their reflective opportunity. When Senator David Hill of New York was told that Democratic candidate William Jennings Bryan was making up to sixteen campaign speeches a day, he wondered pointedly: "When does he think?"

The collocation's popularity is underscored by a Google search showing nearly six million uses over the years. How old is the term? A dictionary of ancient Greek phrases includes *phrontisterion*, a term translated as "thinkery" or "think shop," from the Greek playwright Aristophanes' *The Clouds* (423 B.C.), a usage not counted by the search engine. See SCENARIO.

third-party movement A bolter's extreme.

Third parties engender no warmth in the hearts of most professional politicians. Thomas E. Dewey, who had his troubles first with the American Labor party and then with the Liberal party, both exclusively New York organizations, said that such sectional parties "have proved to be a menace to responsible government elsewhere."

On the national scene, however, Dewey found occasional justification for third parties. Historian Richard Hofstadter noted that their principal role is to provide ideas when the two major parties have stagnated. "Third parties," he wrote, "are like bees: Once they have stung, they die."

The POPULISTS, most successful of the third parties, expressed a radical, primarily rural, revolt against the uncontrolled power of industry in general and the railroad in particular. They won twenty-two electoral votes in 1892 with 8% of the popular vote, as Democrat Grover Cleveland narrowly won his rematch with Benjamin Harrison. In the next election, the Democratic party absorbed the Populists, adopting their platform of unlimited coinage of silver (cheap money) and avowed enmity to unfeeling business interests, but business-minded Republicans behind William McKinley whipped William Jennings Bryan and swept back into power.

The income tax and the direct election of senators were Populist ideas; each came to pass a generation after the party died. Their influence in the West lingered among the Republicans as well, leading to the Progressive revolt against Eastern-dominated Republican conservatism. The break came in the Progressive "Bull Moose" campaign of 1912: Theodore Roosevelt's stand at ARMAGEDDON divided Republicans and elected Woodrow Wilson.

Progressivism was the watchword again when liberals, disgusted with a contest in which both major parties seemed to vie as to which was the more conservative, scored 17% of the popular vote with Senator Robert La Follette of Wisconsin as their candidate. See DON'T WASTE YOUR VOTE.

In 1948 a potpourri of liberals, radicals, and disguised Communists again went to the people, headed by former Vice President Henry Wallace, who told his followers, "When the old parties rot, the people have a right to be heard through a new party." In that same campaign there was still another party, the States Rights Democrats. They hoped that Governor Strom Thurmond of South Carolina, calling for racial segregation and political conservatism, could win enough support to throw the final presidential selection into the House of Representatives where, on a state-by-state count, the South might make its views dominate. This had happened in 1824, denying Andrew Jackson the White House despite his plurality.

That idea occurred in 1968 to Alabama's George Wallace as well. He achieved 9 percent of the vote, taking more from Nixon than from Humphrey, making his 1972 plans a concern to both parties. (See SEND THEM A MESSAGE.) Such was the likelihood of his third-party campaign continuing, before an assassination attempt crippled him, that other splinter movements in the early '70s were automatically called "fourth parties."

John Anderson, a liberal Republican, bolted in 1980 to run to the left of Carter and Reagan, winning a respectable 6.6% of the popular vote. In 1992, billionaire Ross Perot's third party achieved a stunning 19% of the vote cast, the highest percentage since former President Teddy Roosevelt's 27% in his 1912 "Bull Moose" run.

There is always a sore core around which a third-party movement can gather support. Those fearful of change or dissatisfied with its pace often agree with cockroach critic archy, of Don Marquis' *archy and mehitabel*, who—though he could not reach the shift key on the typewriter to make capital letters—answered the Announcer's question "Do you think the time is ripe for launching a third national political party in America?" with "it is more than ripe it is rotten."

See BOLT; SPLINTER PARTY.

third rail An issue so highly charged with emotion among voters that politicians touch it at their peril.

"Social Security—they used to call it the third rail of American politics," said President Bush in 2007. He used that metaphoric warning frequently, at another time concluding "You grab ahold of it, and you get electrified." (He meant "electrocuted.")

The source of this mock-frightening trope was usually given as the former House Speaker Thomas P. "Tip" O'Neill (D-Mass.), though no direct citation could be found.

When the lexicographer advertised for etymological help in his language column, Henry Hubbard, a former White House correspondent for *Newsweek*, came up with the source: Kirk O'Donnell, a senior aide to O'Neill, in May of 1982: "It was said by Kirk O'Donnell to me. From then on, every time I bumped into Kirk, rest his soul, he marveled at how the quote followed him around."

The metaphor—based on the system invented in the 1880s providing electric current to railroad trains running on a line parallel to its wheels' two rails—appeared in *Newsweek*'s issue of May 24, 1982, as "Social Security is the third rail of American politics. Touch it, you're dead." The attribution was to "one Democrat." Next day, the *Boston Globe* noted, "One Democratic aide who used to have nightmares about the subways he rode as a child likens Social Security to the *third rail* of American politics. 'Anyone who tries to touch it gets electrocuted,' he says."

Twenty-five years later, Tom Oliphant of the *Globe*, who was a writer of the *Globe* story, informed the author: "Like all wise pols, Kirk had a passion for anonymity and never offered his wit and wisdom on the record. The line came during a typical, off-year election battle, with the parties playing their traditional Social Security roles—Republicans tinkering, Democrats fulminating. The next year," the reporter added, referring to the reform made after recommendations by the bipartisan commission under the chairmanship of the economist (and later Federal Reserve chairman) Alan Greenspan, "after the Greenspan Commission fix, I asked Kirk how come nobody got electrocuted. Always sharp, he replied that the *third rail* is not like the one in the subway: if a Republican foot and a Democratic foot touch it simultaneously, nothing happens."

The metaphor, now one of the most prevalent in the lexicon of entitlements, is also applied to changes in Medicare (see DOUGHNUT HOLE). But it has become generic: In San Francisco—named after St. Francis of Assisi, famed friend to animals, where 120,000 dogs outnumber small children—controversy rages over regulations to keep animals on leashes. "It's the third rail of San Francisco politics," Supervisor Sean Elsbernd told the *Los Angeles Times* in 2007. "City officials know if they touch the issue, they're going to get hurt."

(The following letter does not really belong in a dictionary, but it will give the reader a sense of the warm feeling an etymologist gets when his research has an unexpectedly welcome impact.)

Dear Mr. Safire,

My name is Kathryn O'Donnell. I am the widow of Kirk O'Donnell. I am writing to thank you for the article you wrote in the New York Times Magazine on February 18th, 2007. Once again, I felt very proud of my late husband. It is nice to know that he is remembered and recognized in ways, both big and small. I could just visualize Kirk talking to people about the article and I know that he would laugh with his friends about how this quote had gotten so much mileage.

The article appeared two days prior to what would have been our thirty fifth wedding anniversary…. what a coincidence to have Kirk appear in such a stunning way. The article also stirred up a flurry of phone calls and emails from friends I had not heard from in a long time. Although bittersweet, for me, the article was a message from Kirk.

With every good wish, Kathryn.

third-rate burglary See NOBODY DROWNED AT WATERGATE.

third term See VOICE FROM THE SEWER; SMOKE SCREEN.

third way Centrist political philosophy espoused by British "New Labor," employing conservative means to reach liberal goals.

"Things Can Only Get Better" was Britain's Labor Party campaign slogan in 1997, as it adopted the name "New Labor" to drive out the Tories. On taking office at 10 Downing Street, the new Prime Minister, Tony Blair, launched what he called "the Third Way." (The phrase had been used for a political alternative since 1935 and was the name of a neutralist-pacifist movement begun in Holland in 1949 against participation in NATO, but few remembered it.) Blair's goal was to strike a domestic political balance: "A false opposition was set up between rights and responsibilities, between compassion and ambition, between the public and private sectors, between an enterprise economy and the attack on poverty and exclusion."

Although an American economist, Jeff Faux, said in 1999 that "the Third Way has become so wide that it is more like a political parking lot than a highway to anywhere in particular," the liberal columnist E.J. Dionne in *The Washington Post* wrote in retrospect, "And with the Third Way, you could have it all. And Blair and Clinton were right in seeing that clearing away those false choices was a necessary condition to routing their conservative adversaries."

Blair stepped down ten years later, his popularity diminished by his unwavering support, on both human-rights and strategic grounds, of the war in Iraq; he was derogated as "Bush's poodle" and as "the Right Honorable Member for Texas North" for maintaining the SPECIAL RELATIONSHIP in foreign policy between Britain and the U.S. during trying times for the American president.

Dionne noted that London's *Daily Mail* had asked, "Is the prime minister really the president's poodle, slavishly willing to jump through any hoops at the request of the White House?" The columnist added, "What makes that quotation interesting is that it's from a critique of Blair's support for *Clinton's* policies toward Iraq, published in December 1998. Say what you will, there is a kind of consistency in Blair's pro-American interventionism."

Blair's decade-long term in office was thought by many on the left to have likely lasting effects. "Social justice arm-in-arm with economic success is not the Third Way," editorialized Australia's *The Age* on his departure, "it's the only way now." See TRIANGULATION.

third world Originally, nations—usually underdeveloped—that were not aligned diplomatically with the FREE WORLD of Western democracies or the "Communist world"; now, the Arab–African–Latin American–Indian bloc, with which the People's Republic of China identifies.

The phrase was originally French (*tiers monde*), in use to describe the neutralists (see NEUTRALIST) in the Cold War. Alfred Sauvy, the French sociologist, was credited with coining the phrase in 1952. As the *Barnhart Dictionary of New English Since 1963* points out, the reason for the archaic *tiers*, rather than the modern French *troisième*, is that the phrase is patterned after *tiers état*, or "Third Estate" (which goes back to the fourteenth century and refers to the commoners as distinguished from the first and second estates, the king and clergy). (See FOURTH ESTATE.) The idea behind *third world* was that it would stand independent of the first and second worlds of established power.

The phrase came into U.S. use in the '60s. "The students, following the gospel of Marcuse, look to the Third World," wrote *New York Times* reporter Philip Shabecoff in a typical late-'60s usage, "to Fidel Castro and Ho Chi Minh, for salvation." Those "Third Worlders" were Africans, Asians, or Arabs. However, with the oil-price increases of the mid-'70s, some third-world countries—Nigeria, Venezuela, Saudi Arabia—became far more wealthy, and lost some popular support in the U.S. In addition, when the "Group of 77" (as 126 nations in the U.N.called themselves) demanded a "new world economic order"—in effect, a redistribution of wealth from HAVE to HAVE-NOT NATIONS— and topped that with a U.N.vote equating Zionism with RACISM, *third world* became a more pejorative label in the U.S.

"The 'Third World' urgently needs to be renamed," wrote Henry Grunwald in the Summer 1993 issue of *Foreign Affairs*, "and not only because the 'Second World' has collapsed. The inadequacy of a label covering everything from dysfunctional non-countries in Africa to emerging industrial powers in South America indicates a lack of press understanding and attention."

With the breakup of the Soviet Union and end of the bipolar geopolitical world, the rise of an economically unified Europe, the emergence of China as a capitalist though totalitarian power challenging democratic Japan, and the dangerous spread of global jihadism, a MULTIPOLAR WORLD created itself. The third world split into have and have-not, disaligned and realigned nations, and parts became the South in a North-South relationship.

those who The amorphous armies of the vaguely venal; a rhetorical device that enables an attacker to ostentatiously avoid naming names.

"There are *those who* say ..." This frequently employed technique in political discourse enables a speaker to lump together moderate adversaries with extremists, thereby discrediting the moderates; and to characterize a opposing position in its most easily attackable terms.

Those who, said with a facial expression between a sneer and a smirk, are never in the right; they are often dangerous, if unwitting, tools of sinister forces; and they are always triumphed over. Their only supporters are *some*, as in "Some say ..." See STRAW MAN.

thought police Hypersensitive censors; vocabulary vigilantes; an attack phrase on intrusive attempts to enforce conformity to POLITICALLY CORRECT ideas.

Newsweek used the term "Thought Police" as the headline of its December 24, 1990, issue, the cover story of which was about political correctness on campus. "After the *Newsweek* story came out," Lynne Cheney, chairman of the National Endowment for the Humanities, told the PBS television interviewer Jim Lehrer, "I was called by more than one representative of the media saying 'we're doing a story about PC; we want you to represent the Thought Police.'"

In his book *Kindly Inquisitors: The New Attacks on Free Thought*, Jonathan Rauch extended the metaphor to thought vigilantes, stressing the unofficial nature of the "police."

The phrase originated as a colloquial name for the Special Higher Police (*Tokubetsu Koto Keisatsu*) whose mission was to imprison political dissenters in Japan before World War II. After the war, in 1945, the Baltimore *Sun* wrote of "an order imposing freedom of speech, thought, religion and assembly on the Japanese people, and requiring the immediate liberation of those imprisoned for political offenses by the so-called 'thought police.'" ("Imposing freedom"? Call the language police.)

It was George Orwell's novel *1984*, which appeared in 1949, that popularized the phrase as the name of the dreaded police force in the fictional totalitarian state, whose function was to suppress freedom of thought. The term was applied during the Cold War to the Soviet secret police. Its current use as an attack phrase is intended to evoke an image of tyranny.

thousand days Phrase associated with the length of the Kennedy Administration, from January 20, 1961, to November 22, 1963, or 1,037 days.

Taken from Kennedy's inaugural address, the phrase was quoted five days after his assassination by President Johnson before a joint session of Congress: "On the twentieth day of January in 1961, John F. Kennedy told his countrymen that our national work would not be finished 'in the first thousand days, nor in the life of this Administration, nor even perhaps in our lifetime on this planet. But,' he said, 'let us begin.' Today, in this moment of new resolve, I would say to all my fellow Americans, let us continue."

Johnson dropped a "one" in front of the "thousand" in quoting Kennedy, probably for rhetorical cause. Kennedy used "one thousand days" to compare with Franklin Roosevelt's use of "one HUNDRED DAYS" as follows: "All this will not be finished in the first one hundred days. Nor will it be finished in the first one thousand days ..."

Arthur Schlesinger, Jr., chose *A Thousand Days* for the title of his book on the Kennedy Administration. See HUNDRED DAYS; "LET US CONTINUE."

thousand points of light Metaphor for volunteerism; community service that costs the taxpayer nothing.

George H.W. Bush introduced the phrase into political metaphor during the 1988 campaign. In his acceptance speech at the Republican National Convention in New Orleans that year, he depicted America as a vast network of service organizations: "We are a nation of communities, of thousands and tens of thousands of ethnic, religious, social, business, labor union, neighborhood, regional and other organizations, all of them varied, voluntary and unique. This is America…a brilliant diversity spread like stars, like a thousand points of light in a broad and peaceful sky."

The elder Bush echoed the theme in his Inaugural Address in January 1989: "And I am speaking of a new engagement in the lives of others—a new activism, hands-on and involved, that gets the job done. I've spoken of a thousand points of light—of all the community organizations that are spread like stars throughout the nation doing good."

The concept was further popularized in a Top 40 country hit by Randy Travis. In that 1991 song about volunteerism, titled "Point of Light," Travis sings: "When you take what's wrong and you try to make it right, you can be a point of light."

Peggy Noonan, Bush's speechwriter who supplied him with the luminous phrase, discussed the term in her 1990 book, *What I Saw at the Revolution*:

> It was my favorite phrase in the speech because its power is born of the fact that it sounds like what it is describing: an expanse of separate yet connected entities sprinkled across a broad and peaceful sky, which is America, the stretched continent. Why stars for communities? I don't know, it was right. Separate, bright and shining, each part of a whole and yet discrete. Why a thousand? I don't know. A thousand clowns, a thousand days—a hundred wasn't enough and a million is too many.

Noonan chronicled the results of searching for the phrase's origins. Suggestions ranged from a Nazi hymnbook to citations from C.S. Lewis and a letter by Vincent Van Gogh. An engineer gave a speech in Venice at the turn of the century urging the city managers to add electricity and fill the city with "a thousand points of light." Of the various possibilities, Noonan suggests that the most likely source was her earlier reading of Thomas Wolfe's novel *The Web and the Rock*, which contains the phrase "a thousand points of friendly light."

Democrats later used the phrase to attack Bush's economic strategy. The *Los Angeles Times* reported in November 1991 about the words of one Democratic candidate at a meeting of the political party in New Hampshire: "'If you are on welfare and food stamps, you can't hardly pay your light bill and be one of the thousand points of light…let alone buy a house or a car.'"

Former Senator Gary Hart wrote in 1993: "Like a prim Anglican bishop delicately stepping over the bodies of the hungry and the homeless, Reagan's successor cynically put forward the homily of something called a thousand points of light. Presumably, this was meant to suggest that the human detritus of rampant laissez-faire could be accounted for if only each buccaneer would put just a farthing more in the Sabbath collection box."

Still, in a gesture of nonpartisanship, the Points of Light Foundation, a national community service organization founded in 1990, continued to be financed in 1993 as a part of President Bill Clinton's own national service initiative.

thou shalt not steal Convention battle cry of 1912 and 1952, directed at candidates named Taft.

"From the outset," said Theodore Roosevelt's campaign manager, Senator Joseph Dixon of Montana, "the scheme to renominate Taft was a scheme to steal the nomination." As most Republican state conventions in 1912 went for President William Howard Taft over former President Theodore Roosevelt, Dixon cried foul. "You will become a deliberate receiver of stolen goods," he charged in an open letter. At the GOP national convention, the national committee leaned hard toward Taft whenever there was a contested delegation: 164 Taft delegates were seated to 19 for Roosevelt in contests. "A fraud," said Roosevelt, "as vulgar, as brazen and as cynically open as any ever committed by the Tweed regime …"He labeled them "stolen delegates" and thundered the Biblical commandment: "Thou shalt not steal!"

It didn't work. Taft got the nomination, Teddy formed a third party to "stand at

ARMAGEDDON" and industrialist Chauncey Depew correctly sized up the situation: "The only question now is which corpse gets the most flowers." Democrat Woodrow Wilson won.

Forty years later, the commandment worked. In the 1952 Eisenhower-Taft clash, the balance of power was held by the Southern delegations whose election was contested. Eisenhower's manager Henry Cabot Lodge said: "In the interest of fair play and decency, we will support at the opening session a resolution to amend the rules and to bar these contested delegates from voting to seat themselves or other contested delegations—regardless of whether they are for us or for Senator Taft."

The "fair play" resolution and "Thou shalt not steal" charge gave the Eisenhower forces their moral issue; the General was quoted as growling about "cattle rustlers." Stephen Hess wrote: "There was a grand irony in charging the two Tafts, William Howard and his son Robert, both with trying to steal presidential nominations. Bob had been called 'Mr. Integrity,' and it was certainly an inherited characteristic. Yet at the 1912 convention and forty years later their opponents contended that the Tafts had secured Southern delegates by foul means."

Politicians are continually on the lookout for slight shadings of immorality by the opposition. Often a public that will shrug off major blunders or serious breaches of morality will become infuriated by a small trick. Winston Churchill, speaking in the House of Commons on the conciliation of South Africa in 1906, put it this way: "In dealing with nationalities, nothing is more fatal than a dodge. Wrongs will be forgiven, sufferings and losses will be forgiven or forgotten, battles will be remembered only as they recall the martial virtues of the combatants; but anything like a trick, will always rankle."

Exodus 20:15 offers "Thou shalt not steal" as the eighth of the 10 Commandments. See ELEVENTH COMMANDMENT for a political addition to the biblical list.

three-eye league A high-status club that can be joined by any politician willing to tour Ireland, Italy, and Israel.

In many big cities, three of the largest—or at least most active—ethnic groups are the Irish, Italians, and Jews. In the fifties, so many urban political figures made the new "Grand Tour" of Ireland, Italy and Israel that the itinerary gained the "Three-Eye" label.

In baseball, the Three-Eye League was a decidedly minor league made up of teams in Illinois, Indiana, and Iowa; it came to typify "bush league" and was spoken of as a kind of Siberia for pitchers who could not find the plate. But in urban politics, a man who hits well in the Three-Eye League belongs on the All-Star team.

three-martini lunch Symbol of tax unfairness.

In the keynote speech at the Democratic National Convention in Miami Beach on July 11, 1972, Florida Governor Reuben Askew zinged the "system" that has "forgotten the average man or woman in America today. What can we expect them to think," he asked rhetorically, "when the business lunch of steak and martinis is tax-deductible, but the workingman's lunch of salami and cheese is not?" The line by speechwriter Roland Page was little noticed at the time, but was destined for two revivals.

George McGovern, who became the 1972 Democratic nominee, picked up the "martini lunch" in his campaign and improved it: "The rich businessman can deduct his three-martini lunch, but you can't take off the price of a baloney sandwich." The applause-getting line became a part of his THE SPEECH, but it was lost in the debacle of his announced "thousand percent support" for a running mate, Senator Thomas Eagleton, that he was in the process of dropping, in a campaign that was lost before it began.

The line survived the McGovern campaign. The picture of the FAT CAT imbibing while the workingman paid appealed to the POPULISM of Jimmy Carter. As the Georgian began his 21-month trek to the 1976 nomination, Carter took the line as his own, beginning with "expense-account lunch" and then adding the *martini* (a gin-and-vermouth cocktail which probably derives its name from the California city of Martinez, but was influenced by an Italian vermouth named Martini and Rossi). Candidate Carter called such a tax system "a disgrace to the human race," which had a nice rhyme; after Carter's victory in November, Senator Edward Kennedy of Massachusetts added: "There are few more vivid symbols of the disgrace of our current tax laws than the martini lunch."

A counterattack began, not from the expected source of inebriated martini-lunchers, but from the Hotel and Restaurant Employees and Bartenders International Union (AFL-CIO), which issued a press release in 1977: "Martini lunches make an appealing villain, but the martinis are made by bartenders and the meals served are served by waiters after being prepared by chefs." When President Carter floated a trial balloon of tax reform in which only half of a business luncheon or similar entertainment could be deducted, *Newsweek* columnist George Will pointed to the irony of the union opposition: "So what is intended as an attack on privilege is opposed by the proletariat." As for himself, the conservative writer argued, "the tax subsidy for the 'Martini lunches' is a defect in the nation's moral system."

NEOCONSERVATIVE Irving Kristol disagreed, writing in *The Wall Street Journal*: "Senator McGovern, in the 1972 campaign, tried—and failed—to make an issue out of the 'two-martini lunch'... apparently, President Carter is convinced that the Senator underestimated the seriousness of the situation... if you spend all your time worrying whether or not a business executive is getting a tax-free martini with his lunch, you might very well fail to pay due attention to the obvious—that is, encouraging businessmen to make profits."

Despite the catchiness of the *martini-lunch* phrase, it was not tax "reform" that most voters wanted, but tax reduction. Resentment in the late '70s was directed not at the rich businessman, but at the tax-guzzling bureaucracy. See TAX REVOLT.

Another use of a cocktail in political rhetoric is a standard gibe at the sitting President's economic policy: "Recipe for a Johnson (or Nixon, Carter, or Bush 41) cocktail: economy on the rocks." For the metaphoric use of delicatessen meats, see BALONEY and SALAMI TACTICS.

Throttlebottom Caricature of a useless, bumbling Vice President.

In the 1931 Kaufman-Ryskind-Gershwin musical satire *Of Thee I Sing*, Vice President Alexander Throttlebottom, played by Victor Moore, had to join a guided tour to get into the White House. Little-known Charles Curtis was Hoover's vice president when this show was written.

The vice presidency has taken its share of abuse. John Adams said: "My country has in its wisdom contrived for me the most insignificant office that ever the invention of man contrived or his imagination conceived.... Today I am nothing, but tomorrow I may be everything."

He may be sure of being ridiculed. In November of 1977 *New Times* magazine headlined an item about Vice President Walter Mondale with this pun: "Throttlebottoming out." Vice President Dan Quayle was the butt of many jokes, including an image of having "a look on his face like a deer caught in the headlights," which he did his best to accept good-naturedly. *The Boston Globe* referred to him as "Dan Quayle, who has reaped his share of the indignity heaped upon heirs to Throttlebottom's throne." Al Gore was ribbed for his woodenness, and what angry partisans threw at Dick Cheney wasn't funny; however, not even Cheney's severest critics called the policy-powerful vice president a Throttlebottom.

For other assessments, see DEAD END, POLITICAL; HEARTBEAT AWAY FROM THE PRESIDENCY; STEPPING-STONE; VEEP.

throw away your vote See DON'T WASTE YOUR VOTE.

thumbsucker Political reporter's derisive term for an analytical story; a think piece, sometimes thoughtful.

From time to time in the early '70s Don Oberdorfer of *The Washington Post* would call this writer at the White House and begin the conversation with "I'm doing a thumbsucker for tomorrow." The term is currently limited to journalists' argot, and perhaps because of its similarity to an obscene word, may not cross over to general use, as has a related term, DOPE STORY.

Newsweek columnist Stewart Alsop, in his 1973 book *Stay of Execution,* used the term: "Walter Lippmann wrote the best straight think-pieces, or thumbsuckers as they are called in the trade, of any journalist of our time."

In December 1977 "The Ear," a gossip column in *The Washington Star,* ran this item about reporter James Wooten: "Jim will become a kind of Haynes Johnson, if you get Ear's meaning. (Say Thumb Suckers if you're in the biz …)." The meaning was that Wooten might write fewer hard-news stories and more stories with a sociological bent, which sometimes require more thought and introspection.

Many reporters and editors use the term with derision, to mean the opposite of *well researched,* as in this 1978 letter from John Sweet, publisher of *U.S. News & World Report* promoting the cover article as "not one of those 'thumb sucker' articles consisting of opinions from futurists, gathered over THREE-MARTINI LUNCHES." A 1990 editorial in *Roll Call* echoed the hooting: "That public cynicism is a fact of life, but, we feel, it's unjustified. It is the handiwork of a class of professional thumb-suckers (journalists, analysts, lawyers, and other public affairs hangers-on) who seem to believe that to bash the American political system is a mark of keen sophistication."

Public officials also use the word to dismiss press speculation. When Vice President Dick Cheney appeared on NBC's *Meet the Press* in September 2006, Tim Russert put on the screen a headline that read "Cheney's power no longer goes unquestioned" and asked "if the treatment and prosecution of terror suspects and of NSA surveillance policy has weakened your influence within the White House." Cheney's reply: "It looks like one of those thumb-suckers that's done periodically, and is probably as valid as the ones that were done saying that I was in charge of everything."

The root of the derision implicit in the word (which comes from "staring at the wall and sucking on your thumb" in jejune judgment) is the contempt tinged with envy that *shoe-leather reporters* feel at the high salaries and high-level access given to writers of high-domed opinion pieces. With the proliferation of cable television panel shows, "talk radio" commentators and the advent of weblogs—all relatively inexpensive to produce—investment in standard newsgathering and writing has fallen off. Walter Isaacson, who had been both an editor of *Time* magazine and president of CNN, said on PBS in 2007: "One of the great pressures we're facing in journalism now is, it's a lot cheaper to hire thumbsuckers and pundits and have talk shows on the air than actually have bureaus and reporters."

In current usage, a background piece or *situationer* provides general information about a topic or geographic area in the news; it is not to be confused with the insightful analysis that can result from a BACKGROUNDER, which a reporter calls a DOPE STORY. Between often ideological *thumbsucking* and usually objective *straight reporting,* a hybrid has developed, which the author occasionally describes as *opinionated reporting,* and defines as "analysis with bite and fresh information." See PUNDIT; TICK-TOCK; JOURNALESE.

thunder on the left Rigorous objection from liberal activists.

"An end to the Vietnam War would change the situation drastically," wrote Louis Heren in the *Times* of London in 1968. "Much of the thunder from the left would die away, and the right, as represented by Mr. George Wallace, would be more clearly identified as anti-racist."

The phrase harkens to days of fierce liberalism, first in England and then in the U.S.; currently it is used mainly in an ironic sense, as if the rumbling were remote. The phrase was the title of a book by Christopher Morley in 1925 and was thus popularized. Professor Irwin Stark of City College of New York directed the author to its origin in *The Dangers of This Mortall Life,* by Sir Eustace Peachtree, who was said to have flourished about 1640: "Among the notionable dictes of antique Rome was the fancy that when men heard thunder on the left the gods had somewhat of special advertisement to impart. Then did the prudent pause and lay down their affaires to study what omen Jove intended."

One might have thought that such a gentleman as Sir Eustace Peachtree had existed, since the source given was *Bartlett's Familiar Quotations* (11th and 12th editions). However, "Kit" Morley liked an occasional practical joke, and the "quotation" placed in *Bartlett's*—which Morley helped edit—was a hoax. It is no longer in recent editions, which is a pity, since it added a human element to a great compilation of quotations, and deserves at least a footnote there.

On the analogy of Morley's title, "thunder on the right" is occasionally used to describe conservative expostulations. When *Time* wrote a piece on this writer in 1977, calling attention to my interest in wordplay as well as right-wing espousals, the headline was "Pun-der on the Right."

ticket The slate of candidates, running as a team.

"The old ticket forever!" wrote Benjamin Franklin's daughter Sarah in 1766, her usage duly noted in 1879. "Its usage in this sense dates back to early colonial times," the lexicographer Charles Ledyard Norton wrote in 1890, "since Mrs. Bache (nee Franklin) would not have used the word in this sense had not its meaning been popularly recognized." Its first *OED* citation is from a 1711 letter by Isaac Norris: "Chester [Pennsylvania] carried their ticket entire."

Tickets discussed elsewhere in this book include BALANCED TICKET, with hopefully broad-based appeal; SPLIT TICKET, a voter selection, as from a Chinese menu, of "one from column A, one from column B." Al Smith joked about being able to win on a LAUNDRY TICKET, while politicians are only half in jest about their imaginary, unbeatable DREAM TICKET. A predecessor to split ticket was *mixed ticket*, now obsolete; *scratched ticket*, where a name was erased on a paper ballot, was made obsolete by the voting machine, which created CHAD.

Political regulars prefer the *straight ticket*, which in voting-machine times became "vote row A all the way." The practice was being described as "straight" over a century ago. "Old Henry," wrote *Harper's* in January 1860, "generally votes a 'straight ticket.'" Lord Bryce, an English observer of American politics, used a variant form in his 1888 *American Commonwealth*: "The electors ... give little thought to the personal qualifications of the candidates, and vote the 'straight-out ticket.'" This variant also occurs in *The Political Text-Book* of 1860: "I know nothing of your straight-out ticket; I know nothing of your Union ticket; I know nothing of Fremont."

Harry Truman used the word to stretch a historical point: "Lincoln had dropped Hannibal Hamlin of Maine because he wanted a Union ticket. Lincoln was elected in 1864 on the American Union ticket and not on the Republican ticket." (To err is Truman, as Martha Taft liked to say: Lincoln was elected in 1864 on the National Union ticket.)

At one time, *ticket* was synonymous with *ballot*; voters cast their *tickets*, or written slips of paper. This sense has been preserved in the current political phrase, *to have the tickets*, meaning "to have enough votes to win."

tick-tock Journalists' argot for a story detailing the chronology leading up to a major announcement or event.

"I'm doing a tick-tock on the new economic policy," Henry Hubbard, White House correspondent for *Newsweek*, told the writer after President Nixon had frozen wages and prices on August 15, 1971.

The elder George Bush misused the onomatopoeic term in 1990 while defending his tour of defense installations during a time of disarmament talk: "I think it was a good trip, and I've read some tick-tock inside here, but it doesn't bother me a bit."

A tick-tock (the metaphor, obviously, of a mechanical clock moving toward a fateful hour) is often written with boldface dates indicating significant meetings or preliminary events, and is more reportorial than a THINK PIECE or THUMBSUCKER.

In 1991, Margaret Tutwiler explained at a State Department briefing: "We're not going to go through a laundry list or a tick-tock, or here are options that we may or may not pick and choose from."

Another term especially associated with newsmagazines is *violin piece*, which is the leading story in the magazine that sets the tone of the week. Usage: "What's the violin this week?" "Crisis of confidence" or "The isolation of the President." A purple-prose assessment of the national mood was featured in newsmagazines in the '30s as if to the accompaniment of a violin; this has been modified in recent times to a general story that is intended to interpret the hot topic or profile the newsmaking celebrity of the week. Though the music is much faster, the term lingers on.

Another time metaphor is *two minutes to midnight* (see DOOMSDAY MACHINE).

tilt Lean toward, give preferred treatment to.

"Tilt toward Pakistan." Columnist Jack Anderson reported in 1971 that Henry Kissinger had passed on this advice from Richard Nixon at a National Security Council meeting on the India-Pakistan dispute about Bangladesh. Mr. Nixon wanted to rebuke the neutralist Indian government and help Mohammed Yahya Khan in Pakistan, who was helping him to arrange his trip to China.

Tilt was a favorite '70s locution, referring not to the warning flashed when a pinball machine is tampered with, but to the angle of "slant." ("A few individuals think and speak for themselves," wrote Hiram Haydn in *The American Scholar* in 1946, "a few newspapers refuse to tilt their headlines and news stories to satisfy their advertisers' slanted views …")

Tilt has a purpose: it is crisper than *lean toward*, and less pejorative than *slant*. Its adoption as part of the diplomatic lingo was evident in this use by Harvard professor Jerome Alan Cohen in a *Foreign Affairs* article in 1976: "Or do the realities of world politics say that the United States should 'lean to one side'—that of Peking? … If so, how, and to what extent, should such a de facto tilt be carried out?"

Wags refer to any hotel in Pisa, Italy, as "the tiltin' Hilton."

timber, presidential A man who could be THE MAN WHO (easily switchable to "the woman who"); one who has the background, personality, and voter appeal to "go all the way" to the White House.

The hardwood metaphor originated with Sir Francis Bacon, whose "Essay on Goodness," written in 1612, was about men whose nature was the opposite of goodness, in whom a "natural malignity" burned. "Such dispositions are the very errors of human nature, and yet they are the fittest timber to make great politics of." He compared these warped men to "knee timber," wood that has grown crooked and has been cut so as to form an angle "that is good for ships that are ordained to be tossed, but not for building houses that shall stand firm."

Political uses of the metaphor in the U.S. go back as far as 1833. The Cleveland *Plain Dealer* grumbled in 1880 that "the situation now so chaotic arises from the fact that there is a superabundance of timber."

Finley Peter Dunne's Mr. Dooley (see DOOLEY, MR.) in his usual rich dialect offered his friend Hennessey this advice: "If ye say about a man that he's good prisidintial timber he'll buy ye a dhrink. If ye say he's good vice-prisidintial timber ye mane that he isn't good enough to be cut up into shingles, an' ye'd betther be careful."

The qualities that make a man's timber "presidential" include the timbre of his voice and the warmth of his smile; courage (his timbers cannot be shivered); either a proven record of vote-getting power or a powerful vote in the opinion polls; age from the 40s (Kennedy) to the 60s (Reagan); a power base in a major state or national renown; nothing in his record that would permanently alienate a major group or region; and AVAILABILITY. The qualities that make a good president—judgment, intelligence, decisiveness, and above all, character—are not always the qualities that make good presidential timber. In that regard, Bacon's point remains a good definition: presidential timber is that which best resists twists and strain—"ordained to be tossed"—but it would be helpful if it could support weight. See SPLINTER GROUP.

time for a change Appeal to unrest and dissatisfaction; Republican slogan in 1944, 1948, and finally—successfully—in 1952.

Thomas E. Dewey said in San Francisco, September 21, 1944: "That's why it's time for a change." In 1946, a zingier phrase—"HAD ENOUGH?"—came on the Republican scene, and "Time for a Change" became a subsidiary slogan in the campaign of 1948. Dewey's running mate, Earl Warren, modified it further in his own speeches, predicting that the American people would turn to the Republicans "not because they want a change, but because they want a chance."

By 1952 the Democrats had been in power for twenty consecutive years. Long before, Democrat Grover Cleveland had made a similar point about long Republican rule: "Parties may be so long in power, and may become so arrogant and careless of the interests of the people, as to grow heedless of their responsibility to their masters." *The New York Times* editorialized in 1952: "The Republicans have pegged their campaign largely on one theme—that it's time for a change because of the 'top to bottom MESS IN WASHINGTON.'"

Democratic candidate Adlai Stevenson, whose grandfather—Grover Cleveland's running mate—had exploited the desire for new faces, felt the pull of the appeal, and fought directly against the phrase: "As divided, as silent as both wings of the Republican Party are on major objectives, on policies to guide the nation, they have wholeheartedly united on one profound proposition: 'It's time for a change.'... They talk of change. These days they do little else but talk of change. But where were the Republicans when the great changes of these twenty years were made? I'll tell you where they were. They were trying to stop the changes."

The desire for a "new face," a "fresh approach," is strong, attracting Democrats to Barack Obama in the 2008 primaries; counter-balancing it is a resistance to make changes, illustrated by phrases like "Experience Counts" and "DON'T CHANGE HORSES." In the British general election of 1964, D. E. Butler and Anthony King quoted a Conservative saying: "The issue at this election is

'time for a change' versus fear of change. Who wins will depend on which feeling is stronger."

Senator Al Gore, at the 1992 Democratic Convention, tried a variation in addressing the first Bush Administration, repeating so the crowd would join in: "It is time...for you...to go." This reminded some of Oliver Cromwell's speech to the "Rump Parliament" in 1653: "Depart, I say, and let us have done with you. In the name of God, go!"

tin box See LITTLE TIN BOX.

tinhorn politician A cheap or "two-bit" pol, often used in conjunction with *tinhorn gambler*, with adjectives interchangeable.

William Allen White, editor of the *Emporia* (Kansas) *Gazette*, coined *tinhorn politician* in an editorial on October 25, 1901. Before that, the adjective *tinhorn* was applied to a gambler in an 1885 issue of the *New Mexican Review*: "We have been greatly annoyed of late by a lot of tin horn gamblers and prostitutes."

New York Mayor Fiorello La Guardia added a note of cheapness to the derogation by using the adjective *two-bit*, a slang term for a quarter-dollar. "The Little Flower" (sobriquet of the well-liked Fusion mayor, translation of his Italian first name) lumped both usages together in frequent blasts at the "tinhorn gamblers and two-bit politicians."

Former Tammany leader Edward Costikyan wrote in 1966: "La Guardia fortified the anti-political-leader bias of the good-government tradition. His tirades against 'tinhorn gamblers' and 'two-bit politicians' deepened the public association between politicians and evildoers. In retrospect, his administration became a myth—a myth which equated good government with the absence of political leaders in government."

An obvious derivation might appear to be from a cheap, or tin, noisemaker—hence, noisy politician of a low variety. However, historian George Willison offered a more plausible explanation in discussing gambling ethics of the early West in *Here They Dug for Gold*: "Chuck-a-luck operators shake their dice in a small churn-like affair of metal—hence the expression 'tinhorn gambler,' for the game is rather looked down on as one for 'chubbers' and chuck-a-luck gamblers are never admitted within the aristocratic circle of faro-dealers."

tipping point See PARADIGM SHIFT.

titular leader The most recently defeated presidential candidate of the party out of power; leader in name, seldom in fact.

Both Thomas E. Dewey and Adlai Stevenson, "titular leaders" of their parties for eight years, felt ambivalent about the phrase. Dewey wrote in 1950: "Who speaks for the party out of power? It has its last nominee for President who is called the 'Titular Head of the Party.' I have held that title in my party now for nearly six years and I still have some doubts about what it means except that I am the last, duly nominated spokesman for my party."

Stevenson said in 1956: "The titular leader has no clear and defined authority within his party. He has no party office, no staff, no funds, nor is there any system of consultation whereby he may be advised of party policy and through which he may help to shape that policy. There are no devices such as the British have developed through which he can communicate directly and responsibly with the leaders of the party in power. Yet he is generally deemed the leading spokesman of his party."

Because there is no "leader of the opposition" in America as in Great Britain, the defeated candidate is often challenged by the wing of the party that felt it could have done better. A year after Willkie's defeat in 1940, Senator Robert A. Taft said that Willkie could not "speak for the Republican party," because there was "no justification in precedent or principle for the view that a defeated candidate for President is the titular leader of the party."

The titular leader, however, does carry a special responsibility to oppose the incumbents. In the late thirties, Republican candidate Alf Landon told Republican Minority Leader Joe Martin that Roosevelt had offered him the post of Secretary of War. "I advised him not to accept," wrote Martin. "He was, after all, the titular head of the Republican Party, and I felt it would be damaging to the Party for him to enter Roosevelt's Cabinet at a time [1940] when we were coming up to a convention and a campaign."

Does a titular leader have any special advantage in recapturing a nomination? Probably not. The 1940 GOP nominee, Wendell Willkie, defeated in the primaries of 1944, dropped out of the race. Thomas E. Dewey lost to Harold Stassen in Wisconsin and Nebraska in 1948, but was able to win in Oregon, enabling him to go into the convention as the favorite and win. Adlai Stevenson in 1956 started to play the same reluctant role that had been so successful for him in 1952, but soon discovered—after primary losses in New Hampshire and Minnesota—that he needed some victories to capture the nomination. He dropped his reluctance, campaigned in Oregon, Florida, and California, and won those primaries and the nomination.

The role of the titular leader, never really defined, is what the man makes it. William Jennings Bryan, who seemed to be a born titular leader, made much of the position and became Woodrow Wilson's Secretary of State. Alfred E. Smith was an outspoken anti-Republican voice between 1928 and 1932 until he found himself losing the mantle of leadership to Franklin Roosevelt. Dewey was the titular leader most responsible for the choice of his successor, fighting for Eisenhower and defeating his own archrival, Robert A. Taft. Richard Nixon was campaigning for governor of California in the midst of his titular leadership and did not really speak for the party; oddly, he assumed that role in the 1966 off-year elections in the midst of Barry Goldwater's titular leadership.

The word has a built-in derogation: *titular* means "holding the title," nominal, "in name only." And should a woman candidate for president be unsuccessful, the phrase is likely to go into hibernation until the party chooses its next presidential STANDARD-BEARER.

to err is Truman See RED HERRING.

to hell with the cheese See FIGHTING THE
PROBLEM.

too little and too late A criticism of inadequacy of resources interminably delayed.

"Too Late" was the caption of a famous
1885 *Punch* cartoon showing the belatedly
dispatched relief column reaching Khartoum
two days after the death of General "Chinese"
Gordon at the hands of the African Mahdi.

The addition of "too little" to the words
made a phrase both balanced and pointed.
Professor Allan Nevins of Columbia was an
early user in an article titled "Germany Dis-
turbs the Peace" in the May 1935 *Current
History*: "The former allies have blundered
in the past by offering Germany too little,
and offering even that too late, until finally
Nazi Germany has become a menace to all
mankind."

The phrase was sharpened and popularized by David Lloyd George, who had
served as Great Britain's Prime Minister
during World War I. On the day after the fall
of Finland—March 13, 1940—the seventy-
seven-year-old statesman told the House of
Commons: "It is the old trouble—too late.
Too late with Czechoslovakia, too late with
Poland, certainly too late with Finland. It is
always too late, or too little, or both."

Throughout the early part of World War II,
the phrase was used to deride Allied defeats
and lack of preparation. Toward the end of
the war, "enough and on time" was used
to explain the reason for Allied successes.
After the war, the phrase was used by an
"out" party to attack policy on the grounds
of inadequacy, which is a political attack
permitting little counterattack. John F. Kennedy, campaigning in 1960, called an Eisenhower embargo on shipments to Cuba "too
little and too late," suggesting that the U.S.
also "attempt to strengthen the non-Batista
democratic anti-Castro forces in exile. ..."
In his memoirs of the Kennedy Administration, Ted Sorensen used the phrase in its
current generic sense: "Kennedy's error in
1960 on the 'MISSILE GAP' had been the result
of the public's being informed too little and
too late—even after the facts were certain—about a danger which he had in good
faith overstated."

The danger of delayed decision was
expressed in different words by Defense
Secretary Charles E. Wilson early in the
Eisenhower Administration. "I have so many
people in my department," he said sadly,
"who keep putting off decisions until the
only thing left to do is the wrong thing."

New York State Comptroller Arthur Levitt
said in 1967 regarding a $2.5 billion trans-
portation bond issue: "Too much, too soon"
(the title of a 1957 autobiography by Diana
Barrymore).

In 2007, as the rest of the world clucked
sympathetically and dithered, President
Bush announced sanctions on Sudan for
continuing what he had earlier described
as its genocide; the AP reported "advocacy
groups and lawmakers wished the president
had been harsher and wondered whether it
was a case of too little, too late for Darfur.
The violence has killed 200,000 people and
forced 2.5 million more from their homes
since it began in February 2003."

The possibilities of this phrase, so much
a part of our political language, are not yet
exhausted. A use may even be found for
"too little, too soon."

too old to cry See CONCESSION SPEECH.

too proud to fight A high-minded Wilsonian defense of neutrality that helped unite
his opposition.

A British ship, the *Lusitania*, was sunk
with many Americans aboard on May 7,
1915, by a German submarine. Three days
later, clinging to his "mediator nation" philosophy, President Wilson said to a group of
newly naturalized citizens: "The example of
America must be the example not merely of
peace because it will not fight, but of peace
because peace is the healing and elevating
influence of the world and strife is not. There
is such a thing as a man being too proud to
fight. There is such a thing as a nation being
so right that it does not need to convince
others by force that it is right ..."

The "too proud to fight" phrase was used
as a gibe at Wilson until his policy changed
and he toured the country urging preparedness for war. Years later, *The Nation*
editor and pacifist Oswald Garrison Villard

claimed authorship: "I supplied the President through Tumulty with a phrase which brought down upon him a storm of abuse and denunciation. The words 'too proud to fight' were mine."

Neither the phrase nor the criticism of it died. In 1961, former Congresswoman and Ambassador Clare Boothe Luce quoted Wilson's statement as an example of how not to keep the peace:

> This was certainly a statement which the embattled French and British heard with dismay and contempt and bitterness. How can a man be proud not to fight while his friends are being killed and even conquered in a war they did not start? America was not too proud to sell guns, make loans, ship supplies to the Allied side, and to heap abuse on Kaiser Bill—a procedure which American morality permitted us nevertheless to call "neutrality," since neutrality also consisted entirely in not joining the fighting until "war came."

tooth fairy See SANTA CLAUS, NOBODY SHOOTS AT.

Topic A The subject at the tip of everybody's tongue; a continuing news story that currently gets top coverage.

The expression appeared in the late '50s and was formalized by the *New York Herald Tribune*, which headed the lead item in its front-page news summary "Topic A." The same attention-getting device has been used in publications as diverse as the New York *Daily News* and *The Texas Monthly*.

A politician ignores Topic A at the peril of being ignored himself. In current usage, PARAMOUNT ISSUE is synonymous with—though more sedate than—*burning question*: both must be addressed by both parties in depth. *Gut issue* is an underlying social phenomenon, like a religious or racial issue, and need never be addressed head-on. *Topic A* is the event or running story that draws attention that day or week—especially among the CHATTERING CLASS—generating arguments, cartoons, and jokes, and requires some attention from a public figure who cannot appear out of touch. It is dealt with "above the fold" of the front page of a newspaper, a

phrase now also applied to the home page of a website.

Curiously, there is no "Topic B."

torch has been passed An allusion to a new generation, or at least the transfer of responsibility to a more vigorous group.

"Let the word go forth from this time and place," said John F. Kennedy at his inaugural, "to friend and foe alike, that the torch has been passed to a new generation of Americans …"

The torch is a favorite political symbol. In 1555, just before being burned at the stake for heresy, English prelate Hugh Latimer said, "Be of good cheer, brother, we shall this day light such a candle in England as, I trust in God, shall never be extinguished."

The passing of the torch, perhaps derived from the passing of a baton in relay races, was popularized in a sentimental World War I poem by John McCrae:

> *Take up our quarrel with the foe:*
> *To you from failing hands we throw*
> *The torch; be yours to hold it high.*
> *If ye break faith with us who die*
> *We shall not sleep, though poppies grow*
> *In Flanders fields.*

The image of passing the torch was reinforced by the practice instituted in 1936 of carrying a flame from Mount Olympus in Greece to the site of the Olympic games.

An incendiary speaker is called a *firebrand*; the statue in New York harbor holds the *torch of liberty*; and the liberation of North Africa in World War II was *Operation Torch*.

totalitarian Highly centralized government, permeating all aspects of the society it controls, repressing internal opposition and promoting a fear and awe of the leadership.

Police state is a properly derogatory synonym for totalitarian government, popularized during the era of Nazi Germany, Fascist Italy, and the Communist Soviet Union.

Totalitarian is to the free world vocabulary what *imperialist* was to Communist terminology: a profound insult needing no further explanation. Walt Whitman Rostow, later an adviser to the Johnson Administration, wrote in 1952:

A totalitarian regime ... can be defined as a state in which the potentialities for control over society by governmental authority are exploited to the limit of available modern techniques— where no significant effort is made to achieve the compromise between the sanctity of the individual and the exigencies of efficient communal life; where the moral weakness of men in the administration of concentrated power is ignored; where the aspiration toward a higher degree of democratic quality is not recognized as a good; and where, conversely, the extreme authority of concentrated power is projected as an intrinsic virtue.

In 1975, French philosopher-columnist Jean-François Revel wrote *The Totalitarian Temptation*, challenging the argument of EUROCOMMUNISTS that they offered "Communism with a human face." He used the example provided by Alexander Solzhenitsyn (see GULAG) to show that severe repression was part of the essence of Communism.

Dictatorships are euphemized as *autocracies*. Friendly dictators are euphemized as *paternalistic*; totalitarian regimes necessary to the pursuance of "realistic" policies of democracies are called *authoritarian*.

The English-language *Moscow Times*, in April 2007 one of the relatively few dissident newspapers allowed to publish in Russia, wrote about the arrest of chess grandmaster and democracy activist Garry Kasparov during a demonstration by anti-Putin protesters: "Of the epithets regularly applied to President Vladimir Putin and his political practices, 'authoritarian' in particular seems to rankle the Kremlin and its supporters. But what other word comes to mind when 9,000 riot police officers are sent out into the streets to handle several thousand protesters? The deliberate targeting of Kasparov and the arbitrary detentions were part of the day's absurd nature. They provide more than a hint of its authoritarian nature, too."

President George W. Bush tied totalitarian ideology to terrorist methodology in a speech to the American Legion in 2006. "This war will end with the defeat of the terrorists and the totalitarians ... Despite their differences, these groups form the outlines of a single movement, a worldwide network of radicals that use terror to kill those who stand in the way of their totalitarian ideology."

See REALISM; S.O.B..

total war Wars involving a general mobilization, destruction of the opposition's productive capacity; a war carried "home" to the enemy.

The phrase was popularized by a book, *Der totale Krieg*, by Nazi General Erich Ludendorff in 1935. The aging general, who had been the chief German strategist in World War I, stressed the need to mobilize the economy of a nation behind a war effort. The German word for this mobilization was *Wehrwirtschaft*, "war economy," based on rearmament that would prepare an economy for the strain of war.

Total, to Ludendorff, did not mean "more ferocious than usual"; it meant the addition of economic and psychological warfare to what had once been a strictly military affair. However, in a 1937 entry in his *Berlin Diary*, correspondent William L. Shirer was prescient: "Total war means the complete and final disappearance of the vanquished from the stage of history!" During World War II, its meaning changed to "all-out effort" and the destruction of civilian population centers.

In current usage, *total war* is sometimes used as a contrast to LIMITED WAR, though it is more often dealt with in the other direction by *all-out* or *nuclear war*, and *World War III*. Since the end of the COLD WAR and the diminution of the prospect of a conflict between superpowers, *global war* has increased in usage, most often expressed as "global war on terror."

As a result of the difficulty of defeating an insurgency or averting Sunni-Shiite civil war in Iraq, a strategy was needed short of *total war* and not quite *limited war*. Thus, *hybrid war* was put forward by some military thinkers, combining Special Forces use against guerilla groups and heavier conventional forces against supply lines and terrorist concentrations (the name possibly concurrent with the rising interest in hybrid automobile engines, fueled by combination of gasoline and electrical energy).

The word *total*, though in decline as a modifier of *war*, has become a favorite oratorical word for politicians favoring "total commitment," "total involvement," "bold new total approaches to problems which must be viewed in their totality." In the '70s the word was turned into a verb to mean "destroy completely in value," as "In the crash, my car was totaled."

tough-minded and tender-minded See DOVES.

tracker Videographer working for one campaign assigned to follow an opposing candidate to catch any slips or BLOOPERS.

"Trackers," reported the *Los Angeles Times* in 2006, "—using inexpensive handheld cameras and having the ability to post clips almost instantly on YouTube and other video-sharing websites—have become a major element in several campaigns."

A tracker's goal is to catch a candidate in an embarrassing moment. In Virginia that year, a tracker working for Democrat James Webb recorded on video a remark made by Republican Senator George Allen describing him, an Indian-American, as "macaca," which was said to be a racial insult despite apologies and protestations from the hapless candidate. The clip, played on computers and then telecast on news programs for the rest of the campaign, cost Allen—who had been leading—his seat in the Senate, and cost the GOP the Senate majority.

In a 2006 Senate campaign in Maryland, a tracker working for Democratic Rep. Ben Cardin recorded his rival, Lt. Gov. Michael Steele, talking to the mother of two soldiers killed in Iraq; Steele called it "an indefensible invasion of privacy … callous disregard for families who have lost a loved one," branding the tracker's work as "ugly, gutter politics." Cardin's spokesman noted that a tracker from the Steele campaign had caught Cardin, the favorite who emerged the winner, at such non-political activities as riding bumper cars at the state fair with his grandchildren.

Surveillance in time of terrorism has become a way of life. In 2007, a sign in a cosmetics store window not far from national monuments in Washington, D.C. (where face-recognition cameras abound), read, "You are secretly photographed 50 times every day," adding, "Why not look your best?"

See TRUTH SQUAD.

trade-off Compromise; the tension that exists between divergent but mutually necessary elements, such as target date and cost.

The word was a favorite of the NEW ECONOMICS and an explanation by Walter Heller is included in that entry. The delicate-balance meaning is limited to the fields of economy and defense, however. To politicians, the word is used as BARGAINING CHIP, an expendable person or issue that can be used to close a negotiation (or make a distasteful deal more palatable by using it as a "sweetener").

In the sense of political compromise, the word is not new. Republicans in 1940 planned to use the youthful Thomas E. Dewey in a cavalier fashion: "The original plan," a Republican leader is supposed to have said, "was to use him as a STALKING HORSE and trade him off later."

trained seals See RUBBER STAMP.

trains ran on time A defense of the Fascist "corporate state" on the basis of its efficiency; now only used derisively.

Whenever a government or political organization abridges personal liberties—giving as its reason the need for "master planning" or "efficiency"—the mid-thirties expression is recalled: "But you have to admit that Mussolini made the Italian trains run on time." Such an admission was not valid. According to Snopes.com, a website that debunks urban legends, "Those who actually lived in Italy during the Mussolini era have borne testimony that the Italian railway's legendary adherence to timetables was far more myth than reality"; historian Victoria de Grazia wrote that "The story that Mussolini made the trains run on time arose in the late

20's and gained credence abroad mainly because of well-heeled British tourists who considered the hopelessly refractory Italians governable only by dictatorial means."

Writing about Boss Ed Crump of Tennessee in 1947, John Gunther made the point vividly:

> Of course the boss has given Memphis first-class government—in some respects. But almost all the creditable items are the equivalent of Mussolini making the trains in Italy "run on time." Perhaps they did run on time, and a good thing too. But at what sacrifice?—at what cost to things much more important? Mr. Crump has made Memphis a "clean" enough city. But it is a community that has not really functioned as a democracy for more than a quarter of a century; a whole generation has grown up without fulfilling the first and simplest duty of citizenship, that of exercising political choice.

See FASCIST.

traitor to his class Epithet applied to Franklin Roosevelt by aristocratic Democrats.

"His background belied his political philosophy," wrote White House correspondent Charles Hurd. "On several occasions he laughed rather grimly at the comment that he was 'a traitor to his class.'"

Roosevelt's "class" included ancestors dating back two hundred years in America; he was educated at Groton and Harvard, and lived like a country squire in fashionable Hyde Park, New York. In the '20s and early '30s, millionaires and socialites were not identified with liberal positions or considered "of the people," a situation since partially rectified. At the time of FDR's election to the presidency, he was probably the wealthiest person ever to hold that office.

Roosevelt's New Deal programs were especially startling to those fellow-patricians who felt he would be "reasonable" once elected; indeed, his pre-election speeches laid heavy stress on budget balancing and efficiency in government. For an idea of the depth of antipathy FDR inspired among members of his "class," see THAT MAN IN THE WHITE HOUSE.

FDR led the way for other men of wealth in politics, particularly in New York State. Herbert Lehman of the banking family, Averell Harriman of the railroad family, Nelson Rockefeller of the oil and banking family, and Robert Kennedy of the Kennedy family have since held high office in the Empire State.

Sir Denis Brogan showed a variation of class distinctions in the U.S. in this way: "There is the famous story of a lively discussion in a smart New York club in which FDR was attacked as being 'a traitor to his class.' A member who was the head of a very old, distinguished and, more important, rich family (he is the father of the present junior Senator from Rhode Island) protested. 'The President is not a traitor to your class; he doesn't belong to it. You are business men. He is a gentleman.'"

trial balloon A testing of public reaction by suggestion of an idea through another person, causing no embarrassment to the balloonist if the reaction is not good.

The idea of placing a political toe in the water—with no commitment to plunge in—by the use of NOT FOR ATTRIBUTION comments to reporters was developed by Theodore Roosevelt. Quincy Howe wrote: "He also originated the 'trial-balloon' technique and gave favored correspondents 'OFF-THE-RECORD' statements that they attributed to 'AUTHORITATIVE SOURCES.' If the statement caught on, Roosevelt would make it his own. If it fell flat, he would drop it."

Pointing out that Teddy Roosevelt had ordered the first White House press room installed (after he noticed a group of rain-soaked newsmen standing disconsolately at the gate), AP correspondent Jack Bell observed: "Roosevelt was a great man for trial balloons. He tried out some of his ideas on the reporters. If they backfired, he denied everything and denounced the newsmen for printing what he had told them."

Before President Bill Clinton's health-care plan was publicly unveiled, rumors streamed from the White House. "Some apparently were Administration trial balloons," noted *Time* in May of 1993, but as Republican objections to what they labeled "Hillarycare" mounted, "many more, or so White House insiders insist, were leaks from the 500-plus members of the Administration's health-care task force."

A subtle alternative to the trial balloon is *putting a ball in the air*, when the balloonist freely admits to being the source. Dean Acheson (then Truman's Undersecretary of State) made a probing address in 1947 that indicated a direction that led to the Marshall Plan, and carefully got White House clearance. "I wanted everyone to understand," said Acheson some years later, "that I was putting a ball in the air and that we had all better be prepared to field it when it came down, because if it just landed, *plunk!* on the ground, it would be a very bad thing." (Of course, it did not; Marshall's seminal foreign-aid address is framed and hangs in the reception room outside the Secretary of State's office today.)

The derivation is not as obvious as it seems. A *trial balloon* is a balloon put up to test the direction and velocity of the wind in balloon ascensions and kite-flying contests. Both kites and balloons, however, have speculative and fraudulent connotations in their history, and this—like LAME DUCK—is probably a political borrowing from business. *Ballooning* a stock meant promoting its rise by spreading false information, a technique now described as *touting*; this was also described at one time as *kite-flying*. Issuing a check with no money in the bank to cover it is still called *kiting* a check (probably because the check, like a kite, is supported only by thin air). That speculative meaning may well have been helped into politics by its financial usage (but that is speculative).

The phrase is probably of French origin. Francis Bacon, Lord Chancellor of England in 1618, later fired for corruption and bribery, was skilled in the manipulation of public opinion. In *Great Englishmen of the Sixteenth Century*, S. Lee wrote in 1907 that "Bacon set forth these views as mere *ballons d'essai*, as straws to show him which way the wind blew."

For methods of launching trial balloons, see BACKGROUNDER; BALLOON GOES UP; DOPE STORY; LEAK.

trial heat A mock election by poll of a limited number of candidates.

"Supposing the election were being held today; of the following candidates, which one would you vote for?" This question is in a survey different from DEPTH POLLING, and many other "issues" polls that have greater influence on candidate strategies.

A trial heat indicates only where one stands on a given day; it does not indicate in what direction public opinion is likely to go if certain issues grow in importance. However, the trial heat may be devastating in a CAN'T-WIN campaign, convincing delegates to switch to another candidate who runs better in a trial heat against an incumbent.

In current use, a *trial heat* is usually between candidates of opposing parties as a general election nears; a *preference poll* is among candidates of a single party during primaries.

In racing and track sports, a trial heat is often an elimination of competitors before a major race; this is not its political meaning, which is why it is sometimes confused with preference poll. See POLLSTER.

triangulation The political strategy of charting a middle course between traditional party positions by adopting or co-opting elements of the opposition's policies.

The word was introduced into the American political lexicon by Dick Morris, Republican pollster who crossed party lines to advise Democratic president Bill Clinton in 1994. Reporting on a meeting with the president in December of that year, Morris wrote in his "tell-all" memoir, *Behind the Oval Office*: "The president needed to take a position that not only blended the best of each party's views but also transcended them to constitute a third force in the debate. I blurted out the strategy in a single word: *triangulate*." Morris wrote that he counseled the president: "Triangulate, create a third position, not just between the old positions of the two parties but above them as well. Identify a new course that accommodates the needs the Republicans address but does it in a way that is uniquely yours."

Waxing philosophic, Morris explained in a 2006 message to the author: "Triangulation is essentially Hegelian in its origin, drawing on his 'thesis v. antithesis, and the resulting synthesis, which is, in turn, challenged by a new antithesis.' It seemed to me in the mid-'90s that the old and shopworn debates about crime, welfare, and balancing the budget had been aired sufficiently by the parties and ideologies, and that the American people were willing to make a verdict, not by choosing one side or the other, but by ordering, a la carte, the parts of each position that appealed most to them."

Surveyors and navigators have used the word *triangulation* since at least 1818 for determining a distant position at the apex of a triangle by measuring the angles at either end of a baseline of known length. Morris used sailing as an example:

> Clinton...consults polls as if they were giant wind socks that tell him which way the wind is blowing. And then he asks the pollster to help him determine which current he should try to harness to move him closer to his destination. He sails with that current until he has gone too far to the left of his destination. He polls again, reverses his tack, and this time aims a little to the right. And he gets there. He ends up just where he wanted to be, in the middle.... To the journalist covering the news of the day as it occurs, without the advantage of perspective, it looks like zigzagging. That's what tacking is. But it's not the zigzag of a FLIP-FLOP. These zigs and zags bring you ever closer to where you want to be.

Most observers interpreted this tactic as a simple lateral maneuver toward the middle of the political spectrum. An AP political analyst described *triangulation* in a November 1995 as "a dressed-up buzz word for centrism, whose banner Clinton carried in the 1992 election. In that year, centrism was presented under phrases such as 'New Paradigm' and the 'Third Way.'" That same month *The Washington Post* posed the rhetorical question, "But what, precisely, is 'triangulation' trying to say?" to which it supplied two answers: "Democrats in Congress use it to describe Clinton's (for them) alarming tendency to abandon party principles in the service of political expediency.... Republicans invoke it as proof of the president's cynical lack of conviction, an alleged willingness to embrace nearly any position suggested by his polling, to cozy up to almost anyone in his quest for short-term political advan-

tage while dividing and confounding his enemies."

Referring to the jockeying for power between British prime minister Tony Blair and his ultimate heir in the Labor Party, chancellor Gordon Brown, *The Washington Post* noted in 2005 that "One biographer has written that Brown dislikes Blair's 'triangulation' strategy—playing off conservatives and old Labor to follow a 'THIRD WAY,' similar to what Bill Clinton did."

Republicans resist being associated with the term. Richard Berke reported in *The New York Times* in 1999: "Gov. George W. Bush of Texas gets no higher praise from President Clinton's devotees than when they applaud the Republican for proving himself a deft triangulator. But asked about his triangulation skills over lunch at the Governor's Mansion in Austin last week, Mr. Bush looked as if he wanted to smash the sweet potato pie into his questioner's face."

Challenging Senator Hillary Clinton in the 2008 primaries, Senator Barack Obama said: "The same old games won't do; triangulating and trimming won't do."

trick See THOU SHALT NOT STEAL.

trickle-down theory The idea that aid to corporations will seep through to employees and irrigate the economy.

William Jennings Bryan drew the metaphor using "leak through" rather than the word *trickle* in his "Cross of Gold" speech in 1896: "There are two ideas of government. There are those who believe that, if you will only legislate to make the well-to-do prosperous, their prosperity will leak through on those below. The Democratic idea, however, has been that if you legislate to make the masses prosperous, their prosperity will find its way up through every class which rests upon them."

In the Hoover-Roosevelt presidential campaign of 1932, with the nation in the grip of the Depression, President Herbert Hoover argued that public relief measures proposed by some Democrats were "playing politics with human misery" and that his program was aimed at restoring prosperity to corporations and banks, which supposedly would in turn reinvigorate the economy. The Democrats derided this as a "trickle-down theory" aimed at "feeding the sparrows by feeding the horses." In October, the *Burlington* (N.C.) *Daily Times* opined that the president "still wants to pour in relief from the top, expecting it all to trickle down to the bottom—from the banker to the breadline."

"The 'trickle down' system was the idea of the late Andrew Mellon," wrote the *Coshocton* (Ohio) *Tribune* in 1938, about the Treasury Secretary during the Harding-Coolidge era, "who believed that if you fed business to the big firms at the top, without taxing them too much, the benefit eventually trickled down to the worker at the bottom … the trickle … was, in fact, only a trickle." The opposing economic theory retained water as the metaphor in the phrase PUMP PRIMING.

At the 1975 Gridiron Dinner, a newsman impersonating presidential press secretary Ron Nessen led a group dressed as cheerleaders serenading President Gerald Ford with this spoof of "Buckle Down, Winsocki":

Trickle down, Winsocki, trickle down
You can win, Winsocki, if you trickle down
Give a tax rebate
To the highest rate
Let it gravitate
And trickle down!

Republicans—often stung by the populist phrase—shy away from it. Reagan pollster Richard Wirthlin said in 1988: "It's much harder to make the trickle-down theory work in politics than in economics." The compound modifier was turned around in 2006 above a *Newsweek* column by Robert Samuelson about what he saw was a growing inequality that threatened the social compact: "Trickle-Up Economics?" See PARTY OF THE PEOPLE; SUPPLY SIDE.

trigger-happy Inclined to a panicky decision on war; bellicose.

Barry Goldwater, tagged as "trigger-happy" early in his primary campaign against Nelson Rockefeller for the 1964 Republican nomination, could not shake it throughout the general election campaign.

His use of DEFOLIATE and stress on "victory" were turned into issues that pictured him as an irresponsible candidate who "shot from the hip" and whose election would plunge the country into nuclear war.

The Democratic advertising agency, Doyle Dane Bernbach Inc., produced two commercials so extreme that they were quickly withdrawn. One pictured a hand reaching toward a nuclear button (see FINGER ON THE BUTTON). Another, which became known as the DAISY SPOT, showed a little girl pulling the petals off a daisy, with a voice of doom in the background counting down the firing of a missile with each petal pulled.

Goldwater characterized this as "the warmonger charge," but Democrats did not need to use the word *warmonger* (see -MONGER); *trigger-happy* was good enough. Art Buchwald wrote a column long after the election about how happy he was that Goldwater had not been elected, because of all the escalation that would have resulted—and he then proceeded to list all Johnson's decisions to escalate. In this vein, economist Pierre Rinfret told a group of economists in 1966 of the woman who said, "They told me if I voted for Goldwater, we'd be at war in six months, and by golly, I voted for Goldwater and we were."

The compound adjective had made a brief political appearance in the previous campaign. When Richard Nixon made clear he would defend the islands of Quemoy and Matsu off the shore of mainland China—an outpost of the Chiang Kai-shek forces in Taiwan—John F. Kennedy called this position "trigger-happy." Ted Sorensen, in retrospect, called this one of the rare occasions Kennedy "stepped over the borders of fair comment." It was also used against Ronald Reagan by the Jimmy Carter campaign in 1980, as part of a general imputation of COWBOY irresponsibility.

The Western allusion made its first political appearance in 1860 as "hair-trigger," in a letter from London written by George M. Dallas, a former senator and vice president who was then minister of the United States at the British court, about "the hair-trigger tendency to religious war." In 1904 it was used to describe Theodore Roosevelt's impulsiveness. Roosevelt himself used the phrase in 1908, predicting a "hair-trigger convention." The word submerged for many years until it was reactivated during World War II.

At that time there were a rash of *happy*'s. The original, *slap-happy*, or dizzy, intoxicated, was closely akin to punch-drunk. The first variations appeared in 1940 ("I'm *snap-happy* since I discovered Kleenex cleans the ... lens of my camera"), *footlight-happy* for "stage-struck," etc. The military applications were legion: *stripe-happy*, *bomb-happy*, *flak-happy*, and in a *Life* magazine of November 1, 1943: "Cadets are taught here to be 'trigger happy': to shoot at anything any time."

As can be seen, the adjective *happy* is like an unstable chemical ready to form a compound with anything. When it joins with a noun, it transforms the noun into a hyphenated adjective, useful information for grammar-happy readers.

tripwire The presence of troops in an area as hostages to peace, an attack on whom would automatically trigger military involvement of the nation from which the token force is drawn.

The expression took on its strategic sense early in the COLD WAR, in connection with the garrison of U.S. troops in Berlin. The troops were placed in that four-power city, an island surrounded by East Germany, not to make a serious defense in case of attack but to provide the *tripwire*, or national commitment to come to their rescue or avenge their loss.

Later the word was used in NATO terminology to justify the presence of 300,000 American armed forces in Europe: not that this force would stop a Soviet offensive to seize Europe, but it would trigger U.S. nuclear response. In PENTAGONESE, this is part of "automaticism," a technique that removes the possibility of a craven response and thus contributes to a DETERRENT. The *Observer* wrote in 1957: "The German electorate are baffled as to whether NATO is meant to defend their soil, or provide the tripwire for a Soviet-American suicide pact."

The term is based on military tactics: a device, strung low along the ground, to be tripped over by an advancing scout, which sets off a signal or an explosion. Still in use, the term appeared in a 1993 *Boston Globe* piece on post–Gulf War relations with Iraq: "In a further warning to Iraq, the United States dispatched a battalion of troops to Kuwait to act as a tripwire against any further Iraqi incursions into Kuwait."

troglodytic Out of the stone age; traditional to the point of seeming prehistoric; like a caveman.

Pronounced "trog-loh-DIH-tik," this adjective comes from *troglodyte*, a term for a primitive cave-dweller, found in English since the mid-1500s. Borrowed from the Greek *troglodytes* (formed from *trogle*, "hole, cave," and *dyein*, "to go into"), the term in the nineteenth century took on a transferred sense, similar to *ape* and *Neanderthal*, of "an uncouth person." Robert Louis Stevenson wrote in his 1886 horror story *The Strange Case of Dr. Jekyll and Mr. Hyde* of the transformed title character: "God bless me, the man seems hardly human! Something troglodytic ... ?"

Politics found it to be a fine exaggeration of *old-fashioned*. The Scottish adventure novelist John Buchan wrote in the 1910 *Blackwell's Magazine* story "A Lucid Interval" about "a respectable, troglodytic peer." In the 1950s, British slang clipped the noun to *trog*, although American usage continues to favor the full term. By 1980, the term gained a sense of "reactionary" or "extremely conservative." *National Journal* reported in 1980 on attempts to modernize public utilities; a House subcommittee staff member, according to the *Journal*, said that this industry has some of "the most troglodytic, traditional utility managers to deal with."

A decade later, the adjective was used as an attack term during a Massachusetts political campaign. *The Boston Globe* quoted a candidate who criticized his opponent's attitude in failing to endorse sex education as "troglodytic."

The word in noun form began losing some of its sting. "Once mocked as MOSSBACKS and 'troglodytes,'" wrote Russell Baker in *The New York Review of Books* in 2007, "conservative journalists were now welcome everywhere, especially on around-the-clock cable news channels desperate for ways to fill their idle hours…Their eagerness to become unabashed political warriors coincided with journalism's transformation into 'media,' a slippery word that usually means 'television,' which usually means 'the entertainment business.'"

See LEFT WING, RIGHT WING.

Trollope ploy See PLOY.

troops Party workers, or those volunteers willing to ring doorbells.

Primary *campaigns* are decided by the *regular* organization's ability to "turn out the *troops*"; the opposing *camp* sets up a *cadre* of *volunteers* who are expected to turn out *troops* of their own. The italicized terms are MILITARY METAPHORS; *troops* has long been gaining preference over *workers*, possibly because of Communist use of the latter or an aura of proud militancy around the former.

Troops is a word in semantic trouble. In one sense, it means "soldiers"; does this exclude sailors and airmen (now grouped as "service personnel")? *Troops* means "a group of," but so does *a troop*; the extent of the number is fuzzy. (It sounds more natural to say "two soldiers" than "two troops.") As a collective noun, it is not construed as singular, as collectives should be: a group *is*, a platoon *is*, a collection of individuals *is*— but troops *are*. One cannot say "The troops is getting restless." A *troop* means both "one soldier" and "a group of soldiers," which is not what a word is supposed to do.

The language has been though this grammatical agony with another military collective, *cohort*, originally a group of soldiers (600 in ancient Rome), but now coming to mean a single ally or crony, so that a politician is surrounded by his *cohorts*, not his "cohort." (Demographers stick to the collective, meaning "a segment of the population.")

Although *troops* in politics is mainly used to mean low-level workers, it means all supporters in a campaign. David Broder,

writing about the political experts gathering around Governor Ronald Reagan in 1967, headlined his column with a military triple metaphor: "Gunning for a Draft: The Reagan Troops." See PARTY FAITHFUL.

trot out the ghosts Speechwriters' term for reference to the past luminaries of the speaker's party and to the past "failures" of the opposition party.

"I stand in direct succession to Woodrow Wilson and Franklin Roosevelt and Harry Truman," candidate John F. Kennedy said often in his version of THE SPEECH. "Mr. Nixon, the Republican leader, stands in direct succession to McKinley, to Coolidge, to Hoover, to Landon and to Dewey." He skipped Eisenhower, also a Republican, but popular.

Republican reference to "the party of Lincoln" is another example of "trotting out the ghosts," although constant quotation of Lincoln by Adlai Stevenson and John Kennedy resulted in watering down of Lincoln's Republican identification, an erosion the GOP combats each year at its Lincoln Day dinners.

Typical of *trotting out the ghosts* was Warren G. Harding's 1912 nomination of William Howard Taft; the future president's speech was, in his phrase, "glorying in retrospection." He hailed Taft as one "as wise and patient as Abraham Lincoln, as modest and dauntless as Ulysses S. Grant, as temperate and peace-loving as Rutherford B. Hayes, as patriotic and intellectual as James A. Garfield, as courtly and generous as Chester A. Arthur, as learned in the law as Benjamin Harrison, as sympathetic and brave as William McKinley, as progressive as his predecessor."

Harding did not mention the name of "his predecessor" because he was Theodore Roosevelt, who had bolted the party and was running against Taft for the nomination. Harding feared that that particular ghost was too lively to trot out. As this is written (post Nixon-Bushes, post Carter-Clinton), the only recent ghost that Democrats can safely trot out is Kennedy and the only suitable spectre for Republicans is Reagan.

true believer Used in friendly fashion, a loyalist and comrade in arms; used by a political opponent, a fanatic.

In current political usage, *true believer* is most often applied to conservatives, seen by them as one who holds firmly to the articles of right-wing faith and considers any compromise of them for political gain to be an abandonment of basic principles. The most frequently used charge made by a true believer is SELLOUT.

In a counterattack, centrists—the BIG TENT advocates—deprecate the divisiveness of "narrow IDEOLOGUES." Returning that fire, partisans embracing the word *principled* who believe a party should "stand for something" insist it offer a CHOICE NOT AN ECHO, avoid the ME-TOOism of TWEEDLEDUM AND TWEEDLEDEE and all such comparisons that show "not a DIME'S WORTH OF DIFFERENCE." The hard-right Howard Phillips, who challenged liberal Republican Edward Brooke in 1978 to the disapproval of party centrists, charged linguistic hypocrisy: "When liberals challenge conservative Republicans, they call it 'base-broadening.' But when conservatives oppose liberal GOP-ers, it is called 'cannibalism.'"

The term is applied to any profoundly principled (a.k.a "rigidly doctrinaire") group. "To the pragmatists such as Chou En-lai," editorialized *The New York Times* in October 1971, "the invitation to the American President was an opportunity to advance China's prestige on the world scene and to deter the preventive war advocates in Moscow. But to the true believers in Peking, the invitation must have seemed a sellout of all China's proclaimed revolutionary principles—as reprehensible in the eyes of those fanatics as was Nikita Khrushchev's visit to the United States in 1959 as President Eisenhower's guest."

But the expression need not reflect either fanaticism or tough-mindedness; a certain affection for steadfastness was in the use of the phrase as the title of a 1953 book by longshoreman-philosopher Eric Hoffer, and in *The Wall Street Journal*'s farewell to Hubert Humphrey on January 16, 1978: "Last of the True Believers?"

One origin is in the Koran, from the seventh century: "O true believers, take your necessary precautions against your enemies, and either go forth to war in separate parties, or go forth all together in a body." Though it is sometimes used today to describe or derogate fundamentalists of any religious faith, it has become more associated with political beliefs. The safest phraseology for both liberals and conservatives is to assert "basic values" that cannot be compromised provided they are not definitively defined.

See IDEOLOGY; LITMUS TEST.

Truman Doctrine See DOCTRINES.

"truth-in" construction A device to build persuasion into the generic name of legislation.

Truth in Packaging legislation caused running controversy in the early sixties. Proponents held that the public needed to be protected from misleading claims on packages of goods, especially regarding weight and bulk; opponents felt such restraints were captious, unnecessary, and a step toward government control of all advertising.

Truth in Lending followed, with proponents seeking to force banks, loan companies, and all suppliers of credit to show borrowers exactly how much the interest charges would add to costs.

The technique of slipping a message in a name (see RIGHT TO WORK) did not begin with *truth in packaging*. Early New Deal legislation included an attempted reform of the Wall Street community. "Undiscriminating people," wrote Raymond Moley, "described the securities bill [of 1933] as the 'Truth in Securities Act.'... But as the year passed, even Roosevelt realized that the Act in its existing form was unworkable ..." This led to the Securities Act of 1934 and the Securities and Exchange Commission. This act continued to be called "Truth in Securities" throughout the '30s, though the designation is no longer current.

Columnist Max Lerner wrote in 1939: "We have a Truth in Securities Act to make sure that there is no rigging of the stock market... are we to have nothing to protect us against the infinitely more dangerous advertising of anti-labor, anti-democratic, anti-Semitic lies? I know that liberals will immediately say: Why could not a Truth in Opinion Act be used against the left as well as the right? The answer is that it is already in use against the left."

A spin-off of *truth in packaging* is *sell-by date*, said of a candidate who has been trotted out once too often: "He has passed his sell-by date."

truth squad A team of officials, usually congressmen, organized to harass an opposition candidate by following close on his or her heels with refutations.

The phrase has a built-in advantage, implying what the opposition leader says is not true. The technique is useful and growing, since it makes the opposition more careful in its charges and gets newspaper space with "the last word" after a candidate has left a city.

John F. Kennedy was dogged by a *truth squad* headed by Republican Senator Hugh Scott of Pennsylvania in the 1960 campaign. Toward the end of the campaign, he used them as a foil: "Now we have five days before this campaign is over. I cannot predict what is going to happen. The 'truth squad' has been ditched. They told the truth once and they don't let them travel around anymore."

The term may have had its origin in the Agriculture Department's "Poison Squad" at the turn of the century. The department's Chief Chemist, Dr. Harvey W. Wiley, had collected a group of young scientists so dedicated to the fight for good food-and-drug legislation that they won the nickname by testing adulterated foods on themselves. Their efforts and Upton Sinclair's novel *The Jungle*, about the adulteration of meat, led to the Pure Food Act of 1906.

Its early use as a political technique was in 1919, when a group of Republican congressmen dogged Woodrow Wilson's steps as he tried to sell the idea of the League of Nations to the American people.

The best squelch was Adlai Stevenson's, who said of a Republican squad following him around in 1956: "A truth squad bears the same relationship to 'truth' as a Fire Department does to 'fire.'"

For a recent refinement of this technique, employing a hand-held video recorder, see TRACKER.

turkey farm Accusation of an agency or department being packed with political cronies and official's relatives gobbling up the taxpayer's funds.

In 1992, *The New York Times* ran an editorial about Washington's slow response to the victims of Hurricane Andrew. Blame was primarily directed to the George H.W. Bush Administration's neglect of the Federal Emergency Management Agency. Staff investigators for the House Appropriations Committee said that FEMA was "widely viewed as a dumping ground" for political appointees, "a turkey farm, if you will."

When Hurricane Katrina, a Category Five storm, struck New Orleans and the Gulf Coast in 2005, much of the city was inundated and the emergency response by federal, state, and local authorities was heavily criticized. FEMA and "turkey farm" were phrases that seemed almost to be fused in media coverage, and the younger President Bush was extensively mocked for praising the FEMA director for doing "a heck of a job."

Rooted in theatrical slang for "flop show," *turkey* became associated in the 1960s with any congenital failure. This fowl derogation (see BIRD METAPHORS) flies in the face of Ben Franklin's suggestion for our national bird; instead of supporting the bald eagle, Franklin preferred the turkey.

See PATRONAGE.

turnarounds Creating a phrase by reversing the construction of a famous saying; or, original rhetorical antithesis.

Franklin Roosevelt in 1932 took a Darwinian phrase and turned it around, saying that the aim of the national economy "should not be the survival of the fittest," but rather "the fitting of as many human beings as possible into the scheme of surviving."

"It has been said of the world's history hitherto," said Abraham Lincoln, "that might makes right. It is for us and for our time to reverse the maxim, and to say that right makes might." He liked that *turnaround*, using it again in his 1860 Cooper Union speech that made him a national candidate: "Let us have faith that right makes might, and in that faith let us to the end dare to do our duty as we understand it."

Republican presidential candidate Wendell Willkie, overwhelmed by FDR's campaign for a third term in 1940 and defeated four years later by Thomas E. Dewey for the GOP nomination, said, "I would rather lose in a cause I knew some day would triumph, than triumph in a cause that I know some day will fail."

Turnarounds, a form of CONTRAPUNTAL CONSTRUCTIONS and *parallel constructions*, are often created for purposes of ridicule: anti-Goldwater partisans paralleled "In Your Heart You Know He's Right" with "In Your Guts You Know He's Nuts." Cartoonist Walt Kelly, in the comic strip *Pogo*, turned around Captain Oliver Perry's famous line with "We have met the enemy and he is us." For other examples, see SPOILS SYSTEM, and the use of "shoo-out" under SHOO-IN.

turnip day See DO-NOTHING CONGRESS; RED HERRING.

turnout The number of voters on Election Day; also, the size of a partisan crowd.

Lip service is always given to the advisability of getting everyone to come to the polls. Franklin D. Roosevelt on election eve in 1940 said on the radio: "Last Saturday night, I said that freedom of speech is of no use to the man who has nothing to say and that freedom of worship is of no use to the man who has lost his God. And tonight I should like to add that a free election is of no use to the man who is too indifferent to vote ..."

But what the working politician really means is the need for his own side to turn out the vote. Systematic party efforts at turnout probably started with Aaron Burr and his Tammany Hall organization in 1800. Using a card index of the voters, members of the Society of Tammany made sure that all the FAITHFUL—now called the *core constituency* or BASE—went to the polls.

The word is applied more generally to the size of crowds. According to *New York*

Post columnist Leonard Lyons, President Lyndon Johnson was touched by the huge assemblage that greeted him at the airport in Seoul, Korea. Johnson later reported he had asked his host how large the crowd was and the President of Korea replied, "Two million! Two million people"—and then continued earnestly, "I'm sorry, President Johnson, but that's all the people I have."

The ability to reach voters considered reliable partisans has been refined by using computer technology. Acolytes of Karl Rove, who in 2000 and 2004 emerged publicly as George W. Bush's political GURU, swore by his "micro-targeting techniques" to turn out the committed voters. When this failed to ensure victory in the midterm election of 2006, in which control of Congress shifted to Democrats, Republican consultant Mike Murphy opined: "The problem wasn't that our voters didn't turn out, it was that our voters alone are not enough...when the 'swing' voters stampede toward your opponent, you are usually toast."

RNC Chairman Ken Mehlman said, "Historically, turnout matters at the margin. If you are losing an election because of an issue or the environment or the candidate, you are not going to win it on turnout."

The need to turn out is sometimes satirized. The early late-night TV comedian Jack Paar liked to quote the "little old lady" who firmly stated, "I never vote. It only encourages them."

See SILENT VOTE; STAY-AT-HOMES; "drop-off voters" in OFF-YEAR.

turn the rascals out See PROVERBS AND AXIOMS, POLITICAL.

Tweedledum and Tweedledee Literary characters used to attack the similarity of the two parties by those who claim to see not a DIME'S WORTH OF DIFFERENCE.

The twinlike characters popularized by Lewis Carroll in 1869 were injected into American political discourse by cartoonist Thomas Nast throughout the 1870s as he caricatured the characters chosen by "Boss" Tweed of Tammany. Long after Nast, the useful device has been brought into political play.

"There is little doubt," wrote Clinton Rossiter in 1960, "that many voters see nothing to choose between the Tweedledumism of the Democrats and Tweedledeeism of the Republicans. Lacking any third choice, they fail to choose at all."

As a Republican candidate attacked by disappointed conservatives as being a "me-tooer" (see ME TOO), Thomas E. Dewey wrote:

> It is only necessary to compare the platforms of both parties in a normal presidential year to find how similar they are. This similarity is highly objectionable to a vociferous few. They rail at both parties, saying they represent nothing but a choice between Tweedledee and Tweedledum. ...
>
> These impractical theorists with a "passion for neatness" demand that our parties be sharply divided, one against the other, in interest, membership, and doctrine. They want to drive all moderates and liberals out of the Republican party and then have the remainder join forces with the conservative groups of the South. Then they would have everything very neatly arranged, indeed. The Democratic party would be the liberal-to-radical party. The Republican party would be the conservative-to-reactionary party. The results would be neatly arranged too. The Republicans would lose every election and the Democrats would win every election.

Tweedledum and Tweedledee are generally assumed to be creations of Lewis Carroll; in his *Through the Looking Glass*, they sing the ditty "The Walrus and the Carpenter." Carroll took them from John Byrom's satire about bickering schools of musicians in the 1750s whose real difference was negligible. The best-known Byrom verse:

> *Some say compared to Bononcini*
> *That Mynheer Handel's but a ninny;*
> *Others aver that he to Handel*
> *Is scarcely fit to hold a candle.*
> *Strange all this difference should be*
> *'Twixt tweedle-dum and tweedle-dee.*

Tweed Ring See TAMMANY TIGER.

twenty years of treason An extreme version of the SOFT ON COMMUNISM charge, referring to the period (1932–52) in which Democrats occupied the White House.

In early 1954 Senator Joseph McCarthy made a series of speeches arranged by the Republican National Committee in nine cities, giving them the title "Twenty Years of Treason." In Charleston, W. Va., he stated the theme: "The issue between the Republicans and Democrats is clearly drawn. It has been deliberately drawn by those who have been in charge of twenty years of treason."

"Dwight Eisenhower," wrote Robert Donovan, "was quick to proclaim his belief in the loyalty of Democrats in disassociating himself from McCarthy's claim that the Roosevelt and Truman administrations represented 'twenty years of treason.'" As the senator demanded information from Administration appointees in hearings, the White House bluntly stated that its rights "cannot be usurped by any individual who may seek to set himself above the laws of our land." The use of *individual* rather than *man* or *person* or even *anyone* is pure Eisenhower style, indicating that he personally composed or edited the statement.

Senator McCarthy promptly responded by toughening his phrase, extending it into the present with "the evidence of treason that has been growing over the past twenty—(*pause*)—twenty-one years."

The accusation is used today mainly in recollections of the McCarthy era, though as late as 1960 the *Bulletin* of the John Birch Society held that the "key" to the advance of world Communism was "treason right within our government and the place to find it is right in Washington."

If this be demagoguery, as it surely was, some made the most of it. The combination of alliteration and neat packaging of the combined Roosevelt-Truman Administrations made *twenty years of treason* a well-turned catchphrase.

A milder form of accusatory retrospection predated McCarthy: a 1936 Republican convention keynote address was punctuated with "three long years!" This slogan threatened to become effective until FDR flattened it with his own account of the Harding-Coolidge-Hoover era: "Nine mocking years with the golden calf and three long years of the scourge ... nine crazy years at the ticker and three long years in the breadline!"

twisting slowly, slowly in the wind Left exposed to political attack; abandoned to the opposition.

The phrase was made a part of the political vocabulary in 1973 by White House Domestic Council director John Ehrlichman, who reported to this lexicographer on its origin: " 'Twisting slowly' is on a recording I made of a phone talk with [John] Dean re [FBI Acting Director] Pat Gray. RN [Richard Nixon] had decided to withdraw his nomination but no one had told Gray, and Pat was going back to the Judiciary Committee and taking punishment day after day. He was a corpse hanging there and RN hadn't yet cut him down for a decent burial. It seemed an apt description."

Ehrlichman, with H.R. Haldeman derogated as "the Berlin wall" isolating the president (as he wished) in the Nixon Administration, was someone the author worked with in the White House and remembers as an intellectual lawyer with a profound grasp of domestic policy and an openmindedness encouraged by an admirably outspoken wife, but also with an unconcern for privacy and an occasional callous streak.

In preparing this fifth edition, I examined his exact words on the tape: "I think we ought to let him hang there," Ehrlichman told John Dean, the president's counsel and participant in the unlawful obstruction. "Let him twist slowly, slowly in the wind." Those words were not a description, as John had later recounted for this dictionary; it was a direction, which Dean obeyed, and which Ehrlichman—to his later dismay—chose to secretly record.

The metaphoric overkill of the phrase—treating an undefended colleague as a corpse dangling in the breeze—is in the grand tradition of political hyperbole, and has been used frequently since, especially regarding confirmation hearings.

The phrase has an ancient "hanging" connotation: in his 1785 edition of *A Dictionary of the Vulgar Tongue*, Captain Frances Grose lists *twisted* as "executed, hanged," and there is a 1725 reference to that lugubrious meaning in the *New Canting Dictionary* (1725). The late slanguist Stuart Berg Flexner, in a letter to the author, suggested: "I find that the trap-door scaffold and the hangman's knot weren't accepted before the nineteenth century, meaning that before this late date victims suffered slow strangulation while out there kicking and twisting at the end of the rope."

The most vivid fictional use of the metaphor (and perhaps Ehrlichman's unconscious source) was in the concluding paragraph of *Brave New World*, the prescient novel written in 1932 by Aldous Huxley: "Just under the crown of the arch dangled a pair of feet...Slowly, very slowly, like two unhurried compass needles, the feet turned towards the right; north, northeast, east, south-east, south, south-south-west; then paused, and, after a few seconds, turned as unhurriedly back towards the left. South-south-west, south, south-east, east ..."

The Ehrlichman phrase rivals SMOKING GUN as fixed in the political lexicon more securely than most other WATERGATE WORDS. In 1976, Britain's *The Economist* explained how Hua Guofeng's rise led to the downfall of Jiang Qing, widow of Chairman Mao Zedong, and titled the story: "How Hua Left Mrs. Mao Twisting in the Wind."

In 1990, R. W. Apple Jr. of *The New York Times* wrote: "April C. Glaspie, the American Ambassador to Baghdad, was on leave when Saddam Hussein attacked on Aug. 2. Many believe she is the leading Foreign Service authority on the Arab world, but she remains in Washington, with little role to play except twisting slowly in the wind."

And in June 2007, when President George W. Bush's Attorney General, Alberto Gonzales, came under sustained fire from the new Democratic majority in Congress over the firing of eight U.S. Attorneys who had been appointed by Bush and served "at the pleasure of the president," *Newsweek* headlined: "Gonzales, the president's lawyer and Texas buddy, is twisting slowly in the wind, facing a vote of no confidence from the Senate." In each of these citations, the editing-out of Ehrlichman's repeated "slowly, slowly" may have served the interests of saving space but drained the power of the metaphor.

twisting the lion's tail Defying Great Britain; speeches originally aimed at nineteenth-century Irish voters; now, any attack on the British government.

Early written references are few, though *Harper's Weekly* in 1872 ran a cartoon showing President Grant with his foot on the British lion's tail. Later, in 1889, Theodore Roosevelt wrote that "just at present our statesmen seem inclined to abandon the tail of the lion and instead we are plucking vigorously at the caudal feathers of that delightful war-fowl, the German eagle—a cousin of our own bald-headed bird of prey" (see BALD EAGLE).

Carl Schurz indicated in 1898 that the phrase was already familiar when he wrote: "for the present attitude of Great Britain will no longer permit the American demagogue to seek popularity by twisting the British Lion's tail."

The phrase is losing its currency as the lion symbol is not as symbolic of the United Kingdom as John Bull.

two-bit politician See TINHORN POLITICIAN.

two cars in every garage See CHICKEN IN EVERY POT.

two-fer See GOFER.

two minutes to midnight See DOOMSDAY MACHINE.

two-party system In American thinking, happy medium between tyrannical one-party control and an anarchic profusion of splinter parties; a system most U.S. politicians speak of with reverence.

"I think it is very important that we have a two-party country," President Lyndon Johnson joked at a press conference in 1964. "I am a fellow that likes small parties, and the Republican party is about the size I like."

Two-party system (representing a practice seldom found outside the U.S. and Great Britain) is a phrase difficult to find in early writings about government, but there are plenty of strong opinions about the general idea. Warnings against parties in general range from George Washington's 1796 "The spirit of party serves always to distract the public councils, and enfeeble the public administration" to the Soviet Union's Nikita Khrushchev in 1957: "After the liquidation of classes we have a monolithic society.

Therefore, why found another party? That would be like voluntarily letting someone put a flea in your shirt."

Most of the comments about the division of political activity by parties, gleefully quoted today by those who plead for more BIPARTISANSHIP in foreign policy and urban affairs, are based on ideological division (as in England and France) rather than administrative division (as in the U.S.). Joseph Addison wrote about a philosophical split in *The Spectator* in 1711: "There can not a greater judgment befall a country than such a dreadful spirit of division as rends a government into two distinct people, and makes them greater strangers and more averse to one another than if they were actually two different nations." The wrench of ideological faction concerned Thomas Jefferson in 1789: "If I could not go to Heaven but with a party I would not go there at all."

Early defenders of the two-party system also spoke mostly of ideological division. "Party divisions," wrote Edmund Burke in 1769, "whether on the whole operating for good or evil, are things inseparable from free government." Horace Walpole wrote in 1760 that "A nation without parties is soon a nation without curiosity," and Disraeli in 1864 held that "Party is organized opinion."

Another reason given for the two-party system was the inherent cleansing process of having INS AND OUTS. Congressman, later autocratic Speaker, Thomas B. Reed put it bluntly in 1880: "The best system is to have one party govern and the other party watch." The "watching," in its active sense, meant keeping it honest and responsive; competition for office bred new programs and advances.

Ideological differences within each major U.S. party are usually greater than the difference between the parties, despite attempts to delineate fundamental schisms of beliefs. Democratic orators have tried to separate themselves—the PARTY OF THE PEOPLE—from the "party of the SPECIAL INTERESTS"; the Republicans have countered with variations of their platform of 1908: "The trend of Democracy is toward Socialism, while the Republican party stands for a wise and regulated individualism. Socialism would destroy wealth; Republicanism would prevent its abuse."

Undoubtedly a general difference exists in the approach, appeal, and personality of the two U.S. parties, but the *two-party system* is more of a means to political power and administration than a means to social revolution. In this sense, the system is much the same as our *adversary system* of criminal justice, in which the truth is expected to win in fair competition.

Coalition is always a danger to the two-party system. FDR's war cabinet brought in Republicans Stimson and Knox; Churchill's deputy was his archrival, Clement Attlee. Wendell Willkie, who ran against FDR in as war loomed in 1940, in his LOYAL OPPOSITION speech, drew the line: "We, who stand ready to serve our country behind our Commander in Chief, nevertheless retain the right, and I will say the duty, to debate the course of our government. Ours is a two-party system. Should we ever permit one party to dominate our lives entirely, democracy would collapse and we would have dictatorship."

To most Americans, the two-party system is a contrasting phrase for *one-party rule* or *single-party domination*. It ranks with FREE ENTERPRISE, the AMERICAN WAY OF LIFE, CHECKS AND BALANCES, and the AMERICAN DREAM as an unassailable political phrase.

Whenever one party wins a particularly lopsided victory, as in 1936, 1964, 1972, and 1984, fears are expressed about the future of the system. Politicians worry about the U.S. adopting a configuration of power such as that in Japan's Diet in most of the post–World War II period, which Yale professor Warren M. Tsuneishi called "the one-and-one-half party system" characterized by "a dominant party that monopolizes power and alone knows how to govern while opposed by a permanent minority group that at times seems 'positively afraid of power.'" Somehow, in the U.S., the pendulum has always managed to swing back, partly because politicians in power too long tend to get arrogant and lazy, and often corrupt, triggering TIME FOR A CHANGE.

A left-handed but intensely practical reason for attaching oneself to one of two parties was given by George Savile, Marquess of Halifax, in 1690: "If there are two parties a man ought to adhere to that which he disliketh least, though in the whole he doth not approve it; for whilst he doth not list himself in one or the other party, he is looked upon as such a straggler that he is fallen upon by both."

See ME TOO; TWEEDLEDUM AND TWEEDLEDEE; PARTISAN; PARTY LOYALTY; THIRD-PARTY MOVEMENT.

U

umbrella symbol Symbol of APPEASEMENT, from the umbrella carried by British Prime Minister Neville Chamberlain on his return from the Munich Conference in September 1938.

A character on Fred Allen's radio program in the early '40s, supposedly afflicted with amnesia and trying—by the slow process of elimination—to figure out who he was, said, "I don't have an umbrella—so I can't be Neville Chamberlain."

The continuing close identification with Chamberlain, appeasement, and umbrellas is illustrated in this passage from historian Eric Goldman's *The Crucial Decade* about Dwight Eisenhower's arrival at an airport: "When the President's plane, the Columbine III, neared the Washington airport, a summer shower was spattering the Capital. Vice-President Richard Nixon issued an instruction to the officials going out to the airport: No umbrellas, the Vice-President said, because people might be reminded of Prime Minister Neville Chamberlain coming back with his umbrella from the Munich appeasement of Hitler."

In the final days before the Democratic nomination in 1960, columnists Rowland Evans and Robert Novak claimed that candidate Lyndon Johnson joined the attack on Joseph P. Kennedy, his rival's father, recalling the former ambassador's reputation for appeasement. "On the very day of the balloting, July 14," they wrote, "Johnson took up the cry: 'I wasn't any Chamberlain-umbrella policy man. I never thought Hitler was right.'"

The umbrella has other political symbolic meanings as well. A presidential program can be an umbrella under which congressional candidates scurry before an election. Not surprisingly, the symbol can be extended from mild protection to military preparedness to pessimism. "The American people," wrote Al Smith in 1931, "never carry an umbrella. They prepare to walk in eternal sunshine."

See PEACE FOR OUR TIME. For other symbols in politics, see CARTOONISTS' SYMBOLS.

un-American Not conforming to the ideology or sharing the same values as the particular American using the term.

The word *American*, as used in the term *un-American*, describes neither a person's nationality (a U.S. citizen) nor point of origin (from the Western Hemisphere). American in this sense is short for AMERICANISM, a creed based on economic opportunity, political freedom, and social mobility.

The Fourth of July is not a national holiday hailing the birth of a nation, like Bastille Day in France; it is more of a commemoration of the realization of an ideology, which Communists tried with May Day.

One who is *un-American* does not, in the accuser's opinion, share that ideology. "This concept of 'un-American activities,' as far as I know, does not have its counterpart in other countries," wrote professor Seymour Martin Lipset. "American patriotism is allegiance to values, to a creed, not solely to a nation. An American political leader could not say, as Winston Churchill did in 1940, that the English Communist Party was composed of Englishmen, and he did not fear an Englishman … this emphasis on ideological conformity to presumably common political values … legitimizes the hunt for 'un-Americans' in our midst."

Its origin may have had its origin in the revolutionary ardor of Alexander Hamilton, alluded to in this 1880 letter by President James Garfield: "More than a hundred years ago, a young student of Columbia College was arguing the ideas of the American Revolution and American Union against the un-American loyalty to monarchy of his college president and professors." Other citations date back to the early nineteenth century.

The word gained political popularity in a reaction against the American, or KNOW-NOTHING, party in the mid-nineteenth century.

The anti-Catholic, anti-Semitic, anti-foreign philosophy of the "Sams" (after UNCLE SAM), styled as American, naturally drew a blast as anti-American, or un-American, as in this 1844 pamphlet: "Misguided men assuming the title Native American, but un-American at heart, breathing destruction on those not born here, denouncing a whole religious community and all professing a particular faith, have been joined with the Whigs."

Republican William Seward added a few years later: "every thing is un-American which makes a distinction of whatever kind, in this country, between the native born American and him whose lot is directed to be cast here by an overruling Providence."

After the collapse of the Know-Nothings, *un-American* took on its antiradical, antinonconformist coloration. *The New York Times* complained in 1870 that its rival, the *New York Tribune*, "stigmatizes its opponent as false to his party, or as 'un-American'—its two favorite and well-worn labels."

The Democratic platform of 1896 held gold bimetallism to be "not only un-American, but anti-American"; soon afterward, editor William Allen White began a generation-long campaign against Bryan's "un-American doctrine of state paternalism." Third-party candidate Robert "Fighting Bob" La Follette in 1924 stressed his Progressive movement's moderation: "We are unalterably opposed to any class government, whether it be the existing dictatorship of plutocracy or the dictatorship of the proletariat. Both are essentially undemocratic and un-American."

The word gained its greatest prominence in the late '30s as the name of a congressional committee, nicknamed by its initials in the sixties, HUAC. *The New Yorker* wrote in 1948:

One questionable thing about the House Committee on un-American Activities is its name. ... The word "un-American," besides beginning with a small letter and gradually working up to a capital, is essentially a foolish, bad word, hardly worth the little hyphen it needs to hold it together. Literally, nothing in this country can be said to be un-American. "Un" means "not," and anything that happens within our borders is American, no matter what its nature, no matter how far off the beam it may be.

The word is used as an epithet casting the person attacked outside the pale of common values; its use, however, carries the built-in boomerang of indicating the user to be intolerant of dissent.

This term still carries a punch. An opinion piece in *Newsday* during the 1992 Presidential campaign: "[George H.W.] Bush at his debate lectern had renewed his innuendo that Bill Clinton's opposition to the Vietnam War and draft avoidance at that time had been un-American, near traitorous." Conservative Barry M. Goldwater wrote a *Washington Post* essay in 1993 in favor of lifting the ban on homosexuals in the military; the headline was "The Gay Ban: Just Plain Un-American."

uncertain trumpet See MUSICAL METAPHORS.

Uncle Sam Symbol for the collective citizenry of the U.S.

In the minds of most Americans, Uncle Sam is a stern-looking man on a World War I recruiting poster by James Montgomery Flagg pointing his finger directly at the viewer and saying: "I want YOU for the U.S. Army."

He was created in the War of 1812. The first written record of his appearance is in *The Troy* (N.Y.) *Post*, September 3, 1813: "'Loss upon loss,' and 'no ill luck stir[r]ing but what lights upon Uncle Sam's shoulders,' exclaim the Government editors, in every part of the Country. ... This cant name for our government has got almost as current as 'John Bull.' The letters U.S. on the government waggons &c are supposed to have given rise to it." (John Bull had a more specific genesis in a 1712 satire by Dr. John Arbuthnot, and is now the cartoonists' symbol—more so than a lion—of Great Britain.)

Forst's *Naval History of the United States* relates that a government inspector of provisions in Troy, New York, named Samuel Wilson was the original Uncle Sam. He was supposed to have been given the nickname during the War of 1812 by workmen in the military stores handling casks labeled "E.A.—U.S.," with Elbert Anderson the name of the contractor. The story is not substantiated.

Charles Ledyard Norton wrote in his 1890 political dictionary: "Uncle Sam is for Americans what John Bull is for the English, save that he is always pictorially represented in exaggerated and impossible habiliments, such as might be worn on the stage by a burlesque actor, and with a personality to match, while the typical John Bull takes life seriously in sober garb, like a 'fine old English gentleman.'"

When Uncle Sam is being described as one unduly taken advantage of, he becomes "Uncle Sugar." To European debtor nations in the 1920s, U.S. stood for "Uncle Shylock," demanding his pound of flesh. Individual Americans were known for a time as BROTHER JONATHAN, after Jonathan Trumbull, aide to General Washington; members of the Know-Nothing party, styled the "American" party, were known as "Sams" after the Uncle Sam symbol. See UN-AMERICAN.

Uncle Sam may bring to mind a small boy's demand that another quit a fight by "saying uncle"; at any rate, when a politician talks about "going to Uncle," he means going to the federal government for aid.

unfinished business Reason often given, after much public and prayerful soul-searching, for running again.

No politician decides to run again because he enjoys the play of power, savors the perks, or because he couldn't make as much in private industry; nor does he or she elect to be reelected because retirement would be boring, the party needs to retain the seat or because too many people are owed too many favors.

On the contrary, reassuming the burdens of office is said to be a great personal sacrifice. His neglected family will gamely go along with his decision because the country, state, or assembly district must come first. Why hang on grimly to the onerous torch rather than pass it on to the next generation of grasping, ambitious, inexperienced YOUNG TURKS who are eager to get their grubby hands on it? The standard reason: "unfinished business."

In 1948, Harry Truman phrased his motive in its classic form: "There was still 'unfinished business' confronting the most successful fifteen years of Democratic administration in the history of the country. ... I also felt, without undue ego, that this was no time for a new and inexperienced hand to take over the government and risk the interruption of our domestic program and put a dangerous strain on our delicately balanced foreign policy."

The antonymic phrase for politicians facing electoral disaster or a scandal about to be revealed is an overpowering "need to spend more time with my family."

unflappable Cool under heat; calm in a crisis; unmoved by furor.

The sobriquet "unflappable Mac" was applied to Harold Macmillan, British Foreign Minister and Prime Minister (1957–63). For a time spanning the Suez crisis to the Profumo affair he retained his reputation for imperturbability in the face of political storms. In 1967 Mayor Jerome Cavanagh of Detroit was described in a profile during the racial riots in his city as "unflappable."

The opening lines from Kipling's poem "If" describe the unflappable public servant: "If you can keep your head / When all about you / Are losing theirs and blaming it on you ..." (A parody of this poem appeared in the form of signs put up in offices by advertising executives in the early '60s: "If you can keep your head when all about you are losing theirs—perhaps you don't understand the gravity of the situation.")

Flap, according to H. L. Mencken, originated with British aviators in World War I as a word for "air raid." The mental picture of the flapping wings of birds when frightened is apt; a political *flap* is a minor crisis, with assurances by professionals that "this, too, shall pass." *Flapdoodle,* or nonsense, can be traced back to the American Civil War.

A frequently used synonym for *flap,* milder than a FEEDING FRENZY or a FIRESTORM, is *brouhaha,* a fifteenth-century French word for "commotion" or "hubbub" which was introduced into English letters by Oliver Wendell Holmes Sr. in 1890. The French word is from *Brou, brou, brou, ha, ha!,* exclaimed noisily by actors entering a scene playing priests disguised as devils in early French farce; the source of the exclamation may be the Hebrew *baruch haba*, "blessed is he who enters."

For the causes of flaps, see FLAP and FALLOUT.

ungovernable What pessimists and farmers consider every major U.S. city to be.

"Is New York City ungovernable?" was a question often asked in the late '60s when strikes, smog, congestion, and what a Carter pollster was later to call a "malaise" afflicted the city dweller. The word was popularized by CBS commentator Eric Sevareid.

Ungovernable soon became an urban-affairs cliche, trotted out in think pieces following each new strike by public employees, along with "crisis of the cities," the title of a series by the *New York Herald Tribune* in the early '60s.

Governance, another word from the same French root, sprouted in academia and became a vogue-word substitute for "government" or "governing." It is used by writers who also like *polity*.

unholy alliance Attack phrase on any political agreement, especially when disparate elements find themselves in opposition to the same thing.

Unholy alliance was Franklin Roosevelt's characterization of the groups backing Wendell Willkie in the 1940 presidential campaign. Both John L. Lewis, head of the United Mine Workers, and the American Communist party opposed Roosevelt for different reasons; he skillfully used their support of Willkie as a KISS OF DEATH. Judge Samuel Rosenman, a close FDR adviser and speechwriter, recalled: "The President, who for years had been called by political enemies a Communist or a tool of the Communists, was now able to turn the tables on his Republican adversary, and attack the alliance of the Communists, the dictatorial labor leader Lewis, and the old-guard reactionary Republican leaders. This opportunity was unique in his political experience, and he cheerfully took full advantage of it." FDR warned:

There is something very ominous in this combination ... within the Republican Party between the extreme reactionary and the extreme radical elements of this country. ... We all know the story of the unfortunate chameleon which turned brown when placed on a brown rug, and turned red when placed on a red rug, but who died a tragic death when they put him on a Scotch plaid. We all know what would happen to Government if it tried to fulfill all the secret understandings and promises made between the conflicting groups which are now backing the Republican Party.

Bernard Schwartz was an energetic counsel for a House subcommittee investigating the Federal Communications Commission in 1958. When he appeared overzealous to members of the subcommittee, he was fired. His subsequent statement illustrates the current usage of the word: "I accuse the majority of this subcommittee, in order to further their own partisan interests, of joining an unholy alliance between business and the White House to obtain a WHITEWASH."

All "unholy" alliances are based on the "Holy Alliance" signed by the kings of Russia, Prussia, and Austria in Paris in 1815.

The phrase is a favorite of "conspiracy theorists," who often connect the little dots that aren't there. (The phrase first attested is *conspiracy theory*, in 1909; the *theorist* phrase is first cited in 1964 by the *OED*.) Lane Kirkland, who headed the AFL-CIO in the '90s and wrote his own literate speeches, liked to say, "I'm against any conspiracy I'm not a part of." See COALITION; STRANGE BEDFELLOWS; VAST RIGHT-WING CONSPIRACY.

unilateralism Going it alone; a foreign policy that proceeds despite the reservations of allies or the reluctance of international organizations to follow the lead of the independent power.

This word started as a variant of the earlier (1844) noun *unilaterality*. The *-ism* variant is first found in print in 1926, when *Public Opinion* urged that "We must ... surmount national and social unilateralism in the domain of the spirit." The combining form *uni-*, meaning "one" (as in the single-wheeled *unicycle*), differentiates this term from *bilateralism's* reciprocity or *multilateralism's* many-sided approach.

Unilateral has been primarily used in politics in the phrase *unilateral disarmament*. Referring to a one-sided decision to destroy weaponry, the term first appeared in a 1929 report in *The Times* of London: "Lord Salisbury agreed that unilateral disarmament had probably reached its limits."

Unilateralism entered American political usage in the '50s. Writing in 1951, a decade before joining the new Kennedy Administration, the historian Arthur Schlesinger Jr. denounced the policy in popularizing its name: "Unilateralism, to coin one more gobbledygook term, has become the new isolationism. Go it alone; meet force with maximum force; there is NO SUBSTITUTE FOR VICTORY; do not worry about consequences: these are the tenets of the new faith." A *Washington Post* article in 1977 quoted Peter Walters, a British shipping magnate, on "the increasing tendency in the United States toward unilateralism and protectionism."

Gaining a pejorative sense of "foreign policy that ignores the views of allies," the term was used by Henry Kissinger in his 1979 book, *The White House Years*: "From an early hostility to the American alliance with Japan,…the Chinese leaders soon came…to view it a guarantee of America's continued interest in the Western Pacific and a rein on Japanese unilateralism."

Asked about the U.S. role in stopping "ethnic cleansing" by Serbia in Bosnia in 1993, Bill Clinton replied: "But I also believe it is imperative that we work with our allies on this. The United States is not in a position to move unilaterally, nor should we." See GO-IT-ALONE; MULTILATERALISM.

uninhibited, robust, and wide-open What the Supreme Court has held debate on public issues has a constitutional right to be.

This ringing tripartite modifier appeared first in a 1964 Supreme Court ruling on freedom of speech. The phrase, part of a twentieth-century bulwark reasserting the First Amendment's prohibition against making law "abridging the freedom of speech or of the press," has been repeatedly used in the decades since that decision to justify both spoken and written freedom.

Associate Justice William J. Brennan Jr. issued the opinion in the libel case of *New York Times Co. v. Sullivan*. Anthony Lewis, who won a Pulitzer Prize for his coverage

of the Supreme Court and later served as a *New York Times* columnist for three decades, described the drafting of the passage in his 1991 book *Make No Law*:

Like most members of the Court, Justice Brennan often asked his law clerks to draft opinions. In this case he did not. He wrote the first draft himself, completing it toward the end of January.… The first draft was not circulated to the other justices. Justice Brennan showed it to his law clerks, and a few days later a second draft was produced. On February 6, 1964, it was circulated to the rest of the Court. There were minor changes in wording throughout.… Eleven days later on February 17, Justice Brennan circulated a third draft among his colleagues. It included many stylistic changes, bringing the form and rhetoric of the opinion significantly closer to its final version.… The second draft's pedestrian statement that "the national commitment to freedom of speech…cannot be foreclosed by 'mere labels'" was transformed in the third to one of the most arresting passages in the final opinion: "thus we consider this case against the background of a profound national commitment to the principle that debate on public issues should be uninhibited, robust, and wide-open, and that it may well include vehement, caustic, and sometimes unpleasantly sharp attacks on government and public officials."

See CHILLING EFFECT.

union A voluntary alliance making one out of many.

Like the few extra vertebrae on the end of the human backbone that used to be the start of a tail, this vestigial term preserves an idea of great political import.

The word *union*, which Americans capitalize when using it to refer to the United States, was first used in an American context in Massachusetts in 1754: "A motion was made that the Commissioners deliver their opinion whether a Union of all the Colonies is not at present absolutely necessary for their security and defense."

Thomas Jefferson in 1775 wrote: "A Committee of Congress is gone to improve our circumstances, so as to bring the Canadians into our Union." It is used almost casually in Article II, Section 3 of the Constitution, directing that the President "shall from time to time give to the Congress information of the state of the Union, and recommend to their consideration such measures as he shall judge necessary and expedient." (Different times, different grammar; in the Founders' English, Congress was construed as plural, followed by the pronoun *their*; today's Americans construe it as singular and say *its*.)

At the time of the Civil War, *Union* became a dramatic word, meaning something worth fighting to preserve and, as an adjective, describing the blue-clad Northern forces. A term for the United States fighters was "Unions," as in this dialect use by Mark Twain in 1874: "When de Unions took dat town...dey all run away and lef' me all by myse'f."

By the late nineteenth century, *Unionist* ceased to mean a supporter of a *federal union* against nullification or secession by a Confederacy; gradually, it changed to mean an alliance of workers organized in a *labor union* to counterbalance the power of management. By the late twentieth century, it had gained yet another divisively unifying meaning: *civil union*, recognition of many of the rights of marriage within a single sex.

Short word, long history; many meanings, reflecting the contradiction of the need for unity in protecting diversity. See STATE OF THE UNION.

United Nations International organization of member states; name coined by FDR.

Roosevelt speechwriter Samuel Rosenman wrote of the bathroom agreement that named the world body:

He [FDR] was also pleased—and proud—that it was he who had suggested the phrase "United Nations" to Churchill. Churchill, in public utterances, had referred to them as "Allied Nations" and "Associated Nations." The President thought of "United Nations," not as an analogy to "United States," but rather as expressive of the fact that the Allies were united in a common purpose. Having hit upon that phrase one day, he immediately had someone wheel him right into Churchill's room, interrupting the Churchillian bath, and the two agreed then and there upon the name. The same name was used three years later to designate the formal worldwide entity, the United Nations Organization.

The British Prime Minister confirmed this in his war memoirs: "The President has chosen the title 'United Nations' for all the Powers now working together. This is much better than 'Alliance,' which places him in constitutional difficulties, or 'Associated Powers,' which is flat."

Bartlett's Familiar Quotations offers the specific passage from Lord Byron's 1812 poetic work *Childe Harold's Pilgrimage* that Churchill quoted to FDR in 1941 to support the term *United Nations*:

Thou fatal Waterloo.
Millions of tongues record thee, and anew
Their children's lips shall echo them and
*   say—*
"Here, where the sword united nations drew,
Our countrymen were warring on that day!"
And this is much, and all which will not pass
*   away.*

Ironically, it was another American President, Woodrow Wilson, who chose *covenant* rather than *agreement* or *treaty* in the Covenant of the League of Nations; he felt that the Old Testament word, recalling God's covenant with Abraham, added a necessary solemnity.

United States of America A great nation's name, which is in coinage dispute.

Claims William E. Woodward (coiner of the verb *debunk*—see BUNK), in his 1945 biography *Tom Paine, America's Godfather*: "To Paine also belongs the honor of naming our country the 'United States of America.' He was the first to use the name in print, and it was his own creation." Just over six months after the Declaration of Independence, on January 13, 1777, Paine brandished the title at Lord Howe. "The United States of America," he wrote in the second issue of *The Crisis*, "will sound as pompously in the world or in history as The Kingdom of Great Britain." (*Pompous* then meant "important," rather than the present meaning, "self-important.")

However, the last paragraph of the 1776 Declaration, delivered to the Continental Congress on June 28 and signed on July 4, 1776, reads "the Representatives of the United States of America." The official naming was authoritative, ignoring Benjamin

Franklin's suggestion of "The United States of North America" (more modestly accurate but perhaps too long). Working with Franklin and John Adams, Thomas Jefferson drafted the declaration over the course of eight days, between June 11 and June 18, 1776, according to Julian Boyd's 1943 *The Declaration of Independence: The Evolution of the Text*.

Evidently, the name was "in the air"; Jon R. Simon of the *Oxford English Dictionary*, digging around the stacks of the Library of Congress, found a letter from Elbridge Gerry, a Massachusetts member of Congress, to General Horatio Gates, George Washington's rival, giving him the good news that capital punishment was in store for all spies "or other enemies of the United States of America." Gerry's letter was dated June 28, 1776, the same day Congress received the Jefferson-Adams-Franklin draft. Further research is hereby invited.

In current usage, the nation's name is referred to as the *U.S.*, which is often written as *US*. The use of all three initials seems corny, as in "the good old U.S.A." It is known familiarly as UNCLE SAM and, to those looking askance at foreign aid, *Uncle Sugar*.

united we stand An early U.S. motto that never quite made it to official status.

John Dickenson wrote "The Patriot's Appeal" in 1776: "Then join hand in hand, brave Americans all—By uniting we stand, by dividing we fall." The State of Kentucky sharpened it to "United we stand; divided we fall" and adopted it as its state motto in 1792.

But the U.S. had already adopted another motto in 1777: *E Pluribus Unum* (From Many, One), first found on the title page of the *Gentleman's Miscellany* in January 1692. Thus was *united we stand* blocked, though many Americans still think it is the translation for *E Pluribus Unum*.

Salmon P. Chase, Lincoln's devout Secretary of the Treasury, placed "In God We Trust" on coins to go with "E Pluribus Unum" and "Liberty," crowding the coin so that there was no space left for "United We Stand." The rear of the Great Seal, published on every dollar bill, contains some Latin slogans known to few citizens: *Annuit Coeptis*

means "He [God] has favored our undertakings" (from Virgil's *Aeneid*, Book IX, verse 625), and *Novus Ordo Seclorum* means "A new order of the ages" (from Virgil's fourth Eclogue). Both mottoes were proposed by Charles Thomson, Secretary of Congress, in a report adopted by the Continental Congress on June 20, 1782. Why? Nobody knows; Edwin S. Costrell, chief of the Historical Division of the U.S. Department of State, informed the author: "In response to your query 'why they appear on the Seal,' I can only conjecture that Thomson, in proposing the mottoes, and the Congress, in adopting them, considered them to be appropriate."

"United we stand, divided we fall" combines two old concepts. "Union is strength" is an old English proverb; the idea is expressed in Shakespeare's *King John*: "This union shall do more than battery can / To our fast-closed gates." "Divide and conquer" (in the original "divide and reign") has a record at least as old as 1633.

"America the Beautiful" is more singable than "The Star-Spangled Banner," which, however, remains the national anthem. Similarly, *United we stand* is stronger and more intelligible than any Latin motto, including the sacrosanct *E Pluribus Unum*; unfortunately, its supporters have been divided.

unleash Chiang A Republican threat to remove restraints on Chiang Kai-shek's Taiwan forces, which it was felt might intimidate "Red China"; the People's Republic of China was not intimidated.

In the late forties and early fifties, there was a strong feeling in the U.S. that the "let the dust settle" policy (see WATCHFUL WAITING) had caused the free world to "lose" China to Communism. To add insult to injury, went this opinion, the anti-Communist Chinese forces on Formosa were being held back from launching an invasion of their homeland.

John Foster Dulles, first Dewey's and then Eisenhower's chief foreign policy adviser, was the American most associated with a promise to "unleash Chiang." When he became President, Eisenhower redeemed the Republican pledge with this statement:

In June 1950, following the aggressive attack on the Republic of Korea, the United States Seventh Fleet was instructed both to prevent attack upon Formosa and also to insure that Formosa should not be used as a base of operations against the Chinese Communist mainland.... I am...issuing instructions that the Seventh Fleet no longer be employed to shield Communist China. Permit me to make crystal clear this order implies no aggressive intent on our part. But we certainly have no obligation to protect a nation fighting us in Korea.

In fact, the Seventh Fleet had been protecting Formosa (now Taiwan) from invasion by China, and not vice versa. The purpose of the removal of the "shield" was to put Communist China on notice that the U.S. might have a surprise in store, and to require deployment of defense forces opposite Formosa on the mainland. But when years slipped by and no action was taken by Chiang's forces—nor was any permitted by the U.S.—the phrase boomeranged, and became a derisive term for foreign policy bluffing.

When the offshore islands of Quemoy and Matsu were bombarded early in 1955 by "Red" China, the Administration took a deliberately vague posture, indicating the U.S. would come to the islands' defense if they were considered necessary to the defense of Formosa. At the same time, a promise was extracted from the Nationalists not to invade the mainland without first informing the U.S. Critics called this "re-leashing Chiang." After the 1972 signing of the Shanghai Communiqué between the U.S. and the People's Republic of China, the phrase was used only in ironic recollection. See Nixon's use of *People's Republic* under GREAT LEAP FORWARD.

The phrase "unleash Chiang" was and is associated with Secretary of State Dulles. Criticizing "journalese" in their *Dictionary of Contemporary American Usage*, Bergen and Cornelia Evans wrote in 1957: "Certain pompous phrases must remain permanently set up in type: *bipartisan foreign policy, act of overt aggression...titular head of the party, diplomat without portfolio...policy of containment*. But to assume such inflated terminology is confined to newspapers is to be as ignorant as unjust. It was not some petty, pretentious scribbler who invented *massive retaliation* and *agonizing reappraisal* or spoke of *unleashing* Chiang Kai-shek." The Evanses left out Dulles's other lively coinages, LIBERATION OF CAPTIVE PEOPLES and BRINKMANSHIP, in their last grouping. A less linguistically colorful successor to Dulles, Dean Rusk, popularized EYEBALL TO EYEBALL.

The *unleash* metaphor was used successfully by British MP, later Prime Minister, Harold Macmillan in 1945: he advocated "the unleashing of production" after the war, playing further on the canine image by urging the Labour party to "let sleeping dogmas lie." See ATTACK DOG.

unpack Punch line of a religious issue joke.

Worries about potential "popery" in the U.S. if Catholic Al Smith were elected in 1928 led to this gag: When Smith lost to Herbert Hoover, he was said to have sent a one-word wire to the Pope in the Vatican: "Unpack."

When a Catholic finally was elected, in 1960, he took a strong position against federal aid to parochial schools. John F. Kennedy, proposing an education bill to Congress, knew it would cause some anger among Catholics. He turned around the old Smith joke: "As all of you know, some circles invented the myth that after Al Smith's defeat in 1928, he sent a one-word telegram to the Pope: 'Unpack.' After my press conference on the school bill, I received a one-word wire from the Pope: 'Pack.'"

After Kennedy was assassinated, blacks were concerned about the racial attitude of the administration of Texan Lyndon Johnson. After his first speech to the joint session of Congress on November 27, 1963, in which he called for civil rights legislation, black comedian Dick Gregory revived the gag: "Twenty million of us unpacked our bags."

un-poor, un-young, un-black See MIDDLE AMERICA.

unthinkable thoughts Proposals too mind-boggling or frightening to discuss, but also a phrase used by those who want to advance schemes that shatter shibboleths.

The oxymoron agitated political parlance when used by nuclear physicist Herman Kahn, who wrote *On Thermonuclear War* in 1959. James Newman in *Scientific American* magazine attacked Kahn's character as well as style of writing in a vitriolic review calling his book "a moral tract on how to justify mass murder." The reviewer's lead was memorable: "Is there really a Herman Kahn? It's hard to believe. Doubts cross one's mind almost from the first page of this deplorable book: no one could write like this; no one could think like this. Perhaps the whole thing is a staff hoax in bad taste."

Perturbed about the fury of the reviewer's onslaught, Kahn wrote the editor of the magazine, Dennis Flanagan, asking him to consider a rebuttal entitled "Thinking about the Unthinkable." Flanagan replied stiffly: "I do not think there is much point in thinking about the unthinkable; surely it is more profitable to think about the thinkable … nuclear war is unthinkable. I should prefer to devote my thoughts to how nuclear war can be prevented."

Kahn, of the Hudson Institute THINK TANK in New York, turned the phrase to his advantage by using it as the title of his 1962 book, in which he wrote:

> It is characteristic of our times that many intelligent and sincere people are willing to argue that it is immoral to think and even more immoral to write in detail about having to fight a thermonuclear war. … In a sense we are acting like those ancient kings who punished messengers who brought them bad news. … In our times, thermonuclear war may seem unthinkable, immoral, insane, hideous, or highly unlikely, but it is not impossible. To act intelligently we must learn as much as we can about the risks. We may thereby be able better to avoid nuclear war.

In current usage the adjective is synonymous with *inconceivable*, with an added pinch of condemnation. *Newsweek* columnist Meg Greenfield brought the phrase home to politicians in 1968: "'Thinking about the unthinkable'—the old nuclear strategist's phrase—has a new meaning in Washington these days," she wrote. "It means thinking about the possibility that the Senate will reject the SALT agreement Jimmy Carter brings home."

Kahn's contradictory coinage surfaced again in Vice President Dick Cheney's response to the sharp questioning of Tim Russert on NBC's *Meet the Press* on the eve of the fifth anniversary of the 9/11 attacks, with criticism mounting of the war in Iraq: "Part of my job is to think about the unthinkable, to focus on what, in fact, the terrorists may have in store for us … the possibility of a cell of al-Qaeda in the midst of one of our own cities with a nuclear weapon or a biological agent. In that case, you'd be … looking at a casualty toll that would rival all the deaths in all the wars fought by Americans in 230 years." That is the "unthinkable" thought that Herman Kahn was among the first to think about—and to share with the public.

up-or-down vote A simple majority vote on a bill or a nominee.

Legislative calls for *up-or-down votes* typically are issued only by those who are sure of winning. The modifying *up-or-down*, with the conjunction insisting on a yea-or-nay decision, is a symptom of majority frustration: an ordinary vote has been prevented by the threat of a FILIBUSTER or some other parliamentary tactic, such as bottling up a bill or nomination in committee.

Senate majority leader Dr. Bill Frist (R-Tenn.) hammered away at the denial of *up-or-down votes* in a 2005 debate: "In the last Congress, for the first time in history, a minority of senators obstructed the principle of a fair up-or-down vote on judicial nominees. That was unprecedented. Never before in 214 years of Senate history had a judicial nominee with majority support been denied an up-or-down vote. … A minority of senators denied up-or-down votes not just once to one nominee, but 18 times to 10 nominees."

Frist switched from "up *or* down" to "up *and* down" in a statement issued before that debate: "Republicans believe in the regular order of fair up and down votes and letting the Senate decide yes or no on judicial confirmations free from procedural gimmicks like the filibuster." (See NUCLEAR OPTION.) Up-*or*-down vote is much more common than up-*and*-down vote. A check of the *Washington Post* archive for 2000–06 turned up 73 examples of the former versus

3 of the latter. Other newspapers had similar ratios.

Are the phrases synonymous? There is a shade of difference: In the nineteenth century, *up-and-down*, applied to a person, meant "plain, direct, unceremonious." Harriet Beecher Stowe wrote in *Oldtown Folks* in 1869: "Miss Debby was a well-preserved, up-and-down, positive, cheery, sprightly maiden lady." The *or* divides the alternatives more sharply, and the meaning of *up-or-down* is not just "direct" but "decisive." Earliest use that I can find in connection with a vote (thanks to the U.S. Senate Historical Office's Dr. Betty K. Koed, and that's her real name) is from the *Hartford Courant* of October 3, 1873, about Connecticut's costly new capitol building: "The state will pay the amount appropriated any way, whether the amendment is voted up or down."

"*Up-or-down* is an unofficial term," a parliamentary source too shy to be identified says, "for a vote *on* the question rather than a vote *with respect to* the question. It's the polar opposite of a motion to TABLE." A vote on the motion to table, explains Ilona Nickels, author of the C-SPAN Congressional Glossary, "is not a vote on an amendment but a vote on whether or not to address it at all. It's that squishy middle that avoids voting on the content and gives politicians a procedural out. They can then say they didn't vote against it, but only voted to table it for now"—and perhaps the language will be changed or the issue be overtaken by events.

Decisiveness and on-the-record accountability are the keys. Thus, *up-or-down* votes may be urged as a means of forcing legislators to take public stands on controversial issues. A senatorial aide in 1981 was quoted as predicting "There will be a major fight in this Congress. The Senate will be asked to vote up or down on gun control."

Accordingly, up-or-down votes can be employed to push bills through the legislative mill without amendments. The Syracuse *Post-Standard* reported in 2003: "The current Republican majority has made no secret of preferring to write legislation in conference and to send it back to each chamber for an up-or-down vote without the prospect of amendments." It is also why, in foreign trade negotiations, chief executives of both parties seek to extend the president's "fast-track authority," which is the right to negotiate complex trade deals, then submit them to Congress for an up-or-down vote, amendment-free. Commentator Lou Dobbs told Larry King on CNN in 2007 why he opposed this: "So-called fast-track authority effectively moves Congress out of real consultation and involvement in trade policies," allowing the president to say "take it or leave it."

On voting to confirm nominees: Don Ritchie, associate historian of the Senate, informs the author that "with nominees, an up-or-down vote means that you don't want anything to block the vote. You can't change the language, as in an amendment, because they're people." If a senator wishes to avoid taking a stand, he or she can vote "present," but not even a senator can amend a nominee.

Synonyms for the compound adjective *up-or-down* are *recorded yea-or-nay* and *roll call*, as well as—informally—a *clean* vote.

up to speed Familiar with the latest details; au courant; briefed and ready to joust with questioners.

A newly appointed cabinet officer is brought *up to speed* by the permanent bureaucracy before his confirmation hearings; a White House aide who has been on vacation or working on a special assignment must be brought *up to speed* by his colleagues when he returns; a president, preparing for a press conference, needs to be brought *up to speed* on a variety of topics that have not been the focus of recent attention.

This phrase was made part of Washington parlance by White House aides with advertising backgrounds in the '60s. One origin is said to be in radio, referring to the need to bring an electrical transcription up to a certain number of revolutions per minute on a turntable before turning up the sound for broadcast, to avoid jarring listeners with a "wow" sound. In television, it was defined in the *Television Dictionary/Handbook for Sponsors* as "Time when the camera and sound mechanisms are ready for filming and moving at the same speed."

National Journal used the term in 1993: "As the Clinton transition team scrambled to get up to speed on Haiti, it seemed like old home week at the State Department."

The opposite of *up to speed* is, curiously, *out of pocket*, a phrase that used to mean "unreimbursed" regarding expenses, but in the '70s came to mean "out of touch," or in its most extreme form of mental fuzziness, "out to lunch." A related term, from moviemaker's lingo, is *off my screen*—that is, "beyond my ken or sphere of interest."

A near-synonym for *up to speed*, in its sense of being ready to go with all in agreement, is *on all fours*. Some say this is rooted in lawyer's lingo—"A phrase used to express the idea that a case at bar is in all points similar to another"—while others hold it is the balance struck by a sprinter at the start of a dash.

used car salesman Symbol of slickness or untrustworthiness.

Nobody trusts a used car salesman, whose job—according to the cruel stereotype—is to cover up defects and make the used look almost new. In politics, the symbol usually appears in the full form of a question, "Would you buy a used car from this man?" Its political usage is sometimes meant to gauge voter confidence in a candidate or elected official, although it is often an attack phrase, designed to elicit the metaphor of any used car that's a "lemon."

The phrase was one of the first used to derogate Richard Nixon early in his California career, and was resuscitated after his downfall. Dan Aykroyd, the *Saturday Night Live* comedian, used the phrase in a 1978 sendup of the first American forced to resign the presidency. Imitating Nixon's voice and posture, Aykroyd assumed the role of a TV pitchman: "There used to be a saying in America, 'Would you buy a used car from this man?'" said Aykroyd-as-Nixon, moving the awkward way Nixon sometimes did during unrehearsed public appearances, arms akimbo. "Well, now

you can. At San Clemente Dodge-Chrysler, we're offering a full range. ..."

To have an impact in the future, the question would have to be euphemized, updated, and politically corrected to "Would you buy a previously owned hybrid vehicle from this person?"

useful idiots of the West Communist derogation of liberals, dubiously sourced to Lenin but later seized upon by hard-liners.

In 1987, West German Chancellor Helmut Kohl, interviewed in *Business Week*, derided "fellow travelers who support this [Soviet] propaganda effort in Western Europe. We call them 'useful idiots.'" Also in that year, Zbigniew Brzezinski used "useful idiots of the West" in deriding "so-called notables who were convened as props for Gorbachev's speech"; those foreign-affairs experts included former Secretaries of State Cyrus R. Vance and Henry A. Kissinger and former U.S. ambassador to the U.N. Jeane Kirkpatrick.

John Vinocur wrote in the *International Herald Tribune*: "Maarten van Traa, the Dutch Socialists' international secretary, insists that the party is not playing the role of the useful idiots for the Russians, a phrase used by Lenin to describe left-liberals and Social Democrats." The phrase has also been used about Central American politics, as in *The New York Times* headline "Lenin's 'Useful Idiots' in Salvador."

Frequently attributed to Lenin, the phrase has not been found in any of his writings. Grant Harris, senior reference librarian at the Library of Congress, said, "We get queries on 'useful idiots of the West' all the time. We have not been able to identify this phrase among his published works." Neither Tass, the Russian news agency, nor Communist Party headquarters in New York City can offer the source.

Harris suggested a source put forth by former Colgate Professor Albert Parry, who reviewed the 1966 book *People and Portraits: A Tragic Cycle*. That book was written by Yuri Annenkov, a painter who was commissioned by the Communist Party in 1921 to do a portrait of Lenin and who had access after Lenin's death to the leader's personal papers at the Lenin Institute in Moscow.

Here is Annenkov's quote, taken supposedly from Lenin's handwritten notes: "To speak the truth is a petit-bourgeois habit. To lie, on the contrary, is often justified by the lie's aim. The whole world's capitalists and their governments, as they pant to win the Soviet market, *will close their eyes* to the above-mentioned reality and will thus transform themselves into *men who are deaf, dumb and blind.* They will give us credits.... They will toil to prepare their own suicide." (The italics, characteristic of Lenin's style, are added from the Russian edition of Annenkov's book.) To translate that into the English "useful idiots of the West" is quite a stretch. That last sentence, however, may be the source of another frequent Lenin attribution, "The capitalists will sell us the rope with which to hang them."

The apocryphal *useful idiots of the West* quotation is more powerful than *unwitting dupe*, but less damaging than the outmoded FELLOW TRAVELER or the discredited COMSYMP.

Utopianism See TECHNOCRAT; WAR TO END WARS.

V

vast right-wing conspiracy An alleged widespread plot to achieve conservative political and social goals; fanciful attack on the effort to discredit and then impeach President Bill Clinton.

Hillary Rodham Clinton popularized the phrase in an interview on NBC's *Today Show* on Jan. 27, 1998. Supporting her husband's denial that he had been involved sexually with Monica Lewinsky, a former White House intern, the then First Lady portrayed the president as the victim of a "feeding frenzy" by conservatives who sought "to undo the results of the last two elections."

"Look at the very people who are involved in this," she said. "They have popped up in other settings. The great story here for anybody willing to find it, write about it, and explain it, is this vast right-wing conspiracy that has been conspiring against my husband since the day he announced for president."

"Bill and I have been accused of everything, including murder," she protested, alluding to questions about the suicide of White House deputy counsel Vince Foster.

Ms. Clinton did not coin the phrase. From the *Detroit News* in 1991: "Thatcher-era Britain produced its own crop of paranoid left-liberal films. … All posited a vast right-wing conspiracy propping up a reactionary government ruthlessly crushing all efforts at opposition under the guise of parliamentary democracy." From a 1995 AP story: "Privately, a senior federal official said that the attack [on the federal building in Oklahoma City] was probably not some kind of vast right-wing conspiracy but the work of maybe five malcontents, only two of whom did any 'heavy lifting.'"

Independent counsel Kenneth Starr was unable to bring criminal charges against the Clintons but sent a report to the House of Representatives in September of 1998 replete with details of the president's relationship with Ms. Lewinsky. Ardent con-servatives then flaunted *vast right-wing conspiracy* as a way of lampooning the Clintons; entrepreneurs offered the phrase on merchandise, and satirist Mark W. Smith wrote *The Vast Right-Wing Conspiracy Handbook*, which came with a card declaring the bearer to be an "official member of the VRWC."

The phrase is not limited to politics. The *Omaha World-Herald* editorialized in 1999: "A former football player for Northwestern University has been charged with perjury— charged with lying to a grand jury about point-fixing in a football game. How far does the vast right-wing conspiracy reach?" And from a 2006 article on CBS television programming by Alessandra Stanley in *The New York Times:* "The network has a track record of bowing to determined lobbyists. It pulled an unflattering portrait of Ronald and Nancy Reagan ('The Reagans') off the CBS schedule in 2003. And it doesn't require a vast right-wing conspiracy to make the network tremble: That same year CBS ditched plans for a reality show based on 'The Beverly Hillbillies' after protests from Appalachian lobby groups."

The phrase is bottomed on the accusation by Senator Joseph McCarthy in 1951 that in delivering China to Communism, U.S. Secretaries of State George C. Marshall and Dean Acheson had been engaged in a "conspiracy on a scale so immense as to dwarf any previous venture in the history of man." The phrases "a conspiracy so immense" and "a conspiracy so vast" became titles of books and articles critical of McCarthy.

See WHITEWATER.

vast wasteland A sweeping criticism of television programming; a gloomy description about the results of any unfulfilled effort.

Newton Minow, a law partner of Adlai Stevenson appointed by John F. Kennedy to be chairman of the Federal Communications Commission, astounded a National

Association of Broadcasters audience in 1961. He said that if anyone watched television from morning to night, "I can assure you that you will observe a vast wasteland." After Minow's talk, a broadcaster told him, "That was the worst speech I ever heard in my whole life." LeRoy Collins, the head of NAB, tried to be kind and assured Minow that the complainer "has no mind of his own. He just repeats everything he hears."

Minow's use of the phrase was taken up immediately because (1) it was directed to an audience in the communications field; (2) that audience is notorious for self-flagellation on artistic grounds while it increases earnings on mediocre programs; and (3) previous phrases of criticism—"boob tube," "idiot box," and "vidiot"—were too frivolous or severe.

Minow's phrase combined a proper forum with, perhaps, a fitting literary source: poet T. S. Eliot's *The Waste Land*. (According to Syracuse University professor Mary Karr, a poet and expert on Eliot's work, the title was supplied by Jessie Weston, author of a book on the Holy Grail legend titled *From Ritual to Romance*. That was why the word *wasteland* was written in its earlier form, *waste land.*)

Joseph P. Kennedy, father of the president, told Minow that "this was the best speech since January 20 [the inaugural address]—give 'em hell—hit 'em again." President Kennedy let Minow take the lead on the subject of television programming. At a press conference July 24, 1962, Kennedy was asked if the introduction of the Telstar communications satellite meant that "the U.S. networks should make a greater effort to do something about the 'vast wasteland'?" Kennedy evaded the question: "I'm going to leave Mr. Minow to argue the wasteland issue, I think."

The phrase continues to be used in this general sense, some recalling the description of television in its pre-cable, pre-Internet era. Former President Eisenhower called President Kennedy's economic program in 1963 "fiscal recklessness" that would lead not to "a free country with bright opportunities but a vast wasteland of debt and financial chaos."

Veep Affectionate nickname for the vice president.

Senate Majority Leader Alben Barkley of Kentucky was a popular choice for Truman's vice president in 1948, after Justice William O. Douglas turned down the nomination. At that time, more and more corporate vice presidents were becoming known as "VPs," and the familiar form *veep*—to describe an informal-minded man—was natural.

Barkley's successor, Richard Nixon, sidestepped the title: "I think *veep* was a term of affection applied to Mr. Barkley and should go out with him." Barkley then appropriated the acronym for a television series, *Meet the Veep*.

Writing about acronyms for *American Speech* quarterly in 1955, Temple University's S. V. Baum predicted: "It is a near certainty that *veep* will pass out of general use and will eventually fall into linguistic obsolescence." Its use did decline for a time, but it remains a useful alternative to *VP* for headline writers and political punsters. *Newsweek*, in a 1967 article on candidates for the Republican vice-presidential nomination, said that Governors Love, Kirk, and Chafee and Senators Tower and Javits were entries in "The Veepstakes."

Asked after the 1992 defeat of the Bush-Quayle ticket if he would go through all the abuse if he had it to do again, Dan Quayle told a small group: "Yes. One out of three makes it to the Presidency." (See HEARTBEAT AWAY FROM THE PRESIDENCY.)

vested interests The wealthy; the powerful; the privileged class; the Establishment.

Great Britain's policy in the nineteenth century was reputed to have been that a great power had only interests, never friends. The interests—*vested, special, predatory, selfish,* and *sinister*—have made few new friends since.

Vested (from its meaning of clothed) legally refers to a consummated—that is, secured and settled—right. The term *vested rights* was used in a political sense by English essayist and historian Thomas Babington Macaulay in 1857: "On one side is a statesman preaching patience, respect for vested rights.... On the other side is a demagogue ranting about the tyranny of capitalists.... Which of the two candidates is likely to be preferred by a working-man who hears his children cry for bread?"

Economists had an affinity for the phrase. American economist and politician Henry George, who died of a stroke, then called *apoplexy*, while running for mayor of New York City in 1897, used the term *vested interests* in urging a single tax on landowners. Essayist Agnes Repplier wrote at the turn of the century that "A world of vested interests is not a world which welcomes the disruptive force of candor." British economist John Maynard Keynes wrote in 1947 in his *General Theory of Employment, Interest and Money*: "I am sure that the power of vested interests is vastly exaggerated compared with the gradual encroachment of ideas...it is ideas, not vested interests, which are dangerous for good or evil."

On the "interest" half of the phrase: English philosopher Jeremy Bentham became suspicious of the "sinister interests" early in the nineteenth century. Prime Minister William Gladstone said, "The interests are always awake while the country often slumbers and sleeps." In 1883 Joseph Chamberlain, defending English radicalism, said that "private interests are like a disciplined regiment while the public good was defended by an unorganized mob."

"The Interests," wrote H. L. Mencken, capitalizing the noun, "were first heard of during the Bryan saturnalia of vituperation at the end of the Nineteenth Century." William Jennings Bryan called them "the predatory interests" in his three campaigns; Robert La Follette attacked "special privilege" at the same time, and the two expressions merged with Theodore Roosevelt's attack on SPECIAL INTERESTS.

Roosevelt, who attacked President Taft as "a tool of the interests," left no group out, hitting equally at "the big special interests and the little special interests." The man who benefited by the Roosevelt-Taft split, Woodrow Wilson, was not above adopting the magic "radical" word: "The business of government is to organize the common interest against the special interests."

Because the word *interest* had a progressive-populist-radical tradition, Republicans as a rule stayed away from it. But Wendell Willkie, campaigning in 1940 first for the nomination and then against FDR, used it in both directions. First, he charged that the Republican Old Guard was "corrupted by vested interests in its own ranks and by reactionary forces. It forgot its own liberal tradition." After he became the nominee, he gave it a new twist in a "petition" to FDR: "Give up this vested interest that you have in the depression, open your eyes to the future, help us to build a New World."

More than anyone, Harry Truman revived the battle cry. He declared in several campaigns that the task of the Democratic party was to take government out of the hands of "the special interests" and return it to "the people"; in 1948, he dipped into Robert La Follette's vocabulary to specify a portion of those interests as "gluttons of privilege."

It has been spoofed: Victor Aloysius ("Just Call Me Vic") Meyers, Lieutenant Governor of Washington during World War II, told reporters: "Habitually I go without a vest so that I can't be accused of standing for the vested interests."

veto See POCKET VETO.

Vice Presidency See DEAD END, POLITICAL; HEARTBEAT AWAY FROM THE PRESIDENCY; RUNNING MATE; STEPPING-STONE; THROTTLEBOTTOM; VEEP.

victory has a hundred fathers Expression made famous by President John F. Kennedy on April 21, 1961—and frequently misquoted—as he acknowledged responsibility for the BAY OF PIGS FIASCO.

At a televised press conference after the disastrous, CIA-directed operation to depose Cuba's Fidel Castro, newsman Sander Vanocur referred to "a certain foreign policy situation" about which no questions were being taken. "In view of the fact that we are taking a propaganda lambasting around the world, why is it not useful, sir, for us to explore with you the real facts behind this, or our motivations?"

"There's an old saying that victory has a hundred fathers, but defeat is an orphan,"

JFK said, adding "Further statements ... are not to conceal responsibility because I'm the responsible officer of the government ... I do not believe such a discussion would benefit us ..." When Kennedy was asked the source of the hundred-fathers expression, he told an aide, "Oh, I don't know; it's just an old saying." *Bartlett's Familiar Quotations* cites a 1942 use by Count Galeazzo Ciano, in *The Ciano Diaries*: "As always, victory finds a hundred fathers but defeat is an orphan."

There are other unsubstantiated sightings. N.Y.C. Transit Commissioner John J. Gilhooley told the author he heard Philippines Ambassador Carlos Romulo use this expression to describe the Korean conflict to Secretary of State John Foster Dulles on an airplane en route to a CIO convention in 1953. Others suggest it was spoken by the character portraying Field Marshal von Rundstedt in the 1951 film *The Desert Fox*. But nothing so far antedates the Ciano usage.

In 1968 Florida Governor Claude Kirk told a Ripon, Wisconsin, audience that the war in Vietnam was "the first in which defeat has a thousand fathers and victory is an orphan."

Which is it—a hundred fathers or a thousand? The answer is a hundred, attested by the Kennedy Library transcript of the press conference. The error is made hundreds—thousands—of times, including in earlier editions of this dictionary. I am indebted to my former *New York Times* colleague, Adam Clymer, for the correction.

Representative Stephen J. Solarz of New York also turned to JFK's figure of speech in 1992, but apparently did not want to derogate orphans: "As you know, victory has a thousand fathers while defeat is an only child."

vicuña coat. See ABOMINABLE NO-MAN; INFLUENCE PEDDLER.

Vietnamization A plan for the extrication of U.S. ground forces from Vietnam, with the concurrent build-up of South Vietnamese forces, so as to provide the South Vietnamese people with what President Nixon called "a reasonable chance for survival."

The predecessor word, used in the later stages of the Johnson Administration by both Democrats and Republicans, was the awkward *de-Americanization*. In 1968, however, this began to be replaced by newsmen and American officials in Saigon with *Vietnamization*.

In a dispatch from Saigon to the *Los Angeles Times* by correspondent Robert Elegant on February 16, 1969, a distinction was drawn:

> In Washington the fashionable term is "de-Americanizing" the Vietnam war. In Saigon, men talk of "Vietnamizing" the allied military machine. The two efforts must obviously go hand-in-hand. The semantic difference is slight, but the actual difference is great. Washington is primarily concerned with reducing the American commitment—with regard to developments on the battlefield and in Paris. For reasons equally apparent, both Americans and Vietnamese in Saigon are primarily concerned with building an effective native military force to cope with Communist forces when the American presence is greatly reduced—and eventually removed.

The word was popularized in the U.S. in 1969 by Secretary of Defense Melvin Laird on *Meet the Press*: "I believe that we can move toward Vietnamizing the war ... by modernizing the forces of the South Vietnamese on a realistic basis." In his November 3 SILENT MAJORITY speech, President Nixon gave the word the presidential imprimatur: "The Vietnamization Plan was launched following Secretary Laird's visit to Vietnam in March. Under the plan, I ordered first a substantial increase in the training and equipment of South Vietnamese forces." He described "our plan for Vietnamization ... a plan in which we will withdraw all of our forces from Vietnam on a schedule in accordance with our program, as the South Vietnamese become strong enough to defend their own freedom."

President Thieu did not like the word. On November 15 he publicly urged the Vietnamese media to avoid using the term because he felt it gave credence to North Vietnamese charges that the U.S. was turning the fighting over to "puppet, mercenary troops."

The *-ization* suffix had been used in diplomacy before. *Balkanization* was used to mean the breakup of an empire into small, usually ineffective, states. The West German newspaper *Die Zeit* used it in a modern context in 1968: "After the Second World War, we witnessed the Communization of the Balkans. Today we witness the Balkanization of Communism." *Normalization* became popular in the diplomatic lexicon in 1971, popularized by Henry Kissinger and usually referring to relations between the U.S. and "mainland" China. A bland, unexciting word was required here, and *normalization* is so bland as to be tranquilizing. The use of the *-ization* suffix can stretch too far: a few of those calling for arming of the Bosnian Muslims in 1993 used "Bosnia-Herzegovinization."

Though U.S. policy in Iraq after REGIME CHANGE in 2003 was—as in Vietnam nearly two generations earlier—to train, equip and gradually turn over the fighting to indigenous troops and police, the term *Iraqi-ization* was too awkward to be promulgated as well as too reminiscent of failure in Vietnam.

See WINDING DOWN; VIETNAM LINGO.

Vietnam lingo Words and phrases left over from the Vietnam war, now only used bitterly or ironically, usually to derogate political and military hawkishness.

Washington writer and slanguist Paul Dickson ran down a farrago of these expressions in 1972: "Among them: 'pacification,' 'light at the end of the tunnel,' 'body count,' 'free-fire zone,' 'hearts and minds of the people'...'kill ration'...'search and destroy' ..." (See VIETNAMIZATION; WINDING DOWN; VIETNAM SYNDROME.) In the investigation of the destruction of the village of My Lai, the term *waste* to mean "kill" was used by Lieutenant William Calley. Linguist Mario Pei traced the use of the word to Middle English, and to Shakespeare's use of the verb as "Would he were wasted, marrow, bones and all."

A reprise of these terms by war correspondent Homer Bigart in *The New Republic* in 1977 shows how they can be used in bitter hindsight, with his editorial point of view regarding *waste*:

Let us rejoice over the demise of some dreary slogans associated with the Vietnam conflict. For the next imbroglio a whole new set of incantations are needed. Our leaders no longer can tell us to get out there and fight to keep the dominoes from falling. Nobody will profess to see the light at the end of the tunnel. There will be no more crusades to win the hearts and minds of people and save them from aggression. One term—"waste"—is not easily shelved. GIs in Vietnam used it as a synonym for kill. When a man was killed he was wasted. A chillingly appropriate term for the 46,229 Americans who fell in action in the Indochina War.

Vietnam syndrome The belief that foreign intervention is unwinnable and therefore a QUAGMIRE to be avoided; the inability to make and follow through with overseas commitments.

Originally the term referred to a mental disorder suffered by Vietnam veterans after returning to the United States. An early user of the psychiatric term in a political sense was Henry Kissinger. From the Pacific *Stars and Stripes* of May 14, 1969: "In a sense, the Paris peace talks have resembled the Vietnam War itself. Optimism has alternated with bewilderment. Henry A. Kissinger, President Nixon's national security adviser, has called this 'the classic Vietnam syndrome.'"

The term soon was lengthened to *post-Vietnam syndrome* in both medical and political contexts. In the former, Boyce Rensberger wrote in *The New York Times* in 1972: "Perhaps the most commonly reported symptoms of what has been called 'post Vietnam syndrome' are a sense of shame and guilt for having participated in a war that the veteran now questions, and the deeply felt anger and distrust of the government that the veteran believes duped and manipulated him."

Politically, the meaning of the phrase was extended to refer to an unwillingness to commit to an unwinnable conflict. *Newsweek* wrote in 1978 about Senator Sam Nunn's legislation allowing the President to call up reservists without a declaration of an emergency: "He argues that such emergency powers are necessary to counter a 'post-Vietnam syndrome' that might otherwise paralyze Congress in times of crisis."

America's fast victory in the Gulf War in 1991 led President George H.W. Bush to say, "It is my hope that when this is over, we will have kicked, once and for all, the so-called Vietnam syndrome."

Former Secretary of State Alexander Haig made the link between the medical and political explicit during a 1998 conference on Vietnam at The Nixon Center in Washington, D.C.: "Shell shock—the Vietnam syndrome is not just a military problem, it's in the body politic itself, in the political leadership of this country."

The historical example of the *Vietnam syndrome* continues to loom large in the national psyche. Karen DeYoung of *The Washington Post* reported in 2007: "Much as the Vietnam Syndrome dogged the foreign and military policies of a generation of U.S. presidents, the Iraq Syndrome has become an ever-present undercurrent in Washington."

The *Vietnam syndrome* (intervention leads to failure) often clashes with the MUNICH ANALOGY (appeasement leads to war).

violin piece See TICK-TOCK.

vision of America See "I SEE" CONSTRUCTION.

vision thing A world-weary acknowledgment that a leader must articulate inspiring goals, usually expressed as a VISION OF AMERICA.

This phrase comes from the elder George Bush. Reporting on political vision in 1987, *National Journal* added parenthetically, "[Bob] Dole calls it 'the V-word,' while Bush awkwardly refers to 'the vision thing.' "

The term is typical of "yuppie" phrases in which attributive nouns modified the noun *thing* (a habit derided by critics as "the 'thing' thing"). The lawyer Terry Eastland said in 1992 that some conservative columnists had become Bush-bashers because "they believe he squandered Ronald Reagan's legacy. Bush is more nearly a nineteenth-century President, a guy who is not good at giving speeches and has disparaged the 'vision thing.' "

The phrase still echoes in the English-speaking world. In 2005, Manuel Quezon III, son of a former president of the Philippines, recalled Bush's "vision thing" in a piece written for the *Philippine Daily Inquirer*: "The catch-phrase 'Strong Republic' was supposed to be President [Gloria] Arroyo's vision thing," Quezon wrote, but it had been "junked long ago and replaced by other 'vision things' . . . the '10-point agenda,' then the 'rule of law' and 'let's move on' and . . . the real one: the 'Fear Factor' . . . the 'brutality' vision thing."

vital center See CENTRIST.

voice from the sewer Any anonymous, disembodied voice in a crowd that seeks to stampede or heckle; particularly, the unidentified voice at a hidden microphone that reassured the 1940 Democratic convention.

Senate Majority Leader Alben Barkley electrified the convention audience with a message from President Roosevelt that at first seemed like a warning not to nominate him for a third term: "The President has never had, and has not today, any desire or purpose to continue in the office of President, to be a candidate for that office, or to be nominated by the convention for that office. He wishes in all earnestness and sincerity to make it clear that all of the delegates to this convention are free to vote for any candidate."

Stunned silence followed. Then a voice on the loudspeaker began the chant, "We want Roosevelt!" and the "draft" began. It turned out that the "voice from the sewer," as it was called, was a member of Chicago Mayor Edward J. Kelley's organization, primed to begin the chant immediately after the Barkley bombshell.

The push for a third Presidential term led to the pun of "third termite." During Ronald Reagan's second term, Bill Curry wrote in the *Los Angeles Times* in 1986: "Unheard of since 1973, when America last had a President serving his second term, the Termite—a usually derogatory reference to a third Presidential term—is again chomping its way into the American political scene." See SPONTANEOUS DEMONSTRATION.

voice of the people See VOX POPULI.

volunteers Unpaid political workers, enthusiastic and vital to a campaign; or, a method of committing troops without formally becoming a belligerent.

The Eisenhower "volunteers" and CITIZENS COMMITTEE gave pep, sparkle, panache, and a sense of idealistic purpose to the Republican campaign of 1952. See AMATEURS; BANDWAGON; RALLY. In 1960 the President, in his administration's final year, wondered aloud to Sherman Adams, "What happened to all those fine young people with stars in their eyes who sailed balloons and rang doorbells for us in 1952?"

Adlai Stevenson also attracted a devoted group of volunteers in his 1952 campaign, but by 1956 the ranks of the starry-eyed had dwindled for him as well. Volunteers are attracted by a candidate's personal CHARISMA, by a desire to participate in the fun (and fresh social and professional contacts) of a campaign, by a desire to do something tangible to advance their political beliefs, and very little by any expectation of appointive office.

Many volunteers come to a headquarters once, get bored if given an assignment they consider beneath their talents, and disappear; others amaze a campaign staff with a zeal that can never really be purchased. Alexis de Tocqueville noted it with some wonderment in his *Democracy in America*: "I have often admired the extreme skill with which the inhabitants of the United States succeed in proposing a common object for the exertions of a great many men and inducing them voluntarily to pursue it."

In its "international warfare" meaning, the word was popularized in the Spanish Civil War. German and Italian troops were dispatched to General Francisco Franco by Hitler and Mussolini under the guise of "volunteers." Foreign nationals supporting Loyalist forces were also called volunteers, but quotation marks did not appear around the word because it was felt in the U.S. that they were genuine idealists, not troops serving the disguised interests of their respective countries. When the Chinese Communists decided to enter the Korean War, they reused this technique and term, which has since become a standard method of intervention, along with "military advisers."

The word *voluntarism*, formed from *voluntary*, appeared in *The Wall Street Journal* in March of 1969 to describe the Nixon Administration's plan "to enlist the help of private groups in solving social problems." It followed the warm press reception to the Kennedy Administration's PEACE CORPS and preceded similar evocations of the power of community self-help which is both uplifting and cost-free to the taxpayer. For the most dramatic call in this regard, see THOUSAND POINTS OF LIGHT.

voodoo economics Derogation of Ronald Reagan's conservative economic philosophy.

The elder George Bush introduced this phrase during the 1980 primaries, campaigning for the Republican nomination. He lost to Reagan, and before the Californian chose Bush as his running mate, conservatives reminded delegates at the GOP national convention that Bush had attacked Reagan's SUPPLY-SIDE theories as "voodoo economics." This was colorful oratory using a term for the religious rites involving sorcery that originated in West Africa (in Ewe, *vodu* means "spirit, demon").

Suggesting witchcraft rather than practicality, *voodoo economics* became linked to Reaganomics (see -NOMICS). John Jacob, president of the Urban League, commented in 1982 that Reaganomics "is giving voodoo a bad name."

The denigrating phrase came back to haunt its originator. When George Bush subsequently ran for vice president on the Reagan ticket in 1980 and 1984, and when he ran on his own in 1988, Democratic detractors pointed out that the Reagan economic policies had once been ridiculed by Bush with this expression. (Another charge of "deep voodoo" was a rhyming play on Bush's label of political trouble with the baby-talk reduplication of "in deep doodoo.")

This phrase did not disappear with Reagan and Bush. In 1993, playing on the redundancy attributed to Yogi Berra ("It's deja vu all over again"), Raymond DeVoe wrote in a market letter critical of populist economics: "Sounds like 'Deja Voodoo' all over again."

The U.S. Ambassador to Zimbabwe in 2005, Christopher Dell, criticized President Robert Mugabe for his "corrupt rule" and "disparaging dismissal of textbook economics" that was causing a crisis in the southern African country. "To argue that they are is simply what the first President Bush long ago in a different context called 'voodoo economics.'" The choice of the phrase had more sinister resonance for that continent's residents than it did when used in the U.S.

vote early and often A self-mocking Election Day greeting by politicians.

This is the sort of line that is ordinarily lost in the mists of election time, but historian James Morgan believed he found the originator in his 1926 book of biographies: the jokester was John Van Buren, New York lawyer, who was the son of President Martin Van Buren. Laurence Urdang and Janet Braunstein, in their *Every Bite a Delight and Other Slogans*, agreed; they say the phrase "appeared in 1848, attributed to John Van Buren."

Bartlett's Familiar Quotations found an early use in a speech in the House of Representatives on March 31, 1858 by William Porcher Miles: "'Vote early and vote often,' the advice openly displayed on the election banners in one of our northern cities."

The context, especially the word *openly*, makes the comment by Rep. Miles seem disapproving of a serious invitation to nefarious electioneering. Contrariwise, as used today, the "slogan" is a cheerful evocation of overt corruption in the distant past. However, the old ways are still recalled: Republican opponents to the "motor-voter" bill in 1993 said that the ability of voters to register at Motor Vehicle Bureaus was an "open invitation to vote early and often."

vote fraud See BALLOT-BOX STUFFING; CEMETERY VOTE.

vote of confidence Legislative reassurance; more generally, any expression of support.

The phrase originated in the British Parliament, where it is a division of the House of Commons in which the government tests its strength. Members of the majority party must vote with their party; if enough defect to lose a vote, the government is expected to call for a general election.

Conversely, if a motion of no confidence is introduced by the opposition in the House of Commons and passes, the result is called a *vote of censure* (although it contains the words "no confidence," it is not referred to as a "vote of no confidence," except in America); in that case, the government *is upset* or *falls*, and an election is called.

When criticism of the conduct of the war rose in 1942, Prime Minister Winston Churchill asked for a vote of confidence, calling the procedure "thoroughly normal, constitutional, and democratic"; after three days of debate, the motion was carried 464 to 1. In effect, Churchill brought the criticism to a head and then mustered support for his policies.

In the U.S., there is no such formal method of saying, "There may be sniping, but when the chips are down, we have a majority." As used in this country, the phrase means some voter expression, such as a special local election or a referendum, that is interpreted as a renewed MANDATE; or a reelection, which is called "a vote of confidence for his policies," or any pat on the back from a group of supporters.

Newsweek reported in 1967 that a group of anti-Reagan voters in California had hopes of forcing a recall election: "They want to make him face an embarrassing 'vote of confidence.'" A similar movement to recall in that state in 2003 saw Governor Gray Davis, a Democrat, recalled, and replaced in a special election by Republican Arnold Schwarzenegger.

vox populi ... vox Dei. "The voice of the people is the voice of God."

The phrase is attributed to Alcuin, in an epistle to Charlemagne, around the year 800. It was used as the text of a sermon by Walter Reynolds, Archbishop of Canterbury, early in the fourteenth century at the coronation of Edward III; the "voice of the people," expressed through the nobles, had dethroned Edward II.

The thought is beautiful and universal; the Japanese language has a parallel proverb: "Heaven has no mouth but it talks through the people." However, the phrase has been used to justify the bending of leadership to the popular will, and in that sense has been attacked, for instance by:

Alexander Hamilton, who said in a speech to the Federal Convention in 1787: "The voice of the people has been said to be the voice of God; and, however generally this maxim has been quoted and believed, it is not true to fact. The people are turbulent and changing; they seldom judge or determine right."

Theodore Roosevelt, who said: "It may be that the voice of the people is the voice of God in fifty-one cases out of a hundred; but in the remaining forty-nine it is quite as likely to be the voice of the devil, or what is still worse, the voice of a fool."

General William Tecumseh Sherman, who wrote in a letter to his wife in 1863: "Vox populi, vox humbug."

Walter Lippmann, who in 1925 gave the phrase a narrower meaning: "I have conceived public opinion to be, not the voice of God, nor the voice of society, but the voice of the interested spectators of action."

Dwight Eisenhower, who, after viewing the film in Paris of Tex McCrary's Madison Square Garden rally of 15,000 people urging him to come home and run in 1952, yelling "We Like Ike!" found the voice unclear, stating publicly: "Even though we agree with the old proverb, 'The voice of the people is the voice of God,' it is not always easy to determine just what that voice is saying. I continue to get letters from certain of my friends who are almost as violent in their urgent recommendations that I do not make an early visit home as those who believe that I should come." (Privately, according to the aviatrix Jacqueline Cochran, who flew the film to Paris to show Eisenhower the crowd reaction, the General said, "Go back and tell them I'll do it." See RALLY.)

The phrase has been used as a barb (Abraham Lincoln was called "Fox populi" by *Vanity Fair* in 1863), as the title of a radio show (*Vox Pop*), and as doggerel in the presidential campaign of 1920:

Cox or Harding, Harding or Cox?
You tell us, populi, you got the vox.

See Mo Udall's reaction to the people's voice under LOSER, SHOW ME A GOOD.

waffle To shift positions as if they were tired feet; to straddle or refuse to commit; to use WEASEL WORDS.

At the time of the six-day Israeli-Arab war in 1967, U.S. Secretary of State Dean Rusk evaded a question from Senator John Sherman Cooper (R-Ky.) regarding a declaration of intent to keep open the Gulf of Aqaba to all international shipping. Rusk said, "That matter has not been finally decided. There are some plusses and minuses. At the present time, no, I cannot give you a final answer."

Chalmers Roberts of the *Los Angeles Times–Washington Post* syndicate reported, "That sort of response led Senators and Representatives to tell reporters afterwards that Rusk had waffled about supporting Israel. One said, 'They just walked around it.'"

Suddenly the rare verb found new admirers. C. L. Sulzberger of *The New York Times* wrote on June 11: "The United States can claim no credit for Israel's swift victory, but the fact of that victory was of strategic benefit to us although our role was confined to waffling."

Newsweek's July 19 issue, written a week before, reported that "many Jews felt that Israel had been forced to go to war because of waffling by the Administration." In a letter dated June 13 to the *Times* of London, Desmond Donnelly, a Labour Member of Parliament, demanded: "Are the Western powers going to act about the Arab refugees or continue to waffle?"

It seemed as if world journalism had been taken over by a chef who had over-ordered waffle mix and told his waiters, "Push waffles." Occasionally when a bellwether reporter uses an out-of-the-ordinary word in a particular context, there follows a brief flurry of usage by other commentators and soon the word returns to limbo.

The word may be derived from *waff*, a Scottish word for "wave," and its dictionary definition is "to flutter or flap like a clumsy bird." Another possible derivation is from *waff*, "to bark and snarl, or to talk foolishly." It does not come from the noun *waffle*, rooted in *wafer*, an indented cake baked in a griddle contraption called a *waffle iron*, whose boxy pattern gives no indication of uncertainty.

In its political use, to *waffle* is synonymous with the verb to *fudge*, which appears also to be taken from the name of a food—in this case a candy—but actually comes from to *fadge*, "to succeed." In Washington, the State Department is called "the fudge factory." Former President Gerald Ford, in a December 1977 breakfast meeting with reporters, was asked about the change in President Carter's position on the Panama Canal, and replied with candor, "I think we both fudged a little on Panama in the campaign." That was a far cry from his charge about Carter in the 1976 campaign: "He wavers, he wanders, he wiggles and he waffles, and he shouldn't be President of the United States."

The word in its non-food sense has spread around the English-speaking world. A "waffle watch" was featured in the Perth *West Australian* in 2006, calling on readers to send in examples of "waffle, obfuscation and balderdash."

waging peace Eisenhower's phrase showing the new nature of foreign relations; it means ideological competition without warfare—no "war" but also no real "peace."

Dwight Eisenhower used the phrase as the title of a volume of his memoirs: he followed *Mandate for Change* with *Waging the Peace*. The technique of substituting the word *peace* for the word *war* is frequently used, often effectively. When the stock market booming in a wartime economy gets news of the likelihood of peace, any market drop is termed a "peace scare"; opponents of the U.S. effort in Vietnam have been called "peacemongers." This continued a linguistic tradition popularized by Napoleon in 1802, who said after the signing of the Treaty of Amiens, "What a beautiful fix we are in now: peace has been declared!"

walking-around money Petty cash pay-offs to precinct workers for undetermined "expenses."

Campaign managers searching for a euphemism to describe payments to door-bell-ringing volunteers came up with *walking-around money* in the early '60s. Managers often feel that a precinct captain should have a few dollars in his pocket to pay for a babysitter, or buy a potential voter a drink, or settle a real or potential parking fine; thus, the cash is distributed for these "anticipated expenses." In fact, rarely are the expenses used other than as recompense for the captain's time, but the phrase is as common as "miscellaneous" on expense accounts.

On June 16, 1976, a *Washington Post* editorial wondered "how much of the $40,000 [spent to defeat Democratic Senator Joseph Tydings in 1970] was spent for 'walking-around money' in Baltimore City on election day."

A synonym is *street money*. The author, a conduit for some of the cash passed to local workers in the 1960 presidential campaign, recalls the two phrases used concurrently: *street money* by the givers, *walkin'-around money* by the recipients. The AP reported in 1976: "The Jimmy Carter campaign gave donations to black ministers who supported him in the California primary and paid out other 'street money' that was not properly accounted for, the *Los Angeles Times* noted." Covering the same story in *The New York Times*, Charles Mohr wrote: "the use of subcontractors, or neighborhood leaders, who are given 'walking around money' is an established part of political life in some cities."

With post-Watergate morality causing many reformers (see GOO-GOO) at that time to frown on such activity, *The Washington Star* reported:

> walking-around money ... is the phrase used to describe the money political candidates give Baltimore political clubs just prior to a city election for all sorts of purposes—like canvass-

ing, poll-watching, the printing of ballots and getting out the vote. It is "mingling money," as one Baltimore politician put it this week ... Whatever the proper definition, Jack Pollack gets the drift. "You give a guy a $50 bill before the election and he does a chore for you. So what?"

The phrase can be used to illustrate what a large sum is not. In a 2007 editorial deriding the Hillary Clinton campaign's payment of $10,000 per month to a black political leader preparing for the Democratic primary in South Carolina, *The Washington Times* wrote: "By historical standards, that may seem high for 'walking around' money in the South, but with the campaign possibly raising $500 million, such payment is 'chump change.'"

The compound adjective should be hyphenated; in pronunciation, the *g* in *walking* is usually clipped.

walking back the cat In diplomacy, retreating from a negotiating position; in intelligence gathering, examining old analyses in light of new information.

Foreign Service officers use this diplomatic slang, which is similar to the "down off the mountaintop" expression of labor leaders faced with the need to reduce demands. (See MOUNTAINTOP.) When President Carter's chief armaments negotiator, Paul Warnke, was criticized for making an unrevealed concession to the Soviets in strategic arms limitation talks, columnists Rowland Evans and Robert Novak wrote in 1977: "The 600-kilometer mystery, therefore, raises suspicions that Paul Warnke will begin 'walking back the cat' on the Carter SALT package, unless checked by the President himself."

A second meaning, in spookspeak, emerged in an 1986 opinion piece in the *Chicago Tribune* discussing the investigation into the troubling past of Austrian and later U.N. leader Kurt Waldheim: "Intelligence agencies are now 'walking back the cat'—reconstructing events and decisions in light of Waldheim's Nazi past and who might have known and made use of it."

wall, political symbol of "General Secretary Gorbachev," said President Ronald Reagan on June 12, 1987, during his visit to the Brandenburg Gate at the Berlin Wall, "if you seek peace—if you seek prosperity for the Soviet Union and Eastern Europe—if you seek liberalization: Come here, to this gate. Mr. Gorbachev, open this gate! Mr. Gorbachev, tear down this wall!"

The Berlin Wall was erected in the city occupied after World War II by the four allied powers (Britain, France, the Soviet Union, and the U.S.) beginning on August 13, 1961, after the rate of refugees fleeing the Communist East German regime arriving in West Berlin had reached 300 per day; more than two million Germans had fled from east to west since 1949, stripping the east of much of its intellectual and entrepreneurial capital. The Western powers in Berlin, caught unaware by its almost overnight construction in that summer of 1961, decided not to react; the Wall became a *de facto* part of the joint occupation of the former German capital, and Berlin ceased to be a portal to the West. Some propaganda advantage was sought by naming it "The Wall of Shame," calling attention to the desire of Germans to leave the oppressive East Germany, a Soviet satellite, and enter prosperous, democratic West Germany. Visiting Western politicians on NONPOLITICAL TRIPS made it a standard part of their itinerary, posing for pictures looking sternly across the barbed wire atop the concrete blocks.

On June 23, 1963, nearly two years after the Wall's construction, President John F. Kennedy was photographed at the site and then made a speech at Berlin City Hall identifying with the spirit of Germans who wished to be free of communism with the line "Ich bin ein Berliner." (Before saying the words "I am a Berliner" in the German language, Kennedy wrote out the phrase in longhand on a card, spelling it "Ish bin ein Bearleener" to be certain he got the pronunciation correct. The card is in his presidential library.)

Kennedy made another use of the wall metaphor on the day before his assassination in 1963, basing it on the act of a child challenging himself to climb a wall by tossing his cap over it: "This nation has tossed its cap over the wall of space—and we have

no choice but to follow it. … With the help of all those who labor in the space endeavor, with the help and support of all Americans, we will climb this wall with safety and with speed—and we shall then explore the wonders on the other side."

A generation later, on June 12, 1987, speaking at the Brandenburg Gate, President Ronald Reagan issued his direct challenge to the Soviet leader, cited above: "Mr. Gorbachev, tear down this wall!" On November 6, 1989—after more than a hundred Germans had been shot dead trying to cross the hated barrier in its 28 years of existence—the jubilation of East Germans able to destroy the wall figuratively, and in some respects literally with their bare hands, came to symbolize the crumbling of imperialist Communism in Europe and the beginning of the end of the COLD WAR.

Was Reagan's speech a catalyst for the dissolution of the Soviet empire, or an exercise in showmanship at a propitious moment? In a 2007 Op-Ed in *The New York Times*, James Mann, a Cold War historian, argued on the twentieth anniversary of the speech that it was neither. "It was an anti-Communist speech that helped preserve support for a conservative president seeking to upgrade American relations with the Soviet Union" which "created the vastly more relaxed climate in which the Soviets sat on their hands when the wall came down … He wasn't trying to land a knockout blow on the Soviet regime, nor was he engaging in mere political theater … he was helping to set the terms for the end of the cold war."

Another use of the wall as a symbol—in this case, a "good" one—was by Thomas Jefferson in a time when the Founders frequently identified freedom and democracy with the will of the Creator. In an 1802 letter to Connecticut's Danbury Baptist Association, Jefferson wrote approvingly about "a wall of separation between Church & State." Writing in 2006, *Newsweek* editor Jon Meacham posed the question that troubled many nonreligious Americans in a largely churchgoing nation: "How, then, do we reconcile matters when that same government, one pledged to defend the rights of nonbelievers, engages in essentially religious activity—the offering of prayers in legislative sessions; the employment, at public expense of military chaplains ... the appointment of days of Thanksgiving on explicitly religious grounds?" His answer: "Chiefly by noting that Jefferson's wall metaphor—one that the Supreme Court picked up again in the middle of the twentieth century—is between church and state, not between religion and politics. Because politics is about people, religion will forever be a force in public life ..."

During the Nixon presidency, presidential aides H. R. Haldeman and John Ehrlichman—because of their Germanic names and assignment to restrain access to the President—became known to critics, as well as to Cabinet members and staffers seeking such access, as "The Berlin Wall."

When Israel in 2003 began constructing a barrier within some of the disputed territory known as the West Bank (of the Jordan River) to deter the entry of Palestinian suicide bombers in the second *intifada*, the term Israelis used was "a security fence." Arab spokesmen called it a *wall*, evoking the Berlin Wall. Physically, the planned 400-mile construction was more than 90% fence but—in certain vulnerable sections—it was a wall, mostly running along the "Green Line" marking a pre-1967 armistice. Israeli Prime Minister Ariel Sharon told the author in an interview that the "Ariel salient," composed of Israeli towns and villages (all called *settlements*, with its colonial connotation, in pro-Arab accounts) along with the heavily populated suburbs of Jerusalem, Israel's capital, "will be on our side of the fence and will always remain part of Israel." Journalists determined to appear evenhanded sought a neutral synonym and took the route chosen in this entry, referring to the combination of fence and wall as a *barrier*.

In 2006, when the influx of Mexican workers into the U.S. became a campaign issue, President Bush sought to compromise between those who wanted to invest heavily in building a barrier along the U.S. southern border and those more inclined to make it possible for "guest workers" to earn

citizenship over a course of years. Legislation to build a 700-mile barrier was passed, but funds to build it were not immediately authorized. In the debate, the word *fence* was, not surprisingly, preferred to *wall*.

On occasion, when the wall metaphor is used, a 1914 poem, "Mending Wall" by Robert Frost, is cited, especially the lines "Before I built a wall I'd ask to know / What I was walling in or walling out."

ward heeler Political hack; hanger-on; hangdog politician.

"As the crowd dispersed into the corridor," *The New York Times* wrote in 1876, "a gentleman happened to say that the gang in the room was composed of Tammany 'heelers,' when a Tammany retainer, taking umbrage at the epithet, knocked the gentleman down."

The gentleman deserved at least some reproof; *heeler* comes from the way a dog is *brought to heel* to follow its master closely. In 1912, *The New Republic* editor Herbert Croly wrote of Mark Hanna, former Ohio Senator and putative GOP kingmaker: "He used to go to the businessmen of his ward, and try to persuade them ... that they, the taxpayers, and not the wardheelers, should rule the city."

Ward is still used in many cities as a political subdivision; *ward heeler* was preceded by *ward politician*, which can be traced to Washington Irving's *Salmagundi* in 1807: "He, however, maintained as mysterious a countenance as a Seventh Ward politician."

The word still has sting to reformers; to regulars, *ward heeler* is a term of fond condescension. The *San Francisco Chronicle* commented in 1993 on Bill Clinton's reluctance to stand by his nominations of women when they came under criticism: "It wasn't sexism that torpedoed [Zoe] Baird and [Kimba] Wood: It's the fact that they didn't raise buckets of billions for Clinton. Ward heelers can expect Clinton to stand by their past transgressions; competent individuals, without industrial-strength fund-raising in their past, live or die by their press."

Occasionally the ward heeler will have defenders, such as Boss Martin Lomasney of Boston: "I think that there's got to be in every ward somebody that any bloke can come to—no matter what he's done—and get help. Help, none of your law and justice, but help." Lomasney is also credited with the sage political advice: "Never write if you can speak; never speak if you can nod; never nod if you can wink."

war-gaming words See FAIL-SAFE; INFRASTRUC-TURE; OPTIONS; OVERKILL; PENTAGONESE; PREVEN-TIVE WAR; SCENARIO; SHOCK AND AWE.

war hawks Bellicose political leaders; an early American phrase that was replaced by *jingoist* and later reappeared as *hawk*.

"In a contest between a hawk and dove," wrote Senator J. William Fulbright, "the hawk has a great advantage, not because it is a better bird but because it is a bigger bird with lethal talons and a highly developed will to use them." The senator, chairman of the Foreign Relations Committee and a leading dove during the Vietnam war, also wrote: "The agitation of the 'war hawks' of 1812, and of the Committee on the Conduct of the War in the 1860s, and the neutrality legislation of the 1930s are among the more striking instances which may be cited from the past of the Congress either forcing or binding the hands of the executive."

War hawk was a coinage of Thomas Jefferson in 1798 ("as for Jefferson," wrote H. L. Mencken, "he produced two of the best bugaboos of all time in his *war hawks* and *monocrats*"). Jefferson wrote to his ally, James Madison, on April 26, 1798: "At present, the war hawks talk of septembrizing [i.e., assassination], deportation, and the examples for quelling sedition set by the French Executive."

The phrase was originally applied to those Federalists, opponents of the Francophile Jefferson, who were ready to risk a war with France. In 1810 the epithet—along with *war dogs*—was revived by Jeffersonian Republican John Randolph against the "war Republicans" accused of seeking a renewal of war with England to expand into Canada and take Florida from Spain, Britain's ally. The group, which succeeded in bringing on the War of 1812, was led by

House Speaker Henry Clay, *the* War Hawk; later in his long career he was to become known as "the Great Pacificator" (see CAN'T-WIN TECHNIQUE).

For the term's reemergence into political parlance during the Cuban missile crisis in 1962, see DOVES. In 1993, during controversy about U.S. entry into the first Persian Gulf war, Senator Joseph I. Lieberman of Connecticut said: "It isn't hawks and doves anymore. It's internationalists and isolationists." He retained that position, though not in those words, in 2006; was defeated for renomination in the Democratic primary by an end-the-war-now candidate; ran as an independent, and won reelection.

When internationalists oppose the use of military power, or when isolationists find reasons to urge intervention, they are sometimes called *dawks*. The aviary metaphor has been extended to poultry: "Nobody is going to 'SWIFT-BOAT' Jim Webb," wrote *Newsweek* admiringly about the Virginia Democrat campaigning for the Senate in 2006. "During Vietnam, he scorned antiwar protestors with the same contempt he shows today for so-called *chicken hawks*, the neocons who never served in the military but were all for invading Iraq." See DOVES, JINGOISM.

war horse A veteran campaigner who has had a battle-scarred career in politics.

Samuel Medary, a leading Ohio editor in the mid-nineteenth century, who is credited with the coinage of "Fifty-Four Forty or Fight," was nicknamed "The War Horse of Democracy." Robert E. Lee affectionately called James Longstreet "my old war horse." The first *OED* citation is from Robert M. Bird's 1837 *Nick of the Woods*: "Ar'nt thee the Pennsylvanny war-horse, the screamer of the meeting-house, the ba'r of Yea-Nay-and-Verily?"

This MILITARY METAPHOR comes from the charger used in battle. "[Thou] didst pick up Andrew Jackson," wrote Herman Melville in *Moby-Dick*, "[and] didst hurl him upon a war-horse."

In the vote-as-you-shot, BLOODY SHIRT politics of Reconstruction, the *war horses* had an edge. In time the phrase came to be an affectionate, occasionally contemptuous name for a veteran politician. "There poured into the city by every train," wrote the *Weekly New Mexican Review* in 1885, "democratic 'war horses' from the four corners of New Mexico."

War horse is in current use, though not as frequent as its synonym, WHEELHORSE, from the horse harnessed nearest the front wheels who follows the lead horse. For other equine expressions in politics, see BOLT; DARK HORSE; FRONT RUNNER; SHOO-IN.

war of national liberation Communist terminology for a "just war" against "colonial" powers, started by a faction within the country and possibly assisted by a Communist neighbor.

Nikita Khrushchev, in a 1961 speech in Moscow, stated: "Liberation wars will continue to exist as long as imperialism exists, as long as colonialism exists. These are revolutionary wars. Such wars are not only admissible but inevitable.... The Communists fully support such just wars and march in the front rank with the peoples waging liberation struggles."

Obviously the meaning of the phrase depends on who is using it. Abraham Lincoln illustrated this dilemma in 1864: "The shepherd drives the wolf from the sheep's throat, for which the sheep thanks the shepherd as his liberator, while the wolf denounces him for the same act as the destroyer of liberty."

The phrase itself was not born in the cold war. MUGWUMP statesman Carl Schurz, opposing the annexation of Hawaii and the Philippines in 1899, reminded President McKinley that the American people who went to war against Spain over Cuba "were indeed willing to wage a war of liberation, but would not have consented to a war of conquest."

war of nerves In political terms, psychological pressure; in diplomacy, threats, and feints to the point of terrorization.

Adolf Hitler dissected the theory in *Mein Kampf*: "At a given sign it unleashes a veritable barrage of lies and slanders against whatever adversary seems most dangerous, until the nerves of the attacked persons break down.... This is a tactic based on precise calculation of all human weaknesses, and its result will lead to success with almost mathematical certainty."

Before Bernard Baruch's use of COLD WAR filled the need for a new phrase, *war of nerves* was used by world leaders to describe the tension building between the Soviet Union and the West. In 1946, upon receipt of George Kennan's CONTAINMENT memorandum (see MR. X), Secretary of State James Byrnes stated that "we must not conduct a war of nerves to achieve strategic ends" and suggested the Soviets not conduct one either. A year later in Britain, Harold Macmillan, worried about what he called the "cordon sanitaire" of satellites in Eastern Europe, warned Parliament that the situation was "only a war of nerves, but a war of nerves may be very dangerous."

On a personal level, a war of nerves was conducted against Justice Felix Frankfurter to get him to resign from the Supreme Court bench in 1953. *The Nation* wrote: "Sen. William Knowland is said to have demanded, as his price for accepting the truce in Korea...the appointment of Governor Warren to the first Supreme Court vacancy.... Recently a curious war of nerves has been launched to induce Justice Frankfurter to resign. It has taken the form of stories that his letter of resignation is on the President's desk, pointed inquiries about his health, a drumbeat insistence in the gossip columns ..."

Frankfurter sent word to Warren through Clint Mosher of the *San Francisco Examiner*: "Tell him I would not want it on my conscience that I had kept him off the Supreme Court." Warren did get the next available seat, but it was not Frankfurter's, who remained on the court for a decade, outlasting five other justices in that time.

A more recent term, with a military ring, is *psywar* or *psychological warfare* (see PROPAGANDA); its practitioners are called *psyops*. The older phrase is still in use: In 1993, after the breakup of the Soviet Union, Georgia announced that it had shot down a Russian warplane. Commented *The Washington Post*: "The downing of the Russian air force fighter plane ... is the most serious incident in a gradually escalating war of nerves between the two former Soviet republics."

War on Poverty President Lyndon Johnson's phrase for his domestic social welfare program, reminiscent of FDR's ONE-THIRD OF A NATION.

England's conservative Edmund Burke foresaw the need and the probable reaction. "Government is a contrivance of human wisdom to provide for human *wants*," he wrote in his 1790 *Reflections on the Revolution in France*. Five years later, he added, "and having looked to Government for bread, on the very first scarcity they will turn and bite the hand that fed them."

In the U.S. in 1879, *Progress and Poverty* by economist Henry George (see VESTED INTERESTS) was one of the biggest nonfiction best sellers of the time.

Herbert Hoover, who earned a reputation after World War I as a man dedicated to the relief of suffering, said in 1928: "We in America today are nearer to the final triumph over poverty than ever before in the history of any land." The stock-market crash came one year later, and newsman Elmer Davis drily called 1930 "the Second Year of the Abolition of Poverty."

It was not until the early '60s, however, that governmental action to alleviate poverty found its slogan. Three books paved the way: John Galbraith's AFFLUENT SOCIETY in 1958, with a provocative chapter on "The New Position of Poverty"; a study directed by economist Leon Keyserling in 1962 called *Poverty and Deprivation in the U.S.—The Plight of Two-Fifths of the Nation*; and most important, in the same year, *The Other America*, a passionate book by Michael Harrington showing how poverty haunts our otherwise affluent society, and translating the statistics into bitter, human terms.

Campaigning in 1960, John F. Kennedy had been impressed by the extent of poverty in West Virginia and elsewhere in Appalachia and used the phrase that was to be the Johnson battle cry: "The war against poverty and degradation is not yet

over." A year earlier Dwight Eisenhower in New Delhi had called for "a successful war against hunger—the sort of war that dignifies and exalts human beings."

President Johnson, in his first address to a joint session of Congress five days after the Kennedy assassination, promised to "carry on the fight against poverty." In a meeting of his staff going over the State of the Union message a month later, he said he was worried about the word *poverty*. "It's not poverty," he said, "it's wastage of resources and human lives"—but nobody came up with a better word, so the President agreed to call it a "poverty" program. In that speech, the phrase became his own: "Unfortunately many Americans live on the outskirts of hope, some because of their poverty and some because of their color, and all too many because of both. Our task is to help replace their despair with unconditional war on poverty in America ..."

By 1966 the phrase was open to attack. Republicans pointed out waste and inefficiency in local programs, and pledged to "take the profit out of poverty." In an economic context, Richard Nixon said the President's unwillingness to cut non-defense spending amounted to "a war on prosperity."

Soon many programs became "wars." Every racketeering crackdown became a "war on crime," even education programs were labeled "wars on ignorance." The author helped persuade Nixon to declare cancer research a "war on cancer," and Ronald Reagan had a "war on drugs." One sloganeer, who refused to let his candidate name a highway safety program a "war on roadhogs," declared he would start a war of his own—a "WAR TO END WARS."

war on terror Conflict with an amorphous, non-governmental enemy.

Addressing a joint session of Congress on September 20, 2001, nine days after the 9/11 attacks on the United States (see 9/11), President George W. Bush said: "Our war on terror begins with al Qaeda, but it does not end there." This stirring call to arms implicitly compared the war with al-Qaeda to World Wars I and II. It also drew on the well-established use of *war* as a metaphor for other kinds of national campaigns such as "war on illiteracy," announced by Bush at a Florida elementary school just the day before 9/11, and WAR ON POVERTY.

War on terror had been employed in various contexts for many years prior to 9/11. As far back as April 2, 1881, *The New York Times* headlined a story about penalties for assassins: "The War on Terrorism; European Measures for Its Extermination." Criminals were also classed as terrorists: The *Decatur* (Ill.) *Daily Review* headed a story about plans to hire an additional 1,000 policemen in Chicago in 1922: "Promise Action in Chicago War on Terror." In 1956, the *Times* reported: "Britain Deports Cyprus Prelate in War on Terror." In 1995, *The Washington Post* referred to "the broad Israeli consensus that the war on terror cannot be pretty."

Strictly speaking, *war on terror* is an inapposite pairing of nouns. *Terror* is not so much an enemy as a tactic—a method of making war. To say that one is conducting a *war on terror* could be like saying that one is conducting a *war on blitzkrieg* or a *war on aerial bombing*. The point may be dismissed as grammatical but is not trivial: When the tactic is substituted for the enemy, ultimate victory becomes elusive. If the conflict were presented as a *war on al-Qaeda*, say, the implication is that the war might be won by destroying that particular terrorist organization. A *war on terror*, however, is open-ended both in scope and length, since a tactic cannot be captured, killed, or otherwise defeated. Such a war may peter out eventually, but will not have a definite ending—an unconditional surrender—that can be recognized with parades. Inherent in such a name is more a requirement for patience and resolve than a promise of decisive victory.

By 2005, with fighting continuing against insurgents in Iraq, American military leaders began to characterize the conflict in other terms. Gen. Richard Myers, chairman of the Joint Chiefs of Staff, told the National Press Club in July that he "objected to the use of the term 'war on terrorism'... violent

extremists [are] the real enemy here and terror is the method they use." Secretary of Defense Donald Rumsfeld also moved away from "war on terror," instead characterizing the conflict as a "global struggle against violent extremism." Recognizing that this struggle might last for generations, Rumsfeld and other administration officials also began calling it *the long war*, making the term all but official in a key Pentagon planning document, the *Quadrennial Defense Review*, released in early 2006.

War on terror was so convenient a phrase that it was difficult to give up, however. Announcing the selection of Robert M. Gates as Rumsfeld's successor in December of 2006, President Bush defined victory in terms of a democratic Iraq that can be "an ally in the war on terror." Gates himself told the Senate committee considering his nomination that Iraq constituted "one of the central fronts in the war on terror."

Former Democratic Senator John Edwards had said when running for vice president in 2004 that "the war on terrorism is absolutely winnable" but when campaigning for the Democratic nomination for president in 2007 pointedly recanted his earlier support and objected to the phrase: "This political language has created a frame that is not accurate and that Bush and his gang have used to justify anything they want to do." But even critics of U.S. policy had trouble finding a more satisfactory phrase. Columnist Peter Beinart wrote in *The Washington Post* that "Replacing 'terror' with 'jihadism' would offend many Muslims...'Jihadi-salafi,' a term used by some scholars, is less offensive and more accurate but unlikely to PLAY IN PEORIA. 'Al-Qaeda' is logical, but experts now consider it more an inspiration than a mass organization. And al-Qaeda-ism doesn't exactly roll off the tongue. The answer is elusive." Under ACRONYMS, POLITICAL, see GWOT.

war party Desperation charge against the Democrats; like DEPRESSION PARTY against Republicans, considered a low blow.

"He kept us out of war" was the proud Democratic slogan in 1916, helping to reelect Woodrow Wilson. "I hate war" was a familiar Franklin Roosevelt line in 1939. By the time of the Vietnam war—the fourth in this century entered under Democratic Administrations—Democrats were understandably touchy about the charge of being the "war party."

Not surprising, then, is the emphasis by Democratic candidates on peace, paralleling the emphasis of Republicans stung by depression on prosperity. Former Eisenhower speechwriter Emmet Hughes wrote about the 1952 campaign: "the irony was this: each party recognized that its popular strength was plainly greater in the sphere where its public record was plainly weaker. Democrats feared popular distrust of their foreign policies as deeply as Republicans feared popular distrust of their domestic policies. Each was haunted by its own caricature—the Democrats as 'the Party of War,' the Republicans as 'the Party of Depression.'"

war room Central command post for directing a military, political, or business campaign.

The political sense of *war room* was popularized by Bill Clinton's campaign organization during his successful run for president in 1992. It was reinforced the following year by the documentary film using the phrase as its title, which focused on the room's two principal denizens, James "the Ragin' Cajun" Carville and George Stephanopoulos.

The Clinton *war room* was located in a large open space, the former newsroom of the *Arkansas Gazette* in Little Rock. Meetings were held twice a day, at 7:00 A.M. and 7:00 P.M., to assess polling information, ads, news, and attacks from the opposition, and to plan responses to unfolding events. The openness of the room fostered a sense of camaraderie and cooperation. To remind everyone what the campaign was about, Carville put a sign on one wall. It had just three lines:

Change vs. More of the Same
The Economy, stupid
Don't forget health care

The candidate's wife, Hillary Rodham Clinton, gave the room its nickname. "Hillary

said it was like a 'war room,' and the name stuck," recalled Bill Clinton in his 2004 memoir, *My Life.*

War rooms originally were for conducting real wars. When Prime Minister Winston Churchill inspected the underground cabinet rooms in central London in 1940, he declared, "This is the room from which I will direct the war." The British also had a *war room* in World War I. Admiral Sir Arthur Wilson wrote in October of 1914 to Churchill, then First Lord of the Admiralty, saying, "I should like to have a room set apart for me near the War room."

Post-Clinton, *war rooms* have appeared in other contexts. When the giant retailer Wal-Mart started feeling heat from critics in 2005, it developed a rapid-response public relations operation housed in a *war room*, its headquarters in Bentonville, Arkansas. Denizens of this room—a stuffy, windowless one—included veterans from both camps in the 2004 presidential campaigns. See also PREBUTTAL and SIT ROOM.

war to end wars An idealistic World War I slogan, now used only cynically.

Like MAKE THE WORLD SAFE FOR DEMOCRACY, this phrase is associated with President Woodrow Wilson and the disillusionment following World War I.

The phrase was not Wilson's. *The War That Will End War* was the title of a 1914 book by British author H. G. Wells; in Bertrand Russell's 1956 *Portraits from Memory*, the philosopher recalled that it was Wells who coined the phrase. George Bernard Shaw, in his 1923 play *Back to Methuselah*, had a character say, "There was a war called the War to End War. In the war that followed it ten years later … seven of the capital cities of Europe were wiped out of existence."

When Neville Chamberlain returned from Munich (see MUNICH ANALOGY) with what he called "PEACE FOR OUR TIME," *The Nation* headlined its issue "A Peace to End Peace." That phrase had been applied before to the Treaty of Versailles.

The phrase has a steady, cynical use meaning "pipedream." In 1967, a gloomy Walter Lippmann described Secretary of

State Dean Rusk in *Newsweek* as "one of the few surviving TRUE BELIEVERS among statesmen, in the great Utopian Delusion which has been employed so extensively by propagandists ever since it was fabricated in the first world war. The delusion is that whatever war we are fighting is a war to end war. Anyone with experience and some toughness of mind knows from the history of the past 50 years that these wars which are supposed to end wars have never, in fact, ended wars. The historical record is quite plain: on the contrary, each of the wars to end wars has set the stage for the next war."

Richard Nixon, in the peroration of his November 3, 1969, SILENT MAJORITY speech, recognized the grandiose nature of the promise and set more realistic sights: "Tonight I do not tell you that the war in Vietnam is the war to end wars. But I do say this: I have initiated a plan which will end this war in a way that will bring us closer to that great goal to which Woodrow Wilson and every American President in our history has been dedicated—the goal of a just and lasting peace ..." See FULL GENERATION OF PEACE.

warts and all See IMAGE.

WASP White Anglo-Saxon Protestant: an ethnic group.

By the time the expression *WASP* (first recorded in 1962) came to be used, White Anglo-Saxon Protestants were no longer the majority of Americans. In urban politics, ticket-balancing to attract the votes of minority groups—Catholics, Jews, Irish, Germans, Puerto Ricans, or blacks—has become accepted. In some circles, *WASP* is used to connote snobbish patrician types, but politicians use it affectionately in the big cities.

Richard Scammon and Ben Wattenberg wrote in 1965:

> Some day someone will write an inspiring piece about one of America's greatest and most colorful minority groups. They came here on crowded ships, were resented by the natives and had to struggle mightily for every advance they made against a hostile environment. Despite these

handicaps, despite even a skin color different from the native Americans, this hardy group prospered and, in prospering, helped build the nation.... The only thing different about the group is that it is the one traditionally viewed as the "American majority." For the minority group described is of course the "White Anglo-Saxon Protestant," further qualified today as "native-born of native parentage." The key point is that neither the WASP-NN, nor any solidified ethnic or religious group constitutes an "American majority."

Accused of being "waspish" toward the press in 1971, Herbert Stein, newly appointed chairman of the Council of Economic Advisers, retorted, "I'm not waspish, I'm Jewish."

waste See VIETNAM LINGO.

waste, fraud, and abuse An easy way to promise to squeeze down spending without offending anyone who might be offended by specific cuts.

As his presidency began, Jimmy Carter said in a fireside television talk of February 2, 1977: "I will support the Congress on its effort to deal with the widespread fraud and waste and abuse in our Medicaid system." His Secretary of Health, Education and Welfare, Joseph Califano, followed with a pledge "to reduce fraud, abuse, and error"; in April of 1978, the AP reported that HEW's inspector general had found that the department had misspent $7.4 billion in fiscal year 1977 "because of waste, fraud and abuse." It was this final formulation, probably by Califano, who recalls the coinage, that became frozen into the budgetary cliché.

In Ronald Reagan's campaign of 1980 that unseated Carter, he promised "I will not tolerate, and will fight with all my strength, the inexcusable waste, fraud and abuse of government programs—many of which are aimed at older Americans."

Newsweek reported in March 1993 that the newly elected President Bill Clinton had "repeatedly said he could pay for extending health coverage to the 36 million uninsured Americans simply by eliminating waste, fraud and abuse in the system, which he estimated to be more than $200 billion."

Columnist Meg Greenfield followed up in July "observing a classic case of the dread big three: waste, fraud and abuse."

Why is WF&A the constant whipping boy? Not all expenditures that fail to deliver are *waste*; many are experiments that by their nature are an administrative gamble. *Fraud* should be easy to deal with, requiring no new approach; it's criminal, and the career Justice Department officials who should be dealing with it do not change with a change of administrations. *Abuse* is the ultimate catch-all of spurious spending control: Abuse of what? Power? That's impeachable. The public trust? That's amorphous. Regulations? That's tilting at bureaucratic windmills.

Nobody is in favor of waste, fraud, and abuse; the denunciation is a cop-out by politicians fearful of getting specific about ending government programs that have voting constituencies.

wasteland See VAST WASTELAND.

watchdog committee A committee that "probes" waste in government operations, or overseas expenditures in agencies like the Central Intelligence Agency or the Atomic Energy Commission.

The "watchdogs of the Treasury," a usage traced back to 1827, were originally those trying to hold down government spending in general; the meaning today has narrowed to trying to cut waste out of specific areas of spending.

In the earlier sense, Representative William S. Holman of Indiana was given the sobriquet "The Watchdog of the Treasury" in the mid-nineteenth century, along with his earlier nickname "The Great Objector" (to appropriations bills in the House).

In the current sense, Senator Lyndon Johnson headed the Defense Preparedness Subcommittee of the Senate Armed Services Committee in 1951, investigating the conduct of the Korean conflict. The same kind of work made Senator Harry Truman famous during World War II. Economic journalist Eliot Janeway wrote a glowing account of "Johnson of the 'Watchdog Committee'" in *The New York Times Magazine* in 1951, and *Newsweek* put Johnson

on its cover with the caption "Watchdog in Chief."

The heroic dogs are still on the job, against great odds. An AP dispatch at the end of 2006: "The inspectors general entrusted to unearth WASTE, FRAUD AND ABUSE in federal agencies are increasingly under attack, as top government officials they scrutinize try to erode the watchdogs' independence and authority." See CANINE METAPHORS; EARMARK; OVERSIGHT; PORK BARREL.

watchful waiting Wise diplomatic restraint, or craven justification for inaction.

President Woodrow Wilson did not want to be drawn into a war with Mexico in 1913. "We shall not," he told Congress, "I believe, be obliged to alter our policy of watchful waiting." President Victoriano Huerta had seized power and murdered the previous president; when he provoked an incident in 1914 by arresting a group of U.S. Marines in Tampico, Wilson sent in troops that took Veracruz.

The phrase had been used by President Grover Cleveland in a letter in 1893 criticizing the U.S. seizure of Hawaii: "There seemed to arise…the precise opportunity for which he was watchfully waiting."

The *watchful* gives purpose to the *waiting*, like a cat on a stakeout in front of a mousehole. The *New York Times* editorialized in 1967: "The United States has an embassy in Port-au-Prince. Its policy is to adopt a 'correct attitude' toward the Duvalier Government. It watches and it waits."

The predecessor phrase was "masterly inactivity" by Sir James Mackintosh (1765–1832), who was also the espouser of "disciplined inaction": "The Commons, faithful to their system, remained in a wise and masterly inactivity."

In opposition to the cautious look-before-you-leap school is the decisive he-who-hesitates-is-lost school. Its favorite recent derogation was "Let the dust settle," an evocation of a 1950s criticism of U.S. China policy. General Albert Wedemeyer's 1947 report to Secretary of State George Marshall during the Truman Administration urged U.S. economic and diplomatic support to China's Nationalist government under Chiang Kai-shek, then fighting a communist takeover.

Wedemeyer recalled in 1983 that his warnings were ignored and the U.S. "adopted a passive 'wait-and-see' or 'let the dust settle' policy with respect to China." This unwillingness to intervene, its critics felt, permitted Mao Zedong's Communists to take over mainland China, and led to the condemnation "Who Lost China?" in U.S. politics.

A subsequent policy phrase within China, reminiscent of "watchful waiting" and "masterly inactivity," was recalled by the economist Milton Friedman in a 2006 *Wall Street Journal* article. He noted the success of Hong Kong's laissez-faire government under British rule in the 1960s administered by John Cowperthwaite, whose approach of economic freedom was described by his successor, Sir Phillip Haddon-Cave, as "positive noninterventionism." After the "handover" to Beijing's rule, that policy has changed, and Friedman observed that "a half-century of 'positive noninterventionism' has made Hong Kong wealthy enough to absorb much abuse from ill-advised government intervention."

The phrase, also used in economic and wine-making contexts, is most often used in medicine: one often recommended course in dealing with slow-developing prostate cancer is "watchful waiting."

waterboarding A form of torture in which the captive is made to believe he is suffocating to death under water.

On May 12, 2004, *The New York Times* reported that "C.I.A. interrogators used graduated levels of force, including a technique known as 'water boarding,' in which a prisoner is strapped down, forcibly pushed under water and made to believe he might drown. These techniques were authorized by a set of secret rules for the interrogation of high-level Al Qaeda prisoners ..."

In 1991, columnist Jack Anderson reported a "Chinese water board torture demonstration" being conducted by the U.S. Navy on its trainees, a simulation unearthed by congressional investigators. This was not to be confused with "Chinese water torture"—the slow dripping of water on the forehead until the victim was driven mad—but was the simulation of drowning known to U.S. forces in the Phillipines during the Spanish-American war. President Theodore Roosevelt in a 1902 letter defended the practice: "The enlisted men began to use the old Filipino method: the water cure. Nobody was seriously damaged."

The "tactic of waterboarding" inflicted on al-Qaeda terrorist Khalid Shaikh Mohammed, suspected of planning the 9/11 attacks that killed more than 3000 Americans, was criticized in 2005 by Senator John McCain, who suffered years of torture in a Vietnamese prison: "To make someone believe that you are killing him by drowning," he wrote, "is no different than holding a pistol to his head and firing a blank. I believe that is torture, very exquisite torture."

Waterboarding, now a one-word verbal noun, became the subject of congressional and internal Administration investigations in 2008, as Americans were forced to come to grips with the need to balance strongly held moral, humanitarian and practical concerns with what many felt were necessarily harsh methods of obtaining information to protect the lives of noncombatants.

Watergate words *Watergate*, like *Teapot Dome*, means everything associated with a scandal that became what President Ford later called "our long national nightmare."

Watergate means a place: the hotel-offices-apartment-house complex in Washington, D.C., facing the Potomac, named after the dockside facility that once occupied the site, into which the "waterbugs" stole to plant a BUG in the offices of the Democratic National Committee.

Watergate also means a time: the period from June 17, 1972, when the break-in was considered merely a madcap "caper," to the near-impeachment, resignation, and pardon of President Nixon, and then back in time to the start of eavesdropping in his Administration by the PLUMBERS.

And *Watergate* means a mood: a time of revulsion against the ENEMIES L ISTS and the LAUNDERING of campaign contributions, of die-hards who protested "double standards" and "ex post facto morality," of tips from Mark Felt, a disgruntled FBI official known only as "Deep Throat" (see FOLLOW THE MONEY), and of condemnation of the men of CREEP who "shredded" and DEEP-SIXED evidence in a COVER-UP.

Watergate came to mean political drama on the grandest scale: of a search for the SMOKING GUN by the "straight arrows," of the FIRESTORM that followed the SATURDAY NIGHT MASSACRE of the "good guys" who finally won, of the STONEWALLING about DIRTY TRICKS and "White House horrors" by the BIG ENCHILADA, of plans to "paper the file" by "team players" who had not been brought UP TO SPEED, of the "black advance," of legalese like "misprision of a felony" and EXECUTIVE PRIVILEGE, of a "sinister force" known only as the OVAL OFFICE capable of producing an 18½-minute GAP.

After the HANGING TOUGH and the "limited, modified hangout route" had led nowhere, the men who had maneuvered themselves between "a rock and a hard place" found themselves TWISTING SLOWLY, SLOWLY IN THE WIND. A few instant revisionists with anti-Nixonian credentials observed that more than a few "abuses of power" had been perpetrated in the name of civil liberty, and that NOBODY DROWNED AT WATERGATE, but that a perspective on the "long national nightmare" was too soon AT THAT POINT IN TIME. It was the golden age of political coinage.

Watergate words continue to be revived. John D. Ehrlichman's statement about a "modified limited hangout" was reworked by the elder President George Bush. According to Rich Jaroslovsky of *The Wall Street Journal*, Bush described a presidential photo session in 1989 as "a modified limited photo op cum statement sans questions." See -GATE CONSTRUCTION.

water's edge Where some believe that partisan politics, in the interests of national foreign policy, is supposed to stop.

Democratic Majority Leader Lyndon Johnson viewed the election in 1956 of a Democratic Congress and a Republican President as an affirmation of the principles of the bipartisanship he had been talking about since 1952. According to columnist Arthur Krock, "As defined by Lyndon Johnson, ...these principles were: Partisan politics stops 'at the water's edge.' The only test of all legislation is whether 'it is good for the country.'"

In 1964, recalling his days as Majority Leader, President Johnson repeated one of his favorite phrases: "I took the position that politics stopped at the water's edge. We had but one President and Commander-in-Chief."

The phrase is closely linked to a BIPARTISAN foreign policy. Architect of that policy, Michigan Republican Senator Arthur Vandenberg, whose 1945 Senate speech marked his repudiation of isolationism, used it in his own 1950 definition to a constituent: "To me 'bipartisan foreign policy' means a mutual effort under our indispensable two-party system to unite our official voice at the water's edge." "What mainly stops at the water's edge," countered historian James MacGregor Burns, "is not party politics in general but congressional party politics in particular. The real 'UNHOLY ALLIANCE' to a good congressional Republican is the historic coalition between the internationalists in both parties."

Describing Harry Truman, historian Richard Neustadt wrote: "He played 'Chief of State' like a gracious host, 'Chief of Party' like an organization politician, 'Chief of Foreign Policy' like a career official anxious to obey his own injunction that 'politics stops at the water's edge.'"

Describing Woodrow Wilson, Winston Churchill sidestepped the use of a cliché by substituting other words: "He did not truly divine the instinct of the American people. First and foremost, all through and last, he was a party man. The spacious philanthropy which he exhaled upon Europe stopped quite sharply at the coasts of his own country."

The phrase, though intimately associated with foreign policy, can be extended to other realms. In 2007, James Hoagland of *The Washington Post* noted that Ségolène Royal, Socialist political leader and mother of four, campaigning against Nicolas Sarkozy to become President of France, was "not getting momentum from an effort to suggest that the world would be a much better place under a sisterhood-in-power of [Germany's Chancellor Angela] Merkel, [America's potential president

Hillary] Clinton and herself … when Royal's camp put out feelers to Clinton's staff last year about a high-profile meeting of the two in New York, a deafening silence persuaded Royal's aides to cancel her trip to the United States. It used to be said that for Americans, foreign policy debates stop at the water's edge. Today, so does political sisterhood."

watershed election A campaign that decides the course of politics for decades; one that is especially memorable, or that proves to be a dividing line between historical periods.

California Lieutenant Governor Robert Finch said in 1967: "The Nixon-Kennedy campaign of 1960 will prove to be the great watershed election of this century."

The word *watershed* entered dictionaries in its metaphoric meaning in the '60s. The literal meaning is a water-storage area making the surrounding region fertile, or providing a city with its water supply. A second meaning is "dividing line" as between drainage areas. The political meaning comes from both the nourishing meaning (of the vital water-holding uplands) and the epochal meaning (a line between two areas, or a moment between two eras).

The political meaning emerges in these examples. Biographer Leo Katcher: "The University of California was one of the great watersheds of experience for Earl Warren." *Times* of London headline, 1965: "Parliament at a Watershed." Treasury Secretary Douglas Dillon, describing 1961–64 as "a watershed in the development of American economic policy." Author Theodore White: "The great revolutionary in the flow of ideas proved to be John Fitzgerald Kennedy.… He was the watershed."

The word crested in the late sixties. In 1968 this writer suggested to candidate Richard Nixon that he adopt the word to describe the forthcoming election, which he did in several speeches. However, in 1969, when *Newsweek* described a conference on Midway Island about Vietnam as "a watershed in the quagmire," editorial writer Meg Greenfield of *The Washington Post* proceeded to blast the shed out of the water:

"I have also become an incurable, even obsessive collector of printed watersheds, of which I believe I now have the best collection in town—watersheds perching on escalation ladders, watersheds embedded in arms spirals, watersheds wrapped (like chicken livers, perhaps) in an enigma. It is not, however, an expression that I would dare to use myself. I came to that drainage basin two years ago and paddled left, into the sunset."

Ms. Greenfield's sandbagging of the watershed flood was widely hailed. "In terms of getting things done," she wrote in a follow-up article, "a number of MOVERS AND SHAKERS stepped forward to reveal their sympathy.… for instance, a principal presidential speechwriter (who had done invaluable pioneer work on the subject in his political lexicon), sent a letter to say that 'watershed' deserved all the opprobrium we could heap upon it, and he added that the term had long since been dropped from the presidential vocabulary."

However, two leading political figures— Dr. Henry Kissinger and then Senate Majority Leader Mike Mansfield—had used the word in the interim. "I was still prepared to issue a rather favorable report," continued Ms. Greenfield, "speaking harshly only to these two offenders. I was only dissuaded from doing so by a sharp-eyed colleague, who asked how I would explain exactly whom I spoke for at *The Washington Post*, which had only recently hailed the Apollo moon adventure as—yes—'a watershed' in history in space … I would be less than candid if I did not report that, at the present time, there is no light at the end of the watershed."

wave of the future Admiring description of TOTALITARIANISM; a phrase used today only to be denied or derogated.

In 1940, poet Anne Morrow Lindbergh, influenced by her isolationist husband Charles Lindbergh, wrote a long essay published as a book with the title *The Wave of the Future*, which many readers took to be an apologia for Fascism.

Working on Roosevelt's third inaugural address, speechwriter Robert Sherwood said to the President, "I certainly wish we could use that terrible phrase, 'the wave of the future.'" Samuel Rosenman recollects FDR calmly saying, "Why not?" and dictating the following: "There are men who believe that democracy, as a form of government and a frame of life, is limited or measured by a kind of mystical and artificial fate—that, for some unexplained reason, tyranny and slavery have become the surging wave of the future—and that freedom is an ebbing tide. But we Americans know that this is not true."

A few months later Interior Secretary Harold Ickes castigated what he called "the wavers of the future" at an "I Am an American Day" rally in New York's Central Park:

> For years we have been told that we are beaten, decayed, and that no part of the world belongs to us any longer. Some amongst us have fallen for this carefully pickled tripe … this calculated poison. Some amongst us have begun to preach that the "wave of the future" has passed over us and left us a wet, dead fish.
>
> Americans, with the aid of our brave allies— yes, let's call them "allies"—the British, can and will build the only future worth having. I mean a future, not of concentration camps, not of physical torture and mental straitjackets, not of sawdust bread or sawdust Caesars—I mean a future when free men will live free lives in dignity and in security. This tide of the future, the democratic future, is ours.

President John Kennedy, speaking to students at the Berkeley campus of the University of California, said: "No one can doubt that the wave of the future is not the conquest of the world by a single dogmatic creed but the liberation of the diverse energies of free nations and free men."

The same technique of setting up *wave of the future* as a strawman phrase, and then knocking it down, has been used often since. In the 1968 campaign Richard Nixon found a sure-fire applause line in "the wave of crime must not become the wave of the future."

The change in more recent generations was to identify Communism rather than Fascism as the "waver." It has not yet been replaced by Jihadism or Islamofascism as the totalitarian threat.

The undulation of the sea, in use politically as GROUNDSWELL, was used metaphorically by Ralph Waldo Emerson in his essay "On Self-Reliance": "Society is a wave. The wave moves onward, but the water of which it is composed does not. … The persons who make up a nation today, next year die, and their experiences with them."

waxworks Dais guests with frozen expressions at a political dinner.

"It's a pleasure to be back up here as a member of the waxworks," defeated senatorial candidate Bernard Shanley told a New Jersey political dinner in 1968. The reference was to Madame (Marie) Tussaud's wax museum, which she set up permanently in London in 1835 after traveling around England with it since her arrival in 1802; it became a landmark with its lifelike representations of historical figures, many from the Reign of Terror during which Madame Tussaud herself was nearly executed but was spared for her talent at making death masks. The museum has since replicated itself in New York, Las Vegas, Hong Kong, and elsewhere. (The author was in 2007 startled to find himself seated next to Abraham Lincoln on a shuttle flight from New York to Washington, D.C., where the lifelike wax figure was being transported for exhibition. Despite eager questioning, it had no comment.)

People who sit on daises, even when thoroughly bored, must appear friendly and interested. The resulting expression is a waxen smile which, when strung out in a line of twenty people, makes "waxworks" an apt description. See RUBBER-CHICKEN CIRCUIT.

weaned on a pickle See MAN ON THE WEDDING CAKE.

we are all Declaration of membership in a group that becomes highly quotable when expressed by an unlikely source.

The first well-known use was unifying rather than surprising. "We have called by different names brethren of the same principle," said Thomas Jefferson in his first inaugural address. "We are all Republicans, we are all Federalists."

When the Prince of Wales (later Edward VII) used it in an 1895 speech in England, it startled the world: "We are all Socialists now-a-days." (Sir Denis Brogan credited this line to Sir William Harcourt.)

And conservative economist Milton Friedman put the NEW ECONOMICS over the top when *Time* magazine used his remark on its cover in 1965: "We are all Keynesians now." Liberal economist Walter Heller commented a year later: "When Milton Friedman, the chief guardian of the laissez-faire tradition in American economics, said not long ago, 'We are all Keynesians now,' the profession said 'Amen.'" Overlooked was the second half of Friedman's remark: "—and there are no longer any Keynesians."

"We are all guilty" was described in 1969 by linguist Mario Pei as "perhaps the most ingenious of all Communistic slogans created to demoralize us by giving us collective and inherited guilt as a substitute for individual responsibility."

weasel words Ambiguous speech; deliberately fuzzy phraseology.

"One of our defects as a nation," said Theodore Roosevelt in 1916, "is a tendency to use what have been called weasel words." He had popularized the phrase as president, and gave this example of what he meant: "You can have universal training, or you can have voluntary training, but when you use the word 'voluntary' to qualify the word 'universal,' you are using a 'weasel word'; it has sucked all the meaning out of 'universal.' The two words flatly contradict one another." (The origin of that metaphor can be found in Shakespeare's *As You Like It*, when "the melancholy Jaques" asks Lord Amiens to continue his singing: "I can suck melancholy out of a song, as a weasel sucks eggs.")

Author Stewart Chaplin explained the phrase in an article about political platforms in a 1900 issue of *The Century Magazine*: "weasel words are words that suck all the life out of the words next to them, just as a weasel sucks an egg and leaves the shell. If you heft the egg afterward it's as light as a feather, and not very filling when you're hungry; but a basketful of them

would make quite a show, and would bamboozle the unwary."

President Franklin D. Roosevelt, according to speechwriter Samuel Rosenman, "was extremely impatient with some of the drafts that came over from the State Department during those years, and with some of the suggested corrections in the drafts he had sent over to them for consideration. He felt that they were too apt to use 'weasel words' (a favored phrase he had borrowed from Theodore Roosevelt); that they made too many reservations and were too diplomatically reserved."

Editor William Allen White, writing about the direct quality of Wendell Willkie in 1940, thought the Republican candidate was making headway because "The American people are tired of the smoothy in politics—even if he is honest. They don't like the oleaginous weasel words with which so many politicians grease their way back when they venture upon a dangerous salient of honesty."

President Nixon, in a meeting with Chinese Premier Zhou Enlai in Beijing in 1972, first used the word in high-level international diplomacy (and presaged the use of COVER-UP in the same sentence): "The conventional way to handle a meeting at the summit like this, while the whole world is watching is to have meetings for several days, which we will have, to have discussions and discover differences, which we will do, and then put out a weasel-worded communiqué, covering up the problems." Nixon then disclaimed such intention.

The colloquial verb *to weasel* means "to renege on a promise," usually for some cowardly reason. In prison slang, it refers to an informer. The Wentworth-Flexner *Dictionary of American Slang* adds that "applied to small, thin males, the word retains its physical connotation." Why the weasel has acquired a cowardly reputation is not known; it is a bold, vicious little beast that kills more than it can eat. In snowy areas, it acquires a white coat and enters judicial metaphors as *ermine*.

President Eisenhower wrote to Ambassador to Italy Clare Boothe Luce in 1953: "I assure you first that, so far as I know, we have no intention of weaseling on our

October 8th decision on Trieste." In that forthright statement, "so far as I know" are weasel words. See REPORTEDLY; WAFFLE.

wedge issue A HOT-BUTTON subject that splits a coalition or constituency.

"Education is the opposite of a wedge issue," *The Washington Post* reported in the last month of the Reagan-Mondale campaign of 1984, which suggests the phrase's appearance earlier. "It is a bridge issue for the diverse Democratic coalition."

In 1989, Eric Alterman, a senior fellow of the World Policy Institute, wrote of Lee Atwater's campaign strategy for George H. W. Bush. Alterman noted the emphasis on Willie Horton, a black man convicted of murder who raped a white woman while on furlough from a Massachusetts prison: "Atwater served notice on two occasions that the Horton furlough would be a central 'wedge' issue for the Republicans."

Stuart Eizenstat, once an adviser to Jimmy Carter, used the term a year later when the elder Bush's White House aides were arguing about the relationship between affirmative action and quotas. He wrote that Republicans in the Bush Administration had "a need to give the Reagan Democrats RED MEAT at a time when the economy is going into the tank, and they see civil rights and quotas as a wedge issue."

James Carville, a Clinton strategist, picked up the phrase in the 1992 campaign. Charging that George Bush's advisers lacked an agenda, Carville said they had to "dust off the Republican manual, which is to go to wedge issues: 'We can't lead the country so maybe we can divide it.'"

Wedge, with Germanic roots, is a forceful verb and noun that improves on the Latin-based POLARIZE and *polarization*. Often used by liberals and moderates, *wedge issue* attacks conservatives who bring up sensitive social subjects like abortion or homosexual rights under the rubric of FAMILY VALUES during a campaign. The wedge, however, is not necessarily racial or exclusive to liberals; politicians on the right see free trade as a wedge issue for dividing global-warming envi-

ronmentalists and labor's auto workers on the left.

But it can be applied to foreign affairs as well: a *Washington Post* editorial in the fall of 2006 criticized President George W. Bush for demanding "that Congress immediately approve his controversial schemes for the detention and trial of foreign terrorists, once again using vital questions of national security as a campaign wedge issue."

The antonym of wedge issue is MAGNET ISSUE. See also BREAD-AND-BUTTER ISSUE; HOT BUTTON; ISSUES, THE; PARAMOUNT ISSUE; POCKET-BOOK ISSUE. (Do you have an issue with the omnipresent substitution of *problem* with *issue*?)

welfare reform See WORKFARE.

welfare state Government that provides economic protection for all its citizens; this is done, say its critics, at the price of individual liberty and removes incentives needed for economic growth.

When British politician Edward Hallett Carr said in 1948, "Let us substitute welfare for wealth as our governing purpose," linguist Simeon Potter delightedly pointed out that the word *wealth* had returned to its original meaning: "weal," "well-being," and "welfare."

Welfare state, which the author believes was publicized by *New Republic* editor Herbert Croly at the turn of the twentieth century, had often been applied to the government of Sweden, and after World War II, particularly to Great Britain. Conservatives in England, accepting many social security programs short of nationalization, often reacted bitterly. In 1951 a reader of *Picture Post* urged Prime Minister Clement Attlee to dismiss "everyone who used the term 'welfare state,' because 'nobody is very well, and the state of the fare is rotten.'"

The phrase had a competitor at the start. *The Servile State* was the title of a 1913 book by Hilaire Belloc, which he defined as "that arrangement of society in which so considerable a number of the families and individuals are constrained by positive law to labor for the advantage of other families and individuals as to stamp the whole community with the mark of such labor." But statism was not ripe for an attack phrase so early; the welfare state triumphed as a proud assertion at first, and later became an epithet.

Current use in the U.S. is as an attack phrase. Those who urge more social welfare legislation rarely use the term; those who oppose it use "welfare state" as synonymous with CREEPING SOCIALISM. The use of *state* in the sense of "society" has a totalitarian connotation: *police state, garrison state, corporate state, state socialism.* (*Society*, contrariwise, is usually upbeat, as in Walter Lippmann's "The Good Society" and Lyndon Johnson's "The Great Society.")

The fire is not only directed at left-wingers. The conservative *Chicago Tribune* said of Eisenhower's 1955 State of the Union message: "Welfare statism and a tender if meddlesome solicitude for every fancied want of a once self-reliant citizenry were pyramided and compounded in this message." In Britain, especially after the advent of Margaret Thatcher as Prime Minister, such compassion was derogated as "the nanny state." See WORKFARE.

Welfare—the word, without the *state*—has had a curious history. From the verbal phrase *wel fare*, "to fare well," it began as a cousin of its turnaround *farewell*, and was used by Shakespeare politically in *Henry VI*, as Warwick advised "study for the people's welfare." In the U.S. the word first appeared in its aid-to-people sense in a 1904 *Century Magazine* article: "the welfare manager ... is a recognized intermediary between the employers and employees of mercantile houses and manufacturing plants."

The name of an island next to Manhattan, in the East River, gives a clue to the fortunes of the word in recent years. Blackwell's Island, the site of a prison, was renamed Welfare Island in the '30s, as some of its facilities were turned to other than penal use. In the '70s, when housing developers wanted to rent out apartments on the island, they insisted on a name change—"welfare" was too evocative of charity and the poor. It is now Roosevelt Island.

Welliver Society See SPEECHWRITER.

Weltanschauung World view.

The use of foreign words for political concepts or practices is usually regarded as pretentious by politicians. News magazines may write of a candidate's *apparat* being concerned with REALPOLITIK, but neither of the words is in the spoken tongue. DÉTENTE made it; *entente* has not been received cordially.

Columnist Joseph Alsop, wrote Douglass Cater in *The Fourth Branch of Government*, "can claim to have a reasoned *Weltanschauung.*" Thermonuclear thinker Herman Kahn countered his critics by saying that "often the reluctance to think about these problems is not caused by the advocacy of any particular *Weltanschauung.* Rather it is based on nothing sounder that a supernatural fear of the magical power of words." See UNTHINKABLE THOUGHTS.

Other German words used tangentially in politics are *Zeitgeist* (spirit of the age), *Schadenfreude* (the guilty pleasure one feels at the sufferings of others), *Weltschmerz* (world-weariness), and *Fingerspitzengefühl* (translated by Hildegard Mahoney as "a sandpapered-fingertip 'feel' for nuances").

we Polked you in 1844, we'll Pierce you in 1852 See SLOGAN; DARK HORSE.

we shall overcome Civil rights chant of the early '60s.

More than any other song, "We Shall Overcome" was the anthem of the civil rights movement led by black "moderates"; it was one of the highlights of the nonviolent 1963 March on Washington and was sung in front of the Lincoln Memorial.

Arthur Schlesinger, Jr., called the tune "an old Baptist hymn." John Anthony Scott in *The Ballad of America* chose "an old spiritual" originating among coal miners of West Virginia in the early New Deal days. *Bartlett's Familiar Quotations* credits the hymn to C. Albert Tindley, born a slave, died in 1933, a minister and hymn writer. Stevenson's *MacMillan Book of Quotations* credits the tune to Mrs. Zilphia Horton, a musician and folklorist who helped run the Highlander Folk School in Tennessee, known for its critical role in the civil rights movement, from the 1930s to her death in 1956, and additional verses to folk singers Pete Seeger, Frank Hamilton, and Guy Carawan in 1962.

The words were familiar to every civil rights marcher:

> *We shall end Jim Crow, we shall end Jim Crow,*
> *We shall end Jim Crow some day, some day;*
> *Oh, deep in my heart, I know that I do believe*
> *We shall end Jim Crow some day.*
> *We shall overcome, we shall overcome,*
> *We shall overcome some day, some day;*
> *Oh, deep in my heart, I know that I do believe*
> *We shall overcome some day.*

President Johnson chose it as his text in a speech to a joint session of Congress in 1965, urging them to adopt a voting rights bill: "It is not just Negroes but really it is all of us who must overcome the crippling legacy of bigotry and injustice. And we shall overcome ... these enemies, too, poverty, disease, and ignorance, we shall overcome."

wets A word attacking liberals or believers in accommodation; Britishism for *doves*.

When West German Chancellor Helmut Kohl was criticized for undercutting American policy in 1989, an unidentified American official told London's *Sunday Telegraph*: "We are used to such NATO antics from the alliance's wets like Belgium and the Netherlands, but to experience a STAB IN THE BACK like this from the Germans really does shake my faith in NATO." The paper's headline read "A 'Stab in the Back' by NATO's New Wets."

In British slang, *wet* has been used as an adjective for "ineffectual" or "inept" since World War I; in American slang, *drip, nerd, dork*, or the Yiddish *nebbish* is used to label that type of person. The *OED* defines the political use of the noun *wet* as "a politician with liberal or middle-of-the-road views on controversial issues (and was applied to members of the Conservative Party opposed to the monetarist policies of Margaret Thatcher)."

Wrote *The Observer* in 1981: "The term 'Wet' was originally used by Mrs. Thatcher, who meant it in the old sense of 'soppy,' as in 'What do you mean the unions won't like it, Jim? Don't be so wet.' It meant feeble, liable to take the easy option, lacking intellectual and political hardness. Like so many insults, it was gleefully adopted by its victims, and so came by its present meaning of liberal, leftish, anti-ideological." (*Soppy* comes from *sop*, a piece of bread or cake dipped in honey, as in *a sop to Cerberus*, the appeasement offered to the three-headed hound guarding the entrance to Hades in Greek mythology. Leftist, dovish politicians range from *dripping wet, sopping wet*, to the extreme, *wringing wet*.)

The antonym for the adjective-turned-noun *wet*, of course, is *dry*. (The same words in United States politics once applied to those for or against the prohibition of alcohol, a long-forgotten controversy except in places like Roxbury, Conn., which put the issue of alcohol sale on the ballot in 2007.) Melbourne's *The Age* commented in 1983 on British politics: "In contrast to the expansionist, protectionist and welfare-oriented Wets, the Dries stand for small government, economic rationality and individual responsibility."

we will bury you An offhand remark by a Russian leader that was taken to be the height of truculence by Westerners.

"Whether you like it or not," Nikita Khrushchev told Western diplomats at a Kremlin reception in November 1956, "history is on our side. We will bury you."

He chose the wrong verb. In context, he appears to have meant "outstrip," "outlast," or "leave you far behind." The reaction to the word he chose, however, was shock and anger: *bury* was a word too close to death. Two years later *Pravda* quoted the Soviet leader in a clarification: "My life would be too short to bury every one of you if this were to occur to me. ... I said that in the course of historical progress and in the historical sense, capitalism would be buried and communism would come to replace capitalism."

One of the Russian leader's favorite expressions was the picturesque peasant threat "We'll show you Kuzka's mother!" (*kuzka* being a kind of grain beetle, and its "mother" being the deeply buried larva); the hopelessly overmatched interpreters gave up and started translating this as the more familiar and comprehensible "We will bury you." (For this eye-opener the lexicographer is grateful to editor and researcher Stephen Dodson.)

Khrushchev was never able to inter the statement. After a while, he took it philosophically. To a group of Westerners in the audience in Yugoslavia, he tacitly accepted the simplistic translation and remarked, "I once said, 'We will bury you,' and I got into trouble with it. Of course we will not bury you with a shovel. Your own working class will bury you."

It was too wide a rhetorical opening for Western politicians to let pass. Six months later, in his first State of the Union message, Lyndon Johnson made a point of it again. "We intend to bury no one—and we do not intend to be buried."

what's good for General Motors…is good for the country A misquotation used to show the supposed big-business bias of the Eisenhower Administration.

Charles E. Wilson, called "Engine Charlie" to distinguish him from the former head of General Electric, Charles E. ("Electric Charlie") Wilson, gave a fairly innocent answer to a question posed by a senator at the hearing before approval of his nomination for Secretary of Defense: "if a situation did arise where you had to make a decision which was extremely adverse to the interests of your stock and General Motors Corporation, or any of these other companies, or extremely adverse to the company, in the interests of the United States Government, could you make that decision?"

Mr. Wilson: "Yes, sir, I could. I cannot conceive of one because for years I thought what was good for our country was good for General Motors, and vice versa. The difference did not exist. Our country is too big. It goes with the welfare of the country. Our contribution to the nation is considerable."

As Eisenhower put it in his memoirs: "This was interpreted and broadcast—it still is—in the form of 'What is good for General Motors is good for the country,' and of course the breast-beaters had a field day."

The construction has become locked into the political lexicon, taking many forms. In 1970 President Nixon told black leader Whitney Young, Jr., shortly before his death: "To paraphrase a former Defense Secretary, what's good for the Urban League is good for the country."

See BIRD DOG … KENNEL DOG.

wheelhorse Dependable party member; a regular.

A wheelhorse in a team is one that bears the most weight; hitched between the shafts, he pulls more of a load than the leader. Like WAR HORSE, the phrase has been used politically for over a century; the Marion (Ohio) *Buckeye Eagle* wrote in 1848 about Lewis Cass that he "has been the very wheel horse on which the party has relied to carry through all their great measures."

Historian Eric Goldman, writing about the struggle to find a vice presidential nominee for Harry Truman in 1948: "Finally a sacrificial victim was found—the faithful party wheelhorse Alben Barkley."

John F. Kennedy used the word in 1960, discussing his early days as a congressman: "We were just worms over in the House—nobody paid much attention to us nationally. And I had come back from the service, not as a Democratic wheelhorse who came up through the ranks. I came in sort of sideways."

wheels within wheels The minutiae of government; the infinitely detailed workings that a leader must not concern himself with, at the peril of wasting the time needed for broad policy.

Wendell L. Willkie, defeated Republican nominee in 1940, gave this phrase political context in a 1943 *Reader's Digest* article titled: "Better Management, Please, Mr. President!" Willkie held that Roosevelt was too "zealous for the accumulation of power and loath to disburse it," and pointed out that the presidency of the United States "is not a small-claims court." His main point: "The President's desk is cluttered and his mind distracted by his concern with the wheels within wheels, the foremen and the subforemen of our gigantic Federal machine. He is his own supervisor and trouble shooter. Broken parts are brought to him for patching and he undertakes to patch them. Bruised feelings are brought for his treatment and he sets about anointing them. No man could do all these things well. No President should try."

The phrase probably comes from the Bible, Ezekiel 1:16: "Their work was as it were a wheel in the middle of a wheel." The expression was used in Shaftesbury's *Characteristicks* in 1709: "Thus we have *Wheels within Wheels*. And in some National Constitutions...we have *one Empire within another*."

Other uses of *wheel* in American slang often applied to politics are *big wheel*, a derogatory term for a man of authority and power, probably derived from "the man at the wheel"; and *wheeler-dealer*, one who acts independently, ruthlessly, and often unethically, probably derived from gambling's roulette wheel (*wheeler*) and card shark (*dealer*).

whip A party leader, chosen in caucus, who makes certain that members are present for important votes, and urges them to vote the way the leadership wants.

The *party whip* must be tough and tactful; he is expected to turn out every member on crucial party-line votes. In recent years in the U.S., the whip's job is considered the best STEPPING-STONE to party congressional leadership.

The word comes from *whipper-in*, a man assigned to keep the hounds from straying in a fox hunt, and was turned into a political word in England in the eighteenth century. Benjamin Disraeli said the Government Chief Whip's office required "consummate knowledge of human nature, the most amiable flexibility, and complete self-control."

In Britain, a *documentary whip* is a weekly agenda sent to Members of Parliament, with attendance requirements underlined. Sir Wilfred Lawson explained that a one-line whip meant "you ought to attend"; a two-line whip meant "you should attend"; a three-line whip meant "you must attend"; and a four-line whip "stay away at your peril."

The official name of the party whip in the U.S. is *assistant floor leader*. Its original whipping-in meaning is illustrated in an observation made by General Maxwell Taylor, who explained the relationship of the Chairman of the Joint Chiefs of Staff to the other chiefs of staff: "a sort of party whip, charged with conveying the official line to the chiefs."

whipsaw Corruptly to accept money from both sides in a dispute.

In lumbering, a *whipsaw*—operated by two men—cuts both ways; in poker, two players in collusion bid up the pot to cheat a third; in the business of bribery, a legislator will *whipsaw* two opposing crooked lobbyists by accepting money for a "fix" from both and then delivering for only one.

Charles Ledyard Norton suggested in 1890 that the term originated in the New York State Legislature (cradle of LULUS). An Albany joke concerns a grafting boss who called two "fixers" into his office and said, "One of you paid me two thousand dollars to get this bill passed. The other paid me one thousand to get it killed. I want to be fair. How about the second guy paying me another thousand—making two even from each—and we'll debate the bill on its merits?"

whirlwind campaign A busy campaign, usually of short duration.

This DISASTER METAPHOR began in the Harrison–Van Buren campaign of 1840. A campaign that "spreads like a prairie fire" was already a political expression, and *whirlwind*—occasionally the result of a prairie fire—was a natural extension. "The prairies are on fire," wrote a Cleveland newspaper in 1840, "and the whirlwind they create will be felt east of the mountains."

In 1896 the *Review of Reviews* reported that William McKinley's FRONT-PORCH CAMPAIGN speeches were carefully prepared in advance, "punctuated with statistics and precise statements of fact which a 'whirlwind campaign' from a platform would not allow."

The phrase is in occasional current use: "Tom Gallagher returned to his political roots in Miami," reported *The Miami Herald* in 2006 about a GOP primary, "where he found welcoming crowds and a bit of good luck, while the whirlwind campaign of opponent Charlie Crist skidded to a close because of airplane trouble and rain." However, Crist blew in first and became Governor.

whispering campaign Word of foul mouth; an organized spreading of gossip, based in truth or not, about a candidate's morality, drinking or gambling habits, hidden influences, or possible mental or physical disability.

"Where there is whispering there is lying" is an English proverb traced back to 1678; John Randolph, fighting the WAR HAWKS in 1811, said his opponents' plan was "to assail me by every species of calumny and whisper, but Parthian-like never to show their faces or give battle on fixed ground." (Cavalrymen in ancient Parthia were known for shooting arrows at the enemy while retreating, remembered as a *Parthian shot*, worn down in usage to *parting shot*.)

In World War I, Germany's long-range naval gun sent shells high above the front lines known to Allied troops as "Whispering Willies," which may have influenced the phrase that first appeared in the presidential campaign of 1920. Democrats James Cox and Franklin D. Roosevelt, burdened by the unpopularity of the departing President Woodrow Wilson, faced Republicans Warren Harding and Calvin Coolidge. In its election issue, *The Nation* magazine suggested one reason that Harding (see OHIO GANG) won: "The scandalous underhandedness of the whispering campaign of the Democrats...only prove[s] the spuriousness of all their protestations of belief in equal rights for black and white."

The phrase *whispering campaign* became famous in the presidential campaign of 1928. In an Edwin Marcus cartoon,

a bigot with a rifle labeled "whispering campaign" was shown hiding behind a large jug labeled "prohibition issue," taking aim at candidate Al Smith. The anti-Catholic rumors (see UNPACK) undoubtedly harmed the New York Governor's candidacy, though he was beaten more by general prosperity and his outspoken opposition to Prohibition, which he said led to bootlegging and crime. After the campaign, Smith wrote: "I was probably the outstanding victim of the last half-century of a whispering campaign." (See HAPPY WARRIOR.)

Reporter Elliott Bell wrote of a similar campaign attacking Franklin Roosevelt as "mentally deranged" in the early New Deal days. "It came out in the course of a Senate investigation that an obscure and misguided publicity man had conceived the idea of undermining the President by a whispering campaign to the effect that his mind was unbalanced."

John F. Kennedy in 1960 suffered from a whispering campaign—unconnected to his Catholicism—about his back ailment. Before the Democratic convention, Lyndon Johnson supporters spread word of Kennedy having the debilitating Addison's disease, which was at first ignored and later brushed off by his doctors as "a mild adrenal deficiency"; the whispers turned out to be true, but the episode is still classified as a *whispering campaign*, suggesting that the meaning comes from the method of dissemination rather than the content. See ROORBACK; SMEAR.

whistleblower A government employee who "goes public" with complaints of mismanagement or corruption in his agency.

On June 13, 1977, the Institute for Policy Studies in Washington called together a "conference on whistleblowing," to focus "on government harassment of workers who publicly disclose mismanagement, illegality and other wrongdoing by agency heads." In December of that year, *Village Voice* writers James Ridgeway and Alexander Cockburn used the expression in print: "Then there is the case of whistle-blower Dr. J. Anthony Morris. He has long argued against government inoculation programs (including the swine-flu-shot fiasco). Morris recently lost his case in the Civil Service Commission."

The figurative blowing of the policeman's whistle can be a reason for, or an excuse for, being fired. After widespread layoffs at the CIA in late 1977, John Kendall of the *Los Angeles Times* wrote about one of those dismissed: "For half his career he says he considered himself a 'whistle blower' who tried to correct perceived faults in the CIA's domestic operations." When the CIA retorted that the man had been fired for insubordination, the ex-employee said he "became a 'whistleblower' to correct [abuses] with full realization he was harming his career."

Whistleblower has a positive connotation (contrary to its predecessor slang term, *whistler*, for "police informer"); the phrase portrays a public servant risking his job by publicly making noise to call attention to a scandal. A related term is *leaker* (see LEAK; PLUMBER), which connotes stealthiness in exposure and describes an employee not willing to risk dismissal by becoming known as a SOURCE.

whistlestopping Going to the people by railroad train with a series of short, ad-lib speeches in small communities, to give the impression of an old-fashioned campaign.

The *Jackson* (Tennessee) *Sun* gave the background of the word in 1952:

> A "whistle-stop," in railroad terms, is a community too small to enjoy a regular scheduled service. Customarily, the passenger trains whiz right by. But if there are passengers to be discharged, shortly before the train approaches the station, the conductor signifies that fact by pulling the signal cord. The engineer responds with two toots of the whistle. Naturally enough, such unscheduled pauses became known as "whistle-stops." The communities were "whistle-stop towns," shortened in the course of time to "whistle-stops."

In March of 1948, the *Wisconsin Rapids Daily Tribune* reported that President Harry Truman "will be following two Tafts, the senator and his wife, Martha, who have scheduled separate whistle-stop tours April 5, 6 and 7." Truman recalled he had discovered a gift for ad-libbing speeches one month later, in May: "My first formal experience at extemporaneous speaking had come just a few weeks before I opened the whistle-stop tour in June. After reading an address to the American Society of Newspaper Editors in April, I decided to talk 'off the cuff' on American relations with Russia. When I finished my remarks about thirty minutes later, I was surprised to get the most enthusiastic applause."

Truman made an old-fashioned back-of-the-platform railroad tour of the nation, ad-libbing seventy-one out of seventy-six speeches. Senator Robert A. Taft, speaking to the Union League Club in Philadelphia, derided the spectacle of an American president "black-guarding Congress at whistle-stops all across the country." That was Taft's blunder; "whistlestop" was an insult to a town, nearly as bad as calling its residents "hicks." Railroad men had stopped calling small stations *whistlestops* years before, preferring *flag stop* or *flag station* so as not to offend the citizens of small towns.

The Democratic National Committee wired the mayors of thirty-five cities through which Truman had passed, asking if they agreed with Taft's slur on their civic importance. "Very poor taste," said the mayor of Gary, Indiana; "Must have the wrong city," replied the mayor of Eugene, Oregon. (For another Republican train disaster, see Thomas Dewey's "idiot engineer" remark under BLOOPER.)

Truman said later about the word *whistlestop*: "You know, that phrase was invented by Senator Taft on October 8, 1948. The Republicans were trying to make fun of my efforts to take the issues in that campaign directly to the people all over the country." He was mistaken about the coinage, but right about the impact. "It was the whole performance at the 'whistle-stops' that was the story," reported the *Berkshire Evening Eagle* (Pittsfield, Mass.) on June 18, 1948, "the talk by the President in his easy, informal colloquial manner ... entirely different from that gained by reading some isolated sentence or two from what he said."

An AP report showed how the word had become locked into politics in this 1952 lead: "Whistlestopper Harry S. Truman lent a hand to Adlai Stevenson here Saturday in the biggest 'whistlestop' of them all." The reference was to New York City.

In 1968, to provide photographers with a heartland-of-America picture, candidate Richard Nixon rented a train to roll through Ohio; it was there that an aide said he spotted a sign that read BRING US TOGETHER.

In the 1976 campaign President Gerald Ford hired a riverboat to cruise into the heart of Jimmy Carter strength in the South; it was called "the whistlefloat." (Evidently any conveyance used by a candidate to reach small towns can be described as a whistle-whatever.) In 1984, *The Wall Street Journal* described President Ronald Reagan, with "the late afternoon sun slanting through the trees, standing on the observation platform of beautiful old U.S. No. 1, the Pullman car used in earlier whistle-stop campaigns by Franklin Roosevelt and Harry Truman." That was more photo-op than whistlestop.

white backlash See BACKLASH.

white hats The good guys.

Liberal members of Washington's permanent establishment drew a distinction among Nixon Administration officials in this Western-movie metaphor, where heroes wear white hats and villains wear black.

"White-hat" status was given Robert Finch, Leonard Garment, Elliot Richardson, Peter Flanigan, Henry Kissinger, George Shultz, and Peter Peterson, among others; viewed as "black hats" by liberal hostesses were John Mitchell, H. R. Haldeman, Murray Chotiner, Charles Colson, and anyone associated with Vice President Agnew.

The phrase was given currency in the late '60s by TV commentator and hostess Barbara Howar, who once invited this writer to a party with the admonition: "Wear your white hat."

The white hat has an ancient political history. In fourteenth-century Flanders, the badge of the democratic party, led by Ghent brewer Jacob von Artevelde, was the white hat. In England, during the administrations of the Duke of Wellington and Robert Peel, radical protesters wore the white hat as a form of derision.

The metaphor lends itself to cartoon treatment. On the cover of *National Journal* in December 1977, a group of black-hatted cloak-and-dagger types were shown marching into the office of reform-minded Director of Central Intelligence Stansfield Turner, and then marching out wearing white hats.

In India, as in the U.S., the white hat is a symbol of political purity. "Before the last few shifts of the sands of Indian politics," wrote *New York Times* correspondent William Borders from New Delhi in 1978, "it was possible to identify Congress Party members by their starchy white 'Gandhi caps,' named after Mohandas K. Gandhi, the independence hero. But now the caps are worn on all sides." See BLACK HATS.

White House The metaphoric center of executive power; or the place where the president of the U.S. is at any moment; or the Executive Mansion in Washington, D.C.

The *White House*, in its figurative and most often used sense, is the presidency. A *White House spokesman* is a presidential spokesman. The extended *White House Office* includes staffers who do not have a pass to get into the President's house.

To Americans, it combines the tradition of Buckingham Palace with Britain's working center of power at 10 Downing Street. Its symbolism is evident in this mid-'60s use by *Ebony* magazine: "There is a joke going the rounds about a telephone conversation between Martin Luther King and John F. Kennedy. Says the President: 'Yes, Dr. King. I know, Dr. King. I understand, Dr. King. But Dr. King—it has always been known as the *White* House!'"

The second sense of the usage, as a dateline, was described by Dwight Eisenhower: "The dateline 'White House' carries a meaning far broader than a mere structure or location; the White House, in newspaper stories, always means the President's headquarters, all the time, even when dispatches identify it as the 'Summer' or the 'Vacation' [or 'western'] White House."

As a specific house, it was known as the *Executive Mansion* (which is its formal title) until its destruction by the British in

1814, when it was rebuilt and painted white and became known informally as the *White House*. Theodore Roosevelt changed the stationery from "Executive Mansion" to "The White House," formalizing the name.

As a place to live, its prisonlike, goldfish-bowl, transient nature gets complaints from its residents. Harry Truman called it "a big white jail"; Theodore Roosevelt said, "You don't live there, you're only Exhibit A to the country." And when a senator joked to Calvin Coolidge, "I wonder who lives there," the President gave it the necessary note of transience: "Nobody. They just come and go."

In calibrating the structure of power, the OVAL OFFICE gets the most attention; then the West Wing (with a sub-category of the SIT ROOM); and finally the most general, the White House. Carter presidential aide Hamilton Jordan informed the author that when he and his colleagues placed phone calls, there was little of the imperious "The White House is on the line"; in fact, he reported that Attorney General Griffin Bell liked to say, "The White House is a building. Don't tell me 'the White House' is calling—I work for the President."

white man's war See RICH MAN'S WAR, POOR MAN'S FIGHT.

white paper A statement of official government policy with background documentation.

In the U.S., a *blue book* is usually a directory of the social elite; in England, it is an extended explanation of government policy, bound in blue covers. (See RED TAPE.) *White Paper* was the English terminology for a report too short to be bound as a blue book, and that phrase was adopted in the U.S.

American political usage leans harder on the background than the policy. (Ted Sorensen: "All the economists in government were to pull together a 'Fact Book' or 'White Paper' on steel to be widely distributed.") *The Washington Post* in 1985 requested evidence from the State Department to support Ronald Reagan's assertion that Nicaragua was "a focal point for the world terrorist network"; the newspaper reported what was received: "The unclassified documents included several recent and not-so-recent public 'white papers' and briefing transcripts that outline Administration views. ..."

Black book is a newer variation. (*Wall Street Journal*, 1967: "Israel published a 'black book' charging that Soviet propaganda paved the way for justifying an Arab attack on Israel.") *White Paper* (usually capitalized) is an official statement with the government rationale; a POSITION PAPER is an unofficial document that can be synonymous with *aide-mémoire* in diplomacy, or may mean a candidate's stand with background; *blue book* is limited to Great Britain and means a lengthy statement of policy; a *black book* is a documented charge or attacking brief, and the *black briefing book* is in some administrations the loose-leaf notebook the president of the U.S. studies before news conferences.

whitewash See SMEAR; WITCH HUNT.

Whitewater Real estate venture in the Ozarks that became the basis for an investigation that roiled the body politic from 1994 to 2000 and resulted in the impeachment of President Bill Clinton.

Whitewater was the name of a 230-acre tract of forested land along the White River in northern Arkansas, purchased in 1978 for some $200,000 by Bill Clinton and Hillary Rodham Clinton in partnership with another couple, James and Susan McDougal. (Clinton was the Arkansas state attorney general at the time.) The plan was to subdivide the parcel into lots for vacation homes, but it never worked out, and the Clintons claimed to have lost more than $68,000 when they sold their shares prior to his inauguration as president in 1993.

New York Times reporter Jeff Gerth raised questions in a series of articles, beginning March 8, 1992, about the propriety of such an investment by a public official. The reporter focused on tax deductions taken by the Clintons and about their connections with Madison Guaranty Savings and Loan, a bank purchased by James

McDougal in 1982 that had to be bailed out at taxpayer expense after it failed in 1989, along with many other S&Ls throughout the nation.

A series of independent counsels—Robert Fiske, Kenneth Starr, and Robert Ray—along with the House and Senate banking committees and a special Senate Whitewater committee investigated the Whitewater affair and surrounding events, including the suicide in 1993 of White House deputy counsel Vince Foster. Fifteen people, among them the McDougals and the governor of Arkansas, Jim Guy Tucker, eventually were convicted on various charges, including fraud, embezzlement, and conspiracy.

The scope of the investigation was expanded in early 1998 by Starr to include allegations that President Clinton had had a sexual relationship with Monica Lewinsky, a White House intern. Clinton's denial of this (see IS IS, MEANING OF) led to his impeachment at the end of the year in the House of Representatives by an essentially party-line vote on charges of perjury and obstruction of justice. The Senate acquitted him after a trial in January 1999, with enough Republican senators breaking ranks so that a majority could not be obtained for either article of impeachment.

The Whitewater investigation concluded in September 2000, six years and $60 million later, when Richard Ray, the last of the independent counsels, released a report stating, "This office determined that the evidence was insufficient to prove to a jury beyond a reasonable doubt that either President or Mrs. Clinton knowingly participated in any criminal conduct." See VAST RIGHT-WING CONSPIRACY.

Whiz Kids The relatively young executive team skilled in the latest management methods, brought to the Defense Department in 1961 by Secretary Robert McNamara.

At 45, McNamara was a member of the original "Whiz Kids" at the Ford Motor Company, one of ten Army Air Force statistical-control experts who came to Ford in a group in 1946 (Arjay Miller, later Ford president, was also a member).

The Ford nickname was picked up by Pentagon officials who resented what they felt was high-handed, ruthless administration by youthful civilians who relied too heavily on "thinking machines."

Meanwhile, back at Ford, *Fortune* magazine reported in 1966: "There's another generation of Whiz Kids at Ford—they're young, unabashedly brainy, boundlessly aggressive, open to new ideas—and they don't want to be called 'Whiz Kids.'"

The McNamara group at the Pentagon often relied on PERT—the Program Evaluation and Review Technique—a computerized decision-indicating method of pointing to the "critical path" that will most efficiently produce a new weapons system. Their espousal of this advanced technique reinforced the "Whiz Kid" image of them held by some military planners.

The word *whiz* came into American slang about 1880, probably as a short form of *wizard*; the phrase grew out of *The Quiz Kids*, a radio program of the forties featuring brilliant youngsters. *Whiz Kids* was probably first applied to the University of Illinois basketball team in the late 1940s.

who gets what, when, and how A frequent definition of politics, stressing its less spiritual rewards.

The phrase was coined by political scientist Harold Lasswell in 1936. Sidney Hillman in the 1944 *Political Primer for All Americans* added an introspective word to the definition: "Politics is the science of how who gets what, when and why."

"The structure of coalition politics," wrote James MacGregor Burns in 1963, "is inevitably the structure of 'who gets what, when and how' in American national politics. As the Madisonian system in being, it is also the structure of slowdown and stalemate in American Government." Burns was using the old definition in the sense of a division of the power of the executive; in most uses, it is a division of the spoils, like "slicing the pie" or "divvying up the melon."

For a more frequent and charitable definition of politics, see ART OF THE POSSIBLE. For the less uplifting side, see SPOILS SYSTEM and PATRONAGE.

whole hog See DYED-IN-THE-WOOL.

who-lost construction A charge of failure to foresee and avert foreign policy disaster.

"The HOT BUTTON ISSUE in the 1950's was 'Who lost China?'" said former president Richard Nixon in 1992. "If Yeltsin goes down, the question 'Who lost Russia?' will be an infinitely more devastating issue in the 1990s."

After Mao Zedong's Communists defeated Chiang Kai-shek's Kuomintang forces in China, conservatives in the U.S. criticized the failure of the Truman Administration, with its "Let the dust settle" policy (see WATCHFUL WAITING), to adequately support the anti-Communist forces, who had been forced to flee to Taiwan. The watchword of the right-wing Sinologists was "Who lost China?"

Although liberals liked to point out that China was not "ours" to lose, the attack phrase stung and put Democrats on the defensive. The construction, with its resonance of foreign-policy failure, was used again after the Bay of Pigs disaster, when Kennedy critics asked, "Who lost Cuba?"

Robert Blackwill, the National Security Council specialist on the Soviet Union during the early years of the elder Bush's Administration, was asked by the author during the Reagan Administration about White House refusal to back the Russian reformers who believed that PERESTROIKA was proceeding too slowly and was a mask for the continuance of Communism. Blackwill explained the continuance of the Reagan-Bush embrace of the current Moscow leadership with "There's the 'who-lost-Gorbachev' problem."

Fred Hiatt, editor of *The Washington Post*'s editorial page, picked up the classic construction, brushed it off, and used it ironically to make his point in the lead of a March 2007 column: "Who lost Russia? As the world's biggest country backslides ever more quickly into authoritarianism, the answer you hear increasingly is: the United States. Curiously, you hear it both from Russians, who simultaneously deny that anything bad has happened and blame America for it; and from Americans, who assume that a few tweaks of policy could have made everything come out differently in Moscow."

who's Polk? See DARK HORSE.

wiggle room Policy space in which to move around; ability to modify one's position and avoid political embarrassment through flexibility.

The sinuous gyrations of the phrase *wiggle room* began in the late '70s. *Business Week* reported in 1978: "Congress has drafted regulatory legislation in a way that gives agencies...as little 'wiggle room' as possible." A week later, *Newsweek* picked up on the phrase: "When it came to plugging Democratic candidates, Rosalynn Carter was sensitive enough to give each a little wiggle room—to dodge clear of her husband's political liabilities."

The undulation has not ceased. Mike Jendrzejczyk, Washington representative of Asia Watch, a human rights group, commented on Clinton Administration expectations for China in a 1993 strategy: "There's an enormous amount of wiggle room." And back to *Business Week* in the summer of 2007: "The Fed has little wiggle room as it tries to figure the balance of risk between inflation and growth." Later that pre-election year, a Marist College poll showed fewer than half of likely voters in the New Hampshire GOP primary "strongly supported" their candidate, which *The New York Times* headlined "Wiggle Room in New Hampshire."

Although the genteelism *wriggle room* sometimes sees print, the word is properly spelled *wiggle*.

wilderness years The "down time" of a politician's career; the difficult years between periods of popular acceptance or success.

A 1983 review in *The Washington Post* chronicles a drama about "a stubborn man, Winston Churchill in the 1930s, 'the wilderness years.'" This term, which expresses trying times for a politician, is a recent metaphor based on a biblical image. In the Hebrew Bible's Numbers 14, God tells Moses of the punishment for his faithless followers who left Egypt for the Promised Land: "And your children shall wander in the wilderness forty years... until your carcases be wasted in the wilderness."

Churchill picked up the term in his early writings; in 1905, he called Prime Minister Gladstone "that strange prophet of Israel who for thirty years had wandered in the wilderness of fiscal heresy"; writing of Moses, Churchill said, "Every prophet has to come from civilization, but every prophet has to go into the wilderness."

Richard Nixon, in the 1960s, often referred to the "wilderness years of de Gaulle and Churchill," comparing them to his own time of wandering in the wastes of public rejection between defeats in 1960 and 1962 and the comeback to victory in 1968. During difficult times in 1987, according to the *Chicago Tribune*, Ronald Reagan remained in the White House, "staffed largely by relative strangers who, unlike such longtime loyalists and family retainers as Michael Deaver, Ed Meese and Lyn Nofziger, were unknown to him in the wilderness years of his quest for the Presidency."

Jerry Brown used the phrase in 1992 in what the *Los Angeles Times* reported as "his so-called 'wilderness' years from 1983 to 1989, following his second gubernatorial term." Such a period of disfavor, however, can prove beneficial. Brown seemed to experience a biblical wandering during those wilderness years, commented the newspaper, "that enabled him to discover through travel, studies and writings a way to integrate his Roman Catholic religious values with political action."

According to Ta-kuang Chang, a New York attorney, a similar term can be found in the Chinese language. "The word *ye* ordinarily means 'wilderness,'" he informed the lexicographer, "but is commonly used in opposition to the word *chao* (meaning 'government' or, literally, 'the emperor's court') to refer to not being in government service and being among the people."

wimp factor Weakness, the noun *wimp* being "a weakling or sissy"; the adjective is *wimpy*; the verb *wimp out* also has a noun form, in the sense of "an ignominious retreat."

George H. W. Bush had to fight the *wimp* label for years prior to becoming president, despite having a distinguished service record in World War II. The AP reported in March of 1987: "Asked about charges that he is a wimp, Bush said 'I was shot down two months after my twentieth birthday, fighting for my country. I didn't detect any wimp factor then.'" When he told supporters that October, "you're going to see a tiger unleashed," the *Los Angeles Times* noted: "This remark appeared aimed a countering the so-called 'wimp factor' that has dogged the vice president in recent years."

Still, his announcement of his candidacy for president was greeted by a cover story in *Newsweek* with the headline, "Bush Battles the Wimp Factor." Bush was not above using the term himself, scribbling a note to Democratic Senator J. James Exon, of Nebraska, as a vote neared on President Ronald Reagan's Strategic Defense (aka Star Wars) Initiative in 1987: "I'm the pit bull of S.D.I., you Ivy League wimp."

Wimp, with its suggestion of weepiness, is one of the stronger attacks that can be made on any male politician—*wimp-baiting*, as it is sometime called. In Bush's case, the attack was reinforced pictorially. Editorial cartoonist Pat Oliphant portrayed him with a purse slung over his shoulder. Garry Trudeau called Bush a "wimp" in his *Doonesbury* strip and said that he had placed his manhood in a blind trust. Jules Feiffer denigrated him in a 1988 *Village Voice* cartoon as "a fake, a fool and a wimp." Characterizing the then vice president's efforts to gain support of conservative Republicans, columnist George Will savaged Bush by comparing him to a woman's canine companion: "The unpleasant sound Bush is emitting as he traipses from one conservative gathering to another is a thin, tinny 'arf'—the sound of a lapdog."

The elder Bush had plenty of company over the years as target of the *wimpiness* attack, many of them Democrats. (Democrats typically are cast as the *Mommy Party*, Republicans as the *Daddy Party*.)

Adlai Stevenson, the Democratic nominee for president in 1952 and 1956, was called "Adelaide"; Senator Walter Mondale, the Democratic candidate in 1984, confronted bumper stickers proclaiming "Mondale Eats Quiche" (Republican politico Ed Rollins said of Mondale that year, "There's no question there's a wimp factor"); Vice President Al Gore, the Democratic candidate in 2000, was ridiculed for allowing a feminist writer to help him refashion himself in "earth tones" as an alpha male; and 2004 candidate John Kerry was disparaged because he "looks French" and seemed to like things French, presumably including quiche.

Wimp is not limited to national politics. *Wimp factor* entered into the 1982 Illinois gubernatorial campaign after the Democratic candidate, former Senator Adlai Stevenson III (son of "Adelaide"), charged that Republican Gov. James Thompson "is saying, 'Me tough guy,' as if to imply I'm some kind of wimp." In California that year, an aide to Democratic Gov. Jerry Brown managed to put down his boss as well as his challenger for the Senate seat, San Diego Mayor Pete Wilson (who won the race), with the rhetorical question: "Why trade a flake for a wimp?" (*Flake* in the slang sense of "offbeat, eccentric" often was applied to Gov. Brown, roundly derogated for marching to the sound of his own drummer.)

Wimp entered the political lexicon on October 15, 1980, when an anonymous prankster at *The Boston Globe* changed the headline for an editorial about President Jimmy Carter's anti-inflation program from the platitudinous "All Must Share the Burden" to an overly acerbic "Mush from the Wimp." *Wimp* may have been influenced by J. Wellington *Wimpy*, Popeye's hamburger-loving friend in the *Thimble Theater* cartoon strip. More likely, it is a clipping of *whimper*. *Wimp*, meaning "young girl or woman," has been dated to the early twentieth century in British college slang. Sinclair Lewis referred to "Wimpish little men with spectacles" in *Arrowsmith*, published in 1925.

Whether or not they wear spectacles, "real men" remember. In June of 1991, well into his third year as president, George

H. W. Bush remarked to Andrew Rosenthal of *The New York Times:* "You're talking to the 'wimp.' You're talking to the guy that had a cover of a national magazine [*Newsweek*], that I'll never forgive, put that label on me."

The Wall Street Journal in 2007, hailing Senator John McCain's character in staunchly defending the younger Bush's perseverance in trying to win an unpopular war, recalled the elder Bush's feisty contretemps with a CBS anchor: "Presidential campaigns often have their defining media moments, for better or worse: think of Teddy Kennedy's fumbling replies to Roger Mudd's Chappaquiddick questions in 1979, or George H.W. Bush shaking off the wimp factor in his 1988 interview with Dan Rather."

windfall profits A sudden financial bonanza to a private firm or individual caused by a change in government policy.

In October 1977 President Jimmy Carter laced into the opponents of his energy program as "war profiteers" whose "windfall profits" constituted the "biggest ripoff in our history."

The word *windfall*, in its sense of an unexpected gift, such as a piece of fruit blown off a tree, has been in the language since the mid-sixteenth century. It was applied politically by Franklin Roosevelt in a message to Congress accompanying the 1936 Revenue Bill; the Supreme Court, in January of that year, had held a processing tax provision of the Agricultural Adjustment Act unconstitutional, and FDR's message was drawn to deny to processors a *windfall* from the tax they had already collected: "The first relates to the taxation of what may well be termed a 'windfall' received by certain taxpayers," wrote President Roosevelt on March 3, 1936. Supporting the Administration bill, Representative John McCormack of Massachusetts said on the House floor that "the tax on unjust enrichment" amounted to a "windfall."

An "excess profits tax" was used in World War I; it is still the formal name for the "windfall profits tax," which remains polemical.

Modifiers for profits have turned from *healthy* or *surging* to *swollen* and *obscene*. These last two are recognized as judgmental, while *windfall* is taken to be descriptive of something unexpected to the producer or retailer and unfair to the consumer.

winding down De-escalating; causing to come to an end gradually.

This was one of the oddest terms to come out of the war in Vietnam. The verb *to wind*, when followed by *up*, means "to conclude"; the noun *windup* means "conclusion." Therefore, the process of VIETNAMIZATION could logically have been called "the winding up of the war in Vietnam." But the term that came into use in 1969, and was ground into a cliché in 1970, was "winding *down* the war."

The metaphor appears to be that of a clock, which is wound up by hand and—in the process of doing its job—runs down, or may be said to "wind down." *Unwind* has a modern meaning of "relax." The trouble with the metaphor in this case is that *winding down* has a passive connotation—that is, one may permit a clock to wind itself down, but no action is taken to remove the tension in the mainspring. However, the term is used here in an active sense.

William Zinsser, in a 1971 issue of *Life* magazine, had some fun with the phrase: "I submit that if science tells us anything, it tells us that man can only wind things up. Indeed, in the long and restless search of *Homo sapiens* for mastery of his physical environment, one invention that continues to elude him is the downwinder."

Whatever the source, the term has come to mean the deliberate, steady pursuit of a policy to reduce the intensity of a war, in the hopes of an honorable extrication. House Speaker Nancy Pelosi, a Democrat urging rapid withdrawal of U.S. troops from Iraq in 2007, returned to that wartime metaphor with "We must work together to wind down this war."

window of opportunity Availability for action or attack.

Space jargon provided the source for the term *launch window* in the mid-1960s.

Walter Sullivan used it in quotation marks when he reported in *The New York Times* in 1967: "The Soviet and American vehicles flew to Venus close together because both were fired during one of the periodic 'windows' for such shots. These are brief periods of time when Venus is overtaking the Earth and relative positions of the two planets are propitious." Through that alignment, an imaginary hole or "window" in the sky allowed rockets to be launched successfully.

Another metaphoric window comes from the positioning of bank tellers at one time behind barred windows. The nation's *credit window* referred to the Federal Reserve's willingness to offer credit; the *gold window* named the Treasury's willingness to convert gold into dollars.

Flying to Camp David on August 13, 1971, aboard "Marine One," the presidential helicopter, the author asked Herbert Stein, the economist strapped in on my right, what the secret weekend meeting was to be about. "Closing the gold window" was the cryptic whisper. The passenger on my left, Paul Volcker—then Assistant Secretary of the Treasury for Monetary Policy, later chairman of the Federal Reserve—asked me what was so hush-hush about the suddenly convened meeting. I replied, not knowing the import of what I had just learned, "No big deal—I'm supposed to write a speech closing the gold window." The tall banker blanched, said "My God!" and put his face in his hands. I learned at the meeting that it meant ending the convertibility of the dollar into gold at $35 an ounce, stopping the outflow of the U.S. gold supply and causing the establishment of a new global economic order.

From these windows came the sense of "small space or short period to get something accomplished." The phrase *window of vulnerability* appeared in the mid-'70s. John Newhouse, a former arms-control official, noted that the term entered the Senate's Salt II hearings during the summer of 1979. Newhouse answered the lexicographer's query contemporaneously: "The phrase describes a time just ahead when improved Soviet missile forces will, in theory, be able to destroy most of America's silo-based Minuteman ICBM's in a literal bolt from the blue."

Ronald Reagan picked up the political usage in 1981. Defending a cut in defense spending, he explained on September 24, 1981, "I'll confess, I was reluctant about this, because of the long way we have to go before the dangerous window of vulnerability confronting us will be appreciably narrowed." See STAR WARS.

In language, art follows life: a *Los Angeles Times* review of a theatrical production in 2006 began: "There may not be a more up-to-the-minute play in town than 'Window of Opportunity,' a comedy-with-plot-twists that dissects the putrid moral innards of a corporate Croesus trying to manipulate his way out of an Enron-like scandal, while indulging in the call girls-a-la-carte lifestyle of a Yale-degreed, White House-connected, Teflon-coated scoundrel."

winds of change A fundamental shift in power or policy; an inexorable current that rushes pass attempts at control by political leaders.

The phrase was popularized in its present context by British Prime Minister Harold Macmillan in an address to the South African Parliament, February 4, 1960, speaking about the future of Africa: "The wind of change is blowing through the Continent. Whether we like it or not, this growth of national consciousness is a political fact."

In an editorial, *The Christian Science Monitor* later congratulated Macmillan (see UNFLAPPABLE) on coining an excellent expression, and pointed to *The Libation-bearers*, written by Aeschylus in 458 B.C.: "Zeus at last may cause our ill winds to change."

As with most memorable phrases, a long history can be traced, which does not detract from the ring of originality. Of course nothing is more changeable than the direction of the wind, but the use of the simple metaphor in the turmoil of African affairs was apt.

An early use of changing winds can be found in "Sweet William's Farewell to Black-Eyed Susan" by English poet John Gay (1685–1732):

We only part to meet again.
Change, as ye list, ye winds; my heart shall be
The faithful compass that still points to thee.

Typical use of the *wind* metaphor in modern times was by Indian Prime Minister Jawaharlal Nehru in 1947: "The masses are awake and they demand their heritage. Strong winds are blowing all over Asia. Let us not be afraid of them but rather welcome them for only with their help can we build the new Asia of our dreams."

Reporter John Gunther of the *Inside* books wrote of the Mormon community in Utah in 1947: "the astringent winds of a new world, which bewilder the older believers, are beating mercilessly at the pillar they drove into the desert." Sixty years later, with the emergence of former Massachusetts governor Mitt Romney, a Mormon, as a candidate for presidential nomination, new attention was paid to these "astringent winds."

Windy, of course, is slang for "long-winded," and is related to "full of hot air." "Winds of doctrine" was used by Milton in *Areopagitica* in 1644: "Though all the winds of doctrine were let loose to play upon the earth, so Truth be in the field, we do injuriously, by licensing and prohibiting, to misdoubt her strength." Philosopher George Santayana used Milton's *Winds of Doctrine* as the title of a book in 1913. In 1934 British Prime Minister Stanley Baldwin said: "There is a wind of nationalism and freedom blowing around the world."

When Harold Macmillan in retirement came to titling his own memoirs in 1966, he accepted the editing of common usage that changed his "wind of change" to "winds" and called his book *The Winds of Change*.

wingnut See MOONBAT.

winning See CAN'T-WIN TECHNIQUE; NO SUBSTITUTE FOR VICTORY; NO-WIN POLICY; ZERO-SUM GAME; PROVERBS AND AXIOMS, POLITICAL; and LOSER, SHOW ME A GOOD.

winning the peace Only victory promise made in LIMITED WARS.

When it became apparent in the late '60s that the cost of victory in South Vietnam would be too high, political emphasis in the U.S. shifted to an honorable settlement. Thus, in the 1968 primary campaign, Richard Nixon pledged to "end the war and win the peace," which caused supporters of George Romney to demand that Nixon make public his "SECRET PLAN to end the war."

The use of the word *win* appealed to those who were distressed at a NO-WIN POLICY and disturbed those who feared that military victory was Nixon's objective. As president, Nixon held to the policy, and occasionally the rhetoric, of "winning a peace"—through a withdrawal that he hoped would give the South Vietnamese "a reasonable chance of survival as a free people."

The phrase was based on the time-honored device of military terms to describe peace (see WAGING PEACE) and is taken directly from Will Rogers' aphorism: "The United States has never lost a war or won a peace." See NEVER LOST A WAR.

wiretap See TAPS AND BUGS.

wish list See ENEMIES LIST.

witch hunt Investigation characterized by hysteria.

Woodrow Wilson's Attorney General, A. Mitchell Palmer, led what was called a "Red hunt" just after World War I, finding "Communists under every bed."

The phrase *witch hunt*—an allusion to the Salem, Massachusetts, witch trials in the seventeenth century—is now applied to investigations considered to be motivated by a desire to capitalize on a popular fear. One of Eisenhower's campaign pledges made on the eve of election in 1952 was that we would engage in no "witch hunts or CHARACTER ASSASSINATION," adding that he would strive to "prevent infiltration of Communists and FELLOW TRAVELERS" into government that straddled the "McCarthy issue."

A *witch hunt*—an attack phrase on an attack—is the opposite of a *whitewash*

(see SMEAR), which is an attack on an exoneration. A witch hunt is a FISHING EXPEDITION with a vengeance.

Controller of the Currency John Heimann, in describing the ground rules for a 1977 investigation of Bert Lance by his office, showed a nice understanding of the Scylla and Charybdis of probes when he told his employees: "I want this to be neither a whitewash nor a witch hunt." Three decades later, a review of a book published in Canada drew on the old Salem image to call attention to the effect on civil liberty of the WAR ON TERROR. Its headline: "The witch-hunt for terrorists: An Ottawa author draws parallels between historic times of fear and paranoia and today's battle against terror."

with all deliberate speed The operative phrase in the U.S. Supreme Court decision striking down segregation in schools. See SEPARATE BUT EQUAL.

On May 17, 1954, in *Brown v. Board of Education*, the Supreme Court directed public schools throughout the U.S. to integrate; a year later, on May 31, 1955, another unanimous Court directed that this be done "with all deliberate speed."

In response to a query from the lexicographer about the 1968 *Green v. County School Board* decision (see ROOT AND BRANCH), Justice William J. Brennan, Jr. wrote: "It's the decision that abandoned the 'all deliberate speed' standard which had been adopted in the second *Brown* decision, *Brown v. Board of Education*, decided May 31, 1955. The pertinent quote from that opinion directs the district courts to enter orders 'as are necessary and proper to admit to public schools on a racially nondiscriminatory basis with all deliberate speed.'

"*Green* discarded this approach," noted Justice Brennan in his letter, "holding that 'The burden on a school board today is to come forward with a plan that promises realistically to work, and promises realistically to work now.'"

The question was soon raised: How speedy is "deliberate"? The Court obviously chose the phrase so as to give some flexibility to the lower courts in determining compliance, and the phrase became the center of legal controversy for the next decade. In 1964, writing for the majority in a decision ordering reopening of Virginia schools that closed rather than integrate, Hugo Black stated: "There has been entirely too much deliberation and not enough speed. The time for mere 'deliberate speed' has run out ..."

The near-oxymoronic phrase can be found in a poem by Francis Thompson, "The Hound of Heaven," written in 1893: "But with unhurrying chase / And unperturbed pace / Deliberate speed, majestic instancy ..."

The Supreme Court, however, probably chose the phrase from a 1912 decision by Justice Oliver Wendell Holmes, in the case of *Virginia v. West Virginia*: "a State cannot be expected to move with the celerity of a private business man; it is enough it proceeds, in the language of the English Chancery, with all deliberate speed."

Drawing on Holmes, Justice Felix Frankfurter used the phrase five times in cases preceding the desegregation decisions. Although scholars assume Justice Holmes knew what he was talking about in attributing the phrase to English Chancery practice, diligent research has failed to come up with a single quotable instance of its use. A fascinating clue was found in a letter from George Gordon, Lord Byron, to his publisher dated April 6, 1819. The poet had often been threatened with Chancery Court action, and in *Don Juan* wrote that his hero was "sole heir to a Chancery suit." Writing to John Murray, Byron complained of a previous exhaustion that obliged him to "reform my 'way of life' which was conducting me from the 'yellow leaf' to the ground with all deliberate speed." Certainty in phrase detection is rare; it can only be assumed that Byron drew the phrase from his Chancery experience.

Two years earlier, Sir Walter Scott's 1817 novel *Rob Roy* recounted a theft of valuable papers: "there was no mode of recovering it but by a suit at law, which was forthwith commenced, and proceeded, as our law-agents assured us, with all deliberate speed."

Much of the above information was provided the author by Supreme Court Justice Potter Stewart and Professor Alwin Thaler of the University of Tennessee. Justice William Brennan's contribution can be found under ROOT AND BRANCH. See also QUOTA.

In 1993, *Newsweek* commented on President Clinton's campaign promise to gay and lesbian groups to lift the military ban on homosexuals: "Even they must have been surprised by what were almost the first words out of his mouth after his election—that he would proceed with all deliberate speed to lift the restriction." (A compromise was struck with a "Don't ask, don't tell" policy.)

The oxymoron of slow speed has appeared in other forms. A more familiar Chancery phrase was "all convenient speed," which can also be found in Shakespeare's *The Merchant of Venice*; just before Shylock's trial, Portia sends Balthasar to consult a lawyer and her messenger assures her, "Madame, I go with all convenient speed."

President Lincoln approached this clash of meanings from another angle in 1861 when asked if he favored the immediate emancipation of the slaves. "It will do no good," he replied, "to go ahead any faster than the country will follow.... You know the old Latin motto, *festina lente*." (That motto, a frequent saying of Augustus Caesar, means "make haste slowly.")

Strictly speaking, *deliberate speed* is not always an oxymoron, a phrase or epigram built on the jarring juxtaposition of opposites, such as "thunderous silence" or "cruel kindness." It does not qualify as a full-fledged oxymoron (a word that columnist William Buckley Jr. liked to use because it sounds like an insult) for the reason that it is possible to have a *speedy deliberation*. See LOYAL OPPOSITION.

women's lib A movement promoting equal rights for women, more militant and culturally successful than similar women's rights and women's suffrage movements in the past; a phrase now taken as a put-down.

Betty Friedan, whose 1963 book *The Feminine Mystique* focused on the emptiness in the lives of suburban women, told the author that the phrase originated with the women of Students for a Democratic Society in the late '60s.

Feminist editor Gloria Steinem, in response to the author's query, confirmed this: "As far as I know, Women's Liberation is a phrase that sprang from the women of SNCC and the women of SDS... I think I first heard it early in 1967. Those women were very active. They went to jail with the men, demonstrated with the men, and earned Ph.D.'s with the men. Yet, when they got back to their organizational meetings they were supposed to make coffee, not revolutionary policy. This made it very clear to them that the revolution they were fighting was not necessarily going to benefit the other half of the human race.

"Shortening the phrase to Women's Lib," continued Ms. Steinem (who did much to popularize the honorific *Ms.*), "is a bit of ridicule perpetrated by the press. Would you say Black Lib? Puerto Rican Lib? I doubt it. The cavalier shortening is a kind of putdown in itself. Because of this, and because of the vast enlargement of the numbers of women involved, women now tend to say 'Women's Movement' rather than 'Women's Liberation'... comparable to 'Civil Rights Movement' as a phrase."

In its unshortened form, *women's liberation* was considered appropriate by many of its leaders. Kate Millett, who wrote *Sexual Politics* in 1970, said, "Women's Liberation is my life."

The attack phrases of the movement are *male chauvinist* (for origin of chauvinist, see SUPERPATRIOTS) and SEXISM.

An attack word on the most militant feminists, popularized in the early 1990s by Rush Limbaugh, the conservative radio polemicist, was *feminazi*. See CONSCIOUSNESS-RAISING.

woodshed, take him to the To punish briskly but gently.

The expression, its first printed citation in 1907, comes from taking a child out of the presence of others—in rural areas, to a woodshed outside the house—for punishment.

When the Reagan Director of the Office of Management and Budget, David Stockman, derided "Reaganomics" as "a Trojan horse" in a series of indiscreet interviews to William Greider of *The Atlantic Monthly* in 1981, the president summoned him to the White House for a meeting. Afterward, Stockman told reporters: "I hesitate to use metaphors after the bad luck I've had in recent days, but I grew up on a farm and I might say, therefore, that my visit to the Oval Office for lunch with the president was more in the nature of a visit to the woodshed after supper." The impression he left with his homely rural metaphor was that a paternal Reagan had properly chastised him but asked him to stay on, which he did until 1985.

In his 1986 memoir, *The Triumph of Politics*, Stockman's account changed. He quoted Reagan as asking, "You have hurt me. Why?" and after Stockman made a 15-minute apology for his derogation of the president's supply-side policy, Stockman quotes Reagan saying that the budget aide was "a victim of sabotage by the press. They're trying to bring you down because of what you have helped us accomplish." In Stockman's belatedly self-serving account, Reagan then told him to "write up a statement" with the help of loyal White House aides upset at his "Trojan horse" figure of speech—a statement that Stockman disavowed five years later as "a countermetaphor. A woodshed story. A self-inflicted public humiliation. So that afternoon I played out the script that the White House public relations men had designed."

A decade later, another budget director gave an equally revealing interview to a breakfast group of reporters. Leon Panetta said the free trade treaty with Mexico, supported by President Clinton, was "dead," and that expensive health reform legislation being prepared by Hillary Clinton should be delayed.

Asked about this, Bill Clinton laughed it off by referring to the Stockman metaphor: "I don't need to take him to the woodshed.... I need for him to sort of get his spirits up."

In 2007, the woodshed metaphor resurfaced when Stockman, a successful investment banker, was indicted for securities fraud. A writer for the liberal Slate online magazine, Jack Shafer, charged angrily that Stockman had admitted in his memoirs that his initial account was a "lie"—that "he never voyaged to the Reagan woodshed"—but that "two decades later, it still holds tighter than any truth." We may never know whether to believe the original assertion or the subsequent disavowal, but we can be certain that a homely metaphor at the right moment will echo though every newsworthy episode in a political figure's life.

-word Combining form used with an initial capital letter to refer euphemistically to an obscenity, a slur, or a political controversy.

This use of this form of initialese became popular during the mid-1980s, when a hyphen before the word *-question* was the more frequent combining form after a capitalized initial. When Gary Hart was asked at a news conference if he had ever committed adultery, many reporters considered such an imputation of immorality to be beyond the pale, recoiling at what was dubbed *the A-question*. After Judge Douglas H. Ginsburg was nominated to the Supreme Court, he was forced to admit that he'd smoked marijuana in the early 1970s and had to withdraw; Sam Donaldson of ABC called that issue "the *M-question*."

In the late '80s, *-word* took center stage. A *Washington Post* editorial noted the reluctance of candidates to talk about raising taxes after Walter Mondale's 1984 defeat: "They've been Mondaled. You say the T-word and you die." An editorial in *The New York Times* commented, "These days the mere mention of the U-word—unemployment—sends shivers through the ranks of Moscow's economic reformers."

This *-word* construction may be rooted in baby-talk euphemism. "The Rating Code office told me a mandatory R went to any film using one of 17 words," said Roy E. Disney, producer of the movie *Pacific High*, in a 1980 interview with the Associated Press. "The picture has four of what my mother calls 'that F-word.'"

The identification of a word by its initial letter expression is used in mock-horror to designate plain terms, as in *L-word* for "liberal." In print, blanks can be left in supposedly dirty words; as *The Washington Post* reported in 1987, "The only way even to begin to do these things is to raise t_____s."

By 1991, the use of *-word* had become so widespread a cliché that *The New York Times* felt compelled to editorialize on the subject. "The Cute Alphabet is filling up fast," it commented in 1991. "'R' has fallen, as in 'the R word,' the nervous euphemism for recession.... Last week President Bush swept up the 'Q' word, applying it to supposed quotas in employment."

The racist *N-word*, when used by non-blacks, remains taboo with most publications. (Black activist Dick Gregory titled his memoir *Nigger!*, which was taken to be an expression of legitimate protest.) The use of the full word, a staple of hip-hop and rap lyrics, was criticized after racist-sexist expressions were used by a white radio commentator in 2007, causing black musical impresarios to urge self-restraint. A federal court soon afterward ruled that the Federal Communications Commission had no authority to ban the live use of the *f-word* and the *s-word* (formerly known as "four-letter words") in their unbowdlerized form. The author does not use them here because they and their arch, initialized euphemisms have become bereft of their shock value.

workers See TROOPS, VOLUNTEERS.

work ethic The idea that work in itself is good for a person, molding character and inspiring a quality of thrift and an understanding of values.

In his 1904 *The Protestant Ethic and the Spirit of Capitalism*, the German sociologist Max Weber pointed to a paradox: although the pursuit of money was once regarded as unworthy of a Christian, and the possession of riches seen long ago as evidence of selfishness, in modern times religion has endowed material success with the aura of godliness. Calvinism's themes of hard work and personal asceticism led to the accumulation of fortunes, which was considered the mark of a good man—thus, went Weber's thesis, "the Puritan stood at the cradle of economic man," providing "good conscience in money making."

At its coinage, then, Weber intended the term *Protestant ethic* (later *Puritan ethic*, or *work ethic*) to be a derogation. It has since gained in stature and is now a compliment, politically popularized in the U.S. in a 1972 Labor Day speech by Richard Nixon. The president was impressed with a memorandum entitled "The Problem of the Blue-Collar Worker," written in 1970 by Assistant Secretary of Labor Jerome Rosow. Inflation and the cost of family education had driven up these workers' cost of living at a time when their income was topping out, the memo showed, and white-collar work had been glamorized while blue-collar jobs were denigrated as menial.

The author, then a White House speech-writer, was assigned a speech on the "dignity of work" to reassure these lower-middle-class ETHNICS that their work was respectable and respected, and—in retrospect—to exploit a resentment at a cultural trend that put too great a stress on intellectual endeavors while patronizing the calloused hand.

A speech was drafted on the work ethic; the president removed references to "Protestant" and broadcast the speech on radio: "As the name implies, the work ethic holds that labor is good in itself; that a man or woman at work not only makes a contribution to his fellow man, but becomes a better person by virtue of the act of working. The work ethic is ingrained in the American character. That is why most of us consider it immoral to be lazy or slothful—even if a person is well off enough not to work." (Here the president wrote in: "—or can avoid work by going on welfare.")

Liberal columnist Max Lerner, with an eye for sociology in politics, noted: "President Nixon's Labor Day sermonette on the work ethic was addressed not only to the traditional audience of union members but also to the South and Midwest, where the language of the work ethic is politically warming, and to the whole middle class which feels that honest work has gone down the drain."

The phrase is in current use, although it can trigger this riposte to politicians who evoke it: "What are you doing about people who have the work ethic but who cannot find jobs?"

workfare Conservative label for welfare reform, stressing an intent to "get people off welfare rolls and onto payrolls."

Harper's magazine in July 1968 discussed the goals of civil-rights leader James Charles Evers: "One of Evers' programs is what he calls workfare; he has said that everybody ought to work for what he gets."

In the late spring of 1969, the Nixon Administration's plan for the overhaul of the welfare system was at an impasse: counselors Arthur Burns and Daniel P. Moynihan differed on the need for a work requirement. George Shultz, then Labor Secretary, came up with a solution that was not a compromise, but a fresh approach: supplementing the incomes of the working poor, to provide an incentive to move from welfare to work.

Inside the government, the plan was originally called *Family Security*, but that was too much like Social Security; *Fair Share* was proposed, but that sounded to conservative members of the Administration too much like FAIR DEAL or *share the wealth*. At a cabinet meeting at Camp David, President Nixon directed some of the discussion of the plan to its name, because he had already decided on substance and wanted its opponents to get their licks in somewhere. *Family Assistance Plan* was decided upon, despite this writer's concern about the initials sounding like an expression—"fap!"—of a harrumphing old cartoon character named Major Hoople.

However, in his nationwide television address on August 8, 1969, the president tried out what his speechwriter believed to be a new word: "In the final analysis, we cannot talk our way out of poverty; we cannot legislate our way out of poverty; but this Nation can work its way out of poverty. What America needs now is not more welfare, but more *workfare*." In his message to

Congress three days later, he used the term again: "This would be the effect of the transformation of welfare into 'workfare,' a new work-rewarding program ..." (The author thought he had coined the word and was able to slip it into the president's speech and message over the objections of the plan's creators, but this "coinage" turns out to have been antedated by Charles Evers, as noted above, a Mississippi candidate for Congress in 1968.)

The emphasis on the work requirement—called "the conservative rhetoric"—was said to offend many liberals who ordinarily might be expected to support the program. Whether the rhetoric was the cause, or a resentment that this major social legislation should be credited to a longtime political adversary underlay it, the welfare reform legislation bogged down in a combination of conservative opposition and liberal lack of enthusiasm. To Moynihan's dismay, it was scorned as "Nixon's Good Deed"; it was brought back into political discourse by President Bill Clinton as "welfare reform."

Welfare, as a word, has fallen far from its heights as one of the basic national purposes described in the Constitution: "to promote the general welfare." See WELFARE STATE.

Work, on the other hand, is doing better all the time, despite the efforts to change *workers* into *employees* and ultimately to bloodless *personnel*. However, the '60s cofounder of the radical Yippies, Abbie Hoffman, called *work* "the only dirty four-letter word in the English language."

working group Committee, or group organized for a single cause or project; substitute for TASK FORCE

Originally *committee* was used for political action, but after it gained a connotation of pettifogging delay it was replaced by *task force* in the '60s. *Board* had its run in the New Deal era, and *council* (economic, domestic, national security) is still doing well. Replacing *task force* has been *group*, taken from British military aviation and later adopted by British business.

By the late 1970s, a gerund was used attributively to describe the activity of this latest designation: *working group*. Perhaps based on the use of *working lunch* for a business meal or *working vacation* to give a patina of activity to a time of relaxation, this phrase was being used in the White House in 1979. The committee working on the Strategic Arms Limitation Talks took the name of "the SALT working group." In 1993, Hillary Clinton and Ira Magaziner of the Clinton Health Care Task Force called many of its subdivisions "working groups." Not many synonyms for *committee* are left; keep an eye on *cluster*. See BLUE-RIBBON PANEL.

working the room/fence Ingratiating oneself with fellow guests; PRESSING THE FLESH of those who come to greet a candidate at an airport or a coffee-klatsch.

To *work* a room is to do a political job on a roomful of people—that is, to make an effort to greet each person individually, squeeze a hand or shoulder, nod sagely at a question, and move along.

Washington Post Style reporters Nancy Collins and Donnie Radcliffe wrote that at a 1977 Pan American reception in Washington, "Rosalynn Carter... instantly began working the room much as she had during the months Jimmy Carter was trying to win the White House." *New York Times* reporter Judith Miller wrote in 1982 that "Henry Kissinger, working the room like a politician, embraced Norman Podhoretz. ..." At a party given in her Georgetown home by Pamela Harriman in 1992, rising media star Tim Russert told media reporter Howard Kurtz: "I got five or six tips I'm pursuing.... I saw my competition working the room just as vigorously."

A more recent coinage is *working the fence*, the habit of politicians greeting the people lined up behind a fence, usually at an airport. When President Ford was shot at twice during a two-week period in 1975, Howard Flieger wrote in *U.S. News & World Report*: "The time is past due for the President and those who aspire to his job to stop 'working the fence.' That is a politician's term to describe the practice of candidates walking along the restraining lines at airports and such public places to shake as many hands and exchange as many greetings as possible.... It produced dramatic pictures for the TV news shows. It has come to be regarded by many politicians as the ultimate common touch—the modern-day equivalent of baby-kissing. And it is foolhardy."

But the practice continues as part of campaigning, and not just in America: *U.S. News* in 1987 described Mikhail Gorbachev as "jailing crooks, firing incompetents, attacking drunkenness, freeing the arts and media, working the fences like an American politician." In recent years an alternate meaning has emerged in the debate about immigration policy to describe the patrol activity of border control agents.

world opinion The moral force, real or imagined, of the anticipated reaction of uncommitted nations, or of leaders not firmly aligned with any regional association or international power group.

The idea is rooted in the Declaration of Independence: "a decent Respect to the Opinions of Mankind requires that they should declare the causes which impel them to the Separation.... To prove this, let Facts be submitted to a candid World." The phrase was probably written by Thomas Jefferson, who used it later: "The good opinion of mankind, like the lever of Archimedes with the given fulcrum, moves the world."

Daniel Webster, speaking to the House of Representatives in 1823 about the Greek revolution, gave the phrase its moral overtones: "Moral causes come into consideration, in proportion as the progress of knowledge is advanced; and the *public opinion* of the civilized world is rapidly gaining an ascendancy over mere brutal force."

After Jefferson, the phrase was most closely associated with President Woodrow Wilson, who used it in his PEACE WITHOUT VICTORY address in January 1917: "The present war must first be ended; but we owe it to candor and to a just regard for the opinion of mankind to say that, so far as our participation in guarantees of future peace is concerned, it makes a great deal of difference in

what way and upon what terms it is ended." In his speech, Wilson used *mankind* as in the Declaration of Independence. Thirteen months earlier, in a letter to Colonel House, he wrote: "If either party to the present war will let us say to the other that they are willing to discuss peace on such terms, it will clearly be our duty to use our utmost *moral* force to oblige the other to parley, and I do not see how they could stand in the *opinion of the world* if they refused."

Dwight Eisenhower, in his SPIRIT OF Geneva speech in 1955, gave a rhetorical, quasi-legal standing to world opinion as a kind of centrist arbiter: "The case of the several leading nations on both sides is on trial before the bar of world opinion."

As can be seen, many political leaders have made obeisances to "the opinion of mankind" and "world opinion" (which is now more frequently used than the Jeffersonian phrase). In practice, however, the requirements of national policy have often led to decisions contrary to the "dictates" of world opinion, as both Pakistan and India did in developing nuclear weapons.

In the twenty-first century, DOVES and REALISTS tend to give great weight to world opinion, while HAWKS and HARD-LINERS, though the lengthy war in Iraq has depleted their ranks, still take a more UNILATERALIST approach. Tony Blankley, writing in the conservative *Pittsburgh Tribune-Review*, warned in 2006 that "world opinion tends—to some extent—to shape American voter opinion. And voter opinion tends to shape American politicians' opinion. Thus over time world opinion may weaken American will to defend itself against the amorphous but deadly Islamist virus."

Ralph Waldo Emerson suggested an otherworldly kind of compromise in 1841: "It is easy in the world to live after the world's opinion; it is easy in solitude to live after our own; but the great man is he who in the midst of the crowd keeps with perfect sweetness the independence of solitude." See GO IT ALONE.

world policeman See POLICEMAN OF THE WORLD.

world view See WELTANSCHAUUNG.

wrap-up See ADVANCE MAN.

write-in A vote requiring the voter, by hand, writing in an unlisted candidate's name, rather than marking a ballot or pulling a lever next to a printed name.

Politicians go to great lengths to make voting easier for the voter. Party symbols (see PARTY EMBLEMS) appear above the line to reassure the nearly illiterate; parties jockey for the first line or column, as if the inside track provides greater speed; "sample ballots" are distributed as literature, with a large arrow pointing to the candidate's name and the rest of the ballot screened with a dull gray overlay. Accordingly, a "write-in"—where the voter has to work, rather than react—is given little chance of winning.

Dwight Eisenhower recalled the Minnesota primary of 1952, which gave a big boost to his candidacy: "The effort to promote a write-in vote had, as with the Madison Square Garden meeting, been opposed by persons who, while participating in the effort to make me a candidate, believed that any write-in effort was doomed to miserable failure and would have a depressing effect." For the result, see POLITICAL MIRACLE; RALLY.

In primary elections, however, a successful write-in campaign occasionally comes to pass. In 1964 in New Hampshire, a late-starting, enthusiastic campaign for former Senator Henry Cabot Lodge upset the well-financed campaigns of Barry Goldwater and Nelson Rockefeller.

The write-in can be used as a symbol of protest. Republican Senator Lincoln Chafee of Rhode Island, a strongly "blue" Democratic state, announced that instead of voting for President George W. Bush in 2004, he had written in the name of George

H.W. Bush, the 41st president. The half-bolting Chafee was defeated anyway in the GOP midterm debacle of 2006.

Write-in victories are likely to remain flukes until the era of Internet voting arrives. See CHAD.

wrong war A criticism of military strategy.

President Harry Truman and General Douglas MacArthur clashed in 1951 over the strategic course to take in Korea. As 200,000 Chinese Communist "VOLUNTEERS" swarmed across the Yalu River to retake North Korea, MacArthur wanted to strike back at China's "PRIVILEGED SANCTUARIES" in force, but the president restrained him. General Omar Bradley, Chairman of the Joint Chiefs of Staff, supported Truman's position before Congress, calling the MacArthur strategy "the wrong war, at the wrong place and at the wrong time, and with the wrong enemy." See the MacArthur response in NO SUBSTITUTE FOR VICTORY.

Critics of a "land war in Asia" (see LET ASIANS FIGHT ASIANS) have often termed this kind of involvement "the wrong war," though no "air war in Asia" is posed as "the right war."

Benjamin Franklin said, "There never was a good war or a bad peace," and educator Charles Eliot Norton, denouncing the Spanish-American War in 1898, said, "If a war be undertaken for the most righteous end, before the resources of peace have been tried and proved vain to secure it, that war has no defense, it is a national crime." The antonym to *wrong war* is *just war*; see WAR OF NATIONAL LIBERATION.

President Johnson used the same construction in a different way, as he appointed a lawyer who was black, Thurgood Marshall, to the U.S. Supreme Court in 1967: "I believe it is the right thing to do, the right time to do it, the right man and the right place."

X

X See MR. X.

Y

yahoo A political brute; or, a rambunctious anti-intellectual; or, a cry of exultation assumed as a corporate name.

Senator Herbert Lehman of New York walked down the Senate aisle to confront Senator Joseph McCarthy, only to be told, "Go back to your seat, old man." Stewart Alsop wrote in his 1968 book, *The Center*: "Thus old Senator Lehman's back, waddling off in retreat, seemed to symbolize the final defeat of decency and the triumph of the yahoos."

In 1970 a reader of *The Washington Post* wrote the editor: "Justice [William O.] Douglas makes a perfect target for the KNOW-NOTHINGS overrunning Washington.... The Yahoos are on the loose. Who is to stop them?"

In 1978, as Washington social pages reported blunders by "the Georgians" on the staff of President Carter, columnist Meg Greenfield wrote in *Newsweek*: "There are far too many Carter Administration Georgians in town who do not play the bumpkin game to lend credibility to the notion that the principal tension here is between a stuffy, decrepit Establishment and a bunch of bare-chested, peanut-feeding Yahoos."

The word comes from Jonathan Swift's *Gulliver's Travels*, written in 1726, coined by him to describe a race of brutes in the form of men who are slaves to the noble breed of *houyhnhnm*, highly intelligent horses (the name derived from the sound of whinnying). *Yahoo!*, with an exclamation point following, is also used as a cheer, similar to *yippee* and *hooray*, and the two senses combined in Edmund Yates's *The Rock Ahead* (1868), describing "a dam low-bred lot, yahooin' all over the place."

The trend is against capitalization in modern political use, which applies the word almost exclusively to anti-intellectual right-wingers (see REDNECK; DINOSAUR WING). In non-political use, the word has been thoroughly identified with the name of a corporation providing a web portal, a search engine, and other Internet services.

Yalta See MUNICH ANALOGY; OPEN COVENANTS.

yardsticks See GUIDELINES.

yellow dog Democrat An unswerving party loyalist; used only as a compliment or self-assertion.

A *yellow dog* is a cur. In labor terminology, a *yellow dog contract* is an agreement signed by employees not to join a union.

But the yellow dog has taken on a different political coloration as a Southern regionalism. When Senator Tom Heflin of Alabama refused to support fellow Democrat Al Smith in the 1928 election and bolted to Herbert Hoover, other Alabamans who disagreed with Heflin popularized the line "I'd vote for a yellow dog if he ran on the Democratic ticket."

This was hardly complimentary to Governor Smith, but it did illustrate the lengths to which some Southern Democrats would go in supporting the ticket. (See CLOTHESPIN VOTE.)

In 2006, *The New York Times* endorsed a local politician opposing Rep. Christopher Shays, a moderate Republican it had long supported, because "his reelection would help empower a party that is long overdue for a shake-up."

Columnist Michael Kinsley observed, "The term 'yellow-dog Democrat' used to mean someone who would vote for any Democrat over any Republican, even if the Democrat were a yellow dog. In recent decades there has been no such person, but this year the dog might have a shot." Shays squeaked through, becoming the only GOP House member left not only from Connecticut, but from all of New England.

The phrase is in active use as a Southern regionalism, an admiring description of a fellow REGULAR. Except for ATTACK DOG, politicians everywhere like a canine association: see FALA SPEECH; BRASS-COLLAR DEMOCRAT; BLUE DOG DEMOCRAT.

yes, but A fault-finding follower; one who supports a principle but refuses to help carry it out.

This was a coinage of Franklin D. Roosevelt's, when he was under fire in 1937 for trying to PURGE the Democratic party of its conservative members. Samuel Rosenman, his unstinting supporter and speechwriter, wrote in *Working with Roosevelt*: "He invented a new word to describe the Congressman who publicly approved a progressive objective but who always found something wrong with any specific proposal to gain that objective—a 'yes-but' fellow."

In 1952 Adlai Stevenson, a close student of Rooseveltian phrases, blasted his opposition in these terms: "The Republicans have a 'me, too' candidate running on a 'yes, but' platform, advised by a 'has been' staff."

The phrase, while never as popular as ME TOO, remains alive. Columnist Flora Lewis, writing with prescience about possible successors to French President Charles de Gaulle in 1967: "Emerging from the shadow of de Gaulle is...the lean, eager face of Valéry Giscard d'Estaing, who says 'yes, but' to de Gaullism to separate his profile from the crowd." Nearly four decades later, National Public Radio's senior news analyst, Daniel Schorr, said about the chances of Senator Hillary Rodham Clinton of gaining the Democratic nomination for president in 2008: "Many Democrats seem to be saying, 'I would vote for her, but I think a lot of other people wouldn't.' That's what you call the 'yes, but...' factor."

you can't beat somebody with nobody
Political proverb used when an "out" party is jubilant over the "in" party's unpopularity, and then is faced with the task of finding a well-known candidate.

Journalist and historian Mark Sullivan wrote in 1930: "When, finally, [Theodore] Roosevelt put his mind upon selecting his successor...he was moved by the axiom of practical politics that says, 'You can't beat somebody with nobody.'" The proverb was current at the turn of the century, and is often attributed to the crusty "Uncle Joe" Cannon, House Speaker from 1903 to 1911. However, Louis Sebold wrote in a 1915 *Boston Daily Globe*: "The logic of the sound political axiom first enunciated by Odell, the most sagacious of New York Republican leaders, 'that you can't beat somebody with nobody,' exactly applies to the conditions confronting the two political parties already planning for the next Presidential campaign." ("Odell" was presumably Benjamin B. Odell, Jr., N.Y. Representative and Governor in the years around 1900.) Republicans chose a somebody—Supreme Court Justice Charles Evans Hughes—but President Woodrow Wilson was reelected thanks to Western strength and a SOLID SOUTH.

Origin of the sage, if obvious, advice may be in a Lincoln anecdote, recorded in biographer-poet Carl Sandburg's writings, related by Everett McKinley Dirksen of Illinois on the floor of the Senate:

When I think of all the comments by persons who seem to think they are better able to do this job in the defense field than is the President of the United States, I think of the Committee on the Conduct of the War, which was established away back in the Civil War days. ... On that committee there was a man named Benjamin Wade, from Ohio. He started out as a canal driver and as a mule skinner. Then he became a teacher, as I recall, and then a lawyer. That qualified him to conduct a war.

He marched down to the White House, shook his finger at Lincoln, and said, "You have to fire General McClellan." Lincoln said, "Well, whom shall I use to replace him?" And Wade said, "Anybody." Lincoln, out of his majestic concepts, said, "I cannot fight a war with anybody; I must have somebody." Away back in those days we had a little of the same attitude which is now apparent.

During the 1992 Presidential campaign, the *Chicago Tribune* applied two clichés of CONVENTIONAL WISDOM to George H.W. Bush and Bill Clinton: "One cliché is that whenever a President is running for reelection, the campaign is a referendum on the incumbent. That has been the case in the past and makes sense, so it's probably true. And if it is, President Bush has already lost the election. But of course he has not, because this cliché runs up against another—you can't beat somebody with nobody—and a little-known candidate with questions about his past isn't going to get elected President." The first cliché prevailed.

See PROVERBS AND AXIOMS, POLITICAL; INS AND OUTS.

you can't fight city hall See GO FIGHT CITY HALL.

you never had it so good The slogan of an "in" party, stressing prosperity.

The Democratic party slogan in the 1952 Stevenson campaign against Eisenhower was "You Never Had It So Good." Those "madly for Adlai" were not enthusiastic about the slogan, since it appeared as a weak defense against the MESS IN WASHINGTON following Harry Truman, who left office with a Gallup rating in the low 20s. See K_1C_2. (In 2007, with George W. Bush's popularity rating sinking into the high 20s, *Newsweek*'s cover showed a famous picture of Harry Truman smiling and walking briskly, under a headline that read: "Wanted: A New Truman.")

Historian Arthur Schlesinger, Jr., looking back in 1965, tried to dissociate his friend Stevenson from the near-universal denigration of the Missouri haberdasher: "In the last days of Truman the party motto had been, 'You never had it so good.' The essence of the party appeal was not to demand exertions but to promise benefits. Stevenson changed all that."

In 1955 the British Conservative party did better with the slogan. The official Tory campaign theme was "Conservative Freedom Works" but the unofficial battle cry was taken from the American campaign three years earlier. British author John Montgomery wrote in *The Fifties*: "Mr. Har-

old Macmillan's statement, that the British people had 'never had it so good,' attracted wide attention. It was, however, only a half-truth. It failed to convince many housewives, struggling against the rising prices of food and other essentials, or brides, or business girls striving to furnish homes, or youngsters attempting to save to get married."

Whenever any political leader asks voters to count their blessings, the criticism heightens, turning "You never had it so good" into an attack phrase on the sloganeer. Lyndon Johnson in 1967 set forth some of the things that were right about America: "We produce more goods, we transport more goods and we use more goods than anyone in the world. We own almost a third of the world's railroad tracks. We own almost two-thirds of the world's automobiles. We own half the trucks in the world. And although we have only about 6 per cent of the population in the world, we have half its wealth."

Columnist James Reston responded: "This, of course, is the old doctrine of 'you-never-had-it-so-good.' ... The Johnson theme will probably do all right, especially since the Republicans have renewed their old game of self-destruction. It is the poor voters who are in trouble, for they are about to be overwhelmed by all the accumulated political rubbish of the centuries."

The derision has not destroyed usage of the slogan. In 2006, Raghuram Rajan, chief economist of the International Monetary Fund, noted that the world was enjoying its fourth consecutive year of growth above 4% and announced: "It would be fair to say to the world, 'You have never had it so good.'" (His version lost flavor in the grammatical correction.)

Young Turks Restive elements within a party seeking control or at least a voice; usually, not always, comparatively young.

The Young Turks were the reformers of the Ottoman Empire, a revolutionary group that seized power in 1908 from the aging sultans; in 1922 the House of Osman gave up and a group of former Young Turks—middle-aged by then—set up a republic. (While Mustafa Kemal, who later took the name Atatürk, had been associated with the Young Turks in his earlier years, the original Young Turks—Enver Pasha, Reshat Bey, and others—had nothing to do with the republic.)

In the U.S., the name was borrowed to describe a group of Republican senators in 1929 who broke with their leadership over tariff legislation. "Spectators of the Senate tariff war last week gasped with surprise," wrote *Time* magazine, "at the sight of a trim new regiment marching briskly and in close order out of the Republican redoubts. These new Republican warriors were called the Young Turks, a band of about 20 who had mutinied against the feeble leadership of the OLD GUARD. For Senators they were young men (average age: 56). As legislative legionnaires they were mostly rookies serving their first Senate enlistment."

During the Bermuda Conference of 1953, Winston Churchill digressed from the agenda to discuss imperialism with Dwight Eisenhower, expressing his doubts about the wisdom of self-government for peoples not yet ready for it. When the American President disagreed with a portion of the Prime Minister's argument, Churchill smiled and said, "You're just like the Young Turks in my government."

Today the phrase is used to describe any faction impatient with delay or defeat, seeking action, reform, change, or plain takeover. Party regulars use it patronizingly, but those so labeled do not resent it. The phrase was eclipsed for a time by ANGRY YOUNG MEN, but has reasserted itself in recent years: *Washington Post* columnist E. J. Dionne, Jr. wrote on the eve of the Democrats assuming majority status in the House in 2007 that "The key to Nancy Pelosi's success as Speaker will be to find a way to bring the OLD BULLS and the Young Turks together."

An unrelated use of the word *turkey* in politics is in *turkey farm*, a place where incompetent but well-connected workers are sent to draw a paycheck and stay out of trouble. See a reference to the Federal Emergency Management Agency under TURKEY FARM.

you're no Jack Kennedy Attack phrase for "don't overestimate yourself."

In the televised debates of the 1988 Presidential campaign, the most powerful blow was struck during the debate between the vice presidential candidates, Dan Quayle and Lloyd Bentsen.

When then-Senator Quayle suggested similarities between his qualifications and those of the youthful former Democratic President—true enough in terms of Senate experience—Senator Bentsen slammed back with a devastating rejoinder: "Senator, I served with Jack Kennedy, I knew Jack Kennedy. Jack Kennedy was a friend of mine. Senator, you're no Jack Kennedy."

That ad-libbed zinger has been reworked often. Uses range from a *New Yorker* art critique of 1991 ("George Moore is no Cézanne") to a 1992 headline of a review for a biography of the Confederacy's president, Jefferson Davis ("He Was No Abe Lincoln"). The most effective recycling of the Bentsen line came from Ronald Reagan delivering a political farewell at the 1992 GOP convention. Noting the middle name of William Jefferson Clinton, the Arkansas Governor just nominated for president by the Democrats, the aging Reagan wryly added, "This fellow they've nominated claims he's the new Thomas Jefferson. Well, let me tell you something. I knew Thomas Jefferson. He was a friend of mine. And, Governor, you're no Thomas Jefferson."

your home is your castle A slogan appealing to whites opposed to residential integration.

George Mahoney, perennial candidate for statewide office in Maryland, had used this slogan in his 1966 campaign. It was picked up by Louise Day Hicks, candidate for mayor of Boston in 1967; both campaigns lost.

"Your Home Is Your Castle—Protect It" was regarded as a CODE WORD phrase by most analysts, playing on the prejudices of voters concerned with property values in their neighborhoods if blacks moved in.

The phrase "a man's home is his castle" into which "not even the king may enter" is taken from a proverb and was codified in English law by Sir Edward Coke in 1604: "For a man's house is his castle, *et domus sua cuique tutissimum refugium*.... Resolved: The house of every man is his castle, and if thieves come to a man's house to rob or murder, and the owner or his servants kill any of the thieves in defence of himself and his house, it is no felony and he shall lose nothing ..."

In recent usage, the proverb has been more the property of opponents of desegregation than of the "gun lobby."

Z

zero-sum game In politics or diplomacy, a confrontation in which a face-saving way out is impossible, and one side wins what the other side loses.

In game theory, pioneered by Professors John von Neumann and Oskar Morgenstern, a game in which the interests of the two players are diametrically opposed is called *zero-sum*—that is, the sum of the winnings is always zero, with one player winning what the other loses. A *non-zero-sum* game is one in which both sides can both win or lose—for example, in a labor-management negotiation, if no agreement is reached and a disruptive strike ensues, both sides have lost. In a successful peace negotiation, considering the savings of not fighting a war, both sides have won, providing the loser is not enslaved.

Game theory is closely studied by national security strategists, and a confrontation to be avoided at all costs is often referred to as a *zero-sum game*, which is a form of NO-WIN POLICY.

Under the headline "US-China relationship not a zero-sum game," the Singapore *Straits Times* wrote in 2006:

> What if the United States were to withdraw from the Western Pacific—would China feel more secure as a result? Or what if China's now booming economy were to implode—would the US become more prosperous as a result? The answer to both questions is "no": No, a US withdrawal from East Asia will not be in China's interest. And no, a collapse of China's economy will not be in America's interest. The US-China relationship, unlike the relationship between the US and the former Soviet Union during the Cold War, cannot be conceived in zero-sum terms.

zinger A barb; or, a punch line; or, a short, stirring conclusion to a speech.

Zing is a word with many slang meanings, from "punch" to "liveliness." In politics, a *zinger* is a verbal jab at an opponent, often on the light side, well short of a denunciation, or "blast." Common usage in this sense: "Give him a zinger in the debate and see if he comes apart."

Senator John McCain, in 2007 taking aim at former Massachusetts governor Mitt Romney's perceived FLIP-FLOPS on abortion rights, immigration, and gun control, drew a delighted comment from the widely read website Wonkette, quoting McCain on his opponent's latest position: "'Maybe I should wait a couple of weeks and see if it changes because its changed in less than a year from his position before,' McCain responded, referring to his rival's immigration stance. 'And maybe his solution will be to get out his small varmint gun and drive those Guatemalans off his lawn.' Wow, that's like three *zingers* in one statement!"

Speechwriters use *zinger* in another sense, that of a moment of uplift or poignancy in a speech, or a punch line likely to trigger applause. When a zinger comes at the very end of a speech or line of thought, it is called a *snapper* (from *snap out of it*). See PERORATION.

zipper problem Drawback to a candidacy owing to rumors of marital infidelity or other louche living.

The phrase *zipper problem* was, until the 1990s, mainly limited a description of the occasional jamming of the interlocking tab that replaced the buttoned fly on trousers and buttons or hooks on the side of skirts.

Early usage in the sense of "loose morals" was in an interview with a celebrated country music star in the *Philadelphia Daily News* in February of 1992: "Garth Brooks said that his *zipper problem* only made his marriage stronger. 'The wife I got back after my infidelity was 15 times the woman I had.'"

The phrase, a less serious or euphemistic formulation than CHARACTER ISSUE, was applied to President Bill Clinton by the *Rocky Mountain News* in September 1998: "Voters knew his *zipper problem* and elected him anyway." London's *Independent* newspaper wrote two years later, "For eight years, Clinton has towered over American politics, 'zipper problem' and all."

Though used freely by journalists and bloggers, the phrase is rarely bandied about by politicians. When asked in early 2004 on background about the presidential chances of a potential candidate, a political figure replied, "He may have a problem." The followup question was "Zipper?" and the reply was a nervous shrug.

zoo plane The least desirable campaign transportation; airborne home of the scorned ANIMALS of television or web technology.

Late in most presidential campaigns, the candidate's aircraft has room only for a press "pool," that handful of reporters who stay close to "the Man"—or "the Candidate" as the case may be—while staying in touch with the accompanying press plane, which lands first at campaign stops to report the arrival and swell the crowd. Often a second press plane is needed to accommodate photographers, television crews, and reporters from less prestigious publications, blogs, or local stations.

The author first heard the expression in the campaign of 1968, when Republican press aide Ronald Ziegler said jokingly to a "pool" reporter who had dared to note a fluff by the candidate: "You'll never get off the zoo plane after this."

Writing in *Fear and Loathing on the Campaign Trail*, his book about the 1972 Nixon-McGovern campaign, Hunter S. Thompson noted "there were no McGovern staffers on the Zoo plane. A few tried to get on it, but the press people had nailed down their own seats and refused to leave them." Columnist Jules Witcover wrote in 1973 about a Republican observer who was discovered on a Democratic campaign plane: "Given campaign press credentials as a representative of the Women's News Service and a freelance book writer, she was shunted to the 'zoo plane'—the No. 2 plane in the McGovern entourage. It was so named by reporters because it mostly carried TV cameramen and technicians—'the animals' in the quasi-affectionate, quasi-snobbish parlance of political campaigns."

See MR. NICE GUY.

Zulu See BRAVO ZULU.

INDEX